HANDBOOK OF CHILD LANGUAGE ACQUISITION

HANDBOOK OF CHILD LANGUAGE ACQUISITION

Edited by

William C. Ritchie

Syracuse University

and

Tej K. Bhatia

Syracuse University

ACADEMIC PRESS

An Imprint of Elsevier

San Diego London Boston New York Sydney Tokyo Toronto

This book is printed on acid-free paper. 

Academic Press
An Imprint of Elsevier
525 B Street, Suite 1900, San Diego, California 92101-4495, USA
http://www.apnet.com

Academic Press Limited
24-28 Oval Road, London NW1 7DX, UK
http://www.hbuk.co.uk/ap/

Library of Congress Catalog Card Number: 98-85528

ISBN-13: 978-0-12-589041-0
ISBN-10: 0-12-589041-9

PRINTED IN THE UNITED STATES OF AMERICA
06 07 08 09 10 EB 9 8 7 6 5 4 3 2

To our families, with love and affection

To Laurie, Jane, and Pete; and to Marnie

To Shobha, Kanika, and Ankit

CONTENTS

CONTRIBUTORS xix
ACKNOWLEDGMENTS xxi

I RESEARCH AND THEORETICAL ISSUES IN CHILD LANGUAGE ACQUISITION

1 Child Language Acquisition: Introduction, Foundations, and Overview

William C. Ritchie
Tej K. Bhatia

I. Introduction 3
II. Issues of Innateness, Maturation, and Modularity in Child Language Acquisition 5
A. Maturation versus Continuity Theories of Acquisition 12
B. A Nonmodular Theory of Acquisition 14
C. Acquisition and Limited Input: The Bioprogram Hypothesis 15
D. Functionalist Approaches to Acquisition 16
E. Another Approach: Connectionism 17
III. Word Learning 18
IV. The Child's Acquisition of Phonology and Pragmatics 19
V. Research Methodology and Applications 21
VI. Modality and the Linguistic Environment in Child Language Acquisition 24

VII. Language Disorders and Impairments: Special Cases of Child Language Acquisition 26
VIII. Conclusion 28
References 28

II ISSUES OF INNATENESS, MATURATION, AND MODULARITY IN CHILD LANGUAGE ACQUISITION

2 On the Nature, Use, and Acquisition of Language
Noam Chomsky

I. On the Nature, Use, and Acquisition of Language 33

3 Maturation and Growth of Grammar
Kenneth Wexler

I. Growth/Maturation, Language Acquisition, and Linguistic Theory 55
II. Growth/Maturation, Biology, and Cognition 69
III. UG-Constrained Maturation and Continuous Development 75
IV. Maturation at the Interface? 78
V. Some Linguistic Developments 79
A. Binding Theory and Interpretation 80
B. Optional Infinitives: The Growth of Finiteness 90
C. A Note on Argument-Chains 101
VI. Conclusion 105
References 105

4 Universal Grammar: The Strong Continuity Hypothesis in First Language Acquisition
Barbara Lust

I. Introduction 111
A. Theory of UG 111
B. Brief History of Empirical Confirmation of UG as a Model of the Initial State 113
II. Indeterminacy in Interpretation of the Theory of UG 117
A. Problems with the Instantaneous Hypothesis (IH) 120
B. Maturation Hypothesis (MH) 122
C. Problems with the Maturational Hypothesis 124

D. Reasons for Failure of the MH 134
E. The Issue of Age 135
III. The Strong Continuity Hypothesis (SCH) 137
A. Relation between UG and Language Development 137
B. Grammatical Mapping: From UG to Specific Language Grammars (SLG) 138
C. UG as "Constraining" the Course of Acquisition 138
D. UG as "Guiding" First Language Acquisition 139
E. UG Can Itself Provide Apparent "Developmental Delay" 139
F. Explanation of Developmental Delay without Offense of SCH 140
G. Recent Revisions of the MH 142
IV. Conclusions 143
References 145

5 The Acquisition of Syntactic Representations: A General Nativist Approach
William O'Grady

I. Background 157
II. Some Assumptions about the Acquisition Process 160
A. Properties of the Grammar 160
B. The Nature of Experience 161
III. The Learnability Problem Reconsidered 164
A. A Simple Categorical Grammar 166
B. The Acquisition Device 169
C. Syntactic Categories 174
D. Hierarchical Structure 183
IV. Conclusion 187
References 189

6 Creole Languages, the Language Bioprogram Hypothesis, and Language Acquisition
Derek Bickerton

I. Origins of the Hypothesis and Its Relevance to Acquisition 195
II. Current Status of the LBH 198
III. What the LBH Predicts for Acquisition 203
IV. The Pace of Normal Syntactic Development 207
V. The LBH versus Other Acquisition Theories 213

VI. Conclusion 216
References 217

7 Functionalist Accounts of the Process of First Language Acquisition

Matthew Rispoli

I. History and Definitions: Functionalism in Linguistics 221
A. Definitions 221
B. Mathesius and the Prague School 222
C. The Chomskyan Revolution 223
D. Neofunctionalism in Linguistics 225
II. Studies of Language Acquisition 232
A. Semantic Analyses and Cognitivist Approaches 233
B. Isolated Functionalist Analyses of First Language Acquisition Phenomena 234
C. Bates and MacWhinney's Competition Model 236
III. Recent Developments 238
A. Silverstein's Critique of Functionalism in Language Acquisition Research 238
B. The Mosaic Acquisition of Grammatical Relations 239
IV. Conclusions 241
References 243

III SEMANTICS AND SYNTAX IN CHILD WORD LEARNING

8 Theories of Word Learning: Rationalist Alternatives to Associationism

Paul Bloom

I. Introduction 249
II. Associationist Theories of Word Learning 250
A. Issue 1: The Nature of Word Meanings 253
B. Issue 2: Establishing Word/Meaning Mappings 258
III. Rationalist Perspectives 260
A. Syntax as a Pointer to Conceptual Type 260

B. Abstract Conceptual Types 264
C. Intentionality 267
IV. Conclusion 272
Appendix: Determining the Syntactic Categories That Words Belong to 272
References 274

9 The Role of Syntax in Verb Learning

Lila R. Gleitman
Jane Gillette

I. Insufficiency of Observation for Verb Learning 280
II. More Power to Verb Learning 282
A. Origins and Motivation 283
B. Form–Meaning Interactions in Verb Learning 284
III. The Zoom Lens Hypothesis 285
IV. The Multiple Frames Hypothesis 288
V. The Potency of Various Evidentiary Sources 288
VI. How the Structures of Sentences Can Aid Vocabulary Acquisition 291
A. Relation of Surface Syntax to Semantics 291
References 293

IV THE CHILD'S ACQUISITION OF PHONOLOGY AND PRAGMATICS

10 Child Phonology, Learnability, and Phonological Theory

B. Elan Dresher

I. Learnability: The Logical versus Developmental Problem of Acquisition 299
II. Some Issues in the Logical Problem of the Acquisition of Phonology 304
A. The Abstractness Controversy 305
B. Nonlinear Phonology 307
C. Underspecification 309
D. Principles and Parameters 314

III. Some Issues in Developmental Phonology 317
A. Methodological Problems in the Analysis of a Child Language 319
B. Discrepancies between Production and Perception 320
C. Models of the Organization of Child Phonology 323
D. Phonological Development as Growth of Complexity 326
E. Accounting for Stages of Development 337
IV. Conclusion: The Fourth Dimension of Complexity 339
References 340

11 The Development of Pragmatics: Learning to Use Language Appropriately

Anat Ninio
Catherine E. Snow

I. Defining the Domain of Pragmatics 347
A. Pragmatics versus Syntax and Semantics in Formal Models 347
B. The Place of Pragmatics in Functionalist Models 349
C. Pragmatics in Developmental Theories 350
II. Developing Communicative Intents and Appropriate Ways of Expressing Them 353
A. Prelinguistic Communicative Abilities 353
B. Communicative Intents Expressed at the Preverbal Stage 354
C. The Continuity Hypothesis 355
D. Transitional Phenomena 355
E. The Pragmatics of Early Single-Word Utterances 356
F. Developmental Trends in the Expression of Communicative Intents in the Early Stages of Speech Use 358
G. Individual Differences in the Earliest Speech Uses 359
H. Developmental Course of Verbal Control of Speech Acts 359
III. Development of Control over Conversational Rules 360
A. Turn Taking 361
B. Topic Selection and Maintenance 362
C. Individual Differences in Conversational Skill 362
IV. Learning to Be Polite 364
V. Learning to Produce Connected Discourse 365
A. Linguistic Devices That Maintain Cross-Utterance Cohesion 366
B. Adaptations to the Audience 367
C. Learning about Genres and Their Structure 368
VI. Endpoint of Pragmatic Development 369
References 370

V RESEARCH METHODOLOGY AND APPLICATIONS

12 Methodology in the Study of Language Acquisition: A Modular Approach

Stephen Crain
Kenneth Wexler

I. Introduction 387
II. Competing Models of the Language Processing System 388
III. Strong Crossover 394
IV. Null Subjects and the Output Omission Model 403
V. Performance Errors versus Nonadult Grammars 407
VI. Minimality and Modularity 410
VII. Statistics and Competing Factors 412
VIII. Inferences about Grammaticality 418
IX. Conclusion 422

13 How Do We Know What Children Know? Problems and Advances in Establishing Scientific Methods for the Study of Language Acquisition and Linguistic Theory

Barbara Lust
Suzanne Flynn
Claire Foley
Yu-Chin Chien

I. Introduction 427
The Structure of This Chapter 428
II. Problems in Determining What Children Know 428
A. What Is the Object of Inquiry? 428
B. Relating Grammar and Behavior 429
C. Indeterminacy of Language Data 430
D. Variability in Estimating Linguistic Knowledge from Language Data 432
III. Foundations for Theory of Research Methodology 434
A. Resolving Theoretical Paradox 434
B. Resolving Indeterminacy and Variability of Language Data 435
C. Experimental Methods 436

IV. Inferring What Children Know from Their Behavior on Tasks 437
A. Current Advances in the Study of Natural Speech 437
B. Experimental Test of Production: Elicited Imitation (EI) 439
C. Experimental Test of Comprehension: Act Out (AO) 439
D. Converging Evidence: Comparing the EI and AO Tasks 440
V. Can Performance Be Bypassed? 443
A. Reduced Behavior Methods 443
B. Examples of Reduced Behavior (RB) Tasks 444
C. Conclusions on Reduced Behavior Tasks 448
D. Converging Evidence 448
VI. Conclusion 450
References 451

14 The CHILDES System

Brian MacWhinney

I. Background 457
II. The Database 458
A. English Data 459
B. Non-English Data 461
C. Narrative Data 463
D. Language Impairments 463
E. Bilingual Acquisition Data 465
F. Books 465
G. Access to the Database 466
H. Reformatting of the Database 466
III. CHAT 467
A. Key Features of CHAT 467
B. How Much CHAT Does a User Need to Know? 468
IV. CLAN 469
A. CLAN for Lexical Analysis 471
B. CLAN for Morphological Analysis 474
C. CLAN for Syntactic Analysis 480
D. CLAN for Discourse and Interactional Analyses 482
E. CLAN for Phonological Analyses 484
F. Utilities 487
G. CHECK 488
V. The Future 489
References 491

VI MODALITY AND THE LINGUISTIC ENVIRONMENT IN CHILD LANGUAGE

15 Input and Language Acquisition

Virginia Valian

I. Three Metaphors 497
II. Forms of Evidence 499
A. Positive Evidence 499
B. Negative Evidence 500
C. Indirect Negative Evidence 502
III. Input Studies 503
IV. Reply Studies 513
V. Intervention Studies 522
VI. Conclusion 525
References 527

16 Modality Effects and Modularity in Language Acquisition: The Acquisition of American Sign Language

Diane Lillo-Martin

I. Introduction and Background 531
II. The First Decade of Research on the Acquisition of American Sign Language 533
A. First Signs 534
B. Early Pronouns 534
C. Early Lexical Development 536
D. The Acquisition of ASL Verbal Morphology and "Spatial Syntax" 536
III. Current Issues: The First Stages 540
A. Manual Babbling 540
B. First Signs 541
C. Lexical Development 544
D. Phonological Development 545
IV. The Acquisition of Morphology and Syntax 546
A. Verbs of Motion and Location (Classifiers) 546
B. Spatial Syntax 549
C. Nonmanual Grammatical Markers 555
V. Modality and Modularity Effects in Language Acquisition 557
VI. Conclusion and Implications 560
References 561

17 The Bilingual Child: Some Issues and Perspectives

Tej K. Bhatia
William C. Ritchie

I. Introduction 569
II. Some Basic Questions 571
A. What Is Bilingualism? 571
B. What/Who Is a Bilingual Child? 572
III. Why Study the Bilingual Child? 576
IV. Key Assumptions and Claims 578
A. Universal Grammar and the Principles-and-Parameters Framework 578
B. The Critical Period Hypothesis and Its Biological Basis 579
C. Acquisition versus Learning 582
V. Input Conditions 582
A. Natural versus Unnatural Setting 583
B. Formal Setting: School and Media 583
C. Age and Time 583
D. Other Input Factors and the Typology of Childhood Bilingualism 585
VI. Input and Stages of Bilingual Language Development 587
A. Separation versus Lack of Separation in Input 587
B. Progression and Regression Phenomena in Bilingual Children 590
VII. Stages in Monolingual and Bilingual Language Development 591
A. Phonological Development 592
B. Vocabulary Development 594
C. Morpho-syntactic Development 596
VIII. The Two Linguistic Systems in Bilingual Children 598
A. The Unitary Hypothesis 599
B. The Dual System Hypothesis 603
IX. Input Poverty and Input Modality 614
X. Code Mixing and Code Switching 618
A. Fusion, Code Mixing, and Code Switching 619
B. Adult and Early Child Language Mixing: Qualitative and Quantitative Differences 620
XI. Bilingual Children and Speech Disorders 627
XII. Conclusions and Future Research 630
A. Theoretical Issues 630
B. Methodological and Analytical Issues 632
References 633

VII LANGUAGE DISORDERS AND IMPAIRMENTS: SPECIAL CASES OF CHILD LANGUAGE ACQUISITION

18 Some Empirical and Theoretical Issues in Disordered Child Phonology

Daniel A. Dinnsen

I. Introduction 647
II. Empirical Characteristics and Theoretical Accounts 648
A. Error Patterns 648
B. Natural Phonology Accounts 651
C. Alternate Accounts 651
D. The Nature of Phonetic Inventories 659
III. Phonological Issues in Clinical Treatment 665
IV. Conclusion 668
References 670

19 Linguistic Perspectives on Specific Language Impairment

Harald Clahsen

I. Introduction 675
II. Linguistic Interpretations of SLI 677
A. The Surface Account 678
B. The Missing Feature Account 679
C. The Rule-Deficit Model of SLI 680
D. The Grammatical Agreement Deficit 681
III. Empirical Results on Grammatical Development in SLI Children 682
A. Person and Number Agreement 683
B. Auxiliaries and Modals 684
C. Case Marking 685
D. Gender Marking 686
E. Noun Plurals 687
F. Tense Making 690
G. Participle Inflection 691
H. Word Order 692
IV. Discussion 693
A. Problems of the Surface Account 694
B. Features and Rules in SLI Children's Grammars 695
C. Evaluating the Missing Agreement Hypothesis 697

V. Summary and Conclusion 700
References 701

LIST OF ABBREVIATIONS 705
AUTHOR INDEX 707
SUBJECT INDEX 721

CONTRIBUTORS

Numbers in parentheses indicate the pages on which the authors' contributions begin.

Tej Bhatia (3, 569), Department of Languages, Literatures and Linguistics, Syracuse University, Syracuse, New York 13244-1160

Derek Bickerton (195), Department of Linguistics, University of Hawaii, Honolulu, Hawaii 96822

Paul Bloom (249), Department of Psychology, University of Arizona, Tucson, Arizona 85721

Yu-Chin Chien (427), Department of Psychology, California State University at San Bernardino, San Bernardino, California

Noam Chomsky (33), Massachusetts Institute of Technology, Cambridge, Massachusetts 02139-3594

Harald Clahsen (675), Department of Linguistics, University of Essex, Colchester C04 35Q, United Kingdom

Stephen Crain (387), Department of Linguistics, University of Maryland at College Park, College Park, Maryland 20742-7505

Daniel A. Dinnsen (647), Department of Linguistics, Indiana University, Bloomington, Indiana 47405

B. Elan Dresher (299), Department of Linguistics, University of Toronto, Toronto, Ontario M5S 3H1, Canada

Suzanne Flynn (427), Foreign Languages and Literatures, Massachusetts Institute of Technology, Cambridge, Massachusetts 02139-3594

Claire Foley (427), English, Foreign Languages, and Philosophy, Morehead State University

Jane Gillette (279), Department of Psychology, University of Pennsylvania, Philadelphia, Pennsylvania 19104

Lila R. Gleitman (279), Department of Psychology, University of Pennsylvania, Philadelphia, Pennsylvania 19104

Diane Lillo-Martin (531), Department of Linguistics and Haskins Laboratory, University of Connecticut, Storrs, Connecticut 06269-1145

Barbara C. Lust (111, 427), Modern Languages, Human Development, Cornell University, Ithaca, New York 14853-4401

Brian MacWhinney (457), Department of Psychology, Carnegie Mellon University, Pittsburgh, Pennsylvania 15213

Anat Ninio (347), Department of Psychology, The Hebrew University, Jerusalem 91905, Israel

William O'Grady (157), Department of Linguistics, University of Hawaii, Honolulu, Hawaii 96822

Matthew Rispoli (221), Department of Speech and Hearing Science, Arizona State University, Tempe, Arizona 85287-0102

William Ritchie (3, 569), Department of Languages, Literatures and Linguistics, Syracuse University, Syracuse, New York 13244-1160

Catherine E. Snow (347), Graduate School of Education, Harvard University, Cambridge, Massachusetts 02138

Virginia Valian (497), Department of Psychology, Hunter College, New York City, New York 10021

Kenneth Wexler (55, 387), Department of Brain and Cognitive Sciences and Department of Linguistics and Philosophy, Massachusetts Institute of Technology, Cambridge, Massachusetts 02139

ACKNOWLEDGMENTS

We have contracted many debts in developing this volume. We are grateful first and foremost to the contributors, without whom, after all, the volume would not exist and without whose cooperation and assistance this undertaking would have been considerably less pleasant than it was. We are particularly grateful to those who took the trouble to update their chapters as the time between their initial submissions and the completion of the full manuscript became extended. Their patience in waiting for the final product has been remarkable.

The volume benefitted immeasurably from the advice and counsel of a number of valued colleagues in the field—most prominently Barbara Lust and Ken Wexler. In addition, the following have offered both moral support and valuable advice in the development of this work: Elizabeth Bates, Derek Bickerton, Noam Chomsky, Annick De Houwer, Dan Slobin, and Catherine Snow. Needless to say, all final decisions were ours and those whom we gratefully acknowledge should bear no burden for any of them.

We are fortunate to have friends, colleagues, and teachers like Braj and Yamuna Kachru, James Gair, Suzanne Flynn, Barbara Lust, Hans Hock, Manindra Verma, Rajeshwari Pandharipande, and S. N. Sridhar. Their support, inspiration, and scholarship mean a great deal to us and have directly influenced this work.

We are grateful as well for the professional assistance and Job-like patience of the staff at Academic Press—particularly the Acquisition Editor Nikki Levy, her Editorial Assistant Barbara Makinster, and the Production Editor Kay Sasser.

PART I

RESEARCH AND THEORETICAL ISSUES IN CHILD LANGUAGE ACQUISITION

CHAPTER 1

CHILD LANGUAGE ACQUISITION: INTRODUCTION, FOUNDATIONS, AND OVERVIEW

William C. Ritchie and Tej K. Bhatia

I. INTRODUCTION

Though speculation and empirical research concerning the character of child language acquisition have a long history,[1] the "cognitive revolution" in psychology and linguistics in the 1960s profoundly affected research in the area, both qualitatively and quantitatively. Qualitatively, the cognitive revolution turned research away from the concrete and detailed description of the linguistic behavior of the child that characterized the immediately preceding research in the field to the study of the cognitive states and processes that underlie language acquisition and use.[2]

[1]Investigation of child language acquisition extends back to ancient times. Two instances of "research" on child language acquisition in the ancient world are a purported "experiment" conducted by the pharaoh Psammetichus (Psamtik) I of Egypt in the seventh century B.C.—later described by the Greek historian Herodotus—and St. Augustine's "recollection" of the process of acquiring the lexicon of his native language described in his fourth–fifth-century A.D. work, *Confessions* (Book I). Psammetichus is reported to have had two children raised in linguistic isolation for the purpose of discovering what the original language was. St. Augustine's account of his learning of words is quoted in part in chapter 8 of the present volume, authored by Paul Bloom.

[2]Though there had been precedents for setting problems in the study of child language acquisition at a more abstract, cognitive level by continental scholars—most notably, Roman Jakobson (e.g., Jakobson, 1941/1968)—much of the research on child language acquisition at midcentury was influenced to a greater or lesser degree by the highly concrete, behaviorist orientation of B. F. Skinner and

The result was a dramatic increase in the depth, specificity, and breadth of accounts of the phenomena of acquisition. Quantitatively, the number of publications in the field grew prodigiously from the early 1960s—when language acquisition was viewed primarily as one element in the overall psychological development of the child—to the 1970s and beyond—when language acquisition came to be seen as an isolable aspect of child development. This growth led to the establishment of two respected professional journals dedicated entirely to the publication of research on language acquisition—*The Journal of Child Language* (Cambridge University Press) in 1973 and *Language Acquisition* (Lawrence A. Erlbaum) in 1990.

A major step in the cognitive revolution with respect to the study of learning was achieved with the recognition that one cannot expect to gain genuine insight into the human ability to learn in a given cognitive domain without a precise characterization of "what is learned." Though we return to more detailed discussion of the issues later in this chapter, we may say that "what is learned" in the case of child language acquisition is the *grammatical structure* and the *pragmatics* of the language of the environment.

Grammatical structure includes the principles of sentence structure for the language (its *syntax*) and those of pronunciation (its *phonology/phonetics*) as well as its vocabulary items (that is, its *lexicon,* including the syntactic, phonological, and semantic properties of each lexical item). Pragmatics subsumes a wide range of principles of language use including (but not limited to) conventions for the expression of communicative intents (or speech acts), such as requesting, warning, or informing, as well as rules for conversational turn taking and politeness and for introducing and maintaining topics in a conversation.

The volume is divided into seven parts reflecting major areas of research in the field. Part I consists of the present introductory chapter. Part II, which includes chapters 2 through 7 by Noam Chomsky, Kenneth Wexler, Barbara Lust, William O'Grady, Derek Bickerton, and Matthew Rispoli, respectively, covers central issues in the study of child language acquisition including those of **innateness, maturation, and modularity** and presents some of the major theoretical orientations in the field.

The chapters in Part II are concerned almost entirely with the child's acquisition of syntax. The next two parts are therefore devoted to three areas of research other than syntax. Part III is concerned with children's **word learning** with research reviews by Paul Bloom (chapter 8) and Lila Gleitman (chapter 9). Part IV includes Elan Dresher's chapter 10 on issues in research on the child's acquisition

---

others. Two events were of major importance in the change from behaviorist to cognitive thinking in research on child language. The first was Chomsky's classic review (Chomsky, 1959) of *Verbal Behavior,* Skinner's major book-length work on the learning and use of language; the second was the detailed longitudinal study of the acquisition of English by three young children conducted over a 17-month period by Roger Brown and others in the early 1960s (Brown, 1973).

of phonology and Anat Ninio and Catherine Snow's review of work on the acquisition of pragmatics in chapter 11.

As mentioned, a great deal of research has been devoted to child language acquisition over the past 35 years. Nonetheless, a great many **research-methodological** issues remain to be addressed and solved. Part V includes three chapters on methodological questions: chapter 12 by Stephen Crain and Kenneth Wexler; chapter 13 by Barbara Lust, Suzanne Flynn, Yu-Chin Chien, and Claire Foley; and chapter 14 by Brian MacWhinney.

Types of **input** to the child, which can vary not only in quality and quantity but in modality as well, and their effects, are examined in Part VI, which contains chapter 15 by Virginia Valian on monolingual spoken input; chapter 16, which is a discussion of the acquisition of a signed (rather than spoken) language; and a treatment of the research on the bilingual child by Tej Bhatia and William Ritchie in chapter 17.

Finally, Part VII explores the study of *language and speech disorders,* which has shed important light on the underlying processes of child language acquisition. Chapter 18, by Daniel Dinnsen, provides a review of research on phonological disorders in children, and Harald Clahsen's chapter 19 treats the complex of production problems that constitute specific language impairment.

II. ISSUES OF INNATENESS, MATURATION, AND MODULARITY IN CHILD LANGUAGE ACQUISITION

Chapter 2 ("On the Nature, Use, and Acquisition of Language"), by Noam Chomsky, provides a historical and conceptual framework for Part II and, in fact, for the rest of the volume. Whether or not one agrees with the position of Chomsky and his colleagues on the central issues in the study of language, of language use, or of language acquisition, or even with their view of the nature of empirical inquiry—and several of the contributors to this volume do not—it seems fair to say that their thinking on these issues has framed much of the debate in the field over the past 30 to 35 years.

In his chapter, Chomsky considers the character and origin of the cognitive revolution (referred to earlier) in which his work on grammatical structure played a central role. More specifically, he notes two conceptual shifts in the study of language since the 1950s. The first, which took place in the late 1950s and early 1960s, altered the focus of research on grammatical structure from the study of behavior to the examination of the mental/cognitive systems underlying behavior—that is, to the investigation of linguistic mental representations, the rule systems that specify these representations, and the mental operations that process them. We discuss the second shift, which occurred in the late 1970s and early 1980s and was specific to research within the generative tradition, later in this discussion.

In his chapter, Chomsky identifies four questions as central to the empirical study of language: (a) What does the speaker/hearer's knowledge of a particular language consist in? (b) How does the speaker/hearer put this knowledge to use in the expression of thought and in the understanding of others who possess the same or similar knowledge? (c) What are the physical mechanisms that instantiate the structures discovered in the abstract investigation of linguistic knowledge and use of that knowledge? and (d) How are knowledge of a particular language and the ability to use it acquired?

An answer to question (a) (a hypothesis about the speaker/hearer's knowledge of a particular language) is a (generative) grammar of the language. Though a full treatment of generative grammatical theory—even at an elementary level—is well beyond the scope of this chapter,[3] a short digression in the form of a set of syntactic examples may make the discussion more concrete. These examples are of particular interest in the present context because the issues of their structure and the acquisition of their grammar are discussed in several chapters in the volume, including Chomsky's chapter. Consider the sentences and nonsentences from English in (1):

(1) a. i. John studies history.
 ii. He studies history.
 b. i. It rains.
 ii. There is a problem.
 c. i. *Studies history.
 ii. *Rains.
 iii. *Is a problem.

In accordance with the native speaker's perceptions, an empirically adequate grammar of English will include rules and principles from which it follows that the examples in (1.a.) and (1.b.) are well formed (grammatical) and those in (1.c.) are ill formed or ungrammatical.

On the other hand, parallel sentences in Spanish (with parallel meanings throughout) have the grammaticality values indicated in (2).

(2) a. i. Juan estudia historia. "Juan studies history."
 ii. ?El estudia historia. "He studies history."
 b. i. *El llueve.
 he/it rains
 ii. *Ahi hay un problema.
 there has a problem
 c. i. Estudia historia. "He/She studies history."

[3]For recent introductory treatments of generative syntactic/semantic theory, see Haegeman (1994), Culicover (1997), and Radford (1997). For an introduction to generative phonology, see Kenstowicz (1994).

ii. Llueve. "It rains."
iii. Hay un problema. "There is a problem."

Focusing on the examples in (2.b.) and (2.c.), note that the grammaticality values are precisely the opposite of the parallel examples in (1.b.) and (l.c.). The grammar of Spanish must therefore differ from that of English in disallowing word sequences like those in (2.b.) and allowing those in (2.c.).[4] Thus the grammar of Spanish allows (in some cases, requires) the subject of a sentence to be "merely understood" or phonetically empty or null, whereas that of English disallows all null subjects. Like the grammar of English, the grammar of French rejects null subjects; the grammar of Italian, like that of Spanish, allows null subjects in sentences like (2.c.i.) and requires them in sentences parallel to (2.c.ii.) and (2.c.iii.). Hence the answer to Chomsky's question (a) consists in a grammar for a given language—in this case English, French, Spanish, or Italian—which makes empirical claims of the sorts discussed previously, and these features of the adult grammars of English, French, Spanish, and Italian are thus the *targets* of children acquiring these languages—"What is learned" in the case of child language acquisition.

Because Chomsky's questions (b) and (c) are of less concern in the present context, we turn immediately to Chomsky's question (d). The central element in an explanation of the facts of language acquisition is a hypothesis about the human genetic endowment in the domain of grammar—that is, about the *initial state* of the language faculty in advance of linguistic experience. Such a hypothesis is referred to as a "universal grammar" (UG)—that is, a theory that imposes limits on the grammars of particular languages, specifying all and only those abstract systems that constitute possibly fully acquired adult grammars of natural languages. For empirical adequacy, the theory must place severe limits on the range of possible grammars. Otherwise, it will fail to account for the speed with which the child acquires the grammatical structure of his or her language.

Returning to our earlier example, the principles of an empirically adequate version of UG must allow for both null-subject grammars, like those of adult Spanish and Italian, and the nonnull-subject grammars of English and French. Assuming, for the sake of the example, that all grammars of natural languages are of either of these two types,[5] UG must also exclude abstract systems that do not have the relevant properties of either of these two types of grammars.

[4]Sentence (2.a.ii.) is of questionable grammaticality unless the subject *el* is contrastively stressed.

[5]The question of what type of language allows null subjects and what type does not is a complicated one. A traditional view is that a language which, like Spanish or Italian, has a rich set of subject-verb agreement markers that identify the subject even when it is absent allows null subjects, whereas a language that lacks such a system of markers (like English or French) does not allow them; more recent theoretical work also takes these observations into account. However, this picture is complicated by the fact that many languages have no subject-verb agreement at all—for example, Chinese and Japanese—but nonetheless allow null subjects. See, for example, Huang (1984) and Jaeggli and Safir (1989) for discussion.

One way in which the task of justifying a particular version of UG has been approached is in the form of *the logical problem of language acquisition* or, as Chomsky refers to it in chapter 2, the specific case of "Plato's problem" that applies to language acquisition. The problem is that the result of language acquisition—the adult grammar—is grossly underdetermined by the linguistic experience of the language learner. The gap between the learner's experience and the resulting grammar, then, is to be filled by UG as an account of the contribution of the learner in the form of his or her genetic endowment in the cognitive domain of grammar—that is, in the form of the human language faculty. In particular, the logical problem of language acquisition is set as the problem of acquisition under an idealization that is radical but has proven extremely fruitful for research—the idealization that the process of language acquisition is instantaneous. Under this idealization, acquisition is treated as if (a) all experience that is relevant to acquisition of the adult grammar is available to the learner, (b) the learner imposes the principles of UG on this experience, and (c) the adult grammar is the instantaneous result.

In approaching the logical problem with respect to specific cases, it is necessary to take into account the fact that the learner's linguistic experience is limited almost entirely to information about which utterances in the environment are grammatical and that little or no information is available about which utterances are ungrammatical (see, e.g., Brown & Hanlon, 1970, for relevant empirical work). In the example of the grammars of English and Spanish, we must assume that a learner of English is exposed to utterances like those in (1.a.) and (1.b.) and therefore assumes them to be grammatical but never receives the information that the utterances in (1.c.) are ungrammatical. Conversely, the learner of Spanish encounters examples like those in (2.a.) and (2.c.) and thus takes them to be grammatical but is never informed by experience that the utterances in (2.b.) are ungrammatical.[6] Hence, the exclusion of the utterances in (1.c.) by the adult grammar of English and the exclusion of the utterances in (1.b.) by the adult grammar of Spanish must be a consequence of some property of UG—that is, the language faculty in the sense of Chomsky's chapter.

Until the late 1970s, UG was formulated as a set of conditions on grammars as rule systems. Under this conception, it was understood that the grammars of Spanish and Italian include a rule of *pro-drop,* which deletes the subjects of sentences under certain conditions, and that the grammars of English and French do not contain this rule. However, as Chomsky reports in his chapter, the formulation of UG as a set of conditions on rule systems allowed for too many rule systems to make the acquisition of a language in a limited time feasible. Thus, in the second con-

[6]It might be countered that the nonoccurrence of utterances like (1.c.) in the learner's English linguistic experience or of (2.b.) in the Spanish learner's experience is sufficient to determine their exclusion by the adult grammars of these languages. However, this is not obvious; after all, many utterances that are perfectly well formed in the language of the environment (in fact, a potential infinity of them) fail to occur as part of the learner's experience.

ceptual shift referred to in Chomsky's chapter, Chomsky (1981) and others reformulated UG as a system of principles that places heavy restrictions on the range of possible grammars of natural languages and at the same time allows for variation among the grammars of languages through a system of parameters or "switches," each of which can be set in a small number of values, each value determining a certain range of properties of grammars and the structures that follow from them. The child's acquisition of a grammar is then understood as consisting in the setting of each parameter of UG in the one of its values that accords with his or her linguistic experience.

Turning once again to our example of English and Spanish, Chomsky (1981) proposed that there is a single parameter (referred to in subsequent work as the null subject parameter) with two values—a null-subject value, which determines the occurrence of null subjects in the grammar of Spanish along with other properties, and a nonnull-subject value that determines the exclusion of null subjects and other properties of the grammar of English.

The logical problem is to be distinguished from *the developmental problem of language acquisition*. The latter is the problem of explaining the process of acquisition in real time in terms of the learner's linguistic experience, his or her capacity of acquisition, and the resulting grammar at each stage of acquisition. Thus, in addition to a characterization of the class of grammars that are available to the learner as possible adult grammars of the language of the environment (that is, UG), a solution to the developmental problem also requires a system of principles or strategies that implements UG and explains the sequence of grammars (whether adultlike or not) that the learner goes through to arrive eventually at the adult grammar. In chapter 2, Chomsky refers to this system of principles as "learning theory" or "growth theory." Within the principles-and-parameters (or, in the terminology of chapter 2, "network-and-switch") framework, the developmental problem will be solved by a learning/growth theory that provides an explanation of the sequence in which the parameters of UG are set in their adult values for the language of the child's environment.

How might the real-time acquisition of the null-subject properties of grammars in our earlier example be accounted for? As Chomsky notes in Chapter 2, Hyams (1986) reported that children who are at an early stage in the acquisition of English show evidence of having grammars that, unlike the adult grammar of English, allow null subjects. Within the principles-and-parameters framework, Chomsky proposed in chapter 2 that all children—no matter what language they are learning—go through an early stage of acquisition when they have grammars determined by the null-subject value of the null subject parameter. If their linguistic experience is compatible with this grammar—that is, the language of the environment is Spanish or Italian—then the child retains the properties of his or her grammar that follow from the null-subject value of the parameter; if the language is English, then the child's linguistic experience (of which utterances like

He studies history, It rains, and *There is a problem* are a part) induces a resetting of the null subject parameter to its nonnull-subject value. Chomsky discusses two major approaches to phenomena like these in chapter 2, and we return to these later.[7]

Many of the issues raised in Chomsky's research program—some addressed explicitly in chapter 2, some discussed elsewhere in the research literature—have occasioned considerable controversy. Here we briefly discuss three of these issues in relation to chapters 3 through 7, all of which address the issues in question in detail.

One aspect of Chomsky's program that was controversial at one time in the past is no longer controversial: It is now widely accepted that much of the structure of any particular language is not a product of experience but, rather, of the human genetic endowment. Hence the process of child acquisition is seen as more a matter of elaborating a structure that is present from birth rather than the accrual of knowledge from scratch. The major issue now is the specific character of the genetic endowment.

First, although the imputation of the theory of adult grammars (that is, UG) to the language acquirer's initial state gives that theory empirical content under an appropriate and productive idealization, the question arises as to how the highly idealized account of language acquisition of which this imputation is a part is to be "de-idealized" in the more realistic study of the actual process of language acquisition—that is, how the developmental problem is to be approached in detail. Chomsky explores two possibilities in his chapter: (a) what he refers to as a "no-growth" theory on one hand and (b) what he calls a "maturation" theory on the other. Under a no-growth theory and the switch-setting account of acquisition, "[learning] theory is negligible or non-existent, so that language acquisition simply involves [immediate] switch setting on the basis of presented data." However, because children do not acquire the features of a language that follow from the setting of a given switch immediately upon exposure to the relevant data, "some independent and extrinsic change in cognitive capacities, say in memory or attention, accounts for the observed stages of growth." Such no-growth accounts of the process of acquisition have come to be known in the research literature as *continuity hypotheses.*

Maturation theories, on the other hand, would allow for the possibility that, for example, some parameter/switch settings (and the structures that follow from them) are biologically unavailable to the child early in life and become available later only after a process of mind/brain maturation has taken place. Accounts of this latter kind have come to be known as *maturational hypotheses.* Kenneth

[7]See chapter 10 by Elan Dresher for discussion of the logical and developmental problems in relation to the acquisition of phonology.

Wexler argues for a maturational hypothesis in chapter 3 and Barbara Lust argues for a particularly strong continuity hypothesis in chapter 4. We return to a more detailed discussion in Section II.A.

Second, Chomsky refers in chapter 2 to the language faculty as "a specific faculty of the mind/brain," "an identifiable system of the human mind/brain"—what he has elsewhere (e.g., Chomsky, 1980, 19986) called an "organ" or "module" of the mind/brain analogous to the physical organs of the body—that is, a system of principles distinct from but interacting with other identifiable systems or "modules" of the mind/brain entering into and, in part, determining human thought and action. Opposed to this *modular* view of the mind and of language as one of its modules is the view that treats grammatical structure as following from principles of general multipurpose cognitive capacities—a *nonmodular* view. These two views of grammatical structure have different implications for the study of child language acquisition. Chapter 5 by William O'Grady argues for a nonmodular account of acquisition (*contra* Chomsky) and we return to a discussion of the issues in Section II.B.

A third variable that enters into theorizing about child language acquisition is the nature of the linguistic input from the environment, the primary linguistic data to which the child is exposed in interaction with speakers of the language. It is assumed that, in the normal case of child language acquisition, input to the child consists of relatively uniform adult speech in a *full* language rather than the highly various and simplified form of, say a pidgin language. What is the outcome of acquisition with a pidgin language as input (as in the case of creolization of a pidgin), and what conclusions can be drawn concerning the human linguistic genetic endowment on the basis of careful study of acquisition cases of this sort? In chapter 6, Derek Bickerton discusses this sort of case in relation to his language bioprogram hypothesis. We return in Section II.C. for further discussion.

Finally, linguistic theory in Chomsky's sense is preeminently a theory of grammatical form in which syntax is generative and central, whereas semantics is interpretive and, relatively speaking, peripheral; and, similarly, pragmatics—though presupposing and dependent on grammatical form and semantic interpretation—is a separate system ("pragmatic competence"—addressed most clearly in Chomsky, 1980, pp. 224–225). Hence, grammatical structure (and to a large extent its acquisition) is explicable independently of semantics and pragmatics. In opposition to Chomsky, some researchers propose that grammatical structure is, at least in part, a product of semantic and pragmatic principles. Positions like Chomsky's are termed *formalist;* approaches of the second type have been termed *functionalist.* Matthew Rispoli reviews functionalist accounts of language structure and of its acquisition in chapter 7. See Section II.D. for further discussion.

In addition to these issues and approaches to them, others have arisen in recent years. We address these additional issues in Section II.E.

A. Maturation versus Continuity Theories of Acquisition

As noted previously, the central problem in a realistic account of the process of child language acquisition within Chomsky's program is that the setting of some "switches" that determines the structures in adult language may occur relatively late in the process of acquisition, whereas the unelaborated assumption that UG is part of the initial state should predict that switch setting (and the appearance of associated structures) would, contrary to fact, occur as soon as the child is exposed to the relevant input. In Wexler's words (chapter 3), "Why should the child only learn at a (much) later date a structure for which the evidence was available much earlier?" (p. 60).

The maturationist's solution to this problem—argued for by Wexler in chapter 3 ("Maturation and Growth of Grammar")—is to claim that, in fact, UG (the theory of adult grammars) is *not* a characterization of the initial state of the language faculty. Rather, in a realistic account of the early stages of the process of acquisition, the theory of grammars that plays a role analogous to UG (in more idealized accounts) differs from UG in particular ways. For example, under Wexler's view (chapter 3; Borer & Wexler, 1987), the child's early grammatical theory ("Proto-UG" in Wexler's terminology) excludes the possibility of NP-movement (A-chains) and therefore excludes those constructions, the derivations of which involve NP-movement in the adult grammar—for example, verbal passives and sentences containing unaccusative verbs like *drop* and *move* in which the surface subject NP is in the object position in more abstract representation—thus accounting for the absence of these structures in the child's early performance. Hence, under maturation hypotheses, the human genetic endowment in the cognitive domain of grammar is, in effect, not a single grammatical theory (that is, UG) but a *sequence* of grammatical theories, each member of the sequence specifying the class of grammars available to the organism at a particular stage in the maturation of the language faculty.[8]

Early discussion of maturation theories (Gleitman, 1981; Pinker, 1981, 1984) expressed concern that allowing variation in the child's grammatical theory might lead to an unconstrained theory of the process, even allowing for the possibility that children's early grammars might look radically different from those of adults just as, for example, tadpoles look radically different from frogs. However, in his chapter (as in Borer & Wexler, 1992), Wexler proposes a solution to this problem in the form of the assumption that no stage of maturation (that is, under our interpretation given earlier, no grammatical theory in the sequence of grammatical theories that characterize the genetic endowment of the organism) allows mental rep-

[8]Note that under this view it is natural to extend the sequence of grammatical theories through the lifetime of the organism, raising the question of precisely what the organism's grammatical theory consists in adulthood for the case of adult (second) language acquisition. See Ritchie and Bhatia (1996) and Schachter (1996) for discussion.

resentations that are not allowed by UG—none of the grammatical theories allow representations that fall outside of UG and UG thus places outer limits on the process of maturation. This approach is called UG constrained maturation (UGCM).

Wexler analyzes research results on binding theory, optional infinitives, and A-chains in terms of UGCM and the minimalist program. He concludes that, although many features of syntactic structure specific to the language of the child's environment are in place extremely early in the child's development (by 2 years of age), those aspects of structure that are maturationally delayed appear to share the property of requiring coordination of the computational system of the minimalist program (the syntactic component in earlier theories) and the conceptual-interpretative component (the semantics) of the developing grammar.

Turning to continuity theories of the acquisition process, Lust (chapter 4, "Universal Grammar: The Strong Continuity Hypothesis in First Language Acquisition") argues against maturation hypotheses (in direct opposition to Wexler) on a number of theoretical, logical, and empirical grounds. Among other issues, she addresses Radford's well-known proposal (e.g., Radford, 1990) that functional categories are absent from early grammars and that they become available maturationally as well as Borer and Wexler's account of passives in English and Hebrew (Borer & Wexler, 1987; referred to previously).

In opposition to the maturation hypothesis, Lust proposes a strong continuity hypothesis (SCH) under which UG is fully available to the child throughout the process of acquisition. Language development is then understood as a process of grammatical mapping from UG to an adult language through the construction of the grammar for that language on the basis of input from the environment. Grammatical mapping subsumes a variety of processes including the integration of modular UG principles, the setting of parameters, the realization of deductive consequences of the setting of parameters, the integration of principles and parameter setting, as well as the morphosyntax and semantics of the lexicon of the ambient language.

Lust argues that UG both constrains and guides the course of acquisition—even in cases where acquisition is gradual. In cases of "delayed" acquisition, she claims for some specific cases that the mapping from UG to the grammar of a specific language requires more time than in others. She refers to empirical results in several areas of syntactic development—binding theory, relative clause structure, control, and directionality—as supporting her case. She argues that, on the SCH account, cases in which language-specific integration of the operation of distinct principles of UG are what cause delay in the process, because UG itself does not determine this integration. She then refers to empirical research on control, relative clauses, anaphora, and various movements in Germanic languages to support her arguments.

Positions concerning grammar development other than the maturation and strong continuity hypotheses have been offered in the research literature. For example, Clahsen and his colleagues (e.g., Clahsen, Eisenbeiss, & Vainikka, 1994) take a position that they refer to as "weak continuity" specifically in relation to the development of phrase structure and morphological case. Clahsen and colleagues attribute to Boser, Lust, Santelman, and Whitman (1992) the view that German-acquiring children have in place certain specific features of German phrase structure by the age of 2 years even though, Clahsen and colleagues claim, the evidence for those features in the children's performance is very weak. Clahsen and colleagues' position is that though the universal principles are available to the child from the beginning of language development, the child gradually attains these structures on the basis of the interaction of these principles with the input.

Additional reference to the maturation/continuity debate is found elsewhere in the volume. Bickerton (chapter 6) argues, on the basis of evidence of more global features of the linguistic performance of children than that adduced by Wexler or Lust, that there is a developmental "explosion" in the quantity and variety of children's utterances around the age of 2 years. In accordance with his language bioprogram hypothesis, Bickerton attributes this radical change in the child's language ability to the operation of an innate bioprogram that specifies a sudden increase in the complexity of the child's grammar at around 2 years of age.

Also, it should be noted that the maturation/continuity debate has been investigated in circumstances other than the standard case of monolingual acquisition. On the basis of the view that a single child acquiring two native language simultaneously constitutes a perfect case of a matched pair for the purpose of studying the ways in which maturation or continuity might reveal themselves in the acquisition of the grammars of two different languages, Paradis and Genesee (1997) argued for a form of weak continuity on the basis of evidence from a group of bilingual children acquiring German and French.

B. A Nonmodular Theory of Acquisition

O'Grady (chapter 5—"The Acquisition of Syntactic Representations: A General Nativist Approach") argues for an account of acquisition that does not require a special endowment for language acquisition in the form of UG (as per Chomsky), but rather derives the facts of language acquisition from principles of general cognitive functioning. O'Grady refers to his (nonmodular) position as a general nativist one and to Chomsky's (modular) view as special nativist. The core of O'Grady's argument is that an account of the facts of acquisition in terms of general properties of cognition is no less satisfactory than one that requires an appeal to a special endowment such as that argued for in Chomsky's program. Hence, O'Grady argues, if it can be shown that a general nativist theory can account for the same range of phenomena that special nativist theories can, then the general nativist account is to be preferred on methodological grounds.

In O'Grady's words, "The goal of the general nativist research program is to provide an account of syntactic development that does not require *syntactic* [emphasis in the original] categories or principles. On this view, then, the inborn acquisition device must consist only of mechanisms that are not inherently linguistic in character; it cannot include UG." (this volume, p. 169). O'Grady's model includes five innate modules, each of which is claimed to be independently necessarily for general cognitive learning. Taking input to consist of pairings of sentence form and meaning as well as lexical form and meaning, O'Grady provides an account of syntactic categories in terms of semantic or conceptual structure. Noting the failures of earlier attempts to derive the major syntactic categories from semantic notions like "action" (verb) and "thing" (noun) or predicate-argument relations, O'Grady proposes that verbs be characterized as denoting events, which are, in turn, linked innately to the concepts expressed linguistically as tense and aspect. Nouns are characterized as having denotations that are individuated in terms of notions of specificity or definiteness as expressed in the determiner system of a language.

C. Acquisition and Limited Input: The Bioprogram Hypothesis

Studies of acquisition are ordinarily concerned with the "normal" case, in which the child is exposed to speech that is the product of a full-blown grammatical structure. As noted previously, even in this case, the child's linguistic experience underdetermines the grammar that he or she acquires. What is the result of acquisition when input to the child is not from a "full" language but the relatively simple and varied structure of a pidgin language? Pidgins are languages that are created by groups of adults for communication under circumstances where no language is shared among the members of the group but communication is nonetheless necessary. In cases where a pidgin language provides a child's linguistic experience, the result of acquisition is termed a creole language.

On the basis of his research on creole languages (e.g., Bickerton, 1973, 1975, 1980) and his work on the phylogenetic evolution of language (Bickerton, 1981, 1990), Derek Bickerton (chapter 6, "Creole Languages, the Language Bioprogram Hypothesis, and Language Acquisition") has proposed his language bioprogram hypothesis—an account of child language acquisition under which an early, essentially syntaxless protolanguage is extended by a syntax bioprogram that "comes on line" through maturation at approximately 2 years of age. From an evolutionary point of view, the protolanguage reflects a phylogenetically earlier stage in the evolution language; hence, under Bickerton's account, language ontogeny recapitulates language phylogeny. The protolanguage stage also exhibits the properties of systems that arise when true linguistic communication breaks down as in the case of the social context in which pidginization occurs. In contrast, creole languages show the effects of the syntax bioprogram even though the pidgin input on the basis of which children acquire (more accurately, create) a creole language is nonuniform and lacking many of the semantic/syntactic distinctions found in creole languages.

For the case of the acquisition of full languages, Bickerton's proposal predicts a major increase in the structural variety and quality of language production around the age of 2 because of the maturation of the syntax bioprogram. In addition to earlier studies of this period of time in the child's development, Bickerton reports the results of an empirical study of the development of five children that documents statistically a spurt in acquisition that occurs at approximately 2 years of age.

D. Functionalist Approaches to Acquisition

The term *functionalist* has been applied in linguistics to a wide range of approaches to the study of grammatical structure and child language acquisition. In grammatical investigation per se the term has been applied to approaches that differ as much as Van Valin's role and reference grammar (RRG) (Foley & Van Valin, 1984; Van Valin & La Polla, 1997) on one hand and MacWhinney and Bates's competition model of linguistic performance (e.g., MacWhinney & Bates, 1989) on the other. Whereas RRG provides an account of linguistic competence that combines semantic, pragmatic, and morphosyntactic information in the mental representation of sentence structure, the competition model is a performance model based on the notion that utterances in a given language are identified in perception and production by native speakers of the language through semantic and structural cues and is not committed to any particular account of competence. In the study of acquisition, approaches as different as Schieffelin's account of the acquisition of case marking in Kaluli (Schieffelin, 1981, 1985) as a function of pragmatic and semantic (as well as morphosyntactic) features of speech utterances on one hand and, again, MacWhinney and Bates's account of acquisition as the establishment of cue validity and strength in a language by speaker/hearers of the language on the other, have been labeled "functionalist." What all of these positions share is the belief that the grammatical forms of any language are in some way determined by their communicative function and/or by features of general human cognition. In addition, all of these approaches oppose Chomsky's formalist position under which grammatical structure is autonomous from semantic, pragmatic, and general-cognitive factors—what Van Valin and La Polla (1997) refer to as a *syntactocentric* position.

In chapter 7 ("Functionalist Accounts of the Process of First Language Acquisition"), Matthew Rispoli adopts a characterization of functionalist grammatical theories—and by extension, functionalist theories of child language acquisition—as including explanations of grammatical structure in which semantic and pragmatic constructs are integral as opposed to formalist theories under which such constructs are extraneous to the explanation of grammatical structure. Rispoli recognizes the centrality of issues concerning the form (or architecture) and content of mental representations of grammatical structure in current theorizing about language, language use, and language acquisition, and he further narrows his notion of functionalism to those approaches that are concerned with low semantic, pragmatic, and morphosyntactic content interact in such representations and how such concerns may reveal something about the architecture of these representations.

One effect of this narrowing of the notion of functionalism is to establish a systematic relationship between functionalist modes of grammatical analysis on one hand and functionalist research on child language acquisition in parallel with the relationship between grammars of particular languages and research on child acquisition within the formalist tradition.

As noted previously, among the modes of grammatical analysis that qualify as functionalist under Rispoli's characterization is RRG, and Rispoli provides a brief summary of its major tenets. Schieffelin's work on the acquisition of case in Kaluli and his own work on the mosaic theory of grammatical relations serve, for Rispoli, as paradigm instances of functionalism in the study of child language acquisition. He notes that other approaches to child language acquisition that have been designated functionalist—including those of Schlesinger (1982), Bowerman (1973), L. Bloom (1973), Karmiloff-Smith (1979), and MacWhinney and Bates (1989)—fall outside of his narrowed notion of functionalism on one or more counts. Rather, their "functionalism" relates to general human cognition rather than semantics or pragmatics, or it is not based on a notion of grammatical representation that differs significantly from that of formalist approaches. He then calls for functionalist research on acquisition to be grounded in independently (e.g., typologically) justified functionalist grammatical theories like RRG.

E. Another Approach: Connectionism

An additional approach to research on child language acquisition that has achieved some prominence in the field and is very different in conception from all of the approaches discussed so far should be mentioned here for completeness, in spite of the fact that it is not represented in this volume with a full chapter treatment. We refer to work within the connectionist framework. Connectionist approaches to acquisition represent linguistic knowledge—say the relationship between a verb and its past tense form as in Rumelhart and McClelland's influential work (Rumelhart & McClelland, 1986)—as a relationship between the input to a network of connected units and the output of the network. In the specific case of Rumelhart and McClelland's study, the "learning" of this relationship takes place when the network receives verb stems as input and computes past tenses for them as output. The output forms are matched to target forms for the verbs and if there are mismatches, a learning algorithm adjusts the network. Discrepancies between output forms and target forms are reduced over time until the error rate is reduced to zero.

For an introductory survey of research of acquisition within the connectionist approach, see Plunkett (1995). Criticisms of connectionist models of learning and cognition are to be found in Fodor and Pylyshyn (1988) and Pinker and Prince (1988).

III. WORD LEARNING

Because the focus of much of the discussion in the field of different theoretical approaches to the study of child language acquisition has been on the acquisition of syntax, the chapters in Part II of the volume are devoted almost entirely to this area of research. Part III and IV of the volume turn to the acquisition of other areas of linguistic structure. Part III is concerned with the acquisition of lexicon (that is, with word learning), and Part IV deals with the acquisition of the sound systems of languages (phonology) and with pragmatics (the principles of language use).

Part III consists of two chapters. Chapter 8 ("Theories of Word Learning: Rationalist Alternatives to Associationism"), authored by Paul Bloom, rejects empiricist views of word learning in favor of a rationalist view under which a variety of factors intrinsic to the organism play central roles in determining the process of word learning; in chapter 9 ("The role of Syntax in Verb Learning"), Lila Gleitman and Jane Gillette report on a series of experiments exploring the particular issue of role of syntactic structure in the acquisition of word meanings for verbs. Chapters 8 and 9 thus offer a discussion of general issues in the research literature of lexical acquisition and a more concentrated treatment of a particular issue, respectively.

Bloom argues convincingly against the traditional empiricist accounts of word learning found in Skinner (1957), Quine (1960), and more recent "cognitivized" accounts of the same type—that is, rule-based versions proposed in terms of Anderson's ACT* model as well as connectionist models. On Bloom's interpretation of these views, a word meaning is an abstraction from perceptual experience and the meanings of words are established by a process of association through perceptual generalization. Bloom argues against both of these positions on the grounds that children have abstract word meanings from the earliest stages of acquisition and even in those cases where a word designates a class of relatively concrete objects, the child does not apply the word on perceptual grounds alone. Against the second position, he cites empirical evidence that children's simultaneous perception of word and object is neither sufficient nor necessary for the acquisition of lexical meanings.

Bloom then presents and argues for the view that factors such as the syntactic structure of sentences in which a word occurs, the conceptual type of word meanings in relation to the learner's naive theories about the environment, and the intentions of adults referring to objects all play a role in the child's acquisition of lexical meanings.

Gleitman and Gillette provide additional support for Bloom's position from the empirical study of the role of syntactic structure in the learning of verb meanings in particular. Unlike nouns, the verbs to which children are exposed early in acquisition have abstract meanings (*think, want*) and when used by adults tend not to be closely linked in time and space to their designata. Hence, Gleitman and Gillette argue, there is a closer relationship between the acquisition of syntactic structure and that of verb meaning than between structure and the acquisition of nouns in two ways—through both the projection of verb complements from verb meaning and the narrowing of the class of possible meanings for a new verb based on its complement structures. On this basis, Gleitman and Gillette argue for two hypotheses concerning verb learning. The *zoom lens hypothesis* claims that, given a linguistic event in association with an extralinguistic event, the child exploits the semantically relevant structural information from the linguistic event to "zoom in on" one from among the various interpretations that are warranted by the extralinguistic event; the *multiple frames hypothesis* states that the child makes use of the full range of syntactic frames in which a given verb occurs in order to arrive at the general character of its meaning. They conclude with a general discussion of how sentence structure aids vocabulary acquisition.

IV. THE CHILD'S ACQUISITION OF PHONOLOGY AND PRAGMATICS

Elan Dresher (chapter 10, "Child Phonology, Learnability, and Phonological Theory") examines a number of issues in the logical and developmental problems of language acquisition in the domain of phonology. Chapter 11 (Anat Ninio and Catherine Snow, "The Development of Pragmatics: Learning to Use Language Appropriately) addresses the acquisition of principles of language use.

As discussed earlier in this chapter, the central assumption in the formulation of the logical problem is the idealization of instantaneous acquisition under which the adult grammar of a language is understood to be the result of the interaction between data from the language on one hand and the principles of UG—the theory of adult grammars—on the other. Though, as mentioned earlier in this chapter, this idealization has been highly productive and has, in fact, been generally assumed in grammatical analysis (though sometimes implicitly), its appropriateness depends on yet another assumption—that all data from the language is available to the learner at the time of acquisition. Any evidence that this latter assumption is false will adversely affect the appropriateness of the idealization. Dresher discusses two credible cases in which the assumption of instantaneity of acquisition will not lead to the best analysis of adult data from a language—either because a learner may (plausibly) retain properties of earlier grammars at later stages of acquisition or because he or she may not have consistent access to all of the relevant data. Dresher concludes that it is the later stages of acquisition, where consistent access to all forms plays a role, that can effect the adult grammar and, hence, the appropriateness of the idealization of instantaneous acquisition.

Dresher then takes up a number of issues in the logical of acquisition with respect to phonology, including the abstractness of underlying forms, nonlinear phonology, the underspecification of phonological representations, and phonological principles and parameters.

Finally, the chapter addresses a variety of questions concerning the developmental problem of phonological acquisition. Included are discussions of methodological problems—the child's inability to provide well-formedness judgments, rapid change in child phonology, gaps in the data, and a high degree of variability in the data, to name a few—and consideration of models of child phonology at a given stage of acquisition and how these models might be interpreted into an account of the development of phonology as growth in complexity.

Ninio and Snow begin by defining the domain of pragmatics in relation to formalist and functionalist approaches to the investigation of language as discussed earlier in this chapter. They distinguish between the truth-conditional theory of meaning, under which meaning is a property of sentences independent of actual contexts of use, and the use-conditional theory of meaning, which ties the concept of linguistic meaningfulness to the communicative use people make of language. They adopt a use-conditional, or functional, approach in their review. Under this approach, linguistic form is seen as a consequence of mapping a communicative intent onto a linguistic expression of that intent.

In accordance with the general research literature in pragmatics (e.g., Levinson, 1983), Ninio and Snow note the variety of linguistic phenomena that come under the heading of "pragmatics" including centrally the study of communicative intents (e.g., requesting, greeting, showing off, and acknowledging), rules of conversation and politeness and of the principles of connected discourse. They then review the research literature on the development of each of these four areas of language use in children.

Ninio and Snow trace the research on communicative intents and their development from the preverbal stages through the one-word stage to the (limited) work on control of speech acts. They note two major trends in the process of learning to express communicative intents: first, from a holistic communicative intent/verbal expression mapping to a more selective mapping and, second, an increasing mastery of the many-to-many mapping from intent to expression.

A number of skills enter into the exercise of conversational rules, including turn taking and topic selection/maintenance. In addition, clear differences exist among individuals with respect to mastery of these skills—among adults as well as children. Ninio and Snow review the acquisition research in each of these areas. With respect to turn taking they find that children master the required skills very early (as early as the one-word stage), at least for dyadic conversation. On the other hand, Ninio and Snow find that the skills involved in topic selection and maintenance may not develop to an adultlike level until after puberty. Individual differences among children appear most sharply between shy children and those with language or reading disabilities on one hand, and those without these characteristics on the other. In addition, Ninio and Snow note development in connectedness between conversational turns in terms of factual relatedness and the ability to take the perspective of interlocutors takes place from the earliest stages to adulthood.

In their survey of research on the development of politeness, Ninio and Snow conclude that children quickly acquire social sensitivity to such matters as power and social distance but development of the linguistic conventions that express these sensitivities in the ambient society takes time.

Ninio and Snow note several issues in the study of the mastery of the devices that connect discourses, including linguistic devices that maintain cross-utterance cohesion, adaptation to the audience, and the structure of genres such as narratives, explanations, and descriptions. Ability to produce and recognize devices of cohesion such as choice of definite rather than indefinite article in second mentions of referents arise as early as 2 years and continue to develop through the early school years. The ability to adapt to the audience also appears quite early but is sometimes revealed in unconventional ways. In some cases, children show mastery of genres—and, in fact, the ability to move from one to another—in the very early stages of acquisition. However, in the case of more culturally determined genres, such as definitions, mastery does not occur until later.

Ninio and Snow complete their review with suggestions for further research on the relationship between the various skills subsumed under pragmatics in the process of development as well as the relationship between the development of the linguistic structures on one hand and pragmatic skills on the other. Finally, they note the importance of the role of the development of pragmatics in determining or driving the development of syntactic/semantic structure.

V. RESEARCH METHODOLOGY AND APPLICATIONS

The central methodological problem in the study of child language acquisition is that of finding ways of eliciting overt linguistic behavior (linguistic performance) that can be brought to bear on hypotheses about the system of tacit knowledge (linguistic competence) that underlies that performance. Not only is the child's performance influenced by many factors other than his or her linguistic competence (e.g., processing constraints, pragmatic considerations [see chapter 11] and experimental noise), but it is inherently variable whereas underlying competence at any stage of acquisition must be assumed to be categorical and invariant. Chapter 12 (Stephen Crain and Kenneth Wexler, "Methodology in the Study of Language Acquisition: A Modular Approach") and chapter 13 (Barbara Lust, Suzanne Flynn, Yu-Chin Chien, and Claire Foley, "How Do We Know What Children Know? Problems and Advances in Establishing Scientific Methods for the Study of Language Acquisition and Linguistic Theory") take complementary positions on these issues. Crain and Wexler propose a refinement of the theoretical basis for interpreting experimental, whereas Lust, Flynn, Chien, and Foley's view is that a greater emphasis on experimental rigor is called for.

The sharing of data among researchers is an important, if not vital, contribution to the development of any field. Chapter 14 (Brian MacWhinney, "The CHILDES System") describes a computer archive of naturally occurring child speech that is widely used in the field and is accessible to the general research community.

As a solution to the problem of the complex causation of the child's linguistic performance, Crain and Wexler argue for a null hypothesis about the child's language processing system—the modularity matching model—under which all of the linguistic abilities of a child are assumed to be those of an adult—that is, in the absence of clear evidence to the contrary, children are assumed to have access to both UG as a system of constraints on possible grammars and a universal parser as the basis for language processing, just as adults do. On this view, the testing of claims about the child's grammatical knowledge is relatively straightforward. For example, if children give evidence of rejecting utterances or utterance interpretations that are excluded by some principle of UG, then this constitutes evidence that they have the constraint in question and if they give evidence of accepting such utterances, then they lack the constraint, though such matters as preference of one reading over another in the case of ambiguous utterances must also be taken account of.

Crain and Wexler contrast the modularity matching model with what they refer to as the competing factors model under which a variety of factors (of which grammatical competence is but one) "compete" in determining the child's response to an experimental task. On this view, children's performance is interpreted in a relative way—for example, if the child rejects a structure violating a principle with higher frequency than one that does not violate the constraint, then the child's performance is taken to confirm the presence of the constraint regardless of the absolute frequency with which the structure is rejected. Crain and Wexler argue on the basis of reinterpretations of two existing studies that the operation of binding theory in children that the modularity matching model is to be preferred over the competing factors model on both empirical and methodological grounds.

In adopting the assumption that the adult's processing capacities are available to the child, Crain and Wexler are also able to argue that the well-known phenomenon of absence of overt subjects in the utterances of children acquiring English (which in its adult form disallows such utterances) has a grammatical rather than a processing basis contrary to arguments of others in the field. They cite empirical evidence to support their assumption.

Lust, Flynn, Chien, and Foley emphasize the need to evaluate children's variable linguistic performance so as to test categorical claims about specific aspects of underlying linguistic competence. They refer to a number of sources of such variability including nonlinguistic cognitive factors such as memory, linguistic factors other than those under investigation, realizations of principles of UG in the grammar of the specific language under investigation, pragmatic factors, and, finally, factors of performance in real time.

Lust, Flynn, Chien, and Foley then describe ways in which the effects of these sources of variability can be diminished. Noting that the theory of UG is hypothesized to impose constraints on variance and to the extent that variance is so constrained, the theory is supported. More particularly, specific principles of UG can be tested through experimental manipulation, statistical treatment, and replication.

The authors then address three forms of data widely used in research on child language acquisition: natural speech, elicited imitation, and act-out tasks. They note a number of recent advances in the analysis of natural speech that make it possible to infer specific grammatical knowledge in the child to a much higher degree than had previously been the case. Having spelled out the specific features of elicited imitation as an experimental test of production and the act-out task as a test of comprehension and differences between them as tests of grammatical knowledge, the authors cite work that indicates a convergence in results between the two kinds of tasks.

Lust, Flynn, Chien, and Foley see some researchers as having claimed that certain tasks, which the authors refer to as "reduced behavior" tasks, are intended to bypass performance to tap the child's linguistic competence directly. Among these are yes/no responses to adult linguistic performances of a certain kind and the truth-value tasks of Crain and McKee (1986) and the infant preference tasks of Hirsch-Pasek and Golinkoff (1991). They argue that these elicitation tasks do not tap grammatical competence directly but are like other tasks in evoking cognitive systems and capacities other than those specific to grammar competence. They conclude by calling for attention to cases of converging evidence among experimental linguistic performance tasks like elicited imitation and act-out tasks on one hand and the reduced behavior tasks on the other as the basis for inferring features of the child's grammatical competence.

The earliest work on child language acquisition influenced by the cognitive revolution of the 1960s relied on natural speech for its data. Since then this form of data has continued to provide an important basis for theorizing in the study of language development. For this reason, the field is very fortunate to have available to it a computer archive containing a wide variety of natural speech corpora—the CHILDES system. Brian MacWhinney, the cocreator of the CHILDES archive, provides a description in Chapter 14 of the main features of the system, including a brief history of how it came about. MacWhinney reports that CHILDES makes available more than 30 corpora of English data, sets of data from 12 languages other than English, 13 corpora of language-impaired productions, and 5 bilingual corpora. He provides instructions for accessing the database as well as a number of different forms of transcription, coding, and data analysis. He concludes with a description of plans for the future development of CHILDES.

VI. MODALITY AND THE LINGUISTIC ENVIRONMENT IN CHILD LANGUAGE ACQUISITION

Though it is clear that the child's experience with the language of the environment plays an important role in the process of language acquisition (as it is *that* language that the child eventually acquires rather than any other!), many issues concerning its exact role remain. Part VI of the volume addresses these issues. Chapter 15 (Virginia Valian, "Input and Language Acquisition") reviews research on the relationship between the child's linguistic environment and the process of acquisition when input is oral-auditory and monolingual. In chapter 16 ("Modality Effects and Modularity in Language Acquisition: The Acquisition of American Sign Language"), Diane Lillo-Martin surveys work on the acquisition of a language when the input is visual-gestural rather than auditory-oral. In chapter 17 ("The Bilingual Child: Some Issues and Perspectives"), Tej Bhatia and William Ritchie take up the case of acquisition in which the input to the child is the product of the linguistic systems underlying two distinct languages rather than one.

Valian begins her chapter by distinguishing among three metaphors of acquisition: the copy, hypothesis-testing, and trigger metaphors. Under the copy metaphor, the child "copies" input from the environment, approximating that input more and more closely as acquisition proceeds. As the term implies, the hypothesis-testing metaphor represents acquisition as a tacit process of hypothesis formulation and testing by the learner in which the hypotheses available to the learner are constrained by UG; environmental input then provides the basis for the learner's acceptance or rejection of a given hypothesis. Finally, on the trigger metaphor, the child tacitly chooses, from a number of alternative specific language structures made available by UG, the best one, given input from the environment. The role of innate structure in the acquisition process is least—and, hence, the role of input is greatest—in the copy theory, whereas the reverse is true of the trigger theory; the hypothesis-testing position lies between the other two.

After outlining these three positions, Valian reviews the distinction among direct and indirect positive evidence and direct and indirect negative evidence and their roles in languages acquisition under the hypothesis-testing and trigger theories. She then reviews experimental work on the role of input in acquisition.

Valian distinguishes among three types of studies that have been performed to determine the role of the environment in acquisition: input, reply, and intervention studies. Studies of the first type seek correlations between types of input and the learner's progress in acquiring the language; those of the second investigate parents' responses to children's well- and ill-formed utterances (including corrections of the child performance); and those of the third kind look for the effects of caretaker manipulation of input to the child in the form of expansions, extensions, and recasts of the child's production.

Valian concludes on the basis of this work that neither input nor reply studies show any correlations between linguistic activity in the child's environment and progress in acquisition. On the other hand, intervention studies, which examined cases in which children were called on to parse input, show more effects on acquisition.

Lillo-Martin develops her review of recent research on the acquisition of American Sign Language (ASL) as an extended argument for the claim that differences between acquisition in the two cases are attributable entirely to be superficial, "phonetic" differences between ASL and spoken languages, and that the deeper, more significant features of acquisition are shared across the two types of language, as would be expected if they are both products of the same module of the human mind.

In support of her position, Lillo-Martin notes a number of similarities (if not identities) between the development of ASL and that of spoken languages. Among these are, first, there is an identifiable stage of manual babbling in the acquisition of ASL parallel to oral babbling in hearing children. Second, even in cases where a sign is highly iconic, an ASL-learning child will treat it in the same way as a child learning a spoken language treats an arbitrary spoken form. Third, children learning ASL acquire morphemically complex signs in which two or more morphemes are produced simultaneously as though the morphemic elements are separate rather than holistically—again, in parallel with children acquiring multimorphemic forms in a spoken language where the morphemes occur sequentially. Fourth, sublexical ("phonological") structure appears to develop from the formationally (that is, anatomically and cognitively) simplest hand configurations to the formationally more complex, parallel to the development of phonological systems in spoken languages. Fifth, and, perhaps, most tellingly, children at a certain point in the acquisition of ASL exhibit constraints on the use of null arguments ("dropped" subjects and objects) in accordance with principles of UG justified on the basis of the careful study of spoken languages in both adults and in children.

Where the visual-manual modality of ASL appears to play a role in its acquisition is in the physical realization ("phonetics") of ASL as opposed to spoken languages. One such case is the appearance of signs at an arguably earlier age than the appearance of words in spoken languages. Another is a delay in the development of verb agreement in ASL where the agreement depends on the learner's memory for analogically (rather than "digitally") distinct locations in the signing space—apparently not a linguistic (or grammatical) constraint but one on general perception and memory.

Bhatia and Ritchie (chapter 17) review issues in the study of child bilingualism ranging from attempts to "define" bilingualism to an observation of the deaf child who uses both a signed language and a spoken language. However, the most central issues in the study of the bilingual child, as in the study of the monolingual child, are the nature of input to the child and the child's development in each language in comparison to that of monolingual children and the fusion or separation of the two language systems in the process of acquisition.

Bhatia and Ritchie describe the two major views of bilingual acquisition. Under the unitary hypothesis (UH), the child begins the process of acquisition of his or her two languages with a single language system and does not fully separate the two language systems until the age of approximately 3 years. Under the dual system hypothesis (DSH), the child separates the two systems from the beginning stages of acquisition. They then review the research in the field, concluding that the available evidence supports the DSH rather than the UH.

The DSH is supported even by cases in which input to the child is mixed—that is, all caretakers use both languages in whatever way is pragmatically and socially appropriate in the ambient society. In fact, Bhatia and Ritchie argue that the unnatural separation of the two languages in input to the child—for example, with one parent consistently speaking one language and the other parent consistently speaking the other—may lead to pragmatically inappropriate performance in the bilingual setting on the part of the child.

With respect to comparison with monolingual children, Bhatia and Ritchie find no solid empirical evidence in the literature that bilingual children differ in any major way from monolingual children acquiring the two languages in question separately, whether in the pace of acquisition or in the course of acquisition.

Other issues treated by Bhatia and Ritchie include, as mentioned previously, the deaf child as bilingual, language mixing in children, and speech disorders and the bilingual child.

VII. LANGUAGE DISORDERS AND IMPAIRMENTS: SPECIAL CASES OF CHILD LANGUAGE ACQUISITION

A great deal can be learned about the capacity for and process of language acquisition in children through the study of ways in which this process becomes disordered. Chapter 18 (Daniel Dinnsen, "Some Empirical and Theoretical Issues in Disordered Child Phonology") surveys recent theoretically informed empirical research on phonological disorders in children, and chapter 19 (Harald Clahsen, "Linguistic Perspectives on Specific Language Impairment") reviews work on the morphological and syntactic disorders associated with specific language impairment (SLI).

Dinnsen presents two modes of analysis found in the research literature on children's phonological disorders—one grounded in the natural phonology framework (Stampe, 1972) and the other in generative phonology (the theory of Chomsky & Halle, 1968, and its descendants). The first approach is based on the view that the child's underlying phonological representations are those of the adult speakers of the ambient language and the child's production is then seen as the result of the application of a small number of innate processes to these underlying representations. The approach based on generative phonology hypothesizes underlying forms in the child's phonology on the basis of the distribution of forms in the child's speech and accounts for the child's phonetic representations as the consequences of phonological rules of the general type found in the phonologies of adult grammars.

Dinnsen gives a number of convincing arguments that the second account carries greater explanatory power and empirical content than the first. In particular he argues that underspecification theory (Archangeli, 1988), which Dresher (chapter 10) also discusses in relation to normal phonological development, provides a suitable account of disordered speech as well.

An important theoretical and practical question in the study of phonological disorders is whether the kinds of disordered speech that are most frequently found must be considered deviant in some essential way or whether they can best be characterized as mere delays in development. Again, Dinnsen provides strong evidence for the latter position.

One aspect of the study of phonological disorders that is not found in the study of normal phonological development is its practical implications and the resulting opportunities for experimentation with child phonology. Because work on disorders is motivated in part by the practical need for programs of intervention that have a theoretically and empirically sound diagnostic basis, such interventions can serve as experiments that test claims about the nature of phonological development. Dinnsen reports the results of a number of such interventions/experiments.

The term *specific language impairment* has been used in the research literature to designate a complex of problems in speech production, primarily involving failure to produce such elements as verbal affixes indicating number and person agreement, modal and other verbal auxiliaries elements, case marking in nouns, and so on. In chapter 19, Clahsen outlines four different proposed accounts of these deficits that are grounded in linguistic analysis rather than psychological assessment as has been traditional in the field. He then surveys the experimental literature on SLI with a view to choosing among these positions. In particular he reviews work on SLI children acquiring a number of languages with respect to subject-verb agreement, modal and aspectual auxiliaries, nominal case marking, gender marking, noun plurals, tense marking on verbs, particle marking and certain features of word order in German and Swedish. Of the four positions that he presents, Clahsen argues for one, which claims that it is specifically agreement relationships within sentences that cause problems for SLI children.

In the process of reviewing the research literature on SLI, Clahsen reports the use of a number of linguistics-based profiling instruments including the Language Assessment Remediation and Screening Procedure (LARSP) developed for English by David Crystal and his colleagues and a number of other recently developed instruments for other languages including Hebrew, Dutch, and German. All of these include developmentally graded linguistic categories. In addition, Clahsen reports that he and his colleagues have developed a software package (COPROF) for the German profile to assist in speeding up the analysis.

VIII. CONCLUSION

In conclusion, research on child language acquisition has undergone rapid and radical change over the past 35 years and promises to continue to do so in the future. No work of this (or any other) sort should be seen as the final word on the issues that are treated here. The present volume should be considered as providing a snapshot of the field at a particular point in its history.

REFERENCES

Archangeli, D. (1988). Aspects of underspecification theory. *Phonology, 5,* 183–207.
Bickerton, D. (1973). On the nature of a creole continuum. *Language, 49,* 640–699.
Bickerton, D. (1975). *Dynamics of a creole continuum.* Cambridge, UK: Cambridge University Press.
Bickerton, D. (1980). Decreolization and the creole continuum. In A. Valdman and A. Highfield (Eds.), *Theoretical orientations in creole studies* (pp. 109–128). New York: Academic Press.
Bickerton, D. (1981). *Roots of language.* Ann Arbor, MI: Karoma.
Bickerton, D. (1990). *Language and species.* Chicago: University of Chicago Press.
Bloom, L. (1973). *One word at a time: The use of single word utterances before syntax.* The Hague: Mouton.
Borer, H., & Wexler, K. (1987). The maturation of syntax. In T. Roeper and E. Williams (Eds.), *Parameter setting* (pp. 123–172). Dordrecht: D. Reidel.
Borer, H., & Wexler, K. (1992). Bi-uniqueness relations and the maturation of grammatical principles. *Natural Language and Linguistic Theory, 10,* 147–189.

Boser, K., Lust, B., Santelman, L., & Whitman, J. (1992). The syntax of V2 in early German grammar: The strong continuity hypothesis. *Proceedings of the North Eastern Linguistic Society 22.* Amherst: Gradual Student Linguistic Organization, University of Massachusetts.

Bowerman, M. (1973). *Early syntactic development.* Cambridge, UK: Cambridge University Press.

Brown, R. (1973). *A first language.* Cambridge, MA: Harvard University Press.

Brown, R., & Hanlon, C. (1970). Derivational complexity and order of acquisition in child speech. In J. Hayes (Ed.), *Cognition and the development of language* (pp. 155–207). New York: Wiley.

Chomsky, N. (1959). Review of *Verbal Behavior* by B. F. Skinner. *Language, 35,* 26–58.

Chomsky, N. (1980). *Rules and representations.* New York: Columbia University Press.

Chomsky, N. (1981). *Lectures on government and binding: The Pisa lectures.* Dordrecht: Foris Publishers.

Chomsky, N. (1986). *Knowledge of language: Its nature origin and use.* New York: Praeger.

Chomsky, N., & Halle, M. (1968). *The sound pattern of English.* New York: Harper & Row.

Clahsen, H., Eisenbeiss, S., & Vainikka, A. (1994). The seeds of structure: A syntactic analysis of case marking. In T. Hoekstra & B. Schwartz (Eds.), *Language acquisition studies in generative grammar* (pp. 85–118). Amsterdam: John Benjamins.

Crain, S., & McKee, C. (1986). Acquisition of structural restrictions on anaphora. In S. Berman, J.-W. Choe, & J. McDonough (Eds.), *Proceedings of the Sixteenth Annual North Eastern Linguistic Society* (pp. 94–110). Amherst, MA: University of Massachusetts Press.

Culicover, P. (1997). *Principles and parameters: An introduction to syntactic theory.* Oxford: Oxford University Press.

Fodor, J., & Pylyshyn, Z. (1988). Connectionism and cognitive architecture: A critical analysis. *Cognition, 28,* 3–71.

Foley, W., & Van Valin, R. (1984). *Functional syntax and universal grammar.* Cambridge, UK: Cambridge University Press.

Gleitman, L. (1981). Maturational determinants of language growth. *Cognition, 10,* 103–114.

Haegeman, L. (1994). *Introduction to government and binding theory* (2nd ed.). Oxford: Basil Blackwell.

Hirsch-Pasek, K., & Golinkoff, R. (1997). *The origins of grammar.* Cambridge, MA: Bradford Books.

Huang, C.-T. J. (1984). On the distribution and reference of empty pronouns. *Linguistic Inquiry, 15,* 531–574.

Hyams, N. (1986). *Language acquisition and the theory of parameters.* Dordrecht: D. Reidel.

Jaeggli, O., & Safir, K. (1989). *The null subject parameter.* Dordrecht: Kluwer.

Jakobson, R. (1968). *Child language, aphasia, and phonological universals.* (A. Keiler, Trans.) The Hague: Mouton. (Original work published in 1941.)

Karmiloff-Smith, A. (1979). *A functional approach to child language.* Cambridge, UK: Cambridge University Press.

Kenstowicz, M. (1994). *Phonology in generative grammar.* Oxford: Basil Blackwell.

Levinson, S. (1983). *Pragmatics.* Cambridge, UK: Cambridge University Press.

MacWhinney, B., & Bates, E. (1989). *The cross-linguistic study of sentence processing.* Cambridge, UK: Cambridge University Press.

McDaniel, D., McKee, C., & Cairns, H. (Eds.). (1996). *Methods for assessing children's syntax.* Cambridge, MA: MIT Press.

Paradis, J., & Genesee, F. (1997). On continuity and the emergence of functional categories in bilingual first-language acquisition. *Language Acquisition, 6,* 91–124.

Pinker, S. (1981). Comments on the paper by Wexler. In C. Baker & J. McCarthy (Eds.), *The logical problem of language acquisition.* Cambridge, MA: MIT Press.

Pinker, S. (1984). *Language learnability and language development.* Cambridge, MA: Harvard University Press.

Pinker, S., & Prince, A. (1988). On language and connectionism: Analysis of a parallel distributed processing model of language acquisition. *Cognition, 28,* 73–193.

Plunkett, K. (1995). Connectionist approaches to language acquisition. In P. Fletcher and B. MacWhinney (Eds.), *The handbook of child language* (pp. 36–72). Oxford: Basil Blackwell.

Quine, W. (1960). *Word and object.* Cambridge, MA: MIT Press.

Radford, A. (1990). *Syntactic theory and the acquisition of English syntax.* Oxford: Basil Blackwell.

Radford, A. (1997). *Syntax: A minimalist approach.* Cambridge, UK: Cambridge University Press.

Ritchie, W., & Bhatia, T. (1996). Second language acquisition: Introduction, foundations, and overview. In W. Ritchie & T. Bhatia (Eds.), *Handbook of second language acquisition* (pp. 1–46). San Diego, CA: Academic Press.

Rumelhart, D., & McClelland, J. (1986). On learning the past tenses of English verbs. In D. Rumelhart, J. McClelland, and the PDP Research Group (Eds.), *Parallel distributed processing, Volume I.* Cambridge, MA: MIT Press.

Schachter, J. (1996). Maturation and the issue of universal grammar in second language acquisition. In W. Ritchie & T. Bhatia (Eds.), *Handbook of second language acquisition* (pp. 159–193). San Diego, CA: Academic Press.

Schieffelin, B. (1981). A developmental study of the pragmatic appropriateness of word order and case marking in Kaluli. In W. Deutsch (Ed.), *The child's construction of grammar.* New York: Academic Press.

Schieffelin, B. (1985). The acquisition of Kaluli. In D. Slobin (Ed.), *The cross-linguistic study of language acquisition, Volume I* (pp. 525–593). Hillsdale, NJ: Erlbaum.

Schlesinger, I. (1982). *Steps to language: Toward a theory of language acquisition.* Hillsdale, NJ: Erlbaum.

Skinner, B. (1957). *Verbal behavior.* New York: Appleton-Century-Crofts.

Stampe, D. (1972). *A dissertation on phonology.* Doctoral dissertation, University of Chicago.

Van Valin, R., & La Polla, R. (1997). *Syntax: Structure, meaning, and function.* Cambridge, UK: Cambridge University Press.

PART II

ISSUES OF INNATENESS, MATURATION, AND MODULARITY IN CHILD LANGUAGE ACQUISITION

CHAPTER 2

ON THE NATURE, USE, AND ACQUISITION OF LANGUAGE[1]

Noam Chomsky

I. ON THE NATURE, USE, AND ACQUISITION OF LANGUAGE

For about 30 years, the study of language—or more accurately, one substantial component of it—has been conducted within a framework that understands linguistics to be a part of psychology, ultimately human biology. This approach attempts to reintroduce into the study of language several concerns that have been central to Western thought for thousands of years and that have deep roots in other traditions as well: questions about the nature and origin of knowledge in particular. This approach has also been concerned to assimilate the study of language to the main body of the natural sciences. This meant, in the first place, abandoning dogmas that are entirely foreign to the natural sciences and that have no place in rational inquiry, the dogmas of the several varieties of behaviorism, for example, which seek to impose *a priori* limits on possible theory construction, a conception that would properly be dismissed as entirely irrational in the natural sciences. It means a frank adherence to mentalism, where we understand talk about the mind to be talk about the brain at an abstract level at which, so we try to demonstrate, principles can be formulated that enter into successful and insightful explanation of linguistic (and other) phenomena that are provided by observation and experiment. Mentalism, in this sense, has no taint of mysticism and carries no dubious ontological burden. Rather, mentalism falls strictly within the standard prac-

[1]This originally appeared in a published series of lectures entitled Language in a Psychological Setting. *Sophia Linguistica*, Special Issue *11*, 1987.

tice of the natural sciences and in fact, is nothing other than the approach of the natural sciences applied to this particular domain.

This work proceeds from the empirical assumption—which is well supported—that there is a specific faculty of the mind/brain that is responsible for the use and acquisition of language, a faculty with distinctive characteristics that is apparently unique to the species in essentials and a common endowment of its members, hence a true species property.

These ideas have developed in the context of what some have called "the cognitive revolution" in psychology, and in fact constituted one major factor contributing to these developments. It is important, I think, to understand clearly just what this revolution sought to accomplish, why it was undertaken, and how it relates to earlier thinking about these topics. The so-called cognitive revolution is concerned with the states of the mind/brain that enter into thought, planning, perception, learning, and action. The mind/brain is considered to be an information-processing system, which forms abstract representations and carries out computations that use and modify them. This approach stands in sharp contrast to the study of the shaping and control of behavior that systematically avoided consideration of the states of the mind/brain that enter into behavior, and sought to establish direct relations between stimulus situations, contingencies of reinforcement, and behavior. This behaviorist approach has proven almost entirely barren, in my view, a fact that is not at all surprising because it refuses in principle to consider the major and essential component of all behavior, namely, the states of the mind/brain.

Consider the problem of learning. We have an organism with a mind/brain that is in a certain state or configuration. The organism is presented with certain sensory inputs, leading to a change in the state of the mind/brain. This process is the process of learning or, perhaps more accurately, mental and cognitive growth. Having attained a new state as a result of this process, the organism now carries out certain actions, in part influenced by the state of the mind/brain that has been attained, though there is much more to the matter, a very important topic that I will not have time to address in these remarks. There is no direct relation between the sensory inputs that led to the change of state of the mind/brain and the actions carried out by the organism, except under highly artificial, uninformative, and very marginal conditions.

There is of course a relation of some kind between sensory inputs and behavior; a child who has not been presented with data of Japanese will not be able to carry out the behavior of speaking Japanese. Presented with appropriate data from Japanese, the child's mind/brain undergoes a significant change; the mind/brain comes to incorporate within itself knowledge of Japanese, which then enables the child to speak and understand Japanese. But there is no direct relation between the data presented to the child and what the child says, and it is hopeless, indeed perverse, to try to predict what the child will say, even in probabilistic terms, on the basis of the sensory data that led to acquisition of knowledge of Japanese. We can study the process by which the sensory data leads to the change of state of the mind/brain, and we may study at least certain aspects of how this attained knowledge is used. But an effort to study the relation between the sensory data and the actual behavior, avoiding the crucial matter of the nature of the mind/brain and the changes it undergoes, is doomed to triviality and failure, as the history of psychology demonstrates very well. The cognitive revolution was based in part on the recognition of such facts as these, drawing conclusions that really should not be controversial, though they are so regarded, a sign of the immaturity of the field, in my view. This change of perspective in the study of psychology, linguistics included, was surely a proper one in essence and, in fact, was long overdue.

Not only was this change of perspective overdue, but it also was much less of a revolution than many believed. In fact, without awareness, the new perspective revived ideas that had been developed quite extensively centuries earlier. In particular, 17th-century science developed a form of cognitive psychology that was quite rich and basically, I think, on the right track. Descartes's major scientific contribution, perhaps, was his rejection of the neo-scholastic idea that perception is a process in which the form of an object imprints itself somehow on the brain, so that if you see a cube, for example, your brain has an actual cube imprinted in it in some fashion. In place of this fallacious conception, Descartes proposed a representational theory of mind. He considered the example of a blind man with a stick, who uses the stick to touch in sequence various parts of a physical object before him, let us say a cube. This sequence of tactile inputs leads the blind man to construct, in his mind/brain, the image of a cube, but the form of the cube is not imprinted in the mind/brain. Rather, the sequence of tactile inputs leads the mind/brain to construct a mental representation of a cube, using its own resources and its own structural principles. Descartes argued that much the same is true of normal vision. A series of patterned stimuli strike the retina, and the mind/brain then forms ideas that provide a conception of the objects of the external world. The mind/brain then carries out various computational processes, as the person thinks about these objects, including processes that enable the person to carry out certain actions involving them: for example, picking up the cube, rotating it, and so on. This is surely the right general approach. It has been revived in recent psychology and physiology, and by now a good deal is known about how the process takes place, including even some understanding of the physical mechanisms involved in the coding and representation of stimuli.

Descartes also observed that if a certain figure, say a triangle, is presented to a person, then what the person will perceive is a triangle, though the presented image is certainly not a Euclidean triangle, but rather some far more complex figure. This will be true, he argued, even if the subject is a child who has had no previous acquaintance with geometrical figures. In a certain sense the point is obvious, because true geometrical figures do not exist in the natural environment in which we grow and live, but we nevertheless perceive figures as distorted geometrical figures, not as exact instances of whatever they may happen to be. Why does the child perceive the object as a distorted triangle, rather than as the very complex figure that it actually is: with one of the lines slightly curved, with two sides not quite touching, and so on? Descartes's answer was that the Euclidean triangle is produced by the mind on the occasion of this stimulation, because the mechanisms of the mind are based on principles of Euclidean geometry and produce these geometrical figures as exemplars or models for the organization of perception, and for learning, drawing them from its own resources and structural principles.

In contrast, empiricists such as David Hume argued that we simply have no idea of a triangle, or a straight line, because we are never presented with perfect images of such objects in the real world. Hume correctly drew the consequences of the empiricist principles that he adopted and developed: in particular, the principle that the mind receives impressions from the outside world and forms associations based on them and that this is all there is to the story. But the consequences that Hume correctly drew from these assumptions are certainly false. Contrary to what he asserted, we do, indeed, have a clear concept of a triangle and a straight line, and we perceive objects of the world in terms of these concepts, just as Descartes argued. The conclusion, then, is that the empiricist assumptions are fundamentally wrong, as a matter of empirical fact, and that the properties of the mind/brain are crucially involved in determining how we perceive and what we perceive. Crucially, we must resort to a representational theory of mind of the Cartesian sort, including the concept of the mind as an information-processing system that computes, forms, and modifies representations; and we must also adopt something like the Cartesian concept of innate ideas, biologically determined properties of the mind/brain that provide a framework for the construction of mental representations, a framework that then enters into our perception and action. Ideas of this sort have been revived in the context of the cognitive revolution of the past generation, and as I mentioned, a good deal is now known about the psychological processes involved and even about the physiological mechanisms: line detectors and so on.

Seventeenth-century psychologists, who we call "philosophers," went far beyond these observations. They developed a rather rich form of what much later came to be called "Gestalt psychology" as similar ideas were rediscovered during this century. These 17th-century thinkers speculated rather plausibly on how we perceive objects around us in terms of structural properties, in terms of our concepts of object and relation, cause and effect, whole and part, symmetry, proportion, the functions served by objects and the characteristic uses to which they are put. We perceive the world around us in this manner, they argued, as a consequence of the organizing activity of the mind, based on its innate structure and the experience that has caused it to assume new and richer forms. "The book of nature is legible only to an intellectual eye," as the 17th-century philosopher Ralph Cudworth argued, developing such ideas as these. Again, these speculations seem to be very much on the right track, and the ideas have been rediscovered and developed in contemporary psychology, in part within the context of the cognitive revolution.

The contemporary cognitive revolution has been considerably influenced by modern science, mathematics, and technology. The mathematical theory of computation, which developed in the 1920s and 1930s particularly, provided the conceptual tools that make it possible to address certain classical problems of representational psychology in a serious way, problems of language in particular. Wilhelm von Humboldt understood, a century and a half ago, that language is a system that makes infinite use of finite means, in his phrase. But he was unable to give a clear account of this correct idea, or to use it as the basis for substantive research into language. The conceptual tools developed in more recent years make it possible for us to overcome these limits and to study the infinite use of finite means with considerable clarity and understanding. Modern generative grammar can be regarded in part as the result of the confluence of the conceptual tools of modern logic and mathematics and the traditional idea, inevitably left vague and unformed, that language is a system that makes infinite use of finite means. A generative grammar of a language is a formal system that states explicitly what are these finite means available to the mind/brain, which can then make infinite, unbounded use of these means. Unfortunately, the classical ideas concerning language and representational psychology had long been forgotten when the cognitive revolution took place in the 1950s, and the connections I am now discussing were discovered only much later, and are still not widely known.

The development of electronic computers has also influenced the cognitive revolution considerably, primarily, in providing useful concepts such as internal representation, modular structure, the software-hardware distinction, and the like, and also, in areas such as vision at least, in making it possible to develop explicit models of cognitive processes that can be tested for accuracy and refined. It is worthy of note that much the same was true of the 17th-century cognitive revolution. The Cartesians were much impressed with the mechanical automata then being constructed by skilled craftsmen, which seemed to mimic certain aspects of the behavior of organisms. These automata were a stimulus to their scientific imagination much in the way that modern electronic computers have contributed to the contemporary cognitive revolution.

Some of these 17th-century ideas, which are now being rediscovered and developed in quite new ways, have much earlier origins. What is probably the world's first psychological experiment is described in the Platonic dialogs when Socrates undertakes to demonstrate that a slave boy, who has had no instruction in geometry, nevertheless knows the truths of geometry. Socrates demonstrated this by what we call the "Socratic method." He asks the slave boy a series of questions, providing him with no information but drawing from the inner resources of the slave boy's mind, and in this way Socrates leads the slave boy to the point where he recognizes the truth of theorems of geometry. This experiment was understood, quite plausibly, to show that the slave boy knew geometry without any experience. Indeed, it is difficult to see what other interpretation can be given. The experiment was, presumably, a kind of thought experiment, but if it were carried out rigorously, as has never been done, the results would probably be more or less as Plato presented them in his literary version of a psychological experiment.

The human mind, in short, somehow incorporates the principles of geometry, and experience only serves to bring them to the point where this innate knowledge can be used. This demonstration also poses a very crucial problem: to explain how the slave boy can have the knowledge he does have, when he has had no relevant experience from which he could derive this knowledge. This is what I have referred to as "Plato's problem." We return to it directly.

The rise of generative grammar in the 1950s, a major factor in the cognitive revolution, also resurrected traditional ideas. The Cartesians, in particular, had applied their ideas on the nature of the mind to the study of language, which was commonly viewed as a kind of "mirror of mind," reflecting the essential properties of mind. Further study of these topics in the 18th and early 19th century enriched these investigations in quite impressive ways, which we are now only beginning to understand. The cognitive revolution of the 1950s, then, should be understood, I believe, as having recovered independently the insights of earlier years, abandoning the barren dogmas that had impeded understanding of these questions for a very long period and then applying these classical ideas, now reconstructed in a new framework, in new ways, and developing them along lines that would not have been possible in an earlier period, thanks to new understanding in the sciences, technology, and mathematics that had developed during this century.

From the point of view adopted in this so-called cognitive revolution, the central problems of the study of language are essentially the following four:

The first question, a preliminary to any further inquiry, is this: What is the system of knowledge incorporated in the mind/brain of a person who speaks and understands a particular language? What constitutes the language that the person has mastered and knows. A theory concerned with this topic for a particular language is called "a grammar of that language" or, in technical terms, "a generative grammar of the language," where the term *generative grammar* means nothing more than a theory of the language that is fully explicit, so that empirical consequences can be derived in it enabling the theory to be tested for accuracy in the manner of the natural sciences. Traditional grammars, in contrast, were inexplicit, relying crucially on the knowledge of language of the reader of the grammar to fill in the enormous gaps that were left unstudied and were not even recognized to be gaps. A traditional grammar, then, is not a theory of the language, but is rather a guide that can be followed by a person who already knows the language. Similarly, a traditional grammar of English written in Japanese is not a theory of English but rather a guide to English that can be used by a speaker of Japanese who already knows the basic principles of language, though unconsciously, and can therefore make use of the hints and examples in the grammar to draw conclusions about English. A generative grammar, in contrast, seeks to make explicit just what this knowledge is that enables the intelligent reader to make use of a grammar. A generative grammar is almost complementary in its concerns to traditional grammar. Thus a traditional grammar or a pedagogic grammar will concentrate on idiosyncratic facts, irregular verbs, and so on; it will give only vague and general hints about sentence structure, relying on the intelligence of the reader—on the reader's innate language faculty—to fill in the gaps. A generative grammar, in contrast, is only marginally concerned with idiosyncracies, but rather with the deeper principles of the language; it is not an arrangement of examples and hints, but a theory of the language, much in the sense in which chemistry is a theory of other objects in the physical world.

To the extent that we can provide at least a partial answer to the first problem, the problem of characterizing the knowledge of language of a person who has come to know that language, we can turn to a second problem: How is this knowledge of language used in thought or expression of thought, in understanding, in organizing behavior, or in such special uses of language as communication, and so on? Here we have to make a crucial conceptual distinction between (a) the language, a certain cognitive system, a system of knowledge incorporated in the mind/brain and described by the linguist's generative grammar and (b) various processing systems of the mind/brain that access this knowledge in one or another way and put it to use.

Assuming some kind of answer to the first and central problem of characterizing the knowledge attained, we can turn to a third problem: to discover the physical mechanisms that exhibit the properties that we discover in the abstract investigation of language and its use, that is, the physical mechanisms of the brain that are involved in the representation of knowledge, and the physical mechanisms of the different systems of the brain that access and process this knowledge. Notice that these are two distinct though related tasks. They are, furthermore, pretty much tasks for the future, and they are very difficult ones, primarily, because for very good ethical reasons, we do not permit direct experimentation that might enable scientists to investigate these mechanisms directly. Notice that in the case of other systems of the mind/brain, such as the visual system, the investigation of mechanisms has proceeded quite far. The reason is that we allow ourselves, rightly or wrongly, to carry out direct experimentation with other organisms: cats, monkeys, and so on. Their visual systems are in many ways like our own, so a good deal can be learned about the physical mechanisms of the human visual system in this way. But it appears that the language faculty is a unique human possession in its essentials, and if we were to discover some other organism that shared this faculty in part, we would probably regard it as quasi-human and refrain from direct experimentation. Consequently, the study of physical mechanisms of the language faculty must be studied in much more indirect ways, either by nonintrusive experiments or by "nature's experiments," such as injury and pathology. Part of the intellectual fascination of the study of language is that it must proceed in such indirect ways, relying very heavily on the abstract level of inquiry, a difficult and challenging task, but one that can be addressed and has much promise.

The fourth problem is to explain how the knowledge of language and ability to use it are acquired. This problem can also be addressed only insofar as we have some grasp of the first problem, of the nature of the knowledge that comes to be mastered. This problem of acquisition arises both for the language—the cognitive system itself—and for the various processing systems that access the language. I will focus attention here on the first of these questions: on acquisition of language. Plainly, the question can be formulated only to the extent that we have some understanding of what is acquired—of what is a language—though as always, inquiry into the acquisition or use or physical basis of some abstract system can and should provide insight into its nature.

The fourth question, the question of how language is acquired, is a special case of Plato's problem: How do we come to have such rich and specific knowledge, or such intricate systems of belief and understanding, when the evidence available to us is so meager? That was the problem that rightly troubled Plato, and it should trouble us as well. It is a question that did not trouble psychologists, linguists, philosophers, and others who thought about the matter for a long, long period, except for a few, who were rather marginal to the main intellectual tradition. This is a sign of the serious intellectual failings of the thought of this era, an interesting topic that I will not pursue here. If a rational Martian scientist were to observe what takes place in a single language community on Earth, he would conclude that knowledge of the language that is used is almost entirely inborn. The fact that this is not true, or at least not entirely true, is extremely puzzling and raises many quite serious problems for psychology and biology, including evolutionary biology.

Recall that Plato had an answer to the problem he posed: We remember the knowledge we have from an earlier existence. This is not a proposal that we would nowadays be inclined to accept in exactly these terms, though we should, in all honesty, be prepared to recognize that it is a far more satisfactory and rational answer than the ones that have been offered in the dominant intellectual traditions of recent centuries, including the Anglo-American empiricist tradition, which simply evaded the problems. To render Plato's answer intelligible, we have to provide a mechanism by which our knowledge is remembered from an earlier existence. If we are disinclined to accept the immortal soul as the mechanism, we will follow Leibniz in assuming that Plato's answer is on the right track, but must be, in his words, "purged of the error of preexistence." In modern terms, that means reconstructing Platonic "remembrance" in terms of the genetic endowment, which specifies the initial state of the language faculty, much as it determines that we will grow arms not wings, undergo sexual maturation at a certain stage of growth if external conditions such as nutritional level permit this internally directed maturational process to take place, and so on. Nothing is known in detail about the mechanisms in any of these cases, but it is now widely and plausibly assumed that this is the place to look. At least, it is widely assumed for physical growth. The fact that similar evidence does not lead to similar rational conclusions in the case of the mind/brain again reflects the serious intellectual inadequacies of recent thought, which has simply refused to approach problems of the mind/brain by the same methods of rational inquiry taken for granted in the physical sciences. This is strikingly true, particularly, of those who falsely believe themselves to be scientific naturalists and who see themselves as defending science against the obscurantists. Exactly the opposite is true, in my opinion, for the reasons that I have briefly indicated.

Putting aside these dogmas, let us approach questions of mind/brain, including questions of language, in the spirit of the natural sciences. We do not know now what are the physical mechanisms of the language faculty, the mechanisms that enter into the representation of knowledge of language and the processing of language. Therefore we must proceed much in the way that 19th-century chemists proceeded when they studied chemical elements, organic molecules, the molecular theory of gases, and so on, all at an abstract level, abstracting away from the unknown physical mechanisms that exhibited the properties that they investigated. In the case of language, abstracting way from unknown mechanisms, we assume that the language faculty has an initial state, genetically determined, common to the species apart from gross pathology, and apparently unique to the human species. We know that this initial state can mature to a number of different steady states—the various attainable languages—as conditions of exposure vary. The process of maturation from the initial state to the steady state of mature knowledge is, to some extent, data driven; exposed to data of English, the mind/brain will incorporate knowledge of English, not Japanese. Furthermore, this process of growth of the language faculty begins remarkably early in life. Recent work indicates that 4-day-old infants can already distinguish somehow between the language spoken in their community and other languages, a most remarkable fact, which shows that the mechanisms of the language faculty begin to operate and to be tuned to the external environment very early in life.

It is fairly clear that the process of maturation to the steady state is deterministic. Language learning is not really something that the child does; it is something that happens to the child placed in an appropriate environment, much as the child's body grows and matures in a predetermined way when provided with appropriate nutrition and environmental stimulation. This is not to say that the nature of the environment is irrelevant. The environment determines how the options left undetermined by universal grammar are fixed, yielding different languages. In a somewhat similar way, the early visual environment determines the density of receptors for horizontal and vertical lines, as has been shown experimentally. Furthermore, the difference between a rich and stimulating environment and an impoverished environment may be substantial, in language acquisition as in physical growth—or more accurately, as in other aspects of physical growth, the acquisition of language being simply one of these aspects. Capacities that are part of our common human endowment can flourish, or can be restricted and suppressed, depending on the conditions provided for their growth.

The point is probably more general. It is a traditional insight, which merits more attention than it receives, that teaching should not be compared to filling a bottle with water, but rather to helping a flower to grow in its own way. As any good teacher knows, the methods of instruction and the range of material covered are matters of small importance as compared with the success achieved in arousing the natural curiosity of the students and stimulating their interest in exploring on their own. What the student learns passively will be quickly forgotten. What students discover for themselves, when their natural curiosity and creative impulses are aroused, will not only be remembered, but will be the basis for further exploration and inquiry and perhaps significant intellectual contributions. The same is true in other domains as well. A truly democratic community is one in which the general public has the opportunity for meaningful and constructive participation in the formation of social policy: in their own immediate community, in the workplace, and in the society at large. A society that excludes large areas of crucial decision making from public control, or a system of governance that merely grants the general public the opportunity to ratify decisions taken by the elite groups that dominate the private society and the state, hardly merits the term *democracy.* The point was made, in another context, by Immanuel Kant, defending the French Revolution during the period of the Terror against those who argued that the masses of the population "are not ripe for freedom." Kant wrote:

> If one accepts this proposition, freedom will never be achieved, for one can not arrive at the maturity for freedom without having already acquired it; one must be free to learn how to make use of one's powers freely and usefully . . . one can achieve reason only through one's own experience and one must be free to be able to undertake them . . . To accept the principle that freedom is worthless for those under one's control and that one has the right to refuse it to them forever, is an infringement of the rights of God himself, who has created man to be free.

Reason, the ability to make use of one's powers freely and usefully, and other human qualities can be achieved only in an environment in which they can flourish. They cannot be taught by coercive means. What is true of physical growth holds quite generally of human maturation and learning.

Returning to the language faculty, learning of language, as noted, is something that happens to the child, without awareness for the most part, just as other processes such as sexual maturation happen to the child. A child does not decide to undergo sexual maturation because it sees others doing so and thinks this would be a good idea, or because it is trained or reinforced. Rather, the process happens in its own inner-directed way, if the environment is appropriate. The course of the process, its timing, and its detailed nature are in part influenced by the environment, by nutritional level, for example, but the process itself is inner directed in its essentials. The same appears to be true of language learning, and of other aspects of cognitive growth as well. The term *learning* is, in fact, a very misleading one, and one that is perhaps best abandoned as a relic of an earlier age, and earlier misunderstandings. Knowledge of language grows in the mind/brain of a child placed in a certain speech community.

Knowledge of language within a speech community is shared to remarkably fine detail, in every aspect of language from pronunciation to interpretation. In each of these aspects, the knowledge attained vastly transcends the evidence available in richness and complexity, and in each of these aspects, the fineness of detail and the precision of knowledge go well beyond anything that can be explained on any imaginable functional grounds, such as the exigencies of communication. For example, children mimic the sounds of the language around them to a level of precision that is well beyond the capacities of adults to hear, and in other domains as well the precision of knowledge and understanding, as well as its scope and richness, are far beyond anything that could be detected in normal human interchange. These properties of normal language can often only be discovered by careful experiment. These are the basic and simplest elements of the problem we face.

We therefore conclude that the initial state of the language faculty can be regarded as in effect a deterministic input-output system that takes presented data as its input and produces a cognitive system as its output—here the output is internalized, represented in the mature mind/brain; it is the steady state of knowledge of some particular language. The initial state of the language faculty can be regarded, in essence, as a language-acquisition device; in mathematical terms, it is a function that maps presented data into a steady state of knowledge attained. This general conclusion allows many specific variants, to some of which I will briefly return, but it is virtually inconceivable that it is wrong in any fundamental way. There has been much debate over this issue in the literature—more accurately, a one-sided debate in which critics argue that the idea has been refuted, with little response from its defenders. The reason for the lack of response is that the criticism must be based on profound confusion, and inspection of the arguments quickly reveals that this is the case, as it must be, given the nature of the problem.

The theory of the initial state—of the language acquisition device—is sometimes called *universal grammar,* adapting a traditional term to a somewhat different conceptual framework. It is commonly assumed that universal grammar, so conceived, determines the class of attainable languages. Let me quote from one recent paper by the two leading researchers in the important new field of mathematical learning theory (Daniel Osherson and Scott Weinstein), a paper on models of language acquisition. They wrote that universal grammar

> imposes restrictions on a [particular] grammar in such a way that the class of [particular] grammars admissible by the theory includes grammars of all and only natural languages, [where] the natural languages are identified with the languages that can be acquired by normal human infants under casual conditions of access to linguistic data.

The first of these propositions is a definition, and a proper and useful one, so it is not open to challenge: We may define a *natural language* as one that accords with the principles of universal grammar. But the second of these propositions need not be correct. The languages attainable under normal conditions of access are those that fall in the intersection of two sets: (a) the set of natural languages made available by the initial state of the language faculty as characterized by universal grammar and (b) the set of learnable systems. If universal grammar permits unlearnable languages, as it might, then they simply will not be learned. Learnability, then, is not a requirement that must be met by the language faculty.

Similarly, parsability—that is, the ability of the mind/brain to assign a structural analysis to a sentence—is not a requirement that must be met by a language, contrary to what is often claimed. In this case, in fact, we know that the claim is false: Every language permits many different categories of expressions that cannot be used or understood, though they are perfectly well formed, a fact that in no way impedes communication. This has been a commonplace for 30 years, but nevertheless, the false claim that languages must be parsable is quite common and is often taken to be a condition of principle that must be met by linguistic theory.

In the case of learnability, the proposition that the natural languages are learnable may very well be true, but if so, that is not a matter of principle, but rather a surprising empirical discovery about natural language. Recent work in linguistics suggests that it probably is true, again, a surprising and important empirical discovery, to which I will briefly return.

There has been a fair amount of confusion about these matters, in part resulting from misinterpretations of observations concerning formal systems, for example, the well-known observation of Stanley Peters and Robert Ritchie that unconstrained transformational grammars can generate all sets that can be specified by finite means, and results on efficient parsability of context-free languages. In both cases, entirely unwarranted conclusions have been drawn about the nature of language. In fact, no conclusions at all can be drawn with regard to language, language learning, or language use on the basis of such considerations as these.

When the study of language is approached in the manner I have just outlined, one would expect a close and fruitful interaction between linguistics proper and the investigation of such topics as language processing and acquisition. To some extent this has happened, but less so than might have been hoped. It is useful to reflect a little about why this has been the case. One reason, I think, is the one just mentioned: Misinterpretation of results about formal systems has caused considerable confusion. Other problems have arisen from a failure to consider carefully the conceptual relations between language and learnability, and between language and processing. One instructive example is the history of what was called "the derivational theory of complexity," the major paradigm of psycholinguistic research in the early days of the cognitive revolution. This theory led to an experimental program. The experiments carried out were tests of a theory with two components:

(a) assumptions about the rule systems of natural language and (b) assumptions about processing. Some of the experimental results confirmed this combination of theories, other disconfirmed it. But care must be taken to determine just which elements of the combination of theories were confirmed or disconfirmed. In practice, where predictions were disconfirmed, it was concluded that the linguistic component of the amalgam was at fault. Although this might be true, and sometimes was as other evidence showed, it was a curious inference, because there was independent evidence supporting the assumptions about language but none whatsoever supporting the assumptions about processing; these assumptions were, furthermore, not particularly plausible except as rough first approximations. Failure to appreciate these facts undermined much subsequent discussion. Similar questions arise with language acquisition. Confirming evidence too, in both areas, is unclear in its import, unless the various factors entering into the predictions are properly sorted out. Where this is done, we have meaningful results; otherwise we do not.

The history of the derivational theory of complexity illustrates other problems that have impeded useful interaction between linguistics and experimental psychology. Early experimental work was designed to test certain ideas about rule systems on the assumption that processing satisfies the conditions of the derivational theory of complexity. By the time the experimental program had been carried out, with mixed results, the theories of rule systems had changed. Many experimental psychologists found this disconcerting. How can we carry out experimental tests of a theory if it is not stable and is subject to change? These reactions led to a noticeable shift in focus to work in areas that are better insulated from theoretical modification elsewhere.

Such reactions pose a number of problems. One problem is a point of logic: To insulate one's work from theoretical modifications elsewhere is to keep to topics of limited significance, close to the surface of phenomena. If one's work is important enough to have consequences beyond its immediate scope, then it cannot be immune to new understanding outside of this scope. For example, it is likely that results on order of acquisition of function words or on turn taking in conversation will be immune to discoveries and new understanding elsewhere; the reason is that the implications are very slight. Relevance, after all, is a two-way street. This reaction to the inevitable changes in theoretical assumptions in a discipline that is alive also reflects a far too limited concept of the work of the experimental psychologist, who is perceived as someone who tests ideas developed elsewhere but does not contribute otherwise to their proper formulation. But research into language should obviously be a cooperative enterprise, which can be informed and advanced by use of evidence of many different kinds. There is no privileged sector of this discipline that provides theories, which are tested by others. One sign that the discipline is approaching a higher level of maturity will be that researchers into language processing and language acquisition will be led to conclusions about the structure of language that can be tested by linguists, using the tools of their specific approach to a common network of problems and concerns. The idea that linguistics should be related to psychology as theoretical physics is related to experimental physics is senseless and untenable and has, I think, been harmful.

Theories of language have indeed undergone significant changes during the period we are now considering—which is to say that the discipline is alive. I think we can identify two major changes of perspective during this period, each with considerable ramifications for the study of language use and acquisition. Let me review these changes briefly, focusing on the three central questions that I mentioned earlier: (a) What is knowledge of language? (b) How is it acquired? and (c) How is it used?

Some 30 years ago the standard answers to these questions would have been something like this.

(a) *What is knowledge of language?* Answer: It is a system of habits, dispositions and abilities. This answer, incidentally, is still widely held, notably by philosophers influenced by Wittgenstein and Quine.

(b) *How is language acquired?* Answer: By conditioning, training, habit formation, and general learning mechanisms such as induction.

(c) *How is language used?* Answer: Language use is the exercise of an ability, like any skill, say, bicycle riding. New forms are produced or understood by analogy to old ones. In fact, the problem posed by production of new forms, the normal situation in language use, was barely noticed. This is quite a remarkable fact, first, because the point is obvious, and second, because it was a major preoccupation of the linguistics of the first cognitive revolution of the 17th century. Here we have a striking example of how ideology blinded scientists to the most obvious of phenomena.

Attention to the most obvious and simplest phenomena suffices to show that these ideas cannot be even close to the truth of the matter and must simply be abandoned. Let me illustrate with a very simple example. Imagine a child learning English who comes to understand the sentence *John ate an apple.* The child then knows that the word *eat* takes two semantic roles, that of the subject (the agent of the action) and that of object (the recipient of the action); it is a typical transitive verb. Suppose that the child now hears the reduced sentence *John ate,* in which the object is missing. Because the verb is transitive, requiring an object, the child will understand the sentence to mean, roughly, "John ate something or other." So far everything is straightforward, if we assume the simple principle that when a semantically required element is missing, the mind understand it to be a kind of empty pronoun meaning something or other. Perhaps an empiricist linguist might be willing to suppose that this principle is available as an innate element of the language faculty.

Consider now a very simple but slightly more complex sentence. Suppose the child comes to understand such sentences as *John is too clever to catch Bill.* Here the verb *catch* also requires a subject and an object, but the subject is missing in this sentence. It therefore has to be supplied by the mind, in the matter of the object of *ate* in *John ate.* By the principle just assumed to account for *John ate,* the sentence should mean "John is so clever that someone or other will not catch Bill." That is a fine meaning, but it is not the meaning of *John is too clever to catch Bill.* Rather, the sentence means "John is so clever that he, *John,* will not catch Bill. The mind does not use the "empty pronoun principle," but rather takes the subject of *catch* to be the same as the subject of *is clever.* Because this is known without instruction or evidence, we must attribute to the mind still a second principle, let us call it the "principle of subject control": The missing subject of the embedded clause is understood to be the same as the subject of the main clause. Our assumptions about the innate resources of the mind must therefore be enriched.

Let us carry the discussion a step further. Suppose we delete *Bill* from the sentence *John is too clever to catch Bill,* so that we have *John is too clever to catch.* By the empty pronoun principle and the subject control principle, the sentence should mean "John is so clever that he, *John,* will not catch someone or other." But the child knows that it does not mean that at all; rather, it means "John is so clever that someone or other will not catch him, *John.*" The child interprets the sentence by some other principle, call it the "inversion principle," which tells us that the object of the embedded sentence is understood to be the same as the subject of the main verb, and the subject of the embedded sentence is an empty pronoun referring to someone or other.

We now have to attribute to the mind/brain three principles: the empty pronoun principle, the subject principle, and the inversion principle. Furthermore, some overarching principle of the mind/brain determines when these principles of interpretation are applied.

Turning to slightly more complicated examples, the mysteries deepen. Consider the sentence *John is too clever to expect anyone to catch.* English speakers at first may find this sentence a bit puzzling, but on reflection (whatever that involves), they understand it to mean that John is so clever that someone does not expect anyone to catch John; that is, it is interpreted by means of the empty pronoun principle and the inversion principle, necessarily. But now compare this sentence—again, *John is too clever to expect anyone to catch*—with an other sentence that is roughly comparable in complexity: *John is too clever to meet anyone who caught.* Here all principles fail; the sentence is complete gibberish. Somehow the computational principles of the language faculty are blocked.

Notice that none of this is the result of training, or even experience. These facts are known without training, without correction of error, without relevant experience, and are known the same way by every speaker of English—and in analogous constructions, other languages. Hence all of this must somehow derive from the inner resources of the mind/brain, from the genetically determined constitution of the language faculty. Clearly the answer cannot be that these resources include the empty pronoun principle, the subject principle, the inversion principle, and some overarching principle that determines when they apply. Rather, we would like to show that the observed facts follow from some deeper principles of the language faculty. This is a typical problem of science, and one that has, in fact, been rather successfully addressed in recent work. But the point here is that the facts show rather clearly that the standard answers to our questions that I have just mentioned cannot be even close to correct.

Notice also that the concept of "analogy" does no work at all. By analogy to *John ate,* the sentence *John is too clever to catch* should mean "John is too clever to catch someone or other." But it does not. Notice also that such examples refute the conception of knowledge of language as a skill or ability. The child does not fail to provide the analogous interpretation because of a failure of ability—because it is too weak or needs more practice. Rather, the computational system of the mind/brain is designed to force certain interpretations for linguistic expressions. To put the matter in the context of the theory of knowledge, our knowledge that expression such-and-such means so-and-so is not justified or grounded in experience, in any useful sense of these terms, is not based on good reasons or reliable procedures, is not derived by induction or any other method. Because these are examples of ordinary propositional knowledge, knowledge that so-and-so, the standard paradigms of epistemology and fixation of belief cannot be correct, and investigation of further examples and other cognitive systems reveals exactly the same thing, so I believe.

I think that these are all important facts, insufficiently appreciated, with quite considerable import. We discover facts of this sort wherever we look, if we are not blinded or misled by dogma.

Recognition of the complete inadequacy of these conceptions led to the first major conceptual change, which was, in many respects, a return to traditional ideas and concerns that had been dismissed or forgotten during the long period when empiricist and behaviorist doctrines prevailed. This shift of focus provided a new set of answers to the central questions:

(a) *What is knowledge of language?* Answer: Language is a computational system, a rule system of some sort. Knowledge of language is knowledge of this rule system.

(b) *How is language acquired?* Answer: The initial state of the language faculty determines possible rules and modes of interaction. Language is acquired by a process of selection of a rule system of an appropriate sort on the basis of direct evidence. Experience yields an inventory of rules, through the language-acquisition device of the language faculty.

(c) *How is language used?* Answer: The use of language is rule-governed behavior. Rules form mental representations, which enter into our speaking and understanding. A sentence is parsed and understood by a systematic search through the rule system of the language in question. The new set of answers constitutes a major component of the cognitive revolution.

This was a significant shift of point of view: from behavior and its products, to the system of knowledge represented in the mind/brain that underlies behavior. Behavior is not the focus of inquiry; rather, it provides evidence concerning the internal system of the mind/brain that is what we are trying to discover—the system that constitutes a particular language and that determines the form, structural properties, and meaning of expressions. More deeply, behavior provides evidence concerning the innate structure of the language faculty. As I mentioned earlier, this shift toward an avowed mentalism is also a shift toward assimilating the study of language to the natural sciences, and it opens up the possibility of a serious investigation of physical mechanisms.

This shift of focus was extremely productive. It led to a rapid increase in the range of empirical phenomena that were brought under investigation, with many new discoveries, including facts, such as those I just illustrated, that had never been noticed before, including quite simple ones. It also led to some degree of success in providing explanations for these facts. But serious difficulties were noticed at once. Basically, these difficulties related to Plato's problem, the problem of acquisition of language. In essence, the problem is that there are too many possible rule systems. Therefore it is hard to explain how children unerringly select one such system rather than another.

This problem set the research agenda for the past 25 years of inquiry into the nature of language, within the framework I am considering here. I will not review the steps that were taken, but rather will turn to the result. In the past several years, a new and somewhat different conception of language has emerged, which yields new answers to our three questions. The initial state of the language faculty consists of a collection of subsystems, or *modules* as they are called, each of which is based on certain very general principles. Each of these principles admits of a certain very limited possibility of variation. We may think of the system as a complex network, associated with a switch box that contains a finite number of switches. The network is invariant, but each switch can be in one of two positions, on or off. Unless the switches are set, nothing happens. But when the switches are set in one of the permissible ways, the system functions, yielding the entire infinite array of interpretation for linguistic expressions. A slight change in switch settings can yield complex and varied phenomenal consequences as its effects filter through the network. There are no rules at all, hence no necessity to learn rules. For example, the possible phrase structures of a language are fixed by general principles and are invariant among languages, but there are some switches to be set. One has to do with order of elements. In English, for example, nouns, verbs, adjectives and prepositions precede their objects; in Japanese, the comparable elements follow their objects. English is what is called a head-first language, Japanese a head-last language. These facts can be determined from very simple sentences, for example, the sentences "John ate an apple" (in English) or "John an apple ate" (in Japanese). To acquire a language, the child's mind must determine how the switches are set, and simple data must suffice to determine the switch settings, as in this case. The theory of language use also undergoes corresponding modifications, which I cannot explore here.

This second conceptual change gives a very different conception of language and knowledge. To mention one example, notice that from the point of view of rule systems, there are an infinite number of languages, because there are infinitely many possible rule systems. But from the network-switch point of view, there are only a finite number of languages, one for each arrangement of switch settings. Because each of the switch settings can be determined from simple data, each of these finite number of languages is learnable. Hence the general principle of learnability theory discussed earlier is in fact partially true: Each natural language is learnable—though it is far from true that the learnable systems are all natural languages. As I mentioned, this is an empirical result, and a very surprising one, not a matter of principle. There is, incidentally, quite intriguing work in mathematical learning theory, which suggests that language acquisition is possible in principle under plausible conditions only if the set of natural languages is indeed finite.

This second conceptual change has, once again, led to a great increase in the range of empirical materials discovered and subjected to serious inquiry within generative grammar, now from a much wider range of languages.

Assuming that this change is pointing in the right direction, what are the consequences for the study of language acquisition? The problem will be to determine how the switches are set and to discover the principles of learning, or maturation, or whatever is responsible for carrying out the transition from the initial state of the language faculty to the steady state of adult competence—that is, for setting the switches of the language faculty. Recall that two factors enter into language acquisition: the nature of the language faculty and the principles of learning theory or, more properly, growth theory. Any evidence about language acquisition must be assessed carefully to determine how it bears on one or the other of these two interacting factors. How can we proceed in studying this question?

Notice that the problems of assessment of evidence and explanation would plainly be simplified if one or the other of these two components—universal grammar or growth theory—does not exist. Each of these positions has been maintained, the first one quite vigorously, the second as a tentative working hypothesis.

Denial of the existence of universal grammar, that is, of the language faculty as an identifiable system of the human mind/brain, is implicit in the empiricist program and is explicit in recent claims about mechanisms of general intelligence or connectionism or theory formation, mechanisms that are allegedly applied to yield our linguistic abilities and other intellectual achievements in an undifferentiated way. No attempt has been made to formulate these alleged mechanisms that seems to offer any real promise. The clearer formulations have been immediately refuted, in some cases refuted in principle, and for reasons that should be familiar the prospects for this program seem very dim. Because there is nothing substantive to discuss, I will disregard this possibility and proceed to the second possibility: that growth theory is negligible or nonexistent, so that language-acquisition simply involves switch setting on the basis of presented data, such as the sentences "John ate an apple" or "John an apple ate." Let us call this the "no-growth theory" of language acquisition.

Obviously, this theory cannot be literally true. During the first few months or perhaps weeks of life, an infant probably is exposed to enough linguistic data to set most parameters, but plainly it has not done so. In fact, the process extends over quite a few years. So to maintain the no-growth theory we would have to argue that some independent and extrinsic change in cognitive capacities, say in memory or attention, accounts for the observed stages of growth.

Such ideas have been advanced with regard to stages of cognitive development in the sense of Jean Piaget and also with regard to the stages of language growth. For example, it has been observed that the transition from so-called telegraphic speech, lacking function words, to normal speech is quite rapid and includes a number of different systems: questions, negations, tag questions, and so on. Furthermore, in the telegraphic speech stage, children understand normal speech better than their own telegraphic speech, and if function words are introduced randomly, the results are unintelligible. This suggests that the children knew the facts of normal speech all along and were using telegraphic speech because of some limitation of attention and memory. When this limitation is overcome in the course of normal growth and maturation, their already acquired knowledge of language can be manifested. But there are some serious problems in assuming this idea in other cases of regular stages of development: for example, the shift from semantic to syntactic categories, the use of color words, the appearance of a true verbal passive construction and other more complex structures, the emergence of semantic properties of control, and so on. *Prima facie,* it seems hard to explain these transitions without appeal to maturational processes that bring principles of universal grammar into operation on some regular schedule in a manner to be described and accounted for in a genetic theory. Of course, what is *prima facie* plausible is not necessarily correct, but the questions that arise are clear enough, and it is an important task to address them, as several investigators are now doing in important recent work.

There is, on the one hand, work by Yukio Otsu, Stephen Crain, and others that seems to show that principles of universal grammar are available as soon as constructions are used in which they would be manifested, and the delay in use of these constructions might be explained in terms of inherent complexity, hence extrinsic factors such as memory.

To take one complex example of much general interest, consider recent work of Nina Hyams on the null-subject property that distinguishes languages like French and English, in which subjects must be overtly expressed, from languages such as Italian and Spanish, in which the subject may be suppressed in the phonetic output. Hyams's work indicates that at an early stage, all children treat their language as if it were a null-subject language. The switch, she has suggested, has what is called an "unmarked setting," or in the more usual terminology, the null-subject parameter has an "unmarked value," a value determined in the absence of data, and this value provides a null-subject language. Italian-speaking children maintain the unmarked value, whereas English-speaking children later change to the marked value of the parameter, setting the switch differently. The question then is, what triggers the change? There is good evidence that positive evidence suffices for language acquisition; that is, correction of error is unnecessary and probably largely irrelevant when it occurs. Assuming so, the answer to the question cannot be that the English-speaking children are explicitly corrected—and indeed, we known that this is not the case. Nor can the answer be that they never hear sentences without subjects, because they hear no evidence for most of what they know. Assuming a no-growth theory, Hyams has suggested that the change is triggered by the presence of overt expletives in English, such elements as *there* in "there is a man in the room," elements that are semantically empty but must be present to satisfy some syntactic principle. The assumption is that universal grammar contains a principle implying that if a language has overt expletives, then it is not a null-subject language. This is, incidentally, an example of a hypothesis about universal grammar deriving from language acquisition studies that might be tested by linguists, rather than the converse, as in the usual practice.

But now we have to ask why the English-speaking children delay in using this evidence. A possible answer might be that extrinsic conditions of memory and attention render these expletives inaccessible at an early stage.

Pursuing a similar idea, Luigi Rizzi suggested that, contrary to Hyams's initial conclusion, the unmarked value for the parameter is overt subject. English-speaking children appear to violate this principle at an early stage, but only because extrinsic considerations suppress the production of such elements as unstressed subject pronouns. Italian-speaking children then select the marked value of the parameter on the basis of direct evidence of subjectless sentences.

A third approach is to reject the no-growth theory and to suppose that the null-subject parameter only becomes available at a certain stage of maturation and is set at the marked null-subject value only if direct evidence of subjectless sentences is presented. At the moment, the question remains open.

Notice that further clarification of these issues might well contribute to our knowledge of the principles and parameters of universal grammar—of the nature of the network and the switches—on the basis of evidence from language acquisition, as we should anticipate as the discipline progresses.

Consider a second example. Sascha Felix has argued against the no-growth theory on the basis of evidence about use of negatives in several languages. Apparently, at the earliest stage, children use sentence-external negation, as in "not John likes milk." This fact already raises problems for a no-growth theory, because natural languages rarely if ever exhibit sentence-external negation. At a later stage, the child shifts to sentence-internal negation, as in "John no likes milk," which is also inconsistent with the evidence from the adult language. Later, the correct form "John doesn't like milk" emerges. Felix pointed out that Stage I, with sentence-external negation, is consistent with Dan Slobin's principle that the learner avoids interruption of linguistic units and hence might be taken to support this principle. But he noted that that leaves unresolved the question why this principle become inoperative at Stage II and is even more radically abandoned at Stage III. A maturational theory seems the most likely candidate for an explanation. Again, further research should contribute to clarifying both the principles of language growth, if they exist, and the actual principles and parameters of universal grammar.

Consider finally a more complex example studied in some detail by Hagit Borer and Kenneth Wexler. They have argued that the results in many languages on acquisition of passives can be explained by a maturational theory, which provides a more sophisticated version of the idea that transformations are acquired step-by-step during language acquisition. Their theory postulates that until a certain stage of development, phrases can only be interpreted in a canonical position in which semantic roles are assigned by principles of universal grammar, thus the position of abstract underlying deep structures, in effect. Thus at this stage, a sentence such as "John was killed" is simply uninterpretable, because *John* is displaced from its canonical position as object of *kill.* Apparent passive forms at this stage, they argue, are in fact adjectives, as in "the door is closed." Later, a device becomes available, through maturation, by which displaced elements can be interpreted through a so-called *chain* formed by a transformation, which links the displaced element to an empty *trace* in the canonical position. Such chains must then meet various conditions of universal grammar, which account for the possibilities of displacement. They argued that the range of available evidence about acquisition of passives can be largely explained on the basis of this assumption: that chains become available at a certain stage of maturation. Again, there are numerous consequences to be explored, and the results should bear directly on the principles of universal grammar as well as growth theory.

If Borer and Wexler are right, one might be tempted to explore a famous suggestion by Roman Jakobson that language acquisition and language loss in aphasia are mirror images: The earlier some items and structures are acquired in language learning, the later they are lost under brain injury. It would then follow that in some kinds of aphasia, we should find that chains are lost while other aspects of phrase structure remain. Evidence to this effect has in fact been presented by Yosef Grodzinsky. This again suggests what might prove to be an intriguing line of inquiry.

These examples barely scratch the surface. A wide range of intriguing questions arise at once if we think through the implications of the principles-and-parameters conception of universal grammar in terms of an invariant network and an associated set of switches, and if we ask how this conception might relate to possible principles of maturation involved in language growth, along with extrinsic factors in cognitive development. I have not had time to consider the question of language processing, but here too the questions look quite different when approached in these terms. And within the study of language proper, many new and exciting questions enter into the research agenda. If the principles-and-parameters approach is correct, it should be possible literally to deduce the properties of each natural language by setting the switches in one or another way and computing the consequences. Typological difference should be a matter of differences in switch settings. Language change should be the result of a change in such a setting; note that a small change might yield a substantial phenomenal difference as its effects filter through the fixed network of modular principles. These are all questions that are now being addressed, in some cases with some success, in other cases with failures that are very suggestive in opening up new lines of inquiry. Furthermore, the class of typologically different languages that have come under investigation, and that seem to be amenable to a coherent and uniform approach, has vastly extended—again, a promising sign.

There are, it seems, real grounds for considerable optimism about the prospects that lie ahead, not only for the study of language proper, but also for the study of cognitive systems of the mind/brain of which language is a fundamental and essential component in the human species.

CHAPTER 3

MATURATION AND GROWTH OF GRAMMAR

Kenneth Wexler

I. GROWTH/MATURATION, LANGUAGE ACQUISITION, AND LINGUISTIC THEORY

A substantial body of research shows that children already know a number of aspects of universal grammar (UG), the biologically given system of grammar in the human brain. Research on a number of topics from binding theory to the details of verbal inflection and verb movement (some of which will be reviewed in the following sections) shows that children know a good deal about UG. A theory which assumes that children do not know UG can hardly be entertained at the present moment, given the empirical results in the literature.

The question remains whether young children know from birth UG in its every detail, or whether in fact they show small deviations from it. Furthermore, the question remains, if there *are* small deviations of certain kinds from UG, how does the change take place to full adult UG?

The purpose of this chapter is to review some of the arguments that children show certain deviations from adult UG and that the change to adult UG takes place via a process of *growth,* guided by the underlying genetic program of language. I would like to emphasize, however, that what is known about child deviations from adult UG make it clear that the deviations are specific and limited. But they must be taken account of if development of language is to be explained. It is important to have a theory of the deviations and of how they change. I myself have spent much research effort at establishing that children know much about UG. It is important to reiterate an argument that some aspects of UG that are not known to a child should not cast any doubt on the conclusion that children have a grammar similar to UG, and that this grammar is the result of a genetic program.

The classic problem of linguistic development (really, the central issue for linguistic theory) breaks up into two related questions: First is the problem of *learnability;* how is it possible for a child to master, naturally and easily, any natural language? Second is the problem of *development;* what accounts for the fact that a child seems to develop linguistic abilities over time? Both problems have to take into account the fact that a child develops different languages depending on linguistic experience, that is, the input language.

To account for the fact that a child develops different languages depending on experience, every account (from linguistic theory to behavioral psychology) invokes at least some component of *learning*. By definition, *learning* means development based on experience, on environmental influences. However, to account for the facts of learnability and development, linguistic theory has insisted that the only possible solution is *innateness,* namely, that a genetic program guides the development of language in the human, and that this program is responsible for most of the details of the ultimate language, as well as of its development. This is the model of what Chomsky has often called the *growth* of language in the child, insisting that *growth* is a better word than *learning* for most of what happens in the development of language.

Everybody can agree that some component of learning is needed, for example, to set language-specific parameters of lexical items. What else is needed? Linguistic theory concludes that to explain how every child exposed to input from one language winds up with an essentially identical language, and one which goes way beyond what is heard in the input, it must be the case that the child has a genetically based program (that is, UG) that determines much of the form of the attained grammar. Moreover, to explain how and why every child goes through many of the same steps in linguistic development, steps that are also not directed by the input, linguistic theory concludes that parts of UG grow in a way that is dictated by the genetic program. Thus we have a model of human grammar development which consists of two parts:

1. A genetic program (UG) guiding grammar growth
2. A learning component for the language-specific aspects of grammar

Borer and Wexler (1987, 1992), in the first modern detailed studies of the UG-related aspects of the temporal properties of the genetic program underlying language development, called the time-related growth of UG *maturation.* We will often continue to use that term here; however, it should be borne in mind that maturation simply means the time-related aspect of the genetic program underlying UG. That is, by definition, *maturation* = *growth,* and to emphasize this fact, we will often call maturational theories, theories of growth/maturation (GM).

This chapter reviews some of the aspects of linguistic growth (= maturation) that have been studied. This first section deals with the conceptual analysis of linguistic growth/maturation, and later sections deal with some particular case studies. It should be emphasized that maturation is hardly a controversial notion in linguistic theory; it has really been the (often implicit) assumption from the start of work in generative grammar, though actually applied in an explanatory manner to actual developmental phenomena for the first time in Borer and Wexler (1987). In this regard, any model that attempted to account for linguistic development without a growth/maturation component would be making a claim that would have to be justified empirically.

Let us flesh this out. The fundamental problem of development is that the child has a different grammar at different ages; the grammar actually *develops*. What accounts for this development? Why is it that the child of 10 days appears to have a different grammar than the child of 2 years?

Of course *some* parts of grammar are *learned*. Thus some parts of what the child of 2;0 knows that the child of 10 days does not know come from experience. Let us put these aside, because all models must account for experience-related aspects of grammar development. However, linguistic theory concludes that most of what an adult knows about grammar is a result of the genetic program called UG; it is *not* learned. Therefore we have to account for the development of the nonlearned aspects of grammar. Linguistic theory has a natural way to account for the development of these nonlearned aspects of grammar; they *grow*. Some aspects of UG grow over time. Both the structural details and the development over time of UG all flow from one genetic program. Because genetic programs (and UG is one of them) play out over time, the conclusion could hardly be otherwise.

It must be emphasized that the claim of linguistic theory that UG is a genetic program does not imply that *all* aspects of UG take a substantial amount of time to develop. It could very well be that much or most of UG is available shortly at birth, but that only certain aspects take longer to develop. It might be that what appear to be large aspects of development result from only small amounts of underlying growth. Just as in the linguistic theory of the adult, the more-inclusive linguistic theory of development can only be evaluated in its precise details. For the developmental aspects of linguistics, the question is, what parts of UG are known to the child when? Again, note that because the basic assumption of linguistic theory is that UG is *not* learned, any parts of UG which are not known to the child at a certain age can *only* develop through linguistic growth/maturation. No other explanation is available; growth/maturation and learning (and combinations of these) are the only two explanations that have ever been offered for the development of any ability, including language.[1]

[1] I am referring only to modern scientific explanations in tune with what is known about biology. Alternatives are, of course, possible, for example, Plato's theory that we know things because we experienced them in a previous life.

Logically, of course, one could question whether the conclusion of linguistic theory that UG is basically not learned, but rather is guided by a genetic program, is correct. If one rejects the genetic program assumption and hypothesizes rather that grammar is learned, then of course it will be possible to question whether maturation/growth of grammar takes place. In my opinion (and in the opinion of linguistic theory in general), the evidence is very large that grammar is basically unlearned. This is not the place to review that evidence, but see work in syntactic theory from at least Chomsky (1965) and work in learnability theory (from Wexler & Hamburger, 1973, to Wexler & Culicover, 1980, and many other references). Thus I will assume that grammar is basically unlearned and therefore grows in the mind/brain.

Although the idea of growth/maturation of grammar is the basic construction of linguistic theory, some other ideas have occasionally been put forth. These ideas almost always depend for their logical coherence on the idea that grammar is learned. Thus, one of the ideas that one often hears is that knowledge of a particular construction is "triggered" by some particular input data. If this is true, then, it is sometimes argued, UG, the developmental program, does not have to specify how the "construction" develops.

Borer and Wexler (1987) argued on empirical grounds that triggering in this sense could not be the basic mechanism of language development. They argued that facts of language development often showed that a particular piece of knowledge of grammar often remained in place for a long period of time (several months or longer in many cases). If the development of that piece of knowledge simply depended on some particular linguistic experience, then why didn't the knowledge develop earlier? Why did it seem to have to wait until the child had achieved a certain competence level? Borer and Wexler dubbed this problem the "triggering problem," and that problem remains at the heart of developmental theory in linguistics.

One might want to argue that evidence is not available to the child at an earlier age, that parents and other speakers systematically withhold linguistic input from children. Thus the parent is responsible for the child's delay in mastery of a certain construction. But Wexler and Culicover (1980) showed in a quite detailed fashion, based on the empirical literature as well as theoretical arguments, that parents and others did not present input to the child in any fashion systematically geared toward language training. For example, parents do not present simpler input to young children. Thus the fields of linguistic theory and of language acquisition have accepted that children's stages of linguistic knowledge do not correspond to particular presentations by adults of input data. Again, this is not the place to review the evidence for this conclusion, but I will assume it, as does linguistic and psycholinguistic theory in general.

Borer and Wexler (1987) concluded that it is the *child* who was responsible for the stages of linguistic development; that is, it is the genetic program (UG) that guides linguistic development. This is the growth/maturation model of linguistic theory, often called the UG model.

Note that arguments that attempt to show that growth/maturation is not part of language development all rely on the assumption that grammatical structures arise in the child by *learning*. For example, the idea that constructions arise at a certain time because they are "triggered" means that the constructions have been "learned." They do not arise as a simple consequence of UG (the genetic program). Rather, they are created by the child as an act of learning. The general problem of learnability (how can precise and uniform structures that go way beyond the evidence available to the child be "learned"?) argues against this conclusion, of course. Nevertheless, it is worth pointing out that arguments against growth/maturation (almost) always demand that linguistic structures arise through "learning," thus contradicting the basic conclusions of linguistic theory and of language acquisition research.

There is one other possibility, at least *a priori*. One could argue that, in fact, aside from the learning of language-specific properties, linguistic knowledge *does not* develop. That is, the child in fact has perfect adult knowledge of grammar from birth, aside from language-particular properties. We can call this assumption *rigidity*.[2] Rigidity states that knowledge of language is unchanging, at least from birth.[3]

Rigidity has a tremendous empirical hurdle to surmount. Because of the very large amount of evidence which shows that children in fact do not have identical linguistic properties as adults, somehow rigidity has to show that this actually is not true. Because all models agree that language particular properties have to be learned, rigidity could attempt to show that in fact children have all adult properties except language-particular ones; that is, that children in fact have all universal linguistic properties. All differences between children and adults would have to then be resolved as the differences between languages, which have to be learned.

Even if rigidity theory could show such a result (we will argue that in fact the evidence is rather strikingly against such a view), it will still have large logical/empirical problems to deal with. In particular, because children show systematic patterns in development that last for awhile, and because these patterns often differ from the language being learned (the input), the question arises as to why children seem to show systematic deviances from the linguistic input, if this input is the ba-

[2]Borer and Wexler (1987) called the proposal of unchanging knowledge *continuity*. But I think that was an unfortunate name, which created some confusion I believe. *Continuity* seems to allow for some development, whereas the idea to be contrasted to growth-maturation is no growth, no change. Thus *rigidity* seems like a better name for the idea.

[3]It is not clear why birth should be the event that marks the beginning of adult knowledge of language; perhaps fertilization of the egg should mark adult knowledge of language according to rigidity theories. At any rate, presumably even proponents of rigidity theory have to assume growth/maturation before birth. Presumably they would assume that this process stops at birth or sometime before birth. So far as I know, no proponent of rigidity theory has suggested exactly when growth/maturation stops, whether at birth or before birth.

sis for the learning that rigidity theory insists is the only driving force of linguistic change. Again, Borer and Wexler's 1987) triggering problem surfaces. Why should children only learn at a (much) later date a structure for which the evidence was available much earlier?

The reply could be that the learning mechanism changes over time. But how does the learning mechanism change? The only answer seems to be growth/maturation. That is, the genetic program for the "learning mechanism" guides its development. Thus, no matter how one attempts to answer otherwise, only growth/maturation at bottom seems to allow for the systematic deviances from adult language that children show.

It is sometimes said that there is a preference for a theory to assume rigidity, that assuming growth/maturation involves an extra stipulation, all other things being equal. In my opinion, this is a fallacious argument. The reason is that all other things are never equal in this case. Assuming rigidity always means that extra learning has to be assumed. That is, if UG (the genetic program) does not specify why a certain structure has a certain nonadult form at a certain age, and why it develops into the adult form at a later age, then only learning can be invoked to explain the development. But because the basic argument of linguistic theory (the Argument from the Poverty of the Stimulus, as Chomsky, 1975, put it; and see Wexler, 1991, for discussion) is that learning *cannot* be invoked to explain development, it is very unlikely in most cases that models of learning can be created to explain the development of the structures. Moreover, the model of learning will have to face the triggering problem; why didn't learning take place earlier? In general, proposals which suggest that it's less stipulation to say that there is no development (i.e., that rigidity holds) do not specify the learning theory and just assume it can happen, thereby ignoring the basic argument of linguistic theory.

I think we can show this very clearly by comparing the situation to the assumption of innateness. Linguistic theory argues that much of UG (for simplicity let's say all of UG) is innate in the child. The argument is that otherwise we cannot explain why all children ultimately develop language. Critics of this approach, not so common these days, but still around, at least in the technical fields themselves (philosophy is another story), often say that the assumption of innateness is dispreferred, because one has to *stipulate* extra knowledge in the child. Because we have to assume that the child can learn *some* pieces of linguistic knowledge (e.g., the language-particular ones), the assumption that there is no innate knowledge of grammar is preferred, everything else being equal, over the assumption that there *is* innate knowledge of grammar.

This is a logically correct argument; it fails immediately, however, because one of its assumptions strongly fails; other things are *not* equal. Linguistic theory and learnability theory have shown in detail that there are many structures of grammar that go way beyond the input and that children nevertheless develop. There is no way for learning to account for the development of these structures. Thus, although it would be a simpler model to assume that children do not have innate structures of UG, empirical considerations immediately force us into assuming that children *do* have innate knowledge of UG. That is, empirical material has forced the field to accept a far more complicated model than behaviorists had, because in behaviorists' model there was no innate knowledge of language. It was not some commonsense notion of simplicity, but the attempt to account for the facts of language in humans, that brought linguistic theory to conclude that there is much innate knowledge of grammar.[4]

Exactly a parallel situation holds with respect to growth/maturation. Perhaps it is simpler to say that children at birth have adult knowledge of every aspect of language, aside from language-particular ones. But as soon as one begins to look at the facts of development, then one cannot accept the argument that there is no development, that rigidity holds. Rigidity is simpler than growth/maturation in *exactly* the same sense as empiricism is simpler than nativism. In both cases, the facts about human language argue that the more complicated theory must hold. There is a genetic program that underlies the development of language; it would be simpler if it were not true, but it *is* true. Thus science arrives at a somewhat more complicated view of the world, and not a necessarily more unsatisfying one.

In my experience, when I make this argument to many scholars who want to argue for rigidity, their reply is that, well, they don't believe in innateness, in nativism, anyway. I believe that, in fact, the failure to accept the nativist foundations of linguistic theory is one and the same in many cases as the failure to accept the nativist foundations of development, that there is a genetic program that determines the structure and timing of grammar in the human mind/brain.[5] This view,

[4]See Batchelder and Wexler (1979) for a discussion of how empiricist theory was more simple than linguistic theory and how this simplicity itself (as opposed to empirical justification) was a strong reason for its long-time hold on the field.

[5]See, for example, Clahsen, Penke, and Parodi (1994) and Vainikka (1994), who hypothesize that the functional categories are learned and thus no genetic program is necessary for their development; they arise from experience. These learning (antigrowth) views fail for exactly the same reasons that learning views have always failed for UG. Namely, no details or even hints at a plausible learning theory are given, a learning theory that would allow the functional categories to be learned. See Wexler and Culicover (1980) and many other learnability references, as well as standard works in linguistic theory, for the argument that the basic constructs of UG are, in fact, encoded in the genetic program. As soon as an attempt is made to give a learning theory for these constructs, any plausible, possibly successful learning theory will wind up incorporating the very concepts that have to be learned in the innate learning mechanism. Thus it is not surprising that the antigrowth views, based on learning, actually do not attempt to state a learning theory. In the absence of any plausible learning theory, the only plausible view to be taken is the growth/maturation/innateness/genetic program view. Although generally accepted in linguistic theory, one often still finds that this view is not accepted in parts, at least, of language acquisition studies, presumably as a holdover from the originally behaviorist foundations of psychology. In recent years, however, the situation has been changing considerably, even in the field of language acquisition, and one now finds that the growth/innateness view is more readily accepted.

essentially the empiricist one, then in fact becomes coherent (though totally failing empirically). The view is that language is learned, there is no innate specifically linguistic structure. Thus developmental facts about language as well as ultimate adult facts must fall out of a constant learning mechanism. No genetic program for language exists.

As I have already pointed out, this chapter is not the place to argue for the nativist foundations for linguistic theory, which I take as established. Thus if the objection to the maturation/growth view of language development is an antinativist one, I will not deal in any detail with that objection.[6] I take it for granted that we are assuming a nativist view of linguistic theory, that UG is genetically determined.

On the view that there *is* a genetic program that constructs UG, we have to ask at exactly which time point a full UG arises. At birth? Why at birth? What is special about birth that makes UG arise then? Before birth? When? After birth? When? (And that is the growth/maturation view anyway). The point is that a theory which *accepts* that UG is determined by a genetic program (the basic postulate and conclusion of linguistic theory) *must* accept that a full UG arises at a certain time, and this time must be after the original fertilization of the egg, as nobody would claim that UG existed in its entirety at that point. Thus on the linguistic theory (innateness) view, a time of full UG must be stipulated. Thus there is no possible simplicity argument for a nongrowth, nonmaturational view. The only question is, when is full adult UG reached? The only possible simplicity argument must be based on a noninnateness theory, because on such an empiricist theory, no genetic program for UG has to be postulated at all and thus no time of emergence of UG has to be postulated. But we have already said that such a noninnateness view totally fails to fit empirical facts.

As there are no simplicity arguments, let us turn to ways to decide between views. All innateness views have to stipulate a time at which full UG emerges. Growth/maturation views make this time at some point after birth. It's not clear what the alternative should be, but presumably rigidity views attribute some special significance to birth. So let's say that rigidity hypothesizes that full adult UG has been achieved at or before birth. We not have to contrast empirically a view which says that full adult UG is achieved somewhat after birth (the growth/maturation hypothesis) with a view which says that full adult UG is achieved no later than birth (the rigidity hypothesis).

In general, children's language *looks* different from adult language. This fact would give *prima facie* support to the growth/maturation model, because rigidity has to assume no difference between early and later grammatical capacity. The typical rigidity move is to say that *grammatical* capacity is the same for young (anytime after birth) and older children, but that there is some other reason that children's early language appears to be different.

[6]For detailed discussions of the learnability foundations of nativism (innateness) of grammar, see Wexler (1979), Wexler and Culicover (1980), and many other references.

Rigidity hypotheses use two standard nongrammatical growth possibilities to account for the fact that young children's language is different from older children's language. First, it may be that children have not learned a language-specific property. Let us call this hypothesis the *learning delay* (*LD*) hypothesis. The idea is that it takes awhile for the learning mechanism to learn particular language-specific properties and that this delay makes children's language look different from adults' language.

The second standard nongrammatical growth possibility that rigidity hypotheses use to account for differences in young children's language from adult language is the assumption that some other, *nongrammatical* delay in children's capacities accounts for language delay. In general, it is suggested that young children have some kind of performance or processing problems, compared to older children and adults, and that, despite the fact that their grammatical capacities are exactly the same as adults' capacities, the performance deficit makes their language look different. Let us call this the *performance delay* (*PD*) idea.

Considering first the learning delay idea, we have already pointed out that it runs afoul of Borer and Wexler's (1987) triggering problem. Why should a particular language-specific property only be learnable at a late age when the data is available at a much earlier age?[7] Thus the learning delay hypothesis does not take account of the central facts of language learnability.

Furthermore, the learning delay idea implies that it takes a substantial amount of time for a child to learn some (maybe most) language-particular properties of grammar. To the extent that this is true, it would be in tune with the LD idea. However, suppose that it turns out that a large number of language-particular properties are learned at a very early age. To the extent that there is no obvious reason why these properties are learned early and other properties are learned late, we would have evidence against the learning delay idea. For, why should certain properties emerge late if the learning mechanism is capable of learning other properties very early? Suppose, for example, that certain very common structures in the input are in fact incorrectly learned by the young child, whereas other structures are in fact learned easily by the same child. What kind of learning mechanism would have these properties? It seems that there could be no such general-purpose learning mechanism. Only a learning mechanism specifically tuned to handling

[7]It is sometimes suggested that the data really *is not* available at an earlier age, because the child does not or cannot *use* the data at an earlier age; there is a difference between language *input* and language *intake*. But this begs the question of *why* the younger child cannot use the data. The growth/maturation model says that reasons of grammatical growth dictate whether or not children can use data to learn a particular language-specific property; the genetic program guides the development of language, including possibly when learning a particular kind of language-specific fact can take place. The only way that rigidity can claim that certain data cannot be used at an earlier age is to claim that some other system (an *intake* system?) matures, thereby confirming the growth/maturation model. See our discussion that follows soon on the performance delay hypothesis; the idea that intake is delayed seems to be a variant of the performance delay hypothesis.

certain kinds of structures at certain ages would have this property. But this is the growth/maturation hypothesis. The learning delay hypothesis can only attribute lateness to properties of a general-purpose learning mechanism, and there does not seem to be such a mechanism that will allow for certain structures that are easily available in the input to be only learned quite late.

As we will show later in this chapter, the facts of language development turn out to show that a very large number of highly detailed language-specific facts (e.g., parameters, "paradigms") are learned extremely early by the child, for example, the child who is just beginning to make multiword utterances around the age of 1;6. Thus there is no general learning delay. The same child will show delay on other structures. There does not seem to be any way that learning delay can account for this kind of pattern of development. The pattern seems much more grammatically specific.

The second way in which rigidity can attempt to account for language delay is PD—performance delay. The idea is that children's grammars are identical to adult grammars (at least with respect to the non-language-specific aspects of grammar), but that children have certain kinds of performance deficits that make it only *appear* as if their grammars are delayed. As soon as their performance matches adult levels, in the PD view, it will be clear that their grammars are also adultlike.

First note the major complication that the PD view brings to the description of linguistic development. One has to assume that children have major difficulties with linguistic performance, difficulties so large that it becomes very difficult to show that they know grammar. As far as I know, there is no evidence at all for such a view. In fact, I have argued in detail (see Crain and Wexler, Chapter 12 of this volume; Thornton and Wexler, in press; and Wexler, 1992, 1994, and 1996) and will argue in some detail later in this chapter that children in fact have no particular problem producing sentences in accordance with their grammar. They not only know grammar, but they obey it. Thus there is no evidence for the view that performance delays are usually the cause of children's nonadult language.

Moreover, note that the PD view brings with it a major question: How does performance become adultlike? As I know of no theory in the literature that attempts to describe children's performance and how it changes via learning, and as any learning approach to changes in performance will run into the same learnability problems that learning approaches to grammatical structure run into, one can only assume that changes in the performance system are due to growth/maturation, and in fact this probably is the standard, if often implicit, assumption of PD accounts.

Thus a PD account must assume that growth/maturation is what lies behind the change in children's performance systems over time. This assumption greatly complicates the theory of language development. What is the theory of children's performance that accounts for their nonadult language behavior? As far as I know, hardly any attempt has been made to answer these questions. Thus PD accounts greatly complicate the theory of language and of language development, compared to the growth/maturation (of grammar) account. Moreover, the PD accounts do not specify the crucial details that are needed to make them work (the theory of performance systems and of how they grow). Third, the PD accounts seem to be empirically wrong in that they depend on it being difficult for children to obey their grammars, a claim that has been shown to be mostly false. Fourth, the PD accounts make the theory of language and of language development far less restrictive, because, especially given the lack of any theory or empirical work on children's performance abilities, almost anything can be said about children's performance. Thus it is extremely difficult to falsify these nonrestrictive PD accounts, because no restrictive theory of children's performance exists. Thus, on at least four grounds, the rigidity hypothesis incorporating PD fails in comparison to the growth/maturation view.

The last point about the lack of restrictiveness of rigidity accounts incorporating PD is worth expanding on. It is sometimes suggested that rigidity is a more restrictive hypothesis than is growth/maturation, because lack of full growth of grammar is not available as an explanation for a particular deficit. It is suggested that the growth/maturation view is unrestrictive because it allows for particular timing of certain grammatical developments.

In my view, exactly the opposite situation holds regarding restrictiveness. It is true that the growth/maturation theory must state particular times that certain properties grow. But so must rigidity, as I have pointed out, as nobody would argue that full UG exists at the moment of fertilization. If birth is taken as the time at which full UG exists, then rigidity cannot use timing of grammatical properties as an explanation.

However, rigidity more than makes up for this restriction by its capacity to assume anything it wants to about children's performance. Thus whenever a child shows any linguistic structure that looks different from an adult's, all that rigidity has to do (and, in practice, does) is to stipulate that it must be a performance problem. Thus the rigidity hypothesis that incorporates performance delay is essentially completely unrestrictive, far more unrestrictive than the growth/maturation hypothesis.[8]

[8]For an example, see Bloom (1990), who stipulates that children have severe memory limitations that force them to drop obligatory constituents out of their sentences in production, what Hyams and Wexler (1993) called the *output omission* model. Moreover, the output omission model assumes that elements are dropped from the *beginning* of a sentence much more than from the final position of the sentence, in contradiction of what is known about children. Note that no justification in terms of psychological properties is given for the asymmetry in memory problems in particular parts of the sentence, except for reference to Yngve (1960), a production model that has been known for a long time to be wrong empirically and for which, moreover, the argument about dropping constituents in the beginning of a sentence does not go through. See Hyams and Wexler (1993) for detailed discussion of these and many other points. The output omission model fails in a very strong and specific way on the empirical data of acquisition, as Hyams and Wexler had shown. But my point here is only to point out that the output omission model is a kind of performance delay model, which assumes large numbers

Of course, any theory can be made more restrictive by creating a restrictive version of the theory, with details filled in. Thus in principle one could create a restrictive performance theory based on empirical details. However, this has not been done, and there is no reason to believe it could be done. There is hardly any evidentiary base on which to create such a theory.

In contrast, the growth/maturation theories that have been created are highly restrictive. They suggest particular aspects of grammar that mature in particular ways and at particular times in a child's development. (For examples of such theories, see Borer & Wexler, 1987, 1992, and the examples I discuss later in this chapter). Moreover, what matures is stated in a formal way and is furthermore based on empirical support. The growth/maturation theories in every way are more restrictive than the performance delay theories.

Thus it is sometimes said that growth/maturation is unrestrictive because one can explain any development by saying it matures. But exactly the same holds for performance delay theories because one can explain any development by saying it was caused by a performance problem that matures. One has to compare the relative restrictiveness of the actual theories, what has been accomplished in the attempt to state such theories. In my opinion, there is no contest. The growth/maturation theories are far more worked out, far more restrictive, far more capable of empirical test than the rigidity theories with performance delay. Of course, future research could change the situation; this is always possible. For the moment we have to go with research that has actually been accomplished; the rigidity hypothesis, given its necessary performance delay component, simply fails the test of restrictiveness. Because I believe the empirical evidence also does not agree with performance delay, I am not optimistic that an empirically adequate restrictive theory based on rigidity can, in fact, be constructed.

Again, it is worth comparing the situation in developmental theory (language acquisition) and in linguistic theory. A very frequent argument against the innateness hypothesis (the hypothesis that much of UG is genetically encoded) in the early days of generative grammar was that it was an unrestrictive hypothesis. The argument went thusly: Because any aspect of adult linguistic knowledge can be

---

of performance properties in a completely unrestricted way, in this case so unrestricted as to fail to meet conditions that are known empirically. It is typical of performance delay models in its appeal to an essentially unrestricted set of stipulations about children's performance abilities and thus illustrates the unrestrictiveness of performance delay models as they have been developed. See Crain and Wexler (Chapter 12 of this volume) for further discussion of this point. What is particularly interesting about many appeals to performance delay in the literature is the general failure to understand that performance is an empirical property, which must be justified on empirical grounds, and is not a condition that can be arbitrarily specified as if it comes for free, no matter what the properties of performance actually are. In this sense, many performance delay models do not take performance seriously as an empirical issue. But it should be obvious that performance considerations must be invoked in exactly the same way that structural considerations are invoked—on the basis of empirical conditions and restrictive theories.

explained by assuming that it is innate (genetically encoded), the innateness hypothesis explains nothing. Given any piece of adult knowledge, simply assume it is innate. Thus the innateness hypothesis is unrestrictive and, in fact, unfalsifiable.

Generative grammar had to do battle with this view for many years, and I am not sure that such a view is completely dead. But notice how wrong it is. As Chomsky frequently pointed out, suppose that it is *true* that a piece of grammar is innately specified (that is, through the genetic program). Then it *is* explanatory to say that that piece of grammar is innately specified. This truism is what was missing from the argument that the innateness hypothesis is nonrestrictive and unfalsifiable.

In fact, linguists and psycholinguists know very well that there are many ways to refute a particular innateness hypothesis. Suppose, for example, that one postulates property A as a property of UG, which all languages must satisfy. Then if it turns out that there is a language that does not satisfy Property A, the hypothesis that Property A is part of UG is false. In practice, it turns out to be difficult to find a particular true theory that specifies exactly what is innate. This is what we would expect in an empirical science. Linguists and psycholinguists falsify particular theories of innateness (of UG) every day. The point that was missing from the claim that the innateness hypothesis is unfalsifiable was that it is not the claim that *something* is innate that is tested. Rather, it's a *particular* hypothesis about what is innate.

The growth/maturation theory has exactly the same status in developmental research. It is *particular* growth/maturation theories that are tested, just as particular theories of UG are tested. If a particular growth/maturation theory claims that Property A is not available at a particular age N, and then a construction is found in some language that has Property A and children of age N are shown to know that construction, then the particular growth/maturation theory is shown to be false. Of course, one might come up with a *different* growth/maturation theory, which gets around the problem. But that is just normal science, just as when a particular theory of UG is shown to be false and one then comes up with a different theory of UG. We do not say that the innateness hypothesis (i.e., the claim that UG exists) is false or untestable. Exactly the same holds for growth/maturation theories.

In fact, a number of papers have attempted to show that particular growth/maturation theories are false on empirical grounds. In particular, these papers take a claim of a particular growth/maturation theory that a particular linguistic construct is not available at a certain age and attempt to show that constructions in some languages have that property and *are* available to children at that age. Thus the logic of how to disconfirm growth/maturation theories is quite clear. In fact, the theories that have been created are quite falsifiable, since, as theories of linguistic development go, they are rather clear and precise. They attempt to tie together a number of developmental phenomena in a general way. Thus the general hypothesis applies to many constructions in many languages. It is relatively easy to falsify such theories if in fact they *are* false. (Again, note the very close similarity to linguistic theory, not an accidental similarity, as growth/maturation theories were constructed in quite conscious imitation of the theoretical methodology of linguistic theory, that is, of science in general—see Borer & Wexler, 1987).

In contrast, rigidity theory, necessarily incorporating a performance delay component, is often quite unfalsifiable, because it is so vague and gives completely free rein to the notion of what might be performance. If no theory of a crucial component of the hypothesis (i.e., of performance in children) exists, then of course the theory is unrestrictive and close to unfalsifiable. This vague and unrestrictive characterization is true of performance delay ideas in general. If they are ever made more precise, perhaps they can be tested. At the moment, they are hardly a competitor for growth/maturation theories.

On the other side, one should bear in mind that the vague and unrestrictive character of rigidity theories is in large measure due to the relatively undeveloped status of processing theory, especially the theory of children's processing. Almost nothing is known about the processing of language in children.[9] One reason for this is that processing theory in adults depends on the assumption that the adult has a particular grammar, as uncovered by linguistic theory, so that processing deviations can be studied on this basis. In children, we have to uncover the nature of their grammars, and that has been the goal of most research in linguistic development. Thus it is difficult to study language processing in children, given that we do not know what their grammars are. If we ever discover methods that allow us to uncover what children's processing/performance abilities are, it might be possible to show that certain features of language delay are due to processing/performance considerations. At the present time most of such claims are not based on any systematic research. We should leave the possibility open. However, it is also extremely important to make clear that any claim that a child's language delay is due to performance considerations must be evaluated with the same seriousness as a claim that a child's language delay is due to grammatical considerations. Perhaps the fact the growth/maturation theories have been able to be stated with a certain amount of specificity and detail and empirical support should count in their favor when compared to rigidity/performance delay theories, which remain rather vague. However, we should keep open the possibility that some day the rigidity/performance delay theories might be specifiable in a more adequate way. Certainly research in this direction could be useful.

We can conclude that the general idea of linguistic theory that grammar grows in the mind/brain is plausible and correct, and that growth/maturation is a plausible mechanism that is responsible for much linguistic change in the child. Thus

[9]Except for a claim that I make that for the most part children's performance systems are like adult systems. See Crain and Wexler (see Chapter 12 of this volume) for a detailed discussion of this point, under the name of *modularity matching*.

developmental and linguistic considerations join together in one conclusion. Growth/maturation is not only compatible with linguistic theory; it also is in many ways expected by linguistic theory.

It is also worth noting Rizzi's (1994) interesting suggestion that if it turns out that in fact there *are* some small deviations in child grammar from adult UG, along the lines of Borer and Wexler's conceptual analysis of maturation, then results in language acquisition will be even *more* interesting for linguistic theory than if rigidity strictly holds. The reason is that it should be very interesting and productive for linguistic theory to see what grammars are the results of small perturbations in UG are like, whereas if rigidity holds, then child grammars will simply be further examples of grammars completely obeying UG, as are the grammars of any natural language. In my view, such examples already exist, and we will discuss them.

II. GROWTH/MATURATION, BIOLOGY, AND COGNITION

I have discussed growth/maturation theories in contrast to the alternative, which is rigidity theory, and shown that, as they have developed at least, growth/maturation theories are more restrictive than rigidity theories and, moreover, are what is expected given the general facts of language acquisition and the learnability problem for linguistic theory. In later sections I will go through some detailed growth/maturational theories of certain aspects of grammar to show why they have these properties and why they are empirically more satisfying. First, however, we should discuss the place of growth/maturational theories in the general context of biology and the study of cognition.

First, growth/maturation *is* biology, in many ways. That is, biology is often looked at as the study of systems that develop, and growth/maturation is in fact what drives change in all living species. Thus it would be extremely odd, a real contradiction to the basic tenets of biology, to find a species that showed no development, no growth, no maturation. Probably it would be considered impossible, in fact.

Now, this would be of no importance to the study of grammatical development and of grammar if we believed that grammar has nothing to do with biology. But the basic tenet of linguistic theory (generative grammar) is that language is a central part of human biology. Grammar is a species-specific, genetically encoded system. Chomsky even suggested that we look upon UG as a (mental) organ. Thus, if we accept the foundations of linguistic theory, the claim that language has all these biological properties, then language must be seen to grow, to mature. There is no other logically coherent way of analyzing language as part of human biology.

Of course, it is possible, as we have pointed out, that the growth/maturation takes place before birth; some aspects of biology mature before birth, some after birth. But in general, in biological systems, in the mammal say, there is growth/maturation after birth. For example, in humans there is a large amount of physical growth in organs after birth. This growth is dictated by the genetic program, it is not something that happens through any kind of learning. For a discussion of the ways in which innateness and growth are typical of biological systems, as well as a discussion of how language growth seems to have the same properties, see Wexler (1990a).

Examples are obvious. In humans, a first set of teeth falls out and is replaced by a second set of teeth, all this as a result of growth/maturation. At a much later age, secondary sexual characteristics emerge, again as the result of growth/maturation. The genetic program guides the development of these features, but it guides them at specific times; the program plays out its results over time. This is characteristic of biology, almost the essence of biology. If grammar is a piece of biology, how could we expect grammar to not show traces of growth processes?

There are cases of even more extreme growth/maturation processes, in which it appears as if species transform in development after birth into very different types of creatures indeed. For example, tadpoles grow into (mature into) frogs. Gleitman (1981) has pointed out that if children do not have grammars, but rather only obey various semantic constraints, as had been proposed in earlier speculations about child language, then it must be the case that the children who develop grammars later are like tadpoles turning into frogs. That is, the young children simply grow a grammar; they do not learn it. Of course, Gleitman's point is exactly right.[10]

It turns out that young children indeed have grammars quite similar to UG; they have what Borer and Wexler (1992) called *Proto-UG,* a grammatical system that deviates in highly specific ways from UG. Thus language development is not like a tadpole turning into a frog. It is more like the addition of some specific properties to a young child's system that already has the basic structure of UG. We do not say neonates are not human because they don't have a second set of teeth or secondary sexual characteristics. UG appears similar. Young children (at least at the ages at which we can so far study it—as young as 1;6 or perhaps a bit earlier) have UG systems with some highly specific variations.[11] Thus young children

[10]It should be pointed out that Gleitman did not accept the conclusion that young children do not have grammars. She was simply making the learnability point that there is no way for children to learn grammar; if they do not have grammar as young children they can only grow into (mature into) adult grammar. Thus she was arguing against the hypothesis that young children do not have grammars because they have not had time to learn them yet.

[11]At ages much younger than about 1;6 we simply do not have any information, due to methodological limitations. But it would not surprise us to discover that even younger children had much of UG. How early this goes, of course, we do not know at present. But there is no reason to believe that methodologies will not become available that will help us to determine the answer to this question. Certainly in recent years, concerted effort has allowed us to show the establishment of central aspects

have human grammar (UG), even though they still have some growing to do from the standpoint of adult UG, not a big surprise given what we know about human maturation in general.

This might appear to be a bit of a complicated picture. Children have central aspects of UG, but there are still variations. But it seems to be that it is no more complicated than what we find in biology in general with respect to all sorts of species-specific abilities. In addition to the previous examples, we can look at other—more cognitive—organs of human biology. Consider vision, for example. It is well known that there are central aspects of the visual system that grow/mature after birth. Nevertheless, much of the human visual system is essentially present in young children. See Wexler (1990a) for some references.

Thus the complications are exactly what we expect in biology, including human biology. The genetic program plays itself out, guiding the development over time of the organism, and certain aspects of development of systems, including centrally important systems, are not complete by the time of birth, but take more time. The idea of complication is only true if birth is looked on as the central time at which growth is complete. But in general growth does not stop at birth. Thus the picture is this: The genetic program guides the development of systems, and some of the development continues after birth. Period. The growth/maturation of UG fits right into this simple, and satisfying, picture. This is perhaps especially true, because we do not have to invoke the tadpole/frog model for UG. Rather, the genetic program begins to develop language in the human brain, and much of it has already been established (at least by 1;6, probably much earlier; see our earlier footnote about methodological limitations so far limiting us to that age). No total transformation of grammar exist; rather, the genetic program continues to play out, finally developing full adult UG.

In many ways, this process, of UG having developed in young children but with some further playing out of the genetic program to go, seems to be naturally called *continuity,* because the idea is that adult UG is continuous with, though not identical to, young children's UG. Unfortunately, the term *continuity* has come to be identified with what I have called rigidity, the notion that UG does not change at all after birth, that there is no genetically based grammar growth process after birth. So as not to confuse the reader, I won't use the term *continuity* for the ideas on growth/maturation presented here, but perhaps the time will come when the term *will* apply to the ideas as presented here.

Meanwhile we need a term for the hypothesis presented in this chapter, that the genetic program constructs UG already in very young children but has not completed its task, and that some properties continue to develop in children, eventual-

---

of UG in much younger children that would have been dreamed about as little as 10 years ago. See later sections of this paper for some details, especially about the inflectional/head/specifier/verb movement systems, which are central to clausal syntax.

ly reaching full UG. Until we can use the term *continuity* for this view, I suggest that we call it the *continuous developmental* (*CD*) view. The notion *development* in CD is meant to capture the idea that there *are* changes in UG as children get older and that these changes are due to growth mechanisms. *Continuous* in CD is meant to capture the idea that the changes modify and add to the basic child system of UG but do not make it into something completely different. Tadpole to frog changes (metamorphosis) would presumably be excluded by the term *continuous development,* but the kinds of developmental changes that I have described in other systems would be included. Note that it is simply an empirical result that UG change in children so far seems best described by the continuous development hypothesis, rather than by the more fundamental changes that seem to occur in the transformation of a tadpole into a frog. Either possibility is compatible with the logic of growth/maturation, as they must be, because both occur in nature. Also study of much younger children (say at 3 months of age) or of other grammatical properties that have not yet been studied may eventually result in showing that in fact there are some more fundamental changes; there might be part of UG that children know nothing or little about.[12] As this does not seem to be the case given what we know so far, I will in this chapter maintain the continuous developmental view.

Note that the continuous development view is *exactly* the view stated in Borer and Wexler (1987, 1992), which assumed that children knew much about UG whereas other properties were in fact somewhat different from UG (I will return to a more explicit formulation in the next section). Because arguments against maturation have generally been against the Borer/Wexler view, they must be arguments against continuous development and in favor of rigidity.

It is sometimes said that growth/maturational theories do not have content or are vague because they do not specify the *physical* mechanism of maturation. But this point is invalid. To specify a theory of a phenomenon at one level, does not mean that the theory has to be specified at another level. For example, one can specify that growth/maturation is the driving force for certain aspects of linguistic development and show that the theory makes certain predictions about development and learning that seem to be true. If one does not have a physical theory of the growth/maturational changes, that in no way invalidates the claims about growth/maturation.

Again, notice that *exactly* the same situation holds of any nativist theory of linguistic development. Linguistic theory assumes that UG is innate, and this is an

[12]Just to take one example almost at random, it has been impossible so far to establish that very young children (let us say, younger than 2 years old) know the structure of logical form. There is also no evidence that they *do not* know the properties of logical form, as far as I know. But the question remains open, pending the development of further methods. There are all sorts of discussions around about what the *null hypothesis* should be about areas where we have no empirical information, and I have contributed to this discussion. Whatever the interest of such discussion, the ultimate answer must be empirical.

important part of UG's explanatory apparatus. But we know nothing at all about the physical mechanisms of this innate structure; linguistic theory does not specify it, and the brain sciences have no idea how to do it. Yet we do not say that the idea that UG is innate is empty, or lacks contents, because we don't know what the physical structures are. The situation with respect to growth/maturation is exactly the same. We know nothing more about the physical basis for the innate structure of UG than we do about the physical basis for the development timing aspects of UG (the growth/maturation part). Of course, we would in each case like to know the physical mechanism. But the truth of innateness, or of growth/maturation, does not depend on knowing the physical basis.

Similarly, common sense and biology agree that walking is growth/maturation driven. Children cannot learn to walk when they are too young. Whatever the status of our knowledge of the physical basis for the growth/maturation explanation of walking, it is accepted that it is growth/maturation driven because of its behavioral properties. (For example, all children seem to have a delay after birth before they can walk, training does not seem to speed walking up considerably, it is hard to imagine what a "learning" explanation could be, other animals can walk at birth, and so on.) Whatever we know today about the physical basis of this maturation, certainly maturation/growth was accepted as a basis for the development of walking way before the foundational physical basis was understood, if in fact it is understood.

The same is true for the development of secondary sexual characteristics or for the growth of new teeth. Certainly a century ago we did not know whatever physical events (hormonal changes and so on) caused these developments and we certainly did not understand the genetic program that caused these events (I don't know if biology knows them today). Nevertheless, the field of biology accepted the developments as driven by growth/maturation. There is no reason that it takes understanding of the physical basis of a maturational event to accept that maturation/growth is indeed the cause of the physical event. Indeed, in biology, where growth/maturation is omnipresent and crucial, the physical basis of the growth/maturation is *rarely* known. Thus the claim that a physical basis for a maturational/growth event must be understood before accepting the claim of growth/maturation is completely unwarranted.

It would not strike me as surprising if a psychologist who believed the standard assumption in traditional American psychology that learning explains all cognitive growth did not believe that growth/maturation is a central developmental mechanism for human grammar. For such a psychologist would not believe that human language was determined by a genetic program, and thus there would be no such program to play out over time. But I do find it surprising that some generative linguists do not easily accept growth/maturation as a central developmental mechanism for human grammar, as, first of all, that is the central idea of linguistic theory, though not always explicitly stated, and second, the essence of the linguistic argument, the learnability argument, leads to growth/maturation as a basic mechanism of developmental change.

Although I cannot completely explain what appears to be a contradiction in the belief of some linguists, let me speculate. The establishment of generative grammar produced a revolution in linguistic thinking that centered around the idea that human language was established as a central aspect of human biology, directed by a genetic program. This view was directly at odds with many years of thinking in structural linguistics (as well as in behaviorist psychology, of course). Although this was the central conceptual change in generative grammar—paired with a central methodological argument, the learnability argument, also known as the Argument from the Poverty of the Stimulus (Chomsky, following Descartes)—it also brought with it a large number of methodological and analytical tools for the analysis of grammar. It may very well be that some linguists have accepted the new tools for the analysis of grammar but have not accepted the basic conceptual argument at the foundations of linguistic theory. That is, some linguists—even ones who appear to be *generative* linguists because they use the modern analytic devices and theories—have not accepted the foundational aspects of generative grammar. Such linguists might still believe that language exists apart from the human brain; it is not determined by the genetic program but has its own existence.[13] They might also accept the idea that this independent, autonomous UG, which is not in the mind, is learned by the human being. If language is not determined by a genetic program, there is no reason to think that it actually grows/matures in the human the way other biological properties of human grow/mature. Of course, the learnability argument must be ignored in order to maintain this view. It might be a failure to accept the radical consequences of linguistic theory—that language is in the individual brain, not in society and not living independently—that leads some linguists to have a reluctance to accept growth/maturation as a central mechanism of linguistic development. For such linguists, language is really not part of human biology. The difficulty with accepting the radical and over-arching changes that generative grammar brought to linguistics may be a consequence of growing pains as linguistics developed from part of the humanities into part of the modern sciences, part of biology (at least conceptually). However, many linguists accept the growth/maturation idea as central to developmental change in language and are completely at home with the view of language as a central aspect of human biology, determined by a genetic program.

The arguments of this section lead us to conclude that growth/maturation is almost necessary given the establishment of human language as part of human biology. In my view, it is particularly satisfying that arguments from (adult) linguistic theory, from the study of language acquisition, and from the study of biology

[13]Such a view is explicitly championed by the *Platonist* linguists and philosophers, for example Jerrold Katz. But most generative linguists do not consciously accept such views.

all lead to the same view—that growth/maturation is a central aspect of developmental change in grammar.

III. UG-CONSTRAINED MATURATION AND CONTINUOUS DEVELOPMENT

We have already mentioned that there is no *learnability* argument against growth/maturation or in favor of only small amounts of development. Because the hypothesis of growth maturation implies that the genetic program guides the development of grammar, the development does not have to be learned. Thus there is no learnability problem. The situation is exactly analogous to the assumption that there is a large innate component to UG. If a property is innate, that means that it develops under the guidance of the genetic program and does not have to be learned; thus there is no learnability problem.

So learnability logic does not dictate that young children have something very close to UG; the tadpole to frog model *could* be true of language. Also it is good that learnability logic does not dictate that young organisms *must* be very similar to older organisms; otherwise, how could this logic be made compatible with the existence of changes like the tadpole to frog?

Nevertheless, we have suggested that empirical considerations (which we will discuss in later sections) show that young children have grammars very much under the influence of UG, although their *Proto-UG* (Borer and Wexler's [1992] term) has some deviance from adult UG. Borer and Wexler (1992) offered a hypothesis that constrained maturational theories, the hypothesis of *UG-constrained maturation.*

(1) *UG-constrained maturation* holds that all child grammatical representations are available in UG.

UG-constrained maturation (UGCM) implies that, whatever a child's grammar, its representations are possible in (adult) UG. Thus a child cannot have a representation that UG does not allow. When the child represents a sentence, that representation must be available in UG, although in fact it might not be the representation that the adult grammar that the child is developing actually gives to that sentence.

Crucially, the implication in (1) is one-way; the converse does not necessarily hold. Namely, it does not follow from UGCM that a UG representation is a possible child representation. According to UGCM, that is the only way in which child UG (Proto-UG, or PUG) differs from (adult) UG. Namely, there might be representations available in UG that are not available in PUG. (For simplicity, here I am only referring to PUG as if it is one thing. Of course, there could be various PUGs, at different ages. UGCM applies to all of them.)

One hypothesis among others given in Borer and Wexler (1987, 1992) is that certain kinds of argument-chains are not available to children who have PUG. That is, children find certain kinds of representations ungrammatical; these are representations that have certain kinds of A-chains in them. Thus there are representations that are available (grammatical) in UG, that are *not* grammatical in PUG. However, on Borer and Wexler's UGCM hypothesis, if a representation is available (grammatical) in PUG, then it is grammatical in UG.

UGCM is a strict *growth* hypothesis. It says that children never have representations that are not compatible with UG. However, they *may* be missing the possibility to have certain representations. Thus if adult UG represents sentence S with representation R(S), and if R(S) is not a representation that is possible in PUG, then either children won't represent S at all, or they will give *another* representation R′(S) to S, where R′(S) *is* possible (grammatical) both in PUG *and* in UG. According to UGCM, they will *never* give a representation R″(S) to S where R″(S) is *not* grammatical in UG.

UGCM is a strict *growth* hypothesis; children will never have representations that have to be made impossible on the way to UG. Roughly, it is like developing secondary sexual characteristics. The organism at a young age does not have structures and capacities that are not available to the organism at an older age. Rather, certain structures and capacities grow (secondary sexual characteristics). But the child does not have structures and capacities that are lost as the child matures. Thus tadpole to frog transformations are ruled out by UGCM; only growth of structures is possible.

To take another example, UGCM seems to be the human property whereby growth/maturation dictates when they have the capacity to walk. It is well known that children can't walk before certain maturational developments have taken place.[14] Thus maturation/growth *adds* capacities (walking), just as UGCM assumes that grammatical capacities are added over time. If something as relatively simple (compared to language) as walking is subject to timing in the genetic program, it seems that something relatively more complicated, like language, should be subject to the same kind of developing timing constraints.

If UGCM does *not* hold, then the child could have grammars that generate representations that are not available to UG. To take a wild example, the child could decide that a way to ask yes/no questions is to delete every other word. This non-UG possibility is ruled out by UGCM.

Thus UGCM is one way of stating a hypothesis that has the property of continuous development that we discussed in the last section. Children have much of UG

[14]Of course, behaviorist psychology, based on learning, did not believe this, and there were in fact experiments attempting to train children to walk at an earlier age. Essentially, these experiments failed and are now taken to show indeed that the commonsense idea that walking is maturational is indeed correct.

(they have many UG representations) and they add other ones as they grow/mature. But they never have structures that are different from UG possibilities.[15]

Borer and Wexler stated UGCM as the result of empirically driven analyses of a number of cases of growth/maturation, because the property held of those cases. In their work there was no reason to ever posit that a child used a non-UG representation. Thus UGCM became a restrictive hypothesis that fit a set of empirical data.

But it is important to reiterate that UGCM is not dictated by learnability logic, the foundations of the field. Because the genetic program guides growth/maturation, learnability logic does not prevent the child from using a non-UG representation and then growing out of it, deleting that representation as possible. To the extent that UGCM is true, it seems to be the result of developmental (genetic program) properties of the organism; humans, in their language growth as well as in other aspects of their growth, do not seem to undergo the kinds of radical changes that the tadpole to frog change contains.

Thus UGCM is an empirical hypothesis that is one way of instantiating continuous development. UGCM is clearly a growth/maturation hypothesis, because it allows for certain UG representations that are not in PUG and because it is allied with the theory that the change from PUG to UG is the result of growth/maturation, as directed by the genetic program of UG.

Borer and Wexler (1992) also presented a particular theory of maturation, one that met the condition of UGCM. They hypothesized that much growth/maturation involves the weakening over time of biunique principles, that is, principles of UG that constrain grammar by requiring a particular one-to-one relation between two structures in the grammar. The theory presented assumed that the elements that go into both sides of the biunique principles can weaken, become less restrictive, over time as the child grows. Thus the child has a kind of strong, let us say canonical, set of structures that go into the principles, whereas after growth, a wider set of noncanonical structure enters into the principles; that is, the child can associate a wider class of elements.

For example, the theta criterion in UG associates an argument position with a

[15]Suppose that the critical period hypothesis is right in some form. The critical period hypothesis states that children can develop language well if they have been exposed to the language by a certain age, but not if they are only first exposed to the language at a later age. In a sense, this gives a child *more* capacity than an adult. If the critical period hypothesis is right, the ability to develop a particular language does *not* follow a strict growth theory, because children are better at this, have more capacities, than do adults. However, this result is in no way antithetical to UGCM. There is no reason to believe that the critical period hypothesis prevents an adult from having a representation; adults have the representations available in UG if they developed the language early enough. The critical period hypothesis, if it is true, rather must be taken to imply that adults have difficulty in learning certain aspects of a particular language. This is a completely different matter than asking what representations are possible for an adult, that is, what UG is.

theta role in a one-to-one fashion. Borer and Wexler (1992) hypothesized that the child has a *proto-theta-criterion,* which associates a *selected* (or subcategorized) position with a theta role in a one-to-one fashion. Thus a patient theta role is associated with grammatical object position. But if the object NP has moved to subject position, as in a *passive* structure, for example, the theta criterion will still be satisfied (the patient theta role is associated with the subject, an argument position), but the proto-theta criterion will be violated because the patient theta role is not associated with its subcategorized (selected) position. Thus an argument-chain of this kind will not be allowed by the child's grammar. See Section 5.3 for a discussion of the empirical consequences of this theory.

Note that the theory that suggests that there is a gradual weakening of biunique principles is a theory that meets UGCM. The child who can deviate from UG only in requiring a stronger, more canonical mapping will never have a representation that UG will not allow, although that child very well might not have a representation that UG *does* allow. We will also discuss whether this theory accounts for the cases of maturation that we present.

One task that we shall set ourselves in the detailed sections that follow is to see to what extent UGCM can be maintained. It is not the *only* way of achieving a continuous development theory of growth/maturation, so it will be important to see whether in fact it can be maintained in a wider set of circumstances. At any rate, the exact status of UGCM (or of the development of biunique principles) does not change the status of growth/maturation as an essential driving force of linguistic development.

IV. MATURATION AT THE INTERFACE?

With the development of the minimalist approach to linguistic theory (Chomsky, 1995), another possibility presents itself. A central construct of minimalism is that much of the central computational system of grammar (Chomsky's term, *CS*) is determined by the interfaces. The two interfaces are the phonetic interface (the interface between phonology and phonetic form, PF) and the conceptual interface (the interface between logical form, LF and the conceptual or interpretive systems). The central computational system CS is a formal, computational system that operates autonomously, but many of its properties are derived from the properties required by the interfaces. In a system that is absolutely minimalist, no further properties would have to be stated about CS; it would just operate on the basis of properties derived for free from the interface requirements. Whether theories can be constructed that meet this goal, of course, is an open question.

I would like to suggest that many properties of the growth/maturation system are in fact growth/maturation of interface properties. The hypothesis is that the coordination of two separate systems might be delayed. In particular, we will be concerned with the interface between the computational system of grammar—the *syntax*—and the conceptual/interpretive system of language. We will examine some cases of growth/maturation that seem amenable to this characterization.

If the hypothesis that interface coordination proves to be at the basis of some aspects of growth/maturation, we can presumably understand it as a general case of coordination of two systems. It is often suggested that it is lack of growth of coordination of systems that is responsible for the appearance of delay in physical/cognitive systems. *Eye-hand coordination* is a classic example. The idea is that the properties of the visual system itself have developed and the properties of the motor system have developed, but the development of the coordination of these two systems is slower than the development of the individual systems.

In particular, we will explore the hypothesis that some late developments are caused by the lack of coordination of the computational system of language (the syntax) and the conceptual/interpretive system of language. If the hypothesis proves to have some value, then it will provide further evidence not only for this characterization of the growth/maturational aspects of language, but also of the modular split between the computational and conceptual/interpretive systems of language. Furthermore, to the extent that the growth of coordination of systems at the interface is the right explanation for some aspects of growth/maturation, then it provides evidence that the individual systems themselves—for example, the computational system (syntax)—developed earlier.

Of course, there is no reason that *all* properties of growth/maturation must be characterizable by the development of interface coordination. At this stage in our understanding of the development of language, the best strategy seems to be to list some hypotheses about development, some theories that characterize the development, and to see how many particular aspects of growth/maturation actually fit within these theories.

V. SOME LINGUISTIC DEVELOPMENTS

In this section we will discuss a number of properties of grammar that develop over time. We will use these illustrations as case studies of linguistic growth, detailing some of their properties and trying to understand them in terms of what kind of growth/maturation takes place. All the structures that we will discuss are well-studied aspects of linguistic development, and there is no room here to detail most of the properties or to discuss the entire literature that has provided evidence concerning the developmental properties of these structures. The idea, rather, will be to see how each of the areas fits into general notions of growth/maturation and what light the developments that take place can shed on growth/maturation theories.

Section A examines aspects of the development of binding theory, particularly in relation to principle B. Section B discusses the development of clausal and inflectional structure. Section C explores the development of structures which contain argument-chains.

A. Binding Theory and Interpretation

Binding theory provides a very nice example for several reasons. First of all, it has been one of the most active experimental areas in language acquisition in the past 15 years. There are many relevant developmental results. Second, binding theory provides a very nice illustration of a linguistic domain that seems to have important properties at the interface of the computational (syntactic) systems of grammar and the conceptual/interpretive system. Thus it is a good area in which to explore the question of the development of interface properties.

Because there has been so much research in binding theory and its development, as we have pointed out we will only discuss some issues that are central from a developmental point of view and in that results relevant to the issue of growth/maturation exist. Also, we will not review the experimental evidence for the results that we discuss, but in most cases we will simply state the result and refer the reader to some of the literature.

Let us state very simple forms of two binding principles, principle A and principle B (Chomsky, 1981). The simple forms will be enough for the work that we need to do; empirical considerations might force the principles to be stated in more complex or different ways but should not basically affect what we have to say about the developmental aspects.

(2) Principle A: An anaphor is bound in its governing category
(3) Principle B: A pronoun is free in its governing category
(4) X *binds* Y (where X and Y are nodes in a phrase marker) if and only if
 a. *X* c-commands Y, and
 b. X is co-indexed with Y
(5) X *c-commands* Y (where X and Y are nodes in a phrase marker) if and only if the first branching node that dominates X also dominates Y
(6) X is *free* in its governing category if and only if X is not bound in its governing category

Anaphors are items like reflexives (*myself, herself,* and so on) and reciprocals (*each other*). As in most of the literature, we will present results only concerning reflexives. Pronouns are items like *she, him, her,* and *I.* Basically, the intuition is that anaphors are items that *must* depend on other items in the structure for their interpretation (the items that c-command them and are coindexed with them), whereas pronouns are items that do not have to receive their interpretation from other items in the structure.

The definition of *binds,* which is used in Principles A and B, is given in (4). It says that X and Y are coindexed, which means that their interpretations (references in many cases) are directly linked, are determined in the same way, and perhaps are the *same* (i.e., the interpretation will be that the reference of X is the same as the reference of Y). Furthermore, if X binds Y, they are in a particular structural configuration; X c-commands Y. (5) gives the definition of c-command.

Principle A (2) thus says that the antecedent of an anaphor (the item that is coindexed with it) must c-command it. Furthermore, the antecedent must be in the same *governing category* as the anaphor. We will not discuss the notion of *governing category* but will simply point out that basically it is a *locality* notion; in most (but not all) cases, the governing category can be taken to be the clause that contains the anaphor. At least this is true if the anaphor is in object position, the structure on which most experiments have been carried out.

Principle B (3), on the other hand, says that pronouns are free in their governing category, where the definition of *free* is given in item 5. In other words, Principle B says that pronouns may *not* have a c-commanding coindexed element in their governing category, which again for our purposes we can take to be the clause that contains the (object) pronoun.

The basic results on the development of principles A and B were developed between the mid-1980s and 1990. Wexler and Chien (1985) showed that children before age 5 knew the c-command aspect of principle A, namely that a reflexive must be c-commanded by its antecedent, and this result has been confirmed in many experimental studies with a number of different types of structure in a number of different languages. Furthermore, Chien and Wexler (1987, 1990) showed that children before age 5 knew the locality aspect of Principle A, that the antecedent of the reflexive must be in its clause, and this too has been confirmed by subsequent research.[16] Thus the basic conclusion of the field has been that the properties of Principle A are known to the young child, at least by age 5 (the earliest ages remain to be studied in a convincing way).

Principle B, on the other hand, has provided what at first appears to be a different picture. Wexler and Chien (1985) (see also Chien and Wexler 1987, 1990, for conformation with additional structures) showed quite systematically that at the very ages at which children displayed excellent knowledge of Principle A, they very often failed on what appeared to be tests of Principle B. For example, in their

[16]In fact, very young children (about 2;6 to 3;6) very often chose a long-distance antecedent for a reflexive, so there was no direct proof of knowledge of the locality property at the earliest ages. Chien and Wexler (1987, 1990) provided experimental evidence and analyses to suggest that it may have been something other than lack of knowledge of the locality property of Principle A that caused this behavior. But the issue remains open, pending further research. It is somewhat difficult to carry out the experiments on very young children, which is perhaps one reason why the issue is not resolved. If Chien and Wexler are in fact wrong, and very young children *do not* in fact know the locality property of Principle A, then there will be further results for a developmental/growth theory to account for.

experiments children would often (let us say 50% of the time for simplicity here, but the percentage varies with age, structure, and experimental method) take *her* to be Cinderella's sister rather than Cinderella in sentences like the following

(7) Cinderella's sister pointed to her.

This interpretation is ruled out by Principle B, because the NP *Cinderella's sister* c-commands the pronoun *her.* Thus the NP *Cinderella's sister* cannot be coindexed with *her,* or Principle B would be violated because the NP is in the same clause (governing category) as the pronoun. In other words, *her* is not free in its governing category in (7) if it is coindexed with the NP *Cinderella's sister.*

This result has been confirmed in a large number of subsequent studies, many of them starting out with the hope of disconfirming it. By now it is an accepted fact in the acquisition literature, probably the most well-studied experimental fact in the literature, especially among facts that seem to go against the adult grammar (for example, see McDaniels, Cairns, & Hsu, 1991). Despite many attempts to show that the fact does not hold, the result in almost every case is the same; children do not appear to follow Principle B.[17] For reviews of the literature on the topic, see Avrutin and Wexler (1992) and Thornton and Wexler (in press).

At first sight, the result might suggest a direct growth/maturational approach to Principle B. Yet Wexler and Chien (1985) did not take this route, though they mentioned it as a possibility. They argued against the maturation of Principle B because the direct underlying constructs of Principle B are so similar to Principle A that it seemed unlikely to them that the rate of maturation of one principle would be significantly ahead of the other principle. Yet Principle A was known to the child, whereas the experiments on principle B showed consistent poor performance on the part of many children for many years, even for some 6-year-old children.

Wexler and Chien (1985) and Montalbetti and Wexler (1985) instead suggested that the problem that the child had was not one of lack of knowledge of Principle B but rather a problem with pragmatic/interpretive knowledge. The idea is that the child *knew* Principle B but did not know (or could not apply) the interpretive principles concerning noncoindexed pronouns. Consider a representation like the following:

(8) a. *Mama Bear$_i$ hugged her$_i$
b. Mama Bear$_i$ hugged her$_j$

In (8a) *Mama Bear* and *her* are coindexed. Principle B thus rules out the representation. In (8b), *Mama Bear* and *her* are not coindexed. Thus *her* can be anybody; it could be Cinderella, for example. In certain situations it could even be

[17]For example, Grimshaw and Rosen (1990) attempted to eliminate what they perceived to be artifacts from some experiments in the literature. Yet their experiment produced identical results to the standard results in the literature. See Avrutin and Wexler (1992), Crain and Wexler (Chapter 12 of this volume), and Thornton and Wexler (in press) for discussion.

Mama Bear.[18] In other words, as is well known in the study of binding theory, contraindexation does *not* imply noncoreference. NPs with different indices may indeed wind up as coreferential.

Wexler and Chien (1985) and Montalbetti and Wexler (1985) followed well-known discussions in the binding theory literature, especially those of Reinhart (1983), in suggesting that the noncoreference that speakers intuit about most instances of sentences like (8) ("Mama Bear hugged her") follows from a combination of the syntactic Principle B (to mark representation (8a) as ungrammatical) and pragmatic/interpretive principles, which prevent representation (8b) from having a *Mama Bear* = *her* interpretation in most cases.[19]

Wexler and Chien (1985) and Montalbetti and Wexler (1985) thus pointed out that a simple test of sentences like (8) could not tell whether children knew Principle B, because children who did poorly on the sentence (taking *her* to be *Mama Bear*) could know Principle B but could be using the noncoindexed representation (8b), thus violating pragmatic/interpretive principles rather than Principle B. They thus suggested that a more appropriate test of Principle B would be one in which the semantics ensured that the only possible interpretation of the sentence was the bound, coindexed one. For example, when a pronoun is bound by a quantifier, the only possible grammatical interpretation is one in which the pronoun and quantifier are coindexed, as in the following example:

(9) a. *every bear$_i$ hugged her$_i$
    b. every bear$_i$ hugged her$_j$

The coindexed representation (9a) is ruled out by principle B, as in (8a). Similarly, Principle B does not rule out the noncoindexed representation (9b). However, by the principles of interpretation, *her* is not (logically) bound by *every bear* in (9b); the sentence cannot mean that every bear hugged herself, no matter what the pragmatic situation.

Thus Wexler and Chien (1985) and Montalbetti and Wexler (1985) argued a child who knew Principle B would reject sentences like (9) (on the coindexed interpretation, meaning that every bear hugged herself), even if the child accepted sentences like (8) on the coreferential interpretation. These authors argued that if indeed children showed this pattern of behavior, then it would demonstrate that they knew Principle B but lacked the pragmatic interpretive knowledge that would rule out the coreferential interpretation of (8b).

[18]For example, one could say "Mama Bear hugged everybody in the room. She even hugged *her*." In this case, *her* is Mama Bear, and the sentence is grammatical. See Chien and Wexler (1990) and Thornton and Wexler (in press) for a fuller discussion.

[19]As Chien and Wexler (1990), Avrutin and Wexler (1992), and Thornton and Wexler (in press) discuss, this assumption, that noncoindexed but coreferential interpretations are ruled out by pragmatic/interpretive principles, is in fact central to all standard lines of investigation in the binding theory, so the Wexler and Chien (1985) assumption was simply congruent with all standard approaches to binding theory.

In other words, Wexler and Chien (1985) and Montalbetti and Wexler (1985) proposed a crucial experiment: study children's behavior on (8) and (9). If they demonstrated excellent behavior on (9), then even if they did not demonstrate excellent behavior on (8) one could conclude that they knew Principle B. Moreover, this experimental result would show a problem with children's knowledge of interpretive/pragmatic rules (what Chien and Wexler, 1990, called Principle P).

The experiment took a number of years to carry out; methods had to be created for studying some detailed structures that had not been studied before. (Note that the result was not known; the prediction concerned entirely unknown data.) Chien and Wexler (1990) succeeded in doing the experiment and obtaining accurate results. The result confirmed that children often violated (8), 5-year olds accepting the coreferential interpretation more than 50% of the time. But the same children rejected (9) on the bound interpretation 86% of the time, that is, fairly close to 100% of the time. Chien and Wexler's study contained four experiments, and even the one experiment that studied the bound interpretations like (9) had a very large number of experimental conditions, which allowed the general claim to be substantiated in some detail. We cannot discuss all these conditions here. But let us just point out that Chien and Wexler showed that children had no trouble understanding bound variable interpretations; they were almost always correct when the quantifier bound a *reflexive,* as in the following example:

(10) every bear hugged herself

Thus children had no trouble with bound variable interpretations. Furthermore, in a later study, Chien and Wexler (1991) systematically demonstrated that children who rejected locally bound pronouns (9) had no trouble in accepting pronouns as bound variables when Principle B did not rule them out. Thus children rejected (9) because of Principle B, not because of any problem with bound variable interpretations.

Again, further investigation by other experimenters confirmed the basic truth of the facts that Chien and Wexler investigated, in particular the error on sentences like (8) and good behavior on sentences like (9). In fact, they have been confirmed in a variety of structures (different types of quantifiers, and so on), in different languages, using different methodologies (see, e.g., Avrutin & Wexler, 1992, 1998; McDaniels et al., 1991).

These developments read a bit like a classic story of theory and experiment in science, something rarely achieved in psycholinguistics. An anomaly appears (poor behavior on pronouns coreferential with a locally c-commanding NP), theory is proposed to account for the anomaly (the distinction between bound and coreferential pronouns), the theory makes a prediction on a subtle type of phenomenon (NP antecedents versus quantified, binding antecedents in development), which has not been studied before, or even thought about, and effort is expended at methodologies to experimentally determine whether the prediction is true, resulting in confirmation of the hypothesis. Perhaps because of this success story for the field, a case of what seemed to be a clear increase in understanding, there has been much interest in this subject, and many experiments carried out and hypotheses investigated.

What we have presented is only the barest outline of the literature on the topic of Principle B and its interpretations in development. See Thornton and Wexler (in press) for a very extensive up-to-date discussion of the literature, both the empirical literature and its interpretations. I have not presented any exact empirical data or results, because that would easily constitute a chapter in itself. But the basic results should be clear.

Now, what of the interpretation and how does it relate to maturation/growth theory? First of all, let us call the delay on sentences like (8) the "apparent Principle B error" effect. Apparent, because the empirical results confirm Wexler and Chien's (1985) original analysis, which predicted that children actually do not make Principle B errors.

The detailed explanation that I will offer follows the one presented in Thornton and Wexler (in press); there are related, but not identical, analyses in Avrutin (1995) and Avrutin and Wexler (1992). Let us start by noting that in addition to the computational system of language (syntax) there is a discourse/pragmatic/interpretive system, and the two systems work together to produce linguistic knowledge. Of relevance to us is the part of the system that governs the interpretation of pronouns. Pronouns must be interpreted; their reference must be made clear. It is the function of the discourse/interpretive system to provide the constraints that make the reference of pronouns clear.

In particular, a pronoun's reference must be made clear to the listener. We will say that a pronoun must be *grounded;* this means that its reference must be made clear.

(11) The grounding principle: An NP must be grounded.

There are basically two ways that an NP can be grounded. On the one hand, the NP itself can point out its referent, as, for example, in the use of a proper name or in the use of a deictic pronoun, in which some act of *pointing* makes the referent clear. Alternatively, an NP can be grounded by being coindexed with another NP that is itself grounded and receiving its reference through this coindexation. See Thornton and Wexler (in press) for a recursive definition of *grounding,* which captures these properties.

Thus a pronoun can be grounded either by some kind of deictic act, in which its reference is made clear in the context, or under coindexation with another NP, such that the reference of the latter NP is transferred to the pronoun. Note that the former method is governed by discourse/pragmatic principles. For grounding by some kind of deixis, it is crucial that the speaker make clear to the listener who or what is being referred to.

Grounding via coindexation is a strictly formal, computational, syntactic process. If a pronoun is coindexed with a referential NP, then the pronoun and NP are coreferential; this is a strict formal outcome, and no knowledge of the world is necessary to arrive at this conclusion. On the other hand, grounding through deixis is a subtle act that involves many cognitive/discourse abilities. In particular, the speaker must find some way to make clear to the listener who or what is being referred to, for there is no syntactic/computational part of the representation that does this.

In particular, a listener, to understand a sentence like (8), must know who *her* refers to. Suppose the sentence is presented in a context in which both Mama Bear and Goldilocks are potential referents. Let's say the experimental situation is like Chien and Wexler's (1990):

(12) a. This is Mama Bear and this is Goldilocks
b. Is Mama Bear hugging her?

The adult is shown a picture, in this case, of Mama Bear hugging herself, Mama Bear (of course, half the time, the child is shown a picture of Mama Bear hugging Goldilocks). The adult will answer no to (12), when presented with a picture of Mama Bear hugging herself. Why? If the adult has a coindexed interpretation like (8a), Principle B rules it out. But why can't the adult take the representation to be as in (8b) and, because the syntax/computational system does not rule out *her* = Mama Bear, why can't the adult accept this interpretation?

The answer presented in Thornton and Wexler (in press) goes like this. When a name is repeated in reference to the same referent as previously mentioned, the name is coindexed with the previous mention; that is how it is grounded. (In Thornton and Wexler's terms, following Heim's, 1988, notation, the second mention of the name does not create a new file card; thus this second use receives its interpretation from its coindexation with the first use of the name.) Thus the NP *Mama Bear* in (12b) is coindexed with the NP *Mama Bear* in (12a). We now ask about the grounding of *her* in (12b). If *her* is grounded by being coindexed with *Mama Bear* in (12a), then via transitivity of indexing, *her* will also be coindexed with *Mama Bear* in (12b). Thus Principle B will be violated. Thus *her* must be grounded in some other way. One way is to coindex *her* with Goldilocks. The adult can accept this and make *her* coindexed with Goldilocks. Suppose *her* is not coindexed with any NP mentioned in the discourse (12). That is, *her* receives an index that is not anyplace else in (12). This is certainly a grammatical representation, because no syntactic principle is violated, surely not Principle B. It would appear that *her* could then refer to any NP, to *Mama Bear,* for example, yielding the unwanted interpretation. But we have to ask about how a noncoindexed *her* is grounded, since the grounding principle requires that every NP be grounded. Because *her* is not coindexed, it can only be grounded via deixis. So the adult knows that deictic grounding can only be carried out through means that make clear to the listener who is being referred to, for example, by pointing or some more complicated substitute (shared understanding, etc.). But in (12) there is no way for the listener to know who *her* is unless it's coindexed with an NP in the utterance, so the adult listener can only ground *her* through coindexation; this is the result of pragmatic/interpretive/discourse knowledge. Thus for the adult, *her* cannot be Mama Bear. Thornton and Wexler (in press) showed how this derivation applies in general to grammaticality judgments of adults concerning principle B context sentences, not only to the experimental situation as here described.

Now consider the child. Following Thornton and Wexler, I assume that the child can make one kind of error; she sometimes thinks that an NP is grounded when in fact it has not been. That is, the child cannot always adequately apply the grounding principle, although she knows the principle. The reason is that the child does not always adequately calculate what a listener can know or infer from the evidence presented. Thus the child *overaccepts* pronouns as grounded, when in fact they are not.

Thus consider such a child presented with (12). The child coindexes the NP *Mama Bear* in (12a) with the NP *Mama Bear* in (12b), thus grounding the latter via coindexation, just as the adult does. Because the child knows Principle B, she cannot coindex *her* with *Mama Bear* in (12a), because then *her* would be coindexed with *Mama Bear* in (12b), violating Principle B. The child can coindex *her* with *Goldilocks,* as can the adult. But the child has one extra option.

Suppose the child makes *her* have a different index from any other NP in (12), that is, different from the index of *Mama Bear* and of *Goldilocks.* This was a grammatical possibility for the adult, but was ruled out by the grounding principle; *her* could not be adequately grounded in (12) without coindexation. But the child, we have assumed, often misapplies the grounding principle. Namely, she thinks that a pronoun is grounded when in fact it is not. That is, she thinks the listener can infer who *her* is even when an adult will not do this because the adult thinks that adequate conditions have not been met for this grounding. In this case, the child can accept *her* as coreferential with *Mama Bear.* The child has accepted a *deictic* reading of *her* even though adequate (for the adult) conditions on deixis have not been presented. The child takes the possibility of *her* being Mama Bear in its (the child's) own mind as enough of a condition for the listener to know that *her* is Mama Bear. Thus the child will accept (8) on the coreferential interpretation, unlike the adult. The child does not violate Principle B, but only violates the grounding principle and violates it not because she does not know it, but because she misapplies it, thinking that a pronoun has been grounded when in fact it has not.

Because we assume that the child knows the grounding principle, but can misapply it by overaccepting pronouns as grounded (but not by refusing to accept pronouns as grounded if they in fact are grounded), we can derive another property of children's behavior in the experiments. Consider a discourse like (12). It is well known that when the picture requires a yes response (i.e., Mama Bear is hugging

Goldilocks), the proportion of yes responses is high, depending on the experiment over 80% and reaching close to 100%. On the other hand, when the picture requires a no response (i.e., Mama Bear is hugging Mama Bear), the proportion of yes responses is not 80 to 100% but much lower, say, around 50%. Why this asymmetry in the two cases? If the child simply failed to apply the grounding principle in the second (mismatch) case, we would expect the child to say yes in these cases, so the yes responses should be about the same as in the match pictures, which violate no principle for the child.

But, as Thornton and Wexler (in press) have shown, because we assume that the child knows the grounding principle, it is reasonable to suppose that she only sometimes misapplies it, that is, the child only sometimes overaccepts a pronoun as grounded when it is not. In these cases, the child can say yes; otherwise the grounding principle will rule out the coreferential but noncoindexed representation of (12). Thus when there is a mismatch (Mama Bear is hugging Mama Bear), only sometimes will the child accept a noncoindexed *her* as grounded; thus only sometimes will the child accept the sentence. But when a picture is shown in which Mama Bear is hugging Goldilocks, then the child can accept this sentence by coindexing *her* with *Goldilocks.* We assume that the child never fails to be able to coindex a pronoun with an NP that in fact (for the adult) has been adequately grounded.[20] Thus the child can always say yes to such a sentence. Thus we get the difference in probabilities in responses for the match and mismatch cases.

Why does the child overaccept pronouns as grounded when in fact they are not? Thornton and Wexler put it as in (13):

(13) The child's problem in the apparent Principle P error stage: The child believes that listeners can infer more from a discourse situation than in fact they can infer, that is, more than is adequately grounded.

That is, children who make apparent Principle B errors simply believe that a listener has more inferential powers than in fact she has; thus they think the referent of a pronoun has been made clear to a listener even though the conditions have not been met that actually do this.

The child's problem then, her lag, is in her ability to make inferences about what speakers and listeners can infer from discourse situations. This is a problem concerning pragmatic/inferential/discourse properties, in particular knowledge about minds and what they can infer. It is in a quite different module from the syntactic/computational/formal module. The latter's principles apply blindly to symbolic representations, without reference to beliefs of speakers. They are purely formal, computational, symbolic. The discourse/pragmatic principles, on the other

[20]Thornton and Wexler (in press) call this property asymmetry of discourse inferencing errors (ADIE). Namely, children will accept pronouns as grounded that in fact are not grounded for an adult, but they will not refuse to accept pronouns as grounded that in fact an adult accepts as grounded. The children accept too wide a class of pronouns as grounded.

hand, directly involve inferences about speakers' and listeners' minds and what they can infer. These are two very different modules.

How does the child become an adult, no longer making apparent Principle B errors? It is difficult to see how learning can explain the change. What is learned? It would have to be what listeners can infer from a situation. It is possible a priori that such learning could occur, but it is difficult to see how. What information would a learner base learning on? Ever since Wexler and Hamburger (1973), the field of linguistically based language acquisition has assumed that negative information is not presented to the learner, that is, the learner does not receive information about what representations are ungrammatical. For a child to learn which pronouns are not grounded, she would have to be told when she made a mistake. Wexler and Hamburger argued that the empirical results showed that such information was not presented. It is possible that such pragmatic situations are an exception, that the child in fact *is* corrected when she overaccepts a pronoun as grounded. But it does not seem very plausible to me; I would rather guess that in many cases an adult will accept a child's utterance that uses an ungrounded pronoun, so at to encourage the child. It is unlikely that the child receives systematic (correct) information as to which pronouns in fact are adequately grounded. Moreover, even if the child *did* receive this information, it is not clear that she has a learning mechanism that can figure out what the conditions are. All the classic learnability problems arise.

Thus it is more likely, as I have argued, that the change in the child is driven by maturation/growth. What, in fact, changes? On the theory that I have presented, what changes is the ability of the child to infer whether a pronoun has been adequately grounded, that is, the ability of the child to infer what other minds can infer from situations. This ability grows with time. Interestingly, it is an ability at the interface of the syntax/computational system of grammar and the discourse/interpretive/conceptual system of grammar. The child must take a syntactic representation (e.g., a pronoun indexed in a certain way) and apply principles of the discourse/pragmatic component (e.g., the grounding principle). It may turn out, as I suggested in Section IV that it in fact is the coordination of separate modules that is late in development. The child knows the syntactic system, as shown by knowledge of Principle B and as shown by the child's rejection of locally bound pronouns. The child knows that grounding principle, as shown by the non-100% acceptance of apparent principle B violations. Perhaps it is the difficulty in coordinating the syntactic and pragmatic/discourse/conceptual modules that lies at the basis of the overacceptance of grounded pronouns.

The child's misapplications of the grounding principle go on for quite awhile; to age 5 or 6 for many children. But if in fact it is the coordination of two systems that is responsible for the delay, perhaps that helps to explain its late development. Furthermore, children differ in the age at which they attain the ability to (almost) always apply the grounding principle correctly. Such a difference in ages at which the ability is attained fits with what is known about growth/maturation in general; there is a variability in when it happens in different children.

At any rate, we see in the apparent principle B errors story a case in which the syntactic/computational system appears to be intact and the problem lies with discourse/pragmatic properties. There is no evidence to date for maturation of principles of the binding theory, but there is evidence for growth/maturation of the ability to apply discourse principles, cognitive principles concerning inferences that can be made about knowledge in other minds.

Moreover, the analysis presented here certainly meets the criterion of UG-constrained maturation discussed in Section III. At no point does the child have a representation that is not constrained by UG. After all, UG is a purely symbolic/computational system. The child does not violate its representations. The child both knows UG principles and applies them correctly. Rather, the child makes errors on those aspects of linguistic knowledge that concern inferences about what other minds know. Such inferences are not part of UG, strictly conceived; they are not part of the computational system of language.

Before ending this discussion I should point out that a number of other properties of the development of syntax and discourse and inferencing can be captured by this story, but I do not have time to go into here. In particular, there is experimental research on verb phrase (VP) ellipsis, and its interaction with the binding theory, in particular, strict and sloppy interpretations, which shows a particular distribution of facts that are best interpretable, in my opinion, by our assumption that it is discourse inferencing properties (about other minds) that the child isn't getting right. See Thornton and Wexler (in press) for a detailed presentation of the experimental and theoretical evidence.

In conclusion, the apparent Principle B errors story shows the value of work in the interaction of linguistic theory and language acquisition. The facts of linguistic development, and the theory developed to explain it, sharpen the distinction between the syntactic and pragmatic modules that work around binding theory. It is a very rich area of developmental linguistics, of which I have presented only some of the central features. A maturational account seems a natural one.

B. Optional Infinitives: The Growth of Finiteness

The Problem of the Development of Inflection

One of the most intensively studied areas of linguistic development in the last 10 years involves the development of finiteness, verbal inflection, agreement, and simple clause structure. Much of the work revolves around the discovery of *optional infinitives* (Wexler 1990b, 1992, 1994). In many respects, this research has uncovered some of the biggest surprises yet in the study of language acquisition. On the one hand, optional infinitives themselves proved to be a surprise, not expected, and the theoretical consequences are still being digested, as we will see, and should tell us a good deal about how language grows in the mind/brain. On the other hand, optional infinitives have proved to be a tool that has allowed us to determine what might be an even *bigger* surprise—namely, that at an extremely young age (before 2;0) the child not only *knows* major and very subtle aspects of both UG and language-specific properties of clause structure, including verbal inflection, verb movement, case, the possibilities of licensing null subjects, and so on, but also *uses* these appropriately in almost all cases. In other words, the child before 2;0 (probably considerably younger, as we will discuss) *does not* make serious mistakes on most of the abstract properties of clause and verbal structure that lie at the heart of so much current syntax. Before the work on optional infinitives this was not generally known and, in fact, was not generally believed, whether by (developmental) psycholinguists or by linguists. In other words, the research of these years has constituted something of a minirevolution in our understanding of the extremely young child's linguistic capacities.

Let me elaborate on why the picture that has emerged is so different from the earlier picture. It is generally agreed, that is, it is everybody's impression, that young children talk funny. Their productions seem quite different from adult productions. Of course, the sentences are shorter; children have less cognitive capacities and know less about the world, so they speak more simply (in cognitive terms). But it is much more than that in people's impressions. The young children seem to make grammatical mistakes; they seem to be deviant in a variety of ways—hard to pin down—from adult speech.

What is to account for this difference? It has generally been agreed that many of the mistakes show some kind of problem with verbal inflection. The verb is in many ways the heart of a sentence, and children seem to make errors on the verb, errors that involve the particular form of the verb, and also errors that involve word order. So it has been generally thought that there are word order and inflectional problems in children. Sometimes it has been suggested that inflection provides more difficulties than word order, but there has rarely been a suggestion that children do not have problems with inflection.

This view has permeated the thinking of scholars working from every viewpoint. This includes linguists and linguistically oriented psycholinguists and not just behaviorists and nonlinguistically oriented cognitive developmentalists. The phenomenology just seemed too clear that there were very often problems in inflectional development to allow us to say that children's knowledge of and/or performance concerning these properties was adultlike.

Of course there were different schools of thought on what constituted the problem. Some scholars though that children just did not know the grammatical properties that constrained inflection and clause structure, that they had to painstakingly learn the general properties of syntax. But perhaps a more popular point of view in linguistic theory and in the developmental psycholinguistics that related to linguistic theory was what I will call the delayed learning of inflections view on the development of inflection. The delayed learning of inflections view assumed that perhaps the children *did* know the general syntax (no evidence was really offered but the hope was expressed that UG is basically known), but had not learned two things. First, the language particular properties of the syntax involving clause structure, verbal inflection and verb movement, and second, the particular phonological form of particular inflections. This latter was crucial to the learning of inflections view—it was thought that children had a very difficult time learning the phonological form of the language-particular inflections and that this problem accounted for much of the so-called funny nature of child speech.

Wexler (1990b, 1992, 1994) argued against the delayed learning of inflections view of early child grammar. He argued that children *did* know the basic UG properties involved in inflection and verb movement. But he also argued against the coherence of the view that children took a very long time to learn the forms of basic verbal inflections. He pointed out that children heard many of these forms thousands of times. Given that the children knew basic UG properties, it would take a very odd learning model to predict that children could not fairly quickly learn the properties of inflection, especially given evidence that there were many things about language that children *could* learn quickly. Furthermore, Wexler presented a large amount of evidence that showed that very young children in a variety of languages *did* know the form and properties of many verbal inflectional items, the basic properties, for example, of agreement morphemes and also the syntactic properties associated with finite inflections (we will return to this point). So Wexler presented arguments against the coherence of the delayed learning of inflections point of view about children's funny productions and also presented a large amount of empirical evidence against this point of view.

Note that the delayed learning of inflections view is a particular instantiation of the learning delay (LD) view that I discussed in Section 1. Its motivation seems to be mostly an attempt to make sense of children's funny talk on the assumption that they basically have UG capacities. In other words, the delayed learning of inflections view is an attempt to maintain rigidity by invoking learning delay, an attempt that I argued in Section 1 was not likely to turn out well. The assumption is that some crucial aspect of grammatical learning is slow and painful and full of errors. The question is, why should it be such given children's rather subtle knowledge of grammar and general ability at manipulating its constructs? Fortunately, the evidence has turned out that the LD view is not correct in this well-studied domain (nor, in my opinion, is it in general true), so that we can maintain a coherent theory.

In general, Wexler showed the children's productions at extremely early ages (before 2;0) agreed with the grammar of verbal inflection and clause structure in the language that they were developing. This result held over a variety of Germanic and Romance languages that Wexler investigated. (Of course we would expect it to hold in general.) Thus the research also showed that children's performance (production) on central aspects of clause structure and verbal inflection was excellent. Given this result, one can also not attempt to save rigidity by invoking the other way out discussed in Section 1—namely performance delay. Simply, there is no delay in children's performance on crucial and subtle and abstract aspects of clause structure and verbal inflection. Given this result, it is very difficult to hypothesize that children talk funny because they have problems in matching their productions to their grammars. Simply put, the evidence shows that child's productions obey (follow) their grammars.

Given that neither learning delay nor performance delay is an accurate characterization of early child grammar with respect to clause structure and inflection, how can we account for children's early funny speech with respect to clause structure and inflection? Wexler (1990b, 1992, 1994, 1996) and many other papers have argued that children basically know the grammar of clause structure and inflection, both the universal and language-particular aspects, but have a particular delay, in one aspect of the grammar/interpretive system, and that this aspect grows/matures. This aspect is not subject to parametric variability in UG, so far as we know, nor does it involve the learning of an inflection. The learning delay and performance delay ideas cannot account for its delay. Thus it is a property that grows over time in the child's brain, directed by the underlying genetic program for language. Rigidity has a very hard time dealing with these facts, because learning delay and performance delay have been shown to not hold empirically, much less even offer a coherent account of development.

Some Evidence on the Optional Infinitive Stage

In the preceding section I made many points based on evidence from the optional infinitive (OI) stage in grammatical development. In this section I would like to illustrate how these points are substantiated in the OI literature. The OI literature has become so rich and is such an active, changing area of language acquisition research that there is no way to do it justice, even in a discussion devoted wholly to the topic. Thus here I will only give a few small examples to illustrate the argumentation and its empirical basis; the literature should be consulted for detailed treatments of many topics.

Following Wexler (1990b, 1992, 1994) in essentials, the optional infinitive stage in child grammar has the following characteristics:

(14) The optional infinitive stage:
  a. The child's grammar allows both finite forms and nonfinite forms of the verb in contexts where the adult requires finite forms only
  b. The child nevertheless knows all the relevant properties of finiteness in the language being required, in particular the precise verb movement properties that depend on finiteness

Consider an example from German, discussed in Wexler (1990b, 1992, 1994) and analyzed in detail in Poeppel and Wexler (1993). Following standard analyses in syntactic theory, German is an SOV/V2 (verb-second) language. This means that the underlying word order is subject-object-V, but that the finite verb in main clauses always moves to the second position in the sentence, usually taken to be the complementizer (C) position, head of the CP, the basic sentence. Another constituent moves into the first position, the spec(ifier) of CP.

Thus nonfinite verbs must remain in final position; they are not attracted to C; only finite verbs move to C. Furthermore, in a main clause, the finite verb (there may only be one finite verb) *must* move to C; the finite verb must be in second position in all sentences.[21]

The OI child shows exactly this pattern; the child deviates from adult grammar in exactly one way, as (14a) states, the child allows the main clause to be nonfinite as well as finite, although the adult always requires that the main clause be finite. However, the child essentially always places the verb in the required position depending on its finiteness; in second position if it is finite, in final position if it is nonfinite. In (15) are the figures from Poeppel and Wexler's study of Andreas, a child of 2;1 whose production data, from Wagner (1985) can be found on the CHILDES database (MacWhinney & Snow, (1985).

(15)

	+finite	−finite
V2/not final	197	6
V final/not V2	11	37

The numbers in (15) represent utterances; each utterance in Andreas's natural production was counted. The columns represent the verbal inflection; it can be determined by inspection of the phonological form of the inflection whether it is finite (tensed) or nonfinite (infinitival inflection). The rows represent word order; V2/not final means that the verb was in second position, which was not final (at least three constituents had to be in each sentence so that this could be determined) and V final/not V2 means that the verb was in final position, not in second position. Note first of all that there were many nonfinite verbs, although these were all main clause utterances in which an adult must give a finite form. This is property (14a) of the OI stage. Furthermore, note the dramatic discrepancy between the word order for finite and nonfinite verbs. Finite verbs almost always show up in second position (roughly 20 to 1), whereas nonfinite verbs almost always show up in final position (roughly 6 to 1). Thus there is a ratio of roughly 120 to 1 difference in the placements of finite and nonfinite verbs. This is the kind of dramatic difference that is rare in cognitive developmental studies; yet the OI literature is full of such dramatic differences; the field has come to expect them.

Furthermore, Poeppel and Wexler counted all utterances that did not easily fit into the pattern against the OI hypothesis and force these utterances into one of the

[21]There are a small number of cases in which the finite verb is in (surface) first position, especially yes/no questions, where it is assumed that Spec, C is filled by a phonetically empty "Question" operator.

disconfirming cells. They provide an analysis of some of these examples that suggests that they are probably performance errors and really should not be counted. Thus the differences are even more dramatic than (15) indicates.

At any rate, tables like (15) have become standard in the field; there is a categorical difference in the placement of finite and nonfinite verbs if the adult grammar has such a difference. We can take the cells that do not agree with the hypothesis as performance errors, at least at a first pass, because they are so infrequent.

Let us take one other example from Wexler (1990b, 1992, 1994), which he took from Pierce (1989, 1992). In French, the finite verb raises up to an inflectional position that precedes negation, whose morphological form is *pas.*[22] Nonfinite verbs do not in general raise. This explanation, in a very informal way, follows Emonds (1976) and Pollock's (1989) explanation of why finite verbs precede *pas* but nonfinite verbs follow *pas*.

French children too often give infinitival forms of the verb (14a). Thus we can create a table which has, for its columns, a determination of whether the main clause verb is finite or nonfinite, as determined by the phonological form of the verb and for its rows an indication of word order; did the verb precede *pas* or follow *pas?* Pierce's (1989) data are given in (16), where this table collapses data over three children over a period starting before 2;0 and ending a bit after 2;0.

(16)

	+finite	−finite
pas verb	11	77
verb pas	185	2

Finite verbs precede *pas* about 17 to 1 whereas nonfinite verbs follow *pas* about 38 to 1, so there is about a $17 \times 38 = 646$ to 1 difference in the relevant ratios, again, an enormous difference by language acquisition or cognitive development or almost any behavioral measure standards. The cells which agree with the OI hypothesis (14b), where finite verbs raise up and nonfinite verbs do not, account for almost all the entries. Only 13 counterexamples exist. Although some of these may be meaningful, the numbers are so small overall that, again, at a first pass we can take the 13 examples as performance errors. Clearly the child's grammar represents finite verbs as preceding *pas* and nonfinite verbs as following *pas.*

Wexler (1990b, 1992, 1994) analyzed data from Danish, Dutch, English, French, German, Norwegian, and Swedish, showing how, in different ways depending on properties of the language, they all fell under the OI hypothesis. Both parts of the OI hypothesis, the OI stage in (14), are crucial: that children's grammars allow nonfinite main verbs although adults do not and that children know the syntactic reflexives of finiteness and nonfiniteness, that is, that verb movement of particular kinds takes place depending on the finiteness values.

[22]The preverbal negative particle *ne* can be ignored for our purposes; it is usually optional, is almost never uttered by the young child, and does not affect the analysis, although it has its own interesting properties.

Since the original description of the OI stage, there has been a large amount of literature on the topic, basically confirming the hypothesis and exploring many further dimensions of it. This is not the place to review those properties. I hope I have given sufficient examples to illustrate the methodology and conclusions. I will concentrate in the remainder of this section on further implications, especially for growth/maturation theories.

First, note that work on the OI stage has demonstrated that children at this very young age know the UG possibilities of verb movement and the kinds of factors that motivate or prevent verb movement. This is illustrated by the fact the children in the various languages move the verbs, they move them to the right position, and furthermore they move only verbs that have the relevant finite features and not nonfinite verbs. This is a remarkable demonstration of abstract syntactic knowledge in children as young as 1;5.[23]

Furthermore, the OI research has established that not only do very young children know the UG possibilities but they know the particular operations that take place in their language (the one they are hearing); they have set the parameters right. Thus German children known that their language is V2, as Poeppel and Wexler (1993) demonstrated (other data go into this analysis, besides [15]; for example, the German children produce a significant proportion of nonsubjects in first position when the finite verb occupies second position, as would be expected in a V2 language). But French children (or English children, etc.) give no hint of having a V2 grammar. Similarly, French children raise the V to the inflection position, past NEG, but English-speaking children do not do this. Wexler (1996) argued for the hypothesis of *very early parameter setting* (*VEPS*):

(17) Very early parameter setting: Children at the very earliest observable age, that is, at the beginning of multiple-word utterances at about 18 months, have set correctly the basic parameters of clause structure and inflection in their language. These include the following:
a. the V to INFL (verb raising) parameter
b. the V2 (verb-second) parameter
c. the parameter regulating verb object order (SVO versus SOV)
d. the null-subject parameter (Does INFL license null subjects?)[24]
e. properties of agreement
f. properties of case

We have given examples of (16a) and (16b). Wexler (1992, 1994) provided evidence concerning SVO versus SOV (16c), for example, in the differences between Swedish (SVO) and German (SOV). But this difference can also be seen by com-

[23]Rohrbacher and Vainikka (1995) showed that the basic Poeppel and Wexler (1993) results held for a child of 17 months.

[24]Of course, some of these parameters might be too grossly stated, for example, the V2 parameter and the null-subject parameter most likely are decomposable into finer properties. As evidence mounts we might be able to show that young children know even finer aspects of their grammars.

paring English and German development. There is nothing in English children like German children's strong tendency to place nonfinite verbs in final position.

We do not have time to discuss the null-subject parameter (16d) here, except to say that the OI literature has demonstrated that children know whether or not they are speaking an Italian-style null-subject language, in which INFL licenses a null subject. See Bromberg and Wexler (1995), Roeper and Rohrbacher (1995), Sano and Hyams (1994), Schutze and Wexler (1996), and Wexler (1995a, 1995b) for evidence for this position concerning English; although children drop subjects quite often in English, basically this is the result of the OI stage, as Wexler (1995a, 1995b) has argued, rather than a mis-set parameter, as originally suggested by Hyams (1986). Rhee and Wexler (1995) demonstrated the effect within Hebrew, depending on that part of the paradigm in which null subjects are licensed. It has long been known that children who speak a null subject language know that indeed it is a null subject language.

Skipping (16e) for the moment, let me just say about case that there is now extensive evidence to show that children in the OI state know the case-marking properties of the appropriate functional categories, that that NOMinative is assigned by AGR and that ACCusative is assigned by the functional category associated with the verb. See Babyonyshev (1993), Schutze (1996), Schutze and Wexler (1996), and Wexler (1995a, 1995b) for relevant evidence and analyses.

Turning to properties of agreement (16e), Wexler (1992, 1994) and Poeppel and Wexler (1993) argued that, contrary to earlier suggestions in the literature, young children (namely those in the OI stage) have grammars that correctly mark agreement. The analysis rested on the appropriate methodology to test the hypothesis. Poeppel and Wexler showed that when a German child used a particular agreement morpheme on the verb, the probability that the subject's features matched the morpheme was close to 1. For example, if the child used third-person singular *-t,* then the probability that the subject was third-person singular was close to 1. Thus the child knew the features of third-person singular *t.*

The reason that it had previously been thought that the child did not know the agreement morphemes was that scholars had usually calculated the inverse probability, for example, the probability that the verb has third-person singular *-t* when the subject is third-person singular. This probability, or the OI analysis, must be significantly less than 1 because there will be many infinitives, more generally nonfinite verbs that do not mark agreement. But if we want to test whether the child knows which morphemes have particular features, we have to check whether the subjects match the morphemes. And they do.

What Grows as the Child Leaves the OI Stage?

The VEPS hypothesis contains quite a remarkable list of properties of inflections that are known to children. The properties they know are both morphophonological and morphosyntactic. They not only know the basic phonological form of the particular inflection, but they know its syntactic properties, whether it triggers verb movement or not and what kind of movement, whether it licenses a null subject, how it agrees with a subject, and what the word order properties are. Given all this, it seems plausible to suppose that even more will be shown to be known to the child as research proceeds.

Moreover, research on the OI stage shows that not only does the child's grammar have the relevant UG and language-specific properties, but the child's performance on these properties is near perfect. In particular, the child's *productions,* her *utterances,* show near perfect performance on the relevant properties. Almost all the data that has gone into the analysis of the OI stage has been production data, for example, the tables presented in (15) and (16). These data show that the child performs almost perfectly in accordance with not only UG but also many crucial language specific properties. There is no performance delay in producing the grammatically appropriate verbal inflections and placing the elements in the correct word order, in appropriately marking nominative and accusative cases, in grammatical (INFL-based) licensing of null subjects or not.

Thus there is no learning delay in a wide variety of parameters of clause structure and verb movement and forms of inflectional morphemes, and there is no performance delay in producing utterances that show the appropriate properties. Children at the youngest ages (in the OI stage) know basic properties of UG, have learned the correct parameter settings for processes that are language-specific, and produce utterances that correspond to these properties.

Why weren't these properties observed earlier? How could it be that linguists and psycholinguists thought, for example, that there was a delay in learning inflections? The reason, I think, aside from a certain theoretical motivation, as discussed earlier, was that the appropriate methodology was not used. It was noticed that children often used incorrect inflections, and the inference from this was that the children just did not know what the correct inflections were. But before contemporary research on the OI stage, no attempt was made to determine if the morphemes showed appropriate syntactic properties. In particular, no attempt was made to see if there was a particular correlation between inflectional form and word order. This is a crucial methodology in research on the OI stage, as illustrated earlier. The correlation shows that children have knowledge of the syntactic properties of particular morphemes, and also that they know the phonological properties of morphemes, because particular (phonologically determined) inflections go in certain word order positions. The correlational methodology is the natural one given the crucial linkage in contemporary linguistic theory of inflectional morphemes (categories) and syntactic processes.

Returning to our main theme, we see that performance delay and learning delay cannot account for the properties of early child grammar, because both performance and learning are so excellent. Children have learned the necessary properties and they do rather well in producing them. So why do early child utterances often seem so odd?

Let us concentrate on the properties of verbal inflection that have been studied in the OI stage. Clearly the most different property of early child grammar in the OI stage is that nonfinite main verbs are allowed. Except in very special semantic contexts, this does not happen in adult utterances. Yet the children use nonfinite main verbs to have ordinary declarative meaning (see Poeppel and Wexler, 1993, for evidence, also Behrens, 1993).

There have been a large number of attempts to work out implementations of the OI stage, and this is not the place to review them. But different implementations agree with Wexler's (1990b, 1992, 1994) proposal that children in the OI stage know the grammatical processes of verb movement and their motivation and the properties of the morphemes of verbal inflection. The crucial point is that what develops over time is *not* a parametric property; it is *not* a point on which grammars can differ in principle, not a point of grammatical variation. Thus we cannot account for the development out of the OI stage by saying that a piece of learning has taken place, a piece of learning that is allowed for in the principle and parameters framework.

It really is a good thing that it is not a parametric property that keeps children in the OI stage, because we have already seen (VEPS) that children have learned parametric properties at a very early age. There is no learning delay in general, so it would be difficult to explain why just one property was subject to a learning delay. The intriguing thing about the OI stage is that what develops is just the kind of property that is *not* subject to variation in various adult grammars.

There is no room here to detail a particular theory of the OI stage but let me briefly mention one proposal that has relevant implications for growth/maturation. Note that one property must hold; TENSE is optional in children's utterances at this age, as Wexler (1990b, 1992, 1994) showed.[25] Wexler (1995a, 1995b) provided a new theory of the OI stage which derives why TENSE is optional. He suggested that what the child in the OI stage does not know is whether the D (determiner) feature is *interpretable* or not, in the sense of Chomsky (1995). For adults, D is always interpretable; for children in the OI stage, it is sometimes interpretable and is sometimes not interpretable.

When D *is* interpretable, for OI children adult finite sentences result. But when D is *not* interpretable for the child, the D feature erases after the subject DP has been raised to TNS. Then there is no way to satisfy the D feature of the AGR inflectional head, and the derivation crashes. Thus the child omits TNS so that the D feature does not have to be checked twice; the noninterpretable D-feature is capable of checking once.[26]

[25] Schutze and Wexler (1996) show, on the basis of the development of Case properties, that AGReement must be optional also.

[26] Actually, either AGR or TNS can delete to satisfy the property that the noninterpretable D-feature can check only once. And, in fact, this result will derive the claim of Schutze and Wexler (1996) and Wexler (1997) that it is necessary for AGR to be optional in order to account for the Case properties of OI grammars.

This D-interpretability theory has a very nice property. Namely, without further assumptions, it allows us to derive the fact that Italian-style null-subject languages, that is, languages in which AGR licenses null-subjects, will not go through the OI stage, a generalization that is argued for by Wexler (1995a, 1995b).[27] I will not go through the derivation here (see Wexler 1995a, 1995b).

The D-interpretability theory locates the cause of the OI stage in the child's lack of complete knowledge of whether D (the determiner feature) is interpretable. If this theory turns out to be correct, it has intriguing properties. In particular, the child is not missing any aspect of the computational system of UG, but rather is missing some knowledge about the interpretability of features. This missing knowledge is knowledge at the interface of the computational system (the syntax) and the interpretive (conceptual) system. If it turns out to be true, it will reinforce our suggestion that much growth/maturation has to do with the coordination of two systems, two modules, namely the computational system of the syntax, and the interpretive/conceptual system. This delay in coordination is similar in this sense to the delay that we suggested held for binding theory—in which the application of the grounding principle is delayed and must grow.

Note that it is really intriguing that what seems to grow in the child is some property that causes TENSE to become obligatory. It is rather difficult to know exactly what in UG causes TENSE to be obligatory. It is not some simple property of syntax, whether government-binding syntax or minimalist syntax. I suspect that nowhere in the pages of Chomsky (1981) or Chomsky (1995) will one find a *principle* that requires that main clauses be finite, that is, have TENSE. In the latter one will find all sorts of properties that check heads against specifiers, features against features, but these will not require TENSE in main clauses, so far as I can tell.[28]

Rather, what requires TENSE in main clauses is probably some kind of grounding or anchoring principle, such as in Enc (1987). The idea of the D-interpretability theory is that children may (perhaps only partially) know this anchoring property of TENSE, but can give it up when necessary in order to find a grammatically convergent derivation, and if they think D can be noninterpretable they will have

[27]Wexler (1992, 1994) suggested that Italian did not go through the null-subject stage, and this was confirmed in detailed work by Guasti (1994). Torrens (1995) showed that Spanish and Catalan, also AGR-licensed null-subject languages, also do not go through the OI stage. Grinstead (1994) also showed the result in Spanish. Sarma (1994) showed that Tamil, a null-subject language, does not go through the OI stage. Rhee and Wexler (1995) showed that within Hebrew, the part of the inflectional paradigm that allows null subjects does not go through the OI stage but the part of the paradigm that does *not* allow null subjects does go through the OI stage. This work is summarized and the generalization relating AGR-licensed null subjects to the lack of an OI stage is made in Wexler (1995a, 1995b).

[28]TENSE is not required to assign Case to subjects. As Wexler (1995a, 1995b) and Schutze and Wexler (1996) showed, Case can be assigned in other ways, without violating UG. And in fact, as Wexler (1995a, 1995b) showed, the subjects of OI's always raise (e.g., to the left of NEG) even when they do not have NOM case. This is understandable given the proposals in Chomsky (1995); subjects raise to check off a D-feature, not for Case reasons. For related acquisition work, see Jonas (1996).

to omit TENSE in order to attain a convergent derivation. Perhaps the children misapply the grounding or anchoring principle and this is why they give OIs. (This idea was proposed in slightly different ways in Hyams, 1996, and in Wexler, 1996). I am suggesting that in a way analogous to the misapplication of the grounding principle for NPs (e.g., pronouns) discussed earlier, the children may think that a nonfinite verbal form is grounded when it really is not. They might overaccept grounding for verbal forms just as they overaccept grounding for pronouns. One reason that I have tried to find another theory to derive the facts from is that the overacceptance of grounding does not in itself seem to explain why AGR-licensed null-subject languages do not go through an OI stage. But perhaps a way can be found to derive this result in a misapplication of grounding theory.

At any rate, it is clear from research on the OI stage that children know all the complicated spec-head checking relations in verbal syntax, and moreover they even know the inflectional forms that correspond to some of these relations. Furthermore, they know the functional categories that instantiate the inflectional relations in the phrase marker, and they know their properties.[29] In addition, children's utterances obey the restrictions imposed by these checking relations.

In contrast to the striking knowledge and performance on these abstract relations in the computational system of grammar (syntax) we find a particular, widespread, systematic delay in some properties at the syntax-conceptual interface. Growth/maturation of this property seems to be what is provided by the genetic program underlying UG.

C. A Note on Argument-Chains

The first topic studied in the modern literature on growth/maturation was the development of certain properties of argument-chains (A-chains). Borer and Wexler (1987) argued that children until a certain age cannot assign theta roles out of position, so that an argument moved to another argument position will not be able to be assigned a theta role, and the derivation will crash. They suggested that the ability to assign theta roles out of position grows/matures in the child, perhaps around age 4. They used this assumption to explain why children did very poorly on verbal passives in English and some other languages, because verbal passives in these languages (not necessarily all languages) involve A-chains. At the same time, Borer and Wexler argued that children at very young ages have no problem

[29] Radford (1990) suggested that young children do not have functional categories and that these categories mature. Empirical work has decisively shown that children in the optional infinitive stage have functional categories (see almost all the papers referenced and many more). Radford's hypothesis had the virtue that its developmental logic was correct. He assumed that if functional categories were missing, they could only develop in the child via the kind of maturation sketched in Borer and Wexler (1987). The objection to his hypothesis is empirical; research on the OI stage has shown that children *do* have functional categories, probably all of them, at least all the commonly studied ones.

with adjectival passives, which are equally difficult conceptually but which do not involve A-chains. Further evidence, which we won't review here, was adduced in Borer and Wexler (1987, 1992).

I wanted to concentrate on newer proposals about growth/maturation. So here let me just very briefly mention some of the studies that have continued the investigation of the possibility of growth/maturation of the ability to assign theta roles out of position and thus to have A-chains of a certain kind.

There has been some positive and negative reaction to those proposals. Some papers have used the result and extended it to other domains. Let me mention here, however, some of the reactions against the paper.

Demuth (1989) argued on the basis of production data that the children who speak Southern Sesotho, a Bantu language, produce verbal passive at a much younger age than do English-speaking children. She tried to use this evidence to argue that the A-chain hypothesis of Borer and Wexler (1987) was wrong.

However, a number of properties make Demuth's claim problematic. First, in my opinion, her evidence concerning children's general knowledge of verbal passive in Sesotho was not large. Second, she gave no syntactic analysis to show that the passive in Sesotho involves an argument-chain. In many languages, the passive, even the verbal passive, may not involve such a chain; see, for example, the argument of Heider (1990) that the German verbal passive does not involve an argument-chain. To establish an A-chain takes subtle syntactic arguments involving escape from various violations, and so forth. Thus there is no particular reason to believe that Southern Sesotho necessarily has an A-chain in the passive. Thus any early knowledge of passive in this language cannot count against the A-chain hypothesis.

Third, if one looks at the examples of passive given in Demuth's paper, they in general seem to have a certain quality—the surface subject (underlying object) always seems to have an affectedness quality to it. They sound like the adversity passives of Japanese or, strikingly, like *get* passives in English—for example, "I got tied up." Suzman's (1990) work on the development of the Zulu passive (Zulu is a related Bantu language) confirms that the early passives have this character, although the language in general does not have this restriction. Why should early passives have this property if the language itself does not have the property? I have suggested that *get* passives are earlier than *be* passives in English possibly because the same kind of A-chain does not exist in *get* passives as in *be* passives.[30]

[30]Crain (1992) claimed to have elicited a number of verbal passives from children younger than the age at which A-chains are supposed to have grown. But inspection of the data, which are fairly limited, shows first that the children were not all that young and second that almost all the passives, especially for the younger children, were *get*-passives. We have no reason to suppose that *get*-passives are more frequent or common in the input than *be*-passives. So the delay in *be*-passives is a mystery. And it must be remembered that the empirical basis for Borer and Wexler's (1987) argument that passive was delayed was the long experimental tradition in developmental psycholinguists that argued that

Sugisaki (1997) has shown in comprehension experiments that Japanese direct verbal passives are delayed relative to adversity passives, despite the greater semantic complexity of the latter. He assumes, following much syntactic literature, that adversity passives do not contain an A-chain, whereas direct passives do; thus the direct passives are delayed due to A-chain maturation. This provides further empirical support for the idea that *get* passives are earlier because they do not contain an A-chain.

Fox and Grodzinsky (1994) have argued, however, that there *is* an A-chain in *get* passives. It may turn out, however, that a refinement of the notion of A-chain is required. This refinement would also have to account for the fact that children are not significantly delayed in raising subjects out of VPs to the specifier of a higher inflectional position. See Borer and Wexler (1992), who first pointed out the possible problem of VP-internal subjects, for the growth/maturation of A-chain hypothesis and a possible solution to it.

The main point is that some theory must be stated that explains why verbal passive is delayed in some languages and not in others, why adjectival passive is not delayed, why certain kinds of passives (e.g., for certain kinds of verbs—see Borer and Wexler, 1987) are delayed and others are not, and related properties. In my opinion, the A-chain theory accounts for more of the properties than any other theory; I know of no competitors at the moment. To produce counterexamples is not to disconfirm a theory; one can only argue against a theory with a better theory. Demuth did not attempt to account for the facts of passive development. Fox, Grodzinsky, and Crain (1995) attempted to account for the delay of verbal passive with *by* phrases in English by suggesting that the *by* phrase represents a kind of clitic doubling and that clitic doubling is delayed. But Torrens and Wexler (1995) show that clitic doubling in general is known to much younger children (by studying clitic doubling in Spanish) so that this explanation cannot be right. And of course, if it *were* right, the best explanation for why clitic-doubling is delayed would be a growth/maturation theory.

Given that the A-chain theory still seems to account for more facts than any other theory, we must consider it until a better theory turns up. Meanwhile, let me briefly mention some recent intriguing confirming work. Borer and Wexler (1992) pointed out that the growth of A-chains hypothesis predicts that young children should misanalyze unaccusative verbs as unergative verbs, because unaccusatives demand an A-chain in their derivation. This hypothesis has proven difficult to test

---

comprehension of *be*-passives was quite delayed. Crain's failure to elicit *be*-passives fits with this tradition of comprehension experiments. See also Fox, Grodzinsky, and Crain (1995) for further evidence relevant to the issues at hand. They attempt to show that children are better at passive than Borer and Wexler (1987, 1992) and the traditional experimental literature in developmental psycholinguistics claim, but despite their efforts, they still find some significant delays. The data are limited, however, and further studies would be welcome.

because one needs to use a diagnostic for unaccusativity (something like *Ne-cliticization* in Italian) and many of these diagnostics are difficult for children.

However, recently, Babyonyshev, Fein, Ganger, Avrutin, Pesetsky, and Wexler (1994) have succeeded in finding a construction in which the idea could be tested. The genitive of negation in Russian is a construction in which genitive case replaces the usually expected nominative case. Namely, in certain negated sentences, direct objects show up in genitive rather than accusative case, and with negated unaccusative verbs (and only unaccusative verbs), the subjects (underlying objects) turn up in genitive case rather than in nominative case. Careful experimentation by these authors showed that Russian children around 4 and 5 years old, however, very often gave nominative case instead of genitive case to these subjects. These same children always gave the correct genitive case for the negated objects. Thus children had no trouble in producing genitive case on negated objects but had a good deal of trouble producing genitive case on negate subjects of unaccusative verbs. This is exactly what would be expected if the children could not represent the unaccusative verbs as unaccusatives, but instead represented them as unergatives. Negated unergatives take nominative subjects.

The result is especially striking because children hear some of these negated unaccusative verbs with genitive subjects very often indeed; they are very common expressions. Thus the children have to go out of their way to produce sentences that they have never heard and against the evidence that they have constantly heard. This is striking evidence of a growth/maturational point of view. Despite a good deal of evidence in the input, the children produce the wrong utterances.

The paper on genitive of negation contains a good deal of data and analysis that I have not had time to go into here. But it is striking that the first research project that succeeded in testing the prediction of the A-chain hypothesis that children would represent unaccusative verbs as unergative verbs found confirming evidence for the hypothesis. The prediction is so against what would be expected *a priori* that the result is indeed notable. Unaccusative verbs are simple everyday verbs with clear semantics in many cases. The children in Russian hear direct evidence concerning their structure (the case facts). So common sense would suggest that children would represent unaccusative verbs correctly. Only a precise hypothesis suggests otherwise. That the precise hypothesis has been confirmed suggests that the A-chain hypothesis may indeed be on the right track.

Before closing this section, we should ask whether the A-chain hypothesis can be related to the general idea of growth/maturation of interface properties. At the moment, no such suggestion has been made in detail. However, the underlying proposal of Borer and Wexler (1992), that the A-chain delay derives from a too-strong biuniqueness relation in the children, a proto-theta criterion, may be relevant. Children demand that a theta role be related to a selected position, not just to any argument. The theta criterion is being looked on in contemporary work on the minimalist approach as an interpretive principle rather than as a principle of the computational system of syntax. So perhaps the delay in A-chains is a delay in being able to ground an NP in a theta role unless the NP is in a canonical position. Possibly this delay too will be able to be seen as an interface problem.

VI. CONCLUSION

This has been a far too brief survey of the conceptual, theoretical, and empirical issues surrounding growth/maturation as an explanation of linguistic development. If I had more space, I would have brought up a number of other topics that have been studied in growth/maturational terms. Let me just summarize my conclusion.

First, linguistic delay cannot be accounted for by any kind of learning delay or performance delay. Children, even at very early ages, are just too good at learning language-specific properties and at producing utterances that conform to their grammars. Second, many aspects of linguistic growth/maturation seem to be properties of coordinating the interface of the computational system of language (the syntax) and the conceptual/interpretive system of grammar. Third, the child knows a good deal about UG, but still deviates in certain respects from it, and these deviances are principled, a consequence of the genetic program of language. The central idea of linguistic theory—that language grows/matures in the brain—seems to be true, as evidenced by the number of cases that have been studied in this regard. The fact that linguistic theory agrees with general biological theory in this regard should be looked upon as a nice moment in the unification of science.

REFERENCES

Avrutin, S. (1995). *Psycholinguistic investigations in the theory of reference.* Unpublished doctoral dissertation, Massachusetts Institute of Technology, Cambridge, MA.

Avrutin, S., & Wexler, K. (1992). Development of principle B in Russian: Coindexation at LF and coreference. *Language Acquisition, 2*(4), 259–306.

Avrutin, S., & Wexler, K. (1998). Children's knowledge of subjunctive clauses. Submitted to *Language Acquisition.*

Babyonyshev, M. (1993). Acquisition of the Russian case system. In C. Phillips (Ed.), *Papers on case and agreement II, MIT Working Papers in Linguistics* (Vol. 19, pp. 1–43). Cambridge, MA: MIT Department of Linguistics and Philosophy.

Babyonyshev, M., Fein, M., Ganger, J., Avrutin, S., Pesetsky, D., & Wexler, K. (1994). *Maturation of A-Chains: Preliminary new evidence from the acquisition of Russian unaccusatives.* Paper presented at the 19th Boston University Conference on Language Development, Boston.

Batchelder, W. H., & Wexler, K. (1979). Suppes' work in the foundations of psychology. In Bogdan, R. J. (Ed.), *Patrick Suppes.* (pp. 149–187). Dordrecht: D. Reidel.
Behrens, H. (1993). *Temporal reverence in German child language.* Doctoral dissertation, University of Amsterdam, The Netherlands.
Bloom, P. (1990). Subjectless sentences in child language. *Linguistic Inquiry, 21*(4), 491–504.
Borer, H., & Wexler, K. (1987). The maturation of syntax. In T. Roeper and E. Williams (Eds.), *Parameter Setting* (pp. 123–172). Dordrecht: D. Reidel.
Borer, H., & Wexler, K. (1992). Bi-unique relations and the maturation of grammatical principles. *Natural Language and Linguistic Theory, 10,* 147–189.
Bromberg, H., & Wexler, K. (1995). Null subjects in child Wh-questions. *MIT Working Papers in Linguistics, 26.* Cambridge, MA: MIT Department of Linguistics and Philosophy.
Chien, Y-C., & Wexler, K. (1987). Children's acquisition of the locality condition for reflexives and pronouns. *Papers and Reports on Child Language Acquisition, (PRCLA),* Stanford University, CA.
Chien, Y-C., & Wexler, K. (1990). Children's knowledge of locality conditions in binding as evidence for the modularity of syntax and pragmatics, *Language Acquisition, 1,* 225–295.
Chien, Y-C., & Wexler, K. (1991). Children's knowledge of pronouns as bound-variables in a long-distance context. In *Papers and Reports on Child Language Development (PRCLD), 30,* 25–38.
Chomsky, N. (1965). *Aspects of the theory of syntax.* Cambridge, MA: MIT Press.
Chomsky, N. (1975). *Reflections on Language.* New York: Pantheon Books.
Chomsky, N. (1981). *Lectures on Government and Binding.* Dordrecht: Foris.
Chomsky, N. (1995). *The Minimalist Program.* Cambridge, MA: MIT Press.
Clahsen, H., Penke, M., & Parodi, T. (1994). Functional categories in early child German. *Language Acquisition, 3*(4), 395–429.
Crain, S. (1992). Language acquisition in the absence of experience. *Behavioral and Brain Sciences, 14,* 597–650.
Crain, S., & Wexler, K. (1999; see Chapter 12 of this volume). Methodology in the study of language acquisition: A modular approach. In W. C. Ritchie & T. K. Bhatia (Eds.), *Handbook of Child Language Acquisition.* San Diego, CA: Academic Press.
Demuth, K. (1989). Maturation and the acquisition of the Sesotho passive. *Language, 65*(1), 56–80.
Emonds, J. (1976). *A transformation approach to English Syntax.* New York: Academic Press.
Enc, M. (1987). Anchoring conditions for tense. *Linguistic Inquiry, 18*(4), 633–657.
Fox, D., & Grodzinsky, Y. (1994). *Children's passive: A view from the* by- *phrase.* Unpublished manuscript, MIT and Tel-Aviv University.
Fox, D., Grodzinsky, Y., & Crain, S. (1995). An experimental study of children's passive. In C. T. Schutze, B. T. Ganger, & K. Broihier (Eds.), *Papers on Language Processing and Acquisition. MIT Working Papers in Linguistics,* 26, 249–264.
Gleitman, L. (1981). Maturational determinants of language growth. *Cognition, 10,* 103–114.

Grimshaw, J., & Rosen, S. (1990). Knowledge and obedience: The developmental status of the Binding Theory. *Linguistic Inquiry, 21*(2), 187–222.
Grinstead, J. (1994). *Tense, agreement and nominative case in child Catalan and Spanish.* Unpublished masters thesis, University of California, Los Angeles.
Guasti, T. (1994). Verb syntax in Italian child Grammar: Finite and nonfinite verbs. *Language Acquisition, 3*(1), 1–40.
Heider, H. (1990). Null subjects and expletives in romance and Germanic Languages. In W. Abraham, W. Kosmeijer, and E. Reuland (Eds.), *Issues in Germanic Syntax.* Berlin: Walter de Gruyter.
Heim, I. (1988). *The semantics of definite and nondefinite noun phrases.* New York: Garland Publishers.
Hyams, N. (1986). *Language acquisition and the theory of parameters.* Dordrecht: Reidel.
Hyams, N. (1996). The underspecification of functional categories in early grammar. In H. Clahsen (Ed.), *Generative prespectives on language acquisition* (pp. 91–128). Amsterdam: John Benjamins Publishing.
Hyams, N., & Wexler, K. (1993). On the grammatical basis of null subjects in child language. *Linguistic Inquiry, 24*(3), 421–459.
Jonas, D. (1996). *Clause structure and verb syntax in Scandinavian and English.* Doctoral dissertation, Harvard University.
MacWhinney, B., & Snow, C. (1985). The child language data exchange system. *Journal of Child Language, 12,* 271–296.
McDaniel, D., Cairns, H., & Hsu, J. (1991). Control principles in the grammar of young children. *Language Acquisition, 1,* 297–336.
Montalbetti, M. M., & Wexler, K. (1985). Binding is linking. *Proceedings of the West Coast Conference on Formal Linguistics, 4,* 228–245.
Pierce, A. (1989). *On the emergence of syntax: A crosslinguistic study.* Doctoral dissertation. Massachusetts Institute of Technology, Cambridge, MA.
Pierce, A. (1992). *Language acquisition and syntactic theory: A comparative analysis of French and English child grammars.* Dordrecht: Kluwer.
Poeppel, D., & Wexler, K. (1993). The full competence hypothesis. *Language, 69*(1), 1–33.
Pollock, J.-Y. (1989). Verb movement, universal grammar and the structure of IP. *Linguistic Inquiry, 20,* 365–424.
Radford, A. (1990). *Syntactic theory and the acquisition of English syntax.* Oxford: Basil Blackwell.
Reinhart, T. (1983). *Anaphora and semantic interpretation.* London: Crumb Helm.
Rhee, J., & Wexler, K. (1995). Optional infinitives in Hebrew. In C. Schuetze, B. Ganger, and K. Broiler (Eds.), *Papers on Language Processing and Acquisition.* MIT *Working Papers in Linguistics, 26,* 383–402.
Rizzi, L. (1994). Some notes on linguistic theory and language development: The case of root infinitives. *Language Acquisition, 3,* 371–394.
Roeper, T., & Rohrbacher, B. (1995). *Null subjects in early child English and the theory of economy of projection.* Unpublished manuscript, University of Massachusetts, Amherst, and University of Pennsylvania.
Rohrbacher, B., & Vainikka, A. (1995). On German verb syntax under age 2. In D. MacLaughlin & S. McEwen (Eds.), *Proceedings of the 19th Annual Boston University*

Conference on Language Development (Vol 2, pp. 487–498). Somerville: Cascadilla Press.

Sano, T., & Hyams, N. (1994). Agreement, finiteness and the development of null arguments. In M. Gonzalez (Ed.), *Proceedings of NELS 24* (pp. 543–558). Amherst: GLSA, University of Massachusetts.

Sarma, V. (1994). *Harmony branches to a syntactic tree? Disagreements over agreement.* Paper presented at NELS 25, North East Linguistic Society, University of Pennsylvania.

Schutze, C. (1996). Evidence for case-related functional projections in early German. In J. Camacho, L. Choueiri, & M. Watanabe (Eds.), *The Proceedings of the 14th West Coast Conference on Formal Linguistics* (pp. 447–461). Stanford: CSLI.

Schutze, C., & Wexler, K. (1996). What case acquisition data have to say about the components of INFL. Talk presented at the WCHSALT Conference, Utrecht University, June 28–30.

Sugisaki, K. (1997). Japanese passives in acquisition. Unpublished manuscript, University of Connecticut, Department of Linguistics.

Suzman, S. M. (1990). *Language acquisition in Zulu.* Doctoral dissertation. University of Witwatersrand, Johannesburg.

Thornton, R., & Wexler, K. (in press). *VP Ellipsis, Binding Theory and Interpretation in Child Grammar.* Cambridge, MA: MIT Press.

Torrens, V. (1995). *The acquisition of syntax in Catalan and Spanish: The functional category inflection.* Doctoral dissertation, University of Barcelona. Spain.

Torrens, V., & Wexler, K. (1995). Clitic doubling in early Spanish. In A. Stringfellow, D. Cahana-Amitay, E. Hughes, & A. Zukowski (Eds.), *Proceedings of the 20th Annual Boston University Conference on Language Development* (Vol. 2, pp. 780–791). Somerville: Cascadilla Press.

Vainikka, A. (1994). Case in the development of English syntax. *Language Acquisition, 3*(3), 257–323.

Wagner, K. (1985). How much do children say in a day? *Journal of Child Language, 12,* 475–487.

Wexler, K. (1990a). Innateness and maturation in linguistic development. *Developmental Psychobiology, 23*(3): 645–660.

Wexler, K. (1990b). On unparsable input in language acquisition. In L. Frazier & J. deVilliers (Eds.), *Language Processing and Language Acquisition.* Dordrecht: Kluwer.

Wexler, K. (1991). On the argument from the poverty of the stimulus. In A. Kasher (Ed.), *The Chomskyan Turn.* Cambridge, UK: Basil Blackwell.

Wexler, K. (1992). Optional infinitives, head movement and the economy of derivation in child grammar. Occasional paper #45. Center for Cognitive Science, Massachusetts Institute of Technology, Cambridge, MA.

Wexler, K. (1994). Optional infinitives, head movement and the economy of derivations. In D. Lightfoot & N. Hornstein (Eds.), *Verb Movement* (pp. 305–382). Cambridge, UK: Cambridge University Press.

Wexler, K. (1995a, September). *Feature-interpretability and optionality in early child grammar.* Paper presented at the Workshop on Optionality, University of Utrecht, The Netherlands.

Wexler, K. (1995b, November). TNS, DET and feature strength and interpretability in early child grammar. Talk presented at the Workshop on Clausal Architecture, Bergamo, Italy.

Wexler, K. (1996). The development of inflection in a biologically based theory of language acquisition. In M. Rice (Ed.), *Toward a Genetics of Language.* Hillsdale, NJ: Lawrence Erlbaum Associates.

Wexler, K. (1997). D-interpretability and interpretation in the OI stage. Talk presented at the Workshop on Interpretation of Root Infinitives and Bare Verbs, Massachusetts Institute of Technology, Cambridge, MA, January 13–14, 1997.

Wexler, K. (in press). The unique checking constraint and the extended projection principle as the explanation for the optional infinitive stage: Very early parameter-setting, maturational mechanisms and variation in grammatical development. Paper presented at GALA 1997, University of Edinburgh, United Kingdom.

Wexler, K., & Chien, Y.-C. (1985). The development of lexical anaphors and pronouns. *Papers and Reports on Child Language Development (PRCLD)* (pp. 138–149). Palo Alto, CA: Stanford University.

Wexler, K., & Culicover, P. (1980). *Formal principles of language acquisition.* Cambridge, MA: MIT Press.

Wexler, K., & Hamburger, H. (1973). On the insufficiency of surface data for the learning of transformational languages. In K. J. J. Hintikka, J. M. E. Moravcsik, & P. Suppes, *Approaches to natural language* (pp. 167–179). Dordrecht: D. Reidel.

Yngve, V. (1960). A model and an hypothesis for language structure. *Proceedings of the American Philosophical Society, 104,* 444–466.

CHAPTER 4

UNIVERSAL GRAMMAR: THE STRONG CONTINUITY HYPOTHESIS IN FIRST LANGUAGE ACQUISITION

Barbara Lust

I. INTRODUCTION

In this chapter, we first introduce the theory of universal grammar (UG) as a model of the initial state, fundamental to the explanation of first language acquisition and briefly review a history of supporting evidence for UG that has accrued over the past several decades (Section I). We then identify an indeterminacy in the interpretation of UG, which characterizes work in the field today (Section II). We provide the outlines of a solution to this indeterminacy, one consistent with a strong continuity view of UG, but one which recognizes real change in children's language knowledge over time and thus does not claim that *all* language knowledge is innate. We argue that this strong theory of UG is both theoretically and empirically motivated (Section III).

A. Theory of UG

For the past several decades, researchers have been compelled by the proposal that a linguistic theory of universal grammar provides a theory of the initial state, as in (1), as well as a theory of linguistic structure that underlies all natural language—that is, a "theory of languages and the expressions they generate" (Chomsky, 1993, p. 1).

(1) a. *In a highly idealized picture of language acquisition, UG is taken to be a characterization of the child's pre-linguistic initial state.*
(Chomsky 1981, p. 7)

b. *UG is a theory of the initial state S_0 of the relevant component of the language faculty.* (Chomsky, 1993, p. 1)

c. *S_0 is the "initial state," prior to any language learning.*
(Chomsky, 1975a, p. 119)

By virtue of its status in (1), the theory of UG has promised that it can explain the human competence for language, that is, explain first language acquisition, for example, (2), and at the same time explain the structural commonalities and differences that are possible across natural languages. This theory of UG formalized a rationalist theory of language acquisition, in which knowledge of language was proposed to be not simply derived by unstructured induction from experience of the environment, but to a large degree determined by the structure of the human mind. The theory of UG formalizes a language faculty, and thus provides a major scientific component of current cognitive science. The explanatory adequacy of the theory of UG has long been proposed to lie in this role, as in (2). (See for example, Chomsky, 1975b/1955–1956, for sustained concern for the problem of "whether the linguist 'plays mathematical games' or 'describes reality'" [p. 103] and concern for "validation for the program of building an objective science of linguistics" [p. 82]).

(2) a. *The problem of internal justification—of explanatory adequacy—is essentially the problem of constructing a theory of language acquisition, an account of the specific innate abilities that make this achievement possible.*
(Chomsky, 1965, p. 27)

b. *In practice, the real problem faced by the linguistic theorist is to devise a system of principles sufficiently restrictive so that it succeeds in accounting for the transition from the initial to the final state, in the case of particular languages.* (1975b, p. 14)

This proposed bidimensional nature of linguistic theory has allowed the development of a scientific basis for linguistic theory. Hypotheses about linguistic structure (which are based on theory-internal argumentation derived from descriptions of a language [or several languages]) now have additional foundations.

(3) *A theory of UG is true if (or to the extent that) it correctly describes the initial state of the language faculty.* (Chomsky & Lasnik, 1991, p. 4)

Because the components of a theory of UG (i.e., formally specified principles and parameters that constitute a theory of natural language) are hypothesized to be biologically programmed in the initial state, as in (4),[1] it follows that hypotheses

[1]We will assume the term *initial state* to refer here to the earliest measurable period of language

about UG that are derived by theory-internal argumentation can, in principle, even be validated by empirical test of their biological foundations.

(4) *Linguistic theory, the theory of UG, construed in the manner just outlined, is an innate property of the human mind. In principle, we should be able to account for it in terms of human biology.* (Chomsky, 1975a, p. 34)

It may be true that the most intense and precise study of UG lies in test of its predictions as a model of the initial state, as we have suggested elsewhere (e.g., Lust, in preparation). This is because UG is a "theory of human I-languages" (Chomsky, 1984, p. 8). Chomsky has formulated this distinction between I- and E-language (where *I* refers to "internal and intensional" or that represented in the mind, and *E* refers to "external and extensional") (e.g., Chomsky, 1986; cf. Kapur, Lust, Harbert, & Martohardjono, 1993, in preparation). Adult language, on the basis of which linguistic theory derives its theoretical formulations and cross-linguistic predictions, always reflects not only UG but also both specific internal grammatical systems in the mind of those who know a specific language and the acoustic, physical data that are spoken and heard. A profound question persists as to the degree UG remains distinct from the specific language grammar of an adult language. (See Chomsky, 1991, p. 450, fn. 21; Flynn & Martohardjono, 1994; and Epstein, Flynn, & Martohardjono, 1996, on this issue.) Profound issues persist on the relation between E-language and I-language (e.g., Koster, 1978, pp. 59–64; Kapur et al., in preparation). Child language also reflects an integration of I- and E-language, but we assume that the closer to the initial state this child language is, the less it is mediated by specific language grammar, and thus the more closely its grammar will reflect UG. In fact, we have argued that universal "constraint on the course of first language acquisition" may provide the most important evidence for UG because it most directly reflects a theory of possible I-language (cf., Lust, 1986, in preparation; Somashekar, 1995; Somashekar, Yamakoshi, Blume, & Foley, 1997). We never expect to find a more direct exemplification of UG. (That is, UG will never simply appear in a unique, direct way, in a particular utterance, a particular structure, a particular language, or a particular grammar.)

B. Brief History of Empirical Confirmation of UG as a Model of the Initial State

Over the past several decades, research has advanced in this interdisciplinary area (linking linguistic theory of UG and the study of the course of first language acquisition). Numerous studies have provided evidence for the essential premise of UG, that is, that knowledge of language is not simply directly induced from the

acquisition, before language experience. Although given current theories of embryology, such a distinct point of existence may not in fact be identifiable, the term provides a useful idealization (cf., Lust, in preparation).

environment. Language acquisition is now known to be robust over radially varied input conditions (e.g., Feldman, Goldin-Meadow, & Gleitman, 1978; Gleitman, Gleitman, Landau, & Wanner, 1988; Goldin-Meadow, 1982; Goldin-Meadow & Feldman, 1977; Landau & Gleitman, 1985). It is modular (e.g., Blank, Gessner, & Esposito, 1979; Caplan, 1992; Curtiss, 1977, 1982; Garrett & Cohen-Sherman, 1989, on Alzheimer's; Smith & Tsimpli, 1995; Yamada, 1990). Carefully controlled scientific research has documented the insufficiency of simple induction to explain language acquisition in the early stages (e.g., Newport, Gleitman, & Gleitman, 1978, studies of the Baby Talk Register).

In terms of acquisition of syntax, experimental research results involving behavioral studies of children's early language acquisition have confirmed critical hypotheses relevant to a theory of UG as a model of the initial state and have led to new, progressively more refined hypotheses. For example, experimental results have confirmed that specifically linguistic principles,—for example, "structure dependence," such as that hypothesized by theory-internal argumentation to characterize UG (e.g., Chomsky, 1988)—do, in fact, constrain first language acquisition (see, for example, Lust, Eisele, & Mazuka, 1992, for review; and Crain & Nakayama, 1986). With results such as these, the field must move from a general position, which once was dominated by the view that children's language is initially determined by general cognitive (i.e., nonlinguistic or pragmatic) learning alone, to one which must now recognize the strength and effects of a language faculty, that is, a linguistic module, coherent with what UG has proposed.[2]

For example, where researchers studying language acquisition had once hypothesized that early child language could be characterized by nonlinguistic principles alone, for example, "linear precedence," or by principles relevant to pragmatic context alone, it must now be recognized that these claims have been disconfirmed by empirical (including experimental) evidence, where these hypotheses were tested, that is, when they were precise enough to be tested (cf. Cohen Sherman, 1987, on a proposed minimal distance principle; Lust, Chien, Chiang, & Eisele, 1996; Lust & Mazuka, 1989; Lust, Flynn, Chien, & Clifford, 1980; Lust, Loveland, & Kornet, 1980; Lust & Clifford, 1986 [the 3-D study on pronoun coreference, which factored out surface distance from depth of embedding of pronoun antecedents]; Chien & Lust, 1983, 1985 [which showed the child overriding pragmatic context where this would offend the grammar of Chinese "equi" constructions]). In fact, the child's use of pragmatics (contrary to underlying gram-

[2]Many of the earlier proposals that attempted to place first language acquisition in a simple manner into a "general framework of cognitive development" identified themselves with the theory of Jean Piaget, the developmental psychologist. However, it should be noted that Piaget himself held a more subtle position. Designing a rationalist theory of the growth of the mind, Piaget admitted that "the rational origin of language presupposes the existence of a fixed nucleus necessary to the elaboration of all languages" (*noyeau fixe* referring to UG) (Piaget in the *Chomsky-Piaget Debate,* Piatelli-Palmarini, 1980, p. 57).

matical knowledge) appears to develop over time, even into adulthood, long after essential grammatical knowledge is evident (e.g., Eisele & Lust, 1996; Foley, Nuñez del Prado, Barbier, & Lust, 1997).

In addition, a wide set of new types of experimental methods has recently allowed testing of infant knowledge, even before the child has overt speech and comprehension, for example, during the first 12 months of life. These experimental results have confirmed the infant's very early sensitivities to structural aspects of language, for example, clause structure, as well as linear order. These results confirm the earliness and the general strength of the infant's linguistically relevant sensitivities to the primary language data (PLD) to which the child is exposed (e.g., Hirsh Pasek et al., 1987, Jusczyk et al., 1983, 1997; Mazuka, 1996; Mehler & Christophe, 1995; Morgan & Demuth, 1996).[3] Several of these results, at the very least, ground the hypothesis that the very young child has very early competence to apply linguistic principles and parameters to the PLD. This research has brought us closer to an answer to the question Chomsky raised early, that is, "What are the initial assumptions concerning the nature of language that the child brings to language learning . . . ?" (1965, p. 27).

In addition, issues of methodology, which provide the foundation for scientific hypothesis testing, have also now been addressed in the area of first language acquisition. We now have a more developed idea of ways in which each type of task which tests language performance in the child (e.g., production, comprehension, or grammaticality judgement task) reflects grammatical competence. We now have a more precise understanding of the way in which variable behavioral performance (in behavioral research) and discrete grammatical competence (in mental representation) interact in behavioral research (cf. Grimshaw & Rosen, 1990; Kaufman, 1988, 1994; Lust, Chien, & Flynn, 1987; McDaniel, McKee & Cairns, 1996). We have evidence from converging methods in hypothesis testing, a result that is essential to the scientific foundations of a field (e.g., Lust, Chien, & Flynn, 1987, cf. also this volume; Lust, Eisele, & Mazuka, 1992). For example, production and comprehension task results have provided converging measures (although not identical) in numerous studies of various aspects of grammatical competence (e.g., Lust, Solan, Flynn, Cross, & Schuetz, 1981; Sherman & Lust, 1993). New methodologies are now being developed to incorporate tests of youngest ages of infancy, as mentioned previously, and they now begin to make these very young ages also susceptible to experimental method (e.g., Hirsh-Pasek and Golinkoff, 1997).

In fact, there are even initial results in the area of biology as to the underpinnings of basic linguistic factors of structure dependence in language knowledge.

[3]This literature includes precise analyses of the acoustic cues that may underlie the infant's early knowledge of the PLD. However, this general acoustic basis to the infant behaviors does not change the point being made here. The fact remains that this growing body of infant research documents that, however achieved, the child does have the competence to map linguistic knowledge (e.g., "clause") to the acoustic stimulus of the PLD.

See, for example, Eisele (1993) and Eisele, Lust, and Arams (1998), which resulted from studies of matched samples of children with discrete neurological damage, discretely limited to left or right hemisphere, who were tested on their comprehension of complex sentences involving negation scope and presupposition in language knowledge. (See also relevant research by Mills, Coffey-Corine, & Neville, 1993, and Neville, Mills, & Lawson, 1992.)

Today, the issues in this interdisciplinary study of UG have advanced to the point where they have become more subtle along each dimension of the theory. In linguistic theory, linguistic research continues to advance in description and theory construction on the basis of cross-linguistic evidence (i.e., adult language data), developing new and more refined hypotheses and continuing to pursue the formulation of the true content of the theory of UG. (For example, Chomsky's minimalist program economizes this theory by eliminating various levels of representation, such as levels of "surface" or "deep" structure, as independent entities, and proposes that the interface between levels characterizes the true I-language representation, [Chomsky, 1993]. It also refines certain aspects of the theory; for example, the theory of phrase structure has become more articulated and its fundamental origins are being sought.)

Similarly, in the study of first language acquisition today, research continues to produce more subtle evidence on the nature of the principles and parameters that actually constrain first language acquisition, the scope of their application, and their nature. For example, moving on from general issues concerning structure dependence, empirical research has now been able to move forward to more precise questions regarding configurational sensitivity in the child. Lust, Suñer, and Whitman (1994) provided a collection of representative studies in the field in the area of configuration of phrase structure. Other research has evaluated the role of the child's configurational sensitivity in very subtle aspects of language knowledge, for example, the differentiation of empty categories and the knowledge of pronominal systems, and mapped the child's structural sensitivities to precise principles and parameters of UG theory. This research has linked children's structural knowledge of long distance dependencies of various types (e.g., Gair, Lust, Sumangala, & Rodrigo, 1989, on control in Sinhalese; Lust, Wakayama, Mazuka, & Snyder, 1985, on differentiation of empty categories in different embedding structures ['*to/nagara*'] in Japanese; Lust, Mangione, & Chien, 1984; Lust, Eisele, & Mazuka, 1992, on Principle C of the binding theory; Cohen, Sherman & Lust, 1993, on control theory; Lust, Chien, Chiang, & Eisele, 1996, on null and lexical pronouns in Chinese; Barbier, 1993, on optional and obligatory scrambling in Dutch; Kornfilt, 1994, on Turkish scrambling; Boser, Santelmann, Lust, & Whitman, 1991a, 199b, on V-raising in German; Santelmann, 1995, on "WH" movement and other XP [or phrasal] movement in Swedish; and Austin, Blume, Parkinson, Nuñez del Prado, & Lust, 1997, and Nuñez del Prado, Foley, Proman, & Lust, 1994, 1997 on pro drop in Spanish; also see Lust, Hermon, & Kornfilt,

1994, and Maxfield & Plunkett, 1991, for examples of overviews regarding acquisition of grammatical dependencies). Various complex structures (e.g., coordination, relativization) have been analyzed in terms of the UG-proposed principles and parameters that underlie their acquisition both within and across languages (e.g., Lust, 1977, Lust & Mervis, 1980, Foley, Nuñez del Prado, Barbier, & Lust, 1992a, 1992b, 1992c, and 1997; Flynn & Lust, 1980). Lust (1983, in preparation) summarized a wide set of cross-linguistic evidence on the precise nature of a phrase structure parameter that appears to guide language acquisition continuously and to closely constrain the child's theory of anaphora as one of its deductive consequences.

In fact, today research in first language acquisition has advanced to the point where, in several studies, acquisition results actually lead the way to distinguishing the "correct theory" of universal grammar (e.g., Gair et al., 1989; Oshima & Lust, 1997; Foley et al., 1992a, 1992b, 1992c, and 1997, on VP ellipsis structures; Nuñez del Prado et al., 1994 and 1997, on pro drop phenomena; Barbier, 1993a, 1995a,b, and 1996a,b, on scrambling and on IP directionality in Dutch; Mazuka & Lust, 1994, on the binding theory in Japanese; Lust, Chien, Chiang, & Eisele, 1996, on pronominals in Chinese). All of these acquisition studies have led to new theoretical proposals regarding the representation of the structures these involve.

II. INDETERMINACY IN INTERPRETATION OF THE THEORY OF UG

As both of the research dimensions of UG continue to develop, and as they begin to merge progressively more closely, we are, as a result, now forced to confront an indeterminacy that has characterized our interpretation of the theory of UG as a model of the initial state. It is an indeterminacy which arises when the theory of UG and the study of first language acquisition merge so closely that the real fact of language development, that is, sequential change in language knowledge over time, must be accounted for (i.e., explained, by the theory).

In fact, this is an indeterminacy that Chomsky himself had foreshadowed very early. In early proposals of the UG paradigm, he stated (5):

(5) *What I am describing is an idealization in which only the moment of acquisition of the correct grammar is considered.* (Chomsky, 1965, fn. 19, p. 202)

For the purposes of theory construction, (5) allowed the linguist to proceed in the construction of a theory of UG, *as if* language acquisition were instantaneous (Chomsky, 1975a). However, at the time, Chomsky realized, and articulated, (6a). More recently he has reiterated this point of view, as in (6b) and (6c).

(6) a. *[I]t might very well be true that a series of successively more detailed and highly structured schemata (corresponding to maturational stages, but perhaps in part themselves determined in form by earlier steps of language acquisition) are applied to the data at successive stages of language acquisition. There are, a priori, many possibilities that can be considered here.* (Chomsky, 1965, p. 202, fn. 19)

b. *[S]pecific subcomponents of the genetic program, coming into operation as the organism matures, determine the specific properties of these systems* (Chomsky, 1980, p. 245)

c. *[I]t seems hard to explain these transitions without appeal to maturational processes that bring principles of universal grammar into operation on some regular schedule in a manner to be described and accounted for in a genetic theory. . . .* (Chomsky, 1988, p. 70)

Note that (5) has been interpreted as licensing an instantaneous hypothesis (IH) and (6) a maturational hypothesis (MH) of UG. On the surface, these two appear to be diametrically opposed interpretations of UG theory. They appear to be opposed with regard to a theory of first language acquisition.

The "instantaneous" hypothesis is consistent with, although not identical to, a continuity hypothesis, which we have articulated elsewhere, and restate generally in (7) (e.g., Boser, Santlemann, Barbier, & Lust, 1995; Lust, 1986, 1994; in preparation; Lust & Martohardjono, 1987; Whitman, Lee, & Lust, 1991).

(7) **Strong Continuity Hypothesis of UG**
UG (where this term refers to the "principles and parameters" which provide the true content of UG) is a model of the Initial State; it is thus available to the child from the beginning. The "initial state" is taken to refer to the onset of first language acquisition, even "before experience" [cf. Chomsky in (1)]. UG remains continuously available throughout the time course of first language acquisition. UG does not itself change during this time course. (cf. fn. 1)

The strong continuity hypothesis (SCH) contradicts the maturational hypothesis (MH) in the following way. According to the SCH, it there are developmental changes in children's language knowledge, they are *not* due to changes in UG.

The MH in (6) is opposed to both (5) and (7). The MH proposes discontinuity of UG, that is, UG is proposed to change over time. As it does so, it gives rise to discrete "stages" of language acquisition, where each stage of child language has a distinct grammar defined in terms of UG, such as "partial UG" grammar. Only some principles, if any, and only some parameters or possibly only some parameter settings, are available at a particular stage. A complete UG is attained only gradually over time. (We discuss variations on this proposal in Section 3.7. See also Section II.C.)

Not surprisingly, given both (5) and (6), various researchers in the field of first language acquisition have varied in terms of their interpretation of the UG paradigm. Hamburger and Crain (1982), for example, reflect an example of the interpretation of child language data in terms of an instantaneous, no-development hypothesis. For example, in their study of children's knowledge of relative clauses in English, Hamburger and Crain (1982) suggested that only aspects of methodology are responsible for the child's apparent lack of knowledge in this area.[4] If methodology is properly developed, the authors suggest, then complete knowledge will be evidenced in the young child, presumably as young as they can be tested. (See also, in this view of the paradigm, Crain & McKee, 1986, who suggested that directionality effects on children's pronoun interpretation are methodological artifacts, and Lasnik & Crain, 1985, who interpret directionality effects on pronouns in child language as analagous to adult translation from one language to another, rather than as reflecting any constraint on, or principles of, grammar or grammar construction, which might reflect UG.)

Alternatively, other researchers have adopted the second hypothesis, for example, (6), which proposes a change in UG principles, for example, (8):

(8) a. *The purpose of this paper is to challenge the continuity hypothesis. In particular, we will propose a theory for the development of certain aspects of linguistic competence. This theory is in contradiction to the continuity hypothesis. It does not assume that the formal principles available to the child are constant through development. Rather, the assumption is that certain principles mature. The principles are not available at certain stages of a child's development, and they are available at a later stage.*

(Borer & Wexler, 1987, p. 124)

b. *When maturation occurs, relevant positive evidence allows the reanalysis of these representations, causing a retreat to the unmarked adult rule.*

(Borer & Wexler, 1987, p. 166)

In (8), the maturation hypothesis is applied to observed facts regarding children's acquisition of the passive construction in English, and it is suggested as an explanation for these facts. It is proposed, there, for example, that "once maturation occurs, the derivation of verbal passives becomes possible" for the child (Borer & Wexler, 1987, p. 139).

Another example of the maturation hypothesis, this one with regard to parameters, appears in research on the "pro drop parameter" (i.e., the possibility for null subjects such as in Spanish or Italian, or lack of it, as in English) (Hyams, 1986). Here biological programming is proposed to limit the child's knowledge of P-setting; it "presets" parameters to unmarked settings. In this proposal, only one pa-

[4]It is worth noting that the Hamburger and Crain (1982) methodology has not yet been tested for replication with a large, controlled sample in contrast to other methods.

rameter setting is available to a child, regardless of input data at the initial stages of child language knowledge. Considering the possibility for pro drop to reflect a positive setting of a pro drop parameter, the proposal holds that children acquiring a non–pro drop language like English hold a false hypothesis about the grammar for their language at initial stages. These children also believe their grammar is [+ pro drop] (biological programming for markedness of parameter values determines this in the initial state). In accord with maturation, biological programming finally releases the child from this false analysis, making the child newly sensitive to certain aspects of input data that now come to act as triggers for parameter resetting in the input data.[5]

Not surprisingly, given (5) through (7), debates persist today on interpretation of the UG paradigm as a theory of language acquisition. Because the theory of language acquisition is essential to a theory of UG, these debates lie at the core of this theory. The essential motivation for these debates lies in what appears to be an essential ambiguity/indeterminacy in the theory of UG as a model of the initial state—(5) versus (6). It also lies in the fact that there is now a new dissatisfaction with merely assuming the idealization in (5). This state of affairs reflects scientific advance in the UG paradigm, but it also challenges it.

Our proposal of the SCH in (7) is distinct from either (5) or (6), as we will clarify. We will suggest that this SCH is the strongest interpretation of the relation between UG theory and first language acquisition and is not incompatible with real change in children's language knowledge. The SCH of UG does not require a claim that there is no development in the child's language knowledge.

A. Problems with the Instantaneous Hypothesis (IH)

The essential problem with the instantaneous hypothesis in (5) is formulated by Chomsky:

(9) *The "simplifying assumption" of "instantaneous" learning of language is "obviously false."* (Chomsky, 1975a, p. 119, 121)

In fact, (5) was not intended to describe a comprehensive theory of language acquisition. It was based on the fact that different orders of data presentation do not seem to significantly affect the nature of completed language acquisition (end states). However, more and more, linguists and psycholinguists working in the UG

[5]This case of the MH differs from the case involving UG principles in (8). In this "pro drop" case, eventual correct parameter setting must involve some specific language experience (triggers for parameter setting) and so cannot be totally maturationally derived. In this case, however, maturation appears to determine when specific language experience can be consulted, because the same data in the input language are available at initial stages of language acquisition but do not act as a trigger for change. If they had, there would be no marked parameter setting. This parameter-setting proposal is then compatible with (8b).

paradigm have come to acknowledge "real change" (i.e., development) during the course of the child's acquisition of language knowledge. They have come to acknowledge this as a domain that the theory of UG must account for if it is to attain explanatory adequacy. Representing a major advance in the theory, current interpretations of UG no longer consider it to be sufficient to maintain merely "a highly idealized picture of language acquisition," as in (1).

According to research, which provided results that were argued to be coherent with the IH, observed change in children's language is usually attributed either to methodological artifacts or to changes in performance or processing rather than change in grammar or knowledge. These proposals have not been totally successful, however. (This is not to deny that there are certainly *some* cases where children's language performance or behaviors *do* reflect performance or processing factors.) No theory of performance or processing has yet been proposed to account fully for the full set of child language facts observed. In addition, limitations in the methods used to attempt to provide evidence for IH may themselves beg the issue of the child's true theory of language, as we argue elsewhere (Lust, Flynn, Foley, & Chien, see chapter 13 of this volume). In general, forced choice yes/no comprehension tasks such as used with young children by researchers who argue for the IH can underdetermine the true state of the child's knowledge, because they provide so little opportunity for the child to reveal the nature of the child's hypotheses as even possibly distinct from the adult's (cf. Lebeaux, 1990, on the Hamburger & Crain, 1982, methodology [see also fn. 4]; and Eisele, 1988, and Eisele & Lust, 1996, for relevant studies).

In addition, in accord with (9), other research suggests that there are real changes in children's language over time in certain domains. These changes in children's language appear to reflect real changes in their grammatical knowledge in some cases. For example, see Hamburger (1980) and Flynn and Lust (1980), as well as Lee (1991), Packard (1982, 1987), Foley (1996), Somashekar (1998), and Lust (1994), for studies that provide evidence for the development of knowledge of lexically headed restrictive relative clause structures. In addition, directionality effects on anaphora in child language have appeared even in the reduced behavior comprehension tasks (e.g., forced choice yes/no judgement tasks) (e.g., Eisele, 1988, Eisele & Lust, 1996); so it is now known that these directionality effects cannot simply be due to methodological artifacts.

Finally, on theoretical grounds, the instantaneous hypothesis begs the issue of the independence and the complex interactions between UG and specific language grammars (SLG). Notice for example, that Hamburger and Crain (1982), who argued for full grammatical knowledge in the child at early ages, must argue not only that children know UG completely, but also that they know the adult English grammar (in this case, the SLG pertaining to English relative clauses (RC) structures) completely. Cross-linguistic variation in grammars of RC makes it obvious that the English RC structure is not fully given in UG (e.g., Andrews, 1985). Thus UG does not predict full knowledge of this structure. In fact, in current theory, the RC structure (like all specific structures) is viewed as "epiphenomenal" (cf., Chomsky, 1993) and as such must be, in a general sense, "derived" from the grammatical phenomena themselves. Thus, if at any time of acquisition [t_n] measured by Hamburger and Crain, children's knowledge of English relative clauses *were* in fact perfect, some component of acquisition of the specific language grammar must have already occurred prior to t_n. This acquisition would remain unexplained.

We then reject the IH as programmatic for the theory and study of language acquisition in its strong form (although at a metalevel of analysis, IH correctly captures the fact that variation in individual orders of experience of particular structures on a day-to-day level does not appear to play a major role in the end state of acquisition.)

B. Maturation Hypothesis (MH)

It would seem initially, then, that given a choice between 5 and 6, Chomsky's maturational hypothesis in (6) would be the most valid interpretation of the UG theory if UG is to be merged closely with the real facts of real time first language acquisition, and thus gain in explanatory adequacy (i.e., if UG is truly to explain first language acquisition, as promised in Section I). We will argue, however, that this conclusion is incorrect.

General MH

In general, it cannot be denied that there is some maturational component to first language acquisition. Lenneberg's developmental milestones for example, track an apparently biologically programmed progression in all children at roughly similar ages from birth, through cooing and babbling to first words and word combinations (Lenneberg, 1967). A surface "length" constraint appears to universally characterize earliest stages of word combinations, regardless of specific language grammar. Surely, this general, universal outline of language acquisition must be under some form of biological, genetic control. Such facts, and an apparent resistance of this early developmental course to variations in adult input (e.g., to the Baby Talk Register or to the variations in input arising from studies of children "in different mental states," that is, with auditory or visual impairments) have led Gleitman, for example, to conclude, "The studies I have sketched are consistent with a maturationally driven acquisition process, with progress relatively independent of exposure time or type" (Gleitman, 1981, p. 110).

This fact, however, which we may term, *general maturation* (GM) must be distinguished from the specific *maturation hypothesis* (MH) stated in (6). The hypothesis in (6)—and the way that various researchers have been interpreting it, for example, (8)—proposes that grammatical knowledge, and in particular, knowledge accounted for by universal grammar (i.e., the specifically linguistic, biologically programmed language faculty), is under genetic control and is only partially, if at all, available at early periods of language development. This claim concerning grammatical knowledge is independent of the general maturation proposal. GM may be true (in fact, certainly is true) even if the specific grammatical hypothesis (MH) in (6) is not.[6]

Specific Grammatical MH

The MH proposed by Chomsky in (6), distinctly refers to maturation of grammatical knowledge.[7] It thus predicts that different grammars (or parts of UG, which constitute distinct grammars) appear under biological control. Children's specific hypotheses *about grammar* are hypothesized, under this interpretation, to differ over time, under biological control. Under this view, biology must not only determine UG content (principles and parameters), but also particular divisions or partial components of UG and ordering of these components of UG. That is, biology must assign to the child distinct grammars *en route* to a full UG. Biology must account for stages of grammatical knowledge, where the stages correspond to distinct grammars that underlie children's language knowledge at distinct times of language acquisition. Under this interpretation, it is also predicted that these ordered stages are independent of the adult model (i.e., the specific adult language to which the child is exposed). They are under biological control, and so they are not determined by, or affected by, the adult language data to which the child is exposed (much like Jakobson's [1972] theory of phonological acquisition). This type of application of the MH can render all learning about language facts unnecessary for the child. New knowledge about language simply "emerges" in a preprogrammed, biologically determined manner (e.g., [8]).[8] It is consistent with real

[6]These two (MH and GM) may interact; for example, one would not expect a child who is still in the cooing stage to acquire complete grammatical knowledge about empty categories in "control" structures. Although, given recent infant research results, such as those offered by Juszyck and others cited earlier, and given the emerging evidence from recent child language research (see the following) for very early grammatical knowledge by infants in many areas, it in fact *is* likely that some knowledge relevant to complex grammar *is* being acquired even at these earliest periods, just as it is for phonology (cf. Mazuka, 1996).

[7]We do not assume that Gleitman's (1981) proposal requires or intends a simple stagewise innate unfolding of "grammatical" knowledge, given her extensive research on the complex interplay between induction and deduction in the acquisition of "representational" knowledge (e.g., Gleitman, et al., 1988). On this point, we do not agree with the interpretation of Gleitman (1981) given by Levy (1983), for example.

[8]More complex models of development are possible here; although in this chapter we will concentrate on the simpler alternatives. For example, the MH as articulated here (and as represented in the current language acquisition literature) is not identical to the discontinuity stagewise developmental theory of Piaget. For Piaget, although clear biological programming and maturation underlay cognitive stages, the course of their emergence was not preprogrammed. This course was acquired through the combination of innate programming and the child's rationalist approach to experience (Piaget's constructive developmental model).

change in a child's language knowledge, but (in the stated form) all such change is viewed as biologically programmed. This biological programming reflects the stagewise unfolding of UG. Although each stage may be partially consistent with UG in some way, it necessarily deviates from the full theory of UG in some way.

In this chapter we are concerned with this more specific interpretation of Chomsky's MH, not with the general MH, which is not debatable.

C. Problems with the Maturational Hypothesis

The specific MH, as sketched in the preceding discussion, raises several critical problems for a theory of UG on both theoretical and empirical grounds. We will suggest that not only does it undermine the explanatory adequacy of a strong theory of UG (as we will argue in Section 2.3.1), but a wide amount of experimental/empirical research has now disconfirmed it in several areas in which it has been proposed to account for specific areas of language acquisition (as we will argue in Section II.C).

Theoretical/Logical Problems for the Maturational Hypothesis

First consider how a typical MH account works for first language acquisition. In a typical account, a particular aspect of child language will be described, such as the absence of passives in much early English child speech, the absence of overt functional categories in early English telegraphic speech, or the absence of subordinate clauses in early English child speech. Children, after all, speak initially in quite simple sentences, for example, (10).

(10) *"Mommy sock"* (age 21 mos., Bloom, 1970)

Then, in order to describe the observed disparity between child and adult speech, a proposal is made that some component of grammar that is involved in the adult form of this sentence is lacking in the child grammar. It is proposed that, by definition, this component is a property of UG; for example, absence of functional categories in child grammar accounts for the absence of overt inflection in child telegraphic speech (Radford, 1990), absence of A-chains in the child's UG accounts for the absence of passives (Borer & Wexler, 1987), and so on. (Because so little is overt in the early child language, like [10], the possibilities for postulating what is absent in the child's knowledge of grammar are essentially limitless.) Then it is proposed by the MH that a maturing UG explains this aspect of first language acquisition, because this component, which is proposed to be missing in child language, is proposed to become available, through maturation, in the adult language (on the basis of which UG has been defined).

There are several problems with this approach.

1. Although it is true that these proposals provide possible descriptions of child language data (typically they do so by using a restricted vocabulary that is con-

sistent with the vocabulary of linguistic theory of UG), in themselves they are not explanatory. This is fundamentally because there is nothing within the theory of UG to explain how and why UG should be so fractionated, why it would appear in parts as it is proposed to do, or why the parts are ordered as they are; for example, why the change should go in one direction, not another; why not functional categories before lexical categories; why not A-chains before A-bar chains. There is nothing within linguistic theory to constrain the content of the child's grammar at t_1 in the observed sequence ($t_1 \ldots t_n$), or the content of any particular state, $t<n$.

In fact, it is only the behavioral facts of first language acquisition that motivate the proposed fractionation and the proposed order of gradual constitution of UG. These behavioral facts may be said to determine or explain the (use of the) theory of UG, not *vice versa.* This approach thus suffers from the logical flaw of *petitio principii.* These partial applications of UG to describe child language data are not, in themselves, theoretically motivated, and they are thus not explanatory in themselves. Used in this way, UG theory cannot be said to explain the developmental changes it is being used to describe.

2. Even more seriously, the previous MH interpretation of UG divorces the theory of UG from a theory of the initial state, as it was defined in (1). On the MH, UG (defined independently by the science of theoretical linguistics on the basis of adult language) arises only gradually, culminating when language acquisition is completed. Therefore, on the MH, the full theory of UG (i.e., the result of theory internal argumentation, which is the core of linguistic science today) characterizes the final state, not the initial state (prior to experience). In this, the MH robs the linguistic theory of UG of its essential scientific force. This is because, as we saw earlier, the independent empirical validity of the theory of UG was proposed to lie in its status as a model of the initial state, for example, (3). If UG only characterizes the end state, then (3) does not have empirical force.

As an indication of this loss of validating power for UG, notice that whereas the theory in (1), *a priori,* allowed the theory of UG to have predictive value for the independent domain of first language acquisition, the MH, by divorcing UG from the initial state, robs it of this predictive value. No longer does the theory of UG make any definite testable predictions for the nature of the initial state or for first language acquisition. This is because any piece of the complete theory of UG could be missing at any time in the initial state, in keeping with the MH. This theory (UG) is totally and accurately reflected only in the end state. But if this is so, then the independent empirical validation in (3) is nullified.

Of course, empirically, it is possible that UG matures (i.e., changes and develops over time). An independent linguistic theory could be developed now to define just which aspects of a complete theory of UG may or may not be missing in the initial state and what sequence or order of emergence the various components have, in accord with (2a) and (2b), for example. Along these lines, the theory of UG could then be said to account for the initial state even if it were only fully realized in the end state. Early grammars could be described by this theory as in some way contained in later grammars.[9]

In this way, the linguistic theory of UG would become, in fact, a theory of development. This, however, would amount to the necessary creation of a metatheory of UG. This metatheory would arguably, in fact, become the real UG itself, if the assumption in (4) is maintained, that is, the assumption that UG is what is biologically programmed. In this case, the task of construction of this metatheory would have to replace the task of UG theory construction as it is presently conceived in the field of linguistics. In addition, the issues we raised in number 1 above would have to be considered in the construction of this meta UG theory. Without the external empirical validation of the constant initial state, how would the new metatheory itself be validated?

It might be counterargued that there is a way in which UG could be said to "characterize the initial state" even though it were not fully realized there. This might be said to be the same way, for example, that we say that the genetic program for the existence of arms or wings or branches on a tree or frogs from tadpoles in some way *exist* in the initial state of the organism, although they are not fully realized there. This biology analogy may be what Chomsky had in mind in (6). This analogy does not answer the argument in number 2, however. It merely again raises the issue in a different form. We can ask the same questions about these obviously biological phenomena. Is the genetic program for the development itself intact in the initial state of the organism? To what degree does the biological program account for the actual developmental course of the emergence of arms, wings, or branches? In fact, recent research in the area of genetics and biochemistry have, on the biological level, led to promising results in this area of biological development. For example, Marx (1987, p. 27) has concluded that in these areas, "The experience of the past few years has . . . shown that the riddles of development are beginning to yield." This positive opinion results from recent research in which a developmental control gene, which "encodes a protein that resembles a growth factor receptor," has been discovered in the fruit fly (Marx, 1987, p. 26). (See also Marx, 1981, 1988, and Gehring, 1987.) Other research results have evidenced a "fos gene as master switch" (based on study of mouse viruses) (*Science,* 1987) and various growth factors resulting from biochemical studies, which "form part of a complex cellular signalling language" (Schmeck, 1988).

It would be possible for the theory of UG to begin to more fully analogize to this area of biological development. Here again, UG would need to become, on analogy, a developmental program, a growth program, not a model of either the initial state or end state of language knowledge, as currently conceived. If so, the methodology of current linguistic theory, (i.e., now based on study of adult language) would have to be substantially revised.

[9]In fact it is not clear that "containment" can describe the developmental facts. For example, it is not true that a grammar that must function devoid of functional categories can be said to be "contained" in a grammar that does not.

In addition, the biology analogy is not precise enough. Specific languages vary in a different way than different arms or different branches do. Specific languages are each in themselves systems, that is, they reflect I-languages, where the systematic differences across these, as well as the commonalities in these systems, must be accounted for in a principled manner. The gaps between genetic program and biological organ and that between genetic program and specific language vary in ways that must be accounted for by the respective theories of their nature and development.

3. In the biology of human cerebral cortex development, there is evidence of developmental change at least up to adolescence. Huttenlocher (1990) for example, reports "growth of dendrites and of synaptic connections" and the elimination of "excess synaptic connections" over this period (Huttenlocher, 1990, p. 517; see also Huttenlocher, 1974, 1984). Clearly these general biological underpinnings underlie general and broad cognitive developmental changes. There is however, at present, no independent motivation (e.g., from biology) wherein one component of universal grammar (e.g., lexical categories) should be predicted to precede another (e.g., functional categories) in grammar, given the observed biological changes. For certain cases where certain developmental changes are observed (e.g., Mills et al., 1993), these are argued to correspond to language experience, not to chronological age; they are argued to be due to development of language knowledge (or language abilities) rather than to general maturational changes. As such, they would reflect result, not cause.

Finally, it is never impossible that some biological foundation will be found for some cognitive or linguistic change. However, the strongest scientific confirmation of UG would involve a case where such biological discoveries, at least in part, are led by hypotheses that derive from linguistic theory.[10] As we argued previously, no such predictions have derived from linguistic theory for the type of change in UG (or gradual emergence of parts of UG) that have been proposed in recent applications of the MH to language acquisition. These proposals are, to date, solely motivated descriptively by observations of language behavior. This does not mean that no possible evidence regarding the nature of UG can arise from independent a-theoretic studies of the biology of cerebral cortex development and descriptive behavioral studies of language development; only that to date, none such exists.[11]

A priori, it is true that independent biological discoveries may occur, and they may ultimately lead linguists to reformulate their theory of UG. However, if these biological facts alone determine what constitutes the theory of UG, then it is the

[10]With regard to certain cognitive developmental changes, for example infant search behaviors related to object concepts, originally discovered by Piaget on the basis of behavioral observations, some of these have been subsequently discovered to have definable biological foundations (e.g., Chugani & Phelps, 1986; Diamond, 1991).

[11]More fundamental issues arise here also. Without a leading linguistic theory, what behaviors should be described?

biology that is explaining UG, not *vice versa.* In this case, the independent theoretical results of linguistic scholarship risk losing their explanatory adequacy.

In some sense, because UG is proposed to be "biologically programmed"—for example, (4)—it *is* in a sense actually claimed to be "explained" by its biological underpinnings. The issue raised here, however, may essentially be one of scientific methodology. Although behavioral description alone could lead to discovery of biological facts regarding language knowledge, it would have to be the case that the formal theoretical model adopted for this behavioral description were accurate in order for biological discoveries to be interpreted in terms of this theory. We have argued, however, in numbers 1 and 2 that once UG is divorced from the initial state, as it is by the MH, there is no way to validate this formalization. Any theoretical formalization (as long as it is consistent with weak generative capacity) is possible as description of any observed language behavior correlating with any biological states. Clearly, then, the strongest search for biological evidence of UG must relate to an independently grounded theory of UG. Only an SCH allows such independent grounding.

4. In general, the MH robs the theory of UG of a possible correlation with linguistic "markedness." The theory of UG, in one form, constitutes a precise theory of markedness in natural language (cf. Gair, 1988, and Kapur et al., 1993, in preparation). If UG only appears sequentially through development in parts and is complete only in adulthood, then it is not clear how facts about first language acquisition can provide converging evidence on what is marked or unmarked in linguistic theory in a theoretically principled way.

Recent Variations on the MH Proposal

Recent interpretations of a theory of UG include some that are more subtle. For example, Cairns, McDaniel, and Hsu (1993) proposed that certain aspects of UG may not be available in the initial state, only because certain learning must take place before they can be accessed. For example, they proposed that initial child grammars lack subordination or embedding and are restricted to coordination. They suggest that the child must learn the semantics of subordinating connectives first; only then will the rest of UG, including subordination, become available. The lack of knowledge of the semantics of the lexicon of subordinating connectives, they proposed, "bleeds" UG. They interpret this proposal as consistent with "continuity of UG" (cf. Cairns et al., 1993, Cohen Sherman & Lust, 1993a,b). This proposal represents an interesting alternative to the syntactic bootstrapping hypothesis (e.g., Gleitman, 1994), in which acquisition of lexicon is to some degree explained by the child's prior knowledge of syntactic structure. In this alternative proposal, on the contrary, acquisition of the semantics of the lexicon is proposed to explain the child's development of syntactic structure.

This type of proposal suffers the same problems as the MH, however. If the order of acquisition (coordination, then subordinating connectives, then syntactic subordination) is determined by the internal structure of the organism, then it is equivalent to a maturation hypothesis. If it is determined by some aspect of the external environment, or some aspect of the data itself, then an independent theory is needed to characterize this graded difficulty. (In fact, the proposal becomes a learning theory in this case.) If the order is determined only because the child appears to demonstrate this order, then again the proposal suffers from *petitio principii.* (See also Gleitman, 1981, and Landau & Gleitman, 1985, on specific difficulties with semantic bootstrapping as a basic mechanism in language acquisition.)

In another recent interpretation of the specific MH in language acquisition, Penner (1994) argued that at certain ages, children cannot access certain aspects of UG, although this UG may exist. Certain aspects of UG are claimed to be "inoperative" in the initial state. Penner has suggested, for example (with regard to the acquisition of question formation in the child), that "COMP may be realized at the initial stage only if it bears an abstract index" (Penner, 1994, p. 205, fn. 4), which we interpret as suggesting that COMP (complementizer) and its projection must exist in the initial state. At the same time, however, Penner 1994 suggested (p. 205, fn. 3): "It is, however, not unreasonable to assume that the integration of language-specific COMP system refers to idiosyncratic properties of inflectional paradigms." It is proposed that the "unavailability of COMP is just a special manifestation of a more general acquisition procedure due to which the unification of A-bar and A-domains is inoperative at the initial stage." If we understand this proposal, it requires no UG maturation. Developmental delay is proposed to lie in the integration of language-specific aspects of the grammar being acquired with UG. At the level of grammatical competence, this is in fact a version of the SCH, not of MH. Developmental data in this Penner proposal must now be accounted for in terms of a separate theory of access, which changes over time, not in terms of UG change. Presumably this developmental aspect of the theory does not pertain to the UG linguistic module. It could result from some performance or processing component. In this case, it is subject to the remarks we raised in Section II.A. (regarding the "instantaneous H"). Alternatively, if we understand this proposal, it is consistent with what we have described as our grammatical mapping hypothesis (Lust, 1994) (cf. Section III below) and a SCH of UG.

In sum, we conclude here that the strongest theory of UG must reject the specific MH on theoretical grounds. Recent variations on the MH do not strengthen it.

Empirical Evidence Regarding the MH

In addition, numerous studies have now investigated specific empirical claims made by particular applications of the MH; and in each case, they have disconfirmed them. We will consider only a few of these here as examples.

Absence of Functional Categories

For example, consider the MH that children's early grammars are deficited, lacking functional categories and functional projections (e.g., C(omplementizer),

D(eterminer), I(nflection). [We assume here that the knowledge of functional categories, which underlies their lexical realization, must be provided by UG. For an interesting alternative, see Tsimpli (1991).] Radford (1990), for example, conducted a wide investigation of early English child language, tracing numerous deficits in children's production of clause and noun phrase (NP) structure to this underlying deficit, thus attempting an explanation of many diverse aspects of the early child speech in these terms. This is exactly the type of analysis that would be necessary to defend a stage in child grammars.[12] (Radford's is perhaps the most developed proposal in a MH framework; cf., also, Lebeaux, 1990, and many others.[13])

Consider the predictions made by the MH for such a discontinuity theory. The MH predicts that the adult model should not fundamentally affect the course of language acquisition, because presumably the underlying biology is a property of the human species and change over time is held not to involve learning (i.e., induction from the environment/input). MH thus predicts universal language acquisition patterns. It also predicts discrete points of change from one stage to another.

With regard to functional categories, cross-linguistic evidence has provided clear and direct evidence for functional categories (FC) in the earliest periods of language acquisition. The evidence ranges from simple description of overt FC in speech, to arguments that the FC underlie grammatical knowledge that is implicit in early child language, such as verb raising, noun classification, differentiation of finiteness in grammar, or syntactic movement (cf. Deprez & Pierce, 1994; Lust, Suñer, & Whitman, 1994; Santelmann, 1995, provide a recent collection of related studies). For example, Sesotho provided examples like (11a) and (11b) (Demuth, 1994); early Italian first language reveals examples like (12) (Hyams, 1984; Nieddu, 1997). Pye (1983) provided (13) for Quiché Mayan, and Varma (1979) provided (14) in Hindi. Numerous other cross-linguistic studies confirm this point, such as (15) (Tamil). See also Levy (1983) regarding Hebrew and Fortescue (1985) regarding Greenlandic. The child studied by Fortescue, for example, (Agissiag, age 2.2) exhibited 13 verbal inflections, 15 nominal inflections, and 24 derivational affixes (cf. Parkinson, in preparation). These cross-linguistic studies all reveal early overt production or they imply knowledge of the grammar of functional categories in early child language.

As Demuth argued, evidence like that in Sesotho acquisition in (11a) and (11b)

[12]Compare here the immense literature in the field of cognitive development that has been devoted to stage theory in other areas of cognition; consider Gelman and Baillargeon (1983) on Piaget's theory, for example, which considers criteria assumed necessary for documenting a stage in knowledge development.

[13]Radford (1994) made a more specific proposal, in which children are proposed to initially have "an immature AGR constituent" (p. 30). Here he calls on Chomsky's recent more differentiated theory of inflectional phrase (IP) structure to account for several aspects of child language. He thus no longer proposes a simple stage with complete absence of functional categories apparently.

shows "that children know the appropriate noun classes to which nominal stems belong, even when the noun itself surfaces with a null functional element" (1994, p. 122).

(11) a. *Sesotho* (2.1 years) (Demuth, 1994, =4)
  (i) ponko *lá*-ne
    (corresponding to the adult: le-phoqo *lá*-ne)
    5-green corn stalk 5Dem-that
    "that green corn stalk"
  (ii) kólo *sá*-ne
    (corresponding to the adult: se-kólo *sá*-ne)
    7-school 7DEM-that
    "that school"

(12) a. *Italian child* (age between 1.10 and 2.4) (Hyams, 1984, p. 59; =4h)
  Guarda il topo piccolino
  (Look at the little [msc sg] mouse)
 b. *Italian* (1.6) (Nieddu, 1997, p. 135, citing data from Volterra, 1976).
  uè hai messo Lole a catta?
  (=Dove *ha*i mess*o* Lole la gatt*a?*)
  (Where have you, Lole, put the cat?)

(13) *Quiché Mayan* (age 2 years) (Pye, 1983, =15, p. 599)
  chat . . . ix . . xa:j
  (=ch-Ø-a-k'a:t-is-a:j)
  (asp-B3-A2-shine-CAUS-TR)
  (Make it shine)

(14) *Hindi* (age 1.5, MLU) (Varma, 1979, p. 168)
  Hari a raha
  Hari come-ing
  (Hari is coming)

(15) *Tamil* (age 2 yrs.) (Raghavendra & Leonard, 1989, p. 320)
  ide aNNaccu -Da -Num
  This switch off: past definitely:ASP must
  (This (cassette player) must definitely be switched off)

On Italian, see also Guasti (1993) who has provided evidence that "Italian children at a young age, distinguish between finite and infinitival verbs" and "have knowledge of the verbal agreement paradigm"; interpreting these empirical results as "evidence that the initial structure of children's sentences includes functional categories, specifically the Inflectional phrase" (1).

Thus, no "universal stage" that includes simple absence of FC has been attested. On the contrary, there is clear influence of the adult model reflected in the cross-linguistic differences in child language representation of functional categories at early periods (See Demuth, 1994; Gerken & McIntosh, 1993; Gerken, Remez, & Landau, 1990; Gerken, 1994, for examples of different attempts to explain the sources of FC omission and cross-linguistic variation.)

In all of these studies, the full inflectional morphology appears to be incomplete, but this incompleteness can clearly not be described in terms of a stage of knowledge in which FC are simply grammatically unavailable.

It might be argued here that different languages may make it possible for children to skip a stage involving absence of FC. But this is exactly the point. In opposition to the assumptions of a maturational model, (and in keeping with the grammatical mapping model discussed in Section 3), distinctions in the adult language model appear to result in when and how functional categories of the specific language grammar are represented in earliest language of the child. If there were a stage in which FC were grammatically impossible because of biological programming, this should not occur; and if the presence of FC is dependent on biological maturation, not on mapping to the adult model, then there is no reason why such cross-linguistic variation should occur.

Other studies have argued not only that knowledge of functional categories characterizes early child language, but that perhaps it even provides the skeletal base for this acquisition, as opposed to lexical categories (e.g., Boser et al., 1991a, 1991b; Boser, 1997; Lust, 1994, for review of evidence relevant to complementizer phrase (CP); Santelmann, 1995, regarding knowledge of Swedish CP; Whitman et al., 1991). In fact, the functional category projection of CP appears to provide the basis for development of complex sentence structure, such as relative clauses. Lee's research on Korean acquisition (1991; cf. Whitman, Lee, & Lust, 1991) provided evidence for this in development of Korean relative clauses, even where adult grammar does not demonstrate the complementizer overtly, for example, (16):

(16) a. *Korean child* (23 months)
[[Mok-ey $[e]_{NP}$ ke-nun] kes] ya?
neck-on wear-pres COMP be-Q?
Is it what you wear on your neck?

Lust (in preparation), in fact, argued that very early parameter setting for phrase structure knowledge occurs with the complementizer, that is, CP head direction (corresponding to a grammar's principal branching direction) and provides the earliest grammatical organization for the young child universally.

Knowledge of CP has also been argued to provide the basis for other knowledge, such as question formation and topicalization. Pro drop phenomena have also recently been linked to the CP domain, (e.g., Roeper & Weissenborn, 1990; Nuñez del Prado, Foley, & Lust, 1993; Nuñez del Prado et al., 1994, 1997, provided experimental evidence for significant cross-linguistic differences in pro drop linked to CP embedding in subordinate clauses even in very young [2-year-old] children.). See also Hyams (1994) for defense of children's knowledge of CP projection.

As Demuth (1994) also noted, change in the production of overt functional categories is not discrete and sudden, as a stage theory would predict, but gradual and highly subject to individual differences. See also Boser and colleagues, 1991a,b, 1995; Boser, 1997, for similar arguments regarding the development of overt "AUX" in some aspects of German child language; and Valian, 1992.

Passive

With regard to the acquisition of passive—motivating the statement supporting the MH in (8)—Pinker, Lebeaux, and Frost (1987) have shown very early evidence for knowledge of the grammatical passive even in English, and for gradual development of productivity of use of the passive, that is not a discrete change as a stage model like the MH would require. In addition, cross-linguistic evidence has shown that the apparently slow productivity of passive in English is highly language-specific. In Sesotho, for example, Demuth (1989, ex. 13b) showed very early evidence of the passive:

(17) 'Na ke-kut-uo-e ke nkhono oaka (Keneuoe, 2.8 years)
pn sm-cut hair/prf-Pass-m by grandmother my
(As for me I've been given a hair cut by my grandmother)

Similarly, Pye and Quixtan Poz reported (1988) that Quiché children are "precocious users of passive and antipassive constructions" (p. 78). See also Jakubowicz (1989) on acquisition of passive in French, providing evidence for 3-year-old French children's knowledge of A-chains. Allen provided evidence for A-chains, (both verbal passive and noun incorporation) in acquisition of Inuktitut as early as 2.0 (Allen, 1994; Allen & Crago, 1993; cf. Parkinson, in preparation). Thus, the initial claims for an MH, in terms of the passive construction, are disconfirmed by empirical evidence just as they were in the case of functional categories.

Stage of Coordination before Subordination

Another area in which a MH has been proposed involves the basic syntax of phrase structure. Here, in accord with a MH, coordinate structures have been proposed to appear in child grammars as a stage before subordination or embedding, as we mentioned earlier (e.g., Cairns et al., 1993; Lebeaux, 1990; Lust, 1981). Here too, recent research has challenged this proposal.

Recent evidence for early knowledge of operator-variable binding defined over complex coordinate structures involving CP (Foley et al., 1992a, 1992b, 1992c, 1997) suggests that grammatical knowledge of coordination is as complex as knowledge of subordination, and that several grammatical principles involving the A-bar system (nonargument system) are evidenced in the very young child's knowledge of coordinate structures. These and other results challenge the developmental staging between coordination and subordination that has been proposed by several versions of the MH. Lust (1994) provided a summary of evidence on this issue. See also C. Koster (1994) for evidence relevant to this argument.

In addition, considering a particular type of grammatical knowledge relative to a particular type of subordination, Cohen Sherman (1983) and Cohen Sherman and Lust (1993a, 1993b) reported results of a study explicitly testing the hypothesis that children do not have the grammatical knowledge relevant to control theory (which involves a particular form of subordination) and are limited at first to coordination in grammar. Their results disconfirm this hypothesis explicitly, where children are experimentally tested on both types of structures.

Again, there is clear evidence of the role of the adult model in early child language. Cross-linguistic research (Gair et al., 1989, 1998) shows very early subordinate structures in a left branching language, namely Sinhalese:

(18) *Sinhalese child* (2,11 yrs,mos)
mamə gedərə gihil*la* kaeaemə kaeaewa
I home go-*la* food eat-past
(Having gone home, I ate)/ (I went home and ate)

Oshima and Lust (1997) and Lust, Wakayama, Mazuka, Otani, and Snyder (1985) provided similar evidence for Japanese subordination.

In summary, then, proposals of a MH in order to account for putative systematic deficits in children's syntactic knowledge related to phrase structure (i.e., proposals that early stages exist in which child grammars are restricted only to coordinate structures) are disconfirmed by empirical evidence as are the MH claims for stages related to FC, or to absence of passive constructions.

Operator-Variable Binding

Other areas in which MH proposals have been made and challenged include operator-variable binding in relative clauses (Guasti & Shlonsky, 1992; cf., Foley, 1996; Foley et al., 1992a, 1992b, 1992c, 1997) and Italian agreement (Borer & Wexler, 1992; cf., McKee & Emiliani, 1992; Nieddu, 1997).

D. Reasons for Failure of the MH

We may ask then why there was failure in the original strong proposals in support of a MH?

On the one hand, these were often based on insufficient investigation of child language data. For example, Radford (1990) had based his reasoning on observations of limited natural speech samples from limited samples of children. For the most part, this proposal did not consult experimental evidence from children of the same age. Although inflectional endings are often missing in early child speech in

English, there is experimental evidence (as well as evidence arising from more extensive, more systematic investigation of natural speech data) that has shown that children acquiring English know about these inflections, i.e., that is, have the grammatical competence for them, even when they are omitted (e.g., Egido, 1983; Gerken, Remez, & Landau 1990; Shipley, Smith, & Gleitman, 1969; Valian, 1992). In addition, the initial data adduced by MH proposals were primarily limited to studies of English language acquisition. These have now been augmented by numerous cross-linguistic studies.

Similar problems arose with regard to early proposals regarding children's knowledge of word order in German, which argued for an early "extended verb final" stage. This claim has now been disconfirmed by more extensive investigation of larger samples of children, consisting of both experimental research and more systematic natural speech investigations (e.g., Boser, 1982, 1997; Boser, Santelmann, Lust, & Whitman, 1991a, 1992b; see also references collected in Lust, Suñer, & Whitman, 1994).

However, we think that the more fundamental reason for the failure of these initial proposals rests in the theoretical problems we raised earlier, which characterize the MH. Namely, in these investigations, only a description of the behavioral data motivated the theoretical MH account that was proposed for the data. These behavioral data alone always underdetermine the possible theoretical analyses. Linguistic theory (i.e., theoretically motivated proposals regarding the content of UG), did not motivate the data analyses on independent grounds, but accommodated it. On the contrary, if the SCH is assumed, specific hypotheses that are derived from linguistic theory can be tested against the data (as in Section I.A., for example). The data can and do provide argumentation for the "correct" theory of UG.

E. The Issue of Age

It may be argued that although experimental evidence disconfirms MH proposals for discontinuity in UG, "real" UG change occurs only earlier, in infancy, before standard experimental methods are possible, for example, during the period when the child is in the first 2 years of life and only just beginning to combine words (e.g., Radford, 1990, 1994a,b, has recently proposed 1½ to 2 years to be the critical period for existence of maturation, constituting possibly a silent stage). During this period, observations on natural speech samples would become the primary evidence for the stage; and, there might not even yet be productive speech. However, for several reasons, we are skeptical that such new evidence will appear to confirm a MH and disconfirm SCH. We mention a few caveats here:

(19) a. Many of the studies cited earlier in this chapter, which disconfirm the MH, have involved children's natural speech from earliest periods of syntactic word combination (e.g., for German in Boser, 1997, and Boser et al., 1993,

or for Swedish in Santelmann, 1995, including children early during the first 2 years). (For related evidence during these ages, see Demuth, 1994, Stromswald, 1990, and Valian, 1992, among others.) No period of grammatical discontinuity has been discovered in these very early naturalistic data (cf., Mazuka, Lust, Wakayama, & Snyder, 1986; and Mehler & Christophe, 1995).

b. Notice that, in general, the farther down in age one pushes the discontinuity hypothesis (DH), the more difficult it becomes to adduce requisite empirical evidence for the DH and against SCH. In fact, such proposals may require that they *not* be subjectable to experimental test, that is, to scientific disconfirmation. This is because observations on natural speech samples alone, without experimental research, can never test for disconfirmation of an hypothesis conclusively (e.g., Lust et al., 1987). (Proposals for a MH that depend on a silent stage would certainly render the proposal without empirical content.)

c. As is well known, the length constraint on children's language (affecting their E-language) is continuously present during these early ages, and the more so the younger the child.[14] As a result, more and more of the child's grammatical knowledge (i.e., I-language knowledge) is reflected at the level of phonetic form (PF) through empty categories or empty constituents. Argumentation regarding these empty elements can require quite subtle empirical and theoretical argumentation (cf. Gerken, Remez, & Landau, 1990, or the Boser, 1992, 1997, and Boser et al., 1991a, 1991b argumentation for the presence of a "null aux" in early child German, for example; or Bloom's 1970 reduction hypothesis.) Frequently, such argumentation has produced evidence for the presence in grammatical knowledge of an apparently missing element in child speech, for example, the "C-zero V-2" position filled by "aux" features in early child German (Boser et al., 1991b). Early attempts to argue for the absence of categories on the basis of mere observed absence of a category in the phonetic form or E-language (i.e., absence in individual utterances by a child) have clearly been shown to have underestimated the child's I-language knowledge. (See Santelmann, 1995, on this issue.)

d. For study relevant to the possible exceptional earliness of parameter setting in infants, even before the first word (including parameter setting involving CP and clausal embedding), see Mazuka (1996) and Jusczyk, Mazuka, and colleagues (1993); compare also Hirsh-Pasek et al. (1987).

e. Finally, the real issue is not age, because children vary greatly in the level of their language both within and across ages. The real issue is whether

[14]This length constraint is still not well understood, but is clearly an empirical fact.

UG is continuously available during periods of real language development, that is, when there are actual changes in the language knowledge of the child. If children show development in certain phenomena, regardless of age, these developmental facts are what need explanation. Changes in language knowledge occur after age 2.0, in phenomena related to relative clauses, control structures, *wh* structures, certain types of passives, and so on. There is no theoretical or empirical motivation for "UG change" (MH) to explain development in one set of cases but not in another (e.g., changes before age 2 but not changes after).

III. THE STRONG CONTINUITY HYPOTHESIS (SCH)

We will assume then, that the null hypothesis must be the strong continuity hypothesis (SCH) with regard to UG. This is the strongest hypothesis on theoretical grounds. It is supported by extensive empirical studies now. No empirical evidence has conclusively disconfirmed it.

There do appear to be real developmental changes in children's knowledge of their languages, however. We turn now to a brief introduction of an alternative UG-based theory of language acquisition, which is consistent with language development, but not with maturation of UG. It maintains the SCH of UG at the same time that it recognizes true development.

A. Relation between UG and Language Development

The SCH (7) must be separated from the IH (5). The SCH does not require assuming IH in the sense that language acquisition is itself viewed as instantaneous. As we noted, the original motivation for the IH was only that different (day-to-day) orders of initial presentation of data did not appear to significantly affect final outcome of acquisition (e.g., Chomsky, 1965). This motivation remains true.

A changing UG is not the only possible theory of a principled relation between UG and language development. It is, in fact, too simplistic. It underestimates the complexity of a complete linguistic theory, and it underestimates the complexity of the child mind with regard to theory construction.

In our work elsewhere, we develop an alternative interpretation of the theory of UG as a model of the initial state. Several empirical studies of specific areas of language acquisition now provide precise examples of this now theoretical paradigm that we term *grammatical mapping* (e.g., Boser, Santelmann, Barbier, & Lust, 1995; Cohen Sherman & Lust, 1993a,b; Foley, 1996; Lust, 1994, in preparation; Somashekar, 1998). We sketch its outlines briefly next.

B. Grammatical Mapping: From UG to Specific Language Grammars (SLG)

In this model, the child is viewed as "mapping" from UG to SLG. The mapping involves the integration of modular UG principles, the setting of parameters,[15] realization of widespread deductive consequences of parameter setting, the integration of principles and parameter setting, and the morphosyntax and semantics of the lexicon in a specific language. The grammatical mapping consults the adult data, to which the child is exposed, albeit indirectly (e.g., Kapur et al., 1993, in preparation). On this theory, the child (equipped with UG) is *mapping to* the adult language through the construction of the grammar for this specific language.

This interpretation of UG is in accord with (20) in which UG is not viewed as identical to the growth of language, but as its framework:

(20) *What many linguists call "universal grammar" may be regarded as a theory of innate mechanisms, an underlying biological matrix that provides a framework within which the growth of language proceeds.*

(Chomsky, 1980, p. 187)

UG is not independent of experience, but determines and constrains how experience is used:

(21) *Proposed principles of universal grammar may be regarded as an abstract partial specification of the genetic program that enables the child to interpret certain events as linguistic experience and to construct a system of rules and principles on the basis of this experience.* (Chomsky, 1980, p. 187)

In fact,

(22) *universal grammar (. . . is of course, not a grammar but rather a system of conditions on the range of possible grammars for possible human languages).*

(Chomsky, 1980, p. 189)

C. UG as "Constraining" the Course of Acquisition

Numerous studies now provide evidence that in several specific areas of language acquisition, UG (where principles and parameters are independently defined by UG theory) continuously "constrains" first language acquisition, even where this acquisition may be gradual (more precisely, where acquisition of specific language grammars or structures may be gradual).

Such evidence exists now in the area of the binding principles (Lust, Eisele, & Mazuka, 1992; Lust, Mazuka, Martohardjono, & Yoon, 1989). It exists in the

[15]At least one parameter, and possibly only one, involves phrase structure head direction (cf., Lust, in preparation). Thus grammatical mapping is not fully determined by P-setting.

area of control theory (cf. Cohen Sherman, 1983; Cohen Sherman & Lust, 1993a,b). It exists with regard to the knowledge of scrambling in Dutch (Barbier, 1993a,b, 1995a,b); verb raising in German (Boser, 1997); and with regard to Wh constructions in Swedish (Santelmann, 1995) as well as in other languages (e.g., Roeper, Weissenborn, & deVilliers in Maxfield & Plunkett, 1991).

We will exemplify with a few examples here.

D. UG as "Guiding" First Language Acquisition

With regard to Principles A and B of the binding theory (BT), some language acquisition data appear on the surface to critically challenge the SCH of UG, because they show a long developmental delay (6 to 8 years) before the child makes correct locality judgments for pronouns in certain experimental designs (e.g., Chien & Wexler, 1990; cf. collection of papers in Lust, Hermon, & Kornfilt, 1994, and introduction to that volume for critical summary). This would appear to suggest that Principle B of the binding theory develops.

However, it has been argued that these acquisition data, in fact, reflect a continuous role of the binding theory applying in a definitional manner to the lexicon of a language. This mapping consults both positive and indirect negative evidence. These acquisition data, thus, do not reflect a contradiction to the BT. They do not require a proposal for the dissociation of the BT in terms of a slower development of Principle B, possibly maturationally derived (i.e., the principle that determines that pronouns must be disjoint in reference with subjects locally, e.g., *"$John_i$ likes him_i") (cf. Lust, Martohardjono, Mazuka, & Yoon, 1989; cf., Jakubowicz, 1989; Mazuka and Lust, 1994). Rather, they reflect the time required for the child mapping from UG to SLG, and a resolution of the SLG lexicon.

A similar ostensible program for SCH exists in the area of acquisition of relative clause structures. Here children appear to evidence true development (e.g., Flynn & Lust, 1981; Hamburger, 1980). Lust (1994) sketched a SCH approach to these developmental facts (cf. Foley, 1996). It is argued there that lexically headed restrictive relatives are a language-specific grammatical phenomenon that is achieved (in languages where required) by a developmental process of "grammatical mapping" from continuous, universal assumptions about phrase structure, through modular interaction with other UG modules (e.g., a module involving "wh" movement) in order to construct the relative clause structures of the specific language grammar being acquired. (See also Somashekar, 1998.)

E. UG Can Itself Provide Apparent "Developmental Delay"

Interestingly, there are also examples where current research shows that the very strength of UG can itself appear to cause developmental "delay" in the acquisition of language-specific or structure-specific phenomena. Cohen, Sherman, and Lust

(1993) (after Cohen Sherman, 1983), for example, argued that a very strong "syntactic minimality" constraint, defined over configuration, and reflecting "structure dependence" and a strong sense of locality (presumably UG-determined) appears to be the source of the young child's error in English with regard to the unique verb *promise,* as in (23):

(23) Mary promised Sarah [to make a cake]

Here the child acquiring English perseveres to 6 to 8 years in an "error" of taking the object to be controller of the EC(PRO) in the embedded clauses (cf. C. Chomsky, 1969)—that is, the child interprets (23) as referring to *Sarah* making a cake. Experimental analyses have now provided evidence that this "error" is structure dependent and linguistically motivated (Cohen Sherman and Lust, 1993a). It reflects grammatical mapping through a strong UG principle of syntax (minimality) to SLG.

Directionality

Elsewhere, we have argued that an apparent "forward directionality constraint" on pronouns in child language (English) is in fact a reflex of combined constraint by phrase structure parameter setting (deriving the right branching grammar of English) and constraint by the binding principles (e.g., Lust, in preparation; Lust & Mazuka, 1989). Critical evidence here is that children acquiring other languages (which are left-branching) (e.g., Chinese, Japanese, Sinhalese) do not show the same forward directionality effects on pronouns that children acquiring English do. The interaction of grammatical principles in a particular language can thus lead to a variety of surface outcomes in child language. These outcomes may appear on the surface to be nongrammatical in nature, because they are not identical to adult language. But, in fact, they reflect the child's UG-based theory construction in grammatical mapping to SLG. (See also Lust, Chien, Chiang, & Eisele, 1996, on Chinese.)

F. Explanation of Developmental Delay without Offense of SCH

Various individual studies of individual phenomena have now discovered evidence with regard to the precise aspect of mapping between UG and specific language grammar, which may be the source of real development in language acquisition.

Interaction of Modular Principles

A common foundation for explanation of development in the preceding studies lies in the child's need to integrate principles of UG, which are modular and which must be integrated in a language-specific manner. UG cannot predetermine this integration. Cohen Sherman and Lust (1993a), for example, traced the source of persistent developmental delays in control structures, such as (23), to the need for language-specific modular integration of UG principles that are each independently intact, but that must be integrated in a language specific manner (e.g., syntactic minimality, finiteness of embedded complement, and lexical aspects of main clause verb). Similar language-specific integration of modular "Wh" principles (A-bar) and phrase structure (X-bar) knowledge was proposed to be necessary for the development of relative clause knowledge (Foley, 1996; Lust, 1994). In the acquisition of anaphora, studied from a cross-linguistic perspective, the integration of parametrically determined phrase structure direction and the binding principles is proposed to continuously constrain the gradual acquisition of language-specific options for free anaphora in a specific language (Lust, 1986, in preparation). Boser, Santelmann, Barbier, and Lust (1995) explicated this grammatical mapping paradigm in a study of various movement phenomena in language acquisition in several Germanic languages.

Integration of Modular UG Principles and Parameters with Lexicon

Several studies have implicated integration of knowledge of lexicon with knowledge of syntactic configuration in language development. For example, this modular integration includes language-specific knowledge of the lexicon (although it is not limited to it) in the Cohen Sherman and Lust (1993a) study of control. A similar proposal is made in Padilla Rivera's 1990 study of acquisition of control into subjunctive complements in Spanish. The integration with language-specific lexicon is also implicated in the study of binding theory acquisition (cf. Jakubowicz, 1989, 1994; Lust, Mazuka, Martohardjono, & Yoon, 1989; Mazuka & Lust, 1994). In addition, the integration with lexicon, as each of the previous studies show, is not necessarily direct and simple, but theoretically complex. A recent study of acquisition of Chinese pronominal systems exemplifies such indirect effects. Here it is argued that the acquisition of certain language-specific properties of Chinese empty categories results in part from gradual acquisition of the pronominal lexicon in Chinese (Lust, Chien, Chiang, & Eisele, 1996).

Interaction of Modular UG and Processing/Performance

In other cases, it has been argued that continuous knowledge of UG with regard to pro-drop parameter setting (e.g., Nuñez del Prado et al., 1994, 1997) interacts not only with other modules of UG (e.g., phrase structure) but also with processing/performance phenomena (e.g., the length constraint), leading to apparent development in children's production of overt/lexical subjects (e.g., Mazuka et al., 1986; Mazuka, Lust, Snyder, & Wakayama, 1995; cf. Austin et al., 1997). See also Mazuka (1998) on this general area.

Grammatical Mapping

In all of the above proposals, grammatical mapping (GM) proceeds on the basis of a continuous UG. Yet, true development is recognized. All knowledge of specific language grammar is not proposed to be innate, contrary to the IH, even if UG is continuously and completely available. Development in this GM theory does not involve the staged tadpole-frog view of the child's UG-determined biology, in contrast to the MH. Development lies in the child's theory construction of a SLG on the basis of innate biological programming of UG (a language faculty), which is continuously and completely available to the child, and which constrains the child's theory construction over time. The child's specific theory construction is based on the child's mapping from the adult language data (PLD) to which the child is exposed to a grammar for these data. This constrained mapping, based on both positive evidence and indirect negative evidence, takes time. No MH, for example, (6), is required to account for development, even when true development in children's language knowledge is evident. This is a fortunate result, because as we have argued, the MH weakens, if not vitiates, the scientific force of a theory of UG. (We leave the reader to the reference listed previously for details regarding this GM paradigm of UG.)

G. Recent Revisions of the MH

The precise manner in which Chomsky's MH (6) is interpreted is being revised now by several of its proponents. In closing, we must consider whether these may save the MH. For example, the statement in Borer and Wexler, (8), has been revised in Chien and Wexler (1990):

(24) *All the instances that Borer and Wexler discussed are instances in which "structures" grow, but principles are in place from the beginning.*
(Chien & Wexler, 1990, p. 154)[16]

This reinterpretation of Chomsky's MH in (6), and of Borer & Wexler in (8), begins to converge with the SCH we have articulated. Specifically, we held the content of UG to be "principles and parameters." Structures are necessarily not only language specific, but they reflect E-language, not I-language and thus do not constitute the direct domain of UG. The statement in (24) thus, would be consistent not with Chomsky's MH in (6), but with the SCH in (7). Chien and Wexler use the term "UG-constrained maturation" for this recent revised proposal. If this statement intends to propose that it is not UG that matures, but something else, then it is in general consistent with our proposal in (7). The issue would depend on what exactly this revised proposal does propose to mature at all. Certainly, specific language structures cannot mature in themselves, because these are, in principle, un-

[16]It is not clear how the original Borer and Wexler proposal that A-chains mature can be made susceptible to this reinterpretation, because although specific chains might be said to characterize specific structures, the limitation in grammatical competence was originally proposed to reflect a principled limitation.

countable if not infinite. Further, as Chomsky proposed recently, "structures" (i.e., specific constructions) have no real status in the theory of UG. Thus, they cannot have content in biological programming. Chomsky (1993, p. 5) proposed, for example, that language-specific constructions are viewed in current linguistic theory "only as taxonomic artifacts, collections of phenomena explained through the interaction of the principles of UG." They thus cannot be biologically programmed in a way that would allow their maturing in any principled way. (Similar issues characterize the related proposal in Wexler, 1992, p. 254, in which it is proposed that "UG constrains every stage of child language development, but certain constructs may not be available at certain ages"; although here the term *constructs* is less clear theoretically than the term *structures,* and so the proposal is more difficult to evaluate theoretically.)

In another recent interpretation of the MH, Atkinson (1993) posited:

(25) *To say that a representational capacity, in this case a grammar including functional categories, matures at t does not entail that the child will exhibit full competence with functional categories at t. He or she has still to determine how the system of functional categories is "realized" in the grammar being acquired, and there is no reason to believe that the complexity of this task will be uniform across grammars.* (Atkinson, 1993, p. 267)

In this way, Atkinson argued that cross-linguistic variation in acquisition facts (e.g., precocious appearance of functional categories in some languages) does not provide disconfirmation of a maturation hypothesis. If (25) is accepted, however, then there is no reason why grammatical competence (UG) need be proposed to mature/change at all, because it is recognized that its presence may coexist with failure to reflect its knowledge in the language. In fact, the proposal in (25) appears in full accord with the nonmaturational hypothesis we articulated earlier, wherein developmental delays are attributed precisely to the mapping between UG and specific language grammars, not to discontinuity in UG.

IV. CONCLUSIONS

We have considered the relation of the linguistic theory of universal grammar to the child's acquisition of a first language in real time. We have argued on theoretical grounds that a maturational hypothesis of UG (one wherein UG is proposed to change over time in order to describe observed developmental changes in the child's language knowledge) weakens the theory of UG and leads to theoretical paradox. We have argued on empirical grounds that there is no evidence for such a maturational hypothesis in several of the areas in which it has been proposed.

Alternatively, we have suggested that on both theoretical and empirical grounds, a strong continuity hypothesis (in which UG characterizes the biologically programmed "initial state" and is continuous across language development) should be maintained. We have suggested that this SCH of UG is consistent with real development in children's knowledge of specific languages, through a grammatical mapping hypothesis, in which a continuous UG guides the child's mapping to a specific language grammar.

One critical consequence of this result is that the study of linguistic theory and the study of first language acquisition can be interpreted as providing converging evidence on the true nature of UG and on the true nature of the language faculty.

We note that one can always say that empirical evidence in favor of SCH (such as we have presented in this chapter) is not conclusive because children *could,* in each case, be deriving ostensibly correct results through a tacit ungrammatical theory or a child grammar distinct from that of adults. In this case, however, the researcher must develop such distinct theories; these theories must operate to replace existent adult grammar of UG but give the same results. Presumably these distinct, redundant systems must cohere with each other across the various language areas studied in the child at a particular time. In addition, it is not clear how or why the child would ever need to abandon these (redundant to adult G) grammatical systems.[17] The coherent linguistic theory of UG, as it is being developed now on theoretical grounds, would be otiose in this endeavor, because the precise effect of the discontinuity theory is to *replace* this UG in the child. Finally, it is not clear, how such alternative redundant grammars could ever be subject to disconfirmation because the linguistic tests applied to a coherent theory of UG will not be applicable to them. In fact, this same possibility could be raised for the adult. Different adults *could* a priori, in the same way, be hypothesized to hold different grammars by which they derive similar language. We assume this proposal would reflect a major weakening of linguistic theory, and we reject it.

Fundamentally, the purpose of this chapter has been to suggest on a priori theoretical grounds as well as on empirical grounds, that there is no motivation for such an endeavor for the child or for the adult. A linguistically significant theory of first language acquisition need not modify UG in real time over the course of language development. In fact, it must not, unless the current linguistic theory of UG were to be fundamentally revised and in itself approach a developmental theory. True development in language knowledge can be accounted for with maintenance of the SCH of UG.

[17]In some cases, it has been proposed that redundant grammars persist to the adult state (Guasti & Shlonsky, 1992). This move, at best, must greatly complicate our theory of the adult grammar, because it allows that linguistic arguments for one analysis of a particular grammatical phenomenon (in the adult language) would never conclusively rule out another.

ACKNOWLEDGMENTS

I thank James Gair, and Noam Chomsky, Sam Epstein, and Suzanne Flynn for critical debate on these issues; Katharina Boser, Claire Foley, Zelmira Nuñez del Prado, David Parkinson, and Lynn Santelmann for critical scholarship in the area, and Jennifer Austin, Yu Chin Chien, Fang Fang Guo, Luis Lopez, Nuria Lopez Ortega, Whitney Postman, and Shamitha Somashekar for provocative discussion of issues raised in this chapter. I thank William Ritchie for "triggering" this chapter.

REFERENCES

Allen, S. (1994). *Acquisition of some mechanisms of transitivity alternation in Arctic Quebec Inuktitut.* Unpublished doctoral dissertation, McGill University, Montreal.

Allen, S., & Crago, M. (1993). Early acquisition of passive morphology in Inuktitut. *Proceedings of 24th Annual Child Language Research Forum.* E. Clark (Ed.) (pp. 112–123). Stanford, CA.

Andrews, A., III. (1985). *Studies in the syntax of relative and comparative clauses.* New York: Garland Publishing.

Atkinson, M. (1993). *Children's syntax.* Oxford, UK: Blackwell.

Austin, J., Blume, M., Parkinson, D., Núñez del Prado, Z., Lust, B. (1997). The Acquisition of Spanish null and overt pronouns: Pragmatic and syntactic factors. In Somashekar, S. et al. (Eds.) *CUWPL. 15,* 160–177.

Barbier, I. (1993a). The structure of IP in German and Dutch: Arguments from first language acquisition. *Proceedings of the 10th Eastern States Conference on Linguistics.*

Barbier, I. (1993b). *Unscrambled objects in the acquisition of Dutch.* Paper presented at the Conference on Generative Approaches to Language Acquisition. University of Durham, England.

Barbier, I. (1995a). *Configuration and movement in Germanic: Studies of first language acquisition of Dutch word-order.* Unpublished Ph.D. thesis, Cornell University.

Barbier, I. (1995b). *The acquisition of embedded clauses with finite verbs in non final position in Dutch* (pp. 147–158). Stanford, CA: Stanford Linguistics Association. Center for Study of Language and Information.

Barbier, I. (1996a). An experimental study of scrambling and object shift in the acquisition of Dutch. *Proceedings of Berne Workshop on the L2 and L2 Acquisition of Clause-Internal Rules: Scrambling and Cliticization.*

Barbier, I. (1996b). The head direction of Dutch VPs: Evidence from LI acquisition. In C. Koster and F. Wijnen (Eds.), *Proceedings of the Groningen Assembly on Language Acquisition* (pp. 97–106). Groningen: Centre for Language and Cognition Groningen.

Blank, M., Gessner, M., & Esposito, A. (1979). Language without communication: A case study. *Journal of Child Language, 2,* 329–352.

Bloom, L. (1970). *Language development, form and function in emerging grammars.* Cambridge, MA: MIT Press.

Borer, H., & Wexler, K. (1987). The maturation of syntax. In T. Roeper & E. Williams (Eds.), *Parameter setting* (pp. 123–172). Dordrecht: Reidel.

Borer, H., & Wexler, K. (1992). Biunique relations and the maturation of grammatical principles. *Natural Language and Linguistic Theory, 10,* 147–189.

Boser, K. (1992). *Early knowledge of verb position in children's acquisition of German: An argument for continuity of universal grammar.* Unpublished MA thesis, Cornell University.

Boser, K. (1997). Verb initial utterances in early child German. In E. Clark (Ed.), *Proceedings of the 27th Stanford Child Language Forum.* Stanford University.

Boser, K., Santelmann, L., Barbier, I., & Lust, B. (1995). Grammatical mapping from UG to language specific grammar: Variation in the acquisition of German, Dutch and Swedish. In D. MacLaughlin & S. McEwen (Eds.), *BUCLD Proceedings.* Boston: Cascadilla Press.

Boser, K., Santelmann, L., Lust, B., & Whitman, J. (1991a). The syntax of CP and V-2 in early German child grammar: The strong continuity hypothesis. *Proceedings of the North Eastern Linguistic Association, 22,* 51–66. University of Massachusetts, Amherst.

Boser, K., Santelmann, L., Lust, B., & Whitman, J. (1991b). *The theoretical significance of auxiliary insertion in early child German.* Paper presented at Boston University Child Language Conference, Boston, MA.

Boser, K., Santelmann, L., & Lust, B. (in preparation). *Obligatory syntax in first language acquisition: Arguments for the "strong continuity hypothesis" from V-2 in early child German.* Unpublished Manuscript, Cornell University.

Cairns, H., McDaniel, D., & Hsu, J. R. (1993). A reply to "Children are in control." *cognition, 48*(2), 193–194.

Caplan, D. (1992). *Language.* Cambridge, MA: MIT Press.

Chien, Y.-C., & Lust, B. (1983). Topic-comment structure and grammatical structure in first language acquisition of Mandarin Chinese: A study of equi-constructions. In Stanford University *Paper and Reports on Child Language Development, 22,* 74–82.

Chien, Y.-C., & Lust, B. (1985). The concepts of topic and subject in first language acquisition of Mandarin Chinese. *Child Development, 56*(6), 1359–1375.

Chien, Y.C., & Wexler, K. (1990). Children's knowledge of locality conditions in binding as evidence for the modularity of syntax and pragmatics. *Language Acquisition, 1*(3), 225–295.

Chomsky, C. (1969). *The acquisition of syntax in children from 5 to 10.* Cambridge, MA: MIT Press.

Chomsky, N. (1965). *Aspects of the theory of syntax.* Cambridge, MA: MIT Press.

Chomsky, N. (1975a). *Reflections on language.* New York: Pantheon.

Chomsky, N. (1975b/1955–1956). *Logical structure of linguistic theory.* New York: Plenum Press.

Chomsky, N. (1980). *Rules and representations.* New York: Columbia University Press.

Chomsky, N. (1981). *Lectures on government and binding.* Dordrecht: Foris.

Chomsky, N. (1984). *Changing perspectives on knowledge and use of language.* Cambridge, MA: MIT Press.

Chomsky, N. (1986). *Knowledge of language: Its nature, origin, and use.* New York: Praeger Scientific.

Chomsky, N. (1987). *Language in a psychological setting. Sophia Linguistica.* Working Papers in Linguistics, number 22. Tokyo, Japan. (See also chapter 1 in this volume).
Chomsky, N. (1988). *Language and problems of knowledge. The Managua lectures.* Cambridge, MA: MIT Press.
Chomsky, N. (1991). Some notes on economy of derivation and representation. In R. Friedin (Ed.), *Principles and parameters in comparative grammar* (pp. 417–454). Cambridge, MA: MIT Press.
Chomsky, N. (1993). A minimalist program for linguistic theory. In K. Hale & S. J. Keyser (Eds.), *The view from building 20* (pp. 1–52). Cambridge, MA: MIT Press.
Chomsky, N., & Lasnik, H. (1991). Principles and parameters theory. In J. Jacobs, A. von Stechow, W. Sternefeld, & T. Vennemann (Eds.), *Handbook of Contemporary Research.* Berlin: deGruyter.
Chugani, H., & Phelps, M. (1986). Maturational changes in cerebral function in infants determined by 18/FDG Positron Emission Tomography. *Science, 231,* 840–843.
Cohen Sherman, J. (1983). *The acquisition of control in complement sentences: The role of structural and lexical factors.* Unpublished doctoral dissertation, Cornell University.
Cohen Sherman, J., & Lust, B. (1993a). Children are in control. *Cognition, 46,* 1–51.
Cohen Sherman, J., & Lust, B. (1993b). A note on continuity of universal grammar: Response to Cairns, McDaniel and Hsu, *Cognition, 48*(2), 195–197.
Crain, S., & McKee, C. (1986). Acquisition of structural restrictions on anaphora. In S. Berman,, J.-W. Choe, & J. McDonough (Eds.), *Proceedings of the Sixteenth Annual North Eastern Linguistic Society.* University of Massachusetts, Amherst, 94–110.
Crain, S., & Nakayama, J. J. (1986). Structure dependence in children's language. *Language, 62,* 522–543.
Curtiss, S. (1977). *Genie.* New York: Academic Press.
Curtiss, S. (1982). Developmental dissociations of language and cognition. In L. Obler & L. Menn (Eds.), *Exceptional language and linguistics* (pp. 285–312). New York: Academic Press.
Demuth, K. (1989). Maturation, continuity, and the acquisition of Sesotho passive. *Language, 65,* 56–80.
Demuth, K. (1992). Accessing functional categories in Sesotho: Interactions at the morpho-syntax interface. In J. Meisel (Ed.), *The acquisition of verb placement: Functional categories and V2 phenomena in language development.* Dordrecht: Kluwer.
Demuth, K. (1994). On the underspecification of functional categories in early grammars. In B. Lust, M. Suñer, & J. Whitman (Eds.), *Syntactic theory and first language acquisition: Cross-linguistic perspectives. Volume 1. Heads, projections and learnability.* Mahwah, NJ: LEA.
Deprez, V., & Pierce, A. (1994). Cross-linguistic evidence for functional projections in early child grammar. In T. Hoekstra & B. Schwartz (Eds.), *Language acquisition studies in generative grammar* (pp. 57–84). Amsterdam/Philadelphia: John Benjamins Publishing Co.
Diamond, A. (1991). Neuropsychological insights into the meaning of object concept development. In S. Carey & R. Gelman (Eds.), *The epigenesis of mind: Essays on biology and cognition* (pp. 67–110). Mahwah, NJ: LEA.
Egido, C. (1983). *The functional role of the closed class vocabulary in children's language processing.* Unpublished doctoral dissertation, MIT.

Eisele, J. (1988). *Meaning and form in children's judgments about language.* Unpublished MA thesis, Cornell University, Ithaca, NY.

Eisele, J. (1993). *The role of negation in determining presuppositions and implications of truth: A study of early hemisphere damage.* Unpublished Ph.D. dissertation, Cornell University.

Eisele, J., Lust, B., & Aram, D. (1998). Presupposition and Implication of Truth: Linguistic Deficits following early Brain Lesions. *Brain and Language, 61,* 376–394.

Eisele, J., & Lust, B. (1996). Children's knowledge about pronouns: A developmental study using a "truth value judgement task." *Child Development, 67,* 3086–3100.

Epstein, S., Flynn, S., & Martohardjono, G. (1996). Second language acquisition: Theoretical and experimental issues in contemporary research. *Behavioral and Brain Sciences, 19,* 677–758.

Feldman, H., Goldin-Meadow, S., & Gleitman, L. (1978). Beyond Herodotus: The creation of language by linguistically deprived deaf children. In A. Lock (Ed.), *Action, gesture and symbol: The emergence of language* (pp. 251–414). New York: Academic Press.

Flynn, S., & Lust, B. (1980). Acquisition of relative clauses. A preliminary report. In W. Harbert (Ed.), *Cornell University Working Papers, 1*(1). Department of Modern Languages and Linguistics, Cornell University, Ithaca, NY.

Flynn, S.,. & Martohardjono, G. (1994). Mapping from the initial state to the final state: The separation of universal principles and language specific principles. In B. Lust, M. Suñer & J. Whitman (Eds.), *Syntactic theory and first language acquisition: Cross-linguistic perspectives. Volume 1. Heads, projections and learnability.* Hillsdale, NJ: Erlbaum.

Foley, C. (1996). *Knowledge of the syntax of operators in the initial state: The acquisition of relative clauses in French and English.* Unpublished doctoral dissertation, Cornell University.

Foley, C., Nuñez del Prado, Z., Barbier, I., & Lust, B. (1992a). *LF representation of pronouns in VP ellipsis: An argument for UG in the initial state.* Paper presented at BU conference on child language development. Boston, MA.

Foley, C., Nuñez del Prado, Z., Barbier, I., & Lust, B. (1992b). *On the strong continuity hypothesis: A study of pronoun coindexing.* Paper presented at LSA, Philadelphia.

Foley, C., Nuñez del Prado, Z., Barbier, I., & Lust, B. (1992c). *Quantifier raising in VP ellipsis.* Paper presented at 'wh' workshop, University of Massachusetts, Amherst.

Foley, C., Nuñez del Prado, Z., Barbier, I. & Lust B. (1997). *Operator variable binding in the "Initial State": An argument from English VP ellipsis.* Cornell University Working Papers in Linguistics. *15.* Papers on language acquisition. Ithaca, NY: Cornell University, 1–19.

Fortescue, M. (1985). Learning to Speak Greenlandic: A Case Study of a two-year-old's morphology in a polysynthetic language. *First Language, 5,* 101–114.

Gair, J. (1988). Kinds of markedness. In S. Flynn and W. O'Neil (Eds.), *Linguistic Theory in Second Language Acquisition* (pp. 225–250), Dordrecht: Kluwer.

Gair, J. (1998). *Studies in South Asian Linguistics.* New York: Oxford.

Gair, J., Lust, B., Sumangala, L., & Rodrigo, M. (1989). Acquisition of null subjects and control in some Sinhala adverbial clauses. In *Papers and Reports on Child Language Development, 28,* 97–106. Stanford University.

Garrett, M., & Cohen-Sherman, J. (1989). *Modular performance systems in normal and aphasic language.* Paper presented at American Association for Advancement of Science, Symposium on Brain and Language, San Francisco.

Gehring, W. J. (1987). Homeo Boxes in the Study of Development. *Science*, 1245–1252.

Gelman, R., & Baillargeon, R. (1983). A review of some Piagetian concepts. In P. Mussen, (Ed.), *Handbook of child psychology* (4th ed., volume 3, pp. 167–230), J. Flavell & E. Markman (Eds.), *Cognitive development*. New York: John Wiley & Sons.

Gerken, L. (1994). Sentential processes in early child language: Evidence from the perception and production of function morphemes. In H. Nusbaum & J. Goodman (Eds.), *The transition from speech sounds to spoken words*. Cambridge, MA: MIT Press.

Gerken, L. (1996). Phonological and distributional information in syntax acquisition. In K. Demuth & J. Morgan (Eds.), *From signal to syntax*. Mahwah, NJ: LEA.

Gerken, L., & McIntosh, B. (1993). Interplay of function morphemes and prosody in early language. *Developmental Psychology, 29*(2), 448–457.

Gerken, L., Remez, R., & Landau, B. (1990). Function morphemes in young children's speech perception and production. *Developmental Psychology, 26*(2), 204–216.

Gleitman, L. (1981). Maturational determinants of language growth. *Cognition, 10*, 103–114.

Gleitman, L. (1994). A picture is worth a thousand words, but that's the problem: The role of syntax in vocabulary acquisition. In B. Lust, J. Whitman, & M. Suñer (Eds.), *Syntactic theory and first language acquisition: Cross linguistic perspectives. Volume I: Heads, projections, and learnability*. Hillsdale, NJ: Erlbaum.

Gleitman, L., Gleitman, H., Landau, R., & Wanner, E. (1988). Where learning begins: Initial representations for language learning. In F. Newmyer (Ed.), *The Cambridge Linguistic Survey. Volume III. Language: Psychological and biological aspects* (pp. 150–193). Cambridge, MA: Cambridge University Press.

Goldin-Meadow, S. (1982). The resilience of recursion: A study of a communication system developed without a conventional language model. In L. Gleitman & E. Wanner (Eds.), *Language acquisition: The state of the art* (pp. 51–77). Cambridge, MA: Cambridge University Press.

Goldin-Meadow, S., & Feldman, H. (1977). The development of language-like communication without a language model. *Science, 22*, 401–403.

Gould, J., & Marler, P. (1987). Learning by instinct. *Scientific American, 256*(1), 74–85.

Grimshaw, J., & Rosen, S. (1990). Knowledge and obedience: The developmental status of the binding theory. *Linguistic Inquiry, 21*(2).

Guasti, M. T. (1993). Verb syntax in Italian child grammar: Finite and nonfinite verbs. *Language Acquisition, 3*(1), 1–40.

Guasti, M. T., & Shlonsky, U. (1992). *The acquisition of French relative clauses reconsidered*. Paper presented at Boston University Conference on Language Development, Boston, Massachusetts.

Hamburger, H. (1980). A deletion ahead of its time. *Cognition, 8*, 389–416.

Hamburger, H., & Crain, S. (1982). Relative acquisition. In S. Kuczaj (Ed.), *Language Development* (Volume 1). Hillsdale, NJ: Erlbaum.

Hirsh-Pasek, K., Kemler-Nelson, D., Jusczyk, P., Wright Cassidy, K. L., Druss, B., & Kennedy, L. (1987). Clauses are perceptual units for young infants. *Cognition, 26*, 269–286.

Hirsh-Pasek, K., & Golinkoff, R. (1997). *The origins of grammar*. Cambridge, MA: Bradford Books.

Huttenlocher, P. R. (1974). Synapse elimination and plasticity in developing human cerebral cortex. *American Journal of Mental Deficiency, 88*, 488–496.

Huttenlocher, P. (1990). Morphometric study of human cerebral cortex development. *Neuropsychologia, 28,* 517–527.

Huttenlocher, P. R. (1974). Dendritic development in neocortex of children with mental defect and infantile spasms. *Neurology, 24,* 203–210.

Hyams, N. (1984). Semantically-based child grammars: Some empirical inadequacies. *Papers and Reports on Child Language Development, 23,* 58–65.

Hyams, N. (1986). *Language Acquisition and the Theory of Parameters.* Dordrecht: Reidel.

Hyams, N. (1994). VP, null arguments and COMP projections. In J. Hoekstra & B. Schwartz (Eds.), *Language acquisition studies in generative grammar.* Amsterdam: John Benjamin Publishing.

Jakobson, R. (1972). *Child Language, aphasia and phonological universals.* The Hague: Mouton. [Original work published 1941.]

Jakubowicz, C. (1989). Maturation or invariance of universal grammar principles in language acquisition. *Probus, 1.3,* 283–340.

Jakubowicz, C. (1994). Reflexives in French and Danish: Morphology, syntax, and acquisition. In B. Lust, G. Hermon, & J. Kornfilt (Eds.), *Syntactic theory and first language acquisition: Cross-linguistic perspectives. Volume 2. Binding, dependencies and learnability.* Hillsdale, NJ: Erlbaum.

Jusczyk, P. (1997). *The Discovery of Spoken Language.* Cambridge, MA: Bradford Books.

Jusczyk, P., Kemler Nelson, D., Hirsh-Pasek, K., Kennedy, L., Woodward, A., & Piwoz, J. (1992). Perception of acoustic correlates of major phrasal units by young infants. *Cognitive Psychology, 24,* 252–293.

Jusczyk, P., & Mazuka, R. (1993). Paper presented at the Society for Research in Child Development.

Kapur, S., Lust, B., Harbert, W., & Martohardjono, G. (1993). Universal grammar and learnability theory: The case of binding domains and the subset principle. In E. Reuland & W. Abraham (Eds.), *Knowledge and language, Volume 3, Issues in Representation and Acquisition* (pp. 185–216). Dordrecht: Kluwer.

Kapur, S., Lust, B., Harbert, W., & Martohardjono, G. (in preparation). On the language faculty and learnability theory. Intensional and extensional principles in the representation and acquisition of binding domains.

Kaufman, D. (1988). Grammatical and cognitive interactions in the study of children's knowledge of binding theory and reference relations. Unpublished Ph.D. dissertation, Temple University, Philadelphia.

Kaufman, D. (1994). Grammatical or pragmatic: Will the real Principle B please stand? In B. Lust, G. Hermon, & J. Kornfilt (Eds.), *Syntactic theory and first language acquisition: Cross-linguistic perspectives. Volume 2. Binding, dependencies and learnability.* Hillsdale, NJ: Erlbaum.

Kornfilt, J. (1994). Some remarks on the interaction of case and word order in Turkish: Implications for acquisition. In B. Lust, M. Suñer, & J. Whitman (Eds.), pp. 159–170.

Koster, C. (1994). Problems with pronoun acquisition. In B. Lust, G. Hermon, & J. Kornfilt (Eds.), *Syntactic theory and first language acquisition: Cross-linguistic perspectives. Volume 2. Binding, dependencies and learnability.* Hillsdale, NJ: Erlbaum.

Koster, J. (1978). *Locality principles in syntax.* Dordrecht: Foris.

Landau, B., & Gleitman, L. (1985). *Language and experience.* Cambridge, MA: Harvard University Press.

Lasnik, H., & Crain, S. (1985). On the acquisition of pronominal reference. *Lingua, 65,* 135–154.
Lebeaux, D. (1990). The grammatical nature of the acquisition sequence: Adjoin-A and the formation of relative clauses. In L. Frazier & J. deVilliers (Eds.), *Language processing and language acquisition* (pp. 13–82). Dordrecht: Kluwer Academic.
Lee, K-O. (1991). On the first language acquisition of relative clauses in Korean: The universal structure of COMP. Korea: Hanshin Publishing.
Lee, K-O., Lust, B., & Whitman, J. (1990). On functional categories in Korean: A study of the first language acquisition of Korean relative clauses. In E-J. Baek (Ed.), *Papers from the Seventh International Conference on Korean Linguistics* (pp. 312–333). University of Toronto Press.
Lenneberg, E. H. (1967). *Biological foundations of language development.* New York: Wiley.
Levy, Y. (1983). It's frogs all the way down. *Cognition, 15,* 75–93.
Lust, B. (1977). Conjunction reduction in child language. *Journal of Child Language, 4*(2), 257–297.
Lust, B. (1981). Constraint on anaphora in early child language: A prediction for a universal. In S. Tavakolian (Ed.), *Linguistic theory and first language acquisition.* Cambridge, MA: MIT.
Lust, B. (1983). On the notion "Principal Branching Direction": A parameter of universal grammar. In Y. Otsu, H. VanRiemsdijk, K. Inoue, A. Kamio & N. Kawasaki (Eds.), *Studies in Generative Grammar and Language Acquisition,* Tokyo Gakugei University, Japan.
Lust, B. (Ed.). (1986). *Studies in the Acquisition of Anaphora. Volume I. Defining the Constraints.* Dordrecht: Reidel Press.
Lust, B. (Ed.). (1987). *Studies in the Acquisition of Anaphora. Volume 2. Applying the Constraints.* Dordrecht: Reidel Press.
Lust, B. (1994). Functional projection of CP and phrase structure parameterization: An argument for the strong continuity hypothesis. In B. Lust, J. Whitman, & M. Suñer (Eds.), *Cross linguistic perspectives. Volume I: Heads, projections, and learnability* (pp. 85–118). Hillsdale, NJ: Erlbaum.
Lust, B. (in preparation). *Universal grammar and the initial state: Cross-linguistic studies of directionality.* Bradford Books/MIT Press.
Lust, B., Barbier, I., Boser, K., Foley, C., Kapur, S., Nuñez del Prado, Z., Suñer, M., & Whitman, J. (1994). General introduction: Syntactic theory and first language acquisition: Cross-linguistic perspectives. In B. Lust, M. Suñer, and J. Whitman (Eds.), *Syntactic theory and first language acquisition: Cross-linguistic perspectives.* Hillsdale, NJ: Erlbaum.
Lust, B., & Chien, Y-C. (1984). The structure of coordination in first language acquisition of Chinese. *Cognition, 17,* 49–83.
Lust, B., Chien, Y-C., Chiang, C-P., & Eisele, J. (1996). Chinese pronominals in universal grammar: A study of linear precedence and command in Chinese and English children's first language acquisition. *Journal of East Asian Linguistics, 5,* 1–47.
Lust, B., Chien, Y-C., & Flynn, S. (1987). What children know: Comparison of experimental methods for the study of first language acquisition. In B. Lust (Ed.), *Studies in the acquisition of anaphora: Volume 2. Applying the constraints* (pp. 271–356). Dordrecht: Reidel Press.
Lust, B., & Clifford, T. (1986). The 3-D study: Effects of depths, distance, and directionality on children's acquisition of anaphora. In B. Lust (Ed.), pp. 203–244.

Lust, B., & Eisele, J. (1991). On the acquisition of syntax in Tamil: A comment on Garman (1974). *Journal of Child Language, 18,* 215–226.

Lust, B., Flynn, S., Chien, Y-C., & Clifford, T. (1980). Coordination: The role of syntactic, pragmatic and processing factors in first language acquisition. *Papers and Reports on Child Language Development, 19,* 79–87.

Lust, B., Flynn, S., Foley, C., & Chien, Y-C. (1999). How do we know what children know? Problems and advances in establishing scientific methods for the study of language acquisition and linguistic theory. M. Ritchie & T. K. Bhatia (Eds.), *Handbook of child language acquisition.* San Diego, CA: Academic Press.

Lust, B., Hermon, G., & Kornfilt, J. (Eds.) (1994). *Syntactic theory and first language acquisition: Cross-linguistic perspectives. Volume 2. Binding, Dependencies and Learnability.* Hillsdale, NJ: Erlbaum.

Lust, B., Kornfilt, J., Hermon, G., Foley, C., Nuñez del Prado, Z., & Kapur, S. (1994). Introduction: Constraining binding, dependencies and learnability: Principles or parameters. In B. Lust, G. Hermon & J. Kornfilt (Eds.), *Syntactic theory and first language acquisition: Cross-linguistic perspectives. Volume 2. Binding, dependencies and learnability* (pp. 1–37). Hillsdale, NJ: Erlbaum.

Lust, B., Loveland, K., & Kornet, R. (1980). The development of anaphora in first language: Syntactic and pragmatic constraints. *Linguistic Analysis, 6*(2), 217–249.

Lust, B., Mangione, L., Chien, Y-C. (1984). The determination of empty categories in first language acquisition of Chinese. In W. Harbert (Ed.), *Cornell University Working Papers in Linguistics, 6,* Ithaca, NY, pp. 151–165.

Lust, B., & Martohardjono, G. (1987). *On the contribution of the binding theory module to a theory of the acquisition of anaphora.* Paper presented at BU conference. Boston, MA.

Lust, B., & Mazuka, R. (1989). Cross-linguistic studies of directionality in first language acquisition: The Japanese data (response to O'Grady, Suzuki-Wei and Cho 1986). *Journal of Child Language, 16,* 665–684.

Lust, B., Eisele, J., & Mazuka, R. (1992, June). The binding theory module: Evidence from first language acquisition for Principle C. *Language, 68*(2), 333–358.

Lust, B., Mazuka, R., Martohardjono, G., & Yoon, J.-M. (1989). On parameter setting in first language acquisition: The case of the binding theory. Paper presented at GLOW, Utrecht.

Lust, B., & Mervis, C. A. (1980). Coordination in the natural speech of young children. *Journal of Child Language, 7*(2), 279–304.

Lust, B., Solan, L., Flynn, S., Cross, C., & Schuetz, E. (1981). A comparison of null and pronominal anaphora in first language acquisition. In *Proceedings of the 11th Annual Meeting of the Northeastern Linguistic Society,* 175–186. [See also B. Lust (Ed.), 1986.]

Lust, B., Suñer, M., & Whitman, J. (Eds.), (1994). *Syntactic theory and first language acquisition: Cross-linguistic perspectives. Volume I. Heads, Projections and Learnability.* Hillsdale, NJ: Erlbaum.

Lust, B., Wakayama, T., Mazuka, R., Otani, K., & Snyder, W. (1985). *Confirmational factors in Japanese anaphora: Evidence from acquisition.* Paper presented at Linguistic Society of America, Seattle,, WA.

McDaniel, D., McKee, C., & Cairns, H. (Eds.). (1996). *Methods for assessing children's syntax.* Cambridge, MA: MIT Press.

McKee, C., & Emiliani, M. (1992). Il clitico: C'e ma non si vede. *Natural Language and Linguistic Theory, 10,* 415–437.

Marx, J. L. (1981). Genes that control development. *Science, 213,* 1485–1488.
Marx, J. L. (1987). Developmental control gene sequenced. *Science, 236,* 26–27.
Marx, J. L. (1988). Symposium focuses on genes in development. *Science, 239,* 1493–1494.
Maxfield, T., & Plunkett, B. (Eds.). (1991). *Papers in the Acquisition of WH.* UMOP Special Edition, University of Massachusetts, Amherst.
Mazuka, R. (1998). *The Development of Language Processing Strategies.* Mahwah, NJ: LEA.
Mazuka, R. (1996). Can a grammatical parameter be set before the first word?: Prosodic contributions to early setting of a grammatical parameter. In J. Morgan & K. Demuth (Eds.), *Signal to syntax.* NJ: LEA. 313–330.
Mazuka, R., & Lust, B. (1994). When is an anaphor not an anaphor. A study of Japanese "zibun." In B. Lust, J. Kornfilt, & G. Hermon (Eds.), *Syntactic theory and first language acquisition: Cross linguistic perspectives. Volume II: Binding, dependencies, and learnability* (pp. 145–175). Hillsdale, NJ: Erlbaum.
Mazuka, R., Lust, B., Snyder, W., & Wakayama, T. (1995). Null subject grammar and phrase structures in early syntax acquisition: A cross-linguistic study of Japanese and English. In C. Jakubowicz (Ed.), *Recherches Linguistiques de Vincennes.* France, Vincennes, *24,* 55–81.
Mazuka, R., Lust, B., Wakayama, T., & Snyder, W. (1986). Distinguishing effects of parameters in early syntax acquisition: A cross-linguistic study of Japanese and English. In Stanford University *Papers and Reports on Child Language Development,* 73–82.
Mehler, J., and Christophe, A. (1995). Maturation and learning of language in the first year of life. In M. Gazzaniga (Ed.) *The Cognitive Neurosciences,* (pp. 943–954). Cambridge, MA: MIT Press.
Mills, D., Coffey-Corine, S., & Neville, H. (1993). Language acquisition and cerebral specialization in 20-mo-old infants. *Journal of Cognitive Neuroscience* 5(3).
Morgan, J., & Demuth, K. (1996). *Signal to syntax.* Mahwah, NJ: LEA.
Neville, H., Mills, D., & Lawson, D. (1992). Fractionating language: Different neural subsystems with different sensitive periods. *Cerebral Cortex, 2,* 224–258.
Newport, E., Gleitman, H., & Gleitman, L. (1978). Mother, I'd rather do it myself: Some effects and noneffects of maternal speech style. In C. Snow & D. Ferguson (Eds.), *Talking to children.* Cambridge, England: Cambridge University Press (pp. 109–150).
Nieddu, P. (1997). The Object Agreement rule in *Passato Prossimo* of Young Italian Children. In *CUWPL 15,* papers on Language Acquisition (pp. 141–159). S. Somashekar et al. (Eds.).
Nuñez del Prado, Z., Foley, C., & Lust, B. (1993). The significance of CP to the pro-drop parameter: An experimental study of Spanish-English comparison. In E. Clark (Ed.), *The Proceedings of the Twenty-fifth Child Language Research Forum, 25,* 146–157. Stanford University, CSLI.
Nuñez del Prado, Z., Foley, C., Proman, R., & Lust, B. (1994). Subordinate CP and pro-drop: Evidence for Degree-n learnability from an experimental study of Spanish and English acquisition. In M. Gonzalez (Ed.), *Proceedings of NELS, 24,* 443–460.
Nuñez del Prado, Z., Foley, C., Proman, R., & Lust, B. (1997). Subordinate CP and pro-drop: Evidence for degree-n learnability. In S. Somashekar et al. (Eds.), *Cornell working papers in linguistics, 15,* 141–159.
Oshima, S., & Lust, B. (1997). Remarks on Anaphora in Japanese Adverbial clauses. In S. Somashekar et al. (Eds.). *CUWPL. 15,* 88–100.

Packard, J. (1982). *The acquisition of modified nominals in Mandarin Chinese.* Unpublished master's thesis, Cornell University.

Packard, J. (1987). The first language acquisition of prenominal modification with "de" in Mandarin. *Journal of Chinese Linguistics,* 31–53.

Padilla Rivera, J. (1990). *On the Definition of Binding Domains.* Dordrecht: Kluwer.

Parkinson, D. (In preparation). *The acquisition of morphology in Inuktitut: Theoretical issues and empirical evidence.* Unpublished doctoral dissertation, Cornell University.

Penner, Z. (1994). Asking questions without CPs? In T. Hoekstra & B. Schwartz (Eds.), *Language acquisition studies in generative grammar* (pp. 177–212). Amsterdam/Philadelphia: John Benjamin Publishing.

Piatelli-Palmarini, M. (Ed.). (1980). *The Chomsky-Piaget Debate.* Cambridge, MA: Harvard University Press.

Pinker, S., Lebeaux, D., & Frost, L. (1987). Productivity and constraints in the acquisition of the passive. *Cognition, 26,* 195–267.

Pizzuto, E., & Casselli, M. C. (1992). The acquisition of Italian morphology: Implication for models of language development. *Journal of Child Language, 19,* 491–557.

Pye, C. (1983). Mayan telegraphese. *Language, 59*(3), 583–604.

Pye, C., & Quixtan Poz, P. (1988). Precocious passives (and antipassives) in Quiche Mayan. *PRCLD.* Stanford University, pp. 71–80.

Radford, A. (1990). *Syntactic theory and the acquisition of English syntax.* Oxford: Basil Blackwell.

Radford, A. (1994a). The nature of children's initial clauses. Unpublished manuscript, Essex University, GB.

Radford, A. (1994b). Tense and agreement variability in child grammars of English. In B. Lust, M. Suñer, & J. Whitman (Eds.), *Syntactic theory and first language acquisition. Volume 1. Heads, projections and learnability.* Hillsdale, NJ: LEA.

Raghavendra, P., & Leonard, L. B. (1989). The acquisition of agglutinating languages: Converging evidence from Tamil. *Journal of Child Language, 16,* 313–322.

Roeper, T., & Weissenborn, J. (1990). How to make parameters work. In L. Frazier & J. deVilliers (Eds.), *Language processing and language acquisition* (pp. 147–162). Dordrecht: Kluwer.

Santelmann, L. (1993). *Wh-question formation in early Swedish: An argument for CP and operator knowledge.* Unpublished manuscript, Cornell University. Paper presented at BU child language conference, Boston.

Santelmann, L. (1995). *The acquisition of verb second grammar in Swedish: WH-questions, topics and verb-raising.* Unpublished doctoral dissertation, Cornell University.

Schmeck, H. M., Jr. (1988). Scientists decipher code that governs life and death of cells. *New York Times,* April 5.

Shipley, E., Smith, C., & Gleitman, L. (1969). A study in the acquisition of language: Free responses to commands. *Language, 45*(2), pp. 347–370.

Smith, N., & Tsimpli, I.-A. (1995). *The Mind of a Savant.* Cambridge: Blackwell.

Somashekar, S. (1995). Indian children's acquisition of pronominals in Hindi 'jab' clauses: Experimental study of comprehension. Unpublished master's thesis. Cornell University, Ithaca, NY.

Somashekar, S. (1998).

Somashekar, S., Yamakoshi, K., Blume, M., & Foley, C. (Eds.). (1997). Cornell Working

Papers in Linguistics, *15. Papers on Language Acquisition,* Ithaca, NY: Cornell University.

Stromswald, K. (1990). *Learnability and the acquisition of auxiliaries.* Unpublished Ph.D. dissertation, MIT.

Tsimpli, I-M. (1991). Functional categories and maturation: The prefunctional stage of language acquisition. *Working Papers in Linguistics, 3,* 123–148. London: University College.

Valian, V. (1992). Categories of first syntax. *be, be-ing,* and nothingness. In J. Meisel (Ed.), *The acquisition of verb placement: Functional categories and V2 phenomena in language acquisition.* Dordrecht: Kluwer.

Varma, T. L. (1979). Stage one speech of a Hindi-speaking child. *Journal of Child Language, 6*(1), 167–174.

Volterra, V. (1976). A few remarks on the use of the past participle in child language. *Italian Linguistics, 2,* 149–157.

Wexler, K. (1992). Some issues in the growth of control. In R. Larson, S. Iatridou, U. Lahiri, & J. Higginbothan (Eds.), *Control and Grammar.* Dordrecht: Kluwer.

Whitman, J., Barbier, I., Boser, K., Kapur, S., Kornfilt, J., & Lust, B. (1994). Introduction: Constraining structural variation and the acquisition problem. In B. Lust, M. Suñer, & J. Whitman (Eds.), *Syntactic theory and first language acquisition: Cross-linguistic perspectives. Volume I. Heads, projections and learnability* (pp. 1–12). Hillsdale, NJ: Erlbaum.

Whitman, J., Lee, K-O., & Lust, B. (1991). Continuity of the principles of Universal Grammar in first language acquisition: The issue of functional categories. *Proceedings of the North Eastern Linguistics Society Annual Meeting, 21* (pp. 383–397). Amherst, MA: University of Massachusetts.

Yamada, J. (1990). *Laura. A case for the modularity of language.* Cambridge, MA: Bradford Books.

CHAPTER 5

THE ACQUISITION OF SYNTACTIC REPRESENTATIONS: A GENERAL NATIVIST APPROACH

William O'Grady

I. BACKGROUND

The study of language acquisition is oriented around the search for the acquisition device—the set of mental mechanisms that operate on experience to produce the body of linguistic knowledge that linguists call a grammar. Because the acquisition device cannot be studied directly, its properties must be inferred by investigating the type of data on which it operates and the type of cognitive system that it ultimately yields. A major result of this research strategy has been the discovery of what is often called the underdetermination problem: experience does not provide enough information to allow discovery of a language's grammar by any known process of learning. From this it is concluded that the information needed to close the gap between the child's experience and the adult grammar must be supplied genetically in the form of inborn knowledge.

There is little controversy in contemporary linguistics over the claim that the human mind is innately structured in a way that makes language acquisition possible. There is simply no other plausible explanation for why human beings—but not chimpanzees, dogs or rabbits—can acquire and use complex grammatical systems. Slobin (1985, p. 1158) observed:

> In one way or another, every modern approach to language acquisition deals with the fact that language is constructed anew by each child, making use of innate capacities of some sort, in interaction with experiences of the physical and social worlds.

As Chomsky (1975, p. 13) has remarked along similar lines, "every 'theory of learning' that is even worth considering incorporates an innateness hypothesis."

Despite this consensus, there is disagreement over the precise contribution of the genetic endowment to the language learning capacity. At least two different positions can be identified. On the one hand, there is the view—referred to here as *special nativism*—that the genetic endowment for language includes a set of inborn mechanisms that are specifically linguistic in character. The most familiar version of this view has been developed in the literature on government and binding (GB) theory, where it is claimed that the acquisition device includes universal grammar (UG), a system of linguistic categories and principles that is shared in some form by all human languages.

In contrast, cognitive psychology offers many examples of what might be called *general nativism,* the view that the innate knowledge required for language acquisition is more general in nature and does not include actual linguistic categories, principles, or strategies. Probably the best known example of a general nativist approach to language was put forward by the late Swiss psychologist Jean Piaget, who held that "language is a product of intelligence"—that is, general cognitive mechanisms—rather than a special set of inborn linguistic principles such as UG (e.g., Inhelder, 1980; Piaget, 1980, p. 167). However, general nativism is not solely a Piagetian enterprise. Indeed, setting aside the little work that is expressly behaviorist or empiricist in orientation, most research on linguistic development that does not endorse the UG model of acquisition assumes some version of general nativism, at least implicitly.[1] Bates and MacWhinney (1988, p. 147) characterize this position as follows:

> The human capacity for language could be both innate and species-specific, and yet involve no mechanisms that evolved specifically and uniquely for language itself. Language could be a new machine constructed entirely out of old parts. The universal properties of grammar may be *indirectly innate,* based on interactions among innate categories and processes that are not specific to language.

Like special nativism, work on general nativism is motivated by the methodological goal that guides all scientific inquiry—the search for ever deeper, ever more general properties and principles. Within special nativism, the leading edge of research in recent years has focused on the search for principles that hold both across languages and across structures. Thus, the idea of a *passivization rule* is rejected in favor of the view that the properties of passive patterns follow from gen-

[1]It is unclear precisely how the work of Slobin (1973, 1982, 1985) and his colleagues should be categorized. The fact that the inborn operating principles that he has posited include reference to syntactic notions such as *word, morpheme,* and the like suggests that his theory is a variety of special nativism. However, Slovin has insisted that he wishes to remain neutral on the extent to which the acquisition device is "specifically tuned to the acquisition of language as opposed to other cognitive systems" (1985, p. 1158).

eral principles that apply to a wide variety of structure types in all languages. In a sense, the general nativist research program simply takes the quest for generality one step further by considering the possibility that the mechanisms responsible for language acquisition and use are not narrowly linguistic in character.

A significant problem with most work that adopts the general nativist perspective is that it either rejects or ignores a major premise of much contemporary research on syntactic development, namely that the end product of the *language acquisition* process is a generative grammar—an explicit system of categories and principles that can provide syntactic representations for all well formed sentences of a language. As a consequence, this work has simply not addressed the central concerns of most syntacticians who take an interest in linguistic development; apart from some discussion of lexical categories (see Section III.C), it has made few proposals about how the generative grammar underlying adult linguistic competence is acquired.

In contrast, the version of general nativism that I have advocated in earlier work (e.g., O'Grady, 1987, 1991) and that I will outline here adopts the standard view that the formation and production of sentences by adult speakers of a language requires a grammar (in addition to other cognitive systems) and that this grammar consists of categories and principles whose emergence must be the central concern of language acquisition research.

In earlier work on general nativism, I vacillated somewhat over precisely what type of grammatical mechanisms are appropriate for this approach to language acquisition. In fact, two competing views are compatible with general nativism (see, e.g., O'Grady, 1987, p. 181): the very strong view that the categories and principles needed for language acquisition are all independently attested outside of language and the weaker view that these categories and principles are not grammatical (i.e., *syntactic*) in the conventional sense. Both views entail that no innate grammatical system exists (that is, no UG), but only the latter leaves open the possibility that linguistic development might make use of nonsyntactic concepts or mechanisms that are not manifested outside of language. I currently believe that the latter view is more plausible (a possibility that I acknowledged in earlier work as well—see, e.g., O'Grady, 1987, p. 193). Although some components of the acquisition device (e.g., those in the computational module described later) are apparently manifested outside the language faculty, some are arguably peculiar to language (for example, many of the notions found in the conceptual module, as will be discussed further). Crucially, however, the acquisition device does not include conventional syntactic notions such as noun or verb or constraints such as Principle A or the Subjacency Condition.

The purpose of this chapter is to outline in some detail a specific proposal concerning a *general nativist* acquisition device, the type of experience on which it operates, and the type of grammar that it yields. To this end, I will begin my discussion by outlining some basic assumptions about the nature of the grammar that the acquisition device must construct and the character of the experience to which it has access. I will then outline the acquisition device that I propose, exploring the nature and status of its various components. Finally, I will examine the way in which this acquisition device can ensure the emergence of a grammar capable of forming the type of syntactic representations appropriate for human language.

II. SOME ASSUMPTIONS ABOUT THE ACQUISITION PROCESS

I adopt the view (assumed at least implicitly by virtually all researchers) that the acquisition device is a function from experience of a particular sort to a grammar of a particular sort. Put another way, the acquisition device is the bridge between children's linguistic experience and the adult grammar that they must ultimately master.

Although the acquisition device cannot be observed directly, the relationship depicted in Figure 5.1 suggests an obvious research strategy: By investigating the properties of experience (the input to the acquisition device) and the nature of the adult grammar (its output), it should be possible to draw significant conclusions about the content and functioning of the acquisition device itself. Our first step, then, must be to outline a set of plausible assumptions about the character of the adult grammar and of the linguistic experience relevant to its acquisition. This information will shed light on the precise extent of the underdetermination problem that the acquisition device must surmount.

A. Properties of the Grammar

The variety, complexity, and instability of contemporary syntactic theory is a familiar source of frustration for acquisition researchers. Although this problem cannot be resolved here, it can be mitigated somewhat by focusing on three components of grammar whose existence and general character is a matter of near consensus in the field.

The first and arguably most basic component of a grammar consists of a small inventory of syntactic categories (N, V, etc.) to which the words of a language are assigned. I will discuss the nature of these categories at greater length later. For now it suffices to assume that such categories exist and are relevant to sentence formation.

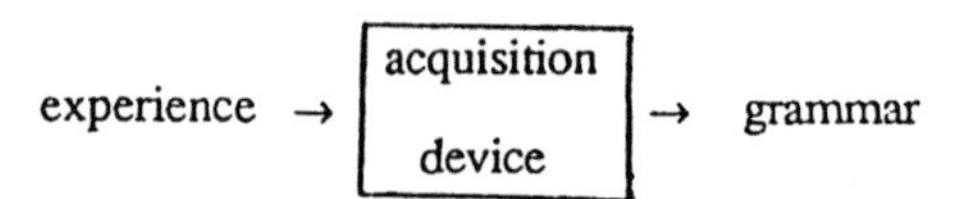

Figure 5.1. The acquisition process.

A second component of syntactic knowledge includes a set of mechanisms that combines words into larger phrases and ultimately sentences. Although these mechanisms are themselves finite, they have the capacity to form an unlimited number of sentences, including utterances that have not previously been heard or produced by the language user. In agreement with the widely held view, I assume that the sentences produced by these mechanisms have structures that meet three conditions: (a) every word and phrase is assigned to a syntactic category, (b) all branching is binary, and (c) there is a subject-object asymmetry in that a verb is structurally closer to its direct object than to its subject. The syntactic representation in (1) exemplifies a structure that meets these conditions. (The symbol X takes the place of the various category labels.)

(1)

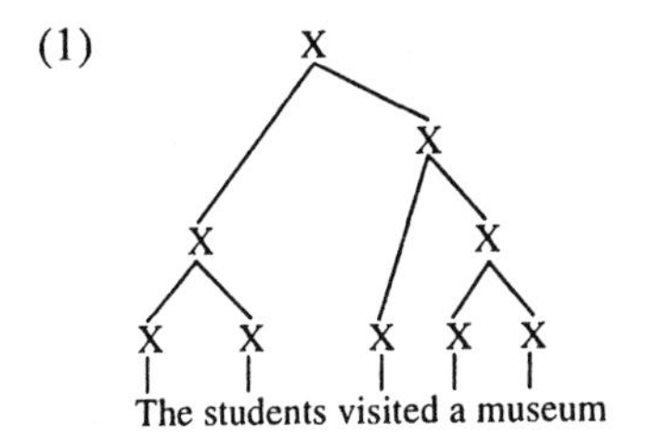

The third and final component of syntactic knowledge assumed here consists of the principles that regulate phenomena such as pronoun interpretation (the binding principles) and the relationship between a gap and the displaced element with which it is associated (island constraints). The precise nature of these principles is the subject of ongoing debate, but this fact need not concern us here. For now, it suffices to note that the principles in question apparently make reference to categorial and configurational features of syntactic structure. It therefore becomes doubly important for the acquisition device to uncover the mechanisms that build syntactic representations satisfying the conditions outlined previously.

What can we conclude from all of this? At the very least, the syntactic system produced by the acquisition device can form abstract representations whose component parts belong to categories of a particular type, are arranged with respect to each other in a particular manner, and are compatible with various structure-sensitive constraints on phenomena such as pronoun interpretation and gap placement. We must now ask how much information, if any, experience provides about these particular syntactic properties.

B. The Nature of Experience

The widely accepted view, also adopted here, is that the experience relevant to language acquisition does not include systematic feedback about the status of sentences produced by the language learner or any information about the ungrammaticality of hypothetical sentences (negative data). Rather, the acquisition device must operate solely on so-called positive data—sentences used by other speakers of the language, subject only to the following condition (similar formulations have been put forward by Gleitman, 1981, p. 115; Macnamara, 1972; Pinker, 1984, p. 29; and Wexler & Culicover, 1980, p. 78; among others):

(2) **The Interpretability Requirement**
The acquisition device requires exposure to utterances whose meaning can be independently determined.

The Interpretability Requirement ensures that the acquisition device receives information about the relationship between form and meaning in the language to which it is exposed. Without such information (e.g., if a child heard language only over the radio), it would obviously be impossible to learn even the most rudimentary features of a language's grammar.

For the Interpretability Requirement to be satisfied, two conditions must be met. First, language learners must have at least a rudimentary vocabulary of content words (e.g., nouns and verbs) before the process of actual syntactic development begins. Precisely how this happens need not concern us here, but the relevant learning presumably takes place during the one-word stage, which is marked by the development of words naming basic objects, actions, and properties in the child's environment.

Second, sentences consisting of these previously learned words must be encountered in contexts in which their propositional meaning can be established without knowledge of the language's syntactic rules. Thus, to take a concrete example, we must assume that a child who already knows the meaning of words such as *dog, cat,* and *chase* is exposed to a sentence such as *The dog is chasing a cat* in a context where it is clear that the dog is the pursuer and the cat is pursued. There is good reason to think that this condition is satisfied, thanks to a practice that is common in adult speech to children. As Snow (1977, p. 41) noted, this speech is largely limited to discussion of "what the child can see and hear, what he has just experienced or is just about to experience, what he might possibly want to know about the current situation. . ." (See also Wexler & Culicover, 1980, p. 79.)

In sum, I assume that the experience crucial to the operation of the acquisition device (at least in the early stages of syntactic development) is an utterance-meaning pair, consisting of a phonetic form (the utterance) and a corresponding semantic representation depicting the meaning of its components parts and their relationship to each other, perhaps in association with a representation of the accompanying real-world context. To illustrate more precisely the use to which this sort of information is put by the acquisition device, it is necessary to have a system of notation capable of representing those aspects of meaning relevant to grammatical development. For expository purposes, I will follow Pinker (1984) in using a modified version of the notation employed within lexical-functional gram-

The sentence's form:	The sentence's meaning:	
[the dog is chasing a cat]	PREDICATE	CHASE (agent, theme)
	TENSE	present
	ASPECT	progressive
	AGENT	DOG [+ def]
	THEME	CAT [- def]

CONTEXT IN WHICH THE CHILD IS EXPOSED TO THE SENTENCE

Figure 5.2. An utterance meeting the interpretability requirement.

mar (e.g., Bresnan, 1982) for representing the relationship between a predicate, its arguments, and modifiers, as well as grammatically relevant semantic features such as tense, aspect, definiteness, number, gender, and so forth. For purposes of illustration, I assume that the phonetic string in Figure 5.2 has been successfully segmented. I also assume that semantic concepts can be matched with words in a fairly direct fashion and that children and caregivers perceive the situation being described in the same way (Gleitman, 1981, pp. 15–116; Gleitman & Wanner, 1982, pp. 10, 12). (Such assumptions are commonplace in the literature on learnability and syntax.) The first line of the semantic representation contains the predicate corresponding to the verb *chase* as well as information about the two arguments that it takes (an agent and a theme). The next two lines specify the tense and aspect of the sentence, whereas the last two lines identify the verb's two arguments and indicate their status with respect to the semantic feature of *definiteness*.

This example helps make precise the extent of the underdetermination problem. As Figure 5.2 illustrates, the experience available to the acquisition device contains no information about syntactic categories (N, V, etc.) or their organization into larger phrases exhibiting binary branching and a subject-object asymmetry. Yet virtually all contemporary syntactic theories agree that the adult grammar forms sentence structures that include word- and phrase-level syntactic categories and that higher-level constraints (such as those on binding and bounding) operate on representations with a binary architecture. This apparent paradox illustrates the degree to which experience can be inadequate as a source of information about the grammar that the acquisition device must construct.

III. THE LEARNABILITY PROBLEM RECONSIDERED

This brings us to the question that is central to the entire field of language acquisition research: How can the grammar for the adult language be identified on the basis of data that contain no direct information about any of its major components? The answer offered by special nativism is the familiar proposal that the acquisition device must include an inborn UG (see Table 5.1) whose component systems include an inventory of syntactic categories (from which each language can draw at least a subset), an X-bar schema that determines the architecture of phrase

TABLE 5.1

The Special Nativist Approach: Some Components of Universal Grammar (based on Chomsky, 1981, 1986)

The Inventory of Syntactic Categories

Lexical Categories	Functional Categories
Noun (N)	Determiner (Det)
Verb (V)	Inflection (Infl)
Adjective (A)	Complementizer (Comp)
Preposition (P)	

The X-Bar Schema

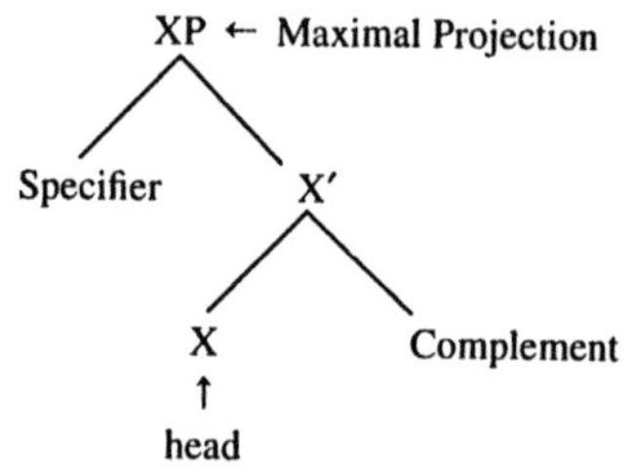

XP ← Maximal Projection

Specifier X′

X Complement

↑

head

Some Regulatory Principles

(3) **Principle A**
A reflexive pronoun must be bound in its governing category.

(4) **Principle B**
A nonreflexive pronoun must be free in its governing category.

(5) **The Empty Category Principle**
An empty category (a "gap") must be properly governed.

structure (word order aside), and the principles that regulate pronoun interpretation, gap placement, and the like.

To assimilate the internal structure of sentence-sized units to the X-bar schema, a certain amount of abstraction is required. As proposed by Chomsky (1986), it is often assumed that sentences take as their head the morpheme-carrying information about tense. Although this morpheme frequently corresponds to an inflectional affix and is therefore dubbed *I* (for inflection), it can also be a model auxiliary verb such as *will, can, may,* and so on. As depicted in (6), the category I takes VP as its complement and the subject of the sentence as its specifier. (A far more abstract representation is assumed in recent work within the minimalist program—e.g., Chomsky 1993.)

(6)

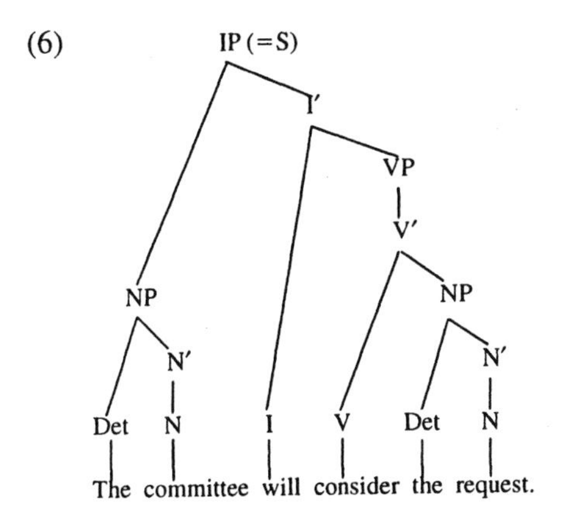

If the type of grammar assumed by proponents of universal grammar is right (i.e., if something like the GB view of syntax is correct), special nativism is inevitable. The syntactic categories, representations, and principles assumed by this theory are simply too far removed from experience to be learnable. If they do in fact exist, they must be supplied by an innate universal grammar, consistent with the central thesis of special nativism.

It seems unlikely that future research will uncover some hitherto unnoticed type of experience that could erase the underdetermination problem. This leaves proponents of general nativism relatively little room to maneuver. Given that the acquisition device cannot (by hypothesis) contain inborn syntactic principles and given that the traditional characterization of experience is correct, work within general nativism must focus on the grammar that results from the language acquisition process. In particular, it must show that this cognitive system is fundamentally different from the GB-type grammar that so evidently requires an inborn UG to ensure its learnability. This is obviously a daunting challenge, and very little work addresses it directly. In what follows, I will extend and refine proposals that have been made in this regard by O'Grady (1987, 1991). (A more complete outline of these proposals can be found in O'Grady, 1997.)

A. A Simple Categorial Grammar

For the purposes of illustration, I will present a simple combinatorial system influenced by traditional and recent work in categorial grammar (see e.g., Bach, 1988; Bar-Hillel, 1953; Dowty, 1982) as well as head-driven phrase structure grammar (e.g., Pollard, 1988). Because of limitations on space, I will focus on the formation of relatively simple sentence structures consisting of a verb and one or more grammatical terms (subject, direct object), ignoring for now modifiers such as adverbs and adjectives. Subsequent sections of the chapter will deal with how the various components of the syntactic system I propose can be acquired.

The two most important features of the sentence-building system I propose are both shared by categorial grammar in general. First, the system builds structure from the bottom up, combining elements to create phrases and ultimately a sentence. Second, a distinction is made between *functor* categories, which require arguments, and *basic* categories, which do not exhibit such argument dependencies. Categories of the latter type include simple nouns (e.g., *Harry* or *car*) and Ss. Table 5.2 introduces some verbal functors; the symbol Na stands for nominal bearing an agent role and Nt for nominal bearing a theme role. (The use of thematic role labels as a shorthand to identify arguments constitutes a departure from mainstream categorial grammar.)

Within this type of system, sentence formation is driven by semantic considerations. In particular, it is assumed that as functor categories combine with arguments of the appropriate number and type, their meanings are amalgamated to form the types of complex meanings conveyed by sentences. The structure in (7) illustrates the syntactic representation that is formed when the intransitive verb *leave* combines with its agent argument.

(7) S (=$V^{<0>}$)

N $V^{<Na>}$

Harry left

This syntactic representation differs from more familiar syntactic representations in two major respects. First, V (not inflection) is taken to be head of S, which is treated simply as a verbal category with no argument dependencies (i.e., S = $V^{<0>}$, as in Keenan & Timberlake, 1988, p. 269); versions of this claim are widely accepted in syntactic frameworks other than GB theory. Second, as in most work in categorial grammar, constituents are marked for category membership, but not

TABLE 5.2

Some Verbal Functors and Their Properties

Category	Dependencies	Symbol	Examples
Unergative Intransitive V	One agent argument	$V^{\langle Na \rangle}$	Run, walk, dance
Unaccusative Intransitive V	One theme argument	$V^{\langle Nt \rangle}$	Fall, faint, die
Transitive V	One agent argument and one theme argument	$V^{\langle Na,Nt \rangle}$	Touch, wash, hit
. . .			

for bar-level; thus, N stands for both noun and noun phrase; V stands for both verb and verb phrase; and so on.[2]

Since the combinatorial operation responsible for sentence formation applies to pairs of elements (that is, a functor and one argument), no more than one dependency can be satisfied at a time. This raises two questions: (a) Which of a transitive verb's two arguments should it combine with first? and (b) What happens to the other argument? The answer to the first question presupposes the existence of an argument hierarchy that regulates the order in which a verbal functor should combine with its arguments (for example, Bresnan & Moshi, 1990; Dowty, 1982; Grimshaw & Mester, 1988; Larson, 1988; Li, 1990). For our purposes, the hierarchy in (8), which stipulates the relative combinatorial order for agents and themes, will suffice.

(8) **The Argument Hierarchy**

theme *first*

. . . ↓

agent *last*

Turning now to the second question, any dependencies that remain after a combinatorial operation has taken place are passed up to the resulting phrase in accordance with the following principle:

(9) **The Inheritance Principle**

Unsatisfied dependencies are inherited upward.

The following example illustrates how this works. (A dotted line represents inheritance.)

[2]On this view, phenomena that are treated in terms of bar level in government and binding theory have to be analyzed in an entirely different way. Space does not permit a discussion of these matters here, but see Kornai and Pullum (1990), Speas (1990), and O'Grady (1989) for some discussions and suggestions.

(10)

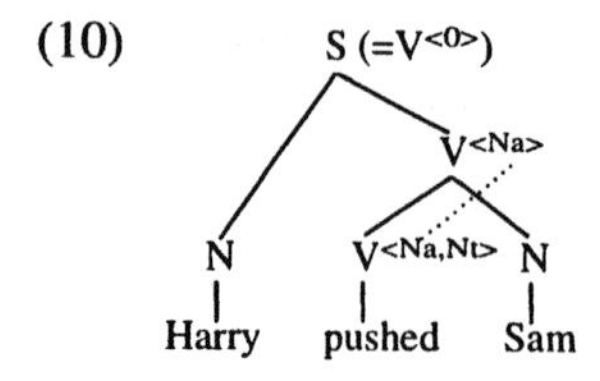

In (10), the transitive verb *push* combines first with the N *Sam.* This satisfies its dependency on a theme argument, leaving the dependency on an agent argument to be inherited by the phrase *pushed Sam.* Combination with the missing argument (*Harry*) then gives S ($V^{<0>}$), the terminal category that results from having satisfied all the dependencies associated with a verbal functor.

The sentence building system presented to this point is neutral with respect to word order. It will just as easily form sentences in which both arguments precede the verb as sentences in which the agent argument occurs preverbally and the theme argument postverbally. To impose the required restrictions, it is assumed that functor categories are *directional* in the sense that they include information not only about the type of category with which they must combine but also about its location. In English, transitive verbs ($V^{<x,y>}$) look rightward for the argument with which they must combine whereas intransitive verbal categories ($V^{<x>}$) look leftward. This ensures that in a simple structure such is (7), the (intransitive) verb will follow rather than precede its subject argument. It also explains why the transitive verb *push* in (10) precedes its theme argument, whereas the resulting phrase *pushed Sam* (an intransitive verbal category because it exhibits a single unsatisfied argument dependency) follows the argument with which it combines.

The proposed sentence building system can easily be extended in other ways as well. For example, the ability to form multiclausal sentences can be introduced by assuming that verbs such as *know, believe,* and the like take an S rather than an N as their theme complement (i.e., they are categories of the type $V^{<Na,St>}$). This gives syntactic representations such as the following:

(11)

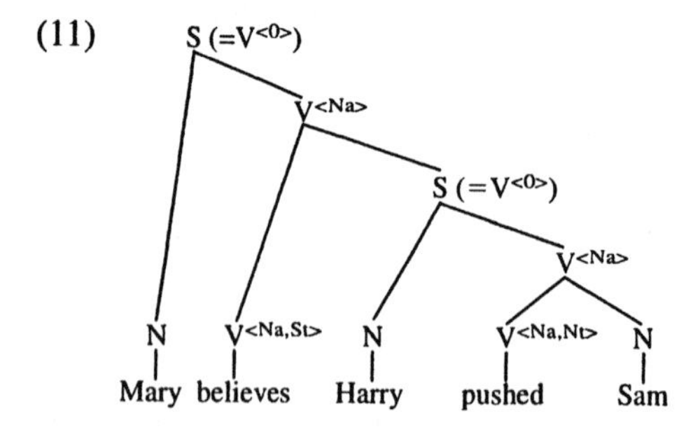

Although sketched only in outline, the system of sentence formation that I propose meets the basic requirements for syntactic representations laid down in Section II.A: Each word and phrase is assigned to a syntactic category, all branching is binary, and the direct object is structurally closer to the verb than is the subject. These structures are thus suitable for the formulation of whatever additional principles might be required to regulate phenomena such as pronoun interpretation or gap placement.

Taking this very simple system as our starting point, we can now begin to consider the nature of the acquisition device that is needed to ensure the appropriate syntactic development in response to experience.

B. The Acquisition Device

The goal of the general nativist research program is to provide an account of syntactic development that does not require inborn *syntactic* categories or principles. On this view, then, the inborn acquisition device must consist only of mechanisms that are not inherently linguistic in character; it cannot include UG. As conceived in O'Grady (1991, 1997), the acquisition device includes several independent modules whose interaction with each other and with experience ultimately gives a grammar (see Table 5.3). Before considering the interaction of these modules, it is first necessary to investigate their individual content and function.

The Perceptual Module

As its name suggests, the perceptual module is concerned with the perception of speech. As such, it is responsible both for the analysis of the auditory distinctions underlying the phonemic contrasts of human language and for attention to the cues that facilitate the segmentation of speech into its component words and morphemes (see Peters, 1985, and Slobin, 1985, for further proposals and discussion).

It remains to be seen to what extent the inborn mechanisms of the perceptual module are specifically linguistic in character (Chomsky, 1980, p. 60; Miller, 1990). At least certain of the operating principles for speech perception proposed by Peters and Slobin are arguably applicable to nonlinguistic stimuli as well (for

TABLE 5.3

Organization of the General Nativist Acquisition Device

Module	Function
Perceptual	Provides a means of dealing with the auditory stimulus
Propositional	Provides a representation of propositional meaning
Conceptual	Provides an inventory of notions relevant to grammatical contrasts: singular-plural, definite-indefinite, past-nonpast, and so on
Computational	Provides the means to carry out combinatorial operations on functors and their arguments
Hypothesis formation	Provides the means to formulate and test hypotheses

example, sensitivity to loudness as well as to initial and final positioning). In addition, it has been noted that the ability to make certain types of auditory distinctions is shared by other species (e.g., chinchillas can make the distinction between /t/ and /d/—Kuhl & Miller, 1975), which suggests that it may not be specifically linguistic in character.

On the other hand, it is not difficult to imagine proposals about the perceptual module that would be inconsistent with a strong version of general nativism. For example, work on the perception of vowel formants, tones, or stress contours may establish the need for perceptual mechanisms that have no nonlinguistic basis. However, as my primary concern here is with sentence structure, I will not consider this possibility or its consequences further in this chapter.

The Propositional Module

A second component of the general nativist acquisition device provides a way to represent meaning in an inborn "language of thought" (for example, Braine, 1987; Fodor, 1975; Slobin, 1985, p. 1192). At the very least, this module must have the power to represent propositions in terms of an internal structure consisting of predicates, modifiers, and arguments bearing a variety of thematic roles. (Consistent with our earlier practice, the formalism used to depict semantic representations is borrowed from lexical-functional grammar.)

(12) *Harry studies astronomy.*

PREDICATE	STUDY (agent, theme)
AGENT	HARRY
THEME	ASTRONOMY

(13) *Fish swim.*

PREDICATE	SWIM (agent)
AGENT	FISH

Because these representations contain no syntactic labels or phrasal constituents, there is no reason to think that the mechanisms responsible for forming them include inborn *syntactic* knowledge. Rather, it is widely assumed that such representations reflect the inborn architecture of cognition that exists independent of language. This is true not only for the predicate concepts themselves, but also for the thematic role labels used to classify their arguments. For example, Jackendoff (1976, p. 149) proposed that the characterization of theta roles is nonlinguistic in nature, drawing on "the study of the innate conception of the physical world and the way in which conceptual structure generalizes to ever wider, more abstract domains." Emonds (1991, p. 423) went even further, suggesting that "theta roles are not part of syntax and are more likely properly associated with the cognitive referents of NPs, and assume significance only in a cognitive psychology for the most part shared by humans and other primates."

The Conceptual Module

A third component of the acquisition device is concerned with the basic notions in terms of which grammatical contrasts are formulated. Obvious examples of these notions include definite-indefinite (underlying the contrast between *the* and *a* in English), past-nonpast (for tense), singular-plural (for the category of number), and masculine-feminine-neuter (underlying the *he-she-it* distinction in the English pronoun system).

Working together, the conceptual and propositional modules provide language learners with a representation of sentence meaning (call it *semantic form*) that includes information about predicate-argument relations and about contrasts such as past-nonpast and definite-indefinite. The sample semantic representations for the two sentences given earlier can thus be revised as follows to include information about grammatical contrasts pertaining to tense and number:

(14) *Harry studies astronomy.*

PREDICATE	STUDY (agent, theme)
TENSE	present
AGENT	HARRY
	[singular]
THEME	ASTRONOMY
	[noncount]

(15) *Fish swim.*

PREDICATE	SWIM (agent)
TENSE	present
AGENT	FISH
	[plural]

At present, there is no definitive list of notions available to the acquisition device, although various proposals have been made—ranging from early work by Nida (1946, p. 166ff) to recent proposals in acquisition theory by Slobin (1985), Bowerman (1985), and Pinker (1989), among others. Although it is still not known whether the contrasts provided by the conceptual module are relevant to nonlinguistic cognitive activity (Pinker, 1989, p. 359, argued that they have little or no such relevance), it is at least clear that they involve something other than formal syntactic notions. They are therefore qualitatively different from the categories and principles that make up UG.

The Computational Module

Still another component of the general nativist acquisition device regulates the formation of structural representations by imposing certain requirements on the combinatorial operations that produce them. The computational module has at least the following three properties.

(16) **binarity:** Its operations apply to pairs of elements.
iterativity: Its operations can reapply without definite limit.
inheritability: Operations that cannot apply at one level are carried up to the next.

The binarity property ensures that syntactic representations are formed by combining pairs of elements, in accordance with the widely held view (e.g., Bach, 1988, p. 22; Kayne, 1983, p. 227n; Larson, 1988, p. 381). The inheritability and iterativity properties permit the inheritance of unsatisfied dependencies and the repeated application of the combinatorial operation needed to satisfy them. The resulting syntactic representations take on the familiar profile depicted in (17).

(17)

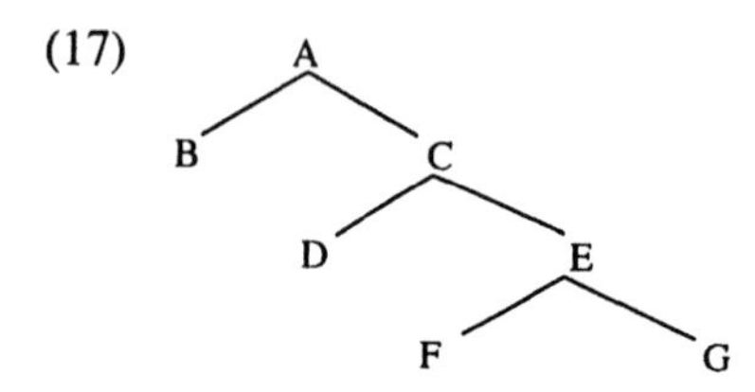

Binarity, inheritability, and iterativity are manifested in arithmetical computation as well. For example, no one calculates cubes in a single step. Rather, the cube of a number x is determined by multiplying x by x and then multiplying the product by x. Given binarity, these operations must take place in separate steps, with the second multiplication operation being inherited upward.[3]

(18)

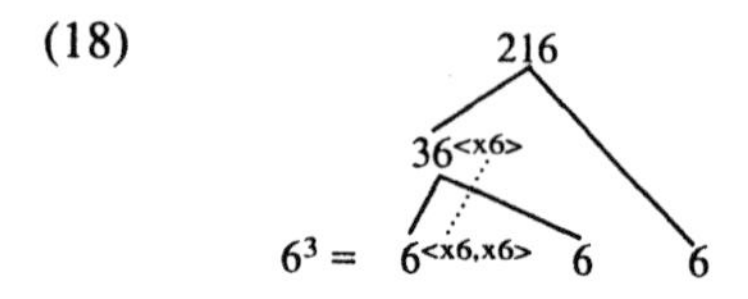

Of course, none of this is meant to imply that children are capable of doing arithmetic at the point when they start to combine words to form phrases.[4] Among other things, arithmetical ability requires an understanding of the notion of number, which is not required for sentence formation. The point here is simply that certain properties of the computational operations employed by language are not unique to that cognitive domain and are (eventually) manifested in other areas. (For a

[3]The *times 6* function is equivalent to the 'multiplication table' of traditional arithmetic (ensuring that $6 \times 2 = 12$, $6 \times 3 = 18$, and so on). It is created by combining the two-place function $\times$ with a number to create a new function that then takes a single additional number as its argument.

[4]Interestingly, though, recent work suggests that a rudimentary ability to add and subtract is in place as early as 5 months of age (Bryant, 1992; Wynn, 1992).

discussion of other similarities between language and arithmetic, see Bach, 1981, and Lenneberg, 1971).

The Hypothesis Formation Module

Finally, the acquisition device includes a module that is responsible for the actual learning of grammatical knowledge. I take learning to be a process of hypothesis formation and testing, consistent with the widely held view. As Pinker (1989, pp. 166–167) remarked: "Despite its many guises, learning can always be analyzed as a set of 'hypotheses' the organism is capable of entertaining and of a 'confirmation function' by which environmental input tells the organism which one to keep." (See also Fodor, 1975, p. 95.)

Hypotheses formation is constrained by the following law. (A similar constraint is embodied in the Limited Functions operating principle of Slobin, 1985, p. 1199, and the Subset Principle of Berwick, 1985, p. 37, and Wexler & Manzini, 1987.)

(19) **The Conservatism Law**
The acquisition device makes use of the available notions to construct the most conservative hypothesis consistent with experience.

The major advantage of the Conservatism Law is that it precludes many potentially uncorrectable overgeneralizations, such as those involving island constraints and binding principles. Consider for example the case of reflexive pronouns, as exemplified by the contrast between (20) and (21).

(20) **Reflexive Pronoun with a Subject Antecedent**
The boy saw himself in the mirror.

(21) **Reflexive Pronoun with a Genitive Antecedent**
*The boy's mother saw himself in the mirror.

The Conservatism Law prevents the acquisition device from reacting to sentences such as (20) by concluding that a reflexive pronoun can take an antecedent anywhere in the sentence. Rather, using whatever notions are relevant to the characterization of pronoun interpretation (a matter on which I do not take a position here), it concludes only that a particular type of NP can serve as antecedent (say, an argument in the same clause). This in turn prevents the grammar from licensing the anaphoric dependency in (21).

Are the components of the hypothesis formation module compatible with general nativism? Hypothesis formation itself is traditionally assumed to be available to nonlinguistic cognitive domains and is thus unproblematic. The generality of the Conservatism Law is less clear, though, and at least one commentator has suggested that the constraint it embodies is "probably specific to the acquisition of language" (Atkinson, 1992, p. 140), a possibility acknowledged by O'Grady (1987, p. 193). However, because the formulation of the Conservatism Law does

TABLE 5.4
Summary of the General Nativist Acquisition Device

Module	Sample Properties
Perceptual	Ends of stimuli are salient, stressed stimuli are salient, . . .
Propositional	Provides representation of propositional meaning in terms of predicates, arguments, and modifiers
Conceptual	Inventory of "grammaticizable" notions: singular-plural, definite-indefinite, past-nonpast, . . .
Computational	Binarity, iterativity, inheritability, . . .
Hypothesis formation	"Learning," Conservatism Law, . . .

not refer to or presuppose any inborn syntactic notions, it seems compatible with at least the spirit of general nativism.

In sum, the theory of general nativism being put forward here posits an inborn acquisition device consisting of the five modules outlined in Table 5.4. As an illustration of how this acquisition device works, I will consider the development of two components of the mature sentence formation system: the inventory of syntactic categories and the mechanisms that combine these categories to form hierarchically structured syntactic representations. (O'Grady, 1997, considers the ontogeny of a structure-sensitive constraint on reflexive pronoun interpretation.)

C. Syntactic Categories

Underlying the question of how the acquisition device identifies the inventory of syntactic categories relevant to human language is the deeper issue of what a syntactic category is. There are essentially two views in the linguistic literature. The first view, which we can call the *prime* theory, treats syntactic categories as formal primitives. (A variant of this view defines syntactic categories in terms of features such as $\pm$N and $\pm$V, which are themselves treated as formal primitives—see, for example, Chomsky, 1981, p. 48). Because primitives cannot be defined in terms of anything more basic, the prime-based theory implies that syntactic categories must be directly supplied to the language learner by the acquisition device. This in turn supports the special nativist view that the genetic endowment for language includes knowledge that is purely syntactic in character.

Contrasting with the prime-based theory is the *reductionist* view, which holds that syntactic categories can be reduced to a more basic set of notions. This is the option that has been explored in the general nativist literature, with at least three separate lines of inquiry being discernable.

First, there have been occasional attempts to reduce syntactic categories to semantic notions such as *action* for verbs, *attribute* for adjectives, and so on. (This sort of approach is to be distinguished from *semantic bootstrapping* (e.g., Pinker,

TABLE 5.5

A Semantic Characterization of Syntactic Categories (Schlesinger, 1982, p. 225)

Category	Corresponding Semantic Notion
Verb	Action
Adjective	Attribute
Noun	Agent or patient

1984), which treats syntactic categories as formal primitives but assigns them prototypical semantic realizations. Schlesinger (1982, 1988), whose work is probably the best example of semantic reductionism (see Table 5.5), tried to circumvent the obvious counterexamples (for example, nonactional verbs and nouns with abstract referents) by proposing that the semantic characterization of syntactic categories is extended (by a process he calls *semantic assimilation*) in response to distributional facts (see also Braine, 1992). Thus, he argued (1988, p. 125ff), words such as *find, see* and *remember* get interpreted as actions (hence, verbs) in part because of the formal similarity between the (SV0) patterns in which they occur and the patterns used to express prototypical agent-action-patient relations. However, this move seems to rob the action concept of any inherent content, thereby jeopardizing the reductionist program. Moreover, it fails to address Maratsos's (1982, 1988) observation that some adjectives (e.g., *helpful* and *quick*) seem more actionlike than some verbs (e.g., *belong* and *exist*) and that words with very similar meanings (e.g., *like* and *fond*) can belong to different syntactic categories. In principle, the acquisition mechanism assumed by Schlesinger could analyze *helpful* as a verb (because of its actional meaning) and then compound the error by applying semantic assimilation to formally similar words (*useful, doubtful,* and so forth), incorrectly adding them to the verb class.

A second type of theory seeks to reduce syntactic categories to distributional properties such as co-occurrence with a determiner or a plural suffix in the case of nouns and co-occurrence with tense in the case of verbs. Starosta (1988, pp. 27–28) presented one of the few contemporary theories of adult linguistic competence that endorses a purely distributional view of categories. A detailed proposal about the acquisition of distributionally defined syntactic categories (see Table 5.6) has been put forward by Maratsos and Chalkley (1981) and Maratsos (1982, 1988) but has met with various objections. One problem, noted by Pinker (1984, p. 49ff), is that it is not clear how the acquisition device selects the distributional properties needed to make the right categorial distinctions in a language. (For example, one would not want the acquisition device to attempt to categorize words on the basis of their initial phoneme, the color of the entities to which they refer, and the like.) Moreover, because many of the distributional properties used by Maratsos are language

TABLE 5.6

A Distributional Characterization of Syntactic Categories (for example, Maratsos, 1982; Maratsos & Chalkley, 1981)

Category	Sample Distributional Properties
N	Occurs in the frames _ *-s* [pl], *the* _
V	Occurs in the frames *don't* _, _ *-ed*[pst],_*-s*[prs]
...	

particular (e.g., occurrence with third person, singular *-s* or with *don't* in the case of English verbs), syntactic categories cannot be given universally valid definitions—an undesirable consequence in the eyes of many syntacticians.

Finally, some theories seek to analyze syntactic categories in terms of predicate-argument relations. This is probably the single most popular approach to syntactic categories in the literature compatible with general nativism. I adopted a variant of this idea in my earlier work (e.g., O'Grady, 1987, 1991), and somewhat similar proposals have been put forward independently by Braine (1987), Berman (1988), and Ninio (1988). The basic idea is simply that categories can be identified in terms of the number and type of arguments they take. For example, O'Grady (1987, 1991) has suggested that nominals take no 'bare' arguments (e.g., *arrival* in **the man arrival*), that intransitive verbs take one (*The man arrived*), transitive verbs take two (*The man brought a friend*), and so on (see Table 5.7). A number of problems undermine this sort of analysis. For one thing, some verbs take no arguments. The English verb *snow,* for example, occurs only with expletive *it* (cf. *It snowed* versus **The sky snowed*), which has no reference and therefore does not count as an argument in the conventional sense. (In some languages, *impersonal* verbs do not even occur with an expletive; Keenan & Timberlake, 1985, p. 422, offer Latin *curritur* "there is running" as an example of this.) Second, there are various contexts in English (and other languages) in which adjectives take NP arguments in the sort of subject-predicate pattern that is usually considered to be diagnostic of the verb class.

TABLE 5.7

A Predicate-Argument Characterization of Syntactic Categories

Category	Status with Respect to Predicate-Argument Contrast
N	Takes no bare arguments (but can serve as an argument itself)
Intransitive V	Takes one bare argument
Transitive V	Takes two bare arguments
...	

(22) a. With [John sick], someone must take over his position.
b. The searchers found [Harry asleep]
c. The committee considers [Sue unfit for the job].

Finally, there are patterns in languages such as Korean and Japanese in which a noun can take arguments of the same number and type as verbs (Tsujimura, 1992).

(23) [(John -i) enehak -ul [$_N$ yenkwu] cwung] . . . (Korean)
(John-Nom) linguistics-Ac research middle
"In the middle of John researching linguistics, . . ."

These and similar facts seriously undermine analyses of syntactic categories based on predicate-argument relations.

A New Proposal

Is there a plausible reductionist analysis of syntactic categories, or must general nativism be abandoned in the case of language's categorial inventory? In O'-Grady (1997), I propose a reductionist theory of syntactic categories that is influenced by all three of the approaches just described. The first step is to draw a sharp distinction between a word's syntactic category and its argument dependencies. Although the latter type of information influences a word's distribution (and therefore has a place in its lexical entry), it does not determine its syntactic category per se. Thus, *curritur* can be a verb in Latin even though it takes no arguments, and *yenkwu* can be a noun in Korean even though its argument dependencies resemble those of a transitive verb.

(24) a. *curritur:* $\mathrm{V}^{<0>}$
b. *yenkwu:* $\mathrm{N}^{<\mathrm{Na,Nt}>}$

It is also possible to accommodate the fact that English *sleep* and *sleepy* can have identical argument dependencies even though they belong to different categories.

(25) a. *sleep:* $\mathrm{V}^{<\mathrm{Nt}>}$
b. *sleepy:* $\mathrm{A}^{<\mathrm{Nt}>}$

What then is a syntactic category? In the theory that I propose, categories are characterized in terms of a set of inborn semantic notions that have direct distributional consequences. Unlike the sort of notions employed in more traditional work (e.g., *thing* and *action*), which are too restrictive and must eventually be expanded to the point of abandonment (see my earlier discussion of Schlesinger's proposal), the notions I use are if anything too broad and their precise boundaries must be stipulated with the help of appropriate distributional criteria. The proposal is probably easiest to illustrate for the V category, whose denotations I take to be instances of *events* in a sense that I will elaborate as I proceed.

I take the criterial property of events to be compatibility with the time-based contrasts encoded by tense or aspect. Thus, a distributional property (co-occurrence with whatever tense and aspect markers a language employs) indicates category membership but that distributional property is important for a semantic reason: Tense and aspect markers are relevant to the identification of the verb category because they are inherently (i.e., innately) linked to the inborn event concept to which the verb category is reduced.

This proposal has a number of advantages. First, all languages apparently express tense or aspect, albeit in different ways (some by affixes, some by free morphemes, some by suprasegmental modifications, and so on). The proposed definition of the verb class is thus a plausible universal, unlike distributional definitions formulated in terms of particular morphemes such as *-ing, not,* and so forth.

Second, by referring to tense and aspect in our definition, we dramatically limit the set of possible distributional properties that the acquisition device must consider in the course of categorizing a verb. Because compatibility with tense and aspect—inborn notions provided by the conceptual module—is taken to be the criterial feature of true events (and hence of verbhood), this is the only distributional property that the acquisition device needs to consider when identifying verbs.

Third, by not equating verbs with actions even as a prototypical correlation (in contrast both to Pinker's semantic bootstrapping proposal and Schlesinger's semantic reductionism), we avoid the prediction that the first verbs to appear during linguistic development should refer to actions. As noted by Maratsos (1988, p. 36), nonactional verbs such as *need, want, know, like* and *sleep* are among the first verbs to be acquired in English. (Yamashita, 1990, reports that *inai*—to not exist—was one of the first verbs acquired by the 2-year old Japanese child she studied.)

Turning now to the noun class, I propose that its members have denotations that can be *individuated*—that is, distinguished in a particular way from other potential referents of the same type. Except for proper names (*Henry, Tokyo*), which are inherently individuating, the most common sign of individuation in the sense intended here is occurrence with morphemes marking specificity/definiteness (e.g., definite articles or their equivalent) or deicticity (such as English *this* and *that*). Thus, when I say *he read the/that book,* I am distinguishing a particular book from other potential referents of that NP. As the examples in (26) help show, compatibility with markers of specificity and deicticity seems to be a viable test of category membership not only for nouns with concrete referents, but also for less prototypical instances of this category.

(26) Individuation in nouns that do not refer to concrete objects

a. **Mass Nouns**
that water, this butter

b. **Abstract Nouns**
these truths, that policy, this responsibility

c. **Nominalizations**
this kick, that jump, this running, the destruction

What makes these words nouns is not that they always denote individuals—that is, actual *individuated* things (for clearly they do not); rather, it is that their denotata are *individuatable*. In many (perhaps most) uses, for instance, mass nouns denote nonindividuated substances and portions (for example, *Water is necessary for life; There is water on the floor*). However, as the examples in (26a) show, the denotata of mass nouns *can* be individuated in the sense of being distinguished from other substances of the same type through the use of deictics. On the view put forward here, this is what justifies assignment of the corresponding words to the noun category. (Nothing in this theory implies that members of the noun category can or must occur with a determiner or deictic in each and every context in which they are used. Co-occurrence with a determiner or deictic in even one context is in principle enough to establish membership in the noun class.)

Like verbs, then, nouns are characterized in terms of a semantic notion (individuatability) that is inherently linked to a particular distributional phenomenon—co-occurrence with markers of definiteness/specificity and deicticity that are used to distinguish their referents from other referents of the same type. The acquisition device therefore *knows* precisely which distributional properties to focus on in order to identify nouns. Moreover, although the precise structural devices that mark individuation differ from language to language, the fact that all languages have mechanisms to represent at least spatial deictic contrasts (Anderson & Keenan, 1985, p. 308) ensures the universal viability of the proposed definition.[5]

Finally, consider the adjective class. Unlike nouns and verbs, this category is not found in all languages (e.g., Dixon, 1982). However, where it does occur, its denotations seem to fall into the class of gradable properties (see also Croft, 1991, p. 132) and are incompatible with tense and aspect contrasts. If this is right, then the criterial distributional characteristic of adjectives will be occurrence with those morphemes that a language uses to indicate gradation (e.g., in English, *-er, very, most,* and so forth) but incompatibility with tense and aspect.[6] As with verbs and nouns, then, the distributional criterion that the acquisition device uses to identify adjectives is determined by the inborn semantic notion to which this category is reduced (gradability).

[5]Languages also have deictic expressions such as *here/there* and *now/then* that occur with verbs rather than nouns. However, there seems to be an important difference. When I say *I slept here,* I am not (normally) using the deictic to distinguish between two sleeping events, one here and another someplace else; rather, I am simply indicating the place where I slept. In contrast, when I say *I slept in this bed,* I use *this* to distinguish a particular bed from others. This is the sort of individuation that is characteristic of the deictic markers that serve as diagnostics for the noun class.

[6]Various matters remain to be worked out. For example, according to this analysis, words such as *mere* and *utter* cannot be adjectives because they are not subject to gradation. Given their special properties (for example, they cannot occur with a copula verb), this conclusion is perhaps not unacceptable. Also problematic is the fact that adjectives can occur with an apparent deictic in structures such as *The car was this/that blue.* However, the role of the deictic here seems to be to compare a particular property with some other (e.g., in the example at hand, to compare the blueness of the car with that of some other object that is in sight). This is quite different from what happens when a deictic appears with a noun and may be closer to gradation than to individuation.

In sum, I propose that the conceptual module of the acquisition device includes an inborn classificatory system that takes each concept that can be encoded by a major lexical item and classifies it as an *individuatable* thing (something that can be individuated), an *event* (a phenomenon that is situated in time), or a time-independent, gradable *property*. Just as the human perceptual system forces classification of every speech sound as either voiced or voiceless with no intermediate options, so the conceptual system requires classification of every concept as an individuatable thing, an event, or a property. On the surface, this seems impractical because many words appear to express concepts that either cannot be unambiguously classified or are likely to be misclassified. (For example, does *helpful* in *We found him helpful* denote a property or an event? Does *debate* in *The debate was boring* denote an individuated thing or an event?) As noted earlier, the notions underlying the categorial system proposed here are deliberately broad and in many cases semantics alone will permit more than one categorization. (This is why near-synonyms such as *like* and *fond* can belong to different categories and why the notion *thirsty* is encoded as an adjective in English and a noun in French.)

However, just as the perceptual module must provide information about the precise acoustic correlates of voicing, so the conceptual module supplies the specific criteria that are to be used to classify denotations. By definition, individuatable concepts must be compatible with markers of specificity/definiteness and deicticity; events must permit tense and aspect contrasts; and properties must be compatible with morphemes encoding gradation. (Another way to state this is to say that the conceptual module treats tense and aspect markers as operators that apply to events, deictics and determiners as operators that apply to individuatable things, and degree morphemes as operators that apply to gradable properties.)

It is easy to imagine definitions of individuatability, eventhood, and propertyhood that would yield different results. (For example, the term *event* is often used in a sense broad enough to include any happening, including the denotations of nominalizations such as *arrival* and *destruction*—which would obviously undermine the classificatory system I have proposed.) By the same logic, of course, one could easily imagine an acoustic criterion for voicing that would yield the wrong result in the case of phonological development. I assume that whatever the merits of such alternative definitions, they cannot be the ones used by the acquisition device in its categorizational operations.

Figure 5.3 summarizes the classificatory operation on which the general nativist

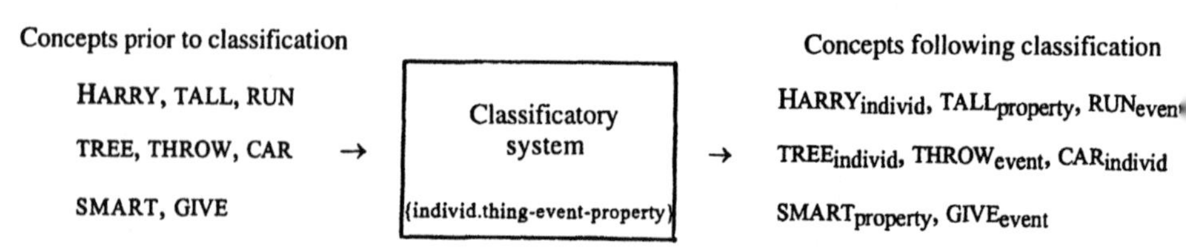

Figure 5.3. Operation of the classificatory system.

TABLE 5.8
Syntactic Categories and Semantic Classes

Category Label	Semantic Class	Corresponding Distributional Properties
N	Individuatable thing	Compatibility with markers of definiteness/specificity and deicticity
V	Event	Compatibility with contrasts involving tense, or aspect
A	Property	Compatibility with markers of gradation, incompatibility with tense and aspect
. . .	. . .	

theory of categories is based. Thanks to the reductionist view of syntactic categories adopted here, the results of this classificatory operation yield syntactic categories: the category labels N, V, and A are nothing more than 'shorthand' for the classes consisting of individuatable things, events, and properties, respectively (see Table 5.8). This theory differs from both semantic bootstrapping and inductivist approaches to category development. Unlike semantic bootstrapping, the general nativist approach takes the view that syntactic categories are fully reducible to more basic semantic notions, not just that some instances of particular categories have semantic correlates (e.g., that prototypical Ns refer to things or prototypical Vs to actions). Moreover, unlike inductivist theories, the general nativist approach does not equate syntactic categories with sets of distributional properties. The latter are used as diagnostics for category membership, but only because they provide tests for classifying words in terms of the contrast among individuatable things, events and properties on which category distinctions are based in the general nativist theory.[7]

One thing that the proposed analysis of syntactic categories does not and cannot do is explain without circularity precisely how individual languages draw their categorial boundaries. (Of course, the prime-based theories associated with special nativism cannot do this either.) In fact, other than a few obvious generalizations (e.g., discrete objects are seen as individuatable and therefore encoded as nouns), little can be said about why particular meanings are treated as instances of one type rather than another in any given language. For example, as noted earlier, there is no way to predict a priori that the concept denoted by *fond* falls into the property class whereas the concept denoted by *like* belongs to the event class. This is because the dividing line between events and properties is not a priori clear—which is why it must be defined with the help of distributional criteria.

[7]Nothing in this theory precludes the subsequent development of alternative strategies for syntactic categorization. For example, once the acquisition device has established that the plural suffix applies only to nouns in English or that verbs occur sentence-finally in Japanese, nothing prevents the use of these criteria for categorizational purposes. The rapidity and efficiency of the categorization process suggests that a number of different criteria for category assignment must eventually be available to language learners, but I will not explore this matter further here.

This seems reasonable. The job of the acquisition device is to discover the grammatical system that a particular language employs, not to explain how it came to be that way in the first place. Because actual languages reflect the often idiosyncratic effects of borrowings, historical change, lexical exceptions, and many other factors, an acquisition device that required a rationale for every phenomenon that it encountered would almost certainly fail. As I have described them, the basic categorial contrasts employed by a language are relatively easy to discover, thanks to the existence of straightforward distributional correlates for each of the semantic notions to which syntactic categories are reduced (see Table 5.8). The question of whether category membership can be predicted and explained in terms of some still deeper set of principles is a matter that extends well beyond acquisition theory and presents a major challenge for all accounts of syntactic categories.

Related Issues

Thus far, we have focused on category assignment as it pertains to the major word-level categories of noun, verb, and adjective. However, as noted in our earlier discussion, phrases too must be categorized. (The question of how phrases are formed in the first place will be addressed in the next section.) For example, we must ensure that the phrase formed by combining an adjective with a noun is a category of the N type, whereas the phrase formed by combining a verb with one or more nominals is a category of the V type. (Recall that we treat S as a verbal projection.)

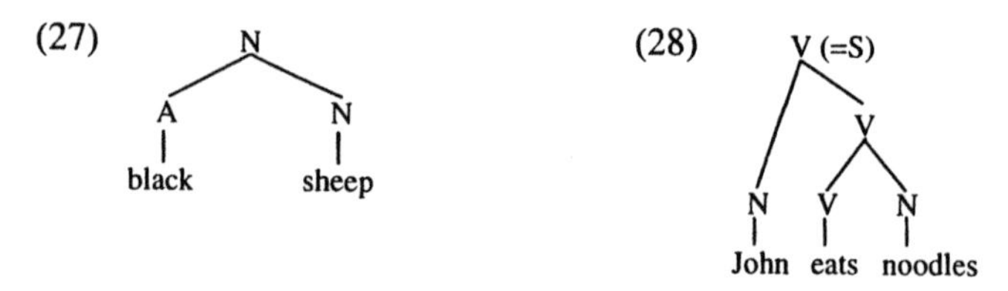

Let us assume not only that syntactic categories have the semantic basis proposed previously, but also that the complex concepts corresponding to the phrases formed by combining two smaller elements must be classified in terms of the same three-way contrast that is applied to word-level concepts. Thus, because a sheep whose color is specified is still a sheep, *black sheep* will be classified as an individuatable thing and the corresponding phrase will therefore be of the N type. Similarly, because an eating event whose theme or agent participants are specified is still an event, phrases such as *eat noodles* and *John eats noodles* should both be treated as categories of the V type. This gives the result depicted in (27) and (28), as desired. (Ninio, 1988, p. 116, independently makes a similar proposal.)

Even with this extension, the proposal I have been outlining presents only the *core* of the categorization system that is required for human language, and it is obvious that various refinements and additions are necessary. For example, a characterization must be found for the adverb category, about which nothing has been said to this point. Members of this category are arguably involved in the expression of properties of events (versus individuatable things), which suggests that they can perhaps be identified with the help of a suitably expanded classificatory operation in the conceptual module.

It is also necessary to consider possible cross-linguistic variation in categorial contrasts. In languages such as Korean and Japanese, for instance, there seems to be no true adjective category because words that pass the tests for gradability also occur with tense and aspect markers. This raises the possibility that the classificatory system proposed here might produce a hybrid category (call it an *adjectival verb*) in such instances. See O'Grady (1996) for a proposal along these lines for Korean.

Still another problem arises in the case of so-called minor categories such as determiners, auxiliary verbs, and prepositions. Various possibilities are worth considering. For example, Croft (1991, p. 113) discussed a semantic analysis for determiners and auxiliaries, whereas Montague (1973, p. 223) treated prepositions as categories that combine with a nominal to create either an adjectival expression (e.g., *a seat* [*near the window*]) or an adverbial expression (*sit* [*near the window*]).

These and other matters are obviously worthy of careful attention. However, limitations on time and space make further consideration of these issues impossible here. I will therefore set them aside for now, and turn my attention to the question of how the acquisition device is able to produce the mechanisms required to form syntactic representations with the appropriate hierarchical properties.

D. Hierarchical Structure

Work within the general nativist tradition has typically had little to say about how the configurational properties of syntactic structure (in particular, binary branching and the subject-object asymmetry) emerge in the course of syntactic development. Setting aside approaches that simply reject these hierarchical properties (e.g., Van Valin, 1991), the dominant view seems to be that at least certain features of a phrase's architecture can be inferred from semantic information. Consistent with this view, a number of authors (e.g., Braine, 1992, p. 93; Schlesinger, 1982) propose that the existence of a syntactic unit consisting of the verb and its object can be attributed to the fact that there is a corresponding action unit in the language of thought.

This proposal has a number of shortcomings. Even granting that there is semantic action constituent, nothing in this proposal ensures that it will be matched with the verb and its object rather than the verb and its subject. (If "reading a book" in *Harry read the book* qualifies as action, then so should "Harry reading.") As Newmeyer (1992, p. 787n) observed, there is little independent evidence that the VP does correspond to a semantic unit; the evidence for a VP constituent comes from syntactic phenomena rather than semantic facts.

A further problem with the semantic approach is that it says nothing about the internal structure of VPs when they consist of more than two elements. In the case of the VP *read it slowly,* for example, should there be a subunit *read it* with which the adverb *slowly* combines or are all three words immediate constituents of the VP? A parallel issue arises in the case of NPs such as *expensive new cars,* because the semantic approach says nothing about whether there should be a subconstituent *new cars* with which the adjective *expensive* combines or whether the two adjectives independently modify the noun.

The version of general nativism that I advocate takes a very different approach to the problem of hierarchical structure. As noted previously, the propositional and conceptual modules jointly provide the language learner with semantic forms such as those in (29) and (30). (As is evident, these representations contain no syntactic categories or structure per se; there is, for example, no semantic unit corresponding to VP.)

(29) a. *John left*

PREDICATE	LEAVE (agent)
TENSE	past
AGENT	JOHN

b. *John fell*

PREDICATE	FALL (theme)
TENSE	past
AGENT	JOHN

(30) *John builds houses*

PREDICATE	BUILD (agent,theme)
TENSE	present
AGENT	JOHN
THEME	HOUSE [+pl]

The single most important piece of information provided by these representations involves the number and type of arguments associated with particular functors (an obvious prerequisite for the formation of complete and coherent sentences). It is possible that this is the first type of information to be uncovered by the acquisition device, yielding preliminary lexical entries such as those in (31). (As before, a = agent and t = theme)

(31) *fall:* <t>
left: <a>
build: <a,t>

As noted by many researchers (e.g., Braine, 1976; Ninio, 1988), early combinatorial patterns typically consist of a predicate (functor) and an argument, but they lack the determiners and tense affixes associated with the emergence of true syntactic categories. This delay is to a certain extent expected: Although the inborn conceptual module can prepare language learners for the fact that compatibility with markers of deicticity, tense, and degree is relevant to categorization, it cannot tell them in advance what form these markers have in any particular language.

For example, before *this* can be used in its intended classificatory role, the acquisition device must determine that it is a deictic—presumably by observing it used in the appropriate way in a semantically transparent sentence that requires no syntactic analysis, in accordance with (2). There is thus room for a stage in syntactic development during which various lexical items have been acquired and are used in combinatorial patterns, but the system of syntactic category distinctions is not yet in place.

At any rate, once the classificatory system becomes operational, it will yield the more complete set of lexical properties exemplified in (32).

(32) **A Fragment of the English Lexicon**
John: N
house: N
left: $V^{<Na>}$
fall: $V^{<Nt>}$
build: $V^{<Na,Nt>}$

Ultimately, it is categories with these properties that are combined to form sentences.

As mentioned in Section III.A, the impetus to combine word-level categories to form phrases and sentences has a semantic basis: As functor categories combine with their arguments, their meanings are amalgamated to form the types of complex meanings typical of human communication. The binary character of phrase structure is guaranteed in advance by innate properties of the computational module (as shown previously). However, to ensure the formation of the right syntactic representations, the acquisition device must identify the relative linear order of functors and their arguments, and it must determine the relative combinatorial order in cases where a single functor has two (or more) arguments. Let us consider each point in turn.

The developmental data suggests that the first syntactic patterns produced by language learners consist largely of two-word utterances, including many subject-verb patterns such as *John left* and *John fell* (inflection and choice of lexical items aside). Sentence formation in such cases is maximally simple because the functor (an intransitive verb) combines with a single argument, whose relative positioning can easily be determined from experience. This results in the formation of the following syntactic representations, assuming the emergence of the relevant categorial contrasts:

(33) a. S (=$V^{<0>}$)
N $V^{<Na>}$
John left

b. S (=$V^{<0>}$)
N $V^{<Nt>}$
John fell

At this point, the hypothesis formation module of the acquisition device can formulate the following generalization:

(34) A $V^{<x>}$ combines with an argument to its left.

Matters are somewhat more complicated in the case of sentences containing three or more constituents. Sentences such as *John builds houses,* which contains a transitive verb, are a case in point. Because of the (innate) binarity property of the computational module, the verb can combine with only one of its arguments at a time. The inheritability and iterativity properties (also inborn) allow the remaining dependency to be passed up to the resulting phrase and to be satisfied by subsequent combination with an appropriate argument. This leaves the acquisition device with the problem of determining which argument the verb should combine with first.

How can this information be inferred? One possibility is that the acquisition device makes use of the word order rule in (34), which was previously inferred from the simple two-word sentences illustrated in (33). Given that a $V^{<x>}$ must combine with an argument to its left, it follows that sentences built around a transitive verb must have the structure in (35a) rather than (35b):

(35) a. b.

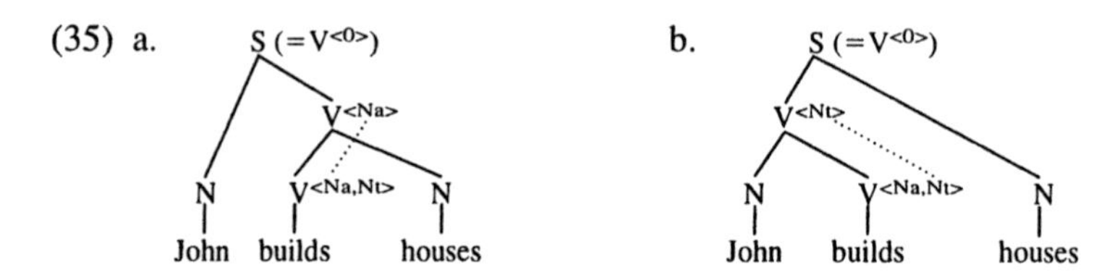

Only in (35a) does a $V^{<x>}$ (the phrase *builds houses*) combine with an argument to its left.

This allows the hypothesis formation module to draw two inferences. The first is simply that a transitive verb (a $V^{<x,y>}$) combines with an argument to its right as in (35a)—a generalization about linear order. Moreover, because that argument corresponds to the theme, it is also possible to infer that a verb combines with its theme argument before its agent argument, giving the content of the argument hierarchy, repeated as follows for convenience:[8]

(8) **The Argument Hierarchy**

theme *first*

... ↓

agent *last*

[8]In languages that use case marking rather than word order to encode grammatical relations, the last argument will be identified by its case affix rather than its linear position. Special problems arise in so-called ergative languages, in which the subject of an intransitive verb does not bear the same case marker as the subject of a transitive verb. However, I will not try to resolve this problem here.

I also say nothing here about the acquisition of VSO sentence structure, which I take to involve a discontinuous verb phrase (e.g., Dowty, 1982; O'Grady, 1987).

The emergence of (8) completes the acquisition of the sentence-building system illustrated here and allows formation of an unlimited number of sentences, each with an appropriate syntactic representation.

In summary, given our inborn computational module, the emergence of sentence structure can be reduced to three simple steps:

1. Identification of the directionality of the $V^{<x>}$ category: It combines with an argument to the left; see (34).
2. Use of the information garnered in step 1 to infer the directionality of the $V^{<x,y>}$ category: It combines with an argument to the right; compare (35a) and (35b).
3. Use of the information garnered in step 2 to infer the content of the argument hierarchy: Theme arguments are less prominent than agents.

The syntactic representations that result from this acquisition procedure differ from the syntactic structures of government and binding theory in various ways. Among other things, their component categories lack the characteristic bar-level designations of GB representations, and S is treated as a projection of V rather than the more abstract category I (inflection). Nonetheless, in these respects the representations advocated here resemble those of various widely used and respected theories, including versions of categorial grammar and phrase structure grammar. Moreover, the proposed representations comply with the widely held view that syntactic structure consists of words and phrases belonging to various category types, that it is binary branching, and that it exhibits a subject-object asymmetry (with the verb structurally closer to the object than to the subject).

Because they provide a plausible analysis of sentence structure, the syntactic representations formed by the general nativist acquisition device should be compatible with a component of the grammar not explored here: the set of principles required to regulate phenomena such as gap placement and pronoun interpretation. The next step in the general nativist research program must address the issue of how these second-order principles and constraints can be discovered by an acquisition device that does not include universal grammar. This is a major concern in my own current research (see, e.g., O'Grady, 1997), but I will not attempt to report on this here. (Bever, 1992, p. 206, implied that he too is exploring this issue.)

IV. CONCLUSION

As stated at the outset, the central goal of contemporary research into linguistic development is to identify the properties of the acquisition device, the inborn system responsible for constructing a grammar in response to the child's experience with language. The majority view within linguistics is that the innate endowment for language includes universal grammar, a system of specifically linguistic categories and principles. Contrasting with this special nativism is the view that the genetic contribution to language acquisition consists of more general sorts of mechanisms and does not include actual syntactic categories or principles. Although this general nativist perspective is often tacitly assumed in the literature on cognitive psychology, it has suffered from a lack of serious proposals about the acquisition of actual syntactic systems.

The goal of this chapter has been to help remedy this deficit by outlining a proposal about how a general nativist acquisition device could provide the core mechanisms involved in the formation of syntactic representations. The particular acquisition device outlined here consists of several independent modules, none of which contains information that is inherently syntactic in character. The interaction of these modules gives a sentence building system that is capable of forming syntactic representations that meet at least minimal criteria for adequacy (i.e., the component words and phrases are assigned to categories, all branching is binary, and there is a subject-object asymmetry).

The proposal that I have made does not claim that the crucial categorial and hierarchical properties of sentence structure are somehow discovered in experience, as might be suggested in an empiricist (i.e., nonnativist) theory. Quite to the contrary, the categories and geometry of syntactic representations follow from inborn principles and properties. However, in contrast with special nativism, these principles and properties are supplied by the various (nonlinguistic) modules that make up the acquisition device and are not specifically syntactic in character.

Despite this difference between special and general varieties of nativism, a striking similarity exists between the two approaches: Both leave relatively little room for actual learning in the conventional sense. This is obviously so in the case of special nativism, which supplies (via UG) both an inventory of syntactic categories and a template (the X-bar schema) to regulate the hierarchical organization of phrase structure. But it is also so, although perhaps in a subtler way, in the version of general nativism outlined here. According to my proposal, the categorial contrasts found in syntactic structure are determined by the innate classificatory system inherent in the conceptual module, whereas the hierarchical properties of sentence structure are largely derived from inborn properties of the computational module (binarity, iterativity, and inheritability). The role of experience is limited to providing information about the meanings and argument dependencies of individual forms, which is necessary in any case, and to supplying data about two very specific syntactic phenomena: the relative ordering of constituents and the combinatorial order imposed by the argument hieraracby, both of which are susceptible to cross-linguistic variation and therefore are not eligible for genetic specification in the first place.[9]

[9]Marantz (1984, p. 196ff) has argued that in some languages a transitive verb combines with the agent argument before the theme.

It must be admitted that at this time there is no full-fledged alternative to special nativism. However, it is at least possible to see the direction in which to proceed in developing such an alternative: Priority must be given to the formulation of specific proposals about how an acquisition device that does not include UG can respond to particular types of linguistic experience by producing a grammatical system that is capable of building plausible syntactic representations. Although recognizing that this chapter constitutes only an initial step in that direction, I believe that it points toward the validity and potential of the general nativist research program.

POSTSCRIPT

This chapter was initially written in 1992. Since that time, work within the minimalist program (e.g., Chomsky 1993) that has grown out of GB theory suggests that the conventional view of UG is being abandoned by those traditionally committed to special nativism in its strongest form. The latest generation of proposed explanatory principles focuses on the notion of economy, demanding short moves that are postponed for as long as possible (*procrastinate*) and that take place only to satisfy requirements of the moved element itself (*greed*). Such principles are broadly computational in character and do not draw on conventional syntactic notions such as subject, governing category, bounding node, and so forth. In this, they are very unlike the inventory of principles making up the sort of universal grammar posited in the first 35 years of work in the special nativist tradition and more like the types of principles associated with the version of general nativism adopted here. This opens the possibility for a rapprochement between general nativist and special nativist conceptions of the nature of the acquisition device, even if there are still substantial disagreements about the specific computational principles and the types of representations to which they apply.

ACKNOWLEDGEMENTS

In the course of writing this chapter, I benefited from discussions with Greg Lee, Kazue Kanno, and Stanley Starosta. I am especially grateful to Kevin Gregg for his detailed feedback and criticism, and to Paul Bloom, Michael Maratsos, Laurent Sagart, Ann Peters, Cathy Wong, Yoshie Yamashita, and Mark Sawyer for helpful comments.

REFERENCES

Anderson, S., Keenan, E. (1985). *Deixis.* In T. Shopen (Ed.), *Language typology and syntactic description* (Vol. 3, *Grammatical categories and the lexicon,* pp. 259–308). New York: Cambridge University Press.

Atkinson, M. (1992). *Children's syntax. An introduction to Principles and Parameters theory.* Cambridge, MA: Blackwell.
Bach, E. (1981). Discontinuous constituents in generalized categorial grammars. In V. Burke & J. Pustejovsky (Eds.), *Proceedings of the Eleventh Annual Meeting of the North Eastern Linguistic Society* (pp. 1–12). Amherst, MA: GLSA.
Bach, E. (1988). Categorial grammars as theories of language. In R. Oehrle, E. Bach, & D. Wheeler (Eds.), *Categorial grammars and natural language structures* (pp. 17–34). Boston: Reidel.
Bar-Hillel, Y. (1953). A quasi-arithmetical notation for syntactic description. *Language, 29,* 47–58.
Bates, E., & MacWhinney, B. (1981). Functionalist approaches to grammar. In E. Wanner & L. Gleitman (Eds.), *Language acquisition: The state of the art.* New York: Cambridge University Press.
Bates, E., & MacWhinney, B. (1988). What is functionalism? *Papers and Reports on Child Language Development, 27,* 137–152.
Berman, R. (1988). Word class distinctions in developing grammars. In Y. Levy, I. Schlesinger, & M. Braine (Eds.), *Categories and processes in language acquisition* (pp. 45–72). Hillsdale, NJ: Erlbaum.
Berwick, R. (1985). *The acquisition of syntactic knowledge.* Cambridge, MA: MIT Press.
Bever, T. (1992). The logical and extrinsic sources of modularity. In M. Gunnar & M. Maratsos (Eds.), *Modularity and constraints in language and cognition* (pp. 179–212). Hillsdale, NJ: Erlbaum.
Bowerman, M. (1985). What shapes children's grammars? In D. Slobin (Ed.), *The crosslinguistic study of language acquisition* (Vol. 2, *Theoretical issues,* pp. 1257–1314). New York: Erlbaum.
Braine, M. (1976). Children's first word combinations. *Monographs of the Society for Research in Child Development, 41* (Serial No. 164, No. 1).
Braine, M. (1987). What is learned in acquiring word classes—A step toward an acquisition theory. In B. MacWhinney (Ed.), *Mechanisms of language acquisition* (pp. 65–87). Hillsdale, NJ: Erlbaum.
Braine, M. (1992). What sort of innate structure is needed to "bootstrap" into syntax? *Cognition, 45,* 77–100.
Bresnan, J. (Ed.). (1982). *The mental representation of grammatical relations.* MIT Press.
Bresnan, J., & Moshi, L. (1990). Object asymmetries in comparative Bantu syntax. *Linguistic Inquiry, 21,* 147–185.
Bryant, P. E. (1992). Arithmetic in the cradle. *Nature, 358,* 712–713.
Chomsky, N. (1975). *Reflections on language.* New York: Pantheon.
Chomsky, N. (1980). *Rules and representations.* New York: Columbia University Press.
Chomsky, N. (1981). *Lectures on government and binding.* Dordrecht: Foris.
Chomsky, N. (1986). *Barriers.* Cambridge, MA: MIT Press.
Chomsky, N. (1993). A minimalist program for linguistic theory. In K. Hale & S. Keyser (Eds.), *The view from Building 20* (pp. 1–52). Cambridge, MA: MIT Press.
Croft, W. (1991). *Syntactic categories and grammatical relations: The cognitive organization of information.* Chicago: University of Chicago Press.
Dixon, R. M. W. (1982). *Where have all the adjectives gone?* The Hague: Mouton.

Dowty, D. (1982). Grammatical relations and Montague grammar. In P. Jacobs & G. Pullum (Eds.), *The nature of syntactic representation* (pp. 79–130). Boston: Reidel.
Emonds, J. (1991). Subcategorization and syntax-based theta role assignment. *Natural Language and Linguistic Theory, 9,* 369–429.
Fodor, J. (1975). *The language of thought.* New York: Crowell.
Gleitman, L. (1981). Maturational determinants of language growth. *Cognition, 10,* 115–126.
Gleitman, L. & Wanner, E. (1982). Language acquisition: The state of the state of the art. In E. Wanner & L. Gleitman (Eds.), *Language acquisition: The state of the art* (pp. 3–48). New York: Cambridge University Press.
Grimshaw, J., & Mester, A. (1988). Light verbs and θ marking. *Linguistic Inquiry, 19,* 205–232.
Inhelder, B. (1980). Language and knowledge in a constructivist framework. In M. Piattelli-Palmarini (Ed.), *Language and learning: The debate between Jean Piaget and Noam Chomsky* (pp. 131–141). Cambridge, MA: Harvard University Press.
Jackendoff, R. (1976). Toward an explanatory semantic representation. *Linguistic Inquiry, 7,* 89–150.
Kayne, R. (1983). Connectedness. *Linguistic Inquiry, 14,* 223–249.
Keenan, E., & Timberlake, A. (1985). Valency affecting rules in extended categorial grammar. *Language Research, 21,* 415–434.
Keenan, E., & Timberlake, A. (1988). Natural language motivations for extending categorial grammar. In R. Oehrle et al. (Eds.), *Categorial grammars and natural language structures* (pp. 265–295). Boston: Reidel.
Kornai, A., & Pullum, G. (1990). The X-bar theory of phrase structure. *Language, 66,* 24–50.
Kuhl, P. K., & Miller, J. D. (1975). Speech perception by the chinchilla: The voiced-voiceless distinction in alveolar plosive consonants. *Science, 190,* 69–72.
Larson, R. (1988). On the double object construction. *Linguistic Inquiry, 19,* 335–392.
Lenneberg, E. (1971). Of language knowledge, apes and brains. *Journal of Psycholinguistic Research, 1,* 1–29.
Li, Y. (1990). On V-V compounds in Chinese. *Natural Language and Linguistic Theory, 8,* 177–207.
Macnamara, J. (1972). Cognitive basis of language learning in infants. *Psychological Review, 79,* 1–13.
Marantz, A. (1984). *On the nature of grammatical relations.* Cambridge, MA: MIT Press.
Maratsos, M. (1982). The child's construction of grammatical categories. In E. Wanner & M. Maratsos (Eds.), *Language acquisition: The state of the art* (pp. 240–266). New York: Cambridge University Press.
Maratsos, M. (1988). The acquisition of formal word classes. In Y. Levy, I. Schlesinger, & M. Braine (Eds.), *Categories and processes in language acquisition* (pp. 31–44). Hillsdale, NJ: Erlbaum.
Maratsos, M. & Chalkley, M. A. (1981). The internal language of children's syntax: The ontogenesis and representation of syntactic categories. In K. Nelson (Ed.), *Children's language* (Vol. 2, pp. 127–214). New York: Gardner Press.
Miller, J. (1990). Speech perception. In D. Osherson & H. Lasnik (Eds.), *An invitation to cognitive science* (Vol. 1, *Language,* pp. 69–93). Cambridge, MA: MIT Press.

Montague, R. (1973). The proper treatment of quantification in ordinary English. In J. Hintikka, J. Moravcsik, & P. Suppes (Eds.), *Approaches to natural language* (pp. 221–242). Boston: Reidel.

Newmeyer, F. (1992). Iconicity and generative grammar. *Language, 68,* 756–796.

Nida, E. (1946). *Morphology: The descriptive analysis of words.* Ann Arbor, MI: University of Michigan Press.

Ninio, A. (1988). On formal grammatical categories in early child language. In Y. Levy, I. Schlesinger, & M. Braine (Eds.), *Categories and processes in language acquisition* (pp. 99–119). Hillsdale, NJ: Erlbaum.

O'Grady, W. (1987). *Principles of grammar and learning.* Chicago: University of Chicago Press.

O'Grady, W. (1989). Two perspectives on learnability. *Behavioral and Brain Sciences, 12,* 354–355.

O'Grady, W. (1991). *Categories and case: The sentence structure of Korean.* Philadelphia: John Benjamins.

O'Grady, W. (1996). The categorial system of Korean: A learnability perspective. In J. Shim, Y. Ko, I. Lee, P. Lee, H. Im, S. Lee, M. Choi, & H. Lee (Eds.), *A Festschrift for Lee Ki-Moon* (pp. 1023–1049). Seoul: Shin-gu.

O'Grady, W. (1997). *Syntactic development.* Chicago: University of Chicago Press.

Peters, A. (1985). Language segmentation: Operating principles for the perception and analysis of language. In D. Slobin (Ed.), The crosslinguistic study of language acquisition (Vol. 2, *Theoretical issues,* pp. 1029–1068). Hillsdale, NJ: Erlbaum.

Piaget, J. (1980). Schemes of action and language learning. In M. Piattelli-Palmarini (Ed.), *Language and learning: The debate between Jean Piaget and Noam Chomsky* (pp. 163–182). Cambridge, MA: Harvard University Press.

Pinker, S. (1984). Language learnability and language development. (Cambridge: Harvard University Press.

Pinker, S. (1989). *Learnability and cognition: The acquisition of argument structure.* Cambridge, MA: MIT Press.

Pollard C. (1988). Categorial grammar and phrase structure grammar: An excursion on the syntax-semantics frontier. In R. Oehrle, E. Bach, & D. Wheeler (Eds.), *Categorial grammars and natural language structures* (pp. 391–415). Boston: Reidel.

Schlesinger, I. (1982). *Steps to language.* Hillsdale, NJ: Erlbaum.

Schlesinger, I. (1988). The origin of relational categories. In Y. Levy, I. Schlesinger, & M. Braine (Eds.), *Categories and processes in language acquisition* (pp. 121–178). Hillsdale, NJ: Erlbaum.

Slobin, D. (1973). Cognitive prerequisites for the development of grammar. In C. Ferguson & D. Slobin (Eds.), *Studies of child language development* (pp. 175–208). New York: Holt, Rinehart & Winston.

Slobin, D. (1982). Universal and particular in the acquisition of language. In E. Wanner & M. Maratsos (Eds.), *Language acquisition: The state of the art* (pp. 128–172). Cambridge University Press.

Slobin, D. (1985). Crosslinguistic evidence for the language-making capacity. In D. Slobin (Ed.) The crosslinguistic study of language acquisition (Vol. 2, *Theoretical issues,* pp. 1157–1256). Hillsdale, NJ: Erlbaum.

Snow, C. (1977). Mothers' speech research: From input to interaction. In C. Snow & C. Fer-

guson (Eds.), *Talking to children: Language input and acquisition* (pp. 31–49). London: Cambridge University Press.
Speas, M. (1990). *Phrase structure in natural language.* Dordrecht: Kluwer.
Starosta, S. (1988). *The case for lexicase: An outline of lexicase grammatical theory.* London: Pinter Publishers.
Tsujimura, N. (1992). Licensing nominal clauses: the case of deverbal nominal in Japanese. *Natural Language and Linguistic Theory, 10,* 477–522.
Van Valin, R. (1991). Functionalist linguistic theory and language acquisition. *First Language, 11,* 7–40.
Wexler, K., & Culicover, P. (1980). *Formal principles of language acquisition.* Cambridge, MA: MIT Press.
Wexler, K., & Rita Manzini, M. (1987). Parameters and learnability in binding theory. In T. Roeper & E. Williams (Eds.), *Parameter setting* (pp. 41–76). Dordrecht: Reidel.
Wynn, K. (1992). Addition and subtraction by human infants. *Nature, 358,* 749–750.
Yamashita, Y. (1990). Syntactic theory and the acquisition of Japanese syntax: Radford's GB approach. *Hawaii Working Papers in Linguistics, 22,* 93–126.

CHAPTER 6

CREOLE LANGUAGES, THE LANGUAGE BIOPROGRAM HYPOTHESIS, AND LANGUAGE ACQUISITION

Derek Bickerton

I. ORIGINS OF THE HYPOTHESIS AND ITS RELEVANCE TO ACQUISITION

A student of acquisition unfamiliar with the literature on creole languages may well wonder what a hypothesis originally designed to explain certain facts about such languages is doing in a volume on acquisition and perhaps be tempted to skip this chapter and get on with "the real stuff." At the same time, one might successfully wager that the same student has often felt puzzlement and frustration at the fact that, even after several decades of thorough research, the question of how children acquire languages is still far from receiving a satisfactory and convincing answer. This chapter seeks to explain why that answer has remained so elusive. But first, some background information should be given.

The language bioprogram hypothesis (LBH) evolved out of the observation by many earlier investigators (Taylor, 1960; Thompson, 1961; Whinnom, 1956) of striking similarities in the semantics and syntax of creole languages, in particular (but by no means limited to) the system of tense and aspect that characterized many of these languages. On the face of things, no obvious reasons for such similarities existed. Creole languages, arising through the nativization of rudimentary contact languages (pidgins) mainly on colonial plantations, differed widely both in their superstrates (which might be English, French, Spanish, Portuguese, Dutch, or even Arabic) and in their substrate languages (drawn from hundreds, if not thousands

Handbook of Child Language Acquisition

of languages in East and West Africa, South Asia, the Pacific Rim, and elsewhere). Some creole languages arose in locations thousands of miles from the nearest similar language, and contact between speakers of different creole languages has been, in general, negligible to nonexistent. Yet the similarities existed and had to be explained.

Explanations based on possible similarities between superstrate languages (Chaudenson, 1979; Hall, 1966) failed because the similarities among creole languages involved features that were absent from the superstrates or with respect to which the superstrates varied. Explanations based on the possibility that a single original, medieval pidgin (or creole) had been diffused globally (Thompson, 1961; Voorhoeve, 1973; Whinnom, 1965) foundered on a variety of linguistic and extralinguistic facts which indicated that in a majority of cases the required transmissions could not have taken place. Explanations based on possible similarities between substrate languages (Alleyne, 1980; Lefebvre, 1986; Sylvain, 1936) fared somewhat better, if only because, with so many potential substrates, it was always possible to find substrates with features similar to those of creole languages. However, substrate theorists failed to produce any satisfactory explanation of why, given that most features of most substrates differed from the creole pattern, the same particular set of features should surface repeatedly in creolization, and they similarly failed to explain the persistance of that set in at least one creole language (in Hawaii), none of whose substrates exhibited the relevant features (Bickerton, 1984).

A paper that appeared nearly two decades ago (Bickerton, 1974) proposed that, contrary to all previous theories, the distinctive pattern of creole features was not inherited from preexisting languages but rather represented the surfacing, in an unusually direct form, of an innate program for the creation of language that formed part of our species' biological endowment. This proposal had clear affinities with the nativist theory proposed earlier by Chomsky (1965, 1972) and indeed that theory had served to suggest the proposal. However, there were (and continue to be) some differences of detail. Chomsky seems to have envisaged a device that could potentially generate a wide range of possible grammars, from which the child would in effect choose on the basis of primary input data. This idea of the potential variability of the innate grammar has been preserved in later versions of the theory, in which principles of universal grammar allow for parametric variation and parameters are set by the child on the basis of input. The LBH, on the other hand, began by envisaging a single, invariant innate grammar that might be subject to modification through relevant experience. The current state of the model, and the respects in which it both agrees with and differs from the current state of the Chomskyan model, will be discussed in Section II.

The LBH had obvious implications for language acquisition, but these were slow to be developed. It was not until seven years after the original paper that its implications were thoroughly explored (Bickerton, 1981). However, as will become apparent, the emphasis in that work tended to deflect attention away from the most crucial questions that the LBH posed for current approaches to acquisition.

Some of the most striking creole similarities involved semantics as much as syntax. In particular, the typical tense-aspect system, in addition to syntactic features—the invariant (1)-tense-(2)-modality-(3)-aspect ordering of preverbal free morphemes—included a high degree of regularity in the meanings/functions of the morphemes concerned (anterior tense, irrealis modality, nonpunctual aspect). In addition, differences in the distribution of tense and aspect morphemes suggested a significant distinction between stative and nonstative verbs, whereas the distribution of articles (including zero forms) suggested a similar semantic distinction between specific and nonspecific reference in nouns. Finally, the tendency of creoles to 'middleize' a wide range of verbs (*X plant the tree yesterday* versus *the tree plant yesterday*) suggested the innateness of a causative-noncausative distinction which, in the absence of morphological marking, was automatically expressed in the syntax by across-the-board alternation between [N V [$_N$Theme]] and [[$_N$Theme] V].

Accordingly, Bickerton (1981) hypothesized that four semantic distinctions—punctual-nonpunctual, specific-nonspecific, stative-nonstative, and causative-noncausative)—(a) formed part of universal grammar, (b) were directly expressed either in the syntax or the grammatical morphology of creoles, (c) led to rapid and errorless acquisition in languages where the distinctions were clearly expressed, and (d) caused creole-like "errors" in languages where their expression was obscured or distorted by other, language-specific factors. Thus, for example, children learning English quickly and errorlessly acquired the morpheme *-ing* (since it was invariant and attached exlusively to nonstative verbs) but made frequent errors with causatives (e.g., *I flatted the box, I'm eating my dolly*) because the causative-noncausative distinction was handled by English in a confusing variety of ways (a restricted range of ergative verbs, lexical alternation, constructions with *make,* and so on).

The claims involving these semantic distinctions looked as if they could be fairly straightforwardly tested, and accordingly the bulk of the acquisition community's response to the LBH has involved testing or contesting these claims (e.g., Cziko, 1986, 1988, 1989; Cziko & Koda, 1987; Mapstone & Harris, 1985; Youssef, 1988). The most that can be said about this literature is that some evidence seemed to support the claims, some seemed to go against them, and no clear resolution was reached. No attempt will be made to summarize the debate here, because the subsequent development of the LBH has made these issues moot, for reasons to be discussed shortly.

It was unfortunate for a variety of reasons that emphasis was placed on primarily semantic claims and that the deeper, syntactic implications of the LBH went largely unnoticed. The most critical question posed by the LBH is, how is it that children acquire a novel language when input is too severely degraded for them to acquire a preexisting language? The second most critical question is, why are the languages acquired by children under the foregoing conditions so strikingly similar to one another? Neither question has been addressed or (with only a handful of exceptions) even recognized by the acquisition community.

Yet, fairly obviously, a theory of acquisition that cannot provide answers to either question cannot constitute an acceptable theory of acquisition. Acquisition theories cannot be permitted to content themselves with providing an account of how languages are acquired under the rich and favorable circumstances of normal generation-to-generation transmission. They must, like any theory of anything, be able to meet the challenge of abnormal circumstances. Indeed, the failure of acquisition studies to go beyond the familiar parent-to-child form of transmission is what largely accounts for the present state of affairs in which a wide variety of theories—some mainly input driven, others emphasizing innate mechanisms of one sort or another—continue to compete with one another. In other fields, it is precisely the challenges of abnormal circumstances that have indicated, among competing theories, which were superficial and which showed genuine explanatory power. In failing to meet the challenge of creolization, acquisition theories have shirked a genuine test of their viability.

However, in order that the acquisition community should deal adequately with this challenge, it seems desirable to present it as clearly and unambiguously as possible. Accordingly, the present state of bioprogram theory and the empirical base on which it rests will be set forth in the section that follows.

II. CURRENT STATUS OF THE LBH

The nature of the bioprogram hypothesis cannot be clearly understood unless the mode of development of creole languages and their relationship to more conventional languages are described in some detail. During the last couple of years, the circumstances surrounding creolization have been illuminated by still-unpublished archival research carried out by Julian Roberts in Hawaii (Roberts, 1991, n.d.). Although the case of Hawaii represents the most recent formation of a creole, it had been widely believed that little documentary evidence could be recovered for the relevant period. Roberts, however, has uncovered upwards of 600 contemporary references, the majority of which incorporate actual citations of current language use. On the basis of this evidence, it is possible to create a picture far more vivid and accurate than any available before of the conditions that preceded and accompanied the emergence of a creole.

During the first century of language contact in Hawaii (1778–1876), the predominant contact language between Hawaiians and non-Hawaiians, as well as between different groups of non-Hawaiians in Hawaii, was not some form of English (as had generally been supposed) but a reduced and in most cases clearly pidginized variety of Hawaiian. Contacts were sufficient to give this pidginized Hawaiian a high degree of stability, including such features as a consistent SVO word order (as opposed to Hawaiian's VSO), replacement of articles by demonstratives, and a highly stereotyped vocabulary marked by reduplication, phonological simplification, and semantic shifts. Conversely, although fluent English was acquired by a few members of the *alii* or ruling caste, and radically reduced forms of English were used sporadically in the ports and between English-speaking masters and their servants, attempts at English never spread to the general population and such attempts remained highly unstable and idiosyncratic with the consequence that no standardized English-based pidgin ever developed.

Numerous comments by contemporary observers attest to the widespread belief that it was easier for English speakers to acquire Hawaiian (or what they fondly imagined was Hawaiian!) than it was for Hawaiians to acquire English (Bishop, 1875; Corwin, 1872; Dutton, 1884; Grant, 1888). Certainly there is abundant evidence that up until the last decade of the 19th century, Hawaiian of some kind was routinely acquired and used by resident Caucasians (and even some who visited for extended periods) and even more universally by non-Caucasian immigrant groups, such as Chinese (who intermarried extensively with Hawaiians) and Pacific Islanders (whose first language was, in some cases, related to Hawaiian).

In 1876 the lowering of U.S. tariffs on Hawaiian sugar caused an explosion in the sugar industry, and massive immigration resulted, first from China and Portugal and later from Japan, the Phillipines, Korea, and other areas. Initially, since plantations labor had been almost exclusively Hawaiian, the task of training these new workers fell to Hawaiians; to this day, a high proportion of the technical vocabulary used in the sugar industry consists of Hawaiian or, in many cases, specifically pidgin-Hawaiian words (Das, 1931). Accordingly, the majority of immigrants acquired (usually pidginized) Hawaiian, whereas many younger residents, especially Hawaiians and part-Hawaiians, acquired at least a smattering of the immigrant languages (Editorial, *The Friend,* April 1886, p. 10., cited in Roberts, n.d.).

However, as more and more English-speaking supervisory personnel were introduced into the islands, pidgin Hawaiian absorbed an increasing number of English words until, by the late 1880s, perhaps the commonest medium of communication was a macaronic pidgin, a largely structureless and highly unstable medium that incorporated Hawaiian and English words in roughly equal proportions, as well as numerous words from other languages involved in the contact situation. Alongside this macaronic pidgin, pidgin Hawaiian continued to be used by earlier arrivals and by those newcomers who were located in predominantly Hawaiian-speaking communities, while a rudimentary English spread (particularly among those catering to the new tourist industry), but it remained, however, a series of idiosyncratic improvisations rather than becoming a stabilized code.

The children of the immigrants, along with Hawaiian children, mostly went to schools at which, in theory, instruction in Hawaiian was rapidly being replaced by instruction in English. However, according to contemporary testimony, "they learn in the schools the English language textbooks as an American child would learn the Latin or Greek languages" (*Papers relating to the mission of James H. Blount,* 1893, p. 19, cited in Roberts, n.d.), while in school playgounds there reigned a state of affairs that, according to one observer, was as if "the curse of Babel had fallen on the school" (*Pacific Commercial Advertiser,* 16 January 1888, p. 2, cited in Roberts, n.d.). Because oral histories from an even later period indicate that many non-Hawaiian as well as Hawaiian children in rural areas (where, of course, all plantations were located) continued to use some form of Hawaiian, we can be reasonably sure that at least until the late 1890s the vast majority of children acquired Hawaiian and used it in intergroup contacts, retaining their own ancestral language for intragroup contacts, and using little if any English, whether pidginized or not.

The availability of Hawaiian seems to have been what prevented the prior emergence of creole in Hawaii. However, in 1893 the Hawaiian monarchy was overthrown, and the following year the islands were annexed by the United States. Eleven years later comes the first recognizable reference to an emerging creole (*Paradise of the Pacific,* December 1904, pp. 43–44, cited in Roberts, n.d.)—a reference to what the observer described as the "I-bin-go" language spoken by newsboys in Honolulu (*bin* is a marker of anterior tense not found in any citations of pidgin Hawaiian, macaronic pidgin, or pidginized English for this or previous periods). Since even nowadays Hawaiian newsboys are mostly in the 10 to 12 age range (and were probably even younger around the turn of the century), this evidence is consistent with the creole having been initiated by children born from around 1893 on. This is supported by the fact that (with the exception noted previously) citations of distinctively creole forms do not begin to appear until 1910 through 1911. The latter date is consistent with children born around the time of the overthrow having reached late adolescence or early manhood around this time and their speech having therefore become salient for the first time in the community at large.

We can therefore conclude that Hawaiian creole began to be created by children around 1895. It thus becomes possible to determine the type of input that those children received, which would typically have ranged from pidgin Hawaiian through macaronic pidgin to fragmentary and idiosyncratic attempts at English. A representative sample of such input (excluding the more heavily Hawaiianized varieties) is given in examples (1) through (10) (examples from Roberts, n.d.):

(1) No sharky, leafy (= leave), no more (Chinese servant, 1890)

(2) Too much work—too warm—some more tomorrow—no use—mahope (= later) (Hawaiian children 1891)

(3) Jap no go outside, all stop here, byumby go Hardrow (Hawaiian policeman to plantation workers, 1891)

(4) Olo laita kapena, kela hulipau no sawe (unidentified seamen, 1893)
"All right captain, the second mate doesn't know"

(5) Luna huhu, too much hanahana, Kahuku no good (Japanese plantation worker, 1894)
"The foreman's bad-tempered, there's too much work, Kahuku (plantation) is no good"

(6) You see, I got wood there, plenty men here no job, come steal (Portuguese, 1895)

(7) Pehea you kaitai, you hanahana allsame lili more, me hanamake you (Chinese plantation worker, c. 1898)
"Why you bastard, if you do that again I'll kill you"

(8) Wassamatta you, bakatari you, pehea you speak allsame (Japanese plantation worker, c. 1898)
"What's the matter with you, you bastard, why do you talk like that?"

(9) Honolulu come; plenty more come; too much good pineapple there. 40 cen' kela (= that), 50 cen' kela, 30 cen' kela (Chinese store owner, 1898)

(10) No pilikia me, go kaukau (Caucasian plantation manager to Japanese woman, c. 1899)
"Don't bother me, go and eat" (or, "I'm going to eat")

A representative sample of the early creole, based (like the earlier non-creole examples) exclusively on contemporary records, is given in examples (11) through (14) (examples again from Roberts, n.d.):

(11) Papa bin lick mama and I wen' help her (Child age 6, 1910)

(12) I got plenty good dress suit for sell now after I been hear Joe Cohen been say no use go Opera House all stuff up, but trouble now find somebody buy this clothes, no? (Japanese old clothes dealer, 1913)

(13) You bin say go up on roof and paint him, but I no hear you say come down. Why you not say when I bin through come down? ("a three-quarter-grown half-white youth," 1913)

(14) I think haole (= Caucasian) man nui huhu (= very angry) for Hawaiian get good job so he get Pakiko (= Portuguese) Pacheco and Pake (= Chinese) Achi for make new charter for give haole job (Hawaiian, 1915)

(15) Bimeby I go look one tenement house on Nuuanu Street (unidentified, 1916).

(16) And sometime my father take me for I go look the horse race with him. Friday I bin go the Kapiolani Park and I see plenty funny thing. Tomorrow I go look the race again (unidentified, 1916)

The question that acquisitionists have to face is simply this: How was it possible for children receiving the input of (1) through (10) to produce the output of (11) through (16)? The regularities we observe in the second set of examples—regularities in the use of *bin* and *go* as tense and modality markers, *one* for specific indefinites and zero for nonspecifics, *for* as a complementizer, and so on—simply do not exist in the first set, although these regularities (down to the exact same morphemes, in some cases) can be documented from dozens of other creoles. But more striking even than these is the fact that the speakers of (11) through (16) produce what Radford (1990) described as D-systems (phrases in which determiners have noun phrases (NPs) as their regular complements), I-systems (systems that require obligatory representation of inflectional heads, such as modals and auxiliaries under statable conditions), and C-systems (systems that require a complementizer position at the beginning of sentences and that require overt complementizers in certain types of sentential embedding). These systems, as Radford pointed out, are central in and essential to an adult syntax. Yet there is no evidence of them in the input that these speakers received.

It is futile to claim that these regularities and this structure must somehow have been drawn from some source not included in examples (1) through (10). Too many of the features that characterize examples (11) through (16) are not present in standard (or even nonstandard) varieties of English, nor are they found in the range of substrate languages (Portuguese, Japanese, Hawaiian, various varieties of Chinese, and so on) that were currently available. It is tempting to argue, with Bruner & Feldman (1982) and a number of subsequent commentators, that children *must have* first acquired the languages of their parents and then somehow transferred structure from these to the nascent creole. But this proposal ignores the fact that any such procedure would have produced not a uniform creole but a series of substrate-influenced creole varieties—Japanese-flavored, Hawaiian-flavored, Portuguese-flavored, and so on. Yet what is so striking about Hawaiian creole, from its earliest attestations to the present, is its high degree of homogeneity. There would simply not have been time for a range of ethnic creoles to develop and then level into a single uniform variety. Even had there been time, such a hypothesis would fail to explain why the outcome of such a leveling process exhibited so many features characteristic of creoles in general.

Writers such as Goodman (1984, 1985) and Holm (1986, 1988) have hypothesized that there must have existed some kind of antecedent English-based pidgin, a pidgin that was fully conventionalized and systematic and that shared a large number of features with the subsequent creole. This pidgin, it has been argued, rather than the heterogeneous collection of varieties represented by examples (1) through (10) or the pidgin data from survivors of the pidgin period recorded in the 1970s and described in Bickerton and Odo (1976) and Bickerton (1981), must have served as the input to the first creole generation and must thus constitute the immediate ancestor of Hawaiian creole. However, no citations of such a stable pidgin have ever been produced, and the complete absence of anything resembling such a pidgin from Roberts's data strongly suggests that no such language ever existed. Examples (1) through (10), fully typical of that data, show that the input to the creole-creating generation was at least as degraded as, and little different from, the material recovered from survivors of the pidgin period in the 1970s.

If no previous variety of language exhibits the features that constitute the grammatical system of examples (11) through (16), then it can only be concluded that the structural regularities of Hawaiian creole, and likewise those of other languages created under similar conditions, were not derived from input but were somehow derived from the language faculties of the children concerned.

III. WHAT THE LBH PREDICTS FOR ACQUISITION

At this point an important distinction between the present and earlier versions of the LBH must be emphasized. According to earlier versions, the human mind contained a blueprint that was *both semantic and syntactic.* It followed logically from this that children acquiring established languages would be expected to acquire semantic distinctions in the following manner:

a. In advance of learning the semantic distinctions of the target language they would initially seek to impose the semantic distinctions of the bioprogram.

b. In case the bioprogram distinctions did not match the target language distinctions, they would only gradually replace the former with the latter.

These were the kinds of claims that the acquisition research of Cziko and others, referred to in Section 1, sought to test. However, as noted earlier, evidence was at best equivocal, and some evidence was clearly inconsistent with such claims. But empirical evidence seldom gives unambiguous signals, and what caused the revision of the LBH were theoretical rather than empirical considerations. First, there is no a priori reason why syntax and semantics should pattern in the same way—indeed, if they are autonomous, as they seem to be, they are rather unlikely to do so. Second, evolutionary considerations suggest a likely disjunction of syntactic and semantic bioprograms.

This second reason deserves further explication, since evolutionary considerations do not yet, unfortunately, form a standard part of linguistic argumentation. The origins-of-language story told in Bickerton (1981) was gradualist and did not fully conform to what is now known of human evolution. A more probable scenario in Bickerton (1990) envisaged a two-stage development of language—first to a protolanguage, lacking syntax and somewhat resembling contemporary pidgins, which exploited semantic distinctions derivable from higher-mammalian perception, and then to a fully syntacticised language, which could exploit a still wider range of semantic distinctions that, likewise, are assumed to have been already present.

Such a model is fully consistent with what is presently known of human evolution and of the relationship between human and nonhuman forms of cognition. Its consequences for the LBH are as follows. The syntactic bioprogram maps theta structure (verbs and their complement of thematic roles) onto a binary-branching hierarchical structure. This process is automatic, neurophysiologically instantiated, and comes on line at approximately age 2. It is invariant and universal. The semantic bioprogram more closely resembles the Chomskyan picture of the syntactic bioprogram. That is to say, it consists of a list of options, among which a child is obliged to choose just those that are instantiated in its target language(s).

These options consist of the features of language that can be grammatically marked (i.e., marked by grammatical morphemes rather than expressed via lexical items). This list is finite and relatively short. It consists of things like number, gender, person, tense, modality, aspect, specificity, possession, object-type (e.g., long/thin versus spherical), transitivity, agency, grammatical function, and so forth. It is assumed that there is a universal list, that languages must choose from this list, and that choices may constrain one another in ways that are far from understood. If there were no such list, then no child could ever correctly determine the meanings of grammatical particles, because the number of semantic distinctions that could *in principle* be grammaticized is all but infinite. A child could not, in a human lifetime, exclude all the options (edibility, dangerousness, part-whole, and so on) that are not in fact grammaticized in any human language and that therefore (one assumes) do not form part of the universal list of grammaticizable distinctions.

In pidgin input, as the examples of (1) through (10) suggest, no semantic distinctions whatsoever are grammaticized—indeed the very concept of grammaticization is quite meaningless in a pidgin context. Thus, the child exposed to a pidgin cannot arrive inductively at any grammaticized semantic distinctions. However, for reasons that remain unclear, it appears that no natural language can avoid grammaticizing *some* semantic distinctions, if only in the form of free grammatical morphemes (as creoles customarily do). Thus there seems no alternative but to assume that there exists a set of *default distinctions,* which will be grammaticized just in case no grammaticized distinctions are present in input.

Accordingly, earlier assumptions about the acquisition of grammaticizable distinctions (given as a and b earlier) need to be revised as follows:

a′. The child reviews target-language input in an attempt to determine which members of the universal list of grammaticizable semantic destinctions are instantiated in the target language.

b′. In case no (or an inadequate number of) such distinctions are grammaticized in target input, the child reverts to the list of default grammaticizations (just those that are repeatedly found among creole languages and that may be required for syntactic more than for semantic reasons).

Further research is clearly needed to establish the contents of the universal list. The contents of the default list are fairly clear from the creole evidence: number, specificity, and identifiablity on noun-phrases (note contrast between *one* and *zero* in (11) through 16) above), anterior tense, irrealis modality and nonpunctual aspect on verb-phrases (note *been* and *go* in (11) through (16), number and person (but not gender) on pronouns, thematic roles (other than agent and theme), purposiveness (note use of *for* in (11) through (16)) and factuality in sentential complements—these all but exhaust the list. As regards acquisition, it follows from this revision that we would not necessarily expect to find children trying to enforce default-list distinctions where other types of allowable distinction are readily available in target language input. If a language has past tense but no anterior tense, children will simply acquire the past tense. If a language does not specifically mark the punctual-nonpunctual distinction but marks other distinctions on verb-phrases that are included in the universal list, children will acquire those target distinctions without ever necessarily trying to replace them by the default distinctions.

However, it is still predicted that where the grammaticized semantic distinctions of the target language conform to the default distinctions (and provided always that the mapping from semantics to lexicon is relatively simple and straightforward), the child will acquire those distinctions early, rapidly, and without error. It is noteworthy, for example, that what is to date the only study of acquisition of a creole language (Adone, 1991) shows early acquisition and a complete absence of errors in the acquisition of Morisyen (also known as Mauritian creole).

The syntactic bioprogram works quite differently from the semantic bioprogram. Here, it is hypothesized that there is an invariant mechanism that operates regardless of input. Whether input is well or ill formed, provided that there *is* some input the syntactic bioprogram will automatically add constituents to one another to form arguments, arguments to verbs to form clauses, and clauses to other clauses to form sentences. Without such a mechanism, the formation of creole languages would be impossible.

This syntactic mechanism is of course universal as well as invariant, and the differences in syntax that arise between different languages are owed to two causes. First is the order of constituents. The syntactic mechanism imposes only vertical (hierarchical) structure, yet language must be expressed in a linear manner. The *horizontalization,* so to speak, of this vertical structure involves fixing the order in which paired constituents (e.g., heads and their complements) can occur in so-called configurational languages or allowing free order for at least some pairs, as in nonconfigurational or *scrambling* languages. It will be clear that a series of pairwise orderings is all that is needed to establish ordering consistencies for all possible constituents in a language, so that this procedure can be largely completed within the so-called two-word stage. It should be equally clear that (because pairs do not constrain the ordering of other pairs) a wide variety of different ordering types can arise from this process, as observational data suggest (the idea that each language sets something called a *head-complement parameter,* often voiced in the generative literature, does not even reach the level of observational adequacy).

The second cause of differences between the syntaxes of natural languages lies in the lexicon. Languages differ unpredictably throughout their lexicons, but the differences that most concern us here lie in the selections they make from the list of possible grammatical morphemes (Do they mark cases? Transitivity? Noun classes? Do they have clitics? Subject agreement? Gender? Long-distance reflexives?—and so on) and the particular properties that particular grammatical morphemes embody. For example, the English morpheme *for* can function as preposition, governing benefactive arguments (*I gave a book to Mary for Bill*) or expressions denoting quantity (*for 10 miles, for 10 minutes, for 10 dollars*), or as complementizer, where a purposive nonfinite clause has an overt subject (e.g., *for us to finish the job*), or as conjunction, with a meaning weakly equivalent to *because* (*I'll go, for there's little point in staying*). It is unlikely that any morpheme in any other language has precisely this distribution of properties.

Children must learn word order, as well as morphemes and their properties, in the old-fashioned sense of *learning* (although the fact that there is a limited number of logically possible orders and an innate universal list of possible properties makes the task considerably easier than it would otherwise be). In the acquisition of established languages, variability of word order and morpheme properties are sufficient to yield a range of grammars no two of which, in the somewhat limited set of 5000 or so natural languages, will be the same.

However, in the case of creole languages, word order is similar if not identical. All known creoles, for example, exhibit the order (S)ubject-(V)erb-(O)bject—which may be due to the fact that in their antecedent pidgins, topics, which are often agents (or themes in nonagentive sentences) tend to precede comments in what could be reinterpreted as a subject-predicate relationship. The contents of the lexicon are naturally less uniform. Some creoles (especially those lexified by Portuguese) have inherited from antecedent languages a distinction between emphatic and nonemphatic pronouns, whereas others have not. Some creoles have inherited a form (e.g., *ki,* from French *qui/que,* almost universal among French creoles) that functions both as (part of a) question word and relative pronoun, whereas others have inherited only a question form (*hu,* reflex of English *who,* can function in questions in English creoles but not as a relative pronoun). Some creoles have inherited case distinctions in the third-person singular pronoun, whereas others have not, and so on. Differences such as these, multiplied by a dozen or two, ensure that the syntaxes of different creoles will not show point-for-point identity. However, the reduction of original input (pidginization) common to creoles ensures that even in the lexicon, similarities will outweigh differences. Thus identity of word order, plus strong similarities among grammatical morphemes and their properties, ensure that the resultant grammars of creole languages will show striking similarity, although not, of course, complete identity.

Given the nature of the syntactic mechanism described and the account of language evolution proposed in Bickerton (1990), a clear prediction can be made with regard to "normal" acquisition. This is that the earliest linguistic efforts of children will not be guided by the syntactic bioprogram, but will rather reflect the protolanguage developed by an earlier species (probably *homo erectus*) and still available to our species when true linguistic communication breaks down (i.e. the pidgin situation). However, at a determinate age the syntactic bioprogram will come on line so to speak, and there will consequently be an exponential increase in the capacity of the child to form structures and in particular to form structures of some degree of grammatical complexity. However, contrary to maturational models, different modules of syntax are not envisaged as coming on line at different times. Rather, a single development is seen as providing all that is necessary both for the acquisition of particular (preexisting) grammars and, if necessary, for the creation of a novel (if far from unique) grammar.

This prediction is not made by any other theory of language acquisition. The extent to which the prediction is in fact fulfilled by children in the course of normal development will be discussed in the next section.

IV. THE PACE OF NORMAL SYNTACTIC DEVELOPMENT

That the pace of syntactic development is uneven has been well known for some time. For instance, in the 1930s, Leopold (1939–1949, Vol. 4, p. 26) made the following observation of his daughter Hildegard at age 2;5

> The last few months have brought enormous progress. At two years she still spoke prevailingly in single words. Six weeks ago she put sentences together haltingly. Now . . . she can express everything and does so in more and more complicated sentences. . . . The decisive step has been taken. All that can follow now is growth in details.

In one of the surprisingly few studies devoted to the time of emergence of complex structures, Limber (1973, p. 165) remarked:

> What I have not been able to do, unfortunately, is to alleviate by explanation any of the astonishment Leopold—or anyone else—is compelled to express upon consideration of the linguistic achievements of these 2-year-old children.

These achievements (which include, according to Limber, the acquisition of infinitivals, conjunctions, embedded questions, and subordinate *if/when*-type clauses prior to 2;4, followed shortly afterward by factive and relative clauses) are all the more astonishing in view of the fact that, up until the start of the second year, progress has been so sluggish. At age two, many children have been producing recognizably linguistic utterances for a period of nine to twelve months and may have remained several months in a stage during which the bulk of utterances consisted merely of pairs of words. Within a few weeks, the child is producing a wide variety of single-clause structures, often showing considerable depth of embedding, and the first complex sentences follow within at most another month or so. Indeed, these may well appear simultaneously, as they do for one child (Seth, see Wilson, 1985) from whom diary as well as audiotaped data were obtained. The schedules most common in the audiotaping or videotaping of children's speech (an hour or so at biweekly, triweekly, or monthly intervals) almost certainly will miss the first appearances of such sentences. Subsequent to this period of high acceleration, the pace of acquisition slackens again as the child engages in a years-long "mopping-up operation" aimed at the more language-specific constructions of the target language.

In Bickerton (1992) the nature of this progress is documented in a longitudinal study of five children between the ages of 18 months and three years. In three of the five (Seth, Cheryl, and Peter), the syntactic acceleration took place around the age of 25 months. This acceleration can be confirmed by a variety of measures (statistics on four of the children are based on samples of 100 utterances taken from each recording session, whereas Cheryl's data are taken from a diary kept by her father, Richard Brislyn). One is the rate at which the percentage of three-word or longer utterances increases. Over the three months prior to the acceleration, rates of increase are either extremely slow (averaging no more than 3% per month in one case) or may actually fall (a decrease in frequency was observed in the other two cases). Subsequently, however, over a two-month period, Seth's percentage increased from 9% to 54% (equivalent to a gain of 22.5% per month), Cheryl's from 14% to 55% (20.5% per month), and Peter's from 9% to 56% (23.5% per month). (It should be noted that, since one- and two-word utterances continue to be found among adults, the *adult* percentage of three-word-plus sentences seldom rises above about 95%.) Indeed, most of this progress was accomplished in much shorter periods: Cheryl from 27% to 55% (28%) in a month, Peter from 9% to 40% (31%) in three weeks, and Seth from 15% to 33% (18%) in two weeks.

A second measure involves the type-token ratio of utterance types. The type-token ratio is low in the early stages of language acquisition, because the child controls a very limited number of structural types. As the child acquires more and more structural types, the ratio of types to tokens increases until it approaches the limit of 100%. For two of the children, the percentage of types in a sample of 100 tokens per period rises from 23% to 45% in a month (Cheryl), from 11% to 28% in a month (Seth), and from 10% to 24% in three weeks (Peter).

A third measure involves the rate at which novel structures are produced. This figure can be determined by calculating the percentage relationship of newly introduced structures to previously used structures at any given period. By this measure, Seth's production of novel structures increases from 50% to 150% in two weeks, Cheryl's from 50% to 225% in four weeks, and Peter's from 150% to 325% in three weeks. What is noteworthy about the higher figures is that they represent peaks of achievement; in the period immediately following the peak, Seth's production rate for new forms falls from 150% to 80%, Cheryl's from 225% to 130%, and Peter's from 325% to 120%. In other words, as claimed in the previous section, the pace of syntactic acquisition declines immediately after the brief peak period of acceleration has been passed.

The measures described here—and a couple of other related measures discussed in Bickerton (1992), which give similar results—are of course quantitative. However, qualitative measures give similar results. Whereas noun phrases containing two constituents (Det N, or Adj N) occurred sporadically from 18 months onwards, none of the children produced three-constituent noun phrases prior to 25 months. At that age, however, there emerged [Det Adj N], [Poss Adj N], and [Adj Adj N], as well as a variety of complex VP structures, equally without precedent—[V [N] [P [Det N]]], [V [P [Det N] [Det N]]], and [V [N] [P [Det Adj N]]], among several others. The appearance of such deeply embedded structures within a space of a few weeks, after several months without any clear evidence of embedding even of the simplest kind, suggests again the sudden appearance of an innate capacity rather than the gradual emergence of an acquired capacity.

The other two children (Eve and Adam, two of the original subjects of Brown, 1973) differ from the previous three only in the timing of onset of their syntactic mechanism. In the case of Eve, onset was unusually early (around 19 months). However, age of onset had little effect on the statistical measures described previously. Eve's three-word-plus utterances went from 7% to 53% over a two-month period (closely matching the figures for Seth), while her type-token ratio went from 11% to 27% over a two-week period, and her percentage of new utterance types rose from 65% to 113% in two weeks and fell again to 40% in a similar period. As regards qualitative measures, Eve produced complex NPs and VPs comparable to those of the other three subjects, but some six months earlier in each case (e.g., [Det Adj N] at 19 rather than 25 months, [P [Det N]] at 18;2 rather than 24;2, and so on). Thus, with one or two minor differences (due largely to the fact that Eve's vocabulary was, quite naturally, considerably smaller than that of the other children at the onset of syntactic acceleration), the pattern of Eve's development did not differ from that of the other three children despite its much earlier onset.

Adam's acceleration, however, happened considerably later than that of the others (after 34 months). Over an eight-month period (26–34 months) Adam showed a gain in the percentage of three-word-plus utterances of only 35%—a gain only slightly larger than that made by Peter in three weeks! The highest gain in type-token ratios is 8% in a month, as compared to gains two to three times greater than this by the other children over equal or shorter periods. Three other statistical measures each have their peaks in a different month (at 30, 32, and 34 months, respectively), whereas for all the other children, all three measures peak in the same month. Also, Adam's measures fluctuated randomly, whereas those of the other children showed an identical pattern—a single rise to a sharp peak, followed by a single fall (for full statistics on all five children, see Bickerton, 1992). With regard to qualitative measures, Adam produced only six complex phrase types over the whole eight-month period, (as opposed to eight to ten types within six weeks or less by each of the other four children) and he produced no biclausal sentences prior to 35;2.

What are we to conclude from these figures? The acceleration by Cheryl, Seth, and Peter at 25 months, and by Eve at 19 months, does not coincide with any significant stage in cognitive or motor development. If the children are in fact engaged in some active (even if unconscious) mode of acquisition, regardless of whether that mode consists of operating strategies, inductive inference, or parameter-setting, there is no logical explanation of why their syntactic capacities should increase so rapidly in so short a time. However, the emergence of an automatic, biologically based capacity—one which, on recognizing the properties of words, mapped them onto a recursive, hierarchical structure—would be completely congruent with the data surveyed.

Acquisitionists to whom this idea is repulsive will doubtless seek to claim Adam, with his much more gradual development, as a counterexample. But if Adam is indeed doing whatever he is supposed to do—setting parameters, testing hypotheses, utilizing operating procedures—and if this is supposed to explain the relative slowness of his development, how are we to account for the development of the other four children (which corresponds, as far as one can tell, to the normal development of the population as a whole)?

Adam's repertoire of utterance types at 27 months, and indeed the whole profile of his development at that age, closely resembles the repertoires and profiles of the other children when they were at a point immediately prior to their syntactic acceleration. There is no reason to suppose that Adam was any less intelligent or slower in overall cognitive development than the other children. Yet within a few weeks of being at Adam's 27-month stage, all the other children were producing a wide range of complex sentences. It took Adam more than eight months to progress to complex sentences. Proposing Adam as a counterexample to the LBH's claims does nothing to explain this fact.

But what of the fact that during those eight months Adam's development did not simply stand still? The answer is that even in the absence of a specialized syntactic mechanism it would be bizarre to expect his development to stand still. After all, Adam, along with other children, acquired certain aspects of language by some means—if the present account is correct, by means of general cognition, presumably assisted by task-specific sound-recognition, word-recognition, and perhaps even category-recognition devices—prior to age 2. These resources do not simply disappear after that age. To the contrary, to the extent that general cognitive abilities increase after 2, the capacity to learn in this way should likewise increase. However, the fact that Adam's discourse was for so long restricted to simple sentences suggests that if the syntactic mechanism had not begun to function at some phase, he might never have attained a mature command of syntax.

But quite apart from such theoretical considerations, there are some striking ways in which Adam's output during the period in question differs from that of children who are acquiring language with the aid of the syntactic mechanism. For instance, Adam produces anomalous utterances at a much higher rate than the other children—nearly 9%, as opposed to 1% or 2% for the others. More striking still, the percentage of anomalous utterances increases with utterance length—only 4% of two-word utterances are anomalous, as opposed to 15% of three-word utterances and 19% of utterances consisting of four or more words. This strongly suggests that Adam is putting words together in ways different from those of other children.

Also, when Adam's longer utterances *are* grammatical, they look suspiciously as if they were formed by simply adding together two-word combinations that he had already heard many times from others and indeed had actually used himself. Of those longer utterances, 74% contained components that Adam had previously used (as against 31% in Peter's output), and 100% contained components that Adam had either used himself or that had been modeled for him by other speakers (as against 72% in the case of Peter). In light of all the evidence, the most likely assumption is that Adam's syntactic mechanism was late in developing and that up until nearly age 3 his acquisition of syntax proceeded in ways quite different from those of the other children.

The hypothesis of an automatic syntax-forming mechanism raises, of course, a variety of questions. We might ask, for instance, what becomes of continuity theory, argued for by Baker (1979), Chomsky (1975), and Pinker (1984), among others on the grounds that parsimony forbids the hypothesis of distinct grammars at distinct developmental stages because the hypothesis of a single underlying grammar is enough to explain normal development. This position has already been challenged from a maturationist position (Borer & Wexler, 1987; Radford, 1990), which sees different modules of the grammar surfacing at different stages of development, and the maturationist position has in its turn been criticised by Crain (1991) for its dubious falsifiability, as well as on empirical grounds.

However, the LBH does not claim discontinuity in grammar types—rather than there is *no* grammar prior to the syntactic acceleration and that this acceleration is only made possible by the onset of a completely mature syntactic capacity. Why this mature *capacity* does not immediately give rise to a mature *syntax* is easily answered: The acquisition of a mature (adult) syntax of any target language depends on the acquisition of the full range of lexical properties (including properties of gaps such as the circumstances under which these are licensed in subjects of tensed sentences) that is specific to that language. This information can only be learned (even if, as claimed earlier, the list of possible properties from which different languages select different menus is somehow innate) and learning takes time.

Another question involves the nature of the syntactic mechanism. What exactly does it accomplish? How, if language has been hypothesized to consist of a variety of modules, can a single mechanism endow its possessor with a mature syntactic capacity? The answer is that up until the syntactic acceleration the child has simply been stringing words together as one strings beads—with few beads per string, at that. The syntactic mechanism that comes on line sometime between the 18th and 36th month begins to map words onto hierarchical, recursive structures by (a) pairwise attachment, beginning with the most deeply embedded verb and its complement (b) attachment of this pair to another unit or pair of units, (c) repetition of the preceding, as often as needed.

Prior to the syntactic acceleration, the bead-stringing process proceeds without any guidance from the thematic component. As Hyams (1986) noted, arguments in subject position are often missing; as Radford (1990) noted these omissions extend to arguments in all other positions. Initially, the mechanism maps only theta positions onto this formal structure (it is assumed that the theta grids of verbs are universal: Any verb that means *sleep* will select one argument, any verb that means *break* will select two, and any verb that means *give* will select three). It is this that gives child language at the commencement of the acceleration the strict configurational pattern and lack of "movement" that have often been noted.

However, the syntactic component is guided not merely by the theta system but also by incoming data. Thus a child learning English must soon realize that pleonastic subjects, raising verbs, full and truncated passives, and other constructions where the mapping of theta roles onto formal structure is far from straightforward have somehow to be accomodated in the grammar. But note that all that is required here is lexical learning, because knowledge of the properties of *it/there, seem, be* + participial *-ed,* and so forth will allow these items to be mapped appropriately onto the formal structure. Note too that it is precisely features of this nature that are missing from creole languages—the original pidgin inputs to these languages included no pleonastic forms, no raising verbs, and no copulas or bound morphemes; thus creoles either lack entirely or have only very recently invented *there is/are*-type presentative constructions, raising constructions, or passive constructions.

Indeed, this is the only respect in which the original creation of creole languages from pidgin input differs from the normal acquisition of established languages. Whether the input to the child consists largely of well-formed sentences (including complex sentences), as is the case in "normal" acquisition, or whether it consists almost entirely of ill-formed sentences (without any complex sentences), as in the case of the first creole generation, is a matter of total indifference to the syntactic mechanism. Give that mechanism any kind of vocabulary, minimally specified for properties like N and V, and it will process that vocabulary into hierarchical structures, complex as well as simple. However, it will pay heed to input, insofar as it *is* sensitive to lexical properties. In the creole case, the mechanism is working with a very limited (pidgin) vocabulary that has very few properties. In the normal case, it has to handle a rich vocabulary with many properties, the precise language-specific distribution of which is idiosyncratic.

Mention of the creole case leads us naturally to consider the problems that are raised for current theories of acquisition by the conjunction of the two empirical areas we have surveyed: the extraordinary rapidity of early syntactic development plus the capacity to create a complex syntax from input that is both limited and ill formed. Acquisition theory has so far avoided facing these problems, an avoidance the consequences of which are discussed in the section that follows.

V. THE LBH VERSUS OTHER ACQUISITION THEORIES

It should be clear that neither of our crucial data—syntactic acceleration and creole formation—can be adequately accounted for by any approach that depends on the quality of input. The best such a theory could hope to do with the first datum is claim that at some point in acquisition, something clicks and the input data with which the child has been struggling for many months, without any very striking success, suddenly falls into place. But *what* clicks and precisely how it clicks are questions that these approaches would be hard put to answer. The second datum presents still more severe problems. Creole languages cannot have been learned from mother (Snow, 1977) because mother did not know the language that was being acquired, and they cannot have been learned by inductive inference (MacWhinney, 1982) because there was no body of well-formed utterances from which structures, especially complex structures, could have been derived.

Approaches such as that of Slobin (1979, 1985), which rely on the child applying to input data a series of strategies or operating procedures (OPs), fare little better. Slobin's claim that children's versions of target languages resemble one another more than adult versions do is observationally correct but fails to explain why, as they diverge toward the adult target, the rate at which they are acquired should first suddenly speed up and subsequently slow down. As regards creolization, OPs like "Pay attention to the ends of words" are of little help when there is nothing at the ends of the words to pay attention to—a state of affairs that characterizes all pidgin input.

More recently, Gleitman (1989) has argued for a process known as *syntactic bootstrapping*—one by which children, far from inferring morphophonemic and syntactic properties from semantics, as had often been claimed, are able to infer semantic properties from morphophonemics. Thus a child might infer that an item belongs to a class of verbs by observing the verb inflections that the item will accept. Syntactic bootstrapping, however, is no more helpful than OPs in accounting for the emergence of creoles, since the first creole generation could not have acquired anything from inflectional morphemes or indeed any bound morphemes—there weren't any. It may indeed be the case that a child in the normal situation finds syntactic bootstrapping useful in acquiring the target language (although the case of Chinese remains dubious!). However, creoles show that syntactic bootstrapping can in no sense form a necessary component of language acquisition.

A variety of models, both inductionist and innatist, have relied on the child adopting some form of of *hypothesis testing* as an acquisition device. But it should be apparent that, at least as regards syntax, hypothesis testing is on a par with syntactic bootstrapping. There is no way in which a child creating a creole language out of pidgin data could form a hypothesis with the least hope that the data would ever either confirm or disconfirm it. Thus, while hypothesis formation (about morphemes and their properties) may perhaps form part of acquisition under normal circumstances, it too cannot possibly form a necessary component of language acquisition.

One might suppose that in acquisition models relying more heavily on innate factors, problems raised by the LBH would diminish, but this does not seem to be the case. Except for maturational models, none of the more nativist theories predict any sudden increments in linguistic capacity, and maturational models usually predict more than one significant increment. As for creolization, nativist theories do no better than inductionist ones. Consider, for example, the proposals of generativists such as Berwick (1985, p. 95), who assumed that the acquisition device must receive "a representative sample of sentences generated by the target grammar in question" and who defined *representative* as meaning that all the grammatical sentences must appear with greater frequency than errors. Berwick explicitly admitted that his model would not work if input from two languages (such as English and Chinese) was randomly mixed—what he called the problem of "Chinese noise." But mixed input (varying proportions of pidgin English, macaronic pidgin, and pidgin Hawaiian) was precisely what was received by the first generation of Hawaiian creole speakers, who still somehow managed to derive from it a homogeneous grammar.

One of the most radical nativist proposals is that of Lightfoot (1989), who, responding to an earlier proposal (Wexler & Culicover, 1980) that grammar could be derived from input limited to *degree-2* sentences (sentences with no more than two depths of embedding), argued that syntax could be acquired from an input of *degree-0* sentences (sentences without any embedding at all). This claim was, at least in part, motivated by a desire, actively expressed in earlier work (Lightfoot,

1984, 1988), to inoculate acquisition theory against "unacceptable" evidence from creoles. However, Lightfoot (1989) was forced to admit that his degree-0 sentences would have to be homogeneous as well as robust—that is, they would have to contain a very high ratio of grammatical to ungrammatical sentences. As Bickerton (1991) pointed out, Lightfoot showed his failure to grasp the nature of the original input to creoles by describing that input, at different points in Lightfoot (1989), as simple but not mixed, and mixed but not simple—a contradiction that his response to Bickerton (1991) (Lightfoot 1991) signally failed to elucidate.

In common with other generativists, Lightfoot has to suppose that the child sets the parameters of a grammar by processing well-formed input from the relevant language, arriving at settings that are normally identical with those found in the grammars of adult speakers of the same language. If this were the case, creoles would either have the same settings as some single preexisting language, take some settings from one language and some from another, or have no settings at all (if children attended exclusively to the pidgin data and ignored other languages spoken around them). As is well known, none of these three alternatives is what happens. A creole language arrives at a set of settings (assuming for the moment that parameter setting is what really happens in acquisition) different from that of any single language available at its time and place of creation, and indeed with settings that may differ from *any* of these in *any* available language. Moreover, the set of settings at which it arrives is virtually identical to the set of settings in dozens of completely unrelated creole languages—a fact that, after two decades, still patiently awaits its orthodox generative explanation.

Unlike Lightfoot, Pinker (1984, p. 357) was prepared to confess the inability of his approach to account for creole acquisition, and he insightfully linked this inadequacy to the input issue: "The theory is fairly data-driven, and at present cannot account in any simple way for the creation of novel grammars under conditions of radically degenerate linguistic input documented by Bickerton (1981)." However, even Pinker was unwilling to draw from this fact the obvious conclusion that a theory of acquisition that cannot account for creole acquisition is about as useful as a theory of medicine that can explain why healthy people stay healthy but not why they fall sick.

Finally, a recent work (Radford, 1990), although still constrained by orthodox generative assumptions, comes closer than any other work within that framework to the conclusions of the LBH. Radford viewed the child as initially in an *acategorial* stage, which yields (at around 20 months) to a *lexical-thematic* stage (at which the child can identify lexical categories and thematic roles, but do little else). However, at around 24 months the child progresses to a *functional-nonthematic* stage, and Radford speculated that "specific types" of language handicap (e.g., language delay or agrammatism) may be characterized by the late onset of (or loss of) functional-nonthematic modules of grammar" (1990, p. 276).

Although Radford spoke specifically of *modules* in the plural, it is clear that he believed (correctly) that several such modules come on line more or less simultaneously. As he himself stated (1990, p. 283):

> The nature of the linguistic development that has taken place in that short period of time is *nothing short of astounding* [emphasis added]. What is particularly striking is that the development is *cross-categorial* [original emphasis] (i.e., it isn't just the D-system, or the I-system which has evolved, but rather a whole range of different functional and nonthematic structures have developed altogether).

With a few vocabulary changes, this account would differ little from the LBH account given previously. In particular, Radford's claim (1990, p. 112) that "Small children speak Small Clauses" and that they lack determiner systems, complementizer systems, inflection systems, case systems, and true empty categories is virtually equivalent to the claim in the present account that small children have no syntax at all. The only major point of difference is on the issue of thematic relations prior to syntactic acceleration. Whether or not the child can distinguish thematic roles prior to this point, it is a plain fact—and one that Radford (1990, pp. 213–218), in discussing the work of Hyams, himself specifically points out—that prior to syntactic acceleration children frequently fail to express all the roles of a verb's theta grid. They leave gaps—gaps that are not recoverable by any regular rule but that have to be filled by the listener on a purely pragmatic, contextual basis. Once the acceleration is under way, all thematic roles in a verb's grid are represented—overtly, at first. There is little evidence for movement, and certainly none for A-movement, at this stage. But it is only natural that an all-arguments-present stage should occur between a randomly inserted-argument stage and the mature stage in which gaps may be left provided they are recoverable under rule. The child has to know that there *are* obligatory theta positions before being able to insert null, but rule-recoverable, categories in those positions.

It may well be that the child tactily understands theta *roles,* as Radford suggested, prior to the syntactic acceleration. Indeed, if the child did not already understand theta roles, it is hard to see how accessing an automatic, purely computational mechanism would bring about understanding. But what the child *does not* understand at this stage are theta *positions,* and it is the expression of theta positions—at first only overtly, later with the option of null-category insertion—that distinguishes the syntactically accelerating child and the adult, on the one hand, from the preacceleration child with a pidginlike protolanguage.

VI. CONCLUSION

The evidence surveyed in the foregoing section highlights the failure of current acquisition theories, whether innatist or inductionist in tendency. This failure is expressed in two principal ways. First, although so far only one acquisitionist (Pinker, 1984) has been honest enough to admit it, current theories of acquisition apply only to the "normal" case in which a child in an intact language community acquires the well-established language of that community from the well-formed input of its parents or other caregivers. None of these theories has anything to say about cases in which a child in a chaotic language community acquires a previously nonexistant language from the ill-formed and indeed largely structureless input of its parents or other caregivers.

This would be bad enough, since the goal of any acquisition theory should be to determine how children acquire *language,* not how they acquire this particular language or that particular language. But existing acquisition theories cannot even account for the course that the normal acquisition of particular languages takes. None has any principled way of explaining that process's sluggish start, its incredibly rapid acceleration, and its subsequent, much slower advance to mastery of a particular, preexisting language variety.

It should be emphasized, however, that the first failure logically begets the second—that is, it is failure to deal with the creole case that makes theories unable to explain normal development in a way that is faithful to the well-established facts of that development. For *the mechanism that creates creole languages is the same mechanism that acquires other kinds of language.* It would be absurd to suppose that there are two acquisition devices, one for normal languages, and a parachute, so to speak, just in case one is accidentally born into a pidgin community. But if indeed a single mechanism is responsible for both processes, then there is no hope of ever understanding normal acquisition until the process that creates creoles is recognized, understood, and allotted its rightful place in acquisition studies.

REFERENCES

Adone, D. (1991). *The acquisition of Mauritian Creole.* Unpublished doctoral dissertation, University of Hamburg, Germany.

Alleyne, M. C. (1980). *Comparative Afro-American.* Ann Arbor, MI: Karoma.

Baker, C. L. (1979). Syntactic theory and the projection problem. *Linguistic Inquiry, 10,* 533–581.

Berwick, R. (1985). *The acquisition of syntactic knowledge.* Cambridge, MA: MIT Press.

Bickerton, D. (1974). Creolization, linguistic universals, natural semantax and the brain. *Working Papers in Linguistics, 6*(3), 124–141, University of Hawaii.

Bickerton, D. (1981). *Roots of language.* Ann Arbor, MI: Karoma.

Bickerton, D. (1984). The language bioprogram hypothesis. *Behavioral and Brain Sciences, 7,* 173–212.

Bickerton, D. (1990). *Language and Species.* Chicago: University of Chicago Press.

Bickerton, D. (1991). Haunted by the specter of creole genesis. *Behavioral and Brain Sciences, 14,* 364–366.

Bickerton, D. (1992). *The instantaneous acquisition of syntax.* Manuscript submitted for publication.
Bickerton, D., & Odo, C. (1976). *General phonology and pidgin syntax.* Final report on NSF Grant No. GS-39748, Vol. 1 [Mimeo]. University of Hawaii.
Bishop, I. B. (1875). *Six months in the Sandwich Islands.* London: J. Murray.
Borer, H., & Wexler, K. (1987). The maturation of syntax. In T. Roeper & E. Williams (Eds.), *Parameter setting* (pp. 123–172). Dordrecht: D. Reidel.
Brown, R. (1973). *A first language: The early stages,* Cambridge, MA: Harvard University Press.
Bruner, J., & Feldman, C. (1982). [Review of *Roots of language*]. *New York Review of Books.*
Chaudenson, R. (1979). A propos de la genese du creole mauricien: Le peuplement de l'Ile de France de 1721 a 1735. *Etudes Creoles, 2,* 43–57.
Chomsky, N. (1965). *Aspects of the theory of syntax.* Cambridge, MA: MIT Press.
Chomsky, N. (1972). *Language and mind* (2nd ed.). New York: Harcourt, Brace, Jovanovich.
Chomsky, N. (1975). *Reflections on language.* New York: Pantheon.
Corwin, E. (1872, October). *Overland Monthly,* 314.
Crain, S. (1991). Language acquisition in the absence of experience. *Behavioral and Brain Sciences, 14,* 597–650.
Cziko, G. (1986). Testing the LBH: A review of children's acquisition of articles. *Language, 62,* 878–898.
Cziko, G. (1988). The LBH. A reply to Youssef, *Journal of Child Language, 15,* 669–671.
Cziko, G. (1989). A review of the state-process and punctual-nonpunctual distinction in children's acquidition of verbs. *First Language, 9,* 1–31.
Cziko, G., & Koda, K. (1987). A Japanese child's use of stative and punctual verbs. *Journal of Child Language, 14,* 99–112.
Das, U. K. (1931). *Terms used on Hawaiian plantations.* Honolulu: Hawaiian Sugar Planters' Association.
Dutton, C. E. (1884, February 9). *The Hawaiian islands and people.* Lecture delivered at the Smithsonian Institution, Washington, DC.
Gleitman, L. (1989, April). The structural sources of verb meaning. Keynote address, Stanford Child Language Conference, Palo Alto, CA.
Goodman, M. (1984). Are creole structures innate? *Behavioral and Brain Sciences, 7,* 193–194.
Goodman, M. (1985). [Review of *Roots of language*]. *International Journal of American Linguistics, 51,* 109–137.
Grant, M. F. (1888). *Scenes in Hawaii.* Toronto: Hart & Co.
Hall, R. A., Jr. (1966). *Pidgin and creole languages.* Ithaca: Cornell University Press.
Holm, J. (1986). Substrate diffusion. In P. Muysken & N. Smith (Eds.), *Substrate versus universals in creole genesis,* 259–78. Amsterdam: Benjamins.
Holm, J. (1988). *Pidgins and Creoles* (Vol. 2). Cambridge University Press.
Hyams, N. (1986). *Language acquisition and the theory of parameters.* Dordrecht: Reidel.
Lefebvre, C. (1986). Relexification in creole genesis revisited: The case of Haitian creole.

In N. Smith & P. Muysken (Eds.), *Substrate versus universals in creole genesis* (pp. 279–300). Amsterdam: Benjamins.

Leopold, W. (1939–1949). *Speech development of a bilingual child.* Evanston, IL: Northwestern University Press.

Lightfoot, D. (1984). The relative richness of triggers and the bioprogram. *Behavioral and Brain Sciences, 7,* 198–199.

Lightfoot, D. (1988). Creoles, triggers and universal grammar. In C. Duncan-Ross et al. (Eds.), *Rhetorica, pragmatica, syntactica: a festschrift for R. P. Stockwell.* London: Croom-Helm.

Lightfoot, D. (1989). The child's trigger experience: Degree-0 learnability. *Behavioral and Brain Sciences,* 15.

Lightfoot, D. (1991). Simple triggers and creoles. *Behavioral and Brain Sciences, 14,* 365–368.

Limber, J. (1973). The genesis of complex sentences. In J. Moore (Ed.), *Cognitive development and the acquisition of meaning* (169–185). New York: Academic Press.

McWhinney, B. (1982). Basic syntactic processes. In S. A. Kuczaj (Ed.), *Language development: Vol. 1, Syntax and semantics* (73–136). Hillside, NJ: Lawrence Erlbaum.

Mapstone, E. R., & Harris, P. L. (1985). Is the English present progressive unique? *Journal of Child Language, 12,* 433–441.

Pinker, S. (1984). *Language learnability and language development.* Cambridge, MA: Harvard University Press.

Radford, A. (1990). *Syntactic theory and the acquisition of English syntax.* Oxford: Basil Blackwell.

Roberts, J. (1991). *Origins of pidgin in Hawaii.* Paper presented at the 17th Austronesian Conference, Honolulu, HA.

Roberts, J. (n.d.). Language and communication in Hawaii between 1809 and 1920. Unpublished manuscript.

Slobin, D. I. (1979). *Psycholinguistics* (2nd ed.). London: Scott Foresman.

Slobin, D. I. (1985). Crosslinguistic evidence for the language-making capacity. In D. I. Slobin (Ed.), *The crosslinguistic study of language acquisition: Vol. 2, Theoretical issues* (1157–1256). Hillsdale, NJ: Lawrence Erlbaum.

Snow, C. E. (1977). Mother's speech research: From input to interaction. In C. E. Snow & C. A. Ferguson (Eds.), *Talking to children: Language input and acquisition* (31–49). Cambridge: Cambridge University Press.

Sylvain, S. (1936). *Le creole haitien, morphologie et syntaxe.* Wetteren, Belgium: de Meester.

Taylor, D. (1960). Language shift of changing relationship? *International Journal of American Linguistics, 26,* 144–161.

Thompson, R. W. (1961). A note on some possible affinities between the creole dialects of the Old World and those of the New. In R. B. LePage (Ed.), *Creole Language Studies* (Vol. 2, pp. 107–113). London: Macmillan.

Voorhoeve, J. (1973). Historical and linguistic evidence in favor of the relexification theory in the formation of creoles. *Language and Society, 2,* 133–145.

Wexler, K., & Culicover, P. (1980). *Formal principles of language acquisition.* Cambridge, MA: MIT Press.

Whinnom, K. (1956). *Spanish contact vernaculars in the Philippine Islands.* Hong Kong: Hong Kong University Press.
Whinnom, K. (1965). The origin of the European-based pidgins and creoles. *Orbis, 14,* 509–527.
Wilson, R. (1985). *The development of the semantics of tense and aspect in the language of a visually impaired child.* Ph.D. dissertation, University of Hawaii.
Youssef, V. (1988). The LBH revisited. *Journal of Child Language, 15,* 451–458.

CHAPTER 7

FUNCTIONALIST ACCOUNTS OF THE PROCESS OF FIRST LANGUAGE ACQUISITION

Matthew Rispoli

I. HISTORY AND DEFINITIONS: FUNCTIONALISM IN LINGUISTICS

A. Definitions

The dichotomy between functionalism and formalism constantly seems to arise in the effort to understand biological and psychological structure. For example, in the history of biological thought, the question of the origin of an organ such as a wing or an eye gives rise to both teleological explanations and mechanistic explanations. The teleological explanations cast the origin of a wing or eye in terms of the organ's purpose, whereas mechanistic explanations cast the origin of the organ in terms of the physical and chemical makeup and processes (Mayr, 1982). Despite the recurrence of functionalist/formalist dichotomies, such a dichotomy in the explanation of language acquisition will resemble dichotomies in other disciplines only in the abstract. Therefore, in order to proceed we must define the two sides of this dichotomy so that it applies straightforwardly to the study of language structure. We will first focus our attention on the dichotomy between functionalism and formalism in linguistics, and attempt to trace the dichotomy through its applications in language acquisition. Let us begin by defining *formalism* in linguistics:

Definition 1. *Formalism* is the explication and explanation of grammatical structure in which semantic and pragmatic constructs are extraneous.

Handbook of Child Language Acquisition

Definition 2. *Functionalism* in linguistics is the explication and explanation of grammatical structure in which semantic and pragmatic constructs are integral.

Some may argue that these definitions are too narrow. For example, some linguists propose that principles of grammar are related to cognitive principles of a variety of types (Langacker, 1986), and some might argue that these cognitive approaches could also be placed under the rubric of functionalism in linguistics (Nichols, 1984). Holding to the definitions presented here, such cognitive approaches cannot be classified as functionalist. The definitions have the advantage of being explicit enough to allow us to trace in detail a history of functionalist approaches in linguistics and language acquisition that has a high degree of unity and coherence. Therefore, we shall adopt these definitions of functionalism and formalism.

The crux of the difference between functionalism and formalism in linguistics lies in the treatments of two components of linguistic knowledge: semantics and pragmatics. If a theory explains a structure through formal principles alone, this theory is formalist in nature. An example would be government and binding theory's approach to case assignment in English, which is based on the structural notion of government (Chomsky, 1981; Haegeman, 1991). In contrast, a functionalist approach to case assignment invokes semantic and pragmatic information, such as Silverstein's (1976) approach to case, in which case is treated as the encoding of intersections of person, animacy, and the inherent lexical content of a noun phrase.

Keeping these definitions of formalism and functionalism in mind, we will trace the history of functionalist approaches to language acquisition. We shall begin this history with functionalist approaches to grammar, focusing on the contribution of these approaches to our understanding of grammatical representation. In this regard, we will also examine the theoretical environment in which this functionalist research was conducted, namely the Chomskyan revolution. We will then examine the way functionalism in linguistic research was translated into functionalist approaches to language acquisition. It will be argued that much of what has been labeled *functionalist* in language acquisition research is, in fact, essentially anti-Chomskyan, but not necessarily functionalist.

B. Mathesius and the Prague School

One of the earliest recognizable characterizations of grammatical structure in which pragmatic constructs are integral comes with the Prague school of structuralism (ca. 1920s). Mathesius's characterization of sentence types in Czech and English, dating back to the 1920s, were published posthumously in English (Mathesius, 1975). Mathesius recognized a level of organization based on pragmatics (although he did not use this term) separate from the morphemic or constituent analysis. In particular, he introduced the theme/rheme contrast, among other constructs. Theme was the element in a sentence that was less informative, whereas rheme was the contrasting element that was more informative. However, the work of the Prague school was never transmitted in a coherent way to scholars in the United States. With a few notable exceptions, functionalist approaches to grammar were absent in the United States until the mid-1970s. But intervening between the 1920s and the 1970s was the Chomskyan revolution.

C. The Chomskyan Revolution

By now the notion that there was a revolution during the 1950s and 1960s has become an accepted piece of standard historiography in linguistics and psychology. Although many contributed to a shift in thinking toward a representational and computational theory of mind, it was Chomsky who catapulted linguistics into the "cognitive revolution" (Gardner, 1987). The effect of the Chomskyan revolution was to set grammar on a firm mentalistic footing. The goal of linguistics was no longer to explicate grammar, but now to reveal the mental properties that were reflected in grammar. In setting the agenda for this new era of linguistic research an important distinction was drawn: the competence/performance distinction. Grammatical structure was indirectly related to the actual production or comprehension of an utterance, which, after all, had to satisfy the exigencies of the communicative situation: time pressure, memory load, noise, and lack of attention. When the researcher attempts to neutralize these sources of interference, by exhaustive reflection, a robust structure to linguistic behavior emerges. This structure, it was argued, was a closer approximation of our knowledge of grammar, or grammatical competence.

Further suggestions were made by Chomsky (1965) concerning an innate set of principles and substantives—which were purely formal in nature—called *universal grammar.* This made the study of child grammar a legitimate topic for linguistic and psychological research. The language acquisition problem became the problem of the ontogenesis of the *mental representation of grammar.* Because grammatical representations were held to be abstract, unrelated to physical reality, it was impossible to conceive of them as arising from the learner's inductive generalizations (Chomsky, 1986).

As linguists and psychologists pondered the question of just what mental properties were reflected in grammar, at least one philosopher proposed that some essential properties of grammar lay at the basis of cognition. In *The Language of Thought,* Fodor (1975) detailed an hypothesis that cognition, like language, had the equivalent of combinatorial semantics and syntactics. Combinatorial systems such as these have at their core a set of simple or atomic representations and a set of complex or molecular representations that can be analyzed in terms of molecular representations and atomic representations (Fodor & Pylyshyn, 1988). The power of this hypothesis and its implications put the study of grammar on a new plane. Grammatical representation was archetypical of cognition as a whole. By identifying the syntax of grammatical representations with the *syntax* of cognition, the form of grammatical representations came under scrutiny. In particular, the combinatorial nature of representations implied that cognitive operations in some way utilized structural descriptions of representations, such descriptions being the embodied equivalent of symbols (Fodor & Pylyshyn, 1988).

It should be borne in mind that during this period of intellectual revolution, roughly from the mid-1950s to the middle 1970s, research in the functionalist tradition, particularly that of the Prague school, was at a near standstill. The reemergence of functionalism, the subject of the following section on neofunctionalism, may have been fostered by a generalized reaction to the formalism of the Chomskyan revolution. However, with there being so many individual researchers labeling their approaches as functionalist in nature, it has never been clear exactly how functionalist approaches relate to the central question of Chomskyan linguistics and psycholinguistics, that is, the question of the mental representation of grammar. As we shall see, this has led to confusion and misunderstanding on the part of developmental psycholinguists.

To comprehend the seeds of this misunderstanding, we must dwell further on the nature of mental representation in general, and in particular, on the nature of the mental representation of grammar. Representations have at least two separate components. The components are the representation's *content and architecture.* The content is a representation's *semantic* content, what the representation is a representation of. The architecture of a representation is the *syntactic* properties of a representation, determining its internal and external constituency (if any) as well as its compatibility with other forms of representation. Take the simple example of a statue of Lincoln and a hologram of Lincoln. The architecture of these representations are radically different. The statue is made of a solid material, and its three-dimensional nature ceases to exist only if the statue ceases to exist. In contrast, the hologram is a projection. Its three-dimensional nature is not tied to the existence of the hologram because it is stored in another form—a non-three-dimensional form. The content of these representations, Lincoln, is the same for both the statue and the hologram.

In the Chomskyan revolution a comprehensive theory of the mental representation of grammar was advanced that encompassed both the content and architecture of representations. Some of the content of these representations initially included (and still do) theoretical entities corresponding to phrase structure constituents and lexical items, to mention a few. The architecture was highly componential. The representation of a sentence was analyzable into discrete components from the initial symbol for a sentence down to the smallest word internal symbol for an individual morpheme. Grammars, conceived of in this format, divided up naturally into larger subsystems, such as phonology, semantics, and syntax. The content of the representations in each of these subsystems is radically different, as common sense would lead one to expect. A phone cannot have the same relationship to the semantic subsystem as does a morpheme.

However, the architecture of the subsystems were hypothesized to be similar across the subsystems, with the basic design of componentiality and recombination retained in phonology, semantics, and syntax. For example generative semantics, an attempt to explicate the semantic component of grammar, had a surprisingly syntactic-looking representational architecture (McCawley, 1976; see Dowty, 1979, chapter 2, for an overview of several architectural possibilities). For example, the prelexical structure of the predicate *x kill y,* was diagrammed by McCawley in a tree diagram format. The tree structure is clearly modeled after syntactic representations prevalent at the time (See Figures 7.1a–c). Each *S* symbol in the tree denotes a possible proposition, with further propositions being constituents of the highest *S.* Each *S* constituent has a predicate, *cause, become,* and so on. The arguments of the predicate, x and y, are arguments of the predicates *cause* and *alive,* respectively. Note that there is no terminal node corresponding to the word *kill* itself. McCawley's proposal was that before the lexicalization of the verb *kill* was possible, successive transformations would have to move component Ss into progressively more inclusive constituents. One cycle of transformation has applied to the tree in Figure 7.1a to produce the tree in Figure 7.1b. The constituent *not alive* corresponds to a word in English: *dead.* Eventually, when all the predicates have been moved into one constituent, as in Figure 7.1c, we can lexicalize the entire set of components into the single word: *kill.* Clearly, the content of the representations in generative semantics was vastly different from the contents of representations in generative syntax, but the architecture of the two components was cast from the same mold.

As we approach the 1970s in this historical overview, it is important to bear in mind the following points. The Chomskyan revolution threw linguistics, and consequently developmental psycholinguistics, irrevocably into the investigation of mental representation. The comprehensive theory of the mental representation proposed by Chomsky during this period (Chomsky, 1957, 1965, 1981) encompassed hypotheses concerning both the content and architecture of grammatical representation. The content included entities of a purely formal nature. The architecture was highly componential, built of discrete elements or symbols. It was into this intellectual context that research self-labeled *functionalist* began to emerge.

D. Neofunctionalism in Linguistics

Almost 20 years after the publication of Chomsky's *Syntactic Structures* (1957), and approximately 10 years after Chomsky's *Aspects of a Theory of Syntax* (1965), in the middle 1970s analyses of grammatical structure began to appear that were explicitly labeled by the authors as *functionalist.* They include the work of Silver-

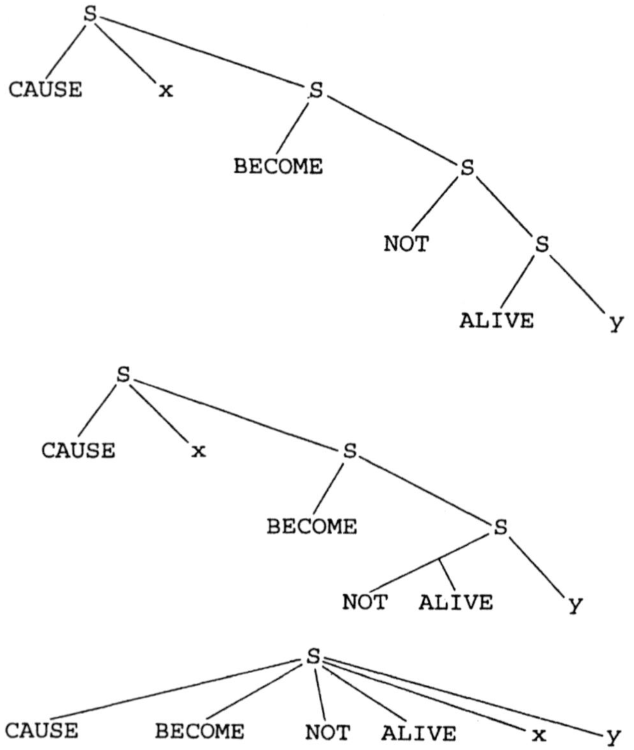

Figure 7.1. (top) Prelexical structure of *x kill y.* (middle) Prelexical structure of *x kill y* after one transformation has applied. (bottom) Prelexical structure of *x kill y* after all transformations have applied.

stein (1976), Dik (1978), Givon (1979), Foley and Van Valin (1984), and Van Valin (in press). Much of this research has been highly focused at particular phenomena in languages quite different from English. As a result, it is not possible to give a single, coherent statement of how this array of functionalist research addresses questions of grammatical representation. However, in keeping with the definition of functionalism given in Section I.A, it should be apparent that the major goal of functionalist research is the precise specification of how semantics, pragmatics, and morphosyntactic content interact in grammatical representation. Although such interactions may be thought of primarily in terms of the content of grammatical representations, it is possible that understanding these interactions will also reveal something nontrivial about the architecture of these representations. To date, the linguists who have been most successful in advancing our understanding of these interactions have been those Joanna Nichols (1984) termed *moderates.*

In her overview and review of neofunctionalist linguistic research, Nichols (1984) distinguished three levels or degrees of functional stance. (a) Conservative research, such as that of Kuno (1980), offers functional analysis to complement formal analysis but does not attempt to change or replace either the basic content or architecture of grammatical representations offered by formal analysis. (b) Moderate functionalist research, most notably by Silverstein (1976) and Foley and Van Valin (1984) calls into question much of the content of formalist grammatical representations by showing the interdependence of semantic, pragmatic, and morphosyntactic representations. They take the approach that the architecture of the representation accomodates the content of the representation to a much greater degree than in formalist analyses. (c) Extreme research, exemplified in the work of Givon (1979), Hopper and Thompson (1980), and Heath (1984), attempts to deny the existence of the basic formalist architecture in its entirety. In Nichols's opinion, extremists have a penchant for radical posturing but have been shy on substantive reanalyses of grammatical representation.

As mentioned previously, it is probably the moderates who have been most successful in specifying that semantic, pragmatic, and morphosyntactic contents interact in grammatical representations. Among the moderate functionalist research reviewed by Nichols (1984), the work of Silverstein (1976) and Foley and Van Valin (1984) are given special prominence. Silverstein's paper *Hierarchy of Features and Ergativity* (1976) presents a novel view of case systems. In this view, grammatical case is a dependent variable, an outcome predictable from the principled interaction of semantic and pragmatic dimensions in specific constructions. The semantic dimensions are (a) agent-patient relations and (b) tense-aspect distinctions (the latter are only briefly mentioned). The major pragmatic dimensions are (a) inherent lexical content and (b) reference-maintaining devices. Inherent lexical content means the uniqueness, specificity, and definiteness of an NP. For example, proper nouns and kin terms are high in inherent lexical content, whereas anaphoric pronouns are low in inherent lexical content. An example of a reference maintaining device is switch reference, a device often found in the languages of Papua-New Guinea. In switch reference, verbs in clause chains (often composed of coordinate clauses) will be affixed for whether the same referent or a different referent continues to be the subject of the clause. In effect, Silverstein proposed a new representation for case based on its compatibility with semantic and pragmatic components of grammar. One might think of the representation of case as a matrix of semantic, pragmatic, and other structural features, such as presented in Figure 7.2. A particular case is, in essence, indexed for these features, making the representational architecture similar to that of a paradigm. In Figure 7.2, we see a portion of a hypothetical case system in which the usual or unmarked form of an agent takes nominative case. However, when the clause has a tense-aspect feature of *perfective,* and the agent is third person, then the agent takes the ergative case.

It should be noted that Silverstein was speaking only of ergative, absolutive, nominative, and accusative cases. These cases are the ones most closely identified with the formalist constructs of the grammatical relations, subject, and object. In

	Tense and Aspect	
Person	Perfective	Imperfective
1st person	nominative	nominative
2nd person	nominative	nominative
3rd person	ergative	nominative

Figure 7.2. Case marking of agents in a matrix of semantic and pragmatic motivating factors in a hypothetical grammar.

that regard, one should note that in the government and binding (GB) framework (Chomsky, 1981) these cases are defined formally, in terms of phrase structure. The GB view of the representation of case is that case is a feature of NPs *assigned by* specific governers of those NPs. Here we see that Silverstein's representation of case is completely different from that of GB, both in terms of the content and architecture of the representation. Silverstein's notion of case has semantic and pragmatic content, and its architecture is matrixlike. The GB notion of case has very little by way of content, case is little more than a feature tagged to an NP, and the architecture needed to determine this feature is totally based on the hierarchical, componential representation of phrase structure.

Foley and Van Valin's *Functional Syntax and Universal Grammar* (1984) offered a reanalysis of clause structure that integrated semantic and pragmatic representations into morphological and syntactic representations to a degree that had not been previously accomplished. The overall theoretical framework was referred to as role and reference grammar (RRG), emphasizing the integration of semantic roles and referential status. Research in RRG has progressed (Van Valin, 1990, in press), but the basic principles developed in Foley and Van Valin (1984) have not changed. We shall briefly review some of those principles here.

To understand the RRG reanalysis of clause structure, one must begin with the representation of the logical (semantic) structure of a predicate, a theory of lexical representation based on Dowty (1979), which in turn is based on the Vendler's (1967) Aktionsart classification of predicates. This classification recognizes four types of predicate: states, achievements, accomplishments, and activities. Briefly put, states are atelic and nondynamic, activities are atelic but dynamic, achievements entail the inception of a state, and accomplishments entail the causation of either a state or an activity. In RRG, thematic roles are partially motivated by the predicate schema. Although space does not allow a detailed exposition of these relationships here, it is important to note that in RRG, the semantic representation of the predicate places restrictions on the type of thematic roles a predicate will have. A second tier of semantically motivated roles are posited in RRG, that of macroroles. Two macroroles exist: *actor* and *undergoer.* Thematic roles are mapped into these macroroles in interaction with the predicate types described earlier. An agent of an activity predicate will always be an actor, a patient in a state predicate will always be an undergoer. Thus, in RRG there is an explicit representational history traceable from the semantics of a predicate to case in morphosyntax.

Case systems are sets of structures motivated by macrorole assignment. Case systems come in three major varieties: nominative/accusative, for example, English; ergative/absolutive, such as Yidin (Dixon, 1979) and active/stative, for example, Acehnese (Durie, 1988). Case systems all have one characteristic in common: In transitive predicates (more exactly: multiple argument accomplishment predicates), actors and undergoers are treated as different roles. Nominative, ergative, and active cases encode actors, whereas accusative, absolutive, and stative cases encode undergoers. Each of the case systems orients single macrorole predicates differently. Single arguments in nominative/accusative languages receive nominative case, and in ergative/absolutive languages receive absolutive case. In active-stative systems, actor arguments of intransitives are given active case, the same case as actors in transitive predicates. Undergoers in intransitives are given stative case, the same case given to undergoers in transitive predicates. None of these systems are considered especially marked or unusual because they all are adapted to the basic task of encoding the actor/undergoer distinction. It is consistent with the RRG framework to expect that all three case orientations are equally acquirable by the child.

In addition to a detailed semantic representation, RRG assumes an independently motivated pragmatic representation. Every sentence has information structure (Lambrecht, 1987). The motivating force behind information structure is the pragmatic distinction between presupposition and assertion. Those constituents of a sentence that are not presupposed are eligible to become part of a sentence's focus, and the partitioning of a sentence into its focal and nonfocal parts is termed *focus* structure (Van Valin, in press). Lambrecht (1987) treats focus as a "formal scope indicator, i.e., as a grammatical signal indicating the scope of the assertion expressed by a sentence or proposition" (p. 374). WH-elements are always the focal elements of a sentence. In English declaratives, the scope of focus is largely expressed by stress. But this in itself is not entirely accurate. Working within the GB framework, Rochemont and Culicover (1990) have shown that extraposition must satisfy certain focality conditions. In sentence 1a the NP, *A boy wearing weird red glasses,* is presented with all subconstituents contiguous in surface structure. In sentence 1b this same NP is broken apart into discontinuous constituents: The phrase *wearing weird red glasses* is extraposed from its original NP source and adjoined to the periphery of the sentence. However, the NP in its discontinuous form cannot be used to answer a *which* question, as can be seen from the discourse in 2. A *which* question presupposes head noun, *boy,* but calls for adjunct modifiers of the head in the response. It appears that English phrase structure is adapted to a certain degree to be compatible with focus structure.

(1) a. *A boy* wearing weird red glasses came.
 b. *A boy* came wearing weird red glasses

(2) a. Which boy came to the party?
 b. ?A boy came wearing weird red glasses.

(3) a. who came to the party?
 b. A boy came wearing weird red glasses.

In many languages, such as Japanese, focus structure distinctions are signaled morphosyntactically (Kuno, 1973). In Japanese the postpositions *wa, mo, ga,* and *o* all signal differences in focus structure. However, *wa* and *mo* are macrorole neutral. That is, they can cooccur with either an actor or an undergoer. In contrast, *o* can only be used with undergoers in transitive predicates, and when so used it must be compatible with certain focality conditions. Similarly, *ga* cannot be used for the undergoer of a transitive (unless in a passive) and must also be compatible with certain focality conditions.

As to morphosyntactic structure, RRG recognizes the basic, substantive morphological classes such as noun and verb, as well as their possible elaborations into NP, VP, and so on (Foley and Van Valin, 1984; Van Valin, in press). However, RRG does not assume Xbar syntax. This is because many languages seem to have a flat structure, without the classic three levels of X°, X′, and X″. In the GB framework, this is called nonconfigurationality, and because nonconfigurationality abounds in the world's languages (Hale, 1983), nonconfigurationality is assumed as unmarked in universal grammar. Various configurational elements, such as VP in English, must be acquired in a language-specific manner.

RRG has adopted this hypothesis about phrase structure because it allows a more coherent integration of semantics (logical structure) and pragmatics (focus structure). These considerations have also led to a radically different representation of the internal structure of the clause, with a *layered* structure rather than a *branching* structure as found in GB. This layered structure is illustrated schematically in Figure 7.3. In nonconfigurational languages such as Navaho (Faltz, 1992; Young & Morgan, 1981), the *nucleus* of the clause is basically the verb stem; the entire verb, with its object and subject agreement prefixes and its mode and aspect prefixes, is considered the *core* of the clause. This can be seen in Figure 7.4, an analysis of the Navajo sentence *naashné* "I am playing." The macroroles and arguments specified in the semantic representation of the predicate (the logical structure) are realized morphologically as elements of the core. As with many nonconfigurational languages, the core of the clause is morphologically a single word. It is characteristic of such languages that the core alone, realized as a single word, is a grammatical, finite sentence. On the other hand, a variety of phrasal adjuncts, such as full NPs for the macroroles, can also appear in a clause type that is expanded at least one more layer, differentiating the clause from the core. We see this in Figure 7.5, the Navajo sentence *Bill naané* "Bill is playing." In GB, *Bill* would

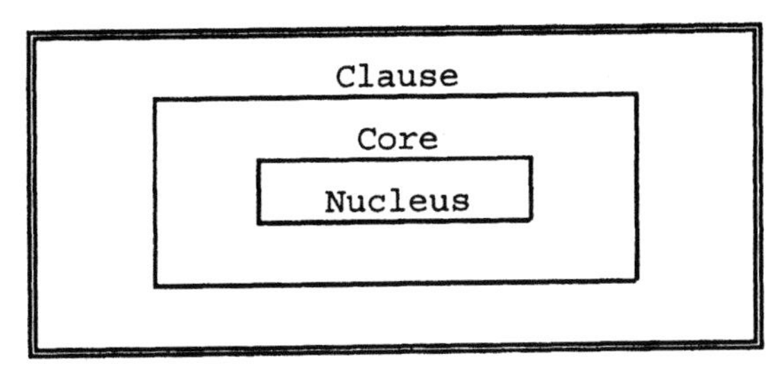

Figure 7.3. Schematic of the layered structure of the clause.

be considered a subject, by virtue of its position in phrase structure (Speas, 1990). However, in RRG it is considered an actor, by virtue of its semantics. There is in fact no separate subject NP constituent in RRG.

Concomitant with expansion from core to clause in nonconfigurational languages are differences in focus structure. For example, the sentence in Figure 7.5—*Bill naané* "Bill is playing"—can be used to answer the question, "Who is playing?" in which the actor role is focal. In contrast, the sentence *naané*—"(He) is playing"—cannot be used to answer an actor focal question. Thus, in articulating the interface of semantic and pragmatic representations with the morphosyntactic representation, RRG has been led to a new hypothesis about the basic form of syntactic representation and its status in universal grammar.

To summarize, moderate functionalists, such as Silverstein (1976) and the RRG group (Foley & Van Valin, 1984; Van Valin, 1990; Van Valin, in press), have begun to provide new hypotheses concerning the architecture of grammatical representation. However, this has not been their primary objective. Rather, their primary objective has been the explication of the interfaces between semantics, pragmatics, and morphosyntax, that is, the explication of mechanisms by which

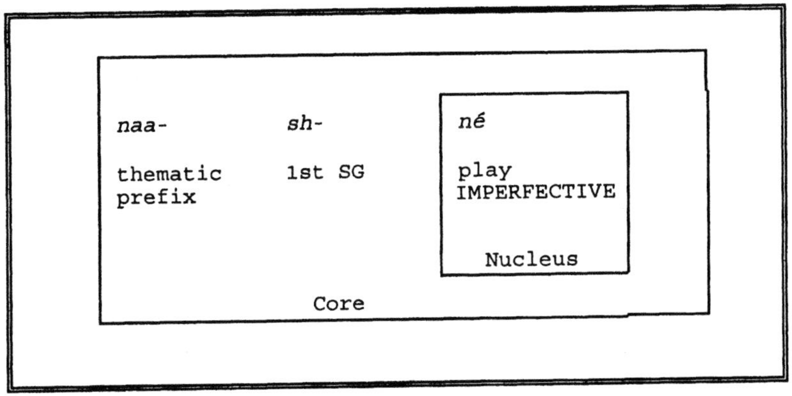

Figure 7.4. The layered structure of a Navajo sentence without overt NPs. *Naashné:* "I am playing."

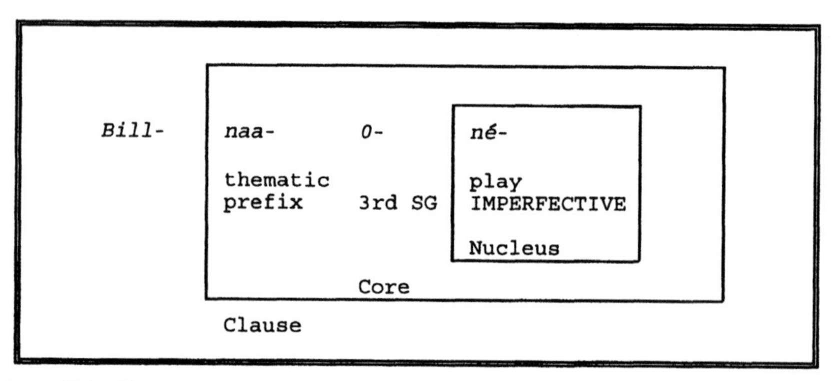

Figure 7.5. The layered structure of a Navajo sentence without an overt NP. *Bill naané:* "Bill is playing."

radically different types of representational content combine to make a grammar. In addition, they have begun to refocus attention on the semantic and pragmatic components of universal grammar. These developments in linguistic theory are of major import to developmental psycholinguists because they speak to the heart of developmental psycholinguistics: the ontogeny and development of grammatical representation.

II. STUDIES OF LANGUAGE ACQUISITION

At this juncture we are ready to shift our attention to the way functionalism in linguistic research has been translated into functionalist approaches to language acquisition. In so doing we must bear in mind that the Chomskyan revolution brought forth a comprehensive theory of both the content and architecture of grammatical representations. We must also keep in mind that functionalist linguistic research has seldom been clear on how it has addressed the central Chomskyan question of mental representation. Only since the late 1970s, with the research of moderate functionalists, has this question begun to be addressed. We must further keep in mind that the moderate functionalists were primarily concerned with the interface of semantics and pragmatics with morphosyntax. In other words, they were concerned with the interface of radically different types of representational content and not with the radical revision of our theories of representational architecture. Unfortunately, much of what has been labeled *functionalist* in language acquisition research is primarily concerned with representational architecture and not with representational content. In this sense, this research is anti-Chomskyan, but not necessarily functionalist, at least as defined at the outset in Section I.A.

A. Semantic Analyses and Cognitivist Approaches

Recall that neofunctionalism, and in particular the research of moderate functionalists, began to emerge in the latter half of the 1970s. In the earlier half of the 1970s, anti-Chomskyan research began to emerge in developmental psycholinguistics. Some of this research was relevant to our history in that the research raised some issues concerning grammatical representation. As will be shown, this work should not be considered functionalist. Examples of this research can be roughly differentiated by their semantic and cognitive foci.

With the publication of Schlesinger's theoretical reanalysis of early child language (Schlesinger, 1971) and Bowerman's research on the acquisition of Finnish (Bowerman, 1973), an hypothesis developed that the structure of early child language was essentially semantic in nature. This is a potentially anti-Chomskyan and antiformalist interpretation of early child language phenomena. Certainly, if the hypothesis were true, it would entail a substantial revision in our understanding of grammatical representation. The hypothesis has been abandoned for at least two reasons. (a) It has been shown that there exist in early child grammars categories based on morphological regularities devoid of semantic content, a particularly vivid example of this capacity underlying the acquisition of grammatical gender systems (Levy, 1983). (b) The hypothesis failed to take into account the possibility of interfaces between semantics and morphosyntax that would allow for simultaneous, dual, and compatible representations. That is, the hypothesis confused the semantic representation with a morphosyntactic one and attempted to replace one with the other. Such confusion led to significant learnability problems (Pinker, 1984; Radford, 1990). We should note, in addition, that such an hypothesis is not functionalist in the sense developed in Section I.A. because it ignores the possibility of yet a third, simultaneously interfacing representation, that of pragmatics or focus structure.

Also during the 1970s there was some movement in the direction of demonstrating the dependence of early child grammar upon cognitive development (Bloom, 1973). This hypothesis too was quietly abandoned as it became increasingly clear that grammatical representation was far too unlike the cognitive metatheory espoused by Piagetians (Piatelli-Palmerini, 1980). Once again, it should be noted, that such so-called cognitivist approaches ignored pragmatics. Cognitivist approaches should not be confused with functionalist approaches, despite the fact that some works espousing the cognitivist hypothesis have in their title the word *function* or *functional* (e.g., Karmiloff-Smith, 1979).

Largely because of their Piagetian basis, cognitivist approaches were often focused on phenomena of the acquisition of European languages. These phenomena have, at times, received reinterpretation in functionalist approaches and are noteworthy for the purposes of our history. Both Antinucci and Miller (1976) and Volterra (1976) traced the development of Italian's passato prossimo. This tense form is coded by an auxiliary verb and a participle. The participle agrees with subject of an intransitive verb if that verb encodes a telic, achievement predicate (Centineo, 1986; Van Valin, 1990), and the direct object of a transitive verb if the object is pronominal. Both Antinucci and Miller and Volterra observed that Italian children overused the agreement pattern, producing agreement when the objects of transitive verbs were lexical rather than pronominal. Volterra noted as well the absence of agreement with pronominal objects. In the children's problems with participial agreement, these researchers saw the children's cognizance of past action developing out of an understanding of present states. These researchers attempted to relate the acquisition of the passato prossimo to alleged cognitive developments. In so doing, however, these researchers accepted the basic formalist account of the participial agreement phenomenon, namely that the participle agrees with subject or object. This constituted a tacit acceptance of the formalist versions of grammatical representation. As we shall see in Section III.B, these researchers failed to note the relationship between the agreement system and the semantic representation. As a result, a possible functionalist interpretation of the phonema was not available to them.

To summarize, in the 1970s two streams of research can be discerned, one focusing on semantics and the other focusing on cognition. These lines of research have largely been abandoned. They were anti-Chomskyan, but not functionalist. They both failed to recognize that semantic, pragmatic, and morphosyntactic grammatical components were developing together, each with their own representational content. It is not surprising that research in both of these streams overlooked the involvement of semantic and pragmatic interfaces in morphosyntactic development.

B. Isolated Functionalist Analyses of First Language Acquisition Phenomena

Since the beginning of the 1980s there have been studies of the development of isolated morphosyntactic phenomena that invoked semantic or pragmatic distinctions. In this respect, these studies have approached a synthesis of functionalist linguistic theory and developmental psycholinguistics.

One study that infused functional analyses into a description of child language phenomena was Schieffelin's (1981, 1985) study of the acquisition of case marking in Kaluli. Kaluli has an ergative-absolutive case system, that is, the so-called subject of an intransitive sentence takes the same case as the so-called object of the transitive sentence (absolutive case). The so-called subject of a transitive sentence is given a special case all its own (ergative case). In order to show the systematicity of case-marking errors found in the acquisition of Kaluli, Schieffelin had to present an analysis of Kaluli grammar that included the pragmatic distinctions of focal scope, drawn from Givon's analysis of negation in Bantu languages and the animacy hierarchy, part of Silverstein's (1976) work on case (subsumed under his theory of inherent lexical content: see Section I.D). As in most cases of ergativity (Dixon, 1979), the ergative case in Kaluli is grammatically restricted. In Kaluli, the restriction is based on focus structure and the animacy hierarchy. Schieffelin showed that 2-year-old Kaluli children acquired the basic distinction between ergative and absolutive case but ignored the animacy hierarchy conditioning of the ergative case. The result was a distinctive pattern of overgeneralization errors of the ergative case postposition. Schieffelin's research stands out as one of the more successful integrations of functionalist theory and developmental psycholinguistics.

It is a well-known fact that children acquiring English replace the nominative case pronoun forms with oblique pronoun case forms, producing such sentences as *my/me want it,* and *her fell* for *I want it* and *She fell,* respectively. Budwig (1989) attempted to account for the distribution of I, me, and my in the subject position of six children's sentences by invoking semantic and pragmatic conditioning. The semantic factor was the construct of *transitivity* as proposed by Hopper and Thompson (1980), and the pragmatic factor was speech-act based. Although no inferential statistical tests were attempted, percentages were presented to show that the three pronoun forms correlated with semantic type. Hopper and Thompson's notion of transitivity, however, is a difficult concept to operationalize. A sentence can be more transitive than another depending on the presence or absence of a number of morphological, syntactic, and semantic features. Aside from problems in operationalization and statistical verification, Budwig's study leaves unanswered important questions about the pronoun case error phenomenon itself. The conditioning semantic and pragmatic factors are geared to an ego-oriented model, but pronoun case errors occur in third-person pronouns as well. Budwig ignored the similarities between errors for the first-person pronouns and third-person pronouns. Moreover, Budwig's analysis suggests that there is systematicity in the distribution of forms once the errors have begun, but the analysis does not address the question of why the errors occur in the first place. Lastly, this study offers no reanalysis of English pronoun case marking, and by avoiding this issue the study tacitly assumes the validity of formalist accounts.

To recapitulate, since the beginning of the 1980s, individual researchers have produced isolated analyses that have, to some degree, integrated functionalist linguistic theory into descriptions or explications of the phenomena. All too few endeavors have managed to show that semantic and pragmatic distinctions are needed to account for the acquisition of syntactic phenomena. One of the more successful pieces of research has been Schieffelin's (1981, 1985) study of the acquisition of the Kaluli case system. Schieffelin demonstrated that the semantic conditioning of the ergative case, in the form of an animacy hierarchy, had to be invoked in order to explain developmental overgeneralization errors. This result lent support to Silverstein's (1976) theory of case as a construction-specific matrix of semantic and pragmatic distinctions. Other endeavors, however, such as Budwig's (1989) analysis of first-person subject pronoun marking, have shown only that forms in a corpus of child language data can be correlated with quasi-semantic distinctions like Hopper and Thompson's (1980) notion of transitivity. By settling only on the demonstration of a correlation, Budwig tacitly accepted formally based theories of morphosyntactic representation. Clearly, functionalist approaches to language acquisition must go beyond mere correlation of form and function. They must show that the interdependence of semantics and pragmatics with morphosyntax is crucial to explaining how grammatical representations are acquired. To do so, one requirement is an explicit theory of the semantics-pragmatics-morphosyntax interface. Unfortunately, as we shall see in the next section, the largest body of so-called functionalist research in developmental psycholinguistics is entirely devoid of such a theory.

C. Bates and MacWhinney's Competition Model

In the study of language acquisition, the largest body of work self-labeled functionalist is the competition model of Bates and MacWhinney (1979, 1982, 1987, 1988, 1989). Prior to joint ventures, both Bates and MacWhinney were separately involved in researching the acquisition of pragmatic competence (Bates, 1976; MacWhinney, 1975). We shall begin our review of their model with Bates' (1976) monograph, *Language and Context: The Acquisition of Pragmatics.* The book itself was not self-labeled *functionalist.* The main foci of the work were the analysis of child language in terms of pragmatic motivations (such as performatives and presupposition) and the attempt to tie emerging pragmatic skills with the Piagetian approach to cognitive development. In some sense we can see this work as arising out of the cognitivist approach outlined in Section II.A. Like most works of that stream, one finds a discouraging tendency to oversimplify morphosyntactic representation. When one looks closely at the discussion of topic-comment and focus structure, as well as definiteness (Bates, 1976, chap. 6), one finds large departures from linguistic functionalism. Bates recognized three types of *subject* (it is never made clear upon what basis this distinction was made): semantic agent, pragmatic topic, and syntactic subject (p. 176). These subjects compete with one another in terms of which sentence constituent will be assigned to them. In a neutral, active, declarative sentence, a single NP can fulfill the role of all three subject types. Marked constructions, such as the English passive, allow speakers to assign different constituents to different subject types. This somewhat dubious taxonomy reoccurs in the later descriptions of the acquisition of grammatical relations by Bates and MacWhinney (1987, 1989). Note that Bates's (1976) research retains the construct of syntactic subject without explaining its origin or development. As such, it is not a true alternative to formalist accounts of the development of grammar. Bates also made a major departure from linguistic functionalism in her conception of the semantics-pragmatics-morphosyntax interface. According to Bates, semantics and pragmatics *compete* (my emphasis) for access to a linear, acoustic-articulatory channel (p. 161). This is a very different approach from, let us say, RRG, in which the interdependence of these grammatical components is seen as a stabile part of the grammatical representation (Foley & Van Valin, 1984). Beginning with Bates and MacWhinney (1979), a self-labeled functionalist approach to language acquisition is proposed. From their earliest writings, Bates and MacWhinney made it plain that the competition model is in no way a theory of grammar, nor was it meant to replace one. Rather, it is proposed as a psychologically based model of performance. As such, it may well be compatible with formalist theories of grammar.

> Performance refers to the actual process of language. . . . As many linguists and psycholinguists have noted, there is no necessary and direct relation between competence and performance models. (Bates & MacWhinney, 1989, p. 3)

> It is also possible, at least in principle, that there may be a rapprochement between a functionalist model of performance and the various rules and representations that have been proposed within the many-times-revised-and-extended school of generative grammar. (Bates & MacWhinney, 1988, p. 149)

The rapprochement of which Bates and MacWhinney spoke concerns the representational content. That is, fundamental constructs of case, phrase structure, and grammatical relations remain unchallenged by the competition model. However, there are serious differences between formalist representational architecture and the representational architecture proposed in the competition model. Bates and MacWhinney do not see grammar as componential and hierarchical. Rather, they see it as essentially probabilistic.

> We argue that the human language processor is also probablistic at its core. In the Competition Model, the adult speaker's knowledge of his native language is represented in a probabilistic form, and probabilities play a fundamental role in the process of language acquisition. (Bates & MacWhinney, 1988, p. 145)

In the preceding quotation, Bates and MacWhinney voice a radical position about the representational architecture. It is one thing to say that there is variability in the observed behavior of a speaker, but it is quite another thing to say that the mental representation of grammar is fundamentally probabilistic. In the former, the observer cannot be absolutely certain ahead of time of the choices a speaker makes, but the speaker's action is the result of at least some set of speaker choices. In the latter, the speaker cannot be sure of what the speaker will say. If taken to its logical conclusion, the Bates and MacWhinney position would hold that the speaker has no real control over the act of speech.

Nichols (1984) classified Bates and MacWhinney (1979, 1982) as extreme functionalists. Nichols also expressed the opinion that Bates and MacWhinney provided no new understanding of grammar. As such, "The 'competition model' is a system of metaobservations rather than a theory or model of language" (Nichols, 1984, p. 114). The competition model offers no reanalyses of grammatical phenomena. When the competition model needs to invoke a construct from grammatical theory, the competition model must import concepts from linguistic theory. A cursory look at the competition model shows that the content of most of the competition model's representational schemas, the *grammogens,* include such terms as *topic, agent, definiteness, transitives,* and *intransitive* (Bates & MacWhinney, 1987, 1989). These terms are not defined by the competition model. They are defined by functionalist linguistic theory. Also incorporated into the competition model are the formalist-derived constructs of case and the grammatical relations of subject and object. In sum, the competition model is a model of performance, with little or no commitment to the particulars of representational content. It is therefore compatible with formalist theories of grammar. Its sole contribution is a set of hypotheses about representational architecture. This has become readily apparent in recent writings. Bates and MacWhinney (1989) have acknowledged that their performance model is neutral to differences in theories of competence, and they have embraced *connectionist* approaches to mental representation, in particular the parallel distributed processing model (Rumelhart, McClelland, & the PDP Research Group, 1986). The competition model was never intended, nor has it ever attempted, to integrate a functionalist theory of grammatical representation with language acquisition theory.

III. RECENT DEVELOPMENTS

A. Silverstein's Critique of Functionalism in Language Acquisition Research

Given the absence of real integration between functionalist analyses of grammatical representation and developmental psycholinguistic research, it is not surprising that Silverstein (1991) took functionalist developmental psycholinguists to task. From Silverstein's perspective, functionalist language acquisition research represents a heterogeneous group of researchers, research agendas proffering a variegated set of empirical studies. The only apparent thread holding this heterogeneity together is "an invocation of factors other than distributional-formal structure itself . . . as vital to the transitions across states of acquisition of distributional-formal structure" (Silverstein, 1991, p. 147). As Silverstein has admitted, there are still some things that functionalist approaches to language acquisition are not. For example, they are clearly opposed to parameter setting approaches, in which the parameters are defined in purely morphosyntactic terms (for example, Hyams,

1986, 1987). Silverstein has been less than sanguine about this range of research suggesting that, far from calling into question the linguistics-based psycholinguistic program, it supports this program. Silverstein wrote, "by tacitly accepting the objects of description and theory in the linguistic programme, . . . this kind of 'functionalism' really confirms the correctness of the overall [formalist approach]" (Silverstein, 1991, p. 146).

In short, functionalist approaches to language acquisition have not offered a true alternative to the system of principles and categories that have evolved in the formalist tradition. Although this may be truly disturbing to those who believe that functionalist approaches to language acquisition present a viable and real alternative to formalists approaches, the following seems undeniable: Functionalist approaches still fall within the broad range of cognitive science. This is especially true of the competition model with its connectionist trappings. Computation is the hallmark of such an approach, not function, or even a synthesis of function and structure.

As noted in the section on neofunctionalism in linguistics, Silverstein's alternative to formal categories based on distribution criteria are *grammatical categories,* namely intersections of semantic and pragmatic distinctions as coded in structure. "Such categories are regularities in the structure of the mapping from domains of linguistic form as generalizable over [a] language to isolable domains of characterizable conceptual content" (Silverstein, 1991, p. 150). Thus, there is structure for Silverstein, but the structure is in the form of a mapping, not a representation per se. The question of representation is left completely open. The explanatory force of such a position is in the indispensability of semantic and pragmatic distinctions.

B. The Mosaic Acquisition of Grammatical Relations

Few scholars have used a functionalist theory of grammatical competence to show that a functionalist theory is superior to formalist theory in explicating the acquisition phenomena. Bates and MacWhinney (1989) regarded theories of grammatical competence as irrelevant, and the studies mentioned in Section 3.1 either tacitly assume formalist theory or are very inexplicit as to what grammatical framework they are assuming. Recently however, Rispoli (1991) has reinterpreted a broad range of apparently unrelated language acquisition phenomena using the role and reference framework (RRG) (Foley & Van Valin, 1984; Van Valin, 1990, in press). Because the principles of RRG are based on robust crosslinguistic typology, it is highly compatible with the comparative approach of Slobin (1985a,b). Rispoli used Slobin's basic comparative approach, but constrained hypotheses about the acquisition of grammatical relations within the RRG theory of grammatical relations. Reviewing acquisition phenomena from Turkish, Kaluli,

Hungarian, Italian (Rispoli, 1991), and, most recently, Georgian (Rispoli, in press), Rispoli asked the following question: When are the morphology and syntax associated with the formalist constructs of *subject* and *object* easy to acquire, and when are they difficult to acquire? Rispoli asked the question, however, from within the RRG perspective in which grammatical relations are well-defined, language-specific constructions built from the intersection of semantic and pragmatic distinctions. This is a radically different perspective from formalist approaches in which *subject* and *object* are primitive, as in lexical functional grammar and relational grammar (Bresnan, 1978; Perlmutter & Postal, 1983), or are defined in phrase structure terms, as in GB (Chomsky, 1981; Haegeman, 1991).

Rispoli (1991, in press) pointed out that, in acquiring languages with split-ergative systems, such as Kaluli (Schieffelin, 1981) and Georgian (Imedadze & Tuite, 1992), children show remarkable conservatism, never confusing the two different case systems coexisting in these languages. The opposing case systems in these languages are structurally distinct. In Kaluli the ergative-absolutive system is encoded in the NP case-marking postpositions, whereas the nominative-accusative system is encoded in verb agreement affixes. In Georgian the active-stative case system and the nominative-accusative case systems are used in different tense-aspect series. This suggests that case systems are acquired locally, in a construction-specific manner, as Silverstein (1976) suggested for the representation of case. Although Rispoli's (1991, in press) emphasis was on the content of grammatical representations, the conclusion that case and agreement systems are acquired mosaically has implications for our understanding of the representational architecture involved. In an effort to deal with the diversity of grammatical relations found cross-linguistically, Pinker (1987) proposed the following. The variety and diversity of morphosyntactic phenomena found in the world's languages were related to primitive, a priori symbols for subject and object (Pinker, 1987). If grammatical relations are acquired in this mosaic manner, the a priori status of subject and object becomes highly questionable.

Rispoli (1991, in press) has gone further by suggesting that there are discernable conditions of grammatical structure that lead to difficulty in the acquisition of grammatical relations. These conditions result from the complexity of the intersection of semantic and pragmatic distinctions encoded by the morphosyntax, in particular the conditions under which these distinctions are *neutralized.* The opposition between two sides of a distinction, A and B, is said to be neutralized when, under grammatically definable conditions, A can only be used. When the grammatical conditions on neutralization *are irrelevant to the distinction,* the pattern of neutralization is difficult to acquire. Such a case is found in the acquisition of the Italian passato prossimo, described in Section 2.1 of this chapter (Antinucci & Miller, 1976; Volterra, 1976). Recall that these researchers attempted to relate the acquisition of the passato prossimo to alleged cognitive developments. In so doing, they failed to note an important relationship between the agreement system and the semantic representation. The essential distinction signaled by the pattern of agreement and nonagreement on the participle of the passato prossimo is one of predicate classes, closely matching basic predicate classes found in RRG (Centineo, 1986; Van Valin, 1990). However, the neutralizing condition, the lexicality of an NP, has little to do with predicate classes. It is therefore not surprising that Italian children should find acquiring the pattern of agreement and nonagreement to be problematic.

Rispoli (1991, in press) also pointed out an additional structural condition that should lead to difficulty in acquisition, that is, *global case marking.* Case marking is said to be global when a single morpheme simultaneously encodes semantic features of both the actor and the undergoer of a transitive sentence. Both Kaluli (Schieffelin, 1981, 1985) and Hungarian (MacWhinney, 1974) have global features (Kaluli in the case system, Hungarian in verb agreement), and these features are the source of trouble for both Kaluli and Hungarian children. Rispoli (1991) referred to the general developmental process by which grammatical relations are constructed over time as *mosaic* because the grammatical relations are themselves composed from smaller parts outlined in RRG. Rispoli concluded that difficulty in acquiring a language-specific system of grammatical relations arises from the complexity and interdependence of the structures involved. Grammatical relations have always been an important aspect of formalist accounts of grammatical competence and language acquisition. By integrating an explicit functionalist reanalysis of grammatical relations with developmental considerations, Rispoli has drawn together a range of developmental phenomena under one explanatory framework. Emerging from this research is the view that grammatical relations are acquired as a mosaic of discrete, smaller components. Thus, grammatical relations as defined by formalist theory are not present in universal grammar.

IV. CONCLUSIONS

Functionalism in the sense of Silverstein (1976, 1991), Foley and Van Valin (1984), and Van Valin (in press) holds that the interdependence of morphosyntax, semantics, and pragmatics is structured and investigatable. However, few developmental psycholinguists have successfully integrated a functionalist theory of grammatical representation into language acquisition research. There have been isolated attempts by developmental psycholinguists to explain acquisition phenomena by introducing semantic and pragmatic considerations, but none have been explicit about their theory of grammatical representation, and some have tacitly assumed formalist theory.

The largest body of developmental research that is self-labeled as *functionalist* is that of Bates and MacWhinney (1979, 1982, 1987, 1988, 1989). However, in metatheoretical statements of their competition model, it has been made evident that their research is aimed only at modeling performance, and that compatibility with particular grammatical frameworks is gratuitous. The competition mode differs from formalist approaches to language acquisition essentially only in architecture, not fundamentally in content. In essence, the competition model makes no commitment concerning the content of grammatical representations, and on this score it cannot be considered a truly functionalist approach to language acquisition.

Functionalist approaches to language acquisition must move beyond correlations of form and function. Correlation does not demonstrate causation. Functionalist approaches to language acquisition must move beyond describing how children use forms. Use in itself tells us nothing directly about either representational content or architecture. What is clearly lacking in developmental psycholinguistics is a functionalist approach to the acquisition of language dealing primarily with the nature of grammatical representations. To present true alternatives to formalist approaches, functionalist research can no longer tacitly assume formally defined grammatical representations or allow itself to be neutral as to the question of the content of grammatical representation. Without focusing anew on the content of grammatical representations, functionalist research runs the risk of being irrelevant to explicating the ontogeny of morphosyntax in particular and grammatical competence in general.

The focus of a functionalist approach to the acquisition of the mental representation of grammar must be the compatibility constraints among semantic, pragmatic, and morphosyntactic representations—that is, the semantic and pragmatic distinctions that constrain case marking, agreement patterns, alpha-movement, and a host of other morphosyntactic phenomena. Many of the phenomena in grammatical acquisition are the result of the child acquiring these constraints. We must uncover and specify the a priori endowment that underlies the content of the semantic and pragmatic components of grammar. A functionalist approach to the acquisition of grammatical competence must show how semantics and pragmatics are an integral part of grammatical representation and play a necessary role in the development of this representation.

The course for providing such a functional alternative is clear. A commitment must be made to a functionalist theory of grammatical competence, such as RRG (Foley & Van Valin, 1984; Van Valin, 1990, in press). The role of such a theory is to provide a detailed, articulate, and sensible account of the interfaces between the semantic and pragmatic components of grammar on the one hand, and the syntactic component on the other (Rispoli, 1991, in press). It is only then that real progress in understanding the acquisition of grammatical competence will be made (Van Valin, 1991). Without such a theory we cannot begin to understand how children acquire the compatibility constraints between these radically different types of representational content. Only in this way will a functionalist approach provide us with hypotheses about the representational architecture of grammar.

REFERENCES

Antinucci, F., & Miller, R. (1976). How do children talk about what happened? *Journal of Child Language, 3,* 167–189.

Bates, E. (1976). *Language and context: The acquisition of pragmatics.* Orlando, FL: Academic Press.

Bates, E., & MacWhinney, B. (1979). A functionalist approach to the acquisition of grammar. In E. Ochs and B. Schieffelin (Eds.), *Developmental pragmatics.* New York: Academic Press.

Bates, E., & MacWhinney, B. (1982). In E. Wanner & L. Gleitman (Eds.), *Language Acquisition: The state of the art.* New York: Cambridge University Press.

Bates, E., & MacWhinney, B. (1987). Language universals, individual variation, and the competition model. In B. MacWhinney (Ed.), *Mechanisms of language acquisition.* Hillsdale, NJ: Erlbaum.

Bates, E., & MacWhinney, B. (1988). What is functionalism? *Papers and Reports on Child Language Development, 27,* 137–152.

Bates, E., & MacWhinney, B. (1989). Functionalism and the competition model. In B. MacWhinney and E. Bates (Eds.), *The crosslinguistic study of sentence processing.* Cambridge, England: Cambridge University Press.

Bloom, L. (1973). *One word at a time: The use of single word* utterances *before* syntax. The Hague: Mouton.

Bowerman, M. (1973). *Early* syntactic *development:* A cross *linguistic* study with *special reference* to *Finnish.* Cambridge, England: Cambridge University Press.

Bresnan, J. (1978). A realistic transformational grammar. In M. Halle, J. Bresnan, & G. Miller (Eds.), *Linguistic theory* and *psychological* reality. Cambridge, MA: MIT Press.

Budwig, N. (1989). The linguistic marking of agentivity and control in child language. *Journal of Child Language, 16,* 263–284.

Centineo, J. (1986). A lexical theory of auxiliary selection in Italian. *Davis Working Papers in Linguistics, 1,* 1–35.

Chomsky, N. (1957). *Syntactic structures.* The Hague: Mouton.

Chomsky, N. (1965). *Aspects of a Theory of Syntax.* Cambridge, MA: MIT Press.

Chomsky, N. (1981). *Lectures on Government and Binding.* Dordrecht: Foris Press.

Chomsky, N. (1986). Aspects of a theory of mind: An interview with Noam Chomsky. *New Ideas in Psychology, 4,* 187–202.

Dik, S. (1978). *Functional Grammar.* Dordrecht: North-Holland.

Dixon, R. (1979). Ergativity. *Language, 55,* 59–138.

Dowty, D. (1979). *Word meaning and Montague grammar.* Dordrecht: Reidel.

Durie, M. (1988). The so-called passive in Acehnese. *Language, 64,* 104–113.

Faltz, L. (1992). *The Navaho verb course.* Unpublished manuscript, Arizona State University.

Fodor, J. (1975). *The Language of thought.* New York: Crowell.
Fodor, J., & Pylyshyn, Z. (1988). Connectionism and cognitive architecture: A critical analysis. *Cognition, 28,* 3–71.
Foley, W., & Van Valin, R. (1984). *Functional syntax and universal grammar.* Cambridge, England: Cambridge University Press.
Gardner, H. (1987). *The Mind's new science: A History of the cognitive revolution.* New York: Basic Books.
Givon, T. (1979). *On understanding grammar.* New York: Academic Press.
Haegeman, L. (1991). *Introduction to government and binding theory.* Oxford, England: Blackwell.
Hale, K. (1983). Walbiri and the grammar of non-configurational languages. *Natural Language and Linguistic Theory, 1,* 5–47.
Heath, J. (1984). Discourse in the field: Clause structure in Ngandi. In J. Nichols & A. Woodbury (Eds.), *Grammar inside and outside the clause: Some views of theory from the field.* Cambridge, England: Cambridge University Press.
Hopper, P., & Thompson, S. (1980). Transitivity. *Language, 56,* 251–299.
Hyams, N. (1986). *Language acquisition and the theory of* parameters. Dordrecht: Reidel.
Hyams, N. (1987). Parameters and syntactic development. In T. Roeper & E. Williams (Eds.), *Parameter setting.* Dordrecht: Reidel.
Imedadze, N., & Tuite, K. (1992). The acquisition of Georgian. In D. Slobin (Ed.), *The crosslinguistic study of language* acquisition (Vol. 4). Hillsdale, NJ: Erlbaum.
Karmiloff-Smith, A. (1979). A *functional approach to child language.* Cambridge, England: Cambridge University Press.
Kuno, S. (1973). *The structure of the Japanese language.* Cambridge, MA: MIT Press.
Kuno, S. (1980). Functional syntax. In E. Moravcsik & J. Wirth (Eds.), *Current approaches to syntax. Syntax and Semantics* (Vol. 13). New York: Academic Press.
Lambrecht, K. (1987). Sentence focus, information structure, and the thetic-categorical distinction. *Berkeley Linguistics Society, 13,* 366–382.
Langacker, R. (1986). *Foundations of cognitive grammar* (Vol. 1). Stanford, CA: Stanford University Press.
Levy, Y. (1983). It's frogs all the way down. *Cognition, 15,* 75–93.
McCawley, J. (1976). Prelexical syntax. In *Grammar and meaning: Papers on syntactic and semantic topics.* New York: Academic Press.
MacWhinney, B. (1974). *How Hungarian children learn to speak.* Unpublished doctoral dissertation, University of California, Berkeley.
MacWhinney, B. (1975). Pragmatic patterns in child syntax. *Papers and Reports on Child Language Development,* 10.
Mathesius, V. (1975). *A functional analysis of present day English on a general linguistic basis.* J. Vachek (Ed.), *Janua Linguarum, Series Practica* (Vol. 208). The Hague: Mouton.
Mayr, E. (1982). *The Growth of biological thought: Diversity, evolution and inheritance.* Cambridge, MA: The Belknap Press of Harvard University Press.
Nichols, J. (1984). Functional Theories of Grammar. *Annual Review of Anthropology, 13,* 97–117.
Perlmutter, D., & Postal, M. (1983). Some proposed laws of basic clause structure. In D. Perlmutter & P. Postal (Eds.), *Studies in Relational Grammar* (Vol. 1). Chicago: University of Chicago Press.

Piatelli-Palmarini, M. (Ed.). (1980). *Language learning: The debate between Jean Piaget and Noam Chomsky.* Cambridge, MA: Harvard University Press.
Pinker, S. (1984). *Language learnability and language development.* Cambridge, MA: Harvard University Press.
Pinker, S. (1987). The bootstrapping problem in language acquisition. In B. MacWhinney (Ed.), *Mechanisms of language development.* Hillsdale, NJ: Erlbaum.
Radford, A. (1990). *Syntactic theory and the acquisition of English syntax: The Nature of early child grammars of English.* Oxford, England: Blackwell.
Rispoli, M. (1994). The mosaic acquisition of grammatical relations. *Journal of Child Language, 18,* 517–551.
Rispoli, M. (1994). Structural dependency. In Y. Levy (Ed.), *Other children, other languages: Issues in the theory of language Acquisition.* Hillsdale, NJ: Erlbaum.
Rochemont, M., & Culicover, P. (1990). *English focus constructions and the theory of grammar.* Cambridge, England: Cambridge University Press.
Rumelhart, D., McClelland, J., & the PDP Research Group. (1986). *Parallel distributed processing: Explorations in the microstructure of cognition.* Cambridge, MA: Bradford Books.
Schieffelin, B. (1981). A developmental study of the pragmatic appropriateness of word order and case marking in Kaluli. In W. Deutsch (Ed.), *The child's construction of grammar.* New York: Academic Press.
Schieffelin, B. (1985). The acquisition of Kaluli. In D. Slobin (Ed.), *The crosslinguistic study of language acquisition: The data.* Hillsdale, NJ: Erlbaum.
Schlesinger, I. (1971). Production of utterances and language acquisition. In D. Slobin (Ed.), *The ontogenesis of grammar.* New York: Academic Press.
Silverstein, M. (1976). Hierarchy of features and ergativity. In R. Dixon (Ed.), *Grammatical categories in Australian languages.* Canberra: AIAS.
Silverstein, M. (1991). A funny thing happened on the way to the form: A functionalist critique of functionalist devleopmentalism. *First Language, 11,* 143–179.
Slobin, D. (1981). The origin of grammatical encoding of events. In W. Deutsch (Ed.), *The child's construction of grammar.* New York: Academic Press.
Slobin, D. (1982). Universal and particular in the acquisition of language. In E. Wanner & L. Gleitman (Eds.), *Language acquisition: State of the art.* Cambridge: Cambridge University Press.
Slobin, D. (1985a). Why study acquisition crosslinguistically? In D. Slobin (Ed.), *The crosslinguistic study of language acquisition: The data.* Hillsdale, NJ: Erlbaum.
Slobin, D. (1985b). Crosslinguistic evidence for the language making capacity. In D. Slobin (Ed.), *The crosslinguistic study of language acquisition: The data.* Hillsdale, NJ: Erlbaum.
Speas, M. (1990). *Phrase* structure *in natural language.* Dordrecht: Kluwer.
Tuite, K. (1987). Some remarks on the acquisition of split ergative patterning. *University of Chicago Working Papers in Linguistics, 3,* 227–236.
Van Valin, R. (1990). Semantic parameters of split intransitvity. *Language.*
Van Valin, R. (1991). Functionalist linguistic theory and language acquisition. *First Language, 11,* 7–40.
Van Valin, R. (1992). A synopsis of role and reference grammar. In R. Van Valin (Ed.), *Advances in Role and* Reference Grammar. Amsterdam: Benjamins.
Vendler, Z. (1967). *Linguistics in philosophy.* Ithaca, NY: Cornell University Press.

Volterra, V. (1976). A few remarks on the use of the past participle in child language. In V. Lo Cascio (Ed.), *Italian Linguistics.* Vol. 2: *On clitic pronominalization.* Lisse: Peter De Ridder Press.

Young, R., & Morgan, W. (1981). The *Navajo language.* Albuquerque, NM: The University of New Mexico Press.

PART III

SEMANTICS AND SYNTAX IN CHILD WORD LEARNING

CHAPTER 8

THEORIES OF WORD LEARNING: RATIONALIST ALTERNATIVES TO ASSOCIATIONISM

Paul Bloom

I. INTRODUCTION

One conception of the nature of word learning was put forth by St. Augustine. Part of it goes as follows:

> When they [my elders] named any thing, and as they spoke turned towards it, I saw and remembered that they called what they would point out by the name they uttered. And that they meant this thing and no other was plain from the motion of their body, the natural language, as it were, of all nations, expressed by the countenance, glances of the eye, gestures of the limbs, and tones of the voice, indicating the affections of the mind, as it pursues, possesses, rejects, or shuns. And thus by constantly hearing words, as they occurred in various sentences, I collected gradually for what they stood; and having broken in my mouth to these signs, I thereby gave utterance to my will. (*Confessions I:* 8)

There are three important claims here. First, as Wittgenstein pointed out when he presented this quote at the beginning of *Philosophical Investigations* (1953), this is a *cognitive* theory. It posits that learning a word involves mapping its sound onto an existing conceptual representation and not onto some behavioral disposition or set of associated percepts. Second, Augustine noted that children learn words as they are used in the context of sentences, instead of adopting the more usual assumption that words are presented to children in isolation. Finally, Au-

Handbook of Child Language Acquisition

gustine suggested that coming to understand the relationship between a word and its referent is an intentional act; the child notices how the speaker's overt behavior indicates "the affections of the mind," and it is this that allows him to infer what the word refers to.

In this chapter, I will defend these claims. More generally, I will review the evidence for a *rationalist* perspective on word learning. This perspective is based on views about the nature of concepts developed by philosophers such as Plato and Descartes and further explored (in quite different ways) by several contemporary scholars whose research I will discuss. The specific focus here will be on a domain central to psychology and epistemology: the learning of names—names for kinds of entities (such as kinds of objects) and names for specific individuals (such as people). In particular, this chapter will outline a theory in which children's sensitivity to sentence-level information, their prelinguistic grasp of concepts, and their capacity to grasp the intentions of others work together to guide their acquisition of the meanings of names.

Many scholars would reject this theory. An alternative perspective posits that early word meanings consist of abstractions from perceptual experience, and that children come to learn these meanings through the process of association. If this is correct, then the complex cognitive capacities posited by Augustine and others are not needed. Before outlining the rationalist perspective, then, I will review this associationist alternative and argue that it fails to explain the nature and acquisition of word meaning.

II. ASSOCIATIONIST THEORIES OF WORD LEARNING

Associationist theories posit that word learning is a process of associating the physical form of a word (usually its sound) with what one is perceiving at the moment the word is used.[1] The child hears the word *dog,* sees a dog in a certain context, and comes to associate the sound with what she is seeing. Over the course of repeated exposure to *dog*-dog pairings, irrelevant features of the experience (such as the particular color of a dog or the type of surface it is standing on) will weaken and disappear, while those aspects of the environment that are present in all contexts in which the word *dog* is used (whatever these are) will become increasingly linked with the linguistic expression. As a result of this process, the child comes to learn the meaning of the new word.

[1]Throughout this chapter, expressions such as *association, associating,* and *associationist* will be used in their technical sense, to refer to notions that arise from the specific learning theory discussed. This should be distinguished from another usage of these words, in which to say "the child forms an association between X and Y" just means that the child comes to understand that there is some relationship between X and Y. In this sense, it is plainly true under any theory of word learning (and therefore totally uninteresting) that children *associate* words with their meanings—because all this means is that children somehow learn the meanings of words.

This view had its origin in the writings of the British empiricists and has been advocated in its most extreme forms by the 20th-century scholars Skinner and Quine. Skinner (1953) construed word learning as primarily the shaping of a distinctive response to a set of stimuli through punishment and reinforcement (i.e., through operant conditioning). To know the word *dog* is to emit the appropriate response—"dog"—to the relevant class of perceptual stimuli (those associated with dogs) and, in older children and adults, to the relevant class of verbal stimuli (such as the question: "What has four legs and barks?").

Similarly, Quine (1960) argued that children's first words map onto "a history of sporadic encounters, a scattered portion of what goes on." Or, as he put it more recently (Quine, 1993), words like *cold* or *milk* are "directly conditioned to the triggering of certain associated sensory receptors." At the onset of word learning, children's generalizations over these sensations are governed solely through an innate similarity space evolved through natural selection. Under this proposal, children do not start off with the ability to make fundamental ontological distinctions. Only through experience—and in particular, language learning—do categories such as individuals, substances, and events come to be formed in the child's mind. For example, Quine proposed that only by learning that some words (count nouns) are preceded by quantifiers like *a* and *many,* whereas others (mass nouns) are not, do children make a conceptual distinction between individuals (such as objects) versus stuff (such as nonsolid substances). Later in development, we come to possess concepts that go beyond perception, such as a concept of fish that does not include whales or a concept of liquid that includes glass. Quine argued, however, that even adults never fully escape this innate "animal" similarity space—a hypothesis that Keil (1989) has dubbed "original sim."

Certain aspects of these views are no longer in fashion. Largely as a result of Chomsky's (1959) critique, the Skinnerian notion that the production of words should be viewed as a conditioned response to certain stimuli has been roundly rejected. Further, empirical studies show that long before the onset of language, children are constrained to interpret their perceptual experience as corresponding to objects that endure over time and space (Spelke, 1988); they possess a "naive physics." With regard to the specific Quinean claim about quantification and the count-mass distinction, it has been found that 2-year olds, who do not yet possess this syntactic contrast, nevertheless make different inductions about word meanings when exposed towards referring to objects versus words referring to nonsolid substances, suggesting that an understanding of the object/substance contrast is not dependent on the acquisition of syntax (Soja, Carey, & Spelke, 1991).

Nevertheless, the theories of Quine and Skinner are of more than historical interest. The position that concepts are, in some interesting sense, abstractions from perceptual experience is perhaps the dominant view in psychology today. Furthermore, many theories of word learning—however cognitive they are in other regards—posit that learning the relationship between the form of a word and its meaning is the result of an associationist process.

Consider, for example, current connectionist models of word learning and conceptual development (e.g., McClelland & Rumelhart, 1986; Smith, 1993; Smith & Gasser, 1993). Researchers from within this perspective assume that to learn a word is to map a phonological string onto some combination of perceptual features, and they posit that this mapping exists as the result of an associationist procedure that involves some sort of correction or feedback. Such models perform statistics on sets of examples, extracting correlations between linguistic input (the phonetic features corresponding to a word) and nonlinguistic experience (the perceptual features corresponding to what the word refers to). One of the presumed merits of these models is that they form perceptual prototypes, a property assumed to be consistent with the psychological evidence as to the nature of word meanings (McClelland & Rumelhart, 1986).

Similar assumptions show up in certain rule-based models. Richards and Goldfarb (1986) use Anderson's rule-based ACT* model (Anderson, 1983) as the foundation of a theory of word learning that is essentially a cognitivized version of operant conditioning. For instance, they propose that children come to know the meaning of the word *car* through repeatedly associating the verbal label ("car") with their experience at the time that the label is used. To the extent that certain features are repeatedly associated with the label, the connection will strengthen, as with *four wheels,* whereas those that are not repeatedly associated with the label will weaken, like *blue.* As a result of this process, children eventually come to associate the label "car" with those features that (arguably) serve to define cars and could be said to have learned the meaning of the word.

Such models differ from the theories of Quine and Skinner in important regards. They assume that the process of strengthening and weakening word-percept associations gives rise to some link between the form of a word and a correlated mental event—not to some behavior. Also, the specific processes through which the associations become adjusted over time are quite sophisticated, particularly in connectionist models, and go far beyond the simple laws of association discussed by British empiricists such as John Locke and later adopted by Quine and Skinner.

Nevertheless, two sets of objections can be raised against current associationist proposals.[2] The first concerns the premise that word meanings are abstractions

[2]Further concerns have also been raised. Fodor and Pylyshyn (1988) have argued that associationist theories cannot adequately characterize the productive and systematic nature of language (see also Pinker & Prince, 1988). This concern will not be addressed here, as it does not directly pertain to word learning procedures proposed by associationists, which are posited to be distinct from those mechanisms that acquire grammar and morphology. However, to the extent that these other aspects of linguistic knowledge play a role in word learning (as argued in Section III.A), any problems that associationist models have in characterizing syntactic structure become relevant. Another concern is that some associationist models (e.g., Smith & Gasser, 1993) require feedback or correction of incorrect performance in order to work. Such feedback does not consistently exist for syntactic development, however (Marcus, 1993) and is unlikely to be essential for word learning.

from perception, and the second focuses on the claim that these meanings are mapped onto words through an associationist learning procedure.

A. Issue 1: The Nature of Word Meanings

Associationist theories posit that word meanings, at least for children, correspond to clusters of sensory or perceptual features. (What counts as *sensory* or *perceptual* can be pretty broad, however. Richards and Goldfarb, 1986, for instance, suggest that features such as *has fuzzy seats* can be reduced to "stored bundles of sensory impression," which is hardly obvious.) This proposal leads to the following research program: Find the correct set of features, describe their interface with sensory systems, and characterize how these features are combined together—this will yield an explanation of the nature of word meanings (for discussion, see Jones & Smith, 1993, and commentators).

It should be noted at the outset that this is not merely the position that competent language users typically possess certain perceptual knowledge. This much is plainly true. For instance, most adult speakers can name objects like dogs and chairs just by seeing them, because they possess mental representations of what these things look like. Associationist theories take the much stronger position that word meaning *reduces* to this sort of perceptual knowledge. The issue, then, is not whether or not people know what dogs look like, it is whether there is ever a stage of lexical development where knowing what a dog looks like is equivalent to possessing the meaning of the word *dog*.[3]

Consider first that regardless of the merits of the perception-as-word-meaning theory, it can only work with those words that refer to entities we can perceive, and which form categories on the basis of perceptual similarity. In particular, it works best for words referring to basic-level object kinds (like *dog* and *cup*) and as a result such words are the focus of most research in word learning. But these words actually make up a small proportion of the words in natural language. Biederman (1987) calculated that there are only about 1500 to 3000 basic-level object names in English—yet the average speaker of English knows roughly 60,000 words (Pinker, 1994a). Similarly, Nelson, Hampson, and Shaw (1993) calculated that most of the high-frequency nouns in English, from the Thorndike and Lorge (1944) word count, are *not* names for people, animals, or things.

Names in natural language are a heterogeneous group. Many have nonmaterial

[3]A related question is whether knowing what a dog looks like is even *necessary* for possessing the meaning of the word *dog*. Unless one is going to argue that blind people have no word meanings, the answer has to be no. In fact, as Landau and Gleitman (1985) have pointed out, blind children have little problem learning word meanings, a phenomenon that is problematic for any perception-based theory of lexical development, given the primacy of vision in how we perceive the world. Also relevant is the fact that blind children successfully acquire words that have been viewed as essentially linked to visual perception, such as color words and the verbs *look* and *see* (Landau & Gleitman, 1985).

referents. For instance, there exist count nouns for psychological entities (*thought, dream, headache*), actions (*kiss, somersault, kick*), events (*war, party, nap*), periods of time (*day, second, month*), interpersonal interactions (*discussion, argument, apology*), university-level teaching environments (*lecture, seminar, tutorial*), humorous speech acts (*joke, pun, quip*), mathematical entities (*number, set, sum*), and so on.

Other words describe kinds of entities that, although material, are not formed on the basis of perceivable qualities. One class of such words consists of names for kinds of people, which includes kinship terms (*uncle, brother, grandmother*), member of different occupations (*provost, undertaker, pilot*), personality types (*wimp, rascal, introvert*), adherents of different political views (*Democrat, anarchist, Marxist*), and members of groups individuated by citizenship, religion, sexual preference, income, and other such properties. Some of these kinds may have a distinctive prototype that can be used for quick-and-dirty identification (such as *grandmother,* see Landau, 1982), but others do not (such as *brother* or *diabetic*). In any case, regardless of the existence of prototypes, one cannot tell whether someone is a grandmother, or a provost, or a pacifist, just by looking.

Other words can refer to both objects and abstractions, with the two usages linked in a systematic way. Chomsky (1988) discussed the example of *book,* which can describe a single physical object (*John's book weighs two pounds*) or some abstract entity that can have a range of physical instantiations (*John wrote a book*) (see also Keil, 1979). Soja (1994) discussed words such as *school* and *church,* which can appear as either count nouns referring to kinds of buildings (*John looked at the school*) or proper names referring to kinds of abstract social institutions (*John goes to school*). Even young children understand both usages of words like *school* and *church* and can use them productively, with appropriate syntactic frames (Soja, 1994).

Other classes of nonobject names exist as well (see the discussion of collective nouns that follows), but most of the names in English fall into one of the three classes discussed previously, either referring to immaterial entities (*idea*), to objects that are individuated by nonperceptual properties (*doctor*), or to both objects and associated abstract entities (*home*). None of these word meanings can be plausibly be learned through a process of abstracting perceptual regularities from the environment.

Although names for basic-level object kinds are among the first words acquired and are considerably more frequent in child language than they are for adults (e.g., Macnamara, 1982; Pinker, 1984), abstract names of the sort previously discussed are also present in the vocabularies of young children from the earliest point of word learning. Nelson and colleagues (1993) examined the speech of 45 children who were each about one year and 9 months of age. They found that only about half of the children's nominals referred to basic-level object kinds; the rest referred to members of other conceptual categories, such as locations (*beach, kitchen*), actions (*kiss, nap*), social roles (*doctor, brother*), natural phenomena (*sky, rain*), and temporal entities (*morning, day*). Other studies looking at even younger children's first nominals (e.g., Bates, Bretherton, & Snyder 1988; Nelson, 1973) have obtained similar results—children do not appear to go through a stage where they are limited to acquiring nouns that refer to things they can see and touch.

Conclusions from spontaneous speech data should be treated with caution, as children may use a word without fully grasping its meaning. And it is quite plausible that when 1- and 2-year olds use words like *day* and *nap* (or words like *cup* and *dog,* for that matter), their corresponding concepts are different from those of adults. But there is no support for the view that when children use such words, they are actually intending to refer to material objects (such that *day* means clock, and *nap* means bed, and so on). If they were, children should produce very odd errors (such as calling a clock *a day*) and none have been observed. In other words, although one cannot infer *full* adult competence from the fact that children use these expressions appropriately, one can safely infer that they do have some grasp of the meaning of at least some abstract names, at least to the extent that they know that they refer to nonmaterial entities.

None of this is to deny that names for basic-level object kinds have a special status in children's lexicons. As noted, names for object kinds occupy a larger proportion of their vocabularies than the vocabularies of adults. There are several reasons why this might be the case. For one thing, a word like *cup* may be conceptually simpler than a word like *day* or *nap,* perhaps because children have more of an understanding of objects and their properties than they do of time and events. Also, a word like *cup* can be acquired through ostension (pointing and naming), and so the link between word and concept might be more accessible for these object names than for other sorts of words. (This is particularly likely if children are biased to favor an object construal when exposed to a new word, as argued by Markman, 1990, and others). A third consideration is that a higher proportion of the nouns in parent-to-child speech refer to concrete entities than in adult-to-adult speech (Hochberg & Pinker, 1984; Pinker, 1984). There are plenty of reasons why object names might be special in lexical development; the point to stress here is that learning *other* sorts of names is also fully within the capacities of young children.

How do children understand basic-level object names? It is often proposed that such names refer to entities identified and represented by virtue of their shape, with other perceptual and nonperceptual properties being less essential. Landau, Smith, and Jones (1988) have applied this argument developmentally, presenting evidence that children possess a *shape bias* causing them to map object names onto categories of objects that share a common shape, as opposed to a common size, color, or texture (see also Landau & Jackendoff, 1993; Landau, Jones, & Smith, 1992).

Children's focus on shape is quite sensible; in many cases, shape is intimately related to the essence of an object kind, due to the tight correspondence between what an object is and how it is shaped. This is especially so for artifacts, by virtue of their intended function (given what a bayonet does, for instance, it had better be pointed). It also applies to natural kinds and parts of natural kinds, where shape is often the result of selectional processes establishing some fit between the animal's phenotype and properties of its environment (it is no accident that a cat's teeth are pointy). More generally, at least for basic-level object kinds, it is a good guess that objects of the same kind will share the same shape and objects of different kinds will have different shapes (Rosch, Mervis, Gray, Johnson, & Boyes-Braem, 1976).

But despite this, shape should not be conflated with word meaning (see also Soja, Carey, & Spelke, 1992). Consider studies carried out by Keil (1989). In one set of experiments (the discovery studies), children and adults were shown a picture of an animal, such as a raccoon, and were told a story in which scientists discovered that this animal had the *deep* properties of a skunk (it had the bones of a skunk, the blood of a skunk, its parents were skunks, etc.). In another set of experiments (the operation studies), subjects were shown a picture of a raccoon and were then told about superficial changes that had been done to it (scientists painted a stripe down its back, put white makeup on its eyes, etc.). Then they were shown a picture of a skunk and told that this is what the animal looked like as the result of the transformations. In both sets of experiments, subjects were asked whether they thought the animal was a raccoon or a skunk.

Preschoolers were found to respond differently from older children and adults. In the discovery studies, they tended to dismiss the deep features (saying that the animal was a raccoon); in the operation studies, they tended to accept the superficial changes (saying that the animal was a skunk). Older children and adults said that the discoveries showed the animal actually was a skunk, and they dismissed the superficial changes in the operation studies. One might be tempted to conclude from this that young children are perception bound—if something looks like a skunk, then it is a skunk, regardless of what has happened to it or what its deeper properties are. Other findings by Keil, however, suggest an alternative interpretation, in which young children do have essentialist notions, just different sorts than adults. Even preschoolers understood (for example), that if you take a raccoon and put it in a skunk costume to make it look like a skunk, it is still a raccoon. Further, no matter how much you change the appearance of a porcupine, young children will not accept that it could change into a cactus: the ontological boundary between animals and nonanimals constrains the transformations that children will accept.

Similar findings of essentialist information overriding superficial features show up in other domains, preschoolers are quite capable of distinguishing real monkeys from toy monkeys, real telephones from toy telephones, and so on (Carey, 1986; Woolley & Wellman, 1990). Intuitions about essences constrain their inferences about what things are; children know that something can look like an X (e.g., have the same shape as typical Xs) but not be an X, while it can look nothing like an X (e.g., have a different shape from typical Xs) but actually be an X. As a result of this, any adequate theory of how children encode the meanings of words must go beyond perceptual features.[4]

Finally, most research on concepts focuses on kinds, but there is some evidence for a similar account with regard to individuals. Sternberg and Allbritton (1992) found empirical support for the proposal that our understanding of proper names has an important indexical or historical component, one that can have priority over superficial features (Donnellan, 1977; Kripke, 1977; Putnam, 1977). For instance, when presented with scenarios of the sort where Dan Quayle changes his name and appearance to those of John F. Kennedy, even nonphilosophically oriented subjects are quite comfortable with the idea that this character is still Quayle, regardless of his new name and appearance.

Liittschwager and Markman (1993) conducted a similar experiment with young children. They showed 3-year olds an object (such as a bear or shoe), named it (*This is Zav*), and then moved it to another location and removed a salient property so as to change its appearance. They then placed a second, perceptually identical object next to this first object and asked the children: *Where's Zav?* The 3-year

[4]In response to these sorts of arguments, Landau and colleagues (1992) and Landau and Jackendoff (1993) have pointed out that our intuitions about concept membership (Is this really an X?) must be distinguished from our use of category names (Can this be called *X*?). It is true that a toy telephone is not really a telephone, but we do use the word *telephone* to describe it. Landau and Jackendoff (1993) noted: "The sixty-foot metal sculpture by Clases Oldenburg that graces downtown Philadelphia is universally recognized as and labeled *the clothespin,* although it clearly violates most of the criterial properties of true clothespins; its shape is the dominating criterion in choosing its name."

But does *clothespin* really mean "clothespin-shaped object"? An alternative is that there exists a linguistic rule allowing for "the . . . matching of a syntactic structure X with a semantic/conceptual structure that is more fully expressed as 'visual representation of X'" (Jackendoff, 1992). Under this view, it is not sameness of shape *per se* that governs the extension of the word *clothespin* to the sculpture, it is the fact that the sculpture is a visual representation of a clothespin (and, like many visual representations, it is the same shape as what it represents). The crucial question, then, is whether representations of X that are *not* the same shape as X can be called *X*. As Soja and colleagues (1992) have pointed out, they plainly can. For instance, one could have a schematic map of an area and denote buildings, people, or other objects with circles and other arbitrary symbols—and one could point to one of the circles and say (for instance) *There is the Psychology building,* even if the Psychology building is not shaped like a circle.

Another example is provided by Millikan (1993), who noted that a 2-year old's drawing may bear no resemblance to a cat yet still be a picture of a cat, because of "the two-year old's intention in drawing it. She intended it to be a cat." Millikan is making the point that representations need not represent by virtue of perceptual similarity, we can extend this example by noting that if you asked the child what she just made, she would coherently say "a cat." In fact, there is evidence that even 3-year olds are capable of using intentional cues (such as what an artist is attending to at the time she is drawing a picture) to name visual representations that bear no particular resemblance to what they depict (Bloom & Markson, 1996). This favors the representational-account of the usage of words that denote things like sculptures, pictures, and toys, and it is problematic for the claim that such words are extended solely on the basis of sameness of shape, even by young children.

olds tended to choose the same object they were first shown, suggesting that they took the proper name as tracking this original entity over space and time, regardless of the change in appearance. Similarly, Xu and Carey (1996) presented evidence that 10-month old infants ignore certain perceptual properties of entities (such as their shape) when tracking them as they move behind a screen; they attend only to spatio-temporal continuity. In particular, if the infants see a truck enter one side of a screen and a duck exit the other side, they ignore the change of appearance and assume that there exists only a single object. These developmental findings are inconsistent with the predictions of a perception based theory of children's understanding of individuals and proper names.

B. Issue 2: Establishing Word/Meaning Mappings

Suppose we were to give up on the notion that word meanings are abstractions from perceptual experience. We might still keep the other premise, which is that children hook up the form of the word with its meaning through a process of association, involving contiguity in space and time.

One famous instance of this is Skinner's theory that proper names are under the stimulus control of their referents. This came under attack by Chomsky (1959), who noted:

> I have often used the words *Eisenhower* and *Moscow,* which I presume are proper nouns if anything is, but have never been "stimulated" by the corresponding objects. . . . Suppose I use the name of a friend who is not present. Is this an instance of a proper noun under the control of the friend as stimulus? Elsewhere it is asserted that a stimulus controls a response in the sense that presence of the stimulus increases the probability of the response. But it is obviously untrue that the probability that a speaker will produce a full name increases when its bearer faces the speaker. Furthermore, how can one's own name be a proper noun in this sense? . . . It appears that the notion of "control" here is merely a misleading paraphrase for the traditional "denote" or "refer."

This is part of a general argument against an associationist theory of word *use,* one based on the fact that our use of words is determined by what we choose to say, not by what we are perceiving or being "stimulated" by. But this point has straightforward implications for a theory of word *learning,* since a reliable correlation between the use of a name and the presence of what it refers to is essential for an associationist learning process to work.

One might argue, however, that although Chomsky might be correct about how adults use words in the presence of other adults, children do learn at least some word meanings by hearing a word while being stimulated by the appropriate object or event, because parents tailor their use of words in the presence of children in special ways. To use Chomsky's example, perhaps when adults speak to children they only use proper names in the presence of their referents—although adults are clearly free to use proper names when their referents are not present and do so when talking to other adults.

Gleitman (1990), however, provided a compelling critique of this position, using the following example as a starting point:

> When, every evening, Mother opens the door upon returning from work, what does the child hear? I would venture that he rarely hears her say *Hello, Alfred, I am opening the door!*, but very often hears *Hello, Alfred, whatcha been doing all day?* Any scheme for learning must have machinery for dealing with the fact that caretaker speech is not a running commentary on scenes and events in view.

This point is worth stressing, because the standard scenario that finds its way into philosophical discussions of word learning is that the child is looking at the cat on the mat and someone points and says: *The cat is on the mat.* But as Gleitman has pointed out, it is not necessarily true that children are exposed to words naming actions at the same time that the actions take place; there is plenty of opening without anyone using the word *opening* and there is plenty of use of the word *opening* without anything being opened.

Gleitman's focus is on verbs, but the same point applies to nominals. Even putting aside those nouns that refer to nonmaterial entities, it is likely that often when a child hears a name for a thing that thing is not going to be around, and most of the time when the thing is around children are not going to hear a name for it. An associationist child who hears *Want a cookie?* while she is looking at her milk is in for some serious problems, but this is exactly how a word like *cookie* tends to be used. There is, of course, *some* correlation between *cookie* and the presence of cookies (see Gleitman & Gillette, chapter 9 of this volume), but it will be imperfect and there will be many mismatches—yet children never appear to think *cookie* means milk, or the child herself, or the child's mother. Somehow they are able to grasp certain aspects of the meaning of the word, often on the basis of a single trial (see Carey, 1978, on "fast mapping").[5]

One might object to this argument on the grounds that it is not every occurrence of a word that matters, but only those in which the adult is intending to name something for the child. After all, there are many occasions where parents purposefully name objects (or pictures of objects) for their children, and children do go through a period where they often explicitly ask adults what things are called. Perhaps it is only these occasions that children use when determining the reference of unfamiliar words, and they ignore adult utterances like *Hello, Alfred, whatcha been doing all day?* and *Want a cookie?*

This proposal is reasonable, but it abandons the associationist premise as it re-

[5]Single-trial learning poses a special difficulty for associationist procedures, as several salient entities are usually present in any single trial (the cookie, the adult, the hand holding the cookie, the plate that the cookie is on, etc.), and so children's ability to learn the correct meaning on a single trial cannot be explained through a procedure of strengthening and weakening of word-world correlations.

quires that children can isolate certain speech acts as instances of *naming,* a capacity that requires considerable inferential capacities. Note also that even for these cases of naming, children do not apply an associative procedure; they do not associate the word with what they are perceiving at the time. As Baldwin (1991) found (see also Section 3.3), they instead actively focus on what the adult is looking at and assume that *this* is what the word refers to, even if they themselves are looking at something else when the word was used. For these reasons, this proposal is not consistent with associationism.

In addition, ostensive presentation of words is unlikely to be necessary for word learning. For one thing, it cannot work with words referring to nonmaterial entities—one cannot point to an idea or a nap or a day. For another, object labeling might not be universal. Middle-class Western parents tend to swamp children with picture books, flash cards, naming games, and so on, but children in other cultures are quite capable of learning words without this sort of extensive social support. Schieffelin (1985), for instance, noted that Kaluli caretakers do not tend to name objects when interacting with children (see also Heath, 1983). In light of this, children must be equipped with the capacity to infer adult intention to refer in conditions more subtle than purposive naming.

III. RATIONALIST PERSPECTIVES

It would be nice at this point to *solve* the problems discussed previously—to outline exactly how children acquire the meanings of words denoting abstract and material kinds and individuals—but what follows is quite a bit more modest. I will instead outline some directions in which solutions might be found, first considering the role of syntactic cues, then turning to some proposals about the nature of possible word meanings within the class of nominals, and finally discussing children's understanding of the intentions of others as it applies to different aspects of word learning.

A. Syntax as a Pointer to Conceptual Type

A useful start is to reject the Quinean premise that we are initially limited to generalization on the basis of perceptual similarity and that only much later do we come to possess different classes of concepts, such as people, objects, substances, actions, and spatial relationships.

This is an excellent premise to give up, largely on the basis of data from children younger than 2 years old. Infants categorize objects as belonging to different kinds: some that are innate, like human faces (Johnson, Dziurawiec, Ellis, & Morton, 1991), others that are learned, like the superordinate category of vehicles (Mandler, 1993). They have a rich understanding of objects and can track them over time and space (Spelke, Breinlinger, Macomber, & Jacobson, 1992), they are sensitive to numerical equivalence between groups of objects and sequences of distinct sounds (Starkey, Spelke, & Gelman, 1990), and they can perform numerical calculations over small numbers of objects (Wynn, 1992). It would be impossible to explain these capacities without attributing to prelinguistic infants an understanding of different types of concepts, such as numerosities, properties, individuals, and kinds of individuals.

A further claim is that there exist mappings between certain conceptual types and syntactic classes. Brown (1957) was the first to propose that such mappings might play a significant role the course of language acquisition. If a word belongs to a specific grammatical category, children could use the mappings to infer the conceptual category it must correspond to.

There is considerable evidence for this proposal. The first empirical test of the hypothesis was by Brown (1957), who showed preschoolers a picture of a strange action performed on a novel substance with a novel object. One group of children was told *Do you know what it means to sib? In this picture, you can see sibbing.* (verb syntax), another group was told *Do you know what a sib is? In this picture, you can see a sib.* (count noun syntax), and the third group was told *Have you seen any sib? In this picture, you can see sib.* (mass noun syntax). Then the children were shown three pictures, one depicting the same action, another depicting the same object, and a third the same substance. They were asked to *show me another picture of sibbing* (or *another picture of a sib,* or *another picture of sib*). Brown found that the preschoolers tended to construe the verb as referring to the action, the count noun as referring to the object, and the mass noun as referring to the substance.

Similarly, Katz, Baker, and Macnamara (1974) found that even some 17-month olds attended to whether a word was used with count noun syntax (*This is a sib*) or noun phrase (NP) syntax (*This is sib*) when determining whether it was a name for a kind of object or a specific individual (see also Gelman & Taylor, 1984; Hall, 1991). Other studies have found that when 3-year olds acquire new words, nouns focus the child on basic-level kinds, whereas adjectives draw children's attention toward properties (Gelman & Markman, 1985; Taylor & Gelman, 1988; Waxman, 1990).

One specific theory about the mappings between semantic types and parts of speech is as follows (Bloom, 1994a, 1994b; Jackendoff, 1991; Macnamara, 1986): A mapping exists between count nouns (words that can follow determiners such as *a* and *many* and that can be pluralized) and the category "Kind of Individual"; another exists between mass nouns (words that can follow determiners like *some* and *much* but that cannot be pluralized and cannot follow determiners such as *a* and *many*) and the category "Kind of Stuff," and a third exists between lexical NPs (words which cannot be quantified at all) and the category of "Individual."[6]

Note that although our notion of *individual* is related to the notion of whole object, it does not reduce to it. The category is intended to be sufficiently broad so as to include names for nonmaterial entities. Also, this is a semantic theory only in the sense that it posits some relationship between grammar and nonlinguistic cognition, not in the sense of relating grammar to the world—these differences in syntax reflect cognitive contrasts, not metaphysical ones. For instance, the same entity or sets of entities in the world could be described with both a count noun and a mass noun, corresponding to different ways of construing that entity (see Bloom, 1994a).

Further studies suggest that children are sensitive to these mappings. In one study, children were shown a pile of small objects, small enough that an adult could name the array with either a plural count noun (like *peas*) or a mass noun (like *rice*). When given a plural count noun to describe the array, preschoolers interpreted the noun as an object name; when given a mass noun, they interpreted it as a substance name (Bloom, 1994a; see also Soja, 1992). This sensitivity to the semantic correlates of count/mass syntax extends even to words that refer to nonmaterial entities: 3-year olds will construe a plural count noun that describes a series of *sounds* as referring to the individual sounds and a mass noun describing the same series as referring to the undifferentiated noise (Bloom 1994a).

Recently, Bloom and Kelemen (1995) found that older children and adults are sensitive to the singular/plural contrast when learning collective nouns, which are nouns that in the singular form refer to groups of discrete objects. When shown a set of five novel objects and told *These are fendles* (plural count noun syntax), most 5-year olds and adults interpret *fendle* as an object name, like *bird.* But when shown the same objects and told *This is a fendle* (singular count noun syntax), most interpret it as a collective noun referring to the whole array, like *flock.*

The preceding discussion has focused on nominals, but similar evidence exists for the acquisition of other kinds of words, including verbs (e.g., Fisher, Hall, Rakowitz, & Gleitman, 1994), adjectives (e.g., Waxman, 1990), number words (Bloom & Wynn, 1998), and prepositions (Landau & Stecker, 1990) (see Bloom, 1996a, for a review). These findings are consistent with the view that children possess several different types of concepts and are sensitive to syntactic cues when determining which of these types a novel word maps onto.

What is the precise role of syntax in word learning? One possible view is that

[6]Being an individual, however, is not enough for an entity to have a proper name. For instance, all objects are individuals (and can be referred to with lexical NPs such as the deictic pronoun *that*), but not all objects get their own names—only those that are importantly unique and *worth* their own names (people, for instance, but not most rocks or forks). Not surprisingly, there exists considerable cultural variation in the application of proper names, especially in more abstract domains, such as names for events (*Canada Day*) and social institutions (*church*) (see Soja, 1994).

syntax completely *solves* the problem of word learning. Perception is unnecessary, because syntactic structure is enough to guide children to the correct meanings of words. But this cannot be right. For one thing, the conceptual contrasts made in the lexicon are much finer-grained than those made by grammar. Syntax might be able to tell the child whether a novel word refers to a specific individual, a kind of individual, or a kind of stuff, but it cannot tell the child *which* specific individual, kind of individual, or kind of stuff. It does not distinguish between *Eisenhower* and *Nixon, dog,* and *quark, caviar* and *spam.* Such precise aspects of word meaning musts be acquired through nonsyntactic means (see Fisher et al., 1994, and Pinker, 1994b, for a discussion of the same issue in the domain of verbs).

It is also unlikely that syntactic information is necessary in order to learn words. Children can learn words prior to understanding language-particular aspects of syntactic structure; for instance, they acquire words like *dog* and *water* before learning the grammatical contrast between count nouns and mass nouns (Soja et al., 1991; Waxman & Markow, 1995). Also, there is some support for the view that children syntactically categorize new words by learning the words' meanings; they categorize *dog* as a count noun because it refers to a solid object, for instance (see the chapter appendix). For this procedure to work, however, the meaning of a word must be accessible to a child prior to knowing its syntax, and thus syntax cannot be necessary for the acquisition of word meaning. Finally, adults and children will sometimes override syntactic cues when they conflict with other sources of information. For instance, when given a mass noun describing a solid object, children will often interpret the noun as naming the kind of object, despite the contrary syntax (Markman & Wachtel, 1988)—possibly because it is difficult for them to construe a solid object as an instance of "stuff" (Bloom, 1994b).

These considerations suggest that the role of syntax is limited to two aspects of word learning. First, assuming that a child has access (through nonsyntactic means) to multiple interpretations of the word, syntax can guide her to the correct meaning. Consider the experiment presented in Bloom (1994a), in which children were exposed to a stimulus created so that it is perceptually ambiguous between a set of objects and a pile of stuff. Three- and 4-year olds were able to use count/mass syntax to determine which of the two interpretations the word actually corresponded to, that is, whether it was an object name or a substance name.

Second, syntax might help children learn words in cases where the meanings of the words are for some reason difficult to access through nonsyntactic means. This occurs, for example, when the child must interpret a word describing a whole object as a solid-substance name instead of as an object name (e.g., *wood* instead of *chair*) or a word describing a substance as a name for the bounded individual composed of that substance instead of as a substance name (e.g., *puddle* instead of *water*) (Gordon, 1985; Soja, 1992). Without the aid of syntax, such words might be extremely difficult to acquire. It might also be that syntax can facilitate the acquisition of words for more abstract notions; Gleitman (1990) has suggested, for instance, that children might acquire mental-state verbs (such as *think*) by noting that they are used with sentential complements.

B. Abstract Conceptual Types

For each semantic type corresponding to a grammatical class, there is the question of its psychological nature. Landau and Jackendoff (1993), for example, presented a detailed theory of the spatial relations encoded by prepositions, and Gentner (1978) has analyzed those aspects of event cognition corresponding to verbs. The discussion that follows focuses on a single conceptual type within nominals: the notion of *individual.* Count nouns, such as *house* and *story* refer to kinds of individuals, where lexical NPs, such as *he* or *Fred,* as well as phrasal NPs headed by count nouns, such as *the dogs* or *a house,* can refer to specific individuals.

Exceedingly little is known about the nature of this category. Many linguistic and philosophical approaches to semantics exploit this notion in one form or another, assuming that certain expressions in natural language (such as names for people) refer to individuals and certain others (such as names for spatial relationships) do not. But there is little discussion as to why this is the case. One might have expected scholars interested in conceptual representation and development to fill the gap, but this work focuses almost exclusively on different types of objects, ignoring names for nonmaterial entities.

It would simplify things if all individuals were objects, but for reasons discussed in Section II, we can reject this proposal. Even 2- and 3-year olds know plenty of count nouns that are not object names, names for kinds of individuals like *puddle, day, party,* and so on, and these form NPs (*that puddle, my party*) that refer to nonmaterial individuals.

What we need then is a broader understanding of the sorts of entities that people naturally think about as individuals. One initial hypothesis is that, at least for some domains, Gestalt principles might help the determine the scope of what can be construed as an individual. These principles were initially posited as generalizations about perceptual grouping (Wertheimer, 1923; see also Palmer, 1992) and they may also serve to define psychologically natural individuals, for some material (and possibly temporal) entities.

Collective nouns are an interesting group with which to explore this possibility. As mentioned previously, these are count nouns where the singular form refers to a group of objects, such as *army, forest, family, bunch, gang, committee, group,* and *flock.* A forest and a bunch may be possible individuals because the objects that make up these individuals—trees and grapes—are grouped together, satisfying the Gestalt principle of proximity. Other collections—like flocks and packs—also share the Gestalt property of common fate, as their component objects move together as a single unit. Could this adherence to Gestalt principles explain why these groups are conceptualized as individuals and described with count nouns in languages such as English?

This hypothesis was explored in a study in which novel collective nouns were taught to adults (Bloom, Keleman, Fountain, & Courtney, 1995). In each trial, the subjects were shown 12 novel objects. Half of the subjects were shown the objects in a single group; the other half were shown the objects in three distinct groups of four objects each. For all subjects, the display was described with a novel plural count noun, for example, *These are fendles.*

In the condition in which the objects fell into three piles, there are two alternatives for what *fendle* might mean, each consistent with the syntax. It could describe the objects (thus there would be 12 fendles) or it could describe the groups (thus there would be three fendles). If Gestalt principles are relevant, adults should favor the collection interpretation when the objects are shown in groups. A second manipulation was the source of the groups; the objects were either taken out of a single bag and placed on the table; or each group was taken out of its own separate bag. The prediction was that when the groups each had its own source, this might further favor the collective interpretation, perhaps as a result of the Gestalt principle of common fate.

Our hypotheses received little support from this study. Regardless of the condition, adults almost always interpreted *fendle* as an object name. Note that adults are *capable* of giving a collective interpretation under similar conditions when this interpretation is forced with a singular count noun (Bloom & Kelemen, 1995). But the Gestalt properties we manipulated in this study were not enough, in the absence of syntactic support, to lead adults to construe the new word as naming the collections of objects.

This failure to find an effect is intriguing. The subjects were clearly perceiving three distinct *groups* of objects, but they apparently had no motivation to construe each of the groups as a distinct individual. This hints at a different sort of analysis of individuation, one that has to do more with explanation and interpretation. In particular, there was nothing interesting about the groups from an explanatory perspective; three groups of objects dumped on a table do not endure over time, they do not interact with each other or with anything else. Given this, perhaps the subjects had no motivation to treat the groups as individuals.

This is not to say that principles of perceptual grouping are irrelevant. It is likely that such principles do play an important role in how people pick out individuals; we are probably sensitive to properties such as proximity and common fate just because entities defined in terms of Gestalt principle are likely to be composed of elements that possess some deeper connection with one another and therefore such entities are likely to be individuals. Given this, Gestalt principles of grouping serve as *cues* to the presence of individuals. This allows for instances (such as in this study) where the Gestalt principles are present but are not sufficient to specify individuals as well as instances where individual exists that need not satisfy the Gestalt principles, as with the individuals denoted by the word *family.*

In fact, a purely Gestalt explanation for collective nouns should have been suspicious in the first place. A forest is not *just* a suitably large number of trees clumped together; if you were to chop down a bunch of redwoods and stack them up inside a stadium, slavishly conforming to the Gestalt principles of proximity and similarity, you would not have a forest. Several people in close proximity are not necessarily a gang, a committee, or even a crowd—more is required. Real collections must have some internal cohesiveness (however abstract) that holds the members together as a single unit.

These considerations motivate a different theory, defended in Bloom (1996b), which is based on the work of scholars such as Carey (1988), Dennett (1987), and Keil (1989): Children and adults possess interpretive systems, sometimes called stances or naive theories. The role of these systems is to explain and predict causal interactions within the environment, and in so doing they posit individuals. In sum,

> *Individuals* are what we posit as primitive entities in our attempt to interpret causal interactions within the (physical, social, cultural, etc.) world.[7]

An ideal example is that of material objects; these are the canonical examples of individuals within the physical domain. As previously noted, infants are predisposed to analyze their sensory input into a world of distinct bounded objects that persist over time (e.g., Spelke, 1988). Construing the environment in terms of bounded objects enduring over time and moving through space is the best way to make sense of what is going on and allows for the most predictive power. Physical objects are some of the first individuals in our mental models of the world, though evidence (Starkey et al., 1990) suggests that infants are also sensitive to some nonmaterial individuals, such as sounds. Similarly, it is possible that infants

[7]One might modify the preceding definition to apply to count nouns (which refer to *kinds* of individuals) and suggest that they refer to categories that are themselves conceptually relevant for the purposes of explanation. That is, just as Fido, as a physical object, is conceptually salient as an individual, there is something about the kind *dog* itself, which contains Fido, that allows one to better understand and predict the behavior of the individuals that fall under that kind (for discussion, see Carey, 1986; Pinker, 1994a; Quine, 1960).

Is it legitimate to propose a notion of *individual* that does not itself appeal to kinds? It is sometimes argued (e.g., Gupta, 1960; Macnamara, 1986; Wiggins, 1980) that every individual requires a supporting kind (or *sortal*) that determines its principles of identity and individuation; there are no untyped individuals. For instance, imagine a lump of clay that is shaped into a statue of Aristotle on Monday and then reshaped into a stature of Augustine on Tuesday. It is clearly the same lump of clay but a different statue, suggesting that the identity of an individual can depend on which kind one construes it as a member of. However, one should also consider that proper names and pronouns typically refer to individuals in a way that is far less restrained. A sentence like *The witch turned Fred into a puff of smoke, and then into a dog, and then back into a person* is perfectly coherent as part of a fairy tale and yet it requires tracking the identity of a single individual through membership in radically different kinds. Similarly, one can ask *What's that?* about a strange object or sound or action, in which the NP *that* is used to refer to (and thus individuate) an individual whose precise kind we are ignorant of. None of this is to deny that individuals differ in their conditions of identity and individuation (surely there are different conditions for people versus countries; see Chomsky, 1992), but it suggests that such conditions might be provided by our more general understanding of the domain that the individual belongs to, as opposed to through our representation of more precise sortals.

are born with a rudimentary notion of the kind of individual *person,* perhaps one that can be triggered through exposure to the human face (Johnson et al., 1991). In such cases, the individuals and kinds of individuals emerge from innate interpretive systems.

For some of the words we learn, however, we must discover the relevant individuals in the course of understanding the nature of different conceptual domains. For instance, it is as the result of our understanding the domains of politics and geography that we come to construe proper names like *France* and *The United Nations* as referring to individuals that causally interact with each other and thus exist as distinct entities within our models of the social and political world.

Recent studies have explored the role of explanation in the acquisition of novel collective nouns (Bloom, 1996b; Bloom et al., 1995). These studies provide contexts in which there is some explanatory motivation to treat a collection of entities as a single individual and compare these to contexts in which no such motivation exists. For instance, when shown three sets of five stationary objects each on a computer screen and told *These are fendles,* we would expect adults to treat *fendle* as an object name, as in the Gestalt study. But if each group of objects is moving independently of the other groups in some regular pattern, this should give the groups some reality as individuals. It would then make sense to view the groups as individuals in their own right because treating each collection of objects as a single individual allows one to better predict and make sense of their motion. Therefore *fendle* should be learnable as a collective noun.

This is precisely what we find; adults give collective interpretation to the groups only when the groups are moving as coherent wholes.[8] Further studies explore precisely why moving groups become so salient as individuals. In particular, there is evidence that this effect is in fact due to the explanatory benefits of viewing these groups as individuals—not due to lower-level perceptual processes of the sort that underlie object perception (Bloom, 1996b). Experiments in progress focus on the role of explanatory factors in how we learn collective nouns that refer to sets of stationary entities (as in *forest*) and sets of entities that have no nontrivial perceptual relationship with one another (as in *family*).

C. Intentionality

What is the role of intentionality in learning words that describe individuals? There is support for the Augustinian view that children do not learn word meanings through association but instead attempt to determine what an adult intends to refer to when she uses a new word (see Macnamara, 1982). In an elegant study,

[8]Along these lines, Dennett (1991) provides an intriguing discussion of the computer program *Life,* pointing out how patterns of pixels on the screen are viewed, by virtue of their systematic patterns of movement, as *real entities.*

16-month olds were presented with a new word by an adult, uttered at a moment when the child was looking at one object and the adult was looking at another (Baldwin, 1991). An associationist theory would predict that children would connect the word to what they were viewing. Instead, when they heard the new word, children looked up, determined the direction of the adult's gaze, followed this gaze, and inferred that the novel word referred to the object of the adult's attention. Thus, cues to what an adult is intending to refer to predominate over salient associations at the time a new word is used.

An implication of this is that children might use knowledge of other's intentions to treat an entity or set of entities as a single individual even in the absence of any other information. Consider, for instance, a 2-year old shown a group of toy soldiers and told "This is an army." Her initial understanding of the meaning of the NP *an army* might just be that it refers to a group of soldiers of a certain approximate numerosity and that the count noun *army* refers to that kind of entity, whatever it is. Later she will come to appreciate what it is about armies that make them coherent social entities, but at this initial stage of learning the word's meaning, just knowing that the array of soldiers is a distinct individual from the perspective of the adult might be sufficient for the child to come to acquire the count noun as a collective name referring to that kind of individual.

This is similar to the claim by Kripke (1977) and others that words can be acquired as rigid designators—as referring to (in the case of NPs) "*that* individual, whatever it is," or (in the case of count nouns), "*that kind* of individual, whatever that kind is." Thus although NPs must refer to entities that play a causal role in some framework (as suggested previously), it is not necessary for the child to know what the role is in order to initially acquire the word—just knowing that it exists from the perspective of others may be enough.

The study by Bloom and Kelemen (1995) provides another example of this. Recall that older children and adults could learn a collective noun by being shown a group of unrelated objects and being told *This is a fendle.* Treating this group of objects as a single individual makes little sense from a conceptual standpoint, so why then are people willing to acquire the word as a collective noun? One explanation is that (a) the syntax requires that *a fendle* must refer to a single individual, and *fendle* must refer to that kind of individual, and (b) it was apparent to the subjects that the experiment's intention was to refer to this set of five objects, because that was what she was pointing at. This led the subjects to take it on faith that the array as some status as an individual even in the absence of other information (for further discussion, see Bloom, 1994b, 1996b).

The issue of the role of intentionality as part of a theory of word learning can be put into a somewhat novel context. Philosophers of art have long speculated about what is and is not an *artwork,* and different definitions (or skeptical arguments against definitions) have been advanced. Debate over the nature of artwork bears some interesting relationships to discussion of word meaning in general, and thus some of these proposals are worth considering here (see Davies, 1991, for review).

Many traditional theories of art posit that an adequate definition of *artwork* would allow one to pass the warehouse test (Kennick, 1958) in which someone armed with the definition could go through a warehouse and, solely by virtue of evidence from her senses, distinguish the artwork from nonartwork because the artwork and only the artwork would have certain physical properties or give rise to certain sensations. Although this requirement might have been adequate for our notion of artwork prior to the middle of the 20th century, it does not currently suffice. Duchamp's *Fountain* is, solely on the basis of what it looks like, indistinguishable from a run-of-the-mill urinal, and no perceptual criteria would allow someone to distinguish the two, yet *Fountain* is an artwork and urinals are not.

Two classes of alternatives have been proposed. One is the so-called institutional theory of art (e.g., Dickie, 1974), which posits that something becomes an artwork by having this status conferred on it by the community of those involved with art, often called "the artworld." The community chooses to confer this status both to traditional works of art, such as the work of Renoir and Beethoven, and to more funky entities such as Duchamp's *Fountain,* conceptual art, performance art, and so on. This focus on the social nature of artwork is motivated in part by Wittgensteinian skepticism about meaning and, more specifically, the concern that recently, just about anything can become art. One response to these points is to suggest that art simply is what the experts say it is.

This view has certain problems, however. It precludes the possibility of art that could exist apart for the social milieu of the artworld, an implication that violates our intuition about what art is. Levinson (1979, p. 233), for instance, considered someone "in a county fair in Nebraska, who sets an assemblage of egg shells and white glue down on the corner of a table for folks to look at. Isn't it possible that she has created art? Yet she and the artworld exist in perfect mutual oblivion." More generally, there does not seem to be anything contradictory in stating that something is an artwork even if the artworld does not recognize it as such, or, conversely, that the artworld could be mistaken in conferring artwork status to an entity. Imagine a case of fraud, where a gullible community of critics is led to believe that Duchamp's shoe (which is actually just his shoe) is *Shoe,* something created by Duchamp with the intent to be displayed as art. There is a strong intuition that the artworld's claim that this is an artwork would not in itself make it so. Instead the artworld would be mistaken, and after the fraud was discovered the aesthetic (and financial) value of the shoe would decrease accordingly. These intuitions suggest that the naive notion of *art* is not equivalent to "whatever entities the artworld views as art" (see also Danto, 1992).

Another class of proposals are intentionalist theories, which posit that something becomes an artwork by virtue of the intent of its creator. A particularly interesting version of this is that of Levinson (1979, 1989, 1993):

> An artwork is a thing (item, object, entity) that has been seriously intended for regard-as-a-work-of-art, i.e., regard in a way *preexisting artworks are or were correctly regarded.* (1989, p. 21)

Levinson noted that the italicized phrase could be given either a transparent or opaque reading. That is, someone could be making art by virtue of intending the object to be regarded in ways such as "with close attention to form," "with awareness of symbolism," and so on; or someone could be making art by virtue of intending the object to be regarded in the same manner as previous artwork has been viewed, whatever that might be.

Through this procedure, the oddest entities can come to be viewed as artwork. Levinson gave the example of Jaspers, who "directs our attention to a pile of wood shavings on the floor, a green 3′ × 5′ index card tacked to his wall, and the fact that Montgomery is the capital of Alabama. He names this set of things *John.* He then says that this his latest artwork." Levinson argued that we are willing to accept this as artwork only to the extent that we can be convinced that this collection has been sincerely intended by Jaspers for regard in a certain way (i.e., one that is associated with how art is typically made and viewed). Obviously our task would be easier if Jaspers had chose to create something more traditional, such as a representational painting or sculpture, but viewing Jasper's "creation" as art *is* possible (at least for some people) and the artwork status of less bizarre constructions, such as those by Picasso or Duchamp or Warhol, is by now relatively uncontroversial (see Danto, 1981 for discussion).

This discussion might seem to take us far afield; surely Jasper's *John* and Duchamp's *Fountain* are exceptional and should be treated as such. Nevertheless, there are reasons why the debate over the proper definition of art can inform theories of word learning and representation. For one thing, different perspectives about the nature of art correspond to different notions of word meaning in general (Fodor, 1993). The traditional views of art (possible artwork = some perceptual or experiential aspects of art objects) mirrors empiricist and associationist views, whereas the institutional view (possible artwork = whatever some community accepts as such) is based on a Wittgenstenian theory that also motivates some word learning theorists (e.g., Nelson, 1985). The intentional-historical theory of Levinson can be viewed as a special case of the rationalist theory: an explicit instance of how people can fix the reference of a term through intuitions about the intent of others.

There are more direct connections, as the acquisition of names for artwork and kinds of artwork is itself an interesting domain. If an adult was to look at Eva Hesse's *Tori,* composed of several pieces of fiberglass and understand that this was intended as an artwork, she would have no problem learning that the proper name refers to this collection, and would be capable using it appropriately, with intuitions about its identity conditions and so on (see also Bloom, 1994b). Unlike other perspectives, a rationalist approach to word learning predicts that young children should also be able to acquire such words, despite the fact that they are not object names and only exist as individuals through the intentions of others.

A further question concerns representations of the meanings of words like *art* (or *artwork*), *drawing, painting, sculpture,* and so on. For adults, such notions are fraught with intentionality, and one can see this without appealing to Jasper's bizarre creation. If I work for months carefully painting a canvas with the conscious intent to proudly display the finished property in an art gallery, the finished product is indisputably a *painting*. But if I were instead to accidentally spill some paint onto a canvas and create the same result, this is not a painting. The same distinction holds for the verb; in the first case, I have *painted* the canvas; in the second, I have not.

Intuitions about intent apply in similar ways with regard to nominals outside the domain of artwork. The most obvious cases are nominals that refer to kinds of individuals linked directly to intentional acts. If I tell you something false, but think that it is true and have no intention to deceive you, it is not a *lie;* if I give you something of mine to hold, but expect it back immediately, it is not a *gift;* if I dig a hole in my yard with the intent to build a pool there, it is not a *trap* (it might be, however, if I was intending to catch a tiger).

The same considerations apply for artifacts; whether or not something is *a toy* or *a weapon* or *a piece of furniture* depends crucially on the intent of the person who made it. Most chairs, for example, can be identified by their shape and size and by noting their current function. But some chairs have unusual shapes (some are shaped like hands, for instance), others cannot be used to sit on (because they are broken or old or poorly designed), and others happen to be exclusively used for other purposes (to pile coats on, for instance). But they are all described as *chairs,* because they share a similar intentional etiology (see Bloom, 1996c, and Chomsky, 1992, for discussion).

Intentionality, then, spills into the acquisition of word meanings in several related ways. Most obviously, as Augustine noted, a sensitivity to the intention of others is used by children to fix the reference of new words. In addition, it can provide an initial understanding of word meaning, even in the absence of other information. At another level, intentionality is a core aspect of the meaning of many (perhaps most) words, most obviously words such as *art* and *painting,* but also names for social institutions like *The United States* and *university,* names for intentional entities like *threat* and *joke,* artifact names like *chair* and *toy,* and so on. The subtlety of our intuitions about the meanings of words like *painting* and *chair,* in the absence of explicit training or instruction, is similar in many regards to our knowledge of abstract properties of grammar and might profit from a similar sort of detailed analysis (see also Chomsky, 1988).

IV. CONCLUSION

The proposal presented in this chapter is that children possess an understanding of different types of concepts at the onset of word learning, these concepts map onto grammatical categories, and children can use syntax to determine the category that a new word belongs to. In particular, count nouns refer to kinds of individuals, where individuals are those entities construed by our interpretive systems as playing an explanatory role in some conceptual domain. Our intuitions about the intentions of others are used to determine the precise individuals that new words refer to. Finally, intentional notions might themselves underlie the meanings of a large class of words in the vocabularies of children and adults.

The issues raised from the standpoint of a rationalist approach are unusual, particularly given the standards of empiricist explanation that are commonplace in discussions of word learning. It is not standard to drag in notions like explanatory role, intentional theories of the nature of artwork, and syntax-semantics mappings to explain how children learn words like *cup* and *Fred.* In fact, the assumption within much of psychology and philosophy has been that one can explain early word learning solely in terms of perceptual primitives and the principles of association—and that the successful theory would be the one that came upon the right primitives and the best characterization of the principles.

It has been argued here that even a cursory look at the words children know and the conditions under which they learn these words reveals that this program is untenable. Most likely, Augustine was correct; one cannot explain the most basic aspects of early word learning without positing substantial innate capacities and without relating the problem of word learning to foundational questions about language, conceptual representation, and social cognition.

APPENDIX: DETERMINING THE SYNTACTIC CATEGORIES THAT WORDS BELONG TO

One premise of this theory is that children can use syntactic cues to determine the semantic status of at least some words in the course of lexical development. In the domain of nominals, they use their knowledge that a word is a count noun, a mass noun, or a lexical NP to infer aspects of its meaning—whether it refers to a kind of individual, a kind of stuff, or an individual. This procedure can only work, however, if children have some prior mechanism with which to learn the grammatical categories that words belong to.

The problem of syntactically categorizing words exists independently of considerations of word learning. Evidence from studies of children's production (e.g., Bloom, 1990; Bloom, Barss, Nicol, & Conway, 1994; Hyams, 1986; Pinker, 1984;

Valian, 1986) and comprehension (e.g., Macnamara, 1982; Naigles, 1990; Soja, 1992) suggests that even 2-year olds possess rules and principles that map over syntactic categories like noun and verb, NP, and VP. Any adequate theory of language development must explain how children solve this assignment problem; how they learn that *dog* is a count noun and not an NP, that *Fred* is an NP and not a verb, and so on.

Older children are able to categorize words using prior knowledge of language, just as adults do. For instance, part of knowledge of English is knowing that the word *kick* is a verb that takes an NP direct object and that the word *many* is a quantifier that co-occurs with plural count nouns. Given this knowledge, a child can infer from hearing *John kicked Fred* that *Fred* is an NP and from hearing *There are many boys* that *boys* is a plural count noun (e.g., Gordon, 1985; Pinker, 1984). This sort of inference does not require any special acquisition mechanism; all children need is some understanding of the syntactic and semantic properties of some existing English words.

This mechanism cannot be sufficient, however, because children must have already learned the syntax of some words in order to use it. One proposal for how children syntactically categorize their first words is that they attend to their meanings (e.g., Bloom, 1994a; Grimshaw, 1981; Macnamara, 1982; Pinker, 1984, 1987; Wexler & Cullicover, 1980). For instance, an object name will be construed as a count noun, a substance name as a mass noun, and a name for a person as a lexical NP. Children's occasional misinterpretations of mass nouns that describe objects as count nouns (e.g., *I see two money*) further suggests that they use semantic cues to categorize new words as count or mass even though this sometimes leads to errors (Bloom, 1994a).

One way in which semantic cues might apply is through children's using the mappings proposed in Section III.A in the opposite direction. Just as knowing the grammatical category of a word can indicate certain aspects of its meaning, knowing a word's meaning can reveal its grammatical category. This method of syntactically categorizing words is sometimes known as *semantic bootstrapping* (Grimshaw, 1981; Pinker, 1984, 1987), although the version presented here (dubbed *semantic competence* in Bloom, 1994a) differs from the Pinker/Grimshaw theory in that it posits that the requisite syntax-semantics mappings are part of knowledge of language, not of an independent language acquisition device.

There is an apparent circularity in claiming that (a) children use syntax to acquire word meaning and (b) they use word meaning to acquire syntax. One solution is that different procedures apply for different words. In particular, children might first acquire the meanings of some words without the help of syntactic cues and use the syntax-semantics mappings to categorize them as nouns, determiners, verbs, and so on. Once children acquire some command of syntactic structure, the mappings can then work in the other direction; syntactic information could then facilitate the acquisition of the meanings of other words. For different perspectives on how syntactic cues to word meaning and semantic cues to word syntax interact with one another, see Bloom (1994a, 1996a), Gleitman (1990), and Pinker (1994b).

ACKNOWLEDGMENTS

This research was supported by grants from the Sloan Foundation and from the Spencer Foundation. I have had a lot of help on this, and would like to thank Felice Bedford, Susan Carey, Noam Chomsky, Jerry Fodor, Lila Gleitman, Bill Ittelson, Jerry Levinson, John Macnamara, Gary Marcus, Mary Peterson, Nancy Soja, Ed Stein, and especially Karen Wynn for discussing these issues with me and for providing comments on a previous draft. None of these people are going to agree with everything I say here, however, and all mistakes are my own.

REFERENCES

Augustine, St. (398/1961). *Confessions.* New York: Penguin Books.

Anderson, J. R. (1983). *The architecture of cognition.* Cambridge, MA: Harvard University Press.

Baldwin, D. A. (1991). Infants' contribution to the achievement of joint reference. *Child Development, 62,* 875–890.

Bates, E., Bretherton, I., & Snyder, L. (1988). *From first words to grammar: Individual differences and dissociable mechanisms.* Cambridge: Cambridge University Press.

Biederman, I. (1987). Recognition-by-components: A theory of human image understanding. *Psychological Review, 94,* 115–147.

Bloom, P. (1990). Syntactic distinctions in child language. *Journal of Child Language, 17,* 343–355.

Bloom, P. (1994a). Semantic competence as an explanation for some transitions in language development. In Y. Levy (Ed.), *Other children, other languages: Issues in the theory of language acquisition.* Hillsdale, NJ: Erlbaum.

Bloom, P. (1994b). Possible names: The role of syntax-semantics mappings in the acquisition of nominals. *Lingua, 92,* 297–329.

Bloom, P. (1996a). Controversies in language acquisition. Word learning and the part of speech. In R. Gelman and T. Au (Eds.), *Handbook of Perceptual and Cognitive Development.* New York: Academic Press.

Bloom, P. (1996b). Possible individuals in language and cognition. *Current Directions in Psychological Science, 5,* 90–94.

Bloom, P. (1996c). Intention, history, and artifact concepts. *Cognition, 60,* 1–29.

Bloom, P., Barss, A., Nicol, J., & Conway, L. (1994). Children's understanding of binding and coreference: Evidence from spontaneous speech *Language, 70,* 53–71.

Bloom, P., & Kelemen, D. (1995). Syntactic cues in the acquisition of collective nouns. *Cognition, 56,* 1–30.

Bloom, P., Kelemen, D., Fountain, A., & Courtney, E. (1995). The acquisition of collective nouns. In D. MacLaughlin and S. McEwen (Eds.), *Proceedings of the 19th Boston University Conference on Language Development.* Boston: Cascadilla Press

Bloom, P., & Markson, L. (1996). The role of intentionality in children's naming of representations. Poster presented at the West Coast Theory of Mind Conference, University of California, Berkeley, May 24–25.

Bloom, P., & Wynn, K. (1998). Linguistic cues to the meanings of number words. *Journal of Child Language, 24,* 511–533.

Brown, R. (1957). Linguistic determinism and the part of speech. *Journal of Abnormal and Social Psychology, 55,* 1–5.

Carey, S. (1978). The child as word learner. In M. Halle, J. Bresnan, & A. Miller (Eds.), *Linguistic Theory and Psychological Reality.* Cambridge, MA: MIT Press.

Carey, S. (1986). *Conceptual change in childhood.* Cambridge, MA: MIT Press.

Carey, S. (1988). Conceptual differences between children and adults, *Mind and Language, 3,* 167–181.

Chomsky, N. (1959). A review of B. F. Skinner's Verbal Behavior. *Language, 35,* 26–58.

Chomsky, N. (1988). *Language and problems of knowledge: The Managua lectures.* Cambridge, MA: MIT Press.

Chomsky, N. (1992). Explaining language use. *Philosophical Topics, 20,* 205–231.

Danto, A. (1981). *The transfiguration of the commonplace.* Cambridge, MA: Harvard University Press.

Danto, A. (1992). The Art World revisited: Comedies of similarity. In A. C. Danto (Ed.), *Beyond the Brillo Box: The visual arts in post-historical perspective.* New York: Farrar, Straus, Giroux.

Davies, S. (1991). *Definitions of art.* Ithaca. NY: Cornell University Press.

Dennett, D. (1987). *The intentional stance.* Cambridge, MA; MIT Press.

Dennett, D. (1991). Real patterns. *Journal of Philosophy, 88,* 27–51.

Dickie, G. (1974). *Art and the aesthetic.* New York: Cornell University Press.

Donnellan, K. S. (1977). Speaking of nothing. In S. P. Schwartz (Ed.), *Naming, necessity, and natural kinds.* Ithaca, NY: Cornell University Press.

Fisher, C., Hall, D. G., Rakowitz, S., & Gleitman, L. (1994). Why it is better to receive than to give: Syntactic and conceptual constraints on vocabulary growth. *Lingua, 92,* 333–375.

Fodor, J. A. (1993). *Déjà vu* all over again: How Danto's aesthetics recapitulates the philosophy of mind. In M. Rollins (Ed.), *Danto and his critics.* Cambridge, MA: Blackwell.

Fodor, J. A., & Pylyshyn, Z. (1988). Connectionism and cognitive architecture: A critical analysis. *Cognition, 28,* 3–71.

Gelman, S. A., & Markman, E. M. (1985). Implicit contrast in adjectives vs. nouns: Implications for word-learning in preschoolers. *Journal of Child Language, 12,* 125–143.

Gelman, S. A., & Taylor, M. (1984). How two-year-old children interpret proper and common names for unfamiliar objects. *Child Development, 55,* 1535–1540.

Gentner, D. (1978). In relational meaning: The acquisition of verb meaning. *Child Development, 49,* 988–998.

Gleitman, L. R. (1990). The structural sources of word meaning. *Language Acquisition, 1,* 3–55.

Gleitman, L. R., & Gillette, J. (this volume). The role of syntax in verb learning.

Gordon, P. (1985). Evaluating the semantic categories hypothesis: The case of the count/mass distinction. *Cognition, 20,* 209–242.

Grimshaw, J. (1981). Form, function, and the language acquisition device. In C. L. Baker & J. McCarthy, (Eds.), *The logical problem of language acquisition.* Cambridge, MA: MIT Press.

Gupta, A. K. (1980). *The logic of common nouns.* New Haven: Yale University Press.

Hall, D. G. (1991). Acquiring proper names for familiar and unfamiliar animate objects: Two-year-olds' word-learning biases. *Child Development, 62,* 1142–1154.

Heath, S. B. (1983). *Ways with words.* Cambridge: Cambridge University Press.

Hochberg, J. G., & Pinker, S. (1984). Syntax-semantics correspondences in parental speech. Unpublished manuscript, Department of Brain and Cognitive Sciences, MIT.

Jackendoff, R. (1991). Parts and boundaries. *Cognition, 41,* 9–45.

Jackendoff, R. (1992). Mme Tussaud meets the binding theory. *Natural language and linguistic theory, 10,* 1–31.

Johnson, M. H., Dziurawiec, S., Ellis, H., & Morton, J. (1991). Newborns' preferential tracking of face-like stimuli and its subsequent decline. *Cognition, 40,* 1–19.

Jones, S. S., & Smith, L. B. (1993). The place of perception in children's concepts. *Cognitive Development, 8,* 113–139.

Hyams, N. (1986). *Language acquisition and the theory of parameters.* Dordrecht: Reidel.

Katz, N., Baker, E., & Macnamara, J. (1974). What's in a name? A study of how children learn common and proper names. *Child Development, 45,* 469–473.

Keil, F. C. (1979). *Semantic and conceptual development: An ontological perspective.* Cambridge, MA: MIT Press.

Keil, F. C. (1989). *Concepts, kinds, and cognitive development.* Cambridge, MA: MIT Press.

Kennick, W. (1958). Does traditional aesthetics rest on a mistake? *Mind, 67,* 317–334.

Kripke, S. (1977). Identity and necessity. In S. P. Schwartz (Ed.), *Naming, necessity, and natural kinds.* Ithaca, NY: Cornell University Press.

Landau, B. (1982). Will the real grandmother please stand up? *Journal of Psycholinguistic Research, 11,* 47–62.

Landau, B., & Gleitman, L. R. (1985). *Language and experience.* Cambridge, MA: Harvard University Press.

Landau, B., & Jackendoff, R. (1993). "What" and "where" in spatial language and spatial cognition. *Behavioral and Brain Sciences, 16,* 217–238.

Landau, B., Jones, S., & Smith, L. B. (1992). Perception, ontology, and naming in young children: Commentary on Soja, Carey, and Spelke. *Cognition, 43,* 85–91.

Landau, B., Smith, L. B., & Jones, S. S. (1988). The importance of shape in early lexical learning. *Cognitive Development, 3,* 299–321.

Landau, B., & Stecker, D. (1990). Objects and places: Syntactic and geometric representations in early lexical learning. *Cognitive Development, 5,* 287–312.

Levinson, J. (1979). Defining art historically. *British Journal of Aesthetics, 19,* 232–250.

Levinson, J. (1989). Refining art historically, *The Journal of Aesthetics and Art Criticism, 47,* 21–33.

Levinson, J. (1993). Extending art historically. *The Journal of Aesthetics and Art Criticism, 51,* 411–423.

Liittschwager, J. C., & Markman, E. M. (1993, March). Young children's understanding of proper versus common nouns. Paper presented at the biennial meeting of the Society for Research in Child Development, New Orleans, LA.

McClelland, J. L., & Rumelhart, D. E. (1986). A distributed model of human learning and memory. In J. McClelland, & D. Rumelhart (Eds), *Parallel Distributed Processing.* Cambridge, MA: MIT Press.
Macnamara, J. (1982). *Names for things: A study of human learning.* Cambridge, MA: MIT Press.
Macnamara, J. (1986). *A border dispute: The place of logic in psychology.* Cambridge, MA: MIT Press.
Mandler, J. (1993). Concept formation in infancy. *Cognitive Development, 8,* 291–318.
Marcus, G. F. (1993). Negative evidence in language acquisition. *Cognition, 46,* 53–85.
Markman, E. M. (1990). Constraints children place on word meanings. *Cognitive Science, 14,* 57–77.
Markman, E. M., & Wachtel, G. F. (1988). Children's use of mutual exclusivity to constrain the meaning of words. *Cognitive Psychology, 20,* 121–157.
Millikan, R. G. (1993). *White queen psychology and other essays for Alice* Cambridge. MA: MIT Press.
Naigles, L. (1990). Children use syntax to learn verb meanings. *Journal of Child Language, 17,* 357–374.
Nelson, K. (1973). Structure and strategy in learning to talk. *Monographs of the Society for Research in Child Development, 38*[1–2, Serial No. 149].
Nelson, K. (1985). *Making sense: The acquisition of shared meaning.* New York: Academic.
Nelson, K., Hampson, J., & Shaw, L. K. (1993). Nouns in early lexicons: Evidence, explanations, and extensions. *Journal of Child Language, 20,* 61–84.
Palmer, S. E. (1992). Common region: A new principle of perceptual grouping. *Cognitive Psychology, 24,* 436–447.
Pinker, S. (1984). *Language learnability and language development.* Cambridge, MA: Harvard University Press.
Pinker, S. (1987). The bootstrapping problem in language acquisition. In B. MacWhinney (Ed.), *Mechanisms of language acquisition.* Hillsdale, NJ: Erlbaum.
Pinker, S. (1994a). *The language instinct.* New York: Morrow.
Pinker, S. (1994b). How could a child use verb syntax to learn verb semantics? *Lingua, 92,* 377–410.
Pinker, S., & Prince, A. (1988). On language and connectionism: Analysis of a Parallel Distributed Processing model of language acquisition. *Cognition, 28,* 73–193.
Putnam, H. (1977). Meaning and reference. In S. P. Schwartz (Ed.), *Naming, necessity, and natural kinds.* Ithaca, NY: Cornell University Press.
Quine, W.V.O. (1960). *Word and object.* Cambridge, MA: MIT Press.
Quine, W.V.O. (1993). In praise of observation sentences. *Journal of Philosophy, 90,* 107–116.
Richards, D. D., & Goldfarb, J. (1986). The episodic memory model of conceptual development: An integrative viewpoint. *Cognitive Development, 1,* 183–219.
Rosch, E., Mervis, C. B., Gray, W. D., Johnson, D. M., & Boyes-Braem, P. (1976). Basic objects in natural categories. *Cognitive Psychology, 8,* 382–439.
Schieffelin, B. B. (1985). The acquisition of Kaluli. In D. I. Slobin (Ed.), *The crosslinguistic study of language acquisition Volume 1: The data.* Hillsdale, NJ: Erlbaum.
Skinner, B. F. (1953). *Verbal Behavior.* New York: Appleton-Century-Crofts.

Smith, L. B. (1993). The concept of same. In H. Reese (Ed.), *Advances in child development & behavior.* New York: Academic.

Smith, L. B., & Gasser, M. (1993). A neural network model of developmental changes in naming behavior. Paper presented at the Society for Research in Child Development, New Orleans, March 25–28.

Soja, N. N. (1992). Inferences about the meanings of nouns: The relationship between perception and syntax, *Cognitive Development, 7,* 29–45.

Soja, N. N. (1994). Evidence for a distinct kind of noun. *Cognition, 51,* 267–284.

Soja, N. N., Carey, S., & Spelke, E. S. (1991). Ontological categories guide young children's inductions of word meaning: Object terms and substance terms. *Cognition, 38,* 179–211.

Soja, N. N., Carey, S., & Spelke, E. S. (1992). Perception, ontology, and word meaning. *Cognition, 45,* 101–107.

Spelke, E. S. (1988). Where perception ends and thinking begins: The apprehension of objects in infancy. In A. Yonas (Ed.), *Minnesota Symposia on Child Psychology* Hillsdale, NJ: Erlbaum.

Spelke, E. S., Breinlinger, K., Macomber, J., & Jacobson, K. (1992). Origins of knowledge. *Psychological Review, 99,* 605–632.

Starkey, P, Spelke, E. S., & Gelman, R. (1990). Numerical abstraction by human infants. *Cognition, 36,* 97–127.

Sternberg, R. J., & Allbritton, D. W. (1992). If Dan Quayle changed his name and appearance to those of John F. Kennedy, who would he be?: Historical versus physical components of meaning. Unpublished manuscript, Yale University.

Taylor, M., & Gelman, S. (1988). Adjectives and nouns: Children's strategies for learning new words. *Child Development, 59,* 411–419.

Thorndike, E. L., & Lorge, I. (1944). *The teacher's word book of 30,000 words.* New York: Bureau of Publications, Teachers College, Columbia University.

Valian, V. (1986). Syntactic categories in the speech of young children. *Developmental Psychology, 22,* 562–579.

Waxman, S. (1990). Linguistic biases and the establishment of conceptual hierarchies: Evidence from preschool children. *Cognitive Development, 5,* 123–150.

Waxman, S. R., & Markow, D. B. (1996). Words as an invitation to form categories: Evidence from 12- to 13-month-old infants. *Cognitive Psychology, 29,* 257–302.

Wertheimer, M. (1923). Untersuchungen zur Lehre von der Gestalt. Reprinted in W. D. Ellis (Ed.), *A sourcebook of Gestalt Psychology.* New York: The Humanities Press, 1950.

Wexler, K., & Cullicover, P. (1980). *Formal principles of language acquisition.* Cambridge, MA: MIT Press.

Wiggins, D. (1980). *Sameness and substance.* Oxford: Blackwell.

Wittgenstein, L. (1953). *Philosophical investigations.* Oxford: Blackwell.

Woolley, J. D., & Wellman, H. M. (1990). Young children's understanding of realities, nonrealities, and appearances. *Child Development, 61,* 946–961.

Wynn, K. (1992). Evidence against empiricist accounts of the origins of numerical knowledge. *Mind and Language, 7,* 315–332.

Xu, F., & Carey, S. (1996). Infants' metaphysics: The case of numerical identity. *Cognitive Psychology, 30,* 111–153.

CHAPTER 9

THE ROLE OF SYNTAX IN VERB LEARNING

Lila R. Gleitman and Jane Gillette

We discuss here the mapping problem for vocabulary acquisition: how word-level concepts are matched with their phonological realizations in the target language. Traditional approaches to this problem assume that, at least at early stages in the acquisition process, children try to line up the utterance of single words with their contingencies in the world. Thus their task would be to discover that *elephant* is most often said in the presence of elephants and rarely said in their absence (Locke, 1690, and many modern sources).

Our recent investigations (Gillette, Gleitman, Gleitman, & Lederer, forthcoming) show how well such a procedure could work in practice for the case of concrete nouns. Adult subjects are shown videotapes of mothers playing with their infants (aged about 18 months, mean length of utterance (MLU) < 2;0) but with the audio turned off. These film clips are long enough for subjects to pick up the pragmatics of the conversation, for example, of a mother showing and describing an elephant puppet to the child, who then takes it and manipulates it. The subjects are told that whenever the mother is uttering the target noun, a beep will sound; their task is to identify the word that she uttered. Subjects perform this task easily, guessing correctly about 50% of the time even on the first video-beep exposure and improving with the addition of more instances. And if any of the maternal usages was deictic, the subjects are virtually perfect in guessing what noun she was saying.

This laboratory situation is radically reduced from the problem that infants face in assigning interpretations to novel words. The subjects are made aware in advance that the target is a noun. These nouns all describe concrete objects that are present in the videotaped scenario and are foci of the mother-child conversation.[1] In light of the task as set for them, the subjects also know that there exists in English a single common word that will fit their observations of these objects in these scenes. Moreover, they are solving for one target noun at a time; their exposures to this item are not complicated by the intervention of any other novel items, so they have no memory problem. In contrast, a child learner might reencounter the new item only after the passage of considerable time, and mingled with other new words.

One further proviso is even more controversial. No doubt arises that the adult subjects can conceptualize the objects in the scenes (e.g., they can represent the concept *elephant*) and can interpret the pragmatics of the mother-child conversation. So built into the claim that these findings are informative for understanding the mapping problem is our assumption that adults and young children are much the same, not only in their data-handling procedures but also in the ways they interpret the everyday world of things, actions, causes, intentions, and so forth (for a recent discussion of this *rationalist perspective,* see P. Bloom, 1994).

Overall, then, the Gillette and Gleitman experiment models the child's vocabulary learning situation in at best a highly idealized fashion. But it does add to a literature demonstrating that maternal usage, at least of highly frequent nouns, is sufficiently faithful to the here and now to support learning by inspecting how the sounds of words match up with present scenes (Bruner, 1975; Ninio, 1980).

This apparent simplicity of the mapping problem for vocabulary acquisition—once purged of the "concept learning" issues—accounts for why it has been something of a stepchild in recent linguistic inquiry into language learning. The task has seemed devoid of any interesting internal structure: merely a matter of associating single words (qua phonological objects) with their standard contexts of use, as in the experiment just described.

The burden of the present discussion is to show that, over the vocabulary at large, this word-to-world pairing procedure is too weak to account fully for mapping. Our claim is that word learning is in general performed by pairing a *sentence* (qua syntactic object) with the observed world.

I. INSUFFICIENCY OF OBSERVATION FOR VERB LEARNING

As a first demonstration of the structural requirement in word learning, we now reconsider the Gillette and Gleitman experiment as it pertains to the acquisition of

[1]This is because only the words the mothers uttered most frequently were used as targets. Because in real life the child is sporadically confronted with the utterance of words in the absence of their referents, the word-to-world matching procedure would necessarily be probabilistic, gaining its power from cross-situational observation (Pinker, 1984).

verbs. The manipulation is the same. The subjects are shown silent videotapes of mother-infant interactions, long enough to reveal the pragmatic contexts for the verbs' use. At the moment that the mother was really uttering some target verb, the beep sounds. Again, only the mothers' most frequent child-directed verbs are tested, and again the subject receives several beep-scenario pairs (that is, pairings of the utterance of the target verb with its observational contingencies) as the basis for his or her guess. Now the results are entirely different from those of the noun experiments. The subjects are helpless. They identify fewer than 10% of the verbs the mother was actually saying.

Once again the experiment has various unrealistic elements, notably that the subjects know all these English verbs in advance and have been told that it is a verb that they are seeking. But this should make their task easier, not harder. One could also object, alluding to the results from a generation of developmental psycholinguists, that children are better language learners (including vocabulary learners) than adults and would therefore do better in this task.

Despite these real contaminants, one effect stands firm: This is the massive *difference* for verbs and nouns in their tractability to this procedure—whereas the nouns were adequately identified from their word (beep) to world (video) contingencies, the verbs were not.

How can we explain the special difficulty of verbs in this manipulation? One factor is that some of the verbs that mothers use *most frequently* to their babies represent concepts that are not straightforwardly observable: *want, know,* and *think* are in the top group in usage frequency. Even some of the more concrete frequent verbs encode some intentional content rather than solely a property of the perceived world, such as *show, see,* and *give.* Another factor, evident upon inspection of these videotapes, is the temporal precision with which the environment matches the utterance. When *elephant* is uttered, overwhelmingly often the elephant is being held, waved, even pointed at. But *push* is usually said well before or after the pushing event takes place (Lederer, Gleitman, & Gleitman, 1995; Tomasello & Kruger, 1992). The verb uses do not line up transparently with their situational contexts, a problem we have called *interleaving:* By the time the mother says *push* ("You pushed the poor elephant down!"), the child is usually *looking* and *smiling* at the consequences of his or her prior pushing action (or the reverse, as when the mother says "Go push the truck"). This makes it hard for the subjects to guess that the beep referred to the pushing act.

If young children are like our adult subjects, they too should have more trouble learning verbs than nouns. And indeed they do. A robust generalization from the vocabulary learning literature is that early vocabularies (the first 50 words) contain few—often no—verbs; and nouns continue to outnumber verbs in productive vocabularies beyond their frequency distribution in maternal speech until the child is past 3 years of age (Gentner, 1978; 1982).

We have mentioned two usage distinctions that can help explain this learning oddity. The first is merely a pragmatic fact of usage with nothing essential to do with the formal or substantive universals of the word classes: Caretakers' most frequent nouns to babies in our corpus are predominantly items that describe observeable objects, whereas their verbs are often abstract: They often say "I think . . . " to their babies, but they rarely say "The thought . . . . " A second and more important factor is that verb use, as opposed to noun use, is not tightly time locked with the extralinguistic contexts and more often refers to the nonpresent. (In fact, in Beckwith, Tinker, & Bloom's [1989] corpus of speech to babies, verbs are used out of context more than a quarter of the time—this includes physical action verbs like *open*).

But there is a third factor—one that we believe holds the primary key to this lexical-class order effect in vocabulary acquisition: Verb acquisition requires access to the phrase structure of the exposure language, and it takes the infant some time to get the structural properties under control.[2]

II. MORE POWER TO VERB LEARNING

Eric Lenneberg (1967) provided the first evidence suggesting a structure-sensitive model for the learning of verbs (and perhaps all classes of words that do not typically express concrete object concepts): The "explosion" of spoken vocabulary, including sudden increase in the range of lexical types, coincides with the appearance of rudimentary (two-word) sentences at approximately the 24th month of life. Perhaps an ability to comprehend the spoken sentence is a requirement for efficient verb learning. It may be that once the child has learned some nouns, she can ask not only "What are the environmental contingencies for the use of this word?" but "What are its environmental contingencies, *as constrained by the structural positions in which it appears* in adult speech?"

For historical reasons that have no present relevance, this approach to vocabulary acquisition has been called *syntactic bootstrapping* (Gleitman, 1990). But because the term itself is something of a misnomer, let us discard it. The idea is that structural information is required by learners—along with the scenario information—to fix the meaning of novel verbs.

[2]The requirement for knowledge of phrase structure in vocabulary learning also should hold for nouns beyond the simplest object terms. A number of authors have recently described the use of syntax-semantics links in the acquisition of abstract nominal categories, for example, mass versus count nouns and proper names. See particularly P. Bloom in chapter 8 of this volume.

A. Origins and Motivation

The first direct demonstration that vocabulary acquisition is sensitive to linguistic context was from Brown (1957), who showed that children would interpret the relation of a novel word to a scene (in this case, a picture) differently depending on available morphological cues: If they heard *the gorp,* they pointed to a visible novel object, but if they heard *gorping* they pointed to the implied action, and so forth. The linguistic cues affected the interpretation of the scene in view, to some extent reversing the causal chain suggested by common sense (namely, that the scene in view determines the interpretation of the linguistic object). The findings hint that learners expect there to be a link between formal properties of language (lexical class membership in this case) and semantic interpretation.

Landau and Gleitman (1985) carried this line further, positing that children use linguistic cues in identifying novel word meanings within as well as across the major lexical classes. Their immediate impetus was a quite startling finding: The first verb in a congenitally blind learner's spoken vocabulary was *see.* Although the exposure conditions for learning this word necessarily differ for blind and sighted, both populations acquire the word as a term of achieved perception, and do so at the same developmental moment.

But such exotica are not really required to show that children acquire aspects of word meaning that do not seem to be warranted by perception and pragmatic inference. Consider a sighted child hearing her mother say "I see a bird over there." Often there will be an occluding object between child and bird. Children come to know that *see* means "see" despite the fact that maternal speech is not a faithful running commentary on events in view.

Related problems in learning from observation alone abound. One is that the listener's focus of attention may differ from that of the speaker's, as when the adult says, "Come take your nap" while the child inspects a cat on a mat. Another is that the scene that accompanies utterance of a verb includes many events, only one of which is encoded by that verb. Consider the plight of the child to whom an adult says, "Do you want some ice cream?" The adult is speaking, smiling, holding and waving the cone, and perhaps pointing to it; it is observably something good to eat, dripping, pink, an object of present desire, and so forth. It requires no empiricist bias (e.g., Quine, 1960) to believe that these interpretive complexities create practical problems in vocabulary learning. None of the aspects of the scene just described is irrelevant to the conversational intent, as this might be reconstructed by a sophisticated observer (which we assume the youngster to be). Yet only one of them is correct to map onto the item *want.* A picture is worth a thousand words, but that's the problem: A thousand words describe the varying aspects of any one picture.

Attempts to circumvent these difficulties involve a probabilistic procedure in which the mapping choice is based on the most frequent word-world match across situations (see Pinker, 1984, for discussion). No one can doubt that cross-situational observation plays a role in vocabulary acquisition, but taken alone it seems to be insufficient. One difficulty has to do with the observed rapidity and relative errorlessness of child vocabulary learning. Children are apparently acquiring five or more new words a day beginning at about the 15th month of life (Carey, 1978). It strains credulity to suppose that they are lucky enough to hear—within a very short time interval—most such words in the variety of informative environments that would be required to parse out the right interpretation.

B. Form–Meaning Interactions in Verb Learning

Inspection of any corpus of natural speech shows that different verbs characteristically occur with different complements, in accord with their differing argument structures. Thus inalienable actions typically are encoded with intransitive structures (*Pinnochio dances*), acts that affect another's state with transitive structures (*Gepetto kisses the puppet*), and so forth. This form-meaning correlation is usually described by saying that the structure is a projection from (aspects of) the verb's meaning; that is, the surface structures are mapped from the argument structure of the verb. Two complementary views of verb learning have recently been put forward, both taking advantage of such relations between verb meaning and sentence structure.

Bootstrapping Complementation Privileges from Knowledge of Verb Meaning

If form-meaning correlations are systematic across the languages of the world (quirks aside), we should expect that children can project the complement structures for a verb whose meaning they have acquired via event observation, rather than having to memorize the structures independently (Grimshaw, 1981; Pinker, 1984). One kind of evidence in support of this hypothesis comes from studies of the invention of language by linguistically deprived youngsters (deaf children of hearing parents who are not exposed to sign language; Goldin-Meadow & Feldman, 1977; Feldman, Goldin-Meadow, & Gleitman, 1978). The self-invented gesture systems of these children appear to conform to the theta criterion (Chomsky, 1981): They gesture one noun in construction with their invented gesture for *dance,* two in construction with *hit,* and three with *give.*[3] Another kind of evidence

[3]Actually, the inferential line that leads to this generalization concerning the isolated deaf children is quite complex. The bulk of data come from two- and three-gesture sentences produced by the children. The number of arguments that show up in the utterance is constrained heavily by this, as L. Bloom (1970) has shown also for young hearing speakers and which has been documented again and again. The number of underlying argument positions in the deaf children's sentences therefore was assessed by a measure that took into account the selective omission of different argument types (in more recent parlance, pro-drop); for this analysis, see Feldman et al. 1978; L. Bloom, 1970).

comes from child errors in complementation; these appear to occur primarily where there are quirks and subtleties in the way the exposure language maps from argument structure to surface structure (Bowerman, 1982). In short, children use their knowledge of a verb's meaning as a basis for projecting the phrase structure of sentences in which it appears.

Bootstrapping Verb Meaning from Knowledge of Verb Complementations

A second learning hypothesis also is consistent with the view that verb clause structure is a projection from verb argument structure: Hearing some new verb in a particular structural environment should constrain its interpretation (Landau & Gleitman, 1985; Gleitman & Gleitman, 1992). Thus hearing *John gorps* increases the likelihood that *gorp* means "smile" and decreases the likelihood that it means "hit," and hearing *John gorps Bill* should imply the reverse. Thus knowledge of the semantic implications of the sentence structure in which a novel verb appears can narrow the search space for its identification. It is this structurally derived narrowing of the hypothesis space for verb meaning on which we now concentrate.

III. THE ZOOM LENS HYPOTHESIS

According to our hypothesis, the first use of structural information is as an online procedure for interpreting a novel verb. Though there may be quite a few salient interpretations of the scene, the learner zooms in on one (or at least fewer) of these by demanding congruence also with the semantic implications of the sentence form. Thus the input is as follows:

(1) The extralinguistic event, as represented by a perceptually and pragmatically sophisticated observer.

paired with

(2) The linguistic event, represented as a novel verb positioned within the parse tree constructed from the adult utterance.

The learner exploits the semantically relevant structural information in (2) to choose among the several interpretations that may be warranted by (1).

An early demonstration is from Naigles (1990). She investigated responses to novel verbs as a function of linguistic introducing circumstances in children under 2 years of age, who had no or few verbs in their spoken vocabularies. In the learning phase of the experiment, the children were shown videotaped action scenes that had two novel salient interpretations. For example, they saw a rabbit pushing down on a duck's head, thus forcing the duck to bend over; simultaneously, both the duck and the rabbit were wheeling their free arm in a broad circle. While watching this scene, half the babies heard "The rabbit is gorping the duck" while the other half heard "The rabbit and the duck are gorping." Then *gorping* might plausibly refer to forcing to bend or to arm wheeling. Subsequently, the scene disappeared and a voice said "Find gorping now! Where's gorping?" At this point, new action scenes appeared, one on a videoscreen to the child's left, the other on a screen to her right. The one on the left showed the rabbit forcing the duck to bend, but with no arm wheeling. The one on the right showed rabbit and duck wheeling their arms, but with no forcing to bend. The measure of learning was the child's visual fixation time on one or the other screen during a six-second interval. Twenty-two of 24 infants tested looked longest at the videoscreen that matched their syntactic introducing circumstances. Evidently the transitive input biased subjects toward something like the cause-to-bend interpretation, whereas the intransitive input biased them toward arm wheeling. Though we cannot know from this manipulation exactly what the children learned about "the meaning of gorp," their interpretation of what they were (relevantly) perceiving during the training phase was clearly affected by the syntax, for the subjects' situations differed in no other way.

More direct evidence of the effect of syntactic context on verb identification comes from studies with 3-year-old learners. This age group is the one in which verb vocabulary (and complex sentence structure) burgeons. These relatively elderly subjects are also useful because they can answer questions about the meanings of novel verbs that they encounter. Fisher, Hall, Rakowitz, and Gleitman (1994) investigated the acquisition of perspective verbs (e.g., *chase/flee, lead/follow*) with children of this age.

Principled difficulties for observation-based learning arise for these verbs, for they come in pairs that vary primarily in the speaker-perspective on a single action or event, and thus their situational concommitants are virtually always the same. This makes them a good testing ground for proposed learning procedures that rely on word-to-world contingencies only. Consider *give* and *get.*[4] Both these verbs describe the same intentional transfer of possession of an object between two individuals. Disentangling them based on the pragmatics of the conversation

[4]Dissociating events where one of these verbs is sensible and the other is not are hard to find, though there are some, for example, while Mary can get a coke from the vending machine, that machine does not "give" it (Pinker, personal communication). But the usefulness of these rare dissociating events for these verbs has to be considered against two facts we just mentioned: (a) Children often learn from a very few exposures, and (b) verbs are often uttered in the absence of their referents and often are not uttered in the presence of their referents. Taken together, these factors imply that (a) a child is unlikely to hear *give* in a usefully dissociating context during the very brief learning interval for this word; (b) for the same reason, the child could not make much of the absence of *give* from conversations about vending machines; and (c) if she has happened to conjecture falsely from prior exposures that *give* means "get," the single mismatching word-event observation, should this occur, can hardly dissuade her and would likely be interpreted as an instance of noise in the database.

would require the listener to gain access to the mental perspective of the speaker—whether she is likely referring to Mary's volitional act of passing the book to John or John's consequent act of getting the book from Mary. Children perhaps can do some mind reading of just this sort by attending to the gist of conversation.

But additional information can come from inspecting the structural positioning of (known) nouns in the sentence heard and comparing these against the scene in view, providing that the learner determines the semantic implications of the sentence structure itself. If that scene shows the book moving from Mary to John, then an adult utterance like

(1) Look!, Ziking!

provides no differentiating information, but if she says

(2) Mary zikes the ball to John

zike likely means *give* (or *throw,* etc.). In contrast, if the sentence is

(3) John zikes the ball from Mary

then *zike* likely means *get* (*or take, receive, catch,* etc.). The potential clues for disentangling this pair are the choice of nominal in subject position, and the choice of a goal (*to*) versus source (*from*) preposition.

Fisher and colleagues showed such scenes/sentences to young children, in a context where a puppet was uttering the sentence: The children were asked to help the experimenter understand some "puppet words" (e.g., *zike*). The structure of the findings was this: If the input sentence to the child was uninformative of the *give/get* distinction, such as example sentence (1), then child and adult subjects showed a bias in interpreting the scene: They were likely to say that it described something like giving rather than getting. This "agency bias" (whoever was subject of the transitive verb was agent of the action) characterized the set of five scenarios tested, including also chasing in preference to fleeing (running away) and so forth.[5] If the input sentence was (2), which matches the bias as to how to interpret the scene, the tendency to respond with a verb that meant something like *give* was further enhanced, in fact, almost categorical. But if the input sentence was (3), which mismatches the perceptual/conceptual bias toward *give,* subjects' modal response became *get* (or one of its relatives, e.g., *take*).

[5]As we will discuss further, the syntactic environment, while narrowing the hypothesis space, still supports a variety of pertinent interpretations, even in the brief videos that these children were shown. Thus one cannot tell whether the rate or trajectory of the ball's motion is encoded in the new verb (as *throw*) or not (as *give*). Therefore, subjects might conjecture either of these as the meaning of *zike.* Moreover, the child subjects seemed loathe to conjecture that this new item was identical to some verb in their vocabulary, perhaps because they believe that there are no synonyms (see, for discussion, Clark, 1987; Markman & Wachtel, in press). Thus they were more likely to respond "making him eat out of a spoon" than "feed" and so forth.

In sum, structural properties of the sentence heard influence the perception of a single scene even in cases where the bias in event representation, taken alone, leads in the opposite direction. Such findings begin to explain why children rarely confuse the perspective verbs despite the fact that they occur in very similar extralinguistic contexts.

IV. THE MULTIPLE FRAMES HYPOTHESIS

In many cases, a surface-structure/situation pair is insufficient or even misleading about a verb's interpretation. For instance, the phrase structure and the typical situation in adult-child discourse are often the same when the adult says "Did you eat your cookie?" as when he says "Do you want a cookie?" In principle, examination of the further syntactic privileges of *eat* and *want* can cue distinctions in their interpretations. For example, *want* occurs with (tenseless) sentence complements, suggesting a mental component of its meaning.

More generally, the range of syntactic frames can provide convergent evidence on the meaning of a verb. "John is ziking the book to Bill" suggests an active verb of transfer (progressive, ditransitive). This would include a broad range of verbs such as *bring, throw, explain,* and so on. But then "John is ziking that the book is boring" narrows the interpretive range to mental verbs. Taken together—and examined against the accompanying scenes—these structural properties suggest mental transfer, whose local interpretation is communication (e.g., *explain;* Zwicky, 1970, Fisher, Gleitman, & Gleitman, 1991).

There is evidence that the linguistic information provided by mothers to their young children is refined enough to support learning from frame ranges. Lederer, Gleitman, and Gleitman (1995) examined lengthy conversations of mothers with babies (MLU < 2). For the 24 most common verbs in these mothers' speech, a verb by syntactic-environment matrix was developed. Within and across mothers, each verb was found to be unique in its syntactic range. Using a procedure devised by Fisher and colleagues (1991), it was shown that degree of overlap in syntactic range predicted the verbs' semantic overlap to a striking extent.

V. THE POTENCY OF VARIOUS EVIDENTIARY SOURCES

So far we have shown some demonstrations with children and adults suggesting that they can use syntactic evidence to aid in the mastery of new verbs. The question remains how much of the burden of verb identification the structure bears;

particularly, the multiple-frame evidence. After all, even if syntactic constraints will affect the observer's interpretation in some carefully constructed laboratory situations, in real life the evidence from extralinguistic and other cues may be so decisive that syntactic deductions rarely if ever come into play.

One indirect but suggestive kind of evidence that multiple-frame information is exploited by learners comes from correlational studies (Naigles & Hoff-Ginsberg, 1993). The idea behind such studies is to inquire how well maternal usage at some point in learning (Time 1) predicts learning by testing the child's progress after some suitable interval (Time 2). Specifically, they investigated the use of common verbs in the speech of mothers to 1- and 2-year olds and then their children's subsequent use of these verbs. The *diversity of syntactic frames* in which verbs appeared in maternal speech at Time 1, with verb frequency in maternal speech partialled out, significantly predicted the frequency with which these verbs appeared in child speech 10 weeks later.

Lederer, Gleitman, and Gleitman (forthcoming) have examined the potential information value of various properties of mothers' speech to infants: its (multiple) extralinguistic contexts, nominal co-occurrences, selectional, and syntactic properties. Which of these attributes of adult speech, taken singly or in various combinations, provide enough information for solving the mapping problem for verbs?

The method was to provide (adult) subjects with large numbers of instances (usually about 50) of the use of some target verb by mothers to 18-month olds, but blocking out one or another potential source of information. For example, some subjects saw 50 or so videotaped film clips of mothers uttering a single common verb but without audio; the procedure was repeated for the 24 most common verbs in these mothers' child-directed speech. Other subjects were told the nouns that occurred with the target verb in each of the 50 maternal sentences. A third group was shown the list of 50 sentences that the mother actually uttered but with all nouns as well as the verb converted to nonsense (e.g., *Rom GORPS that the rivenflak is grum, Can vany GORP the blick?*).

The first finding was that, just as in the Gillette and Gleitman experiment cited earlier, subjects systematically failed to guess the verb from observing its real-world context of use (7% correct identification). In the second condition, subjects did not see the video but were told the co-occurring nouns for each sentence in which the mother uttered that verb: After all, if a verb regularly occurs with nouns describing edibles, maybe it means *eat.* Subjects identified the verb from this kind of information in about 13% of instances.

It is surprising that subjects' mapping performance was so dismal in both the scene and noun conditions. And when new subjects were given both these kinds of information (that is, shown the videos AND told the cooccurring nouns), they still hit upon the target verbs only 28% of the time.

But when subjects were provided with frame-range information—no scenes, no real nouns or verbs, just the set of syntactic structures that the mothers used, with all their content-bearing words converted to nonsense—the subjects identified 52% of the verbs correctly. It appears that syntactic range information is highly informative.

A difficulty with interpreting these results onto the child learning situation is that these subjects (when correct) by definition were identifying old verbs that they knew: Perhaps they just looked up the frame ranges for these known verbs in their mental lexicons rather than using the frames to make semantic deductions. Because of this possibility, the pertinence of the findings to the real learning situation is more easily evaluated by inspecting the 48% of instances where subjects *failed* in this condition (and the 93% of cases where they failed in the scene condition, etc.). The finding is that false guesses given in response to frame-range information were semantically close to the actual verb that the mother had said (as assessed by the Fisher et al., 1991, semantic-similarity procedure); for example, for *think*, the only false guess was *believe*. In contrast, the false guesses offered in response to looking at the scenes in which *think* was actually said were semantically unrelated to this verb (including *run, catch, go, look*, etc.). The frame range information put the subjects into the semantic neighborhood of the target verb. In contrast, false interpretations of scenes do not get the subject close to the mark at all. This latter result raises puzzles for how a cross-situational learning scheme that is blind to syntax might work in practice.

Note that 52% correct identification in the presence of syntactic frame range information only, although it is a significant improvement over 7%, is not good enough if we want to model the fact that verb learning by 3-year olds is a snap. They do not make 48% errors so far as we know, even errors close to the semantic mark. But as we have stressed, our hypothesis is not about a procedure in which the child ignores the scene, or the co-occurring nominals, and attends to syntax alone (as Lederer and colleagues forced their subjects to do in the experiment just described). We have hypothesized a sentence-to-world pairing procedure for verb vocabulary acquisition. Indeed, adding the real nouns to the frames without video in this experiment led to over 75% verb identification; adding back the scene yielded almost perfect performance.

Summarizing these results, scene information and noun contextual information taken alone are quite uninformative (7% and 13% correct identification, respectively), whereas frame range information is highly informative (52% correct identification). But when we combine the information sources, the results look quite different. Once the observer is given access the structure, he or she makes highly efficient use of scene and noun-context information. The reasons why are easy to see. Consider the noun contexts: It does not much help to know that one of the words in an utterance was *hamburger.* But if this word is known to surface as direct object, the meaning of the verb might well be *eat.* (That is, the structural information converts co-occurrence information to selectional information.) Similarly for the videotapes: Once the structure of the sentences uttered in their presence is known, the subject can zoom in on fewer interpretations of the events and states that might be pertinent for the mother to have said of them. So if the child has available—as she does, in real life—multiple paired scenes and sentences, we can at last understand why verb learning is easy.

VI. HOW THE STRUCTURES OF SENTENCES CAN AID VOCABULARY ACQUISITION

We have suggested that the formal medium of phrase structure constrains the semantic content that the sentence is expressing, thus providing clues to the meaning of its verb. One such clue resides in the number of arguments: A noun-phrase position is assigned to each verb argument; this will differentiate *push* from *fall* when viewing a scene where both actions are taking place. Another concerns the positioning of the arguments: The subject of transitives is the agent, differentiating *chase* from *flee*. The case marking and type of the argument also matters, for example, spatial verbs that allow expression of paths and locations typically accept prepositional phrases, and verbs that express mental acts and states appear with sentence complements.

Of course, one cannot converge on the unique construal of a verb from syntactic properties alone. Because the subcategorization properties are the syntactic expressions of their arguments, it is only those aspects of a verb's meaning that have consequences for its argument structure that could be represented syntactically. Many—most—semantic distinctions are not formally expressed with this machinery. The role of the syntax is only to narrow the search space for the meaning, as this latter is revealed by extralinguistic context.

What our experimentation suggests is that this initial narrowing of the hypothesis space by attention to structure is the precondition for using the scene information efficiently to derive the verb's meaning. When babies do not appear to know the phrase structure, they learn few if any verbs (Lenneberg, 1967). When adults and young children are required to identify verbs without phrase structure cues (as when told "Look! Ziking!" or when presented with silent videos of mother-child conversations) again they do not identify target verbs. But the observation of scenes taken together with observation of the structures is sufficient to the task.

A. Relation of Surface Syntax to Semantics

A well-known view is that there are cross-cutting *verb classes*, each defined over some abstract semantic domain (e.g., *mental* or *spatial*) and, therefore, licensing certain structural formats, or frames (see Levin, 1993). We suggest instead that verb frames have semantic implications, and verbs have meanings. Neither the frames nor their semantic implications are part of lexical information: Any verb can appear grammatically in any structural environment. But owing to the meaning of the verb, it may be semantically implausible, and thus rarely or never uttered, in some syntactic contexts. For example, we do not typically say things like "Barbara looked the ball on the table." Arguably, we do not forebear from such utterances because that verb in that sentence would be ungrammatical. Rather, the interpretation of the sentence structure would imply that some external agent (Barbara) caused the ball to go on the table just by looking at it. The improbability of psychokinesis is what makes this verb in this syntactic context rare. This is shown by the fact that if the rare circumstances do occur, *look* can be used unexceptionally in this structure: The rules of baseball make it possible to say (and sports announcers do say) "The shortstop looked the runner back to third base." In this case, moving is immediately caused by the threatening glance, rendering the sentence plausible.

If the view just sketched is correct, verbs have no subcategorization privileges. To take one more example, one does not usually say *Mary danced John* because dancing is ordinarily not externally caused, rather the act of a volitional agent, and this structure implies direct causation of John's dancing by Mary. But one does comfortably say *Gepetto danced Pinnochio* just because here the dancer is a nonvolitional puppet. If there are no subcategorization privileges for individual verbs, then the child never has to learn them.[6]

What the child *must* know are the semantic implications of these structures. There is considerable evidence from the work of a generation of linguists that these semantic-syntactic linkages are to a useful degree universal (see Grimshaw, 1990, for a review and theoretical perspective) and given by nature to the learner (e.g., the evidence from the isolated deaf that we have cited).

Our suggestion is that learners note the frame environments in which verbs characteristically occur, thus deducing the argument structures with which their meanings typically comport. These ranges of typical structures are compatible with only small sets of verb meanings. The phrase structures in turn provide constraints on

[6]We do not deny that there are some quirks in language design—some facts about the complements typical for the use of certain verbs seem arbitrary rather than semantically conditioned. Learners appear to conform to such exceptional usage patterns in the linguistic community fairly well. But the more important facts are that errors by young children are predominantly returns to canonical syntax-semantics complementation (Bowerman, 1982), that sentences containing verbs in disfavored syntactic environments are understood consensually (for some experimental evidence with young children, see Naigles, Gleitman, & Gleitman, 1993), and that novel syntactic environments are often exploited as a device to express irony and the like (e.g., *The general volunteered the private*). If subcategorization frames are rigidly specified in the verb lexicon, there is an awful lot of ungrammaticality in everyday speech, and it is suspiciously understandable.

the interpretation of extralinguistic information, increasing the efficiency of observational learning.

ACKNOWLEDGMENTS

We thank a grant from Steven and Marcia Roth to Lila Gleitman and a NSF Science and Technology Center grant to the University of Pennsylvania, Institute for Research in Cognitive Science, for supporting this work. An earlier version of this article appeared in *The Handbook of Child Language,* P. Fletcher & B. MacWhinney (Eds.), Oxford: Blackwell Publishers.

REFERENCES

Beckwith, R., Tinker, E., & Bloom, L. (1989, October). *The acquisition of non-basic sentences.* Paper presented at the Boston University Conference on Language Development, Boston.

Bloom, L. (1970). *Language development: Form and function in emerging grammars.* Cambridge, MA: MIT Press.

Bloom, P. (1994). Possible names: The role of syntax-semantics mappings in the acquisition of nominals. *Lingua, 92,* 297–332.

Bowerman, M. (1982). Reorganizational processes in lexical and syntactic development. In E. Wanner and L. R. Gleitman (Eds.), *Language acquisition: The state of the art,* New York: Cambridge University Press.

Brown, R. (1957). Linguistics determinism and the part of speech. *Journal of Abnormal and Social Psychology, 55,* 1–5.

Bruner, J. S. (1975). From communication to language: A psychological perspective. *Cognition, 3,* 255–287.

Carey, S. (1978). The child as word learner. In M. Halle, J. Bresnan, & A. Miller (Eds.), *Linguistic theory and psychological reality* (264–293). Cambridge, MA: MIT Press.

Chomsky, N. (1981). *Lectures on government and binding.* Foris: Dordrecht.

Clark, E. V. (1987). The principle of contrast: A constraint in language acquisition. In B. MacWhinney (Ed.), *The 20th Annual Carnegie Symposium on Cognition.* Hillsdale, NJ: Erlbaum.

Feldman, H., Goldin-Meadow, S., & Gleitman, L. R. (1978). Beyond Herodotus: The creation of language by linguistically deprived deaf children. In A. Lock (Ed.), *Action, symbol, and gesture: The emergence of language.* New York: Academic Press.

Fisher, C., Gleitman, L. R., & Gleitman, H. (1991). On the semantic content of subcategorization frames. *Cognitive Psychology, 23,* 331–392.

Fisher, C., Hall, D. G., Rakowitz, S., & Gleitman, L. R. (1994). When it is better to receive than to give: Structural and conceptual cues to verb meaning. *Lingua, 92,* 333–375.

Gentner, D. (1978). On relational meaning: The acquisition of verb meaning. *Child Development, 49,* 988–998.
Gentner, D. (1982). Why nouns are learned before verbs: Linguistic relativity versus natural partitioning. In S. Kuczaj (Ed.), *Language development, Volume 2, Language, thought, and culture.* Hillsdale, NJ: Erlbaum.
Gillette, J. (1992). The acquisition of mental verbs. Unpublished manuscript. University of Pennsylvania.
Gillette, J., Gleitman, H., Gleitman, L., & Lederer, A. (forthcoming). How to learn word meanings.
Gleitman, L. R. (1990). The structural sources of word meaning. *Language Acquisition, 1*(1), 3–55.
Gleitman, L. R., & Gleitman, H. (1992). A picture is worth a thousand words, but that's the problem: The role of syntax in vocabulary acquisition. *Current Directions in Psychological Science, 1*(1), 31–35.
Goldin-Meadow, S., & Feldman, H. (1977). The development of language-like communication without a language model. *Science, 197,* 401–403.
Grimshaw, J. (1981). Form, function, and the language acquisition device. In C. L. Baker & J. McCarthy (Eds.), *The logical problem of language acquisition.* Cambridge, MA: MIT Press.
Grimshaw, J. (1990). *Argument structure: Linguistic Inquiry Monograph 18.* Cambridge, MA: MIT Press.
Landau, B., & Gleitman, L. R. (1985). *Language and experience: Evidence from the blind child.* Cambridge MA: Harvard University Press.
Lederer, A., Gleitman, H., & Gleitman, L. R. (forthcoming). The information structure for verb learning.
Lederer, A., Gleitman, L. R., & Gleitman, H. (1995). Verbs of a feather flock together. In M. Tomasello & W. Merriman (Eds.), *Beyond names for things.* Hillsdale, NJ: Erlbaum.
Lenneberg, E. H. (1967). *Biological foundations of language.* New York: Wiley.
Levin, B. (1993). *English verb classes and alternations: A preliminary investigation.* Chicago: University of Chicago Press.
Locke, J. (1690). *An essay concerning human understanding.* Cleveland, OH: Meridian Books, 1964.
Markman, E. M., & Wachtel, G. F. (1988). Children's use of mutual exclusivity to constrain the meanings of words. *Cognitive Psychology, 20,* 121–157.
Naigles, L. R. (1990). Children use syntax to learn verb meanings. *Journal of Child Language 15*(2), 257–272.
Naigles, L. R., Gleitman, H., & Gleitman, L. R. (1993). Children acquire word meaning components from syntactic evidence. In E. Dromi (Ed.), *Language and cognition: A developmental perspective.* Norwood, NJ: Ablex.
Naigles, L. R., & Hoff-Ginsberg, E. (1993). Input to verb learning: Verb frame diversity in mother's speech predicts children's verb use. Unpublished manuscript, Yale University.
Ninio, A. (1980). Ostensive definition in vocabulary teaching. *Journal of Child Language, 7*(3), 565–574.
Pinker, S. (1984). *Language learnability and language development.* Cambridge, MA: Harvard University Press.

Quine, W.V.O. (1960). *Word and object.* Cambridge, MA: MIT Press.
Tomasello, M., & Kruger, A. C. (1992). Joint attention on actions: Acquiring verbs in ostensive and non-ostensive contexts. *Journal of Child Language, 19,* 1–23.
Zwicky, A. (1970). In a manner of speaking. *Linguistic Inquiry, 2,* 223–233.

PART IV

THE CHILD'S ACQUISITION OF PHONOLOGY AND PRAGMATICS

CHAPTER 10

CHILD PHONOLOGY, LEARNABILITY, AND PHONOLOGICAL THEORY

B. Elan Dresher

I. LEARNABILITY: THE LOGICAL VERSUS DEVELOPMENTAL PROBLEM OF ACQUISITION

To many people, an investigation of language acquisition that does not center on what children do would appear to be a futile enterprise. Nevertheless, there are a number of aspects to the problem of language acquisition, and the relation of child language to these is not always obvious. To begin, it will be useful to make a distinction between what Hornstein and Lightfoot (1981b) have called "the logical problem of acquisition" and what we can call "the developmental problem of acquisition".[1] The logical problem is schematically diagrammed in (1):

(1) The logical problem of language acquistion:

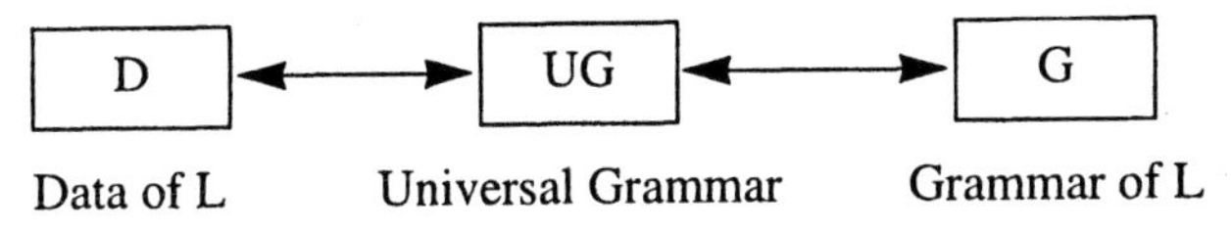

We assume that all humans have an initial set of cognitive principles used to acquire language, collectively called universal grammar (UG); D is the language data

[1]The two approaches to language acquisition correspond to the distinction drawn by Ingram (1989, p. 60) between child language (the developmental problem) and language acquisition (the logical problem). Atkinson (1986) more colorfully characterized scholars pursuing the developmental problem as FLATS (first language acquisition theorists), in contrast to the antonymically named SHARPS who study the logical problem.

of a language, L is the language to which a language learner is exposed, and G is the grammar of the language that is eventually attained by the learner. The logical problem of acquisition can now be characterized as follows: How easily can one learn the grammar G from the set of relevant input data D given UG?

As stated, the logical problem of acquisition pertains to the adult grammar, the final state of knowledge attained by adult native speakers; UG represents the initial state of the learner.[2] In keeping with this adult-centered focus, the diagram in (1) incorporates some idealizations of the acquisition process. One that will be of interest here is what has been called *the idealization of instantaneous acquisition* (Chomsky, 1975, chap. 3; Chomsky & Halle, 1968, chap. 8). According to this idealization, the learner moves from the initial state to the final state in one leap, without any intermediate grammars along the way. This idealization thus abstracts away from the entire developmental sequence of acquisition. In our terms, the developmental problem can be taken to be that of specifying a series of diagrams like (1), representing the various stages of acquisition. Thus, for some stage of acquisition k, a child has grammar G_k projected from a set of data D_k via UG. The logical problem has been stated exclusively in terms of the final stage: G in (1) represents the adult grammar G_f, and D is the final set of relevant data D_f (I will assume for simplicity that UG does not change, though it is possible that it, too, matures in the course of development). The hypothesis suggested by the idealization of instantaneous acquisition is that the early stages do not play a crucial role in determining the final result—that is, that we can consider acquisition *as if* it were instantaneous. If correct, then the final grammar can be viewed as if projected from the final set of data with no significant distortions caused by earlier stages.

The issue is important, because the idealization of instantaneous acquisition is implicitly assumed by virtually all work in descriptive linguistics, not just work in the generative paradigm. To see that this is so, let us consider a typical example of phonological analysis.

Marlett (1981) presented a number of phonological rules of Seri that are sensitive to whether a word begins with a consonant or a vowel. He noted that there exists a set of anomalous vowel-initial words, which behave exceptionally with respect to all such rules in the language. Some of this evidence is summarized in (2), where forms in slant lines represent underlying (phonemic), or lexical, representations, the linguist's hypothesis as to how speakers store the phonological properties of the words of their language; forms in square brackets represent surface (phonetic) representations:

[2] These terms are taken from the debate on language and learning revolving around the different views of Piaget and Chomsky (Piattelli-Palmarini, 1980). Among other differences, the debate can be seen as a clash between a developmental (Piaget) and a logical (Chomsky) approach to the problem of language acquisition.

(2) Anomalous initial vowels in Seri:

	C-Initial	*V-Initial*	*Anomalous*	
a. V deletion	/yo + meke/	/yo + eme/	/yo + amWx/	
	[yomeke]	[yo:me]	[yoamWx]	
	"be lukewarm"	"be used up"	"be brilliant"	distal
b. Epenthesis	/ʔ + ka/	/ʔeme/	/ʔ + amWx/	
	[iʔka]	[ʔeme]	[iʔamWx]	
	"look for"	"be used up"	"be brilliant"	imperative
c. Gemination	/t + meke/	/t + eme/	/t + aX/	
	[tmeke]	[teme]	[ttaX]	
	"be lukewarm"	"be used up"	"be hard"	neutral

In (2a), a rule of vowel deletion removes the second of two adjacent vowels, lengthening the first. The rule applies regularly to /yo + eme/, but not to /yo + amWx/. This rule is one of five vowel deletion rules that are sensitive to whether a root-initial segment is a consonant or a vowel; in each case, the anomalous verbs pattern with the consonant-initial verbs, not with the vowel-initial verbs. In (2b), an /i/ is epenthesized to the left of a sequence consisting of glottal stop followed by a consonant, deriving *ʔika* from /ʔ + ka/. A sequence of glottal stops followed by vowel does not normally occasion epenthesis, as is shown by *ʔeme*. However, the same set of vowel-initial words that do not undergo vowel deletion do undergo epenthesis, hence, *iʔamWx* from /ʔ + amWx/. These last forms are also distinguished in that they cause the gemination of a consonantal prefix other than /ʔ/: thus, we find *ttaX* from /t + aX/. Gemination does not occur before the regular vowel-initial forms or before consonant-initial forms. Finally, the anomalous words pattern with consonant-initial words with respect to a number of allomorphy rules (not shown here).

In his analysis of these data, Marlett (1981) noted that the behavior of the anomalous verbs can be brought under one generalization: These forms, though phonetically beginning with a vowel, act with respect to every relevant phonological process as though they begin with a consonant. He therefore proposed that such forms have an initial consonant in underlying form. This underlying consonant, designated by C in (3), prevents vowel deletion and triggers epenthesis before assimilating to a preceding consonant (causing gemination) or deleting. Marlett was unable, however, to further specify the features of this abstract consonant, as there is no evidence bearing on its nature:

(3) Abstract C analysis:

Underlying forms	/yo + CamWx/	/ʔ + CamWx/	/t + CaX/
Vowel deletion	—	—	—
Vowel epenthesis	—	iʔCamWx	—
Gemination	—	—	ttaX
C deletion	yoamWx	iʔamWx	ttaX
Surface forms	[yoamWx]	[iʔamWx]	[ttaX]

We will return later to some issues raised by this analysis, in particular the abstract nature of the posited unheard consonant. For purposes of the present discussion, let us assume the analysis is correct and consider the position of a learner of Seri who is operating with knowledge of only some of the relevant words. Such a learner might analyze a form like [ttaX] into the underlying morphemes /t + taX/, rather than /t + CaX/; or, extrapolating from a small number of forms, a learner might under- or overgeneralize some of the rules.

How would the analysis be affected if the idealization of instantaneous acquisition is seriously inappropriate? Let's consider the worst-case scenario: suppose that at stage k + 1, a learner does not wipe the slate clean in projecting a grammar from D_{K+1}; rather, suppose the learner preserves some aspects of the grammar of the earlier stage, G_k, leading to some patchwork adjustments. The result, shown in (4), is not the grammar G_{k+1} we would have expected, but rather $G_{k+1'}$, a grammar that deviates from the theoretically expected one (i.e., the grammar we would obtain by applying UG to D_{k+1} afresh) in ways that could not be explained without taking into account earlier stages of acquisition:

(4) Effects of earlier stages on the logical problem of language acquisition:

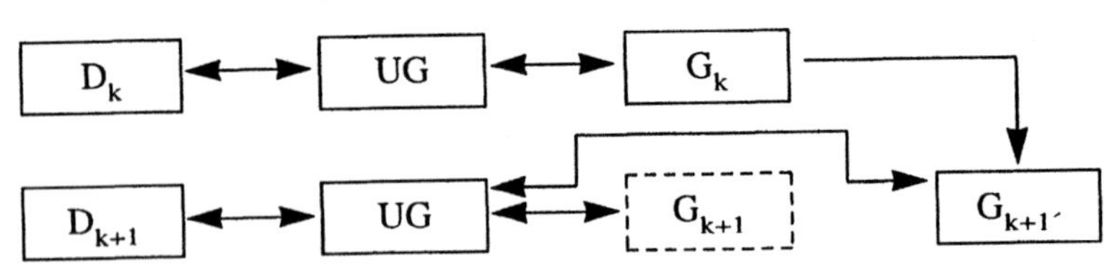

For example, a conservative learner of Seri who is loath to restructure underlying forms might want to retain /taX/ from an earlier stage as the underlying form of the morpheme *be hard*, even after becoming aware that other alternants of the same morpheme do not begin with [t] and that there is a rule of gemination. To account for such forms, a learner could formulate a rule of t-deletion, restricted to a few forms acquired earlier, whereas similar forms acquired later would be assigned an underlying initial C and undergo gemination. The more acquisition is like this, the less tractable the logical problem as given in (1) becomes, because the real final grammar would deviate a great deal from any grammar we could obtain by directly applying UG to D_f.

The fact that learners of the same dialect converge toward very similar adult grammars suggests that the effects of early differences in grammars are minimal. Thus, we find that children, especially at early stages of acquisition, often have phonological rules that have no basis in the language being acquired: for example, many children exhibit consonant harmony in English (see Section III.D), even though adult English has no such processes. There is no evidence that the later grammars of these children are influenced by these early stages.

Sometimes, however, situations arise where crucial evidence bearing on a central aspect of the phonology of a language may be in short supply. Something like this may have occurred in the history of Maori. Modern Maori has the following forms:

(5) Maori alternations (Hale, 1973):

Active	*Passive*	*Gloss*	*Active*	*Passive*	*Gloss*
awhi	awhitia	"embrace"	mau	mauria	"carry"
hopu	hopukia	"catch"	wero	werohia	"stab"
aru	arumia	"follow"	patu	patua	"strike, kill"
tohu	tohuŋia	"point out"	kite	kitea	"see, find"

Kiparsky (1978) pointed out that a clever student of linguistics would observe that if the lexical representations resemble the active forms, it would be impossible to predict the passive, which would have to be formed by suffixing -*Cia*, where C represents a consonant that must be selected idiosyncratically by the stem; whereas if the stems were assigned final consonants that delete in the active forms, a simple and elegant solution is available:

(6) "Clever" solution for Maori (Kiparsky, 1978):
a. Final consonant deletion: Delete a word-final consonant.
b. Passive suffix is -*ia*
c. Derivations:

Underlying	/hopuk + ø	/hopuk + ia/	/patu + ø	/patu + ia/
FCD	hopu	—	—	—
Other rules	—	—	—	patua
Surface	[hopu]	[hopukia]	[patu]	[patua]

As has been much discussed (Hale, 1973; Halle, 1978; Kiparsky, 1978; McCarthy, 1981b), some facts in modern Maori suggest that this analysis may not be the correct one. For example, derived causatives, formed by prefixing /whaka-/, take the passive ending /-tia/ even if the basic verb stem takes a different consonant in the passive: for example, *hopukia,* but *whaka-hoputia;* borrowings from English, even words that end with a consonant, take /-tia/ in the passive; and so on. It has been argued, therefore, that underlying stems have been restructured so that they are vowel final. The passive suffix is becoming -*tia* in the general or default case, and the verbs *hopu, aru,* and so forth are lexically specified to take other consonants: /hopu/ takes /k/, /aru/ takes /m/, and so on.

The simple analysis in (6) is almost certainly correct for the ancestor of the modern language; the modern language, whatever its exact analysis, is considerably more complicated. Why then did the original simple grammar change? Various principles have been proposed, but the change may be in part a consequence of a lack of data at a crucial period in acquisition. Thus, children who know the active form of a verb, say *hopu,* but who have not heard, or do not remember, the passive, can only guess at what consonant, if any, the word might end in. What happens when they want to form the passive? They must develop a default strategy, for example, assign /t/ to a verb, lacking evidence to the contrary. Over time, this default consonant might spread, until verbs with other consonants come to be an ever-decreasing class of exceptional verbs.

This, then, could be an example of a case where the idealization of instantaneous acquisition leads to an incorrect result. We could suppose that a learner of earlier Maori who had access to all the relevant data at the crucial time would arrive at the grammar of (6). But real speakers did not always have access to all the forms, and so they acquired a different grammar, causing (at first) a small change in the language. This change made it even harder for the next generation to acquire (6), leading to further change, until the language has changed in ways that make the original grammar no longer recoverable (Kaye, 1974).

Though there is not a great deal of evidence bearing on this issue, we can make the following hypothesis: The early stages of acquisition, during which the grammars of language learners are most idiosyncratic and most different from the target adult language, have no effect on the grammar eventually acquired. As far as the final result goes, these stages can be ignored for purposes of the logical problem of acquisition, and acquisition is as if it were instantaneous. The later stages of acquisition can affect the final grammar learned; indeed, these stages can cause historical change in the language.[3] If the effects of earlier stages of acquisition are limited in this way, then the logical problem of acquisition remains viable.

II. SOME ISSUES IN THE LOGICAL PROBLEM OF THE ACQUISITION OF PHONOLOGY

As with syntax, consideration of learnability in phonology begins with some general observations about cross-linguistic variation and acquisition. First, in contrast to a once-influential view that languages can vary without limit, we observe that cross-language variation appears to have limits; that is, there exist substantive and formal linguistic universals. Second, Chomsky (1986, 1988) has shown that language learning is a particularly striking example of Plato's problem, the problem of explaining how it is that humans can acquire systems of knowledge that considerably exceed in complexity and richness the input data they are exposed

[3]It is noteworthy also that these examples of "imperfect" learning, which persist into the late stages of acquisition, appear to reflect common tendencies shared by many learners of the same language; see Kiparsky (1982a) and Lahiri and Dresher (1983–1984) for further discussion.

to; that is, the grammars that native speakers internalize are greatly underdetermined by their experience. These two observations can be accounted for if we posit the existence of a rich system of universal grammar which constrains the limits of cross-linguistic variation while informing the process of language acquisition.

In early work in generative grammar, such as *The Sound Pattern of English* (Chomsky & Halle, 1968, henceforth *SPE*), UG was conceived of as allowing a great deal of variation in grammars. The burden of explanation was placed on an evaluation metric: Given a series of grammars all compatible with a set of input data, the evaluation metric assigns a relative value to each grammar, the most highly valued grammar being selected as correct. In the *SPE* theory, the evaluation measure was first a simple feature counter. This metric matched up well with the basic *SPE* theory of phonology, which posits that underlying phonemic representations in the form of feature matrices are converted to surface phonetic forms by a series of partially ordered context-sensitive rewrite rules. The rules have the standard form given in (7), read "A is rewritten as B in the context C_____D":

(7) *SPE* standard rule format:
$A \rightarrow B / C \_\_\_ D$
where A, B, C, and D are sets of features (possibly null) or boundaries.

It quickly became apparent that formal considerations, such as the number of features in a rule, are not the only relevant factors in evaluating grammars. Rules also differ in naturalness, and natural rules are not always simpler (in the sense of having less features) than unnatural ones. As the beginning of an account of such facts, *SPE* proposed to superimpose a theory of markedness, derived from the Prague School, on the formal evaluation measure. Aspects of this theory have been incorporated into various versions of underspecification theory and feature geometry (see Section II.C). It was, however, never made clear how an evaluation metric could be constructed that could successfully choose between entire grammars; between, for example, a grammar with 10 rules that are relatively unnatural and complex and one with 15 rules that are simpler and more natural.

A. The Abstractness Controversy

The first major issue to arise in connection with the learnability of *SPE* phonology concerned the *abstractness* of underlying forms: *SPE* allows underlying forms that may be quite distant from their corresponding surface forms. It was variously suggested that grammars that have too much abstractness are not learnable. For example, the analysis of Seri given in (3) posits an *abstract* underlying segment that never appears in the surface phonetics. Moreover, the rules of vowel deletion and vowel epenthesis are *opaque* (Kiparsky, 1973): They are contradicted at the surface, because vowel deletion does not apply in [yoamWx] though its structural description is met (apparent underapplication), and vowel epenthesis does apply in [iʔamWx] though its structural description is not met (apparent overapplication). Kiparsky hypothesized that surface opacity is one factor that contributes to making a rule hard to learn.

The proponents of various versions of "concrete" phonology (e.g., Braine, 1974; Hooper, 1976) took the position that abstract underlying segments are unlearnable and that surface opacity not only makes a rule hard to learn, but makes it impossible to learn. It was therefore proposed, in various ways, to limit abstractness by ruling out certain kinds of derivations. It is possible that the human language faculty incorporates constraints on abstractness, the way it is subject to other sorts of constraints. However, arguments for abstractness tended to be based not on empirical considerations but on a prioristic notions of what is easy or difficult to learn. For example, Hooper (1976) claimed that a rule cannot be learned if part of its structural description does not exist on the surface; but she gave no evidence why this should be the case. In fact, such assertions assume that we already know what we are trying to discover: the nature of UG in the domain of phonology. Kiparsky (1973) mentioned some other factors that could contribute to making a rule easy or hard to learn, such as the naturalness of the rule. As argued in Dresher (1981b), it is easy to imagine a class of theories of UG that would in many cases require a language learner to posit underlying segments that are not visible at the surface. For example, rules of epenthesis are often motivated by considerations of syllable well-formedness (Broselow, 1982; Itô, 1986). Seri disallows onset clusters whose first member is a glottal stop. Thus, in a form such as /ʔka/, the unsyllabifiable *stranded* /ʔ/ serves as the trigger for epenthesis. If UG highly favors epenthesis in this type of context, then the existence of epenthesis in [iʔamWx] could suggest to the learner that the glottal stop in /ʔamWx/ is also stranded, hence that the onset position before /a/ is occupied by an unheard consonant.

It is of course possible that the grammar of Seri presented in (3) is unlearnable, in which case the preceding analysis must be wrong. This conclusion would be forced by many versions of concrete phonology. It could be proposed, for example, that the anomalous forms do not have an underlying initial consonant but are rather vowel-initial words that are listed as exceptions to a wide array of phonological rules. As Marlett (1981) has pointed out, this type of account misses the generalization that these forms are consistently exceptional in the same way: They act as if they begin with a consonant. Further, such an analysis necessitates numerous complications to lexical entries. In the absence of additional evidence in its favor, we would conclude that it is not as successful a hypothesis about the grammar of Seri as the abstract account.

In both accounts, the anomalous forms appear as exceptional. The difference is that in the abstract analysis, the exceptionality is attributed to a phonological source (an underlying consonant), whereas in concrete accounts it is attributed to a nonphonological source (a set of exception markings associated to lexical items).

The hypothesis of *SPE* is that UG favors the former type of account, a principle that has been called the naturalness condition:

(8) The naturalness condition (Postal, 1968):
Phonological classifications are preferred to morphological or arbitrary classifications at all levels of the phonology.

Theories incorporating some version of the naturalness condition hypothesize that phonological rules are governed by cognitive principles and not just by articulatory or acoustic factors that apply only at the phonetic surface.[4]

If we assume, then, that the opaque grammar posited in (3) is correct after all, it still remains a nontrivial problem to explain how language learners arrive at it. For the main problem with the *SPE* theory is not that it allows abstract grammars, but that it does not sufficiently constrain the choices available to a learner. Imagine a Seri learner who got off on the wrong track, supposing perhaps that [yo:me] derives from /yo + ome/ rather than /yo + eme/. To account for [ʔeme] and [teme], one could posit a rule fronting *o* to *e* after a consonant. A learner would eventually encounter much evidence suggesting that this rule is not correct (e.g., the existence of surface sequences of C*o*), and it is tempting to suppose that the existence of counterexamples would deter the learner from continuing with the fronting hypothesis. We have observed, however, that theories allowing opaque analyses present learners with many superficial counterexamples that can be solved by positing further rules or unseen elements. In our case, for example, the hypothetical learner pursuing the fronting analysis might suppose that an *o* that surfaces after a consonant is derived from some other vowel, say /ö/. It is not clear how learners could extricate themselves from garden paths like these, for it is difficult to distinguish between superficial counterexamples, which a learner must see through, and genuine ones. One solution is to further constrain the types of rules that learners posit, stopping them before they progress too far in the wrong direction.

B. Nonlinear Phonology

The abstractness issue, though never resolved, was pushed into the background in the wake of a number of important developments in generative grammar as a whole, and in phonological theory in particular. At the level of linguistic theory in general, it was recognized that universal grammar was still too unconstrained to give a satisfactory account of universals and acquisition. In phonology, as in syn-

[4]There is an extensive literature on the abstractness controversy; for a sampling of opinions and discussion from various points of view, see Dresher (1981a), Gussmann (1980), and Kenstowicz and Kisseberth (1977, chap. 1) on one side, and Hooper (1976), Linell (1979), and Tranel (1981) on the other.

tax, much research tended in the direction of a more modular conception: rather than treating all phonology with a standard and powerful rule format, it was proposed that the phonology could be divided into different subtheories—a theory of syllables, of stress, of tone, of segment structure—each of which has its own characteristic processes. At the same time, the rather basic phonological representations of *SPE* were enriched by the addition of independent tiers and further structure, in what became known as autosegmental or nonlinear phonology.[5]

An interesting comparison of the learnability issues raised in tiered phonology as opposed to linear phonology is provided by Marlett and Stemberger's (1983) reanalysis of the Seri data discussed earlier. They proposed that a superior analysis is available in the framework of a theory that recognizes different tiers—specifically, a syllable structure tier, a segmental tier, and a CV skeleton (Clements & Keyser, 1983; McCarthy, 1981a), which relates the other tiers—with elements of the different tiers joined by principles of autosegmental association. They propose that the anomalous verbs have an initial onset position that is not associated with any segment. The three types of verbs listed in (2) thus have the representations in (9):

(9) Empty C analysis:

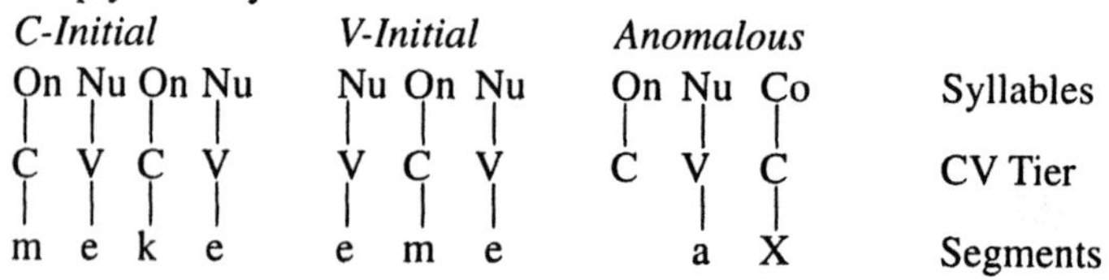

There are empirical differences between the abstract C analysis and the empty C analysis, but we will focus here on the implications for learnability. Marlett and Stemberger commented that, in contrast with the abstract C analysis, the empty C analysis is relatively concrete. For example, the lexical representation of *aX* is as in (10a); the initial C position appears on the surface in the gemination cases, as in (10b):

(10) Lexical and surface representation of *aX:*

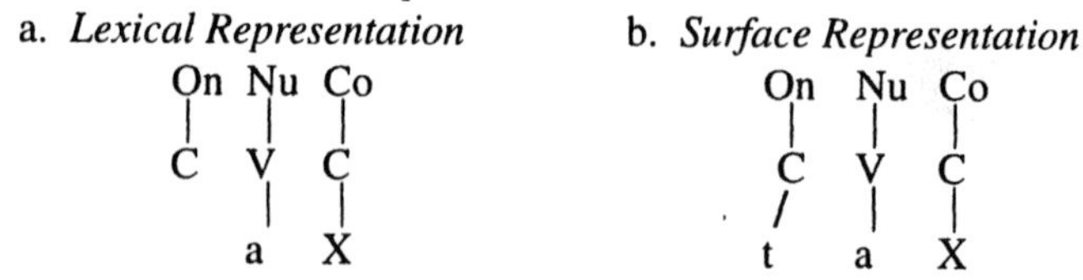

Notice how what must be represented as a *vertical* derivational relationship between an underlying and surface form in linear phonology (the abstract C analy-

[5]Textbooks that provide introductions to nonlinear phonology include Durand (1990), Goldsmith (1990), Katamba (1989), and Kenstowicz (1994). See Kaye (1989) for a lucid introduction aimed at the general reader.

sis) is turned into a *horizontal* relation between the CV tier and the segmental tier in tiered phonology (the empty C analysis). Abstractness is a relation between derivational levels; by enriching phonological representations (by the addition of further structure such as tiers), we can reduce the distance between underlying and surface levels and thereby reduce the degree of abstractness of the analysis. But this fact has little consequence for learnability. To learn that the anomalous verbs in Seri have an initial empty C, one has to discover that these words, though apparently beginning with a vowel, all act as if they begin with a consonant. Therefore, whatever evidence would lead a language learner to posit an empty C given a theory of tiered phonology, UG_T, would lead the learner to posit an abstract C given a linear theory of phonology, UG_L. In either theory, one has to assign a phonological interpretation to the exceptionality of the anomalous words. It follows that the naturalness condition remains important in nonlinear phonology, for without it, the empty C analysis is as unlearnable as the abstract C analysis.[6]

C. Underspecification

A second important innovation in phonological theory illustrated by the Seri example is the possibility of underspecifying certain aspects of the phonological representation. In the theory of *SPE,* segments are considered to be composed of feature matrices in which all features are binary. The possibility of underspecifying such features exists in the *SPE* theory, of course, but it was not much explored, mainly due to the arguments of Stanley (1967) that underspecification would in effect create a ternary feature system: For any feature [F], in addition to the values [+F] and [−F], underspecification would add a third value, [0F]. Stanley showed how misuse of underspecification could lead to spurious generalizations.

The rise of tiered phonology and autosegmental representations led to a renewal of interest in underspecification as a device for expressing observed patterns in phonological systems. Thus, it is a natural consequence of the autosegmental framework that elements need not be represented on all tiers. We have already seen one example, in Seri, of a mismatch between the CV tier and the segmental tier: In the anomalous verbs, a C corresponds to no segmental features in underlying representation.[7] This kind of mismatch was first explored in detail with respect to the phonology of tone (Clements & Ford, 1979; Goldsmith, 1976; Pulleyblank, 1986). For example, a language with two tones, high (H) and low (L), may have three types of morphemes: morphemes that always have a high tone, morphemes

[6]In fact, the abstract C analysis is still available in UG_T, along with the empty C analysis, though in principle there are ways to tell them apart; see Dresher (1985a, 1985b) for further discussion of this issue. Dresher and van der Hulst (1995) discussed problems of learnability raised by a variety of current nonlinear approaches to phonology, including versions of government phonology (Kaye, Lowenstamm, & Vergnaud, 1985) and dependency phonology (Anderson & Ewen, 1987).

[7]A number of other such cases are proposed in Clements and Keyser (1983).

that always have a low tone, and morphemes that are changeable. Such morphemes can be analyzed as being specified for, respectively, H, L, and no tone. Morphemes that lack a tone of their own may then obtain a tone in one of two ways: by spreading of a tone (the marked, or active, tone) from an adjacent morpheme or by default (the unmarked tone).

A number of theories of segmental underspecification have been proposed. Two theories that assume binary features are radical underspecification (RU) and contrastive specification (CS). In RU (Archangeli, 1984; Kiparsky, 1982b; Pulleyblank, 1986), only one value of each feature may be specified in underlying representation, and of these, only unpredictable values may be specified. For example, given the five-vowel system in (11), RU allows the two possibilities in (12), among others. In (12a), the default vowel is /i/, whereas in (12b) it is /e/; other results can be obtained by choosing different underlying specifications:

(11) Five-vowel system: Full specification:

	i	e	a	o	u
high	+	−	−	−	+
low	−	−	+	−	−
back	−	−	+	+	+

(12) Radical underspecification:

(a)

	i	e	a	o	u
high		−		−	
low			+		
back				+	+

[+low] → [−high]
[+low] → [+back]
[ ] → [−low]
[ ] → [+high]
[ ] → [−back]

(b)

	i	e	a	o	u
high	+				+
low			+		
back				+	+

[+low] → [+back]
[ ] → [−high]
[ ] → [−low]
[ ] → [−back]

The rest of the feature values are filled in by rule in the course of the derivation. Archangeli (1988) proposed that UG favors the option in (12a); that is, a language learner would assume (12a) until faced with contrary evidence from the target language.

In contrastive specification (Clements, 1988; Steriade, 1987), it is assumed that only noncontrastive feature values are left blank, whereas features that serve to distinguish segments are specified for both values. For example, in a language where voiced and voiceless obstruents contrast, /p/ would be specified [-voice] and /b/ would be specified [+ voice]; in the absence of voiceless sonorants, however, sonorants would be left unspecified for [voice]. The intuition behind CS is clear enough, though it is often ambiguous as to what the domain of relevant contrast is in any given case, and no algorithm has been proposed by its advocates. An algorithm suggested by Archangeli (1988) is given in (13). Following this algorithm, a CS representation for our five-vowel system would be as in (14):

(13) Pairwise algorithm for CS (Archangeli, 1988):
  a. Fully specify all segments.
  b. Isolate all pairs of segments.
  c. Determine which segment pairs differ by a single feature specification.
  d. Designate such feature specifications as *contrastive* on the members of that pair.
  e. Once all pairs have been examined and appropriate feature specifications have been marked *contrastive,* delete all unmarked feature specifications on each segment.

(14) Contrastive specification

	i	e	a	o	u	Contrasts
high	+	−		−	+	{i,e};{o,u}
low			+	−		{a,o}
back	−	−		+	+	{i,u};{e,o}

[+low] → [−high]
[+high, −back] → [−low]
[+low] → [+back]

Archangeli (1988, p. 192) suggested that learnability considerations favor RU. She observed that the learnability of CS "requires knowledge of the full specification of each segment," so that CS is in this sense segment based, whereas RU is feature based, in that in RU the set of feature specifications forms the inventory of phonological primitives. The argument is incorrect, however, for two reasons. First, it assumes, in the case of RU, that a learner already knows the underlying feature values and the redundancy rules for filling in feature values; because the redundancy rules and the feature values suffice to characterize the system, what is shown is that a learner who has already learned the essentials of the system can go on to learn the rest. Second, CS does not depend on the pairwise algorithm in (13), which Archangeli herself showed to be incorrect, in that it fails in certain configurations where pairs of segments are distinguished by more than one feature. Neither scenario tackles the more fundamental problem of how a language learner arrives at the feature or segmental inventory of the language in the first place.

Imagine a language learner faced with a target language containing the five-vowel system given previously. At an early stage, the learner does not know that there are five vowel phonemes. The learner may well perceive many different vowels from an early age, but would not know how to divide up the vowel space phonemically. One hypothesis, which goes back at least to Jakobson (1941/1968), is that children acquire features through a series of *binary fissions,* in the formulation of

Jakobson and Halle (1956, p. 47); we can call this the continuous dichotomy hypothesis:

(15) Continuous dichotomy hypothesis:

a. In the initial state, all sounds are assumed to be variants of a single phoneme.
b. An initial binary distinction (dichotomy) is made on the basis of one of the universal set of distinctive features.
c. Keep applying the dichotomy to each remaining set until all distinctive sounds have been differentiated.

We suppose that a learner starts off conservatively assuming that there is only one vowel phoneme and that all variation (in vowels, in our example) is allophonic or otherwise conditioned. At some point, the child realizes there are at least two vowel phonemes, perhaps by deciding that at least two vowels are in contrast. Crucially, the contrast is not perceived as a gestalt (contrasting unanalyzable phonemes), but in terms of a single distinctive feature. Suppose the first dichotomy is made on the basis of the feature [low]; then the vowels are partitioned into two sets, a set that is low {a} and a set that is not low {i,e,o,u}. The learner is as yet unaware that there is more than one vowel in the nonlow set (the notation reflects the actual phonemes—for the child, it would be as accurate to notate the sets {a} and {I}, where I represents a nonlow vowel that contrasts with /a/). Further splits subsequently occur in the nonlow set; keeping to our previous example, let us assume these involve first the feature [high] and then [back] until the learner has arrived at the target contrasts.

It is apparent that, in conjunction with a theory of specification, this method will give different results depending on the order in which the dichotomies are made. If we adopt a marking algorithm in the spirit of CS, then whenever a dichotomy is made, all vowels participating in it are specified for the relevant feature. We can convert this procedure into a RU algorithm by one simple modification: At every division, specify only one value of the feature. In our example, when the first cut is made on the basis of [low], /a/ is marked [+ low] and all other potential vowels, conflated at this point into one set, are either designated [-low] (in a CS theory) or are left unspecified (RU). Henceforth, the vowel /a/, being already alone in a set, will not participate in any further divisions and so need not be marked for any other features. The division order [low] > [high] > [back] yields the result in (16a); values in parentheses are omitted in RU:

(16) Continuous dichotomy applied to five-vowel system:

a. [low] > [high] > [back]

	i	e	a	o	u	Contrasts
high	(+)	−		−	(+)	2. {i,u} vs. {e,o}
low	(−)	(−)	+	(−)	(−)	1. {a} vs. {i,e,o,u}
back	(−)	(−)		+	+	3. {i} vs. {u}, {e} vs. {o}

b. [high] > [back] > [low]

	i	e	a	o	u	Contrasts
high	(+)	–	–	–	(+)	1. {i,u} vs. {e,a,o}
low			+	(–)		3. {a} vs. {o}
back	(–)	(–)	+	+	+	2. {i} vs. {u}, {e} vs. {a,o}

Other orders yield different results, because different sets of vowels are participating in relevant contrasts in the different orders. Interestingly, no order gives the equivalent to the pairwise algorithm for CS.

The continuous dichotomy gives slightly different results even for RU, depending on the order of features. Does (16b) violate RU because it has one extra feature specification? It is true that the specification [-high] for /a/ is predictable given that /a/ is [+ low]; but thinking in terms of a learning path, this presupposes that [low] in some way dominates [high], as it does in (16a) where /a/ is not specified for [-high]; but the learner following the path of (16b), say, makes an initial division between high and nonhigh vowels and may not know that the feature [low] will even be needed. Consider, for example, the four-vowel system in (17):

(17) Four-vowel system:

a. Full Specification

	i	e	a	u
high	+	–	–	+
back	–	–	+	+

b. RU

	i	e	a	u
high		–	–	
back			+	+

In such a system, the feature [low] is not required; here it would be correct to designate /a/ as [-high], for this is all that distinguishes it from /u/. An RU learner who makes an initial division on the basis of [high] would be required to designate both /e/ and /a/ as [-high] in (17b); but because such learners do not know at this point how many further divisions there will be, they must do the same in the case of (16b). Therefore, even in RU it is important to consider the relative ranking of the features.[8]

It is tempting to suppose that the ranking of features represents the order in which they are actually acquired. This is not necessarily the case, but it is a reasonable initial hypothesis and one which has obvious implications for a developmental model. We shall consider that aspect of the question in Section III.D.

To the extent that the rank ordering of features is universal, it may reflect dependencies built into the structure of segments. Clements (1985) proposed that features are grouped hierarchically in ways that express dependency relations. This approach to what has become known as feature geometry (McCarthy, 1988; Sagey, 1986) posits that segments may be inherently unspecified for certain features. Avery and Rice (1989), for example, proposed that all features are single-valued and

[8]It is, of course, possible to suppose that a learner revises specifications as more of the segmental system is acquired. Spencer (1986) appears to take such aposition; see Section III.D.2.

grouped together under organizing nodes in hierarchical fashion. In a recent formulation (Rice & Avery, 1995), they proposed the structure in (18):

(18) Segment structure (Rice & Avery, 1995):

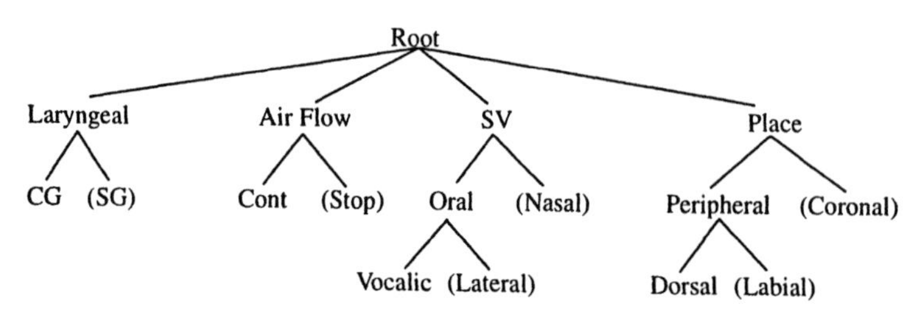

The four organizing nodes are Laryngeal (obstruent voicing, glottalization), Air Flow (manner), SV ("sonorant voicing" or "spontaneous voicing," i.e., sonorant), and Place. Each node has two possible expansions, a marked and unmarked expansion. The unmarked option is in parentheses in (18). Rice and Avery assumed that the unmarked features are default specifications and are not present unless they dominate further contrasts. For example, a segment with a bare SV node (i.e., a sonorant consonant) is interpreted as a nasal; a segment with SV dominating Oral (i.e., a liquid) is interpreted as a lateral. Similarly, a segment with a bare Place node is usually interpreted as having Coronal place; Rice and Avery argued that a Coronal node is only present if a language has contrasts under the Coronal node (such as retroflex versus plain coronals or laminals versus dentals; these features are not indicated in the diagram). We will explore the developmental implications of these various approaches to underspecification in Section III.D.

D. Principles and Parameters

The increasing modularization of phonology and syntax was associated with a new view of the relation between UG and the evaluation metric. As UG is partitioned into increasingly specialized subdomains, the prospect arises that the number of candidate grammars might be relatively small to begin with, putting less burden on the evaluation metric. Chomsky (1981) proposed what has become known as the *principles and parameters* model of UG: Assume that UG contains principles that are not entirely prespecified but that contain a series of open parameters that must be fixed on the basis of experience. Acquisition of grammar, on this approach, becomes largely a matter of correctly fixing the parameters for the grammar one is acquiring.

This approach can be illustrated with respect to the grammar of stress. The metrical theory of stress (Halle & Vergnaud, 1987; Hayes, 1981, 1995; Idsardi, 1992; Liberman, 1975; Liberman & Prince, 1977) proposes that stress is a manifestation of relative prominence of vowels or syllables that are organized into prosodic units that include the metrical foot, word, and phrase. Consider, for example, the pattern of word stress in the Australian language Maranungku, given in (19):

(19) Maranungku stress (Tryon, 1970):
Main stress falls on the first syllable of a word; secondary stresses fall on every second syllable following a stress, e.g., *mérepèt, yángarmàta.*

Maranungku displays a pattern of alternating stress starting from the beginning of the word. In metrical terms, we can characterize the system as in (20); sample words with metrical structure assigned are illustrated in (21):

(20) Maranungku stress in metrical terms:
a. Starting at the left edge of a word, organize syllables into left-headed binary (i.e., trochaic) feet.
b. Group the feet into a left-headed constituent.

(21) Maranungku metrical structures:

```
 x                x                          words      line 2
(x     x)        (x           x)             feet       line 1
(x  x) (x)       (x     x)  (x  x)           syllables  line 0
merepet          yangarmata                  segments
```

In the spirit of the principles and parameters approach, we might surmise that metrical structures can be assembled in a limited number of ways; that is, the general principles governing the form and construction of metrical structure admit of a set of parameters that must be set for each language. Examples of such parameters are listed in (22):

(22) Some metrical parameters:
a. Main stress: The word-level constituent is [left/right]-headed.
b. Feet are [binary/unbounded].
c. Feet are built from the [left/right].
d. Feet are [left/right]-headed.
e. The [left/right]most mark on line X [is not/is] extrametrical.
f. Feet [are/are not] sensitive to the quantity of syllables.
g. Adjacent stresses [are/are not] permitted.
h. Feet [are/are not] iterated across the word.

Although the main stress parameter allows only two options, main stress can occur anywhere in a word, depending on where the line 1 marks are. Parameter (b) determines the maximum constituent size on line 0. If bounded, then there is an upper limit to how big a constituent is; this limit is usually two. Otherwise, there is no fixed limit to size. If feet are bounded, parameter (c) comes into play. Parameter (d) requires feet to be uniformly left-headed or right-headed. If parameter (e) has a positive setting, then a peripheral element at the stipulated level may be ignored for purposes of the stress plane; such an element (a syllable, foot, word, etc.) is said to be extrametrical.

Parameter (f) deals with quantity sensitivity. In many languages, the rules of metrical structure are not concerned with the internal structure of syllables; in such languages, stress is said to be insensitive to quantity (QI). However, many languages have quantity-sensitive (QS) stress systems, which means that they distinguish light and heavy syllables. In such languages, heavy syllables may not occupy a dependent position in a foot; that is, they must be heads. The definition of what a heavy syllable is itself subject to parametric variation (not listed here): in some languages, syllables with long vowels as well as syllables with short vowels that are followed by a consonant (closed syllables) count as heavy, whereas in other languages only syllables with long vowels are heavy.

Parameter (g) reflects the fact that some languages do not allow stresses on successive syllables (stress clash); in such cases, a further set of parameters would come into play that control how stress clashes are avoided or repaired. Finally, parameter (h) allows for the possibility that metrical structure is not iterated across the word, as in Maranungku, but is confined to one edge of the word.

The learner's task is to determine how the parameters are set in the target language. Because the parameters are stated in terms of abstract structures that are not part of the input (heavy and light syllables, bounded and unbounded feet, heads, etc.), the main question for the learning theory is how the learner knows which parts of the input are relevant to each parameter.

One approach (Dresher, 1995; Dresher & Kaye, 1990) is to associate each parameter with invariant triggers, or cues. When we try to construct an explicit learning algorithm of this kind, we quickly discover that the parameters interact in potentially destructive ways. For example, we have seen that the parameter for main stress involves placing a line 2 grid mark on the leftmost or rightmost line 1 mark: if the line 1 marks are not positioned properly, then the main stress parameter cannot be correctly set. It follows that parameters are intrinsically ordered and define a learning path. The parameters must therefore be set in order, or in the equivalent of an order: A parameter cannot be correctly set until the parameters it depends on are. As with feature dependencies, we can hypothesize that this ordering of parameters corresponds to order of acquisition, a matter we will take up in Section III.D.

A different approach to a theory of universal grammar is currently being explored in optimality theory (McCarthy & Prince, 1993; Prince and Smolensky, 1993), which posits that a grammar is a set of ordered violable universal constraints. From underspecified underlying forms, the grammar freely generates many candidate surface forms; the form that is most in harmony with the constraints is selected. It follows from this view of the final adult grammar that a major task of acquisition is to determine the ranking of constraints that obtains in the target language (Tesar & Smolensky, 1998).

The issues discussed previously are a sample of questions that arise in the logical problem of acquisition. These issues all involve learnability in the abstract, considered apart from the facts of phonological development or child language. In the next section, we will turn to the developmental problem of language acquisition.

III. SOME ISSUES IN DEVELOPMENTAL PHONOLOGY

In an ideal world, inquiries into the logical problem of acquisition would dovetail with research on the developmental problem. To this end, we might expect a developmental model of the acquisition of phonology to fill in the sequence of stages from the initial state to the final grammar. For each stage k, we would like to know the relevant input, the principles of UG active at the time, and the grammar G_k, which represents the child's knowledge of the grammar. That is, for each stage k we would like to have a phonological analysis along the lines of analyses done of adult grammar. The task, however, is more difficult, because child phonology presents a number of complexities not present, at least to the same degree, in the study of adult grammar. To name a few: (a) Children's lack of comprehension and patience makes it almost impossible to quiz them about grammatical and ungrammatical forms, the way one might an adult consultant. (b) The child's grammar is typically undergoing rapid change or is liable to do so unpredictably; it is therefore not assured that the investigator can return another time to check on some aspect of the analysis. (c) The preceding problem is exacerbated by the existence of many gaps in the collected data, whose existence may or may not be significant. (d) There are evident discrepancies between a child's perception and production of language, with the latter usually trailing the former by a considerable margin. (e) Partly owing to some of these complexities, child phonology is characterized by a great deal of variability, sometimes unsystematic, and the coexistence of phenomena characteristic of several distinct stages of development.

All these factors contribute to making it difficult to arrive at a clear idea of what the child's knowledge of grammar (i.e., competence) is at any point. Therefore, the study of child phonology has so far contributed little to most of the issues that have been at the center of debate concerning the logical problem of acquisition. To investigate issues of phonological abstractness, for example, it is necessary to consider alternations between variants of morphemes that already presuppose a reasonably advanced vocabulary, whereas most studies of child phonology treat stages of development in which the relevant alternations are not yet being produced. Moreover, it is not obvious how one could bring developmental evidence to bear on this issue. If the child's phonology is the same as the adult's in the relevant respect, it may not add new information; to the extent it is different, then whatever the child's analysis is (assuming we can determine what that is more reliably than we can the adult's), it could be argued that it is different in just the crucial way from the adult grammar, so that no conclusion about the adult grammar can be drawn.

An interesting illustration of this problem is provided by Smith (1973, pp. 180–181) in connection with the status of English [ŋ]. Sapir (1925) argued that English [ŋ] is not a phoneme like /n/ or /m/, but is derived from underlying /n/ by assimilation to a following velar. When this velar is voiceless, it remains, as in *sink* ([sɪŋk]); when it is voiced, it deletes when in syllable-final position; hence, *ring* ([rɪŋ]), but *finger* ([fiŋgər]): This analysis accounts for why [ŋ] does not occur initially (cf. *map, nap,* but "*nap,* like **mbap, *ndap*) and for the systematic lack of [g] syllable-finally after nasals.[9]

Smith observed that [ŋ] does occur in initial position in the speech of his son Amahl (A) at age 2;4 in the word [ŋɛk] *neck,* and that [ŋg] occurs word-finally ([wiŋg], *swing*) and sometimes even word-initially ([ŋgɛk], another rendition of *neck*). Smith concluded from these facts that /ŋ/ is a phoneme in A's grammar, and that there is no evidence that A has a level of representation more abstract than adult surface forms.

Precisely because A's speech is different in crucial ways from the target language, we cannot argue from these facts that [ŋ] is a phoneme in adult English. So proponents and critics of the abstract analysis of [ŋ] are unlikely to be swayed by this evidence. Moreover, it is not obvious that [ŋ] in A's grammar cannot be analyzed as deriving from /ng/, because other aspects of the phonology, such as the rule of *g*-Deletion, are also different. This is not to say that child phonology cannot in principle provide evidence bearing on such issues—just that we should not expect that such evidence will be obvious or self-evident. These facts do bear on establishing the developmental sequence in which generalizations about [ŋ] and related phenomena are apprehended by the child.

If the study of child phonology has not focused mainly on issues relevant to the logical problem of acquisition and the nature of the rules and representations internalized by adult speakers, it is also because researchers have been quite properly absorbed in the study of those aspects of child phonology that make it unique and different from adult grammar. Chief among these differences is the fact that children appear to have their own more or less idiosyncratic rules and representations. Whereas those concerned with the logical problem of acquisition are interested in the largely invisible process of how the child's internalized grammar approaches the adult final state, researchers of the developmental problem are concerned with the outward progress of a child's phonology as it becomes more adultlike over time. Thus, the focus of child phonology has been on the distance between a child's surface forms and the target adult surface forms, not on the web of relations that relate surface forms to each other via underlying lexical representations.

[9]See Borowsky (1986, chap. 2) and I. Smith (1982) for further discussion.

In this section, then, we will briefly survey some of the issues that have been prominent in child phonology research, with a view, where relevant, to relating them to the logical problem of learnability.

A. Methodological Problems in the Analysis of a Child Language

Methodological issues that are not particularly vexing in the study of adult phonology are more problematic in child phonology. Much discussion in Ingram (1989) is devoted to such issues. To take one typical problem: In adult phonology we can usually ascertain what the surface contrasting segments are, whether two sounds in a given language belong to separate phonemes, or whether they are allophones of one phoneme. In child phonology, the situation is not so clear-cut: two sounds may appear to be in complementary distribution or in free variation except for one or two words; or a child may only produce a certain sound in a small number of words. At what point can we say that a child has acquired a new phoneme or a new contrast? What mental representation can we attribute to a child for a word that is pronounced in a great variety of ways? A resolution of such questions is a prerequisite to being able to proceed with an analysis of the child's grammar, or even to giving a coherent description of the facts.

Ferguson and Farwell (1975) studied the development of phonemic oppositions in word-initial position. At each stage, all words beginning with the same phone or set of variant phones were grouped together, the resulting set of word-initial variants being said to constitute a *phone class*. A sample phone class for one of the children they studied, T, at Session VI is given in (23a); the forms on which it is based are given in (23b):

(23) Sample phone classes for T, Session VI (Ferguson & Farwell, 1975):

a. Phone classes:

i. [b ~ β ~ bw ~ p^h ~ ɸ ~ ø]   ii. [p^h]

b. i.

Adult	*Child*
baby	əβeβi ~ əbi ~ bibi
ball	baU
book	əg ~ bʌʔ
bounce	bʌ ~ bɛ ~ bwæ
byebye	p^hædi
paper	ɸetšə ~ bædu

ii.

Adult	*Child*
pat	p^hæt (3x) ~ p^hæ
please	p^he (2x)
purse	p^he (2x)

Phone classes are established in this manner for every chronological stage in a longitudinal series and are then connected across time to form *phone trees*.

Ingram (1989, pp. 201–203) pointed out a number of difficulties in using this procedure to chart the development of phonemic oppositions. He noted that, besides the complexity of the resulting phone trees and the difficulty in interpreting them, phone classes and trees tend to exaggerate the degree of variability in a child's phonological system because of their extreme sensitivity to the variability of a single lexical item. For example, in the first phone class in (23), [β] occurs only in one variant of one lexical item. We might add another problematic aspect of the procedure, which is that it fails to take into account contextual effects that may be systematic. For example, [bw] need not be interpreted as a variant of [b] but may include the realization of the /w/ of *bounce* (/bæwns/, perhaps by metathesis of *bæw* to *bwæ*). Similarly, the lack of an initial consonant in the child's pronunciation of *book* may be due to the influence of the velar consonant; though it is in some sense true that ∅ is thus a possible variant of /b/, it is nevertheless quite misleading in terms of giving a picture of the child's phonemic oppositions.

To provide for a more easily interpretable analysis of phonemic oppositions, which reduces some of the variability introduced by performance and other causes, Ingram proposed to establish a *phonetic type* according to the following rules:

(24) Phonetic types (Ingram, 1989, p. 204):

a. If a phonetic type occurs in a majority of the phonetic tokens, select it.
b. If there are three or more phonetic types, select the one that shares the most segments with the others.
c. If there are two phonetic types, select the one that is not pronounced correctly.
d. If none of the preceding work, select the first phonetic type listed.

The child's forms are then recast in terms of the selected phonetic types, which form the basis of a phonemic analysis. We note that these rules, too, ignore possible contextual effects; in addition, they introduce a certain arbitrariness into the analysis. However, they appear to be intended more as rules of thumb rather than empirically testable principles and are designed for early inventories that may contain numerous gaps and where other diagnostics of the child's system may be lacking.

B. Discrepancies between Production and Perception

An important issue in child phonology concerns the discrepancy between perception and production. In many cases, it is evident that children perceive distinctions that they cannot reproduce.[10] Sometimes, this discrepancy is noted explicitly by the child. For example, Smith (1973, pp. 134–137) reported that his son A would respond correctly when asked to bring a picture of either a *mouth* or a *mouse,* even though he did not distinguish the two in his own pronunciation; that he did not accept [maus] as a pronunciation for *mouth* from his father, even though he pronounced it that way; and similarly rejected [sIp] as a pronunciation for *ship* when it came from an adult, though acknowledging that that is how he said it. Smith further argued that distinctions among segments that do not appear in A's

[10]These cases should be distinguished from those in which children make contrasts that are different from those made in the adult language or that are imperceptible to adults (Macken, 1986; Macken & Barton, 1980).

production nevertheless can be shown to play a role in deriving his output. Smith concluded (1973, p. 206) that the child's competence must be in terms of the adult's surface phonemic system from the time the child begins to speak; indeed, that this is a necessary prerequisite to speaking.

Smith argued that someone who wishes to treat the child as having his own system based on the contrasts evident in production would arrive at a misleading view of the child's competence. For example, Smith observed that at Stage 1, A distinguished the following consonants in his production:[11]

(25) A's consonant phonemes: Stage 1 (Smith, 1973, p.45):

	b	d	g	m	n	ŋ	w	l
sonorant	−	−	−	+	+	+	+	+
nasal	−	−	−	+	+	+	−	−
coronal	−	+	−	−	+	−	−	+
labial	+	−	−	+	−	−	+	−

We might conclude that A's phonological system need refer only to the features in (25); in particular, there is no need to attribute to the child's system the features [voice] or [continuant], because the values of these features are predictable. Nevertheless, Smith argued that these features are needed in an account of A's realization rules:

(26) [voice] in A's phonology (Smith, 1973, pp. 13–14):
  a. A nasal consonant is deleted before any voiceless consonant:
    e.g., bump → [bʌp], tent → [dɛt], meant → [mɛt]
  b. A voiced consonant is deleted after a nasal consonant:
    e.g. mend → [mɛn], finger → [wiŋə]

(27) [continuant] in A's phonology (Smith, 1973, p. 14):
  Alveolar stops /t,d,n/ become velar before a syllabic [l]:
  e.g. puddle → [pʌgəl], but puzzle → [pʌdəl]

If the child's underlying forms are coded only in terms of the features in (25), then the contrasts in (26) are difficult to explain. Consider the minimal pair *mend* and *meant:* if represented using only the features in (25), they should merge; however, they do not, suggesting that the final consonants are distinguished in the child's underlying representations. The examples in (27) are similar, showing that the child distinguishes at some level between a stop and a fricative, though he produces no fricatives at this stage. The form [pʌdəl] for *puzzle* also shows that the child has no motor problem in saying *puddle.*

In contrast to Smith's view that children represent adult words correctly in underlying representations, errors all being due to realization rules that operate in production, Macken (1980), following Braine (1976), argued that there are also

[11] I have changed some of Smith's features, but these changes do not affect the argument.

perceptual miscodings in child language. She suggested that this is the case with respect to words like *puddle:* Rather than attributing to A the rule in (27), she proposed that words of this type tend to be misperceived as having a medial velar, perhaps influenced by the velar *l*. As evidence, she observed that there are a significant number of exceptions to the rule (over 20%): for example, *funnel, tunnel,* pronounced with alveolar /n/, as well as variation between alveolar and velar pronunciations in *cuddle* and *medal,* all from a period when the rule is in force. By contrast, the rule that realizes alveolar fricatives as alveolar stops in *puzzle*-type words has no exceptions. She cited as the most convincing evidence the fact that at the stage where *puddle*-type words start being pronounced with an alveolar consonant, over one-third of words like *pickle,* with underlying medial velar, are pronounced for the first time with alveolar consonants ([pitəl]). She argued that this fact supports the hypothesis that *puddle* words had been miscoded, not created by rule; for then it can be explained why some words that have medial velars in the adult language would also be changed to alveolars.

Braine (1976) argued more generally that though it is clear that children perceive distinctions they do not make, it does not follow that their perception is the same as that of adult speakers. He suggested that a child who is unable to match a feature to an articulation cannot be said to control that feature; that is, if we define a feature as an abstract mental representation having acoustic and articulatory correlates, both must be present to some degree before we can assign the feature to a child's grammar. Returning to the preceding examples, on the Braine-Macken account of *puddle* ~ *puzzle,* we do not need to appeal to a feature [continuant] in the child's underlying representations: *puddle* would simply be represented with a medial velar due to misperception, whereas *puzzle* would have a medial coronal. Of course, we need to have an explicit account of these misperceptions to complete the story. As for *mend* ~ *meant,* Braine suggested that the nasal is perceptually more salient in the first word than in the second, though he does not make an explicit proposal as to how this differential salience is expressed in the child's representations. Spencer (1986, p. 14) suggested a structural account, whereby /n/ is perceived as the head of the coda in *mend,* and /t/ is perceived as the head in *meant.* For the sake of concreteness, we may suppose that A, influenced by his limited syllable structure that does not in any case accommodate consonant clusters at the early stage, perceived the /d/ in *mend* as a part of the closure of the /n/, that is, as a kind of [n^{d}], where this notation does not imply an analysis into distinctive features. By contrast, the /t/ in *meant* evidently has the status of a full consonant, whereas the nasal may have been interpreted as a feature of the vowel or consonant: [ɛ̃]or [^{n}d]. In either case, the nasal feature does not surface.

There is one further point to make: In phonological analyses of adult languages, we often find evidence for the existence of a segment or feature that does not appear as such on the surface. In such cases, however, we require synchronic evidence from the grammar to pin down what the feature is. In the Seri example discussed earlier, for example, we have evidence that certain verbs that begin with vowels on the surface behave as if they begin with consonants (in this case we cannot pinpoint what the consonant is, except that it is not any of the consonants that can surface in word-initial position in Seri). In the same spirit, in order to support attributing a feature contrast to a child whose set of segments does not appear to need it, we must show not only that the child distinguishes between words that would seem to be indistinguishable in terms of the child's own features; it must also be shown that there is evidence bearing on what the extra features are. So if the child distinguishes *meant* and *mend,* it does not follow that the relevant feature is [voice]. It is conceivable that one could show, in some such case, that there is grammar-internal evidence from the child's system for positing a specific *abstract* feature; as far as I am aware, however, Smith's rules do not in general support this.[12]

If this general approach is correct, then, we posit that the child has an auditory impression of adult words, derived from the adult surface forms. This auditory impression may be detailed enough to enable children to distinguish between words that are homophonous in their own speech, but not necessarily on the basis of distinctive features (Ingram, 1974).[13] Auditory forms are mapped into underlying forms coded in terms of distinctive features that are in play at the relevant stage—evidence for what features are in play comes mainly from production. Underlying forms are in turn mapped into phonetic representations.

C. Models of the Organization of Child Phonology

The literature contains a plethora of models of how the phonology of a child might be organized. In this section we will review some of them and attempt to sort out their implications.

We will begin with the model proposed by Smith, which we can diagram as in (28):

(28) Child phonology (based on Smith, 1973):

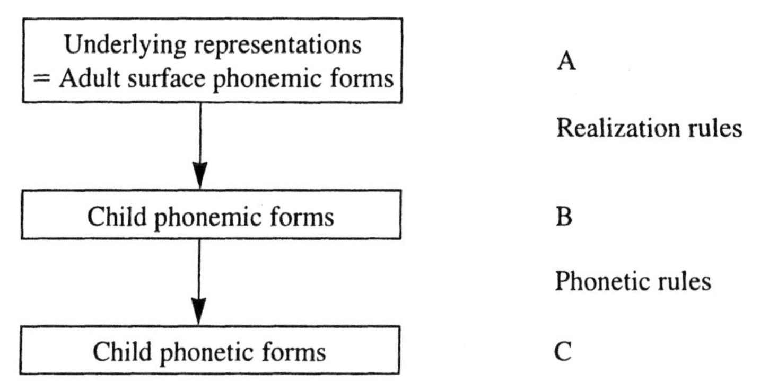

[12]For further discussion, see Wilbur (1981).

[13]See also Ingram (1989, pp. 384–386) and Locke (1986). Waterson (1971) went further in assuming that the child's perception of adult forms is limited

This model is quite different from a model of adult phonology. Adult surface forms—Box A in (28)—are presumably derived from more abstract underlying representations. In most generative theories, surface phonemic representations, either of the adult or the child, do not correspond to any well-defined level of representation.[14] Also, all the realization rules in the diagram are unique to the child—they represent the distance between the adult's quasi-phonemic representations and the child's phonemic representations. The phonetic rules that convert B to C are also largely unique to the child, though some may coincide with adult phonetic rules.

Although Smith wrote that he finds no evidence that a child posits lexical representations more abstract than adult surface forms, we would suppose that at some time a child starts to develop phonological rules and underlying representations of the adult system. A diagram reflecting this assumption is that of Kiparsky and Menn (1977), shown in (29):

(29) Child phonology (Kiparsky & Menn, 1977):

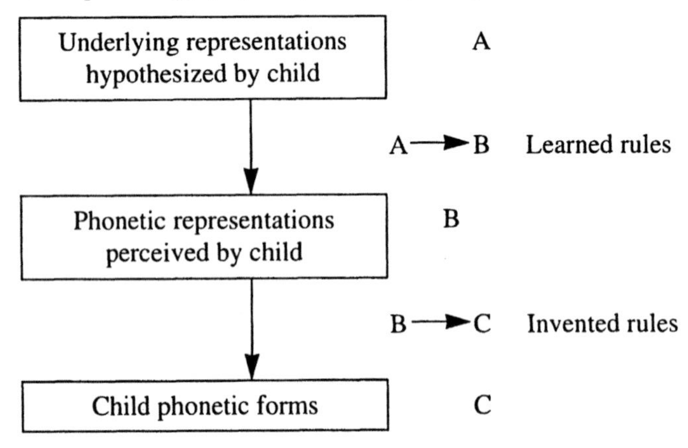

Kiparsky and Menn hypothesized that in the early stages of acquisition, A approximates B, whereas B and C are maximally distinct. As the child's knowledge of the grammar becomes more elaborate, A becomes increasingly different from B and approximates the adult underlying forms. Concurrently, as the child masters the phonetics of the language, the distance between B and C shrinks as the two come to coincide.

[14]Some versions of lexical phonology (Kiparsky, 1982b, 1985; Mohanan, 1982) attribute special status to the output of the lexical component, which is somewhat akin to a classical phonemic level; see Kaisse and Shaw (1985). The notion of adult surface form is not as straightforward as might appear. Lahiri and Marslen-Wilson (1991) have pointed out that surface forms are in fact highly variable, and they argue for abstract underspecified representations even in the adult recognition lexicon; similar considerations are relevant for the child's representations.

This conception differs from Smith's in that it posits no phonemic level apart from the underlying level (A). In common with Smith's model is the idea that child phonology contains a component of invented rules (B → C), unique to the child, whose fate is ultimately to be dispensed with.

Menn (1978, 1983) subsequently revised and elaborated this model as in (30):

(30) Two-lexicon model (Menn, 1978, 1983)

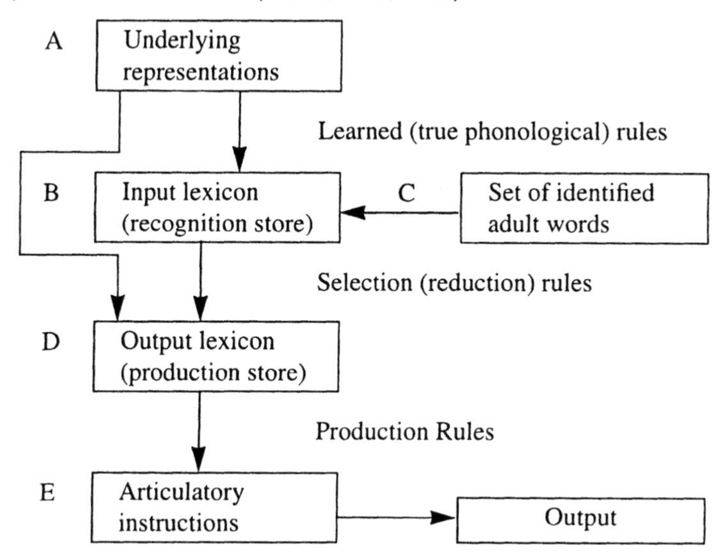

The two-lexicon model is primarily motivated by an attempt to account for the existence of regressive *phonological idioms* or *frozen forms* (Ferguson & Farwell, 1975). For example, Menn (1971) observed the following sequence in the acquisition of Daniel:

(31) Nasal harmony and regressive idioms (Menn, 1971):

	Adult forms	down	stone	beans	dance
a.	First stage	dæwn	don	—	—
b.	Second stage	dæwn	don	minz	næns
c.	Third stage	dæwn ~ næwn	don ~ non	minz	næns

At an early stage (a), Daniel pronounced the frequent words *down* and *stone* with initial obstruents. When he began manifesting a rule of nasal harmony (b), the older forms resisted it, whereas newer forms such as *beans* and *dance* underwent the rule. Still later (c), the holdout regressive idioms began alternating with harmonized forms, which eventually won out (d).

Menn proposed to account for such exceptions by positing, in addition to an input, or recognition, lexicon, an output, or production, lexicon, which contains "the collection of stored information which is required to produce the child's words" (Menn & Matthei, 1992, p. 217). The idea is that a new word enters the input lexicon—from Box C to Box B in (30)—and then is subject to a set of selection rules (B to D), which reduce the input form by filtering out features not in the child's repertoire. These rules may have other functions, such as associating a word with a certain prosodic template. The point is that a word travels this route only once, when it is new. The results of the selection rules are stored in an output lexicon; only the production rules apply on-line. Thus, a word like *down,* acquired at a period before nasal harmony is operative, is stored as [dæwn] (or as a representation that, when applied to articulatory instructions, will result in that form). Nasal harmony enters the grammar as a selection rule, and so applies to new words, but does not affect old ones.

Later, though, nasal harmony does affect older forms; the two-lexicon model leads us to expect that there will be many regressive idioms, but some further mechanism is needed to account for their absence or change to become regular forms. Menn and Metthei (1992) discussed a number of other problems facing a two-lexicon model of this kind. One is the fact that selection rules often appear to apply productively to words and to words in combination (Matthei, 1989). Moreover, new rules of child phonology often do apply across the board, as emphasized by Macken, which again would not be expected if the pronunciation of most forms is stored. Finally, it is not clear how such a grammar develops into the final state, that is, the adult grammar. As much as possible, then, we would assume that the child's grammar resembles the adult grammar in form.

D. Phonological Development as Growth of Complexity

There is a continuing tension between the view that a child's phonology is a mapping from adult surface forms (or something near them) and the view that a child's phonology is a system in itself. Smith (1973) presented both analyses, though he argued in favor of the former, for reasons discussed previously. There is nevertheless something paradoxical about this picture: Whereas the phonological system of a child, seen in its own terms, is in many ways simpler than that of the target language, when regarded as a mapping from adult forms it appears to be more complex in that the child has a set of rules that do not exist in the adult language and that must eventually be discarded. The rationale for these invented rules has been given in terms of the child's need to find a way to say words whose pronunciation present difficulties. A metaphor for this approach is that of training wheels on a bicycle: extra mechanisms added to make the task of balancing easier. As a child becomes more accomplished, the training wheels become less and less conspicuous until they are dispensed with altogether.

Smith (1973) observed that the function of these extra rules of child phonology is to effect various kinds of simplifications. Modifying his own categories somewhat, we can classify them as follows:

(32) Types of simplification effected by realization rules (cf. Smith, 1973, p. 162):
1. Simplification of prosodic structures: syllable and word templates, metrical structures.
2. Simplification of the inventory of features and segments.
3. Reduction of the number of independent specifications in a word by means of consonant and vowel harmony.

A central question is whether these various types of simplification and reduction of structure can be represented in the child's grammar without training wheels, so to speak. A number of researchers, notably Waterson (1978, 1987) and Macken (1978), have taken the approach that the acquisition of phonology should be viewed as a growth of complexity along several dimensions. To the extent that phonological development is the progressive elaboration of the phonological system, reaching its full complexity in the final state, we might imagine that the child's phonology can also be viewed at each stage as lacking some of the complexity of the final state, rather than having extra rules that must be discarded. This idea can be found in one form or other in many writings on child phonology, though there are many different notions as to how it should be worked out. In what follows, we will review the three areas listed in (32) in turn.

Templates

Rather than analyze the various realization rules of child phonology as a series of linear rules, we can understand them to be the results of mapping segmental features onto templates that are much more restricted than the adult templates. These templates may be cast in terms of all units of the prosodic hierarchy (Hayes, 1989; McCarthy & Prince, 1993; Nespor & Vogel, 1986; Selkirk, 1978): Thus, a child might have a word template that allows for at most two syllables, a syllable template that specifies the maximal expansion of a syllable (usually CV at an early stage), and a metrical template that governs the relative prominence of the syllables in a word (often a trochaic pattern, for English and Dutch children at least).[15] The child's problem now is to map representations, based on adult forms that considerably exceed the limited templates of the child, onto these templates. The result is necessarily a loss of information: the child templates cannot accommodate all the individual segments of the underlying representation. Therefore there must be principles that decide how segments are matched up to the templates.

[15]See Allen and Hawkins (1978, 1980), Crystal (1986), and Gerken (1991, 1994).

This sort of mismatch arises in adult phonology as well, although not to the same extent as it does in child language. Semitic languages are well known for their patterned morphology (McCarthy, 1981a): Various morphological categories specify prosodic patterns that must be filled by the segments of the root. Many languages have reduplication processes that can be analyzed as involving the copying of segments from the root onto prespecified prosodic templates,and here, too, there can occur mismatches of segments to available positions (Marantz, 1982; McCarthy & Prince, 1988, 1993).

Syllable patterns, for example, progress developmentally from simple CV syllables to more complex types. In a recent study of 12 Dutch children by Fikkert (1994), all the children begin with CV syllables whose onset is obligatorily a plosive. After this, onsets and codas develop somewhat independently. For onsets, the next stage is one where empty onsets, that is, vowel-initial onsetless syllables, are allowed. This is followed by stages where more types of consonants are permitted into a single onset: Nasals follow plosives for all children, but after that there is much variability in the order in which fricatives, liquids, and glides are introduced. At the same time, the number of onset positions is expanded, first to sequences of plosive followed by liquid or glide in some children or *s* plosive clusters in others. Fikkert proposed that the development of syllable types involves the gradual setting of a series of parameters (cf. Kaye, 1989, pp. 54–58), which govern the number of positions in the syllable and the sonority restrictions imposed on sequences of positions. She observed that /tl/ onset clusters, which are prohibited in Dutch, are nevertheless produced by children until a fairly late stage (e.g., [tlɛi] for adult [trɛin] *train*). She suggested that the prohibition of /tl/ clusters is a constraint (though one shared by a number of languages) of a different nature from the major parameters of syllable structure and is consequently learned later.

Fikkert (1994) also traced the development of metrical structure in the same children, with a view to studying the order in which metrical parameters are set. She showed that parameters become relevant to learners at different stages of development and that the observed sequence thus differs in various ways from what we might have expected in terms of the logical problem of acquisition (e.g., the model of Dresher & Kaye, 1990). For example, the parameter for quantity sensitivity controls the interpretation of which syllables count as heavy and which count as light. Because feet are built on projections from syllable structure, we might expect this parameter to be set early, before the parameters governing the construction of feet. But Fikkert showed that Dutch children already appear to know that feet are generally trochaic and that the last foot in a word is the most prominent one at a stage when they make no distinctions between heavy and light syllables, that is, before quantity sensitivity is relevant to them. Study of such developmental sequences thus sheds further light on the relation between parameters and their cues in the data.

The Acquisition of Distinctive Features and Contrasts

An early and still influential theory of phonological acquisition is that of Jakobson (1941/1968).[16] Jakobson assumed that segments are composed of a set of universal binary distinctive features. Based on the distribution of features in the languages of the world (Trubetzkoy, 1939/1969),[17] Jakobson proposed that there are implicational relations (laws of irreversible solidarity) that hold between features. For example, he observed that no language has fricatives but no stops: The presence of a fricative implies the presence of a stop. The reverse is not true: Some languages have stops but no fricatives. Jakobson observed that the acquisition of fricatives follows that of stops in child language as well. He suggested (1941/1968, p. 51) that in general, there is an "amazingly exact agreement between the chronological succession of these acquisitions and the general laws of irreversible solidarity . . . which govern the synchrony of all the languages of the world." Jakobson thus proposed a theory that ties together the sequence of acquisition with universal relations among features that govern the distribution of segment inventories in the languages of the world.

Jakobson and Halle (1956, p. 41) proposed some predicted developmental sequences; the sequence in (33) concerns oral resonance (primary and secondary place) features. The decimals indicate precedence relations: If one decimal sequence is entirely contained in another sequence, then the contrast corresponding to the former must precede the acquisition of the latter contrast.

(33) Predicted acquisition sequences (Jakobson & Halle, 1956):

Consonants: dental versus labial	0.1
Vowels: narrow versus wide	0.11
Narrow vowels: palatal versus velar	0.111
Wide vowels: palatal versus velar	0.1111
Narrow palatal vowels: rounded versus unrounded	0.1112
Wide palatal vowels: rounded versus unrounded	0.11121
Velar vowels: unrounded versus rounded	0.1113
Consonants: veopalatal versus labial and dental	0.112
Consonants: palatal versus velar	0.1121
Consonants: rounded versus unrounded or pharyngealized versus nonpharyngealized	0.1122
Consonants: palatalized versus nonpalatalized	0.1123

For example, (33) predicts that a contrast between narrow versus wide vowels (equals compact versus diffuse, i.e., /a/ versus a high vowel of low sonority, /I/)

[16]See also Jakobson and Halle (1956) for some revisions. Jakobson's proposals have been much discussed in the literature; see Ingram (1989, pp. 190–197), Kiparsky and Menn (1977), and Menn (1980), among others.

[17]See now also Greenberg (1978) and Maddieson (1984).

must precede the emergence of the contrast between palatal versus velar narrow vowels (/i/ versus /u/), because 0.11 is contained in 0.111. By the same token, the /a/–/I/ contrast is predicted to precede the development of a consonantal contrast between velopalatal versus labial and dental (i.e. /k/ versus /p/ and /t/), because 0.11 is contained in 0.112. But no inplicational relation is predicted to hold between the contrast of palatal versus velar narrow vowels and velopalatal versus labial and dental consonants, because 0.111 is not contained in 0.112. There is no significance to the fact that one decimal is a smaller number than the other; thus, the chart in (33) is equivalent to a branching tree diagram.

As Ingram (1989, pp. 190–197) pointed out, Jakobson's theory of acquisition is more in the nature of a sketch, for it does not deal with all features and does not present detailed analysis of child language data. The theory is more difficult to test than one might think, in part because of the methodological issues discussed above in Section III.A. Another complication is that different contrasts often exist in different positions in the syllable or word, and they often develop differently (Fikkert, 1994; Waterson, 1987). Nevertheless, the central idea has remained influential, and various refinements and elaborations of it have been proposed.

One such model is proposed by Dinnsen *et al.* (1990) and Dinnsen (1992). Dinnsen proposed that commonalities and variation in developing phonetic inventories can be accounted for by the following hierarchy of features:

(34) Feature hierarchy (Dinnsen, 1992):

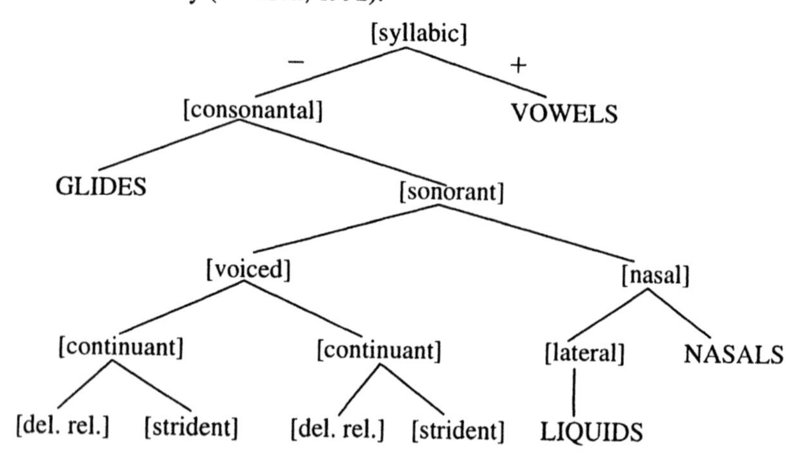

The hierarchy is divided into five levels of increasing articulation. The first level, level A, contains only the features [syllabic], [consonantal], and [sonorant]; Dinnsen has posited the default rules shown in (35):

(35) Level A default rules (Dinnsen, 1992):

1. All consonants are stops.

2. All obstruents are voiceless and unaspirated.
3. All sonorant consonants are nasals.

At Level B, obstruents are differentiated into voiced and voiceless; at Level C, the features [continuant] and [delayed release], if relevant, are added to the obstruents. At Level D, sonorant consonants are divided into liquids and nasals on the basis of the feature [nasal]. Finally, at Level E the liquids are divided into two classes by [lateral], and the full inventory shown in (34) is attained.

The model, like that of Jakobson & Halle, allows for considerable variability within a universal framework. For example, (36) lists two phoneme inventories that both instantiate Level D. Example (36a) is the phoneme inventory of five Quiché children discussed in Pye, Ingram, and List (1987) in the analysis of Ingram (1989, p. 216) (*b'* is an ejective). Example (36b) shows the phoneme inventory of Hildegard at 2;0 (Leopold, 1939–1949, Vol. 1), as analyzed by Moskowitz (1970). Dinnsen's system is also incomplete, as it does not deal with point of articulation or with vowel systems:

(36) Two examples of Level D:

a. Quiché (Ingram, 1989)

(m)	n		
(b')			
p	t	tš	k
			x
w			ʔ
	l		

b. Hildegard (Moskowitz, 1970)

m	n		(ŋ)
b	d		g
p	t	tš	k
		š	h
w		j	
	l		

These accounts of the acquisition of distinctive features can be related to the theories of underspecification discussed in Section II.C. Spencer (1986) proposed a reanalysis of Smith's account of the phonological development of A in terms of autosegmental and underspecification theory, using a version of radical underspecification. He appears to assume, with Smith, that in the child's input lexicon all segments are represented in their fully specifed adult feature specifications. These specifications pass through the filter in (37a) to produce the specifications in (37b). The filter removes specifications for all features except those operating in A's grammar. For example, on this account we assume that the child has a representation at some level of the grammar, in which /s/ and /θ/, say, are fully specified and distinguished by the feature [strident]; this distinction is subsequently filtered out. The filter shrinks in the course of development:

(37) Despecification of A's features (Spencer, 1986):

a. Filter

[+son]→[+son]   [+nas]→[+nas]   [−cor]→[−cor]
[+lab]→[+lab]   [−cons]→[−cons]   [−voc]→[−voc]
[αF]→[0 F]

b. Output of filter

	p/b/f/v	t/d/s/z θ/ð/š/ž	k/g/h	m	n	ŋ	w	l	r/j
son				+	+	+	+	+	+
nas				+	+	+			
cor	−		−	−		−	−		
lab	+			+			+		
cons							−		−
voc	−	−	−	−	−	−	−		−

Alternatively, in the spirit of the approaches of Jakobson and Waterson, we can interpret the filter as representing the limits of the child's elaboration of the feature system, which at this point does not yet include the feature [strident]. As mentioned previously, this does not imply that the child cannot discriminate between words or sounds that contrast in one of the nonrepresented features; however the acoustic difference appears to the child, it does not play a role in the grammar.

The feature matrix of (37b) is essentially that of Smith, given in (25). Spencer goes on to propose that this set of specifications is further reduced (by means that "must for the present remain mysterious") to the radically underspecified matrix in (38a):

(38) Radical underspecification of (37b):

a. Spencer (1986)

	b	d	g	m	n	ŋ	w	l	r/j	i	u
son								+			
nas				+	+	+					
cor			−			−					
lab	+			+			+				+
cons									−	−	−
voc							−		−		

b. Continuous dichotomy with RU, features as ordered:

	b	d	g	m	n	ŋ	w	l	r/j	i	u
cons							−		−	−	−
nas				+	+	+					
son								+			
lab	+			+			+				+
cor			−			−					
voc							−		−		

Aside from the mysterious nature of the despecification in (38a), a lacuna that could be addressed by spelling out the required redundancy rules, this model assumes that the child has, at some level of mental representation, a fully specified set of features, and then proceeds to throw out specifications. Though this is possible, as an initial hypothesis we might assume rather an approach consistent with the continuous dichotomy. Combined with RU, and keeping to the values assumed by Spencer, the continuous dichotomy applying to the features in the listed order yields the results in (38b). These results are very close to those proposed by Spencer; it is of course an empirical issue what the actual specifications are.

Rice and Avery (1995) suggested that acquisition sequences are derived from dependencies built into the geometry of segment structure. They proposed that segmental inventories are elaborated by expanding the feature tree in (18) following two principles:

(39) Principles of segmental elaboration (Rice & Avery, 1995):
  a. Minimality: Initially, the child has minimal structure.
  b. Monotonicity: Inventories are built up in a monotonic fashion.

Together with the structural dependencies, these principles, similar in spirit to the continuous dichotomy, predict that certain oppositions will be acquired in a universally determined order, while still allowing for considerable variation.[18] For example, in terms of place, it is predicted that the first contrast must be between the Peripheral node and the default Place node, Coronal; that is, the first contrast must be between Coronal and Noncoronal (usually interpreted as Labial, the default Peripheral node). It is predicted that a child will not make a systematic contrast between Labial and Dorsal (velar) before contrasting one of these with Coronal. Several sources of variability in developmental sequences are allowed by the model. First, no dependencies are stated to hold between branches of the structure; thus, children may differ as to whether they elaborate the SV node before the Place node, or vice versa. Second, there is some leeway in the interpretation of defaults. For example, a child who expands Place but not SV may distinguish between coronals and noncoronals, but the consonants may be realized as obstruents or sonorants, or as voiced or voiceless. Similarly, a child who adds SV but no nodes under Place makes a contrast between obstruents and sonorants, but has no distinctive place of articulation. Rice and Avery propose that lack of structure allows for more variability than the presence of structure, which constrains articulatory freedom. It follows that early stages of acquisition are characterized by extreme variability.

In terms of Rice and Avery's model, A's Stage 1 consonant system has no expansions of the Laryngeal (voicing distinctions) or Air Flow (obstruent manner) nodes, and only limited expansions of Place and SV, as shown in (40):

[18]Compare Brown (1958, p. 89): "Cognitive development is increasing differentiation." See also Waterson (1971, 1987).

(40) A's Stage 1 in terms of Rice and Avery's model:

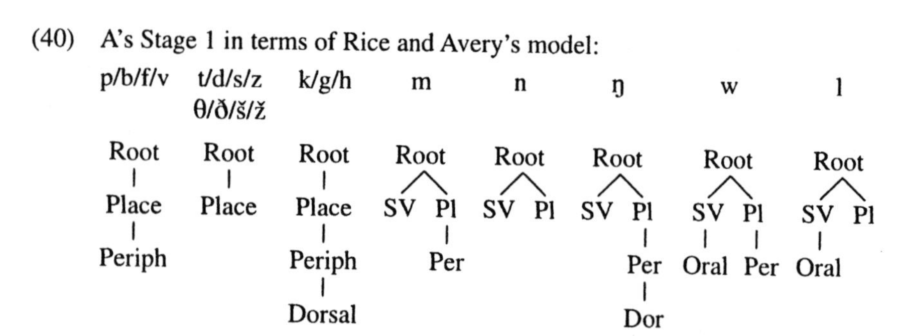

By positing such structures as the input to the child's phonology, we can reflect the distinctive contrasts operative in the child's phonology, as well as continue to view acquisition as a progressive elaboration of the grammar. Thus, the development of segment structure becomes more formally similar to the development of template structures.[19]

Mapping Rules

Even assuming a limited set of distinctive features, children's underlying representations will typically contain more segmental material than can be mapped onto their limited syllable, word, and metrical templates. In such cases, the child has to have principles determining which segments or features will be mapped onto which position, and which will remain unrealized. There remain also many cases where segments that the child can produce in other contexts fail to be realized, even though the relevant template has enough positions to accommodate all the underlying segments. A typical example is that of a child who says [dædi] for *daddy,* but [gʌk] for *duck.* The initial [g] in [gʌk] can be attributed to a rule of consonant harmony, invented by the child; alternatively, its appearance can be interpreted as a manifestation of the third type of limitation listed in (32), namely, a limitation on the number of independent specifications that can be mapped into a template. Thus, the child in the preceding example has the syllable template (CVC) required to produce [dʌk], as well as the alveolar segment [d]; the problem is to produce a [d] when the same syllable or word also contains a velar. Principles that map features onto templates, then, cannot be limited only to cases of mismatch between segments and template positions. Just as templates and segments develop from simple to complex, so, too, do the rules that map segments onto templates.

Macken (1978, 1979, 1992) has proposed that children use two types of templates, which she calls harmony templates and melody templates. With regard to consonants, the dominant element in a harmony template may be position—for example, assuming a template of the form C_1VC_1V, the dominant element is the first consonant for a child who always has progressive (from left to right) harmo-

[19]Developmental data have recently been used to argue for various theories of underspecification; see, for example, Fee (1991), Ingram (1992), Dinnsen (1996), and Stemberger (1993).

ny, no matter what consonants occupy the two positions. Commonly, however, consonants are ranked in terms of a strength hierarchy, where typically coronals are the weakest, and either labials or velars are the strongest.[20] For example, Macken (1992) noted the patterns of a Spanish child whose coronals assimilate to labials and velars from any position:

(41) Consonant harmony (Macken, 1992):

Pattern	*Adult*	*Child*	*Gloss*
Lab Cor	peine	popa	"comb"
Cor Lab	sopa	popa	"soup"
Vel Cor	casa	kaka	"house"
Cor Vel	troca	koka	"truck"

The ubiquity of consonant harmony in child language (Vihman, 1978) poses an interesting problem, however, because consonant harmony is relatively rare in adult languages and tends to be restricted to secondary place features (Shaw, 1991). Lleó (1996) proposed that the underspecified representations of child phonology are consistent with the assumption that consonants and vowels are represented on separate planes (cf. McCarthy, 1989); in a biplanar system, wide-ranging consonant harmony becomes possible, hence accounting for the discrepancy in consonant harmony between child and adult phonology. Levelt (1994), by contrast, presented evidence that cases of apparent consonant harmony in the language of 12 Dutch children can be reanalyzed as assimilation between adjacent consonants and vowels:

(42) C-V interaction (Levelt, 1994):

Pattern	*Adult*	*Child*	*Gloss*
Lab-Round V-Cor	bRot	bop	"bread"
Cor-Round V-Lab	slɔf	pɔf	"slipper"
Lab-Front V-Cor	bɛt	dɛt	"bed"
Cor-Front V-Lab	trɛm	tɛn	"tram"

C-V interaction of this kind is another means of reducing the number of independent specifications in a template.[21]

Melody templates are those in which the (usually two) consonants may differ in place of articulation but must occur in a certain order; in the examples in (43), labial must precede coronal, no matter what the order in the target word:

[20] Strength (or conversely, sonority) hierarchies have been known for a long time to play a role in syllable structure constraints and assimilation. Foley (1977) was one of the first post-*SPE* phonologists to call attention to the importance of strength hierarchies in synchronic and diachronic phonology. In child phonology, see Menn (1975), Macken (1978), and Ingram (1986). Coronals are commonly the "weakest" place of articulation in this respect; see Stemberger and Stoel-Gammon (1991) and the other articles in Paradis and Prunet (1991).

[21] A further possibility is that cases of apparent consonant harmony in child language that cannot be reanalyzed in these terms might be analyzable as copy of the dominant articulator, rather than harmony proper.

(43) Melody template (Macken, 1992):

Pattern	*Adult*	*Child*	*Gloss*
Lab Cor	perro	pedo	"dog"
Cor Lab	sopa	pota	"soup"
	libro	pito	"book"

Similar constraints are reported by Ingram (1974) and Stemberger (1993). In both kinds of templates, the amount of idiosyncratic information conveyed by the phonology of a word is reduced by making predictable some aspect of the phonology that is not in fact predictable in the adult language. Macken (1992, p. 266) noted that such linear constraints do occur in languages, if not in the exact same form: in Tagalog, coronals occur to the right of noncoronals, and [+ cor] [-cor] metathesis is common cross-linguistically.[22]

Matthei (1989) reported on a child who has a template C_1VC_2V, in which C_1 must be at least as sonorous as C_2; the child in question enforced this constraint mainly by a strict selection strategy, attempting mostly words that conform to the required pattern, though some modifications are found in the following data.[23] An asterisk means that the target sequence violates the sonority constraint:

(44) Sonority restrictions (Matthei, 1989):

	a. Within Words		b. Across Words	
Sonority Pattern	*Adult*	*Child*	*Adult*	*Child*
Voiced > Voiceless	diaper	daⁱpə	big tower	bɪ taᵘ
	book	bʊkɔ		
*Voiceless < Voiced	table	tɛpoᵘ	sit down	si taᵘ
	pig	pɪ		
Sonorant > Obstruent	Rafi	rafi	money big	maⁱ bɪ
*Obstruent < Sonorant			big money	mɪ maⁱ

Of special interest is the fact that the same constraint applies to word sequences (44b), indicating that it is not confined to the lexicon.

The development of one aspect of a child's phonological system may have effects on other parts of the system. Waterson (1978) suggested that an increase in the length of an utterance or template may be accompanied by a return to simpler or fewer articulations. In general, then, an increase in complexity in one domain

[22]See Locke (1983, pp. 174–178) for discussion of the anterior-to-posterior progression in adult languages. Locke (pp. 168–174) also saw reflexes of child consonant harmony and other processes of child phonology built into the phonotactics and morpheme structures of adult languages.

[23]A similar example involving vowels is reported by Vihman (1976) for a child learning Estonian, who required that the first vowel be more open (lower) than the second. This constraint was enforced by selection and, where necessary, metathesis; hence, *ema* "mother" became [ami] or [ani], and *isa* "father" became [asi]. This constraint can also be interpreted as requiring that vowel sonority not increase within a word.

may necessitate a temporary decrease in complexity in another.[24] Similarly, Macken (1978) observed an interaction of syllable structure and segmental production in the acquisition of Spanish of J. This child had at an early stage deleted word-final nasal consonants but was subsequently able to pronounce them in monosyllabic CVN words; word-final nasals continued to be deleted in words with more complex syllable structure, however, hence [tɛn] for *tren*, (*train*), but [tu to] for *ratón*, (*mouse*).

Phonological complexity may vary with position. Dresher and van der Hulst (1993) proposed that at each level of the phonology there are heads and dependents, and that heads exhibit the maximum complexity allowed by a grammar. Thus, heads and dependents may be equally complex; but if there is an asymmetry, it will always be the head that is more complex than the dependent. For example, in a series of metrical feet, it may be the case that only the most prominent one (the head) is sensitive to syllable quantity. At the segmental level, stressed vowels are often permitted to be more complex (have more structure) than vowels in unstressed positions. Dresher and van der Hulst suggested that these asymmetries have their origin in the acquisition process, assuming that learners pay particular attention to heads as they expand their initial representations. Such a strategy implies that heads will be expanded before their dependents.

E. Accounting for Stages of Development

The developmental problem of acquisition raises some central questions we have not yet addressed: How do learners arrive at their various intermediate grammars, and what explains their progress from stage to stage? The literature attests to a division between two approaches, the *cognitive* theory (Kiparsky & Menn, 1977; Macken & Ferguson, 1983; Menn, 1983; Menyuk, Menn, & Silber, 1986) on the one side, and the *universalist* theory associated with Jakobson and Chomsky on the other. The cognitive theory views the child as a problem solver, actively seeking ways to communicate in the face of various kinds of limitations and arriving at solutions through trial and error hypothesis testing. This view stresses the variability of child language and the often idiosyncratic nature of the solutions or strategies that children arrive at. The universalist view stresses the commonalities

[24]Though we have been regarding the various components that make up a word (syllable structure, features, mapping rules) as relatively independent, it should be noted that more integrated conceptions have been advanced. Thus, in her account of the system of her child, P, Waterson (1971) recognized a number of distinct structures: for example, labial structures (e.g., *fly* [ßæ/væ/bßæ], *barrow* [bʌwu]) are characterized by labiality at the onset of each syllable, continuance, voiced onsets, an open vowel, and CV syllable structure; sibilant structures (e.g., *fish* [ɪš/ʋš], *brush* [byš]) are monosyllabic and have close vowels, voiced onsets, and syllables ending with a voiceless palato-alveolar sibilant, and so on. We might expect that this degree of cohesion may characterize the very early stages of acquisition of some children, but that the various components become more independent in the course of development.

and universal character of phonology cross-linguistically; if the acquisition of phonology is indeed constrained by a rich universal grammar, we would expect to find it playing a role in the course of acquisition, as well as in the final result. In this model, the emphasis is on innate principles common to all, with variation accounted for by parameters whose values are set on the basis of cues or triggering experiences. To the cognitivists, this model appears rather remote and bloodless, viewing the child as passive rather than actively engaged in a struggle to understand (Campbell, 1988).

The position that one takes on this issue is clearly related to the view one has on the logical problem of acquisition, and on the nature of the grammar that learners ultimately acquire. In practical terms, it is not clear how much empirical content there actually is to this particular debate, however different the two pictures of acquisition appear to be. In the limit, the cognitive model proposes that the child is a little linguist, a scientist engaged in trying to figure out the rules of the ambient grammar. This view is untenable, however, given the vast differences in conditions under which little and big linguists operate. A child, unlike a linguist, has no access to historical or comparative data or to psycholinguistic and other experiments. Most importantly, a child has virtually no access to the type of negative evidence (Lightfoot, 1982, 1989) that linguists routinely rely on to distinguish between accidental and systematic gaps in the data (i.e., between unattested forms that are grammatical but missing accidentally and those that are ungrammatical and ill-formed). Though there are many anecdotes of children actively trying out or practicing various types of linguistic patterns, nobody has yet reported a child struggling with the question of whether distinctive features are binary or single valued, or experimenting with different formalisms for expressing metrical prominence. Moreover, cognitivists (Macken, 1992, p. 267) also recognize that many child rules fall within universal types, even if their details are not predictable.

On the universalist side, we have seen that most universal theories allow much room for variability (sometimes too much, to the extent that the theory is hard to test and makes very weak claims). In addition, there are many aspects of acquisition about which such theories are silent. One concerns a child's cognitive style. Some children are conservative learners, who do not like to attempt words with sounds or patterns that they have not mastered (Ferguson & Farwell, 1975). For such children, selection of words that fit their grammars ("IN words," in terms used by Schwartz & Leonard, 1982) and avoidance (of OUT words) are important strategies. Other children are less discriminating (or more adventurous) and do not hesitate to adapt all sorts of words to their grammar.

In fact, a strict parameter-setting model would lead us to expect a great deal of variation in early stages of acquisition. Ferguson and Farwell (1975) have stressed the importance of individual lexical items in the earliest stages. It is possible that the idiosyncratic templates that some children formulate are inordinately influenced by even one word that, for some reason, is particularly important to the child.

A striking example is reported by Priestly (1977). From the age of 1;10 to 2;2 the author's son developed a productive template of the form C V [j] V C, which, in conjunction with a set of mapping rules, led to forms such as [bajan] for *banana* and [zijan] for *lizard.* Priestly speculated that this pattern may have originated as a simple substitution of the glide [j] for liquids, as shown in [kajat] for *carrot* and [pijow] for *pillow,* creating temporarily a disproportionate number of words with this pattern. Languages with templatic morphology often have prespecified elements in various positions; English is not such a language, but it may have seemed to be one, for a time, to this one child. Because children differ as to what the important words are, they arrive at different templates or mapping rules, just as speakers of different languages attain very different grammars using the same universal principles. As children acquire more words, their input becomes more similar to that of others in the same linguistic community, and their grammars converge.

An interesting variation on the universalist position is that of Stampe (1969, 1973). In his view, the complexity of the adult phonology is attained by suppressing innate universal processes. For example, children learning English have to learn to suppress innate natural processes that voice initial obstruents and devoice final ones. Stampe's approach has not been easy to reconcile with standard versions of generative grammar, but it has obvious affinities with optimality theory.[25]

IV. CONCLUSION: THE FOURTH DIMENSION OF COMPLEXITY

We have been able to touch on only a few issues in the logical and developmental problems of the acquisition of phonology. As should be evident, these problems are largely complementary, and researchers in each area can benefit by applying insights gained in the other. We have observed that much research on the development of phonology can be viewed as studying the development of complexity along three dimensions: prosodic templates, features and segment structure, and rules that map features and segments onto templates. We can integrate this research with main lines of research into the logical problem of acquisition by recognizing a fourth dimension of complexity: the network of sound patterns and relations among lexical items. Just as learners' phonetic surface forms become more complex, so, too, does their understanding of how words and sounds fit into the grammar as a whole. This kind of developing complexity is not as overt as the other dimensions, as it involves changes in learners' lexical representations and cannot be directly observed in production. Nevertheless, it completes the picture of a progression, which begins with a few isolated forms that are part of no larger design, continues through stages of increasingly general and complex patterns, and

[25]For discussion, see Kiparsky and Menn (1977) and Ingram (1989, pp. 386–392).

culminates in the final stage, where the logical and developmental problems of acquisition merge.

REFERENCES

Allen, G. D., & Hawkins, S. (1978). The development of phonological rhythm. In Bell & Hooper (1978), pp. 173–185.

Allen, G. D., & Hawkins, S. (1980). Phonological rhythm: Definition and development. In Yeni-Komshian, Kavanagh, & Ferguson (1980), Vol. 1, pp. 227–256.

Anderson, J. M., & Ewen, C. (1987). *Principles of dependency phonology.* Cambridge: Cambridge University Press.

Archangeli, D. (1984). *Underspecification in Yawelmani phonology and morphology.* Doctoral disseration, MIT, Cambridge, MA. Published by Garland Press, New York, 1988.

Archangeli, D. (1988). Aspects of underspecification theory. *Phonology, 5,* 183–208.

Archibald, J. A. (Ed.) (1995). *Phonological acquisition and phonological theory.* Hillsdale, NJ: Erlbaum.

Atkinson, M. (1986). Learnability. In Fletcher & Garman (1986), pp. 90–108.

Avery, P., & Rice, K. (1989). Segment structure and coronal underspecification. *Phonology, 6,* 179–200.

Baker, C. L., & McCarthy, J. J. (Eds.). (1981). *The logical problem of language acquisition.* Cambridge, MA: MIT Press.

Bell, A., & Hooper, J. B. (Eds.). (1978). *Syllables and segments.* Amsterdam: North-Holland.

Borowsky, T. J. (1986). *Topics in the lexical phonology of English.* Doctoral dissertation, University of Massachusetts, Amherst, MA. Published by Garland Press, New York, 1990.

Braine, M. D. S. (1974). On what might constitute learnable phonology. *Language, 50,* 270–299.

Braine, M. D. S. (1976). Review article: Smith, 1973. *Language, 52,* 489–498.

Broselow, E. (1982). On predicting the interaction of stress and epenthesis. *Glossa, 16,* 115–132.

Brown, R. (1958). How shall a thing be called? *Psychological Review, 65,* 14–21. Reprinted in R. Brown, *Psycholinguistics: Selected Papers by Roger Brown* (pp. 3–15). New York: The Free Press, 1970.

Campbell, R. (1988). On innateness: Nec rasa est, nec omnia tenet. *Toronto Working Papers in Linguistics, 9,* 3–12.

Chomsky, N. (1975). *Reflections on language.* New York: Pantheon.

Chomsky, N. (1981). Principles and parameters in syntactic theory. In Hornstein & Lightfoot (1981a), pp. 32–75.

Chomsky, N. (1986). *Knowledge of language.* New York: Praeger.

Chomsky, N. (1988). *Language and problems of knowledge: The Managua lectures.* Cambridge, MA: MIT Press.

Chomsky, N., & Halle, M. (1968). *The sound pattern of English.* New York: Harper & Row.

Clements, G. N. (1985). The geometry of phonological features. *Phonology Yearbook, 2,* 225–252.
Clements, G. N. (1988). Toward a substantive theory of feature specification. *NELS, 18,* 79–93.
Clements, G. N., & Ford, K. (1979). Kikuyu tone shift and its synchronic consequences. *Linguistic Inquiry, 10,* 179–210.
Clements, G. N., & Keyser, S. J. (1983). *CV phonology.* LI Monograph Series, no. 9. Cambridge, MA: MIT Press.
Crystal, D. (1986). Prosodic development. In Fletcher & Garman (1986), pp. 174–197.
Dinnsen, D. A. (1992). Variation in developing and fully developed phonetic inventories. In Ferguson, Menn, & Stoel-Gammon (1992), pp. 191–210.
Dinnsen, D. A. (1996). Context-sensitive underspecification and the acquisition of phonemic contrasts. *Journal of Child Language, 23,* 57–79.
Dinnsen, D. A., Chin, S. B., Elbert, M., & Powell, T. W. (1990). Some constraints on functionally disordered phonologies: Phonetic inventories and phonotactics. *Journal of Speech and Hearing Research, 33,* 28–37.
Dresher, B. E. (1981a). Abstractness and explanation in phonology. In Hornstein & Lightfoot (1981a), pp. 76–115.
Dresher, B. E. (1981b). On the learnability of abstract phonology. In Baker & McCarthy (1981), pp. 188–210.
Dresher, B. E. (1985a). Constraints on empty positions in tiered phonology. *Cahiers linguistique d'Ottawa, 14,* 1–51.
Dresher, B. E. (1985b). Abstractness, underspecification, and empty skeletal positions. *NELS, 15,* 105–117.
Dresher, B. E. (1995). Changing the learning path: Cues to parameter setting. *Toronto Working Papers in Linguistics, 14*(1), 1–19. Revised version to appear in *Linguistic Inquiry.*
Dresher, B. E., & van der Hulst, H. (1993). Head-dependent asymmetries in phonology. *Toronto Working Papers in Linguistics, 12*(2), 1–17. Revised version in H. van der Hulst & J. van de Weijer (Eds.), *Leiden in last: HIL phonology papers I* (pp. 401–431). The Hague: Holland Academic Graphics.
Dresher, B. E., & van der Hulst, H. (1995). Global determinacy and learnability in phonology. In Archibald (1995), pp. 1–21.
Dresher, B. E., & Kaye, J. D. (1990). A Computational learning model for metrical phonology. *Cognition, 34,* 137–195.
Durand, J. (1990). *Generative and nonlinear phonology.* London: Longmans.
Fee, E. J. (1991). *Underspecification, parameters, and the acquisition of vowels.* Doctoral dissertation, University of British Columbia.
Ferguson, C. A., & Farwell, C. B. (1975). Words and sounds in early language acquisition. *Language, 51,* 419–439.
Ferguson, C. A., Menn, L., & Stoel-Gammon, C. (Eds.). (1992). *Phonological development: Models, research, implications.* Timonium, MD: York Press.
Fikkert, P. (1994). *On the acquisition of prosodic structure* (HIL Dissertations 6). Dordrecht: ICG Printing.
Fletcher, P., & Garman, M. (1986). *Language acquisition: Studies in first language development* (2nd ed.). Cambridge, England: Cambridge University Press.
Foley, J. (1977). *Foundations of theoretical phonology.* Cambridge, England: Cambridge University Press.

Gerkin, L. A. (1991). The metrical basis for children's subjectless sentences. *Journal of Memory and Language, 30,* 431–451.

Gerkin, L. A. (1994). Young children's representation of prosodic phonology: Evidence from English-speakers' weak syllable productions. *Journal of Memory and Language, 33,* 19–38.

Goldsmith, J. A. (1976). *Autosegmental phonology.* Doctoral dissertation, MIT, Cambridge, MA. Published by Garland Press, New York, 1979.

Goldsmith, J. A. (1990). *Autosegmental and metrical phonology.* Oxford: Basil Blackwell.

Greenberg, J. H. (1978). *Universals of human language* (*Vol. 2: Phonology*). Stanford, CA: Stanford University Press.

Gussmann, E. (1980). *Studies in abstract phonology.* Cambridge, MA: MIT Press.

Hale, K. (1973). Deep-surface canonical disparities in relation to analysis and change: An Australian example. In T. Sebeok (Ed.), *Current trends in linguistics* (Vol. 11, pp. 401–458). The Hague: Mouton.

Halle, M. (1978). Formal vs. functional considerations in phonology. *Studies in the Linguistic Sciences, 8,* 123–134.

Halle, M., & Vergnaud, J.-R. (1987). *An essay on stress.* Cambridge, MA: MIT Press.

Hayes, B. (1981). *A metrical theory of stress rules.* Doctoral dissertation, MIT, Cambridge, MA. Published by Garland Press, New York, 1985.

Hayes, B. (1989). The prosodic hierarchy in meter. In P. Kiparsky & G. Youmans (Eds.), *Rhythm and meter* (pp. 201–260). Orlando, FL: Academic Press.

Hayes, B. (1995). *Metrical stress theory: Principles and case studies.* Chicago: University of Chicago Press.

Hooper, J. B. (1976). *An introduction to natural generative phonology.* New York: Academic Press.

Hornstein, N., & Lightfoot, D. (Eds.). (1981a). *Explanation in linguistics.* London: Longman.

Hornstein, N., & Lightfoot, D. (1981b). Introduction. In Hornstein & Lightfoot (1981a), pp. 9–31.

Idsardi, W. (1992). *The computation of prosody.* Doctoral dissertation, MIT, Cambridge, MA.

Ingram, D. (1974). Phonological rules in young children. *Journal of Child Language, 1,* 49–64.

Ingram, D. (1986). Phonological development: Production. In Fletcher & Garman (1986), pp. 223–239.

Ingram, D. (1989). *First language acquisition: Method, description and explanation.* Cambridge, England: Cambridge University Press.

Ingram, D. (1992). Early phonological acquisition: A cross-linguistic perspective. In Ferguson, Menn, & Stoel-Gammon (1992), pp. 423–435.

Itô, J. (1986). *Syllable theory in prosodic phonology.* Doctoral dissertation, University of Massachusetts, Amherst, MA. Published by Garland Press, New York, 1988.

Jakobson, R. (1941/1968). *Child language, aphasia, and phonological universals.* The Hague: Mouton. Translation by A. R. Keiler of *Kindersprache, Aphasie und Allgemeine Lautgesetze.* Uppsala: Uppsala Universitets Årsskrift.

Jakobson, R., & Halle, M. (1956). *Fundamentals of language.* The Hague: Mouton.

Kaisse, E. M., & Shaw, P. A. (1985). On the theory of lexical phonology. *Phonology Yearbook, 2,* 1–30.

Katamba, F. (1989). *An Introduction to phonology.* London: Longman.
Kaye, J. (1974). Opacity and recoverability in phonology. *Canadian Journal of Linguistics, 19,* 134–149.
Kaye, J. (1989). *Phonology: A cognitive view.* Hillsdale, NJ: Erlbaum.
Kaye, J., Lowenstamm, J., & Vergnaud, J.-R. (1985). The internal structure of phonological elements: A theory of charm and government. *Phonology Yearbook, 2,* 305–328.
Kenstowicz, M. (1994). *Phonology in generative grammar.* Cambridge, MA: Blackwell.
Kenstowicz, M., & Kisseberth, C. (1977). *Topics in phonological theory.* New York: Academic Press.
Kiparsky, P. (1973). *Abstractness, opacity, and global rules.* Bloomington: Indiana University Linguistics Club. Also in O. Fujimura (Ed.), *Three dimensions of linguistic theory* (pp. 57–86). Tokyo: TEC.
Kiparsky, P. (1978). Historical linguistics. In W. O. Dingwall (Ed.), *A survey of linguistic science* (pp. 576–649). Stamford, CN: Greylock Publishers. Reprinted in Kiparsky (1982a), 57–80.
Kiparsky, P. (1982a). *Explanation in phonology.* Dordrecht: Foris.
Kiparsky, P. (1982b). Lexical morphology and phonology. In I.-S. Yang (Ed.), *Linguistics in the morning calm* (pp. 3–91). Seoul: Hanshin.
Kiparsky, P. (1985). Some consequences of lexical phonology. *Phonology Yearbook, 2,* 85–138.
Kiparsky, P., & Menn, L. (1977). On the acquisition of phonology. In J. Macnamara (Ed.), *Language learning and thought* (pp. 47–78). New York: Academic Press.
Lahiri, A., & Dresher, B. E. (1983–1984). Diachronic and synchronic implications of declension shifts. *The Linguistic Review, 3,* 141–163.
Lahiri, A., & Marslen-Wilson, W. (1991). The mental representation of lexical form: A phonological approach to the recognition lexicon. *Cognition, 38,* 245–294.
Leopold, W. F. (1939–1949). *Speech development of a bilingual child: A linguist's record* (4 volumes). Evanston, IL: Northwestern University Press.
Levelt, C. C. (1994). *On the acquisition of place* (HIL Dissertations 8). Dordrecht: ICG Printing.
Liberman, M. (1975). *The intonational system of English.* Doctoral dissertation, MIT, Cambridge, MA. Distributed by Indiana University Linguistics Club.
Liberman, M., & Prince, A. (1977). On stress and linguistic rhythm. *Linguistic Inquiry, 8,* 249–336.
Lightfoot, D. (1982). *The language lottery: Toward a biology of grammars.* Cambridge, MA: MIT Press.
Lightfoot, D. (1989). The child's trigger experience: Degree-0 learnability (with commentaries). *Behavioral and Brain Sciences, 12,* 321–375.
Linell, P. (1979). *Psychological reality in phonology: A theoretical study.* Cambridge, England: Cambridge University Press.
Lleó, C. (1996). To spread or not to spread: Different styles in the acquisition of Spanish phonology. In B. Bernhardt, J. Gilbert, & D. Ingram (Eds.), *Proceedings of the UBC international conference on phonological acquistion* (pp. 215–228). Somerville, MA: Cascadilla Press.
Locke, J. L. (1983). *Phonological acquisition and change.* New York: Academic Press.
Locke, J. L. (1986). Speech perception and the emergent lexicon: An ethological approach. In Fletcher & Garman (1986), pp. 240–250.

McCarthy, J. J. (1981a). A prosodic theory of neoconcatenative morphology. *Linguistic Inquiry, 12,* 373–418.
McCarthy, J. J. (1981b). The role of the evaluation metric in the acquisition of phonology. In Baker & McCarthy (1981), pp. 218–248.
McCarthy, J. J. (1988). Feature geometry and dependency: A review. *Phonetica, 43,* 84–108.
McCarthy, J. J. (1989). Linear order in phonological representation. *Linguistic Inquiry, 20,* 71–99.
McCarthy, J. J., & Prince, A. (1988). Quantitative transfer in reduplicative and templatic morphology. *Linguistics in the Morning Calm, 2,* 3–35. Seoul: Hanshin.
McCarthy, J. J., & Prince, A. (1993). *Prosodic morphology I: Constraint interaction and satisfaction.* University of Massachusetts, Amherst, MA, and Rutgers University, New Brunswick, NJ. To appear MIT Press, Cambridge, MA.
Macken, M. A. (1978). Permitted complexity in phonological development. *Lingua, 44,* 219–253.
Macken, M. A. (1979). Developmental reorganization of phonology. *Lingua, 49,* 11–49.
Macken, M. A. (1980). The child's lexical representation: The "*puzzle-puddle-pickle*" evidence. *Journal of Linguistics, 16,* 1–17.
Macken, M. A. (1986). Phonological development: A crosslinguistic perspective. In Fletcher & Garman (1986), pp. 251–268.
Macken, M. A. (1992). Where's phonology? In Ferguson, Menn, & Stoel-Gammon (1992), pp. 249–269.
Macken, M. A., & Barton, D. (1980). A longitudinal study of the acquisition of the voicing contrast in American-English word-initial stops, as measured by voice onset time. *Journal of Child Language, 7,* 41–74.
Macken, M. A., & Ferguson, C. A. (1983). Cognitive aspects of phonological development. In K. E. Nelson (Ed.), *Children's language* (Vol. 4, pp. 255–282). Hillsdale, NJ: Erlbaum.
Maddieson, I. (1984). *Patterns of sounds.* Cambridge: Cambridge University Press.
Marantz, A. (1982). Re reduplication. *Linguistic Inquiry, 13,* 435–482.
Marlett, S. (1981). The abstract consonant in Seri. *Proceedings of the Berkeley Linguistics Society, 7,* University of California at Berkeley, 154–165.
Marlett, S., & Stemberger, J. (1983). Empty consonants in Seri. *Linguistic Inquiry, 14,* 617–639.
Matthei, E. (1989). Crossing boundaries: More evidence for phonological constraints on early multi-word utterances. *Journal of Child Language, 16,* 41–54.
Menn, L. (1971). Phonotactic rules in beginning speech. *Lingua, 26,* 225–241.
Menn, L. (1975). Counter example to "fronting" as a universal of child language. *Journal of Child Language, 2,* 293–296.
Menn, L. (1978). Phonological units in beginning speech. In Bell & Hooper (1978), pp. 157–171.
Menn, L. (1980). Phonological theory and child phonology. In Yeni-Komshian, Kavanaugh, & Ferguson (1980), pp. 23–41.
Menn, L. (1983). Development of articulatory, phonetic, and phonological capabilities. In B. Butterworth (Ed.), *Language production: Development, writing and other language processes* (Vol. II, pp. 3–50). New York: Academic Press.

Menn, L., & Matthei, E. (1992). The "two-lexicon" account of child phonology: Looking back, looking ahead. In Ferguson, Menn, & Stoel-Gammon (1992), pp. 211–247.

Menyuk, P., Menn, L., & Silber, R. (1986). Early strategies of the perception and production of words and sounds. In Fletcher & Garman (1986), pp. 198–222.

Mohanan, K. P. (1982). *Lexical phonology.* Doctoral dissertation, MIT, Cambridge, MA. Published by Reidel, Dordrecht, 1986.

Moskowitz, A. I. (1970). The two-year-old stage in the acquisition of English phonology. *Language, 46,* 426–441.

Nespor, M., & Vogel, I. (1986). *Prosodic phonology.* Dordrecht: Foris.

Paradis, C., & Prunet, J.-F. (1991). *The special status of coronals: Internal and external evidence.* (Phonology and Phonetics 2.). San Diego, CA: Academic Press.

Piattelli-Palmarini, M. (Ed.). (1980). *Language and learning: The debate between Jean Piaget and Noam Chomsky.* Cambridge, MA: Harvard University Press.

Postal, P. (1968). *Aspects of phonological theory.* New York: Harper & Row.

Priestly, T. M. S. (1977). One idiosyncratic strategy in the acquisition of phonology. *Journal of Child Language, 4,* 45–66.

Prince, A., & Smolensky, P. (1993). *Optimality theory: Constraint interaction in generative grammar.* Rutgers University, New Brunswick, NJ, and University of Colorado, Boulder, CO. Technical Report RuCCS TR-2, Rutgers Center for Cognitive Science. To appear MIT Press, Cambridge, MA.

Pulleyblank, D. (1986). *Tone in lexical phonology.* Dordrecht: Reidel.

Pye, C., Ingram, D., & List, H. (1987). A comparison of initial consonant acquisition in English and Quiché. In K. E. Nelson & A. Van Kleeck (Eds.), *Children's language* (Vol. 6, pp. 175–190). Hillsdale, NJ: Erlbaum.

Rice, K., & Avery, P. (1995). *Variability in a deterministic model of language acquisition: A theory of segmental elaboration.* In Archibald (1995), pp 23–42.

Sagey, E. (1986). *The representation of features and relations in nonlinear phonology.* Doctoral dissertation, MIT, Cambridge, MA. Published by Garland Press, New York, 1990.

Sapir, E. (1925). Sound patterns in language. *Language, 1,* 37–51. Reprinted in M. Joos (Ed.), *Readings in Linguistics I* (4th ed., pp. 19–25). Chicago: University of Chicago Press, 1957.

Schwartz, R., & Leonard, L. (1982). Do children pick and choose? An examination of phonological selection and avoidance in early lexical acquisition. *Journal of Child Language, 9,* 319–336.

Selkirk, E. O. (1978). On prosodic structure and its relation to syntactic structure. Bloomington: Indiana University Linguistics Club (1980). Also in T. Fretheim (Ed.), *Nordic prosody II* (pp. 111–140). Trondheim: TAPIR, 1981.

Shaw, P. A. (1991). Consonant harmony systems: The special status of coronal harmony. In Paradis & Prunet (1991), pp. 125–157.

Smith, I. (1982). The English velar nasal. *Linguistics, 20,* 391–409.

Smith, N. V. (1973). *The acquisition of phonology.* Cambridge, England: Cambridge University Press.

Spencer, A. (1986). Towards a theory of phonological development. *Lingua, 68,* 3–38.

Stampe, D. L. (1969). The acquisition of phonemic representation. *CLS, 5,* 433–444.

Stampe, D. L. (1973). *A dissertation on natural phonology.* Doctoral dissertation, University of Chicago, Chicago.

Stanley, R. (1967). Redundancy rules in phonology. *Language, 43,* 393–436.
Stemberger, J. P. (1993). Glottal transparency. *Phonology, 10,* 107–138.
Stemberger, J. P., & Stoel-Gammon, C. (1991). The underspecification of coronals: Evidence from language acquisition and performance errors. In Paradis & Prunet (1991), pp. 181–199.
Steriade, D. (1987). Redundant values. *CLS, 23*(2), 339–362.
Tesar, B., & Smolensky, P. (1998). Learnability in optimality theory. *Linguistic Inquiry, 29,* 229–268.
Tranel, B. (1981). *Concreteness in generative phonology: Evidence from French.* Berkeley, CA: University of California Press.
Trubetzkoy, N. (1939/1969). *Principles of phonology.* Berkeley & Los Angeles: University of California Press. Translation by C. A. M. Baltaxe of *Grundzüge der Phonologie.* Göttingen: Vandenhoeck & Ruprecht, 1958. First appeared as *TCLP* VII. Prague: Prague Linguistic Circle, 1939.
Tryon, D. T. (1970). *An introduction to Maranungku.* (Pacific Linguistic Series B, #14). Canberra: Australian National University.
Vihman, M. (1976). From prespeech to speech: On early phonology. In *Stanford Papers and Reports on Child Language Development, 12,* 23–44.
Vihman, M. (1978). Consonant harmony: Its scope and function in child language. In J. Greenberg (1978).
Waterson, N. (1971). Child phonology: A prosodic view. *Journal of Linguistics, 7,* 179–211. Revised version reprinted in Waterson (1987), pp. 25–52.
Waterson, N. (1978). Growth of complexity in phonological development. In N. Waterson & C. E. Snow (Eds.), *The development of communication* (pp. 415–442). Chichester & New York: John Wiley & Sons. Revised version reprinted in Waterson (1987), pp. 88–107.
Waterson, N. (1987). *Prosodic phonology: The theory and its application to language acquisition and speech processing.* Newcastle upon Tyne: Grevatt & Grevatt.
Wilbur, R. B. (1981). Theoretical phonology and child phonology: Argumentation and implication. In D. L. Goyvaerts (Ed.), *Phonology in the 1980's* (pp. 403–429). Ghent/Belgium: E. Story-Scientia.
Yeni-Komshian, G. H., Kavanaugh, J. F., & Ferguson, C. A. (Eds.). (1980). *Child phonology (Vol. 1: Production and Vol. 2: Perception).* New York: Academic Press.

CHAPTER 11

THE DEVELOPMENT OF PRAGMATICS: LEARNING TO USE LANGUAGE APPROPRIATELY

Anat Ninio and Catherine E. Snow

I. DEFINING THE DOMAIN OF PRAGMATICS

A. Pragmatics versus Syntax and Semantics in Formal Models

Broadly speaking, pragmatics is the study of the use of language in context for the purpose of communication. Thus, developmental pragmatics is concerned with how a child acquires the competencies underlying the rule-governed employment of speech in interpersonal situations. The criteria applied in assessing the pragmatic success of an utterance have to do not with grammaticality (the criterion applied within the domain of syntax) or truthfulness and interpretability (the semantic criteria), but with appropriateness and communicative effectiveness.

This demarcation of the field of developmental pragmatics is, however, far from straightforward or noncontroversial. The status of language use in the study of language is a highly vexed issue within linguistics and the philosophy of language. Indeed, the very distinction between the domain of pragmatics and those of syntax and semantics is itself theory dependent.

The trichotomy of syntax, semantics, and pragmatics originated with Morris (1938), who defined syntax as the study of the formal relations of signs to one another, semantics as the study of the relations of signs to the objects they denote, and pragmatics as the study of the relation between signs and their interpreters, that is, the speaker and the addressee(s). This distinction between the concerns of pragmatics on the one hand and those of semantics and syntax on the other appears in various forms in the writings of many linguists and philosophers of language. It is echoed (with theory-specific distinctions of meaning) in de Saussure's (1922/1983) distinction between language and speech (la langue and la parole), in Chomsky's (1965) distinction between performance and competence, in Austin's (1962) differentiation of illocutionary and locutionary acts, in Searle's (1975) distinction between illocutionary force and propositional content and between literal and indirect speech acts (Searle, 1969), in Grice's (1968, 1969) discrimination of utterer's-meaning and sentence-meaning, in Lemmon's (1966) statements versus sentences, and so forth.

Such a principled distinction between pragmatics and semantics and syntax is the central tenet of formal linguistics. This approach is closely associated with, and mutually reinforcing of, a particular philosophical theory of linguistic meaningfulness, the so-called truth-conditional theory of meaning, identified with such authors as Carnap (1956), Davidson (1979), or Lewis (1972). According to this theory, the sense of sentences is determined by their truth conditions; to know the conditions under which a sentence is true is to now the meaning of the sentence. Linguistic meaning or meaningfulness is a property of sentences, largely independent of actual contexts of use (Davidson, 1979; Wiggins, 1971).

The conception of language this theory supports is one of an autonomous system of fixed symbols and of abstract rules for their lawful combination, all defined independently of their possible contexts of use. The uses people make of the meaningful sentences generated by this system are, properly speaking, extralinguistic; and if these uses are rule-governed, the description of such rules belongs to a separate discipline, such as pragmatics or sociolinguistics. Within this conception, then, the proper concern of pragmatics is the description of phenomena related to the use of meaningful linguistic forms for communicative purposes. Chief among these is the production and comprehension of speech acts—making statements, requesting, promising, and the like. Other phenomena include the regulation of conversational exchange, politeness rules and other culturally conventionalized variations in speech register that convey social meaning and determine appropriateness, the control of presuppositions, and the creation of connected discourse. Linguistics proper, namely syntax and semantics, is confined to concern with the generation of meaningful utterances independent of their potential or actual context of use (cf. Gazdar, 1979; Kempson, 1975; Levinson, 1983). As Chomsky (1990) put it, "there is no reason to single out communication among the many uses to which language is put" (p. 57).

It is however obvious even to the most extremely formalist of linguists that language contains expressions that point to contextual information rather than symbolizing some context-independent abstract concept. These expressions are the deictic or indexical elements of language: pronouns, deictic locatives such as *here* and *there,* deictic temporal terms such as *today* and *tomorrow,* verbs such as *come, go,* and *bring,* and the like. These expressions receive their value from the context of their use; thus, the sentences in which they are used do not have truth conditions (hence, meaning) except as a function of their situated use. Because they are bona fide lexical items, it is impossible to exclude the rules governing the use of such deictic expressions from linguistics proper. However, the treatment of such expressions does not fit well into linguistic theories developed to deal with linguistic entities of apparently context-independent nature. It has therefore been proposed (cf. Bar Hillel, 1954; Kalish, 1967; Montague, 1968) that linguistic theory proper be complemented by a separate pragmatic component dealing with indexical or deictic expressions.

From the formalist point of view, then, pragmatics is already an ill-defined domain, best characterized by means of a list enumerating the various phenomena of inquiry (cf. Levinson, 1983). These use-related phenomena are thought by the formalist to possess varying degrees of affinity with language phenomena proper. Formalists would place on the very boundaries between linguistics and language use deictic expressions, as well as other in-between phenomena such as the grammar of units larger than a single sentence. Speech act production is only slightly more peripheral, because it involves such purely grammatical features as the control of grammatical mood, performative sentence structure, a propositional core, and so on (cf. Lyons, 1981; Searle, 1975). Further away from linguistics proper are the control of presuppositions, politeness rules, and the management of conversational exchanges, in that order. Many would claim these fall in the province of sociolinguistics rather than linguistics proper, and thus even beyond the concerns of pragmatics.

B. The Place of Pragmatics in Functionalist Models

However, the distinction between language and its use underlying the above demarcation of the field is not the only conceptualization possible. An alternative philosophical approach to linguistic meaningfulness with its attendant linguistic metatheory is the so-called use-conditional theory of meaning. This approach ties the concept of linguistic meaningfulness to the communicative use people make of language. The most well-known expression of this viewpoint is the late Wittgenstein's dictum that "for many expressions . . . to know their use is to know their meaning" (1953). According to this approach, the primitive concept from which meaning is derived is one of communication rather than one of truth: The meaning of an utterance is what a speaker has intended overtly to communicate to an addressee (Alston, 1964; Grice, 1957, 1968; Strawson, 1970).

This approach gives logical priority to utterance-meaning over sentence-meaning. The meaningfulness of utterances derives from their use in performing overtly communicative acts. The meaning of sentences is a kind of abstraction from their occasions of use; it is their potential to be used communicatively (Allwood, 1981; Alston, 1964, 1967, 1968; Fillmore, 1971; Grice, 1969). The literal meaning of a sentence may be the meaning element common to all contexts of use, the union of all possible uses or, most probably, the most representative or prototypical use the sentence can be put to (cf. Allwood, 1981; Gibbs, 1984). Likewise, word meaning may be defined as the word's contribution to the use-potential of a sentence (Alston, 1968), or its prototypical conditions of use (Allwood, 1981).

The linguistic theory associated with this philosophical tradition emphasizes the indexical, context-bound nature of all language. Semanticists working in this tradition have shown that the depiction of word meaning as a context-free conglomeration of semantic features is unable to account for such varied semantic phenomena as polysemy, contextual expressions, labeling, and misuse (eg., Anderson & Ortony, 1957; Clark & Gerrig, 1983). Adjustments designed to rescue the formal approach, such as two-stage models for the interpretation of speech acts (e.g., Gordon & Lakoff, 1971; Searle, 1975) and of ironical and metaphorical utterances (Kintsch, 1974; Searle, 1979), have not stood up to theoretical analysis or psycholinguistic experimentation (e.g., Dore & MacDermott, 1982; Gazdar, 1981; Gibbs, 1984; Lakoff, 1982; Rumelhart, 1979; Sperber & Wilson, 1981; Streek, 1980).

Linguistic theories associated with the use-conditional viewpoint are called functional rather than formal (e.g., Dik, 1978; Halliday, 1985). As a generalization, such theories see linguistic forms (words, grammar) as tools for the purpose of communication, namely, sets of subordinate units to be made use of in the construction of decipherable messages. The implicit, internalized linguistic system is thought to consist of "production rules," namely, of procedures for verbally expressing various kinds of communicative intents. Formal rules of language (syntax, morphology, lexicon) appear in this view merely to be components of such a system of production rules (e.g., Bates & MacWhinney, 1979). In the functionalist approach, the boundaries between syntax, semantics, and pragmatics are blurred. What the formalists call linguistic competence proper is but a subset of the "communicative competence" needed to use language meaningfully (Hymes, 1971).

According to this viewpoint, no difference exists between pragmatics and the rest of linguistics. The goal of linguistics is to achieve an understanding of how speakers create interpretable utterances in communicative situations. All boundaries between formal and contextual aspects of language are seen as artificial and ill conceived; the system as a whole is completely contextual and does not possess autonomous components. If it is agreed that the task of pragmatics is the study of language use in context, and if all language is inherently contextualized, then pragmatics is the most general discipline encompassing all aspects of language.

C. Pragmatics in Developmental Theories

Developmental psycholinguists studying the acquisition of pragmatic competence take any of a variety of standpoints—whether explicitly or implicitly—on the general theoretical issue of the nature of the linguistic system. Much work in this field accepts implicitly the separateness of pragmatics, and studies pragmatic development by looking at pragmatic skills more or less in isolation. Other research, though, embodies the assumption that children's initial language is best described in use-conditional terms, whatever the form and nature of the endstate linguistic system. According to this approach, a substratum of social meanings or communicative intents underlies the regularities observed in early single and multiword speech, and the young child's linguistic system consists of realization rules that connect form and function in their speech (e.g., Bates, 1976; Bates, Camaioni, & Volterra, 1975; Bateson, 1975; Benedict, 1979; Braunwald, 1978; Bruner, 1975a; Clark & Clark, 1977; Greenfield & Smith, 1976; Halliday, 1975; Nelson, 1985; Ninio, 1983; Rogdon, Jankowsky, & Alenskas, 1977; Ryan, 1974; Snow, 1979).

Among these studies taking a theoretically intermediate position one could also include studies concerned with the identification of pragmatic factors influencing language acquisition, whether or not such studies operate with an integrated pragmatically based acquisition model. These include investigations of the interactive context of language use in early childhood (Bruner, 1983; Cazden, 1970; Chapman, 1981; Lieven, 1978a, 1978b; Snow, 1977a, 1979), studies concerned with the role of maternal input and scaffolding behavior on the acquisition of linguistic forms (eg., Mervis & Mervis, 1988; Moerk, 1976; Nelson, 1977; Nelson, Denninger, Bonvillian, Kaplan, & Baker, 1984; Ninio, 1985; Ninio & Bruner, 1978; Sachs, Brown, & Salerno, 1976; Snow, 1972, 1977b; Tomasello & Todd, 1983), and, more marginally, studies in which an appeal is made to putative pragmatic reasons for the explanation of acquisition biases (e.g., Benedict, 1979; Stephany, 1986; Wales, 1986). Studies focusing primarily on the interactive context of language acquisition will not be reviewed systematically here (but see Snow, 1995, for a review).

A theoretically radical group of investigators do not consider the early use-conditional language as a transitory stage but explicitly adopt a use-conditional framework for the characterization of endstate language itself. On this approach, the use-based linguistic system postulated for young children is assumed to be in principle, if not in detail, isomorphic and continuous with the full-blown adult system. In the latter, as in the former, meaning is assumed to be use-conditional; the latter, as the former, is thought to consist of rules for the realization of (and comprehension of) communicative messages in verbal form. In these studies the assumption is made that the goal of developmental psycholinguistics is to explain the entirety of language acquisition of functionally effective tools for communication (Bates & MacWhinney, 1979; Halliday, 1975; Ninio, 1994b; Tomasello, 1992; Tough, 1977; van Valin, 1991). These studies adopt as their theoretical framework linguistic theories that do not acknowledge a rigid demarcation of syntax, semantics, and pragmatics, such as Halliday's (1985) Systemic-Functional Grammar, Givon's (1989) Functional Linguistics, Cognitive Linguistics (e.g.,

Lakoff, 1990; Langacker, 1987), or Hudson's (1990) Word Grammar, a communicatively oriented dependency grammar.

The boundaries between this group of studies and the previous one are fuzzy. As long as the target population whose language development is studied are beginning speakers, the theoretical stance taken regarding the ultimate course of development seldom makes a difference in terms of research goals or methodology. There are however exceptions to this generalization; one focal controversy in the field exemplifies the pervasive presence of high-theoretical considerations in the study of early pragmatic competencies. The controversy arose from Bates and colleagues' (1975) claim that, prior to the emergence of language, children perform communicative acts such as requesting by nonverbal means and that the status of these acts is essentially identical to those of illocutionary acts. The later use of verbal means for the expression of the same kind of illocutionary intents is merely the substitution of verbalizations for prior nonverbal behaviors. Dore (1978) criticized this analysis and, relying on Searle's (1969) speech act theory, argued that illocutionary acts incorporate a grammatical component that preverbal communicative acts obviously lack. Therefore, he claimed, prelinguistic communicative skills are necessary but not sufficient for the acquisition of linguistic communication. By themselves, developments in the pragmatic domain cannot provide an explanation for the emergence of speech; substitution of means is not the vehicle of development. Thus, for Dore, children's gradual mastery of types of communicative intents is a separate line of development from the development of language proper, the one not feeding into the other. Indeed, according to Dore, it is not only preverbal communication that is irrelevant to true illocutionary act production but also most of single-word speech; in his publications on the subject (e.g., Dore, 1975) he claimed that even in true verbal utterances carrying illocutionary force, the illocutionary intent is conveyed by nonlinguistic means such as intonation, whereas the words themselves serve only as rudimentary referring expressions naming some random element of the communicative situation. Thus, Dore's studies of the development of speech act production, although superficially similar in their subject matter to Bates' investigations of early pragmatics, actually represent a different viewpoint, one that clearly differentiates between these pragmatic developments and language acquisition proper.

A relatively complete review of empirical work in the domain of pragmatics must abstract from the theoretical differences among the authors on the issues previously identified. In the following, we shall review work on the phenomena that, in our view, constitute the major achievements of language learners within the domain of pragmatics, organizing our review under the following four topics:

1. The acquisition of communicative intents and the development of their linguistic expression, seen as a separate issue from the acquisition of linguistic forms and grammar in the abstract.

2. The development of conversational skills and the acquisition of rules that govern turn taking, interruptions, back channeling, signaling topic relevance or topic switch, and so on.

3. The acquisition of rules of politeness and other culturally determined speech use rules.

4. The development of control over the linguistic devices that govern connected discourse, such as ways to generate cohesion across utterances within a longer discourse and to signal presuppositions, as well as procedures for organizing information into familiar genre-specific forms. We will not review those studies dealing with the acquisition of deictic forms such as pronouns and deictic locatives, which just refer to the pragmatic underpinnings of this kind of knowledge without studying directly the pragmatic aspects of its development (e.g., Charney, 1980; Chiat, 1981, 1986; Clark & Sengul, 1978; de Villiers & de Villiers, 1973; Karmiloff-Smith, 1979; Wales, 1986; Webb & Abramson, 1976).

II. DEVELOPING COMMUNICATIVE INTENTS AND APPROPRIATE WAYS OF EXPRESSING THEM

In this section we shall be concerned with two questions: (a) what type of communicative intents can children express, and (b) how are these intents expressed throughout the course of development? We focus, thus, on children's entry into language via their development of control over rules of expression for speech acts.

A. Prelinguistic Communicative Abilities

Among investigators of early social behavior, there exists wide agreement that infants possess a precocious social understanding that enables them both to emit intentional communicative signals and to interpret the significance of social signals, actions, and events in their environment, prior to understanding speech (Acredolo & Goodwyn, 1988; Antinucci & Parisi, 1975; Bates, 1976; Bronson, 1981; Bruner, 1975a, 1975b, 1978; Carpenter, Mastergeorge, & Coggins, 1983; Carter, 1975a, 1979; Chapman, 1981; Collis & Schaffer, 1975; de Villiers & de Villiers, 1978; Dore, 1974, 1975, 1976, 1978; Eckerman, Whatley, & Kutz, 1975; Edwards, 1978; Golinkoff, 1983; Golinkoff & Gordon, 1983; Harding, 1983; Harding & Golinkoff, 1979; Lewis, Young, Brooks, & Michalson, 1975; Lock, 1980; Moerk, 1975; Rheingold, Hay, & West, 1976; Ross & Kay, 1980; Scoville, 1984; Snow, Dubber, & de Blauw, 1982; Snyder, 1978; Sugarman-Bell, 1978; Vandell, 1977; Zinober & Martlew, 1985). Although this assumption is occasionally attacked by skeptics (e.g., Shatz, 1982), it is supported by a long line of meticulous research into young children's interactive abilities (cf. papers in Feagans, Garvey, & Golinkoff, 1984; Lamb & Sherrod, 1981; Rubin & Ross, 1982). According to some authorities, the possession of communicative intents and the interpretation of others' intents is such a basic human capacity that there is reason to believe that it is a biological disposition or language universal (Dore, 1985; Miller, 1970; Trevarthen, 1977, 1979; Trevarthen & Hubley, 1979).

B. Communicative Intents Expressed at the Preverbal Stage

Even though it is widely agreed that preverbal infants use intentional vocalizations and gestures, such as pointing, gazing, and giving for communicative purposes, there is a relative dearth of systematic information on the types of social meanings they express by such means. The studies that have been conducted fall into three categories. First, there are investigations documenting preverbal infants' gradually evolving participation in specific interactive contexts such as peek-a-boo (Bruner, 1975a; Bruner & Sherwood, 1976; Ratner & Bruner, 1978) or book reading (Ninio & Bruner, 1978). Second, there have been several studies of infants' nonverbal expression of illocutionary-type speech acts in dyadic interaction with their adult caretakers. In one of the earliest studies of this kind, Bates and colleagues (1975) described two broad categories of preverbal precursors to verbally performed speech acts: proto-declaratives, used to direct the other's attention to a focus (the precursors of statements) and proto-imperative, used to bring the other to do something (the antecedents of requests and other directives). Coggins and Carpenter (1978), using a more detailed typology, found the following types of pragmatic behaviors in preverbal children: requesting (object requests, action requests, information requests) greeting, transferring objects, showing off, acknowledging, and answering. Carpenter and colleagues (1983) used seven categories to characterize preverbal communication, including, in addition to the above-mentioned behaviors, protesting, commenting on an action, and commenting on an object. Interestingly, none of the studies in this group mentioned game-embedded meaningful behaviors of the type documented by Bruner and his collaborators among the preverbal communicative acts infants were able to control.

A third category of studies focused on preverbal and early nonverbal communicative behaviors exhibited by infants during interactions with a peer (Bronson, 1981; Dunn & Kendrick, 1982; Eckerman, Whatley, & Kutz, 1975; Lewis et al., 1975). These studies expand the list of early social meanings communicated to include expressions of feelings including sympathy, offers and sharing, compliance and noncompliance or resistance, stage setting, and pretend games.

In all, infants appear to be able to control an impressive array of social meanings and to convey them to others by nonverbal means. These results provide converging evidence on the precocity of the social capacities underlying communication and indicate that communicative exchanges may indeed serve a functional role in children's entry into language.

C. The Continuity Hypothesis

To what extent early language use is built on the preverbal communicative system is as yet an unsettled issue. Some investigators have claimed that children's early language is continuous with their preverbal communicative system, so that early verbalizations are acquired by a process of children's substituting conventional, verbal forms for the expression of the same communicative intents they have been expressing by nonverbal means prior to the emergence of speech (Bates, 1976; Bates et al., 1975; Bruner, 1975b; Carpenter et al., 1983; Carter, 1975a; Halliday, 1975; Lock, 1980; Nelson, 1985; Ninio & Bruner, 1978). Others (e.g., Dore, 1975, 1978) have pointed out that linguistic expressions operate by the uniquely linguistic means of reference and predication, and that a fundamental discontinuity should be acknowledged to exist between preverbal and verbal communication.

Even on this view, however, there is a great measure of continuity in children's communicative behavior. In the first place, it is agreed that many of the intents children express on starting to use speech are identical to the ones previously expressed by nonverbal means. At the least, then, children master the principles of intentional communication as well as the specific social-cognitive concepts underlying some of their earliest verbal utterances before facing the task of acquiring verbal means for expressing them. Second, it is probably true that some early utterances express communicative intents that are novel and are impossible to express by nonverbal means. These intents are emergent consequences of learning language. However, even in these cases the acquisition of forms expressing such intents is possible only because children's precocious communicative abilities at the onset of speech enable them to interpret intents that they themselves cannot express (see Dore, 1975, and Nelson, 1978, for discussions of this issue).

D. Transitional Phenomena

Although some research simply describes early pragmatic capacities, other studies are more process oriented, emphasizing the role of early pragmatics in children's entry into language "proper," and proposing use-conditional theories of acquisition for early speech (e.g., Antinucci & Parisi, 1975; Bates, 1976; Bruner, 1983; Halliday, 1975; Nelson, 1978; Ninio, 1992a; Ninio & Snow, 1988; Ninio & Wheeler, 1984a). For example, Ninio and Snow (1988) proposed that the fundamental learning process by which novel linguistic forms are acquired at the onset of speech is one of pragmatic (rather than semantic) matching, by which children pair an unknown verbal string in the speech addressed to them with their interpretation of the speaker's intended communicative effect.

Various transitional communicative signals have been identified that combine nonverbal and verbal features. Carter (1975a; 1975b; 1979), Dore, Franklin, Miller, and Ramer (1976), and Halliday (1975) have documented an intermediate developmental stage where partly conventionalized vocal signals or proto-words were used. These apparently developed by some process of environmental shaping from spontaneous expressive vocalizations and idiosyncratic communicative signals, but underwent some partial phonetic fixation so that they approximated conventional verbal forms serving similar communicative functions in adult language. (See also Ingram's 1989 discussion of Halliday's findings.) Apparently, the entry into language use is a gradual and relatively protracted process rather than a sudden all-or-none phenomenon.

E. The Pragmatics of Early Single-Word Utterances

Even though children's earliest speech uses have been extensively investigated (cf. Antinucci & Parisi, 1973; Barrett, 1981; Bates, 1979; Carpenter, et al., 1983; Dale, 1980; Dore, 1974; Greenfield & Smith, 1976; Griffiths, 1985; Gruber, 1973; Halliday, 1975; McShane, 1980; Wells, 1985), it is surprisingly difficult to give a list of the kinds of meaningful communicative acts children are able to control verbally at the onset of speech. Investigators disagree on which early speech uses should be considered bona fide communicative acts because each set of pretheoretical assumptions leads to the a prior exclusion of a subset of speech phenomena from the domain under investigation. For example, Halliday (1975) excluded labeling and all other "language practice" from his corpora of early speech; Wells (1985) excluded from pragmatic analysis all self-addressed speech; Dale (1980) omitted from his categories of pragmatic function calling, moves in games, imitation, or expressive exclamations; Dore (1974), McShane (1980), Barrett (1981), and Griffiths (1985) apparently did not regard the production of verbal moves in games true language use; and so forth. The fate of imitations is particularly illuminating. Although Dore (1974), Wells (1985), and Camaioni and Laicardi (1985), for instance, have repeating or imitating as a type of speech act or interpersonal speech use, others studying the communicative or pragmatic meanings of early speech (e.g., Barrett, 1981; Dale, 1980; Greenfield & Smith, 1976; Griffiths, 1985; Halliday, 1975) have explicitly excluded imitations from their database, while still others (Ninio, Snow, Pan, & Rollins, 1994; Ninio & Wheeler, 1984b; Snow, Pan, Herman, & Imbens-Bailey, 1993) assume imitations, like fully spontaneous utterances, can express any of a variety of illocutionary intents.

An overview of the different studies discloses that the phenomenon is not a chance one: The defining characteristic of early speech uses is that they fulfill only partially the criteria defining a prototypical meaningful communicative act. These early utterances are borderline cases on one or more counts: (a) the meanings they express tend to be social rather than, properly speaking, illocutionary, that is, they are nonreferential, playful, or ritual speech uses (Barrett, 1986; Bates, 1979; Braunwald, 1978; Bruner, 1975a; Camaioni and Laicardi, 1985; Corrigan, 1978;

Dore, 1985; Greenfield & Smith, 1976; Harris, Barrett, Jones, & Brookes, 1988; Harrison, 1972; Lock, 1980; Lucariello, Kyratzis, & Engel, 1986; McCune-Nicolich, 1981; Nelson, 1985; Nelson & Lucariello, 1985; Ninio, 1992a, 1992b); (b) the expressions used tend not to be of the major word classes such as verbs, nouns, or adjectives, but, rather, fringe members of the linguistic system such as vocatives, exclamations, interjections, and the like (Benedict, 1979; Dore, 1985; Nelson, 1973; Ninio, 1993b), (c) moreover, even when they do express "serious" pragmatically central meanings such as requests, beginning speakers seldom use any but the most general of pro-words such as pronouns, deictic locatives, pro-verbs, and the like (Barrett, 1981; Clark, 1978; Greenfield & Smith, 1976; Griffiths, 1985; Ninio, 1993b; Weisenberger 1976); (d) rather than being interpersonal, early meaningful speech uses are often directed at the self rather than at another person (Piaget, 1926; Vygotsky, 1978; Wells, 1985); (e) finally, rather than invariably being spontaneously produced, a significant proportion of early utterances are imitations of previous utterances by an interlocutor (e.g., Bates, 1979).

As a broad generalization, it seems that children start to use speech meaningfully by first learning those form-meaning pairings that do not necessitate a simultaneous control of many different novel principles. These speech uses will tend to be supported by familiar interpersonal contexts such as games; they will involve unmarked general forms with a wide range of applicability; and they will involve types of speech uses appropriate for a novice user of the verbal-communicative medium, for example, imitations, language practice, and self-directed speech.

Adding up the information from the different studies of early speech mentioned previously, it appears that the repertoires of specific speech acts early speakers can express verbally are not limited to a definite and recognizable subset of functional uses. Except for the obvious absence of such complex social meanings as explicit promises, predictions, declarations, and the like, most types of illocutionary acts are represented in the combined corpora of the children investigated. By contrast to the theoretically based predictions made by Dore (1975) or Halliday (1975), very young children do engage in the expression of the informative function of language; they do make statements, answer questions, confirm or disagree with a previous speaker's proposition. They may perform at a much lower level of cognition than do adults when it comes to the content discussed (i.e., most early statements concern the immediately observed rather than the distant or the abstract; most arguments regarding the truth of propositions concern the correct name to call a referent rather than more complex issues), but the pragmatic skills involved and demonstrated in the production of the relevant communicative acts are considerable. In sum, the very earliest speech uses documented in young children mirror the pragmatic diversity observed in their prelinguistic communication, although they are limited by the repertoire of means and meanings they can initially control.

F. Developmental Trends in the Expression of Communicative Intents in the Early Stages of Speech Use

Two major developmental trends have been identified in the expression of communicative intents in the single-word period of speech use. The first consists of children's moving from a holistic to a selective type of mapping between their intents and verbal expressions. Various investigators have proposed that at the onset of speech, communicative meaning is packaged into words in a holistic, undifferentiated fashion, either because the concepts underlying children's early words are themselves holistic and undifferentiated (Nelson, 1983, 1985, 1986; Nelson & Lucariello, 1985) or because of specific limitations on their intent-mapping capacities (cf. Barrett, 1978, 1986; Griffiths, 1985). According to this view, selective mapping of analyzed components of communicative intents onto verbal expressions is a later development, typically emerging in the latter part of the single-word period.

The claim that initial mapping is holistic may be found to be too restricted a characterization of children's expressive abilities even during the first period of speech use; wherever they start, though, it is clear that children acquire a more analytic style of verbal expression during the course of development. Early on, children tend to use general, unmarked, nonspecific terms (such as pronouns and other proforms) for the expression of particular communicative functions, whereas later they use a host of more specific terms (such as common nouns and verbs) in the same communicative circumstances (cf. Barrett, 1981; Bloom, 1973; Clark, 1978; Griffiths, 1985; Halliday, 1975; Weisenberger, 1976). Around the middle of the second year, children master the principle of mapping selective elements of their intents to variable expressions encoding the specifics of the communicative situation; earlier they typically mapped their intents to a nonspecific expression functioning as a key word for a broader class of intents (Halliday, 1975; Ninio, 1992b, 1994b).

The second developmental trend is children's mastery of the principle of many-to-many mapping of communicative intents to verbal expressions. It has been pointed out that at the onset of speech, children tend to use a given verbal expression in a single functional context; only later do these forms get defunctionalized (Barrett, 1983; Bates, 1975; Dore, 1985; Greenfield & Smith, 1976; Halliday, 1975; Ingram, 1971; Menn & Haselkorn, 1977; Nelson & Lucariello, 1985). Conversely, beginning speakers apparently operate with some uniqueness principle by which each type of speech function or communicative intent is to be mapped onto a single verbal expression only. The acquisition of multiple mapping rules for the same type of intent is thus a later development, occurring about the same time at the mastery of the variable mapping principle (Ninio, in 1994b). These two trends—defunctionalization of given expressions and the acquisition of two or more forms of mapping for the same type of speech function—lead children from an initial one-to-one mapping of meanings to forms to the many-to-many mapping characterizing the adult linguistic system.

G. Individual Differences in the Earliest Speech Uses

Pronounced individual differences in the type of speech acts first acquired by various groups of children have been documented. Nelson (1973, 1975a, 1975b, 1976, 1978, and see also Della Corte, Benedict, & Klein, 1983) identified two major types of children: expressive children who first acquired expressions appropriate for the verbalization of interpersonal (i.e., regulatory, instrumental, personal, and interactive) language functions and referential children who, in addition to the interpersonal uses, used their earliest vocabulary for informative, heuristic, or mathetic speech functions as well. Referential children acquire many common nouns among their first 50 words, whereas expressive children use pronouns to refer to entities. Before turning to the different interpretations given to this phenomenon, it is worth mentioning that in later replications (e.g., Goldfield, 1987), even more than in Nelson's original sample, most children actually belonged to an intermediate group on the dimension of expressivity/referentiality rather than exhibiting the pure features of either type.

Nelson's interpretation of her findings has been that there exist differences of acquisition style and of pragmatic preference for one kind of speech use. Others (e.g., Pine, 1990; Pine & Lieven, 1990) have raised the possibility that the reported differences are of developmental status, with expressive children lagging behind referential ones. This interpretation is supported by the well-documented use of pronouns rather than common nouns by speakers at the very start of language use (see the previous discussion) and the finding that children start to acquire large numbers of common nouns relatively late in the single-word stage (e.g., Nelson, 1973).

H. Developmental Course of Verbal Control of Speech Acts

Rather little work has been done following children as they expand their repertoire of speech act. Very young children are clearly limited to the production of speech acts that are cognitively accessible and relatively straightforward to express. Thus, for example, in one study we found that various sorts of markings (greetings, transfer forms like *thank you,* notice forms like *uh-oh*) were very common at 14 months, as were prohibitions and expressions indicating attention during discussions of shared, present objects, whereas speech acts such as stating the speaker's intentions or providing affirmative answers to questions only emerged at 20 months, and requesting clarification was still marginal at 32 months (Snow et al., 1993).

A major task for developmental psycholinguists is to generate some basic developmental norms for speech act use, if acquisition of communicative skill is to be systematically charted. An obstacle is the rather chaotic degree of disagreement among various ways of coding speech acts (see Ninio et al., 1994, for a discussion); the lack of an agreed upon comprehensive system has led many to concentrate on subsets of speech acts, such as requests (Corsaro, 1979; Ervin-Tripp & Gordon, 1986). An early attempt to do developmental comparisons of speech act sophistication (Rollins, Pan, Conti-Ramsden, & Snow, in press) found that specifically language-impaired children used a wider variety of speech act types than controls matched on syntactic aspects of language production; these findings suggest that speech act sophistication can be usefully considered separately from syntactic sophistication and that these two domains of language have somewhat different developmental pathways.

III. DEVELOPMENT OF CONTROL OVER CONVERSATIONAL RULES

We focus in this section the development of skills that are specific to conversation—for example, turn taking; maintenance of topic-relevance; eliciting participation from the interlocutor; control over devices for repair, for topic initiation, for topic transition; and so on. Being an effective adult conversationalist is a difficult task precisely because it requires combining control over the semantic and syntactic processes of utterance planning, production and comprehension with control over the pragmatic rules and procedures for turn taking, for ensuring, maintaining, and recognizing topic relevance, for repairing misunderstandings or comprehension breakdowns, and for regulating the local system of proxemics and kinesics. Much of the prior research about adult conversation has focused on the turn-taking system, for example, the pioneering papers by Duncan and Fiske (1977) and by Sacks, Schegloff, and Jefferson (1974), and the many later papers proposing modifications to the notion that smooth conversational exchange is a universal and ubiquitous phenomenon (see Denny, 1985, and Murray, 1985, for reviews). Other work within the conversational analysis tradition has focused on specific conversational subsystems, such as the initiation (Godard, 1977; Scheg loff, 1979) and conclusion of telephone conversations (Clark & French, 1981; Schegloff & Sacks, 1973). Further complexities of conversational competence emerge from analyses of specific conversational genres, for example, ritual insults (Dundes, Leach & Özkök, 1972; Labov, 1972), service encounters (Merrit, 1976), jokes (Sacks, 1974), doctor-patient talk (Coulthard & Ashby, 1976; Mishler, 1984), and therapy sessions (Labov & Fanshel, 1978; Turner, 1972). Much has been written about the kinesic, proxemic, and gaze-control systems competent conversationalists display (e.g., Argyle & Cook, 1976; Birdwhistell, 1970; Hall,

1959, Hinde, 1972; Kendon, 1981; Key, 1975; Knapp, 1972). Attention has been directed to cultural and linguistic differences in the regulation of conversational turn taking and the structuring of conversation events (e.g., Philips, 1976; White, 1989), and to cohesion and mechanisms for determining topic relevance (Halliday & Hasan, 1976; Kintsch & van Dijk, 1978; Tracy, 1983, 1984, and many more), though more often for monologic than for dialogic texts.

These various research efforts have given us some indication of the complex set of skills acquired as the child becomes a competent conversationalist. Like adults, children have to learn the rules of specific conversational genres, such as classroom discourse (Kluwin, 1983; McHoul, 1978; Pride, 1969; Sinclair & Coulthard, 1975). They have to learn that the competent listener has an active role (Hess & Johnston, 1988). Conversational skill may be a particularly important determinant of peer acceptance in school-aged children (Hemphill & Siperstein, 1990). For very young children, most of whose talk occurs in conversational contexts, separating specifically conversational skills from general-language skills is difficult and perhaps somewhat artificial. However, at least theoretically it is possible to identify skills that are specific to the interactive context of conversational exchange—in particular, skills associated with centrally conversational tasks like making small talk rather than with tasks in which information exchange or problem solving is central, and focusing on appropriateness and interactive effectiveness rather than truthfulness or grammaticality (Schley & Snow, 1992).

A. Turn Taking

It is well attested that even very young children are quite good at the turn-taking aspect of conversation, at least in dyadic situations, both with adult interactants and with peers. By the time they are producing their first words, children can typically sustain long bouts of well-timed turn alternations (Kaye & Charney, 1980, 1981; Snow, 1977a); with peers the same pattern appears by at least age 3 (Ervin-Tripp, 1979; Keenan & Klein, 1975). Deaf children acquiring American Sign Language follow similar patterns of development in learning these discourse strategies; Prinz and Prinz (1985) found that deaf children successfully achieved coherency across a multiplicity of sign strings through turn taking, remediating interruptions, obtaining the attention of the addressee, handling topics, and establishing and maintaining eye contact. Young children's turn taking is subject to many more disruptions of order than is that of adults, however, and children under age 5 typically use rather primitive, nonverbal strategies to enter conversations with other children (Corsaro, 1979) and with adults (Sachs, 1982). By about age 4, children show some control over the use of devices such as sentence-initial *and* or repetitive *et puis* (and then) as floor holders to signal that their turn is not yet complete (Jisa, 1984/1985; Peterson & McCabe, 1987).

Of course, many problems of conversational management are eased for young children by the availability of highly cooperative adult conversational partners. Thus, children's violations of some of the rules governing adult conversation are not considered particularly serious, and their frequent difficulties abiding by the Gricean maxims (Grice, 1975) of relevance and quantity are compensated for by adult willingness to engage in extensive repair. Continuation of a conversational topic in adult-child talk is often more a function of adult responsiveness (Bloom, Rocissano & Hood, 1976) than of child topic maintenance behaviors, though improvement in topic maintenance occurs with age. Some of the violations of normal conversational responsiveness by young children may relate to deficits in their ability to comprehend implicitly nominated topics (Bacharach & Luszcz, 1979; Luszcz & Bacharach, 1983), or to other cognitive limitations on control over conversational implicature.

B. Topic Selection and Maintenance

When interacting with peers, children often either fail to maintain a topic (Blank & Franklin, 1980) or else use relatively primitive devices to do so. Keenan and Klein (1975), for example, analyzed conversations between twins to show that exact or partial imitation was a primary device used to maintain coherence across turns. Similarly, Garvey (1975) showed that dyads used both repetition of and ritualized variations on each others' utterances to generate conversational exchanges up through age 5. It is striking in the exchanges Garvey described that cross-turn relevance is sometimes maintained by sound play based cohesion, rather than true topic cohesion. Reliance on imitative devices for maintaining cross-turn cohesion declined from age 2 to age 5 (Benoit, 1982). Explicit marking of cross-utterance relations with "conjuncts" such as *for example, so,* and *anyway* or with "attitudinal" expressions such as *really* or *perhaps* is extremely rare in the speech of 6-year olds, and 12-year olds have not achieved adultlike frequencies of these devices (Scott, 1984). This finding becomes quite important in light of the crucial role such markers are generally assumed to play in introducing nuances of politeness, deniability, and connectedness in adult conversation (Wardhaugh, 1985). Children may rely on relatively primitive devices for linking their own conversational contributions to those of their partners because of an inability to think of anything else to say. Similarly, the relatively passive role often assumed by young children in conversation with adults may derive from their ignorance of the standard, culturally determined list of topics that organizes casual conversation for adults (Kellermann, Broetzmann, Lim, & Kitao, 1989).

C. Individual Differences in Conversational Skill

Most children develop conversational skill relatively easily and automatically. Shy children may show deficits as conversationalists; Evans (1987) compared interactions of reticent children to those of nonreticent children and found that, in addition to speaking less, reticent children also engaged in less complex speech than their peers, using shorter utterances, single topic turns, and fewer narratives and decontextualized descriptions of nonpresent objects. Furthermore, there is evidence that children with language or reading disabilities (Bryan, Donahue, Pearl, & Storm, 1981; Donahue, 1984; Donahue, Pearl, & Bryan, 1980, 1983) and mildly retarded children (Hemphill, 1987; Hemphill & Siperstein, 1990) show problems interacting with peers that may be traceable to lack of control over the subtleties of conversational skill. Bryan, Donahue, and their colleagues found that in unstructured conversations, poor conversationalists could get along by virtue of responding to the conversational initiatives of their more skilled peers, but when they were made responsible for the conversation by use of an interview task their deficiencies were revealed. Mentally retarded children showed more problems than language-matched normally developing children with topic control, conversational assertiveness, topic initiation, and fluency, but they had few problems with topic transitions, requests for clarifications, and replies to initiations (Hemphill, 1987). Furthermore, because the turn-taking system for interviews is more constrained than for mundane conversations (Greatbatch, 1988), one might expect this task to reduce the impact of difficulties with turn taking per se (and thus perhaps reveal other sorts of problems) as a source of conversational ineffectiveness.

Schley and Snow (1992) found that children rated higher as conversational partners (a) used open-ended questions and questions contingent upon previous utterances more often, (b) avoided silent pauses of more than a short duration, and (c) successfully elicited elaborated responses from the adult interlocutor. Conversational skill was not related, however, to other types of disfluencies, including word choice and grammatical self-corrections, repetitions, interruptions, and vocal hesitations. Their findings echo those of Dorval and Eckerman (1984), who carried out one of the few studies of age differences in conversational skill that looked at conversations among peers. Dorval and Eckerman found large differences in the degree to which the talk engaged in related to topics at hand, as well as in the nature of the relations among turns. Their youngest subjects, second graders, produced the highest proportion of unrelated conversational turns. Ninth graders were producing a substantial proportion of factually related turns; the twelfth graders and the adults increasingly incorporated perspective-related turns (those that take into account the perspective of the person being discussed) into their discussions. These findings extend to peer-peer conversations earlier observations by Bloom and colleagues (1976) on degree of relatedness in adjacent conversational turns. Bloom and colleagues had found the percent of children's utterances that were on the same topic as immediately preceding adult utterances and also added new information rose from 21% during Stage 1 (MLU under 1.5, ages 19 to 23 months) to 46% at Stage 5 (MLU above 3.5, ages 35 to 38 months). These findings suggest that one major component of development in conversation is learning to make responses related to the previous turn, whereas Dorval and Eckerman (1984) make clear that older children continue to improve in topic coherency and to achieve coherency in increasingly sophisticated ways. The linguistic task of achieving coherence is one children face in their narratives and in other single-party discourses, not just in conversational exchange.

Conversational skill can play a central role in a child's access to social interaction with peers (Corsaro, 1979), in determining peer acceptance (Hemphill & Siperstein, 1990), in second language learners' access to input in their target language (Krashen, 1980), and in making a positive impression on teachers and other powerful adults (Evans, 1987); clearly there is much more to be known about the factors that relate its development.

IV. LEARNING TO BE POLITE

Being polite involves having acquired a complex set of culturally specific rules for how other members of the group should be treated. This involves knowing how they should be addressed, what their wants, needs, and desires are, and how one's own wants, needs and desires should be expressed without violating others' rights. In a sense, serious theories of politeness are theories of all human social interaction! Starting from Brown and Levinson's (1987) model of polite interaction, it quickly become clear that politeness is a system that regulates what is said and how it is said in all sorts of interactions.

A developmentally early accomplishment that falls squarely within the domain of politeness is producing greetings. Brown and Levinson have pointed out that a greeting is a face-threatening act, because it requires a response from the addressee, and because it puts the speaker's face at risk of injury in case the greeting is not returned. Greif and Gleason (1980) have documented the degree of effort parents put into ensuring their children provide greetings and other formulaic markings like *thank you.* Snow, Perlman, Gleason, and Hooshyar (1990) found that mothers of children with Down's syndrome model such forms more frequently and more exaggeratedly than parents of children developing normally, suggesting the importance attached to socialization of such responses.

Much of the work that has focused specifically on the development of politeness in English has described within naturally occurring interactions parental modeling, explicit correction, hinting, and other techniques used to teach children correct behavior (e.g., Becker, 1988, 1990). This work has in general defined the range of behaviors subsumed under the category of "politeness" rather narrowly, focusing on issues like saying *please* and *thank you,* apologizing, avoiding slang and rude words, and responding to questions but not interrupting. Observations of children growing up in Japan, though, generate far richer data about socialization for politeness, because Japanese requires specific lexical and grammatical forms in polite speech and because Japanese politeness relies extensively on indirectness. Clancy (1986) has described how Japanese mothers explain to their children that visitors may not be expressing themselves directly, that is, that children should offer food again after a refusal, or should stop making requests of the visitor even if the requests are complied with.

Children demonstrate quite early their sensitivity to the dimensions of power and social distance that regulate linguistic forms. For example, children as young as 2 years old are more likely to use imperatives with peers and requests to adults (Corsaro, 1979). However, full knowledge of the linguistic conventions that appropriately signal the dimensions of distance and power may take several years to acquire. Typically, for example, when induced to make requests that should be more "polite" (e.g., addressed to an older person), young children simply add forms like *please;* only after about age 5 do they choose indirect forms (do you mind if . . .) or other mitigators of directness like *I hate to bother you but . . .* (Bates, 1976; Becker, 1982, 1986).

Much work that is relevant to the broad notion of politeness endorsed here has been done under the rubric "language socialization." Language socialization studies focus on how children learn to become effective members of their cultures, which involves acquiring the rules about how to speak in a variety of social interactive settings. Learning which members of the group require deference and which can be treated linguistically as equals, for example, is a product of language socialization, as is learning which address forms are appropriate for each category, learning how males and females talk differently, learning which are the socially valued dialect forms, and learning to participate in speech events such as doing the dozens, telling about one's day at the dinner table, taking a turn at sharing time, or making small talk. Useful examples of language socialization studies can be found in Schieffelin and Ochs (1986), Ochs (1988), Schieffelin (1990), and Goldfield and Snow (1992).

A major theme that deserves emphasis in understanding children's development of politeness is that the basic social system that politeness rules rely on is in place before the linguistic structures that express politeness are acquired. Acquiring politeness—like acquiring the effective expression of speech acts or the appropriate turn-taking and topic-maintenance behavior of mature conversationalists—presupposes a relatively sophisticated social understanding. Evidence suggests that understanding the social structure is not the child's greatest challenge in becoming polite; rather, the challenge is to acquire the varied and subtle linguistic tactics used to express the underlying social dimensions.

V. LEARNING TO PRODUCE CONNECTED DISCOURSE

In their early conversational exchanges, children are exposed to and display cross-turn topic cohesion and expansion; subsequent utterances in conversation build on earlier ones and are interpretable because of rules governing how those cross-turn relationships are signaled linguistically. Simple examples include the use of definite articles in noun phrases for mutually identifiable referents and indefinite articles in noun phrases that introduce referents novel to the listener. Thus, once a referent (e.g., "I saw a dog walking down the street") has been introduced into a conversation, subsequent mentions must use definite referring expressions (e.g., *the dog, that creature, it*). One of the skills children must develop as they get older is that of putting utterances together such that their cross-utterance relevance is clear within single-speaker productions—producing connected discourse autonomously.

In addition to connecting utterances in extended discourse forms, children must learn about the genres of connected discourse: the conventions that characterize various sorts of narratives, explanations, descriptions, and so on. Learning about these genre forms continues well into adulthood: graduate students typically require considerable training in the pragmatics of scientific written or oral presentations. The vast majority of work on the development of connected discourse has focused on narrative, though some work on explanations, descriptions, and school-specific forms like definitions has been done.

A major domain of pragmatic challenge children face in producing relatively autonomous discourse forms has to do with the speaker-audience relationship. In the conversational exchanges in which very young children express their communicative intents, the speaker-hearer relation is quite straightforward: There is face-to-face interaction and speaker and hearer share physical, historical, and social contexts such that the child can presume background knowledge is shared. As children get older they are increasingly asked to communicate to audiences that are distant, either physically (e.g., talking to grandma on the phone), historically (making new friends with whom no past experience is shared), or socially (talking in social roles that involve nonreciprocal relationships or unequal social status, such as patient to pediatrician, student to teacher, customer to clerk). The pragmatic skills involved in communicating effectively during such exchanges while maintaining mutual respect involve control of extremely complex linguistic devices.

A. Linguistic Devices That Maintain Cross-Utterance Cohesion

In dyadic conversations, a major mechanism for maintaining cross-utterance cohesion is ellipsis (a: Where did you go? b: The movies. a: Who with? b: Harvey.) In autonomous productions, though, referential cohesive links are much more common, that is, using pronouns or deictic elements anaphorically, repeating or paraphrasing nouns, and using clusters of nouns that have thematic relations. Children's use of these referential cohesive ties increases between ages 2 and 3½ (Peterson & Dodsworth, 1991) and continues to increase during the early school years (McCutcheon & Perfetti, 1982; Stenning & Mitchell, 1985). Children as young as 2 years old, though, maintained focus on particular referents quite effectively, keeping track of an average of three different referents through an average of four mentions each, in stories that averaged 12 clauses in length (Bennett-Kastor, 1983). Bennett-Kastor also found that 5-year olds had a rather sharp increase in number of referents and number of mentions, thus producing much more coherent stories. Children in this preschool age range, though, produce a fairly high proportion of ambiguous noun phrases or omit required noun phrases (Peterson & Dodsworth, 1991); whereas noun phrase omissions decrease between ages 2 and 4, even school-aged children continue to introduce referents ambiguously in their oral productions and their written texts.

B. Adaptations to the Audience

A first task in interaction is to determine what knowledge is shared between speaker and audience. Young children often seem to think that listeners know more than they actually do—perhaps because the children are used to conversing with mothers, who do know quite a lot about their lives. Children's inadequacies as providers of information are particularly visible in the wisely used referential communication tasks, where their failings include not demanding enough information when they are functioning as listeners as well as not providing enough when functioning as describers (see Ricard & Snow, 1990). On the other hand, even rather young children will respond with more detail and greater specificity when told, for example, that a picture description is meant for someone who cannot see the picture being described (De Temple, Wu, & Snow, 1991; Ricard & Snow, 1990; Wu, De Temple, Herman, & Snow, 1994). Children as young as 4 years old will spontaneously clarify references to individuals or objects they think their interlocutors do not know, for example, "I told Mindy—she's a kid at my preschool . . . " (Sachs, Anselmi, & McCollam, 1990).

It has long been reported that children use definite articles inappropriately to introduce referents not known to the interlocutor (e.g., Karmiloff-Smith, 1979; Maratsos, 1976). This is observed almost exclusively in experimental settings, though, where the child's basis for prediction may be somewhat weak; in settings where the child has a good basis for predicting the interlocutor's state of knowledge, such errors are rare (Stevenson, 1988). Furthermore, even in adult conversation, the indefinite noun phrase is not the only appropriate form for introducing referents. In a structured setting where children aged 7 to 13 were trying to coordinate instructions from maps that differed in some details, unshared knowledge was indicated, not by using the conventional indefinite article ("Turn right at a church"), but using questions ("Do you see the church?") increasingly as children got older (Anderson, Clark, & Mullin, 1991). It seems that children from quite a young age do respond to their audience's needs, but that they do not necessarily do so in conventional ways and they often need help determining exactly what those needs are.

C. Learning about Genres and Their Structure

Quite early children show linguistic differentiation between various narrative forms. For example, by the age of 3 they already use present indicative verbs and generic nominals and pronouns in script productions, thus distinguishing these from past experience narratives that contain specific nominals and past tense for event clauses (Hudson & Nelson, 1986; Nelson, 1986). By the age of 5 children can signal fairly reliably the distinction between background information or setting and events within past experience or fantasy narratives, using progressive or perfect forms for the background information (Hicks, 1991). Children can linguistically signal movement from casual talk into fantasy narratives as young as 2, and become increasingly adept at managing movement into and out of narrative talk during the preschool years (Hudson & Shapiro, 1991). Even mildly retarded children are quite good at many of these skills (Hemphill, Picardi, & Tager-Flusberg, 1991).

Stories have a particular structure—not just "once upon a time" and "the end," but also the requirements of a setting or orientation session, some complicating events, a high point, a resolution, in some versions a coda or explicit statement of the moral. Anglo-American children acquire knowledge of this structure between the ages of 3 and 10 (Botvin & Sutton-Smith, 1977; Peterson & McCabe, 1983), the same age period when Japanese children learn the very different structure of three brief related episodes culturally prescribed for their narratives (Minami & McCabe, 1991). Acquisition of these culturally defined structures for various genres of narrative might seem beyond the realm of pragmatic development, but such structures ensure the communicative effectiveness of narratives; stories that deviate from the expected structure are hard to understand or to get the point of.

In addition to their plot structure though, narratives make their point through the inclusion of evaluations, or clauses that explicitly express the speaker's point of view about the events. Children include evaluations in their narratives from the age of 3 (Peterson & McCabe, 1983; Umiker-Sebeok, 1979). However, younger children tend to use certain categories of evaluations (hedges, negatives, quoted speech, and causals) relatively more than older children and adults, and they tend to underuse the category of emotional states (Bamberg & Damrad-Frye, 1991). Furthermore, when 5-year olds did refer to emotional states, they tended to do so under control of specific episodes in the narrative, whereas adults referred to emotions in ways governed by the overall structure of the story—ensuring, for example, that everyone ends up happy at the end of the story!

Other language forms like definitions also have a culturally prescribed structure; Snow (1990) has studied extensively the growth in children's ability to give definitions during the age period 5 to 12, as have Watson (1985), McGhee-Bidlack (1991), and others. Many 5-year olds, when asked for a definition, give a little description or narrative instead; by the age of about 10, middle-class children give formal definitions that include a superordinate and a restrictive relative clause almost all the time, at least for concrete nouns. The communicative effectiveness of older children's formal definitions is often not greater than that of younger children's informal definitions; the psycholinguistic problem of casting the necessary information into the prescribed genre becomes the domain of development.

VI. ENDPOINT OF PRAGMATIC DEVELOPMENT

One difference between the domain of pragmatics and most of the other domains subsumed under the topic "language acquisition" is that the others have a fairly clear end point, and by late childhood or at least early adulthood learners are seen to have "finished" the task of acquisition. Pragmatics is a domain more like the lexicon, in which continued development can occur throughout the life span. Kemper, Kynette, Rash, O'Brien, & Sprott (1989) found, for example, that elderly speakers' narratives were more memorable and effective than those of younger, middle-aged comparison groups. Continued growth in areas like politeness and communicative effectiveness is probably within the realm of possibility for most adults.

Several issues in the domain of pragmatics remain ripe for continued study. One has to do with the definition and structure of the domain itself: To what degree do the various aspects of pragmatics we have discussed together here—conversational skill, politeness, skill with connected discourse—really go together in development? Does precocious sophistication with a variety of speech acts predict better storytelling or conversational skill at later ages? Do pragmatic demands faced by older children—for example, keeping referents straight in storytelling or being clear about temporal relations among events—generate skills with the syntactic or morphological rules needed to be pragmatically effective?

Another relatively unexplored question has to do with the relation between acquisition of the linguistic structures that are recruited for pragmatics and of the social cognitions that underly appropriate social behavior. We have suggested that children are socially relatively precocious, though their acquisition of the linguistic rules that normally encode the social knowledge may be considerably delayed. Why are the linguistic structures so hard, if the social knowledge underlying their use is present?

Finally, of course, a major unresolved issue is the degree to which pragmatic acquisition is a motor running the system of language acquisition or a somewhat separate (perhaps even peripheral) strand of development. Karmiloff-Smith (1979), Hicks (1991), and others have argued that increased pragmatic challenge drives children to reanalyze and extend their syntactic and lexical resources. On the other hand, high-functioning children with autism can achieve quite astonishing levels of syntactic and lexical competence while nonetheless displaying severe impairments in pragmatic appropriateness, suggesting that pragmatic demands are not the only route to grammatical sophistication. To approach the question of how pragmatic skills relate to other domains of language, we need to develop basic developmental indices for various domains of pragmatics, as well as a database that would enable us to relate descriptors of pragmatic development to information about development in other domains.

ACKNOWLEDGMENTS

Work on this paper has been supported by the National Institute for Child Health and Human Development through HD 23388 to Catherine Snow and by the Israel Foundation Trustees through funding of Ninio's work.

REFERENCES

Acredolo, L., & Goodwyn, S. (1988). Symbolic gesturing in normal infants. *Child Development, 59,* 450–466.

Allwood, J. (1981). On the distinction between semantics and pragmatics. In W. Klein and W. Levelt (Eds.), *Crossing the boundaries in linguistics* (pp. 174–189). Boston: D. Reidel Publishing.

Alston, W. P. (1964). *The philosophy of language.* Englewood Cliffs, NJ: Prentice-Hall.

Alston, W. P. (1967). Meaning. In P. Edwards (Ed.), *The encyclopedia of philosophy.* New York: Macmillan & The Free Press.

Alston, W. P. (1968). Meaning and use. In G.H.R. Parkinson (Ed.), *The theory of meaning* (pp. 141–165). Oxford: Oxford University Press.

Anderson, A., Clark, A., & Mullin, J. (1991). Introducing information in dialogues: Forms of introduction chosen by young speakers and the responses elicited from young listeners. *Journal of Child Language, 18,* 663–688.

Anderson, J. R., & Ortony, A. (1975). On putting apples into bottles—A problem of polysemy. *Cognitive Psychology, 7,* 167–180.

Antinucci, F., & Parisi, D. (1973). Early language acquisition: A model and some data. In C. Ferguson & D. Slobin (Eds.), *Studies in child language development.* New York: Holt, Rinehart & Winston.

Antinucci, F., & Parisi, D. (1975). Early semantic development in child language. In E. H. Lennenberg & E. Lennenberg (Eds.), *Foundations of language development: A multidisciplinary approach, Vol. 1.* New York: Academic Press.

Argyle, M., & Cook, M. (1976). *Gaze and mutual gaze.* Cambridge, England: Cambridge University Press.

Austin, J. L. (1962). *How to do things with words.* New York: Oxford University Press.

Bacharach, V., & Luszcz, M. (1979). Communicative competence in young children: The use of implicit linguistic information. *Child Development, 50,* 260–263.

Bamberg, M., & Damrad-Frye, R. (1991). On the ability to provide evaluative comments: Further explorations of children's narrative competencies. *Journal of Child Language, 18,* 689–710.

Bar-Hillel, Y. (1954). Indexical expression. *Mind, 63,* 359–379.

Barrett, M. D. (1978). Lexical development and overextension in child language. *Journal of Child Language, 5,* 205–219.

Barrett, M. D. (1981). The communicative functions of early child language. *Linguistics, 19,* 273–305.

Barrett, M. D. (1983). The early acquisition and development of the meanings of action-related words. In T. B. Seiler & W. Wannenmacher (Eds.), *Concept development and the development of word meaning.* Berlin: Springer.

Barrett, M. D. (1986). Early semantic representations and early word-usage. In S. A. Kuczay & M. D. Barrett (Eds.), *The development of early word meaning.* New York: Springer.

Bates, E. (1976). *Language and context: Studies in the acquisition of pragmatics.* New York: Academic Press.

Bates, E. (1979). *The emergence of symbols.* New York: Academic Press.

Bates, E., Camaioni, L., & Volterra, V. (1975). The acquisition of performatives prior to speech. *Merrill-Palmer Quarterly, 21,* 205–226.

Bates, E., & MacWhinney, B. (1979). A functionalist approach to the acquisition of grammar. In E. Ochs & B. Schieffelin, (Eds.), *Developmental pragmatics.* New York: Academic Press.

Bateson, M. C. (1975). Mother-infant exchanges: The epigenesis of conversational interaction. In D. Aaronson & R. W. Rieber (Eds.), *Developmental psycholinguistics and communication disorders.* New York: The New York Academy of Sciences.

Becker, J. (1982). Children's strategic use of requests to mark and manipulate social status. In S. Kuczaj (Ed.), *Language development: Language, thought, and culture* (Vol. 2, pp. 1–35). Hillsdale, NJ: Erlbaum.

Becker, J. (1986). Bossy and nice requests: Children's production and interpretation. *Merrill-Palmer Quarterly, 32,* 393–413.

Becker, J. (1988). The success of parents' indirect techniques for teaching preschoolers pragmatic skills. *First Language, 8,* 173–181.

Becker, J. (1990). Processes in the acquisition of pragmatic competence. In G. Conti-Ramsden & C. Snow (Eds.), *Children's Language, Vol. 7.* Hillsdale, NJ: Erlbaum.

Benedict, H. (1979). Early lexical development: Comprehension and production. *Journal of Child Language, 6,* 183–200.

Bennett-Kastor, T. (1983). Noun phrases and coherence in child narratives. *Journal of Child Language, 10,* 135–150.

Benoit, P. (1982). Formal coherence production in children's discourse. *First Language, 2,* 161–180.

Birdwhistell, R. L. (1970). *Kinesics and context: Essays on body motion communication,* Philadelphia: University of Pennsylvania Press.

Blank, M., & Franklin, M. (1980). Dialogue with preschoolers: A cognitively-based system of assessment. *Applied Psycholinguistics, 1,* 127–150.

Bloom, L. (1973). *One word at a time: The use of single word utterances before syntax.* The Hague: Mouton.

Bloom, L., Rocissano, L., & Hood, L. (1976). Adult-child discourse: Developmental interaction between information processing and linguistic knowledge. *Cognitive Psychology, 8,* 521–552.

Botvin, G., & Sutton-Smith, B. (1977). The development of complexity in children's fantasy narratives. *Developmental Psychology, 13,* 377–388.

Braunwald, S. R. (1978). Context, word and meaning: Towards a communicational analysis of lexical acquisition. In A. Lock (Ed.), *Action, gesture and symbol.* London: Academic Press.

Bronson, W. (1981). *Toddlers' behaviors with agemates: Issues of interaction, cognition, and affects (Monographs on Infancy, Vol. 1).* Norwood, NJ: Ablex.

Brown, P., & Levinson, S. (1987). *Politeness: Some universals in language usage.* Cambridge, England: Cambridge University Press.

Bruner, J. S. (1975a). From communication to language: A psychological perspective. *Cognition, 3,* 255–287.

Bruner, J. S. (1975b). The ontogenesis of speech acts. *Journal of Child Language, 2,* 1–19.

Bruner, J. S. (1978). On prelinguistic prerequisites of speech. In R. N. Campbell & P. T. Smith (Eds.), *Recent advances in the psychology of language* (Vol. 4a., pp. 194–214). New York: Plenum Press.

Bruner, J. S. (1983). *Child's talk.* New York: Norton.

Bruner, J. S., & Sherwood, V. (1976). Early rule structure: The case of peekaboo. In J. S. Bruner, A. Jolly, & K. Sylva (Eds.), *Play: Its role in evolution and development.* London: Penguin Books.

Bryan, T., Donahue, M., Pearl, R., & Sturm, C. (1981). Learning disabled children's conversational skills: The "TV Talk Show." *Learning Disability Quarterly 4,* 250–259.

Camaioni, L., & Laicardi, C. (1985). Early social games and the acquisition of language. *British Journal of Developmental Psychology, 3,* 31–39.

Carnap, R. (1956). *Meaning and necessity* (2nd ed.). Chicago: University of Chicago Press.

Carpenter, R. L., Mastergeorge, A. M., & Coggins, T. E. (1983). The acquisition of communicative intentions in infants eight to fifteen months of age. *Language and Speech, 26,* 101–116.

Carter, A. L. (1975a). The transformation of sensorimotor morphemes into words: A case study of the development of "here" and "there." *Papers and Reports on Child Language Development, 10,* 31–48.

Carter, A. L. (1975b). The transformation of sensorimotor morphemes into words: A case study of the development of "more" and "mine." *Journal of Child Language, 2,* 233–250.

Carter, A. L. (1979). Prespeech meaning relations: An outline of one infant's sensorimotor morpheme development. In P. Fletcher & M. Garman (Ed.), *Language acquisition* (pp. 71–92). Cambridge, England: Cambridge University Press.

Cazden, C. (1970). The neglected situation in child language research and education. *Journal of Social Issues, 25,* 35–60.

Chapman, R. (1981). Mother-child interaction in the second year of life: Its role in language development. In R. Schiefelbusch & D. Bricker (Eds.), *Early language: Acquisition and intervention.* Baltimore: University Park Press.

Charney, R. (1980). Speech roles and the development of personal pronouns. *Journal of Child Language, 6,* 69–80.

Chiat, S. (1981). Context-specificity and generalization in the acquisition of pronominal distinctions. *Journal of Child Language, 8,* 75–91.

Chiat, S. (1986). Personal pronouns. In P. Fletcher & M. Garman (Eds.), *Language acquisition* (2nd edition, pp. 339–355). Cambridge, England: Cambridge University Press.

Chomsky, N. (1965). *Aspects of the theory of syntax.* Cambridge, MA: MIT Press.

Chomsky, M. (1990). Language and mind. In D. Mellor (Ed.), *Ways of communicating: The Darwin College lectures.* Cambridge, England: Cambridge University Press.

Clancy, P. (1986). The acquisition of communicative style in Japanese. In B. Schieffelin & E. Ochs (Eds.), *Language socialization across cultures* (pp. 213–250). Cambridge, England: Cambridge University Press.

Clark, E. V. (1978). Strategies for communicating. *Child Development, 49,* 953–959.

Clark, E. V., & Sengul, C. (1978). Strategies in the acquisition of deixis. *Journal of Child Language, 5,* 457–475.

Clark, H. H., & Clark, E. V. (1977). *Psychology and language: An introduction to psycholinguistics.* New York: Harcourt Brace.

Clark, H. H., & French, J. W. (1981). Telephone goodbyes. *Language in Society 10,* 1–19.

Clark, H. H., & Gerrig, R. J. (1983). Understanding old words with new meanings. *Journal of Verbal Learning and Verbal Behavior, 22,* 591–608.

Coggins, T. E., & Carpenter, R. (1978). The Communicative Intention Inventory: A system for observing and coding children's early intentional communication. *Applied Psycholinguistics, 2,* 235–251.

Collis, G., & Schaffer, H. R. (1975). Synchronization of visual attention in mother-infant pairs. *Journal of Child Psychology and Psychiatry, 16,* 315–320.

Corrigan, R. (1978). Language development a related to Stage 6 object permanence development. *Journal of Child Language, 5,* 173–189.

Corsaro, W. (1979). "We're friends, right?" Children's use of access rituals in a nursery school. *Language in Society 8,* 315–336.

Coulthard, R. M., & Ashby, M. C. (1976). A linguistic description of doctor–patient interviews. In M. Wadsworth and D. Robinson (Eds.), *Studies in everyday medical life.* London: Martin Robertson.

Dale, P. S. (1980). Is early pragmatic development measurable? *Journal of Child Language, 7,* 1–12.

Davidson, D. (1979). Truth and meaning. *Synthese, 17,* 304–323.

Della Corte, M., Benedict, H., & Klein, D. (1983). The relationship of pragmatic dimensions of mothers' speech to the referential-expressive distinction. *Journal of Child Language, 10,* 35–43.

Denny, R. (1985). Marking the interaction order. *Language in Society, 14,* 41–62.

De Temple, J., Wu, H. F., & Snow, C. E. (1991). Papa Pig just left for Pigtown: Length, explicitness, complexity, and narrativity of picture descriptions under varying instructions. *Discourse Processes, 14,* 469–495.

de Villiers, J. G., & de Villiers, P. A. (1973). Development of the use of word order in comprehension. *Journal of Psycholinguistic Research, 2,*331–341.

de Villiers, J. G., & de Villiers, P. A. (1978). *Language acquisition.* Cambridge, MA: Harvard University Press.

Dik, S. C. (1978). *Functional grammar.* London: Academic Press.
Donahue, M. (1984). Learning disabled children's conversational competence: An attempt to activate the inactive listener. *Applied Psycholinguistics 5*(1), 21–36.
Donahue, M., Pearl, R., & Bryan, T. (1980). Conversational competence in learning disabled children: Responses to inadequate messages. *Applied Psycholinguistics, 1,* 387–403.
Donahue, M., Pearl, R., & Bryan, T. (1983). Communicative competence in learning disabled children. In K. D. Gadow & I. Bialer (Eds.), *Advances in learning and behavior disabilities, Vol. 2,* (pp. 49–84). Greenwich, CT: JAI Press.
Dore, J. (1974). A pragmatic description of early language development. *Journal of Psycholinguistic Research, 3,* 343–350.
Dore, J. (1975). Holophrases, speech acts and language universals. *Journal of Child Language, 2,* 21–40.
Dore, J. (1976). Children's illocutionary acts. In R. Freedle (Ed.), *Discourse relations: Comprehension and production.* Hillsdale, NJ: Erlbaum.
Dore, J. (1978). Conditions on the acquisition of speech acts. In I. Markova (Ed.), *The social context of language.* Chichester, England: Wiley.
Dore, J. (1985). Holophrases revisited: their "logical" development from dialog. In M. D. Barrett (Ed.), *Children's single-word speech.* New York: Wiley.
Dore, J., Franklin, M. B., Miller, R. T., & Ramer, A. L. H. (1976). Transitional phenomena in early language acquisition. *Journal of Child Language, 3,* 13–28.
Dore, J., & McDermott, R. P. (1982). Linguistic indeterminacy and social context in utterance interpretation. *Language, 58,* 374–398.
Dorval, B., & Eckerman, C. O. (1984). Developmental trends in the quality of conversation achieved by small groups of acquainted peers. *Monographs of the Society for Research in Child Development, 49*(2), Serial #206.
Duncan, S., & Fiske, D. (1977). *Face-to-face interaction.* Hillsdale, NJ: Erlbaum.
Dundes, A., Leach, J. W., & Özkök, B. (1972). The strategy of Turkish boys' verbal dueling rhymes. In J. J. Gumperz and D. Hymes, (Eds.), *Directions in sociolinguistics: The ethnography of communication.* New York: Holt, Rinehart and Winston.
Dunn, J., & Kendrick, C. (1982). *Siblings: Love, envy and understanding.* Cambridge, MA: Harvard University Press.
Eckerman, C., & Stein, M. (1982). The toddler's emerging interactive skills. In K. H. Rubin & H. S. Ross (Eds.), *Peer relations and social skills in childhood.* New York: Springer-Verlag.
Eckerman, C. O., Whatley, J. L., & Kutz, S. L. (1975). Growth of social play with peers during the second year of life. *Developmental Psychology, 11,* 42–49.
Edwards, D. (1978). Social relations and early language. In A. Lock (Ed.), *Action, gesture and symbol.* London: Academic Press.
Ervin-Tripp, S. (1979). Children's verbal turn-taking. In. E. Ochs & B. Schieffelin (Eds.), *Developmental pragmatics.* New York: Academic Press.
Ervin-Tripp, S., & Gordon, D. (1986). The development of requests. In R. L. Schiefelbusch (Ed.), *Language competence: Assessment and intervention* (pp. 61–95). San Diego, CA: College Hill.
Evans, M. A. (1987). Discourse characteristics of reticent children. *Applied Psycholinguistics 8*(2), 171–184.
Feagans, L., Garvey, G. J., & Golinkoff, R. (Eds.). (1984). *The origins and growth of communication.* Norwood, NJ: Ablex.

Fillmore, C. J. (1971). Verbs of judging: An exercise in semantic description. In C. J. Fillmore & D. T. Langendoen (Eds.), *Studies in linguistic semantics* (p. 273–289). New York: Holt, Rinehart & Winston.

Garvey, C. (1975). Requests and responses in children's speech. *Journal of Child Language, 2,* 41–63.

Gazdar, G. (1979). *Pragmatics: Implicature, presupposition and logical form.* New York: Academic Press.

Gazdar, G. (1981). Speech act assignment. In A. K. Joshi, B. L. Weber, & I. A. Sag (Eds.), *Elements of discourse understanding* (pp. 64–83. Cambridge, England: Cambridge University Press.

Gibbs, R. W. (1984). Literal meaning and psychological reality. *Cognitive Science, 8,* 275–304.

Givon, T. (1989). *Mind, code, and context.* Hillsdale, NJ: Erlbaum.

Gleason, J. B., Perlman, R., & Greif, E. (1984). What's the magic word: Learning language through politeness routines. *Discourse Processes, 7,* 493–902.

Godard, D. (1977). Same setting, different norms: Phone call beginnings in France and the United States. *Language in Society 6,* 209–219.

Goldfield, B. (1987). The contributions of child and caregiver to referential and expressive language. *Applied Psycholinguistics, 8,* 267–280.

Goldfield, B., & Snow, C. E. (1992). Who's cousin Arthur's daddy?: The acquisition of knowledge about kinship. *First Language, 12,* 187–205.

Golinkoff, R. M. (1983). The preverbal negotiation of failed messages: Insights into the transition period. In R. M. Golinkoff (Ed.), *The transition from prelinguistic to linguistic communication* (pp. 57–78). Hillsdale, NJ: Erlbaum.

Golinkoff, R. M., & Gordon, L. (1983). In the beginning was the word: A history of the study of language acquisition. In R. M. Golinkoff (Ed.), *The transition from prelinguistic to linguistic communication.* Hillsdale, NJ: Erlbaum.

Gordon, D., & Lakoff, C. (1971). Conversational postulates. *Papers from the seventh regional meeting* (pp. 63–84). Chicago: Chicago Linguistic Society.

Greatbatch, D. (1988). A turn-taking system for British news interviews. *Language in society, 15,* 401–430.

Greenfield, P. M., & Smith, J. H. (1976). *The structure of communication in early language development.* New York: Academic Press.

Greif, E., & Gleason, J. B. (1980). Hi, thanks and good-bye: More routine information. *Language in society, 9,* 159–167.

Grice, H. P. (1957). Meaning. *Philosophical Review, 66,* 377–388.

Grice, H. P. (1968). Utterer's meaning, sentence-meaning, and word-meaning. *Foundations of Language, 4,* 225–242.

Grice, H. P. (1969). Utterer's meaning and intentions. *The Philosophical Review, 78,* 147–177.

Grice, H. P. (1975). Logic and conversation. In P. Cole & J. L. Morgan (Eds.),*Syntax and Semantics, Vol. 3: Speech acts.* New York: Academic Press.

Griffiths, P. (1985). The communicative functions of children's single-word speech. In M. Barrett (Ed.), *Children's single-word speech.* New York: Wiley.

Gruber, J. (1973). Correlations between the syntactic construction of the child and adult. In C. Ferguson & D. Slobin (Eds.), *Studies in child language development.* New York: Holt, Rinehart & Winston.

Hall, E. T. (1959). *The silent language.* New York: Doubleday.
Halliday, M., & Hasan, R. (1976). *Cohesion in English.* London: Longman.
Halliday, M.A.K. (1975). *Learning to mean—Explorations in the development of language.* London: Edward Arnold.
Halliday, M.A.K. (1985). *An introduction to functional grammar.* London: Edward Arnold.
Harding, C. G. (1983). Setting the stage for language acquisition: communication development in the first year. In R. M. Golinkoff (Ed.). *The transition from prelinguistic to linguistic communication.* Hillsdale, NJ: Erlbaum.
Harding, C. G., & Golinkoff, R. M. (1979). The origins of intentional vocalizations in prelinguistic infants. *Child Development, 50,* 33–40.
Harris, M., Barrett, M., Jones, D., & Brookes, S. (1988). Linguistic input and early word meaning. *Journal of Child Language, 15,* 77–94.
Harrison, B. (1972). *Meaning and structure: An essay in the philosophy of language.* New York: Harper & Row.
Hemphill, L. (1987, April). *Conversational abilities in mentally retarded and normally developing children.* Paper presented at the biennial meeting of the Society for Research in Child Development, Baltimore, MD.
Hemphill, L., Picardi, N., & Tager-Flusberg, H. (1991). Narrative as an index of communicative competence in mildly mentally retarded children. *Applied Psycholinguistics, 12,* 263–279.
Hemphill, L. & Siperstein, G. N. (1990). Conversational competence and peer response to mildly retarded children. *Journal of Educational Psychology, 82*(1), 1–7.
Hess, L. J., & Johnston, J. R. (1988). Acquisition of back channel listener response to adequate messages. *Discourse Processes 11,* 319–355.
Hicks, D. (1991). Kinds of texts: Genre skills among first graders from two communities. In S. McCabe & C. Peterson (Eds.), *Developing narrative structure* (p. 55–88). Hillsdale, NJ: Erlbaum.
Hinde, R. (Ed.). (1972). *Non-verbal communication.* Cambridge, England: Cambridge University Press.
Hudson, J., & Nelson, K. (1986). Repeated encounters of a similar kind: Effects of familiarity on children's autobiographical memory. *Cognitive Development, 1,* 232–271.Hudson, J., & Shapiro, L. (1991). From knowing to telling: The development of children's scripts, stories, and personal narratives. In A. McCabe & C. Peterson (Eds.), *Developing narrative structure* (pp. 89–136). Hillsdale, NJ: Erlbaum.
Hudson, R. A. (1990). *English word grammar.* Oxford: Basil Blackwell.
Hymes, D. (1971). *Towards communicative competence.* Philadelphia: University of Pennsylvania Press.
Ingram, D. (1971). Transitivity in child language. *Language, 47,* 889–910.
Ingram, D. (1989). *First language acquisition.* Cambridge, England: Cambridge University Press.
Jisa, H. (1984/1985). Use of *et pis* ("and then"). *First Language 5,* 169–184.
Kalish, D. (1967). Semantics. In D. Edwards (Ed.), *Encyclopdia of philosophy VII* (pp. 348–258). New York: Collier MacMillan.
Karmiloff-Smith, A. (1979). *A functional approach to child language.* Cambridge, England: Cambridge University Press.
Kaye, K., & Charney, R. (1980). How mothers maintain dialogue with two-year-olds. In D. R. Olson (Ed.),*The social foundations of language and thought.* New York: Norton.

Kaye, K., & Charney, R. (1981). Conversational assymetry between mothers and children. *Journal of Child Language, 8,* 35–50.
Keenan, E. O., & Klein, E. (1975). Conversational competence in children. *Journal of Child Language, 1,* 163–184.
Kellerman, K., Broetzmann, S., Lim, T.-S., & Kitao, K. (1989). The conversation MOP: Scenes in the stream of discourse. *Discourse Processes 12,* 27–62.
Kemper, S., Kynette, D., Rash, S., O'Brien, K., & Sprott, R. (1989). Life-span changes to adults' language: Effects of memory and genre. *Applied Psycholinguistics* 10, 49–66.
Kempson, R. M. (1975). *Presupposition and the delimitation of semantics.* Cambridge, England: Cambridge University Press.
Kendon, A. (Ed.). (1981). *Nonverbal communication, interaction, and gesture.* The Hague: Mouton Publishers.
Key, M. R. (1975). *Paralinguistics and kinesics: Nonverbal communication.* Metuchen, NJ: Scarecrow Press.
Kintsch, W. (1974). *The representation of meaning in memory.* Hillsdale, NJ: Erlbaum.
Kintsch, W., & van Dijk, T. (1978). Toward a model of text comprehension and production. *Psychological Review, 85,* 363–394.
Kluwin, T. N. (1983). Discourse in deaf classrooms: The structure of teaching episodes. *Discourse Processes, 6,* 275–93.
Knapp, M. L. (1972). *Nonverbal communication in human interaction.* New York: The Free Press.
Krashen, S. (1980). The input hypothesis. *Georgetown University Roundtable on Language and Linguistics, 1980.* Washington, DC: Georgetown University Press.
Labov, W. (1972). *Sociolinguistic patterns.* Philadelphia: University of Pennsylvania Press.
Labov, W., & Fanshel, D. (1978). *Therapeutic discourse: Psychotherapy as conversation.* New York: Academic Press.
Lakoff, G. (1982). Categories and cognitive models. *Berkeley Cognitive Science Report.* University of California, Berkeley.
Lakoff, G. (1990). The invariance hypothesis: Is abstract reason based on image schemas? *Cognitive Linguistics, 1,* 39–74.
Lamb, M. E., & Sherrod, L. R. (1983). (Eds.). *Infant social cognition.* Hillsdale, NJ: Erlbaum.
Langacker, R. (1987). *Foundations of cognitive grammar.* Stanford, CA: Stanford University Press.
Lemmon, E. J. (1966). Sentences, statements, and propositions. In B. Williams & A. Montefiore (Eds.), *British analytical philosophy* (pp. 87–107). London: Routledge & Kegan Paul.
Levinson, S. C. (1983). *Pragmatics.* Cambridge, England: Cambridge University Press.
Lewis, D. (1972). General semantics. In D. Davidson & G. Harman, (Eds.), *Semantics of natural language* (pp. 169–218). Boston: D. Reidel Publishing.
Lewis, M., Young, G., Brooks, J., & Michalson, L. (1975). The beginning of friendship. In M. Lewis & L. A. Rosenbloom (Eds.), *Friendship and peer relations.* New York: Wiley.
Lieven, E. V. M. (1978a). Conversations between mothers and young children: Individual differences and their possible implications for the study of language learning. In N. Waterson & C. Snow (Eds.), *The development of communication.* Chichester, England: John Wiley & sons.

Lieven, E.V.M. (1978b). Turn-taking and pragmatics: Two issues in early child language. In R. N. Campbell & P. T. Smith (Eds.), *Recent advances in the psychology of language: Language development and mother-child interaction.* New York: Plenum.

Lock, A. (1980). *The guided reinvention of language.* London: Academic Press.

Lucariello, J., Kyratzis, A., & Engel, S. (1986). In K. Nelson (Ed.), *Event knowledge: Structure and function in development.* Hillsdale, NJ: Erlbaum.

Lusczc, M., & Bacharach, V. (1983). The emergence of communicative competence: Detection of conversational topics. *Journal of Child Language, 10,* 623–637.

Lyons, J. (1981). *Language, meaning and context.* London: Fontana.

McCune-Nicolich, L. (1981). The cognitive basis of relational words in the single word period. *Journal of Child Language, 8,* 15–34.

McCutchen, D., & Perfetti, C. A. (1982). Coherence and connectedness in the development of discourse production. *Text, 2,* 113–139.

McGhee-Bidlack, B. (1991). The development of noun definitions: A metalinguistic analysis. *Journal of Child Language, 18,* 417–434.

McHoul, A. (1978). The organization of turns at formal talk in the classroom. *Language in Society, 7,* 183–213.

McShane, J. (1980). *Learning to talk.* Cambridge, England: Cambridge University Press

Maratsos, M. (1976). *The use of definite and indefinite reference in young children.* Cambridge, England: Cambridge University Press.

Menn, L., & Haselkorn, S. (1977). Now you see it, now you don't: Tracing the development of communicative competence. In J. Kegl (Ed.), *Proceedings of the Seventh Annual Meeting of the Northeast Linguistic Society.*

Merrit, M. (1976). On questions following questions in service encounters. *Language in Society, 5,* 315–357.

Mervis, C., & Mervis, C. (1988). Role of adult input in young children's category evolution: An observational study. *Journal of Child Language, 15,* 257–272.

Miller, G. A. (1970, June). Four philosophical problems of psycholinguists. *Philosophy of Science,* 183–199.

Minami, M., & McCabe, A. (1991). *Haiku* as a discourse regulation device: A stanza analysis of Japanese children's personal narratives. *Language in Society, 20*(4), 577–599.

Mishler, E. (1984). *The discourse of medicine: Dialectics of medical interviews.* Norwood, NJ: Ablex.

Moerk, E. L. (1975). Verbal interaction between children and their mothers during the preschool years. *Developmental Psychology, 11,* 788–794

Moerk, E. L. (1976). Processes of language teaching and training in the interaction of mother–child dyads. *Child Development, 47,* 1064–1078.

Montague, R. (1968). Pragmatics. In R. Klibansky (Ed.), *Contemporary philosophy* (pp. 102–122). Florence: La Nuova Italia Editrice.

Morris, C. (1938). Foundations of the theory of signs. In. O. Neurath (Ed.), *International encyclopedia of unified science 1* (pp. 77–138). Chicago: University of Chicago Press.

Murray, S. O. (1985). Toward a model of members' methods for recognizing interruptions. *Language in Society, 14,* 31–40.

Nelson, K. (1973). Structure and strategy in learning to talk. *Monograph of the Society for Research in Child Development, 38,* (1–2 Serial No.).

Nelson, K. (1975a). Individual differences in early semantic and syntactic development. *Annals of the New York Academy of Sciences, 263,* 132–139.

Nelson, K. (1975b). The nominal shift in semantic-syntactic development. *Cognitive Psychology, 7,* 461–479.
Nelson, K. (1976). Some attributes of adjectives used by young children. *Cognition, 4,* 13–30.
Nelson, K. (1978). Early speech in its communicative context. In F. D. Minifie & L. L. Lloyd (Eds.), *Communicative and cognitive abilities—Early behavioral assessment* (pp. 443–473). Baltimore: University Park Press.
Nelson, K. (1983). The derivation of concepts and categories from event representations. In E. Skolnick (Ed.), *New trends in conceptual representation: Challenges to Piaget's theory.* Hillsdale, NJ: Erlbaum.
Nelson, K. (1985). *Making sense: The acquisition of shared meaning.* New York: Academic Press.
Nelson, K. (1986). *Event knowledge: Structure and function in development.* Hillsdale, NJ: Erlbaum.
Nelson, K., & Lucariello, J. (1985). The development of meaning in first words. In M. Barrett (Ed.), *Children's single-word speech.* New York: Wiley.
Nelson, K. E. (1977). Facilitating children's syntax acquisition. *Developmental Psychology, 13* 101–107.
Nelson, K. E., Denninger, M. S., Bonvillian, J. D., Kaplan, B. J., & Baker, N. D. (1984). Maternal input adjustment and non-adjustments as related to children's linguistic advances and to language acquisition theories. In A. D. Pelligrini & T. D. Yawkey (Eds.), *The development of oral and written languages: Readings in developmental applied linguistics* (pp. 31–56). New York: Ablex.
Ninio, A. (1983, May). *A pragmatic approach to early language acquisition.* Paper presented at the Study Group on Crosscultural and Crosslinguistic Aspects of Native Language Acquisition. The Institute for Advanced Studies, Jerusalem.
Ninio, A. (1985). The meaning of children's first words: Evidence from the input. *Journal of Pragmatics, 9,* 527–546.
Ninio, A. (1992a). The relation of children's single word utterances to single word utterances in the input. *Journal of Child Language, 19,* 87–110.
Ninio, A. (1992b). Is early speech situational? An examination of some current theories about the relation of early utterances to the context. In D. Messer & G. Turner, (Eds.), *Critical influences on language development* (pp. 23–39). New York: Macmillan.
Ninio, A. (1993). On the fringes of the system: Children's acquisition of syntactically isolated forms at the onset of speech. *First Language, 13,* 291–313.
Ninio, A. (1994a). Predicting the order of acquisition of three-word constructions by the complexity of their dependency structure. *First Language, 14,* 119–152.
Ninio, A. (1994b). Expression of communicative intents in the single-word period and the vocabulary spurt. In K. Nelson & Z. Reger (Eds.), *Children's Language* (Vol. 8, pp. 103–124). Hillsdale, NJ: Erlbaum.
Ninio, A., & Bruner, J. S. (1978). The achievement and antecedents of labelling. *Journal of Child Language, 5,* 1–15.
Ninio, A., & Snow, C. (1988). Language acquisition through language use: The functional sources of children's early utterances. In Y. Levi, I. Schlesinger, & M.D.S. Braine (Eds.), *Perspectives on a theory of language acquisition* (pp. 11–30). Hillsdale, NJ: Erlbaum.

Ninio, A., Snow, C. E., Pan, B. A., & Rollins, P. (1994). Classifying communicative acts in children's interactions. *Journal of Communications Disorders, 27,* 158–187.

Ninio, A., & Wheeler, P. (1984a). Functions of speech in mother-infant interaction. In L. Feagans, G. J. Garvey, & R. Golinkoff (Eds.), The origins and growth of communication. Norwood, NJ: Ablex.

Ninio, A., & Wheeler, P. (1984b). A manual for classifying verbal communicative acts in mother-infant interaction. *Working Papers in Developmental Psychology, No. 1.* Jerusalem: The Martin and Vivian Levin Center, Hebrew University. Reprinted as *Transcript Analysis, 1986, 3,* 1–82.

Ochs, E. (1988). *Culture and language development: Language acquisition and language socialization in a Samoan village.* Cambridge, England: Cambridge University Press.

Peterson, C., & Dodsworth, P. (1991). A longitudinal analysis of young children's cohesion and noun specification in narratives. *Journal of Child Language, 18,* 397–415.

Peterson, C., & McCabe, A. (1983). *Developmental psycholinguistics: Three ways of looking at a child's narrative.* New York Plenum.

Peterson, C., & McCabe, A. (1987). The connective *and. First Language, 8,* 19–28.

Phillips, S. (1976). Some sources of cultural variability in the regulation of talk. *Language in Society, 5,* 81–95.

Piaget, J. (1926). *The language and thought of the child.* London: Routledge & Kegan Paul.

Pine, J. (1990). *Individual differences in early language development and their relationship to maternal style.* Unpublished doctoral dissertation, University of Manchester.

Pine, J. & Lieven, E. (1990). Referential style at thirteen months. Why age-defined cross-sectional measures are inappropriate for the study of strategy differences in early language development. *Journal of Child Language, 17,* 625–631.

Pride, J. B. (1969). Analysing classroom procedures. In H. Fraser and W. R. O'Donnell (Eds.), *Applied Linguistics and the Teaching of English,* London: Longman.

Prinz, P. M., & Prinz, E. A. (1985). If only you could hear what I see: Discourse development in Sign Language. *Discourse Processes, 8,* 1–19.

Ratner, N., & Bruner, J. S. (1978). Games, social exchange and the acquisition of language. *Journal of Child Language, 5,* 391–401.

Rheingold, H. L., Hay, D. F., & West, M. J. (1976). Sharing in the second year of life. *Child Development, 47,* 1148–1158.

Ricard, R., & Snow, C. E. (1990). Language skill in and out of context: Evidence from children's picture description. *Journal of Applied Developmental Psychology, 11,* 251–266.

Rogdon, M., Jankowsky, W., & Alenskas, L. (1977). A multi-functional approach to single-word usage. *Journal of Child Language, 4,* 23–44.

Rollins, P., Pan, B., Conti-Ramsden, G., & Snow, C. E. (in press). Communicative skills in specific language impaired children: A comparison with their language-matched siblings. *Journal of Communications Disorders.*

Ross, H. S., & Kay, D. A. (1980). The origins of social games. In K. H. Rubin (Ed.) *Children's play: New directions for child development* (Vol. 9). San Francisco: Jossey-Bass.

Rubin, K. H., & Ross, H. S. (Eds.). (1982). *Peer relations and social skills in childhood.* New York: Springer-Verlag.

Rumelhart, D. E. (1979). Some problems with the notion of literal meaning. In A. Ortony (Ed.), *Metaphor and thought* (pp. 78–90). Cambridge, England: Cambridge University Press.
Ryan, J. (1974). Early language development: towards a communicational analysis. In M.P.M. Richards (Ed.), *The integration of a child into a social world*. London: Cambridge University Press.
Sachs, J. (1982). Don't interrupt!": Preschoolers' entry into ongoing conversations. In C. E. Johnson & C. L. Thew (Eds.), *Proceedings of the Second International Congress for the Study of Child Language, Vol. 1*. Washington, DC: University Press of America.
Sachs, J., Anselmi, D., & McCollam, K. (1990, July). *Young children's awareness of presupposition based on community awareness*. Paper presented at the International Association for the Study of Child Language, Budapest.
Sachs, J., Brown, R., & Salerno, R. A. (1976). Adults' speech to children. In W. von Raffler-Engel & Y. Lebrun (Eds.), *Baby talk and infant speech*. Lisse, Netherlands: Swetz & Zeitlinger.
Sacks, H. (1974). An analysis of the course of a joke's telling in conversation. In R. Bauman and J. Sherzer (Eds.), *Explorations in the Ethnography of Speaking*, Cambridge, England: Cambridge University Press.
Sacks, H., Schegloff, E., & Jefferson, G. (1974). A simplest systematics for the organization of turn-taking for conversation. *Language, 50*, 596–735.
Saussure, F. de (1922/1983). *Course in general linguistics*. London: Duckworth.
Schegloff, E. (1979). Identification and recognition in telephone conversation openings. In G. Psathas (Ed.), *Everyday Language: Studies in Ethnomethodology*. New York: Irvington.
Schegloff, E., & Sacks, H. (1973). Opening up closings. *Semiotics, 8*, 289–327.
Schieffelin, B. (1990). *The give and take of everyday life: Language socialization of Kaluli children*. Cambridge, England: Cambridge University Press.
Schieffelin, B., & Ochs, E. (Eds.). (1986). *Language socialization across cultures*. Cambridge, England: Cambridge University Press.
Schley, S., & Snow, C. (1992). The conversational skills of school-aged children. *Social Development, 1*, 18–35.
Scott, C. (1984). Adverbial connectivity in conversations of children 6 to 12. *Journal of Child Language, 11*, 423–452.
Scoville, R. (1984). Development of the intention to communicate: The eye of the beholder. In L. Feagans, G. J. Garvey, & R. Golinkoff (Eds.), *The origins and growth of communication*. Norwood, NJ: Ablex.
Searle, J. R. (1969). *Speech acts*. Cambridge, England: Cambridge University Press.
Searle, J. R. (1975). Indirect speech acts. In P. Cole & J. L. Morgan (Eds.), *Syntax and semantics. Vol. 3: Speech acts*. New York: Academic Press.
Searle, J. R. (1979). Metaphor. In A. Ortony (Ed.), *Metaphor and thought* (pp. 92–123). Cambridge, England: Cambridge University Press.
Shatz, M. (1982). On mechanisms of language acquisition: Can features of the communicative environment account for development? In E. Wanner & L. R. Gleitman (Eds.), *Language acquisition: The state of the art*. Cambridge, England: Cambridge University Press.

Sinclair, J., & Coulthard, R. M. (1975). *Towards an analysis of discourse: The English used by teachers and pupils.* London: Oxford University Press.

Snow, C. E. (1972). Mothers' speech to children learning language. *Child Development, 43,* 549–565.

Snow, C. E. (1977a). The development of conversation between mothers and babies. *Journal of Child Language, 4* 1–122.

Snow, C. E. (1977b). Mothers' speech research: from input to interaction. In C. E. Snow & C. Ferguson (Eds.), *Talking to children.* Cambridge, England: Cambridge University Press.

Snow, C. E. (1979). The role of social interaction in language acquisition. In W. A. Collins (Ed.), *Minnesota Symposia on Child Psychology* (Vol. 12, pp. 157–182). Hillsdale, NJ: Erlbaum.

Snow, C. E. (1990). The development of definitional skill. *Journal of Child Language, 17,* 697–710.

Snow, C. E. (1995). Issues in the study of input: Fine-tuning, universality, individual and developmental differences, and necessary causes. In P. Fletcher & B. MacWhinney (Eds.), *Handbook of Child Language.* London: Cambridge University Press.

Snow, C. E., Dubber, C., & de Blauw, A. (1982). Routines in parent-child interaction. In L. Feagans & D. Farran (Eds.), *The language of children reared in poverty: Implications for evaluation and intervention.* New York: Academic Press.

Snow, C. E., Pan, B., Herman, J., & Imbens-Bailey, A. (1993). Learning how to say what one means: A longitudinal study of children's speech act use. Unpublished manuscript, Harvard Graduate School of Education.

Snow, C. E., Perlmann, R., Gleason, J. B., & Hooshyar, N. (1990). Developmental perspectives on politeness: Sources of children's knowledge. *Journal of Pragmatics, 14,* 289–305.

Snyder, L. D. (1978). Communicative and cognitive abilities and disabilities in the sensorimotor period. *Merrill-Palmer Quarterly, 24,* 161–180.

Sperber, D., & Wilson, D. (1981). Irony and the use/mention distinction. In P. Cole (Ed.) *Radical pragmatics* (pp. 295– 318). New York: Academic Press.

Stenning, K., & Michell, L. (1985). Learning how to tell a good story: The development of content and language in children's telling of one tale. *Discourse Processes, 8,* 261–279.

Stephany, U. (1986). Modality. In P. Fletcher & M. Garman (Eds.), *Language acquisition* (2nd ed., pp. 375–400). Cambridge, England: Cambridge University Press.

Stevenson, R. (1988). *Models of language development.* Milton Keynes: Open University.

Strawson, P. F. (1970). *Meaning and truth.* Oxford: Clarendon.

Streeck, J. (1980). Speech acts in interaction: A critique of Searle. *Discourse Processes, 3,* 133–154.

Sugarman-Bell, S. (1978). Some organizational aspects of pre-verbal communication. In I. Markova (Ed.), *The social context of language.* Chichester, England: John Wiley & Sons.

Tomasello, M. (1992). *First verbs: A case study of early grammatical development.* Cambridge, England: Cambridge University Press.

Tomasello, M., & Todd, J. (1983). Joint attention and early lexical acquisition style. *First Language, 4,* 197–212.

Tough, J. (1977). *The development of meaning.* New York: Halsted Press.

Tracy, K. (1983). The issue-event distinction: A rule of conversation and its scope convention. *Human Communication Research, 9,* 320–334.

Tracy, K. (1984). Staying on topic: An explication of conversational relevance. *Discourse Processes, 7,* 447–464.

Trevarthen, C. B. (1977). Descriptive analyses of infant communicative behavior. In H. R. Schaffer, (Ed.), *Studies in mother-infant interaction: The Loch Lamond Symposium.* London: Academic Press.

Trevarthen, C. B. (1979). Instincts for human understanding and for cultural cooperation: Their development in infancy. In M. von Cranach, K. Foppa, W. Lepenies, & D. Ploog (Eds.), *Human ethology: Claims and limits of a new discipline.* Cambridge, England: Cambridge University Press.

Trevarthen, C., & Hubley, P. (1979). Secondary intersubjectivity. In A. Lock (Ed.), *Action, gesture and symbol.* London: Academic Press.

Turner, R. (1972). Some formal properties of therapy talk. In D. Sudnow (Ed.), *Studies in social interaction.* New York: The Free Press.

Umiker-Sebeok, D. J. (1979). Preschool children's intraconversational narratives. *Journal of Child Language, 6,* 91–109.

van Valin, R. (1991). Functionalist linguistic theory and language acquisition *First Language, 31* 7–40.

Vandell, D. L. (1977). *Boy toddlers' social interaction with mothers, fathers, and peers.* Unpublished doctoral dissertation, Boston University, Boston.

Vygotsky, L. (1978). *Mind in society: The development of higher psychological processes.* M. Cole, Ed. Cambridge, MA: Harvard University Press.

Wales, R. (1986). Deixis. In P. Fletcher & M. Garman (Eds.), *Language acquisition* (2nd ed. 401–428). Cambridge, England: Cambridge University Press.

Wardhaugh, R. (1985). *How conversation works.* Oxford: Basil Blackwell/Andre Deutsch.

Watson, R. (1985). Towards a theory of definition. *Journal of Child Language, 12,* 181–197.

Webb, P. A., & Abramson, A. (1976). Stages of egocentrism in children's use of "this" and "that": A different point of view. *Journal of Child Language, 3,* 349–367.

Weisenberger, J. L. (1976). A choice of words: Two-year-old speech from a situational point of view. *Journal of Child Language, 3,* 275–281.

Wells, G. (1985). *Language development in the pre-school years.* Cambridge, England: Cambridge University Press.

White, S. (1989). Backchannels across cultures: A study of Americans and Japanese. *Language in Society, 18,* 59–76.

Wiggins, D. (1971). On sentence-sense, word-sense and difference of word-sense. In D. D. Steinberg, & L. A. Jakobovits (Eds.), *Semantics* (pp. 14–34). Cambridge, England: Cambridge University Press.

Wittgenstein, L. (1953). *Philosophical investigations.* Oxford: Basil Blackwell.

Wu, H. F., De Temple, J. M., Herman, J. A., & Snow, C. E. (1994). L'animal qui fait oink! oink!: Bilingual children's oral and written picture descriptions in English and French under varying circumstances. *Discourse Processes, 18,* 141–164.

Zinober, B. W., & Martlew, M. (1985). The development of communicative gestures. In M. Barrett (Ed.), *Children's single-word speech* (pp. 183–215). New York: Wiley.

PART V

RESEARCH METHODOLOGY AND APPLICATIONS

CHAPTER 12

METHODOLOGY IN THE STUDY OF LANGUAGE ACQUISITION: A MODULAR APPROACH

Stephen Crain and Kenneth Wexler

I. INTRODUCTION

The study of language acquisition within the framework of generative grammar has advanced rapidly in the last decade, reaching a new level of maturity. Research has profited from discussion of both theoretical and empirical issues. In particular, the argument from the poverty of the stimulus (and its implications for language learnability and innateness) has provided a firm theoretical foundation for much recent empirical work. Accordingly, a fundamental goal of current empirical investigations is to understand language learnability as well as language development.

The development of a new set of theoretical ideas in a field often has important ramifications for research methodology. After all, methodology is intertwined with theory in nontrivial ways. It might very well happen, however, that the development of appropriate experimental methodology does not keep pace with advances in theory. In our opinion, exactly this state of affairs characterizes much of the contemporary study of generative-based language acquisition. The conceptual and theoretical framework of generative grammar, including its arguments concerning learnability and innateness, have been incorporated into the study of language acquisition. In many cases, however, methodologies appropriate to traditional models of *language learning* continue to be used, although the theoretical model underlying the research is generative.

Handbook of Child Language Acquisition

The purpose of this chapter is to investigate the methodological desiderata for the study of language acquisition within the generative framework. In pursuit of this goal, we offer a model of the language apparatus that is responsive to the issues of learnability and innateness. The model guides us toward an understanding of the methodologies that are needed to study generative-based language acquisition; it is also instructive in explaining why the methodologies used by traditional empiricist-based models of language acquisition should not be imported wholesale for this endeavor. We will not discuss the reasons for thinking that the generative framework, including the arguments concerning learnability and innateness, is itself correct. There is a large literature on this topic; we will simply assume its correctness.

To focus our discussion, we consider three examples from the generative-based language acquisition literature. Although we are critical of the methodological strategies used in these researches, we should stress that we agree with much of the theoretical underpinnings of the authors of the papers we criticize. In particular, the authors assume that there is a level of grammatical representation that is largely innate in the child. Because traditional empiricist-based studies of language development do not share this most basic assumption about the theoretical basis of language acquisition, it should be understood that such studies are even further removed from the issues we raise concerning the relationship of method and theory.

II. COMPETING MODELS OF THE LANGUAGE PROCESSING SYSTEM

The model we advocate makes two fundamental assumptions. First, it assumes that the human language processing system is modular. Broadly speaking, the language apparatus is modular in the sense that it is supported by special brain structures and it operates according to principles that are specific to it and not shared by other cognitive systems. In particular, language structure is not penetrated by general cognitive mechanisms that are used to represent and process real-world knowledge (see Fodor, 1983). As a consequence, considerations about the plausibility of sentences, for example, do not influence the grammatical representations that people construct for them. This is why people can readily judge sentences to be funny or false. To take a simple example, when we read or hear a sentence like *Mice chase cats,* we do not attempt to put the words together to make the sentence express a true proposition; if we did we would interpret the sentence *Mice chase cats* to mean that cats chase mice. Instead, we take the writer or speaker to have said something false.

We would extend the notion of modularity. In our view, the architecture within the language processing system is also modular; the primitives and principles of the phonology, syntax, and semantics are represented in autonomous subcomponents of the language processing system. We will call this representational modularity.[1]

Besides representational modularity, there is a second fundamental assumption of the model we advocate. On this model, the language processing system of a child is essentially the same as that of an adult.[2] One of the main goals of recent work has been to verify this claim, at least about the acquisition of syntactic knowledge, and to explain any differences between child and adult grammar that are revealed in these studies. Maximizing the similarities between children's cognitive systems and those of adults is needed in part to explain the learnability problem—why all children successfully converge on an adult linguistic system despite the considerable latitude in their linguistic experience. To the extent that the cognitive mechanisms of children and adults can be shown to be similar, the problem of learnability does not arise.

More generally, these joint assumptions form the basis for a model of the language processing system that we call the modularity matching model. By the modularity matching model, we mean that the principles of any module for a child are essentially identical to the principles of the corresponding module for an adult.

According to the modularity matching (MM) model, all of the linguistic abilities of a child are the same as an adult's. Not only do we assume that children have access to universal grammar, just as adults do, we also make the more controversial assumption that children are equivalent to adults in the mechanisms they use to process language; that is, they have access to a universal parser. The assumption of equivalence in the processing capabilities of children and adults is not generally accepted, even within the generative approach to language acquisition. We take this to be the null hypothesis, however. To show that a child's linguistic system is different from an adult's, it is necessary to prove that the null hypothesis is wrong, whether this concerns knowledge of syntax or semantics, or the properties of any performance mechanism.

There is another view of the relation between behavior and mind. This view has its roots in classical empiricist psychology. The alternative to the modularity matching model views linguistic behavior as determined by a competition among dif-

[1]There is another sense of modularity, which can be called processing modularity. On this view, the subcomponents of the language faculty do not interact in computing and processing grammatical representations. Rather, structural descriptions (more often than not, partial structural descriptions) are first computed at lower levels of representation and the results are then transferred to higher levels (for more details, see Crain, & Shankweiler, 1991; Crain, Shankweiler, Macaruso, & Bar-Shalom, 1990). Crucially, the operations at higher levels do not influence the representations that are constructed at lower levels.

[2]As we conceive it, in addition to principles of grammar, the language processing system encompasses the system of verbal working memory and the mechanisms used in parsing sentences and in resolving ambiguities.

ferent variables. From this perspective, no one component of the language apparatus, not even grammar, has a special status such that it preempts other factors. Instead, the principles of grammar can be overridden by other forces contributing to behavior. We call this viewpoint the competing factors model. To take an example, many proponents of the competing factors model maintain that children have a bias to interpret a sentence so as to make it true in a discourse context; this bias weighs in against the interpretation given by children's grammatical principles if the sentence is false on this interpretation. This would not happen on the modularity matching model.[3]

According to one class of competing factors models, principles of universal grammar are not counted among the contributors to behavior. We have in mind connectionist models of acquisition and processing (e.g., MacWhinney & Bates, 1990). On such models, linguistic behavior is determined by a competition among cues present in the input. However, some proponents of competing factors models invoke linguistic principles and hold many of the basic assumptions of the generative framework, including the assumption that many linguistic principles are innately specified.

It seems to us that all variants of the competing factors (CF) model are inconsistent with the assumptions about the modular architecture of the language faculty that underlie current linguistic and psycholinguistic theory.[4] Yet the CF model remains a popular view, probably the majority view. We believe that its methodological assumptions underlie most psycholinguistic research, including both studies of language acquisition and studies of adult sentence processing. Its sway is so strong that even people who are convinced by the particular arguments of linguistic theory nevertheless retreat to the CF model when they interpret the findings of their experimental investigations of psycholinguistic issues.

Here is the major methodological assumption of the competing factors model as it appears in the literature on language acquisition: Suppose that there are two structures, X and Y, that are similar but not identical. If children perform better on structure X than on structure Y, then this proves that children know something that distinguishes X from Y. In particular, suppose that structure X is ruled out by a grammatical principle of universal grammar, call it Principle R, but that structure Y is consistent with the principles of universal grammar. If children reject structure X significantly more often (in a statistical sense) than they reject structure Y, then the CF model concludes that children know Principle R.

At first glance this position appears reasonable. It leads to certain unwarranted

[3]There is one circumstance in which biases such as this play a role on the modularity matching model—namely, in the interpretation of ambiguous sentences. On the competing factors model, however, such biases also contribute to the interpretation of unambiguous sentences; not so on the modularity matching model.

[4]We are specifically referring here to the widely held assumption of representational modularity, an assumption that connects psycholinguistics to linguistic theory.

conclusions, however. For example, suppose that children accept structure X quite often, despite its ungrammaticality. This does not matter, according to the competing factors model. As long as children reject structure X significantly more often than structure Y, then they know Principle R. This is because all behavior, including linguistic behavior, is viewed as a probabilistic weighted sum. In the sum total of different probabilistic factors, the influence of factors extraneous to grammar may sometimes be enough to make ungrammatical structure X acceptable for children. Principle R is just one among many factors that influence behavior. If the weights come out one way, then Principle R may contribute to a particular behavior, but it can be easily suppressed if other factors are weighted more heavily on a particular occasion.

The modularity matching model rejects such arguments. As we saw, the MM model assumes that children and adults have in common a modular mental architecture, with corresponding principles in each module. According to the MM model, if children know Principle R, they should behave in conformity with it, just as adults do.

In many of the experiments we discuss, a sentence is presented to a child in a certain context. If children can parse the sentence and relate it appropriately to the context, then they will know whether or not the derivation is grammatical or violates a principle of grammar. Therefore, children should reject sentences that are ungrammatical according to Principle R. Furthermore, if children understand the experimental task and are cooperative, then it is expected, on the MM model, that they will perform perfectly (up to the level of noise that is present in the experiment). In short, the fundamental difference between the competing factors model and the modularity matching model is that there is no notion of grammaticality in any absolute sense on the competing factors model, with grammar having priority over other factors, as it does on the modularity matching model.

The principal motivation for adopting the competing factors model seems to be the view that it manages to exonerate grammatical knowledge as the source of differences in behavior between children and adults. By laying the blame elsewhere, it is thought that the CF model brings child grammar more in line with the expectations of universal grammar—that children adhere to universal linguistic principles throughout the course of language development. Though the motivation is beyond reproach, we think that it is generally unwise to relax the limits on what can count as an explanation of children's nonadult responses to linguistic stimuli. By allowing children to differ from adults in processing (in order to attribute grammatical knowledge to them), the CF model threatens to open up a Pandora's box of possible processing explanations. Moreover, the CF model often fails to confront the key issue concerning the linguistic phenomenon under discussion: How do children's processing systems change so as to converge on the adult system?

The minimalist assumptions of the modularity matching model leave little room to maneuver in explaining children's nonadult linguistic behavior. Of course, there will be differences in the behavior and knowledge of children and adults, and these will have to be accounted for. One place to look for an explanation is within the theory of universal grammar itself. It is consistent with the generative framework for children to sometimes hypothesize grammatical representations that are not characteristic of their target language. Parameters are one source of such deviations. Another source is maturation. According to the MM model, however, the internal representations that children assign to sentences must be compatible with the theory of universal grammar. This is necessary in light of the problems of learnability that would otherwise arise. In addition, when researchers offer an analysis of children's linguistic behavior, the representation that is hypothesized should be consistent with all the other evidence in the literature about what children know. So, for example, a proposal that children fail to comprehend pronouns in the adult-like manner because they lack the structural notion of c-command is highly unlikely, as there is a considerable body of evidence showing that c-command constrains children's responses in interpreting sentences with anaphors and referring expressions. Essentially, the grammars of children can differ from the target grammar only in ways that adult grammars can differ from each other. Put simply, children's grammatical hypotheses are constrained by Universal Grammar (see, e.g., Borer & Wexler, 1987; Crain, 1991).

In certain cases, children will produce errors that cannot be explained by linguistic theory. How can the modularity matching model explain such errors without resorting to competing factors? One of the main sources of children's errors are flaws in experimental design. Errors occur in experimental situations that force children to violate either one kind of linguistic principle or another. In these circumstances, children are forced to choose which kind of principle to violate. But if children choose to violate a syntactic principle—say, in order to provide a pragmatically felicitous response—they should not be said to lack syntactic knowledge. Indeed, when placed in situations that are pragmatically felicitous, children should adhere to syntactic principles and should reject sentences that do not conform to them. Typically, syntactic and pragmatic principles are at odds only in infelicitous experimental circumstances; in ordinary circumstances, linguistic principles are not in competition. In sum, this source of errors in children's behavior is artifactual and should not serve as the basis for a model of the language apparatus as it functions in most real-life circumstances.

Another source of children's performance errors can be found in the nonlinguistic demands of an experimental task. Many psychological tasks require building and executing a variety of cognitive algorithms, only some of which are linguistic. In certain circumstances, the complexity of the nonlinguistic components of the task may exceed the child's cognitive ability. This can happen, for example, if the child must formulate a highly complex response plan in order to act out the meaning of a sentence with the props available in the experimental workspace. In such circumstances, analyses that have been made within the language module may be obscured by the complexity of nonlinguistic processes (see Hamburger & Crain, 1987). Errors that derive from this source, however, should not weigh in assessing children's linguistic knowledge or in modeling their language processing system, because the components of the language apparatus are not permitted to contribute to the child's behavior as they would normally. Even consistent nonadult responses in such circumstances should not be construed as evidence of nonadult language processing in the child, for example, within the syntax. If the goal is to investigate child syntax, then it is important to strip away extraneous sources of errors such as those due to response planning. This is accomplished by reducing the cognitive complexity of the response plan the child is required to formulate in the task. Only then can it be determined whether or not the child's analysis of the linguistic input is similar to that of an adult.[5]

Admittedly, the modularity matching model may be incorrect, and it may turn out that there are differences in the linguistic behavior of children and adults that derive from sources within the language processing system; for example, there may be maturation of verbal working memory (see Baddeley & Hitch, 1974). Processing explanations of observed differences between children and adults should be advanced with caution, however. Just as the MM model rejects the position that children have inherently different grammars from those of adults, it also rejects the view that children differ in fundamental ways from adults in their mechanisms for processing sentences. This assumption, too, follows from a concern with the problem of learnability. If the processing system of a child has radically different properties from that of an adult, then the question of learnability arises; namely, how does the child achieve the adult system?

There is one circumstance in which nonlinguistic factors play a role in language processing according to the modularity matching model. These factors are brought into play when children (and adults) are confronted with sentences that are structurally ambiguous. When principles of linguistic theory make multiple representations available for a sentence, the human sentence processing device (i.e., the parser) resolves the ambiguity by engaging the services of real-world knowledge or by consulting the mental model of the current discourse context.[6] In resolving ambiguities, the language processing system attempts to identify a linguistic analysis that makes the sentence true. This explains the bias to say yes to either reading of an ambiguous sentence in an appropriate context; a bias that is mani-

[5]Children may also make errors if, for some reason, they cannot assign any grammatical representation to a sentence, perhaps because they cannot comprehend the sentence because it is too long or too complex. In such cases, children may well invoke nonlinguistic factors in interpreting the sentence and attempt to assign it an interpretation that makes it true in the discourse context. It follows from the assumption of module matching, however, that these sources of errors will have a similar effect on adults.

[6]In resolving ambiguities, one's mental model of the discourse context has priority over real-world knowledge. This ensures that the parser pursues a linguistic representation that successfully refers to entities and events under discussion, regardless of their a priori plausibility.

fested by both children and adults. It should be clear, however, that nonlinguistic factors are not competing with grammatical principles even in the resolution of structural ambiguities. Multiple representations are computed within the language processing system without regard to nonlinguistic factors. It should also be clear that such a bias is not invoked for unambiguous sentences, according to the MM model. If a sentence has a single grammatical representation, then this determines whether the sentence is true or false. Children (or adults) who say that a sentence is true when their grammars tell them the opposite are not behaving in accordance with the competing factors model; they are simply being uncooperative.

This concludes our introductory remarks on the alternative models of linguistic behavior discussed in this chapter. We are convinced that the modularity matching model is superior to the competing factors model. Nevertheless, most researchers in language acquisition, even researchers working within the generative framework, seem to adopt the methodological assumptions of the CF model when they analyze the findings of their experimental research. We believe that the methodology of the competing factors model is inconsistent with the spirit of the generative framework and with its implicit assumptions about the character of mental architecture.

The next section begins a detailed critique of the theoretical underpinnings of the competing factors model. Our strategy is to compare the CF model and the MM model by examining research that presents the strongest possible case against our own position. For this reason, we focus on three studies conducted by researchers in the area of language acquisition who accept the basic precepts of generative grammar. Our discussion is therefore directed at the methodological assumptions of these researchers and not at their theoretical assumptions. All of the researchers we review adopt the methodological stance of the CF model when they attempt to explain children's less-than-perfect (or nonadult) performance. This underscores our point that the vestiges of classical empiricist psychology can be found in current research within the generative-based framework. Another goal of this chapter is to examine the empirical adequacy of the CF model. We conclude that the CF model receives little, if any, empirical support from the studies we discuss.

III. STRONG CROSSOVER

The first study, by McDaniel and McKee (1993), was designed to investigate children's knowledge of the constraint on interpreting *crossover questions* such as (1). The Wh-phrase in (1) *crosses over* the pronoun as it moves from its site of origin (indicated by "*e*") to a position at the beginning of the sentence. For adult speakers, the pronoun in (1) cannot refer to more than a single individual, as it could if it were interpreted as a bound pronoun, as in (2). The absence of the multiple referent interpretation of the pronoun in (1) is called the strong crossover effect. The reason that the pronoun can refer to more than a single individual in (2) is that it can be interpreted as a variable, bound by the Wh-phrase. On this interpretation, (2) can be paraphrased as "Which person(s) x are such that x thinks x has a hat." If there were no constraint on crossover questions like (1), this question could be assigned the same meaning(s) as the bound pronoun question (2), where the pronoun may be interpreted as referring to multiple referents.

(1) Who does he think *e* has a hat?
(2) Who thinks he has a hat?

Based on the results of a study comparing questions like (1) and (2), Roeper and his colleagues concluded that children do not know the constraint on crossover questions (de Villiers, Roeper, & Vainikka, 1990; Roeper, 1986; Roeper, Rooth, Malish, & Akayama, 1984). Roeper and his colleagues claimed that the children in their study interpreted questions such as (1) and (2) in the same way, with the pronoun bound by the Wh-phrase in questions of both types. In fact, there is little empirical support for this claim. The relevant finding would have been evidence that children assigned multiple referent answers to crossover questions such as (1), as well as to bound pronoun questions such as (2). But, in fact, few children responded in this fashion, preferring the deictic interpretation of the pronoun in both types of questions, as McDaniel and McKee observe (also see Crain & Thornton, 1998; Thornton, 1990; Thornton and Crain, 1994).

Children's comprehension of crossover questions such as (1) and bound pronoun questions such as (2) was investigated by McDaniel and McKee (1993) using a different experimental technique. They had children judge the appropriateness of particular answers to both kinds of questions. On a typical trial, one experimenter acted out a scenario with toy figures and props while two puppets (played by a second experimenter) and the child looked on. After acting out the scenario, the first puppet asked the second one a question about what happened. That puppet's reply, although true of the scenario, was either appropriate to the question or not. The child's task was to judge which it was, appropriate or not. The critical contrast in the experiment was children's responses to the following types of questions/answer pairs.

(3) Type III: Question: Who said he was under the blanket?
Answer: He did and he did.

Type IV: Question: Who did he say was under the blanket?
Answer: *He did and he did.

As McDaniel and McKee observed, the multiple referent answer ("He did and he did") is not appropriate for Type IV questions (as indicated by the asterisk). Whereas the pronoun can be bound in Type III questions, the pronoun in Type IV questions cannot be bound; that is, the Type IV questions display strong crossover effects for adults.

The goal of the McDaniel and McKee study was to determine whether children manifest strong crossover effects. Lacking the constraint on crossover questions, children would be expected to permit a multiple referent answer to Type IV as well as Type III questions. Children had the opportunity to demonstrate knowledge of the constraint by rejecting the multiple referent answer ("He did and he did") as inappropriate for Type IV questions while accepting it as appropriate for Type III questions. In the absence of the constraint, children would be expected to accept or reject Type III and Type IV questions equally often, as Roeper and colleagues claimed.

Results of the McDaniel and McKee study were given for 13 children. There was also a control group of 13 adults. Both adults and children gave the same pattern of responses for the most part. Both groups judged multiple referent answers to Type III questions to be appropriate at least 90% of the time. The rate of accuracy for Type IV targets was much lower, however. Children incorrectly judged multiple referent answers to the Type IV questions to be appropriate 54% of the time; adults accepted them 62% of the time.

McDaniel and McKee considered a child to know the grammatical principle under investigation if she accepted the multiple referent answer at least once less often in response to Type IV questions than in response to Type III questions. They argue that if children did not have knowledge of the constraint on strong crossover, they would treat both question/answer pairs in the same way. Many children did not, in fact, treat both types of trials in the same way. As a group, they gave 36% fewer "yes" responses to Type IV questions than to Type III questions, a difference that was significant by the sign test ($p < .05$). Adults, too, treated the two types differently, accepting Type IV questions 34% less often, a difference that was also significant by the sign test.

The methodological assumptions of the competing factors model lie clearly at the heart of the inference by McDaniel and McKee that even a low level of correct performance by children and adults on Type IV trials is indicative of knowledge of the constraint on strong crossover. This explains why McDaniel and McKee pointed to the difference between the level of correct responses to Type III versus Type IV questions rather than to a comparison of the level of performance on the Type IV questions (46%) to the level of performance predicted by the underlying model of universal grammar, which is 100%.

To buttress their conclusion that children know the constraint on crossover questions, McDaniel and McKee pointed to the similar pattern of responses by children and adults. They reasoned as follows. First, it can be taken for granted that adults know the constraint. Embracing the competing factors model, the next assumption is that knowledge does not entail perfect performance, even for adults. For both children and adults, linguistic behavior is taken to be an aggregate of a large number of forces, only one of which is grammatical knowledge. The principles of grammar have no privileged status and can easily be violated; their effects can be seen only statistically. In concluding, McDaniel and McKee clearly stated their adherence to the CF model:

> Since the adult group, though not perfect, did show knowledge of strong crossover, we were able to use their performance as an indication of how the grammatical principle ruling out strong crossover works in this task. (p. 289)

Viewed from this perspective, all that is required to infer that children have knowledge of a constraint is evidence that they display a similar pattern of behavior to that of adults, whose knowledge is not in question.

To summarize the main findings, the mean level of performance for the child subjects was 46% correct responses to the Type IV crossover questions; the adult controls performed slightly worse, with 38% correct responses to the crossover questions. Despite these high error rates (i.e., overacceptance of the multiple referent answer) by both groups, McDaniel and McKee claimed that the findings demonstrate that children know the constraint on strong crossover. As McDaniel and McKee stated, children's knowledge of the constraint on strong crossover "is shown by [their] distinction between Types III and IV, which was significant and as great as the distinction made by adults" (p. 289). Residual failures for both groups are attributed to performance factors, and should not be taken as an indication of a lack of grammatical competence, according to McDaniel and McKee.

In our view, the findings from the McDaniel and McKee study do not support the competing factors model; neither do they demonstrate children's knowledge of the constraint on crossover questions. The point of the study was see whether or not children interpret crossover questions (Type IV) and bound variable questions (Type III) in the same way. McDaniel and McKee concluded that neither children nor adults interpreted them in the same way. They base this conclusion on the results of a statistical test, the sign test. But the sign test only considers individuals who demonstrated a positive or a negative difference in performance on Type III and Type IV question/answer pairs. On the sign test, individuals who do not differ in performance are removed from the calculation. As Siegel (1956) stated:

> All tied cases are dropped from the analysis for the sign test, and the N is correspondingly reduced." (p. 71)

This makes it clear how the adult group could show a significant difference between Type III and Type IV questions on the sign test, even though 6 of the 13 adults gave "yes" responses to both question types on all trials. The responses of these 6 adults did not contribute to the statistical test.

Given the research question, it is evident that individuals who responded in exactly the same way to both question types should have been counted. What is called for, then, is a statistical test that assesses the significance of changes in performance by individuals (such as the McNemar test or the binomial test). We have applied the binomial test to the McDaniel and McKee data, and the result was that neither group differed significantly from chance performance (at the .05 level) in distinguishing between Type III and Type IV questions.[7]

There is an even more fundamental problem in comparing the patterns of correct responses by children and adults to Type III versus Type IV questions. Such comparisons may only lead to valid inferences about children's underlying knowledge in certain circumstances. To infer that children know the constraint on crossover questions, despite a low level of performance, it is crucial that the pattern of responses by both children and adults forms a particular geometric contour—namely, one that is consistent with the competing factors model. In the absence of such a contour, the inference fails, as we will now show.

The competing factors model predicts that subjects' responses will approximate a binomial distribution surrounding some mean value of correct responses (i.e., answering no to Type IV questions). The distribution of subjects' responses should be *unimodal,* with the proportions tapering down from the mode. As we saw, the CF model expects children (and adults) to behave according to some statistical combination of factors. These factors should be the same for all subjects, except for minimal differences due to noise. If children know a grammatical constraint, but are affected in varying degrees by other performance factors, then there should be one group behavior; that is, responses should vary only probabilistically (randomly). We would expect almost no subjects to show all "yes" or all "no" responses.

Suppose that the pattern of responses by children and adults is similar but does not conform to the predictions of the competing factors model. For instance, suppose that the pattern of performance by both groups shows a *bimodal* distribution, according to which some subjects in each group distinguish between Type III questions and Type IV questions, but others do not. In this case, there would not be a single group behavior; rather, there would be two patterns of responses within each group.

If both groups displayed a bimodal distribution, it would not be valid to infer that children have the same grammatical knowledge as adults. At one end of the distribution would be a group of children (and adults) who distinguished between the Type III questions and Type IV questions, correctly accepting the multiple referent answer to the Type III questions but rejecting it for Type IV questions. We could infer that this group of children have knowledge of the constraint on crossover questions, regardless of the existence of a group of adults who performed similarly. This brings us to the other hypothetical group of children. This group allowed a multiple referent answer to both Type III and Type IV questions.

[7]This does not mean that we accept the conclusion of Roeper and colleagues that children do not know the constraint on crossover questions, for reasons discussed toward the end of the section.

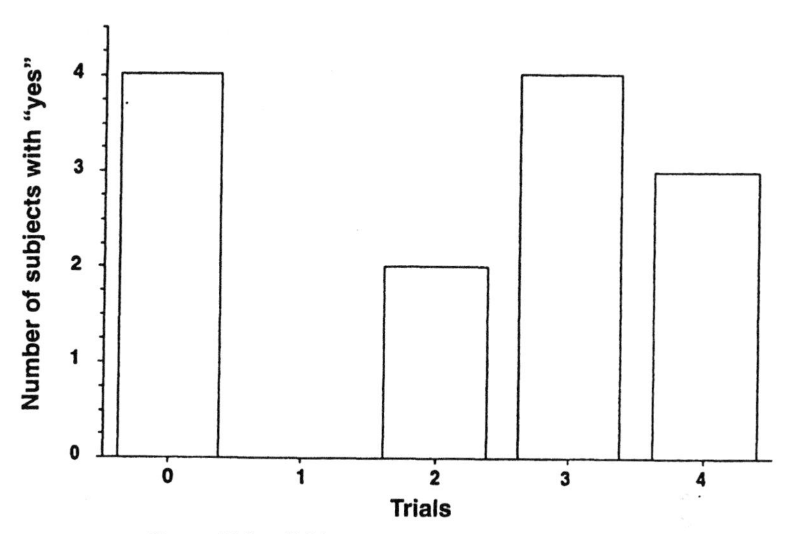

Figure 12.1. Children's response to Type IV sentences.

Clearly, it does not follow from the fact that there was also a group of adults who failed to distinguish the two question types, but who can be assumed to know the constraint governing Type IV questions, that these children know the constraint.

As these observations indicate, it is necessary to look at the data by individual subjects if we are to evaluate the argument made by McDaniel and McKee. A histogram of children's responses is given in Figure 12.1. It is clear from Figure 12.1 that the individual subject data do not exhibit the pattern of behavior predicted by the competing factors model. As we noted, the CF model predicts that each child should reject the Type IV questions roughly half of the time. Four children rejected all Type IV questions; three children accepted them all, and four children accepted three out of four of them. Therefore, the distribution of children's behavior on Type IV trials in Figure 12.1 is *bi*modal, not *uni*modal. Figure 12.1 also makes clear just how poorly some children fared with the Type IV trials. Seven of the thirteen subjects responded correctly at most once on the four trials. That means that this group of children incorrectly accepted multiple referent answers to Type IV questions 86% of the time. Four of these seven children contributed a positive score on the sign test, however, because they accepted Type III question/answer pairs even more often.

Intuitively, the findings are easy to interpret. Only four subjects exhibited knowledge of the constraint on strong crossover on this task. The other nine subjects are spread at the opposite end of the distribution. As Figure 12.2 shows, adults are even more clearly divided into two groups, and even fewer demonstrated competence in the present study.

It appears that the majority of the subjects, both children and adults, did not base

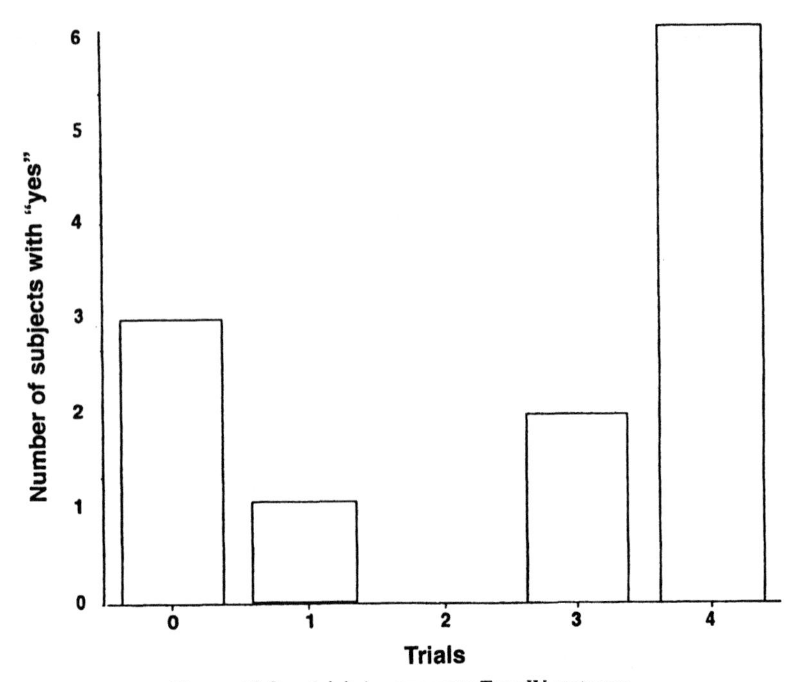

Figure 12.2. Adults' responses to Type IV sentences.

their responses on grammatical considerations. The conclusion we would draw is that some real factor divides the subjects into different groups. The factor that is relevant is not experimental noise, however, because noise should distribute equally across all subjects (i.e., it should be normally distributed). Apparently, the other factor was a bias by subjects to answer yes if they did not understand a given trial of the experiment. The nine children who did not respond with a high degree of accuracy have a probability of .78 of saying yes. As Figure 12.1 shows, this bias does indeed approximate a normal distribution. It is probably correct to distinguish the pattern of responses by these nine children to Type IV trials (which is normally distributed) from their pattern of responses to Type III trials, where most children consistently said yes. But the responses of these nine children to Type IV trials should also be distinguished from the genuine rejection of Type IV trials, which results in "no" responses. This pattern was characteristic of only four children. If there is no way for subjects to display knowledge in some experimental task, they have no alternative but to devise a strategy for responding. It appears that the experiment by McDaniel and McKee had precisely this effect on many child and adult subjects.

We can show more precisely that the distribution of responses over the 13 children does not follow the binomial, unimodal distribution predicted by the competing factors model. Recall that four children gave "no" responses on all four trials. We can calculate the probability that four or more children give "no" responses on all four trials, given the binomial model. If this probability is less than some accepted significance probability, say .05, then this will constitute a significant demonstration that the binomial model does not hold and thus that McDaniel and McKee's CF model is not supported by their own data. Assuming a binomial distribution with the probability of saying no at .46, as in the present data, we have calculated the probability of four or more (of thirteen) children saying no. The likelihood of this occurring is less than .005, a highly significant deviation from the binomial model.

Suppose, contrary to fact, that children (and adults) had performed according to the expectations of the competing factors model in the McDaniel and McKee study. That is, suppose both groups had displayed a binomial, unimodal distribution of responses. Even in this case, we should be cautious in attributing to children knowledge of the constraint on crossover questions. The observation that subjects behave differently on two structures does not in itself show that they know the principles underlying both structures. In particular, if a structure is ungrammatical, it must be shown that subjects consider it ungrammatical.[8] Suppose, for example, that children frowned more often when they heard one sentence than when they heard another sentence. There is no reason to think that this difference in behavior represents a difference in grammatical status of the two sentences. It may simply be that children failed to understand one of the sentences. Knowing that two types of sentences are not treated in the same way by subjects does not tell us about the grammatical properties they assign to each type of sentence.

To take another example, suppose that children showed a difference on the same two types of sentences in an experiment using a different dependent measure, say reaction time. All that we could conclude would be that there is a difference for the children between the two types of sentences. We would not conclude that children know the syntactic and semantic properties of the sentences. Even if the pattern of reaction time differences by children mimicked that of adults, it would be ill advised to attribute the same underlying knowledge to children without additional confirmation from more direct tests of grammatical competence. Yet this was precisely the conclusion reached by McDaniel and McKee, based on a comparison of levels of performance by children and adults on a task that even failed to provide clear evidence of adult competence.

[8]This does not mean that we expect 100% consistent responses by children. In certain experiments, some of them described in later sections of the chapter, we would expect that children's behavior would be much less than this. This might be true, for example, if the sentence were ambiguous and both readings were presented to the child. However, that is clearly not the case in Type IV sentences in the McDaniel and McKee study. There is only one grammatical reading for this sentence, and that is not the reading that is presented. Only an ungrammatical reading is presented. Therefore we expect the children to consistently reject Type IV sentences.

In light of these observations, we should ask why it is justified to use reaction time measures in studies of adult sentence processing. The reason is that grammatical competence is not at issue in such studies. It is justified to assume that adults have all and only the correct grammatical analyses available to them. Therefore, tasks may be used that only indirectly tap grammatical competence, such as measures of reaction time. Clarity is sacrificed in looking at the particular syntactic and semantic properties being represented in order to determine the time course of the availability of alternative sources of information. In studies of children's language development, by contrast, grammatical competence is precisely what is at issue. And, as we have argued, knowing that two types of sentences are not treated in the same way by subjects does not tell us about the properties that they assign to each type of sentence. To demonstrate children's knowledge of universal grammar (UG) principles, it must be established that their pattern of responses conforms to the model—that is, to the relevant principles of UG. To conclude that the constraint on strong crossover is innate, for example, it must be shown that *all* (or at least the vast majority of) children who are tested adhere to the constraint. As we have seen, only four children satisfied this criterion in the McDaniel and McKee study.

Adherents of the competing factors model might reply that certain measures, such as the proportion of correct rejections, are not arbitrary measures of children's knowledge of the different grammatical status of two structures. Rather, they might contend, a higher proportion of children's rejections of structure X than rejections of structure Y is a direct reflection of their knowledge of a grammatical constraint on structure X. This conclusion would follow, however, only if some independent reason could be given for believing that grammatical knowledge was the basis for children's judgments in the experiment. Otherwise, we could be confident that the basis for the judgments was grammaticality only if both children and adults consistently judge structure X to be ungrammatical.

What can we conclude from the experiment by McDaniel and McKee? They showed that children (and adults) do not always respond to questions with bound pronouns in the same way as they do to questions that are subject to the constraint on strong crossover. From this, McDaniel and McKee infer that children know the constraint. It is an implication of the modularity matching model, however, that the experiment by McDaniel and McKee does not demonstrate that children know the constraint on strong crossover. Clearly, something about the McDaniel and McKee task prevented many subjects from displaying their full grammatical competence. This follows from that fact that even many adults performed poorly, often accepting the ungrammatical Type IV trials. On the MM model, by contrast, both adults and children with knowledge of a grammatical principle will perform almost perfectly, at least if the experiment is constructed properly. In the present case, grammatical competence dictates that a subject should consistently accept multiple reference answers to Type III questions and should consistently reject such answers to Type IV questions (subject only to a minimal amount of distortion due to inattention, lack of cooperation, and so on that both child and adult subjects bring to the task).

We might ask why McDaniel and McKee reached the conclusion that a relative difference in behavior on two sentences is sufficient to show that a grammatical property is known, even though subjects in general perform quite poorly in an absolute sense. A point that we raised earlier is relevant here, namely, that the *relative difference* methodology is appropriate for an older class of model, one in which grammatical knowledge is represented as a continuum of behavior, not as a structural, categorical entity. If grammatical knowledge is represented, say, as habit strength, then it would be appropriate to ask whether children have more habit strength in rejecting Type IV trials than in rejecting ones of Type III. What has happened is that the older-style methodology has been carried over into a study based on a newer theoretical framework, where it is no longer appropriate.

Before moving to the next topic, we wish to point out that we do believe that children know the constraint on strong crossover; our point is a methodological one—that the experiment by McDaniel and McKee does not show that children know the constraint. To demonstrate children's knowledge, another kind of experiment must be done. In fact, such an experiment has been done, using a modified truth-value judgment task (see Crain, 1991; Thornton, 1990). In this study, question/answer pairs like (4) and (5) were presented.

(4) I know who he thinks has the best smile. Grover and Yogi Bear.
(5) I know who thinks he has the best smile. Grover and Yogi Bear.

The finding was that children rejected a multiple referent answer to (embedded) crossover questions such as (4) over 90% of the time, but they accepted a multiple referent answer to bound pronoun questions such as (5) half of the time. The high rate of rejection of a multiple referent answer to embedded crossover questions demonstrates children's knowledge of the constraint on strong crossover. The rejection rate drops dramatically for questions such as (5), which allow a multiple referent answer. The reason children reject question/answer pairs as often as they do is evidence that they have a preference for interpreting the pronoun in (5) deictically. In the context, (5) was false on this interpretation (for further discussion also see Crain & Thornton, 1998).

IV. NULL SUBJECTS AND THE OUTPUT OMISSION MODEL

In this section we compare two different approaches to the well-known phenomenon of young children's subjectless sentences. One approach, by Hyams (1986), follows the general methodological stance of the modularity matching model. Hyams argued that children's subjectless sentences represent a stage in which children are speaking a null-subject language. There have been several challenges to this linguistically based account of null-subject phenomenon, however. The alternative accounts appeal to processing and memory considerations to explain children's subjectless sentences. We will examine one of these proposals in this section, namely, the proposal advanced by Bloom (1990; 1993), which we take to be based on a competing factors model (cf. Valian, 1992).

We have two purposes in comparing the modularity matching model and Bloom's model. First, we want to see how well the two models do in predicting the data concerning children's null-subject production (see Hyams & Wexler, 1993, for a fuller analysis). Second, we want to demonstrate how the MM model and the competing factors model may be compared when the relevant data are children's spontaneous productions.

The relevant data concern the choice of subject type in the null-subject stage. Three possibilities exist: lexical subjects, pronominal subjects, and null subjects. We ask first what the modularity matching model says about the development progression of these types of subjects. The MM model assumes that the young child has a null-subject grammar; children's subjectless sentences are simply a reflection of this grammar. Moreover, the MM model assumes that the child will use null subjects in precisely those contexts where an adult speaking a null-subject language will use them. In null subject languages, lexical subjects are typically used in the same contexts as lexical subjects are used in non-null-subject languages. However, speakers of null subject languages do not use pronouns in the same contexts where speakers of non-null-subject languages use pronouns. In null-subject languages, for example, overt pronouns are used in situations involving contrastive stress. So the MM assumes that English-speaking children in the null-subject stage also use pronouns in these special contexts; otherwise they use null subjects.

The modularity matching model assumes that at some stage the English-speaking child switches to a non-null-subject grammar. At this point, contexts in which the child had earlier produced a null subject will now elicit a pronoun in subject position. Therefore we expect that developmentally the child will produce a greater proportion of pronouns in subject position as she advances from one stage to the next. Lexical subjects are unaffected by the process; as we pointed out, they will be used in essentially the same contexts in both null-subject and non-null-subject languages. Therefore we expect the proportion of lexical subjects to remain roughly constant.[9] The proportion of null subjects, of course, will decrease as they are being replaced by pronouns. Thus the following predictions are made by the MM model: Developmentally, lexical subjects will remain constant, pronominal sub-

[9]By *constant,* we mean that the observed levels of performance do not systematically increase or decrease across sessions. Of course, in any speech sample extending over an hour, say, the proportions might vary, because situational context will determine whether a lexical subject or some other form will be chosen, and these contexts will vary.

jects will increase, and null subjects will decrease. It is a well-known property of the null-subject stage that object NPs are rarely omitted. Object NPs have nothing to do with the parameter yielding a null-subject language, so the MM model expects no systematic change in the proportion of lexical and pronominal objects as the child passes from the null-subject to the non-null-subject stage.

Now we can ask about the predictions of the model advanced by Bloom. According to Bloom, memory problems cause children learning English (and other languages) to omit subjects in their output. We will therefore call his account the output omission model. The output omission model (OOM) provides a very different picture of development than that presented by the modular model. The central idea is that the child does not have a null-subject grammar; rather he has the adult English grammar. Therefore when the child produces a null subject, he has actually, in his internal representation, selected a non-null subject. These internally selected subjects come in one of two forms, they are either lexical subjects or pronominal subjects. Under memory pressure, these subjects are sometimes dropped. Because lexical subjects are more demanding of memory resources than are pronouns, lexical subjects are expected to be dropped more often than pronominal subjects.[10]

Children omit subjects, according to the output omission model, because their memory capacities are even more limited than those of adults. Because the basic statistical phenomenon is that subjects are dropped far more often than objects, the memory difficulty must be asymmetrical, according to OOM; the beginning of a sentence is associated with greater memory difficulty than the middle or the end of a sentence.

At the earliest stages of development, memory pressures are greatest. This means that lexical subjects will be omitted more frequently at earlier stages than at later stages. So OOM predicts that the proportion of lexical subjects that are produced will increase with age.[11] For exactly the same reason, OOM predicts that the proportion of pronominal subjects in child language will increase with age. Be-

[10]The assumption that lexical subjects are dropped more often than are pronominal subjects is entailed by the presentation of the model and the evidence that Bloom used to support OOM. In particular, Bloom showed that VP length is longer for pronominal than for lexical subjects and longer for sentences with no overt subject than for pronominal subjects. Bloom argued that these results show that lexical subjects are more sensitive to memory pressure than are pronominal subjects. As Hyams & Wexler (1993) argued, the likeliest candidate for a processing model that allows for such a result is a planning model. When a long VP is being planned, memory pressures (on production) are created. Lexical subjects are more sensitive to these memory pressures than are pronominal subjects (because they are phonetically heavy, presumably). Hyams and Wexler (1993) showed that a similar VP length pattern holds for adult Italian. Therefore, the facts about VP length in early child grammar can be explained by the modularity matching model as well; we would expect the child in the null-subject stage to show whatever properties exist for languages such as Italian.

[11]This assumes that the proportion of lexical subjects that are selected does not systematically vary with age. There is evidence for this assumption to which we will return.

Adam	P(l-s)	P(p-s)	P(l-o)	P(p-o)
06	.33	.11	.50	.44
08	.23	.20	.68	.29
10	.35	.20	.68	.21
12	.14	.20	.61	.31
14	.15	.15	.44	.43
16	.12	.52	.33	.54
18	.16	.60	.43	.43
20	.11	.77	.74	.20
Eve				
02	.11	.29	.58	.21
04	.12	.37	.62	.27
06	.57	.14	.70	.19
08	.47	.26	.65	.21
10	.31	.37	.75	.18
12	.21	.68	.62	.32
14	.13	.74	.89	.07
16	.23	.70	.80	.19

Figure 12.3. Occurrence of lexical and pronominal subjects and objects in Adam and Eve.

cause OOM also assumes that lexical subjects are dropped more often than pronominal subjects (because they are longer), it predicts that the increase of the proportion of pronominal subjects should be more gradual than the increase of the proportion of lexical subjects. Suppose, for example, that the child at the youngest age produces lexical over pronominal subjects by a factor of 3 to 1. As the child grows older, memory pressures lessen and fewer subjects are omitted. Because the younger child omitted lexical subjects more often than pronominal subjects, these omitted lexical subjects will be produced relatively more often than pronominal subjects. Thus OOM predicts that the ratio of lexical subjects to pronominal subjects for the older child will be even more than for the younger child; that is, it will be greater than 3 to 1 in our example.

What are the data? Much of the discussion centers on the findings for two children from the Brown (1973) corpus, Adam and Eve. As Figure 12.3 indicates, the results are the same for both children. The proportion of lexical subjects stays fairly constant for both children, but the proportion of pronominal subjects increases with age. This means that the ratio of lexical to pronominal subjects decreases with age. The proportion of null subjects also decreases with age. As for objects, the proportion of lexical objects and pronominal objects remains roughly steady.[12]

How do the alternative models fare with the data? All of the facts are as predicted by the modularity matching model. Thus, the MM model provides a good fit to the data, at the level of precision that can be obtained using samples of lon-

[12]Figure 12.3 presents portions of the data from two of the figures presented in Hyams and Wexler (1993).

gitudinal data. The output omission model fares less well. First, OOM predicted that the proportion of lexical subjects would increase with development. This is clearly contradicted by the data, which shows a fairly constant proportion of lexical subjects across age. Like the MM model, OOM predicted that the proportion of pronominal subjects would increase with age, and this does occur. Where OOM provides another poor fit to the facts, however, is in the changes over time in the ratio of lexical to pronominal subjects. OOM predicted that this ratio would increase, but in fact it decreases, and the disparity in the ratio is very large. For example, Adam showed a 3 to 1 ratio of lexical to pronominal subjects at the earliest age. We showed that OOM predicts that this ratio should increase, that is, it should be larger than 3 to 1, for a later age. In fact, at the oldest age, an age when there are only 3% omitted subjects, the ratio of lexical to pronominal subjects is less than 1 to 2; the ratio that OOM predicted to be greater than 3 to 1 turns out to be less than 1 to 2; the ratio predicted by OOM is off by a factor greater than 6. We could attempt to make OOM fit the data better by assuming that lexical subjects were selected less frequently, as compared to pronominal subjects, as the child grew older. But, as Hyams & Wexler (1993) have shown, this assumption would entail that the same process would go on for objects. The fact that the frequency of lexical and pronominal objects remains roughly constant shows that this explanation cannot be maintained.[13]

The intuition is clear: Pronominal subjects come to replace null subjects as the child moves from the null-subject to the non-null-subject stage. Minimalist assumptions lead us to expect that the frequency of lexical subjects will remain constant, because their properties are not affected by the shift from null-subject to non-null-subject grammars. The reason that the proportion of lexical to pronominal subjects greatly decreases is that pronouns come in massively as null subjects drop out. For example, at the earliest stage Adam gives 11% pronominal subjects and gives 67% pronominal subjects at the latest stage. The figures for Eve are 29% at the earliest age and 82% at the latest age.

V. PERFORMANCE ERRORS VERSUS NONADULT GRAMMARS

Given the difficulties with a model like OOM we should ask, why does it seem to have been attractive prima facie? It seems to us that the attraction was that it claimed that not only do very young children know UG principles and parametric options but, furthermore, at an early age they choose the correct grammatical options for the language they are learning. That is, despite appearances to the con-

[13]Bloom (1993) commented on some of these criticisms as they were developed in Hyams and Wexler (1993). None of the rebuttal, however, appears to change the status of any of the central empirical points raised by Hyams and Wexler.

trary (i.e., children omit subjects in their speech), young children know UG and, furthermore, they know that subjects cannot be null in English.

It might appear that an approach such as this is even more minimalist than one that assumes that English-speaking children have a null-subject grammar. There is no question of resetting a parameter value if it is already set correctly. Bloom stated the matter as follows:

> Given that 2-year-olds acquiring English are exposed to a non-null subject language, this implies that they should know that subjects are obligatory. Consequently, utterances such as *Want water* must be the result of performance factors, not deficient linguistic knowledge. (p. 721)

The statement by Bloom indicates that he has adopted an idea of continuity that differs in important respects from the one that has been generally assumed in the literature. The standard notion of continuity is that children's grammars are constrained by universal grammar (e.g., Borer & Wexler, 1987; Crain, 1991; Pinker, 1984). The conception of continuity that Bloom has adopted seems to require the child grammar to match the adult input as closely as possible. Although this perspective on language development is not at odds with UG, there is no a priori reason to expect children's grammatical hypotheses to be closely tied to their linguistic experience. Not only is the existence of nonadult grammatical structures consistent with UG, it has often been argued that this is one of the main sources of evidence that children are following UG. As a matter of fact, moreover, there is abundant evidence of children's grammars exhibiting properties of UG that are not exhibited by the language that they are learning (i.e., the adult language).

One example is the medial-wh phenomenon in children learning English (Thornton, 1990; Thornton & Crain, 1994); children around the age of 3 or 4 often, sometimes consistently, put in a medial Wh-word in a long-distance question, for example, (7) instead of the adult (6):

(6) What do you think pigs eat?
(7) What do you think what pigs eat?

Structures like (7) are attested in dialects of German and other languages; the claim of continuity is satisfied even though the child makes a nonadult (for English) construction. Continuity is satisfied because the child's constructions satisfy UG.

A second example concerns children's asking of negative questions. It turns out that children even as old as 5 often form nonadult negative wh-object and adjunct questions and nonadult negative yes/no questions. Thus, they ask Wh-questions such as (8b) instead of the adult (8a), and they ask yes/no questions such as (9b) instead of the adult (9a) (see Guasti, Thornton, & Wexler, 1995; Thornton, 1993):

(8) a. What doesn't Big Bird like?
b. What does Big Bird doesn't like?

(9) a. Doesn't Grover like the ice cream?
b. Does Grover doesn't like the ice cream?

Note that the (b) forms in (8) and (9) are not in the adult language. Guasti, Thornton, and Wexler (1995) have argued that children's questions are nevertheless UG-compatible. No principles of UG are violated: The auxiliary verb raises to COMP, as in adult questions in English, whereas negation does not raise, a characteristic of certain dialects of Italian. Thus the claim is that children have replaced the correct form (for the language that provides the input) by an incorrect, but UG-compatible form.

It would be easy to make up examples of possible child grammars that do not satisfy universal grammar, but these are not found very often in child grammars. One possibility is the *optional infinitive* stage in very young children (Wexler, 1994). French children (see, e.g., Pierce, 1992) often produce infinitival forms such as (10b) instead of the finite form in (10a), which is found in the input.

(10) a. Marie parle.
b. Marie parler.

If it is impossible in UG for a declarative sentence to be infinitival rather than tensed, then the appearance of infinitival root sentences like (10b) appears to contradict continuity. The theory of what underlies the optional infinitive stage is still being extensively discussed, and it may turn out that it is possible to give a UG-consistent analysis of it. Whatever the ultimate truth turns out to be, however, it is clear that child grammars differ from UG at most in small ways and, perhaps, not at all, as maintained by the continuity hypothesis.

The present discussion also makes clear that child grammar may differ from the target grammar in ways that are not anticipated and cannot be explained by the output omission model. This model would be hard-pressed to explain the fact that children insert extra Wh-elements into their grammars, as in the discussion of (6–7). Likewise, it cannot explain why children insert an extra auxiliary into their negative questions, as in the discussion of (8–9). It also cannot explain the widespread use of root infinitivals in children's grammars, as these sentences are also different from the input.[14] Note that the form in (10b) involves the *insertion* of material, another instance of a general phenomenon that is predicted not to occur according to the output omission model.[15] These empirical phenomena of insertion or deviation show quite clearly that children create grammars with properties that are not found in the adult input but that are, nevertheless, consistent with UG.

[14]In some languages, in contrast to English, there is a visible infinitival morpheme instead of the finite morpheme found in the input, as (10) illustrates.

[15]It seems to us that something like the output omission model underlies the idea that morphemes like third-person singular *-s* in English is dropped, yielding "she like me" instead of "she likes me" (Brown, 1973).

In sum, there is no a priori argument against the possibility that a child might create a grammar that allows the possibility of null subjects even if the input language does not allow null subjects. Given that the child's grammar-creation process is driven not only by the input but also by an internal program that is constrained by UG, this is indeed a quite real possibility. Furthermore, it is what we find in many other cases, as we have just shown. Although it might be plausible at first sight to understand the omission of subjects in child English as a performance phenomenon, there is no way to understand these other phenomena in the same way, as output omission. Therefore, there is no a priori reason to favor a performance explanation for the null-subject phenomenon in child language.

VI. MINIMALITY AND MODULARITY

We should ask whether the output omission model is consistent with the assumptions of minimality and modularity that characterize the modularity matching model. As we argued at the beginning of the chapter, these assumptions apply to the processing module as well as to the grammar. If the processing component that has to be assumed for the child is radically different from that of the adult, then the modularity matching model is incorrect. This is a real possibility, of course, but it is not the null hypothesis. If the MM model turns out to be incorrect, however, then we will have to explain how the significant change from child to adult takes place, either by learning or by maturation. If not by maturation, the learnability problem will be difficult to solve, as shown repeatedly in the learnability literature.

Against this backdrop, let us reconsider the basic tenets of the output omission model. The essential feature of the model is that children omit constituents when the processor is put under stress due to unusual demands on verbal working memory. As Hyams and Wexler pointed out, however, there is no evidence that adults do the same. So far as we know, when extreme demands are made on the memory resources of adults, they generally pause. Occasionally, adults even construct a nonfelicitous utterance. But there is no evidence of the systematic omission of constituents under the stress of memory. Apparently, children and adults have different processing systems on the output omission model.

Why don't adults omit constituents under the pressure of memory limitations? It is clear that there are effects of memory pressure in adults, such as garden-path effects, difficulties with center-embedded sentences, problems in starting an utterance, and so on. But we do not see the kind of systematic omission of constituents that occurs in children. Thus we have to assume that if constituent-omission is characteristic of the child production mechanism, then the adult production mechanism is systematically different from the child mechanism.

One way out of this dilemma would be to say that children's processing systems are qualitatively different from adults' systems; whereas children drop subjects as a response to memory pressure, adults hesitate. Granting that adults do not show null subjects as the result of memory or computational problems, it is conceivable (although unlikely) that if adults were placed under even more memory pressure they would drop subjects (and not other constituents). In a way, nature has provided means of putting adults under such extreme pressure. For example, Broca's aphasics are known to have extreme memory problems, and sometimes their sentence production is labored. If extreme memory problems (such as we would have to assume children have, if OOM were correct) caused the existence of null subjects in production, then we would expect null subjects in production to be part of the symptom complex of Broca's aphasics. However, null subjects are not characteristic of the speech of Broca's aphasics; rather, Broca's aphasics typically drop out function words.

The output omission model is at odds with the modularity matching model in another respect. One consequence of modularity is that there is no direct interplay of the primitives and principles in computing and executing representations. Therefore we must assume that in children there is no direct interplay between the primitives and principles in computing and executing representations. Approaches which assume that child productions are distortions of adult productions contradict this assumption of modularity.

In the output omission model, the lack of phonetic execution of the subject NP is correlated with the length of the VPs that children produce (i.e., the VP gets shorter on average, moving from null subjects to pronominal subjects to lexical subjects). What OOM must assume, therefore, is that the cause of the lack of phonetic execution of the subject NP is the planning process for the VP. That is, with a longer planning process (i.e., a longer VP) there is more difficulty in executing the subject, which has already been computed. OOM therefore must assume that the module responsible for the computation of representations (the planning of the VP) directly affects the operation of the module responsible for execution. Greater complexity in the computation module instructs a subprocess (pronunciation of the subject), which is carried out in a completely different module (the execution module). This type of interaction of modules does not occur in the adult language processing system. As we pointed out, when adults experience difficulty in planning a sentence, they hesitate; they do not drop constituents. In other words, difficulty in the computation of representations (the planning process) delays the operation of the execution process. In adults, however, the internal operations of one module (the execution module) are not directly influenced by the exigencies of another module (the computation module).

In this section we have shown that the explanation of null subjects in children as due to memory pressure violates both minimalism and modularity. Not only are there empirical problems associated with such violations, there are also learnability problems. How can the child develop a modular processing system, in which the computation module does not instruct subprocesses in the execution module? It seems highly unlikely that a child could learn that subsystems of language processing are modular. It is possible that modular adult systems of representations could mature from systems with radically different properties; presumably, this is what models such as OOM are forced to assume.

There are methodological morals to be drawn from the present discussion: Hypotheses are meant to solve problems. The continuity hypothesis, for example, is meant to solve the problem of learnability. But if continuity applies only to one component (e.g., the grammatical component) and not to other components (e.g., the processing component) then the problem of learnability is not solved in general; rather, it is just shifted to another domain. There is nothing special about grammar as an object of study such that we should abandon assumptions of continuity as they pertain to processing components that would explain learnability of the grammatical component. As part of a scientific approach to the physical world, we should invoke continuity in order to understand any of the properties of the physical world, including the property that all normal children master both the grammatical and performance components of language early in the course of language development.

VII. STATISTICS AND COMPETING FACTORS

This section considers another example of the competing factors model at work in the study of children's linguistic knowledge. The study to be discussed is by Grimshaw and Rosen (1990), who investigated the development of binding theory (BT), in particular the principle that governs the anaphoric relations of pronouns, Principle B. On each trial of the Grimshaw and Rosen (G&R) study, children were shown a video of puppets acting out a scene; then a puppet being controlled by the experimenter said what he thought had happened in the video. The puppet's commentary contained the target sentence, as illustrated in (11).

(11) I saw Big Bird doing something with Ernie. Big Bird patted him.

The video corresponding to (11) showed Big Bird patting Ernie. In this example, the test sentence *Big Bird patted him* is a grammatically correct description of the video. Grimshaw and Rosen therefore call such sentences BT-grammatical.

Sentences like (12) were also presented:

(12) Big Bird was standing with Ernie. Big Bird hit him.

In the video corresponding to (12), Big Bird was standing near Ernie, hitting himself. Because Principle B rules out this interpretation of the test sentence in (12), *Big Bird hit him,* G&R call these sentences BT-ungrammatical.

Grimshaw and Rosen found that children said yes to BT-grammatical sentences such as (11) 83% of the time. However, children accepted BT-ungrammatical sentences such as (12) less often, only 42% of the time.[16] This same pattern has been observed in many other experimental investigations of Principle B.[17]

Broadly speaking, the related findings in the literature have been interpreted in one of two ways. One interpretation is that children know the relevant principle of UG, Principle B of the binding theory, but lack knowledge of some other factor, let us call it Principle P. The counterproposal, offered by Grimshaw and Rosen, is that the findings do not entail the absence of any aspect of competence in children's grammars.

Grimshaw and Rosen introduced a different way of analyzing the data. The analysis is concerned with the difference in children's behavior in response to the BT-grammatical and BT-ungrammatical sentences. This last fact had been the basis for the conclusion drawn by other experimenters that there is something missing in children's understanding of such sentences. G&R rejected this conclusion. Rather, they argued that the difference in behavior on the two kinds of sentences shows that children know the BT principle governing pronouns. As they put it:

> a subject who does not know the principles should accept all sentences (regardless of whether they are grammatical or ungrammatical according to the adult grammar).... Subjects do not have to be particularly successful in their treatment of BT-ungrammatical sentences; to demonstrate knowledge, it is only necessary for children to treat the two classes of sentences in a systematically different way. In other words, children need not obey the Binding Theory in order to demonstrate knowledge of the Binding Theory. (p. 189)

We disagree. According to the modularity matching model, children who know the principles of binding theory are expected to achieve a high level of correct performance in studies that provide a valid assessment of children's linguistic competence.

Much of the discussion by Grimshaw and Rosen makes it clear that the basic model they assume is close in spirit to the modularity matching model. For example, their explanations of children's behavior are often concerned with the question of whether children are being forced to violate one or another constraint, and are therefore led to choose which one to violate. For example, G&R pointed out that in some studies:

> Subjects must choose between accepting a pronoun with no antecedent in the discourse and violating the Binding Theory. (p. 199).

[16]This is quite close to the percentage of incorrect responses reported in Chien and Wexler (1990).

[17]Grimshaw and Rosen used a truth-value judgment task, with simple Principle B cases. In the Chien and Wexler (1990) research, children were asked whether the test sentences described the pictures.

In this regard, their discussion follows the lines of other discussion in the literature on the acquisition of binding theory, including attempts to establish that children know Principle B. To eliminate this contributing factor, G&R made sure there was a linguistic antecedent in the discourse in their study, as had been the practice in other studies (e.g., Chien and Wexler, 1990; Wexler and Chien, 1985).

Grimshaw and Rosen's theoretical and methodological stance is sometimes at odds with the spirit of the modularity matching model, however. At several points they produced particularly clear statements of the methodological stance of the competing factors model. For example, they wrote in their conclusion:

> The inevitable screening effects of processing demands and other performance factors do not prevent us from establishing the character of linguistic knowledge; they just make it more challenging. In the example considered in this article, an analysis of these performance factors makes it possible to see, if only dimly, through the performance filter. (p. 217)

As we have seen, the modularity matching model maintains that *processing demands* and *performance factors* are not different for children and for adults. If we can attain a clear look at linguistic theory through the performance *filter* for adults, there is no reason why we cannot do the same with children, according to the MM model.[18]

The foundational assumptions of the Grimshaw and Rosen paper are therefore mixed; sometimes they seem to assume a competing factors model and sometimes they seem to assume a modularity matching model. The statistical analysis they propose is clearly based on the CF model, however. To establish that children have a certain aspect of linguistic knowledge, they contend, subjects are required to succeed only to a significant degree; grammar can be suppressed, probabilistically, by competing factors. This viewpoint, which is consistent with the CF model but not with the MM model, underlies the G&R argument that a difference in performance on BT-grammatical and BT-ungrammatical sentences is sufficient to demonstrate knowledge, regardless of the absolute values of a subject's performance.

We disagree with this use of statistics to test children's knowledge of linguistic principles. In our view, adopting this research strategy confuses children's preferences in interpreting ambiguous sentences and their knowledge of linguistic principles. At issue in many studies of children's knowledge is the question of whether they know that a particular interpretation cannot be given to a certain type of sentence. If children lack the relevant linguistic knowledge, then they should allow the test sentences to be interpreted in ways that are ruled out by the linguistic principle. That is, the sentences under investigation should be *ambiguous* for children who lack the relevant linguistic knowledge. The problem in adopting the

[18]In fact, Chien and Wexler (1990) argued that the lack of certain pragmatic capacities made true syntactic principles (binding theory) shine through even more clearly for children, because the syntactic principles were not distorted by certain pragmatic considerations.

methodological stance of the CF model arises because the alternative interpretations of an ambiguous sentence are not necessarily equally easy to access.

Several examples in the literature support our claim that children exhibit systematic preferences in interpreting ambiguous sentences. We will cite just one example, from an experiment designed to test children's knowledge of bound pronouns (Thornton, 1990). In the experiment, children were given question/answer pairs such as (13).

(13) I know who said he has the best smile. Grover and Yogi Bear.

Example (13) was presented as a description of a story that had been acted out in front of the child. The context corresponding to the story were ambiguous. The context was a contest to see who had the best smile. Among the competitors were Grover, Yogi Bear, and a Ninja Turtle. The judge of the competition was last year's winner, The Joker. In the end, The Joker judges the Ninja Turtle to be the winner of this year's contest. Grover and Yogi Bear protest, and the story ends with each of these characters saying that he, himself, has the best smile.

Several children frequently rejected (13) as a description of the situation. When asked to explain "What really happened?" these children indicated that The Joker, not Grover, had said that the Ninja Turtle had the best smile. Notice that this response is consistent with one interpretation of (13), according to which the pronoun refers to the Ninja Turtle. Apparently, these children had some difficulty accessing the alternative, bound pronoun reading, according to which both Grover and Yogi Bear think that they have the best smile.[19] We would not conclude from this finding, however, that these children lack the bound pronoun interpretation of (13), because both a "yes" and a "no" response is correct. It seems more likely that these children have a preference for the deictic interpretation of a pronoun in this construction.[20]

The logic is the same in interpreting the findings of tests of children's knowledge of linguistic principles. If children lack knowledge of certain linguistic principles, then sentences that would otherwise be governed by a principle of the target grammar should be ambiguous for children, whereas these sentences will be unambiguous for adults. If children frequently reject sentences on the interpretation that is prohibited by a constraint, this is only circumstantial evidence that the constraint is part of their grammars. The possibility remains that the sentence is ambiguous for children, but that the adult interpretation is favored. This is the main reason why we reject the methodological stance of the competing factors model—if we adopt it, we are unable to tease apart behavior that reveals knowledge of linguistic principles from behavior that reveals preferences among alternative interpretations.

[19]Other tests of the availability of bound pronouns confirm this (see Crain & Thornton, 1998).

[20]We noted earlier than children have a bias toward responding yes whenever possible. It now seems clear that the weight of this bias may not be sufficient to override children's preferences in interpreting sentences that are ambiguous to them.

Against this backdrop, we now return to Grimshaw and Rosen's statistical argument that children know Principle B because they succeed in rejecting BT-ungrammatical sentences at a higher level than they reject BT-grammatical sentences. Here is our view of the situation. Children who lack knowledge of Principle B will assign an interpretation that adults do not allow, in addition to the interpretation(s) that they have in common with adults. In other words, BT-ungrammatical sentences such as *Big Bird patted him* will be ambiguous for these children. Let us call the deictic interpretation of the pronoun, which both children and adults assign, Reading A. The children under discussion will also permit an interpretation of such sentences according to which there is coreference between a pronoun and a local c-commanding antecedent (despite contraindexation). Let us call this, Reading B. Finally, let us suppose that children have a preference for Reading A.

First, consider the discourse context in (14).

(14) I saw Big Bird doing something with Ernie. Big Bird patted him.
Context: Big Bird is patting Ernie.

Based on our assumptions, children will accept the test sentences on Reading A in (14) because the context is consistent with their preferred interpretation. Although they also permit Reading B, two forces combine to suppress it: (a) a bias to say yes and (b) the preference for Reading A. Therefore, children will respond yes at a high rate.

Now consider the discourse context in (15).

(15) Big Bird was standing with Ernie. Big Bird hit him.
Context: Big Bird is hitting himself.

Children's dispreferred interpretation is more salient in the context associated with (15). Because children retain their preference for Reading A, however, they will not consistently accept the test sentence in (15) as a correct description of the context. The perceptual salience of Reading B, and children's bias to say yes, will both be offset to some degree by their preference for Reading A. Therefore, children will not accept the test sentence to the same extent as they accepted the test sentence in (14), where their preferred interpretation is made salient by the context. In sum, the lower level of acceptance of Reading B is exactly what we expect, based on our assumption that children favor Reading A over Reading B. Therefore, it is not warranted to infer that children lack Reading B, as G&R contended.

According to the modularity matching model, we can infer that children have knowledge of Principle B only if they perform with near-total accuracy, as adults do, in discourse contexts such as (14) and (15). This follows from the basic architecture of the model. Both children and adults have grammatical modules, processing modules, and perhaps other modules. When a child or an adult is confronted with sentences that are grammatically ambiguous, the processing and the other modules can create preferences for one reading or another. But it is a clear prediction of the MM model that neither children nor adults will accept an ungrammatical utterance.

The modularity matching model assumes that adults will also have the potential of saying no to an interpretation that is grammatical for them if there is another grammatical interpretation that they strongly prefer. It is easy to demonstrate that this is true. To take one example from the language acquisition literature, consider research on long-distance and local binding of Chinese possessive reflexives (Chien, Wexler, & Chang 1993). In Chinese, reflexives may be bound either by a local antecedent or by a long-distance antecedent. Thus in (16) either *Mickey Mouse* (long-distance) or *Donald Duck* (local) may be an antecedent for *ziji-de* (*self's*), as determined by grammaticality judgments. (We present here only the English translation; the experiment was done in Chinese).

(16) Mickey Mouse is dreaming that Donald Duck is holding self's picture.

Chien, Wexler, and Chang used a truth-value judgment task to study children's knowledge of this possibility and, as a control, ran adults on exactly the same task. A picture was presented in which Mickey Mouse was dreaming that Donald Duck was holding a picture. In the long-distance case, Donald Duck was holding Mickey Mouse's picture but not Donald Duck's picture, which was just hanging there. In the local case, Donald Duck was holding Donald Duck's picture but not Mickey Mouse's picture, which was just hanging there.

When presented with the local reading, adults said yes 86.5% and no 13.5% of the time. However, when presented with the long-distance reading, adults said yes 38.5% and no 61.5% of the time. Thus, adults rejected a grammatical reading 61.5% of the time. As Chien, Wexler, and Chang argued, the findings reflect a strong preference for the local reading despite the grammaticality of the long-distance reading.[21] Thus adults also show the capacity to reject sentences that are grammatical if they prefer an alternative interpretation. Again, rejection does not imply ungrammaticality when alternative readings are available. On the other hand, if the model predicts that no alternative analysis is available, then we expect there to be few "no" responses (10% or less as a rule of thumb, leaving room for performance errors, lack of attention, and noise of other kinds). In evaluating observed differences between children's and adults' responses to some linguistic stimuli, the same standards should be used in attributing the differences either to children's grammatical knowledge or to their performance mechanisms. To attribute an error to children's grammars, performance explanations should be dispensed with. Similarly, in attributing an error to performance factors, it is prudent to offer evidence of grammatical competence. This is done by showing that the 'error' is greatly reduced or eliminated in contexts that control for the performance factor in question.

[21]Basically children followed the same pattern of results, but we will not discuss the details here.

The conclusions we have reached about the predictions of the modularity matching model become important in the consideration of inferences to be drawn in many language acquisition experiments. For example, we have seen that children accept coreference between a pronoun and a local antecedent in discourses such as (17) about 50% of the time, in the context of a picture in which Donald Duck was tickling himself.

(17) This is Donald Duck and this is Mickey Mouse. Is Donald tickling him?

The preceding analysis suggests that the conclusion to draw is that the interpretation in which Donald Duck is tickling Donald Duck is grammatical for the child.

How would the modularity matching model respond to this state of affairs? It must take seriously the evidence that children lack some kind of knowledge. What children lack could be some aspect of grammatical knowledge that can reasonably be expected to emerge late in the course of language development. Many researchers have pursued this line, proposing that children lack certain interpretive/pragmatic knowledge (Avrutin & Wexler, 1992; Chien & Wexler, 1990; Grodzinsky & Reinhart, 1993; Montalbetti & Wexler, 1985; Wexler & Chien, 1985, among others).[22] It must be admitted, however, that the conclusion that children are lacking grammatical knowledge of any kind constitutes a retreat from the strongest version of the modularity matching model, though it remains consistent with modularity.[23] Although the deficit may be limited to the nonsyntactic component of the grammar, it is nevertheless a deficit, as compared to the knowledge of adults. Moreover, it remains to explain how this knowledge is attained. Whatever the nature of the grammatical deficit, children permit an interpretation that adults do not permit. This constitutes a learnability problem if we assume that children do not encounter the kind of evidence (in this case, negative semantic evidence) that is needed to expunge the incorrect hypothesis from their grammars.

VIII. INFERENCES ABOUT GRAMMATICALITY

It is well known in the study of linguistics that even judgments of grammaticality in adults must be treated with caution; we do not always know what behav-

[22]Grodzinsky and Reinhart suggested that the children do poorly because they cannot determine whether two representations have the same meaning, due to some kind of memory or processing limi tation. We do not see any obvious way to maintain the position taken by Grodzinsky and Reinhart, despite its advantages from the perspective of language learnability. For example, it is our experience that children know that one conjunct of a conjoined sentence is true and one conjunct is false depending on their contents. They can explicitly talk about the truth values of the conjuncts, pointing out that one is true and one is false. In short, children seem able to compare representations quite well.

[23]It may even add to the argument for modularity in children, as Chien and Wexler (1990) have argued, because the breakdown occurs along the natural seams of grammar.

ioral and cognitive processes underlie this behavior. In many cases, perhaps most cases, we can infer from a judgment of grammaticality that a sentence is grammatical for the person who is judging (and vice versa for ungrammaticality), but there are quite well-known cases where this is not completely true. In the study of language acquisition, where most behaviors that we extract from the child are not direct judgments of grammaticality, the relation between behavior and inferences of grammaticality are at least as indirect. Nevertheless, the results in the field have demonstrated that we are quite often in the position to draw quite reasonable and grounded inferences.

In this section we would like to demonstrate some complexities of inferences concerning grammaticality and competence in the child. We will illustrate via the use of the truth-value judgment task (Crain & McKee, 1985; Crain & Thornton, 1998), a task which has been used quite often in the study of child syntax and semantics. The points that we make concerning the analysis of this task can also be made about other methods commonly used in the study of language acquisition, for example act-out tasks. The reason that we concentrate on the truth-value judgment task is that it is our impression that many scholars use the task in a way to suggest that there is no question about how to infer competence from behavior. In our judgment, results using the truth-value judgment task, as any other behavioral task, must be subject to careful analysis based on a model of the underlying competence. There is no royal road from behavior to theory.

Let us start with one of the virtues of the truth-value judgment task. Suppose a sentence has more than one interpretation, syntactic or semantic. That is, the sentence is ambiguous. The truth-value judgment task can be used to determine whether children have each of the alternative meanings of the sentence in question. Many other tasks are not able to achieve similar results. For example, one classical technique to study what the child's analysis of particular sentences is the act-out task. The child is asked to make toy figures perform the actions mentioned in the sentence. Suppose that a child knows that the sentence is ambiguous, that is, the child can analyze the sentence both ways. But suppose also that the child has a preferred analysis. This preference may be based on a large number of different factors, for example, processing considerations, strategies, situational preferences, or syntactic or semantic complexity of particular readings. It is well known that even adults have such preferences. Studies have shown that in tasks that mimic actual language use, adults often get just one reading of a sentence; it is difficult to make the alternative reading appear. In the right situation, of course, an adult can judge that both readings are possible, and use either reading. But in any given situation, one reading might strongly predominate.

Therefore if we use an act-out task in studying ambiguous sentences, we might find that the children always, or almost always, act out just one reading. This might be true even if the preference for one reading is slight, because this small preference might prevail on the vast majority of trials. Therefore the method might fail to give evidence for the alternative reading. Nevertheless it would clearly be wrong to infer that the child did not know the alternative analysis of the sentence.

The truth-value judgment task is an aid in this situation. In this task, we present a context from which the child can directly infer a specific interpretation of the sentence; then we ask if the sentence is true or false. The assumption is that presenting the child with such contexts gives a boost to this interpretation in the child's mind, thereby making it easier for the child to generate the interpretation. Especially if the preference on interpretation A over interpretation B is slight, we expect that presenting context corresponding to interpretation B boosts its availability to the point that the child will generate it. There are at least two reasons for this expectation. First, the reading is actually presented in a context, rather than the child having to generate it. Second, we assume that the child actively attempts to find a match between the sentence and the context. That is, the child prefers to say yes if possible. We therefore expect that the truth-value judgment task boosts the availability of the alternative reading. Thus, using this task should allow us to obtain evidence for both readings, if the child actually has both readings.

Let us give a simple example. Consider sentence (18).

(18) For him to touch the lion would make the zebra happy.

Responding to sentences such as (18) in an act-out task (where children had to make toy animals act out the action), Tavakolian (1978) found that 75% of the time the children had a third animal, neither the lion nor the zebra, touch the lion. Solan (1983) argued that this shows that children's grammars did not allow for backward anaphora (with the pronoun preceding a coreferential NP); that is, there was a directionality constraint on anaphora in children's grammars, unlike the kinds of constraints that exist in adult grammars.

Suppose, however, that the apparent nonavailability of backward anaphora is actually just the result of a preference for forward anaphora, a preference in fact that might also show itself in adult processing. Because this preference would probably influence every trial, we would expect to see a strong bias against backward anaphora in an act-out task. The truth-value judgment task, on the other hand, might be expected to boost the availability of the backward interpretation.

Using a truth-value judgment task on sentences containing backward anaphora, Crain and McKee (1985) presented such sentences to children and asked them if they were true or false of the situation (in contexts in which an alternative interpretation was equally available). Children said yes 75% of the time to backward anaphora sentences; that is, they allowed coreference between a pronoun and a following NP 75% of the time. Of course, it is always essential in using the truth-value judgment task to demonstrate that children will consistently say no to similar sentences that are ungrammatical for the child (and for the adult). This was also done in this experiment, using Principle C violations. We can conclude that children's grammars allow backward anaphora, just as adults' grammars do. By boosting the availability of the backward reading, the truth-value judgment task allowed us to demonstrate the existence of a reading that is nonpreferred.

We might ask in this last experiment why children only said yes 75% of the time when presented with a backward anaphora sentence for which yes was an appropriate answer. The answer is clear; the other reading, in which the pronoun had an external referent, was still possible. By presenting the backward anaphora reading, its availability was boosted; however, 25% of the time the reading that came to children's minds was the external reading, and they therefore said no to the backward anaphora reading. There is no absolute guarantee that making an interpretation available will cause the child to generate that interpretation. Similarly, if a sentence is ambiguous for a child, we cannot take "no" responses to a presentation of one reading in the truth-value judgment task as evidence that a reading cannot be generated by the child. Rather, the preference for the alternative reading might be great enough that even the presentation of a reading does not make it readily available to children (or adults). In the present example we saw that children said no 25% of the time when a backward anaphora sentence was presented.

It is quite possible that the child will even say no considerably more often than this to a presented interpretation if the sentence is ambiguous and the other interpretation is highly preferred. This puts a limit on the effectiveness of the truth-value judgment task. It is not always possible to tell whether a child's pattern of responses is indicative of a strong preference for one reading of an ambiguous sentence or evi-dence of a genuine grammatical prohibition against the other reading. There are ways to overcome this limitation in certain cases, but we will not pursue the matter further here (see Crain & Thornton, 1998).

The need to distinguish preferences and principles has not taken hold in the literature, even among researchers who work within the generative framework. A notable exception is the work of Helen Cairns (e.g., see Cairns, McDaniel, Hsu, & Rapp, 1994). Perhaps the following remarks will help to explain why. Generally, people use ambiguous sentences in contexts that are consistent with only one of their interpretations; it is rare for a sentence to be used in a context that is appropriate for more than one of its interpretations. Although such circumstances are rare, consider an ambiguous sentence for which one interpretation would be strongly preferred, if the context were consistent with both interpretations. In certain instances in ordinary life, the sentence will be used in contexts that are consistent only with the dispreferred interpretation. In such contexts, the perceiver is compelled to disregard the preferred interpretation, and seek out the alternative interpretation. This may take some cognitive effort, but apparently it is something perceivers manage quite well for the most part. In ordinary contexts, then, the perceiver can correctly understand a sentence, whichever interpretation is intended by the speaker, although the cognitive demands may be greater in certain contexts than in others.

Children's linguistic knowledge is rarely tested in ordinary contexts, however. In experiments with children, the contexts that researchers construct are generally consistent with more than one interpretation of the test sentence. One is the adult interpretation; the other is the interpretation prohibited by the principle being investigated. Lacking the principle, children may have access to both interpretations of the test sentence, but they could still favor one over the other. Suppose that children favor the interpretation that is consistent with the adult grammar. If the sentence is false on this interpretation in the (ambiguous) experimental contexts, then children may reject it, because it is false on the interpretation that comes most easily to them. Therefore, we cannot infer from children's "no" responses that they do not command the interpretation associated with the "yes" response. The interpretation associated with the "yes" response may just be less accessible.

IX. CONCLUSION

In this chapter we have argued for the modularity matching model of language acquisition, and we have argued against the competing factors model. As we saw, according to the CF model, all that is required to demonstrate knowledge of a linguistic principle is conformity to the principle at a level significantly above chance. From a theoretical standpoint, the problem with the CF model is that it introduces additional degrees of freedom beyond those of the modularity matching model. On the CF model, language is viewed as a large set of tendencies, so that knowledge of language amounts to certain statistical tendencies in behavior. Therefore, showing that the statistical behavior of children is different for different constructions shows that they have learned adult capacities of grammar. The particular versions of the CF model that we discussed all claimed that grammar is just one linguistic ability that competes with other aspects of linguistic ability to yield a statistical portrait in behavior.

We have tried to illustrate the methodological problems with this approach. Basically, adherence to the CF model makes it difficult to distinguish between a child's knowledge of a constraint and a lack of such knowledge. In the absence of a constraint, children should judge sentences otherwise governed by the constraint to be ambiguous. But, one meaning of an ambiguous sentence may be more accessible than another. It is well-established that adults have systematic preferences for certain interpretations of ambiguities over others; surely this is true for children as well. If this is true, however, then it could turn out that children exhibit a systematic preference for the interpretation that is consistent with the adult grammar, even in cases where they also allow the interpretation ruled out by the constraint in the adult grammar. If children's dispreferred reading is the one prohibited by the constraint being investigated, then it is easy to mistake children's preferences for assigning a semantic interpretation as knowledge of a linguistic principle. This renders the methodological stance of the CF model inappropriate for competence-based theories of language acquisition within the generative framework.

ACKNOWLEDGMENTS

We wish to express our gratitude to the following people for helpful commentary: Sergey Avrutin, Paul Bloom, Carole Boster, Helen Cairns, Laura Conway, Peter Culicover, Nina Hyams, David Lightfoot, Diane Lillo-Martin, Dana McDaniel, Cecile McKee, Mineharu Nakayama, Luigi Rizzi, Sara Rosen, John Rosen, Donald Shankweiler, and, especially, Rosalind Thornton. Portions of this research were presented by Stephen Crain at the 1993 SISSA Conference: Crosslinguistic Acquisition Studies, Trieste, Italy. In addition, the modularity matching model was the foundation for lectures given by Stephen Crain at the 1993 Summer Institute of the Linguistic Society of America at the Ohio State University. The research was supported, in part, by a National Institute of Child Health and Human Development grant to Haskins Laboratories (HD-01994).

REFERENCES

Avrutin, S., & Wexler, K. (1992). Development of Principle B in Russian: Coindexation at LF and coreference. *Language Acquisition, 2*(1), 259–306.

Baddeley, A., & Hitch, G. (1974). Working memory. In G. H. Bower (Ed.), *The psychology of learning and motivation* (Vol. 8). New York: Academic Press.

Bloom, P. (1990). Subjectless sentences in child grammar. *Linguistic Inquiry, 21,* 491–504.

Bloom, P. (1993). Grammatical continuity in language development: The case of subjectless sentences. *Linguistic Inquiry, 24,* 721–734.

Borer, H., & Wexler, K. (1987). The maturation of syntax. In T. Roeper & E. Williams (Eds.), *Parameter setting.* Dordrecht: Reidel.

Brown, R. (1973). *A first language: The early stages.* Cambridge, MA: Harvard University Press.

Cairns, H., McDaniel, D., Hsu, J. R., & Rapp, M. (1994). A longitudinal study of principles of control and pronominal reference in child English. *Language, 70,* 260–288.

Chien, Y., & Wexler, K. (1990). Children's knowledge of locality conditions in binding as evidence for the modularity of syntax and pragmatics. *Language Acquisition, 1*(3): 225–295.

Chien, Y., Wexler, K., & Chang, H. (1993). Children's development of long-distance binding in Chinese. *Journal of East Asian Linguistics, 2,* 229–259.

Crain, S. (1991). Language acquisition in the absence of experience. *Behavioral and Brain Sciences, 14*(4): 597–650.

Crain, S., & McKee, C. (1985). The acquisition of structural restrictions on anaphora. *Proceedings of NELS 16*. Amherst, MA: GLSA.

Crain, S., & Shankweiler, D. (1991). Modularity and learning to read. In I. G. Mattingly & M. Studdert-Kennedy (Eds.), *Modularity and the motor theory of speech perception* (pp. 375–392). Hillsdale, NJ: Erlbaum.

Crain, S., Shankweiler, D., Macaruso, P., & Bar-Shalom, E. (1990). Working memory and comprehension of spoken sentences: Investigations of children with reading disorder. In G. Vallar & T. Shallice (Eds.), *Neuropsychological disorders of short-term memory* (pp. 477–508). Cambridge, England: Cambridge University Press.

Crain, S., & Thornton, R. (1998). *Investigations in Universal Grammar: A guide to experiments on the acquisition of syntax and semantics.* Cambridge, MA: The MIT Press.

de Villiers, J., Roeper, T., & Vainikka, A. (1990). The acquisition of long-distance rules. In L. Frazier & J. de Villiers (Eds.), *Language processing and language acquisition.* Dordrecht: Reidel.

Fodor, J. (1983). *The modularity of mind.* Cambridge, MA: MIT Press.

Grimshaw, J., & Rosen, S. T. (1990). Knowledge and obedience: The developmental status of the binding theory. *Linguistic Inquiry, 21*(2), 187–222.

Grodzinsky, Y., & Reinhart, T. (1993). The innateness of binding and the development of coreference: A reply to Grimshaw and Rosen. *Linguistic Inquiry, 24*(1), 69–103.

Guasti, M. T., Thornton, R., & Wexler, K. (1995). Negation in children's questions: The case of English. *Proceedings of the 19th Annual Boston University Conference on Language Development.* Somerville, MA: Cascadilla Press.

Hamburger, H., & Crain, S. (1987). Plans and semantics in human processing of language. *Cognitive Science, 11,* 101–136.

Hyams, N. (1986). *Language acquisition and the theory of parameters.* Dordrecht: Reidel.

Hyams, N., & Wexler, K. (1993). On the grammatical basis of null subjects in child language. *Linguistic Inquiry, 24,* 421–459.

McDaniel, D., & McKee, C. (1993). Which children did they show know strong crossover? In H. Goodluck & M. Rochemont (Eds.), *Island Constraints.* Dordrecht: Kluwer Academic Publishers, 275–294.

MacWhinney, B., & Bates, E. (1990). *Crosslinguistic studies of sentence processing.* Cambridge, England: Cambridge University Press.

Montalbetti, M., & Wexler, K. (1985). Binding is linking. *Proceedings of the West Coast Conference on Formal Linguistics, 4,* 228–245.

Pierce, A. (1992). *Language acquisition and syntactic theory: Comparative analysis of French and English child grammars.* Dordrecht: Kluwer.

Pinker, S. (1984). *Language Learnability and Language Development.* Cambridge, MA: Harvard University Press.

Roeper, T. (1986). How children acquire bound variables. In B. Lust (Ed.), *Studies in the Acquisition of Anaphora* (Vol. 1). Dordrecht: Reidel.

Roeper, T., Rooth, M., Malish, T., & Akayama, S. (1984). The problem of empty categories and bound variables in language acquisition. Unpublished manuscript, University of Massachusetts, Amherst.

Siegel, S. (1956). *Nonparametric statistics for the behavioral sciences.* New York: McGraw-Hill.

Solan, L. (1983). *Pronominal reference: Child language and the theory of grammar.* Dordrecht: Reidel.

Tavakolian, S. (1978). Children's comprehension of pronominal subjects and missing subjects in complicated sentences. In H. Goodluck & L. Solan (Eds.), *Papers in the structure and development of child language.* University of Massachusetts Occasional Papers in Linguistics (Vol. 4).

Thornton, R. (1990). *Adventures in long-distance moving: The acquisition of complex Wh-questions.* Unpublished Ph.D. dissertation, University of Connecticut.

Thornton, R. (1993). *Children who don't raise the negative.* Paper presented at the LSA Annual Meeting, Los Angeles, CA.

Thornton, R., & Crain, S. (1994). Successful cyclic movement. In T. Hoekstra and B. Schwartz (Eds.), *Language Acquisition Studies in Generative Grammar.* Amsterdam: Johns Benjamins.

Valian, V. (1992). Syntactic subjects in the early speech of American and Italian children. *Cognition, 40,* 21–81.

Wexler, K., & Chien, Y. (1985). The development of lexical anaphors and pronouns. *Papers and Reports on Child Language Development* (Vol. 24). Palo Alto, CA: Stanford University Press.

Wexler, K. (1994). Finiteness and head movement in early child grammars. In D. Lightfoot & N. Hornstein (Eds.), *Verb movement.* Cambridge, England: Cambridge University Press.

CHAPTER 13

HOW DO WE KNOW WHAT CHILDREN KNOW?
Problems and Advances in Establishing Scientific Methods for the Study of Language Acquistion and Linguistic Theory

Barbara Lust, Suzanne Flynn, Claire Foley, and Yu-Chin Chien

I. INTRODUCTION

Current linguistic theory, particularly a theory of universal grammar (UG), makes significant predictions for the study of first language acquisition. As the linguistic theory of UG develops, it generates more refined hypotheses regarding linguistic knowledge. This theory, like any theory in science, however, is only as strong as its predictiveness, and its predictions are only as strong as the methodology that allows them to be tested. Current studies of first language acquisition that work within a theory of UG must confront fundamental issues regarding methodology in this field. Various methods provide data that can "only serve as the grounds for inference about what constitutes the linguistic consciousness that provides the basis for language use" (Chomsky, 1964, p. 132).[1] The question is, when is this inference valid, and how can we find the strongest possible grounds for this inference?

[1]Chomsky here appears to intend the term *consciousness* to refer to *competence.*

Handbook of Child Language Acquisition

The Structure of This Chapter

In Section II of this chapter, we will introduce several problems that characterize the interpretation of language data and the study of children's linguistic knowledge. These problems have confounded researchers' ability to discover the true nature of developmental change in the child's language knowledge (cf. Lust, chapter 4 of this volume). In the rest of this chapter, we suggest ways to confront these problems. To this end, Section III presents the basis for developing a theory of research methodology in this area, one that assumes fundamental properties of scientific inquiry in behavioral science, as well as in formal linguistic theory. Given these assumptions, Section IV and V discuss current advances in research methodology, which can now confront central problems in the study of language acquisition.

II. PROBLEMS IN DETERMINING WHAT CHILDREN KNOW

Chomsky suggested very early:

> The attempt to write a grammar for a child raises all of the unsolved problems of constructing a grammar for adult speech, multiplied by some rather large factor. (1964, p. 129)

We will suggest in this chapter that essential problems regarding linguistic methodology in the study of the child's language knowledge do not differ in nature from those that characterize the study of the adult's linguistic competence. They appear confounded in the study of the child for reasons not directly related to these problems.

One large factor that differentiates the child from the adult is that some aspects of the child's language knowledge may be assumed to be changing (i.e., developing). This issue does not affect the nature of psycholinguistic methodology, however, which must assess grammatical knowledge at single points of time, just as in the adult.

A. What Is the Object of Inquiry?

Grammar Is Not Subject to Statistical Analysis: Behavior Is

The object of inquiry—that is, grammar—is not a statistically analyzable phenomenon. It is not continuous and not continuously variable, but discrete, like mathematics. Linguistic categories and rules for their combination, for example, "are absolutes which admit of no compromise" (Joos, 1966, p. 351).

At the same time, behavior with language, such as an occurrence in real time of production or comprehension of language, is essentially variable. It is subject to the principles of the social sciences and is statistically analyzable on the basis of these continuously variable data. The discrete object of inquiry, grammar, must be inferred.

Complexity of Natural Language Knowledge

The full extent of the problem in assessing children's grammatical knowledge through any methods can be seen when we recognize the complexity of language knowledge. We must distinguish between I-language (that which is represented internally in the mind), E-language (external phenomena commonly referred to as *language*) and data (the actual acoustic phenomena in utterances spoken or understood). (See Chomsky, 1986, and Kapur, Lust, Harbert, & Martohardjono, 1992). In addition, current linguistic theory distinguishes between I-language (which involves a specific language grammar (SLG) that is represented internally in the mind of a particular speaker or hearer) and UG (a theory of possible I-languages) that underlies all specific language grammars. In current linguistic theory, UG is the true object of scientific inquiry. It provides a model of the *initial state* (e.g., Chomsky, 1981, 1986).

Given this complexity, conclusions regarding knowledge of UG on the basis of any type of performance in a single specific language by a particular individual at a particular point in time is always indeterminate with regard to UG, and evidence regarding UG is always confounded with SLG.[2] E-language and I-language are always confounded in any performance with language. Inference regarding grammatical knowledge in the child, as well as in the adult, must acknowledge these distinctions.

B. Relating Grammar and Behavior

Because language behavior is essentially variable, evidence regarding knowledge of grammatical factors on the basis of behavior will always involve significant contrasts of degree, not absolute success with one grammatical condition in a particular sentence and absolute failure with another. Although essential to behavioral science, this premise of assumed behavioral variance is not always applied in the field of first language acquisition.[3] If it were the case that when children (or adults) have grammatical knowledge, then their performance on a task that tests this grammatical knowledge were always perfect, then their performance

[2]Kapur and colleagues (in prep.), Lust (in prep.), and Boser and colleagues (1992) provide examples of attempts to take these distinctions into account. Boser and colleagues (1995), Foley (1996) and Lust (1994 and chapter 4 of this volume) pursue theories of acquisition based on these distinctions. See Flynn and Martohardjono (1994) on the issue of the separability of UG from specific language grammar in language knowledge.

[3]See the contrast between discussions in Grimshaw & Rosen (1990) and Grodzinsky & Reinhart (1993), for example.

would show no variance, If we held this view, however, we would underestimate or ignore the complexity of linguistic theory of language knowledge, as well as the psychological reality of language behavior occurring in real time.

Formulation of Hypotheses: An Apparent Paradox

Before we begin to analyze the relation between grammatical knowledge and behavior, we must first confront a basic paradox that appears to characterize a linguistically guided study of first language acquisition. A linguistic model of grammatical competence is necessary to characterize the grammatical component of what must be acquired by the child and to test the nature of what the child seems to know about language. At the same time, however, the specific aim of the study of first language acquisition is to explain how language knowledge is acquired. Essentially, the field seeks an explanation of the transition from S_o (an initial state at which language is not known) to S_n (a state at which language is known). Here, n must be > 0 and thus $S_o \neq S_n$. Given that the adult linguistic model characterizes the competence of S_n, this adult model cannot characterize the competence of S_o. To assume that it does is necessarily false. It is false logically because $S_o \neq S_n$. It is also false in the sense that various specific language grammars (e.g., Tulu or Indonesian) cannot preexist at S_o. To assume that the adult linguistic model does simply characterize the initial state would beg the issue of language acquisition and vitiate its explanation. However, if the adult linguistic model of competence cannot be simply assumed at S_o, then how can hypotheses, and consequently data analyses, regarding language knowledge in the child at S_o (or at any $S_i < S_n$) be formulated in linguistic terms that characterize S_n?

This important question has led some scholars (e.g., Clark, 1983; Donaldson, 1978) to overlook consistency between child language (S_o) and adult grammar (S_n). These approaches sometimes abdicate hypothesis formation and analyses of child language that make reference to adult grammar. They may also abdicate the use of experimental method, which is led by linguistically guided theoretical hypotheses, in the study of first language acquisition.

C. Indeterminacy of Language Data

In addition, we must presume that the relation between linguistic knowledge and behavioral data will always be to some degree indeterminate.

Competence and Performance

Just as linguistic research in the adult seeks to characterize the true nature of grammar (competence) on the basis of language data resulting from behavior in real time with language (i.e., adult performance with language) in conjunction with analyses of linguistic theory, so also developmental psycholinguistic research must pursue the assessment of possibly changing grammatical knowledge in the child (competence) through the measurement and analyses of various modes of language behavior—principally, *speaking* and *understanding*—in combination with analyses of linguistic theory. The language functions that these behaviors reflect (i.e., language *production* and *comprehension*) constitute language performance. They are essentially variable.

Grammaticality Judgments

On some views, the form of data that most directly reveals grammatical competence in the adult is a judgment about a particular sentence as grammatically acceptable or not.

Grammaticality judgments, however, reflect a type of performance and thus are subject to the variability that characterizes all performance. Subjects (whether adult or child) making a grammaticality judgment must process, store, and comprehend a particular sentence that they hear, analyze its meaning and its form, and judge whether the sentence is possible in any interpretation. Judgment about a sentence may reflect a judgment about any aspect of this language knowledge, from pragmatics to syntax.

Because it involves performance, this method is not a direct and unique measure of grammatical competence. It is not stable, even with adults. (See Levelt, 1974, p. 14f, and Schütze, 1996, for example.) Because grammaticality judgments apply to specific utterances, that is, to specific language data, they do not directly reflect I-language or a theory of possible I-languages (namely, universal grammar).

In addition, grammaticality judgments do not easily allow a standardized experimental procedure with large samples of young children. Brown (1973) reported a child's classic "pop goes the weasel" response by a young child to this task. Sinclair, Jarvella, and Levelt (1978) provided evidence that the competence required for such metalinguistic judgments only gradually develops (cf. Brown, 1973; Clark, 1983; Fraser, Bellugi, & Brown, 1963; & Maratsos, 1983). In addition, young children's judgments have been found not to be consistently *grammatically* based. At best, they can reveal any aspect of the complexity of language knowledge. (See McDaniel, McKee, & Cairns, 1996, for recent discussion.)[4]

Natural Speech

For very young children, researchers must frequently resort to study of observations of natural speech as the basis for their inference regarding the child's knowledge. Particular utterances by particular children (e.g., Adam, Eve, and Sarah, in Brown, 1973) have often been argued to cohere with particular theories of grammatical knowledge and thus are used in a demonstrative manner.

[4]See also Gleitman, Gleitman, and Shipley (1972), who report some initial success with this method of grammaticality judgment with children. They study the relative roles of grammatical and semantic factors in determining children's metalinguistic judgments. See also Pratt, Tunmer, and Bowey (1984) for evidence on these factors with older children (5 and 6 years old) and for evidence of these children's differential metalinguistic ability when given different types of grammatical violation.

However, what occurs in natural speech does not immediately define grammar in the child, just as it does not in the adult. As had been observed very early:

> In actual speech, the highest probability must be assigned to broken and interrupted fragments of sentences or two sentences which begin in one way and end in a different, totally incompatible way. (Chomsky, 1964, p. 132)

In addition, even when an utterance looks grammatical in terms of some adult analysis of the surface string, it is never possible to know, by mere observation of a single utterance, the actual underlying structure of the utterance, not to mention the grammar that generated that structure. A single utterance alone will not provide evidence for what is systematic about grammatical knowledge and will always allow multiple possible formal representations.

Grammatical constraints on possible structures will never be directly evidenced by the occurrence of any utterance or set of utterances. Even more seriously, no particular utterance will in itself instantiate UG, that is, the set of fundamental principles and parameters that constrain all possible theories of grammar (I-languages) and by hypothesis constitute the *initial state.* In addition, given a change of circumstances (time, pragmatic conditions, and different focus), a child, like an adult, may produce a different set of utterances. Problems of *rich interpretation* of what a child *means* by a particular utterance are well known (Bloom, 1970; Brown, 1973). See Berk (1996) for further discussion.

In these ways, any particular sample of natural speech must essentially underdetermine any principles or constraints that might be a part of a child's grammar.

D. Variability in Estimating Linguistic Knowledge from Language Data

Across all tasks and methods, the relation between grammatical knowledge and behavioral data is intrinsically variable. Several distinct sources of variability must be recognized.

Variability Reflecting Cognitive Modularity

Nonlinguistic variables, for example, those involved in real time on-line processing of language, mediate all language behavior and provide variance. In the child it must be assumed that variables relevant to processing may be developing, for example, memory, attention, or speech timing (Cooper, 1977). However, it should be noted that an exact science of these variables (e.g., what constitutes memory, how it interacts with other cognitive functions, and how it develops) is still not well developed. For example, in many ways, child memory is not essentially deficited (cf. Chi, 1978, for example).[5] In addition, the ability to structure a

[5]See Blake, Quarto, Austin, & Vingiles, 1984; Brainerd and Kingman, 1985; Ceci and Howe, 1978; Piaget and Inhelder, 1973; and Squire, 1986 for example.

stimulus (e.g., to structure a list of items) may determine the ability to remember it, not vice versa. Grammar provides the essential *structure* for language. Thus, these variables (i.e., grammatical knowledge and processing variables such as memory for language) cannot be studied totally independently.

Variability Reflecting Linguistic Modularity

The modularity involved in the theory of UG itself provides the basis for further essential variance. Consider for example, an apparently simple sentence, as in (1).

(1) The girl loves the child.

Like all sentences, this one is infinitely ambiguous. Its interpretation depends on a discourse domain through which the reference of the Noun Phrases (NPs) is determined. Its interpretation also depends on possible idiosyncrasies of the lexicon, for example, the range of reference allowed in English to a term such as *girl* and that related to the definite (as opposed to indefinite) determiner *the,* as well as that accorded to the verbal lexicon. Each of these ambiguities will reflect language-specific variation (e.g., in the lexicon) but also subject-specific variation (deriving from belief systems of the individual subject). Like all sentences, this one also obeys a myriad of grammatical/syntactic principles, which derive from different modules of UG, for example, those related to phrase structure as well as those related to binding theory. In this case, Principle C of the binding theory [i.e., the principle determining that an NP may not be c-commanded in a local domain by a NP to which it is coreferential] determines that *the girl* and *the child* are not coreferential. Because these various syntactic principles (e.g., those related to phrase structure and those related to the binding theory) are modular in UG, they must be integrated. Their integration in a specific language grammar cannot be predetermined nor can their integration in a particular sentence. (See Cohen Sherman & Lust, 1993; Boser et al., 1995; and Foley, 1996, for theory of acquisition that involves integration of modular UG components.) Test of knowledge of a particular aspect of grammar in even a simple sentence like (1) will always involve many independent aspects of grammar, other than the one being tested.

Variability Reflecting Language-Specific Grammar

Each syntactic principle involved in any sentence has language-specific components through which it has been filtered. In sentence (1), for example, these principles minimally involve the left-headed parameter of English phrase structure (which determines that the verb precedes the object, as opposed to Japanese, for example), the language-specific system of definite reference linked to the determiner (as opposed to Chinese, for example, where there are no determiners), and the language-specific lexicon of definite NPs as it relates to the binding theory (cf. Lasnik, 1989). The integration of each of the modular UG principles must be achieved through the language-specific grammar. Any particular judgment of grammaticality of a sentence like such as (1), or a particular production or comprehension of such a sentence, will thus necessarily reflect complex knowledge, wherein UG is mediated by the specific language grammar.

Variability Reflecting Language-Specific Pragmatic Factors

Language-specific pragmatic factors will also interact in any particular sentence interpretation (cf. Austin et al., 1996; Boser, 1996; Demuth, 1990; Eisele & Lust, 1996). For example, Austin and colleagues (1996) and Boser (1996) showed how existence of null arguments in child language (e.g., *pro drop*) must be mapped differently to pragmatic facts in Spanish, German, and English.

Variability Reflecting Real-Time Behavior

In addition, as with all performance, slips in memory, attention, misanalysis, and preoccupation are additional factors that will affect every particular language behavior in real time (see also Mazuka & Lust, 1990 for argument that there are principled relations between language knowledge and processing).

III. FOUNDATIONS FOR THEORY OF RESEARCH METHODOLOGY

How then, given these numerous sources of necessary variance, the indeterminacy of all language data, and the complexity of language knowledge, can language behavior be interpreted to be evidence that significantly grounds inference regarding grammatical knowledge that is not variant (which in turn can be related to UG)?

In this section, we lay the foundations for methods to overcome the problems we isolated previously.

A. Resolving Theoretical Paradox

First, the apparent paradox specified in Section 2.2.1 is not real. Given current linguistic theory (e.g., Chomsky 1981, 1986, 1988, and later) and the complexity of language knowledge recognized in Section 2.1.2, UG is a model of fundamental linguistic principles and parameters that characterize the so-called initial state and determine the core grammar of the specific language being acquired (cf. Lust, in prep, and chapter 4 of this volume). UG is not equivalent to a specific language grammar or even to a particular core grammar. Thus we can assume these UG principles, and test them, without begging the essential questions of language acquisition.

The critical predicted empirical consequences of UG as a characterization of the human competence for language are that it may serve to restrict and guide children's hypotheses during first language acquisition (cf. Lust, 1986, in prep). UG does not completely determine the end state.

Through the theory of UG, researchers may seek to formalize linguistically determined principles and parameters that may *constrain* the process of first language acquisition. These principles and parameters are predicted to determine the child's sensitivity to dimensions of language variation and their hypotheses regarding possible language variation. Researchers may test for empirical evidence of these in early acquisition data. Characterizing these constraints on children's hypotheses is focal to the characterization of initial language competence and to the eventual explanation of first language acquisition, without begging the essential issues of acquisition.

B. Resolving Indeterminacy and Variability of Language Data

Mere description of particular behaviors is of limited use. Analysis of properties of the *course* and *nature* of acquisition computed over individual behaviors, however, can provide data that indirectly reflect abstract principles and parameters of initial and universal grammatical competence.

Evaluation of Constraint

Evidence for *constraint* on first language acquisition must (a) compare what children do *not* do in language as well as what they do and (b) evaluate restrictions on the *course* of acquisition over time. For example, if very young children do not take certain options for specific language variation that older children do take, this may evidence a *constrained* acquisition process. In certain cases, we may expect younger children (who are closer to the initial state) to be more restricted in their grammatical hypotheses than older children (cf. Somashekar et al., 1995, for an example). This is because specific language grammars, which are acquired over time, may expand or modulate constraints given by UG. In other cases, UG constraint may be continuous across development (Lust, Eisele, & Mazuka, 1992). (c) Finally, the research paradigm of UG predicts that (at least some) observed constraints in child language may be precisely linked to hypothesized grammatical factors and linguistic theory (cf. Lust, Eisele, & Mazuka, 1992; Somashekar et al., 1995).[6]

[6]This is not to deny that in some instances, language development may include the "development" of restrictions. For example, Lust, Chien, Chiang, and Eisele (1996) found that a *directionality* (linear precedence) principle on lexical pronouns in Chinese is only developmentally achieved. This linear precedence principle, they concluded, is not given by UG.

C. Experimental Methods

Given that all behavioral data is variable and underestimates linguistic knowledge, reliable methodology must (a) constrain and (b) identify and disambiguate the sources of behavioral variance in evaluating child language knowledge.

Manipulation of Linguistically Precise Factors

Experimental methods, including controlled experimental designs, allow test of specific hypothesized linguistic factors as components of grammatical competence that may provide the source of observed constraints on behavior.

Scientific Assumption for Validating Inference from Experimental Data: Assessment of Variance

If linguistic factors that are varied in experimental design of a language task are significant in a child's grammatical competence, then we can assume that the child's behavioral variance on the task will be constrained by these factors to a degree significantly beyond chance. In an experimental design that can measure and evaluate variance, significantly constrained variance can be taken as evidence that children, in their performance, are consulting the experimental linguistic factor that has been manipulated. We can therefore assume that critical data in the study of grammatical competence in the child (or adult) consists of a significant *pattern of behavioral variance* that is constrained by precisely defined linguistic factors.

Statistical Methods

As in other behavioral sciences, the range and pattern of behavioral variance in language across children as well as within children can and must be quantitatively assessed for difference from chance through the use of statistical methods. As with all experimental design, error in interpretation of these statistical results can be controlled by statistical significance level and sample size. In particular, larger sample sizes increase the probability of detecting "real" effects, which may go undetected with smaller samples (avoiding Type II error). Adopting a stringent significance level can reduce the probability that observed variation in experimental data that is actually due to chance, or to extraneous factors, is falsely attributed to a hypothesized grammatical factor (avoiding Type I error).

In addition, empirical results must allow *replication* (cf. Lust, 1981). The following statement of concern, as reported in the journal *Science*, applies to the study of first language acquisition, as it does to all scientific research:

> The implications of not reproducing experiments are severe. Much of what is published goes unchallenged, may be untrue, and probably nobody knows. Does anybody care? (Neufeld, 1986, p. 11)

IV. INFERRING WHAT CHILDREN KNOW FROM THEIR BEHAVIOR ON TASKS

A. Current Advances in the Study of Natural Speech

Recently, researchers have strengthened the methods of analysis on which grammatical knowledge is inferred from observations of children's natural speech. More rigorous recent methods, although not experimental, involve not only more extensive sampling but more thorough, comprehensive analyses of a child's extended corpus of speech at a particular time, analysis of the productivity or generalizability of a child's constructions, and precise linguistic analyses of utterances in conjunction with precise context analyses. (See Boser, 1996; Boser, Lust, Santelmann, & Whitman, 1991; Deprez & Pierce, 1993; Santelmann, 1995; Stromswald, K., 1990; Valian, 1992; and Weissenborn, 1994 for examples of such analytic methods.) Current methods have also insisted on larger samples of children and have also initiated systematic methods for cross-linguistic study of children in order to begin to dissociate UG from specific language grammar.[7] More recently, Berk (1996) developed methods for triggering richer natural speech samples, in connection with linguistic hypotheses, providing a wider range of syntax in the child's utterances.

These newer methods also insist on more comprehensive linguistic evidence of the systematicity of children's grammars in order to infer grammatical knowledge. (See the papers collected in Lust et al., eds., 1994a,b, for examples of such argumentation.) For example, if a child's knowledge of complementizer phrase (CP) in phrase structure is hypothesized, then converging evidence may be sought from knowledge of various grammatical processes that operate on this structure (topicalization, question formation, etc.) (Santelmann, 1995, articulated this position; also see Boser, 1996).

These more comprehensive and systematic linguistic analyses have significantly strengthened inference of children's knowledge of grammar on the basis of the observed data from child natural language, even strengthening inference regarding what does *not* occur, and thus grounding inference on knowledge of constraints. For example, Boser (1989) and Boser and colleagues (1991) argued that "null" auxiliaries occurred in utterances within a child's corpus at the same time as did overt auxiliaries. This supports other arguments that grammatical competence (for the auxiliary) must be intact even when in performance, the knowledge is sometimes reflected in null elements, such as (2) where the child first uses an overt Aux, and subsequently omits one in a single discourse.

[7]For example, see Boser et al. (1995) on German, Swedish, and Dutch contrasts in young children's natural speech and Whitman, Lee, & Lust (1991).

(2) Child: Der affe *ist* pusputt
The ape *is* broken.
Adult: Was ist kaputt? Der arm ab?
What is broken? The arm off?
Child: Affe, der niedere arm gemache, der affe putt gemacht.
Ape, the lower arm made-part, the ape broken made-part.
(JH, 2,7; Boser, Lust, Santleman, & Whitman, 1992)

For another example, earlier work had considered observations of utterances such as (3) to instantiate an early German child grammar that differed from the adult grammar in being verb final during an early stage and in lacking verb raising, which characterizes the adult grammar (e.g., Clahsen, 1982). Boser (1989) reasoned that these utterances were essentially ambiguous as to whether they were V-2 (correct for adult) or V-final.

(3) Wau-wau bellt
bow-wow barks
(("The) dog barks.") KS (1,11) Boser corpus

To test this issue, Boser systematically analyzed natural speech samples from 30 German children, first eliminating these ambiguous two-word utterances and then concentrating on all others with verbs. These data (together with extensive empirical analyses) revealed that there was no early stage of German child language in which the grammar was primarily verb final and inconsistent with the adult's with regard to verb raising (Boser, 1996; Boser et al., 1991). Similarly, cross-linguistic data and systematic, comparative analyses of these revealed that there was no universal stage of lack of verb-raising knowledge in the child (Boser et al., 1995). (See also Demuth, 1994, for an example of similar arguments for continuity of grammatical knowledge on the basis of extended cross-linguistic analyses, including analyses of Sesotho and Valian, 1991, for such arguments on the basis of a systematic contrast of extensive Italian and English acquisition data.)

Thus, extending the natural speech database to larger systematically and richer samples (more utterances from more children and more languages) and systematizing analyses, in connection with hypotheses derived from linguistic theory, can and does lead to strengthened hypotheses, to more constrained inference about the grammatical knowledge of children and the nature of its development, and to the isolation of UG from SLG in the researcher's inference.

Strengthening of Inference from Natural Speech by Experimental Methods

Inference from limited observations of natural speech can also be critically supported, disconfirmed, or corrected by related evidence from experimentation.

Convergence of Natural Speech and Experimental Methods

Systematic analyses of natural speech have been found to provide evidence that converges with that from experimental methods. We briefly review several of these experimental methods. (Examples can be found in Boser's experimental results, 1996, which converged with her natural speech analyses. See also Lust & Mervis, 1980, based on earlier experimental studies of Lust, 1977, and Austin et al., 1996, 1997, for study of natural speech, converging with the experimental study by Nuñez del Prado, Foley, & Lust, 1993; Nũnez del Prado, Foley, Proman, & Lust, 1994; and Berk's 1996 study of natural speech, converging with experimental work by Santelmann, Berk, Austin, Somashekar, & Lust, 1996. See Lust, Chien, & Flynn, 1987, for review of earlier converging studies.)

B. Experimental Test of Production: Elicited Imitation (EI)

We have argued elsewhere (Lust, Chien, & Flynn, 1987; Lust, Flynn, & Foley, 1996, for example) that experimental production tasks (in particular, an experimentally controlled version of elicited imitation [EI]) may provide one of the most direct and scientifically controlled methods to ground inference regarding the child's knowledge of specific factors of grammatical competence, especially syntactic factors.

This method, which is accessible to very young children, is founded on the fact that the child's imitation of sentences (beyond a minimal length and structure) is not simply processed by rote but is actively reconstructed through the child's syntactic and semantic systems—that is, it is interpreted, analyzed, and reconstructed actively in terms of the child's own grammar. Thus children's imitation behaviors reflect their own analytic and reconstructed representations of the adult's stimulus sentence and mirror the child's grammar. Unlike in natural speech data, the child's target is clearly revealed in the EI task.

The EI task can be designed to focus on hypothesized syntactic principles or parameters. For example, principles of linear order and constituent structure (as well as other grammatical factors) can be controlled and varied experimentally in the stimulus sentences (e.g., Lust & Wakayama, 1981, or Barbier, 1995).

Like all behaviors on all language tasks, EI also involves performance factors. Length (syllable, morpheme, and word length), as well as all aspects of the lexicon and possible interpretations, must be carefully controlled, as they must be assumed to interact in determining performance variance in the EI task (cf. Lust & Eisele, 1991).

C. Experimental Test of Comprehension: Act Out (AO)

The act out (AO) task has been developed as a test of children's language comprehension. (See, for example, Ferreiro, Othenin-Girard, Chipman, & Sinclair, 1976; Goodluck & Solan, 1978; McDaniel, McKee, Cairns, 1996; Sinclair et al.,

1976.) This task usually involves providing the child with a set of toy dolls and props and asking the child to demonstrate the meaning (show the story) of sentences through simple actions. In these actions, the child must provide evidence that he or she has reconstructed the subject-predicate structure of the stimulus sentence. Typically, written transcripts (or videotapes) record children's behavior. Stimulus sentences in this task can be varied in grammatical structure (both syntactic and semantic) and designed with the same experimental controls as experimental tasks involving production, for example, EI. AO data can be quantitatively assessed with regard to the degree of correctness under assumptions similar to those used in the EI task. That is, if the child's grammar matches the grammar of the stimulus sentence, then the child can and does successfully represent the stimulus sentence by mapping from its form to its meaning, all other processing factors being equal. If the child *understands* the sentence (grammar maps from form to meaning), it is assumed that the child can and will correctly act out meaning (all other factors being equal). On the contrary, if the child's grammar is constrained, certain stimulus sentences that offend this grammatical constraint will not be accessible to representation by the child grammar, and therefore the child's understanding of the sentence will be disrupted. In addition, AO data can allow evaluation of other properties related to interpretation (e.g., coreference judgments in studies of anaphora). (For example: did the child use the same doll or different dolls in interpreting a proform [e.g., a pronoun or an empty category] and a name in the sentence?)

Designs for AO tasks must be carefully controlled for other factors that can determine ostensibly correct performance without accessing grammar. These cues may be semantic or pragmatic or simply involve general cognition. Zurif (1980) made this clear, for example, in his study of comprehension tests with aphasic patients. Only subtle linguistic designs that deliberately bypassed a possible pragmatic solution revealed systematic syntactic deficits in his aphasia subjects. Indeed, in normal adult comprehension, a constant interaction of syntactic analysis with pragmatic and semantic analyses must be assumed to be involved in sentence comprehension, just as for the child, in any comprehension task, as we showed previously.

D. Converging Evidence: Comparing the EI and AO Tasks

Grammatical factors that actually characterize a child's competence must be robust enough to surpass variance due to either type of behavior (comprehension or production). Numerous studies have now documented converging evidence across EI and AO tasks, where both are designed to assess the same abstract experimental factors. Several issues must be addressed in making these comparisons across tasks, however.

Production versus Comprehension

Each type of task involves its own complexity, which determines behavioral variance.

The EI Task versus the AO Task

The psycholinguistic structure of the AO task, like the EI task, requires the child to (a) hear and perceive the stimulus sentence, (b) represent it in memory and store it over time, and (c) interpret its meaning in the process of encoding and storage. In addition, in the AO test the child must (d) view the set of dolls and props given and assess their physical characteristics with regard to the sentence predicates, (e) re-encode the interpreted sentence and in doing so assess the given physical materials in the given context (e.g., location and identification terms of the particular dolls and props given), and (f) physically represent this meaning motorically and isomorphically by sequential activities with the dolls and props in space and time.

Analysis of the full structure of the act-out task, (a)–(f), shows that the mapping between the mental representation of the stimulus, which involves grammatical competence (a, b, c) and the behavior reflecting this structure (f) is quite indirect—noticeably more indirect than it is in the EI task data. Instead of (d)–(f), the child in EI converts the stored representation to production of linearly sequential and grouped linguistic units (namely, a sentence utterance, involving integrated linearity and constituent structure). In EI, production and perception are in the same mode (oral) and thus are more immediately related. The AO data (f) does not in itself consist of linguistic behavior (namely, it consists of physical activities with available dolls), unlike the EI task. Thus, by necessity, AO data will be more indirectly related to grammatical competence than will specifically linguistic data, such as language production, as in EI. In addition, the time between stimulus and response, particularly the completed response in (f), is typically significantly longer in the AO comprehension task than in the EI task. Thus AO involves memory and other intervening behavioral variables to a greater degree. The pragmatic context of the AO (set of physical objects the child is exposed to) provides another intervening set of variables. The pragmatic context avails the child of a possible pragmatic basis for response to the task, one that may not require full syntactic computation of the grammar of the stimulus sentence. (For example, the mere presence of dolls and props itself suggests a number of possible activities for the child to choose.)

At the same time, however, in the AO task, because the child attempts to reconstruct the full subject-predicate structure of a clause or complex sentence, this behavior indirectly reflects the child's knowledge of the syntax of the sentence. Experimental design, response scoring and statistical analysis for the act-out task can and must specifically assess the degree to which variable AO responses are not independent of syntactic computation, but determined by it.

Examples of Converging Evidence between Comprehension and Production Tasks

When both tasks (AO and EI) investigate the same grammatical factors under similarly controlled conditions, preferably using the same children as subjects, the range and pattern of variance in behaviors can be compared across tasks with regard to these factors. If each task is measuring grammatical competence validly, one would predict each task to provide evidence of the hypothesized grammatical principles or constraints, each in its own way. At the same time, given the basic differences in the nature of these tasks, one does not expect totally identical results across them.

For example, Cohen Sherman and Lust (1993) (see also Cohen Sherman, 1983) studied the acquisition of control structures such as (4) using both EI and AO tests. In AO, Cohen Sherman found that children assign improper control to structures like often choosing *Tom* as the antecedent for the null subject of the embedded clause, contrary to the adult. The same study showed that children have more difficulty imitating these structures than object control verbs, such as *John told Tom to go,* where the object, *Tom,* is the correct antecedent. In fact, In EI, they frequently converted syntactic type of complement of the stimulus sentence in accord with their interpretation, spontaneously changing sentences with verbs like *tell* to infinitive complements, but changing sentences with *promise* away from this structure. (Cohen Sherman's design showed that this result was not due to any intrinsic difference in difficulty of *promise* as a lexical item.)

(4) "John promised Tom 0 to go"

As another example of convergence, Lust et al. (1986) found that children acquiring English assign a free *pronominal* interpretation to sentences with null subjects in subordinate clauses with tenseless verbs such as (5):

(5) "*John*$_i$ saw *Tom*$_j$ when $0_{i,*j}$ going to school"

That is, in AO, they varied their choice of the antecedent of the null subject in the "when" clause depending on pragmatic context, just as they did for a lexical pronoun in this position, as shown in (6), even though the null subject should have been obligatorily bound to the subject (in adult grammar) in (5). In EI, children were found to actually convert the null subject, as in (5), to a lexical pronoun and to tense the verb of the embedded clause, thus confirming that the syntactic representation on the basis of which they were *comprehending* or *interpreting* the administered sentence in (5), was actually like (6). Here the pronoun is, in fact, free:

(6) "*John*$_i$ saw *Tom*$_j$ when *he*$_{i,j}$ was going to school"

Such results confirm that production (EI) and comprehension (AO) tasks both reveal grammatical competence in their own way and yet produce converging results.[8]

The AO and EI tasks are differentially sensitive to specific factors involved in

[8]See also Lust, Mazuka, and Eisele (1992) for a summary of related converging evidence across EI and AO tasks in the area of the acquisition of the binding theory. See Chien and Lust (1985) on the acquisition of Chinese *equi* constructions which document convergence between imitation and comprehension data.

language knowledge. They vary in the directness with which they reveal various factors of this knowledge and in the manner in which they do so (cf. Lust, Chien, & Flynn, 1987, pp. 333–335). In general, although both AO and EI tasks reveal general cognitive factors involved in language knowledge, the AO task appears to reveal these cognitive factors more directly. This is consistent with the structure of the AO task reviewed earlier. In addition, because the AO task is more sensitive to factors such as pragmatic context, the effects of grammatical factors may be modulated more by nongrammatical factors in the AO task than in the EI task. For example, pragmatic context specifically modulated anaphora *directionality* effects in the AO task, but not in the EI task (Lust, Loveland, and Kornet, 1980). Certain grammatical factors may be more directly revealed by the EI task.

V. CAN PERFORMANCE BE BYPASSED?

A. Reduced Behavior Methods

All of the preceding methods attempt to infer grammatical competence on the basis of some performance (overt behavior) with language by the child, combined with analysis of the mental structure of the particular task used, theoretical foundations for experimental designs, and statistical analyses of children's responses.

Recently, an alternative approach to research methodology in the area of language acquisition has attempted to bypass children's performance with language and to access their grammatical competence more directly. This approach, which may be called a *reduced behavior* (RB) approach to experimental tasks, is reflected in the work of Crain (1991) and Crain and Thornton (1991), although early studies (e.g., Fraser, Bellugi, & Brown, 1963) have explored similar methods.[9] This RB approach attempts to limit the overt behaviors required by the child in a task. For example, a child may be asked for a simple yes/no response regarding an adult's performance with language, in a *forced-choice* situation.

The motivation for this alternative approach must be appreciated. A researcher is interested in inferring grammatical competence, not in studying performance per se, and such RB methods are economical to administer and score.

However, it is not possible to bypass performance in the assessment of grammatical knowledge. First, this forced choice response is itself a form of behavior, although it is itself nonlinguistic behavior. Although the behavior elicited from the child is reduced, the elicited responses still involve a form of performance. They are subject to chance. Second, by distancing the child's responses from any overt behaviors that more directly reflect language (e.g., producing or acting out utterances), these methods can weaken the validity of inference on the basis of the

[9]See Eisele and Lust (1996) for analysis and critique of an earlier forced-choice task.

child's response as an indication of the child's grammatical competence. They may not detect true aspects of the child's competence, especially when this may deviate from the adult researcher's hypothesis, because the task allows no possibility for the child's behavior to evidence such variation. Only the experimenter's hypothesis is investigated and this is simply assumed to be accessible to the child.

Responses to these RB techniques, like all behaviors with language, can and do provide the basis for some valid inferences regarding grammatical knowledge, but also some that are related to pragmatics, not grammar (cf. Eisele & Lust, 1996). However, RB tasks can be combined with other methods regarding children's language knowledge and can provide converging evidence on grammatical knowledge.

B. Examples of Reduced Behavior (RB) Tasks

Truth Value Judgment Task (TVJT)

One such *reduced behavior* task (applied recently by Crain & McKee, 1986) is termed a *truth value judgment task* (*TVJT*). In this task, the adult acted out interpretation of sentences through toy-moving behaviors. The child was asked only to respond yes or no, indicating whether the adult's act out of the sentence was acceptable, according to the child's perception. (For example, the child was asked to "feed a rag" to an onlooking doll, if the adult's interpretation was considered unacceptable.)

This TVJT task has sometimes been considered a *grammaticality judgment* task (e.g., Grodzinsky & Reinhart, 1993). However, it is in fact a comprehension task. The child is asked to view a scene that reflects a particular adult interpretation of a sentence and to judge whether this interpretation is a possible one for the sentence, thus giving a semantic judgment of truth or falsity.

In this task, the child may reject the depiction of a particular adult interpretation for a variety of reasons. Because comprehension of the sentence is being evaluated, this judgment is presumably mediated not only by grammatical knowledge, but also by pragmatic and semantic knowledge, just as in other comprehension tasks discussed earlier (such as tasks where the child provides the act out).

Crain and McKee (1986) reported that when they administered this task to children, results confirmed children's knowledge of the UG principle of structure dependence, but showed no *directionality* effects (or any other language-specific grammatical effects). They suggest on the basis of this evidence that child grammar was identical to adult grammar with regard to the principle of UG under consideration. In addition, they appeared to conclude that no specific language grammar effects (or their development) appear, suggesting that the task tapped UG directly. (Results were reported as group percents of acceptance or rejection of particular sentences.) It was implied that this type of test of comprehension could and did more directly access the child's grammatical competence by bypassing the child behavior or performance, which is typically required in other comprehension tasks (such as the AO task) or production tasks such as EI.

As in the AO task, interpretation of results from this TVJ task—that is, the researcher's inference of the child's grammatical competence and of UG on the grounds of the binary yes/no behaviors attained in this task—is highly complex.[10] The child must (a) hold the initial sentence in mind, presumably having analyzed its syntax and certain possible semantic interpretations in order to do so; (b) understand the general structure of an AO task, now performed by the adult; (c) observe, analyze, and interpret the adult's act-out behavior in the pragmatic context to which it is exposed, considering it as only one possible interpretation (e.g., in the Crain & McKee, 1986, study, children see an animal eating ice cream within a fenced in area); (d) hold this pragmatic rendition of a particular semantic interpretation in mind while (e) presumably generating its own interpretation of the sentence; (f) compare and contrast possible interpretations vis à vis the child's initial syntactic and semantic representation of the sentence; (g) make a semantic judgment of truth or falsity regarding the possibility for the observed adult interpretation, given this optional representation. The induced nonlinguistic behavior (a simple yes or no) is the only empirical evidence that the researcher has regarding any aspect of this process in the child, and it is the only evidence on which to make an inference regarding the child's knowledge of grammar. Statistical significance of variance in numbers of Y/N answers in this forced choice behavior provides the only data grounding the researcher's inference.

The yes/no response in this task is only indirectly linked to the nature of the child's grammar, in particular to the child's grammatical representation of the original stimulus sentence. This representation is only one of the components, (a) through (g), of the cognitive process that the child's yes/no response may reflect.

In such a task, it is not that the child is not *performing*, only that the performance is less overt than in the preceding tasks. In essence, the researcher cannot be certain why the child is saying yes or no—that is, it is not clear what component of the complex cognitive task that the child is performing is determining the response.

Statistical analyses are required to evaluate whether the amount of Y/N judgments varied significantly as opposed to chance, because given the binary response possibilities (Y/N), the "correct" response is expected to a certain degree given chance alone.

In addition, the pragmatic context to which the child is exposed will necessari-

[10]We will leave aside here the obvious need to control the administration of this TVJ Task, that is, to control adult's context in the act-out task and questioning of the child, test for replication and generalization, and so on (cf. Eisele, 1988, and Eisele and Lust, 1996). Administration of the task would have to avoid adult interference, such as leading questions that may focus the child on one aspect of meaning over another; and the interview techniques would have to be standardized across subjects so that the group results were susceptible to parametric statistics.

ly affect the acceptance or nonacceptance of a particular act-out event by the adult and thus would need to be carefully controlled or tested for its independent effects, and generalization over such contexts would have to be tested. (cf. Eisele, 1988). As with all comprehension tasks, the researchers must extricate the pragmatic factors from syntactic factors as possible determinants of the child's response.

Even with all possible controls, however, the TVJT does not give direct access to the child's actual syntactic representation of the stimulus sentence being tested. The child's grammatical representation of the stimulus sentence can vary widely and still be consistent with a Y or N response on this task. Inference regarding the child's syntactic representation cannot therefore be conclusive on the basis of forced choice responses in the TVJT. Moreover, because the task (by design) only demonstrates and allows the child's judgment on certain selected adult interpretations, the task would not allow the researcher to discover child-particular interpretations (or the syntactic representations they may be based on) that the adult may not have thought of.

Even if a child performs totally and consistently "correctly" on such a RB TVJ task, with no variance observed at any age, and if all interacting factors could be dissociated, the result would still be indeterminate. The result would be in accord with the specific language grammar of the language constructions being tested; but it would in essence beg the issue of how the child achieved the mapping from UG to SLG, the essential question of first language acquisition. Like all behavioral measures, the TVJT does not give direct evidence on UG.

Infant Preference Tasks

Experimentation with very young infants has developed greatly in the past few decades (e.g., the work of Hirsh-Pasek & Golinkoff, 1991; Jusczyk et al., 1992; Mandel, Nelson, & Jusczyk, 1995), with methods that necessarily involve reduced behavior tasks because the infant may not yet produce or understand language *per se.* For example, Golinkoff, Hirsh-Pasek, Cauley, and Gordon (1987) and Hirsh-Pasek and Golinkoff (1991) described a "preferential looking paradigm" (adapted from infant perception studies, e.g., Spelke, 1979) used with infants as young as mean age 1.4.5 to test infants' knowledge of nouns and verbs. In this method, infants may be presented with two video screens and an audio stimulus, which corresponds to only one of the screens. The infant is expected to accomplish an intermodal matching between these by a head turn. In another version of this paradigm, preferential *listening* (e.g., Hirsh-Pasek et al., 1987), infants were presented with a choice between two auditory stimuli (one with natural intonational breaks at clause boundaries and one that had breaks offending these boundaries).

These techniques provide important extensions of research methods to developmental age groups that are often not susceptible to other experimental methods, and they have begun to reveal important sensitivities to language stimuli in the infant even before she or he can speak or at very early periods of language acquisition. However, these methods also necessarily must always underdetermine the precise nature of children's grammatical competence, because they generally involve only various aspects of binary head-turn behaviors, which are themselves not linguistic. Thus these methods reflect the issues raised earlier in other reduced behavior tasks. In some cases, they test infants' comprehension (e.g., in 1-year olds or older) and thus reflect the complexities of comprehension methods in general, raised earlier.

In the infant-preference tasks, attained data are essentially statistical, not linguistic. The infants' behaviors (e.g., amount of looking or listening time or direction of head turn) are not directly related to their linguistic competence, but significance of variance in one or more of these measures is used to ground the researcher's inference that one of the variables that the experimenter has varied in the stimulus to which the infant is exposed (e.g., across two video screens) may provide a source for the infant's behavior.

Often it is not clear which aspect of the infants' binary behaviors will differ significantly given different stimuli. For example, in Hirsh-Pasek and colleagues' 1987 study of constituent structure, which varied auditory stimulus in terms of natural or unnatural breaks in clause structure, direction of head turn did not vary significantly with different stimuli, but amount of listening time did. In another application of these procedures (e.g., Naigles & Gelman, 1995), which studied children's (mean age 1.9 and 2.3) overextensions in lexical acquisition with a preferential-looking paradigm, critical behavioral variance to be evaluated involved a comparison between looking preference on control and test trials. Data measurements included "number of first looks" at screens ("Where's the dog?"), "duration of first look," and "total visual fixation," involving mean looking times. All three measures were reported to differ significantly in some conditions, showing "a demonstrated, significant preference for the matching screen." (p. 40). During certain trials, however, total visual fixation yielded significant preferences, but the number and duration of first look measures did not" (p. 42). In another application of the visual preference paradigm (Golinkoff, Hirsh-Pasek, Cauley, & Gordon, 1987) with infants (mean age 2.4), an ability to match word-order variations in auditory stimuli to one of two video screens was tested (e.g., "Where's *Big Bird* tickling *Cookie Monster?*" or "Where's *Cookie Monster* tickling *Big Bird?*"). Dependent variables were relativized ["calculated on the mean of the first three test trials and the mean of the last three test trials," (p. 38)]. The authors reported that the match received significantly more visual fixation than the nonmatch (p. 41). A significant interaction was found with the performance variable of *block* however; that is, infants "developed a preference for the 'wining side'" (p. 41) and frequently did not switch when this was changed. Individual subject variance was also attained (19/24 Ss "watched the match more than the non-match," p. 42). These facts show how indirect is the relation of the behavior to the stimulus in these tasks.

Even when behavior does vary significantly (e.g., there are significantly more head turns in one direction than another), the exact properties of the stimulus to which the child is responding in its preference remains a critical open issue in this particular research paradigm. The true motivation for a head turn or length of time looking or listening must remain indeterminate in these behaviors and can only be resolved by experimental designs that seek to dissociate confounding factors (cf. Jusczyk et al., 1992, and Hirsh-Pasek et al., 1987, whose experimental designs separate the properties of acoustic prosody from linguistic clause in the stimulus).

More direct inference regarding a child's precise grammatical competence must await the child's actual linguistic behaviors, that is, speech production or comprehension. Here the child overtly constructs sentence structure and more overtly reveals grammatical knowledge. However, indirect inference regarding the infant's general sensitivities to various properties of language stimuli, which these new infant-preference methods allow, can provide a necessary link to a continuous theory of language development, beginning even before the child is speaking.

C. Conclusions on Reduced Behavior Tasks

The basic point we wish to make here is the following. The critical issue is not simply that "results from tests that rely on object manipulation or other forms of child action may well be underestimating children's linguistic sophistication" (Golinkoff et al., 1987, p. 25), which is often taken to motivate RB approaches to methodology. Rather, all behaviors with language, whether reduced or not, can at best only provide the grounds for the researcher's inference regarding the subjects' (child or adult) grammatical knowledge. Systematic, theoretically motivated experimental design and scientific analyses of behavioral variance must in all cases aid the researcher in attaining validity in this inference. With each method, the source and nature of this variance will differ, but it will always exist.

Methods that reduce children's direct or overt behaviors with language in an attempt to bypass performance and access competence directly do not do so without cost. In fact, by imposing adult interpretations on reduced behaviors, they run the risk of underdetermining the child's complex linguistic competence, if they are used alone.

D. Converging Evidence

Converging evidence across RB and other tasks can most strongly ground an inference regarding specific aspects of grammatical competence in the child, in spite of the fact that all tasks also to some degree tap nonsyntactic aspects of language knowledge, performance, and aspects of language-specific grammars as well as UG.

For example, Eisele (1988) and Eisele and Lust (1996) tested a range of sentence structures with pronouns, which varied in directionality and structure, on a controlled truth value judgment task (a reduced behavior task), where the sentence types had been previously tested in an act-out task (as well as in EI). The experimental sentences overlapped in design with those tested by Crain and McKee (1986) as well as Lust, Loveland, and Kornet (1980). Eisele controlled and varied pragmatic context in the TVJ task (using pictures in an experimental design) and corrected for chance responding (which was observed to be highest in the youngest [3-year-old] children) and rigorously controlled administration procedures.

Although there was some random responding and some pragmatic based responding, especially in the younger children in the TVJT, the overall statistical results in the TVJ task replicated those in the AO task. Not only did the factor of structure dependence replicate as significant in the TVJ task, but so did an effect of the factor of pronoun directionality. For example, Eisele found that children showed evidence for "structural" constraint by Principle C (a UG principle) in comprehension of pronouns, as found in previous AO (and EI) tasks. In addition, Eisele found that in a TVJT, children accepted significantly fewer coreference contexts (pictures) for sentences with backward pronouns than for those with forward pronouns, even when in adult grammar both are completely acceptable. Specific directionality effects cannot be a direct property of UG. This suggests that properties relating to specific language grammar are accessed in this TVJ task, just as in other tasks, and they interact with the specific UG principle being tested by the researcher. (See Lust, Eisele, & Mazuka, 1992, for review.)

This is conclusively shown through Eisele's test of adults. In the TVJT, Eisele and Lust (1996) found that adults also showed a significant forward pronoun directionality preference. Adults accepted fewer than 40% of pictures with disjoint reference when sentences had a forward pronoun, even when this was perfectly grammatical. (For example, in a sentence like "*John* sat down when *he* played the violin," adults said "no" to a picture with [John sitting down and Sam playing the violin] more than 60% of the time, although this is a perfectly grammatical interpretation for the sentence.) This clearly shows that this TVJT, like all tasks reviewed earlier, taps performance with language and the complexity of language knowledge, as well as the precise factors of universal grammatical competence that the researcher is testing. In this case, as in other comprehension tasks, pragmatics interacts with grammatical knowledge to determine performance. Pragmatics determines that disjoint reference is not felicitous here, even though grammatical principles allow it. (Another recent use of the TVJT in related study of pronoun direction and structure in Chinese has also provided results that replicate results attained through AO (and EI) tests (Lust, Chien, Chiang, & Eisele, 1996).

Recent study of verb phrase (VP) ellipsis structures like (7) also showed converging evidence across TVJT and AO tests of comprehension (Foley, Nuñez del Prado, Barbier, & Lust, 1992, 1997).

(7) Big Bird scratched his arm and Ernie did too.
   a. BB scratched BB's arm and E scratched E's arm.
   b. BB scratched BB's arm and E scratched BB's arm.

The two tasks (TVJT and AO) converged in providing evidence that a bound variable reading for these ambiguous sentences—such as (7a)—was the unmarked, most predominant one for children, as opposed to (7b). However, each task contributed differently to this result. The AO task additionally revealed grammatical readings that were spontaneously generated by the children, which the adult researchers had not anticipated, and the TVJT revealed further evidence that children had the option for a second possible interpretation, when the adult predetermined it and made it available to the child. (Some children in the TVJT performed only one reading, however; just as some children performed only one in AO.)

VI. CONCLUSION

In this chapter we have attempted to clarify assumptions regarding current developments in methodology in the study of first language acquisition, in the belief that clarification of these assumptions can significantly move this field to a more developed scientific status where experiment and theory can most fruitfully interact.

We have argued that all language behaviors (whether complex or reduced) are intrinsically variable and all only indirectly indicate linguistic competence (UG), a mental construct, which is categorical and discrete. The language behaviors provide only grounds for inference of grammatical competence. In addition, UG and grammatical computation related to specific language grammar (SLG) are always confounded in any language behavior. UG is not directly accessible.

However, we have argued that, in spite of this indirectness, current methodologies in the study of first language acquisition can and do scientifically test specific hypotheses regarding linguistic theory and the discrete nature of UG. Methods must be subject to rigorous scientific requirements. It is necessary to control research design, statistically interpret behavioral variance, and theoretically evaluate modular components of UG and of SLG, study multiple aspects of language use, and use larger samples of children. Converging evidence across multiple methods (both experimental and naturalistic) is the most powerful approach to hypothesis testing regarding linguistic competence in the child, as in the adult. When such methods combine with precise, theoretically driven, systematic analyses both of what does and does not occur, and evaluate this against assumed behavioral variance, they can provide strong grounding of inference regarding the child's linguistic competence, just as for the adult's. Converging evidence (using a variety of such controlled methods) across numerous languages can provide most conclusive evidence regarding the content of a theory of UG, which is hypothesized to underlie all possible natural languages and various specific language grammars (e.g., Flynn & Martohardjono, 1994) and to characterize the *initial state* as well as every point of language development.

ACKNOWLEDGMENTS

Related papers (e.g., Lust, Chien, & Flynn, 1987) were prepared with the partial support of NSF grants BNS 8318983, BNS 8206328, and BNS 7825115 and a Cornell University College of Human Ecology small grant. We thank James Gair and Marion Potts, Katharina Boser, Lynn Santelmann, Jennifer Austin, David Parkinson, and Isabella Barbier for comments on the manuscript and on its issues.

This paper develops ideas discussed earlier in Lust, B., Chien, Y.-C., and Flynn, S. (1987), "What Children Know: Methods for the Study of First Language Acquisition, in Lust, B. (Ed.), *Studies in the Acquisition of Anaphora, Vol. 2, Applying the Constraints.* Reidel: Dordrecht, Holland.

REFERENCES

Austin, J., Blume, M., Nuñez del Prado, Z., Parkinson, D., Proman, R., & Lust, B. (1996). Current challenges to the parameter-setting paradigm: The pro-drop parameter. In C. Koster & F. Wijnen (Eds.), *Proceedings of Groningen Assembly on Language Acquisition,* 87–97.

Austin, J., Blume, M., Parkinson, D., Nuñez del Prado, Z., & Lust, B. (1997). The status of pro-drop in the initial state: Results from new analyses of Spanish. In A. Perez-Leroux & W. Glass, (Eds.), *Contemporary Perspectives on the Acquisition of Spanish, Vol. 1. Developing grammars* (pp. 37–54). Boston: Cascadilla Press.

Barbier, I. (1995). *Configuration and movement in Germanic: Studies of first language acquisition of Dutch word-order.* Unpublished doctoral dissertation, Cornell University, Ithaca, NY.

Berk, S. (1996). *What does why what trigger?* Unpublished honors thesis, Cornell University, Ithaca, NY.

Blake, J., Quarto, G., Austin, W., & Vingiles, Z. (1984). Memory capacity and language complexity. *Ms.* Toronto, Canada: York University.

Bloom, L. (1970). *Language development: Form and function in emerging grammars.* Cambridge, MA: Cambridge University Press.

Boser, K. (1989). *Acquisition of German word order.* Unpublished honors thesis, Cornell University, Ithaca, NY.

Boser, K. (1996). *Syntactic and pragmatic factors in the first language acquisition of German word order.* Unpublished doctoral dissertation, Cornell University, Ithaca, NY.

Boser, K., Lust, B., Santelmann, L., & Whitman, J. (1991). *The theoretical significance of auxiliaries in early child German grammar.* Paper presented at the Boston University Conference on Language Development, Boston.

Boser, K., Lust, B., Santelmann, L., & Whitman, J. (1992). The syntax of CP and V-2 in early German child grammar: The strong continuity hypothesis. *Proceedings of the North Eastern Linguistics Association, 22,* 51–66.

Boser, K., Santelmann, L., Barbier, I., & Lust, B. (1995). Grammatical mapping from UG to language specific grammars: Deriving variation in the acquisition of German, Dutch and Swedish. In D. McLaughlin & S. McEwen (Eds.), *Proceedings of 1994 19th Annual Boston University Conference on Language Development, Boston,* 130–142.

Brainerd, C. J., & Kingman, J. (1985). On the independence of short-term memory and working memory in cognitive development. *Cognitive Psychology, 17,* 210–247.

Brown, R. (1973). *A first language.* Cambridge: Harvard University Press.

Ceci, S. J., & Howe, M. J. A. (1978). Semantic knowledge as a determinant of developmental differences in recall. *Journal of Experimental Child Psychology, 26,* 230–245.

Chi, S. (1978). Knowledge structures and memory development. In R. Siegler (Ed.), *Children's thinking: What develops?* (pp. 73–96). Hillsdale, NJ: Erlbaum.

Chien, Y.-C., & Lust, B. (1985). The concept of topic and subject in first language acquisition of Mandarin Chinese. *Child Development, 56,* 1359–1375.

Chomsky, N. (1964). Experimental Approaches. In J. P. B. Allen & P. van Buren (Eds.), *Chomsky: Selected readings* (Rev. ed. 1971; 129–134). Oxford: Oxford University Press.

Chomsky, N. (1981). *Lectures on government and binding.* Dordrecht: Foris.

Chomsky, N. (1986). *Knowledge of language: Its nature, origin and use.* New York: Praeger.

Chomsky, N. (1987). Language in a psychological setting. *Sophia linguistica.* Tokyo, Japan: Sophia University.

Chomsky, N. (1988). *Language and problems of knowledge.* Cambridge, MA: MIT Press.

Clahsen, H. (1982). *Spracher werb in der kindheit.* Tuebingan: Narr.

Clark, R. (1983). Theory and method in child language research: Are we assuming too much? In S. Kuczaj II (Ed.), *Language development: Vol. I. syntax and semantics* (pp. 1–36). Hillsdale, NY: Erlbaum.

Cohen Sherman, J. (1983). *The acquisition of control in complement sentences: The role of structural and lexical factors.* Unpublished doctoral dissertation, Cornell University, Ithaca, NY.

Cohen Sherman, J., & Lust, B. (1986). Syntactic and lexical constraints on the acquisition of control in complement sentences. In B. Lust (Ed.), *Studies in the acquisition of anaphora: Vol. 1. Defining the constraints* (pp. 279–310). Dordrecht: Reidel Press.

Cohen Sherman, J., & Lust, B. (1993) Children are in control. *Cognition, 46,* 1–51.

Cooper, W. E. (1977). The development of speech timing. In S. J. Segalowitz & F. A. Gruber (Eds.), *Language development and neurological theory* (pp. 357–373). New York: Academic Press.

Crain, S. (1991). Language acquisition in the absence of experience. In *Behavioral and Brain Sciences, 14.* (Reprinted in *Language Acquisition,* P. Bloom, Ed., 1994, Cambridge, MA: MIT Press)

Crain, S., & McKee, C. (1986). Acquisition of structural restrictions on anaphora. In

S. Berman, J.-W. Choe, & J. McDonough (Eds.), *Proceedings of the Sixteenth Annual North Eastern Linguistic Society,* 94–110.

Crain, S., & Thornton, R. (1991). Recharting the course of language acquisition: Studies in elicited production. In N. Krasnegor, Duane Rumbaugh, R. Schiefelbusch, & Michael Studdert-Kennedy (Eds.), *Biological and behavioral determinants of language development.* Hillsdale, NJ: Erlbaum.

Demuth, K. (1990). Subject, topic and Sesotho passive. *Journal of Child Language, 17,* 67–84.

Demuth, K. (1994). On the underspecification of functional categories in early grammars. In B. Lust, M. Suñer, & J. Whitman (Eds.), *Syntactic theory and first language acquisition: Cross-linguistic perspectives.* In B. Lust (Ed.), Vol. I, *Heads, projections and learnability,* pp. 119–134. Hillsdale, NJ: Erlbaum.

Deprez, V., & Pierce, A. (1993). Negation and functional projections in early grammar. *Linguistic Inquiry, 24,* 25–68.

Donaldson, M. (1978). *Children's minds.* London, England: Fontana.

Eisele, J. (1988). *Meaning and form in children's judgments about language.* Unpublished master's thesis, Cornell University, Ithaca, NY.

Eisele, J., & Lust, B. (1996). Children's knowledge about pronouns: A developmental study using a "Truth Value Judgment Task." *Child Development, 67,* 3086–3100.

Ferreiro, E., Othenin-Girard, C., Chipman, H., & Sinclair, H. (1976). How do children handle relative clauses? *Archives de psychologie, SLIV,* 229–233.

Flynn, S., & Martohardjono, G. (1994). Mapping from the initial state to the final state: The separation of universal principles and language-specific properties. In B. Lust, M. Suñer, & J. Whitman (Vol. Eds.), *Syntactic theory and first language acquisition: Cross-linguistic perspectives: Vol. I. Heads, projections, and learnability* (pp. 319–335). Hillsdale, NJ: Erlbaum.

Foley, C. (1996). *Knowledge of the syntax of operators in the initial state: The acquisition of relative clauses in French and English.* Unpublished doctoral dissertation, Cornell University, Ithaca, NY.

Foley, C., Nuñez del Prado, Z., Barbier, I., & Lust, B. (1992). *LF representation of pronouns in VP ellipsis: An argument for UG in the initial state.* Paper presented at the Boston University Conference in Language Development, Boston, MA.

Foley, C., Nuñez del Prado, Z., Barbier, I., & Lust, B. (1997). Operator variable binding in the initial state: An argument from VP ellipsis. In S. Somashekar, K. Yamakoshi, M. Blume, & C. Foley (Eds.), *Cornell Working Papers in Linguistics, 15,* 1–19.

Fraser, C., Bellugi, U., & Brown, R. (1963). Control of grammar in imitation, comprehension, and production. *Journal of Verbal Learning and Verbal Behavior, 2,* 121–135.

Gleitman, L., Gleitman, H., & Shipley, E. (1972). The emergence of the child as grammarian. *Cognition, 1,* 137–164.

Golinkoff, R. H., Hirsh-Pasek, K., Cauley, K., & Gordon, L. (1987). The eyes have it: Lexical and syntactic comprehension in a new paradigm. *Journal of Child Language, 14,* 23–45.

Goodluck, H., & Solan, L. (Eds.). (1978). *Papers in the structure and development of child language, Occasional papers in Linguistics.* Amherst, MA: University of Massachusetts.

Grimshaw, J., & Rosen, S. (1990). Knowledge and obedience. *Linguistic Inquiry, 21,* 187–222.

Grodzinsky, Y., & Reinhart, T. (1993). The innateness of binding and coreference. *Linguistic Inquiry, 24*(1), 69–102.

Hirsh-Pasek, K., & Golinkoff, R. (1991). Language Comprehension: A new look at some old themes. In N. Krasnegor, D. Rumbaugh, R. Schiefelbusch, & M. Studdert-Kennedy, (Eds.), *Biological and behavioral determinants of language development* (pp. 301–320). Hillsdale: NJ: Erlbaum.

Hirsh-Pasek, K., Nelson, D., Jusczyk, P., Cassidy, K., Druss, B., & Kennedy, L. (1987). Clauses are perceptual units for young infants. *Cognition, 26,* 269–286.

Joos, M. (1966). Description of language design. *Readings in linguistics* (Vol. I, pp. 349–356). Chicago: University of Chicago Press.

Jusczyk, P., Hirsch-Pasek, K., Nelson, D., Kennedy, L., Woodward, A., & Piwoz, J. (1992). Perception of acoustic correlates of major phrasal units by young infants. *Cognitive Psychology, 24,* 252–293.

Kapur, S., Lust, B., Harbert, W., & Martohardjono, G. (1992). Universal grammar and learnability theory: The case of binding domains and the subset principle. In Reuland, E., & Abraham, W. (Eds.), *Knowledge and language: Vol. 3. Issues in representation and acquisition* (pp. 185–216): Dordrecht: Kluwer.

Kapur, S., Lust, B., Harbert, W., & Martohardjono, G. (in prep). *On relating UG and learnability theory: Intensional and extensional principles in the representation and acquisition of binding domains.* Unpublished manuscript.

Levelt, W. J. M. (1974). *Formal grammars in linguistics and psycholinguistics: Vol. 3. Psycholinguistic applications.* The Hague: Mouton.

Lasnik, H. (1989). *Essays on anaphora.* Dordrecht: Kluwer.

Lust, B. (1977). Conjunction reduction in child language. *Journal of Child Language, 42*(2), 257–297.

Lust, B. (1981). On coordinating studies of coordination: Problems of method and theory in first language acquisition. A reply to Ardery. *Journal of Child Language, 8*(2), 459–470.

Lust, B. (1986). *Studies in the acquisition of anaphora.* Dordrecht: Foris.

Lust, B. (1994). Functional projection of CP and phrase structure parameterization: An argument for the strong continuity hypothesis. In B. Lust, J. Whitman, M. Suñer (Eds.), *Cross linguistic perspectives: Vol. I. Heads, projections, and learnability* (pp. 85–118). Hillsdale, NJ: Erlbaum.

Lust, B. (1999). Universal grammar: The strong continuity hypothesis in first language acquisition. In W. C. Ritchie & T. K. Bhatia (Eds.), *Handbook of Child Language Acquisition.* San Diego: Academic Press.

Lust, B. (in prep). *Universal Grammar and the Initial State: Cross-linguistic studies of directionality.* Cambridge, MA: Bradford Books/MIT Press.

Lust, B., Chien, Y.-C., Chiang, Chi-Pang, & Eisele, J. (1996). Chinese pronominals in Universal Grammar: A study of linear precedence and command in Chinese and English children's first language acquisition. *Journal of East Asian Linguistics, 5,* 1–47.

Lust, B., Chien, Y.-C., & Flynn, S. (1987). What children know. In B. Lust (Ed.), *Studies in the acquisition of anaphora: Vol. 2. Applying the Constraints* (pp. 271–356). Dordrecht: Reidel Press.

Lust, B., & Eisele, J. (1991). On the acquisition of syntax in Tamil: A comment on Garman. *Journal of Child Language, 18,* 215–226.

Lust, B., Flynn, S., & Foley, C. (1996). What children know about what they say: Elicited imitation as a research method. In D. McDaniel, C. McKee, & H. Cairns, (Eds.), *Methods for Assessing Children's Syntax* (pp. 55–76). Cambridge, MA: MIT Press.

Lust, B., Loveland, K., & Kornet, R. (1980). The development of anaphora in first language: Syntactic and pragmatic constraints. *Linguistic Analysis, 6,* 217–249.

Lust, B., Eisele, J., & Mazuka, R. (1992). The binding theory module: Evidence from first language acquisition for Principle C. *Language, 68*(2), 333–358.

Lust, B., & Mervis, C. (1980). Coordination in the natural speech of young children. *Journal of Child Language, 7*(2), 279–304.

Lust, B., Herman, G., & Kornfilt, J. (Eds.). (1994a). *Syntactic theory and first language acquisition: Cross-linguistic perspectives, Vol. 2. Binding, dependencies, and learnability.* Hillsdale, NJ: LEA.

Lust, B., Suñer, M., and Whitman, J. (Eds.). (1994b). *Syntactic theory and first language acquisition: Cross-linguistic perspectives, Vol. 1. Heads, projections, and learnability.* Hillsdale, NJ: LEA.

Lust, B., & Wakayama, T. (1981). Word order in Japanese first language acquisition. In P. Dale & D. Ingram (Eds.), *Child language: An international perspective* (pp. 73–90). Baltimore: University Park Press.

McDaniel, D., McKee, C., & Cairns, H. (Eds.). (1996). *Methods for assessing children's syntax.* Cambridge, MA: MIT Press.

Mandel, D. R., Nelson, D., & Jusczyk, P. (1995). *Infants remember the order of words in a spoken sentence.* Unpublished manuscript. University of Buffalo at Buffalo.

Maratsos, M. (1983). Some current issues in the study of the acquisition of grammar. In P. Mussen (Ed.), *Handbook of Child Psychology, 3,* 707–786.

Mazuka, R., & Lust, B. (1990). On parameter-setting and parsing: Predictions for acquisition. In L. Frazier & J. de Villers (Eds.), *Language processing and acquisition* (pp. 163–206). Dordrecht: Kluwer.

Naigles, L., & Gelman, S. (1995). Overextensions in comprehension and production revisited: Preferential-looking in a study of "dog," "cat," and "cow." *Journal of Child Language, 22,* 19–46.

Neufeld, Arthur, H. (1986). Reproducing Results. *Science, 3*(11).

Nuñez del Prado, Z., Foley, C., & Lust, B. (1993). The significance of CP to the pro-drop parameter: An experimental study of Spanish-English comparison. In E. Clark (Ed.), *The Proceedings of the Twenty-fifth Child Language Research Forum,* 146–157.

Nuñez del Prado, Z., Foley, C., Proman, R., & Lust, B. (1994). Subordinate CP and pro-drop: Evidence for degree-n learnability from an experimental study of Spanish and English acquisition. *Proceedings of NELS 24* (Vol. 2), 443–460).

Piaget, J., Inhelder, B. (1973). *Memory and intelligence.* New York: Basic Books.

Pratt, C., Tunmer, W. E., & Bowey, J. A. (1984). Children's capacity to correct grammatical violations in sentences. *Journal of Child Language, 11,* 129–141.

Santelmann, L. (1995). *The acquisition of verb second grammar in child Swedish: Continuity of universal grammar in wh-questions, topicalization and verb raising.* Unpublished doctoral dissertation, Cornell University, Ithaca, NY.

Santelmann, L., Berk, S., Austin, J., Somashekar, S., & Lust, B. (1996). Dissociating movement and inflection: A continuity account of subject-aux inversion. Paper presented at the Linguistic Society of America, San Diego, CA.

Schütze, C. T. (1996). *The Empirical Base of Linguistics.* Chicago: The University of Chicago Press.
Sherman, Janet Cohen—See Cohen Sherman, Janet
Sinclair, H., Berthoud-Papandropoulou, J., Bronckart, J. P., Chipman, H., Ferreiro, E., & Rappe DuCher, E. (1976). Recherches en psycholinguistique genetique. *Archives de psychologie,* 44, 157–175.
Sinclair, H., Jarvella, R. J., & Levelt, J. M. (Eds.). (1978). *The child's conception of language.* Berlin: Springer-Verlag.
Somashekar, S., Lust, B., Gair, J., Bhatia, T., Sharma, V., & Khare, J. (1995). Pronominals in Hindi "jab" clauses: Experimental test of children's comprehension. Paper presented at SALA, University of Texas, Austin, TX.
Spelke, L. (1979). Processing bimodally specified events in infancy. *Developmental Psychology, 15,* 626–636.
Squire, L. R. (1986). Mechanisms of memory. *Science, 232,* 1612–1619.
Stromswald, K. (1990). *Learnability and the acquisition of auxiliaries.* Unpublished doctoral dissertation, Cambridge, MA.
Valian, V. (1991). Syntactic subjects in the early speech of American and Italian children. *Cognition, 40,* 21–81.
Valian, V. (1992). Categories of first syntax. In J. Meisel (Ed.), *The acquisition of verb placement: Functional categories and V2 phenomena in language development* (pp. 401–422). Dordrecht: Kluwer.
Weissenborn, J. (1994). Constraining the child's grammar: Local well-formedness in the development of verb movement in German and French. In B. Lust, M. Suñer, & J. Whitman (Eds.), *Syntactic theory and first language acquisition: Cross-linguistic perspectives: Vol. I. Heads, projections and learnability.* Hillsdale, NJ: Erlbaum.
Whitman, J., Lee, K-O., & Lust, B. (1991). Continuity of the principles of Universal Grammar in first language acquisition: The issue of functional categories. *Proceedings of the North Eastern Linguistics Society Annual Meeting, 21, Amherst: University of Massachusetts,* 383–397.
Zurif, K. (1980). Language mechanisms: A neuropsychological perspective. *American Scientist, 68,* 305–311.

CHAPTER 14

THE CHILDES SYSTEM

Brian MacWhinney

Child language research thrives on naturalistic data—data collected from spontaneous interactions in naturally occurring situations. However, the process of collecting, transcribing, and analyzing naturalistic data is extremely time-consuming and often quite unreliable. To improve this process, the Child Language Data Exchange System (CHILDES) has developed tools that facilitate the sharing of transcript data, increase the reliability of transcription, and automate the process of data analysis. These new tools, described in detail in MacWhinney (1995), are bringing about significant changes in the way research is conducted in the field of child language. This chapter reviews the background to the formation of the CHILDES system, the shape of the basic CHILDES tools, and the relation of particular tools to particular research goals. It concludes with a presentation of extensions to the system that will be developed during the coming decade.

I. BACKGROUND

The dream of establishing an archive of child language transcript data has a long history, and there were several individual efforts along such lines early on. For example, Roger Brown's (1973) transcripts from the children called Adam, Eve, and Sarah were typed onto stencils from which multiple copies were duplicated. The extra copies have been lent to and analyzed by a wide variety of researchers—some of them (Moerk, 1983) attempting to disprove the conclusions drawn from those data by Brown himself! In addition, of course, to the copies lent out or given away for use by other researchers, a master copy—never lent and in principle never marked on—has been retained in Roger Brown's files as the ultimate historical archive. In this traditional model, everyone took his copy of the transcript home, developed his or her own coding scheme, applied it (usually by making pencil markings directly on the transcript), wrote a paper about the results, and, if very polite, sent a copy to Brown. The original database remained untouched. The nature of each individual's coding scheme and the relationship among any set of different coding schemes could never be fully plumbed.

The dissemination of mimeographed and photocopied transcript data allowed us to see more clearly the limitations involved in our analytic techniques. As we began to compare handwritten and typewritten transcripts, problems in transcription methodology, coding schemes, and cross-investigator reliability became more apparent. But, just as these new problems were arising, a major technological opportunity also was emerging. Microcomputer word-processing systems allowed researchers to enter transcript data into computer files, which could then be easily duplicated, edited, and analyzed by standard data-processing techniques. The possibility of utilizing shared transcription formats, shared codes, and shared analysis programs started to glimmer on the horizon. The idea of a data exchange system for the study of child language development slowly began to emerge.

In 1984 a meeting of 16 child language researchers formally launched the CHILDES system with Brian MacWhinney and Catherine Snow as codirectors. The initial focus of the CHILDES project was on the collection of a nonstandardized database of computerized corpora. Between 1984 and 1986, our work focused on the assembly of a large computerized database of transcripts. As the database grew, it soon became apparent that researchers needed more than a disparate set of corpora transcribed in a confusing diversity of styles. They needed a consistent set of standards both for the analysis of old data and for the collection and transcription of new corpora. During the period from 1986 to 1991, the CHILDES system addressed these needs by developing three separate, but integrated, tools. The first tool is the database itself, the second tool is the CHAT transcription and coding format, and the third tool is the CLAN package of analysis programs. These three tools are presented in detail in MacWhinney (1991) and illustrated through practical examples in Sokolov and Snow (forthcoming). Researchers who plan to make use of the CHILDES tools will want to consult both of these resources.

The three major components of the CHILDES system are the database, the CHAT transcription systems, and the CLAN programs. The next three sections describe these three basic tools.

II. THE DATABASE

The first major tool in the CHILDES workbench is the database itself. The importance of the database can perhaps best be understood by considering the dilemma facing a researcher who wishes to test a detailed theoretical prediction on naturalistic samples. Perhaps the researcher wants to examine the interaction between language type and pronoun omission in order to evaluate the claims of parameter-setting models. Gathering new data that are ideal for the testing of a hypothesis may require months or even years of work. However, conducting the analysis on a small and unrepresentative sample may lead to incorrect conclusions. Because child language data are so time-consuming to collect and process, it may be unfeasible to undertake certain kinds of studies of great potential theoretical interest. For example, studies of individual differences in the process of language acquisition require both an intensive longitudinal analysis and large numbers of subjects—a combination that is practically impossible for a single researcher or a small research team. As a result, conclusions about differences in child language have been based on the analysis of as few as two children and rarely on groups larger than 25. A similar problem arises when linguistic or psycholinguistic theory makes predictions regarding the occurrence and distribution of rare events such as dative passives or certain types of NP-movement. Because of the rarity of such events, large amounts of data must be examined to find out exactly how often they occur in the input and in the child's speech.

Using the CHILDES database, a researcher can access data from a number of research projects that can be used to test a variety of hypotheses. The CHILDES database includes a wide variety of language samples from a wide range of ages and situations. Although more than half of the data come from English speakers, there is also a significant component of non-English data. All of the major corpora have been formatted into the CHAT standard and have been checked for syntactic accuracy. The total size of the database is now approximately 140 million characters (140 MB). The corpora are divided into six major directories: English, non-English, narratives, language impairments, bilingual acquisition, and books.

A. English Data

The directory of transcripts from normal English-speaking children constitutes about half of the total CHILDES database. The subdirectories are named for the contributors of the data. Except where noted, the data are from American children. All of the English files have been checked for correct use of the CHAT transcription conventions through use of the Check program.

Bates: This subdirectory contains data collected by Elizabeth Bates from videotape recordings of play sessions with a group of 20 children first at 20 months and then at 28 months. The children were recorded in three contexts in the laboratory with their mothers: free play, snack time, and storytelling.

Bernstein-Ratner: These data were collected by Nan Bernstein-Ratner from nine children aged 1;1 to 1;11. There are three samples from each child at three time points, all transcribed from high-quality reel-to-reel audiotapes in UNIBET notation. In addition to the transcripts with the children are interviews with the mothers.

Bloom: This subdirectory contains the appendix to Bloom (1970) "One Word at a Time" with language samples from Lois Bloom's daughter Allison between ages 1;4 and 2;10. The subdirectory also contains a large corpus of longitudinal data from Bloom's subject Peter between ages 1;9 and 3;1.

Bohannon: This subdirectory contains transcripts collected by Neil Bohannon from one child aged 2;8 interacting with 17 different adults.

Braine: This subdirectory contains a short set of early utterances reported in Braine (1976). Three of the children are English speakers, one is a Hebrew speaker, and three are Samoan speakers.

Brown: This subdirectory contains three large longitudinal corpora from Adam, Eve, and Sarah collected by Roger Brown and his students. Adam was studied from 2;3 to 4;10; Eve from 1;6 to 2;3; and Sarah from 2;3 to 5;1. We have also tagged these corpora for part of speech and the tagged version of the corpora will eventually be included in the database.

Carterette and Jones: This subdirectory contains the complete text of "Informal Speech" by Edward Carterette and Margaret Jones. Conversations with first, third-, and fifth-grade California school children and adults are transcribed orthographically on the main line and in UNIBET phonemic notation on the %pho line.

Clark: This subdirectory contains data from a longitudinal study of a child between age 2;2 and 3;2 by Eve Clark. The transcripts pay close attention to repetitions, hesitations, and retracings.

Evans: This subdirectory contains transcripts contributed by Mary Evans from 16 dyads of first graders at play.

Fletcher: This subdirectory contains transcripts from 72 British children ages 3, 5, and 7 collected by Paul Fletcher and colleagues.

Garvey: This subdirectory contains 48 files of dialogues between two children with no experimenter present. Each dyad is taken from a larger triad, so that there are files with A and B, B and C, and C and A from each triad. There are 16 triads in all. The children range in age from 3;0 to 5;7. The transcriptions are exceptionally rich in situational commentary.

Gathercole: This subdirectory contains cross-sectional data from a total of 16 children divided into four age groups in the period between 2 and 6 years. The children were observed at school while eating lunch with an experimenter present. The study contains a detailed description of actions and situational changes.

Gleason: This subdirectory contains data collected by Jean Berko-Gleason from 24 subjects aged 2;1 to 5;2. The children are recorded in interactions with (1) their mother, (2) their father, and (3) at the dinner table.

Haggerty: This file contains material from an article published in 1929 that reports the exact conversation carried on in the length of one day by the author's daughter at age 2;7.

Hall: This subdirectory contains a large corpus of data collected by Bill Hall from 38 4-year olds in a variety of situations. The target children were from four groups: white working class, black working class, white professional, and black professional.

Higginson: This subdirectory contains data from 17 hours of early language interactions recorded by Roy Higginson. The three children are aged 1;10 to 2;11, 0;11, and 1;3 to 1;9.

Howe: This subdirectory contains data from 16 Scottish mother-child pairs in their homes in Glasgow collected by Christine Howe. The ages of the children are between 1;6 and 2;2.

Korman: This subdirectory contains the speech of British mothers to infants during the first year.

Kuczaj: This subdirectory contains data from a large longitudinal study of Stan Kuczaj's son Abe from 2;4 to 5;0.

MacWhinney: This subdirectory contains data from a longitudinal study of Brian MacWhinney's sons Ross and Mark from 1;2 to 5;0. Data were also collected from 5;0 to 9;0, but these sessions are not yet transcribed.

Peters/Wilson. This subdirectory contains transcripts from Robert Wilson's son Seth from 1;7 to 4;1. Seth was visually disabled.

Sachs: This subdirectory contains a longitudinal study of Jacqueline Sachs' daughter Naomi from 1;2 to 4;9. Only partial data are available from 1;2 to 1;8.

Snow: This subdirectory contains a longitudinal study of Catherine Snow's son Nathaniel from 2;5 to 3;9.

Suppes: This subdirectory contains a longitudinal study of Patrick Suppes's subject Nina from age 1;11 to 3;3.

VanHouten: This subdirectory contains data from Lori VanHouten comparing adolescent and older mothers and their children at ages 2;0 and 3;0.

Warren-Leubecker: This subdirectory contains data collected by Amye Warren-Leubecker from 20 children interacting either with their mothers or their fathers. One group of children is aged 1;6 to 3;1 and the other group is aged 4;6 to 6;2.

Wells: This extensive corpus from Gordon Wells contains 299 files from 32 British children aged 1;6 to 5;0. The samples were recorded by taperecorders that turned on for 90-second intervals and then automatically turned off.

Wisc: This corpus of mother-child play in a laboratory context from 48 2-year olds was donated by Robin Chapman and Jon Miller of the University of Wisconsin.

B. Non-English Data

With the exception of the data from Afrikaans, Polish, and Tamil, the various non-English data sets have no English glosses or morphemic codings. Therefore, they are currently most useful to researchers who are familiar with the languages involved. All of the data are in CHAT and have passed through the CHECK program without error, although a few of the datasets make use of additional codes found in a "00depadd" file.

Afrikaans: Jan Vorster of the South African Human Sciences Research Council contributed a large syntactically-coded corpus of data from children between 1;6 and 3;6 learning Afrikaans. The data do not have English glosses, but they do have extensive syntactic coding which makes them well suited for syntactic analysis.

Danish: Kim Plunkett of Oxford University contributed longitudinal data from two children learning Danish.

Dutch: This subdirectory contains two corpora. The first is a longitudinal study of a single child between 1;9 and 1;11 from Steven Gillis of the University of Antwerp. Additional files from this child, covering a broader age range, will eventually be available. The second corpus is a longitudinal study of three children by Loekie Elbers and Frank Wijnen of the University of Utrecht. The two boys and one girl in this study are in the age range of 2;3 to 3;1.

French: This subdirectory contains a longitudinal study of a single child by Christian Champaud of the CNRS in Paris, a longitudinal study of a single child by Madeleine Leveillé of the CNRS in Paris, and a group study by Jean Rondal of the University of Liège.

German: This subdirectory contains three corpora. The first is a set of transcripts from 13 children between ages 1;5 and 14;10 from Klaus Wagner of the University of Dortmund. The second is a set of protocols taken from older children by Jürgen Weissenborn of the Max-Planck Institut in the context of experimental ellicitations of route descriptions. The third corpus includes transcripts of noncontinuous interactions collected by Henning Wode of the University of Kiel from his four children with a chief focus on his youngest son and daughter.

Hebrew: Ruth Berman of Tel-Aviv University has contributed a longitudinal study of a Hebrew-learning child named Naama between 1;7 and 2;6 and cross-sectional transcripts for children from ages 1 to 6. A third corpus from Dorit Ravid is a longitudinal study of her daughter Sivan from 1;11 to 6;11.

Hungarian: Brian MacWhinney has donated transcripts of five Hungarian children aged 1;5 to 3;3. The children were recorded in a free play context in their nursery school.

Italian: Elena Pizzuto of the CNR in Rome has contributed data in CHAT from a longitudinal study of a single child. The research team located in Pisa at the Center for Computational Linguistics and the Stella Maris Institute has donated data from two girls and one boy ages 1;8 to 2;11.

Polish: Richard Weist of SUNY Fredonia has contributed data from four children learning Polish. The data are coded morphemically in a way that is very useful for comparative analysis.

Spanish: Jose Linaza of the University of Madrid has contributed data from a longitudinal case study of a child between ages 2;0 and 4;0.

Tamil: R. Narasimhan and R. Vaidyanathan of the Tata Institute in Bombay have contributed a longitudinal study of a Tamil child between ages 0;9 and 2;9.

Turkish: There are two corpora for Turkish. One is a set of interviews from children aged 2;0 to 4;8 donated by Dan Slobin. The second is a set of "Frog Story" descriptions donated by Ayhan Aksu-Koc. The children in both data sets are cross-sectionally sampled.

C. Narrative Data

The data in this directory are narratives, currently mostly derived from retellings of stories in books and movies.

Gopnik: The files in this directory were contributed by Myrna Gopnik. They are stories elicited by teachers from children between the ages of 2 and 5.

Hicks: The data in this subdirectory were contributed by Deborah Hicks. They were elicited by showing the silent film *The Red Balloon* to children in grades K through 2 and asking them to then tell the story in each of three different genres. The data are coded for a variety of anaphoric devices.

D. Language Impairments

In the past few years, quite a few corpora on language disorders and impairments have been added to the database. All of these corpora are in CHAT and have passed through the Check program.

Bliss: This subdirectory contains a set of interviews with seven language-impaired children and their matched normal controls collected by Lynn Bliss at Wayne State University and formatted in CHAT.

Brinton/Fujiki: This corpus has spontaneous language samples from 65 young-adult Down's syndrome subjects in a half-hour interview format with an adult male experimenter.

CAP: This subdirectory contains transcripts gathered from 60 English, German, and Hungarian aphasics in the Comparative Aphasia Project directed by Elizabeth Bates. The transcripts are in CHAT format and large segments have full morphemic coding and error coding.

Conti-Ramsden: This subdirectory contains transcripts of five British specifically language-impaired preschool children interacting separately with their mothers, their fathers, and a normally developing MLU-matched younger sibling. The data are in CHAT and were contributed by Gina Conti-Ramsden of the University of Manchester. Control transcripts from the sibling interacting with the mother and the father are also included.

Evans: This corpus includes data collected by Julia Evans from 25 elementary-school-aged children (15 males and 10 females) ages 8;0 to 11;0 that meet Stark and Tallal's (1981) exclusionary criteria as specifically language Impaired (SLI).

There are chronologically age matched (within 6 months) and expressive language matched (based on MLU) for each of the 25 children. A 30-minute spontaneous language sample was collected for each child in an adult-child dyadic interaction with the same female experimenter. Only subjects from white middle-class families were included to control for potential variations in conversational patterns relative to economic level. The Four Factor Index of Social Status (Hollingshead, 1975) was completed for each subject. To control for the effects of birth order all normal language controls were either first-born or only children. The children with SLI all were previously diagnosed as language disordered by a certified speech-language Pathologist and were receiving therapy in the schools. All children had taken or were given the AAPS, the CELF-R, the PPVT-R, and the WISC-R. To rule out potential differences in results due to differences in social maturation and personality, the Child Behavioral Checklist (CBCL) (Achenbach, 1978) was administered to all 25 children to provide social competence and behavior profiles.

Feldman: This corpus includes longitudinal data collected by Heidi Feldman for 58 children with brain damage (46 with PVL; 12 with infarctions) and 21 normal language controls. Of the 46 children with PVL, 38 have bilateral lesions, 4 have right-hemisphere lesions, and 4 have left-hemisphere lesions. For the 12 subjects with infarctions, 8 have right-hemisphere lesions and 4 have left-hemisphere lesions. From ages 15 to 48 months, data were collected every 3 months using a set of tasks designed to elicited spontaneous discourse with their parents. From ages 4 years to 7 years, data were collected yearly employing both freeplay tasks and narrative tasks. The language samples collected for ages 4 to 7 are with a female experimenter. The normal language controls for the 15- to 48-month data collection are nine children born prematurely with no underlying brain damage. The normal language controls for the 4- to 7-year data collection are the subject's siblings. Sibling data have been collected when the child is at an age that is a chronological age match for the subject. In addition to collecting spontaneous language samples, standardized cognitive and language measures have been administered yearly.

Fey: This corpus includes data collected by Marc Fey from 93 language-impaired school-aged children. Approximately half of the transcripts meet the strict criteria for SLI by having a nonverbal IQ greater than 85. The remaining subjects have nonverbal IQ between 75 and 85. Fifteen-minute spontaneous language samples were collected for all subjects in an adult-child dyadic interaction.

Hargrove: This subdirectory contains a set of interviews collected by Patricia Hargrove between a speech therapist and six language-impaired children in the age range of 3 to 6.

Holland: This subdirectory contains a set of interviews collected by Audrey Holland from 40 recovering stroke patients who are suffering aphasic symptoms.

Hooshyar: This subdirectory contains files collected by Nahid Hooshyar of the Southwest Family Institute from 30 Down's syndrome children between the ages of 4 and 8.

Rondal: This subdirectory contains data collected from 21 Down's syndrome children in Minnesota by Jean Rondal of the University of Liège.

Tager-Flusberg: The subjects for Helen Tager-Flusberg's longitudinal corpus include six autistic children and six children with Down's syndrome matched on age and MLU at the start of the study. The autistic children were diagnosed based on Rutter's criteria, which was consistent with the DSM-III criteria. IQ scores were assessed using the Leiter International Performance Scale (Leiter, 1969). The IQ scores for five of the six autistic children fell in the normal to low-normal range. The Down's syndrome children were matched based on chronological age and language level as measured by MLU. Spontaneous language samples were collected with the child and his or her mother during bimonthly visits to the children's homes over a period of between 12 and 26 months.

E. Bilingual Acquisition Data

DeHouwer: Annick De Houwer of the University of Antwerp has donated a corpus of transcripts collected between ages 2;7 and 3;4 from a girl who learned English and Dutch simultaneously.

Deuchar: Margaret Deuchar of the University of Cambridge has donated a corpus of transcripts collected between ages 1;3 and 2;6 from a girl who learned English and Spanish simultaneously.

Guthrie: This subdirectory contains data collected by Larry Guthrie of the Far West Laboratory from three first-grade classrooms of immigrant children in San Francisco.

Hayashi: Mariko Hayashi of the University of Århus has donated a corpus of transcripts collected between ages 1;0 and 2;5 from a girl who learned Japanese and Danish simultaneously.

Snow: This subdirectory contains picture descriptions and word definitions in both English and Spanish from 190 Puerto Rican children in second- through sixth-grade bilingual classrooms transcribed in minCHAT format. The picture descriptions are coded for explicitness and narrativity. Similar data from an additional 18 fifth graders who are not in bilingual programs and from 14 third graders who are monolingual Spanish speakers are also included. These data have been contributed by Catherine Snow.

F. Books

The database also includes the complete text of several books and articles. We have obtained permissions from the publishers to include these books in the database. This directory also includes an extensive computerized bibliography of research in child language development. These materials are not in CHAT.

CHILDES/Bib: With support from CHILDES, Roy Higginson of Iowa State

University used a variety of existing resources to compile a rich computerized bibliography of research in child language development that can be searched with the CLAN program called BIBFIND (Higginson & MacWhinney, 1990).

Cornell: This directory includes small passages from a wide variety of written sources that form the bulk of the Cornell Corpus of Donald Hayes (1988).

Isaacs: This subdirectory contains the complete text of *Intellectual Growth in Young Children* by Susan Isaacs (1930) and *Social Development in Young Children* by Isaacs (1933). The author records interesting interactions with upper-middle class British children, often in nearly verbatim form.

Stern: This corpus contains the diary notes on German child language acquisition produced by Clara and Wilhelm Stern at the turn of the century.

Weir: This subdirectory contains the phonetic transcriptions from the appendix to *Language in the Crib* by Weir (1962).

G. Access to the Database

Membership in CHILDES is open. However, members are asked to abide by the rules of the system. In particular, users should not distribute copies of programs or files without permission, they should abide by the stated wishes of the contributors of the data, and they should acknowledge properly all uses of the data and the programs. Any article that uses the data from a particular corpus must cite a reference from the contributor of that corpus.

There are two levels of membership in the system: passive membership and contributing membership. All members can have passive access to the database and tools through HTTP or CD-ROM. Members who have contributed data or who plan to contribute data can receive further documentation and assistance in using the programs. To access the database on the Web go to Http//childes.psy.cmv.edu.

H. Reformatting of the Database

All of the current corpora are in good CHAT format. However, only a few of the most recent corpora were entered directly into CHAT. The process of converting the older corpora into CHAT required years of careful work. Some corpora had to be scanned into computer files from typewritten sheets. Other corpora were already computerized, but in a wide variety of transcription systems. For each of these datasets, we had to translate the project-specific codes and formats into CHAT. Several sets of files were translated from SALT (Miller & Chapman, 1983) using the SALTIN program. For other corpora, special-purpose reformatting programs had to be written. The fact that these transcripts now all pass through CHECK without error means that all of the files now have correct headers, correct listings of participants, and correct matches of coding tiers to main lines. Each main line has only one utterance and every utterance ends with a legal terminator.

There are no incorrect symbols in the middle of words and all paired delimiters are correctly matched. However, we cannot yet guarantee that the files are consistently coded on the level of individual words. This level of consistency checking remains a goal for our future work with the database.

III. CHAT

The most conceptually difficult task we faced in developing the CHILDES system was the formulation of the CHAT transcription system. From 1984 to 1990, during the period which we now refer to as the period of proto-CHAT, we explored a variety of transcription forms. In 1990 we began to finalize the shape of CHAT until it reached the more stable form published in the manual (MacWhinney, 1995). Users have expressed happiness with the current status of CHAT and the fact that virtually no changes have been made to the basic conventions since 1990. The finalization of CHAT allowed us to sharpen the workings of the CLAN CHECK program so that it now constitutes a computational implementation of the whole CHAT system.

No coding or transcription system can ever fully satisfy all the needs of all researchers. Nor can any transcription system ever hope to fully capture the richness of interactional behavior. Despite its inevitable limitations, the availability of CHAT as a *lingua franca* for transcription both within the Program Project and within the general field of child language research has already led to solid improvements in data exchange, data analysis, and scientific precision.

A. Key Features of CHAT

The CHAT system is designed to function on at least two levels. The simplest form of CHAT is called minCHAT. Use of minCHAT requires a minimum of coding decisions. This type of transcription looks very much like the intuitive types of transcription generally in use in child language and discourse analysis. A fragment of a file in minCHAT looks like this:

```
@Begin
@Participants:  ROS Ross Child BRI Brian Father
*ROS:           why isn't Mommy coming?
%com:           Mother usually picks Ross up around 4P.M.
*BRI:           don't worry.
*BRI:           she'll be here soon.
*ROS:           good.
@End
```

There are several points to note about this fragment. First, all of the characters in this fragments are ASCII characters. The @Begin and @End lines are used to guarantee that the file was not destroyed or shortened during copying between systems. Each line begins with a three-letter speaker code, a colon, and then a tab. Each line has only one utterance. However, if the utterance is longer than one line, it may continue onto the next line. A new utterance must be given a new speaker code. Commentary lines and other coding lines are indicated by the % symbol.

Beyond the level of minCHAT, there are a variety of advanced options that allow the user to attain increasing levels of precision in transcription and coding. Some of the major specifications available in the full CHAT system are the following:

1. *File headers:* CHAT specifies a set of 24 standard file headers such as "Age of Child," "Birth of Child," "Participants," "Location," and "Date" that document a variety of facts about the participants and the recording.
2. *Word forms:* CHAT specifies particular ways of transcribing learner forms, unidentifiable material, and incomplete words. It also provides conventions for standardizing spellings of shortenings, assimilations, interactional markers, colloquial forms, baby talk, and certain dialectal variants.
3. *Morphemes:* CHAT provides a system for morphemicization of complex words. Without such morphemicization, mean length of utterance is computer based on words, as defined orthographically.
4. *Tone units:* CHAT provides a system for marking tone units, pauses, and contours.
5. *Terminators:* CHAT provides a set of symbols for marking utterance terminations and conversational linkings.
6. *Scoping:* CHAT uses a scoping convention to indicate stretches of overlaps, metalinguistic reference, retracings, and other complex patterns.
7. *Dependent tiers:* CHAT provides definitions for 14 coding tiers. Coding for three of these dependent tiers have been worked out in detail.
   a. *Phonological coding:* CHAT provides a single-character phonemic transcription system for English and several other languages called UNIBET. It also provides an ASCII translation for the extended IPA symbol set called PHONASCII. These systems were devised by George Allen of Purdue University.
   b. *Error coding:* CHAT provides a full system for coding speech errors.
   c. *Morphemic coding:* CHAT provides a system for morphemic and syntactic coding or interlinear glossing.

The full CHAT system is covered in MacWhinney (1995).

B. How Much CHAT Does a User Need to Know?

CHILDES users fall into two groups. One group of researchers wants to examine corpora but has little interest in collecting and transcribing new data. Another group of researchers wants to collect and transcribe new data and may be only marginally interested in analyzing old data. Typically, linguists and computer scientists fall into the first category and developmental psychologists and students of language disorders fall into the second category. Researchers in the second group who are using CHAT to transcribe new data soon come to realize that they need to learn all of the core CHAT conventions. Although these users may begin by using minCHAT, they will eventually gain familiarity with all of the conventions used on the main line, as well as with those dependent tier codes relevant to their particular research goals.

Users who are focusing on the analysis of old data may think that they do not need to master all of CHAT. For example, a researcher who wants to track the development of personal pronouns in the Brown corpora may think it sufficient to simply look for strings such as *he* and *it*. However, this type of casual use of the database is fairly dangerous. For example, users need to understand that, in the Brown corpora, the forms *dem* and *dese* are often used as spelling variants for *them* and *these*. Failure to track such variants could lead to underestimates of early pronoun usage. There are dozens of correspondences of this type that researchers need to understand if they are to make accurate use of the database.

When users start to use more detailed analysis programs such as MLU or DSS, the need to understand symbols for omitted elements and repetitions becomes increasingly important. For example, users need to understand that some corpora have been morphemicized in accord with the standards of chapter 6 and that others have not. Users also need to understand how symbols for missing elements or retracings can affect both lexical and syntactic analyses. It is possible that, in many cases, users could reach correct conclusions without a full understanding of the core features of CHAT. However, it is impossible to guarantee that this will happen. It is clear that the best recommendation to CHILDES users is to try to learn as much of CHAT as possible. If a researcher makes erroneous use of the database, these errors cannot be attributed to the CHILDES system, but only to the researcher who has failed to fully learn the system. Reviewers of articles based on the use of CHILDES data need to be convinced that the researcher fully understood the shape of the database and the inevitable limitations of any empirical dataset.

IV. CLAN

The third major tool in the CHILDES workbench is the CLAN package of analysis programs. The CLAN (Child Language Analysis) programs were written in the C programming language by Leonid Spektor at Carnegie Mellon University. The programs benefited from work done by Jeffrey Sokolov, Bill Tuthill, and Mitzi Morris, as well as from the SALT systematization developed by Jon Miller and Robin Chapman (Miller & Chapman, 1983).

CLAN commands include the program name, a set of options, and the names of the files being analyzed. For example the command

freq +f*.cha

runs the FREQ program on all the files in a given directory with the .cha extension. The +f switch indicates that the output of each analysis should be written to a file on the disk. Unless specifically given a file extension name, the FREQ program will figure out names for the new files. Many of the programs have quite a few possible options. Each option is explained in detail in the manual. In addition, you can get a brief list of options for a program by just typing the name of that program with no further options. For example, if you type *freq*, these options will be displayed:

- Freq creates a frequency word count
- For complete documentation on freq, type: help freq
- Usage: freq [c o dN fS k m pF rN sS tS u y zN] filename(s)
- +c: find capitalized words only
- +o: sort output by descending frequency
- +d: outputs all selected words, corresponding frequencies, and line numbers
- +d1: outputs word with no frequency information. in KWAL or COMBO format
- +d2: sends output to a file for STATEFREQ. Must include speaker specifications
- +d3: sends statistics only to STATEFREQ. Must include speaker specifications
- +d4: outputs only type/token information
- +fS: send to file (program will derive filename)
- −f: send output to the screen or pipe
- +k: treat upper and lower case as different
- +m: store output file(s) in the directories of input file(s)
- +pF: define punctuation set according to file F
- +rN: if N = 1 then "get(s)" goes to "gets", 2 − "get(s), 3 − "get"
- +sS: either word S or words in file @S to search for in a given input file
- −sS: either word S or words in file @S to be exclude from a given input file
- +tS: include tier code S
- −tS: exclude tier code S
- +u: merge all specified files together.
- +y: work on non-CHAT format files (default CHAT format)
- +zN: compute statistics on a specified range of input data

The programs have been designed to support five basic types of linguistic analysis (Crystal, 1982; Crystal, Fletcher, & Garman, 1989): lexical analysis, morphological analysis, syntactic analysis, discourse analysis, and phonological analysis. Let us look at how CLAN can be used to test hypotheses in each of these five areas.

A. CLAN for Lexical Analysis

The easiest types of CLAN analyses are those which look at the frequencies and distributions of particular word forms. For example, it is a simple matter to trace the use of a word like *under* or a group of words such as the locative prepositions. The analysis can be done on either a single file or a group of files. For example, let us suppose that we want to trace the use of personal pronouns in the three children studied by Roger Brown. We would construct a file including all of the personal pronouns with one pronoun on each line and call this file "pronouns." We would then use the FREQ command to count the occurrences of the pronouns in a file with a command like this:

freq +spronouns +t*ADA adam01.cha

The switch +t*ADA is included in order to limit the tally to only the utterances spoken by the child. If we also want the frequencies of the words spoken by the mother, we would use this command:

freq +spronouns +t*MOT adam01.cha

If we want to extend our analysis to all of the files in the directory, we can use the wild card:

freq +spronouns +t*ADA adam*.cha

If we want the collection of files to be treated as a single large file, we can add another switch:

freq +spronouns +t*ADA +u adam*.cha

The FREQ command is powerful and quite flexible, permitting a large number of possible analyses. The outputs of these analyses can be sent to either the screen or to files. The names of the output files can be controlled. For example, one might want to maintain a group of output files with the extension .mot for the frequencies of the mother's speech. These can be kept in a separate directory for further analysis.

The second major tool for conducting lexical analyses is the KWAL program, which outputs not merely the frequencies of matching items, but also all the full context of the item. For example, the KWAL command that searches for the word *chalk* in the sample.cha file will produce this output:

```
kwal + schalk sample.cha
kwal is conducting analyses on:
ALL speaker tiers
**************************
From file <sample.cha>
------------------------
***File sample.cha. Line 39. Keyword: chalk
*MOT: is there any delicious chalk?
------------------------
***File sample.cha. Line 51. Keyword: chalk
*MOT: do-'nt you eat wonderful chalk.
------------------------
***File sample.cha. Line 54. Keyword: chalk
*MOT: it's not good to want chalk.
```

It is possible to include still further previous and following context using additional switches.

Frequency Analyses

With tools like FREQ and KWAL, one can easily construct frequency analyses for individual children at specified ages. Many such counts have been produced. However, it is more difficult to move up to the next level of generalization on which a frequency count is constructed across children and ages. First, one would want to tabulate frequency data for the speech of children separately from the speech of adults. And one would not want to automatically combine data from children of different ages. Moreover, we would not want to merge data from children with language disorders together with data from normally developing children. Differences in social class, gender, and educational level may lead one to make further separations. Also it is important to distinguish language used in different situational contexts. When one finishes looking at all the distinctions that could potentially be made, it becomes clear that one needs to think of the construction of a lexical database in very dynamic terms.

Such a database could be constructed using FREQ and other CLAN tools, but this work would be fairly tedious and slow. What we plan to do to address this problem is to build a file with every lexical item in the entire database and attach to each item a set of pointers to the position of the item in every file in which it occurs. These key files and pointer files will be stored along with the database on a CD-ROM. Using the pointers from the master word list to the individual occurrences of words, the user can construct specific probes of this database configured both on facts about the child and facts about the words being searched. The program that matches these searches to the pointer file will be called LEX. Using LEX, it will be possible, for example, to track the frequency of a group of evaluative words contained in a separate file in 2-year olds separated into males and females. And the same search can also yield the frequency values for these words in the adult input. Although we may want to publish hard-copy frequency counts based on some searches through this database, the definitive form of the lexical frequency analysis will be contained in the program itself.

Once the LEX tool is completed, the path will be open to the construction of three additional tools. The first of these is a simple extension of the current KWAL program. Currently, researchers who want to track down the exact occurrences of particular words must rely on the use of the +d option in FREQ or must make repeated analyses using KWAL and keep separate track of line numbers. With the new LEX system, instead of running through files sequentially, KWAL will be able to rely on the pointers in the master file to make direct access to items in the database.

Lexical Field Analyses

A second type of lexical research focuses attention not on the entire lexicon, but on particular lexical fields. Using the +s@file switch with FREQ and KWAL, such analyses can already be computed with the current version of CLAN. Completion of the LEX facility will further facilitate the analysis of lexical fields. For example, using the lexical database, we will be able to examine the development of selected lexical fields in the style of the PRISM analysis of Crystal (1982) and Crystal, Fletcher, and Garman (1976). This analysis tracks the child's developing use of content words in 239 lexical subfields. Examples of these fields include farm tools, units of weight measurement, and musical instruments. These 239 fields can be merged into a set of 61 categories which can, in turn, be merged into nine high-level fields. Bodin and Snow (1993) showed how analyses of this type can be conducted on the CHILDES database. Likely candidates for intensive examination include mental verbs, morality words, temporal adverbs, subordinating conjunctions, and complex verbs.

Other important semantic fields include closed class items such as pronouns, determiners, quantifiers, and modals. As Brown (1973), Lahey (1988), and many others have noted, these high-frequency, closed-class items each express important semantic and pragmatic functions that provide us with separate information about the state of the child's language and cognitive functioning. For example, Antinucci and Miller (1976), Cromer (1991), Slobin (1986), and Weist, Wysocka, Witkowska-Stadnik, Buczowska, & Konieczna (1984) argued that tense markings and temporal adverbs are not controlled until the child first masters the relevant conceptual categories.

It is also possible to track basic semantic relations (Bloom, 1975; Lahey, 1988; Leonard, 1976; Retherford, Schwartz, & Chapman, 1981) by studying the closed-class lexical items that mark these relations. In particular, we can follow these correspondences between semantic relations and lexical expressions:

Relation	Lexical Expressions
Locative	in, on, under, through, by, at
Negation	can't, no, not, wont, none
Demonstrative	this, that
Recurrence	more, again, another
Possession	possessive suffix, of, mone, hers, her
Adverbial	-ly
Quantifier	one, two, more, some
Recipient	to
Beneficiary	for
Comitative	with
Instrument	with, by

Lexical Rarity Index

A third measure that can be developed through use of the LEX facility is the lexical rarity index (LRI). Currently, the major index of lexical diversity is the type-token ratio (TTR) of Templin (1957). A more interesting measure would focus on the relative dispersion in a transcript of words that are generally rare in some comparison data set. The more that a child uses words that are considered rare, the higher the lexical rarity index. If most of the words are common and frequent, the LRI will be low. To compute various forms of this index, the LRI program would rely on values provided by LEX.

Another easy way of tracking the emergence of longer words is to use the WDLEN program, which provides a simple histogram of word lengths in a file along with the location of the longest words.

B. CLAN for Morphological Analysis

Many of the most important questions in child language require the detailed study of specific morphosyntactic constructions. For example, the debate on the role of connectionist simulations of language learning (MacWhinney & Leinbach, 1991; MacWhinney, Leinbach, Taraban, & McDonald, 1989; Marcus, et al., 1991; Pinker & Prince, 1988; Plunkett & Sinha, 1992) has focused attention on early uses and overregularizations of the regular and irregular past tense markings in English. A full resolution of this debate will require intensive study of the acquisition of these markings not just in English, but in a wide variety of languages at a wide sampling of ages. Similarly, the testing of hypotheses about parameter setting within generative theory (Hyams, 1986; Pizzuto & Caselli, 1993; Valian, 1991; Wexler, 1986) often depends on a careful study of pronominal markings, reflexives, and wh-words.

During the earliest stages of language learning, the most obvious developments are those involving the acquisition of particular grammatical markings. The study of the acquisition of grammatical markers in English has been heavily shaped by Brown's (1973) intensive study of the acquisition of 14 grammatical morphemes in Adam, Eve, and Sarah and the cross-sectional follow-up by de Villiers and de Villiers (1973). Since Brown's original analysis, there have been scores of studies tracking these same morphemes in second-language learners, normally developing children, and children with language disorders. There have also been many studies of comparable sets of morphemes in other languages.

The 14 morphemes studied by Brown include the progressive, the plural, the regular past, the irregular past, *in*, *on*, the regular third-person singular, the irregular third-person singular, articles, the uncontracted copula, the contracted copula, the possessive, the contracted auxiliary, and the uncontracted auxiliary. Brown's framework for morpheme analysis has been extended in systems such as the LARSP procedure by Crystal, Fletcher, and Garman (1976), the DSS procedure by Lee (1974), the ASS procedure of Miller (1981), and the IPSyn procedure of Scarborough, Rescorla, Tager-Flusberg, Fowler, and Sudhalter (1991). Other markers tracked in LARSP, ASS, and DSS include the superlative, the comparative, the adverbial ending *-ly*, the uncontracted negative, the contracted negative, the regular past participle, the irregular past participle, and various nominalizing suffixes.

Within the CHILDES framework, De Acedo (de Acedo, 1993) showed how CHAT and CLAN can be used to study the Spanish child's learning of grammatical markers. In the next two sections, we discuss several CLAN tools for the study of morphological structure.

Morphological Analysis from the Main Line

Chapter 6 of the CHILDES manual describes a system for coding the presence of grammatical markers on the main line. For example, the word *cats* can be coded as *cat-s*. This coding then allows users to search for all instances of the plural marker *-s*. The basic lexical tools of FREQ and KWAL can be used to do this. This system provides direct access to the basic grammatical morphemes of English. However, only grammatical markers are coded directly. In a more complex language, such as Italian or Hungarian, a simple system of this type will quickly break down. Moreover, many analyses of morphological and syntactic structure require the construction of a more complete morphological analysis.

MOR—Automatic Morphological Analysis

The more extensive coding needed for many projects requires a complete construction of a part-of-speech analysis for each word on the main line. This analysis is placed on a separate tier called the %mor tier. The coding of the %mor tier is done in accord with the guidelines specified in chapter 14 of the CHILDES manual. Once a complete %mor tier is available, a vast range of morphological and syntactic analyses become possible. However, hand coding of a %mor tier for the entire CHILDES database would require perhaps 20 years of work and would be extremely error-prone and non-correctable. If the standards for morphological coding changed in the middle of this project, the coder would have to start over again from the beginning. It would be difficult to imagine a more tedious and frustrating task—the hand coder's equivalent of Sisyphus and his stone.

The alternative to hand coding is automatic coding. Over the past three years, we have worked on the construction of an automatic coding program for CHAT files. This program, called MOR, was first developed in LISP by Roland Hausser (1990), modified for C by Carolyn Ellis, and then completely rewritten by Mitzi Morris with assistance from Leonid Spektor. Although the MOR system is designed to be transportable to all languages, it is currently only fully elaborated for English and German. The language-independent part of MOR is the core processing engine. All of the language-specific aspects of the systems are built into files that can be modified by the user. In the remarks that follow, we will first focus on ways in which a user can apply the system for English.

How to Run MOR

The MOR program takes a CHAT main line and automatically inserts a %mor line together with the appropriate morphological codes for each word on the main line. The basic MOR command is much like the other commands in CLAN. For example, you can run MOR in its default configuration with this type of command:

```
mor sample.cha
```

However, MOR is unlike the other CLAN programs in one crucial regard. Although you can run MOR on any CLAN file, in order to get a well-formed %mor line, you often need to engage in significant *extra work*. We have tried to minimize the additional work you need to do when working with MOR, but it would misleading for us to suggest that no additional work is required. In particular, users of MOR will often need to spend a great deal of time engaging in the processes of (a) lexicon building and (b) ambiguity resolution.

Files Used by MOR

Before we examine ways of dealing with lexicon building and ambiguity resolution, let us take a quick look at the files that support a MOR analysis. For MOR to run successfully, four files must be present in either the library directory or the current working directory. Although you do not need to have a detailed understanding of the functioning of these files, it will help you to have a view of the shape of these basic building blocks. The default names for the four basic files are eng.ar, eng.cr, eng.lex, and eng.clo. These four files contain the following information:

1. *Allomorphic rules.* The rules that describe allomorphic variations are called *arules.*
2. *Concatenation rules.* The rules that describe allowable concatenations are called *crules.*
3. *Closed class items.* The eng.clo file contains the closed class words and suffixes of English. Because this group forms such a tight closed set, the user will seldom have to modify this file.
4. *Open class items.* The default name of the open class lexicon for English is eng.lex. This file is what we call the *disk lexicon.* Words in the disk lexicon are listed in their canonical form, along with category information.

MOR uses the eng.ar, eng.lex, and eng.clo files to produce a *run-time lexicon,* which is significantly more complete than eng.lex alone. When analyzing input files, MOR uses the run-time lexicon together with the eng.cr file. As a user, you do not need to concern yourself with the actual shape of the run-time lexicon, and you will usually not have to touch either the arules, crules, or drules. Your main concern will be with the process of adding or removing entries from the main open class lexicon file—eng.lex. If all of the words in your files can be located in the eng.lex file, running of MOR is totally trivial. You simply run:

mor filename

But matters are seldom this simple, because most files will have many words that are not found in eng.lex and you will need to refine the eng.lex file until all missing words are inserted. Therefore, the main task involved for most users of MOR is the building of the lexicon file.

Lexicon Building—Finding Missing Words

To see whether MOR correctly recognizes all of the words in your transcripts, you can first run MOR on all of your files and then run this KWAL command on the .mor files you have produced:

kwal +t%mor +s"?|*" *.mor

If KWAL finds no question marks on the %mor line, then you know that all the words have been recognized by MOR. If there are question marks in your *.mor output files, you will probably want to correct this problem by running MOR in the interactive update mode. If you know from the outset that your file includes many words that will not be found in eng.lex, you can directly begin the process of lexicon building by running this FREQ command:

freq +d1 +u +k *.cha > output.frq

This produces a simple list of all the words in your transcript in a form useful for interactive MOR lexicon building. The +d1 option outputs words without frequencies. The +k option is needed to distinguish between *Bill* and *bill.* The redirection arrow sends the output to a file we have called output.frq. Next you can run MOR again using the +s option with a filename added, as in this example:

mor +xl output.frq

MOR will use eng.lex to attempt to analyze each word in the output.frq file. If it cannot analyze the word, it will enter it in a output file of lexical entry templates with the name output.ulx. Then you need to look at the words in the output.ulx file, using an editor. Some may be misspellings and will have to be corrected in the original file. Others will be new words for which you will have to enter a part-of-speech characterization. When you are finished, you should rename the output.ulx file to output.lex. Then you can run MOR again in this form:

mor +loutput *.cha

If all has gone smoothly, MOR will now be able to enter a part-of-speech characterization for every word in the transcripts.

The Structure of eng.lex

Users of MOR may want to understand the way in which entries in the disk lexicon (eng.lex) are structured. The disk lexicon contains truly irregular forms of a word, as well as citation forms. For example, the verb *go* is stored in eng.lex, along with the past tense *went,* because this form is a suppletive form and is not subject to regular rules. The disk lexicon contains any number of lexical entries, stored at most one entry per line. A lexical entry may be broken across several lines by placing the continuation character backslash (\) at the end of the line. The lexicon may be annotated with comments, which will not be processed. A comment begins with the percent sign % and ends with a newline.

A lexical entry consists of the surface form of the word, followed by category information about the word expressed as a set of feature-value pairs. Each feature-value pair is enclosed in square brackets and the full set of feature-value pairs is enclosed in curly braces. All entries must contain a feature-value pair that identifies the syntactic category to which the word belongs, consisting of the feature *scat* with an appropriate value. Words that belong to several categories will be followed by several sets of feature structures, each separated by a backslash. Category information is optionally followed by information about the stem. If the surface form of the word is not the citation form of the word, then the citation form, surrounded by quotes, should follow the category information. If the word contains fused morphemes, these should be given as well, using the & symbol as the morpheme separator. The following are examples of lexical entries:

```
can   {[scat v:aux]}\
            {[scat n}
a     {[scat det]}
an    {[scat det]}      "a"
go    {[scat v][ir +]}
went  {[scat v][tense past]}    "go&PAST"
```

When adding new entries to eng.lex it is usually sufficient to enter the citation form of the word, along with the syntactic category information.

Ambiguity Resolution

MOR automatically generates a %mor tier of the type described in chapter 14. As stipulated in chapter 14, retraced material, comments, and excluded words are not coded on the %mor line produced by MOR. Words are labeled by their syntactic category, followed by the separator "|," followed by the word itself, broken down into its constituent morphemes.

```
*CHI:  the people are making cakes.
%mor:  det|the n|people v:aux|be&PRES v|make-ING n|cake-PL.
```

In this particular example, none of the words have ambiguous forms. However, it is often the case that some of the basic words in English have two or more part-of-speech readings. For example, the word *back* can be a noun, a verb, a preposition, an adjective, or an adverb. The " ^" character denotes the alternative readings for each word on the main tier.

```
*CHI:  I want to go back.
%mor:  pro|I v|want inf|to^prep|to
    v|go adv|back^n|back^v|back.
```

The entries in the eng.clo file maintain these ambiguities. However, open class words in the eng.lex file are only coded in their most common part-of-speech form. The problem of noun-verb ambiguity will eventually be addressed through use of the PARS program, which is currently being developed. Those ambiguities which remain in a MOR transcript after the drules and the PARS program has operated can be removed by using MOR in its ambiguity resolution mode. The program locates each of the various ambiguous words one by one and asks the user to select one of the possible meanings.

MOR for Other Languages

To maximize the portability of the MOR system to other languages, we have developed a general scheme for representing arules and crules. This means that a researcher can adapt MOR for a new language without doing any programming at all. However, the researcher/linguist needs to construct (a) a list of the stems of the language with their parts of speech, (b) a set of arules for allomorphic variations in spelling, and (c) a set of crules for possible combinations of stems with affixes. Building these files will require a major one-time dedication of effort from at least one researcher for every language. Once the basic work of constructing the rules files and the core lexicon files is done, then further work with MOR in that language will be no more difficult than it currently is for English. However, construction of new rules files is an extremely complex process, and construction of a closed class and open class lexicon will also take a great deal of time. Although no programming is required, the linguist building these files must have a thorough understanding of the MOR program and the morphology of the language involved. Complete documentation for the construction of the rules files is available from Carnegie Mellon and will also be included in the next edition of the CHILDES manual.

C. CLAN for Syntactic Analysis

Once a %mor line has been constructed, either through use of MOR or through hand coding, a variety of additional morphosyntactic analyses are then available. Instead of analyzing the lexical items on the main line, programs can now analyze the fuller morphosyntactic representation on the %mor line. The simpler forms of analysis can still be done using FREQ and KWAL. However, several other programs add additional power for morphosyntactic analysis. The MLU program can compute the basic mean length of utterance index in a variety of ways (Rollins, 1993). COMBO extends the power of FREQ and KWAL by permitting more complete Boolean string matching. For example, if the user wants to search for all instances of a relative pronoun followed eventually by an auxiliary verb, it is possible to compose this search string in COMBO. Certain types of matching between the main line and the %mor line can be achieved using the +s switch in the MODREP program. In addition, the COOCCUR program can be used to tabulate sequences of syntactic structures appearing on the %mor line.

More complex analyses of syntactic development require us to deal with structures defined in terms of traditional syntactic categories such as subject, object, and main verb. Among the most important syntactic structures examined by procedures such as LARSP, ASS, IPSyn, and DSS are these:

Structure	Example
Art + N	the dog
Adj + N	good boy
Adj + Adj + N	my new car
Art + Adj + N	the new car
Adj/Art + N + V	my bike fall
V + Adj/Art + N	want more cookie
N + poss + N	John's wallet
Adv + Adj	too hot
Prep + NP	at the school
N + Cop + PrejAdj	we are nice
N + Cop + PredN	we are monsters
Aux + V	is coming
Aux + Aux + V	will be coming
Mod + V	can come
Q + V	who ate it?
Q + Aux + V	who is coming?
tag	isn't it
aux + N	are you going?
S + V	baby fall
V + O	drink coffee
S + V + O	you play this
X + conj + X	boy and girl, red and blue
V + to + V	want to swim
let/help + V	let's play
V + Comp	I know you want it
Sent + Conj + Sent	I'll push and you row.
V + I + O	read me the book
N + SRel	the one you have in the bag
N + ORel	the one that eats corn
S + Rel + V	the one I like best is the monster
passive	he is kicked by the raccoon
Neg + N	no dog
Neg + V	can't come
PP + PP	under the bridge by the river
comparative	better than Bill

Several of these structures also define some of the semantic relations that have been emphasized in previous literature. These include recipient (direct object), agent (subject in actives), verb, and object.

The discussion in this section has focused on the construction of indicators for development in English. However, these same tools can also be usefully applied to basic issues in crosslinguistic analysis. Once we have collected a large database of transcripts in other languages and created a full %mor tier encoding, we can ask some of the basic questions in crosslinguistic analyses. Are there underlying similarities in the distribution of semantic relations and grammatical markings used by children at the beginning of language learning? Exactly which markings show the greatest language-specific divergences from the general pattern? How are grammatical relations marked as ergative in one language handled in another language? Under what circumstances do children tend to omit subject pronouns, articles, and other grammatical markers?

D. CLAN for Discourse and Interactional Analyses

Many researchers want to track the ways in which discourse influences the expression of topic, anaphora, tense, mood, narrative voice, ellipsis, embedding, and word order (Halliday & Hasan, 1976; MacWhinney, 1985). To do this, researchers need to track shifts in narrative voice, transitions between discourse blocks, and foreground-background relations in discourse. They are also interested in the ways in which particular speech acts from one participant give rise to responsive or nonresponsive speech acts in the other participant. CLAN provides several powerful tools for examining the structures of interactions and narrations.

Coder's Editor

The most important CLAN tool for data coding is the Coder's Editor, which is a new program in CLAN 2.0. CED can lead to truly remarkable improvements in the accuracy, reliability, and efficiency of transcript coding. If you have ever spent a significant amount of time-coding transcripts or if you plan to do such coding in the future, you should definitely consider using CED.

CED provides the user with not only a complete text editor, but also a systematic way of entering user-determined codes into dependent tiers in CHAT files. The program works in two modes: coder mode and editor mode. Initially, you are in editor mode, and you can stay in this mode until you learn the basic editing commands. The basic commands have been configured so that both WordPerfect and EMACS keystroke equivalents are available. If you prefer some other set of keystrokes, the commands can be rebound.

In the coding mode, CED relies on a codes.lst file created by the user to set up a hierarchical coding menu. It then moves through the file line by line asking the coder to select a set of codes for each utterance. For example, a codes.lst list such as

```
$MOT
:POS
    :Que
    :Res
:NEG
$CHI
```

would be a shorter way of specifying the following codes:

$MOT:POS:Que
$MOT:POS:Res
$MOT:NEG:Que
$MOT:NEG:Res
$CHI:POS:Que
$CHI:POS:Res
$CHI:NEG:Que
$CHI:NEG:Res

This coding system would require the coder to make three quick cursor movements for each utterance in order to compose a code such as $CHI:NEG:Res.

Chains and Sequences

Once a file has been fully coded in CED, a variety of additional analyses become possible. The standard tools of FREQ, KWAL, and COMBO can be used to trace frequencies of particular codes. However, it is also possible to use the CHAINS, DIST, and KEYMAP programs to trace out sequences of particular codes. For example, KEYMAP will create a contingency table for all the types of codes that follow some specified code or group of codes. It can be used, for example, to trace the extent to which a mother's question is followed by an answer from the child, as opposed to some irrelevant utterance or no response at all. DIST lists the average distances between words or codes. CHAINS looks at sequences of codes across utterances. Typically, the chains being tracked are between and within speaker sequences of speech acts, reference types, or topics. The output is a table that maps, for example, chains in which there is no shift of topic and places where the topic shifts. Wolf, Moreton, and Camp (1993) apply chains to transcripts that have been coded for discourse units. Yet another perspective on the shape of the discourse can be computed by using the MLT program, which computes the mean length of the turn for each speaker.

Recasts

Currently there is only one CLAN program that focuses on the lexical and syntactic match between successive utterances. The is the CHIP program developed by Jeffrey Sokolov and Leonid Spektor. CHIP is useful for tracking the extent to which one speaker repeats, corrects, or expands upon the speech of the previous speaker. Sokolov and Moreton (1993) and Post (1993) have used it successfully to demonstrate the availability of useful instructional feedback to the language-learning child.

Discourse Display

There is more to a transcript than a series of codes and symbols. The superficial form of a transcript can also lead us to adopt a particular perspective on an interaction and to entertain particular hypotheses regarding developments in communicative strategies. For example, if we code our data in columns with the child on the left, we come to think of the child as driving or directing the conversation. If we decide instead to place the parents' utterances in the left column, we then tend to view the child as more reactive or scaffolded. Ochs (1979) noted that such apparently simple decisions as the placement of a speaker into a particular column can both reflect and shape the nature of our theories of language development. Because it is important for the analyst to be able to see a single transcript in many different ways, we have written three new CLAN programs that provide alternative views onto the data. The basic principle underlying these data display programs is the motto of "different files for different styles." The display programs—COLUMNS, LINES, and SLIDE—are designed to facilitate the alternative ways of viewing turns and overlaps.

The COLUMNS program produces CHAT files in a multicolumn form that is useful for explorations of turn taking, scaffolding, and sequencing. COLUMNS allows the user to break up the one-column format of standard CHAT into several smaller columns. For example, the standard 80-character column could be broken up into four columns of 20 characters each. One column could be used for the child, one for the parent, one for situational descriptions, and one for coding. The user has control over the assignment of tiers to columns, the placement of the columns, and the width of each separate column. As in the case of files produced by SLIDE, files produced by COLUMNS are useful for exploratory purposes, but are no longer legal CHAT files and cannot be reliably used with the CLAN programs.

E. CLAN for Phonological Analyses

Despite all the care that has gone into the formulation of CHAT, transcription of child language data remains a fairly imprecise business. No matter how carefully one tries to capture the child's utterances in a standardized transcription system, something is always missing. The CHAT main line induces the transcriber to view utterances in terms of standard lexical items. However, this emphasis tends to force the interpretation of nonstandard child-based forms in terms of standard adult lexical items. This morphemic emphasis on the main line can be counterbalanced by including a rich phonological transcript on the %pho line. As Peters, Fahn, Glover, Harley, Sawyer, and Shimura (1990) have argued, the inclusion of a complete CHAT %pho line is the best way to convey the actual content of the child's utterances, particularly at the youngest ages. CHAT provides two systems for transcribing utterances on the %pho tier. For coarse transcription, researchers can use the UNIBET systems that have been developed for English and several other languages. For a finer level of phonetic transcription, researchers can use the PHONASCII rendition of IPA notation.

Analysis of the %pho Line

The construction of a complete %pho tier for even a few hours of data is a formidable task. Verification of the reliability of that transcription is an even bigger problem. However, once this tier is produced, CLAN provides several programs to facilitate analysis. The two programs that are most adapted to this analysis are PHONFREQ, which computes the frequencies of various segments, separating out consonants and vowels by their various syllable positions, and MODREP, which matches %pho tier symbols with the corresponding main line text. For more precise control of MODREP, it is possible to create a separate %mod line, in which each segment on the %pho corresponds to exactly one segment on the %mod line.

Linking to a Digitized Record

Although inclusion of a complete %pho line is a powerful tool, even this form of two-tier transcription misrepresents the full dynamics of the actual audio record. If the original audiotapes are still in good condition, one can use them to continue to verify utterances. But there is no way to quickly access a particular point on an audiotape for a particular utterance. Instead, one has to either listen through a whole tape from beginning to end or else try to use tape markings and fast-forward buttons to track down an utterance. The same situation arises when the interaction is on videotape.

Computer technology now provides us with a dramatic new way of creating a direct, immediately accessible link between the audio recording and the CHAT transcript. The system we have developed at Carnegie Mellon, called Talking Transcripts, uses fast optical erasable disks, a 16-bit digitizer board, and the Macintosh operating system to forge these direct links. Once a large sound file has been written to disk, we use CED to control access to the file during the coding of a new transcript. Although this process requires some additional time setting up the basic digitization, this investment pays for itself in facilitating high-quality transcription. Each utterance can be played back exactly and immediately without having to use a reverse button or foot pedal.

As a user of this new system, I have found that having the actual audio record directly available gave me a much enhanced sense of an immediate relation between the transcript and the actual interaction. It is difficult to describe verbally the vivid quality of this immediate link, but the impact on the transcriber is quite dramatic. Having the actual sound directly available does not diminish the importance of accurate transcription, because the CLAN programs must still continue to rely on the CHAT transcript. However, the immediate availability of the sound frees the transcriber from the fear of making irrevocable mistakes, because the ongoing availability of the audio record means that codes can always be rechecked for reliability.

Phonological Analysis with a Digitized Record

Now that we have a link between the CHAT %pho line and digitized speech, the way is now open for us to design an entire Phonologist's Workbench grounded on the immediate availability of actual sound. The new programs for phonological analysis that we now plan to write include the following:

1. *Inventory analysis:* We will extend the PHONFREQ program so that it can compute the numbers of uses of a segment across either types or tokens of strings on the %pho line. The program will also be structured so that the inventories can be grouped by distinctive features such as place, manner, articulation, or groups such as consonants versus vowels. The ratio of consonants to vowels will be computed. Summary statistics will include raw frequencies and percentage frequency of occurrence for individual segments. Nonoccurrences in a transcript of any of the standard segments of English will be flagged.
2. *Length:* The MLU program will be used to compute mean length of utterance in syllables. This can be done from the %pho line, using syllable boundaries as delimiters.
3. *Variability:* The MODREP program will be made to compute the types and tokens of the various phonetic realizations for a single target word, a single target phoneme, or a single target cluster. For example, for all the target words with the segment /p/, the program will list the corresponding child forms. Conversely, the researcher can look at all the child forms containing a /p/ and find the target forms from which they derive.
4. *Homonymy:* Homonymy refers to a child's use of a single phonetic string to refer to a large number of target words. For example, the child may say "bo" for *bow, boat, boy, bone,* and so on. The MODREP program will calculate the degree of homonymy observed by comparing the child's string types coded on the %pho tier with the corresponding target forms coded on the %mod tier.
5. *Correctness:* To determine correctness, the child's pronunciation (%pho line) must be compared with the target (%mod line). The MODREP program will be modified to compute the number of correct productions of the adult target word, segment, or cluster. For example, the percentage consonants correct (PCC) will be computed in this way.
6. *Phonetic product per utterance:* This index (Bauer, 1988; Nelson & Bauer, 1991) will be computed by a new CLAN program called PHOP. The index computes the phonetic complexity of the utterance as a function of the number of place of articulation contrasts realized. This index is low if every-

thing is at one place of articulation; it is high if all points of articulation are used.

7. *Phonological process analysis:* Phonological process analyses search for systematic patterns of sound omission, substitution, and word formation that children make in their simplified productions of adult speech. Thus, such processes refers to classes of sounds rather than individual sounds. Process analysis must be based on the comparison of the %pho and %mod tiers. The Clan Analysis of Phonology, or CAP, will examine rates of consonant deletion, voicing changes, gliding, stopping, cluster simplification, and syllable deletion. In addition, nondevelopmental error will be identified and calculated (Shriberg, 1990).
8. *PHONASCII and UNIBET code modifications:* PHONASCII and UNIBET codes will be modified or elaborated to enable cross-tier analysis.
9. *Automatic phonetic transcription of high-frequency words:* To facilitate phonetic and phonological transcription of corpora, we will develop an on-line users reference to provide automatic phonological coding of the 2000 most frequently used words in the English language to facilitate phonetic transcription of naturalistic speech data (e.g., words such as *and* and *the* will not have to be redundantly transcribed each time they occur.
10. *Phonologist's reference:* To help beginning phonologists and to stabilize reliability for trained phonologists, we will have available a complete set of digitized speech samples for each phonological symbol used in either UNIBET or PHONASCII.
11. *Transcription playback:* The same phonological database used by the Phonologist's Reference can be used to playback the sounds of candidate transcriptions.

Alongside the development of programs to support these analyses, we will also be working to broaden the CHILDES database of phonological transcripts. Very few computerized transcripts are currently available, so we can reasonably start from scratch in this area. Because we are starting from scratch, we can require that all transcripts in the CHILDES phonological database be accompanied by good-quality tape recordings, which will be digitized at Carnegie Mellon and then distributed through CD-ROM.

F. Utilities

CLAN also includes a variety of features to make life easier when manipulating files and transcripts. The CHSTRING program can be used to make simple string replacements across collections of files. The CAPWD program prints all capitalized words. The GEM program is designed to allow the user to place important passages into a file for later analysis. Using a text editor, the user marks the passages to be stored. GEM then uses these marks to determine what should be excised and placed in the gems file. A good example of the use of GEM with FREQ can be found in Post (1993). For users working with files from SALT, the SALTIN program helps in the conversion to CHAT. The LINES program allows users to mark their CHAT files with line numbers. DATES can be used to compute a child's age, given the current date and the child's birthdate.

G. CHECK

It is difficult to overestimate the importance of the CHECK program. Although CHECK performs no analysis and computes no numbers, it is perhaps the most important of the CLAN programs, particularly for researchers who are entering new data. By running new transcripts through CHECK, transcribers can avoid errors and guarantee adherence to the CHAT standards.

It is important to use CHECK early in the transcription process. If it is used early, error types will be noted before they begin to replicate. If CHECK produces too many errors, the +d1 option can be used to cut down warnings to one of each type. When using the +d1 option, it is helpful to know that there are 46 different error messages produced by CHECK. What the +d1 option guarantees is that you will only get one complaint for each of these types of errors: missing line beginnings, missing tabs, missing colons, missing @Begin, missing @End, missing @Participants line, nonstandard participant roles, missing roles, incorrect tier names, duplicate speaker declarations, missing speaker identifications, delimiters in words, unmatched paired delimiters, missing main tiers, undeclared codes, illegal date entries, illegal time entries, multiple utterances per line, undeclared prefixes, undeclared suffixes, duplicate coding tiers, missing terminators, extra terminators, and incorrect pairings of @Bg and @Eg markers.

Ideally, CHECK only needs to rely on the standard depfile. CHECK uses the codes in the depfile as its guide to understanding what CHAT codes should be permitted on which tiers. The depfile we distribute is, in effect, a summary of the CHAT system given in the manual. Sometimes users have good reasons for making exceptions to CHAT conventions. To override the definitions given in the depfile without having to tinker with that file, we have added the capacity to create a 00depadd file. This file then also provides an overt record of additions or modifications to CHAT required for particular corpora. For example, if you need to allow for equals signs on the @Comment line and for words with suffixes on the @Bgd line, you could create a 00depadd file with these two lines:

```
@Bgd:       *-*
@Comment:   =
```

If the depfile has a code that is too permissive, such as $*, you will want to remove this before entering the more specific codes in your 00depadd file. In general, it is still best to focus on using CHECK early in the process of transcription, before you begin to accumulate errors. Whenever possible, it is best to use only the standard depfile, but sometimes there will be reasons for extending CHAT by using a 00depadd file.

CHECK only examines files for their compliance to the syntactic specifications of CHAT. An important second type of checking can be achieved by using FREQ to create a unified frequency count for an entire corpus. This is best done with this command:

freq +u +f*.cha

This command will produce a single file with all the words you used on the main lines of all your files. You can then go over these words to check for spelling errors and other inconsistencies. A useful clue in looking for spelling errors is to search for words with a frequency of 1. If you use FREQ with the +o option, you can immediately find all the words with a frequency of 1 together at the end of the printout. Once your preliminary cleanup is done, you may want to repeat the same analysis using the +t% and −t* options so you can check for errors in the codes on the dependent tiers. Alternatively, you can provide CHECK with a complete listing of your codes by creating a 00depadd file.

V. THE FUTURE

If the CHILDES database is to continue to grow, we must continue to receive extensive cooperation from individual scientists. Researchers who use the CHILDES tools to collect new data have the responsibility to contribute these new data to the database. In particular, researchers whose work has benefited from government support have a clear obligation to contribute to scientific progress by adding their data to the database. In fields such as the sequencing of proteins in DNA, researchers, journals, and the government have set the requirement that only data which are publicly available in the Human Genome database can be published. A similar policy for language development studies would ensure the stable and continued development of the CHILDES database. Until such a policy is developed, voluntary acceptance of these responsibilities will guarantee continued growth of the database.

We expect that new additions to the CHILDES database will no longer require reformatting, because they will be transcribed in CHAT from the start. Already, we are starting to receive most new data files in CHAT format. Soon we expect this to become the norm. The database will also continue to grow beyond its original scope. The first corpora included in the database were on first language acquisition by normal English-speaking children. In the future, the database will grow to include large components of second language acquisition data, adult interactional data, and a variety of data from children with language disorders. The numbers of languages represented will continue to grow. As the database grows, it will be important to distinguish between the CHILDES system, the Aphasia Language Data Exchange System (ALDES), the Second Language Acquisition Data Exchange System (SLADES), and the overall Language Data Exchange System (LANDES).

As multimedia computational resources become increasingly available, the CHILDES database will shift from its current concentration on ASCII transcripts to a focus on transcripts accompanied by digitized audio and video. Links between events in the audio and video records will be tied to an increasingly rich set of links in the transcript. These "hot" links will be increasingly dynamic, allowing the user to move around through the audio and video records using the transcript as the navigational map. The full digitization of the interaction will allow the observer to enter into the interaction as an explorer. This is not the virtual reality of video adventures. The scientist is not seeking to change reality or to interact with reality. Instead, the goal is to explore reality by viewing an interaction repeatedly from many different perspectives. These new ways of viewing a transcript will be important for phonological and grammatical analyses, but their most important impact will be on the analysis of interactional structure and discourse. Having full video and audio immediately available from the transcript will draw increased attention to codes for marking synchronies between intonational patterns, gestural markings, and lexical expressions in ongoing interactional relations.

The construction of this new multimedia transcript world would allow us to begin work on the successor to the CHILDES project. This is the Human Speech Genome project. One of the first goals of the Speech Genome project would be the collection, digitization, transcription, parsing, and coding of complete speech records for all the verbal interaction of a set of perhaps a dozen young children from differing language backgrounds. They might include, for example, a child learning ASL, a child with early focal lesions, a child growing up bilingual, and children with varying family situations. The multimedia records will allow us to fully characterize and explore all of the linguistic input to these children during the crucial years for language learning. We will then be in a position to know exactly what happens during the normal course of language acquisition. We can examine exactly how differences in the input to the child lead to differences in the patterns of language development. We will have precise data on the first uses of forms and how those first uses blend into regular control. We will be able to track all types of errors and first usages with great precision.

Alongside this rich new observational database, the increased power of computational simulations will allow us to construct computational models of the language learning process that embody a variety of theoretical ideas. By testing these models against the facts of language learning embodied in the speech genome, we can both refine the models and guide the search for new empirical data to be included in the multimedia database of the future.

ACKNOWLEDGMENTS

This work was supported from 1984 to 1988 by grants from the John D. and Catherine T. MacArthur Foundation, the National Science Foundation, and the National Institutes of Health. Since 1987, the CHILDES project has been supported by grants from the National Institutes of Health (NICHHD). For full acknowledgments and thanks to the dozens of researchers who have helped on this project, please consult pages viii and ix of MacWhinney, 1991. The CLAN programs were developed by Leonid Spektor. Mitzi Morris wrote the DSS and MOR programs with extensive help from Julia Evans, Leonid Spektor, Roland Hausser, Carolyn Ellis, and Kim Plunkett. Nan Bernstein-Ratner collaborated in the development of guidelines for the creation of a phonological analysis system. Ideas regarding the Talking Transcripts project came from Helmut Feldweg and Sven Strömqvist. Joy Moreton, Catherine Snow, Barbara Pan, and Lowry Hemphill helped test and design the CHAINS and CED programs. Important suggestions for modifications of CHAT coding came from Judi Fenson, Frank Wijnen, Giuseppe Cappelli, Mary MacWhinney, Shanley Allen, and Julia Evans. Roy Higginson was the chief compiler of the CHILDES/BIB system.

REFERENCES

Achenbach, T. (1978). The child behavior profile: I. Boys aged 6–11. *Journal of Consulting and Clinical Psychology, 46,* 478–488.

Antinucci, F., & Miller, R. (1976). *How children talk about what happened.* City: 167–189.

Bauer, H. (1988). The ethologic model of phonetic development: I. Phonetic contrast estimators. *Clinical Linguistics and Phonetics, 2,* 347–380.

Bloom, L. (1970). *Language development: Form and function in emerging grammars.* Cambridge, MA: MIT Press.

Bloom, L. (1975). Language development. In F. Horowitz (Ed.), *Review of child development research.* Chicago: University of Chicago Press.

Bodin, L., & Snow, C. (1993). What kind of a birdie is this? Learning to use superordinates. In J. Sokolov & C. Snow (Eds.), *Handbook of research in language development using CHILDES.* Hillsdale, NJ: Erlbaum.

Braine, M. D. S. (1976). Children's first word combinations. *Monographs of the Society for Research in Child Development, 41.*

Brown, R. (1973). *A first language: The early stages.* Cambridge, MA: Harvard.

Cromer, R. (1991). *Language and thought in normal and handicapped children.* Oxford: Blackwell.

Crystal, D. (1982). *Profiling linguistic disability.* London: Edward Arnold.

Crystal, D., Fletcher, P., & Garman, M. (1976). *The grammatical analysis of language disability.* London: Edward Arnold.
Crystal, D., Fletcher, P., & Garman, M. (1989). *The grammatical analysis of language disability.* (2nd ed.). London: Cole and Whurr.
de Acedo, B. (1993). Early morphological development: The acquisition of articles in Spanish. In J. Sokolov & C. Snow (Eds.), *Handbook of research in language development using CHILDES.* Hillsdale, NJ: Erlbaum.
de Villiers, J., & de Villiers, P. (1973). A cross-sectional study of the acquisition of grammatical morphemes in child speech. *Journal of Psycholinguistic Research, 2,* 267–278.
Ervin-Tripp, S. (1979). Children's verbal turn-taking. In E. Ochs & B. Schieffelin (Eds.), *Developmental pragmatics.* New York: Academic Press.
Halliday, M., & Hasan, R. (1976). *Cohesion in English.* London: Longman.
Hausser, R. (1990). Principles of computational morphology. *Computational Linguistics, 47.*
Hayes, D. P. (1988). Speaking and writing: Distinct patterns of word choice. *Journal of Memory and Language, 27,* 572–585.
Higginson, R., & MacWhinney, B. (1990). *CHILDES/BIB: An annotated bibliography of child language and language disorders.* Hillsdale, NJ: Erlbaum.
Hollingshead, A. (1975). *Four Factor Index of Social Status.* Unpublished manuscript, University of Michigan.
Hyams, N. (1986). *Language acquisition and the theory of parameters.* Dordrecht: D. Reidel.
Isaacs, S. (1930). *Intellectual growth in young children.* London: Routledge and Kegan Paul.
Isaacs, S. (1933). *Social development in young children.* London: Routledge and Kegan Paul.
Lahey, M. (1988). *Language disorders and language development.* New York: Macmillan.
Lee, L. (1974). *Developmental sentence analysis.* Evanston, IL: Northwestern University Press.
Leiter, R. G. (1969). *The Leiter International Performance Scale.* Chicago: Stoelting.
Leonard, L. (1976). *Meaning in child language.* New York: Grune and Stratton.
MacWhinney, B. (1985). Grammatical devices for sharing points. In R. Schiefelbusch (Ed.), *Communicative competence: Acquisition and intervention.* Baltimore: University Park Press.
MacWhinney, B. (1992). *The CHILDES Database* (2nd ed.). Dublin, OH: Discovery Systems.
MacWhinney, B. (1995). *The CHILDES project: Tools for analyzing talk.* Hillsdale, NJ: Erlbaum.
MacWhinney, B., & Leinbach, J. (1991). Implementations are not conceptualizations: Revising the verb learning model. *Cognition, 29,* 121–157.
MacWhinney, B., Leinbach, J., Taraban, R., & McDonald, J. (1989). Language learning: Cues or rules? *Journal of Memory and Language, 28,* 255–277.
Marcus, G., Ullman, M., Pinker, S., Hollander, M., Rosen, T., & Xu, F. (1991). Overregularization. *Monographs of the Society for Research in Child Development.*
Miller, J. (1981). *Assessing language production in children: Experimental procedures.* Baltimore: University Park Press.

Miller, J., & Chapman, R. (1983). *SALT: Systematic Analysis of Language Transcripts, User's Manual.* Madison, WI: University of Wisconsin Press.

Moerk, E. (1983). *The mother of Eve—as a first language teacher.* Norwood, NJ: ABLEX.

Nelson, L., & Bauer, H. (1991). Speech and language production at age 2: Evidence for tradeoffs between linguistic and phonetic processing. *Journal of Speech and Hearing Research, 34,* 879–892.

Ochs, E. (1979). Transcription as theory. In E. Ochs, & B. Schieffelin (Eds.), *Developmental pragmatics.* New York: Academic.

Peters, A., Fahn, R., Glover, G., Harley, H., Sawyer, M., & Shimura, A. (1990). *Keeping close to the data: A two-tier computer-coding schema for the analysis of morphological development.* Unpublished manuscript, University of Hawaii, HA.

Pinker, S., & Prince, A. (1988). On language and connectionism: Analysis of a parallel distributed processing model of language acquisition. *Cognition, 29,* 73–193.

Pizzuto, E., & Caselli, M. (1993). The acquisition of Italian morphology: Implications for models of language development. *Journal of Child Language.*

Plunkett, K., & Sinha, C. (1992). Connectionism and developmental theory. *British Journal of Development Psychology, 10,* 209–254.

Post, K. (1993). Negative evidence. In J. Sokolov & C. Snow (Eds.), *Handbook of research in language development using CHILDES.* Hillsdale, NJ: Erlbaum.

Retherford, K., Schwartz, B., & Chapman, R. (1981). Semantic roles and residual grammatical categories in mother and child speech: Who tunes into whom? *Journal of Child Language, 8,* 583–608.

Rollins, P. (1993). Language profiles of children with specific language impairment. In J. Sokolov & C. Snow (Eds.), *Handbook of research in language development using CHILDES.* Hillsdale, NJ: Erlbaum.

Rutter, M. (1978). Diagnosis and definition. In M. Rutter & E. Schopler (Eds.), *Autism: A reappraisal of concepts and treatment.* New York: Plenum.

Scarborough, H., Rescorla, L., Tager-Flusberg, H., Fowler, A., & Sudhalter, V. (1991). The relation of utterance length to grammatical complexity in normal and language-disordered groups. *Applied Psycholinguistics, 12,* 23–45.

Shriberg, L. (1990). *Programs to examine phonetic and phonologic evaluation records.* Hillsdale, NJ: Erlbaum.

Slobin, D. (1986). Crosslinguistic evidence for the language-making capacity. In D. Slobin (Ed.), *The crosslinguistic study of language acquisition. Volume 2: Theoretical issues.* Hillsdale, NJ: Erlbaum.

Sokolov, J., & Moreton, J. (1993). Individual differences in linguistic imitativeness. In J. Sokolov & C. Snow (Eds.), *Handbook of research in language development using CHILDES.* Hillsdale, NJ: Erlbaum.

Sokolov, J., & Snow, C. (forthcoming). *Handbook of research in language development using CHILDES.* Hillsdale, NJ: Erlbaum.

Stark, R., & Tallal, P. (1981). Selection of children with specific language deficits. *Journal of Speech and Hearing Disorders, 46,* 114–133.

Templin, M. (1957). *Certain language skills in children.* Minneapolis, MN: University of Minnesota Press.

Valian, V. (1991). Syntactic subjects in the early speech of American and Italian children. *Cognition, 40,* 21–81.

Weir, R. (1962). *Language in the crib.* The Hague: Mouton.

Weist, R., Wysocka, H., Witkowska-Stadnik, K., Buczowska, E., & Konieczna, E. (1984). The defective tense hypothesis: On the emergence of tense and aspect in child Polish. *Journal of Child Language, 11,* 347–374.

Wexler, K. (1986). Parameter-setting in language acquisition. In B. MacWhinney (Ed.), *Mechanisms of language acquisition.* Hillsdale, NJ: Erlbaum.

Wolf, D., Moreton, J., & Camp, L. (1993). Children's acquisition of different kinds of narrative discourse: Genres and lines of talk. In J. Sokolov & C. Snow (Eds.), *Handbook of research in language development using CHILDES.* Hillsdale, NJ: Erlbaum.

PART VI

MODALITY AND THE LINGUISTIC ENVIRONMENT IN CHILD LANGUAGE

CHAPTER 15

INPUT AND LANGUAGE ACQUISITION

Virginia Valian

I. THREE METAPHORS

Three metaphors illustrate different conceptions of how input—usually parental speech—influences language acquisition. The first is a copy metaphor. The child copies what she hears, imperfectly at first and with greater precision as development proceeds, guided by input cues. The second is a hypothesis-testing metaphor. The child forms and tests hypotheses which may be innate or developed later; input serves as evidence confirming or disconfirming those hypotheses. The third is a trigger metaphor. The child is innately set to choose between two alternatives; input tips the choice one way or the other. Each metaphor incorporates a different picture of the child's innate structure and learning mechanism. Although the metaphors can apply to several aspects of acquisition, the focus in this chapter is syntax.

On the *copy metaphor,* the child gradually aligns her speech with that of her language community. Some biological substrate is necessary, as well as some predisposition to learn, but the focus is on an active role for input. Input embodies what the end state should look like and shapes—by an as yet ill-understood mechanism—an approximation of that state. Copy theories assume little linguistic knowledge in the initial state and fairly shallow linguistic knowledge at the end state. Much of the empirical work reviewed here on input and reply studies was initially motivated by the copy metaphor. The aim was to demonstrate that the input was both richer and cleaner than nativists had supposed, thus reducing the need for extensive innate knowledge.

The *hypothesis-testing metaphor* provides a different picture of acquisition.

Here, acquisition is nonconscious theory construction. The child forms and tests hypotheses about what structures exist in her language. Input is implicitly evaluated by the child in a way similar to the way experimental data are explicitly evaluated by scientists in theory construction, including an appreciation for the fact that the data may be misleading. On this metaphor, the child is not copying the input but is developing a theory that will explain the regularities in the input. Input is important but neither shapes nor molds the child. Hypothesis-testing theories vary in what kind of innate linguistic knowledge they assume the child has. The version I will concentrate on assumes an innate endowment consisting of the linguistic universals.

A brief discussion of universals will be useful to clarify what universals are and how they relate to different conceptions of language acquisition. Some universals are absolute. One example is that, in every language, a tensed verb has a subject. Other universals, referred to as parameters, are relative. An example of this is that the subject of a tensed verb can take one of two values. In some languages, such as English, the subject must be overt and explicit, as in (1), whereas in other languages, such as Italian, the subject can take an abstract, unpronounced form that appears null, as in (2). The direct English equivalent of (2), namely (3), is ungrammatical (and for that reason is marked with a star or asterisk). Hypothesis testing assumes the child innately knows that she must choose between the two possible values of the parameter concerning subjects and must make similar choices for the other dimensions of language.

(1) she is eating pasta
(2) mangia pasta
(3) * is eating pasta

The *trigger metaphor* has commonalities with hypothesis testing (for discussion and a new conception of triggers, see Fodor, 1998) but assumes more innate knowledge and a narrower and more restricted role for input. It is primarily used to explain how the child establishes parametric values and is thus more limited in its scope than copy or hypothesis-testing metaphors. On the trigger metaphor the child neither copies the input nor evaluates it. Rather, a given piece of input "triggers" the correct parametric value. Learning, as usually conceived, is not how language is acquired. Some writers, such as Goodluck (1991), have considered parameter setting and hypothesis testing to be two different names for the same model. However, the models do appear to differ in what kind of acquisition mechanism they entertain, even if they are alike in what innate endowment they assume.

The three metaphors do not exhaust the possible ways that input might affect language acquisition. But they summarize the principal *cognitive* roles that input could play. The main *motivational* role that input could play is to facilitate language acquisition by making the environment conducive to learning. Anyone who has attempted to learn another language after puberty finds that some circumstances encourage learning whereas others make it almost impossible. A smile from a native speaker rewards one's efforts, and a frown makes one stumble. Comparable influences may be at work in first language acquisition. They are, however, outside the focus of this chapter. The focus here is the impact of input on the *cognition,* rather than the *motivation,* of language acquisition.

Each of the three metaphors is considerably more complex than this brief introduction suggests. To develop them further requires looking at the data on the role of input in language acquisition. Data come from three types of studies. In *input studies* investigators examine characteristics of parental speech to children and correlate those characteristics with the child's development. The basic question is what features of the input affect the style or rate of acquisition. In *reply studies* investigators examine characteristics of parents' replies to children's speech in order to determine whether and how parents might subtly inform children that their speech is flawed and should be corrected. In *intervention studies* experimenters provide children with specially designed input in order to determine what features of input are most important in acquisition and how much flexibility there is in the acquisition process.

I will review the empirical data after discussing several terms concerning input that have come into common parlance via the linguistics and learnability literatures. The terms are *positive evidence, negative evidence,* and *indirect negative evidence.*

II. FORMS OF EVIDENCE

A. Positive Evidence

Positive evidence is sequences of words, or word strings (a string of words may or may not be grammatical), perhaps analyzed in whole or in part. Positive evidence confirms *or* disconfirms a parameter setting or a generalization. Positive evidence can be illustrated using the null subject parameter.

A child who is learning English will encounter sentences like (4). The subject of the sentence, *it,* is sometimes called expletive *it,* or dummy *it,* because it does not refer to anything. The *it* seems to be there solely to occupy the subject position. Expletive *it* does not exist in languages such as Italian and Chinese. Sentences like (4), as well as (1), are positive evidence.

(4) it seems that she likes pasta

Sentences like (4) are relevant to the null subject parameter, because the child who hears them has evidence that her language is not a null subject language. If the child had begun acquisition with the null subject value as the preset value, the evidence from (4) would help to disconfirm that value and force a resetting to the other value. If the child had begun with the English-type setting, she would remain with that setting; the evidence would help to confirm that setting. Sentences with an expletive subject are positive evidence whether they disconfirm or confirm a parameter setting.

The term *positive evidence* can be confusing because the linguistic use is specialized. In a philosophy of science, or theory-construction, perspective, positive evidence is evidence that confirms a hypothesis, and negative evidence is evidence that disconfirms a hypothesis. In hypothesis testing, the term *evidence* is a completely theory-relative term. For one hypothesis a given piece of data is positive because it confirms the hypothesis, and for another it is negative because it disconfirms the hypothesis.

Linguists also refer to positive evidence as *primary linguistic data* and take it to be the only data that the child has at her disposal. That is, the linguist sees the child's input as consisting only of strings of words, plus whatever structural analysis the child can attach to those strings. From the perspective of hypothesis-testing, there are no a priori limits on the type of data the child will use as evidence. Her hypotheses determine what counts as evidence.

Whereas Chomsky (1965) proposed that the child's data consisted of strings, whether grammatical or ungrammatical (perhaps with associated structural descriptions), some authors specifically define positive evidence as grammatical strings (e.g., Berwick, 1985, pp. 85–86; Berwick also, however, recognized that the data may be noisy, pp. 94–96), and others are not specific about the composition of positive evidence. In general linguists and learnability theorists idealize the input as grammatical. But a psychologically plausible model of acquisition must include procedures for reducing the potential for harm that nongrammatical input poses.

To summarize, positive evidence consists of strings plus whatever syntactic analysis the child can attach to those strings. The strings, sometimes in combination with universal principles, entrench or dislodge a parameter setting or generalization. The hypothesis-testing theorist attaches a different meaning to positive evidence than does the linguist or learnability theorist; it is evidence of any sort, word strings or otherwise, that confirms a hypothesis. Positive evidence, as the linguist construes it, clearly exists. The child is surrounded by speech. *Input studies* (see the following) examine the role of positive evidence in children's language development. We do not know how the child makes use of speech, nor do we know if speech is the only datum the child attends to. Most linguistic accounts assume that it is.

B. Negative Evidence

Negative evidence, as linguists use the term, is information that a sequence of words, such as (3), is not in the language (e.g., 3) or is ungrammatical. It is a string which, as it were, is marked with an *.

There are various ways that a string could be tagged as ungrammatical in the input. If the child produced something ungrammatical, the parent could explicitly label it as incorrect, and even provide the correct alternative. The parent, for example, could say (5) to the child. Although many parents believe that they do just that, all studies that have investigated parental reactions show that parents of 2-year-olds do not overtly correct their children's speech (Brown & Hanlon, 1970; Demetras, Post, & Snow, 1986; Hirsh-Pasek, Treiman, & Schneiderman, 1984). Explicit correction is rare at any age and tends not to occur at all for children younger than 4 years old.

(5) don't say *Want banana;* say *I want a banana*

Nor do adults produce ungrammatical strings for children and then label them as ungrammatical. Parents might tell their children not to repeat a swear word they have just uttered, but they do not tell them not to repeat an ungrammatical string they (or others) have just uttered. It is agreed that explicit negative evidence is not available to children who are at the onset of learning language.

Generally, when linguists and psychologists speak of negative evidence they are referring to strings that have been tagged, in some way, as ungrammatical. Sometimes negative evidence refers to input in which each string is labeled as grammatical or ungrammatical. If ungrammatical strings are tagged as such, the remainder must be grammatical. That way of speaking about input is also described as informant presentation. It is as if a native speaker of the language informed one about the grammatical status of each string that one heard. (See Gold, 1967, for a learnability discussion of the different consequences of text [positive evidence only] versus informant [negative evidence as well] presentation.)

Negative evidence is not the opposite of positive evidence, except that positive evidence is an unlabeled string whereas negative evidence is a string the grammaticality of which is labeled. Input that is unlabeled with respect to its grammaticality—purely positive evidence—is less informative than input in which the ungrammatical strings are labeled as such. If negative evidence existed it would serve the dual functions of protecting the child from possibly being misled by ungrammatical data and giving the child information that a generalization is incorrect.

In large part because of Brown and Hanlon's (1970) findings, linguists have assumed that the only evidence available to the child is positive evidence. One consequence of the assumption of positive evidence only is that the child's initial parameter settings and generalizations are required to be such that positive evidence can overturn them if they are wrong for the language the child happens to be born into.

Several investigators, however, have suggested that parents provide children with more subtle and implicit forms of negative evidence (Bohannon & Stanowicz, 1988; Demetras et al., 1986; Hirsh-Pasek et al., 1984; Penner, 1987). Parents indicate by their requests for clarification, corrective repetitions, or failures to continue the conversation that a child's utterance is ungrammatical. The child can decode such parental cues, and tag their faulty utterance as ungrammatical. *Reply studies* (see the following) examine the existence and role of such cues. Those cues, if verified, would constitute implicit negative evidence.

From a hypothesis-testing perspective, negative evidence has a different definition than the linguistic one. Negative evidence is data of any sort that disconfirm a hypothesis. What the linguist calls negative evidence the hypothesis-tester would classify as positive evidence, negative evidence, or no evidence at all, depending on its relation to the hypothesis being tested. Discovering that a string is ungrammatical could confirm a child's hypothesis about the nature of his language, could disconfirm it, or could be irrelevant to it, depending on what the hypothesis was.

C. Indirect Negative Evidence

Indirect negative evidence is the absence of a string which is "expected" to occur (Chomsky, 1981). Conceptually, it is the opposite of positive evidence and is unrelated to explicit or implicit negative evidence. Positive evidence is the presence of a string; indirect negative evidence is the absence of a (predicted) string. Because the set of absent strings is infinite, the qualification *expected* or *predicted* is necessary. Only the absent strings that the child expects to occur are indirect negative evidence. Thus, the question of whether indirect negative evidence exists turns on the question of whether the child has expectations.

To understand how indirect negative evidence is used, consider again the null subject parameter. Imagine that it is innately set for all children to the nonnull setting (the setting that requires overt subjects). The child therefore *expects* to hear expletive subjects, in the sense that her grammar predicts their presence. If her language were in fact Italian, she would never hear a sentence with an expletive subject. The absence of the expected input would constitute indirect negative evidence. Continued absence could thus result in a resetting of the parameter to the correct value (Chomsky, 1981; Lasnik, 1989). The child would infer that the absence of the expected strings was due to their ungrammaticality. The child could thus tag the absent sentences as ungrammatical, making them a form of negative evidence.

From a hypothesis-testing perspective, indirect negative evidence is indeed negative evidence. If the child has a hypothesis that a form is grammatical and will therefore occur occasionally and the form fails to occur, the child will infer that her hypothesis is incorrect and will alter it accordingly. (Hypothesis testing allows for other forms of negative evidence as well, such as the existence of a form that is contrary to prediction.) The category of indirect negative evidence is thus the only category where the linguist's usage and the hypothesis tester's usage coincide.

Having considering three metaphors for language acquisition and definitions of different types of evidence, we can now review the data on the nature of parental speech to children.

III. INPUT STUDIES

In input studies investigators tape-record child-parent (usually child-mother) pairs at a minimum of two different intervals, which can be referred to as Time 1 and Time 2. Typically, Time 1 is very early in development. The child is 2;0 (2 years, 0 months) or even younger, and the child's average utterance length (mean length of utterance, or MLU, measured in morphemes, whether bound or free; see Brown, 1973) is 1.5 morphemes or even fewer. Time 2, depending on the study, is anywhere from two to nine months after Time 1. At each time investigators measure a variety of characteristics of both the parent's speech and the child's speech.

Investigators are thus looking at the input to determine what the features of the child's positive evidence are, and how those features correlate with the child's development. The basic question input studies ask is whether there are any features of the parent's speech at Time 1 that predict how much progress the child will make in language development between Time 1 and Time 2. The basic answer, which will be elaborated later, is no. The inconsistencies among the findings, the small number of significant correlations, and the relatively large percentage of uninterpretable findings all suggest that those relations that have been reported are due to chance (Scarborough & Wyckoff, 1986; Schwartz & Camerata, 1985).

There are major conceptual, design, and statistical issues in input research, such as the choice of child and parental variables to measure, the size of each parent-child corpus, and problems introduced by variability among children at their initial measuring point (Furrow & Nelson, 1986; Furrow, Nelson & Benedict, 1979; Gleitman, Newport, & Gleitman, 1984; Newport, Gleitman, & Gleitman, 1977; Scarborough & Wyckoff, 1986; Schwartz & Camerata, 1985). The reader is referred to the sources just mentioned for extensive discussion of such issues.

Compared to speech to other adults, parental speech to children is shorter, is more intelligible, has fewer declaratives and more questions, and has fewer clauses per utterance (Newport et al., 1977; Snow, 1977). A natural first step in looking at the effects of input is to examine whether those special aspects of speech to children facilitate children's linguistic development. In addition to such features, there are other features of parents' speech, such as how frequently verbs are used, which are easy to measure and which might be relevant in acquisition, even if they are not especially characteristic of speech to children.

Scarborough and Wyckoff's (1986) study provides examples of commonly measured parental and child variables. Scarborough and Wyckoff looked at 17 features of parental speech and 5 features of children's speech. The measures of parental speech included the average length of the parents' utterances, how frequently parents produce different types of utterances (e.g., declaratives, imperatives, questions), how frequently parents use different parts of speech (e.g., verbs, pronouns), and how frequently parents expand their children's utterances or repeat their own utterances. The parental variables are heterogeneous, in that some, such as verbs per utterance, involve structural properties; others, such as self-repetitions, involve discourse properties. In most cases, parental frequency of usage is the way a variable is measured.

The measures of children's language development, like the parental measures, are heterogeneous and typically involve frequency of usage. Progress in verbs, for example, is measured by the increase in how often the child uses a verb. The implicit assumption is that the more often the child includes a verb in an utterance, the greater the child's understanding of the syntactic and semantic properties of verbs. The child variables include average length of utterance, number of verbs per utterance, number of noun phrases per utterance, number of auxiliaries (auxs) per verb phrase, and noun inflections (plurals and possessives).

Newport and colleagues (1977, whose data were reanalyzed in Gleitman et al., 1984) motivated their choices of parental measures in part by taking variables that might be predicted to be important if one followed the logic implicit in foreign language teaching, where, for example, students first receive exposure to single-clause, affirmative, declarative sentences. The idea would be that language learning proceeds, as does other learning, from short, simple, basic structures to longer, more complex structures. That commonsense reasoning was explicitly subscribed to by Furrow and colleagues (1979) and can be seen as a version of the copy metaphor. First give the learner something easy to copy, and then progressively provide more complicated material to copy.

Newport and colleagues (1977) noted a difficulty with the simple-to-complex model. It seems unlikely that the model embodied in foreign language teaching is a good one for first language acquisition. (It may not be a good idea for foreign language learning, either.) Further, as Newport and colleagues pointed out, simplicity is not easy to define. There is no theory-neutral way of defining some structures as easy and others as complex. Imperatives, for example, are short and might therefore be considered simple. But imperatives also leave the subject *understood* and therefore might be considered more complex.

Many of the parental variables roughly fit the simple-first hypothesis. Declaratives are simpler than questions, single-clause utterances are simpler than multi-clause utterances, short utterances are (generally) simpler than long utterances. One might also propose that measures like verbs/utterance or nouns/utterance measure complexity: the fewer the simpler.

But, even though questions are syntactically more complex than declaratives, they might be more attention-getting and thus be better input. Finally, not having a verb in an utterance makes it simpler in the sense that the utterance will probably be shorter but makes it more complex in that the meaning might be harder to discern. Also, because full grammaticality requires a verb, presenting a child with a large number of verbless utterances may mislead a child into thinking verbs are optional.

Versions of the copy metaphor animated a number of early studies, but because it, like the other metaphors, makes no explicit predictions about what features of the adult input would facilitate or retard language development, most studies have been exploratory, looking to see if any input variables affect acquisition.

Four studies, because they use similar measures of parental and child speech, form a good database from which to determine whether any aspects of parental speech benefit or hinder the development of children's syntax. Furrow and colleagues (1979) investigated 7 child-mother pairs. Gleitman and colleagues (1984) reported on 12 child-mother pairs, divided into two groups of 6 on the basis of the children's age. Scarborough and Wyckoff (1986) included 9 child-mother pairs. Hoff-Ginsberg (1986) had the largest sample, 22 child-mother pairs.

Scarborough and Wyckoff's (1986) study is a good starting point for examining effects of input on language development. As already mentioned, they used many of the same variables used in other studies, thus allowing a close replication. In addition, the children they examined were as similar as possible at Time 1. Children in other studies have been considerably more varied at Time 1, thus introducing various statistical problems in interpreting later differences in their development. At Time 1 all of Scarborough and Wyckoff's children were 2;0, and their MLUs (measured in words) varied within the narrow range of 1.30 to 1.42, with an average MLU of 1.36. Time 2 for the children was six months later.

Scarborough and Wyckoff (1986) computed correlations between features of the adult input and children's development to determine, for example, whether greater parental use of questions at Time 1 resulted in more auxiliaries in the child's speech at Time 2 (a result that had been reported earlier). For the parents, 13 syntactic variables (ignoring the breakdown of yes/no questions) and 2 discourse variables were measured at Time 1. Children's increase from Time 1 to Time 2 was measured for 5 syntactic variables: MLU, verbs/utterance, NPs/utterance, Auxiliaries/VP, and inflections/NP. Because every adult variable was correlated with every child variable, that produced 75 correlations. Of those 75, 2 (2.6%) were significant at the .05 level, slightly fewer than the number one would expect by chance. Scarborough and Wyckoff's data suggest only chance effects.[1]

[1]In assessing the results for Scarborough and Wyckoff (1986) and for Gleitman and colleagues (1984), I have used the significance levels for their full corpora, not their split-half correlations. Following Furrow and Nelson (1986), I agree that the calculation of two separate split-half correlations serves only to reduce the database, and the small number of observations per parent-child pair is already a problem. If one were to use Scarborough and Wyckoff's split-half data, none of their results would be significant.

Statistical issues loom large in interpreting effects of input. Without a clear set of predictions, investigators are forced to examine every possible relation between the adult and child variables measured. But the larger the number of relations computed, the greater the likelihood that one will find spurious correlations. Thus, it is necessary to control in some way for that likelihood. One common solution is to take a conventional significance level, such as .05 (meaning that the result would occur 5/100ths of the time by chance), and divide it by the number of tests performed to obtain a new significance level. That would require Scarborough and Wyckoff (1986) to obtain correlations significant at the .0007 level, and none of their correlations came close to that level. Another procedure is to de-

Hoff-Ginsberg's (1986) child sample, at Time 1, ranged in age from 2;0 to 2;6, with an average age of 2;2, and ranged in MLU from 1.5 to 2.82, with an average of 2.05. Thus, both the age range and MLU range were wider compared to Scarborough and Wyckoff's (1986) sample. Hoff-Ginsberg used many of the same parental and child variables as Scarborough and Wyckoff. She observed the child-parent pairs on four occasions, each separated by two months. She computed three sets of 60 correlations between adult variables at Time 1 and child variables at Times 2, 3, and 4, for a total of 180 computations. At Time 4 (six months later), which was Time 2 in several other studies, seven correlations (12%) were significant at the .05 level or better, about double what one would expect by chance. (Hoff-Ginsberg adopted a stricter significance level of .01, to take into account the large number of correlations she was computing; two correlations at Time 4 met that criterion.)

Hoff-Ginsberg's data might thus be interpreted as showing a positive effect of input on rate of language development. But consider the nonreplication of significant findings from Times 2 to 4. Across the entire group of 180 correlations, 14 (7.8%) were significant at the .05 level (of which 6 were significant at the .01 level), slightly higher than one would expect by chance. Only 1 correlation—that between parental use of NPs/utterance and child use of NPs/utterance—appeared in more than one set of correlations. Because there is no theoretical explanation for such inconsistencies over different measuring points, I interpret them as chance effects.

The lack of consistency of effects within Hoff-Ginsberg's study is duplicated by a lack of consistency across studies. Despite the high overlap in the child and par-

---

termine how many effects would be due to chance at conventional levels and attend to the results only if a much larger number of correlations were significant. In Scarborough and Wyckoff's case, 3.75 correlations (75 × 5%) would be expected by chance. They had 2, which again suggests chance effects. All effects, then, must be evaluated against the background of the number of tests performed.

An additional complication in input studies is that in general the sample size has been low. For Scarborough and Wyckoff ($n = 9$), correlations more extreme than ±.66 were necessary for significance. For Furrow and colleagues ($n = 7$), correlations more extreme than ±.75 were required. For L. Gleitman and colleagues ($n = 6$ in each of two groups), partial correlations more extreme than ±.88 were necessary. Thus, although many of the reports of correlations appear numerically high, they fail to reach significance. As a result, one might be tempted to attend results more extreme than say, ±.50, whether they are significant or not. Or one might not require significance at the .05 level.

Other data, however, suggest that it would be a mistake to adopt laxer criteria. Hoff-Ginsberg (1986), whose sample size was 22, only needed correlations more extreme than ±.42 for significance at the .05 level, two-tailed. But few of her correlations were significant (see the following discussion for more detail), and the highest was .56. It seems likely that the population correlations are genuinely small, and that increasing the size of the sample will only reduce the size of the observed correlations. For those reasons, and because of the large number of correlations being calculated, it seems desirable to require *at least* the conventional significance level of .05. I have accordingly ignored findings that do not reach that conventional level, two-tailed.

ent variables measured in the four studies we are comparing (Furrow et al., 1979; Gleitman et al., 1984; Hoff-Ginsberg, 1986; Scarborough & Wyckoff, 1986), there was dramatically little overlap in findings. Not a single correlation is significant in all four studies, or even in any three studies. In fact, only two significant correlations match in any two studies.

We will examine those two correlations in depth to see how they might be explained. The first finding is that greater parental usage of yes/no questions (apparently including both those questions in which the auxiliary was inverted and those in which it was not) correlates positively with increase in children's use of auxiliaries in Furrow and associates (1979) and for the older of Gleitman and colleagues' (1984) two groups. One possible explanation is that questions are more likely than declaratives to include an auxiliary—the aux *do* only appears in questions (and negatives); the aux is often the first word and could therefore be salient. Both factors could lead to a highlighting of auxiliaries in the input, in turn resulting in faster growth of auxiliaries by the child.

The correlation between parental use of yes/no questions and children's growth of auxiliaries has often been mentioned as a robust finding, but it in fact has not replicated from study to study. Richards and Robinson (1993) noted that *intonation* yes/no questions were significantly correlated with auxiliary development in three studies (Furrow et al., 1979; Barnes, Gutfreund, Satterly, & Wells, 1983; Hoff-Ginsberg, 1986).[2] Intonation questions are those that omit the auxiliary, as in *that your bike?*.

The possible rationale just discussed for a connection between high parental use of yes/no questions and children's development of auxiliaries—namely, increased salience of the auxiliary when it appears at the beginning of an utterance—cannot explain the correlation with intonation yes/no questions, because the auxiliary is absent there. Those correlations are thus something of an embarrassment for a salience hypothesis.

Richards (1990) reanalyzed the data of Barnes and colleagues and included all speech directed toward the child, whether by parents, other adults, siblings, or peers. He also reclassified various input utterances, in particular using a stricter criterion for yes/no questions. His reanalysis showed that inverted yes/no questions in the input did predict auxiliary development nine months later, while intonation yes/no questions did not. Richards and Robinson (1993) cautiously noted, however, that other studies have been inconsistent in that finding. On balance, then, there is no reliable relation across studies between inverted input questions and children's auxiliary development. The finding of a correlation between parental questions and children's increased use of auxiliaries has no obvious explanation and is most likely to be a chance effect.

[2]I do not review the data from Barnes and colleagues (1983) because of the variability of their sample at Time 1. The children's ages ranged from 1;6 to 2;9 and their MLUs ranged from 1.0 to 2.21.

The second finding that matches in two studies is that parents' use of imperatives is negatively correlated with children's increase in verb usage (Hoff-Ginsberg, 1986, at Time 4; the younger of Gleitman and colleagues', 1984, two groups). That finding is also an embarrassment for a salience hypothesis. Just as children's aux use should increase with increased parental use of inverted questions, children's verb use should increase with increased parental use of imperatives. In both cases the relevant word is highlighted at the beginning of the parental utterance—auxs for questions and verbs for imperatives. Yet in the former case the relation, if it exists at all, is positive and in the latter the relation, if it exists at all, is negative.

The comparison of the effects of yes/no questions and imperatives is important for several reasons. Investigators do not want to have to rely on post-hoc explanations for each significant correlation. What would lend credibility to the sporadic findings of input effects would be a unifying explanation, like salience. If salience of an item in the input is hypothesized to lead to faster learning of that item by the child, that theory can be tested by comparing the effects of input utterances in which an item is salient with those in which it is not salient. If the child learns auxiliaries more rapidly because the input more often presents them at the beginning of a sentence, then the child should learn verbs more rapidly if the input more often presents them at the beginning of a sentence. Finding contradictory results in the two cases suggests that the salience hypothesis is false, or that the input effects are unreliable, or both. Conversely, if auxiliary salience is important to learning, then a large number of declaratives with auxiliaries should be negatively correlated with children's auxiliary development. That particular relation has never been tested.

Richards and Robinson (1993), in an attempt to test a salience hypothesis, used exactly the logic just described. They focused on the verb *be* used as a main verb and hypothesized that the more input children received in which *be* was salient (as in a greater proportion of inverted yes/no questions or as the final word of a sentence), the greater the children's later use of *be* would be. Correspondingly, they predicted that some input would *not* correlate with children's development of the use of *be*. For example, use of auxiliaries in yes/no questions should not correlate with *be* development, because auxiliaries are a different category from main verb *be*. Unfortunately, they did not predict any negative relationships, such as between use of *be* in non-salient positions and children's development in use of *be*.

Richards and Robinson (1993) analyzed data collected by Barnes and associates (1983), restricting the analysis to 33 children between 1;9 and 2;0 and with an MLU range between 1.30 and 2.05. There were four tapings at three-month intervals. They included as input all utterances addressed to the child, whether by parent, adult, sibling, or peer, and examined the effects of 15 different variables. They correlated the input at Time 1 with the child's use of *be* at Times 2, 3, and 4. Because children produce both full and contracted forms of *be*, the two were examined separately. For full child forms, then, Richards and Robinson computed 45 correlations, and for contracted child forms they computed another 45 correlations.

There were no significant correlations among the 45 computed for children's full forms, even at Time 4, when children were producing a fair number of full forms. Of the 45 computed for contracted forms, 2 were significant at the .05 level, two-tailed, which is what one would expect by chance. (An additional 4 were significant at the .10 level, but 13% is only slightly above what one would expect by chance at the .10 level.) Richards and Robinson (1993) suggested, however, that the number of significant correlations, though they perhaps suggest null findings, has to be considered in the light of their pattern of predictions.

In particular, Richards and Robinson (1993) noted that the correlations they predicted would not be significant were not, and of the 5 which they predicted would be significant, 3 were. Richards and Robinson have been cautious about the reliability and generalizability of their findings. But even more caution may be needed. Given that most input studies find few correlations, predicting the absence of a correlation is not making a very strong prediction. The absence of a correlation is the norm, and although 3 of the 5 predicted correlations were confirmed, only 1 was significant at the .05 level or better. Thus, rather than 60% of the predictions being borne out, 20% were. (Further, another significant correlation had not been predicted, although Richards and Robinson have a plausible post-hoc explanation for it.) Taken all in all, the salience hypothesis has little evidence of its favor.

One might suggest that, across all studies, it would be fruitful to look for similarities in the direction and strength of correlations and relax the criteria for accepting significant correlations. Even so, one finds that inconsistencies in strength and even in direction of findings are more common than similarities. Take, for example, parental MLU. Gleitman and colleagues (1984) showed a strong positive relation between it and increased use of auxiliaries for the younger of the two groups of children whom they observed. Scarborough and Wyckoff (1986) reported an insignificant positive correlation between those two variables. Furrow and colleagues (1979) reported an insignificant negative correlation, and Hoff-Ginsberg (1986) showed correlations close to zero at all three time periods. Parental MLU appears unrelated to children's development of auxiliaries.

As another example, Furrow and colleagues (1979) showed a strong negative relation between parental MLU and children's MLU, children's verbs/utterance, and children's NPs/utterance. Other investigators show no relation or, in one case, a strong *positive* relation between parental MLU and children's increase in NPs/utterance (Hoff-Ginsberg, Time 4, 1986). Such inconsistencies with very basic measures suggest that the strong effects that are reported are chance effects.

Even individual correlations are hard to understand. Furrow and colleagues (1979) reported that the more verbs parents use, the *slower* is the children's rate of increase in use of verbs. Scarborough and Wyckoff's (1986) strongest correlation is uninterpretable. The more inverted yes/or questions a parent uses, the greater the increase in children's noun inflections. Gleitman and colleagues (1984) found that the more *un*intelligible the parents' speech was, the more rapid was the child's increase in number of verbs per utterance. The correlation was an astonishing .99. Taken all in all, the studies suggest no relation between the parental and child variables that have been measured.

Hampson and Nelson (1993) have suggested that the effects of input may only be evident very early in language development, and only for some children. Hampson and Nelson visited 45 children first when they were 13 months and then when they were 20 months. They found that some features of parental speech predicted children's MLU development, but only for children who were characterized as nonexpressive (i.e., used nouns for more than 40% of their vocabulary). They suggest that the noneffects so frequently observed are due both to looking at children who are too old and to looking at children as a whole, rather than at subgroups of children.

The most important implication of Hampson and Nelson's (1993) results is that, even where effects of parental input are found, they are minimal. The nonexpressive and expressive children they observed were equal in their MLU development; neither group progressed faster than the other. Further, the parents in the two groups were very similar in their provision of different types of input. The finding is that, within the nonexpressive group, greater or lesser provision of certain features of the input predicted the children's MLU development, whereas in the expressive group development was unrelated to the input. Some children may depend on certain features of the input more than other children, and for those children only, having more of those features will result in faster development.

If Hampson and Nelson (1993) are correct, one would not expect syntax development to be affected by parental input, because little syntax is present at the early ages at which they have found effects. It may be, however, that, for older children, there are other consistent individual differences, so that if one could partition the older children, parental effects would emerge. It remains to be seen to what extent individual differences will be important in accounting for the effects or noneffects of parental input.

To summarize, there is no evidence that any of the syntactic input variables has any effect on any child measure. The few correlations that have been reported appear best explained as chance effects. Scarborough and Wyckoff (1986) noted that parental input may so plentifully contain the examples children need to learn language that the variations in parental frequency are of no consequence. The child may need a certain low level of input examples in order to learn language, which every environment provides. More input, beyond the necessary minimum, may be irrelevant.

Thus far the discussion has focused on syntactic properties of parents' utterances, but inconsistencies also hold for the effects of discourse properties of parental input. Many investigators have noted parents' tendency to repeat part or all of a child's utterance, with additional material that looks syntactically informative. For example, the child might say (6), and the parent might reply with (7), repeating the child's utterance and adding the missing verb. Such parental responses have gone by various names and have had different operational definitions, including *expansions* (Brown, 1973) and *recasts* (Baker & Nelson, 1984). There is also a category called *extensions* (e.g., Barnes et al., 1983), in which the parent might reuse an important lexical item the child had used, but add significantly to it.

(6) that the last one
(7) yes, that's the last one

Gleitman and colleagues (1984) reported that the more expansions parents used, the larger the increase in children's auxiliaries, but only for their younger age group. Scarborough and Wyckoff (1986) and Hoff-Ginsberg (1986) reported no effects of expansions on any aspect of children's development. Barnes and associates (1983) reported that extensions, but *not* expansions, correlated with a more rapid increase in children's MLU (but not with other child measures). Here, too, the scattered significant results appear to be chance effects.

In addition to repeating part or all of the child's utterance, parents sometimes repeat part or all of their own utterance. Ringing the syntactic changes on a theme could be informative to the child. Again, results are contradictory. Hoff-Ginsberg (1986) reported that parental self-repetition was positively related to children's development of MLU and VPs/utterance at Time 2 (but not at Times 3 and 4); Scarborough and Wyckoff (1986) showed no relation; Gleitman and colleagues (1984) showed a strong negative correlation between parental self-repetition and children's development of MLU and Auxs/VP for their younger group. Again, the pattern of results is what one would expect on the basis of chance.

On balance, what is overwhelming is the absence of interpretable effects within each study and the absence of consistent effects across studies (see Pine, 1994, for a similar conclusion). Given the data, affirming that any of the measured parental variables is relevant to any of the measured child variables is unjustified (though see Sokolov & Snow, 1994, for the opposite conclusion). At a minimum, we can conclude that investigators have been looking in the wrong place for effects of input. We know that input has *some* effect, because children grow up to speak the language of their community. But the mystery of how children make use of input will not be elucidated by continuing to look at measures like parental MLU or parental verbs per utterance.

Recall that almost none of the syntactic variables in the input have had any theoretical rationale. Some variables, such as low MLU, are characteristic of parental speech. Others, such as number of verb phrases per utterance, are easy to measure. But, aside from the notions of *simplicity* and *salience,* there has been no conceptual justification for choosing those input variables. We have already seen that what counts as simple input depends on one's yardstick. From one point of view, short utterances are simple, but from another utterances that clearly display the syntactic parts of a sentence are simple. Salience is also difficult to define. On general cognitive grounds one might propose that having an element at the beginning or end of a string of words will make it salient (Richards & Robinson, 1993; Slobin, 1973). That would certainly be the case if the string of words were an unstructured list. But the language-learning 2-year old is probably treating a string of words as a structured and meaningful utterance. In such a case salience will be determined by linguistic as well as by cognitive principles.

If we return to the three metaphors with which we began, we can see that the copy metaphor has dominated research on input effects. With the discovery that parental speech to children was shorter, cleaner, and clearer than adult-to-adult speech, investigators hypothesized that clean and clear input could render at least some innate knowledge unnecessary (Furrow et al., 1979). Although that idea is still current (e.g., Bates & Elman, 1996), it involves a misunderstanding of the main justification for nativism. The justification is not that the input is noisy but that the input is impoverished. The poverty-of-the-stimulus argument was most recently and succinctly restated by Clark, Gleitman, and Kroch (1997). Language data do not come with instructions on how to analyze them, as the inability of chimpanzees to master a syntactic system makes clear. A learning device can only learn what its structure permits it to learn.

That should not, however, be interpreted to mean that input carries no information for the child. The learner's structure allows it to analyze the input. Without input, learners do not create a full syntactic system. The work of Goldin-Meadow and her colleagues demonstrates that young deaf children who are not exposed to sign language create sign combinations that have a more sophisticated structure than the rudimentary signs of their parents (see, e.g., Goldin-Meadow & Mylander, 1988; Goldin-Meadow, Mylander, & Butcher, 1995). Nevertheless, such children do not create a full syntax. There are limitations to what children can develop in the absence of language input. Innate knowledge is necessary to organize language input; structured input is necessary for the development of full linguistic knowledge.

Thus, although input studies have produced no robust findings, we should not draw the conclusion that input is unimportant. Rather, we must conclude that we have not discovered how to examine the interaction between the learner and the input. From the null findings, we know we must look at measures of adult and child speech other than the global ones examined so far.

The hypothesis-testing and trigger metaphors are alike in treating input in terms of how it will bear on particular choices the child makes about language. For that reason, the focus will be on individual structures and the data needed to understand their structure. For example, the child must learn about subjects and determine whether the target language is similar to English or Italian. Both metaphors suggest that certain information in the input will be important. Expletive *it,* as in (4), will be one important piece of information, because it only occurs in languages like English (Hyams, 1986; Valian, 1994).

For the trigger metaphor, a single instance of *it* in the input could be enough to trigger the English setting of the parameter, making frequency largely irrelevant. All that matters is that the input provide some baseline number of examples, which is guaranteed if the child is exposed to a native speaker because all native speakers will automatically use a variety of sentence structures.

For the hypothesis-testing metaphor, a single instance is unlikely to be enough input. The child is testing hypotheses against evidence. A single instance could be a random occurrence that does not correctly represent the language. Frequency is likely to be important in the hypothesis-testing metaphor because the more opportunities the child has to confirm or disconfirm hypotheses, the faster the confirmation process will be.

Some research has suggested that sheer amount of input is relevant to acquisition (Barnes et al., 1983; Gathercole, 1986; Huttenlocher, Haight, Bryk, Seltzer, & Lyons, 1991; Naigles & Hoff-Ginsberg, 1988), especially vocabulary acquisition. But no input studies have specifically looked at the frequency of a particular form hypothesized to be important in acquisition of a particular structure, rather than a particular lexical item. We also do not know whether absolute or relative frequency of input is important (Hoff-Ginsberg, 1992). Input studies have not provided data that would allow one to test hypothesis-testing or trigger metaphors of acquisition.

IV. REPLY STUDIES

Despite the limitations and problems in correlational studies, satisfactory alternatives are not obvious. One alternative is parental reply studies, which examine the responses parents make to children's well- and ill-formed utterances. The goal of such studies is to determine whether parents give children useful clues about which of their utterances are ungrammatical and about how to make appropriate changes in their grammar. The search is for subtle forms of negative evidence.

If the child could determine from adult replies that her grammatical utterances were in fact grammatical and her ungrammatical utterances were in fact ungrammatical, the possibility for a direct didactic influence of feedback would be supported. Like any learner, the child who can tell that she has produced something incorrect is in a better position to figure out how to make corrections. Such a picture of language acquisition could be seen as a copy + correction metaphor. The learner tries to copy the input; when the child succeeds the parent signals that the child was successful, and when the child fails the parent signals that an error was made.

Recall that parents do not explicitly approve or disapprove of 2-year olds' grammatical or ungrammatical utterances. When parents correct children, they correct the factual content of the child's utterance, not its grammaticality (Brown & Hanlon, 1970; Demetras et al., 1986; Hirsh-Pasek et al., 1984). But although adults do not *explicitly* correct children's syntactic errors, they might *implicitly* correct them. That is the interest of reply studies, which look to see whether parents provide children, almost always 2-year olds, with implicit clues. Exactly how the child would learn how to change her grammar on the basis of such clues is unclear, but the first step is to determine whether parents do differentiate between children's grammatical and ungrammatical utterances.

Penner (1987) and Bohannon and Stanowicz (1988) have reported that parents repeat verbatim children's grammatical utterances more than their ungrammatical ones, though some verbatim repetition occurs to each. That finding makes intuitive sense. Parents should be very unlikely to repeat verbatim an utterance that they as native speakers would regard as outside the language.

Penner (1987), Bohannon and Stanowicz (1988), and Furrow, Baillie, and McLaren (1993) have all reported that parents expand or recast children's ungrammatical utterances more than grammatical ones. Again, some expansions occur to both types of utterances. Hirsh-Pasek and colleagues (1984) reported that parents repeated children's ungrammatical utterances more than grammatical ones. Because they included parental expansions in their definition of repetition, their results could primarily be reflecting the effects of expansions. That consistent finding also makes intuitive sense.

Demetras and colleagues (1986) did not examine parental expansions, but did look at how frequently replies of four children's parents continued the conversation, or moved it on, and found that "move-ons" were more frequent to well-formed utterances than to ill-formed ones. That finding has since been replicated by Furrow and colleagues, 1993, with three child-parent pairs. The framework that Demetras and colleagues (1986) provided allows one to understand such a pattern. The child's ill-formed utterance is less likely to be understood by an adult than a well-formed one. Parents will be more likely to expand in some way on the ungrammatical utterance, perhaps in order to establish the child's meaning. Correspondingly, they will be more likely to continue the conversation if the child has spoken grammatically.

Taken at face value, then, the reports of how parents reply to children support the notion that parents treat grammatical and ungrammatical child utterances differently. The reports also provide a communicative framework for understanding how such differential responses could come about. Although the work leaves open how the child would utilize the parental replies to change her grammar, it does suggest that there are frequency asymmetries in parental replies that children could exploit.

There are, however, reasons to doubt the findings. Close examination of the previous studies reveals that different coding schemes were used from one study to the next in determining what counts as a grammatical child utterance and what counts as a parental repetition or expansion. As a result, it is difficult to compare the previous studies to establish whether parents do or do not distinguish children's grammatical and ungrammatical utterances. Similar terms are used from study to study, but they do not refer to the same entities.

More important, the categories used for classifying children's utterances and parental replies may have produced artifactual results. The importance of how one defines grammaticality is obvious. If investigators call strings that are not grammatical grammatical, the results will be different than if they call those same strings not grammatical. Similarly, how one defines repetition or expansion will be crucial. Given the critical importance of the classifications schemes, it may seem surprising that there is not more uniformity from study to study. But the reasons for differences in how investigators code grammaticality become clear as soon as one attempts a classification.

The first issue concerns *kind* of grammaticality. Some investigators (e.g., Demetras et al., 1986) have considered an utterance ill formed if there was *any* type of infelicity, whether phonological, semantic, pragmatic, or syntactic. Others (e.g., Penner, 1987) have focused on syntactic ill-formedness. Parents might well respond differently to different types of infelicities. Only by separately comparing responses to different types can the investigator decide whether they can safely be combined, but no studies have compared responses to different types of errors. For that reason, it is not possible to meaningfully compare studies that merge types of ungrammaticality with those that are confined to syntax.

The second issue concerns *criteria* for grammaticality. Even in studies that are confined to syntactic definitions of well-formedness there are problems in classifying utterances. Although there are many clear cases of grammatical and ungrammatical utterances, there are many unclear cases. Grammaticality is not an everyday commonsense notion. Recourse to some theory is necessary in order to direct the coding scheme.

The most difficult utterances to classify can be illustrated by reference to the following fictitious postcard: "Arrived in Italy on their independence day. What a mistake! Searched for a hotel for hours. Restaurants closed. Still, had a glorious time—impossible not to in Italy. Wish you were here. Come, too, next time?" On a strict definition of grammaticality, in which a string must be a complete sentence in order to be grammatical, not a single string in our postcard is grammatical. Subjects are missing, main and auxiliary verbs are missing, determiners are missing. Yet each "sentence" is *acceptable* in the postcard context.

Everyday speech contexts also allow a relaxation of grammatical constraints.

Adults say things like (8) through (11). In (8), a subject is missing; in (9), both a subject and auxiliary are missing; in (10), the word *what* is missing; in (11), the determiner is missing.

(8) want lunch now?
(9) feeling tired?
(10) time is it?
(11) computer's down again

Adults also produce fragments that are otherwise grammatical as answers to questions, such as responding to (12) with (13). Answers like (13) are acceptable, even if not fully grammatical.

(12) when are you going to California?
(13) on Thursday

Most linguistic theories equate grammaticality with sentencehood. Any string of words that is a sentence is grammatical, and any string of words that is not a sentence is not grammatical. A sentence must have a subject NP (although that subject does not have to be overtly expressed in all languages) and a verb. Depending on the verb, an object NP may or may not also be required. Depending on the noun, a determiner may or may not be required.

How should acceptable examples be handled? Most investigators, beginning with Brown and Hanlon (1970), have classified acceptable utterances as grammatical. They have done so because adults produce utterances of that type. According to a strict syntactic definition, however, acceptable utterances are not completely grammatical.

Nor, of course, are they ungrammatical in the same way that, say, (14) or (15) are. Acceptable utterances occupy a middle ground. No context will render (14) or (15) acceptable. But there are contexts that render the other examples acceptable, even if it is sometimes hard to specify what they are.

(14) * Mary the saw ball
(15) * to whom did they disappear before speaking?
[Base form: they disappeared before speaking to whom?]

A coding system should reflect, on the one hand, the difference between fully grammatical utterances and acceptable ones, and, on the other hand, the difference between out-and-out ungrammatical utterances and acceptable ones. That means a trichotomous division rather than a dichotomous one, a division in which acceptable utterances are a category of their own. Prudence alone would dictate a trichotomy, because with it one is in a position to examine the relations among the three categories, how they change as a function of the child's age and MLU, and whether parents respond differentially to the three types.

If acceptable utterances act exactly like grammatical utterances, the two categories should intercorrelate highly and should be responded to similarly by adults. In that case merger of the two categories is appropriate. But if the categories reflect different aspects of language knowledge and use, the patterns of correlations should be different, and the categories should be kept separate in subsequent analyses.

One reason to think acceptable utterances are *not* like grammatical ones is that most acceptable child and adult utterances are fragments that are typically answers to questions. A parent might reply differently to a child when participating in a sequence of questions and answers than when participating in other types of discourses. If children's acceptable utterances are combined with their grammatical ones, and if parents reply differently to acceptable utterances than they do to either grammatical or ungrammatical ones—because of the special discourse properties of acceptable utterances—then parents may appear to be distinguishing grammatical and ungrammatical utterances when they are doing no such thing.

If acceptable utterances are tabulated separately, it is possible to compare parental responses to purely grammatical, purely ungrammatical, and acceptable child utterances. If parents genuinely distinguish grammatical and ungrammatical utterances, there should be evidence of that even when acceptable utterances are removed. Further, the pattern of replies to acceptable utterances should be the same as that to grammatical utterances.

An in-depth look at children's utterances shows that even a three-part division of grammatical, ungrammatical, and acceptable is insufficient. Children at very low MLUs (e.g., below MLU 2.0) produce a large number of utterances consisting solely of single nouns. The syntactic status of single nouns is very difficult to determine. For that reason some investigators (Brown & Hanlon, 1970; Hirsh-Pasek et al., 1984) eliminate all one-word utterances from analysis. Especially at low MLUs, however, single nouns are a large percentage of children's productions. Eliminating single nouns means eliminating more than a quarter of some children's productions. A better solution to eliminating single nouns is to place them in a separate category.

Finally, both children and their parents produce imitations. Those too are also hard to classify, because imitations are not necessarily the direct output of the speaker's grammar. Imitations, too, should go into a separate category. If those recommendations are followed, there will be five major categories of usable child utterances: grammatical, ungrammatical, acceptable, single nouns, and imitations.

Valian (in press) examined spontaneous speech from 21 child-mother pairs. The children ranged in age from 1;10 to 2;8. The coding scheme developed in my laboratory established the five categories just described. We also developed a coding scheme for classifying adults' replies. The aim of that scheme was to reduce the likelihood of inflating differential responding to children's grammatical and ungrammatical speech. We separated verbatim repetition from *structurally similar replies*. Structurally similar replies could either expand *or* reduce the child's utterance while keeping the basic vocabulary and syntactic structure the same. That category is similar to others' categories of repetition or expansion (see Valian, in press, for more detail).

The principal findings (Valian, in press) were that parents did *not* respond differently to children's fully grammatical and ungrammatical utterances, but they *did* respond differently to acceptable utterances. For example, parents repeated verbatim children's fully grammatical utterances about 5% of the time and repeated children's errors about 2% of the time, a nonsignificant difference. But they repeated acceptable utterances verbatim about 10% of the time, significantly different from both fully grammatical and ungrammatical utterances. Recall that previous work classified acceptable utterances as grammatical and found that parents repeated grammatical utterances more than ungrammatical ones. That finding appears to have been an artifact of scoring. Acceptable utterances play a special discourse role, often being part of question-answer games between child and parent. The parent's repetition is part of the game.

Parents gave a structurally similar response to children's grammatical utterances about 34% of the time, and to ungrammatical utterances about 39% of the time, again a nonsignificant difference. But they gave a structurally similar response approximately 24% of the time to acceptable utterances. Again, recall that previous work found that parents expanded or provided implicit corrections more often to ungrammatical than grammatical utterances. If acceptable utterances are included with grammatical ones, that will reduce the apparent amount of structurally similar responding to grammatical utterances.

In sum, parents do not appear to distinguish between children's grammatical and ungrammatical utterances. What the linguist calls negative evidence does not exist in either explicit or implicit form. Previous reports to the contrary are due to artifacts (see Valian, in press, for more detail). Children cannot exploit parental differential responding in order to determine which of their utterances is grammatical or ungrammatical, because parents do not differentially respond.

Even if parents did respond differentially, children could not in principle make use of the types of differences that have been reported. Assume (counterfactually) that parents do provide structurally similar responses more frequently to ungrammatical utterances than to grammatical ones. On that scenario, the child produces an utterance the grammaticality of which he is unsure, and the parent gives a structurally similar reply. From that response the child cannot tell whether the parent's repetition belongs to the smaller group of grammatical utterances that get altered or the larger group of ungrammatical ones that get altered. The child could not, in principle, make use of frequency asymmetries. (See Gordon, 1990; Penner, 1987; and Pinker, 1988, for similar points.) Therefore, the didactic role of parental feedback cannot possibly be one involving frequency asymmetries for different types of responses. Such asymmetries do not exist, and that is just as well because the child would not be able to make use of them even if they did.

Demetras and colleagues (1986) and Bohannon, MacWhinney, and Snow

(1990) have objected to criticisms of the value of implicit parental corrections. Demetras and colleagues state that children learn other pieces of grammatical information that are not categorical. For example, they point out that although determiners occur before nouns, they do not always occur—some nouns are bare. Similarly, although *-ed* occurs after verbs, some verbs have no endings. Yet children learn to distinguish them. The observations are correct, but do not meet the criticism. Even if the syntactic markers are not omnipresent, they are reliable. When they do occur, they are good indicators. In that respect, they are unlike parental expansions, which are not reliable indicators.

The second response Demetras and colleagues (1986) made was directly addressed to the criticism. They noted that some markers, such as the *-s* ending, are present on both nouns and verbs, yet the child learns to distinguish nouns and verbs. But that response presupposes that the child would be able to learn the difference between nouns and verbs if the only marker either of them had was a marker that they shared. The presupposition is unproved and could well be false. Even if the presupposition were true, the response would still not meet the criticism because the child would not be learning the difference between nouns and verbs on the basis of the *-s* ending, but despite the confusion engendered by the shared ending.

Bohannon and associates (1990), also addressing the criticism, alluded to probability learning, in which only a subset of an organism's responses receive correction. That allusion is not relevant to the criticism. The criticism is not that only a subset of the child's *ungrammatical* utterances are expanded, but that a subset of the *grammatical* ones are also expanded.

Probability learning has been investigated in animal learning experiments. An animal is reinforced according to two different schedules for pressing two distinct bars, one on the left and one on the right. The animal already knows the difference between the left-hand bar and the right-hand bar. The animal is not learning how to tell the difference between the two bars, but is learning something about how often each produces a reward when pressed. In that situation the animal ends up pressing both bars, spending more time on the bar with the greater probability of reinforcement (referred to as the matching law, Herrnstein, 1970).

The analogue to the animal's left-hand bar and right-hand bar is the child's grammatical and ungrammatical speech. The analogy presupposes that the child has already distinguished grammatical and ungrammatical utterances. But if that is the case, the parental difference in expansions is not teaching the child what is grammatical. More important, probability learning shows that an organism's likely response to having two behaviors reinforced at different rates is to produce those two behaviors at different rates, corresponding to the reinforcement rates. On that model, the child would never eliminate, or even come close to eliminating, ungrammatical utterances.

A separate criticism of implicit negative evidence concerns the mechanism. The child is supposed to compare the syntactic structure of her utterance with the syntactic structure of the parental response. From a mismatch the child concludes that her utterance was in error and she changes her grammar so that it fits the adult reply. Parents present their children with a large number of structurally similar responses, just under a third of all parental replies (Valian, in press). Those structurally similar responses include additions, substitutions, reductions, and changes of sentence type, *as well as* corrections. There is no simple way that a child can distinguish a correction from, for example, an addition (Grimshaw, 1986; Valian, 1986, in press).

Say the child produces a determiner-noun sequence and the adult repeats it, but inserts an adjective. The child must *not* conclude that the parent's addition of an adjective is a correction and signifies that adjectives are required in noun phrases. But that situation is formally identical to one in which the child produces a subject NP followed by an object NP, and the adult repeats the child's utterance, but inserts a copula. In that case, the child *should* conclude that verbs are necessary in sentences.

The insertion of an adjective is just an addition; the insertion of a copula is a correction. But the child cannot distinguish the two cases unless he already knows or suspects that adjectives are optional in noun phrases and already knows or suspects that verbs are mandatory in sentences. Yet if he already knows or suspects that, then the so-called corrective input is not informing the child that his utterance was ungrammatical. Rather, it is supplying the child who already hypothesizes that an utterance is ungrammatical with the correct means of producing it. Therefore, the didactic role of this type of corrective parental feedback cannot be to inform the child that an utterance is ungrammatical.

A naturalistic study has attempted to demonstrate that children benefit from parents' implicitly corrective responses. Farrar (1992) looked at parental responses to specific morphemes in the children's speech. The responses could be (a) a corrective recast, in which the parent corrected a specific error in the child's previous utterance, (b) a noncorrective recast, in which the parent recast what the child said but did not correct it, (c) a topic continuation that modeled a target morpheme but was not a correction, or (d) a topic change that modeled a target morpheme. The first type of response could occur only to ungrammatical child strings, but the final three types could occur to ungrammatical or grammatical strings. Each type of parental response is somewhat more distant from the original child utterance than the preceding.

Three types of children's responses could follow an adult response. First, the child could imitate the adult's response, thereby indicating a benefit of the adult's response. Second, the child could repeat her original utterance, thereby indicating a lack of benefit of the adult's response. Third, the child could make a response of some other sort, again indicating a lack of benefit. Each response type was analyzed separately.

Farrar (1992) reported that children's imitations of the adult are most likely to follow a corrective recast, next to follow a noncorrective recast, next to follow a topic continuation. Children are very unlikely to imitate the adult if the adult makes a topic change. Farrar interpreted that result as showing that children attend to and probably benefit from parents' implicit corrections.

What Farrar's (1992) data also show, however, is that the same pattern holds to the same degree for children's repetitions of their own utterance. The child is most likely to repeat its own—incorrect—utterance following a parental corrective recast. (Complementary results are found for the category of children's other responses: They are most likely to follow a parental change of topic.)

The result of interest looks like an artifact. Children are most likely to repeat either their own utterance or their parent's reply if the parent's response is maximally *similar* to the child's original utterance. They are most likely to produce a different response if the parent's response is maximally *different* from the child's original utterance. It is as if, when the parent provides a corrective recast, the child is saying, "Okay, my parent seems stuck for some reason; let me help her by repeating what just happened." The child randomly chooses either the parent's response or her own original as the form to repeat. When, instead, the parent provides a topic change, it is as if the child says, "Ah, that's interesting, let's follow up on that." The data provide no evidence that the child changes her speech to copy the adult model.

Scherer and Olswang (1984) reported that children are more likely to imitate adult expansions than other adult replies. That result is consistent with Farrar's (1992), and suggests that there is something about a highly similar adult response that causes children to stay focused at that particular point. There is, however, no evidence that such a focus benefits children's language learning.

Morgan, Bonamo, and Travis (1995) performed an in-depth analysis of articles (such as *the* and *a*) in child-parent interchanges for three children. They examined the children's increase in the use of articles and the connection between that increase and parental replies that implicitly corrected the child's utterance by including an article when the child had failed to use one. They found no relation or a *negative* relation between how often parents replied with an article and the children's rate of improvement. They similarly found no relation between children's acquisition of *wh*-questions and parental implicit corrections. Children's short- and long-term development appeared unrelated to rate of corrections (but see Bohannon, Padgett, Nelson, & Mark, 1996, for a challenge to that conclusion).

As with input studies, work in reply studies was motivated by the question of whether the input could guide the child's acquisition by providing implicit negative evidence. The results, I have suggested, are again largely null. It appears that neither explicit nor implicit negative evidence exists, however otherwise informative parental replies may be. The data argue against a copy metaphor and are largely irrelevant to hypothesis-testing and parameter-setting theories of acquisition. Despite the null results so far, we cannot conclude the parental replies provide the child with no useful information. Instead, as with input, we should conclude that the particular child and adult variables we have examined are not the right ones and that the questions have not been framed in the right way.

V. INTERVENTION STUDIES

A logical way of examining effects of inputs is to manipulate the child's input and see whether the child benefits from the manipulation. (Researchers try to make sure that effects will not be harmful, but either neutral or beneficial.) The omnipresence of expansions in parental speech was noticed early on in the study of language acquisition. Cazden (1965) was the first to expose children to a concentrated dose of expansions in order to determine whether children's acquisition would be accelerated. She, and later, Feldman (1971), found no benefits from adult expansions of child utterances.

Cazden (1988) more recently noted that her study contrasted expansions with extensions and thus, in effect, used the wrong control. One group of children received expansions of their utterances, and the other received topic extensions. Expansions had been predicted to accelerate children's language development. But because both forms of reply were semantically related to the child's prior utterance, they may both have been effective to the same extent, and thus no difference would be observed between the two groups. That, however, would only support a diffuse motivational impact of parental input. The children were interested in parsing any reply which was directly related to their utterance, and both expansions and extensions fit that definition. (Because Cazden, 1965, did not target specific constructions to recast, and did not measure development of specific constructions, the dependent variables may also have been insensitive measures.)

Nelson (1977) obtained positive results in accelerating children's production of specific new syntactic structures, by using recasts of child utterances and by modeling new forms. Baker and Nelson (1984), using a small sample and a lengthy training period (and no control group), tried to distinguish the effects of simple modeling and recasting; they found both to be effective, with recasting more so. If the results are taken at face value, they support the position that the child can learn auto-didactically, but will benefit slightly more from feedback that is directly related to her own utterance. Again, this supports the diffuse interpretation of the didactic role of parental feedback. Children will attempt to parse a certain amount of ambient input, and thus can learn language without any special feedback. If parental replies are directly related to the child's utterance, that increases the likelihood that the child will attempt to parse the input and therefore increase the speed of learning.

Just how ineffective high ambient frequency of a form may be is apparent from a study by Shatz, Hoff-Ginsberg, and MacIver (1989). They modeled the modal *could* to 2-year olds who were producing few if any modals. The children heard 60 sentences using *could* in each of six play sessions spaced a week apart. Over a six-week period, then, the children heard 360 *could*s. The children who heard *could* did not produce more modals or more auxiliaries in post-intervention sessions than did children who heard no *could*s at all. Even the production of *could* itself appeared unaffected. (The experiment includes subgroups among whom there were differences, but no subgroup differed from the control group.) The problem here may have been the use of a single example (*could*), rather than multiple examples of a particular structure. However, at the least, the study shows that under some circumstances children are impervious to input.

On the other hand, some studies demonstrate that input can be strikingly effective. Roth (1984) successfully taught relative clauses to children aged 3;6 to 4;6, using only 24 sentences, 8 presented at each of three training sessions. She required children to listen to a sentence, listen again and watch while the experimenter used toys to act out the events described in the sentence, and then listen again and act out the sentence themselves. Children's comprehension of relatives increased from 16% to over 50%. Children in a control condition, who received the same type of training, but on coordinate structures, showed no increase in comprehension of relatives. The features of the experiment—having the child watch the experimenter act out the sentence and having the child herself then act out the sentence—undoubtedly increased the likelihood of the child's attempting to parse the input.

de Villiers (1984) successfully used an elicited imitation task to accelerate comprehension and production of passives. She trained 3-year olds who failed a comprehension test on passives by having the children imitate passives that described pictures they were shown. The children heard and imitated 20 sentences. They were also asked to describe other pictures, with no instructions given as to the form of description. A few days later they imitated the original 20 sentences again and described a second new set of pictures. Finally, a few days later, the children were given the initial comprehension test. The children passed the comprehension test they had previously failed and also spontaneously produced passives in describing the pictures during the training sessions. The control group failed the comprehension test both times and did not spontaneously produce passives. Again, elicited imitation probably increases the likelihood that children will actively try to process what they are hearing. The fact that the children spontaneously produced passives further suggests that they were in fact actively trying to assign a structure to the passives they were hearing.

In sum, in some cases massive exposure to a form has been ineffective (Shatz et al., 1989), in other cases effective (Baker & Nelson, 1984); in yet other cases, minimal exposure has been effective (de Villiers, 1984; Roth, 1984). One generalization that appears to cover all the studies is that situations that encourage the child to filter the input through her grammar will facilitate language development more than situations that do not.

Although controls in intervention studies have also been problematic, there is more evidence here in favor of distinct effects of input than in input studies. The facts that successful studies target a particular structure and concentrate the input relative to that target may both be important. The fact that a child *can* use specially provided input is, however, not the same as demonstrating that the child needs such input to acquire language in a timely way (Marcus, 1993) or that the child operates in the same way on the more diluted input she receives in everyday life.

Thus, although the results of laboratory intervention studies are promising and suggestive, it is not clear how they work when they do work, nor why they do not work at other times.

Interestingly, cross-cultural reports (see a brief review in Cazden, 1988) indicate that parental speech to children, although very different in some ways from culture to culture, uses structurally similar replies, elicited imitation sequences, or both. All cultures studied thus far do something that encourages children to parse their input. The encouragement is not intentional, but is a byproduct of other parent practices. (Gordon, 1990, suggested that there are cultures in which adults do not interact conversationally with children, let alone provide tacit encouragement for children to filter the speech they hear through their grammar, but as Bohannon et al., 1990, noted, Gordon only appealed to a single quote by a single parent.)

Middle- and upper-middle-class white parents in technologically advanced societies use expansion-like replies very frequently. Although we do not know how common such replies are across different cultures, it would be as ethnocentrically presumptuous and premature to suppose that only economically secure, technologically advanced peoples respond to children with expansion-like replies as it would be to suppose that such replies are universal.

Recent cross-cultural studies show both that expansion-like replies are not confined to white middle-class Westerners and that a variety of conversational styles with children exist. Watson-Gegeo and Gegeo (1986), for example, have described the parental speech of the Kwara'ae, a "Melanesian people of Malaita in the Solomon Islands, speaking an Austronesian language" (p. 17). In the three villages Watson-Gegeo and Gegeo studied, the "populations are very poor and . . . support themselves primarily through subsistence gardening" (p. 18). Although they present no figures, Watson-Gegeo and Gegeo stated that "between age 9 months and about 2½ years, heavy use of the caregiver speech register and repetitions of infant utterances and of the caregiver's own utterances characterize caregiver-infant interactions" (p. 19). In short, Kwara'ae parents provide repetitions and expansions.

Elicited imitation is also cross-culturally common. Schieffelin & Ochs (1983) reported that Kaluli mothers (the Kaluli are a people in Papua New Guinea) sit alongside their children and interact with others in a group on behalf of the children. The mother will produce a sentence and then say to the child, *say like that.* The Kaluli appear to train features of language via a natural form of elicited imitation. The Kwara'ae also make extensive use of elicited imitation (Watson-Gegeo & Gegeo, 1986), as do the Basotho (Demuth, 1986).

Middle-class white parents in our culture use a limited form of elicited imitation, primarily as a way of introducing lexical items (*That's a bicycle. Say "bicycle."*). The percentage of elicited imitation attempts in adult speech toward children has not been reported, and thus its role in parental speech in general is difficult to assess. Because observers have been struck by both the frequency and the length of elicited imitation routines, however, we may assume that elicited imitation is more common in cultures other than middle-class white Western ones.

Elicited imitation is as close as one can come to direct linguistic tuition and simultaneously maintain an agreeable social interaction. Unfortunately, there are no data as yet on the relation between naturally occurring elicited imitation and syntax development. The de Villiers (1984) experiment, however, does reinforce the idea that elicited imitation is an effective means of facilitating language acquisition.

In sum, under experimental conditions in which children receive massed exposure to particular structures and are encouraged to parse the utterances they hear (e.g., by imitating them or by acting them out), children demonstrate that they can utilize input very effectively and make rapid improvements in their grammars. In the natural situation, there is little evidence available one way or the other. It is noteworthy, however, that many cultures have ways of responding to children that encourage the children to parse the input they receive.

VI. CONCLUSION

From the input studies we know that the variables that have been measured do not correlate reliably with children's syntactic development. Two reasons for the nonfindings are possible. First, the variables that have been measured have had no theoretical motivation. The best way to look at input effects is (a) to target a particular developing structure (such as syntactic subjects or inversion in *wh*-questions) or target a particular category (such as auxiliaries), (b) to have a hypothesis about the necessary and sufficient input for development of that structure or category, and then (c) to examine the relation between the hypothesized relevant input and development of the structure or category. Future studies may take that approach.

Second, it is possible that natural variation in input is too small to affect syntax development. The natural environment seldom offers extremes in linguistic input. When impoverished input or extremely rich input occurs, it is likely to be accompanied by other kinds of impoverishment or enrichment. That makes it difficult to separate linguistic effects from more general cognitive and motivational effects. However, the sheer amount of parental speech (Huttenlocher et al., 1991) has correlated with children's vocabulary development, and the amount of particular forms in the environment (e.g., the present and past participle, Gathercole, 1986) has correlated with acquisition of those forms.

From reply studies we have little evidence that parents distinguish between children's well- and ill-formed speech, despite earlier results suggesting such effects. Parental replies may well be syntactically useful to the child, but they cannot be useful in the manner originally envisioned. Children cannot determine, from a single parental reply, what the status of their own utterance is.

From intervention studies we have evidence that input—sometimes very small amounts of input—can be effectively used by the child to acquire new structures. Studies which require the child to imitate the input or act it out show rapid gains.

Intervention studies have the most potential for isolating input effects and providing sensitive and precise information about the role of input. They allow the investigator to provide different types of input in different circumstances. Although such studies are extremely time-consuming and difficult to perform, they can repay their investment by allowing one to test fine-grained models of how input works.

Consider again, for example, the design of the study examining the development of auxiliaries (Shatz et al., 1989). It compared the efficacy of presenting *could* in medial position alone, in first position alone, and half in each position, against a control group which heard no examples of *could.* In principle, such a design could tell us whether the position of the auxiliary in the input matters. Although the study found that no group outperformed the control group, I have suggested that that was for two reasons. First, modeling of more than one auxiliary may be necessary; second, the children were not required to parse the input. A similar study using mixed auxiliaries and requiring the children to repeat the experimenter's sentences might have found different results.

In sum, from the past two decades of research on input, we have learned a lot about where not to look. Because of that research, the next two decades should be more fruitful.

ACKNOWLEDGMENTS

Preparation of this manuscript was supported in part by a grant from the National Institute of Child Health and Human Development (HD-24369) and in part by a grant from The City University of New York PSC-CUNY Research Award Program. Portions of the manuscript have been adapted from Valian (in press). Address correspondence to: Virginia

Valian, Department of Psychology, Hunter College, 695 Park Avenue, New York City, New York 10021.

REFERENCES

Baker, N. D., & Nelson, K. E. (1984). Recasting and related conversational techniques for triggering syntactic advances by young children. *First Language, 5,* 3–22.

Barnes, S. Gutfreund, M., Satterly, D., & Wells, D. (1983). Characteristics of adult speech which predict children's language development. *Journal of Child Language, 10,* 65–84.

Bates, E., & Elman, J. (1996). Learning rediscovered. *Science, 274,* 1849–1850.

Berwick, R. C. (1985). *The acquisition of syntactic knowledge.* Cambridge, MA: MIT Press.

Bohannon, J. N., MacWhinney, B., & Snow, C. (1990). No negative evidence revisited: Beyond learnability or who has to prove what to whom. *Developmental Psychology, 24,* 221–226.

Bohannon, J. N., Padgett, R. J., Nelson, K. E., & Mark, M. (1996). Useful evidence on negative evidence. *Developmental Psychology, 32,* 551–555.

Bohannon, J. N., & Stanowicz, L. (1988). The issue of negative evidence: Adult responses to children's language errors. *Developmental Psychology, 24,* 684–689.

Brown, R. (1973). *A first language.* Cambridge, MA: Harvard University Press.

Brown, R., & Hanlon, C. (1970). Derivational complexity and order of acquisition in child speech. In J. R. Hayes (Ed.), *Cognition and the development of language* (pp. 11–53). New York: Wiley.

Cazden, C. B. (1965). *Environmental assistance to the child's acquisition of grammar.* Unpublished doctoral dissertation, Harvard University.

Cazden, C. B. (1988). Environmental assistance revisited: variation and functional equivalence. In F. S. Kessel (Ed.), *The development of language and language researchers: essays in honor of Roger Brown* (pp. 281–297). Hillsdale, NY: Erlbaum.

Chomsky, N. (1965). *Aspects of the theory of syntax.* Cambridge, MA: MIT Press.

Chomsky, N. (1981). *Lectures on government and binding.* Dordrecht: Foris.

Clark, R., Gleitman, L., & Kroch, A. (1997). Letter to the editor. *Science, 276,* 1179.

Demetras, M. J., Post, K. N., & Snow, C. E. (1986). Feedback to first language learners: The role of repetitions and clarification questions. *Journal of Child Language, 13,* 275–292.

Demuth, K. (1986). Prompting routines in the language socialization of Basotho. In B. B. Schieffelin & E. Ochs (Eds.), *Language socialization across cultures* (pp. 51–79). Cambridge, England: Cambridge University Press.

de Villiers, J. G. (1984). *Learning the passive from models: Some contradictory data.* Paper presented at the Boston University Conference on Language Development, Boston.

Farrar, M. J. (1992). Negative evidence and grammatical morpheme acquisition. *Developmental Psychology, 28,* 90–98.

Feldman, C. (1971). *The effects of various types of adult responses in the syntactic acquisition of two- to three-year-olds.* Unpublished paper. University of Chicago, Chicago.
Fodor, J. D. (1998). Unambiguous triggers. *Linguistic Inquiry, 29,* 1–36.
Furrow, D., Baillie, C., & McLaren, J. (1993). Differential responding to two- and three-year-olds' utterances: The roles of grammaticality and ambiguity. *Journal of Child Language, 20,* 363–375.
Furrow, D., & Nelson, K. (1986). A further look at the motherese hypothesis: A reply to Gleitman, Newport, & Gleitman. *Journal of Child Language, 13,* 163–176.
Furrow, D., Nelson, K., & Benedict, H. (1979). Mothers' speech to children and syntactic development: Some simple relationships. *Journal of Child Language, 6,* 423–442.
Gathercole, V. C. (1986). The acquisition of the present perfect: Explaining differences in the speech of Scottish and American children. *Journal of Child Language, 13,* 537–560.
Gleitman, L., Newport, E. L., & Gleitman, H. (1984). The current status of the motherese hypothesis. *Journal of Child Language, 11,* 43–79.
Gold, M. E. (1967). Language identification in the limit. *Information and Control, 10,* 447–474.
Goldin-Meadow, S., & Mylander, C. (1998). Spontaneous sign systems created by deaf children in two cultures. *Nature, 391,* 279–281.
Goldin-Meadow, S., Mylander, C., & Butcher, C. (1995). The resilience of combinatorial structure at the word level: Morphology in self-styled gesture systems. *Cognition, 56,* 195–262.
Goodluck, H. (1991). *Language acquisition: A linguistic introduction.* Oxford: Blackwell.
Gordon, P. (1990). Learnability and feedback. *Developmental Psychology, 26,* 217–220.
Grimshaw, J. (1986). *Linguistic mistakes: The role of negative evidence in language learning.* Paper presented at the Boston University Conference on Language Development, Boston.
Hampson, J., & Nelson, K. (1993). The relation of maternal language to variation in rate and style of language acquisition. *Journal of Child Language, 20,* 313–342.
Herrnstein, R. J. (1970). On the law of effect. *Journal of the Experimental Analysis of Behavior, 13,* 243–266.
Hirsh-Pasek, K., Treiman, R., & Schneiderman, M. (1984). Brown & Hanlon revisited: Mothers' sensitivity to ungrammatical forms. *Journal of Child Language, 11,* 81–88.
Hoff-Ginsberg, E. (1986). Maternal speech and the child's development of syntax. *Developmental Psychology, 22,* 155–163.
Hoff-Ginsberg, E. (1992). Input frequency. *First Language, 12,* 233–244.
Huttenlocher, J., Haight, W., Bryk, A., Seltzer, M., & Lyons, T. (1991). Early vocabulary growth: Relation to language input and gender. *Developmental Psychology, 27,* 236–248.
Hyams, N. (1986). *Language acquisition and the theory of parameters.* Dordrecht: Reidel.
Lasnik, H. (1989). On certain substitutes for negative data. In R. Matthews & W. Demopoulous (Eds.), *Learnability and linguistic theory* (pp. 89–105). Dordrecht: Kluwer/Academic Press.
Marcus, G. F. (1993). Negative evidence in language acquisition. *Cognition, 46,* 53–85.
Morgan, J. L., Bonamo, K. M., & Travis, L. L. (1995). Negative evidence on negative evidence. *Developmental Psychology, 31,* 180–197.

Naigles, L. R., & Hoff-Ginsberg, E. (1998). Why are some verbs learned before other verbs? Effects of input frequency and structure on children's early verb use. *Journal of Child Language, 25,* 95–120.
Nelson, K. E. (1977). Facilitating children's syntax acquisition. *Developmental Psychology, 13,* 101–107.
Newport, E., Gleitman, L. R., & Gleitman, H. (1977). Mother, I'd rather do it myself: Some effects and non-effects of maternal speech style. In C. E. Snow & C. A. Ferguson (Eds.), *Talking to children: Language input and acquisition.* New York: Cambridge University Press.
Penner, S. (1987). Parental responses to grammatical and ungrammatical child utterances. *Child Development, 58,* 376–384.
Pine, J. M. (1994). The language of primary caregivers. In C. Gallaway & B. J. Richards (Eds.), *Input and interaction in language acquisition* (pp. 15–37). Cambridge, England: Cambridge University Press.
Richards, B. (1990). *Language development and individual differences: A study of auxiliary verb learning.* Cambridge, England: Cambridge University Press.
Richards, B., & Robinson, P. (1993). Environmental correlates of child copula verb growth. *Journal of Child Language, 20,* 343–362.
Roth, F. P. (1984). Accelerating language learning in young children. *Journal of Child Language, 11,* 89–107.
Scarborough, H., & Wyckoff, J. (1986). Mother, I'd still rather do it myself: Some further non-effects of "motherese." *Journal of Child Language, 13,* 431–437.
Scherer, N. J., & Olswang, L. B. (1984). Role of mothers' expansions in stimulating children's language production. *Journal of Speech and Hearing Research, 27,* 387–396.
Schieffelin, B. B., & Ochs, E. (1983). A cultural perspective on the transition from prelinguistic to linguistic communication. In R. M. Golinkoff (Ed.), *The transition from prelinguistic to linguistic communication.* Hillsdale, NJ: Erlbaum.
Schwartz, R. G., & Camarata, S. (1985). Examining relationships between input and language development: Some statistical issues. *Journal of Child Language, 12,* 199–207.
Shatz, M., Hoff-Ginsberg, E., & MacIver, D. (1989). Induction and the acquisition of English auxiliaries: The effects of differentially enriched input. *Journal of Child Language, 16,* 121–140.
Slobin, D. I., (1973). Cognitive prerequisites for the development of grammar. In C. A. Ferguson & D. I. Slobin (Eds.), *Studies of child language development.* NY: Holt, Rinehart, and Winston.
Snow, C. E. (1977). Mothers' speech research: From input to interaction. In C. E. Snow & C. A. Ferguson (Eds.), *Talking to children: Language input and acquisition* (pp. 31–49). Cambridge, England: Cambridge University Press.
Sokolov, J. L., & Snow, C. E. (1994). The changing role of negative evidence in theories of language development. In C. Gallaway & B. J. Richards (Eds.), *Input and interaction in language acquisition* (pp. 38–55). Cambridge, England: Cambridge University Press.
Valian, V. (1986). *The input to language acquisition.* Paper presented at the Boston University Conference on Language Development, Boston.
Valian, V. (1994). Children's postulation of null subjects: Parameter setting and language acquisition. In B. Lust, G. Hermon, & J. Kornfilt (Eds.), *Syntactic theory and first lan-*

guage acquisition: Crosslinguistic perspectives. Vol. 2: Binding, dependencies, and learnability (pp. 273–286). Hillsdale, NJ: Erlbaum.

Valian, V. (in press). *Input and innateness: Controversies in language acquisition.* Cambridge, MA: Bradford Books/MIT Press.

Watson-Gegeo, K. A., & Gegeo, D. W. (1986). Calling-out and repeating routines in Kwara'ae children's language socialization. In B. B. Schieffelin & E. Ochs (Eds.), *Language socialization across cultures* (pp. 17–50). Cambridge, England: Cambridge University Press.

CHAPTER 16

MODALITY EFFECTS AND MODULARITY IN LANGUAGE ACQUISITION: THE ACQUISITION OF AMERICAN SIGN LANGUAGE

Diane Lillo-Martin

I. INTRODUCTION AND BACKGROUND

There have been two main themes in studies on the acquisition of American Sign Language (ASL) over the past 20 years. One is exemplified in the following quotation:

> The purpose of this paper is to argue for the inherent interest to linguistic theory of the acquisition of sign language by deaf children. (Gee & Goodhart, 1985, p. 291)

The second theme is related to the first, although in some instantiations the two could be considered contradictory. Two relevant quotes follow:

> One might have every reason to believe that such surface differences between signed and spoken languages might influence the course of language acquisition. . . . the change in transmission system (from the ear to the eye, from the vocal apparatus to the hand) might in itself be expected to influence the course of acquisition. (Bellugi & Klima, 1982, p. 3)

> [T]he modality in which the language is conveyed plays a significant role in language learning. (Reilly, McIntire, & Bellugi, 1991, p. 22)

It might be thought that the modality difference between signed and spoken languages makes signed languages *un*interesting to linguistic theory. What responsibility should linguistic theory have to a communication system that does not even use speech, a feature that many have considered a fundamental property of language? Yet, if modality effects do play a pervasive role in the acquisition of signed languages, then linguistic theory should be interested. Numerous recent studies of the structure of ASL have shown convincingly that ASL has the characteristics of natural language and should be accounted for within a general theory of language (see, e.g., Klima & Bellugi, 1979; Wilbur, 1987). Thus, if the acquisition of ASL is significantly different from the acquisition of spoken languages, linguistic theory should well wonder why. However, if modality is, in the end, merely a surface effect—if in fundamental ways signed languages and spoken languages are structured and acquired similarly—then this too should be interesting for linguistic theory, as it broadens the database on which to build the theory, testing it, sharpening it, supporting whichever theory can incorporate the similarities *and* the differences between speech and sign.

First, some common misconceptions about sign language need to be cleared up. ASL is the visual-manual language used by most Deaf[1] people in the United States and Canada. It is not a universal language, nor is it a representation of English. The rules of ASL syntax, morphology, phonology, and so on have been studied in numerous articles (though there is need for many more); some of this research will be summarized as needed for the presentation of the acquisition research that follows.[2]

Only 5 to 10% of deaf children at most are in a position to learn ASL as a native language from Deaf, signing parents; 90 to 95% of deaf children have hearing parents (Schein & Delk, 1974). However, a large percentage of deaf adults consider some form of sign as their primary mode of communication. Most of them learned to sign at school; in some cases, they learned from other Deaf students who were from Deaf families, from Deaf staff members at their school, or from hearing teachers fluent in ASL. In many other cases, they learned sign from hearing teachers using a manual form of English or a mixture of a signed English system with aspects of ASL (see Reilly & McIntire, 1980), or from other Deaf students who learned from such models. In these cases, *sign* might not equal *ASL.* Many factors can potentially influence the acquisition of ASL by Deaf children without Deaf parents, especially regarding the amount and type of input presented. For this reason, the bulk of research on the acquisition of ASL has been conducted with Deaf children of Deaf parents (often abbreviated DCDP), and this chapter will only be concerned with this group. The subjects in the studies reported here are Deaf (or hearing) children with Deaf parents, who are learning ASL as a native language.[3]

[1]It has become relatively common practice to capitalize the word *Deaf* when referring to the cultural group who have, among other characteristics, impaired hearing and who use American Sign Language with each other. People with similar degrees of hearing loss who are not part of this linguistic minority would be referred to as *deaf.* See Padden and Humphries (1988) citing Woodward (1972).

[2]In this literature, it has become common practice to transcribe ASL using English glosses to approximate the meaning of each sign; this gloss is written in all caps. It is important to bear in mind, however, that these are merely glosses; they stand for a sign that has its own particular hand configuration, location, and movement and is used in sentences according to the syntactic rules of ASL.

Linguistic research on the structure of ASL began about 30 years ago, with the publication of *Sign Language Structure* by William C. Stokoe (Stokoe, 1960). Studies of the acquisition of ASL begin perhaps 10 years later. In 1985, an excellent review article of studies on the acquisition of ASL to that date was published by Elissa Newport and Richard Meier (Newport and Meier, 1985).[4] Because this article is rather comprehensive and easily obtainable, this chapter will not, for the most part, duplicate it. Instead, the focus here will be on research published since the Newport and Meier paper was written and not referred to there. For readers unfamiliar with this background, Section II presents a short summary of some of the research presented in Newport and Meier, especially when it concerns topics that have continued to be investigated since their chapter was written.

Some research has been conducted on the structure and acquisition of sign languages other than ASL, though ASL remains the most widely studied. Unfortunately, such studies will not be included in this review, except in cases that directly compare the acquisition of ASL with the acquisition of another sign language. Clearly, for the claims in this chapter to be maintained—especially those claims about modality effects and the nature of the language apparatus—support will have to be found in studies of the acquisition of other sign languages. Such studies are eagerly anticipated.

II. THE FIRST DECADE OF RESEARCH ON THE ACQUISITION OF AMERICAN SIGN LANGUAGE

In summarizing their earliest chapter, Newport & Meier (1990, p. 3) stated:

> [A] synoptic perspective on acquisition in the two language modalities reveals that children acquire sign and speech in much the same fashion and on much the same schedule. (Newport & Meier, 1985)

[3]Many interesting issues arise from consideration of language acquisition in deaf children without Deaf parents. In the most severe cases, essentially no usable linguistic input is available for the first several years of the child's life. In such cases, the children often develop home sign systems—relatively patterned use of gestures that are idiosyncratic to each family (though often related to "natural" gestures, or iconic in various ways). See Goldin-Meadow and Mylander (1990) for a recent review of studies in this area. Many other deaf children of hearing parents receive sign language input and learn ASL but beginning at a later point in development. Some studies have been conducted with such children, concentrating on the differences between their course of development and that of DCDP. See Gee and Goodhart (1985) for a discussion of the issues related to this subject group. See also, among others, Mounty (1986), Newport and Supalla (1987), Galvan (1988), and Mayberry and Eichen (1991). For an interesting study of the effects that such late learners have (and do not have) on the acquisition of ASL by their children, see Singleton (1989).

[4]Other helpful summaries have been presented by Hoffmeister and Wilbur (1980), Hoffmeister (1982), Deuchar (1984), Kyle and Woll (1985), Wilbur (1987), Bellugi (1988), Bellugi and colleagues (1988), and Meier (1991).

Indeed, the milestones that children pass by in first language acquisition are remarkably similar for signed and spoken languages. This said, it is important to point out two caveats: (a) there may be an important difference between modalities in the earliest stages (to be discussed more immediately and in Section III) and (b) at the time of Newport and Meier's review, it was appropriate for them to say "virtually no work has been done to date on the acquisition of ASL syntax" (p. 927) (cf. Section IV). This summary with these caveats tell us that more work is needed in the investigation of the acquisition of ASL and that such effort is likely to pay off.

A. First Signs

The first major issue which Newport and Meier addressed concerns the timing of the first signs. A number of studies had found that young children's first signs seemed to occur significantly earlier than the average age reported for first spoken words. According to some reports, this advantage for signs amounted to as much as six to seven months difference, quite significant during the first year of life. If this difference in the timing of first signs held up in continued studies, it would certainly require explanation. In fact, the earliest studies not only claimed an advantage for the production of the first signs, they also claimed that the first 10- and sometimes 50-sign vocabularies were advanced, and similarly the first 2-sign combinations occurred before the first 2-word combinations. This much of a difference for the acquisition of sign versus speech would need further exploration. However, by the time of the Newport and Meier chapter, the strength of this claim was already under some scrutiny. Because additional work was published later, which helps to clarify the issue, if not to settle it, this will be discussed in more detail in Section III.B.

B. Early Pronouns

One of the first signs to appear in the Deaf child's productions is an indexical point. Pointing occurs in the early gestures of both children learning ASL and children learning to speak, and it serves as a linguistic unit—a pronoun—in ASL, so it is an especially interesting phenomenon to study for the light it can shed on possible reorganizations between prelinguistic and linguistic forms of communication. Laura Petitto thus studied the acquisition of personal pronouns in Deaf children learning ASL. The first stages of her work are summarized by Newport and Meier; see also Petitto (1983, 1987, 1988, 1990) for more recent discussion. Because the later references expand on (rather than alter) the conclusions summarized by Newport and Meier, I will review the more recent work along with the discussion by Newport and Meier here.

Pronouns for *me* and *you* are produced in ASL by pointing to the intended referent—the same gesture as the nonlinguistic point that often accompanies speech. Because this gesture is highly iconic, it might be expected that the acquisition of first- and second-person pronouns in ASL would be relatively effortless. In comparison, hearing children learning spoken languages often go through a stage of confusing the reference of the words *me* or *you*. This is most likely because the meanings of these words shift in discourse, but children apparently initially treat them as names.

Petitto found that Deaf children also initially treat the signs for *me* and *you* as names, despite their iconicity. She found that at the age of 6 to 12 months, Deaf and hearing children point to themselves and others as a way to investigate and explore their surroundings. However, although points to objects continue, from ages 12 to 18 months the two Deaf children whom Petitto studied ceased pointing to people. Following this, at 21 to 23 months, the Deaf children went through a phase of using the sign YOU for ME (one child consistently, the other child inconsistently), just like the pronoun reversal errors often found in hearing children. They also made other errors with personal and possessive pronouns. Petitto argued that at this time, the indexical pointing had changed from a prelinguistic gesture to a linguistic unit, and like other linguistic units being acquired at that time, the children were treating this unit as a name with consistent reference rather than shifting reference. When hearing and Deaf children go through this phase of pronoun reversal errors, they often avoid using first- or second-person pronouns and produce names instead. Finally, by 25 to 27 months, Petitto's subjects correctly produced personal pronouns.

Two other more recent studies have also supported Petitto's conclusions. Pizzuto (1990) studied one Deaf child and found that deictic personal pronouns were not produced until 20 months. Furthermore, the first pronouns of this child also displayed a few ME for YOU substitution errors, at the beginning of use of deictic pronouns. Unlike pronouns, points for demonstratives and locatives occurred at 15 and 18 months, respectively. Jackson (1984, 1989) studied a hearing child of Deaf parents, learning ASL and spoken English simultaneously. She found *you* = *me* substitution errors in both speech and sign at 28 months, although they were not systematic. She found additional errors in the development of possessive pronouns, not limited to pronoun reversals. In ASL, possessive pronouns use the same locations as personal pronouns, but a different handshape. One interesting error Jackson's subject displayed in possessives concerned the direction of the agreement. Instead of moving the possessive pronoun toward the location of the possessor, she directed it to the possessed object. Because possessor agreement is found in some languages, Jackson concluded, "Thus, Cari's errors concerning what deixis to code in her ASL possessive constructions are not linguistically unusual forms, but are types of constructions allowed across languages. They do not happen to be the options exercised by the languages she was learning" (Jackson, 1984, p. 42).

There are two reasons for theoretical interest in Petitto's result. First, it shows that the high iconicity of some ASL signs seems not to affect the time-course of language acquisition. As Pizzuto (1990) pointed out, the acquisition of these forms does not "seem to be significantly influenced by the modality in which communication and language take place" (p. 152). This point will be repeated later. Second, Petitto used her result to argue against proposals that early gestures form a sort of continuum into first words. For example, Bates, Benigni, Bretherton, Camaioni, & Volterra (1979) argued that the young child's pointing and other gestures are generated by the same cognitive mechanism that underlies naming. In this view, the apparent break between prelinguistic gestures and linguistic naming is an artifact of modality. Alternatively, in sign languages, where gestures and words take place in one and the same modality, this position would not expect a drastic break between prelinguistic and linguistic forms. According to Petitto's results, however, there is a clear break between prelinguistic and linguistic forms. This casts doubts on the proposal that a single cognitive mechanism underlies both prelinguistic gesturing and linguistic naming.

C. Early Lexical Development

Other signs that children acquire in the early stages of sign language acquisition, like the first words of speech in many languages, take the form of uninflected common nouns and verbs referring to things and actions common in the child's daily life. The child learning ASL has yet to acquire the rich verbal morphology and use it appropriately in syntax. Instead, first signs in ASL are typically *citation* forms, that is, uninflected roots or unanalyzed amalgams if they appear inflected. Semantically, they capture the range of concepts common to young children in their home environments (Newport & Meier cited Newport & Ashbrook, 1977; see also Bonvillian & Folven, 1993; Petitto & Charron, 1987).

D. The Acquisition of ASL Verbal Morphology and "Spatial Syntax"

The verbal morphology of ASL includes markers for agreement with subject and object, aspect marking, and classifiers used in verbs of motion and location. The acquisition of these morphological forms has been studied and reviewed in Newport and Meier's chapter. Here, I will discuss the former and latter. Both topics have also received attention since Newport and Meier was written, so the discussion will be continued in Section IV.

Verb Agreement and Anaphoric Reference

A digression should be made here to describe the system of agreement morphology and anaphoric pronouns used in ASL (see Padden, 1983, 1990, among other sources). A verb root is specified lexically for its hand configuration and general location and movement, but for verbs that can be inflected to agree with subjects and objects,[5] specific verb location and movement are supplied by agreement. An example will help to illustrate. The verb for *give* is produced by moving a hand that is closed as if holding a piece of paper or other thin object, in the neutral space in front of the signer. If the verb is used in a sentence meaning "I give (something) to you," then the hand moves from a position near the location of the signer (I) to a position near the location of the addressee (you). If it means "you give (something) to me," the movement goes in the opposite direction: from *you* to *me.* In general, verbs that inflect for subject and object agreement thus move from a location designating the subject to a location designating the object.[6] The location designating a referent will be a location near that referent, if he or she is present; in this case, I will discuss agreement with present referents. If the referent is not present, an arbitrary location in the signing space will be chosen to designate that referent, and that arbitrary location will be used for verb agreement and pronouns. These arbitrary locations are usually on the right and left side of the signer, chosen to maximize perceptual saliency; however, in some cases the locations are representative of real spatial locations. The association of referents with these locations can be done in a number of ways, including naming the referent and then pointing to the location, eye gaze in the direction of the location, or verb agreement using this location with an overtly named referent.

The sign for *give* was used as an example of verb agreement, because the resulting form is rather iconic: the sign as inflected for "I give to you" takes almost the same form as I would take in handing something to you; likewise, although "you give to me" is not signed in the same way as it would be pantomimed, nevertheless the reference is quite clear once one knows the system. Even the forms for nonpresent referents are rather transparent, especially for a verb like *give.* In other verbs, the iconicity or transparency is diminished; for example, the verb *hate* takes the form of the thumb contacting the middle finger while the other fingers are extended; the middle finger is released from the thumb while the hand moves in the direction of the location designating the object.

Once a location has been marked to designate a particular referent, that location can then be used for anaphoric pronouns as well as verb agreement. Thus, if Sally is associated with a location on the signer's right, then subsequent uses of this location in the verb agreement will indicate whether Sally is the subject or object of the inflected verb. In addition, an indexic point can be directed at that location to serve as the pronoun *she.*[7] To use such pronouns and verb agreement appropri-

[5]Not all verbs participate in the agreement system. Verbs that cannot be inflected for subject and object agreement generally can still be marked for aspect; Padden called these "plain" verbs.

[6]A small class of verbs is sometimes referred to as backwards verbs. These verbs move from the location of the object to the location of the subject.

[7]Unlike the English pronoun, the ASL pronoun does not indicate gender. However, it does more than the English third-person pronoun in that it picks out a particular referent (in this case, Sally) rather than a class of referents (e.g., third-person singular female). For more on this particular characteristic of ASL pronouns, see Lillo-Martin and Klima (1990) and Meier (1990).

ately, Deaf children need to learn (a) to associate a referent with a location, (b) to use different locations for different referents (except when a group of referents is being referred to or, in some cases, for possession), (c) to use verb agreement or pronouns with nonpresent referents, and (d) to remember the association of referents with locations over a stretch of discourse. This complex system of locations and the verb agreement and pronouns directed to these locations is called "spatial syntax" by some researchers.

A number of studies have examined the acquisition of this system of verb agreement and pronominal reference, as summarized by Newport and Meier. One in-depth study of verb agreement with present referents was undertaken by Richard Meier (Meier, 1982, 1987), who asked in particular whether the iconic or transparent nature of some verb forms would make them easier to acquire than others. He used studies of spontaneous productions in 3 Deaf children aged 1;6 to 3;9, and elicited imitation in 10 Deaf children aged 3;1 to 7;0. He found that the iconic and transparent verb forms were not acquired any earlier than the more abstract forms, and that the whole ASL system was not acquired earlier than comparable agreement systems in spoken languages. At the earliest ages (less than 2 years), Deaf children use mostly verbs that do not participate in the agreement system. As they begin using verbs that can be modified (age 2;0 to 2;6), they produce only uninflected verb forms, with a short movement in neutral space not picking out any particular referents. The verb agreement system is not acquired until around the age of 3;0 to 3;6. This is similar to the age at which children acquire verb agreement in nonagglutinative spoken languages, but in fact later than the acquisition of verb agreement in other languages (such as Turkish). Note that Meier studied the acquisition of verb agreement for present referents only—that is, situations in which the verb agrees with a subject or object physically present in the discourse. In Section IV.B I will discuss more recent studies of the acquisition of this verb agreement system.

The use of verb agreement with nonpresent referents comes substantially later than verb agreement with present referents. In Ruth Loew's longitudinal study of one Deaf child's use of verb agreement with nonpresent referents, she found that consistent and correct use of this system does not occur until the age of 4;9 (Loew, 1984). Similar results were found by Robert Hoffmeister (Hoffmeister, 1978, 1987) in his longitudinal study. Newport and Meier consider this a result of the additional abstraction and association of nonpresent referents with locations in the signing space, rather than a failure to identify agreement in the two situations. This point will also be discussed further in Section IV.B, together with more recent studies.

Loew's and Hoffmeister's studies found that once children begin using verb agreement with nonpresent referents and associating referents with locations, they initially make some interesting errors. For example, from 3;6 to 3;11 the child used some forms marked with agreement; however, all the referents of a story might be associated with one location in space. Further uses of verb agreement or anaphoric pronouns picking out this location fail to distinguish between the various referents. Later errors include the use of different, but inconsistent locations within one story. Loew called this use of spatial loci contrastive, as opposed to the adult use, which distinctly identifies referents. By 4;0 to 4;4, these subjects used what Hoffmeister called "semi-real world forms"; that is, an object in the discourse situation would serve as a substitute for the nonpresent referent, and the location of the present referent would be used for agreement and pronouns. Occasionally abstract locations would be associated with referents, or verb agreement would be used with multiple locations, but many errors would remain. It was not until 4;6 to 4;9 that these subjects were able to use this system accurately in their discourse and storytelling.

Newport and Meier suggested that this acquisition pattern "suggest[s] that the errors arise from difficulties inherent in establishing and maintaining abstract spatial loci" (p. 905), rather than separate acquisition of verb agreement with present versus nonpresent referents. In Section IV.B, I will present data that bears on this point and discuss it more fully.

Verbs of Motion and Location

ASL has a rich system of classifiers that are used in verbs of motion and location. The term *classifier* refers to the hand configuration used to represent a semantic class of referents, such as upright beings or land and water vehicles. Hand configuration is not usually morphemic; only in these classifier constructions and some other morphological processes in ASL (such as number incorporation) does the hand configuration by itself convey meaning. These classifier handshapes are combined with movement roots to produce verbs of motion and location. In many cases, the resulting form appears *mimetic* or analog; however, Supalla (1982, 1986) has convincingly argued that they consist of complex combinations of a limited number of morphemes.

Ted Supalla, in addition to his study of the structure of verbs of motion and location, examined their acquisition by three Deaf children from 2;4 to 5;11. Other studies of this construction reviewed by Newport and Meier include Ellenberger and Steyaert (1978), Kantor (1980), and Newport (1981). These studies find that children acquire the structures of verbs of motion and location piece by piece, morphemically rather than holistically. The youngest children use limited movement roots, and frequently use the incorrect classifier handshape and omit morphemes for manner of movement or secondary objects. At around 3, children use some correct combinations of handshapes and movements, but combinations of movement roots or movement plus manner are absent. Interestingly, a few months later children sometimes produce two roots in sequence, rather than simultaneously; for example, one child produced linear and arc movements sequentially, meaning "to move (straight) downward followed by a jump," rather than the target simultaneous combination of these morphemes, which would mean "to jump downward." By the age of 5;6, most complex verbs of motion and location are produced correctly, although errors do remain. In sum, Newport and Meier stated, "All of these patterns suggest that young children are not acquiring ASL verbs of motion in an analog or holistic fashion, but rather are acquiring them morpheme by morpheme, just as in the acquisition of morphologically complex spoken languages" (p. 901).

Most of the issues that were reviewed by Newport and Meier have continued to be of interest to researchers in the acquisition of ASL. Further work in each of the areas just discussed will be brought up in the sections that follow. For more details on the earlier studies, the reader is referred to Newport and Meier's very helpful summary and the original sources.

III. CURRENT ISSUES: THE FIRST STAGES

A. Manual Babbling

The acquisition of ASL received national attention in 1991 when Laura Petitto and Paula Marentette published a cover story in *Science* (Petitto & Marentette, 1991). The paper made the claim that Deaf children, exposed to a natural sign language from birth, "babble" manually in much the same way that hearing children babble orally, at around the same age, 10 months. This claim led to front-page newspaper headlines such as "Deaf Babies Use Their Hands to Babble, Researcher Finds" (*New York Times*, 3/22/91). Why was there so much attention paid to this research (when, sadly, most language acquisition research is ignored or garbled by the popular press)? Apparently, this work brought home the message that similarities in the development of signed and spoken languages reveal the falsity of the idea that language = speech and reinforce the plausibility of some biological foundations for language, present at birth in all humans.

Petitto and Marentette were not the first to claim that children learning ASL babble manually. Newport and Meier cited two works making this claim, one as early as 1979. However, they stated, "there are no detailed studies of this behavior, so the precise phonological status of this babbling (e.g., is it phonologically restricted to those forms which are permissible in gestural languages generally, or in ASL in particular?) is unknown" (1985, p. 888). Petitto and Marentette are able to answer this question in part. Their detailed study found that Deaf children exposed to sign language, but not hearing children exposed only to spoken language, manually babble systematically using syllables that are possible phonetic units in signed languages. Furthermore, they state (in a footnote) that Deaf children exposed to Langue des Signes Québécoise (LSQ)[8] babble using the same syllabic

[8]LSQ is the sign language used by French Deaf people in parts of Quebec and in some other parts of Canada. It is apparently distinct from ASL and LSF, the sign language used in France.

units as children exposed to ASL: thus, "[j]ust as hearing infants do not babble in specific languages, deaf infants do not babble in ASL or any other sign language" (p. 1496).

Besides the point that Deaf children do babble manually, one of the most interesting claims that Petitto and Marentette made is that hearing children, in general, do not. They show that using the same criteria to classify manual babbling in both the hearing and Deaf children, the hearing children produce manual babbles in at most 15% of manual activities; in contrast, the Deaf children produce manual babbles in 32 to 71% of their manual activities. Petitto and Marentette have claimed that the Deaf children's vocal babbling is similar to the hearing children's manual babbling: with little variation in form and a reduced set of phonetic units. They state, "[t]hat infants produce occasional babbling forms in the modality that does not carry linguistic input appears to be the vestige of their potential to have produced language in either modality" (p. 1496).

This study makes it clear why developmental psycholinguists should be interested in the acquisition of ASL—for the same reason that readers of the *New York Times* should be—and it sets the stage for future studies of the earliest stages of language acquisition. Future work should include studies of more, younger children (Petitto and Marentette studied two Deaf children at the ages of 10, 12, and 14 months), and it should provide additional detailed information regarding the questions concerning the phonology of sign babbling and the characteristics of the prelinguistic gestures of young hearing children.[9] With more extensive studies Petitto and Marentette's strong claims about the equipotentiality of language in either modality can be defended.

B. First Signs

For hearing children, vocal babbling develops into first words. Although estimates vary, first words tend to appear at 10 to 12 months; the first 10-word vocabulary is achieved at an average age of 15 months (Nelson, 1973). Given the overall summary that the development of spoken languages and the development of sign languages follow remarkably similar courses, it is surprising to find that numerous studies have claimed an advantage for the acquisition of the first signs compared to first words. In some studies, it has been claimed that the first signs are produced as early as 5 months (Schlesinger & Meadow, 1972).

The strongest, most consistent claims for earlier first signs compared to first spoken words comes from a series of studies done by John Bonvillian, Michael Orlansky, and their colleagues (Bonvillian & Folven, 1990, 1993; Bonvillian, Or-

[9]In an unpublished poster presentation, Willerman and Meier (1992) reported on such a study in progress. Their study includes several younger children, both Deaf and hearing. They found that hearing children do produce a large amount of manual babbling, including some of the complex manual babbling forms that Petitto and Marentette found only for Deaf babies.

lansky, & Folven, 1990; Bonvillian, Orlansky, Novack, Folven, & Holley-Wilcox, 1985; Orlansky & Bonvillian, 1985). Bonvillian and colleagues reported on two studies of children learning ASL from Deaf, signing parents. In the first project, 9 children were studied (8 of them had normal hearing, one was Deaf); in the second, 13 children were studied (12 hearing, 1 Deaf).[10] Using parents' reports plus monthly videotape sessions, these studies found that the first signs were produced at an average age of 8.5 months; the first 10-sign vocabularies were obtained by an average age of 13.3 months (Bonvillian & Folven, 1993). An additional study that also claims early first signs is Siple and Akamatsu (1991); interestingly, Siple and Akamatsu studied a pair of twins (one hearing, one Deaf), and still found precocious first signs, despite the fact that twins are often found to be slightly language delayed (Siple & Akamatsu cited, among others, Day, 1932).

Newport and Meier reviewed the earliest studies on the appearance of first signs in their 1985 chapter, and concluded that

> young children, whether deaf or hearing, may be capable of first language use at somewhat earlier ages than has previously been supposed, if they have access to a modality which favors their earliest attempts. . . . From this perspective, it is spoken language onset which is slightly delayed (rather than signed language onset which is slightly advanced), relative to when the child is cognitively and linguistically capable of controlling the first lexical usages. (p. 889).

Later, Newport, & Meier expanded on this possibility in a review including additional studies of the timing of first signs and words (Newport & Meier, 1990). They summarized their review by saying, "We have defended the claim that there are indeed differences across the two language modalities in the emergence of language milestones" (p. 18). However, they acknowledged that there is still controversy regarding the accuracy of this claim. The controversy mainly concerns whether the studies claiming early sign use might be overattributing *word* status to early gestures akin to the early nonlinguistic communicative gestures used by hearing children with no sign language input. Although they make very different claims with regard to the development of first signs, Petitto (1988) and Volterra and Caselli (1985) both argued that more stringent criteria need to be applied when determining when a gesture *counts* as a sign (word).[11]

Petitto (1988; Petitto & Charron, 1987) has claimed from the study of Deaf chil-

[10]Bonvillian and his colleagues included hearing children as well as Deaf children, as long as at least one parent was Deaf and ASL was considered the most dominant language used at home. Although they do not report extensively on the hearing children's development of spoken English, they do say that the precocious appearance of signs compared to spoken words was present even for those hearing children with one hearing parent. The difference between sign and speech usually disappeared by age 2, they reported.

[11]Other researchers who do not find earlier signs than words include Ackerman, Kyle, Woll, and Ezra (1990), who studied Deaf and hearing children learning British Sign Language and English, and Gaustad (1988), who, like Siple and Akamatsu, studied twins, one Deaf and one hearing.

dren learning ASL and LSQ, and hearing children learning English and French, that when rigorous criteria are adopted, no differences appear in the emergence of first spoken words versus signs. In particular, Petitto was concerned with the linguistic status of early communicative gestures and argued that both Deaf and hearing children produce such gestures as pointing, "natural" gestures (reaching, raising the hands, etc.), instrumental gestures with and without objects, and iconic gestures (e.g., twisting the hands as if opening a jar); but Petitto argued that none of these communicative gestures are linguistic. To determine whether a gesture has the characteristics of naming, Petitto argued that the form of a gesture must be distinct from the object or action to which it refers; the scope of the referring relations must include a single, consistent form to designate a class or kind; and the function of the name is to assign an object to a category (this summary is necessarily very sketchy; see Petitto, 1988 for more detail). In her study, Petitto used these criteria for both Deaf and hearing children's gestures and vocalizations; she found that only the Deaf children used gestures linguistically, and that both the Deaf children's first signs and the hearing children's first words occurred at the same time, around 12 months. It should be pointed out that Petitto used once-monthly videotape sessions with particular elicitation protocols. Although this is much more exacting than Bonvillian's use of parental reports (with videotaped visits), it is likely to underestimate children's proficiency (cf. Newport & Meier, 1990, citing Nelson, 1973).

Bonvillian and colleagues, aware of the necessity for caution in over attributing linguistic status to early gestures, excluded waving, pointing, and other gestures common to Deaf and hearing children in their second study. Still they found almost the same average age at onset of signing across the two studies (8.2 months in the first study, 8.6 months in the second). However, they note that "initial sign production occurred within a nonreferential context—the signs emitted typically were either imitations of others' productions or requests for action. Not until these children were, on the average, 12.6 months old . . . did they begin to use signs referentially" (Bonvillian & Folven, 1993, p. 240). Thus, it seems that Bonvillian and colleagues are not in disagreement with Petitto regarding the age at first referential sign use. The disagreement concerns earlier gestures—whether they indicate an earlier onset for sign language compared to spoken language. Noting this, Meier and Newport stated, "For our own purposes, a modality difference even in nonsymbolic early usages would be interesting" (p. 7).

If there is not a difference between signed and spoken language development for *referential* sign/word use, what implications does this have for theories of language acquisition? As mentioned earlier, Newport & Meier found the possibility that sign languages are begun earlier than spoken languages a potential source of information regarding the mechanism(s) by which linguistic milestones are achieved. They suggested that the linguistic and cognitive underpinnings for the first lexical items are in place at the same time, regardless of whether a manual or vocal language will be acquired. However, the development of peripheral factors such as articulatory and perceptual mechanisms for sign and speech may differ. In particular, although children may be ready to begin using language by an age of 8 to 10 months, perhaps control over the vocal apparatus (or perceptual apparatus)—at least sufficient control to produce recognizable words—simply takes longer to attain than similar control over the large muscles of the hands and arms. The fact that both Bonvillian's study and Petitto's study found similar ages for referential sign use supports this conclusion. Apparently, the mechanism underlying the deepest linguistic abilities does develop in step, regardless of modality.

C. Lexical Development

It is a misconception to think that ASL signs are pictures in the air, but it should be recognized that some signs are iconic, or have an iconic base. This includes some common nouns, such as TREE (in which the forearm is extended vertically, with the fingers of the open hand extended; this calls to mind the trunk and branches of a deciduous tree); as well as verbs such as DRINK (a cupped hand moves up at the mouth); and adjectives such as BIG (the two hands, fingers outstretched and palms facing, move away from each other in the neutral space in front of the signer's body). Despite the presence of some iconic signs, naive adults could only guess the meaning of 10% of 90 common ASL signs in one study; in another, their multiple-choice guesses for the meanings of signs were no better than chance (Klima & Bellugi, 1979). Would perhaps the iconicity of some ASL signs make these signs the earliest or easiest to acquire?

A number of researchers have asked whether the iconicity of ASL signs affects their acquisition. Perhaps children learning sign languages will acquire iconic signs more quickly than noniconic signs. In fact, it has been suggested that this might underlie the apparently earlier acquisition of first signs compared to first words. However, every researcher who has examined this has concluded, with Pizzuto (1985), that

> the child does not exploit to her advantage the iconic-indexical features that observers have found in the ASL . . . lexicon. Thus it would appear that the iconic-indexical features inherent in a formal linguistic system are irrelevant to language learning processes. (p. 53)

Bonvillian and colleagues found that only one-third of the first signs that the children they studied produced were iconic (Bonvillian & Folven, 1993). Petitto (1988) even found that young children do not comprehend the iconic gestures which they themselves produce. Thus, it seems that iconicity is irrelevant to the acquisition of the first words. As we have seen in Section II, and will see in Section IV, it also is ignored in the acquisition of other aspects of ASL grammar.

Unlike the claims for the first signs and the first 10-sign vocabularies, it appears that the first 50-sign vocabulary is not acquired drastically earlier than the first 50 spoken words. Bonvillian and colleagues found the 50th sign in the 18th month on average; similar findings with children learning a spoken language place 50 words in the 19th month (Nelson, 1973). Thus, the sign advantage (if there is one) diminishes as acquisition proceeds. Given this difference, it is not surprising that the course of the acquisition of the first 50 words or signs differs, according to Bonvillian and colleagues. For children learning a spoken language, there is a later start, and a large increase in the number of words acquired during the month in which the 50th word is achieved. For children learning sign, since the start is earlier, the increase in vocabulary during the month marking the 50th word is much less dramatic—only about half as many new signs are added in this month compared to spoken language acquisition (Bonvillian & Folven, 1993). At about the same time as this milestone, children learning both signed and spoken languages put together two words into early sentences, and syntax begins.

D. Phonological Development

The term *phonology* when applied to studies of sign language applies not to the patterns of sounds (*phones*), but to the patterns of sublexical, meaningless units. Although recent studies of the phonological structure of ASL have become rather advanced (see, e.g., Coulter, 1993), relatively few studies of the development of ASL phonology have been made. Those that have been published have concentrated on examining when children show command of the basic units of individual ASL signs: handshapes, locations, and movements.

The earliest work in phonological development concentrated on accuracy in hand configuration (see review in Newport & Meier, 1985; also Boyes-Braem, 1990; McIntire, 1977). According to these earlier models, children are expected to develop ASL handshapes in part by their anatomical and cognitive complexity. In support of this model, young children were found to use first the subset of ASL hand configurations that are formationally simplest. These hand configurations are also unmarked phonologically in the language; for example, they are the allowable hand configurations for the base (nonactive) hand in two-handed signs in which each hand uses a different hand configuration (Battison, 1974).

More recent work has looked beyond hand configurations used by the youngest signers. Siedlecki and Bonvillian (1993a, 1993b) examined several aspects of children's acquisition of sign phonology. They found that location was the first aspect of signs to be acquired; even the first signs produced by children learning ASL (less than 14 months of age) had accurate locations 84% of the time. Movements were accurate less often—only 61% of the time on average for children from 5 to 18 months of age. Handshapes were accurate the least often—only 43% of the youngest children's handshapes were accurate; even at 16 to 18 months, only 58% of handshapes were accurate. In their analysis of patterns of hand deletion, Siedlecki and Bonvillian (1993b) again found a prominent role for location. They found that one hand of a two-handed sign was deleted more frequently if the deletion left information about the location of the sign intact; for example, a two-handed sign modeled with both hands using the same configuration on the face might be produced by a Deaf child with only one hand. In this example, location information (as well as information about the configuration of the missing hand) is recoverable from the hand that remains.

Schick (1990b) took a different approach. She looked at older (4;5 to 9;0) children's accuracy in handshape productions during a classifier production task (see also Section IV.A). The predictions made by Boyes-Braem and McIntire would be that as these children produce morphologically complex forms, they may revert to less marked handshapes—that is, hand configurations acquired at the earliest stages. However, contrary to this prediction, Schick found that substitutions came from hand configurations classified as equally complex or even more complex than the target handshape according to Boyes-Braem's model. Schick interpreted these findings as showing that "handshape simplification did not support notions of anatomical complexity" (p. 37). Rather, Schick focused on the morphosyntactic complexity of the utterances leading to the handshape errors. Because the children were able to produce the handshapes under investigation in morphosyntactically simpler forms, this leads to a consideration of these errors within the context of the acquisition of classifier morphology, so they will be discussed more later. Note also that (as she pointed out) the children Schick studied were considerably older than those that Boyes-Braem and McIntire studied; perhaps their anatomical models are still appropriate for the youngest children.

IV. THE ACQUISITION OF MORPHOLOGY AND SYNTAX

A. Verbs of Motion and Location (Classifiers)

As discussed in Section II, Supalla conducted a major study of the acquisition of ASL verbs of motion and location, which was reviewed by Newport and Meier. Since their review, three additional studies have been reported that bear on the development of this complex morphological system.

Brenda Schick studied the development of verbs of motion and location in Deaf children aged 4;5 to 9;0 (Schick, 1987, 1990c). She used a classifier elicitation task, in which the children had to describe the scene on a picture accurately enough for her to choose a matching card. These pictures were most felicitously described using classifiers to indicate spatial relationships; in addition, the experimenter produced classifier constructions in turn with the children, encouraging their use of this structure. Using this method, Schick collected a large number of classifier predicates from each of 24 children; these predicates differed in the category of classifier used, the particular hand configuration needed, and the morphosyntactic complexity of the utterance. (See Schick, 1990a, for the morphosyntactic analysis used here.)

Schick found that accurate classifier handshapes were produced most often for what she has called CLASS predicates. These are the classifiers that represent semantic classes, such as people or four-legged animals. She attributed the relative ease of acquisition of CLASS handshapes to their morphological simplicity: the handshape represents one semantic class and has no handshape-internal morphemes. When combined with a movement root (as in the forms elicited), a CLASS predicate represents a subject with an intransitive verb (e.g., CL:G-MOVE-FORWARD "a person went forward").

The second-most accurate classifier predicates were produced with SASS handshapes. SASS (for size-and-shape-specifier) handshapes represent aspects of the physical dimensions of the referent; they are more complex than CLASS handshapes morphologically, in that a single handshape might represent both shape (e.g., circle) and depth (e.g., a long cylinder). A SASS handshape with a movement root produces an inanimate predicate adjective (e.g., 2hCL:C-SPREAD-APART "be a long, deep cylinder").

The most difficult classifiers for the children in Schick's study were HANDLE classifiers, which represent the size or shape of a referent by indicating how it is held by a human hand. These have multimorphemic handshapes, like SASS classifiers, and combine with movement roots to produce transitive, agentive predicates (e.g., 2hCL:S-MOVE-UPWARD "lift a long, shallow cylinder").

The progression of difficulty for handshapes shows that the different classifier morphemes are acquired differentially and that both semantic and syntactic factors play a role in determining sequence of acquisition. Furthermore, the sequence of acquisition for location morphemes did not parallel the sequence for handshape morphemes, again supporting the hypothesis that these forms are acquired morphologically rather than holistically (cf. Section II). Location morphemes were produced most accurately in HANDLE classifiers. Schick attributed this to a proposed linguistic difference between HANDLE versus CLASS and SASS predicates: whereas the CLASS and SASS predicates use space to represent space, Schick analyzed the HANDLE predicates as transitive verbs with regular verbal inflection.[12] According to this analysis, the acquisition of the use of space in one domain of ASL syntax does not cross over automatically into other domains; rather, the morphologically relevant spatial locations used in verb agreement are acquired differently from those same locations when used with predicates representing space directly.

If correct, this analysis may bear on a current debate in the literature on ASL

[12]This analysis is inconsistent with that of Padden (1983), who analyzed the inflections on verbs of movement and location (her "spatial" verbs) as different from verb agreement with other "agreement" verbs. Whereas Shick maintained a distinction between abstract and location agreement, Padden argued that verbs like GIVE-BY-HAND (which incorporates a HANDLE classifier) are spatial verbs—that is, verbs that agree with locations rather than arguments.

structure. Although most researchers have made a distinction between spatial, *mapping* uses of linguistic space, and arbitrary *referential* uses of space, Liddell (1990, 1992) argued that in most cases the two are manifestations of the same linguistic use of space; in particular, Liddell argued that essentially all linguistic uses of space are mapping. In contrast, Poizner, Klima, and Bellugi (1987) have argued for the distinction between these uses of space, and they have shown that they break down differentially in signers with right or left hemisphere brain damage. If Schick's conclusion that the two types of space are acquired differentially is correct, it provides psycholinguistic evidence along with that of Poizner and colleagues for a distinction.

Another study which examined Deaf children's fluency with verbs of motion and location was conducted by Hamilton and Lillo-Martin (1986). One concern of this study was to compare DCDP with DCHP (ages 7 to 10) in their ability to imitate short sentences containing verbs of motion and location. It was found that the DCDP made many fewer errors than DCHP, and the few errors that the DCDP made led Hamilton and Lillo-Martin to conclude, "The errors made by the [DCDP], as opposed to those made by the [DCHP], indicate that the [DCDP] are making a structural analysis and are mastering the system" (p. 47), as opposed to acquiring the system holistically or analogically. In this way, these results corroborate those of Supalla's earlier study.

A third study that bears on the development of the classifier system examined children's acquisition of ASL word formation devices. Lillo-Martin (1988) presented Deaf children with two tests of their ability to create new words. The results showed that very different results were found when different methods were used.

The first word formation test was the People and Machines test. Twenty-four Deaf children ages 3 to 10 were asked, "What do you call a person who X's," or "What do you call a machine that X's," where "X" might be feeds babies, tears paper, laughs, and so on. Given this type of presentation, the children used mainly word-based word formation devices, such as compounding (e.g., LAUGH^MACHINE), affixation (e.g., FEED-ER), and derivation (e.g., READ[D:noun]). The youngest children, perhaps following a principle of formal simplicity (cf. Clark & Berman, 1984), mostly used derivation, as the derived forms require the least change to the input (furthermore, it should be noted that their derivations did not necessarily use the correct movement patterns found in the adult grammar).

Rather different results were found in the Invented Objects test, in which 34 Deaf children ages 2 to 10 were shown pictures of made-up objects or people using these objects. They were asked, "What is this thing?" or "What is he or she doing?" Compounds and extensions of existing signs were used, but now compositional responses making use of the ASL classifiers were also frequently used. SASS and HANDLE classifiers (in Schick's terms) can be used in descriptions or neologisms that clearly refer to the strange objects or activities used in this experiment. Even 2- and 3-year-old subjects produced innovative forms using SASS and

HANDLE classifiers. Thus, although development was found in the precision and frequency of these forms, it is clear that they are available as word-formation devices even to young children.

In sum, it is clear that children acquire the complex morphology of verbs of motion and location morphologically, not holistically. Various factors affect the course of acquisition, including the sequence encountered and the errors made. These factors are mainly linguistic in nature—factors such as morphological and syntactic complexity—and they show that the child's approach to these constructions is analytic, not analogic.

B. Spatial Syntax

As discussed in Section II, several studies have examined the acquisition of verb agreement and pronominal anaphora in ASL. However, these studies have been conducted with relatively few subjects, and they have left open some questions. Several studies have since been conducted to address some of these questions, although much interesting work remains to be done.

The Comprehension of Referent Association and Verb Agreement

One of the first questions to be addressed concerns the apparent difference between children's use of verb agreement with present referents, and its use with nonpresent referents. Recall that Newport and Meier attributed this difference to the difficulty of establishing and maintaining abstract loci for nonpresent referents. This step, necessary for the felicitous use of verb agreement with nonpresent referents, certainly seems more cognitively demanding than using the locations of present referents. It is doubtless reasonable to ask whether young children even understand the association of referents with abstract locations. Tests of the comprehension of this association and of verb agreement were presented in Lillo-Martin, Bellugi, Struxness, and O'Grady (1985) and in Bellugi, vanHoek, Lillo-Martin, and O'Grady (1988).

The first test looked simply at how well young Deaf children understand the abstract association between a referent and a location in signing space. The tester signed a sequence such as "BOY $HERE_a$, GIRL $HERE_b$"; in some cases three objects were used. (The different subscripts indicate that different locations are used.) A sequence of a noun followed by an indexic point to a location in space is one way to designate a location for a referent—the most explicit way possible. Following this simple sequence, the child was asked, "WHERE BOY?" or "WHAT $HERE_a$?" The results showed that the youngest subjects, less than 3 years old, did not understand the abstract association. They would look for a real boy when asked the test question. However, even 3-year olds were able to understand the association: they answered WHERE questions with about 80% accuracy. Their errors seemed to reflect memory shortcomings rather than an lack of understanding of the issue, because they made more errors on the tasks that required the most memory—that is, they performed better on the items with two objects than with three, and they performed better on the WHERE questions (which require only a point as a response) than on the WHAT questions (which require a referent).

Thus, the results of this test indicate that it is not simply a matter of not comprehending the association of referents with locations that prohibits young Deaf children (at least by age 3) from producing verb agreement with nonpresent referents. What, then, of their comprehension of such verb agreement? A series of tests presented in Lillo-Martin and colleagues (1985) and Bellugi and colleagues (1988) looked at children's comprehension of verb agreement. In these studies, it was found that a total of 43 Deaf children ages 3 to 10 did not show a high level of comprehension of verb agreement with nonpresent referents until the age of 5, when they obtained about 80% accuracy (at ceiling for these tests, which included picture choice and act-out tests). Thus, despite an understanding of the basics of the spatial syntax system—including associating referents with locations and use of agreement with present referents—the Deaf children in these studies failed to comprehend the agreement with nonpresent referents until age 5.

Like Newport and Meier, however, I believe the problems that the children are encountering have to do with performance, and with the memory burden that agreement with nonpresent referents poses, rather than with competence in the rules followed by this system. Newport and Meier pointed out that the acquisition of verb agreement with nonpresent referents does not "recapitulat[e] the acquisition of real-world verb agreement" (1985, p. 905), in its pattern of development. Rather, once abstract loci "are correctly established and maintained, verb agreement with these loci is immediately correct" (p. 906). Further evidence for this position comes from the fact that by the age of around 3;0 to 3;6, when the verb agreement system has been acquired with present referents, the children's productions even with nonpresent referents show that they respect certain conditions on the use of null arguments associated with agreement. This will be discussed in more depth later in this section.

The "Paint" and "Balloon" Stories: Studies of Production

An additional large body of data has been examined for the acquisition of verb agreement, pronouns, and other aspects of the spatial syntax. These data were generated by asking young Deaf children to tell stories. In many of the studies to be discussed, children were shown two separate picture books with no words, each displaying a short story. The children were first asked to describe each picture individually, then, after seeing the whole book, they were asked to retell the story from memory. The two stories are described here briefly. One, the balloon story, was adopted from Karmiloff-Smith (1985). This story shows a boy walking down a neighborhood street. He encounters a balloon man, who gives him a balloon. After walking happily with the balloon, the boy lets go, and the balloon flies away.

Finally, the boy continues walking, crying. The second story is the paint story. In this story, two children are sitting at a kitchen table, painting. The boy paints on the girl's face, and then the girl paints on the boy's face. Next, the boy pours a container (of paint or water) on the girl's face, and the girl pours on the boy's face. Finally, the mother, who has been blithely washing dishes in the background all this time, turns around, sees the children, and scolds them. These two stories have proved to be excellent elicitation aids. They encourage the children to use ASL spatial syntax. Some additional tasks were also used in the following studies, as described next.

One study using data from these stories looked at children's development of verb agreement, pronouns, and cross-sentential cohesion. Ursula Bellugi and colleagues (Bellugi, Lillo-Martin, O'Grady, & vanHoek, 1990) described four stages in children's storytelling based on these elicited narratives.

In Period One, at around 2 years of age, children use short, isolated sentences without any of the trappings of the spatial syntax. This is the stage at which children use only uninflected forms, even with present referents; word order is used to convey grammatical relations.

In Period Two, $2\frac{1}{2}$- to $3\frac{1}{2}$-year-old children use verb agreement with present referents only. This result was demonstrated in the earlier studies as well. Here, it is replicated with additional subjects; furthermore, it is reinforced by the finding that in storytelling, children will sometimes use the pictures in the book as *present referents.* By producing a verb such as PAINT as if it agrees with a present subject and object—that is, the pictures of the boy and girl on the page—the children show that they have command of the rules for the verb agreement system, but need a crutch for nonpresent referents. Furthermore, at this stage children's stories don't cohere—there is no clear continuity from one utterance to the next.

In Period Three, ages $3\frac{1}{2}$ to 5, the children's stories do have the coherence missing from the earlier stage. However, the sentences, in general, do not use the spatial syntactic marking. Because not all verbs mark agreement in ASL, it is possible to use word order to convey grammatical relations in a sentence devoid of spatial manipulation. However, these children were doing so even with verbs that do mark agreement, and thus should be inflected. Later in this period, children begin to use the verb agreement with nonpresent referents, but, like the subject Loew studied, they may stack or use inconsistent locations for each referent. This makes individual sentences grammatical, but across the narrative each location should be associated with a consistent referent (unless the referent has been changed explicitly).

Only by Period Four, age 5 to 6, is the cross-sentential use of verb agreement and anaphoric pronouns accurate in these children's productions. Of course, some may go on to be fluent and entertaining storytellers, whereas others may not achieve such refinement; but by this time, the basics of the system are used.

Overall, then, Bellugi and colleagues found support for the results of Meier, Loew, and others, with a much larger group of children. Further investigation of paint and balloon stories revealed still more interesting phenomena in children's development of spatial syntax.

Karen vanHoek and colleagues (vanHoek, O'Grady, Bellugi, & Norman, 1987) found that eight children between the ages of 3;0 and 5;6 produced novel morphological forms when telling the paint story. These forms used space, but not in the grammaticized ways allowed in adult ASL. For example, some of the children used the right versus the left side of the face to distinguish referents. Thus, they signed PAINT on the right side of the face to mean "he paints on her face," and PAINT on the left side of the face meant "she paints on his face." Although it is possible to sign PAINT on one's own face to mean "paint on someone's face," it is not possible to distinguish two referents on different sides of the face. vanHoek and colleagues said, "[t]he children are thus taking a basic organizational principle of ASL's spatial morphology and giving it a novel instantiation."

When PAINT is signed on one's own face to mean "paint on someone's face," an additional layer of ASL's spatial syntax is invoked. This layer, often called referential shift, uses a change in body or head position, eye gaze, or other nonmanual marking to indicate a change in the association between locations and referents (hence, referential shift). The 3- to 5-year-old children in the study summarized above should have used this referential shift with their PAINT-FACE sign, which they did not. By invoking the referential shift, PAINT on one's own face does not mean "painted *me* on the face"—it just means "painted on the face." Furthermore, it becomes intransitive; to express an object, the location-incorporated verb must be used in a serial verb construction, with a regular transitive verb (without body location) preceding it. Referential shift is used in perspective shift, direct quotation, serial verbs, and other constructions. How do children learn to use referential shift?

This was explored by vanHoek and colleagues in another study (vanHoek, O'-Grady, Bellugi, & Norman, 1989), which used the paint stories and an additional elicitation procedure. As seen previously, up until age 5 Deaf children incorporate the body location (body classifier) in sentences without the required shift, and they use the incorporated verb as a transitive, rather than intransitive, form. Five- and six-year olds cease making this error. Instead, they simply omit the body location or use a separate nominal to indicate where the painting took place. Seven- to ten-year olds finally use the serial verb construction, but they too fail to include the shift. Only 10-year olds used the serial verb construction with the shift.

On the other hand, the referential shift was used by children in discourse, to indicate perspective shift or direct quotation, much earlier than it was used in serial verbs. This looks similar to the problem in verb agreement: a morphosyntactically complex construction is acquired and used in one context, but not extended to another applicable context.

Why should these differences occur? In a third study, vanHoek and colleagues (vanHoek, O'Grady, Bellugi, & Norman, 1990) analyzed the children's paint stories again, attempting to discover why the spatial syntax is so relatively late in development, compared with other aspects of syntactic acquisition. They hypothesized that intra-sentential reference might be in place before cross-sentential reference, and they tested this hypothesis by comparing the development of nonspatial and spatial aspects of reference at the sentential and narrative levels.

This hypothesis was supported. The children's narratives were categorized by levels, according to the consistency of nonspatial reference (e.g., naming) and spatial reference. It was found that the two developed in parallel. As one example, they studied a 4-year old for whom they had longitudinal data in depth and concluded,

> We thus find a striking similarity between Maxine's use of referential loci and her signaling of reference and reference switches. At the sentential level, reference is clear and spatial indexing is used appropriately. It is at the level of the overall narrative, what we might call the discourse level of structure, that she still has not acquired full fluency with either system.

Five months later, this subject had consistency for both reference and space at the discourse level.

Parameter Setting: The Use of Null Arguments in ASL

Given the rich morphological agreement found in ASL, it might be expected that null arguments (subject or object not overtly expressed using a separate lexical item) would be allowed. This turns out to be the case, although it is somewhat complicated due to the splitting of the verb lexicon into verbs that can and cannot be marked for agreement (for the analysis to be presented here, see Lillo-Martin, 1986; also Kegl, 1986; but cf. Aarons, Bahan, Kegl, & Neidle, 1992).

For verbs that are marked with subject and object agreement, these arguments can be null. Furthermore, the behavior of these null arguments, especially in extraction, shows them to behave like null pronominals, or *pro* (cf. Jaeggli & Safir, 1989; McCloskey & Hale, 1984; Rizzi, 1986). It should be noted that *pro* is licensed and identified by verb agreement, so even a verb that can be inflected does not allow pronominal null arguments if it is not inflected (subject agreement is optional).

However, it is not the case that null arguments are never found with verbs that are not marked for agreement. Rather, these verbs seem to allow null arguments of the type found in Chinese and other "discourse-oriented" languages (Huang, 1984). The null arguments refer to a discourse topic, and do not display pronominal characteristics. Like Chinese, ASL has been called "discourse oriented," and the typological characteristics of such a language are found in ASL (most noticeably, topic prominence).

Given the abundance of null arguments found in ASL, how does the Deaf child sort them out? This question was studied by Lillo-Martin (1991). The paint and balloon stories of 23 Deaf children ages 1;7 to 8;11 were examined, as well as an elicited imitation test with 18 children ages 2;11 to 10;8. It was found that the Deaf children's appropriate use of null arguments was intimately tied with their development of verb agreement, as noted in the preceding discussion.

Children in the earliest stages, using no verb agreement or spatial syntax, used null arguments freely. In this way, they are like children learning a language such as English. Although English does not allow null arguments, young children frequently omit the subject (and much less frequently, the object) in their early sentences. Because English does not have a rich enough verb agreement system, and does not pattern as a discourse-oriented language, it seems that early null subjects are unidentified (Hyams, 1986; but cf. Hyams, 1991).

However, an interesting change takes place at around 3 years of age. From the earlier studies cited, it is known that Deaf children acquire and use the verb agreement system with present referents at around 3;0 to 3;6. At the same age, verb agreement is not used with nonpresent referents. In their stories, which involve nonpresent referents, they turn at this age to using almost all overt arguments. If they used many null arguments with verbs not marked for agreement, they would violate the requirement that null arguments be identified. Because they do not use these null arguments, it seems that this requirement is respected at this age. Perhaps this is related to the development of verb agreement with present referents: it seems that children at this age do use null arguments with present referents, when they use verb agreement and their null arguments are thus identified. Hence, their stories show that by age 3, Deaf children understand both that null arguments are allowed in ASL, and that they must be identified. Because the stories with nonpresent referents do not show verb agreement, they also do not show null arguments.

To be more precise, it should be pointed out that children's stories at this age are not completely devoid of null arguments. They do occasionally use null arguments identified by a discourse topic. However, they do not make up for the lack of null arguments with agreement-marked verbs. The children's utterances give the impression of an overuse of overt arguments, especially repeated names.

Once the children learn to use verb agreement with nonpresent referents, they correctly use null arguments in these sentences. There is a short period marked by errors in both agreement and null arguments, as the children learn to associate referents with locations differentially. However, it is clear that appropriate use of null arguments comes in step with appropriate use of verb agreement.

If one looked exclusively at the development of adultlike use of null arguments, one might be tempted to say that the Deaf children go back and forth between a parameter setting that allows null arguments and one that does not. Such a pattern would not be consistent with the idea of parameter setting as throwing a switch in one direction or another. However, I have argued that it is important to consider the use of null arguments together with the development of the verb agreement system. In so doing, it becomes clear that the Deaf children in fact do not go back and forth in parameter setting, but they do experience a delay in their correct verb agreement use with nonpresent referents. This analysis places the locus of children's delayed acquisition within the morphology and the lexicon, rather than in syntactic parameter setting, which is expected to occur relatively rapidly and effortlessly.[13]

C. Nonmanual Grammatical Markers

As noted earlier, in 1985 Newport and Meier stated that essentially no work had been done on aspects of the acquisition of ASL syntax. Now, some years later, a few studies have been published, though more are desperately needed. A very interesting set of studies was undertaken by Judy Reilly, Marina McIntire, and Ursula Bellugi. These studies focus on the acquisition of the nonmanual facial behaviors that mark certain kinds of structures in ASL.

As Reilly and colleagues pointed out, facial behaviors serve several purposes in signing. As with the facial gestures made by hearing people while they are talking, a number of affective facial gestures accompany ASL signs. Reilly, McIntire, and Bellugi assumed that these uses of affect as a "complement to language" would develop much as they do in hearing children. Indeed, they found that 1-year olds use facial expressions to report their own present state; as they mature, affective facial expressions take on increasing complexity and decontextualization. No radical reanalysis is shown in the gradual development of affective facial expressions (Reilly, McIntire, & Bellugi, 1990b).

In contrast, grammaticized facial expressions take a different route. There are specific facial expressions that accompany signs for affective states. From 1;6 to 2;3, Deaf children use these signs with these facial expressions—as amalgams, unanalyzed units of face + hands. Around the age of 2;5, a reanalysis occurs. Now, the facial expression may be missing from such a sign, or even a different facial expression might be used (such as smiling while signing SAD). By age 4, the facial expressions are used correctly again, and the timing of the onset and offset of the facial gesture marks it as linguistic rather than affective. There is a sharp break in the development of these facial behaviors. The first linguistic behaviors have been led into by the previously existing nonlinguistic units; Reilly and colleagues claimed, "children use their pre-linguistically productive affective knowledge of facial expression as a bridge into its linguistic use" (Reilly, McIntire, & Bellugi, 1990a, p. 374). Once into linguistic use, however, the forms need to be analyzed and applied by rule to the appropriate signs.

[13]An interesting report on the use of null arguments by Deaf children learning Sign Language of the Netherlands was presented by Coerts and Mills (1992). They found use of both null subjects and null objects in the two children they studied. Like the results of Lillo-Martin (1991) and Wang, Lillo-Martin, Best, and Levitt (1992), this indicates that young children exposed to a language that allows null objects will use them from an early age (as opposed to their infrequent use, compared with null subjects, by children learning a language that does not allow them, like English).

As a third type of acquisition, Reilly and colleagues consider the acquisition of facial gestures which mark syntactic units (Reilly et al., 1990a; Reilly et al., 1991). For example, conditionals are marked by a specific facial gesture, including raised eyebrows, which co-occurs with the antecedent, and an eye-blink and head thrust during the pause between the antecedent and the consequent. Conditionals may be marked by the facial behavior alone; alternatively, a manual sign for IF or SUPPOSE may be used to mark the antecedent.

Fourteen Deaf children ages 3;3 to 8;4 were studied in a set of comprehension and production tasks. It was found that manual marking preceded facial gestures in both comprehension and production. For 3-year olds, conditional sentences were comprehended one-third of the time when a manual marker was present; but none of the sentences with conditionals marked only on the face were comprehended. Similarly, in the one-third of the trials in which the 3-year olds produced conditionals, every case had a manual marker, and no nonmanual markers were used. By age 5, both manual and nonmanual conditionals were comprehended and produced; although the facial expression was not always completely accurate.

Reilly and McIntire (1991) found similar results in a study of the acquisition of the facial expressions used in questions. Wh-words were used by the children in questions as early as 1;6, but the whq facial expression was not used until 3;6. This does not seem to be due to the children's inability to produce these facial expressions. At the same time (1;3), Deaf children can use the yes/no question facial expression appropriately (although the yes/no facial expression uses raised brows, whereas the wh-question facial expression uses furrowed brows). Unlike wh-questions, yes/no questions have no manual marker. And of course, the Deaf children have long since used facial expressions for affect and to accompany affective signs.

What makes the manual markers used first in wh-questions, whereas the facial expression is used for yes/no questions? Reilly and colleagues (1991) cited Slobin's operating principle of unifunctionality: "if a single form signals two similar but distinct meanings, the child will initially seek distinctive means to mark the two notions" (p. 19). Reilly and colleagues suggested that children apply this principle to use the face only for marking yes/no questions. Because wh-questions have a distinctive marker, it will be used to distinguish them from yes/no questions.

This application of Slobin's principle to the acquisition of facial versus manual marking led Reilly and colleagues to the quote cited at the beginning of this chapter, repeated here:

> [T]he modality in which the language is conveyed plays a significant role in language learning. (Reilly et al., 1991, p. 22)

How much does the modality affect language learning—or the organization of language grammar, its localization and processing by the brain, its other fundamental properties? This question is intricately related to the modularity hypothesis, for only certain (limited) modality effects are expected under a modular view of language. Although the topic is too vast to consider all of its implications here, we turn now to a discussion of the effects of modality—and modularity—in language acquisition.

V. MODALITY AND MODULARITY EFFECTS IN LANGUAGE ACQUISITION

The modularity hypothesis, as made well known by Fodor (1983) contends that language is a cognitive system distinct from other cognitive systems. Although the same base of horizontal faculties (memory, attention, etc.) may be tapped by language and other cognitive functions, Fodor argued that language is processed independently of these other systems. In Fodor's terms, language is an *input system,* like vision, audition, touch, and so on, and specialized processors deal with input in any of these systems rapidly, automatically, and without influence from higher-level systems. Once this specialized processor is done with the input, it gets sent to higher levels, where it can be used in decision making, contemplating, and manipulating, or any of numerous other cognitive functions.

The Chomskian version of modularity (see, e.g., Chomsky, 1981) differed some from Fodor's. For the present purposes, let us consider Chomsky's proposals regarding the modularity of the internal structure of the language processor. According to Chomsky, the various subcomponents of the language mechanism are also modular, feeding from phonological processing to syntactic processing to semantic processing. Like the modularity of the language processor as a whole, this means that the various levels work independently, using their own particular rules and mechanisms. Furthermore, the higher levels do not affect the processing of the lower levels.

Given the properties of signed languages discussed earlier—their essential similarities in function and form to spoken languages—I believe that most versions of modularity would have the following expectations regarding modality. Certainly, at the higher levels of organization, such as syntax and semantics, modality should not affect language structure or processing. Why should this be so? If one and the same language mechanism underlies both signed and spoken languages—which seems plausible, given their similarities in structure, acquisition, and, as we have not discussed here, brain organization and processing (see, e.g., Emmorey, 1993; Poizner et al., 1987)—then this mechanism—let us call it Universal Grammar—would not make a distinction between modalities once the input has entered the system.

What about the lower levels—phonology and phonetics? Clearly, at some point the modality must play a role, because the input comes from either the eyes or the ears. How soon can this input be translated into an amodal form that can be processed by Universal Grammar? Apparently, this takes place very soon. The phonological structures of signed and spoken languages have been found to be remarkably similar. Although some authors would not agree, many sign phonologists have found that using the tools and models for representation of spoken languages has been very effective for the analysis of signed languages (see, for examples, papers in Coulter, 1993; bear in mind however, that it would be incorrect to claim that there is consensus in this view). Thus, under the view developed here, even the phonological component of universal grammar is stated abstractly enough for both signed and spoken languages to be included.

Sandler (1993) drew an alternative conclusion. Because the input forms are distinct between signed and spoken languages, and the labels and specific hierarchy needed for sign language phonology are different from those needed for spoken language phonology, Sandler concluded that a Fodorian module "cannot contain sign language, and that, since sign languages are languages, there can be no language module of this sort" (p. 331). An alternative view of modularity, which Sandler dubbed the grammatical form module, would claim that "The principal requirement of the language module . . . is that grammatical forms, constraints, and rules . . . be unique to the module" (p. 345). Although she granted that such a module might accurately explain both signed and spoken languages, Sandler worried that with this view of modularity as a research paradigm, "important and potentially revealing questions go unasked" (p. 347).

Sandler posed many important and potentially revealing questions—a challenge, indeed—for the view of modularity advocated here. However, I believe that it is not necessary to depart from a Fodorian modularity hypothesis in order to accommodate the facts about signed languages. In fact, I believe the modularity hypothesis is supported by the facts about signed languages. For the present chapter, I will focus on the facts about language acquisition.[14]

How many modality effects were found in the present review of the literature on the acquisition of sign languages? Note that many anticipated modality effects were not found. One possible modality effect that was studied by many researchers involved iconicity. Because aspects of the ASL lexical and morphological system are iconic, it is possible that they would be acquired more easily than noniconic equivalents in spoken languages, or nonequivalent counterparts in ASL. However, some individual lexical items, deictic pronouns, and verb agreement, all of which display some degree of iconicity, were found *not* to be acquired more easily because of iconicity. Rather, these aspects of ASL were consistently found to be acquired in parallel to spoken languages.

What about the aspects that led Reilly and colleagues (1991) to claim that

[14]A more in-depth consideration of sign language and the modularity hypothesis is in preparation.

modality does affect language acquisition? Recall that their claim concerned the acquisition of grammaticized facial expressions. They found that Deaf children use manual markers for conditionals and wh-questions before they acquire the facial markers, even though the facial marker is obligatory while the manual marker is optional. They applied Slobin's operating principle of unifunctionality to explain why the children appropriately used facial gestures for yes/no questions while failing to use them for wh-questions. Then, they asked, why does the child use the manual markers before the facial markers, instead of the other way around? Clearly, because the facial markers are used for yes/no questions (as well as affective signs and to show the child's own affective states), it is not because the child has not yet acquired control over facial gestures. Rather, they hypothesized, "it appears that their *first* hypothesis may be that hands are for language and faces are for affect" (Reilly et al., 1991, p. 20). Once language acquisition is under way, they propose that children learning ASL must invoke a new operating principle, applicable only for the acquisition of signed languages: "Pay attention to faces for linguistically significant information" (p. 22).

If the acquisition of signed languages requires new operating principles (or principles of UG) not needed for spoken languages, then it would seem that, as Reilly and colleagues claim, the modality plays a significant role in language learning. However, I would like to propose that the significance of the role of modality is limited to phonetics. The difference between hands and faces that Reilly and colleagues found for wh-questions versus yes/no questions can be accounted for using the same principle of unifunctionality they cited. Rather than use the face for multiple functions (yes/no questions, wh-questions, and conditionals), different means are used to mark each function: the face for yes/no questions and independent lexical items for wh-questions and conditionals. Because there are no independent lexical items for signaling yes/no questions, it is this construction that is marked by the face. Reilly and colleagues also noted that young Deaf children use the topic-marker facial expression before using the same raised eyebrows in conditionals. Here again, it is topics which are marked with the face, because there is no lexical sign to mark topics; unifunctionality leads the children to choose a manual marker for conditionals rather than use the same raised eyebrows.

The operating principle proposed by Reilly and colleagues, pay attention to faces, can still be applied in the acquisition of sign language, but now its role is phonetic. Perhaps this view is not really far off from that intended by Reilly and colleagues. After all, they also said,

> Taken together, the accumulated studies suggest that deaf children use strategies in acquiring ASL that are strikingly similar to those found in the acquisition of spoken languages, despite the radical differences between signed and spoken language. In addition, our study demonstrates the remarkable breadth of the language learning mechanism in its ability to process these unusual behaviors as grammatical units. (1991, p. 20)

At the phonetic level, that is, the level indicating the modality of linguistic input, modality necessarily plays a role.[15] Because of this role, a true modality effect in language acquisition is possible: the effect (if real) of earlier first signs than first spoken words. As Meier and Newport argued, this effect is plausibly due not to a difference in the maturation of the linguistic component, or of the cognitive requirements for language, but to a difference in the maturation of the articulatory or perceptual mechanisms used for signed versus spoken languages.

There is still room for real modality effects in the structure and acquisition of ASL syntax. Liddell (1992) claimed that in the so-called spatial syntax, as well as verbs of motion and location, although movements can be morphologically analyzed (as claimed by Supalla, 1982), locations cannot. His claim is that the locations which were described earlier as "associated with" referents, are analogically representative of real locations, and thus, not analyzable. If correct, this would seem to be a modality effect on the structure of ASL, as by the time input reached the syntactic level, modality should be irrelevant, according to the preceding discussion. As such, it might also have an affect on language acquisition.

In this regard, it is instructive to recall the studies discussed earlier regarding the acquisition of ASL spatial syntax and verbs of motion and location. In every case discussed, the conclusion was drawn that these structures of ASL are acquired morphologically. The time course of acquisition, as well as the types of errors encountered, led the researchers to claim that morphology, not iconicity (or an analog representation of real space) guided language acquisition. However, it is clear that more work needs to be done to address this question specifically. As Schick (1990c) put it, "These data suggest that the key to characterizing and assessing ASL acquisition lies in the nature of the use of syntactic space" (p. 370).

VI. CONCLUSION AND IMPLICATIONS

It is hoped that the goal of making the acquisition of sign language by Deaf children of interest to linguistic theory has been met. It is clear that much work remains to be done, in the collection of much more data on the acquisition of sign languages and in its application to linguistic theory. New theories, new methodologies, new subject groups, and even replications of existing studies are sorely needed. Current work is in progress in the areas of early stages, phonological de-

[15]Despite this modality effect, there may even be similarities between signed and spoken languages in the specialized nature of the phonetic processor for language. Liberman and Mattingly (1985), among others, have argued that the phonetic processor for spoken language is specialized and preemptive; thus, speech is perceived differently from other nonlinguistic sounds. Whether there is a parallel special processor for signed languages is of considerable interest. (See discussion in Mattingly & Studdert-Kennedy, 1991.)

velopment, and syntactic development (at least), and the results of these studies will help in the construction of theories of language acquisition.

The question of modality effects in language acquisition has not, of course, been settled. Such effects are immensely interesting, for they help to sharpen the distinctions between language, communication, and other cognitive systems. In current studies of the acquisition of spoken languages, it has been found that in-depth studies of one language can be a substantial source of data; but comparisons across languages are also vital. The same must be true for signed languages as well: it will be essentially impossible to distinguish modality effects from typology effects until a number of sign languages other than ASL have also been studied. It is gratifying to know that many such studies are currently underway.

The conclusion drawn by other summaries of the acquisition of ASL can be repeated here: Signed languages are acquired in much the same way as spoken languages. The same sequences of steps are found at roughly the same ages; the same types of errors are found and not found. This lends credence to further studies of sign language development, further comparisons with the development of particular spoken languages, and further use of sign language data to sharpen theories of language. Only by including signed languages in the empirical database that a theory must explain will the goal of constructing a theory of language be met.

ACKNOWLEDGMENT

The preparation of this chapter was supported in part by National Institutes of Health Grant NIDCD #DC00183.

REFERENCES

Aarons, D., Bahan, B., Kegl, J., & Neidle, C. (1992). Clausal structure and a tier for grammatical marking in American Sign Language. *Nordic Journal of Linguistics, 15*(2), 103–142.

Ackerman, J., Kyle, J., Woll, B., & Ezra, M. (1990). Lexical acquisition in sign and speech: Evidence from a longitudinal study of infants in deaf families. In C. Lucas (Ed.), *Sign language research: Theoretical issues* (pp. 337–345). Washington, DC: Gallaudet University Press.

Bates, E., Benigni, L., Bretherton, I., Camaioni, L., & Volterra, V. (1979). *The emergence of symbols: Cognition and communication in infancy.* New York: Academic Press.

Battison, R. (1974). Phonological deletion in American Sign Language. *Sign Language Studies, 5,* 1–19.

Bellugi, U. (1988). The acquisition of a spatial language. In F. S. Kessel (Ed.), *The devel-*

opment of language and language researchers: Essays in honor of Roger Brown (pp. 153–185). Hillsdale, NJ: Erlbaum.

Bellugi, U., & Klima, E. S. (1982). The acquisition of three morphological systems in American Sign Language. *Papers and Reports on Child Language Development, 21,* 1–35.

Bellugi, U., Lillo-Martin, D., O'Grady, L., & vanHoek, K. (1990). The development of spatialized syntactic mechanisms in American Sign Language. In W. H. Edmondson & F. Karlsson (Eds.), *SLR '87: Papers from the Fourth International Symposium on Sign Language Research* (pp. 183–189). Hamburg: Signum-Verlag.

Bellugi, U., vanHoek, K., Lillo-Martin, D., & O'Grady, L. (1988). The acquisition of syntax and space in young deaf signers. In D. Bishop & K. Mogford (Eds.), *Language development in exceptional circumstances* (pp. 132–149). Edinburgh: Churchill Livingstone.

Bonvillian, J. D., & Folven, R. J. (1990). The onset of signing in young children. In W. H. Edmondson & F. Karlsson (Eds.), *SLR '87: Papers from the Fourth International Symposium on Sign Language Research* (pp. 183–189). Hamburg: Signum-Verlag.

Bonvillian, J. D., & Folven, R. J. (1993). Sign language acquisition: Developmental aspects. In M. Marschark & M. D. Clark (Eds.), *Psychological perspectives on deafness* (pp. 229–265). Hillsdale, NJ: Erlbaum.

Bonvillian, J. D., Orlansky, M. D., & Folven, R. J. (1990). Early sign language acquisition: Implications for theories of language acquisition. In V. Volterra & C. J. Erting (Eds.), *From gesture to language in hearing and deaf children* (pp. 219–232). Berlin: Springer-Verlag.

Bonvillian, J. D., Orlansky, M. D., Novack, L. L., Folven, R. J., & Holley-Wilcox, P. (1985). Language, cognitive, and cherological development: The first steps in sign language acquisition. In W. Stokoe & V. Volterra (Eds.), *SLR '83: Proceedings of the Third International Symposium on Sign Language Research* (pp. 10–22). Silver Spring, MD: Linstok Press.

Boyes-Braem, P. (1990). Acquisition of the handshape in American Sign Language: A preliminary analysis. In V. Volterra & C. J. Erting (Eds.), *From gesture to language in hearing and deaf children* (pp. 107–127). Berlin: Springer-Verlag.

Chomsky, N. (1981). *Lectures on government and binding.* Dordrecht: Foris.

Clark, E., & Berman, R. (1984). Structure and use in the acquisition of word-formation. *Language, 60,* 542–590.

Coerts, J., & Mills, A. (1992). Early sign combinations of deaf children in sign language of the Netherlands. In I. Ahlgren, B. Bergman, & M. Brennan (Eds.), *Proceedings of the Fifth International Symposium on Sign Language Research.*

Coulter, G. (Ed.). (1993). *Phonetics and phonology, Volume 3: Current issues in ASL phonology.* San Diego: Academic Press.

Day, E. J. (1932). The development of language in twins: I. A comparison of twins and single children. *Child Development, 3,* 179–199.

Deuchar, M. (1984). *Brittish sign language.* London: Routledge & Kegan Paul.

Ellenberger, R. L., & Steyaert, M. (1978). A child's representation of action in American Sign Language. In P. Siple (Ed.), *Understanding language through sign language research* (pp. 261–269). New York: Academic Press.

Emmorey, K. (1993). Processing a dynamic visual-spatial language: Psycholinguistic studies of American Sign Language. *Journal of Psycholinguistic Research, 22,* 153–188.

Fodor, J. A. (1983). *The modularity of mind.* Cambridge, MA: MIT Press.

Galvan, D. (1988). *The acquisition of three morphological subsystems in American Sign Language by deaf children with deaf or hearing parents.* Ph.D. dissertation, University of California, Berkeley.

Gaustad, M. G. (1988). Development of vocal and signed communication in deaf and hearing twins of deaf parents. In M. Strong (Ed.), *Language learning and deafness* (pp. 220–260). Cambridge, England: Cambridge University Press.

Gee, J. P., & Goodhart, W. (1985). Nativization, linguistic theory, and deaf language acquisition. *Sign Language Studies, 49,* 291–342.

Goldin-Meadow, S., & Mylander, C. (1990). Beyond the input given: The child's role in the acquisition of language. *Language, 66*(2), 323–355.

Hamilton, H., & Lillo-Martin, D. (1986). Imitative production of ASL verbs of movement and location: A comparative study. *Sign Language Studies, 50,* 29–57.

Hoffmeister, R. J. (1978). *The development of demonstrative pronouns, locatives, and personal pronouns in the acquisition of American Sign Language by deaf children of deaf parents.* Ph.D. dissertation, University of Minnesota.

Hoffmeister, R. J. (1982). Acquisition of signed languages by deaf children. In H. Hoeman & R. Wilbur (Eds.), *Communication in two societies.* Washington, DC: Gallaudet College Press.

Hoffmeister, R. J. (1987). The acquisition of pronominal anaphora in ASL by deaf children. In B. Lust (Ed.), *Studies in the acquisition of anaphora. Vol. II: Applying the constraints* (pp. 171–187). Dordrecht: D. Reidel.

Hoffmeister, R. J., & Wilbur, R. (1980). The acquisition of sign language. In H. Lane & F. Grosjean (Eds.), *Recent perspectives on American sign language* (pp. 61–78). Hillsdale, NJ: Erlbaum.

Huang, C. T. J. (1984). On the distribution and reference of empty pronouns. *Linguistic Inquiry, 15,* 531–574.

Hyams, N. (1986). *Language acquisition and the theory of parameters.* Dordrecht: Reidel.

Hyams, N. (1991). A reanalysis of null subjects in child language. In J. Weissenborn, H. Goodluck, & T. Roeper (Eds.), *Theoretical issues in language acquisition* (pp. 249–267). Hillsdale, NJ: Erlbaum.

Jackson, C. A. (1984). *Language acquisition in two modalities: Person deixis and negation in American Sign Language and English.* Master's thesis, University of California, Los Angeles.

Jackson, C. A. (1989). Language acquisition in two modalities: The role of nonlinguistic cues in linguistic mastery. *Sign Language Studies, 62,* 1–22.

Jaeggli, O., & Safir, K. (Eds.). (1989). *The null subject parameter.* Dordrecht: Kluwer Academic Publishers.

Kantor, R. (1980). The acquisition of classifiers in American Sign Language. *Sign Language Studies, 28,* 193–208.

Karmiloff-Smith, A. (1985). Language and cognitive processes from a developmental perspective. *Language and Cognitive Processes, 1,* 61–85.

Kegl, J. A. (1986). Clitics in American Sign Language. In H. Borer (Eds.), *Syntax and semantics, Volume 19: The syntax of pronominal clitics* (pp. 285–309). New York: Academic Press.

Klima, E. S., & Bellugi, U. (1979). *The signs of language.* Cambridge, MA: Harvard University Press.

Kyle, J. G., & Woll, B. (1985). *Sign language: The study of deaf people and their language.* Cambridge: Cambridge University Press.

Liberman, A. M., & Mattingly, I. G. (1985). The motor theory of speech perception revised. *Cognition, 21,* 1–36.

Liddell, S. K. (1990). Four functions of a locus: Reexamining the structure of space in ASL. In C. Lucas (Ed.), *Sign language research: Theoretical issues* (pp. 176–198). Washington, DC: Gallaudet University Press.

Liddell, S. K. (1992). *Discrete and continuous in four classes of ASL signs.* Presented at the Fourth International Conference on Theoretical Issues in Sign Language Research, San Diego, CA.

Lillo-Martin, D. (1986). Two kinds of null arguments in American Sign Language. *Natural Language and Linguistic Theory, 4,* 415–444.

Lillo-Martin, D. (1988). Children's new sign creations. In M. Strong (Eds.), *Language learning and deafness* (pp. 162–183). Cambridge, England: Cambridge University Press.

Lillo-Martin, D. (1991). *Universal grammar and American Sign Language: Setting the null argument parameters.* Dordrecht: Kluwer Academic Publishers.

Lillo-Martin, D., Bellugi, U., Struxness, L., & O'Grady, M. (1985). The acquisition of spatially organized syntax. *Papers and Reports on Child Language Development, 24,* 70–78.

Lillo-Martin, D., & Klima, E. S. (1990). Pointing out differences: ASL pronouns in syntactic theory. In S. D. Fischer & P. Siple (Eds.), *Theoretical issues in sign language research, Volume 1: Linguistics* (pp. 191–210). Chicago: University of Chicago Press.

Loew, R. (1984). *Roles and reference in American Sign Language: A developmental perspective.* Ph.D. dissertation, University of Minnesota.

McCloskey, J., & Hale, K. (1984). The syntax of person-number inflection in modern Irish. *Natural Language and Linguistic Theory, 1,* 487–533.

McIntire, M. L. (1977). The acquisition of American Sign Language hand configurations. *Sign Language Studies, 16,* 247–266.

Mattingly, I. G., & Studdert-Kennedy, M. (Eds.). (1991). *Modularity and the motor theory of speech perception.* Hillsdale, NJ: Erlbaum.

Mayberry, R. I., & Eichen, E. B. (1991). The long-lasting advantage of learning sign language in childhood: Another look at the critical period for language acquisition. *Journal of Memory and Language, 30*(4), 486–512.

Meier, R. P. (1982). *Icons, analogues, and morphemes: The acquisition of verb agreement in ASL.* Ph.D. dissertation, University of California, San Diego.

Meier, R. P. (1987). Elicited imitation of verb agreement in American Sign Language: Iconically or morphologically determined? *Journal of Memory and Language, 26,* 362–376.

Meier, R. P. (1990). Person deixis in American Sign Language. In S. D. Fischer & P. Siple (Eds.), *Theoretical issues in sign language research. Volume 1: Linguistics* (pp. 175–190). Chicago: University of Chicago Press.

Meier, R. P. (1991). Language acquisition by deaf children. *American Scientist, 79,* 60–70.

Mounty, J. L. (1986). *Nativization and input in the language development of two deaf children of hearing parents.* Ed.D. dissertation, Boston University.

Nelson, K. (1973). Structure and strategy in learning to talk. *Monographs of the Society for Research in Child Development, 38*(1–2).

Newport, E., & Meier, R. (1985). The acquisition of American Sign Language. In D. Slobin (Ed.), *The cross-linguistic study of language acquisition* (pp. 881–938). Hillsdale, NJ: Erlbaum.

Newport, E. L., & Meier, R. P. (1990). Out of the hands of babes: On a possible sign advantage in language acquisition. *Language, 66,* 1–23.

Newport, E. L. (1981). Constraints on structure: Evidence from American Sign Language and language learning. In W. A. Collins (Ed.), *Aspects of the development of competence, Minnesota Symposia on Child Psychology.* Hillsdale, NJ: Erlbaum.

Newport, E. L., & Ashbrook, E. (1977). The emergence of semantic relations in American Sign Language. *Papers and Reports on Child Language Development, 13,* 16–21.

Newport, E. L., & Supalla, T. (1987). *A critical period effect in the acquisition of a primary language.* Unpublished manuscript.

Orlansky, M. D., & Bonvillian, J. D. (1985). Sign language acquisition: Language development in children of deaf parents and implications for other populations. *Merrill-Palmer Quarterly, 31,* 127–143.

Padden, C., & Humphries, T. (1988). *Deaf in America: Voices from a culture.* Cambridge, MA: Harvard University Press.

Padden, C. A. (1983). *Interaction of morphology and syntax in American Sign Language.* Ph.D. dissertation, University of California, San Diego.

Padden, C. A. (1990). The relation between space and grammar in ASL verb morphology. In C. Lucas (Ed.), *Sign language research: Theoretical issues* (pp. 118–132). Washington, DC: Gallaudet University Press.

Petitto, L. A. (1983). *From gesture to symbol: The relationship between form and meaning in the acquisition of personal pronouns in American Sign Language.* Ph.D. dissertation, Harvard University.

Petitto, L. A. (1987). On the autonomy of language and gesture: Evidence from the acquisition of personal pronouns in American Sign Language. *Cognition, 27,* 1–52.

Petitto, L. A. (1988). "Language" in the prelinguistic child. In F. S. Kessel (Ed.), *The development of language and language researchers* (pp. 187–221). Hillsdale, NJ: Erlbaum.

Petitto, L. A. (1990). The transition from gesture to symbol in American Sign Language. In V. Volterra & C. J. Erting (Eds.), *From gesture to language in hearing and deaf children* (pp. 153–161). Berlin: Springer-Verlag.

Petitto, L. A., & Charron, F. (1987). *Semantic categories in the acquisition of Langue des Signes Quebecoise (LSQ) and American Sign Language (ASL).* Presented at the 12th Annual Boston University Conference on Child Language Development.

Petitto, L. A., & Marentette, P. F. (1991). Babbling in the manual mode: Evidence for the ontogeny of language. *Science, 251,* 1493–1496.

Pizzuto, E. (1985). Sign languages, iconic indexical features and language learning processes. In W. Stokoe & V. Volterra (Eds.), *SLR '83: Proceedings of the Third International Symposium on Sign Language Research* (pp. 48–54). Silver Spring, MD: Linstok Press.

Pizzuto, E. (1990). The early development of deixis in American Sign Language: What is the point? In V. Volterra & C. J. Erting (Eds.), *From gesture to language in hearing and deaf children* (pp. 142–152). Berlin: Springer-Verlag.

Poizner, H., Klima, E. S., & Bellugi, U. (1987). *What the hands reveal about the brain.* Cambridge, MA: MIT Press.

Reilly, J. S., & McIntire, M. L. (1980). American Sign Language and Pidgin Sign English: What's the difference? *Sign Language Studies, 27,* 151–192.
Reilly, J. S., & McIntire, M. L. (1991). WHERE SHOE: The acquisition of wh-questions in American Sign Language. *Papers and Reports in Child Language Development, 30,* 104–111.
Reilly, J. S., McIntire, M. L., & Bellugi, U. (1990a). The acquisition of conditionals in American Sign Language: Grammaticized facial expressions. *Applied Psycholinguistics, 11*(4), 369–392.
Reilly, J. S., McIntire, M. L., & Bellugi, U. (1990b). Faces: The relationship between language and affect. In V. Volterra & C. J. Erting (Eds.), *From gesture to language in hearing and deaf children* (pp. 128–141). Berlin: Springer-Verlag.
Reilly, J. S., McIntire, M. L., & Bellugi, U. (1991). Baby face: A new perspective on universals in language acquisition. In P. Siple & S. D. Fischer (Eds.), *Theoretical issues in sign language research. Volume 2: Psychology* (pp. 9–23). Chicago: University of Chicago Press.
Rizzi, L. (1986). Null objects in Italian and the theory of *pro. Linguistic Inquiry, 17,* 501–557.
Sandler, W. (1993). Sign language and modularity. *Lingua, 89,* 315–351.
Schein, J., & Delk, T. (1974). *The deaf population of the United States.* Washington, DC: National Association of the Deaf.
Schick, B. S. (1987). *The acquisition of classifier predicates in American Sign Language.* Ph.D. dissertation, Purdue University.
Schick, B. S. (1990a). Classifier predicates in American Sign Language. *International Journal of Sign Linguistics, 1,* 15–40.
Schick, B. S. (1990b). The effects of morphological complexity on phonological simplification in ASL. *Sign Language Studies, 66,* 25–41.
Schick, B. S. (1990c). The effects of morphosyntactic structure on the acquisition of classifier predicates in ASL. In C. Lucas (Ed.), *Sign language research: Theoretical issues* (pp. 358–374). Washington, DC: Gallaudet University Press.
Schlesinger, H. S., & Meadow, K. P. (1972). *Sound and sign: Childhood deafness and mental health.* Berkeley: University of California Press.
Siedlecki, T., & Bonvillian, J. D. (1993a). Location, handshape, & movement: Young children's acquisition of the formational aspects of American Sign Language. *Sign Language Studies, 78,* 31–52.
Siedlecki, T., & Bonvillian, J. D. (1993b). Phonological deletion revisited: Errors in young children's two-handed signs. *Sign Language Studies, 80,* 223–242.
Singleton, J. L. (1989). *Restructuring of language from impoverished input: Evidence for linguistic compensation.* Ph.D. dissertation, University of Illinois at Urbana-Champaign.
Siple, P., & Akamatsu, C. T. (1991). Emergence of American Sign Language in a set of fraternal twins. In P. Siple & S. D. Fischer (Eds.), *Theoretical issues in sign language research, Volume 2: Psychology* (pp. 25–40). Chicago: University of Chicago Press.
Stokoe, W. C. (1960). Sign language structure: An outline of the visual communication systems of the American deaf. *Studies in linguistics: Occasional papers, Vol. 8.* Buffalo, NY: University of Buffalo.
Supalla, T. (1982). *Structure and acquisition of verbs of motion and location in American Sign Language.* Ph.D. dissertation, University of California, San Diego.

Supalla, T. (1986). The classifier system in American Sign Language. In C. Craig (Ed.), *Noun classes and categorization* (pp. 181–214). Philadelphia: John Benjamins.
vanHoek, K., O'Grady, L., Bellugi, U., & Norman, F. (1987). Innovative spatial morphology in deaf children's signing. *Papers and Reports on Child Language Development.*
vanHoek, K., O'Grady, L., Bellugi, U., & Norman, F. (1989). The acquisition of perspective shift and serial verbs. *Papers and Reports on Child Language Development.*
vanHoek, K., O'Grady, L., Bellugi, U., & Norman, F. (1990). Spatial and nonspatial referential cohesion. *Papers and Reports on Child Language Development.*
Volterra, V., & Caselli, M. C. C. (1985). From gestures and vocalizations to signs and words. In W. Stokoe & V. Volterra (Eds.), *SLR '83: Proceedings of the Third International Symposium on Sign Language Research* (pp. 1–9). Silver Spring, MD: Linstok Press.
Wang, Q., Lillo-Martin, D., Best, C. T., & Levitt, A. (1992). Null subject versus null object: Some evidence from the acquisition of Chinese and English. *Language Acquisition, 2*(3), 221–254.
Wilbur, R. B. (1987). *American Sign Language: Linguistic and applied dimensions.* Boston: College-Hill Press.
Willerman, R., & Meier, R. P. (1992). *Manual babbling in deaf and hearing infants.* Poster presented at the Fourth International Conference on Theoretical Issues in Sign Language Research, San Diego, CA.
Woodward, J. (1972). Implications for sociolinguistics research among the deaf. *Sign Language Studies, 1,* 1–7.

CHAPTER 17

THE BILINGUAL CHILD: SOME ISSUES AND PERSPECTIVES

Tej K. Bhatia and William C. Ritchie

I. INTRODUCTION

After Werner Leopold's assertion in the late 1940s that "Child language and infant bilingualism have so far only received marginal consideration from most linguistic scholars" (Leopold 1948, p. 1), there was, initially, a slow but steady growth in research on child language. Since the cognitive revolution of the 1960s, an explosion of research on child language acquisition has taken place. However, in the process of this growth, more often than not, research on the bilingual child has taken a back seat to the study of monolingual children. Romaine (1989, p. 165) and many others have observed that the research on child language is predominantly devoted to the monolingual child and that, too, to English. This neglect of bilingual children is readily evident just from the sheer number of studies devoted to this topic in comparison with those of monolingual children. One estimate is that out of about six hundred studies devoted to child language acquisition, only about ten works deal systematically with the bilingual child.

There are a number of reasons for this neglect, but the following two are noteworthy: First, the view has predominated that the phenomena of bilingualism are, in general, highly complex and therefore their study must await the satisfactory development of a theory of monolingual language acquisition. In other words, a better understanding of monolingualism is the key to an understanding of bilingualism in general, and the bilingual child in particular. Second, there are fundamental conceptual problems with bilingualism including the definition and measurement of the phenomenon. Therefore, so the argument goes, it is not wise to invest time and energy in the study of the bilingual child. In spite of these apparent obstacles, there is currently a renewed interest in childhood bilingualism. The main reasons for this new and encouraging development fall into two categories: theoretical and applied. As regards the theoretical reasons, the interest in the theory of grammars in contact and in universal grammar has grown rapidly in recent times, thus changing the nature of research on childhood bilingualism—which was predominantly descriptive as recently as the early 1990s. Applied reasons deal mostly with the effects of bilingualism on language development, socio-political aspects of educational practices, and changing perspectives on global and minority communities.

The main aim of this chapter is to present a comprehensive account of the complex nature of childhood bilingualism, ranging from its formal to its socio-psychological dimensions. At the same time, we attempt to present main trends in the study of early childhood bilingualism, while taking note of the major theoretical, analytical, and methodological findings and issues concerning language development in the bilingual child with a particular focus on the work of the last decade or so. Although we make some reference to the classic, monumental studies of Leopold and other early researchers when they are deemed appropriate for our discussion, no review article with goals such as those stated can provide a sufficient description of them to develop an appropriate appreciation of this research (and its context), on which the succeeding childhood bilingualism research capitalized. Therefore, readers interested in such details are referred to the original classic works. Also, it should be stressed that no attempt is made here to review the theoretical developments and important findings prior to the 1980s, as they are easily accessible from the following important works: Redlinger (1979), Lindholm (1980), Wode (1981) and McLaughlin (1984b).

Following Chomsky (1986 and elsewhere) we take the central questions in the study of language to be the following four: What constitutes the knowledge of a particular language? How is this knowledge put to use in the production and recognition of speech? How is it acquired? How is it represented in the brain? Though these are generally conceived of as questions about monolinguals, we set them with respect to bilinguals as well: How are the bilingual's two (or more) systems of linguistic knowledge organized both separately and in relation to each other? How does possession of two systems of linguistic knowledge affect the mental processes that underlie speech recognition and production? How do the two systems interact at various stages in the attainment of bilinguality? Finally, how are the two systems represented in the brain as indicated by the ways in which various forms of brain damage affect linguistic performance in the two languages? In addition to these questions, research on bilingualism must address the problems of the effects of bilingualism on cognitive functioning and on the social determinants of various forms of bilingual linguistic behavior. These questions will be addressed either directly or indirectly with special reference to the bilingual child.

This chapter presents a state-of-the-art review of research on childhood bilingualism. Section II deals with the problems of defining bilingualism, whereas Section III outlines the reasons for studying this topic. Key assumptions and claims regarding language development are sketched in Section IV. Sections V and VI deal with the input and input conditions under which bilingual language development takes place. A comparative look at language development in monolingual and bilingual children is outlined in Section VII. The central issue of the formal relationship between two linguistic systems in bilingual children together with initial and final stages of the two grammars is detailed in Section VIII. The question of bilingual language development in deaf children is addressed in Section IX. Language mixing in children and speech disorders are treated in Sections X and XI, respectively. Finally, Section XII presents some concluding remarks and needs for future research.

II. SOME BASIC QUESTIONS

A. What Is Bilingualism?

When it comes to defining bilingualism, one is instantly reminded of the expression, so close yet so far away. There is no widely accepted definition or measure of bilingualism and bilinguals, including bilingualism in children. Not only in our society in general but in the linguistic sciences as well, bilinguals are subject to more severe evaluationary and categorical judgments than monolinguals. The rich range of characterizations of bilinguals found in the research literature—scales, categories and dichotomies such as receptive versus productive, early versus late, fluent and nonfluent, functional and nonfunctional, balanced and unbalanced, primary versus secondary, partial and complete, coordinate and compound, and so on—confirm our claim. Although all these terms are equally applicable to monolinguals, as no monolingual native speaker has equal control over all varieties of his or her language, definitional terms and classificatory labels in the linguistic literature are more charitable to monolinguals than to bilinguals.

Throughout this chapter, unless mentioned otherwise, we will use the working definition of bilingualism offered by Bloomfield (1933, p. 56), "native-like control of two languages." Other scholars have suggested that the criterion for bilingualism should be native control of both languages. However, full native control of two languages represents an ideal form of bilingualism that is rarely achieved. Therefore, the term "native-like control" is used in the sense of a balanced bilingual with an appropriate pragmatic dominance of one language—distinct from the term "balance" in the absolute sense. (For more details about the conceptual problems of defining and measuring bilingualism, see Bhatia & Ritchie, 1996a; Romaine, 1996.)

The fact that some deaf children have near-native control of two languages (a spoken/written language and a sign language) and are therefore bilingual under the usual definition is often neglected in deaf education and bilingual research, as is evident in the following remarks: "In deaf education today, 'signs' are recognized to a small degree, yet their place remains unclear. 'Signs' are allowed as long as they accompany and assist vocal language communication" (Bouvet, 1990, p. 230). This chapter does not exclude sign languages used by deaf children as languages, and therefore recognizes that a child who has nativelike control of both a spoken/written language and a signed language is a bilingual in the true sense.

B. What/Who Is a Bilingual Child?

In distinguishing the study of monolingual children from that of bilingual children, it is necessary to take into account the following four critical features of bilingual language acquisition: (a) the amount and type of input from each of the two languages, (b) the possibility of an asymmetry or dominance of one language over the other, (c) the interaction or separation of the two linguistic systems, and (d) socio-psychological factors in bilingual acquisition and use.

Amount and Type of Input from Each Language

The primary linguistic data for a monolingual child consists in ambient linguistic evidence grounded in the grammar of a single language while two languages serve as the input source for a bilingual child. Hence, input in the case of a monolingual child is relatively uniform and homogeneous. Heterogeneity of linguistic input constitutes the defining feature of bilingual acquisition. Furthermore, the input to the bilingual children is always divided, so that the quantity of his or her exposure to each language is much smaller at any given time than that of the monolingual child and, in addition, the input from each language is intermittent with that from the other.

What is also noteworthy about the input source of the bilingual child is that it is either separate (two sources—father speaking one language and mother another; two groups with two distinct languages, thus diglossic) or mixed (both mother and father and all other sources alternating between the two languages). The various input-related differences are shown diagrammatically in Figure 17.1. Depending on the degree and manner of exposure to input from birth, each bilingual child represents a different point on that continuum, which gives rise to different results for the acquisition process in each child.

From the viewpoint of input language, amount of input, input type, and temporal exposure, the bilingual child is not just a clone of two monolingual children. However, as we will show later, in spite of these differences, if these variables stay constant, early bilinguals are remarkably close to two monolinguals in terms of the

Monolingual Child
Single Input

L_a Input → UG → Output

Bilingual Child

L_a
Separate Input → UG → Output
L_b

Single/Separate but mixed input

Figure 17.1. Input conditions for monolinguals and bilinguals.

development of formal features and mechanisms of language acquisition (i.e., in the development of phonology and syntax; see Section VII for details).

Asymmetry/Dominance between the Two Systems

As might already be self-evident from our discussion of the definition of bilingualism, when the two language systems are fully developed to form the linguistic and pragmatic competence of an adult bilingual, they do not form a symmetrical relationship. Due to socio-psychological factors (some members of the society favoring one linguistic system over the other) or temporal and input relationships (lack of equal exposure to the two languages from birth), one system invariably holds the upper hand over the other and in that sense an asymmetrical dominance relationship is found between the two participating linguistic systems. Consequently, one of the bilingual child's languages becomes dominant though he or she is competent in both.

There are two aspects of this dominance: grammar dominance and discourse dominance:

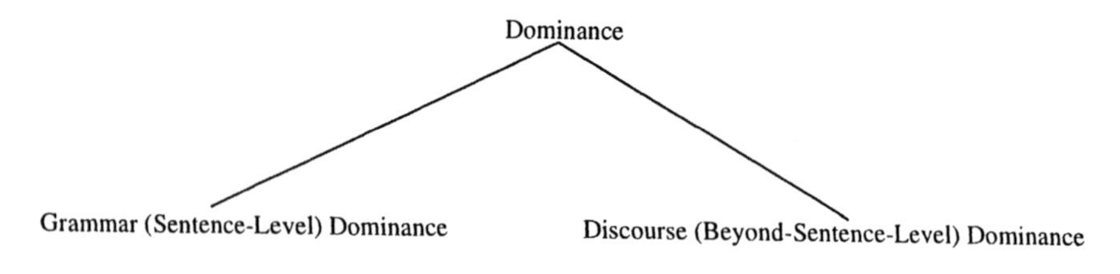

If a bilingual child is not exposed to both languages from birth, the consequence may be the dominance of one language over the other due to differentiated exposure over time. This may result in a delay in the development of either or both languages compared to the development of each language found separately in monolinguals. Such delays give rise to what is sometimes referred to in the research literature as "semilingualism," "subtractive bilingualism," "double semilingualism," or "interference." The limiting case of linguistic dominance is the attrition or loss of the nondominant system (see Halmari, 1992; Seliger, 1989, 1996).

As regards discourse dominance, one language may be seen by the bilingual as more appropriate or better suited in a given situation with respect to audience, topic, situation, and so on. The different usage of the two languages is subject to different domain and function allocations. That is why a bilingual child may feel more comfortable talking to a particular individual in one language rather than another or might find one language better suited to a particular task or activity (e.g., playing with toy characters). Although one cannot rule out the notion of equal status of the two linguistic systems in some contexts for a bilingual child, the dominance of one system cannot be denied in the overall interactional domain of a bilingual child. For additional discussion of the complexity of dominance, see the next section.

Interaction and Separation of the Two Linguistic Systems

Like any other bilingual, the bilingual child is not only capable of keeping the two linguistic systems separate once his or her grammatical competence reaches its ultimate point, but he or she can also employ these two systems interactively. The result is code mixing and code switching behavior on the part of bilinguals whether they are children or adults. This behavior is discussed in detail in Section X.

Interaction and separation modes can be represented as in Figure 17.2 (Grosjean, to appear). The interaction or separation of two linguistic systems—that is, the activation of both languages or the activation of one language and suppression of the other, respectively—results in the complex bilingual verbal behavior illustrated in Figure 17.2 The figure represents the two languages of a bilingual (i.e., Languages A and B in the figure) in each one of a sequence of states as a square

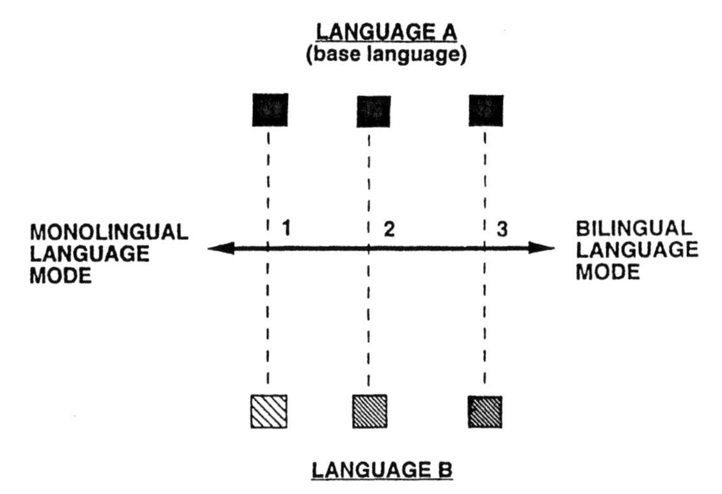

Figure 17.2. Interaction of the two languages of a bilingual.

located on the top and the bottom of the figure and their level of activation is represented by the degree of darkness of the square: black for the fully active Language A, while shades ranging from a very light gray at the left end of the sequence to almost black at the right end for the less active Language B. The dotted lines show three hypothetical positions (Number 1–3) for the same speaker. In all positions, the speaker is using Language A as the main language of communication (the base or matrix language) and this language is, therefore, most active (black square) throughout the sequence. In Position 1, the speaker is in a monolingual mode: Language A is fully activated whereas Language B is fully deactivated. This mode is found when a bilingual interacts with a monolingual speaker of the active language or deals with a topic or situation where only one language is seen as suitable and the other is not. In Position 2, the speaker is in an intermediate mode. Language A is still the more active language but Language B is also partly activated—for example, when the bilingual is interacting with a person with limited knowledge of the other language. In Position 3, the speaker is toward the more bilingual end of the continuum, where both languages are activated, but Language B is slightly less active than Language A; both interlocutors are fully bilingual. By extending this sequence to a Position 4 one could represent a case in which both languages are equally active and shifting occurs between the two languages whenever deemed necessary with respect to topic, interlocutor, and so on.

Socio-Psychological Factors: Progression and Regression Phenomena

Depending on changes in socio-psychological factors, the bilingual child may exhibit regression and progression of the two participating linguistic systems. For example, in Leopold's classic longitudinal case study (Leopold, 1939–1949), when Hildegard was in Germany her English retreated to such an extent that she could use it only to count. Her experience in playing transactional games in English with her mother become so frustrating that she finally had to admit, sadly, "Mutti, ich kann gar nicht mehr englisch sprechen" (English translation: "Mommy, I can't speak English at all any more."). However, the same child on her return to the United States revived her English without much struggle and later on her German begins to yield in favor of English. The accounts of other bilingual children show that, in the case of extreme culture shock, one system may be totally turned off (cf. input deprivation in the case of deaf children of hearing parents, see Section IX).

These four properties, which distinguish bilingual from monolingual language acquisition, set the stage for variable linguistic performance both within each of the child's two languages and between them. Such variability has, in the past, led society to ask whether or not bilingual children suffer somehow from social and intellectual disadvantages in comparison with their monolingual peers. However, answers to this and other similar questions are beyond the scope of this chapter.[1] Instead, we will move to the question of why researchers should study the bilingual child at all.

III. WHY STUDY THE BILINGUAL CHILD?

The proliferation of terms used to refer to bilingual children highlights the complexity of bilingualism in children and adults alike. These terms refer to a variety of factors (age, context of acquisition, etc.; see Section V) essential to the characterization of the complex influences on differential language use and acquisition in the bilingual. Though many earlier myths about a putative causal link between bilingualism on one hand and linguistic and cognitive deficits among bilingual children on the other have been discredited (see, e.g., Peal & Lambert, 1962, for early discussion), the complex interaction of the variables involved in the acquisition of two languages by children is still far from clear. Given these circumstances, one might be tempted to conclude that the topic of the bilingual child is too fluid to be worthy of systematic investigation. On the contrary, the work reviewed in this chapter provides ample evidence that such a conclusion would be premature, misguided, and unnecessarily pessimistic.

In fact, there is good reason to believe that the study of the bilingual child can

[1]For questions and answers on this and similar topics, see Peal and Lambert (1962), Cummins (1978), Saunders (1988, pp. 5–6, 14–25), Hakuta & Diaz (1985), Hakuta (1986, preface), and many others.

help to solve certain methodological problems in areas of research that are currently more intensively pursued. As was pointed out in the opening paragraphs of this chapter, the bilingual child has taken a back seat to the monolingual child in child acquisition research. In cross-linguistic studies that aim at examining the role of language-specific and language-universal factors in language acquisition, there may be methodological justification for preferring the study of the monolingual child over that of the bilingual child. One might argue that a bilingual child is exposed to a wide variety of socio-psychological factors in the process of acquiring two languages that add confounding variables that cannot be held constant in carrying out a meaningful comparison between the language development patterns found in both bilingual and monolingual children.

On the other hand, De Houwer (1990, p. 1) argued convincingly that the study of bilingual children offers a unique opportunity to resolve general issues in the study of language acquisition. Her argument is that a child growing up with two languages constitutes the "perfect matched pair," because the number of possible variables affecting the acquisition of each of the two language is "reduced to a minimum." Because the acquisition of two systems is taking place in a single organism, nonlinguistic cognitive factors are held constant for the acquisition of both languages. Levy (1985), Meisel (1990b), Hayashi (1992), and others have come to the same conclusion concerning the theoretical importance of the careful study of the bilingual child.[2]

Furthermore, careful consideration of the phenomena of bilingualism leads to a reexamination of notions such as that of "native speaker" that are currently applied in linguistic theory and child language research. For example, Ferguson (1992) noted that, in the usual case, those exposed to a given language from birth (i.e., its native speakers) maintain control over its "future structure and use by their own usage and their beliefs about the language." (p. xvi). However, Ferguson described the case of Swahili, where the usage of those who are native speakers and descendants of native speakers has been replaced by a new, standard Swahili, the structure and use of which is dictated by nonnative and new native speakers as a consequence of widespread bilingualism and the rise of new power structures. In this case, who counts as a native speaker of Swahili?[3]

Given this theoretical and methodological background, the importance of these

[2]In an article that appeared too late to be reviewed in detail in this chapter, Paradis and Genesee (1997) gave a similar arguement for the importance of evidence from the study of bilingual children in choosing between continuity and maturation (growth) theories of child language acquisition (see chapters 1 through 4 of this volume for general discussion). Specifically, they found the acquisition of the functional categories "Inflection" and "Determiner" in their two French-English bilingual children to be compatible with continuity but not with maturation.

[3]Other problems with the notion of "native speaker" exist in some cases of bilingual individuals. The first author of this chapter was first exposed to Multani, a regional variety of Panjabi. However, at the age of 4 years he was moved to a Hindi-speaking area. As an adult he is less secure in Multani than

issues in the practical educational and clinical response to childhood bilingualism can hardly be overestimated. Assessment methods and measures used by educators and clinicians are still largely monolingual and monocultural. Therefore, the validity of these methods is questionable and basic research on the bilingual child should be expected to make significant contributions in this area (see Cheng, 1996; Miller, 1984).

In addition, in view of the current (and likely future) rapid growth of global communication, it is hardly necessary to point out that the majority of the population of the world conducts its day-to-day activities, not in one but more than one language. Not only is bilingual verbal behavior a natural outcome of global language contact, it is, once established, as natural as eating, drinking or walking (see Grosjean, 1982, and many others). This means that any research program that neglects the bilingual child unnecessarily restricts the scope of research on child language acquisition.

IV. KEY ASSUMPTIONS AND CLAIMS

Before we begin to discuss language development among bilingual children and how children become bilingual, it is crucial to summarize key assumptions, hypotheses, and claims about language acquisition in general and bilingual children in particular.

A. Universal Grammar and the Principles-and-Parameters Framework

Since the mentalistic revolution in linguistics in the 1960s, there has been unanimous agreement among linguists that the human child is born to speak. Mysteriously, every normal child regardless of its race, gender, color, or geography is capable at birth of acquiring any human language. What is even more intriguing is that children can acquire languages with amazing ease and efficiency. The reason that children can acquire human language with such ease is that humans are "prewired" to acquire human languages. This innate prewiring takes the form of a system of principles that determine the range of biologically possible systems of grammatical knowledge for any human language. The term for this innate system in theoretical studies is universal grammar (UG).

In the process of acquiring language, the role of input is important but limited. Universal principles of grammatical structure and principles of learning guide lan-

---

in Hindi, of which he would now regard himself to be a native speaker. Such cases call for a more nuanced notion of "native speaker" than is currently used.

guage development and all input does is trigger appropriate values for innately given parameters, these parameter values being specific to the language to which the child is exposed (for more detail, see Section VIII).

B. The Critical Period Hypothesis and Its Biological Basis

It has frequently been observed that normal children acquire a language (whether first, second, third, or a language learned later) completely and relatively effortlessly, whereas adults are seldom able to do so in spite of considerable effort and motivation. To explain this and other observations about age-related differences in language acquisition and recovery from aphasia, Lenneberg (1967) proposed the critical period hypothesis, which claims that there is a period in the maturation of the human organism, lasting from approximately two years to puberty, during which effortless and complete language acquisition is possible on the basis of exposure to primary linguistic data and before and after which it is not possible (see also Penfield & Roberts, 1959; Long, 1990; and Schachter, 1996, for recent discussion of maturational effects on late language acquisition).

Lenneberg proposed that the end of the critical period is determined by a loss of brain plasticity—in particular by the completion of the lateralization of the language function in the left hemisphere. However, the lateralization claim was criticized convincingly early on by Harshman and Krashen (1972), Krashen (1973), and others on the basis of evidence that lateralization of the language function occurs by 5 years of age or earlier.

Recent work by Helen Neville and her colleagues using event-related brain potentials (ERPs) as evidence (e.g., Neville, Coffee, Lawson, Fischer, Emmorey, & Bellugi, 1997; Neville, Mills, & Lawson, 1992) explores a possible brain-maturational basis for differences in sentence processing between early-acquired and late-acquired languages. Weber-Fox and Neville (1996) tested 61 native speakers of Chinese who had first been exposed to English at ages ranging from birth to more than 16 years of age. They used a measure of ERP during the subjects' performance of grammaticality judgments on four different types of sentences that included both semantic and syntactic violations in addition to well-formed control sentences.

In association with the processing of (lexical-) semantically control (well-formed) and anomalous sentences, they found strong similarities among monolinguals, early bilinguals (onset of the second language between birth and 10 years of age), and late bilinguals (for whom onset of the second language was at 11 years of age and beyond), with respect to ERP configurations in parietal and anterior temporal regions of the brain. On the other hand, a number of ERP *dis*similarities appeared in the processing by the same subjects of sentences that were either well-formed or anomalous with respect to both language-universal and language-specific syntactic constraints, including language-specific phrase structure principles and universal constraints on wh-movement. These dissimilarities were found in the concentration of activity in the left anterior temporal region of the brain, where monolinguals and early bilinguals showed considerably more concentrated activity during the processing of these syntactic properties than did the late bilinguals. Weber-Fox and Neville concluded that reduction in the ability to attain the syntax of a second language after puberty is due to brain-maturational events producing these differences in concentrated activity. Other aspects of sentence processing—specifically, the processing of lexical semantics—are left relatively unaffected by these maturational processes.

If, as suggested in Section II.A above, we take a bilingual to be one who has nativelike control of two languages, then, clearly, a person who has acquired his or her second language after puberty is extremely unlikely to qualify, given the apparent existence of a critical period ending at that age. But are there critical periods for aspects of grammatical structure that end *before* puberty? Some research by Weber-Fox and Neville and others suggested that there are such critical periods.

Weber-Fox and Neville (1996) not only found differences between prepubertals and pubertal/postpubertal bilinguals in the processing of syntactic constraints (as discussed earlier), they also found differences among early and late prepubertals in the processing of different kinds of syntactic constraints. In particular, the ERP patterns for phrase structure violations and controls were affected in subjects first exposed as early as 4 years of age and for a specificity constraint on wh-movement at 11 years. These results suggest that there are multiple critical periods for language acquisition, some of which end prepubertally (see, e.g., Seliger, 1978, for discussion of multiple critical periods).

Clearly, behavioral evidence for prepubertal critical periods is of considerable importance in the study of child bilingualism as well. In fact, two studies by Johnson and Newport (1989, 1991) bear directly on this issue.[4] Johnson and Newport (1989) reported a study of the ultimate attainment of certain language-specific structures of English by native speakers of Chinese and Korean. These subjects were chosen because of the typological dissimilarity between Chinese and Korean on one hand and English on the other, the purpose being to reduce as much as possible any facilitating effects from the first language. The subjects, who were selected from the student and faculty population of an American university, were divided into four categories according to their age of first exposure to English: 4 to 7 years, 8 to 10, 11 to 15, and 16 and beyond. Native controls were included among

[4]It should be noted that Weber-Fox and Neville ran behavioral tests on their subjects in conjunction with the studies of ERPs referred to in the text. However, the results from some of their tests for subjacency are questionable as indicators of loss of subjacency in late bilinguals because lower performance on these tests was based mostly in rejection of well-formed control sentences rather than on sentences in which subjacency was violated.

the subjects as well. All subjects were presented aurally with 276 utterances, approximately half of which were grammatical and half ungrammatical with respect to 12 language-specific features of English morphology and syntax: plural, third-person singular, and present progressive morphology and the syntax of determiners, pronoun case and agreement, particle movement, subcategorization, auxiliaries, yes/no questions, wh-questions, and word order. Whereas the performance on this task by subjects who were first exposed to English between 3 and 7 years of age did not differ significantly from that of native speakers on any of the 12 structures, the performance of those who were first exposed at age 8 or beyond showed what they interpret as maturational effects with respect to specific grammatical structures. Those in the 8 to 10 group differed significantly from natives only in their mastery of determiners; those in the 11 to 15 group showed a significant difference from native speakers not only in their mastery of determiners but in plural and past-tense morphology and in subcategorization and a number of other areas as well.

Having investigated the ultimate attainment of language-specific structures, Johnson and Newport turned their attention (Johnson & Newport, 1991) to possible maturational effects on the implementation of a universal condition on wh-movement—the subjacency condition, which distinguishes the grammaticality of (1b) from the ungrammaticality of (1c), where both are related to (1a).

(1) a. The policemen [who found Cathy] should get a reward.
 b. What should the policeman [who found Cathy] get ____?
 c. *Who should the policemen [who found ____] get a reward?

The results of Johnson and Newport (1991) show a continuous decline in performance from native through adult acquisition though the 4 to 7 first-exposure group did not differ significantly in performance from native speakers. On the other hand, those with first exposure at 8 years and beyond show a significant decrease in performance with respect to subjacency.

Though a full review of the literature on early critical periods is beyond the scope of this chapter, the work of Johnson and Newport suggests that children up to the age of 7 years are indistinguishable from native speakers in the acquisition of the structures and conditions that they investigated. If these results are replicated for other structures and conditions, then one would be justified in claiming that any child first exposed to a second language before the age of 7 who subsequently received sufficient input (with "sufficiency of input" to be determined empirically) qualifies as a bilingual with respect to grammatical competence.

Finally, we recognize that the capacity for the acquisition of aspects of language use other than grammatical competence may have different maturational timetables. Nonetheless, we propose the kind of results and analysis discussed here as a model for the investigation of other aspects of bilingual acquisition and performance with respect to distinguishing true bilinguals from nonbilinguals.

C. Acquisition versus Learning

Some second language acquisition researchers (most prominently, Krashen [e.g., 1981]) have argued for a distinction between two types of language development: a subconscious process resulting in tacit knowledge of the language (*language acquisition*) and a more conscious process (*language learning*) that is claimed to result in a conscious system that serves as the basis for monitoring utterance representations for well-formedness during the process of sentence production. Language acquisition in this sense is the process found in children under the ordinary circumstances of natural exposure to primary linguistic data. Language learning, on the other hand, is thought to be found most typically in adults developing a language in the formal environment of the classroom. The capacity for language learning is claimed by some to arise only at puberty, perhaps as a consequence of the onset of Piagetian formal operations (Krashen, 1982), whereas the capacity for language acquisition is at its height during the critical period (from approximately 2 years of age to puberty as noted earlier).

The acquisition/learning distinction in the form proposed in Krashen's work (and described briefly earlier) has been severely criticized in the second-language research literature (Gregg, 1984 and many others) as lacking specific empirical content. On the other hand, Schwartz and Gubala-Ryzak (1992) and Schwartz (1993) have argued convincingly that—in a specific, well-studied case—negative evidence in the form of classroom instructions to avoid particular structures in a second language is generalized by 10- and 11-year olds in a way that is quite distinct from the ways in which principles of UG are generalized. This suggests that the internalized results of such instructions have a character that is quite different from the principles of UG as they are instantiated in the tacit knowledge of particular languages—a difference which is, arguably, related to the acquisition/learning distinction in some form.[5]

V. INPUT CONDITIONS

We have touched on the question of input in Section II.A. Input types in bilingual child language acquisition are determined by a number of factors, which are outlined in this section. Although the question of the role of these factors in determining exactly how input is manifested is not clear at this point in research, nevertheless it is clear that some factors are more critical than others. Among other things, careful consideration of the research literature on child bilingualism shows

[5]See Emonds (1986) and Sobin (1994, 1997), who argued for the existence of self-editing operations ("virusses") in native speakers that constitute the mental representations of prescriptive rules and may be "learned" in something like Krashen's sense.

that some basic phenomena such as parent language are addressed in a very informal or anecdotal fashion in this research. This is an important methodological flaw, which can prove to be misleading in the interpretation of results obtained from language acquisition studies on childhood bilingualism and our understanding of the typology of bilingual children.

A. Natural versus Unnatural Setting

In societies such as that of India—where bilingualism is viewed as natural and is widely encouraged, approved, and applauded by society and stimulated further by government educational policies—linguistic groups or communities do not have to take special measures to ensure that children receive input from two languages on a regular basis. However, in settings where the language of a minority group is distinct from that of the majority community, which does not view the (minority) family language as valuable (such as in the United States), minority families and communities must adopt strategies of linguistic interaction to ensure the flow of input from the family language as well as from the majority community language. One such strategy—which we will refer to as the "domain allocation strategy"—restricts the use of one language to one social agent or social setting and the other language to other social situations. The various versions of this strategy are the following: (a) one-parent/one-language (the child's mother speaks one language, the child's father speaks the other; adopted by Leopold, 1939–1949), (b) one-place/one-language (e.g., use of the family language in the living room and the other language elsewhere), (c) a language/time approach, and (d) a topic-related approach. Because domain allocation is, at least sometimes, the by-product of an unnatural environment (e.g., home only, Sunday school only), it leads to a pattern of input for childhood bilingualism that is different from that provided by a more natural environment.

B. Formal Setting: School and Media

The result of exposing the child to a second language only by means of formal teaching in schools is sometimes referred as late bilingualism. Skutnabb-Kangas (1984) drew a dichotomy between natural and school bilingualism. We prefer the term "school language" to designate a language that the child has acquired formally in an institutional setting.

C. Age and Time

Other factors such as age and amount of exposure to the two languages lead to differences in the pattern of childhood bilingualism. The terms *simultaneous* and *sequential* are widely used in the linguistic literature to refer to two different sets of conditions for the development of bilingualism. The process of acquisition whereby the child has more or less equal exposure to both languages from birth is referred to as *simultaneous* (with the term *birth* to be taken in a somewhat vague and fluid sense). Similarly, the term *sequential* indicates that the child is exposed to one language first and the second language sometime later. The terms *early* and *late* bilingualism have also been used to refer to this distinction. The term *early bilingualism* is associated with simultaneous infant or early childhood bilingualism. *Late bilingualism* is also used to distinguish between those sequential bilinguals who attain their second language at a relatively young age from those who acquire a second language as adults.

In spite of the fact that researchers are in almost unanimous agreement about the importance of the difference between simultaneous and sequential bilingualism for theoretical and methodological reasons, this distinction has become the object of more rigorous scrutiny only recently because there is no consensus among scholars about the exact line of demarcation between the two. McLaughlin (1984a) proposed the third birthday as a cutoff point to distinguish between the simultaneous and successive acquisition of two languages. That is, a child exposed to two languages any time before the age of 3 years constitutes a case of simultaneous acquisition and afterwards it is viewed as an instance of successive acquisition. In proposing this distinction, McLaughlin admitted that such a demarcation point is arbitrary. Padilla and Lindholm (1984) rejected this arbitrary criterion and favored birth as the determining point for the distinction between simultaneous and successive or consecutive language acquisition. However, Padilla and Lindholm's criterion is clearly equally arbitrary because, like any such distinction, it is subject to empirical investigation to show that, in fact, a child exposed to the second language after, say, 6 months shows a different pattern of language acquisition and use from a child who is exposed to the second language from birth and that this difference in pattern is traceable to differences in age of onset of exposure to the second language.

De Houwer (1995) rejected terms such as *simultaneous* in referring to the acquisition of two languages. Her main reason is that the term has been used "with different meanings by different authors." It is not readily clear when a researcher states that a child is "simultaneously exposed to two languages" whether exposure to both languages took place soon after birth or whether exposure to one of the languages was delayed until some time between birth and age 3. For this reason, she has favored the use of Meisel's term "Bilingual First Language Acquisition" (BFLA) to refer to the process of acquisition in a child exposed to two languages from birth. On the analogy of this term, she proposed to use "Bilingual Second Language Acquisition" (BSLA) to mean that a second language exposure starts "no earlier than one month after birth, but before the age two." (De Houwer, 1995, p. 223).

The notion of BSLA is not free from problems—specifically, it carries the danger of being confused with adult second language acquisition—though the suggestion clearly lies in the right direction. Although the distinction De Houwer is attempting to draw is in need of empirical support, the determination of the time of exposure to the second language is an important one for the interpretation and comparison of results in establishing the influence of the age of onset and subsequent length of exposure on the language development pattern of the bilingual child. To eliminate the potential ambiguity involving the terms "Bilingual First Language" and "Bilingual Second Language," we propose the use of the terms "Child First Language(s)" (CFL) and "Child Second Language" (CSL) instead to eliminate redundancy and the potential ambiguity present in the terms proposed by Meisel.

On the somewhat arbitrary view that the child's utterances are truly linguistic only when they clearly carry semantic content, we choose full exposure to two languages by the one-word stage as our criterion for simultaneous acquisition with the understanding that a more significant empirical basis for distinguishing simultaneous from sequential acquisition may be found in the future—perhaps in terms of one or more (prepubertal) critical periods as suggested in Section IV.B. (See Section IV.B for more, detailed discussion of this issue.)

D. Other Input Factors and the Typology of Childhood Bilingualism

Having noted the importance of time exposure to the first and second language of the child, let us examine some other factors that can influence the pattern of language input to the bilingual child and consequently influence his or her language acquisition process. A number of external factors such as migration, schooling, nationalism and political federalism, intermarriages, urbanization, linguistic plurality in the region, family and community, perception of ethnic languages, and bilingualism (See Grosjean 1982, chapter 1, for details) play important but varying roles in determining the nature of the linguistic input provided to a child. Although the exact role of these influences in child language development is far from clear, Romaine (1989, pp. 166–168) identified three important factors in input for bilingual language acquisition: (a) the language(s) that parents employ in their interaction with their child(ren), (b) the parents' native language(s), and (c) the extent to which the parent's language(s) reflect the language(s) of the community. Although the role of the parent language is important, it needs to be put into proper perspective. We should point out in passing that the linguistic literature takes a very simplistic and ethnocentric approach to the role of parents' language(s) and in the process attaches too much importance to the role of the parents' language on one hand and underestimates the role of the languages of the other members of the family, particularly in those traditional societies where joint families are still the norm. Furthermore, the literature often fails to take into account the actual situation even in changing western societies. The following discussion will further clarify the point that we are making.

Consider the profile of a bilingual child growing up in India. Nair (1984) dealt with the language development of a bilingual child in New Delhi, India. In addition to his parents, the child lived in a house with grandparents, uncle, and aunt as well as nonfamily members employed by the family to work in the house. His father spoke Bengali and his mother, Malayalam, and both had been educated in the United Kingdom for several years; Hindi and English served as link languages between the two parents. The other languages to which the child was exposed were the following: standard Hindi, Harayanavi (a dialect of Hindi), Indian English, Punjabi, and Oriya. The greatest exposure was to standard Hindi and educated Indian English. Although the language of the parents—who spoke mixed languages and code switched between their native languages and English—is important, what is a more important factor is the method of child rearing in India. Almost immediately after the birth of the child, the mother's mother-in-law usually takes charge of the child, particularly during the first 40 days, in which the mother's role is to feed the child and rest. The child sleeps with his paternal grandmother. The child is under the supervision of the grandmother most of the time. This pattern continues even after the first 40 days if both parents work. In this way the child is exposed more to the language of the grandparents or the other caretakers or household employees than to the language of the parents.

Similarly, the children of the first author of this chapter spent more time in day care (from 8 in the morning to 5:30 in the evening)—where caretakers spoke primarily English and some French—than they did with their English- and Hindi-speaking parents. In short, one should not lose sight of the fact that the language of the parents may play a lesser role in those traditional societies where joint families are still very strong and those western societies where new economic realities are emerging. Thus, what is critical is the actual pattern of the input exposure rather than either the language of the parents or even the dominant language of the community.

De Houwer (1995, pp. 224–225) made a similar point:

> [I]t is not enough to know what language each person used with the child, but in addition it is important to find out approximately *how much time* [our emphasis] the main input carriers each spent with the child. If, for instance, in a claimed one parent/one language situation the child's father hardly ever spent any time with his young baby, and if the father was the sole input carrier of his language, then, it is doubtful that the child actually regularly heard two languages spoken from an earlier age onwards.

Hence, it is not sufficient to know the dominant language of the community but the language that was actually used with a child. If, for instance, one analyzes the linguistic pattern of Delhi, English is ranked quite low among the languages spoken there overall. However, English is quite dominant among educated residents and among those families whose members do not share Hindi as a language. In the absence of an actual analysis of who is talking to a child, when, for how long, and why and in what linguistic form, one might arrive at misleading conclusions about the input language. (For an overview of the linguistic situation in India and the context of multilingualism there, see Bhatia, 1982.)

On the basis of the three factors mentioned earlier together with the pure versus mixed nature of bilingual language input, Romaine (1989, pp. 166–168) proposed the following six types of childhood bilingualism based on an overview of studies devoted to childhood bilingualism.

Type 1 "one person—one language"
Type 2 "Non-dominant home language"
Type 3 "Non-dominant home language without community support"
Type 4 "Double non-dominant home language without community support"
Type 5 "Non-native parents"
Type 6 "Mixed languages"

The analysis of the pattern of bilingualism of the Indian bilingual child studied by Nair (1984) reveals that the actual pattern is more complex than is envisioned by the preceding typology. She reported that the case of her subject incorporates features of Type 2 (parents have different languages—Bengali and Malayalam), of Type 4 (community language is Hindi), and of Type 6 (parents code-mix and code-switch with English). It should also be noted that the differential use of more than one language reported by Nair gave the child's linguistic input a mosaic-like character. In short, in this case we witness much more complexity than is envisioned in the present literature.

VI. INPUT AND STAGES OF BILINGUAL LANGUAGE DEVELOPMENT

In this section we will examine some central issues pertaining to the relationship between input and bilingual language acquisition.

A. Separation versus Lack of Separation in Input

There are two major aspects of bilingual linguistic competence. Not only can bilinguals keep the two linguistic systems separate, but they can also mix them in a skillful fashion. Because the bilingual child's input can range from mixed (code-mixed or pidgin-creole types) to the neatly separated output of separate linguistic systems (in the case of a one-parent/one-language environment), the question arises as to how the bilingual child arrives at separate linguistic systems from mixed input. What, if anything, can caretakers do to promote the acquisition of separate systems? The underlying assumption has been that if caretakers keep the two systems apart, then the task of separating the two languages will be made easier for the child. For this reason, it has been argued by many researchers that adoption of a one parent/one language strategy is the best way to ensure problem-free language development in bilingual children. Among the notable proponents of this input separation condition are Bain and Yu (1980), Kielhöfer and Jonekeit (1983), Clyne (1987), Lebrun and Paradis (1984), Karniol (1992), and others. Clyne terms this method "the interlocutor principle." Bain and Yu (1980, p. 313) go to the extent of setting the time frame for language separation. According to them, if the languages are "kept distinctly apart by the parents over approximately the first three and a half years of the child's life, native-like control of both languages tends to accrue." (de Houwer, 1995, pp. 225–226). The strong proponents of this approach go on to warn that mixed input may lead to a stuttering disorder in bilingual children (Karniol, 1992; Lebrun & Paradis, 1984).

We would like to take issue with this approach and the claims made about the adverse effects of mixed input on bilingual children. First, it is misleading to claim that only the separation of input from the two languages leads to nativelike control of both of them. In fact, such an input condition may create a socially unnatural setting for language use, which can lead to a failure to acquire pragmatic competence on the part of bilingual children. They may develop nativelike control over two languages in terms of linguistic competence; however, they may fall short of sociolinguistic or pragmatic competence in the two target languages. This is self-evident from the remarks of Hildegard (4;0), "Mother, do all dads speak German?" (Leopold, 1978, p. 28). Therefore, one parent/one language has its own serious limitations.

Second, studies on adult code switching indicate that language mixing is the rule and not the exception, even though adults may deny mixing the two languages. As Idiazábal (1984) pointed out, mixed input is inevitable because the separation of the two input languages is impossible in the absolute sense and thus the one-parent/one-language input condition is not feasible. This observation is confirmed by Goodz, Bilodeau, and Legaré (1988) and Goodz's (1989) findings on the context of childhood bilingualism. Their recordings of the spontaneous conversations between the parents in bilingual families and their children revealed frequent use of mixed input by parents even though they reported the use of a single and separate language by each of them. In other words, reports of the use of one parent/one language do not assure the total separation of the two languages in actual practice.

Third, a number of studies show that failure to keep to the one-language/one-parent principle does not result in any linguistic deficiency in the child's use of the two languages. Garcia (1983) studied Spanish-English preschoolers who received English-Spanish mixed input from their mother but showed very little incidence of code switching and experienced no difficulty in keeping the two systems separate. The study by Nair (1984) of a bilingual child in India (referred to earlier) indicates that this child also received mixed input and his parents did not speak Hindi natively, yet the child seems to separate Hindi and English very systematically with ease, with the Hindi system always ahead of English during the development stages. (See Sections VII and VIII for detailed discussion.)

Fourth, the claim that the total separation of the two linguistic systems as an input condition best facilitates the acquisition of native competence in the two languages is too strong. It overlooks a significant portion of the global bilingual situation where mixed input is more natural than linguistically separated input. This is particularly true of nonwestern societies. There is no evidence of linguistic retardation or stuttering among those bilingual children who receive mixed input.

Fifth, the view that language separation in input is a necessary condition to ensure the child's native control over the two linguistic systems also underestimates his or her intrinsic ability to separate the two language systems. It is quite clear that children acquiring two languages do not rely on superficial and overt factors such as one parent/one language to separate their languages. They rely on their innate ability to perform tacit structural analyses of the two participating systems and can thus effectively separate them. As will be discussed in Section VIII, several studies indicate that bilingual children exhibit more formal and analytical linguistic awareness than monolingual children. It seems unlikely that children in general and bilingual children in particular who are capable of unconsciously utilizing the principles and parameters of UG and of setting and resetting parametric values simply fail to distinguish between the two linguistic systems from a mixed input. Nair's study and some studies prior to hers reveal that bilingual children who receive mixed input do in fact employ formal features to distinguish the two systems.

Sixth, as noted earlier, much of the linguistic research literature on the bilingual child views the question of input in terms of an either/or paradigm: Either bilinguals receive separate input or they receive mixed input. Studies on the verbal behavior of adult bilinguals reveal that bilinguals do not subscribe to either language separation or language mixing on either a totally random or an arbitrary basis. On the contrary there are linguistic and nonlinguistic determinants of language mixing or language separation. Hence, even when the child's input is mixed, the mixture is not arbitrary but systematic so that the child is apparently able to sort the languages out.

For these reasons, current views of input, that is, either separate or mixed, would appear to be simplistic. We would like to claim that both separate and mixed input will form a natural part of the input to a bilingual child. The critical question is not whether a bilingual receives separate or mixed input but under what conditions both types of input serve as sociolinguistically realistic input. Because we claim that a bilingual child is likely to receive both mixed and separate input types, the child will be able to make use of his or her rich input sources as well as his or her intrinsic cognitive/linguistic capacities to separate the two languages. The only exception will be those cases where parents either speak only pidgin or creole languages or are not balanced bilinguals.

B. Progression and Regression Phenomena in Bilingual Children

The findings of several diary studies and other studies of bilingual child language acquisition (e.g., Burling, 1959; Leopold, 1939–1949; and others) reveal that with a change in input conditions, bilingual children can retrieve one language and fail to retrieve another in terms of at least linguistic performance—that is, they can either "turn off" or "turn on" one of their languages, as was the case with Leopold's daughter, Hildegard.

If conditions for the turning on of one language and the turning off of the other are prolonged, one language may progress and the other language may regress (or delay) to the extent that the child might experience total language loss—at least at the performance level.[6] Although very little empirical work has been done to isolate the minimal input requirements for promoting or sustaining grammatical competence in a particular language, there are two major schools of thought on this subject.

Input Quantity and Quality

Researchers such as Kessler (1984, p. 35), Idaizábal (1984), Schlyter (1993), Hoffman (1985), Lanza (1990, p. 441), Romaine (1989, p. 169), Schlyter and Westholm (1991), and Saunders (1988, p. 162) stress the value of the quantity of input. (See Sections 5 and 6 for more details.) The more input a child receives in a particular language the more it ensures the active use of that language and vice versa. Although Döpke (1988, p. 103) stressed that quality of input takes precedence over quantity, she does not propose criteria for defining *quality;* however, we would like to claim that one of the determinants of quality of input is "on-line input" to trigger relevant parameters (i.e., readily available in input, particularly in a natural setting; cf. the effect of on-line input deprivation on deaf children of hearing parents, see Section IX; see Section VIII for some discussion of the notion of a parameter trigger). The interaction between a child and a caretaker is critical for the normal growth of language among deaf children. Some studies (e.g., Bouvet, 1990) show that when the parents of a deaf child discover the child's disability, the experience is so traumatic that they shut him or her out of social interaction with them and thus deprive the child of communicative input. Consequently, in some cases the language growth of a deaf child of hearing parents may lag seriously behind that of deaf children whose parents are deaf. Unlike hearing par-

[6]Recall Hidegard's comment cited in Section II.B above not being able to speak English after she had spent time in Germany.

ents, deaf parents never deprive their children of normal verbal and nonverbal interaction because deaf parents do not associate deafness with muteness (Bouvet, 1990).

In addition, any notion of input quality must take into account the interactional pattern between the caretaker and the child and its sensitivity to positive and negative evidence presented by the caretaker or parents.

Positive and Negative Evidence and Social Attitudes

Unlike the monolingual child, the bilingual child has to accomplish the challenging task of sorting out negative and positive evidence, because such evidence is sometimes colored by the prescriptive attitudes of parents and caretakers about language mixing. Some parents signal children that their use of mixed speech constitutes a "wrong" choice of language and, consequently, discourage the use of mixed utterances while they themselves unconsciously use mixed speech. In the process, parents frustrate the genuine, socio-psychologically grounded communicative needs of bilingual children. Such conflicting and contradictory experiences may well become a deterrent to bilingual language development and may result in bilingual language delay or attrition. Prolonged exposure to conditions such as the parents' inaccurate perception of their own communicative style and the child's can lead to monolingualism (Döpke, 1986) and can serve as a major determinant of the final success of a bilingual upbringing.

Positive and negative evidence that is provided by sociolinguistically realistic conditions, on the other hand, will promote the rate and accuracy of bilingual language acquisition. Lanza (1990), Garcia (1983), and Goodz and colleagues (1988, p. 228) have shown that some parents are more successful and perceptive in providing sociolinguistically realistic evidence to children than others. Garcia (1983, p. 143) observed that Spanish-dominant mothers in his study used mixed utterances as a clarificatory or paraphrasing device to promote acquisition and production in both English and Spanish on the part of bilingual children. Similarly, in their study of 13 English/French children and their parents, Goodz and colleagues (1988) found language switching to function as an attention getter, as well as a disciplinary and emphatic device. (See Section X for details on language mixing.)

VII. STAGES IN MONOLINGUAL AND BILINGUAL LANGUAGE DEVELOPMENT

Bilingual children exhibit the same major stages of acquisition as monolingual children: the babbling stage, followed by the one-word, two-word, and multiple-word stages. No study has suggested that the sequence of such stages is different in bilingual children from that in monolinguals. Furthermore, the correlation of these stages with age also remains largely undisturbed. According to Meisel (1986, p. 64) there is no reason to believe that the underlying principles and mechanism of language development among bilinguals are qualitatively different from those found in monolinguals. The order of morpho-syntactic and phonological development and the acquisition strategies described in the classic descriptive works of Slobin (1973), Brown (1973), and others—semantic overextension and underextension of lexical items, substitutions, avoidance, and the general direction of acquisition from unmarked to marked linguistic structures—is essentially the same both for monolingual and bilingual children.

However, researchers are divided over whether monolingual and bilingual acquisition mechanisms are similar in more detailed respects. Some argue that although both monolingual and bilingual children have equal access to universal grammar, numerous factors must be taken into account when making comparisons between the language development of monolingual and bilingual children. Linguistic input, analytical maturity, and other factors mentioned in the foregoing sections might differentiate bilingual from monolingual acquisition (see Section VIII for details). Furthermore, mixed input, unique to bilingual children, might open a different path of language development. Before we go further into the question of similarities and dissimilarities of language development between monolingual and bilingual children, some major salient findings of the research are reviewed in this section.

A. Phonological Development

Most of the research devoted to phonological development among bilingual children reveals a striking resemblence between monolingual and bilingual development. One such parallelism can best be characterized in terms of Jakobson's theory of opposition (Jakobson, 1967). According to this theory "what is important is not single sounds but the distinctions among sounds," which leads the child through a series of binary splits leading to the acquisition of sound classes in a universal order. Leopold found that the sound system in the language development of his daughter was governed by phonemic rather than phonetic considerations. Related to the theory of opposition is the theory of markedness. The phonological development of both monolinguals and bilinguals is generally in agreement with the claims made by the theory of markedness, that is, unmarked elements precede marked elements.

In spite of these parallelisms, there is no doubt that the task that a bilingual child has to undertake is more complex and challenging in terms of both qualitative and quantitative load than the task of a monolingual child. The bilingual child's ability to separate two languages is critical in arriving at appropriate language-specific phonological systems for his or her two languages. This additional task calls for tacit strategies that are exclusive to bilingual children. Consider, once again, the case of the language acquisition pattern of the Hindi-English bilingual child investigated by Nair (1984), referred to earlier. Her study shows that the phonological development in the bilingual child was similar to that in monolingual children of English and Hindi separately, in spite of the fact that the bilingual child (referred to in the study as "*V*") was not raised in a one-parent/one-language environment. Therefore, no nonlinguistic clues were accessible to the child to separate Hindi from English. Cues such as syllable length, phonotactic structures, place, and manner of articulation were employed by the child to sort out Hindi from English. Nair presents evidence that these cues came into operation right from the onset of the one-word stage. At this stage the English lexical output was overwhelmingly monosyllabic, whereas the Hindi lexicon was primarily disyllabic. In addition, the English monosyllabic vocabulary exhibited CVC structure, whereas the disyllabic Hindi vocabulary was restricted to CVCV structure. Much of the early Hindi vocabulary favored dental segments, whereas the English lexicon was more varied in segment type. In other words, even in the absence of overt language separation, it seems that the phonological development of bilingual children shows that the two systems are largely acquired separately, thus no interference is experienced.

As might be expected, separation is also found in those bilinguals who are raised in one-parent/one-language situation (see Hoffmann, 1985; Oksaar, 1970; Ronjat, 1913; Ruke-Dravina, 1965). Ingram (1981) suggested that the use of formal devices for early language differentiation is valid for bilingual children acquiring very different languages. A reexamination of the phonological data from Leopold by Paradis (1996) shows evidence for differentiation in bilingual children acquiring similar languages, namely, German and English in the case of Hildegard. Paradis showed that Hildegard seems to follow two separate paths in her acquisition of German and English prosodic structure from age 1;6 to 2;0. This finding not only provides a striking parallel with Ingram's 2-year-old subject, whose English lexicon consisted of more closed syllables; and Italian lexicon comprised of more open multisyllables and more reduplicated forms, but also with Nair's study.

If the language input to the child exhibits a dominance relation—that is, the child receives more input from one language than the other—the phenomenon of interference or delay may affect the phonological development of the child as was the case in Fantini's son Mario's English development (Fantini, 1985). Because Mario's first use of English lagged more than a year, Spanish emerged as the primary language and the onset of the subordinate language—English—was delayed and gained momentum only after the Spanish system was firmly in place. Therefore, it is not surprising that the child's earlier English words were colored with Spanish phonology (Fantini 1985, p. 134). Similarly, Burling (1959) revealed that his son Stephen's English sound system was delayed and developed later than the Garo phonological system because of the dominance of Garo in the child's input. At the age of 2;9, separation of English and Garo took place but the consonant system never became differentiated. Garo consonants continued to be substituted for English consonants. The English consonantal system developed fully at the age of 3;6, when the family returned the United States from the Garo Hills in Assam, India.

B. Vocabulary Development

The early acquisition of vocabulary by children is a fascinating and complex process. This process is constrained by a number of factors, including the child's cognitive development, socialization practices in the child's community, and his or her linguistic capacity. Although once again one witnesses the existence of the same processes (e.g., overextension and underextension of the meanings of lexical items) in both bilingual and monolingual children, an alternate acquisition route is accessible to bilingual children but remains inaccessible to monolingual children (i.e., input from a second language). This difference plays an important role in the differences found in the acquisition of vocabulary by monolingual and bilingual children. Furthermore, it appears that the different strategic paths adopted by bilinguals also play an important role in the rate and structural type of vocabulary acquisition.

Let us examine vocabulary acquisition by the Hindi-English child described in Nair's study, *V. V* received equal exposure to both Hindi and English "in all environments" and thus the nature of his bilingualism was simultaneous and mixed. The data collected was from *V* between the ages 1;6 and 2;1. The investigator remarks that during the period 1;1 to 1;2, *V* spoke his first words. Over the next few months "his attempts at articulation proceeded at a moderate pace." At the age of 18 months *V*'s lexicon underwent the sudden explosion found in many other well-studied children (see, e.g., Dromi, 1987) as more than 100 words became an active part of the child's vocabulary and a clear syllabic pattern began to emerge. Table 17.1 gives the distribution of vocabulary at the one-word, holophrastic stage. From Table 17.1 it is clear that structural considerations shaped *V*'s acquisition of language-specific vocabulary. Also, as Table 17.2 reveals, *V*'s monosyllabic words favored a closed-syllable pattern over an open-syllabic pattern. Disyllabic words showed the complementary tendency, that is, disyllabic words favor an open syl-

TABLE 17.1
Distribution of *V*'s Vocabulary at the One-Word Stage

	Words	Monosyllabic	Disyllabic
English	38	34	4
Hindi	33	12	21
Baby talk/names	31	1	30

TABLE 17.2

Open and Closed Syllables in *V*'s Monosyllabic and Disyllabic Words

	Monosyllabic	Disyllabic
Open-vowel ending	15	47
Closed-consonantal ending	32	8

lable. Nair claims that the child's production strategy followed four rules.[7] Out of these, three rules applied to monosyllabic words, whereas the fourth rule was reserved for disyllabic words.

By the age of 2;0, *V* had added 83 words to his English lexicon and 80 to his Hindi vocabulary. Once again *V*'s vocabulary follows the same structural pattern. The lexical developmental pattern to this point is summarized in Table 17.3. Note that the tendency to assimilate English words to a monosyllabic structure and Hindi words to disyllabic form is continued at this later stage.

Another remarkable feature of this study is the absence of word-internal mixing or "blending." Blending has been considered to be evidence for an undifferentiated language system (Volterra & Taeschner, 1978). The conspicuous absence of blending in *V*'s speech is especially striking because, as mentioned previously, *V* received mixed input from his parents and caretakers. The absence of blendings lends further support to Meisel's claim that "an individual exposed to two languages from an early age should be capable of separating the two grammatical systems without going through a phase of temporary confusion" (Meisel, 1989, p. 35) and "the task of acquiring the two grammatical systems simultaneously will be easier if the child focuses his attention on problems of form rather than relying on semantic-pragmatic strategies alone" (Meisel 1989, p. 36).

[7]These four rules are as follows:

Rule 1: In monosyllabic CVC structures, obey principles of consonant harmony and cluster reduction (Smith, 1973), for example, *broke, gate* → [ko:k], [te:t]).

Rule 1b: Partial harmony wherever coda is voiced plosive *d* or *g* (*dog, bread* → [kog], [ted]).

Rule 2: In monosyllabic CVC structures, obey principles of consonant harmony consistent with the replacement of a voiced consonant by another voiced consonant (*bath, drink* → [da:th], [gink]).

Rule 1 and 2 are not compatible and relate to English vocabulary exclusively.

Rule 3: In monosyllabic CVC structures where the coda consonant is the *n* and/or the onset is fricative or glide, replace the onset consonant with the plosive *t* or *k*—*phone, fan, pen, rain, soap* → [to:n]/[ko:n], [tæn], [ten], [te:n], [to:p].

Rule 4: In disyllabic structures of the CV+CV and CVC+(C)V, delete onset of first syllable only for disyllabic: roTi, paTTa → [o:Ti], [əTi]; exception ThanDa → [ThənDa]. (Recall that all disyllabic words are Hindi words.)

TABLE 17.3
V's Lexical Development at 2;0

	Monosyllabic		Disyllabic		Polysyllabic	
	Old	New	Old	New	Old	New
English	34	44	4	25	0	14
Hindi	12	9	21	64	0	7
BT and PN	1	0	30	0	0	17

Note. BT = emotive words; PN = proper names.

C. Morpho-syntactic Development

Earlier studies (Carrow, 1971; Imedadze, 1967; Kessler, 1971, 1972; Leopol 1939–1949; Raffler-Engel, 1965; and others) suggest that the order of syntact development in bilingual children parallels that of L1 monolingual developmer Leopold showed that, like monolinguals, his daughter underwent a one-word sta during which there was no syntactic structure. The onset of the two-word stage b gan at the age of 1;8, at which time grammatical relations began to emerge throu the combining of a subject with a predicate. The verb-object pattern started emerge a month later. The SVO pattern together with a simple adjective-noun pa tern were in place by the time Hildegard was 2 years old. The learning of Engli morphological and syntactic patterns progressed rapidly after this period. Prep sitions, articles, auxiliaries verbs, and present and past-tense agreement develop at the age of 2;3. At the age of 2;4, plural marking and the combining of lexical e ements to form coherent utterances were quite frequent. In short, English synta tic and morphological patterns were perfected after the second year.

During this stage Hildegard's German syntax was stagnant. But it flourish suddenly when the child spent half a year in Germany at the end of her fifth ye First the child experienced some interference from English where English and Ge man structure differ significantly (in verb infinitives, etc.), but Leopold report that such interference was corrected quickly. Kessler (1971) found that simult neous Italian-English children acquired structures shared by both languages in a proximately the same sequence and at the same rate as monolinguals. A languag specific complex structure developed later than a structure that is less complex a is shared by both languages. These findings are consistent with other studies th support the position that bilingual children follow the same underlying principl and basic acquisition sequences as monolinguals (see Mikes, 1967; Swain, 197

Some recent studies depart from the preceding descriptive studies in their th oretical and comparative orientation but attempt to address the same question wit in the framework of linguistic theory. The main concern of these notable studi by Meisel (1985, 1986, 1989) and De Houwer (1990) is to examine whether gra matical categories emerge at the same time and in the same fashion in monolingual and bilingual children. By comparing the language development of a bilingual child systematically with language development in monolinguals, they aim to gain insights into the language processes that underlie language acquisition. By studying particularly the semantic-pragmatic principles that play a critical role during the child's early language development, Meisel attempted to find out whether these principles apply in the same fashion in bilinguals as in monolinguals. His study is devoted to the language development of two French-German bilinguals during the period from age 1;0 to 4;0, focusing on the emergence of word order and case markers. On the basis of his study of bilingual syntactic development, Meisel challenged the traditional conception that early differences in use of two languages cannot be characterized as syntactic in nature. The noteworthy difference between the monolinguals and bilinguals is that the bilinguals favored SOV word order in German utterances more rapidly than other possible orders. Similarly, the second position of the verb, which is a distinctive characteristic of German, occurred earlier in bilinguals than in monolinguals. Similarly, Meisel (1989) observed that German bilinguals had an edge over German monolinguals because they were able to acquire morphological markers of syntactic functions such as case earlier than monolinguals.[8]

De Houwer's work (De Houwer, 1990) is devoted to the morphosyntactic development of her Dutch-English bilingual subject Kate, from age 2;7 to 3;4. The morpho-syntactic features examined by this study are the following: gender, plural formation, diminutive suffixes, noun phrases with an adjective as head, verbal forms and verb phrases, word order, and different clause types. The comparison with Dutch and English monolinguals reveals that, in spite of many qualitative and quantitative differences, Kate's bilingual syntactic development "proceeds in a language-dependent manner" (De Houwer, 1990, p. 304) and closely resembles 3-year-old monolingual language in Dutch and English. Shortly after the age 3;0, Kate's syntactic system becomes more diversified and complex. Although the actual contents of Kate's "speech production is quite language-specific, there appears to be a mechanism at work here that concerns both languages at once" (De Houwer 1990, p. 308). In this respect, bilinguals function more or less like "parallel processors" in the sense that the grammars of the two languages develop in a parallel manner.

As regards the question of delay in bilinguals, some studies such as Burling (1959), Vihman (1982), Fantini (1976), and Murrell (1966) have suggested that there is a delay in the acquisition of inflectional morphology because morphology follows the development of syntax. Other studies such as Imedadze (1967), which examines the simultaneous acquisition of Russian and Georgian, report no such

[8]Meisel pointed out that he could not generalize his finding to French because no comparable data were available.

delay. The concepts are learned simultaneously in both languages, for example, the instrumental case markers were learned first in Georgian and three days later appeared in Russian. The only difference was if one pattern seemed less complex than the corresponding pattern in the other language, the less complex form precedes the more complex form.

VIII. THE TWO LINGUISTIC SYSTEMS IN BILINGUAL CHILDREN

During the past two decades the central issue in the field of bilingual language acquisition has been whether or not bilingual children separate the two linguistic systems exemplified in their input during the initial stages of speech production. There is no doubt that eventually separation does take place with the result that the two systems become autonomous from each other. The question is whether, during the initial stages, bilinguals separate the two systems. The two main hypotheses that have attracted attention in research have been termed the unitary hypothesis (also called the single or initial one-system hypothesis) and the dual system hypothesis (also called the independent development or autonomous hypothesis).

A third position should also be mentioned. This position raises the fundamental conceptual problem of what constitutes evidence for either of these two hypotheses in the speech of early bilinguals. As Romaine noted, "It is often difficult to decide what counts as evidence for differentiation." (1989, p. 186). For this and other reasons many scholars (e.g., Klausen, Subritzky, & Hayashi, 1993; Wode, 1990) question the wisdom of entertaining this classical question until the notion of system is clear. Nonetheless, we believe that the significant increase in the specificity of claims made by grammatical theory about the structures of particular languages over the last number of years has made it possible to pose this question in a significant way for many areas of linguistic structure. Hence, though we have already reviewed some evidence that the child separates the phonological systems of his or her two languages very early on in the process of acquisition, it is worthwhile examining the evidence in somewhat more detail.

According to the unitary hypothesis, bilingual children begin the acquisition process with one language system, which later separates into two language systems. Volterra and Taeschner (1978), Swain (1972), Redlinger and Park (1980), Taeschner (1983), Vihman (1982, 1985, 1986), Genesee (1989), Klausen and Hayashi (1990), and Toribio and Brown (1994) all subscribe to this hypothesis, which is diagrammatically represented in Figure 17.3.

The proponents of the dual system hypothesis claim that children do not go through an initial stage or stages of treating the two languages as one but differentiate the two linguistic systems as early as age 2;0 or before. This hypothesis is diagrammatically represented in Figure 17.4. The main proponents of this hy-

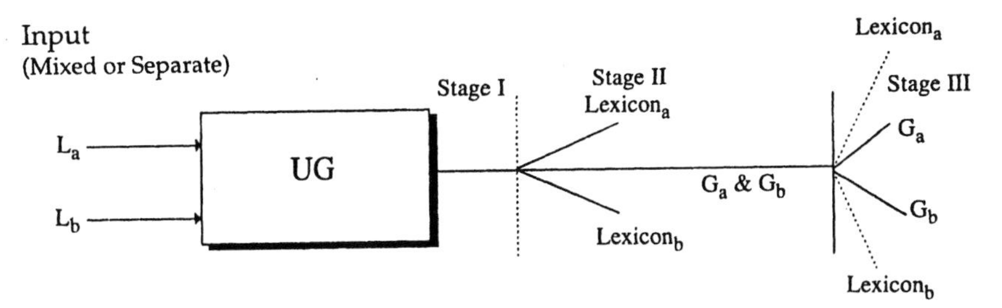

Figure 17.3. The unitary hypothesis.

pothesis are Padilla and Liebman (1975), Bergman (1976), Lindholm and Padilla (1978), Pye (1986), De Houwer (1987, 1990), Meisel (1989, 1994), and Nicoladis (1994), among others.

Before we examine the adequacy of these hypotheses, let us detail some of the more salient features and consequences of these hypotheses and evidence presented to support them.

A. The Unitary Hypothesis

Although the stage was set in the works of Leopold (1939–1949) and Swain (1972), it was the study by Volterra and Taeschner (1978) which sparked the main interest in this hypothesis. Volterra and Taeschner claimed that bilingual children go through a stage of "language confusion" before they finally arrive at the stage of language separation. They attempt to capture the process of language differentiation by way of a three-stage model. This model was later elaborated in Taeschner (1983).

Stage I: During this stage the child's lexicon is hybrid in the sense that the child does not appear to differentiate between the lexicons of the two languages and, hence, has a single lexicon made up of items from the lexicons of both languages; no translational equivalents or synonyms are found in the child's vocabulary.

Figure 17.4. The dual system hypothesis.

Volterra and Taeschner's (1978) two bilingual subjects at the ages of 1;10 and 1;6 were claimed to have such a hybrid list of about 137 words with no translational equivalents.

Stage II: During this stage the slow separation of the lexicons of the two language systems takes place. Cross-linguistic synonyms are introduced but the child applies the same set of syntactic rules to both languages.

Stage III: The two languages are separated in terms of both vocabulary and syntax.

Discussions of Stage I phenomena by Leopold (1978), Grosjean (1982), Saunders (1982, pp. 44–48), Arnberg (1987, pp. 69–70), and others made similar observations, lending support to the proposed three-stage model. For example, in the best-documented classic case—Hildegard—Leopold claimed that during her first two years, his subject combined her two languages into one system and was therefore not really bilingual. Her speech sounds belonged to a unified set undifferentiated by language. She mixed English and German words and failed to distinguish between the two while speaking to German or English monolinguals. In addition to the lack of translational equivalents and presence of interference, language mixing is presented as evidence for the unitary hypothesis.

Findings of recent research have challenged the arguments that were extended in favor of the three-stage model.

Stage-I Lack of Translational Equivalents

There has been a good deal of criticism leveled against the unitary hypothesis on both methodological and empirical grounds. On methodological grounds, De Houwer (1995) has argued that the absence of translational pairs at the performance level during the one-word stage does not mean the child lacks translational pairs in terms of competence. There can be many reasons for the lack of translational pairs in production. First, if an appropriate linguistic and pragmatic context is not provided by an investigator, it is unnatural to expect a child to respond to the context in two languages. There is sufficient evidence to claim that Volterra and Taeschner (1978) and Taeschner (1983) overlooked this possibility; thus, it would not be surprising to find the absence of translational pairs in the speech of bilingual children, even if the unitary hypothesis is false.

According to De Houwer (1990, p. 31), a careful analysis of the Volterra and Taeschner (1978) and Taeschner (1983) studies reveals that they suffer from a number of other methodological drawbacks and inconsistencies. For example, the duration of each recording is stated to be 30 minutes in Volterra and Taeschner (1978) but 45 minutes in Taeschner (1983). Most importantly, the audio-recording method employed for data collection, "even if [the recordings] are supplemented by careful notes, cannot furnish the level of detail required for later accurate interpretation of various aspects of recorded interactions" (De Houwer 1990, p. 31).

Interlocutor constraints (the presence of the German-speaking interlocutor most of the time) may also have contributed to such gaps. De Houwer went on to claim that even if one accepts Volterra and Taeschner's conclusion about the lack of translational pairs at face value, "it is still possible that such equivalents might have turned up in recorded conversations with the children's main Italian-speaking interlocutor" (De Houwer, 1995, p. 231).

Similarly, Leopold's claim about the presence of the single system is not free from methodological drawbacks. The lack of translational pairs in Hildegard's speech might be due to the fact that Leopold himself recorded the data and that he might have created the well-known problem of the "observer's paradox" (Labov 1972, p. 209) in addition to the intrinsic limitations of the diary methodology.

Besides these methodological shortcomings, a reanalysis of the Stage I data from Taeschner (1983, pp. 25–26) by Quay (1993) indicates some counterevidence to the claim by Volterra and Taeschner that there were no translational pairs in their data. Quay's analysis shows that Taeschner's subjects did in fact use quite a few such pairs. The subject, Lisa, used six pairs out of 64 words whereas Giulia used more than twice the number that Lisa did (i.e., 14 out of 73 words). Furthermore, the data obtained from Quay's study show the presence of equivalent pairs. In a carefully designed study, which was sound on methodological and sociolinguistic grounds, Quay found that her Spanish-English subject did make use of dual input and at the age of 1;5 used 18 pairs out of a total of 47 words. The very high incidence of pairs can be credited to methodology (used of toys, books, etc.), which enabled the investigator to create contexts appropriate for the use of language pairs on the part of the bilingual child.

Although the Nair study of the Hindi-English bilingual child *V* (Nair, 1984)—referred to previously—is short on methodological details, our analysis of *V*'s one-word stage at age 1;7 indicates that out of *V*'s total of 66 vocabulary items, seven are pairs. The pairs fall essentially in the domain of basic vocabulary—the words for food items (*bread* and *water*), body parts (e.g., *eyes*), basic verbs (*come* and *go*), adjectives (*hot*), and the negative marker (*not*). Another interesting pair is *car/auto*—although both are from English, it cannot be ruled out that *auto* (3-wheeler) is used in the sense used by monolingual Hindi-speaking children. In other words, regardless of their origin, the two words have membership in both languages at the synchronic and functional levels. At first glance this pair can be interpreted as what Hayashi (1992) termed a "gap in the input"; however Hindi *auto* and English *auto* seem to constitute a pair, because the word *auto* belongs to both Hindi and English.

A note of caution is in order at this point that the overt use of a pair drawn from two languages does not necessarily constitute evidence for language differentiation. The daughter of the first author of this chapter used an apparent Hindi-English translational pair for *water* at a very early age—approximately 1;0 to 1;5; however, careful observation of her usage showed that she used the Hindi equivalent only to refer either to a very large body of water such as a lake or a flowing body of water (e.g., a spring), referring to water otherwise with the English word *water.* The first time she used the Hindi word, *paanii* "water," she was very excited to see a big spring in the Adirondack region of New York State (*Daddy, paanii*). The second time she used this word was when she saw Lake Ontario. The Hindi word was pronounced with the intonation of excitement and surprise. The child had had very little exposure to Hindi, because she had been in day care—where only English was spoken—from 8 A.M. to 5 P.M. for almost six days a week since the age of three months. It is quite clear, then, that she was actually monolingual at that point and that *paanii* and *water* were simply two items in a single (essentially English) lexicon. This case is typical of acquisition in accordance with the uniqueness principle, originally proposed by Wexler (1981), under which the child assumes that, in the normal or unmarked case, a given form in the language has a single meaning and each meaning is associated with a single form.

Pye (1986) questioned the claim made by Vihman (1985) that her son underwent Stage I as stated in Volterra and Taeschner (1978). On the basis of his reanalysis of "mixed language" data presented by Vihman, Pye (1986) concluded that it is "premature" to arrive at Vihman's decision in favor of the unitary hypothesis. Genesee (1989, p. 166) supported Pye's view by remarking that Vihman's analysis is either incomplete or questionable. In short, the existence of Stage I has come under heavy fire by recent research and appears questionable.

Stage-II Fusion

Recall that during the proposed Stage II, the child applies "the same syntactic rules to both languages" in spite of the separation of the two lexicons (Volterra & Taeschner, 1978, p. 311). As in the case of Stage I, the existence of Stage II has been challenged on theoretical, analytical, and methodological grounds. The studies in question are those of Meisel and Mahlau (1988), Meisel (1989), and some recent theory-driven studies conducted within the government and binding model.

According to Meisel the characterization of this stage is particularly vague and full of contradictory statements. For example, the stages are not marked chronologically. The stages for Volterra and Taeschner's subject Lisa's speech production bear the following age ranges.

Stage I 1;6–1;11
Stage II 2;5–3;3
Stage III 2;9–3;11

Lisa continued to mix vocabulary (i.e., drawing vocabulary from both languages and showing a lack of translational equivalents from each language) at the age of 2;5 and beyond, yet she is supposed to be at the stage in which she should have developed lexical separation. The overlapping of stages of acquisition and age opens Volterra and Taeschner's argument for the unitary hypothesis to a charge of circularity. If a particular syntactic development occurs at the age of 2;9, it can be treated as an example of presence or absence of syntactic differentiation at the same time. A case in point is the placement of adjectives in Italian examples, which is supposed to show the use of one syntax; however, this usage occurs at the age of 2;9 and even much later—even after the onset of the proposed Stage III. Similarly, Lisa was in Stage II when her use of negative structures, according to Volterra and Taeschner (1978, p. 324), resembled the negative structures of monolingual children in each language. The use of the parallel structures in the two languages does not constitute evidence for a lack of language differentiation. Such statements are internally inconsistent, which leads one to doubt seriously the evidence presented in favor of Stage II. Similarly, Volterra and Taeschner's argument about the phenomenon of interference as evidence of fusion or lack of language differentiation is not valid. Interference may show the interdependence of two distinct systems as well as it does the lack of two systems.

Nor does the unitary hypothesis gain support from consideration of the early development of phonology. Ingram (1981), for example, examined the speech production of an Italian-English girl at the age of 2;0. On the basis of his analysis he rejected the unitary hypothesis and arrived at the conclusion that possession of two distinct phonological systems enabled the child to keep the two languages separate. Similarly, in addition to our discussion of Nair's (1984) subject *V* in Section VII.A, careful analysis of the Hindi-English data from Nair reveals that *V* reserved retroflex sounds or disyllabicity only for the Hindi lexicon starting from the one-word stage, providing further evidence against the existence of a Stage II.

B. The Dual System Hypothesis

Having shown that the unitary hypothesis has come under serious attack in recent times, let us turn our attention to the dual system hypothesis (DSH). In this section we will review the findings of a wide variety of studies, some of which exclusively aim at testing the DSH. The studies conducted in a one-parent/one-language environment as well as those treating a mixed input environment will be considered. Needless to say, if findings from the latter studies in particular support the DSH, these findings will constitute the strongest evidence in its favor.

One-Parent/One-Language Studies

From a cursory glance at Table 17.4 listing the bilingual acquisition studies that have been reported in the research literature, it becomes readily clear that these studies lack diversity and are overwhelmingly devoted to the Indo-European languages of Western Europe. Clearly, more diversified research in terms of input languages and regions is called for.

Idaizábal (1988, 1991) and Deuchar (1992) examined the development of bound

TABLE 17.4
Bilingual Acquisition Studies

Input Condition	Languages	Subject's Age Range	Study
One-parent/one language	German-French	1:6–3;6	Berkele (1983)
		1;11–4;6	*Klinge (1990)
		1;0–4;0	*Meisel (1985, 1986, 1989, 1990a, 1990b)
		1;6–5;0	*Meisel and Müller (1992), Müller (1990a, 1990b)
		1;1–3;8	Parodi (1990)
		1;11–3;5	*Schlyter (1990)
		1;9–3;5	Koehn (1989)
	Dutch-English	2;7–3;4	De Houwer (1987a, 1987b, 1988, 1990)
	Spanish-English	1;7–3;4	Deuchar (1989, 1992)
	Basque-Spanish	1;11–3;2	Idaizábal (1988, 1991)
Mixed	Igbo-English	3;0	Nwokah (1984)
	Spanish-English	3;0–4;2	Garcia (1983)
	Hindi-English	1;6–2;1	Nair (1984)
Mixed/one-parent/ one-language	French-English	1;11–3;3	*Paradis and Genesee (1996)

Note. *Indicates that the studies utilized different subject(s), covering different age ranges within the age-range indicated.

morphology in the production of noun and verb phrases, respectively, at the multiple word stage. Their findings are uniform in their conclusion that bound morphology developed in a language-specific manner, thus lending support to the DSH. Similarly, De Houwer (1990, p. 149) showed that "the plural morphemes do not travel between the languages but are language-specific. This is but a first instance of the general *principle of morphological language stability*" (emphasis in the original). Many studies demonstrate that bilingual children begin to use language-specific subject-verb agreement from the two-word stage. The evidence is from Spanish-English (e.g., Deuchar, 1992), German-French (e.g., Meisel, 1989), and Dutch-English (e.g., De Houwer, 1987b, 1990) bilingual children and others as well.

It is also reported in some studies that bilinguals adopt two separate paths in other respects in the process of language development. For instance, the separate development of articles (Berkele, 1983), plurality (Koehn, 1989), gender, tag questions and indirect object (De Houwer, 1987a, 1987b, 1990), tense-aspect systems (Schlyter, 1990), and grammatical agreement systems (De Houwer, 1990, p. 279) are attributed to different formal means adopted by bilingual children.

TABLE 17.5
V's Multiword Productions at 2;0

	English SVO		Hindi SOV	
(2) [=Nair (2)]	me	come	you	a:o
			you	come
			"you come"	
(3) [=Nair (3)]	me	car	me	ju:ta
			me	shoes
			"my shoes"	
(4) [=Nair (5)]	pli:dz	milk	(more) jam	do
	please	milk	(more) jam	give
	"Please (give me) milk"		"Give more jam"	

This finding gains further support, once again, from Nair's work on the Hindi-English bilingual child *V.* Recall that *V* used a syllabification strategy to keep his two languages separate. Monosyllabic lexical items were identified as English and disyllabic items as Hindi. Although the relationship between the subject's two languages is not the focus of Nair's study, she does show that at the multiword stage (1;7), two different word orders develop—SVO order for English and SOV for Hindi. Most of the examples given in her Table VII (Nair, 1984, p. 77) are subject to different interpretations because of language mixing data. Nevertheless, our analysis of her data indicates that some examples convincingly show the emergence of the two different word orders. Consider the following examples in Table 17.5, which Nair labeled as English SVO order and Hindi SOV order produced by *V* at the multiword stage (2;0). The first two items, Examples (2) and (3), clearly do not exhibit language-specific syntactic word order, because the expected word order for these particular examples would be the same in Hindi or in English. It cannot be ruled out in (2) that the two-verb forms (i.e., the English verb *come* and the Hindi verb *a:o*) might still be in a state of free variation. Unless evidence for the existence of different Hindi verb forms with the Hindi verb *a:* ("come") is presented to rule out the possibility that the child is not using the *a:o* form as a single unit, the claim that the word order here is language specific is premature. Similarly, just because the Hindi word *ju:ta* is used in (3) does not mean that the word order in question is Hindi. This is particularly true if the sample data is not exclusively from one language. This is an important methodological point that De Houwer makes. The following remark is instructive in this regard: "the database for probing the structural relationships between a young child's two languages should ideally consist of utterances with lexical items from one language only" (De Houwer, 1995, p. 236).

Although the Hindi example in (4) does follow the Hindi OV order with the subject argument deleted, it cannot be ruled out that the surface word order is the result of the young children's use of topicalization, which is widely attested in monolingual children regardless of the language being acquired. However, in our view, the following example does support convincingly the view that *V* has developed two separate and specific word orders for English and Hindi:

(5) [=Nair (1)] ju/tum i: dit
You/you [Hindi] eat this
"you eat this"

The postverbal positioning of the object demonstrative pronoun provides evidence for the emergence of the English word order; because Hindi is a topic-prominent language (Li & Thompson, 1976), *it* as the object argument will not be overt unless it is used contrastively. The following sentences, on the other hand, lend support to the claim for adult Hindi word order in *V*'s output:

(6) je ənki hæ.
this monkey is
"This is a monkey."

(7) je bəra nene nai hæ
this big milk not is
"This is not big milk."

Because Hindi is an SOV language, the use of the postpositions by *V* lends support to the claim that a separate system is emerging for Hindi.

Our analysis of the Hindi vocabulary at the age of 2:0 indicates that there is in fact evidence for Hindi postpositions. *V* uttered the following two-word utterance:

(8) [=Nair's (12), p. 66]
pe:T me
stomach in
"in one's stomach"

Although one cannot rule out the possibility that the Hindi phrase could be a formulaic expression and that the child is unable to map postpositions with their semantic content, the example presented in (9) suggests that this is not the case:

(9) [=Nair's (49), p. 67]
is me
this in
"in this"

The minimal pair presented in (8) and (9) clearly show that not only has the child developed the precise content of the postposition, but he has also chosen the appropriate oblique form of the demonstrative pronoun. Hindi postpositions induce overt case marking in their (preceding) objects. The Hindi demonstrative pronoun *ye/is* 'this' has two case forms. When *ye/is* is not followed by any postposition, it is said to be in the "simple case" and its phonetic shape is *je* (or *ye* in the adult structure). However, when it is followed by a postposition, it is inflected with "oblique case" and has the phonetic shape *is*. In example (9), *V* has produced the appropriate oblique form of the pronoun. In other words, the presence of a postposition induces oblique case marking in the adult language and the presence of a postposition in the bilingual child's sentence also triggers the oblique case marking, hence matching the structural prerequisite for the oblique case specific to the structure of Hindi.

Perhaps one of the most fascinating examples of morphosyntactic development in the Hindi-English bilingual child is the acquisition of the Hindi compound verb structure. Before we turn to a detailed discussion of *V*'s acquisition of Hindi compound verbs, some remarks are in order concerning the nature of such verbs in adult Hindi, a structure that is not found in English. Consider the following Hindi sentence:

(10) vo aa jaa-egaa
he come go-fut. msg
"He will come back, arrive."

In the compound verb structure two verbs such as *aa* "come" and *jaa* "go" in (10) are clustered in a single phrase. However, the meaning of the sentence is not merely a conjunctive meaning rendered by the juxtapositioning of verbs; rather, the meaning of the main verb *aa* "come" is modulated and the "helping verb" *jaanaa* "to go" is the carrier of tense information in the sentence. As a helping verb, *jaa* loses its literal meaning and adds the meaning "transformation of a state or action, completeness or finality" to that of the main verb. Table 17.6 further highlights the contrast between simple and main verbs and compound verbs involving *jaa:*

Let us consider another example of the compound verb construction, this time with *denaa* lit. "to give" as the helping verb. When one gives something, the beneficiary of the action is someone other than the speaker. That is exactly what is added to the main verb by *denaa* when it is used as a helping verb in a compound verb construction, that is, to perform the action designated by the main verb for others. Similarly, consider another verb *lenaa* "to take." When this verb is used as a helping verb it loses its literal meaning and indicates that the beneficiary of the action designated by the main verb is the speaker himself or herself.

Against this background let us examine the one-word and two-word utterances produced by *V.*

(11) a. Simple verb [=Nair (3), p. 66]
do
"give"

TABLE 17.6

Simple and Compound Hindi Verbs Involving *jaa*

Simple Verbs		Compound Verbs		
aanaa	"to come"	aa	jaanaa	"to come back, arrive"
khaanaa	"to eat"	khaa	jaanaa	"to eat up"
piinaa	"to drink"	pii	jaanaa	"to drink up"
samajhnaa	"to understand"	samajh	jaanaa	"to understand fully"
honaa	"to be"	ho	jaanaa	"to become"
bhuulnaa	"to forget"	bhuul	jaanaa	"to forget completely"

b. Compound verbs
  i. [=Nair (18), p. 66]
     kar do
     do give
     "Do it" (for the benefit of someone other than the speaker)
  ii. [=Nair (30), p 67]
     tʃoR do
     leave give
     "Leave/let go"
  iii. [=Nair (65), p 68]
     rakh do
     keep give
     "keep (it)" (for the benefit of someone other than the speaker)

(12) a. Simple verb [=Nair (58)]
     zao
     "go"
  b. Compound verb [=Nair (21)]
     kha: zao
     eat go
     "eat up"

Comparison of (11a) with the examples in (11b) and (12a) with (12b) reveals that *V* has developed an adultlike contrast between simple and compound verbs in Hindi. This contrast is present only in the Hindi language and at no point in *V*'s development (early or late) did English lexical items occur as either main verb or helping verb in the compound verb construction. In addition, Hindi tag questions, negation and question formation, develop along the lines of the corresponding adult Hindi structures, thus supporting the DSH at the expense of the unitary hypothesis. Garcia (1983, p. 40), whose subject received mixed input (as opposed to one-parent/one-language input), found the same pattern of development—the morphosyntactic structure of his subject's two languages (Spanish and English) developed separately between the ages 3;0 and 4;2.

Autonomous or Interdependent Systems

In a carefully designed and theoretically grounded study within the framework of government and binding, Paradis and Genesee (1996) set out to examine the relationship of a bilingual child's two languages. The main concern of this study was to determine whether the two systems develop autonomously or interdependently from the age of two onward. To seek an answer to this question, they conducted a longitudinal investigation of the speech production of three French/English bilingual children between the ages of 2 and 3 years. Paradis and Genesee argued that if the two language systems are interdependent, then evidence of transfer between the two languages,[9] and of acceleration or delay in acquisition of one or the other of the two languages, should be found in their subjects' speech production. To test their hypothesis, the acquisition of the functional category INFL (representing finiteness/nonfiniteness and subject agreement in sentences of French and English and other languages as well) was selected. The results indicated no sign of transfer, or of acceleration or delay, in the performance or the acquisition of the bilingual children. The dual system hypothesis (DSH) therefore received convincing support from the study.

To represent the full impact of Paradis and Genesee's important results, it will be necessary to provide some background information concerning the analysis of INFL in adult French and English and to review basic work on the separate, monolingual acquisition of features of INFL in French and English. We now turn to this task.

Using Chomsky's (1981, 1991) principles-and-parameters approach as their theoretical framework, Déprez and Pierce (1993, 1994) and Pierce (1989, 1992) demonstrated that French and English monolingual children differ from each other in three important ways: emergence and use of finite verbs, negation, and distribution of pronominal subjects. For instance, French-speaking children are capable of producing most of their utterances with inflected or finite verbs as young as the age 2;0, whereas English-speaking children do not produce finite verbs until about age 3;0. In other words, at about age 2, a French child is capable of alternating between finite and nonfinite utterances. In contrast, finiteness is absent in the English-speaking child. These differences are as distinct at deeper levels of analysis as they are at the surface. They are interrelated within the UG framework

[9]Bunenik (1978), Imedadze (1967), Swain and Wache (1975), and Vihman (1982) have reported instances of transfer whereas De Houwer (1990) found no evidence of transfer in her 3-year-old subject, Kate. Paradis and Genesee argued that researchers reporting the incidence of interference fail to show how systematic and frequent the constructions with transferred elements are, nor do they provide information on the alternation of these mixed constructions with single-language constructions of similar meaning where the transferred elements were not present. In the absence of this information, there is no way to determine whether such cases were examples of episodic interference or code mixing or examples of true interdependence (Paradis & Genesee, 1996, p. 3).

and are thus attributable to the abstract grammatical properties of each language. They can be explained by means of differences in the values of the verb movement parameter between English and French, according to some versions of the principles-and-parameter approach (e.g., Chomsky, 1991; Deprez & Pierce, 1993, 1994), to which we now proceed.

Inflectional verb affixation (representing tense and subject-verb agreement) is the result of movement of some type in both adult native French and adult native English and movement must take place in order for a verb to bear tense and agreement inflection, which is crucial to the well-formedness of sentences. This verb movement behaves differently in French and English. In accordance with principles discussed in Emonds (1978) and Pollock (1989), French verbs undergo raising to the INFL position, whereas in English the INFL affixes (realized as *-s* and *-ed*) undergo lowering to the verb position with the exception of the semantically light verbs *have* and *be* (which do undergo raising) and modals (which are base-generated in INFL). The D-structure adopted for both French and English by Paradis and Genesee (1996) is given in (13) (the "NegP" and "Neg" nodes are optional):

(13)

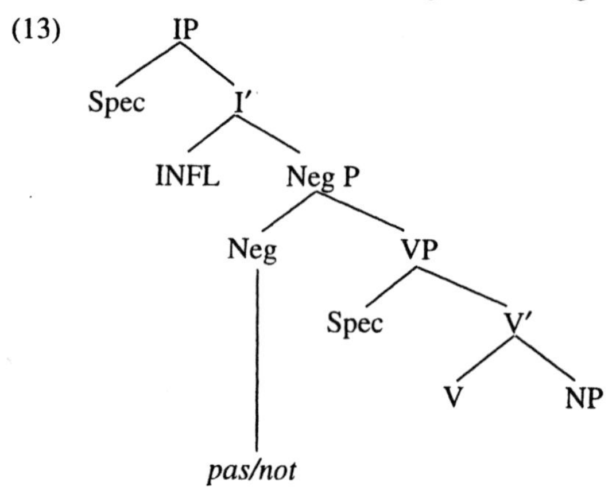

By verb raising we obtain the French structure as in (14) and affix lowering yields the English structure, as shown diagrammatically in (15):

(14) Adult native French verb raising

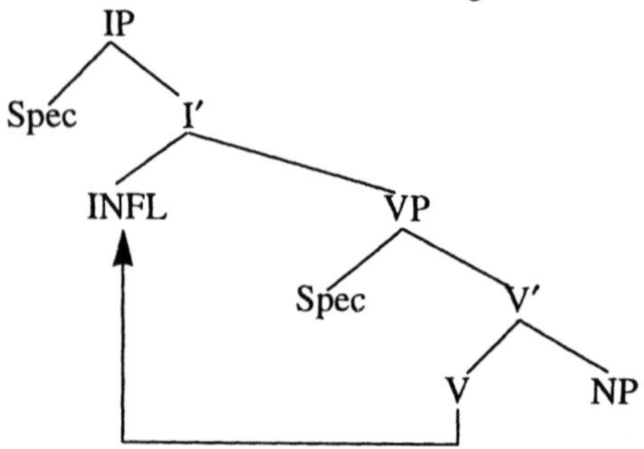

(15) Adult native English affix lowering

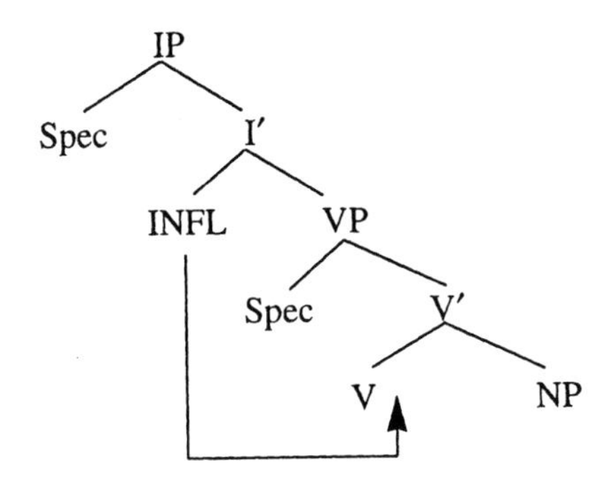

In the case of negative constructions, in English, Neg (i.e., *not*) blocks the lowering of INFL to V—a highly complex process (see the following)—and an application of "*do*-support" is necessary to carry the affixes *-s* and *-ed;* on the other hand, the raising of the verb over the Neg in French (i.e., *pas*) is not blocked.

Under the assumptions of the principles-and-parameters framework, the setting of the verb movement parameter in either its French value or its English value in the process of acquisition is determined by the primary linguistic data to which the child is exposed. In particular, the setting of a parameter in one of its values requires a "triggering" experience, which may consist in evidence for one or more of the structural properties clustered together under either one value of the parameter or the other.

Let us turn now to the monolingual development of these structures in child syntax. The works by Déprez and Pierce (1993, 1994) and by Pierce (1989, 1992) hypothesize that during the initial stage there is no movement in child syntax. Therefore, they predict (and find) nonfinite verbs both in French and English children in the early stages of acquisition. Verb raising is a relatively simple process and French is slightly richer than English in its verb morphology; therefore, finiteness emerges earlier in French children than in English. In contrast, affix lowering is a complex process and English is not as morphologically rich a language as French; therefore, finiteness develops later in English-speaking children.

As regards the developmental differences in negation, Déprez and Pierce's (1993, 1994) and Pierce's (1992) data show that the earlier negatives develop in a complementary fashion in French children: The negative particle *pas* is placed in sentence-initial position with nonfinite verbs (16a) but appears in the postverbal position with finite verbs, as in adult French (16b). English negation is first placed in the sentence-initial position (16c) and later after the subject as in (16d) with nonfinite verbs, neither structure being adultlike.

(16) a. pas chercher les voitures (Phillippe 2;1)
not look-for the cars
"No look for cars."

b. ca tourne pas (Phillippe 2;1)
that turns not
"That isn't turning."
c. No Leila have a turn (Nina 2;1)
d. me no go home (Peter 2;1)

These differences can be explained in terms of two kinds of movements. The first kind of movement, exemplified in the structure of (16b), raises the verb from its D-structure position in VP to INFL over NegP as in adult French (14). The second kind of movement is subject raising and accounts for the difference between (16c) and (16d). Déprez and Pierce assumed that subject NPs originate in [Spec, VP] at D-structure and must move to [Spec, IP] at S-structure over NegP in structures that contain Neg in order to receive Case from INFL (see, e.g., Koopman & Sportiche, 1991, for evidence and arguments). In English (16c), the subject is an unraised, VP-internal subject, whereas in (16d) the subject has undergone raising to [Spec, IP]. In the case where neither the subject nor the verb is raised, the negative marker appears in initial position as in (16c).

In French there are two kinds of pronouns: weak (*je, tu, il, elle, on, nous, vous, ils, elles*) and strong (*moi, toi, lui, elle, eux, elles*). In child French, weak pronouns appear only with finite subjects whereas strong pronouns can occur with both finite and nonfinite verbs. There is no such restriction in English nor is the distinction of weak and strong pronouns valid for English-speaking children. These differences are accounted for by assuming that the weak pronouns are not NPs but, rather, are agreement clitics, part of INFL. In contrast, English pronouns are NPs as are the French strong pronouns. (See Pierce, 1992, for further details.) These three distinctive properties of child French and child English can be accounted for by the hypothesis that French children acquire the properties of INFL earlier than English children do. These differences in the properties of INFL in English and French and the resulting differences in the pacing of the monolingual acquisition of French and of English make the case of French-English child bilingualism a powerful test to examine the question of autonomous development of two languages in the bilingual child (in accordance with the DSH) or interdependent development (according to the unitary hypothesis).

In an application of this test, Paradis and Genesee (1996) reported the language development at three different intervals of three French-English bilinguals who were raised, according to their parents, in a one-parent/one-language environment. However, it later came to light that the parents did not restrict themselves to the one-parent/one-language regimen. In particular, they were in the habit of code mixing intrasententially, so the subjects actually received mixed input. The input pattern and time intervals are summarized in Table 17.7. Figure 17.5 presents the acquisition rate and the pattern of finiteness by the bilingual children: As Figure 17.5 indicates, the proportion of finite utterances is greater in French at each interval and the development of French did not accelerate the rate of the develop-

TABLE 17.7
Input Patterns and Time Intervals

Child	Age			Input Pattern
	Interval 1	Interval 2	Interval 3	
William	2:2	2:10	3:3	More exposure to English than French
Gene	1:11	2:7	3:1	Exposed to both languages equally, French slight edge
Olivier	1:11	2:6	2:10	Interval 1 and 2 more French; Interval 3 more English

Source: Paradis and Genesee, 1996, p. 11.

ment of the finite utterances in English in any serious way in comparison with the rate of acquisition of finite structures by English monolingual children. The slow rate of the development of finiteness in English was predicted based on the complexity of affix lowering, assuming that the language acquisition of the bilingual children follows the path of English monolinguals.

Similarly, postverbal negation in French is an indicator of finite verbs and verb raising. The absence of these structures in the English of these subjects is evidence against interference from French. Both trends were attested by the French-English bilinguals. Not only were no postverbal negatives produced by the bilinguals in their English sentences, postverbal negatives with finite verbs predominated in the French of the subjects. It is also clear that these bilingual children used subject raising to produce sentence-initial and sentence-medial negation in English. The rate of sentence-initial and sentence-medial negation was comparable to that of English monolingual children. No delay was experienced by bilinguals in this regard, which rules out the dependency of these children's English on their French.

Likewise, the use of pronominal subjects by the three bilingual children showed a similar proportion of pronominal subjects with finite and nonfinite utterances with pronominal subjects in English, whereas virtually 100% of their pronominal (weak) subjects in French occur in finite sentences. This led Paradis and Genesee (1996) to claim that these children are aware of the clitic status of French pronominal (weak) subjects and the NP status of English pronominal subjects.

In summary, the acquisition of finiteness, negation, and pronominal subjects in these bilinguals follows the same pattern and the same rate as those of monolinguals in each language, which lends solid support to DSH or "autonomous" system hypothesis. This shows that the amount of input or learning is not critical to the rate of language development of bilinguals. The triggering of the movement parameter by primary linguistic data leads to the acquisition of the language-specific structural properties of INFL, which leads, in turn, to an appropriate monolingual-like rate of acquisition.

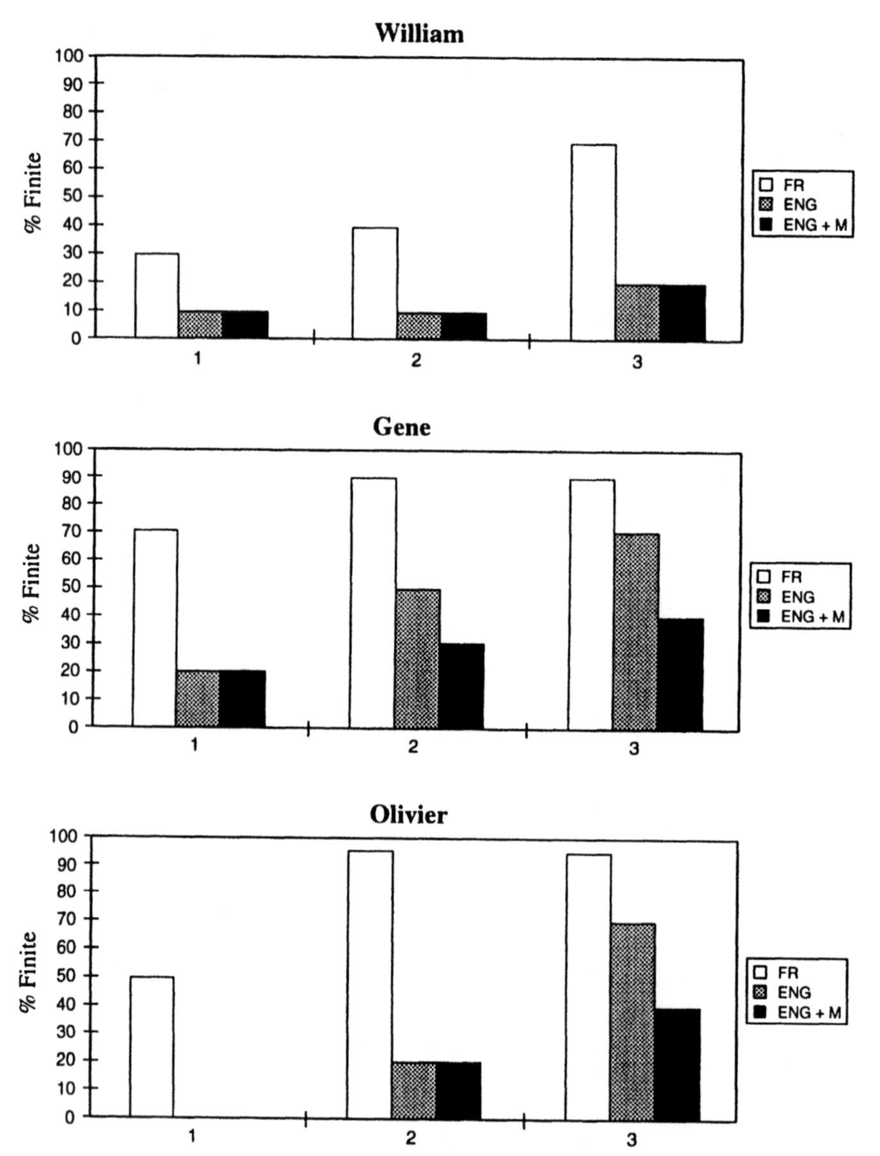

Figure 17.5. Acquisition rate and finiteness pattern in bilingual children. Redrawn from Paradis and Genesee (1996), p. 13.

IX. INPUT POVERTY AND INPUT MODALITY

There is considerable evidence which suggests that many deaf children of deaf parents eventually become bilinguals and biculturals in the sense that they acquire a spoken language in addition to a sign language (see Bouvet, 1990). The deaf parents of deaf children do not deprive their children of bimodal input, that is, visual as well as spoken. However, as noted previously, the hearing parents of deaf children often react by shutting off oral as well as nonoral input, particularly during the critical period of language development. In such cases, the language development of deaf children of hearing parents suffers a setback or lag.

Because the deaf parents of a deaf child do not associate deafness with muteness and therefore sign and speak simultaneously (when they are able to), the deaf child is the beneficiary of a visual language (sign language) and a spoken language as well. The evidence also suggests that such children in turn receive ample input that can be characterized as "mixed input"—a mixture of spoken and visual language. On the receiving end, children nevertheless experience a poverty of spoken language input depending on the degree of their hearing loss and the age at which the hearing loss has taken place. Consequently, the rate of language acquisition varies widely in deaf children.

As regards the acquisition of L1, a deaf child acquires a visual-gestural language as effortlessly and unconsciously as a hearing child acquires an oral-aural language. Despite differences in modality, sign languages instantiate the same properties found in spoken languages. Newport and Meier (1985), Lillo-Martin (see chapter 16 of this volume), and others have observed that a deaf child undergoes the same stages in the development of American Sign Language (ASL) as a hearing child undergoes in the acquisition of a spoken language—the one-word and two-word stages, and the emergence of vocabulary, phonology, morphology, and syntax.[10]

In relation to the deaf children of hearing parents, it is claimed that 90 to 95% of them do not learn ASL from their parents but are exposed to the language from their peers. Naturally, then, their ASL development takes place in the absence of a parental or caretaker model and, thus, shows delays as well as certain characteristics of pidgin languages. In such cases it is hard to determine what the child's native language is. In fact, Berent (1988, 1996) has described their acquisition as "L1.5 acquisition," splitting the difference between L1 and L2 acquisition.

The works of Cooper and Rosenstein (1966), Myklebust (1964), Goda (1964), and Branon (1968) show that deaf children (ages 8 to 18) with severe and profound deafness occurring before age 2 or 3 (called "prelingual deafness") produce shorter, simpler sentences with overuse of nouns, relative to hearing subjects. They used no indefinite pronouns, auxiliary verbs, quantifiers, prepositions, conjunctions, and interjections. In short, they experienced considerable difficulty in the acquisition of function elements as opposed to content elements.

The study by Quigley and King (1980), devoted to the acquisition of English by

[10]One area of slight difference in the acquisition of a spoken language observed by Meier and Newport (1990) is that of vocabulary, where the first signs appear earlier than the first words.

deaf learners and hearing children, reports full parallelism between hearing and deaf children in the acquisition of English syntax, the only difference being that in deaf children syntactic development takes place at a much slower rate than in hearing children. Radford (1988, 1990) observed that young hearing children's early syntactic developments can be characterized by the lack of functional category C (complementizer), I (inflection), and D (determiner, including articles and the possessive marker *'s*). If hearing children acquire thematic categories before functional categories, we might expect the presence of the same pattern among deaf children. The findings of Berent (1983, 1988), Power and Quigley (1973), Wilbur, Goodhart, and Montadon (1983)—see Berent (1996) for review—support the presence of this developmental pattern. In fact, it seems that deaf learners resist functional categories indefinitely.[11]

Berent and Samar (1990) further found that certain structures of English are more learnable than others by deaf learners. For instance, adverbial clauses are more easily acquired than relative clauses. Employing the insights of the theory of markedness, their results revealed more successful acquisition of unmarked structures than the marked ones. Their follow-up studies (Samar & Berent, 1991, 1993) revealed that deaf learners with low English language proficiency showed the acquisition of some movements such as in passive sentences but failed to acquire movement in *be* structures. Samar and Berent attributed such acquisitional failure to poverty of input during the critical stages of language development. In terms of the subset principle (Berwick, 1985; Wexler & Manzini, 1987), they concluded that deaf learners tend to learn languages that are "smaller" than full spoken languages.

Let us now return to the question of language development among those deaf children who either do not receive nativelike input or do not receive any input at all. Ross and Newport (1996) reported data from a case study of a deaf child they call "Simon" who had deaf parents (Singleton & Newport, 1994). Simon's parents did not learn ASL until the mid or late teens. Simon's language acquisition environment is particularly interesting for the following two reasons: (a) Simon was exposed to nonnative ASL input from birth, that is, input from his parental models, and (b) at school his peers did not use ASL or any other sign language and there was no arrangement for him to learn ASL. The specific issues that Ross and Newport aimed at investigating were the following: (a) How close did Simon come to nativelike proficiency as compared to children with native input? (b) How long did it take for Simon to develop this level of proficiency? (c) Was Simon's development complete by the age of 7;11 or did it continue after that time?

To answer these questions, Ross and Newport analyzed Simon's performance

[11]Déprez and Pierce (1993), Poeppel and Wexler (1993), Hyams (1992), and others have argued against Radford's position. If one accepts these criticisms of Radford, then, clearly, some other specific explanation must be sought for the phenomena reported in Quigley and King (1980) and in Berent (1996).

TABLE 17.8
Simon's Input and Output of Classifier Morphemes and Movement Morphemes (Percentage Correct at 7;11)

	Movement	Classifier
Input:		
Mother	75%	42
Father	69	45
(Native Adult	94	82)
Output:		
Simon	88	50
(Native Children	81	69)

Note. Adapted from Ross and Newport (1995), p. 638.

in the acquisition and use of ASL verbs of motion, which are highly multimorphemic. The study focused on two kinds of verbal morphemes: motion morphemes consisting of five morpheme classes (path, manner, direction, and two location morphemes) and classifier morphemes of two kinds (central object classifier and secondary object classifier). (For more details on the two kinds of morphemes, see Supalla, 1982.) Simon was tested at several stages in his development in comparison with children who had received input from native signers. Table 17.8 summarizes the percentage of correct (=consistent) morphemes produced in the verbs of motion production (VMP) part of the ASL Test Battery by Simon's parents (hence in Simon's input)—in comparison with adult native signers—and in Simon's output at age 7;11 in comparison with three children the same age who had received native input. Simon's performance on movement morphemes at 7;11 equals (in fact, slightly surpasses) that of native children at the same age, whereas he is significantly less successful in his use of classifiers at that age than are native signers.

What is Simon's developmental pattern for classifiers like before and after 7;11? The results obtained from the developmental pattern of movement morphemes as analyzed in Ross and Newport (1995) show that, in general, Simon's acquisition pattern closely resembles that of native input children. The course of his acquisition of classifiers also resembles that of natives up to the age of 4;6 to 4;8 as is evident from Figure 17.6. Between 4;6 to 4;8 and 9;1, however, native-input children improved significantly in the use of classifiers, whereas Simon's performance hits a point of stagnation at 4:6 to 4;8. The underlying reasons for this nonnative performance, as claimed by Ross and Newport (1996), are the relative complexity of the classifier system and highly inconsistent input from his parents, who are non-

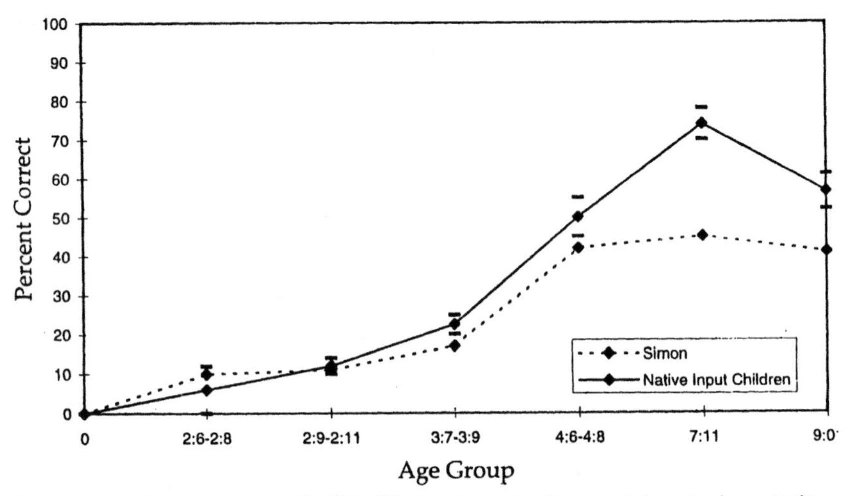

Figure 17.6. Percent correct for CLASSIFIER morphemes for Simon and the native input. Redrawı from Ross and Newport (1995: 642).

native signers. These two factors prevented the child from discovering regulari- ties.

In other words, under certain conditions (consistency of input and relative sim- plicity of target structures) children demonstrate their innate capacity for creoliz- ing nonnative input. Simon's acquisition of classifiers indicates that this capacit) is not free of limitations. Factors such as the complexity of target structures to- gether with an inability to capture regularities from inconsistent input place limi- tations on the child's capacity to creolize nonnative input. This limitation can oc- cur even at a young age. Although research dealing with poverty of input anc nonnative input has registered some interesting results, the complexity of the phe- nomena cannot be underestimated. More research is needed to arrive at definitc conclusions about the interaction of variables such as maturity/continuity, chil- dren's ability to creolize nonnative input, the degree of consistency of input, anc the complexity of target structures.

X. CODE MIXING AND CODE SWITCHING

In Section 8 we discussed the issue of language differentiation in bilingual chil dren during the initial stages of language development. The issue of the onset o language differentiation in simultaneous bilinguals is also central to the two fun damental questions about children's ability to separate and integrate the two lin guistic systems: (a) Can bilingual children mix the two (apparently distinct) languages at the age of two? (b) If they can, how is this mixing different from adult language mixing, both in qualitative and quantitative terms? The proponents of the unitary hypothesis (Leopold, 1978; Redlinger & Park, 1980; Swain, 1972; Taeschner, 1983; Vihman, 1985, 1986; Volterra & Taeschner, 1978) claim that bilingual children start out using elements from the two languages indifferently and redundantly before separating the two systems. On their view, the separation of the two systems occurs between the ages of 3 and 4—first at the lexical level and then at the structural level, as noted previously. On this view, children's early language mixing (before 3;0) is therefore nothing but a reflection of their failure to separate the two systems and is seen as a sign of the "fusion" of the two systems; this mixing is thus understood to be "deficient" in some way and therefore not equatable with an adult's language mixing.

According to the supporters of the dual system hypothesis (Bergman, 1976; De Houwer, 1987a,b, 1995; Lindholm & Padilla, 1978; Meisel, 1989, 1992; Padilla & Liebman, 1975; Pye, 1986), children do not go through an initial stage of treating the two systems as if they were one system, but begin to distinguish them immediately. In fact, their sociolinguistic competence—in particular, their ability to choose the appropriate language for a given interlocutor and context—precedes the acquisition of formal rules (see Döpke, 1992; Lanza, 1992). Döpke's study of the language development of a child between the ages of 2;0 and 2;5 (claimed to have been raised in a one-parent/one-language environment) reveals that the child's ability to perceive two languages as distinct systems might manifest itself in a number of ways—for example, sound distinction and language production. In terms of language production alone, a wide variety of evidence—much of it reviewed in Section VII.B—can be provided to support the claim that even at the age of 2;0 children differentiate between the two systems. Even the appearance of an "inappropriate language" choice may reflect the child's preference for one system over the other contrary to his or her parents' discourse strategy (i.e., a mother's preference for English over German and mixed input).

Before we go further into the debate of language mixing among early bilinguals, some remarks are in order about the definitions and concepts involving language mixing. In addition, we present seminal findings and trends in research on code mixing among adults in order to provide a comparative perspective on the phenomenon of childhood code mixing.

A. Fusion, Code Mixing, and Code Switching

As pointed out earlier, a particular type of language mixing is found in children in the early stages of acquisition that is attributed by supporters of the unitary hypothesis to what Meisel refers to as "fusion" of the two systems—that is, the child's "failure in separating the two grammars" (Meisel, 1994, p. 414). Because such mixing is claimed to arise from a single language system composed of elements from two languages, it differs (in at least this respect) from mature or adult-like code-mixing (CM) and code switching (CS), which are products of the interaction of two separate, fully developed language systems. Therefore, it is crucial to draw a distinction between CM/CS on one hand and other, related phenomenon on the other.

We use the term CM to refer to intrasentential language mixing and the term CS for the intersentential mixing in bilinguals. The two terms are applied in the following fashion: CM refers to the mixing of various linguistic units (morphemes, words, modifiers, phrases, clauses and sentences) primarily from two participating grammatical systems within a sentence. In other words, CM is intrasentential and is constrained by grammatical principles and may be motivated by socio-psychological motivations. CS refers to the mixing of various linguistic units (morphemes, words, modifiers, phrases, clauses, and sentences) primarily from two participating grammatical systems across sentence boundaries within a speech event. In other words, CS is intersentential and may be subject to certain discourse principles. It is also motivated by socio-psychological motivations.

The distinction between CM and CS is controversial. For some linguists this distinction is purely terminological, whereas for others the distinction is profound because it has implications for the grammar of CM and CS. For a review of this controversy and for the distinction between CM/CS and the other related phenomena such as borrowing, pidginization, creolization, and diglossia, see Bhatia and Ritchie (1996a, pp. 629–638).

B. Adult and Early Child Language Mixing: Qualitative and Quantitative Differences

To understand the qualitative and quantitative differences between early CM by children and adultlike CM, it is imperative to examine the structural properties of the two types of CM. With the exception of a handful of studies, in particular the notable study by Meisel (1992), very little attention has been paid to CM by children before the age of 3;0. In addition to the severe scarcity of studies of CM during the earliest phase, there is also a relative dearth of studies devoted specifically to the grammatical properties of CM among children. Some notable exceptions are Bergman (1976), Lindholm and Padilla (1978), Redlinger and Park (1980), Taeschner (1983), Vihman (1985), Peterson (1988), De Houwer (1990), Lanza (1990), and Veh (1990). In contrast, the treatment of the grammar of adult CM has mushroomed during the past two decades (see Bhatia & Ritchie, 1996a, for review.)

Code Mixing: The Early Stages

Let us consider the question of the grammar of children's earliest CM by investigating its structural properties, that is, what kinds of linguistic elements are mixed/switched by children? Studies devoted to childhood language mixing show that CM of syntactic categories by children, like adults, is not a random phenomenon. Nouns and noun phrases are the most favored categories as compared to other major categories such as verbs (e.g., McClure 1977, Lindholm & Padilla, 1978, Redlinger & Park, 1980, Kielhöfer & Jonekeit, 1983; among others). For instance, in their study of five Spanish-English children, Lindholm and Padilla (1978) found the following incidence of mixing from English into Spanish and from Spanish into English: nouns (71 English-into-Spanish/12 Spanish-into-English), verbs (3/3), adjectives (2/0), conjunction (5/3), and phrasal mixes (4/8). Redlinger and Park found no cases of phrasal mixing in their study of three bilingual children. The incidence of noun and verb mixing was at a seven to one ratio in favor of nouns. A total absence of mixed functional categories is also notable.

These findings differ from Vihman (1985) who found that her Estonian-English speaking bilingual child favored verbs slightly over nouns (i.e., 24 verbs and 23 nouns). The study also claimed that the subject mixed 24 function words. Although this finding stands in sharp contrast with other studies, which found an almost complete absence of mixed function words, a close examination of Vihman's data reveals that she defined the term "function word" in a somewhat idiosyncratic and broad-based fashion. In her definition, function words include any word except nouns, verbs, and adjectives.

In spite of some disagreements about the presence or the absence of function words in early mixing by bilingual children—based in large part on a terminological difference—it is clear that child mixing shows a distributional pattern that depends crucially on the syntactic properties of the mixed elements—specifically, the syntactic categories of the mixed elements.

Although no systematic quantitative studies of adult language mixing have been carried out (with the exception of McConvell, 1988), from the data presented and the constraints positied for adult CM (see Bhatia & Ritchie, 1996a, for review and discussion) the pattern of nominal mixing favored by children over verbs is similar to that of adult mixing. However, Lanza (1992, p. 640) found that her 2-year-old subject, Siri, who was acquiring Norwegian and English simultaneously in Norway, exhibited the mixing of pronouns (73 = 43.5%) and adverbs (38 = 22.6%) at a higher rate than nouns (26 = 15.5%) at the multiword stage (age 2;0 to 2;7). The reason for the different pattern can be attributed to the phenomenon of "language dominance" to which we will return later.

Meisel (1992) presented empirical findings from a longitudinal study of two children investigated as part of the DUFDE project,[12] which is devoted to the longitudinal study of two children. Both children were learning French and German

[12]DUFDE stands for Deutsche und Französisch—Doppelter Erstspracherwerb (German-French—Simultaneous Acquisition of Two First Languages). The research group DUFDE videotaped the interaction of the 13 children with adults and occasionally with children every two weeks. Each recording lasted for 60 minutes, half in German and half in French, following the one person–one language technique—that is, one researcher used only French and the other only German in their interaction with children.

and were growing up in middle-class families in Hamburg, Germany, at the ti of the study.[13] The study focuses on their speech patterns during the early peri of acquisition (1;4 to 3;0). The male subject, *Iv*, appears to be French dominant i tially, whereas the female subject, *A*, was to begin with exposure to a balanced l guage input from French and German. However, after the age 2;6, German beg to be dominant in her case.

The qualitative pattern of mixing revealed that a limited number of lexical ite accounted for a majority of the mixes. As for mixing of German into French, following types of lexical items figure prominently: yes-no markers (*ja/n* "yes/no"); deictic marker (*da/das/dies* "there/that/this"); particles (*auf/zu/ab* " (open)/closed/off"); adverbials (*alle* "all gone"); expressions such as *doch* "y indeed I do" and *auch* "me too." Both children shared this pattern.

Almost the same pattern is witnessed with regard to the mixing of French i German. This shows that communicative needs motivate children to mix lexi items expressing deictic reference, assertion, negation, completion, and so on.

As regards the other grammatical categories—adjectives, nouns, verbs, and verbs—German nouns (e.g., those meaning 'car,' 'bed') are mixed fairly f quently into French and vice versa. German adjectives were restricted to th glossable as those meaning 'hot' and 'good' whereas French adjectives mixed w 'little,' 'beautiful,' 'too small,' and 'red.' Only *Iv* mixed German adverbials a verbs into French. He used adverbs of location and direction: *darin* "into that," *rauf* "on top of that," *raus* "out," *drin* "inside," *darunter* "under that," and *un* "down there." He used only one adverb from French in his German utteranc Most of the mixing at this stage seems not to require the kind of skillful cohes of grammatical structures that is witnessed in adult mixing.

Meisel observed that the language mixing described above occurred during one-word stage. From 2;6 for *A* and 2;3 for *Iv*, mixing undergoes qualitat changes. By 2;3,5 *Iv* uses multiword switches, as is evident from the following amples: *ich will NONOURS.* "I want TEDDY," and *l'eau, DE SCHI*

[13]No recordings were made between ages 1;10,18 to 2;0,10 because the family of the children w to Madagascar on a family vacation. Also, the first recording was excluded from Meisel's study cause it contained no incidence of language mixing. The term *dominance* is used in a wide variet ways. The various dimensions of dominance need to be spelled out in bilingual language acquisi studies, for example, weaker language in sequential language acquisition, socio-political conditi (prestige, etc.), and preference for a language in family interaction. The interaction of dominance CM also need further investigation (e.g., Bentahila & Davies, 1992b).

As regards early language mixing by bilingual children, some important gains have been mad the result of the examination of the grammatical and sociolinguistic properties of the languages volved. A number of questions dealing with the qualitative and quantitative differences between a and children language mixing behavior await more definitive answers. After bilingual children de op differentiation of linguistic competence in the two languages, the incidence of language mi increases or decreases in comparison to language mixing prior to language differentiation, though findings are still not conclusive.

SCHWIMMT l'eau "the water, THE SHIP SWIMS (on) the water." Note that the noun determiner is still missing in the first example and the preposition is absent in the second example.

As regards French mixing into German, the first nominal mixes are restricted to single nouns. By 2;0,2 the following two patterns involving more than one noun surface: *das* N "that (is) N" with N in French, and N – V where there is a mix between N and V. By 2;3,5 a more complex structure with *das*– noun sequences such as *das UN AUTRE FIL* "this (is) ANOTHER THREAD." By this time, mixing between determiner and noun on one hand, and subject and verb on the other begins to surface. By 2;4 one finds French verbs are combined with German objects.

Constraints on Early CM by Children

The view that the grammar of adult CM is unpredictable or random was discredited in the late 1970s and early 1980s when it was observed by several researchers (see Bhatia & Ritchie, 1996a, for review) that fluent bilinguals were able to make consistent acceptability judgements about CM utterances. Attempts began at that time to capture constraints on CM in adults within existing theoretical frameworks and approaches. These approaches can be classified into three groups (a) typological, (b) categorical (i.e., referring to grammatical categories), and (c) constituency relationships grounded in different theoretical models such as government-binding (GB) theory and its ancestral and descendant versions. A comprehensive treatment of these constraints is beyond the scope of this chapter; therefore, we will not go further into them here (for review, see Bhatia & Ritchie, 1996a, pp. 640–657).

Meisel (1994) observed that every constraint on CM ever proposed has been challenged on empirical grounds, citing counterexamples for each case. Because proposed constraints such as the government constraint (Di Sciullo, Muysken, & Singh, 1986) make correct predictions for a wide variety of clear cases and because these constraints are formulated in terms of independently motivated principles embedded in relatively successful explanatory theories of grammatical structure, even a fairly large number of apparent counterexamples should not lead us to reject them prematurely. Instead, "a sound research strategy appears to be to examine whether it might be possible to reformulate a constraint in a more adequate fashion and/or to scrutinize the data to determine whether they indeed represent counterexamples" (Meisel, 1992, p. 420). He observed that contrary to the predictions of the government constraint, switches do occur between subject and verb, although they are less frequent than object and verb switching. Similarly, switches before COMP, which are ruled out by the government constraint, do occur. The research approach proposed by Meisel led him to reformulate the government constraint in order to remedy shortcomings (also see Bhatia & Ritchie, 1996a, pp. 648–651, for the shortcomings of the government constraint with special reference to CM and the complex verb phenomenon in South Asian languages). Relying on m-command as the definition of *government,* he made room for INFL among the set of governors in order to account for "coherence" involving the unity of lexical items in VP. The other possible governors noted by Meisel are COMP for VPs and DET for nominals.

Following Radford's theory of early grammatical development (e.g., Radford, 1990, and others; however, see footnote 11), it was mentioned earlier that the functional categories develop later than lexical categories in both deaf children and normal children; therefore, it is natural to expect that bilingual children will exercise adultlike grammatical constraints on CM only after the full development of functional categories such as INFL and COMP. Regarding the language development of the two children discussed earlier, Meisel reported that the functional categories emerged at 2;4 to 2;5 for *Iv* and at age 2;6 for *A*. Before this age wherever there is an appearance of the violation of constraints such as the government constraint, according to Meisel, these instances are simply cases of nonapplicability of grammatical constraints rather than violations of them. From the point in acquisition when the functional categories emerge, switching begins to occur regularly between determiner and noun, as is evident from the following examples:

(17) a. moi je va à la KUCHE (Iv 3;1,3)
me I goes to the kitchen
"I go to the kitchen."
b. il y a beaucoup de BERGE (Iv 3;1,3)
it there has many of mountains
"There are many mountains."

Mixing of an entire prepositional phrase or noun is permitted by the children in both the subject and the verb complement position, as is evident from the following three sentences:

(18) on va maintenant ZUM KRANKENWAGEN (Iv 2;11,21)
we go now to-the ambulance
"We now go to the ambulance."

(19) je veux MILCH (A 3;7,2)
I want milk
"I want milk."

(20) DU DU, aimes ca la soupe (Iv 2;8,15)
you you like that the soup
"Do you like that soup."

Sentences such as (19) and (20) present problems for the government constraint as posited originally by Di Sciullo and colleagues. However, they will be accounted for by the reformulated version of the government constraint proposed by Meisel. Except for certain performance level problems or violations, Meisel found "no violation of grammatical constraints" once children clearly had access to functional categories in their language development stage.

Our analysis of Nair's data does not support this conclusion. In her study of the language development of the bilingual child *V*, Nair claimed that the child has clearly developed language differentiation by the age 24 months. Our analysis of the data indicates that the INFL system both for Hindi and English is clearly being differentiated by the child, as is evident from the earlier discussion. However, the CM employed by *V* violates another constraint on adult CM, as we will argue using the examples in (21) as evidence:

(21) English-*Hindi*

a. I sit-*egaa* no.
   I sit-will neg
   "I will not sit."

b. you *idhal* sit ho *jaao*.
   you here sit be go-imperative
   "You sit down here."

c. *ikko* on-der *karo*
   this on-there do-imp.
   "Put this on that." (lit. "Do this there.")

The mixing of the English verb *sit* (21b) and (21c) is similar to adult CM. As Bhatia and Ritchie (1996b) and Ritchie and Bhatia (1996) show, English verbs cannot switch with attached Hindi tense-aspect marking in the speech of adult bilinguals. However, such a switch is possible if the Hindi tense-aspect marker is carried by a Hindi verb such as *kar* "do" or *ho* "be" and the switched verb appears in the complement of this light verb. The mixing found in (21b) and (21c) is adultlike; however, sentences such as (21a) are not the FHC and thus are not permitted by Hindi-English adult bilinguals. This shows that in spite of the development of language differentiation and acquisition of the INFL system, the CM employed by *V* falls short of its adult counterpart and is still in the developmental stages. Similarly, *V* uses Hindi bound morphemes with nonfinite verbs, as in the following example:

(22) Hindi-*English*

ju *buy*-ke aao.
you buy-having come-imp
"Come, after you buy (it)." (lit. "Having bought this, come.")

Sentences such as (22) are judged ungrammatical by the Hindi-English bilingual adult, because the English verb "buy" is not accompanied by the Hindi light verb, *kar* (i.e., *buy kar ke* "having bought" is well formed). These results suggest that although constraints on CM in bilingual adults are grounded in grammatical competence, development of these constraints is delayed to a point beyond that at which the requisite aspects of competence are acquired.

Dominance, Fusion, and CM

As pointed out earlier, Lanza (1992, p. 640) observed that the CM pattern of the Norwegian-English bilingual child Siri was different in a number of ways: (a) She mixed more pronouns and adverbs than most other bilingual children, who mix nouns more often than they do words in other syntactic categories; (b) The pattern of mixing bound morphemes is what can be characterized as "asymmetrical": English lexical morphemes co-occur with both English and Norwegian bound morphemes (e.g., *looker, looks* both meaning "looks") whereas Norwegian lexical morphemes co-occur only with Norwegian bound morphemes (e.g., *husker* "looks"). In other words, Norwegian stems do not co-occur with English bound morphemes, e.g., **husks* ("swings"). Following Petersen (1988), Lanza attributed this asymmetry or directionality of mixing to Siri's dominance in Norwegian. In another case of language dominance, our analysis of Nair's *V* shows unidirectional mixing. Hindi tense-aspect marking is used with English stems; however, English tense-aspect marking is never used with Hindi verbal stems. This pattern of mixing Hindi bound morphemes with English lexical elements is not restricted to the tense-aspect bound morpheme but is also valid for participial bound morphemes too (e.g., *buy ke* "Having bought"). Though dominance is not necessarily a natural consequence of bilingual first-language acquisition, some children do turn out to be balanced at an early age (see, for example, De Houwer, 1990, and Meisel, 1989).

In addition to directionality of mixing, it is noted that Siri employs more mixing with her Norwegian-speaking father than with her English-speaking mother. This seems to be counterintuitive because Siri appears to be dominant in Norwegian, so she would be expected to mix more with her mother than with her father. How might we explain this apparent contradiction in Siri's CM behavior? Lanza attributes this anomaly to the different discourse patterns of Siri's mother and father. An examination of the conversational exchanges between mother and daughter reveals that whenever Siri mixes Norwegian into her English, she receives a negative response from her mother. The discourse strategy of the mother is to treat Siri's utterances as uninterpretable whenever she mixes Norwegian with her English. A comparison to the father's discourse style reveals that whenever Siri mixes English in her Norwegian, her father responds positively. (For the actual discourse samples, see Lanza, 1992, p. 647–648.) This appears to explain why Siri employs more mixing with her father than with her mother despite her dominance in Norwegian.

Siri's case shows that dominance should not be viewed as static. Dominance is found in children and adults alike and it should not be equated with "fusion," that is, the inability to separate the two systems. In other words, dominance might result from a variety of factors, including differential rate in the growth of the two languages even if the child is exposed to both languages from early on (as in the case of Nair's subject *V*), discourse (parent/caretaker's discourse style), and other social factors (societal prestige/preference for one language over the other, attitudes toward mixing, etc.).

When and Why Children Code Mix or Code Switch

The discussion in the preceding section sheds light on the linguistic and sociolinguistic motivations for CM among early bilingual children. Although the universe of children's discourse is bound to be different from that of adults, there are many shared linguistic and sociolinguistic factors which prompt children and adults alike to code-mix or code-switch, including the following: semantic domain (Kwan-Terry, 1992; De Houwer, 1990), complexity (an item less complex or salient in one language), stylistic effect (Youssef, 1991), clarification, elaboration, input difference (mixed versus separate; Bentahila & Davies, 1992a; Genesee, 1989; Goodz, 1989), relief strategy, that is, a linguistic item being temporarily unavailable in one language (Saunders, 1988); interlocutor identification, discourse strategy of participants/topics (Kielhöfer, 1987; Lanza, 1990, 1992), addressee's perceived linguistic capability and speaker's own linguistic ability (Bentahila & Davies, 1992a; De Houwer, 1987b, 1990; Garcia, 1983; Kielhöfer, 1987; Kwan-Terry, 1992; Stavans, 1990), other sociopsychological reasons (attitudes, societal values, e.g., De Houwer, 1990, Marcon & Coon, 1983), and personality (Hoffman, 1985; Romaine, 1989), and so on.

XI. BILINGUAL CHILDREN AND SPEECH DISORDERS

Like monolingual children and adults, bilingual children may suffer from speech/language disorders such as physiological problems (e.g., clipped lips, cleft palate), malnutrition (speech delays), brain damage (aphasia), and others. During the past two decades or so, there is renewed interest in the study of the brain organization of two or more languages using speech/language breakdown in bilinguals as evidence. Although there is a growing body of research on adult bilingual aphasia, childhood aphasia has received very little attention in comparison. (For a review of bilingual aphasia, see Obler & Hannigan, 1996, and Bhatia & Ritchie, 1996a, pp. 670–674). In this section we will focus on disorders that are not obvious and are often the result of deep-rooted misconceptions about the detrimental effect of bilingualism and the social categorization of languages or dialects. As a result of these misconceptions, bilingual children are often mistakenly labeled as children with speech disorders. One of the most important sources of such a misdiagnosis is the language-mixing behavior of bilingual children and adults.

It is often observed that bilingual children may use their language inappropriately from the adult point of view (see Döpke, 1992). The kinds of bilingual behavior often labeled inappropriate can manifest themselves in two important ways:

first, in the choice of an inappropriate language and, second, in combining the two languages within a sentence in a manner that is different from the adult usage. Perecman (1984) examined the incidence of language mixing in the case of a polyglot aphasic. The patient in question, H. B., was an 80-year-old male who was born in Cameroon, West Africa. He learned German as a native language from his parents, French as a second language, and, finally, English as a third language when he settled in the United States in 1923 at the age of 18. In 1980, he developed aphasia at the age of 75 as the result of a car accident. According to Perecman, the patient suffered from language mixing—particularly "utterance level mixing"—which in Perecman's view reflected a linguistic deficit; the other "symptom" identified is termed "spontaneous translation" by Perecman, which seems to be equivalent to inappropriate language choice.

Our analysis of Perecman's evidence indicates that what she identifies as a sign of language deficit turns out, in fact, to be a normal case of language switch, provided one takes the socio-psychological factors that govern language switch or language choice in bilingual discourse into account (see Bhatia & Ritchie, 1996a, pp. 672–674).

We have already mentioned that in the context of early bilingual children, language differentiation is a prerequisite for normal CM or CS. If, in spite of language differentiation, one witnesses a case of apparently inappropriate language mixing, it calls for a careful analysis of socio-psychological factors before establishing inappropriate language mixing on the part of bilingual children. Let us consider the language switching behavior of the son of the first author of this chapter when he was 3-years old. By this time he had developed language differentiation—in particular, separate negative particles for Hindi and English, which he matched appropriately with the selected language. One day when he was sick and his father was taking care of him, he engaged in a form of CM that appeared odd with respect to the context in which it took place. Whenever he was asked a yes-no question in English, contrary to expectations, he answered 'no' most of the time by using the Hindi negative marker, *nahii,* rather than the English negative particle, *no.* His consistent use of a Hindi yes-no response to an English yes-no question appeared to be a violation of language matching; however, our analysis showed that the child had decided to use the Hindi negator to soften the negative force of his responses. He explicitly asked if his father was being specially kind to him due to his illness on that day; obviously, he was trying to be nice in return by choosing the Hindi negative marker, which he perceived as more intimate and softer in rejection than the corresponding English negative marker. The point is that the apparent inappropriate language choice turned out to be a case of a child's quite sophisticated sociolinguistic competence. Evidence for mixing or switching that appears to violate linguistic and/or sociolinguistic principles should be characterized as odd only if no other explanation can be found.

Although most bilinguals (adults and children alike) exhibit rule-governed behavior in CM and CS, which requires a sophisticated employment of linguistic and sociolinguistic grammatical knowledge, due to the long global history of prescriptivism, CM and CS are often equated with language deficit. Meisel (1992, p. 417) pointed out that the language deficit hypothesis predicts a U-shaped developmental pattern in the frequency of mixes in the course of early bilingual development. High frequency of mixing due to limited competence in both languages should be expected to decrease as the child acquires knowledge about the two lexicons and two grammars. But it may increase again, once the child has acquired sufficient knowledge to use adultlike CM/CS. This test, together with the other examples discussed in this section and the preceding section, can be used by educators, language teachers, speech therapists, and linguists to distinguish normal CM/CS behavior from odd or developmentally inadequate CM/CS among bilingual children. In other words, language mixing which stems from limited or deteriorating language competence in either both or one of the two languages (e.g., Halmari, 1992; Seliger, 1989) needs to be separated from skillful language mixing in bilingual children as well as adults. Otherwise, numerous bilingual children will continue to be misidentified as "children with a linguistic disability" on the basis of what is otherwise normal language mixing behavior. Also, the long held belief that intrasentential mixing either among children or adults is a reflection of language deficit is misconceived in the light of the past two decades of research on CM.

It is a common observation that bilingual children as well as adults can shift from one language to another effortlessly and smoothly without any conscious effort. Against this background it is interesting to observe that there is a long tradition of associating bilingual children with stuttering. Such an observation was pioneered by the French doctors Pichon and Borel-Maisonny, who published a book on stuttering in 1937 (see Hoffman, 1991, p. 141). They found that 14% of their subjects who stuttered were bilinguals. Their conclusion that bilingualism somehow caused stuttering was further reinforced independently by another study by Travis, Johnson, and Shover (1937), who claimed that the incidence of stuttering was higher in bilinguals than in monolinguals (2.8% in bilinguals versus 1.8% in monolinguals). A recent study by Karniol (1992) devoted to the development of a Hebrew-English bilingual child who started stuttering in both languages at the age 2;1 attributes stuttering to syntactic overload. The study concludes that when the parents allowed the child to abandon the use of the second language, the child became a nonstutterer.

Lebrun and Paradis (1984) reassessed the claims of the French studies and found a number of methodological shortcomings, concluding that no correlation between bilingualism and stuttering can be substantiated. The studies that tend to establish a cause-effect relationship between bilingualism and a speech disorder are implicitly or explicitly guided by two invalid assumptions: (a) bilingualism is detrimental to language or personality development in the individual and to a sense of unity in a society at large, and (b) bilingualism induces language or information overload. Both of these assumptions have been discredited as is evident from the discussion in this chapter. What is important is the fact that bilinguals are often subjected to more severe evaluation than monolinguals and the speech communities or parents' discourse strategies that emphasize language separation (e.g., imposing one-person one-language or discouraging mixing) can prove to be extremely traumatic for bilingual children and can take a serious toll on the verbal performance of the child. Although more cross-linguistic studies are needed, we would like to claim that children growing up in a mixed-input environment are less likely to suffer from stuttering than those developing in societies that emphasize language separation.

XII. CONCLUSIONS AND FUTURE RESEARCH

Although remarkable progress has been made over the past two decades in our understanding of bilingualism in general and of childhood bilingualism in particular, the latter phenomenon—which is, ironically, still feared in many families as well as some social and professional circles—is capable of contributing significantly to our understanding of first language acquisition on one hand and of an otherwise neglected dimension of human linguistic creativity on the other. Therefore, its value in the study of language in general—ranging from theoretical linguistics to neuro- and educational linguistics—can hardly be overestimated.

Nonetheless, many problems in the theoretical, analytical, and methodological basis of such studies remain to be solved. Grosjean (to appear) summarized areas of linguistic, psycholinguistic, language development, and neurolinguistic research devoted to bilingualism in general and the bilingual child in particular where investigation has led to conflicting results on central issues. He has attributed these conflicting outcomes to a certain lack of conceptual and methodological clarity in much of the research on bilingualism. He has claimed that the most widely accepted view of bilinguals (which he termed a "fractional view") includes an underestimation of the capacity of bilinguals to acquire and distinguish two languages, an over reliance on monolingual theories of language, and an absence of the methodological depth required to analyze issues pertaining specifically to the study of bilingualism, all of which contribute to contradictory claims and results.

We will conclude this chapter with a brief discussion of some of these problems, which will, in turn, set the stage for future research on this topic.

A. Theoretical Issues

Unitary versus Dual Systems

The central issue of the onset of language differentiation in simultaneous bilinguals—detailed in Section VIII—is still a matter of debate due to unresolved competing hypotheses.

The unitary hypothesis is, initially, a highly plausible claim about bilingual acquisition: First, it implies a fundamental difference between the process of monolingual acquisition on one hand and that of bilingual acquisition on the other, an attractive position in view of the clear differences in input in the two cases. Second, the quite general operation of the uniqueness principle in language acquisition quite generally suggests that bilingual children might initially adopt a single lexicon and grammar for *all* of the input to which they are exposed, regardless of its source.

Nevertheless, the research reviewed in Section VIII clearly supports the DSH at the expense of the unitary hypothesis. Even at the one-word stage the evidence indicates that the child separates lexical items according to syllable structure. At later stages, the morphosyntactic structures of the two languages develop separately in a way that resembles closely the way in which monolingual child acquire each language independently. In addition, language mixing appears to reflect separate systems interacting in much the same way they do in code mixing and switching in older bilinguals where the two languages are clearly separated.

Though the phonological and morphosyntactic evidence for the DSH seems clear, a closer examination of so-called translational equivalents in the child's lexicon may cloud the issue. Recall that proponents of the unitary hypothesis cite the absence of forms constituting translational equivalents in the child's speech as support for that hypothesis, whereas its opponents claim to have found such forms. These latter forms, however, may be translational equivalents *only* from the point of view of the adult speakers of the two languages involved. What is required is evidence that they function as translational equivalents *in the child's lexicon(s)*. Recalling the anecdote concerning the use of Hindi *paanii* "water" by the daughter of this chapter's first author to refer only to large natural bodies of water, it may be that lexical items in a bilingual child's lexicon that are interpreted by opponents of the unitary hypothesis as translationally equivalent are not equivalent for the child. If so, then the unitary hypothesis gains support—at least for the very earliest stages of bilingual development.

Input

Future studies need to scrutinize bilingual input (Section VI) in a more systematic way. What are the similarities and differences, if there are any, among bilingual children in terms of language development depending on the complementarity (separate input) and noncomplementarity (mixed input) of their linguistic environment? The role of different types of inputs in bilingual children needs to be examined more systematically in order for researchers to gain deeper insights into the process of language development in bilingual children.

Simultaneous versus Sequential Acquisition

The issue of distinguishing the child's first language from the second one (or simultaneous acquisition from sequential acquisition)—Section V.C—is still being determined on an arbitrary basis. A more empirically grounded solution to this problem would be the adoption of criteria based on the concept of critical period or critical periods to distinguish between the first and the second language of the child. In other words, the question of whether different time periods provide insights into child's critical periods which, in turn, determine substantive and qualitative differences in the acquisition of the child's two languages needs to be investigated.

Language Mixing

The phenomena of language mixing in children—Section IX—deserves more attention by the proponents of the unitary hypothesis. Is language mixing during the putative "fusion" stage different from the language mixing after Stage III under that hypothesis (that is, after the differentiation of the lexicons as well as the structures of the two languages)? If yes, what evidence separates the two types of mixing? As regards constraints on code mixing, the government constraint needs further investigation to examine more widely the claims made by the m-command version of government proposed by Meisel (1994)—or, perhaps, its descendant notion(s) of locality within the minimalist program.

Other Issues: Socio-Psychological Factors

The determinants of the regression and progression of language in bilingual children—Section VI.B—need to go beyond generic explanations such as culture and language shock or cultural acceptance or rejection in order to shed more light on the underlying mechanisms of performance-related aspects of what is observed with respect to the differential loss and regain of facility in the two languages by the child.

B. Methodological and Analytical Issues

Analytical problems such as those pointed out earlier during our discussion of Stage I under the unitary hypothesis in Section VIII.A—particularly, those regarding translational equivalence and the uniqueness principle—and terminological differences need careful scrutiny if the problem of drawing conflicting conclusions about the phenomena found at that putative stage is to be avoided.

On methodological grounds, as we mentioned in Section VI.A, it is not sufficient to report the language of the parents but, rather, a comprehensive reporting of those participants who provide input to a bilingual child is needed. Over-reliance in research on reports of the language of parents may not provide a faithful picture of the social and linguistic environment of the bilingual child. Input conditions (linguistic and sociolinguistic) and the actual nature of input (as opposed to reports by parents) need to be carefully documented in order to gain better insights into bilingual child language development.

Grosjean (to appear) is certainly a step in the right direction, which can lead researchers to deal with the conceptual problems (e.g., the characterization of bilinguals) and methodological problems (e.g., subject-selection and the type of information critical for future researchers) that continue to take a negative toll on research on bilingualism in general and on the bilingual child in particular. The guidelines and the framework that Grosjean presented can provide some relief for researchers coping with the conflicting research findings, the methodological pitfalls, and the conceptual mazes to be found in the study of the bilingual child.

ACKNOWLEDGMENTS

We are grateful to Annick De Houwer and Elissa Newport for their insightful comments on the earlier version of this chapter.

REFERENCES

Arnberg, L. (1987). *Raising children bilingually: The pre-school years.* Clevedon, UK: Multilingual Matters.

Bain, B., & Yu, A. (1980). Cognitive consequences of raising children bilingually: "One parent, one language." *Canadian Journal of Psychology, 34,* 304–313.

Bentahila, A., & Davies, E. E. (1992a). *Two languages, three varieties: A look at some bilingual children's code-switching.* Paper presented at the International Colloquium on Early Bilingualism, Amsterdam.

Bentahila, A., & Davies, E. E. (1992b). Code-switching and dominance. In R. J. Harris (Ed.), *Cognitive processing in bilinguals* (pp. 443–458). Amsterdam: Elsevier.

Berent, G. (1983). Control judgements by deaf adults and by second language learners. *Language Learning, 33,* 37–53.

Berent, G. (1988). An assessment of syntactic capabilities. In M. Strong (Ed.), *Language learning and deafness* (pp. 133–161). Cambridge: Cambridge University Press.

Berent, G. (1996). The acquisition of English syntax by deaf learners. In W. Ritchie & T. Bhatia (Eds.), *Handbook of second language acquisition* (pp. 469–506). San Diego, CA: Academic Press.

Berent, G., & Samar, V. J. (1990). The psychological reality of the subset principle: Evidence from the governing categories of prelingually deaf adults. *Language, 66,* 714–741.

Bergman, C. R. (1976). Interference vs. interdependent development in infant bilingualism. In D. Keller, R. Teschner, & S. Viera (Eds.), *Bilingualism in the bicentennial and beyond* (pp. 86–96). New York: Bilingual Press/Editorial Bilingüe.

Berkele, G. (1983). *Die entwicklung des ausdrucks von objektreferenz am beispiel der determinanten. Eine empirische untersuchung zum spracherwerb bilingualer kinder*

(Französisch-Deutsch). [The development of the expression of object reference using determiners. An empirical investigation concerning the language acquisition of bilingual children (French/German)]. MA thesis, University of Hamburg.

Berwick, R. (1985). *The acquisition of syntactic knowledge.* Cambridge, MA: MIT Press.

Bhatia, T. (1982). English and the vernaculars of India: Contact and change. *Applied Linguistics, 3*(3), 235–245.

Bhatia, T., & Ritchie, W. (1996a). Bilingual language mixing, universal grammar, and second language acquisition. In W. C. Ritchie & T. K. Bhatia (Eds.), *Handbook of second language acquisition* (pp. 627–688). San Diego, CA: Academic Press.

Bhatia, T., & Ritchie, W. (1996b). Light verbs in code-switched utterances: Derivational economy in I-language or incongruence in production? In A. Stringfellow, D. Chana-Amitay, E. Hughes, & A. Zukowski (Eds.), *Proceedings of the 20th Annual Boston University Conference on Language Development, Vol. 1* (pp. 52–62). Somerville, MA: Cascadilla Press.

Bloomfield, L. (1933). *Language.* New York: Holt, Rinehart and Winston.

Borer, H., & Wexler, K. (1987). The maturation of syntax. In T. Roeper & E. Williams (Eds.), *Parameter setting* (pp. 123–172). Dordrecht: Foris.

Bouvet, D. (1990). *The path to language: Bilingual education for deaf children.* Clevedon, UK: Multilingual Matters Ltd.

Branon, J. (1968). Linguistic word classes in the spoken language of normal, hard-of-hearing, and deaf children. *Journal of Speech and Hearing Research, 11,* 279–287.

Brown, R. (1973). *A first language.* Cambridge, MA: Harvard University Press.

Bunenik, V. (1978). The acquisition of Czech in the English environment. In M. Paradis (Ed.), *Aspects of bilingualism* (pp. 3–12). Columbia, SC: Hornbeam Press.

Burling, R. (1959). Language development of a Garo- and English-speaking child. *Word, 15,* 48–68.

Carrow, E. (1971). Comprehension of English and Spanish by pre-school Mexican-American Children. *Modern Language Journal, 55,* 299–307.

Cheng, L. (Ed.). (1996). Beyond bilingualism: Language acquisition and disorders—A global perspective. *Topics in Language Disorders, 16*(4).

Chomsky, N. (1981). *Lectures on government and binding: The Pisa lectures.* Dordrecht: Foris Publishers.

Chomsky, N. (1986). *Knowledge of language.* New York: Praeger.

Chomsky, N. (1991). Some notes on economy of derivation and representation. In R. Freidin (Ed.), *Principles and parameters in comparative grammar* (pp. 417–454). Cambridge, MA: MIT Press.

Clyne, M. (1987). Constraints on code-switching: How universal are they? *Linguistics, 25,* 739–764.

Cooper, R., & Rosenstein, J. (1966). Language acquisition of deaf children. *The Volta Review, 68,* 58–67.

Cummins, J. (1978). Bilingualism and the development of metalinguistic awareness. *Journal of Cross-Cultural Psychology, 9,* 131–149.

De Houwer, A. (1987a). Gender marking in a young Dutch-English bilingual child. *Proceedings of the 1987 Child Language Seminar* (pp. 53–65). York: University of York.

De Houwer, A. (1987b). Two at a time: An exploration of how children acquire two languages from Birth. Ph.D dissertation, Vrije Universiteit Brussels.

De Houwer, A. (1988). Word order patterns in the speech productions of a three-year-old. *ABLA Papers, 12,* 189–206.
De Houwer, A. (1990). *The acquisition of two languages from birth: A case study.* Cambridge, England: Cambridge University Press.
De Houwer, A. (1995). Bilingual language acquisition. In P. Fletcher & B. MacWhinney (Eds.), *Handbook of child language* (pp. 219–250). Oxford: Basil Blackwell Ltd.
Déprez, V., & Pierce, A. (1993). Negation and functional head projections in early grammar. *Linguistic Inquiry, 24,* 25–67.
Déprez, V., & Pierce, A. (1994). Crosslinguistic evidence for functional projections in early child grammar. In T. Hoekstra & B. Schwartz (Eds.), *Language acquisition studies in generative grammar* (pp. 57–83). Philadelphia: Benjamins.
Deuchar, M. (1989). ESRC report on project "Infant bilingualism: One system or two?" Unpublished manuscript.
Deuchar, M. (1992). Bilingual acquisition of the voicing contrast in word-initial stop consonants in English and Spanish. *Cognitive science research paper 213.* Brighton: University of Sussex.
Di Sciullo, A., Muysken, P., & Singh, R. (1986). Government and code-mixing. *Journal of Linguistics, 22,* 1–24.
Döpke, S. (1986). Discourse structures in bilingual families. *Journal of Multilingual and Multicultural Development, 7,* 493–507.
Döpke, S. (1988). The role of parental teaching techniques in bilingual German-English families. *International Journal of the Sociology of Language, 72,* 101–113.
Döpke, S. (1992). A bilingual child's struggle to comply with the "one parent-one language" rule. *Journal of Multilingual and Multicultural Development, 13*(6), 467–485.
Dromi, E. (1987). *Early lexical development.* Cambridge, UK: Cambridge University Press.
Emonds, J. (1978). The verbal complex V′-Vn French. *Linguistic Inquiry, 9*(2), 151–175.
Emonds, J. (1986). Grammatically deviant prestige constructions. In M. Brame, H. Contreras, and F. J. Newmeyer (Eds.), *A festschrift for Sol Saporta* (pp. 93–129). Seattle, WA: Noit Amrofer Publishing Co.
Fantini, A. (1976). *Language acquisition of a bilingual child: A sociolinguistic perspective.* Battleboro, VT: The Experimental Press.
Fantini, A. (1985). *Language acquisition of a bilingual child: A sociolinguistic perspective (to age ten).* Clevedon, UK: Multilingual Matters Ltd.
Felix, S. (1987). *Cognition and language growth.* Dordrecht: Foris.
Ferguson, C. (1992). Foreword. In B. Kachru (Ed.), *The other tongue* (pp. vii–xi). Urbana, IL: University of Illinois Press.
Garcia, E. (1983). *Early childhood bilingualism.* Albuquerque, NM: University of New Mexico Press.
Genesee, F. (1989). Early language development, one language or two? *Journal of Child Language, 16,* 161–179.
Goda, S. (1964). Spoken syntax of normal, deaf, and retarded adolescents. *Journal of Verbal Learning and Verbal Behavior, 3,* 401–405.
Goodz, N. (1989). Parental language mixing in bilingual families. *Infant Mental Health Journal, 10,* 25–44.
Goodz, N., Bilodeau, L., & Legaré, M. (1988). *Variables influencing parental language*

mixing to children in bilingual families. Paper presented at the International Conference on Infant Studies, Paris.

Gregg, K. (1984). Krashen's monitor and Occam's razor. *Applied Linguistics, 5,* 79–100.

Grosjean, F. (1982). *Life with two languages.* Cambridge, MA: Harvard University Press.

Grosjean, F. (to appear). *Studying bilinguals: Methodological and conceptual issues.* Manuscript, Université Neuchatel.

Hakuta, K. (1986). *Mirror of language.* New York: Basic Books.

Hakuta, K., & Diaz, R. (1985). The relationship between degree of bilingualism and cognitive abilities. In K. Nelson (Ed.), *Children's language* (pp. 319–344). Hillsdale, NJ: Erlbaum.

Halmari, H. (1992). Code-switching strategies as a mirror of language loss: A case study of two child bilinguals. *SLRF 1992 Proceedings,* 200–215.

Harshman, R., & Krashen, S. (1972). An "unbiased" procedure for comparing degree of lateralization of dichotically presented stimuli. *Journal of the Acoustical Society of America, 52,* 174.

Hayashi, M. (1992). *A longitudinal investigation of language development in bilingual children.* Ph.D dissertation, University of Aarhus, Risskov.

Hoffman, C. (1985). Language acquisition in two trilingual children. *Journal of Multilingual and Multicultural Development, 6,* 479–495.

Hoffman, C. (1991). *An introduction to bilingualism.* London: Longman.

Hyams, N. (1986). *Language acquisition and theory of parameters.* Dordrecht: Foris.

Hyams, N. (1992). The genesis of clausal structure. In J. Meisel (Ed.), *The acquisition of verb placement* (pp. 371–400). Dordrecht: Kluwer Academic Publishers.

Idaizábal, I. (1984). Conciencia bilingüe del nino bilingüe [Bilingual awareness of the bilingual child]. In M. Siguan (Ed.), *Adquisición precoz de una segunda lengua* [Early acquisition of a second language] (pp. 55–63). Barcelona: Publications i edicions de la universitat de Barcelona.

Idaizábal, I. (1988). *First verbal productions of a bilingual child learning Basque and Spanish simultaneously.* An analysis of noun phrase. Manuscript.

Idaizábal, I. (1991). *Evolucion nominal en un nino bilingüe vasco-hispanofono* [The evolution of nominal determination in a Basque/Spanish bilingual child]. Paper presented at the Ist International Conference on Spanish in Contact with Other Languages. Los Angeles: University of Southern California.

Imedadze, N. (1967). On the psychological nature of child speech formation under conditions of exposure to two languages. *International Journal of Psychology, 2,* 129–132.

Ingram, D. (1981). The emerging phonological system of an Italian-English bilingual child. *Journal of Italian Linguistics, 2,* 995–1013.

Jakobson, R. (1967). *Child language, aphasia, and phonological universals* (A. R. Keiler, Trans.). The Hague: Mouton & Co. (Original work published in 1941.)

Johnson, J., & Newport, E. (1989). Critical period effects in second language learning: The influence of maturational state on the acquisition of English as a second language. *Cognitive Psychology, 21,* 60–99.

Johnson, J., & Newport, E. (1991). Critical period effects on universal properties of language: The status of subjacency in the acquisition of a second language. *Cognition, 39,* 215–258.

Karniol, R. (1992). Stuttering out of bilingualism. *First Language, 12,* 3–36.

Kessler, C. (1971). *The acquisition of syntax in bilingual children.* Washington: Georgetown University Press.
Kessler, C. (1972). Syntactic constraints in child bilingualism. *Language Learning, 22,* 221–223.
Kessler, C. (1984). Language acquisition in bilingual children. In N. Miller (Ed.), *Bilingualism and language disability: Assessment and remedy* (pp. 26–54). London: Croom Helm.
Kielhöfer, B. (1987). Le "bon" changement de langue et le "mauvais" mélange de langues [Good code-switching and bad code-mixing]. In G. Lüdi (Ed.), *Devenir bilingue-parler bilingue* [Becoming bilingual—Bilingual speech] (pp. 135–155). Tübingen: Niemeyer.
Kielhöfer, B., & Jonekeit, S. (1983). *Zweisprachige kindererziehung* [Bringing children up bilingually]. Tübingen: Stauffenburg.
Klausen, T., & Hayashi, M. (1990). A cross linguistic study of the development of bilingualism—reorganization in early lexical development. *The European Journal of Intercultural Studies, 1,* 31–41.
Klausen, T., Subritzky, M., & Hayashi, M. (1993). Initial production of inflections in bilingual children. In G. Turner & D. Messer (Eds.), *Critical influences on child language acquisition and development* (pp. 65–92). London: Macmillan.
Klinge, S. (1990). Prepositions in bilingual language acquisition. In J. Meisel (Ed.), *Two first languages: Early grammatical development in bilingual children* (pp. 123–156). Dordrecht: Foris.
Koehn, C. (1989). *Der erwerb de pluralmarkierungen durch bilinguale kinder (Französisch/Deutsch). Eine empirische untersuchung* [The acquisition of plural marking by bilingual children (French/German). An empirical investigation]. Master's thesis, University of Hamburg.
Koopman, H., & D. Sportiche. (1991). The position of subjects. *Lingua, 85,* 211–258.
Krashen, S. (1973). Lateralization, language learning, and the critical period. *Language Learning, 23,* 63–74.
Krashen, S. (1981). *Second language acquisition and second language learning.* Oxford: Pergamon Press.
Krashen, S. (1982). Accounting for child-adult differences in second language rate and attainment. In S. Krashen, R. Scarcella, & M. Long (Eds.), *Child-adult differences in second language acquisition* (pp. 202–226). Rowley, MA: Newbury House.
Kwan-Terry, A. (1992). Code-switching and code-mixing: The case of a child learning English and Chinese simultaneously. *Journal of Multilingual and Multicultural Development, 13,* 243–259.
Labov, W. (1972). *Sociolinguistic patterns.* Philadelphia: University of Pennsylvania Press.
Lanza, E. (1990). *Language mixing in infant bilingualism, a sociolinguistic perspective.* Ph.D dissertation, Georgetown University, Washington.
Lanza, E. (1992). Can bilingual two-year-olds code-switch? *Journal of Child Language, 19,* 633–658.
Lebrun, Y., & Paradis, M. (1984). To be or not to be an early bilingual? In Y. Lebrun & M. Paradis (Eds.), *Early bilingualism and child development* (pp. 9–18). Amsterdam: Swets and Zeitlinger.
Lenneberg, E. (1967). *Biological foundations of language.* New York: Wiley Press.

Leopold, W. (1939–1949). *Speech development of a bilingual child: A linguist's record* (4 volumes). Evanston, IL: Northwestern University Press.

Leopold, W. (1948). The study of child language and infant bilingualism. *Word, 4,* 1–17.

Leopold, W. (1978). A child's learning of two languages. In E. Hatch (Ed.), *Second language acquisition: A book of readings* (pp. 23–32). Rowley, MA: Newbury House.

Levy, Y. (1985). Theoretical gains from the study of bilingualism: A case report. *Language Learning, 35,* 541–554.

Li, C., & Thompson, S. (1976). Subjrect and topic: A new typology of language. In C. Li (Ed.), *Subject and topic* (pp. 457–489). New York: Academic Press.

Lindholm, K. (1980). Bilingual children: Some interpretations of cognitive and linguistic development. In K. Nelson (Ed.), *Children's language* (pp. 215–266). New York: Gardner Press.

Lindholm, K., & Padilla, A. (1978). Language mixing in bilingual children. *Journal of Child Language, 5,* 327–335.

Long, M. (1990). Maturational constraints on language development. *Studies in Second Language Acquisition, 12*(3), 251–285.

McClure, E. (1977). Aspects of code-switching in the discourse of bilingual Mexican-American children. In M. Saville-Troike (Ed.), *Linguistics and anthropology: Georgetown University roundtable on languages and linguistics* (pp. 93–115). Washington: Georgetown University Press.

McConvell, P. (1988). MIX-IM-UP: Aboriginal code-switching, old and new. In M. Heller (Ed.), *Code-switching: Anthropological and sociological perspectives* (pp. 97–151). Berlin: Mouton-de Gruyter.

McLaughlin, B. (1984a). Early bilingualism: Methodological and theoretical issues. In M. Paradis & Y. Lebrun (Eds.), *Early bilingualism and child development* (pp. 19–45). Lisse: Swets and Zeitlinger.

McLaughlin, B. (1984b). *Second-language acquisition in Childhood* (Vol. 1, Preschool Children). Hillsdale, NJ: Erlbaum.

Marcon, R., & Coon, R. (1983). Communication styles of bilingual preschoolers in preferred and non-preferred languages. *Journal of Genetic Psychology, 142,* 189–202.

Meier, R. P., & Newport, E. L. (1990). Out of the hands of babes: On a possible sign advantage in language acquisition, *Language, 66,* 1–23.

Meisel, J. M. (1985). Les phases initiales du develppment des notions temporelles, aspectuelles et de modes d'action. *Lingua, 66,* 321–374.

Meisel, J. M. (1986). Word order and case marking in early child language. Evidence from simultaneous acquisition of two first languages: French and German. *Linguistics, 24,* 123–183.

Meisel, J. (1989). Early differentiation of languages in bilingual children. In K. Hyltenstam & L. Obler (Eds.), *Bilingualism across the lifespan: Aspects of acquisition, maturity and loss* (pp. 13–40). Cambridge: Cambridge University Press.

Meisel, J. M. (1990a). Grammatical development in the simultaneous acquisition of two first languages. In J. M. Meisel (Ed.), *Two first languages: Early grammatical development in bilingual children* (pp. 5–22). Dordrecht: Foris.

Meisel, J. M. (1990b). INFL-ection: Subjects and subject-verb agreement. In J. M. Meisel (Ed.), *Two first languages: Early grammatical development in bilingual children* (pp. 237–298). Dordrecht: Foris.

Meisel, J. M. (Ed.). (1992). *The acquisition of verb placement: functional categories and V2 phenomena.* Dordrecht: Kluwer.

Meisel, J. M. (1994). Code-switching in young bilingual children. *Studies in Second Language Acquisition, 16,* 413–439.

Meisel, J. M., & Mahlau, A. (1988). La acquisicion simultanea de dos primeras lenguas. Discussion general e implicaciones para el estudio del bilingüismo en euzkadi [The simultaneous acquisition of two first languages. General discussion and implications for the study of bilingualism in the Basque county]. *Actas del II congreso sobre la Lengua Vasca, Tomo III* [Proceedings of the Second Basque World Congress: Congress on the Basque Language]. Vitoria: Servicio de publicaciones del Gobierno Vasco.

Meisel, J. M., & Müller, N. (1992). Finiteness and verb placement in early child grammars. Evidence from simultaneous acquisition of two first languages: French and German. In J. M. Meisel (Ed.), *The acquisition of verb placement: Functional categories and V2 phenomena in language acquisition* (pp. 109–138). Dordrecht: Kluwer.

Mikes, M. (1967). Some issues of lexical development in early bi-and trilinguals. In G. Conti-Ramsden & C. Snow (Eds.), *Children's language* (Vol. 7, pp. 103–120). Hillsdale, NJ: Erlbaum.

Miller, N. (1984). *Bilingualism and language disability.* London: Croom Helm.

Müller, N. (1990a). Developing two gender assignment systems simultaneously. In J. M. Meisel (Ed.), *Two first languages: Early grammatical development in bilingual children* (pp. 193–236). Dordrecht: Foris.

Müller, N. (1990b). Erwerb de wrotstellung in Französichen und Deutschen. Zur distribution von finitheitsmerkmalen in der grammatik bilingualer kinder [The acquisition of word order in French and German. On the distribution of markings of the finite/nonfinite distinction in the grammar of bilingual children]. In M. Rothweiler (Ed.), *Spracherwerb und grammatik linguistische untersuchungen zum erwerb von syntax und morphologie* [Language-acquisition and grammar. Linguistic investigations of the acquisition of syntax and morphology] (pp. 127–151). Oplanden: Westdeutscher Verlag.

Murrell, M. (1966). Language acquisition in a trilingual environment. *Studia Linguistica, 20,* 9–35.

Myklebust, H. R. (1964). *The psychology of deafness: Sensory deprivation, learning, and adjustment.* New York: Grune & Stratton.

Nair, R. B. (1984). Monosyllabic English or disyllabic Hindi? Language acquisition in a bilingual child. *Indian Linguistics, 54,* 51–90.

Neville, H., Coffey, S., Lawson, D., Fischer, A., Emmorey, K., & Bellugi, U. (1997). Neural systems mediating American sign language: Effects of sensory experience and age of acquisition. *Brain & Language, 57,* 285–308.

Neville, H., Mills, D., & Lawson, D. (1992). Fractionating language: Different neural subsystems with different sensitive periods. *Cerebral Cortex, 2,* 244–258.

Newport, E. L., & Meier, R. P. (1985). The acquisition of American Sign Language. In D. Slobin (Ed.), *The crosslinguistic study of language acquisition: Vol. 1. The data* (pp. 881–938). Hillsdale, NJ: Erlbaum.

Nicoladis, E. (1994). *Code-mixing in young bilingual children.* Ph.D dissertation, McGill University, Montreal.

Nwokah, E. (1984). Simultaneous and sequential acquisition in Nigerian children. *First Language, 5,* 57–73.

Obler, L., & Hannigan, S. (1996). Neurolinguistics of second language acquisition and use. In W. C. Ritchie & T. K. Bhatia (Eds.), *Handbook of second language acquisition* (pp. 509–523). San Diego, CA: Academic Press.
Oksaar, E. (1970). Zum spracherwerb des kindes in zweisprachiger umgebung. *Folio Linguistica, 4,* 330–358.
Padilla, A., & Liebman, E. (1975). Language acquisition in the bilingual child. *Bilingual Review, 2,* 34–55.
Padilla & Lindholm (1984). Child bilingualism: The same old issues revisited. In J. Martinez & R. Mendoza (Eds.), *Chicago Psychology* (pp. 369–408). Orlando, FL: Academic Press.
Paradis, J. (1996). Phonological differentiation in a bilingual child: Hildegard revisited. In A. Stringfellow, D. Chana-Amitay, E. Hughes, & A. Zukowski (Eds.), *Proceedings of the 20th Annual Boston University Conference on Language Development, Vol. 1* (pp. 528–539). Somerville, MA: Cascadilla Press.
Paradis, J., & Genesee, F. (1996). Syntactic acquisition in bilingual children: Autonomous or interdependent? *Studies in Second Language Acquisition, 18,* 1–25.
Paradis, J., & Genesee, F. (1997). On continuity and the emergence of functional categories in bilingual first-language acquisition. *Language Acquisition, 6,* 91–124.
Parodi, T. (1990). The acquisition of word order regularities and case morphology. In J. M. Meisel (Ed.), *Two first languages: Early grammatical development in bilingual children* (pp. 157–192). Dordrecht: Foris.
Peal, E., & Lambert, W. E. (1962). Relation of bilingualism to intelligence. *Psychological Monographs, 76,* 1–23.
Penfield, W., & Roberts, L. (1959). *Speech and brain mechanisms.* Princeton, NJ: Princeton University Press.
Perecman, E. (1984). Spontaneous translation and language mixing in a polyglot aphasic. *Brain and Language, 23,* 43–63.
Peterson, J. (1988). Word-internal code-switching constraints in a bilingual child's grammar. *Linguistics, 26,* 479–493.
Pierce, A. (1989). On the emergence of syntax: A crosslinguistic study. Ph.D dissertation, MIT, Cambridge, MA.
Pierce, A. (1992). *Language acquisition and syntactic theory.* Dordrecht: Kluwer.
Poeppel, D., & Wexler, K. (1993). The full competence hypothesis of clause structure in early German. *Language, 69,* 1–33.
Pollock, J.-Y. (1989). Verb movement, universal grammar, and the structure of IP. *Linguistic Inquiry, 20*(2), 365–424.
Power, D. J., & Quigley, S. P. (1973). Deaf children's acquisition of the passive voice. *Journal of Speech and Hearing Research, 16,* 5–11.
Pye, C. (1986). One lexicon or two? An alternative interpretation of early bilingual speech. *Journal of Child Language, 13,* 591–593.
Quay, S. (1993). *Bilingual evidence against the principle of contrast.* Paper presented at the 67th Annual Meeting of the Linguistic Society of America, Los Angeles.
Quigley, S. P., & King, C. M. (1980). Syntactic performance of hearing impaired and normal hearing individuals. *Applied Psycholinguistics, 1,* 329–356.
Radford, A. (1988). Small children's small clauses. *Transactions of the Philological Society, 86,* 1–43.

Radford, A. (1990). *Syntactic theory and the acquisition of syntax.* Oxford: Oxford University Press.
Raffler-Engel, W. (1965). Del bilinguismo infantile. *Arch. Glottologico Italiano, 50,* 175–180.
Redlinger, W. E. (1979). Early developmental bilingualism, a review of literature. *The Bilingual Review, 6,* 11–30.
Redlinger, W. E., & Park T. (1980). Language mixing in young bilinguals. *Journal of Child Language, 7,* 337–352.
Ritchie, W., and Bhatia, T. (1996). Code-switching, grammar, and sentence production: The problem of dummy verbs. In C. Koster & F. Wijnen (Eds.), *Proceedings of the 1995 Groningen Assembly on Language Acquisition (GALA)* (pp. 313–324). Groningen: Centre for Language and Cognition Groningen.
Romaine, S. (1989). *Bilingualism.* Oxford: Blackwell.
Romaine, S. (1996). Bilingualism. In W. C. Ritchie & T. K. Bhatia (Eds.), *Handbook of second language acquisition* (pp. 571–604). San Diego, CA: Academic Press.
Ronjat, J. (1913). Le développment du langage observé chez un enfant bilingue. Paris: Champion.
Ross, D. S., & Newport, E. L. (1996). The development of language from non-native linguistic input. *The Proceedings of the 20th Annual Boston University Conference on Language Development,* 634–645.
Ruke-Dravina, V. (1965). The process of acquisition of apical/r/ and uvular/r/ in the speech of children. *Linguistics, 17,* 56–68.
Samar, V. J., & Berent, G. P. (1991). BE is a raising verb: Psycholinguistic evidence. *Journal of Psycholinguistic Research, 20,* 419–443.
Samar, V. J., & Berent, G. P. (1993). Is *be* a raising verb in the mental English grammars of congenitally deaf adults? In A. Crochetiere, J.-C. Boulangger, & C. Quellon (Eds.), *Actes du XVe Congres International des Linguistes* [Proceedings of the 15th International Congress of Linguistics] (Vol. 3, pp. 529–532). Sainte-Foy, Quebec, Canada: Presse de l'Université Laval.
Saunders, G. (1982). *Bilingual children: Guidance for the family.* Clevedon, UK: Multilingual Matters Ltd.
Saunders, G. (1988). *Bilingual children: From birth to teens.* Clevedon, UK: Multilingual Matters.
Schachter, J. (1996). Maturation and the issue of universal grammar in second language acquisition. In W. C. Ritchie & T. K. Bhatia (Eds.), *Handbook of second language acquisition* (pp. 159–193). San Diego, CA: Academic Press.
Schlyter, S. (1990). The acquisition of tense and aspect. In J. M. Meisel (Ed.), *Two first languages: Early grammatical development in bilingual children* (pp. 87–122). Dordrecht: Foris.
Schlyter, S. (1993). The weaker language in bilingual Swedish-French children. In K. Hyltenstam & A. Viberg (Eds.), *Progression and regression in language: Sociocultural, neuropsychological and linguistic perspectives* (pp. 289–308). Cambridge: Cambridge University Press.
Schlyter, S., & Westholm, L. (1991). Interaction familiale et développment des deux langues chez des enfants bilingues [Family interaction and development of two languages in bilingual children]. In C. Russier, H. Stoffel, & D. Véronique (Eds.), *Inter-*

actions en langue étrangère [Interactions in a foreign language] (pp. 193–201). Aix-en-Provence: Publications de l'Université de Provence.

Schwartz, B. (1993). On explicit and negative data effecting and affecting *competence* and *linguistic behavior. Studies in Second Language Acquisition, 15,* 147–163.

Schwartz, B., & Gubala-Ryzak, M. (1992). Learnability and grammar reorganization in L2: Against negative evidence causing the unlearning of verb movement. *Second Language Research, 8,* 1–38.

Seliger, H. (1978). Implications of a multiple critical periods hypothesis for second language learning. In W. Ritchie (Ed.), *Second language acquisition research* (pp. 11–19). New York: Academic Press.

Seliger, H. (1989). Deterioration and creativity in childhood bilingualism. In K. Hyltenstam & L. Obler (Eds.), *Bilingualism across the lifespan: Aspects of acquisition, maturity and loss* (pp. 173–184). Cambridge: Cambridge University Press.

Seliger, H. (1996). Primary language attrition in the context of bilingualism. In W. C. Ritchie & T. K. Bhatia (Eds.), *Handbook of second language acquisition* (pp. 605–626). San Diego, CA: Academic Press.

Singleton, J. & Newport, E. (1994). *When learners surpass their models: The acquisition of American Sign Language from impoverished input.* Unpublished manuscript, University of Illinois.

Skutnabb-Kangas, T. (1984). *Bilingualism or not.* Clevedon, UK: Multilingual Matters Ltd.

Slobin, D. (1973). Cognitive prerequisites for the development of grammar. In C. Ferguson & D. Slobin (Eds.), *Studies of child language development.* New York: Holt, Rinehart & Winston.

Smith, N. (1973). *The acquisition of phonology: A case study.* Cambridge, UK: Cambridge University Press.

Sobin, N. (1994). An acceptable ungrammatical construction. In S. D. Lima, R. L. Corrigan, & G. K. Ivereson (Eds.), *The reality of linguistic rules* (pp. 51–65). Amsterdam: John Benjamins.

Sobin, N. (1997). Agreement, default rules, and grammatical virusses. *Linguistic Inquiry, 28,* 318–343.

Stavans, A. (1990). *Code-switching in children acquiring English, Spanish and Hebrew: A case study.* Ph.D dissertation, University of Pittsburgh, Pittsburgh.

Supalla, T. (1982). *Structure and acquisition of verbs of motion in American Sign Language.* Ph.D dissertation, University of California, San Diego.

Swain, M. (1972). *Bilingualism as a first language.* Ph.D dissertation, University of California, Irvine.

Swain, M., & Wache, M. (1975). Linguistic interaction: Case study of a bilingual child. *Language Sciences, 37,* 17–22.

Taeschner, T. (1983). *The sun is feminine: A study on language acquisition in bilingual children.* Berlin: Springer Verlag.

Toribio, A., & Brown, B. (1994). Feature checking and the syntax of language contact. In D. MacLaughlin & S. McEwen (Eds.), *Proceedings of the 19th Boston University Conference on Language Development* (pp. 629–642). Somerville, MA: Cascadilla Press.

Travis, I., Johnson, E., & Shover, J. (1937). The relation of bilingualism to stuttering. *Journal of Speech Disorder, 2,* 185–189.

Veh, B. (1990). Syntaktische aspekte des code-switching bei bilingualen kindern (Französisch-Deutsch) im vorschulalter. MA thesis, University of Hamburg.

Vihman, M. (1982). The acquisition of morphology by a bilingual child, a whole-word approach. *Applied Psycholinguistics, 3,* 141–160.

Vihman, M. (1985). Language differentiation by the bilingual infant. *Journal of Child Language, 12,* 297–324.

Vihman, M. (1986). More on language differentiation. *Journal of Child Language, 13,* 595–597.

Volterra, V., & Taeschner, T. (1978). The acquisition and development of language by bilingual children. *Journal of Child Language, 5,* 311–326.

Weber-Fox, C., & Neville, H. (1996). Maturational constraints on functional specializations for language processing: ERP and behavioral evidence in bilingual speakers. *Journal of Cognitive Neuroscience, 8,* 231–256.

Wexler, K. (1981). Some issues in the theory of learnability. In C. Baker and J. McCarthy (Eds.), *The logical problem of language acquisition* (pp. 30–52). Cambridge, MA: MIT Press.

Wexler, K., & Manzini, R. (1987). Parameters and learnability. In T. Roeper & E. Williams (Eds.), *Parameter setting* (pp. 41–76). Dordrecht: Foris.

Wilbur, R., Goodhart, W., & Montandon, A. (1983). Comprehension of nine syntactic structures by hearing-impaired students. *The Volta Review, 85,* 328–345.

Wode, H. (1981). *Learning a second language: An integrated view of second language acquisition.* Tübingen: Narr.

Wode, H. (1990). *But grandpa always goes like this . . . or, The ontogeny of code-switching.* Papers for the Workshop on Impact and Consequences (pp. 17–50). Brussels: ESF Network on Code-Switching and Language Contact.

Youssef, V. (1991). "Can I put—I want a slippers to put on": Young children's development of request forms in code-switching environment. *Journal of Child Language, 18,* 609–624.

PART VII

LANGUAGE DISORDERS AND IMPAIRMENTS: SPECIAL CASES OF CHILD LANGUAGE ACQUISITION

CHAPTER 18

SOME EMPIRICAL AND THEORETICAL ISSUES IN DISORDERED CHILD PHONOLOGY

Daniel A. Dinnsen

I. INTRODUCTION

Most children acquire the sound system of the surrounding speech community in a relatively short time frame and without any specific instruction. There are, however, many other children who appear to have failed in this regard and often require clinical intervention to bring their speech into conformity with the target system. Their speech typically exhibits one or more errors (relative to the target sound system) persisting well beyond established developmental norms. The number or type of errors may render their speech unintelligible. In such cases, a phonological disorder is presumed to be involved, especially in the absence of any organic etiology. But what is a phonological disorder? What types of errors characterize a disorder? Are those errors different from the errors that occur in early stages of normal acquisition? That is, do phonological disorders represent a delay in the normal acquisition process, or do they constitute a deviant system, one that violates structures or principles evident in other developing or fully developed sound systems? What is the relevance of phonological disorders to theories of acquisition or to phonological theory? This chapter addresses these questions through an examination of the empirical characteristics and theoretical accounts of phonological disorders.

Linguistic research on phonological disorders has focused on issues relating to description or to the clinical treatment of those disorders with both applied and theoretical perspectives. On the applied side, because phonological descriptions

Handbook of Child Language Acquisition

make claims about a speaker's internalized grammar, they are essential to the assessment and remediation of a disorder. That is, a phonological description should tell the speech-language pathologist what the child has internalized about the target system and what the child has yet to learn. Treatment can then be structured to modify those aspects of the phonology that do not conform to the target system. On the theoretical side, these phonological descriptions make claims about the organization and structural characteristics of a disordered system. Although these systems may be considered disordered in some sense, they are nonetheless naturally occurring, first acquired varieties of a sound system. As such, descriptions of phonological disorders are potentially relevant to phonological theory because they provide an additional source for insight into the acquisition process and an additional testing ground for claims about possible sound systems. Also, although clinical treatment has the practical goal of bringing a child's phonology into conformity with the target system, it provides an opportunity to induce and observe change in a phonological system with the benefit of certain experimental controls and in a relatively short time frame, especially when compared to the normal course of language change. Clinical treatment can thus serve our theoretical concerns through the experimental manipulation of linguistic variables to test hypotheses.

II. EMPIRICAL CHARACTERISTICS AND THEORETICAL ACCOUNTS

The theoretical frameworks of natural phonology (Donegan & Stampe, 1979; Stampe, 1972) and generative phonology (Chomsky & Halle, 1968) have guided the descriptions of phonological disorders, although the two frameworks entail very different assumptions and make rather different claims about the nature of these systems. The primary focus has been on children's pronunciation errors, which have been found to be relatively systematic. Several common error patterns have been identified, which will be exemplified next, followed by a discussion of the different theoretical accounts. The adequacy of the frameworks can be evaluated against observed individual differences of various sorts. These error patterns also appear to be related in part to the nature of the children's underlying representations and their phonetic inventories.

A. Error Patterns

Substitutions

One general class of errors is associated with the reduced character of the phonetic inventory in these systems. That is, certain sounds or sound classes that occur in the target system do not occur in the child's system or may only occur in certain contexts. This more limited phonetic repertoire results in some characteristic substitution patterns. At least three general substitution patterns have been identified. One common pattern is the substitution of glides for liquid consonants. The data in (1) are from a child, Subject 46, age 5;2 (years;months),[1] who excludes [r] and [l] from his phonetic inventory and substitutes the glide [w] for both liquid consonants in all contexts.

(1) Subject 46 (age5;2): Substitution of [w] for target liquids

a. [w] for target /r/

[wid] "read"	[tawi] "starry"	[tʃɛw] "chair"
[weɪn] "rain"		
[waɪd] "ride"		

b. [w] for target /l/

[wif] "leaf"	[hiəwi] "hilly"	[mɛw] "smell"
[wɛg] "leg"	[dʒɛwi] "jelly"	[teɪw] "tail"

Another common error pattern is the substitution of stops for fricatives. The data in (2) are from a child, Subject 29, age 4;11, who excludes all fricatives, except for [v] and [ð], from his phonetic inventory and substitutes obstruent stops of roughly the same place of articulation.

(2) Subject 29 (age 4;11): Stops for target fricatives

a. Target /f/

[pɛdʊ] "feather"	[lipi] "leafy"	[naɪp] "knife"
[peɪt] "face"	[tapiŋ] "coughing"	[læp] "laugh"

b. Target /θ/

[tʌm] "thumb"	[titi] "teethy"	[tut] "tooth"
[to] "throw"		

c. Target /s/

[tʌ̃] "sun"	[duti] "juicy"	[jɛt] "yes"
[top] "soap"	[aɪti] "icy"	[maʊːt] "mouse"

d. Target /z/

[dibwə] "zebra"	[nɔɪdi] "noisy"	[bʌd̥] "buzz"
[du] "zoo"	[wodi] "rosy"	[toɬd̥] "toes"

e. Target /ʃ/

[tɛmpu] "shampoo"	[bwʌtiŋ] "brushing"	[plæt] "splash"
[tu] "shoe"	[watin] "washing"	[wʌt] "wash"

[1] All data reported herein are, unless otherwise noted, drawn from the Indiana University archival study of the phonological systems and learning patterns of young children (age 3;4 to 6;8) with nonorganic speech disorders. Subjects are consistently identified by number across our published reports.

The substitution of alveolars for velars is another common error problem. Th data in (3) are from a child, Subject 34, age 5;5, who excludes velars from her phc netic inventory and moreover substitutes alveolar stops.

(3) Subject 34 (age 5;5): Substitution of alveolars for velars

a. Target /k/

[tɪdz] "kids"	[dʌti] "ducky"	[dʌt] "duck"
[tæts] "catch"	[wati] "rocky"	[wat] "rock"
[teɪdz] "cage"		
[tʌp] "cup"		

b. Target /g/

[deɪt] "gate"	[pɪdi] "piggie"	[pɪd] "pig"
[dʌn] "gun"	[fɔdi] "froggie"	[bæd] "bag"
[dʌm] "gum"		

c. Target /ŋ/

[itɪn] "eating"

[tinz] "kings"

Omissions

In addition to the preceding substitutions, the omission of final consonants also a common error pattern. The data in (4) are from a child, Subject 28, age 4;1 who omits word final obstruent stops (left column), even though these same sounc can and do occur in other word positions (right column).

(4) Subject 28 (age 4;11): Omission of final consonants

a. Target /p/

[kʌ] "cup"	[pai] "pie"
[di] "jeep"	[pi] "peach"

b. Target /b/

[tʌ] "tub"	[baɪ] "bite"
[wo] "robe"	[bæ] "back"

c. Target /t/

[i] "eat"	[tu] "tooth"
[waɪ] "light"	[to] "toes"

d. Target /d/

[wi] "read"	[dɪ] "dish"
[haɪ] "hide"	[da] "dog"

e. Target /k/

[dʌ] "duck"	[kɔ] "cars"
[bʊ] "book"	[ko] "cold"

f. Target /g/

[bɪ] "big"	[gɪə] "gift"
[bæ] "bag"	[geɪ] "gate"

B. Natural Phonology Accounts

Based on the framework of natural phonology, these error patterns have been characterized as the result of natural processes (e.g., Edwards & Shriberg, 1983; Grunwell, 1982; Hodson & Paden, 1981; Ingram, 1989; Stoel-Gammon & Dunn, 1985). The theory provides for a limited set of innate processes that presumably find their bases in phonetics and are viewed as simplifying in nature, converting the child's internalized representations (which are assumed to be essentially adult-like) into their corresponding errored phonetic forms. Thus, to account for the substitutions in (1), it is claimed that a "gliding" process changes liquid consonants into glides. The substitutions in (2) are accounted for by a "stopping" process, which changes fricatives into stops. The substitutions in (3) are accounted for by a "fronting" process, which changes velars into alveolars. Finally, the error pattern in (4) is accounted for by a "final consonant deletion" process. These and other natural processes maintain that there is a specifiable relationship of systematic correspondence between the target adult system and the child's system. The framework is essentially relational in nature, characterizing phonological disorders as derivable from the target system via substitution processes. The problem for the child is not with the internalized representation but rather with the need to suppress the natural processes that presumably yield the error patterns. The common, recurring character of these error patterns in both normal and disordered acquisition has been taken as support for the correctness of the theory's claims (e.g., Hodson & Paden, 1981; Locke, 1980, 1983).

C. Alternate Accounts

Underspecification and Abstractness

Many aspects of these natural process accounts are problematic. First, the claim that the children's underlying representations are adultlike is highly abstract. That is, the child is attributed with knowledge of segment types that may never occur phonetically in his or her system. Although liquid consonants, fricatives, and velars are posited in each of the cases cited, the associated natural processes absolutely neutralize the presumed underlying distinctions between liquids and glides, between fricatives and stops, and between velars and alveolars. Second, less abstract accounts of these error patterns are available (Dinnsen, 1993) within an alternate theoretical framework, namely underspecification theory (Archangeli, 1988). That is, the substitution patterns can be accounted for without attributing to the child knowledge of distinctions that never occur in the child's system and without assuming any necessary correspondence between the target system and the child's system. Specifically, these substitutions can be seen as a reflection of underspecification. That is, certain properties of segments need not be specified, but rather can be filled in by (universal) rules. Thus, if liquid consonants have not yet been acquired, glides would be the expected substitutes for liquids if it is assumed that the underspecified or default value for nonnasal sonorants is [-consonantal]. Note that liquids are not "changed into" glides, because no liquid consonants are posited in such cases. Rather, it is claimed that the child has internalized just those features that are common to glides and liquids, namely their nonnasal sonorant character and, for purposes of realization, appeals to a feature fill-in rule that provides the [-consonantal] specification by default for all such segments. Similarly, if manner of articulation is assumed to be underspecified in a child's system, stops will be substituted for fricatives because the default value for manner is [-continuant]. Finally, alveolars would be the natural substitute for velars if it is assumed that coronals are the underspecified place of articulation (Paradis & Prunet, 1991).

The Nature of Underlying Representations and Rules

The natural process approach also fails to provide an adequate account for the error pattern involving the omission of final consonants exemplified in (4). A close examination of this error pattern reveals several systematic individual differences that cannot be accounted for if it is assumed that all children exhibiting this error pattern have underlying knowledge of those presumably deleted final consonants. Specifically, it has been found (Dinnsen, Elbert, & Weismer, 1981; Dinnsen & Maxwell, 1981) that for some children the omitted final consonant alternates with a word-medial consonant in morphophonemically related forms, whereas for other children the omitted consonant does not alternate. For example, children with the alternation have forms like [dΛ] *duck* ~ [dΛki] *ducky*. However, the other children with no such alternation have forms like [dΛ] *duck* ~ [dΛi] *ducky*. The children who do not alternate fail to provide any evidence that they know about the omitted consonant, even in the word-medial contexts where the consonant should appear if the consonant is represented underlying and the rule only applies in absolute final position. A general constraint seems to hold which prevents consonants from occurring post-vocalically at all levels of representation. Their underlying representations thus would not include consonants in a context that could undergo a process of deletion. The crucial difference, then, distinguishing the two subtypes of final consonant omissions rests on the nature of the children's underlying representations. Those forms that alternate provide evidence for adultlike underlying representations with the final consonant being deleted by rule. Those that do not alternate have underlying representations that are different from those of the adult system, at least with respect to morpheme-final consonants.

Attributing this difference in the error pattern to differences in the nature of underlying representations is supported by findings from acoustic analyses and experimental studies of learning patterns. On the basis of instrumental phonetic measurements of vowel durations in words produced by three children who omitted final consonants, Weismer, Dinnsen, and Elbert (1981) reported that two of these children exhibited an alternation between word-medial consonants and null word-finally and also maintained a systematic difference in vowel length corresponding to the voicing of the omitted final consonant. That is, vowels were long before omitted voiced consonants and short before omitted voiceless consonants, as might be expected if the consonants were present. The third child of the study, however, did not show an alternation with the omitted final consonants and also failed to exhibit any systematic difference in vowel length before omitted finals, which is what would be expected if the child had no knowledge of morpheme-final consonants. The examination of children's learning patterns has also supported the claim that children differ in the nature of their underlying representations. That is, in another study relating to this error pattern, Dinnsen and Elbert (1984) found that individual differences in children's learning patterns corresponded to differences in the nature of their underlying representations. Although all the children in that study omitted word-final consonants prior to any clinical intervention, there were differences within and across children in terms of which consonants exhibited an alternation. For example, for any given child, only certain target consonants would alternate with null word-finally, whereas other target consonants were omitted in both word-medial and word-final positions. As a result, children were credited with target-appropriate knowledge of only those omitted consonants that alternated. In the course of a single-subject multiple-baseline experimental design, each child received treatment on final consonants, independent of the nature of the child's underlying representations. The learning patterns within and across children following treatment showed the greatest improvements on those target final consonants that had realizations in morphophonemically related forms. In other words, the greatest improvements were seen in target sounds that were represented as adultlike at the underlying level prior to treatment.

There is another characteristic class of errors that cannot be explained within a natural process approach or any other approach that assumes the uniform adultlike character of these children's underlying representations. To illustrate this, consider the data in (5) reported by Williams and Dinnsen (1987) for a child, N. E., age 4;6, who substituted alveolars for velars sometimes as in (3) but also substituted velars for alveolars other times.

(5) Subject N. E. (age 4;6) (Williams & Dinnsen, 1987)
a. Correct production of labials
[bɪ] "big"
[buʔ] "boot"
b. Correct production of alveolars
[dɪʊ] "deer"
[dɛ] "dress"
c. Substitution of alveolars for velars
[tɛi] "catching"
[te] "cage"
[deʔ] "gate"

d. Correct production of velars
[ko] "comb"
[goʔ] "goat"
e. Substitution of velars for alveolars
[ka] "Tom"
[guʰ] "tooth"
[ga] "dog"

The problem is that there appear to be two error patterns that allow words only sometimes to be realized correctly with the target-appropriate consonants. A natural process approach could account for this by postulating two contradictory processes, "fronting" and "backing," both of which would have to apply inconsistently. Such an account, however, misses the generalization that alveolars and velars in this child's system occurred in complementary distribution and were thus allophones of the same phoneme. The fact is that alveolars occurred always and only before front vowels, and velars before back vowels. If alveolar and velar consonants are indeed taken as allophones of the same phoneme, then at least some of this child's underlying representations must be different from those of the adult system. Specifically, although labials would be represented as contrasting with nonlabial consonants, no place of articulation contrast would be specified among the nonlabial consonants in the child's system, contrary to what is required for the target system. Given this underspecified character of the nonlabials and a feature geometry framework that allows consonants and vowels to interact in particular ways (e.g., Clements & Hume, 1995; Gierut, Cho, & Dinnsen, 1993), the occurrence of alveolars and velars would be predicted from the spread of vowel place features to the underspecified place node of the adjacent consonant. Likewise, because the consonant place feature would be specified for labials, the vowel place features would not be able to spread to the consonant. Figure 18.1 illustrates (a) the spread of the place node, and thus the specified [coronal] feature of a front vowel, to the underspecified consonant to the left, to yield an alveolar consonant; (b) the spread of the specified [dorsal] feature of a back vowel to the underspecified consonant to the left, to yield a velar consonant; and (c) the absence of spreading, when, for example, a front vowel follows a consonant that is already specified for the [labial] place feature.

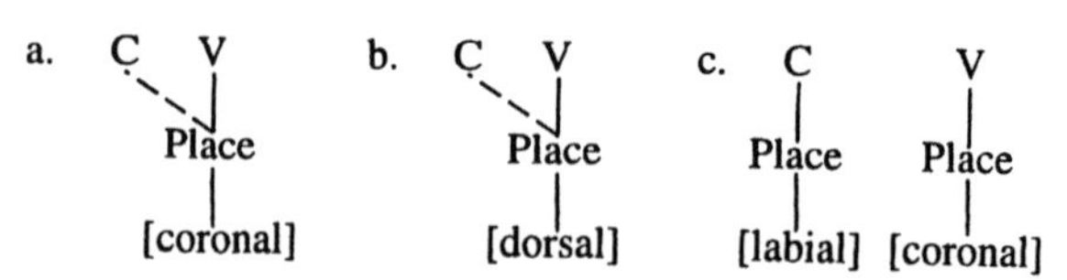

Figure 18.1. An underspecification and feature geometry account of consonant and vowel interactions.

Under this analysis, alveolars will be realized correctly in just those cases where they happen to occur before front vowels in the target system. Likewise, velars will be produced correctly in just those cases where velars occur before back vowels in the target system. On the other hand, these consonants will be produced in error when words in the target system require velars before front vowels and alveolars before back vowels. This analysis has the interesting characteristic of yielding some correct productions for the "wrong" reasons. That is, even though it is claimed that the underlying representations are not adultlike in the case of nonlabial consonants, the child's allophonic rule, which is totally independent of the target system, converts those non-adultlike underlying representations into correct productions in certain instances. From a clinical perspective, then, even correct productions at times warrant concern. In fact, correct productions of this sort may even inhibit the elimination of the error pattern. That is, because alveolars and velars are allophones in this child's system, a restructuring or "phonemic split" is called for that would associate these sounds with different phonemes. It is well established in second language acquisition that it is especially difficult to effect a phonemic split (Lado, 1957).

Other error patterns associated with phonological disorders similar to that just described are reported by Camarata and Gandour (1984) and by Gierut (1986, 1989). For a further discussion and characterization (within underspecification theory) of these error patterns in normally developing and phonologically disordered systems, see Dinnsen (1996a, 1996b) and Dinnsen and Chin (1995). These cases all have in common the complementary distribution (or allophonic status) of sounds that are phonemic in the target system and thus require the postulation of some non-adultlike underlying representations. The case reported by Gierut (1989) is especially problematic for relational approaches, which assume that it is possible to specify a correspondence between the target system and the child's disordered system. The child in her study, A. J., age 4;11, exhibited an allophonic relationship between [f] and [s], the only fricatives in the child's system. As might have been expected from other such cases, target /f/ and /s/ were realized correctly sometimes but other times were incorrectly substituted for one another. An allophonic rule, which does not resemble any process sanctioned within the framework of natural phonology, was required to account for the distributional facts and the apparent inconsistency in substitutions. More importantly, however, no systematic relationship could be established between the child's sounds and the target sounds. For example, as can be seen in (6), target fricatives were not always realized as fricatives by the child, nor did all the child's fricatives correspond with fricatives in the target system. More specifically, sometimes, but not always, target stops and affricates were realized as one of the child's two possible fricatives (6f), and some target fricatives were realized as stops sometimes (6e) and fricatives other times (6a–d).

(6) Subject A.J. (age 4;11) (Gierut, 1986, 1989)
 a. [f] for target /f/
  [fes] "face" [fæt] "fat"
 b. [s] for target /s/
  [maʊs] "mouse" [bwæs] "grass"
 c. [f] for target /s/
  [fɛdʊ] "seven" [fit] "seat"
 d. [s] for target /f/
  [kɔs] "cough" [ɔs] "off"
 e. Stop for target fricative
  [tɪk] "sick" [ti] "feet"
 f. Fricative for target stop or affricate
  [aɪs] "light" [was] "watch"

Even though the child's allophonic rule could predict the observed variation in the place of articulation of his fricatives, the rule could not be extended to predict a correspondence between place in the target system and place in the child's system. The child system was thus largely independent of the target system. For a somewhat different type of nonsystematic correspondence, see also Dinnsen, Barlow, and Morrisette (1997) and Leonard and Brown (1984). The existence of any nonsystematic correspondences or allophonic phenomena of this sort strongly motivates analytical frameworks that examine phonological disorders independently of the target system.

Once it is recognized that phonological disorders are independent and cannot simply be derived from the target system, a richer characterization of the problem is permitted within and across children. The problem can be with the nature of the underlying representations or the rules that mediate between underlying and phonetic representations. The focal point of the problem will have different empirical consequences. Errors of one sort can thus arise from adultlike underlying representations when a rule is internalized that is not characteristic of the target system, as seen earlier in one subtype of final consonant omissions. Errors of a different sort arise if non-adultlike underlying representations are internalized, as seen in the other subtype of final consonant omissions. Under other circumstances, both correct and incorrect phonetic representations can arise from non-adultlike underlying representations that are operated on by a rule, as seen especially in the case of allophonic phenomena, as in (5). In addition to the types of phenomena noted earlier, Dinnsen and Chin (1993) provided evidence of several other possible relationships between underlying and phonetic representations. For example, errors can result even if some aspects of a child's underlying representations are adultlike and no rule operates on those representations. This occurs if the child has failed to learn a necessary rule of the target system. The data in (7) from Subject 29, age 4;11, illustrate adultlike underlying representations with respect to the [voice] feature of initial obstruents but the failure to aspirate voiceless stops as required by the English allophonic aspiration rule.

(7) Subject 29 (age 4;11)

pɪg "pig"	[tut] "tooth"
[paɪ] "pie"	[tʌb] "tub"
but also	
[bɪg] "big"	[dɔg] "dog"
[bæg] "bag"	[dʌk] "duck"

Such an error pattern is clinically interesting because most treatment programs are designed to introduce contrastive properties of pronunciation (e.g., Elbert, Rockman, & Saltzman, 1980; Ferrier & Davis, 1973; Fey & Stalker, 1986), rather than the correct phonetic implementation of noncontrastive properties. In this particular case, the child already demonstrates knowledge of the contrast and only needs to learn the allophonic rule. It is not known if such errors require clinical intervention. It may be that errors of a certain type will be resolved spontaneously. If, however, this type of error pattern persists and treatment proves necessary, it still remains to be determined how allophonic rules are to be taught.

Under yet other circumstances, both correct and incorrect phonetic representations can arise when a child has internalized non-adultlike underlying representations and has additionally failed to learn a rule of the target system. The data in (8) from Subject 21, age 4;5, illustrate the correct realization of the plural morpheme in some cases but an incorrect realization in other cases.

(8) Subject 21 (age 4;5)

a. Correct realization of plural morpheme

[dɪps] "chips"	[gats] "cats"	[geɪks] "cakes"

b. Incorrect realization of plural morpheme

[taʊs] "toes"	[gaɪvs] "caves"	[gaʊms] "combs"

Because for this child, the plural morpheme does not alternate, being realized as [s] in all contexts, the underlying representation would likely be taken to be the same as the phonetic representation, and no rule would be postulated. A standard account of plurals in English, however, assumes the underlying representation to be /-z/ with a rule of progressive devoicing yielding an alternation. It is especially striking that the underlying representation was incorrectly internalized and did not exhibit an alternation because the child had knowledge of the contrast between /s/ and /z/ in final position in other forms. Clinically, this situation calls for the child to learn a rule of English, namely the rule of progressive devoicing, and to restructure his underlying representations. It is unknown how difficult this may be for a child, especially compared with the situation illustrated in (7). That is, in the latter case, the rule to be learned is neutralizing, and in the former case it is allophonic. This difference may also interact with the need to restructure underlying representations in the latter case but not in the former.

For additional examples revealing the independence of disordered systems, see Gierut (1985) and Maxwell (1979, 1981). For accounts of other phenomena in disordered systems, cast within underspecification or feature geometry frameworks, see Bernhardt and Gilbert (1992), Chin (1993), Chin and Dinnsen (1991, 1992), Dinnsen (1995), Dinnsen and colleagues (1997).

In sum, descriptive accounts of errors have revealed that not all errors are equal and not all correct productions are necessarily correct. A given error pattern, such as final consonant omission, can arise for different phonological reasons. In one case, the error can be attributed to adultlike underlying representations but an incorrectly internalized rule of deletion, and in another case, the error can come about simply from non-adultlike underlying representations. Correct productions that are not really correct can also come about for different phonological reasons but in all such cases the correct productions can also be related to a superficial error pattern. These involve cases where a child has internalized non-adultlike underlying representations either with an allophonic rule that is not appropriate for English, as in (5), or without a rule that is necessary for English, as in (7).

An essential component in any of these characterizations of phonological disorders is the nature of a child's underlying representations, which apparently can vary between being adultlike for some children in some instances and being non-adultlike for the same and other children in other instances. This has implications for models of the lexicon, especially given the apparent independence of disordered systems. Maxwell (1984) provided an overview and evaluation of some of the different models that have been proposed for normally developing and disordered systems. The standard assumption about the nature of the lexicon in fully developed sound systems has been that the lexicon, like all aspects of grammar, is neutral with respect to the speaker/hearer. Such a model has been adopted by some (e.g., Donegan & Stampe, 1979; Smith 1973) for normally developing systems. Others (e.g., Braine, 1976; Menn, 1978; Spencer, 1986) have adopted a dual lexicon model, which represents perceptual information in one lexicon and production information in the other lexicon. This was intended to account for the observation that children's perceptual abilities generally appear to develop in advance of their production abilities. In addition, the two lexicons would be related to one another by correspondence rules similar to the processes of natural phonology. Such rules were intended to account for the presumed systematic relationship between the target system (represented in the perceptual lexicon) and the child's phonetic output (represented in the production lexicon). Such a model entails considerable duplication across the two lexicons (cf. Iverson & Wheeler, 1987). More importantly, however, the dual lexicon model is a relational account, which attempts to characterize the child's system as a simple derivative of the target system. The range of variation and the nonsystematic correspondences evident in phonologically disordered systems argue against such a model of the lexicon. See Dinnsen (1993, 1995) and Dinnsen and colleagues (1996) for an alternate account of these phenomena in developing systems, which adopts a more conventional model of the lexicon within a modified framework of underspecification theory. This model differentiates lexical items that the child perceives to be different, but does not necessarily represent those differences exactly as in the target system. These differential representations come about from different combinations of specified and underspecified features and are sufficient to account for the correspondences that do occur.

D. The Nature of Phonetic Inventories

Variation and Typological Characteristics

The preceding characterization of phonological disorders allows for certain observed individual differences by making crucial reference to the nature of children's underlying representations and to the nature of the rules that mediate between levels of representation. There is also considerable individual variation in the constitution of these children's phonetic inventories that must be accounted for (see, for example, Ingram, 1980; Schwartz, Leonard, Folger, & Wilcox, 1980). In a study of the consonantal phonetic inventories of 40 phonologically disordered children (ages 3;4 to 6;8), Dinnsen, Chin, Elbert, and Powell (1989) observed variation along several dimensions. The number of consonants and glides in any given inventory ranged from 9 to 26, not all of which were target English sounds. Inventories differed in terms of available manners of articulation; but in those inventories in which fricatives occurred, no one fricative was common to all. Also, a voicing distinction was not always evident for all occurring places and manners of articulation. In addition, inventories differed in terms of the occurrence of liquid consonants. That is, some inventories excluded liquids altogether, others included one or the other liquid, and finally others included both liquids. Some inventories included many sounds but few feature distinctions, whereas other inventories included few sounds but many distinctions.

Despite this variation, a principle emerged that appears to govern these inventories cross-sectionally and longitudinally and yields a typological characterization. The principle specifies an implicational relationship among various feature distinctions that appear to be necessary as defining characteristics for these inventories. That is, all inventories could be uniquely assigned to one of five characteristic types, each representing a particular level of complexity. The simplest type of inventory (Level A) included only obstruent stops, nasals, and glides. Labial and alveolar consonants occurred, but there was no voice or manner distinction among the obstruents, and liquid consonants were also excluded. These inventories were thus characterized by necessary distinctions within major class features such as [sonorant] and place features such as [coronal]. Features relating to voice, manner, and nasality were entirely predictable. The next more complex type of inventory (Level B) differed from Level A inventories simply by the inclusion of a voice distinction among the obstruents. The featural characteristics of Levels A and B were retained in the next more complex type of inventory (Level C), while also including a manner distinction among the obstruents. That is, fricatives (and affricates) also occurred in these inventories. The next more complex type of inventory (Level D) retained the featural characteristics of the simpler inventories but included in addition one liquid consonant, either [l] or [r], but not both. These inventories were thus characterized by a necessary distinction among the sonorant consonants, expressed in terms of the feature [nasal], yielding nasal and nonnasal sonorant consonants. The most complex type of inventory (Level E) retained all the characteristics of the simpler inventories while including a stridency distinction among the fricatives or a laterality distinction among the liquid consonants. The stridency distinction was typified by the inclusion of both [s] and [θ] or [z] and [ð]. The laterality distinction was evidenced by the occurrence of both [r] and [l].

This is not to say that all the inventories associated with a particular level of complexity were identical, but rather that certain feature distinctions were shared by all inventories of a given level. The display in (9) expresses the implicational relationships among the relevant feature distinctions and defines the levels of inventory complexity with arrows pointing in the direction of implied features.

(9) Implicational relationships among feature distinctions

Level A	<	Level B	<	Level C	<	Level D	<	Level E
[sonorant]		[voice]		[continuant]		[nasal]		[strident]
[coronal]								and/or
								[lateral]

The claim of this principle as it relates to the phonetic inventories of phonologically disordered systems is as follows: Any inventory with a stridency or laterality distinction (Level E) will also include a distinction among sonorant consonants (i.e., will include nasals and a liquid). Moreover, any inventory that includes nasals and a liquid (Level D) will also include a manner distinction among obstruents (i.e., will include at least some fricatives). In addition, any inventory that includes a manner distinction (Level C) will also include a voice distinction among at least some obstruents. Finally, any inventory that includes a voice distinction (Level B) will also include a major class distinction and a place distinction between labials and alveolars. There are, of course, many other possible feature distinctions not specified by this principle. This undetermined character of the principle allows, however, for variation in terms of any features not stipulated and thus accounts for some of the observed individual differences. For example, although some inventories may exhibit a manner distinction, the principle makes no claim about which fricatives must occur; and children do vary in this regard. Also, although many inventories exhibit a voice distinction, the principle makes no claim about which consonants must be distinguished by this feature; and children once again vary in this regard.

The principle does nonetheless represent a severe constraint on the constitution of these inventories that can be tested in various ways. In a follow-up study (Dinnsen, Chin, & Elbert, 1992), it was found that this principle holds as a constraint both cross-sectionally and longitudinally as an account of the changes in the same children's inventories following treatment. Of all the logically possible ways that these inventories might have changed following treatment, all conformed to the principle and could be assigned to one of the five levels of complexity. Tyler and Figurski (1994) provided a further test of the principle in an experimental treatment study. In that study, two children (ages 2;8 and 2;10) presented relatively simple Level B inventories, excluding all fricatives, affricates, and liquid consonants. Each child was taught one sound representing different distinctions and different implicational relationships as specified by the principle. For example, one child was taught the fricative [s], which was intended to introduce the manner distinction associated with Level C. The other child was taught the liquid [l], which was intended to introduce the nasal/nonnasal distinction associated with Level D. The child taught the fricative did not learn any fricatives but did add a few other consonants associated with simpler levels. Interestingly, however, the child taught the implicationally more complex distinction acquired that distinction with the addition of [l] to the inventory but also acquired implicationally necessary (but untreated) fricatives and affricates associated with the Level C manner distinction. In addition to validating this specific principle, these findings have broader clinical implications in terms of the selection of treatment targets and the projection of learning. That is, this and other studies (Dinnsen & Elbert, 1984; Elbert, Dinnsen, & Powell, 1984; Gierut, 1991; Gierut, Morrisette, Hughes, & Rowland, 1996; Gierut & Neumann, 1992; Powell, 1991) suggest that, in those cases where implicational relationships can be established, treatment focused on implicationally more complex properties (or, in some sense, harder) can be expected to have the greatest overall impact on the system, yielding improvements in untreated but implicationally related (or easier) aspects of the system. This is especially significant because it calls for a radical departure from conventional clinical practice, which recommends that treatment targets be selected in a developmental sequence (e.g., Hodson & Paden, 1983; Shriberg & Kwiatkowski, 1982; Smit, Hand, Freilinger, Bernthal, & Bird, 1990).

Descriptions of the phonetic inventories of phonologically disordered systems provide a basis for comparison with normally developing systems. In general, phonologically disordered inventories have been found to resemble those of younger normally developing children, suggesting that the disorder may be one of delay rather than deviance (Ingram, 1989). In fact, the principle illustrated in (9) has as well been found to hold longitudinally (and cross-sectionally) for normally developing inventories (Dinnsen, 1992). However, Ingram (1990) has argued, based on an analysis of the inventories of 35 normal and 35 phonologically disordered children, that the two groups are fundamentally different in terms of the occurrence of voice and place distinctions. That is, he observed a general tendency (not an absolute) for children with disordered phonologies to exhibit voicing distinctions in advance of place distinctions with the reverse trend noted for children with normally developing phonologies. He attributed this difference to the presumed difficulties associated with achieving the supralaryngeal control of articulators required to produce the various place distinctions. This seems to suggest that a majority of the children in the disordered group may not have a phonological problem but rather suffer from some sort of deficiency or limitation of the motor system that impedes supralaryngeal articulations. The presumed motor problem would, however, have to be assumed to be something more than the normal motor immaturity associated with earlier stages of development because the normal group would otherwise also be expected to exhibit voicing distinctions in advance of place distinctions. Gierut (1994) offered an alternate phonological account of the facts that appeals to a principle of cyclicity, which has the effect of introducing voice (laryngeal) and place (supralaryngeal) distinctions in an alternating fashion. Any apparent differences between the two groups of children (normal and disordered) would reduce simply to their being in different phases of the cycle or their having gone through the cycle a different number of times at the point the observation is made. The disordered group would thus be characterized as delayed, but not fundamentally different.

Subtle Acoustic Differentiations

The reduced or limited phonetic inventories of disordered systems presumably result in widespread homonymy or phonemic mergers (Ingram, 1989; Locke, 1979). To the extent that this claim is based on listeners' judgments without the benefit of supporting instrumental analyses, it may not be entirely accurate and may seriously underestimate the child's phonological knowledge. For an overview of instrumental studies of normally developing and phonologically disordered systems, see Weismer (1984).

Maxwell and Weismer (1982) examined the phonological system of a child, Matthew, age 3;11, who appeared to exclude from his inventory all obstruents except [b] and [d]. No voice or manner distinctions were evident among the obstruents. The many target distinctions among nonlabial consonants were all collapsed into [d], as illustrated in (Figure 18.2).

Based on instrumental measurements of voice onset time (VOT), Maxwell and Weismer found that this child actually made a three-way distinction in his [d] realizations. That is, target /d/'s were differentiated from other target voiced obstruents, and these two categories were moreover differentiated from target voiceless obstruents. While the measured differences were statistically significant, the

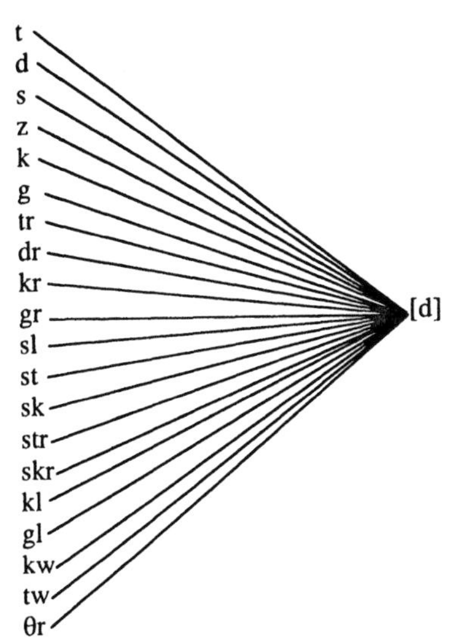

Figure 18.2. An apparent merger of target English distinctions in the speech of Matthew (aged 3;11) (Maxwell & Weismer, 1982).

magnitude of the difference was small, rendering the percept of only one category, namely /d/. Listeners' judgments would thus underestimate what this child knows about the target system. Similar results are reported by Forrest and Rockman (1988) in their study of three phonologically disordered children, who ranged in age from 3;6 to 4;8 and were judged to produce voiced stops in word-initial position for target voiced and voiceless obstruents. It was found that two of the three children produced statistically significant differences in VOT corresponding to the target distinction. For the third child, an examination of VOT along with other common acoustic correlates of voicing failed to establish a voice contrast in the system. These general findings are consistent with those reported by Macken and Barton (1980) for younger, normally developing children acquiring the voice contrast. That is, they identified several stages in the acquisition of the voice distinction. In the earliest stage, no contrast is evident. In the second stage, the child makes a small, but statistically significant, difference in VOT, yielding a voice contrast. But because the difference falls within the English voiced phoneme boundary, listeners do not perceive the difference. In subsequent stages, the VOT differences are increased to approximate adult values. These stages of normal acquisition are thus instantiated cross-sectionally by somewhat older phonologically disordered children.

Other studies have examined the spectral characteristics of apparent mergers and have yielded similar results (Forrest, Weismer, Hodge, Dinnsen, & Elbert,

1990; Hoffman, Stager, & Daniloff, 1983). Forrest and colleagues examined the apparent merger of the place distinction for four phonologically disordered children (ages 3;6 to 6;6), who substituted alveolars for velars as was exemplified in (3). All the children excluded velars from their inventories. The spectral characteristics of these children's alveolar stops were analyzed to determine whether any subtle acoustic differences could be found to correspond to the target place distinction. Children differed, but one of the four did in fact systematically differentiate target alveolars from target velars in terms of spectral properties similar to those used by phonologically normal children of the same age. Interestingly, within a few months of the initial analysis, this same child acquired correct productions of velars even though no treatment was provided on that class of sounds. It may well be that this child's knowledge of the distinction as revealed through the acoustic analysis reflected an early stage in the normal acquisition process, possibly serving as a predictor of change.

A clinical treatment study by Tyler, Edwards, and Saxman (1990) attempted to determine the role of such subtle acoustic differentiations in children's learning patterns. The four phonologically disordered children in their study ranged in age from 4;10 to 5;3 and were all judged to merge the distinction between target voiced and voiceless consonants. Instrumental measurements of VOT revealed that two of the children did maintain systematic differences between target voiced and voiceless consonants, whereas the other two children did not. Three of the children received conventional treatment focusing on the initial voice contrast; the fourth child was intended to serve as a control and thus received no treatment. Only one of the three children receiving treatment evidenced some knowledge of the target voice distinction prior to treatment as determined by the acoustic analysis. That one child achieved correct productions of voiced and voiceless obstruents faster and with higher levels of accuracy than did the two children who evidenced no prior (acoustic) knowledge of the contrast. The child who received no treatment made no perceptible improvement, despite the fact that the acoustic analysis established some prior knowledge of the contrast. These results suggest that knowledge of a phonological distinction, even if implemented only as a subtle acoustic difference, may facilitate the correct realization of the contrast, especially if treatment is focused on that contrast. Knowledge of the contrast is, however, apparently not sufficient to ensure correct realizations, as the one child who was not treated did not improve. It does appear in any case that treatment can exploit the existence of even subtle acoustic differences to select treatment sounds and predict areas of improvement.

In sum, instrumental acoustic analyses have in various cases revealed subtle acoustic differences in seemingly homophonous forms, indicating that that child has some knowledge of the target distinction, even if implemented differently. Such distinctions may be precursors of correct realizations as seen in normal development and may thus facilitate clinical treatment on the target distinction. This is in contrast to the "equivalence classification problem" (Flege, 1987), which presumably confronts second-language learners. That is, second-language learners apparently find it very difficult to achieve authentic target language phonetic realizations of a sound if the native language has a phonetically similar sound. Normally developing and phonologically disordered children who make subtle acoustic differences in accord with target phonological distinctions are, like second-language learners, expected to shift their production values to the phonetically similar, but different, values of the target system. This may be less of a problem for the two groups of children because their phonetic realizations of the distinction may be less well established.

III. PHONOLOGICAL ISSUES IN CLINICAL TREATMENT

The fact that phonologically disordered children often require clinical intervention to bring their speech into conformity with the target system confronts many phonological issues pertinent to the structure of treatment itself, to phonological theory, to the phonological characterization of the disordered system, and to the projection of phonological learning. In addition to the practical concerns of treatment, treatment can be structured as an experiment that manipulates phonological variables to test or validate particular claims or principles. Single subject multiple baseline (within or across subjects) experimental designs (McReynolds & Kearns, 1983) are especially suited to the clinical setting because conventional treatment and treatment experiments are sensitive to individual differences. Observations can be made about aspects of the child's system through probes (nonimitative naming of a set of pictures) over time (before, during, and after treatment) to assess the impact of treatment on the system. The sound or distinction selected for treatment is normally presented to the child in a few nonprobe words until a particular level of accuracy is achieved on that more limited set. With appropriate controls, changes in the pronunciation of untreated words on the probe list can be attributed to the treatment, although not all changes will necessarily be in the treated class of sounds (e.g., Costello & Onstine, 1976; Elbert & McReynolds, 1978). In fact, changes in the untreated aspects of the system tend to be the most interesting from a phonological perspective inasmuch as they reveal principled phonological relationships among sounds or underlying knowledge of the sounds on the part of the child.

These points are illustrated in a number of studies. For example, although the principle referred to in (9) was formulated as a theoretical constraint based on descriptions of observed variation in phonetic inventories, we saw that this phonological principle found support in the experimental manipulation achieved through treatment (Tyler & Figurski, 1994). The validation of the principle also made explicit the implications of the principle for treatment, both in terms of the selection of treatment targets and the projection of learning. That is, a sound selected for treatment from the implicationally more complex end of the hierarchy can be expected to have the greatest overall consequences for learning other untreated sounds, especially sounds implied by the treated sound. On the other hand, a sound selected for treatment from the opposite (unmarked) end of the implicational hierarchy would not necessarily facilitate the learning of any other sounds.

As we saw previously, the descriptive accounts of phonologically disordered systems have claimed that children differ in terms of what they know about the target system, especially as reflected in the nature of their underlying representations. These claims of differential phonological knowledge have been independently validated in an experimental treatment study (Gierut, Elbert, & Dinnsen, 1987). In that study, the phonological systems of six children, ranging in age from 3;7 to 4;6, were described within the theoretical framework of standard generative phonology. The descriptions maintained that each child exhibited some errors that could be attributed to adultlike underlying representations and other errors to non-adultlike underlying representations. Errors involving the exclusion of a sound either from all word positions or from a single word position with no alternations were assumed to be associated with non-adultlike underlying representations in at least those word positions. In all other cases, errors involving alternations were assumed to be associated with adultlike underlying representations. To assess the validity of this distinction and its potential impact on the children's subsequent learning, an experiment was designed that placed the children into two different treatment groups. One group of three children began treatment on target sounds that were assumed to be represented differently from the adult system at the underlying level, and the other group of three began treatment on sounds that were in error but represented in an adultlike fashion at the underlying level. Two different learning patterns emerged that corresponded to the two groups. The group of children receiving treatment on adultlike underlying representations showed improvements in the treated aspects of their systems with limited or no improvements in other untreated properties. On the other hand, the children receiving treatment on non-adultlike underlying representations achieved high levels of performance across the entire system, on both treated and untreated properties. The different learning patterns support such descriptive claims about the nature of children's underlying representations. These findings also have direct implications for structuring treatment and projecting learning. That is, treatment focused on the remediation of non-adultlike underlying representations can be expected to have the greatest overall consequences for the child's system.

A very basic phonological issue involved in the structure of treatment relates to the presentation of the new sound or distinction to be taught. For example, because substitution errors presumably result in homonymy, a standard treatment method has been developed that appeals to minimal pairs by presenting to the child the target treatment sound in one word and the contrasting substitute sound in another word (e.g., Ferrier & Davis, 1973; Weiner, 1981). Thus, a child who substitutes [t] for /k/ as exemplified in (3) would be presented with pairs of words such as "*t*op" and "*c*op" to make explicit to the child that there is a contrast in the target system that he or she has been merging. Although this form of treatment seems reasonable, it does embody several questionable phonological assumptions. First, it assumes that the substitution errors are systematic. As we saw earlier, however, not all errors can be related to the target system in a regular manner. In such cases, the targeted sound would have to be contrasted with any number of other sounds. The second questionable assumption relates to the salience of the distinction that would be presented in the minimal pair. That is, the difference between a target sound and its error substitute tends to be small, involving only one or at most a few feature differences. Additionally, the nature of the feature differences tends to relate to lower level distinctions, including voice, place, or manner. This approach to treatment thus requires the child to recognize and act upon a relatively small phonological difference that moreover may not even be relevant to all aspects of the error. In a series of experimental studies (Gierut, 1989, 1990, 1991, 1992; Gierut & Neumann, 1992), these and other aspects of the structure of treatment were investigated. Several important findings emerged. First, in a comparison with conventional minimal pair contrast treatment, it was found that greater improvement results if a new sound is contrasted with a correctly produced sound that is unrelated to the error pattern. This effect was augmented if the contrasting sounds were maximally opposed in terms of the number and types of feature distinctions. For example, in the case of the child who substitutes [t] for /k/, target /k/ might be presented in contrast to target /m/, which is produced correctly by the child, but which differs from /k/ by many features, including voice and place as well as a major class feature. Additionally, it was found that even greater improvements occur if two new sounds are contrasted with one another, and those sounds are maximally opposed in terms of at least a major class feature. It thus is not necessary to contrast a new sound with a correctly produced sound already in the child's system. The nature of the difference between sounds appears to be a very important factor in projecting a child's learning. Although these findings are directly relevant to clinical concerns, they also support the fundamental and necessary distinction made in phonological theory between major class features and other phonological features (see Stevens & Keyser, 1989).

In sum, virtually all aspects of treatment entail crucial appeal to phonological constructs, principles, or claims. Effective treatment depends first on an accurate assessment. An accurate assessment apparently requires a phonological description from a theoretical framework that allows for individual differences in the child's underlying phonological knowledge. The selection of treatment targets, the mode of presenting treatment sounds, and even the projection of what will be learned can be based on principled relationships among sounds or on a child's underlying knowledge of sounds. Treatment also provides an opportunity for the experimental evaluation or testing of these phonological principles and claims.

IV. CONCLUSION

The results from descriptive studies reveal phonological disorders to be highly structured, intricate, and relatively independent systems that exhibit individual differences in the nature of underlying representations, rules, and phonetic inventories. The variation evident in these systems compares with that observed in other developing and fully developed sound systems. Phonological disorders thus do not appear to violate principles governing language generally. Rather, they appear to represent delays in the normal acquisition process. Given the delayed nature of these systems, they may provide an even clearer picture of the acquisition process. That is, changes in normal acquisition may occur so rapidly and at such an early stage of development that they may go unnoticed. The disordered system on the other hand may afford a slow motion view of these changes. Also, the somewhat older age of the children with disorders eliminates some of the methodological difficulties often encountered in working with younger children. Phonological disorders are moreover amenable to experimental manipulation to test hypotheses through clinical treatment in ways that other normally developing systems are not. Treatment can thus stimulate changes in a system on demand and in a specified time frame for observation.

The issues considered here have been cast within derivational models of phonology, which assume that there are rules (or processes) which convert underlying representations into phonetic representations. These issues and findings should prove equally relevant and challenging to recent nonderivational constraint-based theories such as optimality theory (e.g., Prince & Smolensky, 1993). In such a framework, a ranked set of universal constraints selects for any given input (or underlying representation) an optimal output from among all possible output candidates. Because the constraints are presumed to be universal, the only elements of grammar that are free to vary are the input representations and the constraint rankings. The nature of children's underlying representations (a focal point of this chapter) thus remains a fundamental issue. There is relatively little published optimality work available on normal acquisition (e.g., Gnanadesikan, 1996; Goad, 1996; Pater & Paradis, 1996; Smolensky, 1996) and even less so on disorders (e.g., Barlow, 1996). Much of this work has assumed that children's underlying representations are adultlike. The consequence is that children's substitution patterns must then be attributed to particular constraint rankings. Constraints are of two general types: (a) faithfulness constraints, which require the input and output to correspond, and (b) well-formedness (or markedness) constraints, which favor unmarked outputs. It has been suggested that many of the substitution errors in early stages of development are attributable to well-formedness constraints being more highly ranked than faithfulness constraints (e.g., Gnanadesikan, 1996). For example, because children often acquire fricatives late, replacing them with stops, one possible highly ranked well-formedness constraint might be *[+continuant], which would be interpreted to disfavor fricatives in any output candidate. This constraint would be more highly ranked than some faithfulness constraint that required the feature [+continuant] to be parsed in the output. Even though a stop is unfaithful as an output for a fricative input, the violation of the faithfulness constraint is less serious, allowing a stop to be selected as an optimal output. A subsequent stage of development where the error pattern has been eliminated would be characterized by the opposite constraint ranking. Change comes about then from constraint reranking with faithfulness constraints more highly ranked than well-formedness constraints. If children's underlying representations are adultlike, such rerankings might be expected to result in across-the-board change. Interestingly, however, a close examination of change in children's systems has generally found that change proceeds gradually with evidence of lexical diffusion (e.g., Dinnsen 1996a,b; Macken, 1980). The intermediate stage of development, which exhibits both the emergence of target appropriate realizations in some lexical items and the persistence of the error pattern in other lexical items, is suggestive of a ranking paradox. The alternative may reside in adopting a different assumption about the nature of children's underlying representations. That is, if children's underlying representations are assumed to be underspecified as sketched in this chapter and elsewhere, faithfulness constraints can remain highly ranked with change attributable to changes in the underlying specification of affected lexical items. For example, then, the emergence of fricatives would come about from particular lexical items becoming specified underlyingly for the feature [+continuant] and a highly ranked faithfulness constraint that requires underlying features to be parsed in the output. The persistence of the original error pattern would remain attributable to underspecified inputs and the same highly ranked faithfulness constraints that favor certain features over others in outputs if those features are not in the input. That is, the feature [−continuant] would be favored over [+continuant]. By such an account, what changes is the underlying specification of just those lexical items that change phonetically. Continuity in the grammars is thus preserved across stages of development. For a fuller discussion of these issues in derivational and constraint-based approaches to acquisition, especially as relates to interacting error patterns, see Dinnsen and Barlow (1998). Also, although the constraints are presumed to be universal, their substance is as yet far from being agreed upon. Further research on acquisition phenomena should offer some insight into these constraints and their rankings.

ACKNOWLEDGMENTS

I am especially grateful to Jessica Barlow, Steven Chin, and Judith Gierut for their many helpful comments on an earlier draft of this chapter. This work was supported in part by grants from the National Institutes of Health, DC00260 and DC01694.

REFERENCES

Archangeli, D. (1988). Aspects of underspecification theory. *Phonology, 5,* 183–207.

Barlow, J. A. (1996). The development of on-glides in American English. In A. Stringfellow, D. Cahana-Amitay, E. Hughes, & A. Zukowski (Eds.), *Proceedings of the 20th Annual Boston University Conference on Language Development* (pp. 40–51). Somerville, MA: Cascadilla Press.

Bernhardt, B., & Gilbert, J. (1992). Applying linguistic theory to speech-language pathology: The case for nonliner phonology. *Clinical Linguistics & Phonetics, 6,* 123–145.

Braine, M. D. (1976). Review of *The acquisition of phonology* (N. V. Smith). *Language, 52,* 489–498.

Camarata, S., & Gandour, J. (1984). On describing idiosyncratic phonological systems. *Journal of Speech and Hearing Disorders, 49,* 262–265.

Chin, S. B. (1993). *The organization and specification of features in functionally disordered phonologies.* Doctoral dissertation, Indiana University.

Chin, S. B., & Dinnsen, D. A. (1991). Feature geometry in disordered phonologies. *Clinical Linguistics & Phonetics, 5,* 329–337.

Chin, S. B., & Dinnsen, D. A. (1992). Consonant clusters in disordered speech: Constraints and correspondence patterns. *Journal of Child Language, 19,* 259–285.

Chomsky, N., & Halle, M. (1968). *The sound pattern of English.* New York: Harper & Row.

Clements, G. N., & Hume, E. V. (1995). The internal organization of speech sounds. In J. A. Goldsmith (Ed.), *The handbook of phonological theory* (pp. 245–306). Cambridge, MA: Blackwell.

Costello, J., & Onstine, J. (1976). The modification of multiple articulation errors based on distinctive feature theory. *Journal of Speech and Hearing Disorders, 41,* 199–215.

Dinnsen, D. A. (1992). Variation in developing and fully developed phonetic inventories. In C. A. Ferguson, L. Menn, & C. Stoel-Gammon (Eds.), *Phonological development: Theories, research, implications* (pp. 191–210). Parkton, MD: York Press.

Dinnsen, D. A. (1993). Underspecification in phonological disorders. In M. Eid & G. Iverson (Eds.), *Principles and predictions: The analysis of natural language. Papers in honor of Gerald Sanders* (pp. 287–304). Amsterdam/Philadelphia: John Benjamins.

Dinnsen, D. A. (1995, November). *The manner node reconsidered.* Presented at the 20th Annual Boston University Conference on Language Development, Boston, MA.

Dinnsen, D. A. (1996a). Context effects in the acquisition of fricatives. In B. Bernhartdt, D. Ingram, & J. Gilbert (Eds.), *Proceedings of the UBC International Conference on Phonological Acquisition* (pp. 136–148). Somerville, MA: Cascadilla Press.

Dinnsen, D. A. (1996b). Context-sensitive underspecification and the acquisition of phonemic contrasts. *Journal of Child Language, 23,* 57–79.

Dinnsen, D. A., & Barlow, J. A. (1998). On the characterization of a chain shift in normal and delayed phonological acquisition. *Journal of Child Language, 25,* 61–94.

Dinnsen, D. A., Barlow, J. A., & Morrisette, M. L. (1997). Long-distance place assimilation with an interacting error pattern in phonological acquisition. *Clinical Linguistics & Phonetics, 11,* 319–338.

Dinnsen, D. A., & Chin, S. B. (1993). Individual differences in phonological disorders and implications for a theory of acquisition. In F. R. Eckman (Ed.), *Confluence: Linguistics, L2 acquisition, speech pathology* (pp. 139–154). Amsterdam/Philadelphia: John Benjamins.

Dinnsen, D. A., & Chin, S. B. (1995). On the natural domain of phonological disorders. In J. Archibald (Ed.), *Phonological acquisition and phonological theory* (pp. 135–150). Hillsdale, NJ: Erlbaum.

Dinnsen, D. A., Chin, S. B., & Elbert, M. (1992). On the lawfulness of change in phonetic inventories. *Lingua, 86,* 207–222.

Dinnsen, D. A., Chin, S. B., Elbert, M., & Powell, T. W. (1989). Some constraints on functionally disordered phonologies: Phonetic inventories and phonotactics. *Journal of Speech and Hearing Research, 33,* 28–37.

Dinnsen, D. A., & Elbert, M. (1984). On the relationship between phonology and learning. In M. Elbert, D. A. Dinnsen, & G. Weismer (Eds.), *Phonological theory and the misarticulating child* (*ASHA Monographs Number 22*) (pp. 59–68). Rockville, MD: American Speech-Language-Hearing Association.

Dinnsen, D. A., Elbert, M., & Weismer, G. (1981). Some typological properties of functional misarticulation systems. In W. O. Dressler (Ed.), *Phonologica 1980* (pp. 83–88). Innsbruck: Innsbruck Beiträge zur Sprachwissenschaft.

Dinnsen, D. A., & Maxwell, E. M. (1981). Some phonology problems from functional speech disorders. *Innovations in Linguistics Education, 2,* 79–98.

Donegan, P. J., & Stampe, D. (1979). The study of natural phonology. In D. A. Dinnsen (Ed.), *Current approaches to phonological theory* (pp. 126–173). Bloomington, IN: Indiana University Press.

Edwards, M. L., & Shriberg, L. D. (1983). *Phonology: Applications in communicative disorders.* San Diego, CA: College-Hill Press.

Elbert, M., Dinnsen, D. A., & Powell, T. W. (1984). On the prediction of phonologic generalization learning patterns. *Journal of Speech and Hearing Disorders, 49,* 309–317.

Elbert, M., & McReynolds, L. V. (1978). An experimental analysis of misarticulating children's generalization. *Journal of Speech and Hearing Research, 21,* 136–150.

Elbert, M., Rockman, B., and Saltzman, D. (1980). *Contrasts: The use of minimal pairs in articulation training.* Austin, TX: Exception Resources.

Ferrier, E., & Davis, M. (1973). A lexical approach to the remediation of sound omissions. *Journal of Speech and Hearing Disorders, 38,* 126–130.

Fey, M. E., & Stalker, C. H. (1986). A hypothesis-testing approach to treatment of a child with an idiosyncratic (morpho)phonological system. *Journal of Speech and Hearing Disorders, 51,* 324–336.

Flege, J. E. (1987). Effects of equivalence classification on the production of foreign language speech sounds. In A. James & J. Leather (Eds.), *Sound patterns in second language acquisition* (pp. 9–39). Dordrecht: Foris Publications.

Forrest, K., & Rockman, B. K. (1988). Acoustic and perceptual analyses of word-initial stop consonants in phonologically disordered children. *Journal of Speech and Hearing Research, 31,* 449–459.

Forrest, K., Weismer, G., Hodge, M., Dinnsen, D. A., & Elbert, M. (1990). Statistical analysis of word-initial /k/ and /t/ produced by normal and phonologically disordered children. *Clinical Linguistics & Phonetics, 4,* 327–340.

Gierut, J. A. (1985). *On the relationship between phonological knowledge and generalization learning in misarticulating children.* Unpublished doctoral dissertation, Indiana University.

Gierut, J. A. (1986). Sound change: A phonemic split in a misarticulating child. *Applied Psycholinguistics, 7,* 57–68.

Gierut, J. A. (1989). Describing developing systems: A surrebuttal. *Applied Psycholinguistics, 10,* 469–473.

Gierut, J. A. (1990). Differential learning of phonological oppositions. *Journal of Speech and Hearing Research, 33,* 540–549.

Gierut, J. A. (1991). Homonymy in phonological change. *Clinical Linguistics & Phonetics, 5,* 119–137.

Gierut, J. A. (1992). The conditions and course of clinically-induced phonological change. *Journal of Speech and Hearing Research, 35,* 1049–1063.

Gierut, J. A. (1994). Cyclicity in the acquisition of phonemic distinctions. *Lingua, 94,* 1–23.

Gierut, J. A., Cho, M.-H., & Dinnsen, D. A. (1993). Geometric accounts of consonant-vowel interactions in developing systems. *Clinical Linguistics & Phonetics, 7,* 219–236.

Gierut, J. A., Elbert, M., & Dinnsen, D. A. (1987). A functional analysis of phonological knowledge and generalization learning in misarticulating children. *Journal of Speech and Hearing Research, 30,* 462–479.

Gierut, J. A., Morrisette, M. L., Hughes, M. T., & Rowland, S. (1996). Phonological treatment efficacy and developmental norms. *Language, Speech, and Hearing Services in Schools, 27,* 215–230.

Gierut, J. A., & Neumann, H. J. (1992). Teaching and learning /θ/: A non-confound. *Clinical Linguistics & Phonetics, 6,* 191–200.

Gnanadesikan, A. E. (1996). Child phonology in optimality theory: Ranking markedness and faithfulness constraints. In A. Stringfellow, D. Cahana-Amitay, E. Hughes, & A. Zukowski (Eds.), *Proceedings of the 20th Annual Boston University Conference on Language Development* (pp. 237–248). Somerville, MA: Cascadilla Press.

Goad, H. (1996). Consonant harmony in child language: Evidence against coronal underspecification. In B. Bernhardt, D. Ingram, & J. Gilbert (Eds.), *Proceedings of the UBC International Conference on Phonological Acquisition* (pp. 187–200). Somerville, MA: Cascadilla Press.

Grunwell, P. (1982). *Clinical phonology.* Rockville, MD: Aspen Systems.

Hodson, B., & Paden, E. (1981). Phonological processes which characterize intelligible and unintelligible speech in early childhood. *Journal of Speech and Hearing Disorders, 46,* 369–373.

Hodson, B., & Paden, E. (1983). *Targeting intelligible speech.* Boston: College-Hill.

Hoffman, P. R., Stager, S., & Daniloff, R. G. (1983). Perception and production of misarticulated /r/. *Journal of Speech and Hearing Disorders, 48,* 210–215.

Ingram, D. (1980). A comparative study of phonological development in normal and linguistically delayed children. In *Proceedings of the First Annual Wisconsin Symposium on Research in Child Language Disorders, Volume 1* (pp. 23–33). Madison, WI: University of Wisconsin-Madison, Department of Communicative Disorders.

Ingram, D. (1989). *Phonological disability in children* (2nd ed.). London: Cole & Whurr.

Ingram, D. (1990, November). *The acquisition of the feature [voice] in normal and phonologically delayed English children.* Paper presented at the American Speech-Language-Hearing Convention, Seattle, WA.

Iverson, G. K., & Wheeler, D. W. (1987). Hierarchical structures in child phonology. *Lingua, 73,* 271–285.

Lado, R. (1957). *Linguistics across cultures.* Ann Arbor, MI: University of Michigan Press.

Leonard, L. B., & Brown, B. L. (1984). Nature and boundaries of phonologic categories: A case study of an unusual phonologic pattern in a language-impaired child. *Journal of Speech and Hearing Disorders, 49,* 419–428.

Locke, J. L. (1979). Homonymy and sound change in the child's acquisition of phonology. In N. Lass (Ed.), *Speech and language: Advances in basic research and practice* (Vol. 2, pp. 257–282). New York: Academic Press.

Locke, J. L. (1980). The prediction of child speech errors: Implications for a theory of acquisition. In G. H. Yeni-Komshian, J. F. Kavanagh, & C. A. Ferguson (Eds.), *Child phonology, Volume 1: Production* (pp. 193–209). New York: Academic Press.

Locke, J. L. (1983). *Phonological acquisition and change.* New York: Academic Press.

Macken, M. A. (1980). The child's lexical representation: The "puzzle-puddle-pickle" evidence. *Journal of Linguistics, 16,* 1–17.

Macken, M. A., & D. Barton. (1980). The acquisition of the voicing contrast in English: A study of voice onset time in word initial stop consonants. *Journal of Child Language, 7,* 41–74.

McReynolds, L. V., & Kearns, K. P. (1983). *Single subject experimental designs in communicative disorders.* Baltimore: University Park Press.

Maxwell, E. M. (1979). Competing analyses of a deviant phonology. *Glossa, 13,* 181–214.

Maxwell, E. M. (1981). *A study of misarticulation from a linguistic perspective.* Unpublished doctoral dissertation, Indiana University.

Maxwell, E. M. (1984). On determining underlying representations of children: A critique of the current theories. In M. Elbert, D. A. Dinnsen, & G. Weismer (Eds.), *Phonological theory and the misarticulating child (ASHA Monographs Number 22)* (pp. 18–29). Rockville, MD: American Speech-Language-Hearing Association, pp. 18–29.

Maxwell, E. M., & Weismer, G. (1982). The contribution of phonological, acoustic and perceptual techniques to the characterization of a misarticulating child's voice contrast for stops. *Applied Psycholinguistics, 3,* 29–43.

Menn, L. (1978). Phonological units in beginning speech. In A. Bell & J. Bybee Hooper (Eds.), *Syllables and segments.* Amsterdam: North-Holland.

Paradis, C., & Prunet, J.-F. (Eds.). (1991). *The special status of coronals: Internal and external evidence. (Phonetics and Phonology* 2). San Diego, CA: Academic Press.

Pater, J., & Paradis, J. (1996). Truncation without templates in child phonology. In A. Stringfellow, Cahana-Amitay, E. Hughes, & A. Zukowski (Eds.), *Proceedings of the*

20th Annual Boston University Conference on Language Development (pp. 540–552). Somerville, MA: Cascadilla Press.

Powell, T. W. (1991). Planning for phonological generalization: An approach to treatment target selection. *American Journal of Speech-Language Pathology: A Journal of Clinical Practice, 1,* 21–27.

Prince, A., & Smolensky, P. (1993). *Optimality Theory: Constraint interaction in generative grammar.* Technical Report #2 of the Rutgers Center for Cognitive Science, Rutgers University.

Schwartz, R. G., Leonard, L. B., Folger, M. K., & Wilcox, M. J. (1980). Early phonological behavior in normal-speaking and language disordered children: Evidence for a synergistic view of linguistic disorders. *Journal of Speech and Hearing Research, 6,* 277–290.

Shriberg, L., & Kwiatkowski, J. (1982). Phonological disorders II: A conceptual framework for management. *Journal of Speech and Hearing Disorders, 47,* 242–256.

Smit, A. B., Hand, L., Freilinger, J. J., Bernthal, J. E., & Bird, A. (1990). The Iowa Articulation Norms Project and its Nebraska replication. *Journal of Speech and Hearing Disorders, 55,* 779–798.

Smith, N. V. (1973). *The acquisition of phonology: A case study.* Cambridge: Cambridge University Press.

Smolensky, P. (1996). On the comprehension/production dilemma in child language. *Linguistic Inquiry, 27,* 720–731.

Spencer, A. (1986). Toward a theory of phonological development. *Lingua, 68,* 3–38.

Stampe, D. (1972). *A dissertation on natural phonology.* Doctoral dissertation, University of Chicago.

Stevens, K. N., & Keyser, S. J. (1989). Primary features and their enhancement in consonants. *Language, 65,* 81–106.

Stoel-Gammon, C., & Dunn, C. (1985). *Normal and disordered phonology in children.* Baltimore: University Park Press.

Tyler, A. A., Edwards, M. L., & Saxman, J. H. (1990). Acoustic validation of phonological knowledge and its relationship to treatment. *Journal of Speech and Hearing Disorders, 55,* 251–261.

Tyler, A. A., & Figurski, G. R. (1994). Phonetic inventory changes after treating distinctions along an implicational hierarchy. *Clinical Linguistics & Phonetics, 8,* 91–108.

Weiner, F. F. (1981). Treatment of phonological disability using the method of meaningful minimal contrast: Two case studies. *Journal of Speech and Hearing Disorders, 46,* 97–103.

Weismer, G. (1984). Acoustic analysis strategies for the refinement of phonological analysis. In M. Elbert, D. A. Dinnsen, & G. Weismer (Eds.), *Phonological theory and the misarticulating child* (*ASHA Monographs Number 22*) (pp. 30–52). Rockville, MD: American Speech-Language-Hearing Association.

Weismer, G., Dinnsen, D. A., & Elbert, M. (1981). A study of the voicing distinction associated with omitted, word-final stops. *Journal of Speech and Hearing Disorders, 46,* 320–328.

Williams, A. L., & Dinnsen, D. A. (1987). A problem of allophonic variation in a speech disordered child. *Innovations in Linguistics Education, 5,* 85–90.

CHAPTER 19

LINGUISTIC PERSPECTIVES ON SPECIFIC LANGUAGE IMPAIRMENT

Harald Clahsen

I. INTRODUCTION

In the clinical literature, the notions of dysphasia and specific language impairment (SLI) are used as cover terms for delays or disorders of the normal acquisition of grammar without any clear primary deficit, that is, despite their linguistic problems, SLI children and adults seem to have normal nonverbal IQs, no hearing deficits, and no obvious emotional or behavioral disturbances. Because these clinical criteria are relatively broad, it is to be expected that the syndrome of SLI does not cover a homogeneous population and that there are several different subtypes of SLI.

In this chapter, I will summarize results of linguistic investigations of SLI. I will focus on showing in what ways linguistic studies can contribute to our theoretical understanding of SLI. The investigation of child language disorders has traditionally been a domain of medicine, psychology, and educational disciplines. In accordance with the dominant research paradigm used in studies on child language disorders, some salient linguistic properties from the children's language are selected and then are correlated with various nonlinguistic features, such as general intelligence, auditory perception, hierarchical structuring abilities, and so on. The results are etiological typologies in which factors such as brain damage, genetic impairments, mental handicaps, and environmental disturbances are listed as the potential causes of the children's linguistic problems (cf., e.g., Becker & Sovak, 1975, p. 108). Under this approach, an explanation is given by deriving linguistic behavior from nonlinguistic deficits. A linguistic approach, however, introduces a different way of looking at child language disorders. Linguistics, particularly generative linguistics, regards grammar—that is, syntax and morphology—as a cognitive domain that is to a certain extent autonomous from nonlinguistic systems. A linguistic approach allows one to explain disorders or delays of grammatical developmental in terms of selective deficits of the language faculty itself. Because grammatical problems are the core property of SLI, it is worth exploring SLI from a linguistic perspective.

A second reason for investigating SLI from a linguistic point of view is that the study of SLI may provide insights into the process of language acquisition in general. In normal language acquisition, the various components of grammatical knowledge largely develop parallel to each other, and the extent to which each component is autonomous cannot always be determined clearly. Suppose that SLI or a subgroup of SLI patients is characterized by selective damages of an otherwise normal system for language acquisition. This would allow us to show how far the system could develop, if, for example, syntactic representations are intact, but the acquisition of inflection is disturbed. This would provide insights into the extent to which the development of syntactic knowledge takes place independently of the acquisition of inflection.

Finally, linguistic investigations of SLI contribute to improving the diagnosis of SLI. Linguists have developed assessment procedures that are based on comprehensive linguistic analyses of the spontaneous speech of SLI subjects and can be used in routine clinical practice. The profiling approach appears to me to be the most promising way of spontaneous speech diagnosis. Linguistic profiles provide a detailed assessment of grammatical disability and suggest a remedial approach. The best-known profile is the Language Assessment Remediation and Screening Procedure (LARSP, Crystal, Fletcher, & Garman, 1976). Recently, the profiling approach has been applied to languages other than English—compare Berman, Rom, and Hirsch (1982) for the Hebrew profile HARSP, Admiraal-Berg, Bol, Kuiken, and Verway-de Jongh (1984) as well as Verhulst-Schlichting (1982) for the Dutch profile, and Clahsen (1986) for the German profile. The most important characteristic of profiles is that the linguistic categories are graded developmentally, that is, in terms of their emergence in normal language acquisition. The LARSP profile, for example, consists of a set of seven age-related developmental stages based on a descriptive synthesis of the L1/English acquisition literature, and, at each stage, the profile gives the most commonly used structures that have been documented in empirical studies on normal English child language. Thus, profiles are not just descriptions of the linguistic patterns of disordered language, but, more importantly, the procedure provides a way of identifying the developmental level of grammar an individual SLI child has achieved. In the speech therapy profession, linguistic profiles are considered to be too time-consuming to be applied as a diagnostic tool in routine clinical practice. To improve the practical value of the procedure, we developed a software package for the German profile, COPROF (Clahsen & Hansen, 1991), which, due to a semiautomatic linguistic analysis, enables the clinician to administer a profiling analysis much faster than before.

This chapter concentrates on the linguistic explanations of SLI. The next section briefly summarizes the major linguistically based approaches to SLI that have been proposed in the literature. Later sections summarize empirical results of various linguistic studies on SLI, focusing on studies of grammatical phenomena and mostly based on production data. My conclusion will be that the empirical results currently available support the view that SLI typically involves selective deficits in establishing grammatical agreement processes.

II. LINGUISTIC INTERPRETATIONS OF SLI

In recent years, the linguistic problems of SLI children have been the subject of various research studies in various disciplines. Basically, two different approaches have been taken in these studies: (a) *linguistic approaches,* which try to explain observed language impairments by assuming disruptions of the normal development of central grammatical modules, for example, problems with syntactic features, and so on, and (b) *psychological approaches,* which try to explain SLI in terms of processing impairments, for example, auditory processing problems (Tallal & Stark, 1981), impairments in hierarchical structuring abilities (Cromer, 1978), or severe restrictions in short-term memory capacity (Kamhi, Catts, Raner, Apel, & Gentry, 1988). Overviews of psychological approaches to SLI can be found for example in Bishop (1992), among others. This discussion focuses on the linguistic interpretations of SLI.

The general working hypothesis shared among linguistic investigations of SLI is that, due to (selective) deficits of the language acquisition device, the normal development of grammatical representations is disrupted in SLI. Furthermore, there seems to be a consensus that SLI children have problems in the area of grammatical morphology. Linguistic studies on SLI stress that inflectional morphology—that is, grammatical function words and bound morphemes encoding case, gender, number, person, and so on—is impaired in SLI. SLI children often omit these elements or use them incorrectly. It also seems that in SLI children, the development of inflectional morphology comes to standstill at an early stage, and that beyond that point the acquisition process cannot advance without difficulties. By contrast, it is controversial whether SLI involves deficits in phrase structure and word order, too (cf. e.g., Grimm & Weinert, 1990). We will come back to this controversy in the subsequent sections.

Among the linguistic interpretations of SLI, the following approaches are discussed most extensively in current SLI research:

- *The surface deficit* (Leonard Bertolini, Caselli, McGregor, & Sabbadini, 1992), according to which SLI children are said to have difficulties acquiring grammatical morphemes with low phonetic substance.
- *The missing feature deficit* (Gopnik, 1990a, 1990b), according to which syntactic features (tense, person, number, etc.) are said to be absent from the grammars of SLI individuals.
- *The rule-deficit model* (Gopnik & Crago, 1991), according to which SLI subjects do not have access to regular rules of inflection.
- *The grammatical agreement deficit* (Clahsen, 1989, 1991), according to which SLI children have problems establishing agreement relations between two elements in phrase structure in which one element asymmetrically controls the other.

In the following sections, these approaches and the main empirical findings on which they are based will be briefly summarized.

A. The Surface Account

Leonard's account of SLI involves three major features that are supposed to explain SLI children's problems with inflectional morphology: (a) perceptual limitations, (b) language-particular familiarity/nonfamiliarity with inflectional morphology, and (c) problems in paradigm building.

First, children's problems with inflectional morphology result from *perceptual limitations:* the linguistic input for SLI children is filtered in such a way that closed-class items with low phonetic substance will not become available to the language-learning mechanism. Thus, many of the errors made by SLI children affect nonsyllabic consonantal segments and unstressed syllables. Leonard, Sabbadini, Volterra, and Leonard (1987) found, for example, that English-speaking SLI children show high error rates of the *-s* plural, the possessive *-s,* the third-person singular *-s,* the past-tense *-ed,* and contracted forms of *to be.* Moreover, articles, the infinitive marker *to* and the complementizer *that* are often left out. The common property of these morphemes is that they have low phonetic substance, and it could be—as suggested by Leonard and his collaborators—that SLI children's problems with these elements are due to perceptual limitations.

Second, SLI children have problems building *morphological paradigms.* Leonard and colleagues found that SLI children are not generally unable to process unstressed nonsyllabic consonantal segments; rather, their problems seem to be restricted to those forms that are part of morphological paradigms in the adult language. Thus, English-speaking SLI children are able to process the final segment of the word *dance,* but this segment does not seem to be available to them as an inflectional morpheme, for example in *he keep-s.* Leonard and colleagues have attributed this contrast to the additional demands of paradigm building, which require a child to place an inflectional morpheme into the appropriate cell for the tense/agreement paradigm.

The third feature of Leonard's account is that the linguistic properties of SLI depend on *surface structure properties of the particular language*. In highly inflected languages (morphologically "rich" in Leonard's terms) in which both high frequency and the obligatory nature of morphological information tunes the child in to morphology in general, we find fewer omissions and errors of closed-class items in SLI children, even of those with low phonetic substance, whereas in languages with less complex inflectional systems, unstressed nonsyllabic inflectional morphemes are most often omitted by SLI children. For example, Rom and Leonard (1990) found that Hebrew SLI children were more likely to produce present and past-tense inflections than English SLI children of comparable language level. They have argued that this difference results from the difference in morphological richness between the two languages: Hebrew is more highly inflected than English and therefore Hebrew children are generally more tuned in to morphology than are English children.

B. The Missing Feature Account

According to the missing feature account (Gopnik, 1990a, 1990b), the grammars of SLI children and adults lack syntactic features. Although grammatical notions such as tense, aspect, gender, and so on are accessible to them, SLI children and adults are said to be unable to produce and to comprehend the overt markings of these notions at the level of morphosyntax. Thus, under this account, past-time events may be expressed in SLI—for example, through adverbials such as *yesterday* and so on—but the system of past-tense inflection is said to be absent. This does not mean that SLI children will never produce past-tense inflections. Instead, the missing feature account argues that in SLI, syntactic features will not be used to systematically mark grammatical notions. For example, an SLI child might use past-tense forms to refer to present-tense events and present-tense forms to refer to past-time events. Similarly, they may use the plural *-s* on singular nouns (*a boys, one boys*) and incorrect zero marking when referring to plural nouns (*two boy*). Gopnik concluded that the grammars of SLI individuals lack representations of these features.

The missing feature account was originally developed to describe the language of one SLI child who was bilingual in French and English (Gopnik, 1990a) and who made similar feature-related errors in both languages. In more recent work (Gopnik 1990b, Gopnik & Crago, 1991), the missing feature account was extended to characterize the language of a single extended family in which there seemed to be a dominant pattern of inheritance of SLI. Gopnik and Crago (1991) carried out a set of experiments with the members of this family to support the missing feature account. In one task, for example, the subjects were prompted to change the tense forms of the verbs. The SLI subjects gave semantically relevant answers, for example, by using appropriate adverbials, but seldom produced the required past-tense forms. By contrast, Gopnik did not find any deficit in her SLI subjects in tasks involving knowledge of verb argument structure. They were, for example, able to produce sentences with three-place predicates and to detect the ungrammaticality of sentences such as **he gives it.*

C. The Rule-Deficit Model of SLI

In an attempt to modify their conceptual view of SLI, Gopnik and her collaborators (Gopnik, 1994; Gopnik & Crago, 1991) connected their approach to linguistic theories of inflection, specifically to the so-called hybrid model of English past-tense morphology proposed by Pinker and Prince (1991). According to this model, inflectional systems involve qualitative differences between regular and irregular morphology. Language-unimpaired children and adults are said to possess two distinct psychological mechanisms for inflection: a symbol-manipulating rule system allowing productive on-line concatenation of affixes to stems and an associative system that involves memory-based retrieval processes of stored items. Pinker and his collaborators use the hybrid model of inflection to explain the distribution of overregularizations in language acquisition and to account for regular/irregular distinctions in adult processing experiments.

In applying the hybrid model to SLI, Gopnik and her colleagues claimed that SLI individuals' ability to learn inflectional rules is impaired relative to their ability to memorize and store individual words. We may call this variant *the rule-deficit model of SLI.* Thus, in SLI knowledge of inflection is believed to be restricted to an associative memory network for irregulars, whereas symbolic rules of regular inflection are claimed to be absent. Gopnik and Crago (1991) observed that some of their SLI subjects performed correctly on a comprehension task that involved responding to commands such as *Point to the book* versus *Point to the books.* If the meanings of noun plurals were inaccessible to them, as predicted by the missing feature hypothesis, one would expect SLI subjects to perform randomly on this task. Similarly, Gopnik and Crago observed that some of their SLI subjects were able to produce some past-tense forms correctly. Again, if syntactic features were totally absent from the grammars of these speakers, this should not be possible. Gopnik and Crago explained these findings by assuming that regular inflectional forms were treated as if they were irregular, that is, they were stored in memory, rather than productively generated. To support this idea, they reported that there were practically no overregularizations of plural or past-tense affixes in their data that would indicate productive use of these affixes. This was taken to indicate that the SLI individuals did not have access to regular rules of inflection.

D. The Grammatical Agreement Deficit

According to this account, SLI children have problems establishing a relation that is essential in natural language grammars—the relation of agreement. This missing agreement account emerged from our project on German-speaking children and has not yet been systematically tested from a cross-linguistic perspective. However, some results from recent SLI studies indicate that it might also hold for languages other than German.

There are of course different ways of theoretically defining the notion of grammatical agreement. In our previous research, we adopted the notion of agreement from generalized phrase structure grammar (GPSG) (cf. Gazdar, Klein, Pullman, & Sag, 1985). In GPSG, a clear distinction is made between the level of phrase-structure configuration and the level of control and percolation of grammatical features. Phrase-structure geometry is determined by principles of X-bar syntax, that is, by configurational rules of immediate dominance and linear precedence. The most important principle in GPSG determining the choice of grammatical features is the control-agreement principle (Gazdar et al., 1985, p. 89). In this view, agreement is an asymmetrical relation between two categories, where one is a functor and the other is an argument controlling the functor.

According to the missing agreement account, SLI can be characterized in terms of a selective impairment of an otherwise intact grammatical system. If the missing agreement hypothesis is correct, the following linguistic phenomena should cause problems for SLI children:

- *Subject-verb agreement,* such as the third-person singular *-s* in English or the person and number suffixes that appear on finite verbs in Italian and German.
- *Auxiliaries,* that is, the finite forms of to be and to have that co-occur with participles, gerunds, and so on.
- *Overt structural case markers,* such as the accusative case of the direct object in German.
- *Gender marking on determiners and adjectives,* for example, as in German.

Consider, for example, subject-verb agreement. In terms of the control-agreement principle (CAP), person and number are not primary features of finite verbs. They are only realized on finite verbs (= the functor), but they provide information about the subject and, in this way, can be said to be controlled by the subject (= the argument). Therefore, given that the CAP is not accessible to SLI children, subject-verb agreement should be impaired in SLI. Similarly, auxiliaries in English and German are lexical fillers of subject-verb agreement features, and, if the missing agreement account of SLI is correct, these children should have problems with auxiliaries.

Structural case marking also falls under the CAP. In a language with morph logical case marking, such as in German, structural case is realized on NPs, but is a syntactic feature of lexical and or functional categories (V, Infl, Det). Thus, Government-Binding theory (Chomsky, 1981), it is assumed that structural ca markers are assigned under Specifier-head agreement. For example, the posse sive genitive *-s* in English and German is assigned to the possessor phrase in tl same fashion as nominative case is assigned to the subject and objective case assigned to the direct object, namely from the corresponding head category—th is, from D° for the possessive *-s*, from I° for nominative case, and from Agr-O° f objective case (cf., e.g., Ouhalla 1991). Therefore, German-speaking SLI subjec should have problems acquiring the overt structural case markers of adult Germa

Gender is a lexical feature of nouns, but in German it is morphologically rea ized on determiners and adjectives, and not on nouns. Thus, gender marking ca be subsumed under the general notion of control agreement. By contrast, notio such as definiteness are inherent features of determiners and can be acquired eve without the CAP, for example through semantic bootstrapping. Therefore, v would expect that SLI children have definite and indefinite articles and other d terminers, but that they have problems with the use of correct gender markings (determiners.

In contrast to the subsystems of inflection mentioned previously, noun plura in English and German, past-tense marking in English, and particle inflection German do not fall under the control-agreement principle, because rather than b ing controlled by an argument category, these are marked directly on the noun verb and contribute to its meaning (along with other features). Therefore, we e pect that these areas should be unimpaired in SLI children. In addition, we expe SLI children not to have any genuine word-order difficulties. They should not hav any problems acquiring the correct placement of, for example, articles in relatio to NPs, prepositions in relation to their complements, and other kinds of co stituent-internal word order.

III. EMPIRICAL RESULTS ON GRAMMATICAL DEVELOPMENT IN SLI CHILDREN

This section summarizes empirical findings from various studies dealing wi the development of syntax and inflectional morphology in SLI children. Becau most of the SLI studies have been done on English and German, the focus he will be on these two languages, but, occasionally, findings from other languag will be included. In the next section, the empirical results will be taken to eval ate the proposed explanations of SLI mentioned earlier.

A. Person and Number Agreement

Studies from different languages (English, German, Italian) show that person and number agreement is impaired in SLI.

In studies on English-speaking SLI children, it was found that subject-verb agreement causes major difficulties. Leonard and colleagues (1992) reported, based on a cross-sectional study with 10 English-speaking SLI children (age range: 3;8 to 5;7 years), that the mean percentage of correct usage of the third-person agreement marker was 34%. Leonard and colleagues compared this figure with two groups of normal controls: (a) a group of 10 normally developing children of the same age and (b) 10 normal controls matched for mean length of utterance (MLU). Both comparisons revealed significant differences: The age controls had over 90% correct agreement and the MLU controls 59%. These findings are consistent with Rice and Ötting's (1993) findings. In a study with 81 SLI children and 92 normal controls, they found that the SLI children's correct usage was 36%, whereas the MLU-based control group's mean was 54%; this difference is again statistically significant.

The evidence on Italian-speaking SLI children is mixed. Leonard and colleagues (1992) examined two forms of the Italian subject-verb agreement system, the third singular and the third plural, in the speech of 15 SLI children (age range: 4;0 to 6;0 years), 15 normal children of similar ages and 15 normal children matched for MLU. The SLI children performed significantly worse in the third plural, but not in the third singular. The SLI children's mean of correct usage in obligatory contexts were 49.9% for the third plural (82.3% for MLU controls), but 92.7% for third sing. (93.1% for MLU controls). Leonard and colleagues did not provide any information on how Italian-speaking SLI children encode first- and second-person agreement and no frequencies of correct/incorrect occurrences. Leonard and colleagues mentioned that in many of the third-plural errors, the children used third-singular forms. Extrapolating from that, it might be that third-singular forms also occur in first- and second-person contexts. In this case, the high percentage of correct third singular in third person contexts would be accidental and misleading. Therefore, the high correctness value for third singular is difficult to evaluate. All that can be concluded from Leonard and colleagues' investigation of Italian-speaking SLI children is that the full paradigm of subject-verb agreement of adult Italian does not seem to be available to SLI children.

Several studies examined subject-verb agreement in German-speaking SLI children. Based on cross-sectional and longitudinal data, Clahsen (1991, p. 165ff.) found that only one child out of ten SLI children examined (mean age: 5;6; range: 3;2 to 9;6) acquired the correct paradigm for person and number inflection on the finite verb; in this child (Petra), subject-verb agreement emerged at the age of about 4 years, that is, considerably later than in normal children (cf. Clahsen & Penke, 1992). None of the other nine children acquired the system of subject-verb agreement during the period of observation. Typically, these children used zero affixation or *-n* forms (= infinitives) irrespective of the person and number of the subject. Consequently, the rates of correct overt marking of these forms are rather low. Moreover, only a limited set of affixes occurs in the children's utterances; in particular, the second-person singular suffix *-st* is not acquired, although this affix is the only unique form in the German agreement paradigm.

Similar results were obtained in a longitudinal study with 19 SLI children (mean age: 5;4; range: 3;11 to 6;11) studied over a period of one year (cf. Rothweiler & Clahsen, 1994). It was found that 11 out of these 19 children had problems acquiring the subject-verb agreement paradigm. In this regard, they differed considerably from MLU-matched language-unimpaired controls. The suffix *-st* is rarely used by these 11 SLI children—in less than 50% of the obligatory contexts—and the infinitive form *-n* is often used as a default affix to replace finite verb forms (mean rate of incorrect *-n* = 60%, weighing each of the 11 SLI children equally). During the period of observation, 2 out of these 11 children acquired the subject-verb agreement system including *-st* and showed a significant decrease of the use of default *-n* forms; however, the acquisition of subject-verb agreement in these 2 children is considerably delayed in comparison to MLU-matched language-unimpaired children. The remaining 9 SLI children did not acquire subject-verb agreement during the period of observation.

Subject-verb agreement was also examined in Kaltenbacher and Lindner's (1990) study of three German-speaking SLI children. They studied two children cross-sectionally at the age of 6;8 years and found that one child had correct person and number agreement, whereas the other child most often used sentences without finite verb forms. The third child was studied longitudinally for one year, from age 4;8 to age 5;8. Kaltenbacher and Lindner found that subject-verb agreement emerged during this period, that is, considerably later than in normal children.

B. Auxiliaries and Modals

In studies on English-speaking SLI children, it has been noticed that many errors of negation and question formation reflect difficulties with the auxiliary system (Johnston & Kamhi, 1984). Typically, English-speaking SLI children are more likely than normal controls to provide, in a clause, a verb stem that is uninflected for agreement and not premodified by an auxiliary (Fletcher & Peters, 1984). Leonard and colleagues (1992) examined the use of the copula in 10 English-speaking SLI children and found that in only 41% of obligatory contexts the copula was correctly supplied, a statistically significant difference to normally developing children controlled for MLU and chronological age.

Bol and de Jong (1992) examined omissions of auxiliaries in 16 Dutch-speaking SLI children and 16 normal controls matched for MLU. Overall, they did not find any significant group differences in production of auxiliaries between the SLI and the normal children. However, an individual subject analysis revealed that 6 SLI children omitted 40% of auxiliaries in obligatory contexts, whereas the other 10 SLI children did not omit auxiliaries at all. Thus, mean scores for groups are not particularly revealing for the sample of SLI children studied by Bol and de Jong. What their data suggest is that a subgroup of the SLI children they examined has considerable difficulty with the use of auxiliaries.

In several studies on German-speaking SLI children, it has been reported that these children have considerable difficulty with auxiliaries, but not with modals and lexical verbs (V°). This is the distribution of verbal elements found in the 10 SLI children studied in Clahsen (1991). All the children used modal verbs, but auxiliaries and copulas were rare and were omitted in most of the obligatory contexts. Moreover, the longitudinal data from these children indicate that the overall proportion of omissions of verbal elements decreases over time, but that the omission rates for auxiliaries and copulas remained high (= over 50%) throughout the whole period of observation.

Similar observations were made by Puschmann (1989) in a longitudinal study with four German-speaking SLI children (mean age: 5;9; range: 5;4 to 6;7) studied over one year. Puschmann found that lexical verbs and modals are used by all the children, even at the earliest point of observation, but that auxiliaries and copulas are much less frequent and are often omitted.

In sum, the data indicate that many (but not all) SLI children have difficulty acquiring the subject-verb agreement system of the adult language. This includes person and number affixes on main verbs as well as auxiliaries and copulas.

C. Case Marking

Studies on German-speaking SLI children suggest that the acquisition of morphological case marking is impaired in SLI. The data from 10 SLI children presented in Clahsen (1991) show that, contrary to what is required in German, these children only have a binary case system with nominative forms and either accusatives or datives. None of the children studied produced both accusatives and datives. Moreover, there were only very few instances of the genitive suffix *-s* for possessives; in most cases, the genitive suffix was left out. In the case markings produced, we find many errors—for example, accusative forms instead of datives and vice versa, and sometimes even accusative or dative forms instead of nominatives (see also Clahsen, 1989). In addition, there were no instances of case agreement within NPs. Rather, case marking is only supplied once, in most cases on the article, which results in agreement errors.

Collings (1989) examined longitudinal data from 12 SLI children (mean age: 5;8 range; 3;2 to 6;11) with respect to case markings. He found that most accusative and dative case markings occurred in personal pronouns. These forms are suppletives and are probably stored in memory. However, regular case affixes on determiners were only observed in 5 out of 12 children in a few scattered examples. Two types of nonpronominal case markings were found: (a) cliticized forms on prepositions (*im* "in the," *am* "at the"); (b) the affix *-n* on the determiner or attributive adjective. None of the children acquired case agreement within the DP (= concord), as for example in ***deinem miserablem Wein*** "your-Dat. miserable-Dat. wine"; at most, the case marker occurred once in the DP, either on the determiner or on the adjective. The case affix *-n* is used in contexts requiring acc. and dat., leading to case errors. Some children used this affix even for subjects (see Collings, Puschmann, & Rothweiler, 1989, and Rothweiler, 1988, for similar results).

Taken together, these results show that SLI children have difficulties acquiring case inflections. The longitudinal data indicate that although case-marked pronouns are used more frequently at later recordings, regular case affixation remains to be problematic for SLI children.

The acquisition of case marking by SLI children in languages other than German has not yet been investigated. The only study that I am aware of is Loeb and Leonard's (1991) report that English-speaking SLI children show less use of nominative case marking (and subject-verb agreement) than the normative comparison group. However, English is not the ideal test case to determine the availability of morphological case marking to SLI children. What would be required to evaluate the results on German cross-linguistically is evidence from case-marking languages.

D. Gender Marking

With respect to gender marking, we may rely on results from SLI studies on Italian and German.

Leonard and colleagues' (1992) results on 15 Italian-speaking SLI children are mixed. They examined three properties that are linked to gender marking in Italian: (a) article errors and (b) errors in the use of clitic object pronouns and (c) errors in adjective + noun patterns. In Italian, articles, clitic object pronouns, and adjectives are marked for gender and number. They found significant differences between the SLI group and the normal (MLU-matched) control group for (a) and (b), but not for (c): only 41.4% of the articles and 41.3% of the object clitics were correctly supplied by the SLI children, but 82.8% and 66.3% for the normal children; most of the errors were omissions. However, in adjective + noun patterns they found high correctness rates for SLI children (96.5% correct) and no significant differences to normal children (99.2% correct). It is not clear what we may conclude from these observations. It could be that the high error rates for articles and clitics reflect the children's difficulty with gender or number marking. But the high correctness values for adjective + noun patterns indicates that gender (and number) marking on adjectives seems possible. Because Leonard and colleagues did not present a distributional analysis of the gender markings that occurred in their data, it is hard to decide whether correct gender marking was in fact productive for each child or whether the percentages result from a small number of types that are perhaps stored rather than analyzed internally. We will have to leave these questions open.

With respect to German-speaking SLI children, Clahsen (1991, p. 132) showed that all the 10 SLI children examined used definite and indefinite articles as well as possessive pronouns or quantifiers. However, most of these children neutralized gender distinctions of adult German by using gender-neutral articles: *de* for definite and *ein* for indefinite noun phrases. Other children, who had different gender-marked articles, produced many errors. Furthermore, the longitudinal data available in Clahsen (1991) indicated that the inventory of article forms can be extended during development, without gender oppositions being established. This contrasts with what is known from language-unimpaired children. Around the age of 3;0, omissions of articles in obligatory contexts are rare, and determiners are treated as grammatical function words by language-unimpaired children (see Clahsen, 1982). Gender errors occur seldom throughout, and least of all in the use of definite articles. According to Mills (1985, p. 172ff.), the acquisition of gender oppositions is completed by age 3;0 in language-unimpaired German-speaking children.

Kaltenbacher and Lindner (1990) found that one of the three SLI children they studied created a rather simplified determiner system and that out of the three genders of adult German, the child only used the high-frequency form *die* "the-fem." of the definite article plus the invariant gender-neutral from *ein* "a" of the indefinite article. They also found that after one year of observation, at age 5;8, this child did not show correct gender marking on definite articles.

Collings and colleagues (1989, p. 129ff.) reported, on the basis of a case study with one SLI child studied form age 6;1 to 6;11, that the child produced many errors with respect to gender agreement between adjectives and nouns in NPs; in most cases, the adjective is left uninflected, in contrast to what is required in adult German (**schön tisch* instead of *schön-er tisch* 'nice-masc. table-[+ masc.]'). This contrasts with Leonard and colleagues' (1992) findings on Italian SLI children. Notice, however, that the option chosen by German SLI children, namely to leave out the gender marking on the adjective, would violate word-structure properties of Italian—nouns, verbs and adjectives can never appear as bare stems in Italian. Given that SLI children are not known to grossly go against such constraints, Italian children would not be expected to omit gender markings from adjectives.

E. Noun Plurals

The acquisition of noun plurals in SLI subjects has been examined in several studies from a variety of languages. Most studies found that noun plurals are not severely impaired in SLI.

On the basis of a longitudinal study with 19 SLI children, Clahsen, Rothweiler, Woest, & Marcus (1992) found that their rates for correct use of plural marking were similar to those of normal controls, that is, over 90%. Moreover, the SLI children clearly distinguished between irregular plural affixes, which are restricted in use, and regular default affixes, which are used in overregularizations. Finally, it was found that subtle grammatical constraints, namely the accessibility of regular and irregular inflection to the process of noun compounding, were obeyed by SLI children in the same way as by normal children. The regular default plural must not occur within compounds, irregular plurals, however, are possible within compounds. Clahsen and colleagues argued that SLI children do not just have the surface markings for noun plurals in German, but that the rather abstract, perhaps universal, grammatical constraints that govern the interaction of plural inflection with other morphological processes are also available to SLI children.

The acquisition of German noun plurals by SLI children has also been investigated in Veit (1986), Holtz (1988), and Schöler and Kany (1989). The results of these studies are only based on elicitation and comprehension tests, however. Most of the tests were adaptations of the procedure originally developed by Berko (1958). The tests revealed higher error rates for SLI children than for normal controls. The dominant type of error for the SLI children was the use of singular forms in plural contexts. In these studies, the preference for singular forms in the test is taken to be a reflection of the children's linguistic deficit. Schöler and Kany (1989), for example, claim that due to a deficit in auditory processing it is difficult for SLI children to discover the plural allomorphs of German and to establish analogies between the various forms.

However, this claim is not particularly convincing, for the following reasons. First, it is left unclear in these studies in what ways an auditory processing deficit could affect the acquisition of the plural system. Second, the observation made in previous studies, namely that the use of singulars in plural contexts is characteristic of SLI, has only been tested with elicitation data, and it is therefore unclear whether it holds outside the elicitation test. To check these findings, Clahsen, Rothweiler, Woest, and Marcus (1992) administered an elicitation test along the lines of Berko (1958) and compared the results with those from spontaneous speech samples of the same children. They found that the test results were clearly different from the use of plural markings in spontaneous speech. The most frequent error type in the test is singular forms; this confirms the findings mentioned earlier. In spontaneous speech, however, such forms are significantly rarer, $t(12) = 3.52$, $p < .0005$, two tailed. Notice, for example, that some children repeated singular forms in the test that they correctly produced in spontaneous speech. This suggests that the test results do not give a realistic picture of children's ability to mark plural. Previous studies with language-unimpaired children also show that in the Berko-test zero plural marking is the dominant error type, both for real words and nonsense words. A comparison of Berko's original data with the children studied in Brown (1973) shows, for example, that language-unimpaired children provide affixes far less often in elicitation tests than they do in spontaneous speech. Therefore, I think that the preference of singular forms in the plural test is not a direct reflection of the SLI children's grammatical impairment, but that the high rates of zero plural marking are an artifact of the particular testing procedure.[1]

Taken together, these findings suggest that the acquisition of German noun plurals is not impaired in SLI. We found generally correct plural marking for most of the SLI children, and the same error types as with normal children.

In several SLI studies on English it has been argued that the regular *-s* plural causes problems for English-speaking SLI children. These studies are discussed at length in Ötting (1992). Gopnik and Crago (1991), for example, carried out Berko's elicitation test with English-speaking SLI subjects and found a clear preference for singular forms. They also found some cases in which plural forms were used in singular contexts, for example, *a cups* (Gopnik & Crago, 1991, p. 13). To account for these observations, Gopnik argued that SLI subjects are "feature-blind" and, specifically, that the feature NUMBER is not accessible to them. If this account were correct, we would expect to find several occurrences of plural forms in singular contexts. However, such cases were in fact extremely rare, both in Gopnik and Crago's data and in our data from German-speaking SLI children. In our whole corpus of SLI children we found that only 1.2% (8/665) of the forms with plural affixes occurred in singular contexts. This figure is comparable to that of normal children. Thus, the use of plural forms in singular contexts cannot be due to a specific SLI deficit. Our comparative data from the plural test and spontaneous speech samples suggest that it is rather an artifact of the testing situation.

Leonard and colleagues (1992) reported that the mean percentage of plural use in obligatory contexts was 68% for the 10 SLI children they studied and 96% for the 10 normal (MLU-matched) controls, a statistically significant difference. However, as Ötting (1992, p. 28) observed, the mean scores reported by Leonard and colleagues (1992) are ambiguous. Leonard and colleagues (1992) did not present an individual subject analysis, but in Leonard and colleagues (1987) such data were provided for 8 of the 10 children studied. Ötting (1992) compared these data with figures for correct plurals from normal children on an individual subject basis. She found that the SLI children had either mastered the plural suffix, or their MLUs were so low that mastery could not be expected.

[1]The mechanism responsible for that is unclear, but we might speculate, for example, that in the elicitation experiment, in particular the younger children do not fully understand the task because the newly introduced item attracts their attention. Instead, the children might concentrate on the new words and simply repeat them without attending to the grammatical task. In addition, a strategy to avoid saying plurals of unfamiliar words may also increase the rate of no marking errors in both German and English elicitation experiments.

In a detailed study involving 55 children (18 SLI and 37 normals), Ötting (1992) examined the acquisition of English noun plurals and plurals inside compounds. Her major findings are that both the SLI children and the MLU controls correctly applied the regular plural suffix to regular nouns in obligatory contexts (SLI = 90%, MLU controls = 94%) and productively overapplied it to irregular nouns and to novel nouns. Moreover, they respected the regular-versus-irregular distinction in nominal compounds in English (*mice-eater* versus **rats-eater*) in the same way as normally developing children. Rice and Ötting (1993) obtained similar findings in a study with 81 SLI children around the age of 5 years. They found that the SLI children produced 83% correct plural markings in obligatory contexts, only 16% zero markings in plural contexts and the same number of plural overregularizations as a group of linguistically normal MLU-matched children. Rice and Ötting concluded that the system of noun plurals in English is not impaired in SLI.

F. Tense Making

The acquisition of the English past-tense system has been examined in several SLI studies. For example, Gopnik (1994) administered an experimental task to English-speaking SLI subjects in which a sentence was presented in one tense, and the subject was prompted to produce an analogous sentence in another tense. The answers given by the SLI subjects were always semantically relevant, but rarely involved a change of the tense of the verb. Typically, the SLI subjects produced an unmarked form of the stimulus verb. For example, one subject was given the stimulus sentence "*Everyday he walks eight miles. Yesterday he ______.*" The subject responded: *walk.* They also had difficulty in a related rating test to correctly judge the grammaticality with respect to tense marking. The most striking observation was that in contrast to normals the SLI subjects judged the stem form of the verb in past-tense contexts to be acceptable. In addition, Gopnik kept notebooks for the full school year from two SLI children. Here she found that irregular past-tense forms were correct significantly more often than regular verbs. Gopnik interpreted these findings in terms of the rule-deficit model: The language-impaired subjects do not construct a symbolic rule for deriving past-tense forms for regular verbs, but rather store these forms (like irregulars) in memory. Thus, they are like normals with irregular past-tense forms, but impaired with respect to regular *-ed* forms.

Leonard and colleagues (1992) obtained similar results in their study with 10 English-speaking SLI children. They found that the regular past-tense ending *-ed* was only supplied in 32.3% of the obligatory contexts by SLI children, but in 64.8% by normal MLU-matched children. By contrast, Leonard and colleagues did not find significant differences between SLI children and MLU controls in terms of their use of irregular past-tense forms: 65% correct for SLI children, 76.9% for normal controls. The most frequent error in these cases was the use of present-tense forms in past-tense contexts. These results are similar to Gopnik's and support the idea that SLI subjects have difficulty with the regular past-tense rule. However, one finding from Leonard and colleagues casts some doubt on Gopnik's rule-deficit model: approximately 20% of the SLI children's errors on irregular past were overregularizations, for example, **drawed picture.* These forms cannot be stored and suggest that at least some of the SLI children studied by Leonard and colleagues have the *-ed* rule.

G. Participle Inflection

In adult and in child German, simple past-tense forms are rarely used in spoken discourse. Instead, events in the past are expressed through what is traditionally called the present perfect. Like in English, German present-perfect forms consist of a finite auxiliary (*haben* "to have" or *sein* "to be") and a nonfinite participle form.

Clahsen and Rothweiler (1993) carried out a detailed analysis of participle inflection based on longitudinal data from 19 German-speaking SLI children and found high rates of overt participle marking throughout the entire period of observation; this holds for the SLI children (mean = 91.2%) as well as for three normally developing MLU controls (mean = 83.4%). Moreover, the error rates of the SLI children are within the same range as those of the normal controls, that is, below 10%. Finally, the same kinds of errors were found for both SLI children and normal controls. Apart from occasional cases of zero suffixation (= below 10%), the only source of errors is that strong verbs in German are categorized by the children as regular verbs, and are suffixed with the default affix *-t* instead of the irregular affix *-n,* for example, **gegeht* instead of *gegangen* ("gone") or **gebratet* instead of *gebraten* ("fried"). There are no errors in the stems of irregular participles; examples such as **gefanden* instead of *gefunden* ("found") do not occur. Moreover, all irregular participles, that is, those with ablaut stems, are suffixed with *-n* as required in German; there are no errors such as **geganget, *gefundet,* and so on. Finally, regular participles are correctly suffixed with *-t,* and not with the irregular affix *-n.*

In general, the data indicate that despite occasional errors, the children's system of participle inflection is identical to that of adults. Participles for which the children have identified marked roots (*trunk* "drunk," *ritt* "ridd-en," etc.) are either suffixed with the irregular *-n* or, in rare cases, occur without a participle suffix. Overregularizations occur in cases in which the child has not yet discovered the marked verb roots. Moreover, just like in the adult language, the restricted *-n* suffixation rule blocks the default *-t* rule from marked verb roots. Thus, in overregularization errors *-t* is combined with unmarked present-tense stems.

Summarizing, Clahsen and Rothweiler (1993) found that the SLI children they have studied generally have correct participle marking and the same error types as normal children. This contrasts with problems these children have in other areas of verbal inflection, specifically person and number agreement. Taken together, these observations suggest that SLI children do not have a general deficit with inflectional morphology.

H. Word Order

The acquisition of word order, specifically of verb placement, has been an important focus of research in studies on German-speaking SLI subjects. In addition, we can rely on Hansson and Nettelbladt's (1990) study on Swedish.

On the basis of data from 10 SLI children, Clahsen (1991) found no constituent-internal word-order errors in NPs, PPs, and APs. By contrast, none of the 10 children had generalized V2, that is, the syntactic rule of adult German that moves all finite verbs to the second structural position in main clauses.[2] Quantitative analyses revealed that the proportions of verb-second and verb-final patterns varied, but that verb-final patterns were dominant for most of the children (mean = 64%, range: 36% to 84% counting each child equally). More important, qualitative differences were found between verb-final patterns on the one hand and verb-initial and verb-second patterns on the other hand. Verb-final patterns are typically used with uninflected verbal elements (stems), infinitives and participles, whereas the first or second verb position is dominantly covered by a restricted class of finite verbal elements, that is, modals and auxiliaries as well as some verbs inflected with the suffix *-t,* plus some imperatives. These asymmetries between verb-final and verb-second patterns were found in 9 out of 10 children. One child, Petra, diverged from this distribution in that she produced verb-final patterns for both nonfinite and finite verbs in root clauses. Recall from Section III.A that Petra was the only child studied in Clahsen (1991) who acquired subject-verb agreement during the period of observation. However, in contrast to normal children, she did not raise finite verbs to the V2 position. Rather, the V2-position is filled with a restricted set of (finite) verbs only, particularly with modals, while other kinds of finite verbs remain in clause-final position. A case similar to Petra was reported in Kaltenbacher and Lindner (1990, p. 7). Clahsen (1991) discussed different accounts for the specific pattern found in Petra.[3]

[2]In German main clauses, all finite verbs appear in the second structural position, whereas in embedded clauses, they are in final position. Nonfinite verbs always appear in clause-final position. In syntactic analyses of adult German, the clause-final position is normally taken to be the basic pattern, whereas the main clause word order is said to be a derived pattern, resulting from a rule that moves all finite verbs to the second structural position. This rule is called generalized verb-second (V2). In contrast to other word-order properties of German, the V2 rule crucially depends on morphological features of the verb, namely the finiteness features PERSON and NUMBER.

[3]The most realistic explanation involves assuming that I-to-C movement is not possible in Petra's grammar (perhaps due to a lack of the finiteness operator [+F], which is normally part of the feature grid of C^0 in adult German (cf. Platzack & Holmberg, 1989) and in this way triggers verb-second), and that the few modals that occur in V2 are base-generated in this position.

Grimm (1987) and Grimm and Weinert (1990), based on longitudinal data from eight German-speaking SLI children (age 3;9 to 4;8), found that in 69% of the sentences produced by the SLI children either the verb or the subject was in clause-final position, resulting in incorrect word order patterns in 53% of the cases (Grimm, 1987). Similar results were obtained in a sentence-imitation task that was carried out with the same set of eight SLI children. Grimm and Weinert (1990) found that in 61% of the presented stimuli, the SLI children changed the given word orders to incorrect patterns, typically to subject–object–verb (SOV). These figures for verb-final patterns are within the same distribution as those found in Clahsen (1991), suggesting that the children studied by Grimm and Weinert do not have generalized V2 either.

Collings and colleagues (1989) studied one SLI child (Dieter) longitudinally from age 6;1 to 6;11. They showed that Dieter acquired generalized verb-second in the final recording, at age 6;11, that is, about 4 years later than language-unimpaired children (Clahsen and Penke, 1992). Before that point, verb-final patterns were clearly dominant (see Table 8, Collings et al., p. 139). Interestingly, Dieter did not acquire subject-verb agreement throughout the whole period of observation. Even at age 6;11, when he had V2, Dieter still did not use the second person singular suffix *-st,* and produced many sentences with the infinitive ending *-n* replacing a finite verb form. In contrast to what is known from language-unimpaired children, these verb forms, which are nonfinite in terms of their morphological shape, appeared in the V2 position. Collings and colleagues argued that this child must have acquired the V2 rule without having access to the finite/nonfinite distinction.

Overall, these results indicate that generalized V2, as in adult German, is hard to acquire for SLI children. Most SLI children lack regular subject-verb agreement and, consequently, do not have generalized V2. Some SLI children (Petra, Dieter) seem to acquire a version of V2 that diverges from the one in adult German.

In their study with five Swedish SLI children, Hansson and Nettelbladt (1990) found that one of the most frequent errors in these children were verb-second violations and that these errors correlate with the omission of TENSE affixes on finite verbs. Adult Swedish is similar to German in that both are rigid V2 languages, but finite verbs in Swedish are marked for TENSE only, rather than for subject–verb agreement. Thus, similar to most German SLI children, the problems Swedish SLI children have with the V2 rule seem to be a secondary effect of their problems with creating finite verb forms, rather than a genuine syntactic deficit.

IV. DISCUSSION

In this section, I will discuss the four theoretical approaches to SLI that were presented in Section II in light of the empirical results mentioned in Section III.

A. Problems of the Surface Account

In attempting to evaluate Leonard's account, I will focus on two questions: (a) Is this account empirically adequate, that is, does it account for the data, and (b) does it provide an explanation of the observed linguistic properties of the language of SLI children?

Leonard's surface account predicts that inflectional morphemes that have low phonetic substance will either be omitted or cause morphological errors in the speech of SLI children. However, several findings indicate that this prediction does not hold.

Rice and Ötting (1993) found that English-speaking SLI children were unimpaired as far as their use of the plural *-s* is concerned. By contrast, the SLI children performed much worse in the use of the third-person singular *-s:* the percentage of correct usage in obligatory contexts was 36%, whereas the group mean of the control group was 54%, a statistically significant difference ($t = 2.63$, $p < .01$). Thus, there is a clear difference in the SLI data between the use of *-s* in noun plurals and its use as a subject-verb-agreement marker. This holds despite the fact that phonetically, the plural and the agreement morpheme are identical. Consequently, Rice and Ötting rejected the surface account. Low phonetic substance and subsequent problems in morphological paradigm building cannot be the reason for the missing agreement in SLI children, when the same phonetic form, *-s,* is available for plural marking.

A similar asymmetry holds for German-speaking SLI children. Clahsen and colleagues (1992) found generally correct plural marking for most of the children and the same error types as with normal children. On the other hand, they found that subject–verb agreement is severely impaired in German-speaking SLI children, although some of the noun plural suffixes and the agreement suffixes are phonetically identical, for example, the form *-n,* which occurs as a noun plural morpheme as well as a subject-verb-agreement marker for first- and third-person plural. Thus, the surface account fails to explain the asymmetry between noun plurals and agreement inflection in SLI children, and it incorrectly predicts that different kinds of inflectional morphemes that have the same phonetic substance are equally disturbed.

With respect to the explanatory value of the surface account, I think that the three elements of the surface account—perceptual limitations, language-particular familiarity with inflection, and problems in paradigm building—do not provide a theory-based explanation of the observed impairments. First, it remains unclear in Leonard's account what the perceptual limitations are that SLI children are said to have, that is, why is it that SLI children do not perceive or misperceive inflectional morphemes that have low phonetic substance?

Second, it might very well be the case that language-particular properties may account for characteristics of SLI. One might wonder, for example, what the properties of SLI in an isolating language such as Chinese are like. If SLI really is a surface-based deficit of inflectional morphology, then it should not exist in Chinese at all, simply because this language does not have any inflectional morphology. What Leonard claims is restricted to SLI in fusional languages, namely that the disturbances of inflection in SLI are inversely linked to the degree of fusion of a particular language, so that the more inflections there are in a particular language the less is impaired in SLI. This seems to be self-evident and amounts to saying: the more you hear, the more you get.

Third, the only linguistic notion that plays a role in Leonard's account of SLI is the notion of morphological paradigms. Perceptual limitations plus certain deficits in paradigm building are supposed to explain why SLI children are impaired in the area of inflectional morphology rather than in phoneme perception in general. The supposed deficits in paradigm building, however, are not made explicit: What kind of linguistic knowledge is represented in paradigms? It is far from clear whether only inflection is represented in paradigms and whether inflection as a whole is paradigmatic.

To explain SLI children's problems with inflectional morphology as a result of perceptual limitations, one would want to have a theory of the relation between phonetic perception and inflection that would make it possible to derive specific and falsifiable predictions concerning the linguistic properties of SLI. Similarly, to explain SLI as a result of deficits in paradigm building, a theory of morphological paradigms is required. Leonard does not refer to such theories. As it stands, Leonard's claims about SLI are descriptive generalizations about the data rather than elements of a theoretical account of SLI.

B. Features and Rules in SLI Children's Grammars

Gopnik and Crago's (1991) idea, that SLI subjects do not have symbolic rules of inflection and store all inflected words even those that are rule-based in the adult language, could not be confirmed in other studies.

Leonard and colleagues (1992) found that 20% of the past-tense errors that English-speaking SLI children produced in obligatory contexts for irregulars were overregularizations of the *-ed* rule. In this regard, the SLI children did not differ from MLU-matched controls. With respect to noun plurals, Ötting (1992) found similar overregularization rates of the regular *-s* plural for SLI children and for normal controls. This contrasts with the claims of the rule-deficit model and suggests (a) that SLI children's regular plural forms are rule governed and (b) that the lack of overregularizations in Gopnik's data might result from sampling errors.

In our studies on noun plurals and participle marking in German-speaking SLI children, we obtained similar results. In both areas we found qualitative distinctions between regular and irregular affixes in both normally developing and SLI children: regular affixes were overapplied and were omitted from compounds, irregular affixes were not overapplied and did occur inside compounds. Moreover, we found similar overregularization rates and rates of correct marking for SLI and normal children suggesting that SLI children's pluralization and participle marking abilities and the grammatical organization of regular and irregular inflection are equivalent to those of language-unimpaired children.

Gopnik's initial idea (published in her 1990a article) that SLI subjects lack grammatical features completely is also not maintainable for most SLI subjects. In German-speaking SLI children, gender and number agreement in noun phrases as well as subject-verb agreement were often in error, whereas other kinds of inflectional morphology, for example, rules of participle formation and noun plurals, were unimpaired (Clahsen, 1989, Clahsen et al. 1992, Clahsen & Rothweiler 1993). Rice and Ötting (1993) obtained similar findings for English-speaking SLI children: The plural *-s* was still part of their subjects' grammars, whereas the third-person singular *-s* was missing. These results go against the missing feature account, because under this account one would expect global deficits in inflectional morphology. The data, however, seem to indicate that the impairments of SLI individuals are more narrowly restricted to certain subareas of the grammar rather than to inflectional morphology as a whole.

On the other hand, several studies indicate that, at least with respect to comprehension, the deficit of SLI subjects may go beyond grammatical morphology and may include impairments to processes of grammatical linking, that is, the mapping of thematic roles onto syntactic functions. Van der Lely and Harris (1990) found that English-speaking SLI children have significant problems in comprehending reversible passive sentences. Similarly, Leonard, Sabbadini, Leonard, and Volterra (1988) reported that Italian SLI children often omit obligatory objects, which results in argument structure violations. In a study explicitly designed to determine the availability of processes of grammatical linking, Van der Lely (1994) administered act-out tasks and comprehension experiments with six English-speaking SLI children. Her main finding was that SLI children did not differ from the normal controls in the semantic bootstrapping task, that is, in forming a representation of verb argument structure on the basis of contextual information. However, where no contextual information was given in the experiment and the children had to rely on the morphosyntactic contexts to infer the meaning of a novel verb, the SLI children performed much worse than the normal controls. Thus, the SLI children behaved as if they lacked linking rules. These findings contrast with Gopnik's view that thematic role assignment is intact in SLI subjects.

These empirical problems suggest that the missing feature hypothesis as it has originally been proposed does not adequately account for the SLI data. It is too narrow because it has nothing to say about the SLI subjects' problems with, for example, reversible passive sentences, and it is too unconstrained because it does not explain the selective impairments that were found, for example, in German-speaking SLI children.

To develop the missing feature idea further, one might connect it with theories of syntactic phrase structure and characterize the impairments of SLI in terms of incomplete phrase-structure representations. Suppose that SLI children are able to create the same set of functional and lexical categories as language-unimpaired children, but that the syntactic features that are normally part of the feature grid of functional categories are absent in the phrase-structure trees of SLI subjects. Thus, the phrase-structure representations would be unimpaired in terms of categorical features. However, in SLI, the specific values of syntactic features like agreement (= person, gender, number), tense (= past, present, future), and so on may not be present. In other words, the functional categories Infl and Det would not contain specific features such as [+ past], [+ third-person], [+ masculine], but the value of these features would be deleted in SLI.

If this underspecification account is correct, SLI individuals should be able to distinguish between nominal and verbal categories, and they should not affix a nominal ending, for example, a case marker, onto a verb. However, given that the syntactic features of functional categories are underspecified, SLI children should be unable to supply correct tense, agreement, or case endings (see Grodzinsky, 1990, for a similar idea with respect to agrammatism in Broca's aphasics). Of course, this version of the missing feature hypothesis must be tested against the data. My suspicion is that at least the first prediction, that nominal endings are not affixed to verbs and vice versa, holds, which indicates that basic categorial features such as the distinction between the nominal and the verbal domain are maintained in SLI.

C. Evaluating the Missing Agreement Hypothesis

Recall that according to the missing agreement idea, SLI children have problems establishing agreement relations in grammar. In previous studies, we made use of the control-agreement principle to characterize those areas of grammar that are impaired in SLI. It is true that the missing agreement account has originally been developed for German, on the basis of the findings in Clahsen (1989). Nevertheless, the general picture that emerges from the more recent empirical findings reported in Section III supports this hypothesis. We saw that SLI children have problems with subject-verb agreement and agreement within noun phrases, as well as with case and gender marking and with auxiliaries. Word order, however, does not seem to be disturbed. For example, word order within constituents is usually correct. In addition, we found that SLI children do not have difficulty acquiring other parts of inflectional morphology, for example, noun plurals and the system of participle inflection. In these areas, the SLI children are equivalent to language-unimpaired children, both qualitatively, for example, in terms of types of errors, and quantitatively, that is, in terms of rates of correct marking, zero marking, and overregularizations.

However, some linguistic properties that have been observed in SLI subjects seem to fall outside of the range of the missing agreement account, namely (a) the lack of the general V2 rule in German-speaking SLI children, (b) the problems of English-speaking SLI children with reversible passives, and (c) the difficulties of English-speaking SLI children with TENSE.

Verb-Second

In several studies, it has been found that German-speaking SLI children frequently use verb-final patterns in main clauses rather than the correct V2 patterns. Grimm and Weinert (1990, p. 224) argued that the frequent use of verb-final patterns in German-speaking SLI children represents a problem of dealing with word order per se. In addition, they quote some sample utterances from different children with auxiliaries or modals in clause-final position and separable prefix verbs in second position which, they claim, never occur in normal development (p. 221), and they argue that these "deviant syntactic structures are the result of insufficient language processing" (p. 225).

I think that this conclusion is premature and that the claims on which it is based are incorrect. First, verb-final patterns are not deviant in German. Rather, verb-final is the normal position of nonfinite verbs in German. Thus, the general figures presented in Grimm and Weinert indicating that SLI children prefer the verb-final pattern do not mean that word order per se is impaired. Second, with respect to their claim that SLI children produce deviant sentences with finite verbs appearing in clause-final positions and nonfinite verbs in second position, neither Grimm and Weinert (1990) nor Grimm (1987) present any quantitative figures indicating how many such cases occurred in the data. It is true that SLI children sometimes produce such "deviant" word orders, but (a) such cases have also been reported for normal children (see, e.g., Fritzenschaft, Gawlitzek-Maiwald, Tracy, & Winkler, 1990), and (b) the figures presented in Clahsen (1991) and Clahsen and Penke (1992) indicate that such word-order patterns are extremely rare in both SLI children and normal controls, that is, less than 10%. Third, the idea that word-order "errors" result from deficits of language processing, specifically from the SLI children's "difficulties in separating units that are semantically linked and in placing separated parts in different positions" (Grimm & Weinert, 1990, p. 225) does not explain their preference for the verb-final pattern. If Grimm and Weinert were right, we would expect verb placement to be random.

How can the findings on word order be explained under the missing agreement hypothesis? If the missing agreement account is correct, we would not expect to find any genuine word-order problems in SLI. The data indicate that although word order in general is correct, the acquisition of the V2 rule is impaired in SLI. I suggest that this results from the fact that in German verb-second is indirectly connected to subject-verb agreement: V2 applies to all verbs that are specified for person and number features. Therefore V2 can only be used as a generalized movement rule if the grammar has a productive subject-verb agreement paradigm. As mentioned previously, SLI children do not have a general paradigm of person and number inflection. Thus, their grammars do not allow them to generate a corresponding finite form for any given verb. Instead, these children only have a small set of (stored) finite verb forms, for example, modals, a restricted class of verbs appearing with the suffix *-t* and a few auxiliaries. The missing agreement account correctly predicts that for this restricted class of verbal elements, V2 is possible, but that generalized V2 as in adult German, with all main clauses having a finite verb form in the second structural position, is not possible for SLI children.

Reversible Passives

The second observation that does not immediately follow from the missing agreement account is the SLI children's problems with grammatical linking, that is, with rules mapping thematic roles onto syntactic functions. This has been shown for English-speaking SLI children, who were, for example, unable to correctly comprehend reversible passive sentences with novel verbs (cf. Van der Lely & Harris, 1990, among others). The missing agreement account does not explain these observations. Rather, the comprehension problems observed in these studies are reminiscent of findings with Broca's aphasics. Grodzinsky (1990), for example, found that agrammatics performed at chance level in reversible passive sentences and above chance in the corresponding active sentences. For these findings, Grodzinsky offered an explanation in terms of defective feature specifications of phrase-structure representations. The syntactic features of movement rules are deleted in agrammatics' phrase-structure trees, and NPs in nonthematic positions are assigned by default. Thus, in a sentence such as *John was killed by Bill* the NP *John* is identified as the external argument of the verb *kill,* and because the movement trace that is normally part of the feature specification of this NP in a passive sentence is unavailable under agrammatism, *John* is assigned the theta role that occupies the position of the external argument in the theta grid of the verb *to kill,* that is, the role of agent. Although Grodzinsky was careful enough to restrict his account to agrammatic comprehension, it may also hold for other language deficits including SLI. It remains to be seen whether this account is applicable to SLI subjects.

Past-Tense Marking

The third nonpredicted finding are the difficulties of English-speaking SLI children with TENSE. Past-tense marking in English does not fall under the control-agreement principle. TENSE is directly marked on the verb rather than being controlled by some other sentential element. Thus, if the missing agreement account holds, we would not expect to find any impairments of past-tense marking in English-speaking SLI children. The available data, however, show quite clearly that this prediction does not hold; that regular past-tense marking is impaired was found in several SLI studies on English-speaking SLI children. Similarly, Swedish-speaking SLI children often fail to produce finite verb forms (Hansson & Nettelbladt, 1990). Because adult Swedish does not have subject-verb agreement at all, this can only mean that these children have difficulty marking verbs for TENSE.

How can these results on tense marking be reconciled with the results on German participle inflection reported in Section III.G? Although past-tense marking seems to cause major problems for English-speaking SLI children, particularly the regular *-ed* rule, participle inflection in German-speaking SLI children seems to be unimpaired, both the default affix and the irregular inflections. If this difference can be maintained and the two groups of SLI children are comparable, then we might speculate that SLI involves impairments in the control of the grammatical feature TENSE. In English, this impairment is rather obvious and easier to discover than in German, because in English past-time events are normally encoded with verbs that are marked for [+ past], whereas in spoken German a sentence referring to a past-time event does not contain the feature [+ past] in surface structure. Therefore, the children's problems with TENSE marking cannot be seen directly from the German data.

One can imagine grammatical theories in which TENSE is viewed as a functor-argument (or agreement) relation (see, e.g., Campbell, 1991). If this can be maintained, TENSE might fall under the notion of control-agreement, and we would expect to find impairments of tense marking in SLI children. However, these grammatical theories have not yet been worked out, and the nature of the SLI children's problems with TENSE is unclear. The results on English indicate that irregular past-tense inflection seems to be possible in SLI, but that regular past-tense marking is impaired. Moreover, the past-tense forms that are used by English-speaking SLI children seem to be restricted to past-tense contexts. Taken together, this suggests that the deficit underlying the children's problems with tense marking is selective rather than global. It does not seem to be the case that the feature TENSE is absent from the children's grammar as is clear from the correct use of irregulars. However, why obligatory (regular) tense marking is problematic for SLI children, and whether this is independent of the other linguistic problems that have been observed in SLI children, remains to be seen.

V. SUMMARY AND CONCLUSION

The focus of this chapter was on linguistic studies of specific language impairment. Linguistics, particularly generative linguistics, regards the development of grammar as largely autonomous from developments in other cognitive domains, and thus allows us to explore whether the linguistic problems of SLI children are explicable in terms of selective deficits within the language faculty itself. In this way, a linguistic perspective introduces a new way of looking at language development disorders not available from those disciplines that are traditionally concerned with SLI. In addition, linguistic studies help to improve the diagnosis of SLI, through detailed descriptions of the grammatical systems of SLI children and adults.

Empirical results from various SLI studies were summarized, focusing on grammatical phenomena, particularly inflection and word order. The results were drawn mainly from SLI studies on English and German plus some additional findings on Italian-, Swedish- and Dutch-speaking SLI children. The descriptive findings were discussed with respect to four current linguistic approaches to SLI. Leonard's surface account of SLI has empirical and conceptual problems; it does not explain observed differences in the availability of homophonous affixes, for example, the plural *-s* versus the third-person singular *-s* in English-speaking SLI children. Gopnik predicted global disturbances of inflectional morphology; in one version of her theory, syntactic features are absent, in the other more recent version regular inflectional rules are absent. Several studies, however, found that inflectional morphology is selectively impaired in SLI (see, e.g., Clahsen et al., 1992; Clahsen & Rothweiler, 1993; Rice and Ötting, 1992). Most of the empirical results are consistent with the missing agreement hypothesis. However, some findings could not be captured by the proposed characterization, particularly the difficulties of English-speaking SLI children with past tense marking and reversible passives. Further research is needed to determine whether these difficulties and the children's problems with grammatical agreement have a common source or whether they are independent of one another.

ACKNOWLEDGMENTS

While I was working on this article in 1992, my research was supported by German Science Foundation gramts Cl 97/5-1, Cl 97/1.1-1.2 and grant Wu 86/9.1-9.4. I also acknowledge the American Council of Learned Societies (ACLS) and the German Academic Exchange Council (DAAD) for a grant jointly given to Steven Pinker (MIT) and me for collaborative work on the acquisition of inflection. I thank the members of our research group, in particular Nigel Duffield and Martina Penke, for comments and criticisms on earlier versions of this article.

REFERENCES

Admiraal-Berg, C., Bol, G., Kuiken, F., and Verwey-de Jongh, T. (1984). *Handleiding voor een grammaticale analyse van taalontwikkelingsstoornissen.* Unpublished manuscript, University of Amsterdam.

Becker, K.-P., & Sovak, M. (1975). *Handbuch der logopädie.* Köln: Kiepenheuer & Witsch.
Berko, J. (1958). The child's learning of English morphology. *Word, 14,* 150–177.
Berman, R., Rom, A., & Hirsch, M. (1982). *Working with HARSP: Hebrew adaptation of LARSP.* Unpublished manuscript, University of Tel-Aviv.
Bishop, D. (1992). The underlying source of specific language impairment. *Journal of Child Psychology and Psychiatry, 33,* 1, 3–66.
Bol, G., & de Jong, J. (1992). *Auxiliary verbs in Dutch SLI children.* Unpublished manuscript, University of Groningen.
Brown, R. (1973). *A first language: The early stages.* Cambridge, MA: Harvard University Press.
Campbell, R. (1991). Tense and agreement in different tenses. *The Linguistic Review, 8,* 159–183.
Chomsky, N. (1981). *Lectures on government and binding.* Dordrecht: Foris.
Clahsen, H. (1982). *Spracherwerb in der Kindheit.* Tübingen: Narr.
Clahsen, H. (1986). *Die Profilanalyse.* Berlin: Marhold.
Clahsen, H. (1989). The grammatical characterization of development dysphasia. *Linguistics, 27,* 897–920.
Clahsen, H. (1991). *Child language and developmental dysphasia. Linguistic studies of the acquisition of German.* Amsterdam: Benjamins.
Clahsen, H., & Hansen, D. (1991). *COPROF (Computer-unterstützte Profilanalyse).* Cologne: Focus.
Clahsen, H., & Penke, M. (1992). The acquisition of agreement morphology and its syntactic consequences. In J. Meisel (Ed.), *The acquisition of verb placement* (pp. 181–223). Dordrecht: Kluwer.
Clahsen, H., Rothweiler, M., Woest, A., & Marcus, G. F. (1992). Regular and irregular inflection in the acquisition of German noun plurals. *Cognition, 45,* 225–255.
Clahsen, H., & Rothweiler, M. (1993). Inflectional rules in children's grammars. In G. Booij & J. van Marle (Eds.), *Yearbook of Morphology 1992* (pp. 255–288). Dordrecht: Foris.
Collings, A. (1989). *Zum Kasuserwerb beim Dysgrammatismus.* Unpublished manuscript, University of Düsseldorf.
Collins, A., Puschmann, B., & Rothweiler, R. (1989). Dysgrammatismus. Ein Defizitder grammatischen Kongruenz. *Neurolinguistik, 3,* 127–143.
Cromer, R. (1978). The basis of childhood dysphasia: A linguistic approach. In M. Wyke (Ed.), *Developmental dysphasia* (pp. 85–134). New York: Academic Press.
Crystal, D., Fletcher, P., & Garman, M. (1976). *The grammatical analysis of language disability.* London: Edward Arnold.
Fletcher, P., & Peters, J. (1984). Characterising language impairment in children: An exploratory study. *Language Testing, 1,* 33–49.
Fritzenschaft, A., Gawlitzek-Maiwald, I., Tracy, R., & Winkler, S. (1990). Wege zur komplexen syntax. *Zeitschrift zür Sprachwissenschaft, 9,* 52–134.
Gazdar, G., Klein, E., Pullum, G., & Sag, I. (1985). *Generalized phrase structure grammar.* Cambridge, MA: Harvard University Press.
Gopnik, M. (1990a). Feature blindness: A case study. *Language Acquisition, 1,* 139–164.
Gopnik, M. (1990b). Feature-blind grammar and dysphasia. *Nature, 344,* 715.
Gopnik, M. (1994). Impairments of tense in a familial language disorder. *Journal of Neurolinguistics, 8,* 109–133.

Gopnik, M., & Crago, M. (1991). Familial aggregation of a developmental language disorder. *Cognition, 39*(1), 1–50.

Grimm, H. (1987). Developmental dysphasia: New theoretical perspectives and empirical results. *The German Journal of Psychology, 11,* 8–22.

Grimm, H., & Weinert, S. (1990). Is the syntax development of dysphasic children deviant and why? New findings to an old question. *Journal of Speech and Hearing Research, 33,* 220–228.

Grodzinsky, Y. (1990). *Theoretical perspectives on language deficits.* Cambridge, MA: MIT Press.

Hansson, K., & Nettelbladt, U. (1990). *Comparison between Swedish children with normal and disordered language development regarding word order patterns and use of grammatical markers.* Paper presented at the Second Conference of the European Group for Child Language Disorders, Röros, Norway.

Holtz, A. (1988). Untersuchungen zur Entwicklung der Pluralmorphologie bei sprachbehinderten Kindern. *Ulmer Publikationen zure Sprachbehindertenpädagogik,* 5.

Johnston, J., & Kamhi, A. (1984). Syntactic and semantic aspects of the utterances of language-impaired children: The same can be less. *Merrill-Palmer Quarterly, 30,* 65–85.

Kaltenbacher, E., & Lindner, K. (1990). *Some aspects of delayed and deviant development in German children with specific language impairment.* Paper presented at the Second Conference of the European Group for Child Disorders, Röros, Norway.

Kamhi, A., Catts, H., Rauer, D., Apel, K., & Gentry, B. (1988). Phonological and spatial processing abilities in language- and reading-inpaired children. *Journal of Speech and Hearing Disorders, 53,* 316–327.

Leonard, L., Bertolini, U., Caselli, M., McGregor, K., & Sabbadini, L. (1992). Two accounts of morphological deficits in children with specific language impairment. *Language Acquisition,* 2(2), 151–179.

Leonard, L., Sabbadini, L., Leonard, J., & Volterra, V. (1987). Specific language impairment in children: A cross-linguistic study. *Brain and Language, 32,* 233–252.

Leonard, L., Sabbadini, L., Volterra, V., & Leonard, J. (1988). Some influences on the grammar of English- and Italian-speaking children with specific language impairment. *Applied Psycholinguistics, 9,* 39–57.

Loeb, D., & Leonard, L. (1991). Subject case marking and verb morphology in normally-developing and specifically-language-impaired children. *Journal of Speech and Hearing Research, 34,* 340–346.

Mills, A. (1985). The acquisition of German. In D. Slobin (Ed.), *The cross-linguistic study of language acquisition* (pp. 141–254). Hillsdale, NJ: Erlbaum.

Ötting, J. (1992). *Language-impaired and normally developing children's acquisition of English plural.* Unpublished Ph.D. dissertation, University of Kansas.

Ouhalla, J. (1991, March). *Functional categories and the head parameter.* Glow Colloquium, Leiden.

Pinker, S., & Prince, A. (1991). Regular and irregular morphology and the psychological status of rules of grammar. *Proceedings of the 17th Annual Meeting of the Berkeley Linguistics Society,* Berkeley, CA.

Platzack, C., & Homberg, A. (1989). The role of AGR and finiteness. *Working Papers in Scandinavian Syntax, 43,* 51–76.

Puschmann, B. (1989). *Worarten, Konstituentenstruktur und Genus beim Dysgrammatismus.* Unpublished manuscript, University of Düsseldorf.

Rice, M., & Ötting, J. (1993). Morphological deficits of SLI children: Evaluation of number marking and agreement. *Journal of Speech and Hearing Research, 36,* 1246–1257.

Rom, A., & Leonard, L. (1990). Interpreting deficits in grammatical morphology in specifically language-impaired children: Preliminary evidence from Hebrew. *Clinical Linguistics and Phonetics, 4,* 93–105.

Rothweiler, M. (1988). Ein Fall von Dysgrammatismus—Eine linguistische Analyse. *Frühförderung Interdisziplinär, 3,* 114–124.

Rothweiler, M., & Clahsen, H. (1994). Dissociations in SLI children's inflectional systems: A study of participle inflection and subject-verb agreement. *Scandinavian Journal of Logopedics & Phoniatrics, 18,* 169–179.

Schöler, H., & Kany, W. (1989). Lernprozesse beim Erwerb von Flexionsmorphemen: Ein Vergleich sprachbehinderter mit sprachunauffälligen Kindern am Beispiel der Pluralmarkierung. In G. Kegel (Ed.). *Sprechwissenschaft und Psycholinguistik,* 3 (pp. 123–175). Opladen: Westdeutscher Verlag.

Tallal, P., & Stark, R. (1981). Speech acoustic-cure discrimination abilities of normally developing and language-impaired children. *Journal of the Acoustical Society of America, 69,* 568–574.

Van der Lely, H. (1994). Canonical linking rules: Forward versus reverse linking in normally developing and specifically language impaired children. *Cognition, 51,* 29–72.

Van der Lely, H., & Harris, M. (1990). Comprehension of reversible sentences in specifically language impaired children. *Journal of Speech and Hearing Disorders, 55,* 101–117.

Veit, S. (1986). Das Verständnis von Plural- und Komparativ-formen bei (entwicklungs)dysgrammatischen Kindern im Vorschulalter. In G. Kegel et al. (Eds.), *Sprachwissenschaft und Psycholinguistik* (pp. 217–286). Opladen: Westdeutscher Verlag.

Verhulst-Schlichting, L. (1982). *Handleiding bij de voorlopige nederlandse versie van de LARSP profielkaart.* Unpublished manuscript, University of Utrecht.

LIST OF ABBREVIATIONS

AGR	agreement (in Government and Binding [GB] theory)
ACT	Anderson's model
AO	act out comprehension task
ASL	American Sign Language
AUX	auxiliary (in GB theory)
BFLA	bilingual first language acquisition
BSLA	bilingual second language acquisition
CAP	control–agreement principle
CF	competing factors model
CFL	child first language(s)
COMP/C	Complementizer (in GB theory)
CP	Complementizer Phrase (in GB theory)
CS	contrastive specification
CSL	child second language(s)
Det/D	Determiner (in GB theory)
DP	Determiner Phrase (in GB theory)
EI	elicited imitation
ERP	event-related brain potentials
GB	Government and Binding theory
HARSP	Hebrew Assessment Remediation and Screening Procedure
INFL	Inflection (in GB theory)
IP	Inflectional Phrase (in GB theory)
LARSP	Language Assessment Remediation and Screening Procedure
LBP	language bioprogram
LSQ	Langue des Signes Québécoise
MM	modularity matching model
Neg	negation
NOM	nominative (in GB theory).
OOM	output ommission model
RB	reduced behavior
RRG	role and reference grammar

RU	radical underspecification
SCH	strong continuity hypothesis
SLI	Specific Language Impairment
SOV	subject–object–verb order
SPEC	specifier (in GB theory).
SVO	subject–verb–object order
TNS	tense (in GB theory).
TVJT	truth value judgement task
UG	Universal Grammar
UGCM	universal grammar constrained maturation
VEPS	Very Early Parameter Setting
VOT	voice onset time
X-bar	phrase structure (in GB theory).

AUTHOR INDEX

A

Aarons, D., 553
Abramson, A., 353
Achenbach, T., 464
Ackerman, J., 553
Acredolo, L., 353
Admiraal-Berg, C., 676
Adone, D., 205
Akamatsu, C., 542
Akayama, S., 395
Alenskas, L., 351
Allbritton, D., 257
Allen, G., 327
Allen, S., 133
Alleyne, M., 196
Allwood, J., 350
Alston, W., 349, 350
Anderson, J., 11, 252, 350, 367
Anderson, S., 179
Andrews, A., 11
Anselmi, D., 367
Antinucci, F., 233–234, 240, 353, 355, 356, 476
Arams, D., 116
Archangeli, D., 310, 311, 651
Argyle, M., 360
Arnberg, L., 600
Ashbrook, E., 536
Ashby, M., 360
Atkinson, M., 143, 173, 299
Augustine, St., 3, 249, 271
Austin, J., 141, 434, 439
Austin, W., 432
Avery, P., 15, 314, 333
Avrutin, S., 82–85, 104, 418

B

Babyonyshev, M., 97, 104
Bach, E., 166, 172
Bacharach, V., 362
Baddeley, A., 393
Bahan, B., 553
Baillargeon, R., 130
Baillie, C., 514
Bain, B., 588
Baker, C., 211
Baker, E., 261
Baker, N., 351, 511, 522, 523
Baldwin, D., 260, 268
Bamberg, M., 368
Bar-Hillel, Y., 166, 349
Bar-Shalom, E., 389
Barbier, I., 115, 117, 137, 139, 141, 449
Barlow, J., 656, 668, 669
Barnes, S., 507–508, 511, 512
Barrett, M., 356–358
Barss, A., 272
Barton, D., 663
Batchelder, W., 61
Bates, E., 16–17, 158, 213, 236–239, 242, 255, 350–358, 365, 390, 512, 536
Bateson, M., 351

Battison, R., 15
Bauer, H., 486
Becker, J., 364, 365
Becker, K.-P., 675
Beckwith, R., 282
Behrens, H., 99
Bellugi, U., 431, 443, 531–533, 544, 548–552, 555, 579
Benedict, H., 351, 359, 503
Benigni, L., 536
Bennett-Kastor, T., 367
Benoit, P., 362
Bentahila, A., 622, 627
Berent, G., 615–616
Bergman, C., 619–620
Berk, S., 432, 439
Berkele, G., 604
Berko, J., 364, 688
Berman, R., 176, 548, 676
Bernhardt, B., 658
Bernthal, J., 661
Bertolini, U., 678
Berwick, R., 173, 214, 500
Best, C., 555
Bever, T., 187
Bhatia, T., 5, 12, 24, 26, 435, 571, 587, 620–621, 625, 627, 632
Bickerton, D., 4, 11, 14–16, 196–197, 202–203, 207–209, 215
Biederman, I., 253
Bilodeau, L., 588
Bird, A., 661
Birdwhistell, R., 360
Bishop, I., 199
Bishop, D., 677
Blake, J., 432
Blank, M., 114, 362
Bloom, L., 17, 124, 136, 282, 284, 358, 361, 363, 460, 473
Bloom, P., 3, 4, 18–19, 65, 233, 257, 261–263, 265–268, 271–274, 280, 404, 405, 407
Bloomfield, L., 571
Blume, M., 113, 116, 432
Bodin, L., 473
Bohannon, J., 501, 514, 519
Bol, G., 676, 684
Bonamo, K., 521
Bonvillian, J., 351, 536, 541–546
Borer, H., 12–13, 53, 56–60, 63, 65–70, 72, 75–78, 101–104, 119, 124, 134, 142, 211, 392, 408
Borowsky, T., 318
Boser, K., 14, 116, 118, 132–133, 135–137, 141, 429, 434, 435, 437–439
Botvin, G., 368
Bouvet, D., 572, 590, 591, 615
Bowerman, M., 17, 233, 292
Bowey, J., 431
Boyes-Braem, P., 256
Braine, M., 170, 175–176, 183–184, 306, 321, 322, 658
Brainerd, C., 432
Branon, J., 615
Braunwald, S., 351, 356
Breinlinger, K., 261
Bresnan, J., 163, 167, 240
Bretherton, I., 6, 255
Broetzmann, S., 362
Bromberg, H., 97
Bronson, W., 353, 354
Brookes, S., 357
Brooks, J., 353
Broselow, E., 306
Brown, R., 4, 8, 209, 261, 283, 333, 351, 364, 406, 409, 431, 432, 443, 457, 458, 473, 475, 501, 503, 511, 516, 517, 592, 598, 689
Bruner, J., 202, 280, 351, 353–356
Bryan, T., 363
Bryk, A., 513
Buczowska, E., 473
Butcher, C., 512
Budwig, N., 235, 236
Bunenik, V., 609
Burling, R., 590, 593, 597
Burton, D., 320

C

Cairns, H., 82, 84, 128, 421, 439
Camaioni, L., 351, 356, 536
Camerata, S., 503, 655
Camp, L., 483
Campbell, R., 338
Caplan, D., 114
Carey, S., 251, 256, 258–259, 266, 284
Carnap, R., 348
Carpenter, R., 353–356
Carrow, E., 596
Carter, A., 353, 355
Caselli, M., 474, 542, 678
Cauley, K., 446, 447

Cazden, C., 351, 522, 524
Ceci, S., 432
Centineo, J., 234, 241
Chalkley, M., 175–176
Chang, H., 417
Chapman, R., 351, 353, 466, 469, 473
Charney, R., 353, 361
Charron, F., 536, 542
Chaudenson, R., 196
Cheng, L., 578
Chi, S., 432
Chiang, C.-P., 114, 116, 117, 140–141, 435, 449
Chiat, S., 353
Chien, Y.-C., 22–23, 81–86, 115–117, 121, 139–142, 413, 414, 417, 418, 435, 439, 442, 443
Chin, S., 655, 656, 658, 661
Chipman, H., 439
Cho, M.-H., 654
Chomsky, C., 140
Chomsky, N., 3–14, 16, 27, 56, 58, 60, 69, 74, 78, 80, 99, 100, 111–117, 120–122, 126, 130, 137–138, 142–143, 158, 165, 169, 174, 189, 196, 211, 222, 223, 225, 228, 240, 251, 254, 258, 259, 266, 271, 284, 300, 304, 305, 314, 337, 348, 427–429, 432, 434, 500, 502, 558, 609, 610, 648
Christophe, A., 115, 136
Chugani, H., 127
Clahsen, H., 5, 14, 27–28, 61, 676–678, 683–685, 687–688, 691–694, 696–698, 701
Clancy, P., 364
Clark, A., 367
Clark, E., 350, 351, 347, 358, 548
Clark, H., 350, 360
Clark, R., 287, 430, 431, 512
Clements, G., 308–310, 313, 654
Clifford, T., 114
Clyne, M., 588
Coerts, J., 555
Coffee, S., 579
Coffey-Corine, S., 116
Coggins, T., 353, 354
Cohen Sherman, J., 114, 128, 134, 137, 139–141, 442
Collings, A., 685–687
Collis, G., 353
Conti-Ramsden, G., 360
Conway, L., 272
Cook, M., 360
Coon, R., 627
Cooper, R., 615
Cooper, W., 432
Corrigan, R., 356
Corsaro, W., 360, 361, 364, 365
Corwin, E., 199
Costello, J., 665
Coulter, G., 545, 558
Courtney, E., 265
Couthard, R., 360, 361
Crago, M., 133, 678–680, 689, 695
Crain, S., 5, 22, 51, 64, 66, 68, 82, 102, 103, 114, 119, 121, 122, 211, 389, 392, 393, 395, 404, 408, 419, 420, 431, 443–445, 449, 450
Croft, W., 179
Cromer, R., 473, 677
Cross, C., 115
Crystal, D., 28, 327, 470, 473, 475, 676
Cudworth, R., 36
Culicover, P., 6, 58, 61, 62, 162, 214, 229, 273
Cummins, J., 576
Curtiss, S., 114
Cziko, G., 197, 203

D

Dale, P., 356
Damrad-Frye, R., 368
Daniloff, R., 664
Danto, A., 269, 270
Das, U., 199
Davidson, D., 348
Davies, E., 622, 627
Davies, S., 269
Davis, M., 657, 667
Day, E., 542
de Acedo, B., 475
de Blauw, A., 353
De Houwer, A., 577, 584–586, 588, 596, 597, 599–601, 604–605, 609, 619–620, 626–627
de Jong, J., 684
Dell Corte, M., 359
Demetras, M., 501, 514, 515, 518, 519
Demuth, K., 102, 103, 115, 130–133, 136, 434, 438, 525
Dennett, D., 266, 267
Denninger, M., 351
Déprez, V., 130, 437, 609–612, 616

de Saussure, F., 348
Descartes, R., 35, 36, 74, 250
De Temple, J., 367
Deuchar, M., 533, 603–604
de Villiers, J., 139, 353, 395, 477, 523, 525
de Villiers, P., 353, 475
Diaz, R., 576
Dickie, G., 269
Dik, S., 226, 350
Dimond, A., 127
Dinnsen, D., 5, 27, 330, 334, 651–654, 656, 658, 659, 661–663, 666, 669
Di Sciullo, A., 623
Dixon, R., 179, 229, 235
Dodsworth, P., 366, 367
Donahue, M., 363
Donaldson, M., 430
Donegan, P., 648, 658
Donnellan, K., 257
Döpke, S., 590, 591, 619, 627
Dore, J., 352–358
Dorval, B., 363
Dowty, D., 166–167, 186, 225, 228
Dresher, B. E., 4, 10, 19, 27, 304, 306–307, 309, 328, 337, 338
Dromi, E., 594
Dubber, C., 353
Duncan, S., 360
Dundes, A., 360
Dunn, C., 651
Dunn, J., 354
Durand, J., 308
Durie, M., 229
Dutton, C., 199
Dzierawiec, S., 260

E

Eckerman, C., 353, 354
Edwards, D., 353
Edwards, M., 651, 664
Egido, C., 135
Eichen, E., 533
Eisele, J., 114–117, 121, 138, 140–141, 434, 435, 442–446, 448, 449
Eisenbeiss, S., 14
Elbert, M., 652, 653, 657, 661, 663, 665, 666
Ellenberger, R., 539
Ellis, H., 260
Elman, J., 512
Emiliani, M., 134
Emmorey, K., 557, 579
Emonds, J., 94, 170, 582, 610
Enc, M., 100
Engel, S., 357
Erwin-Tripp, S., 360, 361, 486
Esposito, A., 114
Evans, M., 362, 364
Ewen, C., 309
Ezra, M., 553

F

Fahn, R., 484
Faltz, L., 230
Fanshel, D., 360
Fantini, A., 593, 597
Farrar, M., 520–521
Farwell, C., 319, 325
Feagans, L., 353
Fee, E., 334
Fein, R., 104
Feldman, C., 202, 522
Feldman, H., 114, 284
Felix, S., 52, 53
Ferguson, C., 319, 325, 337, 338
Ferguson, S., 577
Ferreiro, E., 439, 657, 667
Fey, M., 657
Figurski, G., 661, 665
Fikkert, P., 329, 330
Fillmore, C., 349
Fischer, A., 579
Fisher, C., 262, 263, 286–288, 290
Fiske, D., 360
Flege, J., 665
Fletcher, P., 470, 473, 475, 676
Flynn, S., 5, 22–23, 114, 115, 117, 121, 139, 439, 450
Fodor, J., 18, 173, 223–224, 252, 270, 388, 498, 557
Foley, C., 5, 16, 22, 113, 115, 117, 121, 132–134, 139, 141, 226–228, 230–231, 237, 241–242, 335, 429, 439, 443, 449
Foley, J., 335
Folger, M., 659
Folven, R., 536, 541–545
Ford, K., 309
Forrest, K., 663

Fortescue, M., 130
Fountain, A., 265
Fowler, A., 475
Fox, D., 103
Franklin, M., 355, 362
Fraser, C., 431, 443
Frelinger, J., 661
French, J., 360
Fritzenschaft, A., 698
Frost, L., 133
Furrow, D., 503, 504, 507, 509, 514

G

Gair, J., 116, 117, 128, 134
Galvan, D., 533
Gandour, J., 655
Ganger, J., 104
Garcia, E., 588, 591, 604, 627
Gardener, H., 223
Garman, M., 470, 473, 475, 676
Garrett, M., 114
Garvey, C., 362
Garvey, G., 354
Gasser, M., 252
Gathercole, V., 513, 526
Gaustad, M., 542
Gawlitzek-Maiwald, I., 698
Gazdar, G., 348, 681
Gee, J., 531, 533
Gegeo, D., 524–525
Gehring, W., 126
Gelman, R., 130
Gelman, S., 261, 447
Genesee, F., 14, 577, 598, 602, 604, 609, 612–614, 627
Gentner, D., 264, 282
Gerken, L., 132, 135, 136, 327
Gerrig, R., 350
Gessner, M., 114
Gibbs, R., 350
Gierut, J., 654, 658, 661–662, 666–667
Gilbert, J., 658
Gillette, J., 18–19, 259, 279, 289
Givon, T., 226, 227, 234, 351
Gleason, J., 364
Gleitman, H., 281, 285, 288, 289, 292, 431, 503
Gleitman, L., 4, 12, 18–19, 70114, 122, 123, 128, 129, 135, 162–163, 213, 253, 259, 262, 263, 274, 279–286, 288, 289, 292, 431, 503, 505–512
Glover, G., 484
Gnanadesikan, A., 22, 669
Goad, H., 668
Goda, S., 615
Godard, D., 360
Gold, M., 501
Goldfarb, J., 252, 253
Goldfield, B., 359, 365
Goldin-Meadow, S., 114, 284, 512, 533
Goldsmith, J., 308, 309
Golinkoff, R., 23, 115, 353, 354, 446, 448
Goodhart, W., 531, 533, 616
Goodluck, H., 439, 498
Goodman, M., 202
Goodwyn, S., 353
Goodz, N., 588, 591, 627
Gopnik, M., 678–680, 689, 695, 696
Gordon, D., 350, 360
Gordon, L., 353, 446–447
Gordon, P., 263, 273, 518, 524
Grant, M., 199
Gray, W., 256
Greatbatch, D., 363
Greenberg, J., 329
Greenfield, P., 351, 356–358
Gregg, K., 582
Greif, E., 364
Grice, H., 349, 362
Griffiths, P., 356–358
Grimm, W., 677, 693, 698
Grimshaw, J., 82, 115, 167, 273, 284, 292, 412–414, 416, 429, 520
Grodzinsky, Y., 53, 103, 418, 429, 697, 699
Grosjean, F., 574, 578, 585, 600, 630
Gruber, J., 356
Grunwell, P., 651
Guasti, M., 131, 134, 144, 408–409
Guasti, T., 100
Gubala-Ryzak, M., 582
Gupta, A., 266
Gussmann, E., 307
Gutfrend, M., 507

H

Haegeman, L., 6, 222, 240
Haight, W., 513
Hakuta, K., 576

Hale, K., 230, 303, 553
Hall, D., 261, 262, 286
Hall, E., 360
Hall, R., 196
Halle, M., 27, 300, 303, 304, 312, 314, 328, 648
Halliday, M., 350, 351, 355–358, 361, 484
Halmari, H., 574, 629
Hamburger, H., 58, 89, 119, 121, 122, 139, 393
Hamilton, H., 531
Hampson, J., 253, 510
Hand, L., 661
Hanlon, C., 8, 501, 516–517
Hannigan, S., 627
Hansen, D., 677
Hansson, K., 18, 693, 700
Harbert, W., 113
Harding, C., 353
Harley, H., 484
Harris, M., 357, 699
Harris, P., 197
Harrison, B., 357
Harshman, R., 579
Hasan, R., 361, 484
Haselkorn, S., 358
Hausser, R., 476
Hawkins, S., 327
Hay, D., 353
Hayashi, M., 577, 598, 601
Hayes, B., 314, 327
Hayes, D., 466
Heath, J., 227
Heath, S., 260
Heider, H., 102
Heim, I., 86
Hemphill, L., 361, 363, 364, 368
Herman, J., 356, 367
Hermon, G., 116, 139
Herodotus, 3
Herrnstein, R., 519
Hess, L., 361
Hicks, D., 368, 369
Higginson, R., 466
Hinde, R., 361
Hirsch, M., 676
Hirsch-Pasek, K., 23, 115, 136, 446–448, 501, 514, 517
Hitch, G., 393
Hochberg, J., 255
Hodge, M., 663
Hodson, B., 651, 661
Hoff-Ginsberg, E., 289, 505–509, 511, 513, 526
Hoffman, P., 590, 593, 627, 629, 664
Hoffmeister, R., 533, 538
Holley-Wilcox, P., 542
Hollingshead, A., 464
Holm, J., 202
Holmberg, A., 692
Holtz, A., 688
Hood, L., 361
Hooper, J., 306, 307
Hooshyar, N., 364
Hopper, P., 227, 235–236
Hornstein, N., 299
Howe, M., 432
Hsu, J., 82, 128, 421
Huang, C., 7, 553
Hubley, P., 354
Hudson, J., 368
Hudson, R., 352
Hughes, M., 661
Hume, D., 36
Hume, E., 654
Humpharies, T., 532
Hutton-Locher, J., 513, 526
Huttonlocher, P., 127
Hyams, N., 52, 65, 97, 101, 119, 130, 131, 133, 212, 216, 238, 272, 403–407, 410, 477, 513, 554, 616
Hymes, D., 350

I

Idaizábal, I., 588, 590, 603, 604
Idsardi, W., 314
Imbens-Bailey, A., 356
Imedadze, N., 240, 596–597, 609
Ingram, D., 299, 319, 323, 328, 330, 331, 334–336, 339, 356, 358, 593, 651, 659, 661, 662
Inhelder, B., 158, 432
Isaacs, S., 466
Ito, J., 306
Iverson, G., 658

J

Jackendoff, R., 170, 255, 257, 261, 264
Jackson, C., 535
Jacobson, K., 261

Jaeggli, O., 7, 553
Jakobson, R., 3, 53, 311, 329, 330, 332, 337, 592
Jakubowicz, C., 133, 139, 141
Jankowsky, W., 351
Jarvella, R., 431
Jefferson, G., 360
Jisa, H., 361
Johnson, E., 629
Johnson, J., 361, 580–581
Johnson, M., 256, 260, 267
Johnston, J., 684
Jonas, D., 100
Jonekeit, S., 588, 621
Jones, D., 357
Jones, S., 253, 255
Joos, M., 428
Jusczyk, P., 115, 136, 446, 448

K

Kaisse, E., 324
Kalish, D., 349
Kaltenbacher, E., 684, 687
Kamhi, A., 677, 684
Kant, I., 42
Kantro, R., 539
Kany, W., 688
Kaplan, B., 351
Kapur, S., 113, 128, 138, 429
Karmiloff-Smith, A., 13, 17, 353, 367, 369, 550
Karniol, R., 588, 629
Katamba, F., 308
Katz, J., 73
Katz, N., 261
Kaufman, D., 115
Kay, D., 353
Kaye, J., 304, 308, 309, 328
Kaye, K., 361
Kayne, R., 172
Keenan, E., 166, 176, 179, 361, 362
Kegl, J., 553
Keil, F., 251, 254, 256, 266
Keleman, D., 262, 265, 268
Kellermann, K., 362
Kemper, S., 369
Kempson, R., 348
Kendon, A., 361
Kendrick, C., 354
Kennick, W., 269
Kenstowicz, M., 6, 307, 308
Kessler, C., 590, 596
Key, M., 361
Keyser, S., 308, 309, 667
Kielhöfer, B., 588, 621, 627
King, C., 615–616
Kingman, J., 432
Kintsch, W., 350, 361
Kiparsky, P., 303–306, 310, 324, 329, 337, 339
Kisseberth, C., 307
Kitao, K., 362
Klausen, T., 598
Klein, D., 359
Klein, E., 361, 362, 681
Klima, E., 531, 532, 537, 544, 548
Klinge, S., 604
Kluwin, T., 361
Knapp, M., 361
Koda, K., 197
Koehn, C., 604
Konieczna, E., 473
Koopman, H., 612
Kornai, A., 167
Kornet, R., 114, 443, 449
Kornfilt, J., 116, 139
Koster, C., 113, 134
Krashen, S., 364, 579
Kripke, S., 257, 268
Kroch, A., 512
Kruger, A., 281
Kuhl, P., 170
Kuiken, F., 676
Kuno, S., 227, 230
Kutz, S., 353, 354
Kwan-Terry, A., 627
Kwiatkowski, J., 15
Kyartzis, A., 357
Kyle, J., 533, 553
Kynette, D., 369

L

La Polla, R., 16
Labov, W., 360
Lado, R., 655
Lahey, H., 473
Lahiri, A., 304, 324
Laicardi, C., 356

Lakoff, G., 350, 351
Lamb, M., 354
Lambert, W., 576
Lambrecht, K., 229
Landau, B., 114, 129, 136, 253–255, 257, 262, 264, 283, 285
Langacker, R., 352
Lanza, E., 590, 619–621, 626–627
Larson, R., 167, 172
Lasnik, H., 2, 119, 433, 502
Lawson, D., 116, 579
Leach, J., 360
Lebeaux, D., 121, 130, 133
Lebrun, Y., 588, 629
Lederer, A., 281, 288–290
Lee, K.-O., 118, 121, 132
Lee, L., 475
Lefebvre, C., 196
Legaré, M., 588
Leibniz, G., 40
Leinbach, J., 474
Leiter, R., 465
Lenneberg, E., 122, 282, 291, 579
Leonard, L., 131, 338, 473, 659, 678, 679, 683, 684, 686, 689–690, 694–696
Leopold, W., 202, 331, 569, 576, 583, 588, 590, 592, 596, 599–601, 619
Levelt, C., 335
Levelt, J., 431
Levin, B., 292
Levinson, J., 269, 270
Levinson, S., 20, 348, 349, 364
Levitt, A., 555
Levy, Y., 123, 130, 233, 577
Lewis, D., 348, 353, 354
Li, C., 606
Li, Y., 167
Liberman, A., 560
Liberman, M., 314
Liddell, S., 548, 560
Liebman, E., 599, 619
Lieven, E., 351, 359
Lightfoot, D., 214, 215, 299, 338
Lillo-Martin, D., 24, 25, 531, 537, 549–551, 553, 555, 615
Lim, T.-S., 362
Limber, J., 207
Lindholm, K., 570, 584, 599, 619–621
Lindner, K., 684, 687, 692
Linell, P., 307
List, H., 331
Littschwager, J., 257
Lléo, C., 335
Lock, A., 353, 355, 357
Locke, J., 252, 279, 323, 336, 651, 662
Loeb, D., 686
Long, M., 579
Lorge, I., 253
Loveland, K., 114, 443, 449
Lowenstamm, J., 309
Lucariello, J., 357–358
Lust, B., 4, 5, 11, 13–14, 22–23, 113–118, 121 128, 130, 132, 134–141, 428, 429, 434–437, 439, 442–444, 448, 449
Luszcz, M., 362
Lyons, J., 349
Lyons, T., 513

M

MacIver, D., 526
Macken, M., 320, 321, 326, 327, 334–338, 663 669
Macnamara, J., 162, 254, 261, 266, 267, 273
Macomber, J., 261
MacWhinney, B., 5, 16–17, 23–24, 94, 158, 213, 236–239, 241–242, 350–351, 390, 458, 466, 468, 474, 484, 519
Maddieson, I., 329
Mahlau, A., 602
Malish, T., 395
Mandler, J., 261
Manzini, R., 173, 616
Mapstone, E., 197
Marantz, A., 188, 328
Maratsos, M., 175–176, 178, 367, 431
Marcon, R., 627
Marcus, G., 474, 524, 688
Marentette, P., 540, 541
Mark, M., 521
Markman, E., 255, 257, 261, 263, 287
Markow, D., 263
Markson, L., 257
Marlett, S., 300, 301, 306, 308
Marslen-Wilson, W., 324
Martlew, M., 353
Martohardjono, G., 113, 118, 138–139, 141, 429, 451
Mastergeorge, A., 353

Mathesius, V., 222
Mattingly, I., 560
Maxfield, J., 116, 139
Maxwell, E., 652, 658, 662–663
Mayberry, R., 533
Mayer, E., 220
Mazuka, R., 114–117, 134, 136, 138–141, 435, 442, 449
McCabe, A., 361, 368
McCarthy, J., 303, 308, 313, 316, 327–328
McCawley, J., 225
McClelland, J., 17, 238, 252
McCloskey, J., 553
McClure, E., 621
McCollam, K., 367
McConvell, P., 621
McCune-Nicolich, L., 357
McDaniel, D., 82, 84, 115, 128, 394–403, 421, 431, 439
McDonald, J., 474
McGhee-Bidlack, B., 368
McGregor, K., 678
McHoul, A., 361
McIntire, M., 531–532, 555–556
McKee, C., 23, 115, 119, 134, 394–403, 419, 420, 431, 439, 444–445, 449
McLaren, J., 514
McLaughlin, B., 570, 584
McReynold, L., 665
McShane, J., 356
Mehler, J., 115, 136
Meier, R., 533, 4,6, 537–543, 550, 551, 555, 560, 615
Meisel, J., 577, 584, 592, 595–597, 599, 602, 604, 619–624, 626, 632
Menn, L., 324–326, 329, 335, 337, 339, 358, 658
Menyuk, P., 337
Mervis, C., 117, 256, 351, 439
Mester, A., 167
Metthei, E., 326, 336
Michalson, L., 353
Michell, L., 366
Mikes, M., 596
Miller, G., 354
Miller, J., 169–170, 469, 475, 677
Miller, N., 578
Miller, R., 233–234, 240, 355, 473
Millikan, R., 257
Mills, A., 555, 687
Mills, D., 116, 127, 579
Minami, M., 368
Mishler, E., 360
Mitchell, L., 366
Moerk, E., 351, 353, 457
Mohanan, K., 324
Montadon, A., 616
Montague, R., 183, 349
Montalbetti, M., 82–84, 418
Moreton, J., 483
Morgan, J., 115, 521
Morgan, W., 230
Morris, C., 347
Morrisette, M., 656, 661
Morton, J., 261
Moshi, L., 167
Moskowitz, A., 331
Mounty, J., 533
Müller, N., 604
Mullin, J., 367
Murrell, M., 597
Muysken, P., 623
Myklebust, H., 615
Mylander, C., 512, 533

N

Naigles, L., 273, 285, 289, 292, 447, 513
Nair, R., 586, 587, 589, 593–595, 601, 603–608, 624, 626
Nakayama, J., 114
Neidle, C., 553
Nelson, D., 446
Nelson, K., 253–255, 270, 351, 355, 357–359, 368, 503, 510–511, 522, 523, 541, 545
Nelson, L., 486
Nespor, M., 327
Nettelblad, U., 692, 693, 700
Neufeld, A., 436
Neumann, H., 661, 667
Neville, H., 116, 579, 580
Newmeyer, F., 183
Newport, E., 114, 503–504, 533, 534, 536, 538–540, 542–543, 550, 555, 560, 580–581, 616–618
Nichols, J., 226, 237
Nicol, J., 272
Nicoladis, E., 599
Nida, E., 171

Nieddu, P., 130, 131, 134
Ninio, A., 5, 20–21, 176, 182, 184, 280, 351, 354–358
Norman, F., 552
Novack, L., 542
Nuñez del Prado, Z., 115–117, 132, 141, 439, 449
Nwokah, E., 614

O

O'Brien, K., 369
O'Grady, M., 549, 551, 552
O'Grady, W., 4, 11, 14–15, 159, 169, 173–174, 176–177, 183, 186, 187
Obler, L., 627
Ochs, E., 365, 484, 524
Odo, C., 202
Öksaar, E., 588
Ölswang, L., 521
Onstine, J., 665
Orlansky, M., 542
Ortny, A., 350
Osherson, D., 43
Oshima, S., 117, 134
Othenin-Girard, C., 439
Otsu, Y., 51
Ouhalla, J., 682
Otting, J., 683, 689, 690, 694–696, 701
Ozkök, B., 360

P

Packard, J., 121
Padden, C., 532, 536, 537, 547, 651, 661
Padgett, R., 25
Padilla, A., 570, 584, 599, 619–621
Padilla Rivera, J., 141
Palmer, S., 264
Pan, B., 10, 360
Panner, S., 5, 514–515, 518
Paradis, C., 335
Paradis, J., 668
Paradis, M., 14, 577, 588, 593, 598, 602, 604, 609, 612–614, 627, 629
Parisi, D., 353, 355, 356
Park, T., 598, 619
Parkinson, D., 116, 130, 133
Parodi, T., 61, 614
Pater, J., 668
Peal, E., 576
Pearl, R., 363
Penfield, W., 579
Penke, M., 9, 61, 693, 698
Penner, Z., 129
Perecman, E., 628
Perfetti, C., 366
Perlman, R., 364
Perlmutter, D., 240
Pesetsky, D., 104
Peters, A., 169, 484
Peterson, C., 361, 366–368
Peterson, J., 620
Petitto, L., 534, 536, 540–543
Phelps, M., 127
Philips, S., 361
Piaget, J., 51, 114, 123, 130, 158, 300, 357, 432
Piatelli-Palmerini, M., 233, 300
Picardi, N., 368
Pierce, A., 95, 130, 409, 436, 609–612, 616
Pine, J., 359, 511
Pinker, S., 12, 18, 133, 162, 171, 173–175, 178, 211, 233, 240, 252–255, 263, 266, 272–274, 280, 284, 286, 408, 474, 518
Pizzuto, E., 474, 535, 536, 544
Plato, 37, 38, 40, 57, 250
Platzack, C., 692
Plunkett, B., 18, 116, 139
Plunkett, K., 18, 474
Poeppel, D., 93, 94, 96, 97, 99, 616
Poizner, H., 548, 557
Pollard, C., 166
Pollock, D., 95
Pollock, J.-Y., 610
Post, K., 483, 488, 501
Postal, P., 240, 307
Powell, T., 661
Power, D., 616
Pratt, C., 431
Pride, J., 361
Priestly, T., 339
Prince, A., 18, 252, 314, 316, 327, 328, 474, 668, 680
Prinz, E., 361
Prinz, P., 361
Proman, R., 116
Prunet, J.-F., 335, 652
Pullam, G., 167
Pulleyblank, D., 309, 310

Pullman, G., 681
Puschmann, B., 685
Putnam, H., 257
Pye, C., 130, 131, 133, 331, 602
Pylyshyn, Z., 18, 223–224, 252

Q

Quarto, G., 432
Quay, S., 601
Quigley, S., 615–616
Quine, W., 18, 251, 252, 266, 283
Quixtan Poz, P., 133

R

Radford, A., 6, 13, 101, 124, 130, 134, 135, 202, 211, 212, 215, 216, 233, 616, 624
Raffler-Engel, W., 596
Raghavendra, P., 131
Rakowitz, S., 262, 286
Ramez, R., 136, 355
Rapp, M., 421
Rash, S., 369
Ratner, N., 354
Redlinger, W., 570, 598, 619
Reilly, J., 531, 532, 555, 556, 558, 559
Reinhart, T., 418, 429, 444
Rescorla, L., 475
Retherford, K., 473
Rhee, J., 97, 100
Rheingold, H., 353
Ricard, R., 367
Rice, K., 15, 314
Rice, M., 683, 690, 694, 696, 701
Richards, B., 507–509, 512
Richards, D., 252, 253
Rispoli, M., 4, 11, 16
Ritchie, R., 5, 12, 26, 44, 239–242
Ritchie, W., 571, 620, 621, 625, 627, 632
Rizzi, L., 52, 69, 553
Roberts, J., 198–201
Roberts, L., 579
Robinson, P., 507–509, 512
Rochemont, M., 229
Rocissano, L., 15
Rockman, B., 657, 663
Rodrigo, M., 116
Roeper, T., 132, 139, 395–396, 398
Rogdon, M., 351
Rohrbacher, B., 96, 97
Rollins, P., 356, 360, 482
Rom, A., 676, 679
Romaine, S., 569, 571, 585, 587, 590, 598, 627
Ronjat, J., 593
Rooth, M., 395
Rosch, E., 256
Rosen, S., 82, 115, 412–414, 416, 429
Rosenstein, J., 615
Ross, D., 616–618
Ross, H., 353, 354
Roth, F., 523
Rothweiler, M., 684, 688, 691, 696, 701
Rowland, S., 661
Rubin, K., 354
Ruke-Dravina, V., 493
Rumelhart, D., 17, 238, 252
Ryan, J., 351

S

Sabbadini, L., 678
Sach, J., 351, 361, 367
Sacks, H., 360
Safir, K., 7, 553
Sagey, E., 313
Salerno, R., 351
Saltzman, D., 657
Samar, V., 616
Sano, T., 97
Santelmann, L., 14, 116, 118, 130, 132, 136–137, 141, 437, 439
Sapir, E., 318
Sarma, V., 100
Satterly, D., 507
Saunders, G., 576, 590, 600, 627
Sawyer, M., 484
Saxman, J., 664
Scarborough, H., 475, 503, 505, 509–511
Schachter, J., 12, 579
Schaffer, H., 353
Schegloff, E., 360
Scherer, N., 521
Schick, B., 546, 547, 560
Schieffelin, B., 16, 234–235, 241, 260, 365, 524
Schlesinger, I., 17, 175, 177, 178, 183, 233
Schley, S., 361, 363

Schlyter, S., 590, 604
Schmeck, H., 16
Schneiderman, M., 501
Schöler, H., 688
Schuetz, E., 115
Schutze, C., 97, 100, 431
Schwartz, B., 473, 582
Schwartz, R., 338, 503, 659
Scott, C., 362
Scoville, R., 353
Searle, J., 349, 350, 352
Seliger, H., 574, 580, 629
Selkirk, E., 327
Selzer, M., 513
Sengul, C., 353
Shankweiler, D., 389
Shapiro, L., 368
Shatz, M., 353, 523, 526
Shaw, P., 324, 335
Shaw, L., 253
Sherman, J., 115, 139
Sherrod, L., 354
Sherwood, V., 354
Shimura, A., 484
Shipley, E., 135, 431
Shlonsky, U., 134, 144
Shover, J., 629
Shriber, L., 489
Siedlecki, H., 545
Siegel, S., 397
Silber, R., 337
Silverstein, M., 222, 226–228, 231, 235, 238–241
Sinclair, J., 361
Sinclair, H., 439
Singh, R., 623
Sinha, C., 474
Siperstein, G., 361, 363, 364
Siple, P., 542
Skinner, B., 3, 18, 251, 252, 258
Skutnabb-Kangas, T., 583
Slobin, D., 53, 157–158, 169–171, 173, 213, 239, 473, 512, 556, 592
Smit, A., 661
Smith, I., 114, 135, 318
Smith, J., 351, 356–358
Smith, L., 252, 253, 255
Smith, N., 318–321, 323–326, 331, 332, 595, 658
Smolensky, P., 316, 668
Snow, C., 5, 20, 21, 94, 162, 213, 351, 353, 355–356, 359–361, 363–365, 367, 368, 458, 473, 501, 503, 511, 519
Snyder, L., 255, 353
Sobin, N., 582
Socrates, 37
Soja, N., 251, 256, 262–263, 273
Sokolov, J., 458, 483, 511
Solan, L., 115, 439
Somashekar, S., 113, 435, 439
Sovak, M., 675
Speas, M., 231
Spelke, E., 251, 256, 261, 266
Spelke, L., 446
Spenser, A., 313, 323, 331–333, 658
Sportiche, D., 612
Sprott, R., 369
Squire, L., 432
Stage, S., 664
Stalker, C., 657
Stampe, D., 27, 339, 648, 658
Stanley, P., 44
Stanley, R., 309
Stanowicz, L., 501, 514
Stark, R., 463, 677
Starkey, P., 261, 266
Starosta, S., 175
Stavans, A., 627
Stecker, D., 262
Stein, M., 354
Stemberger, J., 308, 334, 335
Stenning, K., 366
Stephany, U., 351
Steriade, D., 310
Sternberg, R., 257
Stevens, K., 667
Stevenson, R., 367
Steyaert, M., 539
Stoel-Gammon, C., 335, 651
Stowell, T., 700
Strawson, P., 349
Strokoe, W., 3
Stromswald, K., 136, 437
Struxness, L., 19
Studdert-Kennedy, M., 560
Sturm, C., 363
Subritzky, M., 598
Sudhalter, V., 475

Sugarman-Bell, S., 353
Sumangala, L., 116
Suñer, M., 116, 130, 135
Supalla, T., 533, 539, 560, 617
Sutton-Smith, B., 368
Suzman, S., 102
Swain, M., 596, 598, 599, 609, 619
Sylvain, S., 196
Synder, W., 134, 136, 141

T

Taeschner, T., 595, 598–603, 619–620
Tager-Flusberg, H., 368, 475
Tallal, P., 463, 677
Taraban, R., 477
Tavakoliam, S., 420
Taylor, D., 195
Taylor, M., 261
Templin, M., 474
Tesar, B., 316
Thompson, R., 195, 196
Thompson, S., 227, 235–236, 606
Thorndike, E., 253
Thornton, R., 64, 82, 83, 85, 88, 90, 395, 404, 408–409, 415, 419, 443
Timberlake, A., 166, 176
Tinker, E., 282
Todd, J., 351
Tomasello, M., 351
Tomasello, W., 281
Toribio, A., 598
Torrens, V., 100, 103
Tough, J., 351
Tracy, K., 361
Tracy, R., 698
Tranel, B., 307
Travis, I., 629
Travis, L., 521
Treiman, R., 501
Trevarthen, C., 354
Trubetzkoy, N., 328
Tryon, D., 315
Tsimpli, I.-M., 114, 130
Tuite, K., 240
Tunmer, W., 431
Turner, R., 360
Tyler, A., 661, 664–665

U

Umiker-Sebeok, D., 368

V

Vainikka, A., 14, 61, 96
Valian, V., 5, 24, 135–136, 273, 395, 404, 437–438, 474, 477, 513, 518, 520
Vandell, D., 353
van der Hulst, H., 309, 337
Van der Lely, H., 696, 699
Van Dijk, T., 361
van Hoek, K., 549–552
Van Valin, R., 16, 183, 226–231, 234, 237, 241–242, 351
Varma, T., 130, 131
Veh, B., 620
Veit, S., 678
Vendler, Z., 228
Vergnaud, J., 309, 314
Verhulst-Schlichting, L., 676
Verway-de Jongh, T., 676
Vihman, M., 335, 336, 597, 598, 602, 609, 619–621
Vingiles, Z., 432
Vogel, I., 327
Volterra, V., 233–234, 240, 351, 536, 542, 595, 598–603, 619, 678, 696
Voorhoeve, J., 196
Vygotsky, L., 357

W

Wache, M., 609
Wachtel, G., 263, 287
Wagner, K., 94
Wakayama, T., 134, 136, 141, 439
Wales, R., 351, 353
Wang, Q., 555
Wanner, E., 114, 163
Wardhaugh, R., 362
Waterson, N., 323, 327, 330, 332–333, 336
Waterson, P., 337
Watson, R., 368
Watson-Gegeo, K., 524–525
Waxman, S., 261, 262

Webb, P., 353
Weber-Fox, C., 579, 580
Weinstein, S., 43
Weir, R., 466
Weisenberger, J., 357, 358
Weismer, G., 652, 662, 663, 667
Weissenborn, J., 132, 139, 437
Weist, R., 473
Wellman, H., 256
Wells, D., 507
Wells, G., 356, 357
Wertheimer, M., 264
West, M., 353
Westholm, L., 590
Wexler, K., 4–5, 11–14, 22–23, 53, 56–66, 68, 70, 72, 75–86, 88–90, 92–97, 99–104, 119, 124, 134, 142, 162, 173, 211, 214, 392, 404–410, 413, 414, 417–418, 474, 602, 616
Whatley, J., 353, 354
Wheeler, D., 658
Wheeler, P., 355, 356
Whinnom, K., 195, 196
White, S., 361
Whitman, J., 14, 116, 118, 130, 132, 135, 437
Wiggins, D., 348
Wilbur, R., 323, 532–533, 616
Wilcox, M., 13
Willerman, R., 541
Williams, A., 653
Wilson, R., 209
Winkler, S., 698
Witkowsha-Stadnik, K., 473
Wittgenstein, L., 249, 349
Wode, H., 570, 598
Woest, A., 688
Wolf, D., 483
Woll, B., 553
Wolley, J., 256
Woodward, J., 532
Wu, F., 367
Wyckoff, J., 503, 505, 509–511
Wynn, K., 261, 262
Wysocka, H., 473

X

Xu, F., 258

Y

Yamada, J., 114
Yamakoshi, K., 113
Yamashita, Y., 178
Yngve, V., 65
Yoon, J., 139, 141
Young, G., 353
Young, R., 230
Youssef, V., 197, 627
Yu, A., 588

Z

Zinober, M., 353
Zurif, K., 440
Zwicky, A., 288

SUBJECT INDEX

A

A-bar system, 133
A-chains, (argument chains), 12–13, 100, 102–105, 124–126, 133, 140, 142
A-domains, 129
Abstractness controversy, 305–307
Acceptable utterances and discourse functions, 518
Acehnese, 229
Acquisition, 20–21, 40, 46, 48
  absence of syntactic devices, 212
  adverbs, 473
  and age, 580, 584–585
  and environment, 41
  and limited input, 15–16
  and modules of the initial state, 49
  and pragmatic factors, 216
  approaches,
    connectionist models, 17–18, 390
    constraint-based vs. derivation-based approach, 669
    formalist vs. functionalist approach, 239–242
    functionalist approach, 222, 232–234, 238–241
  biological basis of, 579–580, *see also* Critical period
  capacity, 211
  developmental problem, 9, 10, 19, 317
  device, 157, 169–177
    and universal grammar, 169
    computational module, 171–173, 188
    conceptual module, 171, 177–180
    hypothesis formation module, 173–177
    interpretability requirement, 162
    perceptual module, 169–170
    propositional module, 170
  from pidgin to creole, 119
  functional-nonthematic, 215
  in children vs. adults, 679
  individual differences,
    development, 365–366
    in pragmatic preferences, 359
  lexical–thematic stage, 215
  linguistic vs. social knowledge, 369
  logical problem of, 9, 10, 19, 299–304
    effects of earlier stages, 302
    phonological issues, 304
  longitudinal studies, 208
  monolingual vs. bilingual child, 591–598
  normal vs. delay, 683–693
  novel structures, 208
  null to non-null subject, 403
  of audience-adaptation, 367
  of cohesion, 366–367
  of discourse plot structure, 368
  of distinctive features and contrast, 329–334
  of empty trace, 53
  of genres, 368–369
  of grammar and its two parts, 56
  of negation, 53
  of passives, 53
  of politeness, 364–365

Acquisition (*cont.*)
of pragmatics,
end-point, 369–370
of social distance, 363
phonological feature hierarchy, 330
prior to syntactic acceleration, 212
process, 160–161, 435
stages, 41, 118, 133, 135, 143, 211
coordination before subordination, 133
early vs. final stages, 300–304
extended verb final, 135
optional infinitive stage, 93–100
prelinguistic, 250
structural complexity, 241
the idealization of instantaneous, 300
true functionalist studies, 234–238, 242
Acquisition vs. learning, 582
Afrikaans, 461, 462
Age, acquisition, and hearing loss, 615
Age and acquisition, 135–137, 207–212, 281
deaf children and sign language acquisition, 538–544, 561
discourse development, 365–366
stages of deaf vs. hearing, 561
topic maintenance, 362
words, 254–257, 261
Agency, 204
Agent, 163, 167, 182, 184, 188, 238, 291
Agent-patient, 227
AGR, 97, 99–101, 130
D-feature of, 99
Agrammatics, 699
Agreement, 90, 97, 131, 206, 681–685, 697–700
abstract vs. location, 547–549
differences, English vs. French child, 610
morphemes, acquisition of, 97
subject–object, 537, 553
Agreement and bilingual child, 581, 604
ALDES, Aphasic Language Data Exchange System, 490
Alpha-movement, 242
Alzheimer's and Universal Grammar, 114
American Sign Language (ASL), 24–28, 531, 615–618; *see also* Complexity; Chapter 16
and babbling, 25
and bilingualism, 26
and English, 532
and handshapes, 545–546
and iconicity, 25, 543, 558
and language delay, 26
and linguistics theory, 531
and null argument, 25
and other sign languages, 533
and spoken language, 25
as visual–manual system, 532
classifier morphemes of, 617–618
history of, 533
learning of, 543
movement morphemes of, 617–618
sublexical structure of, 25
test battery, 617
visual–manual modality of, 25
Analysis, empty C, 308, 309
Analysis, empty C vs. abstract C, 308
Analytical approach, 549
Anaphora,
backward, 420
child's theory, 117, 141
Anaphors, 80, 96
Anglo-American empiricist tradition, 40
Animacy, 222
hierarchy, 235
Analogical approach, 549
Antecedents, long-distance, 81
Aphasia, childhood, 627
Aphasic, Broca, 411, 697
Arabic, 195
Argument, bare, 176
Argument hierarchy, 167, 177, 186–188
Articles and bilingual child, 604
Aspect, 163, 178, 179, 204, 205
imperfective, 228
in ASL, 537
perfective, 227, 228
Association, definition of, 250
Asymmetry, subject-object, 161, 183, 187
Audience-adaptation, development of, 367
Auditory processing, 688
Autism, 369–370
AUX, 133, 136
Auxiliaries and bilingual child, 581

B

Babbling
in deaf, 541
in deaf vs. hearing children, 540, 543

manual, 540–541
vocal, 541
Baby talk, 114, 122, 594
Bantu languages, 102
Basque, 604
Behavior and grammatical factors, 429, 450
Behavior, complex and reduced, 450
Behaviorism, 3
Bengali, 586, 587
Bilingual brain, regions of, 579–581
Bilingual (child), 5
acquisition vs. learning, 582
and age, 583–585
and cognitive deficit, 576
and input modality, 24–26
and language confusion, 599
and language loss, 590
and linguistic deficit, 576
and subcategorization, 581
and speech disorders, 627–630
and stuttering, 629
deaf, 590–591, 614–618
definition of, 572–573
early vs. late, 579–585
language delay, 593, 597, 607, 613, 615, 627
language problems in, 588–590
typology of, 585–587
Bilingual child, language acquisition
agreement, 581, 604
and 'one-parent/one-language' strategy, 583, 587–590, 603
and caretaker's language, 586–590, 615
and discourse allocation strategy, 583, 587–590
and interaction and separation of two languages, 574–575, 587–590, 618–627
and interference, 600, 603
and role of semantic-pragmatic factors, 595
and school and media role, 583
and type of language dominance, 574, 626–627
article, 604
auxiliaries, 581
case, 581
determiner, 581
factors of, 582–587
first language, 584
gender, 604
indirect object, 604
input separation condition, 588–590
mixed input condition, 588–591, 604–618
morpho-syntactic development, 596–598
number, 581, 604
particle movement, 581
phonological development, 592–594, 603
positive and negative evidence, 591
pragmatic competence, 588
progression and regression of language, 576, 590, 632
second language, 584
sequence of stages, 591
sequential, 583–584, 631–632
simultaneous, 583–584, 618, 631–632
stages of, 587–598
subjacency, 580–581
syllabic structure, 594–596, 603
tag question, 604
tense–aspect system, 604
vocabulary development, 594–596
word order, 581
yes–no questions, 581
Bilingual child, language mixing
code mixing
constraints on, 623–625
dominance and fusion, 626–627, 632
early stages of, 620–623
motivations for, 627
code switching
and parent's code switching, 591, 619
in 588, 591, 618–627
vs. code mixing, 619–620
vs. fusion, 619–620, 632
Bilingual child language separation
autonomous vs. interdependent systems, 609–614
role of formal devices, 593–594, 603
Unitary Hypothesis, 26, 598–603, 619–627, 630–631
methodological problems, 600–603, 619
Dual hypothesis, 26, 603–614, 630–631
Bilingual child language processing, 579–581
Bilingual child research, 569, 576–578
developments before 1980s, 570
methodological and analytical issues, 632–633
methodological issues, 599–608
problems of studying, 569–570
questions, 570, 581
theoretical issues, 630–632
Bilingual children and analytical maturity, 592

Bilingualism
and deaf children, 572
bilingualism, definition of, 569, 571
event-related brain potentials (ERPs), 579–580
subtractive, *see* Bilingual child, type of language dominance
types of, 583–587
Bilingualism and American Sign Language, 26
Bilingualism, semi-, *see* Bilingual child, type of language dominance
Binarity, 172, 185, 188
Binary branching hierarchical structure, 204
Binary diffusion, 311
Binding, long distance vs. local, 417
Binding, operator-variable, 133, 134
Binding, principles, 138
Binding Theory, 13, 80
Binding principles, 80
Bioprogram hypothesis (LBP), 11, 14–16, 195–196
and other acquisition theories, 213–216
current state, 198–203
language acquisition, 195–198, 203–207
predictions, 203–207
Biuniqueness principle, 77, 78
its gradual weakening, 78
Blending, 595
Blind children, 283
Bootstrapping, 213
and verb complementation, 285
and verb meaning, 284–285
syntactic, 214, 282
Borrowing, 620
Brain damage and specific language impairment (SLI), 675
Brain organization, of language, 557–558
Branching, 161, 183, 187
British Sign Language, 542

C

C-command, 80, 392, 416
C-system, 202
Capacity, 96–97
morphophonological, 97
morphosyntactic, 97
Caretaker's speech, 259
preference, 282
Case, 96, 98–100
accusative, 104
active, 229
and bilingual child, 581
ergative-absolutive, 229, 234, 235
genitive, 104
NOM, 100
nominative, 104, 229
system, 229, 235, 239, 240
theory of, 235
Catalan, 100
Category, 159, 163
adjective, 179
conceptual, 254
empty, 116, 136, 164
events, 251
functional, 682
functor, 166
hybrid, 183
individuals, 251
lexical, 125, 127, 682
linguistic and their development, 676
minor, 183
noun, 178–179
of "Individual," 262
of recognition, 210
phrase-level, 182
substances, 251
syntactic, 164, 174, 176
verb, 178–179
word-level, 182
Causative-noncausative, 196
Causatives, derived, 303
CHILDES, child language data exchange system, 457–491
access to data, 466
CHECK program for transcription and CHAT standards, 467, 488–489
future research, 489–491
history, 457–458
reformatting data base, 466–467
tools
bilingual acquisition data, 465
CHAT
key features of, 467–468
transcription and coding, 458
CLAN
ambiguity resolution, 479

discourse and interactional analyses, 483–484
frequency analyses, 472–474
irregular forms, 480
lexical analysis, 471–474
lexical building, 476–478
lexical rarity index, 474
lexical (semantic) field analyses, 473–474
morphological analysis, 474–480
other languages, 480
phonological analysis, 484–487
program analysis, 458
semantic relation analyses, 481
syntactic analysis, 480–482
CLAN's utilities, 487–488
data base, 458–459
data from books, 465–466
English data base, 459–461
language impairment data, 463–465
narrative data, 463
non-English data base, 461–463
user's knowledge, 471
Chinese, 7, 114, 117, 140–141, 202, 214, 433, 435, 442, 553, 579, 580, 695
Chomskyan revolution, 222–223, 232
Clarification, 501
Class
closed, 477
errors, 678–679
open, 477
Classificatory schemes, 515
Clinical intervention
and phonetic inventories, 665
for teaching of new sounds, 666
for traditional vs. single subject multiple baseline, 665
for treatment of untreated forms, 665
Clitic doubling, delay, 103
Cliticization, 104
Clitics, 206
Code mixing, *see also* Bilingual child, language mixing, code switching
and other related phenomena, 619–620
vs. language deficiency, 619, 627–630
Coding
errors, 468
morphemic, 468–469
phonological, 470
scheme, 515
Cognition
and language, parallelism, 223
stage theory, 130
Cognitive psychology, 158
history, 35, 37
Cognitive revolution, 3, 5–7, 223
and electronic age, 37
Cognitive theory, 249
Communication effectiveness
role of grammaticality and semantics, 347
Comparative Aphasia Project, 463
Competence
communicative, 350
competence vs. performance, 430–431
Competition model of linguistic performance, 16, 236–238
Complement, 164
phrase, 132, 133
Complementizer (C), 129
position, 94
Complementizer phrase (CP),
head of, 94
specifier of, 94
Complexity
anatomical, 545
cognitive, 545
morphological, 546, 549
of American Sign Language, 545–546
phonological development, 326–337, 339
syntactic, 549
Comprehension, 430, 523, 549
deaf children, 547–550
Computer application,
CD-Rom, 466, 472
talking transcripts, 485
Conjunction, subordinating, 473
Connectionism, 17–18, 238
Connective, subordination, 128
Consciousness vs. competence, 427
Constraint,
functional head, 625, 632
syntactic minimality, 140
universal grammar, 22
Contact languages, *see* Pidgin; Creole
Context, *see* Pragmatics
Continuity hypothesis, 211; *see also* Preverbal stage, to verbal stage
strong, 13; *see also* Chapter 4
the term, 71, 72
weak, 14

Continuous development, 72
Contrast, 171, 182
  spatial deictic, 179, 180
Control–agreement principle (CAP), 681
Control theory, 116, 134, 139
Conversational rules
  development of, 360
Conversational skills
  individual differences, 362–364
Coordination, 117, 128, 133, 134
COPROF, 677
Correction
  by parents, 501
Count nouns
  actions, 254
  events, 254
  humorous speech acts, 254
  interpersonal interaction, 254
  mathematical entities, 254
  periods of time, 254
  psychological entities, 254
  university-level teaching environment, 254
Creole
  development, Children's role, 200, 203
  Hawaiian, 196, 198, 200, 201, 203
  Mauritian, 205
Creole languages, 195
  acquisition of, 196–217
  grammatical morphology, 196
  similarities among, 196–198
  theories of origin, 196
  word order of, 206
Creolization, 11, 15–16, 620
Critical period(s), 579–582, 585

D

D (determiner)-feature, 99
D-interpretability theory, 100
D-system, 202, 216
Danish, 437, 462
data
  language impairment, 463–465
  negative, 162, 499–500
  positive, 162, 500–502
  spontaneous speech, 255
deaf children, 283–284, 532–560; *see also* Bilingualism and deaf children; Input poverty
  language acquisition,
    and new learning principles, 559
    classifier in, 539, 546–549
    classifiers
      ASL, 547–549
      CLASS, 547
      HANDLE, 547–549
      SASS, 547, 548
    comprehension, 547–550
    stages of, 615
Deafness, prelinguistic, 615
Default distinction, 204
Deficit, *see also* Chapters 18 and 19
  accusative marking, 685
  article, 679
  auditory processing, 688
  auxiliaries, 681
  auxiliaries and modals, 684–685
  case marking, 682
  dative marking, 685
  finiteness, 693
  gender, 681, 686–687
  gender marking, 682
  inflectional morphology, 678–682, 691–695
  irregular verbs, 690, 700
  missing feature, 678–680, 694–695
  negation, 684
  overt structural case marking, 681, 685–686
  participle inflection, 691–692
  past tense marking, 699–700
  person, 686–687
  plural marking, 687–690
  plural vs. subject–verb marking asymmetry, 694
  question formation, 684
  reversible passive, 699
  rule–deficit model, 678–680, 695–697
  subject–verb agreement, 681, 683–685, 697–700
  surface, 678
  syntactic, 682
  tense marking, 690–691
  the grammatical agreement, 678, 681–685, 697–700
  verb argument, 680
  verb-second, 698–699
Definiteness, 171, 179, 180, 238
Deictics, 179, 348
Deixis, ASL, 535
Delay, developmental, 129, 139–141

Derivation, vertical, 308
Determiner, 130, 179, 184
  and bilingual child, 581
Developmental pragmatics, 347
Developmental theories, pragmatics in, 350–351
Devices, reference, 227
Differences, in style, 359
Diglossia, 620
Directionality, 117, 119, 138, 140, 168, 187, 444
Discontinuity hypothesis, 136
Discourse, *see* Politeness; Conversational skills
Discourse acquisition,
  chains and sequences, 483
  cohesion, 366–367
  context, 393
  development of, 365–366
  genres, development of, 368–369
  inferencing, 88
  plot structure development, 368
  speech acts, 4, 20–21
  system, 83–86, 88–90
  turn taking, 4, 21
Disorders, *see* Specific language impairment; Down's syndrome
Disorder, phonological, 627
  accurate assessment of, 667
  allophonic rule, 656, 666
  alternative accounts, 651–659
  and children vs. adult derivational relationship, 651–656
  and clinical intervention, 665
  and complementary distribution, 655
  and delay vs. deviance, 661–662, 668
  and equivalence classification problem, 665
  and faithfulness vs. well-formedness constraints, 669
  and independence of disordered systems, 657–658
  and motor system, 662
  and natural phonology accounts, 651
  and optimality theory, 668
  and principle of cyclicity, 662
  and production vs. perceptual storage, 658
  and underspecification theory, 27, 659
  clinically interesting, 657
  constraint ranking of, 668
  difference in voice onset time (VOT), 663
  difference in spectral characteristics, 664
  dual lexicon model, 658
  error patterns, 648–650
  homophonous forms, 664, 667
  omissions, 650
  stages of, 669
  substitutions, 648–651, 666, 668–669
  subtle acoustic differentiations, 662–665
  underlying deletion, 652–653
  underspecification, 653–655
  underspecification and abstractness, 651–659
Do-support, 611
Domains, pragmatics vs. syntax/semantics, 347
Down's syndrome, 465
Dutch, 95, 116, 117, 139, 195, 327, 329, 604, 684
Dysphasia, *see* Specific language impairment (SLI)

E

E-languages, 113, 136
Early stages,
  and grammar, 12
  and speech acts, 357
  development of communicative contents, 358–359
  from general to specific, 358
  individual difference, 359
  multiple mapping, 358
  non-referential speech, 356
  single-word utterances, pragmatics of, 356
  uniqueness principle, 358
Ellipsis, 90
  verb phrase, 117
English, 4, 7–9, 24, 41, 49, 95–97, 100, 102, 130, 135, 140, 168, 171, 176–178, 195, 198, 214, 222, 226, 229, 235, 236, 253–254, 264, 301, 302, 318, 327, 364, 404–405, 408, 433, 434, 442, 459–461, 475, 477, 481, 513, 537, 543, 569, 576, 580, 586–596, 600–615, 619, 621–622, 625–629, 657–659, 663, 676–701
Errors, 86–89, 91, 140, 175, 196, 235, 392, 422, 520, 678–701; *see also* Disorders
  backing process, 654
  clinical, 647, 665–668
  complexity hierarchy, 660
  deaf children's, 535, 538–539, 548–532
  definite article, 367
  final consonant deletion process, 651, 652

Errors (*cont.*)
fronting process, 651, 654
gliding process, 651
inflections, 91, 95
rate, 678
stopping process, 651
unaccusative as unergative, 103
verb-final, 692, 698
verb-initial, 692
verb-second, 692
vs. disorder, 647–648
word order, 692–693, 698
Estonian, 336, 621
Event, 180
Evidence
experimental, 132
indirect negative, 502, 519
negative, 25, 500–502
negative vs. positive, 501, 518
positive, 25, 499
short supply, 303
Experience, nature of, 157, 160–161
Explanations, teleological, 220
Expressive vs. referential children, 359

F

False guess, 290
Feature(s)
checking, 100
despecification, 331–332
distinctive, 329–334
geometry, 313
perceptual, 252
ranking ordering, 313
Feedback, 252
Finiteness, 130, 131, 141
acquisition of, 90, 93–98
English vs. French child, 609–614
First language(s), 585
Fluency, deaf children, 548
Formalism
definition of, 220
vs. functionalism, 220
French, 7, 14, 95, 96, 133, 195, 206, 409, 543, 586, 591, 597, 604, 609–614, 621–622, 628–629, 679
Frozen forms, 325
Functional categories, 13, 124, 127, 129–130, 132–134, 143
absence of, 129
acquisition of, 97, 100
Functionalism, definition of, 222
Functionalist approaches, 11, 16–17, ch. 7

G

Garo, 593
GB theory, 167, 187, 189, 228, 229, 412; *see also* almost all chapters
Gender, 204, 206
and bilingual child, 604
Genetic impairment and specific language impairment (SLI), 675
Georgian, 240, 598
German, 14, 93, 95–97, 102, 133, 135, 139, 408, 434, 437, 462–463, 478, 576, 588, 593, 597–598, 600–601, 619, 621, 628, 676–701
Germanic languages, 92, 141
Gesture, 542–543; *see also* American Sign Language
grammaticized facial expressions, 555
instrumental, 543
linguistic status of, 543
natural, 543
Gradation, 179, 180
Grammar
and cognitive principles, 222
and interface, 78, 105
categorical, 166–169
child vs. adult, 55, 59–62, 94, 95
computational system of, 78, 79, 100, 105
Generalized Phrase Structure (GPSG), 681–682
Government-Binding, 165
interpretive/conceptual, 100, 105
role and reference (RRG), 228, 229, 231, 239, 242
traditional vs. generative, 38, 39
transformational, 44
verb final, 438
verb raising, 438
Grammatical function, 204
Grammatical mapping, 137–142
Grammatical module, disturbance in, 677

Grammatical principles, 4
Grammatical relations, 227, 241
  difficulty of acquisition, 240–241
  mosaic acquisition, 241
Grammaticality, 515
  and sentencehood criteria, 516
  grammaticality criteria, 515
  relaxation of constraints, 515–516
  vs. ungrammaticality and acceptability, 517
Grammaticization, 204
Grammaticized facial expressions, 555
Grammogens, 238
Greek, 200
Greenlandic, 130
Growth theory, 9

H

Handshape, Boyes-Braem's model, 546
Harmony, consonantal, 335
Haryanavi, 586
Hawaiian, 199, 200, 202
  in education, 200
Head, 164, 166
Hebrew, 97, 100, 130, 462, 629
Hebrew Assessment Remediation and Screening Procedure (HARSP), 676
Hindi, 130, 131, 577, 578, 586, 587, 589, 594–596, 601–608, 625–626, 628
Horizontalization, 205
Human speech genome project, 490
Hungarian, 241, 462, 463, 475
Hungarian aphasic data, 463
Hypotheses formulation paradox, 430
Hypothesis
  early stage of phonological development, 304–317
  continuous dichotomy, 312
  testing, 214
  testing metaphor, 24–25, 497–498

I

I-languages, 113, 127, 136
I-system, 202
Igbo, 604
Imperatives, by parents, 508
Indirect object and bilingual child, 604
Indirectness, by Japanese mothers, 364
Individual differences, 133
  normal vs. mentally retarded, 363, 364
  notion of, 266
Inductionist theories, 214, 216
Infinitives, optional, 90, 93–98
INFL, 609
Inflection (I), 130, 134, 187
Inflectional morphology, 132
  and perceptual limitation, 678, 694–695
  and specific language impairment (SLI), 677–679, 694–695
Inflectional phrase (IP), 130, 131
Inheritability, 172, 188
Initial speech, grammar of, 128
Innateness, 50, 100, 157, 185, 188
  and learning mechanism, 60–74
  Cartesian view of, 36, 38
  indirect, 158
  issue, 4–12
  mentalistic view of, 34
  of grammatical system, 159
  Plato's problem, 38, 40, 49
Innateness hypothesis, *see also* Language bio-program hypothesis
  Chomskyan and language bioprogram, 196–198, 204, 213–216
Input, 5, 120, 202, 206, 214–215, 287, 339
  and accelerating children's production and comprehension, 522–523
  and beyond, 60
  and children's parsing, 524
  and cognitive role, 498–499
  and disordered phonology, 668
  and motivational role, 498–499
  and salience hypothesis, 508, 511
  and UG, 58, 59
  class, 524–525
  cross cultural studies, 524–525
  expansion, 511
  extension vs. expansion, 522
  filtration, 678
  in natural environment, 525
  intervention studies, 499, 522–526
    and input effects, 526
    and problem of control, 524

Input (*cont.*)
language,
amount and type of, 572–573
and bilingualism, 572
and child-rearing practices, 585
and language problems, 588–590
conditions, 582–587, 604, 614–618
conditions and deaf children, 614–618
dominance of, 573
mixed, 588, 612
monolingual vs. bilingual child, 573
online, 590
pidgin, 213
poverty, 614–618
quality and quantity, 590–591, 631
separation vs. lack of separation of, 588–590, 618
sociolinguistically realistic, 589–591
vs. pidgin and creoles, 587, 590
manipulation of children's, 522
modality, 24–26, 614–618
modeling and recasting effects, 522
mother's, 213
parent/mother/care-taker, 217
quality, 213
quantity, 513
recast, 511
replies
and probability learning, 519
expansion-type, 521
frequencies, 518
nature of children's responses, 520–521
studies, 502, 513–522, 526
role
and language acquisition, 497
copy + correction metaphor, 513
copy metaphor/theories, 497, 504
hypothesis-testing metaphor, 497–498, 500, 502, 513
trigger metaphor, 498, 513
sensory, 34
simple to complex model, 504
studies, 499, 500, 503–513
and child–parent pairs, 503
and conceptual issue, 503
and statistical issues, 503, 505
design issue, 503
issue in, 503
systems, 557–560
unintelligible, 510
Input, limited, 15; *see also* Pidgin and Creole
Instantaneous hypothesis, 118, 120–122, 141–142
Intelligence and specific language impairment (SLI), 675
Interaction, C–V, 335
Interactivity, 172, 188
Interface
properties, growth/maturation of, 104, 105
semantic, pragmatic and morphosyntactic, 234, 235
Interference, *see* Bilingual child, type of language dominance; Transfer
Interpretation
new/novel verbs, 282
new/unfamiliar words, 255, 259, 265
structural and pragmatic factors in, 285–288
Inuktitut, 133
IPA and ASCII translation, 487
IQ, and language impairment, 464
Italian, 7–9, 52, 97, 100, 104, 119, 130–131, 134, 233, 234, 240, 405, 438, 462, 475, 513, 593, 596, 603, 683, 686, 696

J

Japanese, 7, 34, 41, 49, 102–103, 116–117, 140, 178, 183, 202, 230
Judgments, wellformedness, 20

K

Kaluli, 16–17, 234–235, 239–241, 260, 524–525
Kinship terms, 254
Knowledge, changes over time, 111
Korean, 177, 183, 580
Kwara, 524–525

L

Language
and cognitive revolution, 34–36, 46
and intelligence, 158
and mind, 11
as a cognitive system, 37, 39
behavior, production and comprehension, 430

bioprogram hypothesis (LBP), syntactic, 204–207
complexity, emergence of complex structures, 207–208
conception of, syntax, semantic and pragmatic distinction, 348
deficit hypothesis and U-shaped language development, 629
definition of, 44
delay, 63–64, 66, 92–93, 98, 102–103, 105, 210, 676; *see also* Disorders; Deficit, specific language impairment (SLI)
development, 56, 59–74; *see also* Acquisition
normal, 207–213, 216–217
stages of, 51, 53, 58, 93, 95
disorders, 5, 27
and diagnosis, 27
learning
computational models, 490–491
mechanism, 678
mentalistic vs. behavioristic view, 33–38
mixing, *see* Code mixing/code switching
mixing, adult vs. early childhood, 620
modality, 532, 541
phylogeny, 15
production, 430, 523
profiles, automatic and COPROF, 677
sign, misconceptions, 532, 543
signed vs. spoken, 531–532, 558–561
stages of cognitive development, 51
type
C-zero V, 112, 136
discourse-oriented, 553
head-first, head-last, 49
left branching, 134, 140
morphologically rich, 679
nonconfigurational, 205
non-null subjects, 403
null subject, 403
SOV, 693
V2, 693
verb-final, 94
verb-second, 93, 94
VSO, 199
use, 46, 48
and linguistic knowledge, 39
delay, 51
memory, 51
traditional vs. generative treatment, 38, 39
Language acquisition
and maturation, 40, 41
and sensory input, 34
device, 43
no-growth theory, 51, 52
semantic and cognitive approaches, 233–234
studies, in ancient times, 3
the initial stage, 43, 49
two factors, 49
Language Assessment Remediation and Screening Procedure (LARSP), 28, 676
Languages, *see* Creole
Langue des Signes Québécoise (LSQ), 540
learning of, 541
Latin, 176–177, 200
Law, Conservatism, 173–174
Learnability, 4, 19, 56, 57, 59–79, 99, 499
and changes over time, 60
and clause structure, 92, 99
and language acquisition, 44
and learning delay hypothesis, 63, 64, 66, 92, 93, 98, 100, 102–105
and verb inflection, 92
and verb movement, 92
capacity, 158, 163
cognitive, 15
output omission model, 65
performance delay hypothesis, 63, 65, 66, 68, 98, 105
problem, 164–166
logical vs. developmental problem of acquisition, 299–304
vs. growth/acquisition, 56, 57, 71, 387
vs. non-learnability, 56, 57, 59–79
Learner's experience, 8
Learning
and maturation, 42
imperfect, 304; *see also* Children's errors
the term, 43
theory, 9
mathematical, 43
Lexical
content, 222, 227
pronouns, 116
Lexicon/vocabulary, 4, 18–19; *see also* Word learning
Licensing, 98–99
Linguistic competence vs. performance, 21, 223
Linguistic knowledge
and its characterization, 39, 41, 46, 48

Linguistic knowledge (*cont.*)
and problems, 39
and 19th-century chemists, 41
competence vs. performance, 223
pragmatic, 222
semantic, 222
Linguistic theory
and its biological basis, 105
bidimensional nature, 112
Linguistic performance, competition model of, 21; *see also* Production
Linguistics, neofunctionalism in, 225–233, 239
Listening, preferential, 446–448
Long-distance dependencies, 116

M

M-command, 624, 632
Macroroles, actor and undergoer, 228, 229
Malayalam, 586, 587
Maori, 303–304
Mapping
adult vs. children, 280
concept on words, 279
fast, 259
form-meaning, 357
gramaticality, 137–142
multiple, 358
semantic types and parts of speech, 261–262
syntax-semantics, 292–293
thematic and macroroles, 228–229
utterance-meaning vs. sentence meaning, 349–350, 359
word-meaning, 258–260
word-world, 279–291
Mapping rules, 334–337
feature, 334–337, 339
Maranungku, 315, 316
Markedness, 128, 227, 230
and deaf learners, 616
and phonological development, 592
theory of, 305
Maturation models/hypothesis, 118, 119, 120, 122–124, 127, 132–144, 214
and cerebral cortex development, 127
and learning, 42
and role of biology, 69–74, 105
child vs. adult, 132
empirical evidence, 129–134
physical mechanism, 72
problems, 124–128
recent revisions, 142
stages, 52–54
theories, 56, 64–74, 93, 100–101, 103–104
universal grammar-constrained, 75–79
vs. continuity, 4, 10, 12–14
vs. continuity theories, 10, 12–14
Meaning, *see also* Semantics, Speech acts, and Pragmatics
propositional, 162
Melanesian, 524
Memory, 549, 686
and processing, 411
and specific language impairment (SLI), 677
associative network, 680
Mental
handicaps, specific language impairment (SLI), 675
mechanism, 157
models of the world, 266
Mentalistic revolution, 578
Metalinguistic ability, 431
Metathesis, 336
Methodological problem
and child phonology, 319
children linguistic knowledge, 428
interpretation of data, 428
interpreting children's meaning, 432
of competing factors, 389, 396–397
resolving indeterminacy and variability, 435
resolving theoretical paradox, 434–435
Methodology, 97–98, 119, 121
advances in natural speech, 437–438
analytical methods, 437–438
assessment of variance, 436
bimodal distribution, 398–400
changing children's grammar, 428
comparative analyses, 436
competing factors model (CF), 389–394, 396–403, 410–412, 414, 422, 423
comprehension task, 23
controlled methods, 450
converge evidence, 440–442, 450
convergence of natural speech and experimental methods, 439, 450
data
behavioristic, 135
experimental, 22
indeterminacy, 430
natural speech, 134–135

elicitation and act out task comparison tasks, 440, 441
evaluation of constraint, 435
experiment methods, 436, 450
free pronominal interpretation, 442
generative-based language acquisition, 388
grammar construction, children vs. adults, 428–430
grammatical judgements, 431
inconsistency in children's, 431
incompatibility with theory, 387–388
infant preference tasks, 446–448
inferences about grammaticality, 418–422
inferencing, 437–438
limitations, 70–71, 74
minimal pairs, 321–323
minimality and modularity, 410–412
modularity matching model (MM), 22, 389–394, 403–407, 410, 414–418, 422
natural speech, 431
samples, 134–135
natural speech data, 23–24
output omission model (OOM), 405–407, 410–412
performance errors vs. non-adult grammars, 407–410
practices and input language, 585
production vs. comprehension, 440–443
psycholinguistic, 428
reaction time differences, between children and adults, 401
reduced behavior (RB) task, 23, 444–450
relative difference, 403
replication, 436
sources of variability, 23
statistical
analysis, unreliability of, 428, 445, 450
methods, 436
test, 397
statistics and competing factors, 412–418
statistics use as an unreliable indicator, 414
superiority of modularity matching model (MM), 394
test, 444–450
binomial, 398
comprehension, Act Out (AO), 439, 445–450
experimental, 23
McNemar, 398
production, elicited imitation (EI), 439, 445–450
sign, 397
statistical, 397
theory of, 434–437
truth value judgement task (TVJT), 419, 444–450
types of question–answer pairs, 395–397
underdetermination, 157
unimodal distribution, 398–400
use of puppets, 412
variability, 432
language-specific grammar, 433–435
language-specific pragmatics, 434–435
real time, 434
Metrical structure, Maranungku, 315
Mind, 203
and Euclidean geometry, 36
general nativist view, *see* Non-modular view
rationalist view, 114
special nativist view, *see* Modular view
Minimalist Program, 13, 78
Modality, 204, 205, *see also* American Sign Language (ASL)
and the linguistic environment, 24–26
language learning, 556–560
Modals, 473
Models
normal vs. disordered system, 658
organization of child phonology, 323–326
Modularity, 557–560
hypotheses, 557
in phonology and syntax, 314
issue, 4, 11
matching, 68
notion of, 388–389
processing, 389
Modules, *see* I-system and D-system
Morpheme
bound, 214
grammatical, 206
inflectional, 214
Morphological paradigms and specific language impairment (SLI), 678
Morphosyntax, 138
Motor system and disordered phonology, 662
Movement, 130, 141, 616
Movement, A-, 216
Movement, alpha, 242
Multani, 577
Multiple-word stage and parameter setting, 96

N

Names, non-object, 254
Naming, 253, 260, 534–535
Native speaker, 6
  self-editing by, 582
  "viruses," 582
Nativism
  general, 158–159, 169–170, 174, 180, 181, 184, 187
    a strong version, 170
  general vs. special differences, 188
  special, 158, 181
Nativist
  approach, 497
  theories, 196, 214
Navaho, 230–232
NEG, 100
Negation
  developmental differences, French vs. English child, 611–614
  genitive of, 104
  in Bantu languages, 234
  particles, 95
  scope of, 116
Network-and-switch, 9, 49–50
Neutralization, grammatical conditions on, 240
New/novel words, 279; *see also* Word learning
No-growth theory, 10, *see also* Continuity theory
Nodes
  air flow, 314
  laryngeal, 314, 333
  place, 314
  spontaneous voicing, 314
Nominalization, 178
Non-argument system, 133
Nonconfigurationality, 230
Non-modular theory, 11, 14–15
Norwegian, 95, 621, 626
Noun
  abstract, 178
  basic-level object kind, 253–255
  incorporation, 133
  mass, 178
  material, occupations, 254
  prototypical, 181
NP movement, *see* A-chains
Null
  argument, 553–554
  hypothesis, 22
  -subject, 555, *see also* Pro-drop
    acquisition of, 97, 100
  -subject language, 6–10, 52, 499
Number, 171, 175–176, 204, 262
  and bilingual child, 581, 604

O

Observer's paradox, 602
One-word stage and categorization problem, 517
Opacity, 305
Operating procedures, 213
Oppositions
  phonemic, 319
  phonetic, 320
Optional infinitives, 13
  hypothesis, 90–97, 100, 101
Oriya, 586
Overgeneralization, 680, 691, 694–695

P

Papua-New Guinea languages, 227
Parameter, 64
  head-complement, 206
  headedness, 433
  metrical, 315
  mis-setting, 97
  null-subject, 6–10, 96–97, 100, 430–407, 499, 502
  setting, 13, 98–99, 136, 138, 210
    in sign language, 553
    null-subject, 52
    very early, 96
  the verb-raising, 96
  the verb-second, 96
  verb and object order, 96
Parental vs. caretaker model, 615
Parent replies, contrastive expansion, 522
Parents
  deaf, 532
  deaf and hearing children, 535
Parents' input
  correction
    grammatical learning, 519, 520
    implicit vs. explicit, 514, 522

of articles, 521
simple-first hypothesis, 504
treatment of child's grammatical vs. ungrammatical asymmetries, 509–518
vs. children language development, 507
Particle movement and bilingual child, 581
Passive, 101–102, 124, 133–134, 137
adversity, 103
delay of, 103
be-type, 102, 103
be-type, delay, 102
in English, 101–102, 119, 124, 133
in German, 102
in Japanese, 102
in Zulu, 102
structure, 158
get-type, 102, 103
suffix, 303
verbal, 133
delay of, 103
Perception
as word meaning theory, 253
of stress, 170
of tones, 170
of vowel formants, 170
Perceptual experience and word meaning, 250, 258–260
Performance, 23
errors, 392, 394
factors, 439
children vs. adults, 414
system, 68, 92, 93
Person, 204, 222
Phonetic inventory
individual variation, 659
typology, level A–E, 659–662
Phonological
acquisition, 123
child vs. adult, 318
issues, 317–326
normal vs. disordered, 662
production and perception discrepancies, 320
stages of, 321–323, 337
rules in children, 300
abstract C analysis, 301
consonant harmony, 302
epenthesis, 301, 305
gemination, 301
V deletion, 301, 305
Phonology, 4–5, 18–21
concrete, 306
nonlinear, 307–309
Phrase structure deficit, 677
Physiological and cognitive systems, delay of, 79
Piagetian formal operation, 582
Pidgin, 11, 15–16, 195, 201–203
English-based, 199, 202, 214
Hawaiian, 199, 214
macaronic, 199, 214
Pidginization, 620
Plato's problem, 8, 38, 40–41
Polish, 461–462
Politeness, 4, 21
development of, 364–365
Portuguese, 195, 202
Possession, 204
Power, concept of, 363
Pragmatics, 19–21, 348
acquisition of, *see* Chapter 11
competence, 4, 5, 11, 18–21
domain of, 347
end-point development, 369–370
factors and new words, 285–288
speech acts, 348
Prelinguistic stage
and communicative abilities, 353
and concept understanding, 250, 272
Presupposition, 116
Preverbal stage
communicative intent at, 354
interactivity, 354
non-verbal expression of speech acts, 354
social meaning, 354
to verbal stage, 355–356
Primary language data (PLD), 115, 142; *see also* Evidence, positive
Principle
grounding, 85–87, 100–101
inheritance, 167–169
minimal-distance, 114
modularity, 140
second-order, 187
the inversion, 47
the subject, 47
Principle (of the Binding Theory), 161
A, 80–81, 139, 159, 164
B, 80–88, 139, 164, 412–414, 416
errors, 85, 90
its maturation, 82–90

Principle (of the Binding theory) (*cont.*)
  C, 116, 420, 449
  P, 84, 88
  the empty pronoun, 47
Principles and Parameters, 9, 159, 434, 578–579, 609
  and stress grammar, 314–317
  in phonology, 314–317
Procedure, semantic similarity, 290
Processing
  constraints, 22
  demands, children vs. adults, 414
Pro-drop, 117, 119, 120, 132, 434; *see also* Null-subject
  in Spanish, 116, 119
  languages, 8
  parameter, 119, 120, 141
Production
  deaf children, 550–553
Projection, maximal, 164
Pronoun, 79–84, 101, 116, 473
  forward, 449
  reflexive, 173
  weak vs. strong, 612–614
Proto-theta criterion, 104
Punctual-nonpunctual aspect, 196
Punjabi, 577, 586

Q

Qualities, perceivable, 260
Quantifiers, 83–84, 473
Question
  and bilingual child, 581
  cross-over, 394, 401–402
    strong cross-over, 395, 399
  empty operator, 94
  negative, 408
  vs. declaratives, 504
  yes/no-type, 94
Quiché, 331
Quiché Mayan, 130, 131, 133

R

Reductionist theory, of syntactic categories, 176–182
Reduplication, 199
Reference
  and naming, 553
  intra-sentential, 553
Referents, 254
  material, *see* Nouns, material
  Skinner's theory, 258
Reflexives, long-distance, 206
Regularities, 498
Relations, agent–action–patient, 175
Relative clauses, 121–122
Relativization, 117, 119, 134
Replies, coding scheme for parent and child replies, 517–518
Representation
  architecture, 224–225, 232
  atomic, 223
  content, 224, 237
  lexical, 308
  molecular, 223
  morphosyntactic, 226, 227
  pragmatic, 226, 227
  semantic content, 224, 226, 227
  surface, 308
Research methodology and applications, 5, 21–24; *see also* Chapters 12–14
Romance languages, 92
Rule
  allomorphic, 477
  and naturalness condition, 307
  concatenation, 477
  level A default, 330–331
  level A–E, 331
  SPE format, 305
Russian, 104, 597, 598

S

Scrambling, 117, 139
  in Turkish, 116
Second language(s), 585
Segment structure, 314, 339
  and organizing nodes, 314
Segmental
  contrastive specification (CS), 310–314, 332
  elaboration principles, 333
  radical underspecification (RU), 310–314, 332
  underspecification, 309–314

Semantic
  and pragmatic competition, 237
  assimilation, 175
  bootstrapping, 129, 174, 178, 181
  distinction, 205
  distinction, in creoles, 196
  domains, 292
  feature, 163
  reductionism, 175
  shift, 199
Semantics, 128, 138
Sensory receptors, 251
Sentence
  degree, 196, 214, 215
  fragmentation and grammaticality, 515
Sesotho, 102, 130, 133, 438
Sighted children, 283
Sign, 5
  referential, 543
Sign language, 614–618; *see also* Input modality
  American, *see* Chapter 16
  British, 542
  iconicity and language acquisition, 536
Sign language acquisition, 534–560
  and babbling, 540–541
  and parameter setting, 553
  classifier morphology, 546–549
  classifier system, 548
  early lexicon, 536
  early pronouns, 534, 550
  first signs, 534, 541–544
  issues in, 540–546
  lexicon/words, 544–545
  morphology and syntax, 546–557
  nonmanual grammatical markers, 555–557
  phonetics and phonology, 557–560
  phonological development, 545–546
  spatial syntax, 549–553
  verb agreement and anaphoric reference, 536–539, 550, 553–554
  verbal morphology and spatial syntax, 536–539, 549, 560
  verbs of motion and location, 539–540
  verbs of motion and location (classifiers), 546–549
  wh-questions, 556, 559
  yes–no questions, 559–560
Simplicity, 511
Simplification, 199
  types of, 327
Sinhala, 116, 134, 140
SLADES, Second Language Data Exchange System, 490
Small clauses, 216
Social distance, concept of, 363
Sociolinguistics, 348
Spanish, 6–9, 100, 103, 116, 141, 335, 434, 462, 475, 588, 593, 601, 609, 621
Speaker/hearer's knowledge, 6
Spec-head checking, 101
Special cases (of acquisition), 27
Specificity, 204
  specific-nonspecific, 196, 202
Specific language impairment (SLI), 27
  approaches, 676–677
  auditory perception, 675
  auditory processing, 688
  auxiliaries and modal deficit, 684–685, 692
  brain damage, 675
  case marking, 685–686
  causes, 675
  deficit, reversible passive, 699
  diagnosis, 676
  education, 675
  environment, 675
  feature omission, 679–680, 695–697
  gender marking, 686–687
  genetic impairment, 675
  grammatical agreement deficit, 681–682, 697–700
  grammatical development, 682–693
  intelligence, 675
  language acquisition process, 676
  language deficit, 676
  linguistic profiles, 676
  linguistics, 675
  medicine, 675
  mental handicaps, 675
  particle inflection, 691–692, 694
  past tense marking, 699–700
  person, number deficit, 684, 692, 695–696
  plural marking, 687–690
  psychological approach, 677
  psychology, 675
  rule-deficit model, 678–680, 695–697
  subject–verb agreement, 685, 697–700
  surface structure, 679
  tense marking, 690–691
  verb-second, 698–699
  word order deficit, 692–693, 698–700

Specifier, 164
Speech
acts, 237, 482
development of, 359–360
production and comprehension of, 348
disorders, 627–630
language pathologist, 648
spoken, 5
telegraphic, 51, 124
unintelligibility of, 647
Stage, *see also* Babbling
optional infinitive, 409
three-word, 209
two-word, 206
Stative-nonstative, 196
Stimulus, poverty of, 60, 74
Stress, in Maranungku, 315
Structualism, the Prague school of, 222–224
Structural linguistics and behavioristic view of language, 74, 76
Structure
building, 166
focus, 230, 235
hierarchical, 183–187
morphosyntactic, 229–230
prelexical, 226
schema of layered, 231, 232
Stuttering, 629
Style, differences, 359
Subcategorization and bilingual child, 581
Subjacency, 159
and bilingual child, 580–581
Subject
null, 404
null vs. nonnull, 7, 9
pragmatic topic, 236
semantic agent, 236
syntactic, 236
three types, 236
VP-internal, 103
Subordination, 128, 133, 134
Substitution, 546
Suppressing universal feature, child vs. adult, 339
Suprasegmental, 178
Swahili, 577
Swedish, 95–96, 116, 132, 136, 139, 437, 692, 693, 700, 701
Syllable, 540
Dutch vs. English children, 327–328
System
non-argument, 133
of grammar, computational, 100
of grammar, conceptual/interpretive, 100

T

Tag question and bilingual child, 604
Tagalog, 336
Tamil, 100, 117, 131, 461–462
Task
classifier elicitation task, 546
comprehension, 115, 121
grammaticality judgment, 115
imitation, 523
production, 115
semantic bootstrapping, 696
sentence imitation, 693
sound recognition, 210
Telegraphic speech, 51, 124
Template, melody/prosodic, 327–328, 336
Tense (TNS), 99–101, 163, 165, 171, 175, 178–179, 184, 204–205
Tense-aspect system, 227, 228
and bilingual child, 604
in creoles, 196
Test
comprehension, 688
elicitation, 688
invented objects, 548
Thematic role, 170, 216, 228
assignment, 696
Theme, 163, 167, 182, 184, 206
Theory of language
formalist models, 347–349
functionalist models, 349–350
pragmatics in, 347–349
use-conditional, 349–350
Theta
role, 101, 104, 216
structures, 204
system, 212
Thought and language, 170
Topic, 238
prominence, 553, 606
selection and maintenance, 362
Transcripts, multimedia, 490

Transfer, 609; *see also* Language dominance
mental, 288
Transformation, 226
and word learning, 256
Transitivity, 204
Tree, phone, 319
Trigger metaphor, 24–25
Turkish, 116, 239, 463, 538
Turn taking
acquisition, 361–362
devices, 362

U

Underspecification, theories of, 334, 651–655
Uniqueness principle, 602
Universal grammar (UG), 43–44, 52, 230
access to monolingual and bilingual children, 592
and child language development, 111, 137–139, 144
and Empty C analysis, 309
and innateness, 56–57, 65–67
and language specific properties, 91, 93
and markedness theory, 128
and pragmatics, 114
and speech comprehension studies, 115
and theory of opposition, 592
as constraining acquisition, 138–139
biological basis of, 123, 126–128, 142
bleeding of, 128
children's knowledge of, 55, 72–79, 92, 93, 96, 105
cognitive principles, 299
computational module, 159
continuous development view, 72–79
development, process of, 59–71, 100
discontinuity in, 135, 136, 143
E-languages, 429
experimental results, 114
full-growth of, 60–62, 65
growth vs. no-growth/rigidity theories, 59–74, 96
history of initial state, 113–117
I-languages, 429, 432
theory of, 113, 127, 136
indeterminacy of, 111, 117–122
initial state of, 7, 111–113, 143, 429, 432
input condition on, 114
maturation of, 57, 96, 101
model of acquisition, 158
modularity, 54, 114, 139–142
variability in cognitive, 432–433
variability in linguistic, 433
optimality theory, 316
parameter setting, 498
and value setting, 498
variability, 93
very early, 96–99
principles and parameters of, 51–54, 314–317, 338
proto form of, 70, 75
strong continuity hypothesis, 117–120, 128, 129, 135–144
theory of, 111–113, 136, 427
to specific language grammar, also grammatical mapping, 137, 140–144
trigger problem, 58, 59
variation, 71, 339

V

Verb, 283
acquisition of, 279–293
agreement and reference association, 549–554
complex, 473
compound, 607
finite, 94, 95, 99
intransitive, 176, 178, 185
light, 625
lowering, 611
mental, 473
movement, 96–99
non-finite, 94, 95, 97, 99
pas, 95
prototypical, 181
raising, 116, 130, 139, 610–611
by children, 96
transitive, 168, 176, 178, 186
unaccusative, 12, 103–104
intransitive, 167
unergative intransitive, 167
Verbal inflection, 90, 98–100
Verbal stimuli, 251
Very Early Parameter Setting (VEPS), 96–99

Vision, 71, 79
  and visual system, 37, 39
Vocabulary, *see* Word learning, lexicon
Vocalization, 543
Voice and place distinction and disordered phonology, 662
Voice onset time (VOT), 662–663
Vowel system typology, 310–313

W

Wh-elements, 229, 408
Wh-movement, 116
Wh-principles, 141
Wh-questions, 525
Wh-structures, 137, 139
Word
  and concepts, 261
  categorization
    semantic bootstrapping, 273
    semantic competence, 273
  content, 162
  morality, 473
  objects and abstractions, 254
  recognition, 210
  types and syntactic classes, 251
Word learning, 18–19
  adjectives, 262
  and beyond perceptual features, 257
  and Gestalt principles, 264–267
  and perception-boundedness, 256
  and role of
    environment, 265
    intentionality, 267–271
    linguistic context, 283–284
    syntax, 260–264, 291
  and syntactic competence, 272–274
  approaches
    rationalist, 250, 260–271, 280
    rationalist vs. empirist, 18–19
  by matching (absence of referent), 280
  by transformations, 256
  collective nouns, 264
  conceptual, 280
  early vocabularies, 27281
  essential information, 256
  issues
    nature of meaning, 253–258
    word-meaning mapping, 258–260
  meaning of the verb, gorp, 286
  mental transfer, 288
  models/theories
    Anderson's ACT* model, 18
    associationist theories, 250–260
    connectionist model, 252
    intentional-historical theory of, 270
    multiple frames hypothesis, 19
    rule-based models, 252
    Wittgenstenian theory, 270
    Zoom Lens hypothesis, 285–288
  mother–child conversation, 280
  names of art work, 270–271
  nouns, 250–262, 264
  nouns vs. verbs, 18–19, 281–291
  prepositions, 262
  puppet words, 287
  sameness of shape, 257
  shape-bias in, 255
  single-trial, 258
  two-word stage, 282
  verb, perspective, 286
  verbs, 262, 264, 281, 286
Word order, 94, 98, 206, 207, 605
  acquisition, 94, 97, 98
  and bilingual child, 581, 603–609
  deficit, 677, 698–700
  SOV, 94, 96
  SVO, 96
  underlying, 94

X

X-bar, 141, 164, 165, 188, 230
X-bar syntax, 681

Y

Yes-no questions
  and bilingual child, 581
  by parents, 507
Yidin, 229